"Gentry and Wellum offer a third way, a via media, between covenant theology and dispensationalism, arguing that both of these theological systems are not informed sufficiently by biblical theology. Certainly we cannot understand the Scriptures without comprehending 'the whole counsel of God,' and here we find incisive exegesis and biblical theology at its best. This book is a must read and will be part of the conversation for many years to come."

> **Thomas R. Schreiner**, James Buchanan Harrison Professor of New Testament Interpretation, The Southern Baptist Theological Seminary

"*Kingdom through Covenant* is hermeneutically sensitive, exegetically rigorous, and theologically rich—a first-rate biblical theology that addresses both the message and structure of the whole Bible from the ground up. Gentry and Wellum have produced what will become one of the standard texts in the field. For anyone who wishes to tread the path of biblical revelation, this text is a faithful guide."

> **Miles V. Van Pelt**, Alan Belcher Professor of Old Testament and Biblical Languages and Director, Summer Institute for Biblical Languages, Reformed Theological Seminary

"What do you get when you cross a world-class Bible scholar and a first-rate systematic theologian? You get 800-plus pages of power-packed biblical goodness. You get the forest and quite a few of the trees. This is not the first volume that has attempted to mediate the dispensational/covenant theology divide, but it may be the culminating presentation of that discussion—just as Bach was not the first Baroque composer but its highest moment. Gentry and Wellum's proposal of *Kingdom through Covenant* should be read by all parties, but I won't be surprised to learn in twenty years that this volume provided the foundation for how a generation of anyone who advocates regenerate church membership puts their Bible together."

> **Jonathan Leeman**, Editorial Director, 9Marks; author, *Church and the Surprising Offense of God's Love*

"Gentry and Wellum have provided a welcome addition to the current number of books on biblical theology. What makes their contribution unique is the marriage of historical exegesis, biblical theology, and systematic theology. *Kingdom through Covenant* brims with exegetical insights, biblical theological drama, and sound systematic theological conclusions. Particularly important is the viable alternative they offer to the covenantal and dispensational hermeneutical frameworks. I enthusiastically recommend this book!"

> **Stephen G. Dempster**, Professor of Religious Studies, Crandall University

"The relationship between the covenants of Scripture is rightly considered to be central to the interpretation of the Bible. That there is some degree of continuity is obvious, for it is the same God—the God of Abraham, Isaac, and Jacob as well as the Father of our Lord Jesus Christ—who has revealed himself and his will in the covenants. That there is, however, also significant discontinuity also seems patent since Scripture itself talks about a new covenant and the old one passing away. What has changed and what has not? Utterly vital questions to which this new book by Gentry and Wellum gives satisfying and sound answers. Because of the importance of this subject and the exegetical and theological skill of the authors, their answers deserve a wide hearing. Highly recommended!"

Michael A. G. Haykin, Professor of Church History and Biblical Spirituality, The Southern Baptist Theological Seminary

"*Kingdom through Covenant* is directly applicable to a pastor faithfully seeking understanding of God's Word as it reveals the structure that supports the narrative of God's message throughout time. The study of the covenants provides a framework for understanding and applying the message of the Bible to life in the new covenant community. I have found this study personally transforming, and enriching in my teaching ministry."

Joseph Lumbrix, Pastor, Mount Olivet Baptist Church, Willisburg, Kentucky

"This impressive volume makes a significant contribution to our understanding of the nature of the biblical covenants. Meticulously researched, clearly written, and boldly argued, the 'progressive covenantalism' thesis—a *via media* between dispensational and covenantal theology—combines exegetical depth with theological rigor in the service of covenant faithfulness. The result is penetrating reflections on theology proper, Christology, ecclesiology, and eschatology. Even at points of disagreement, all who teach the Scriptures to others will find here a rich treasure trove of whole-Bible theological thinking and an invaluable resource to return to again and again."

David Gibson, Minister, Trinity Church, Aberdeen, Scotland; coauthor, *Rich: The Reality of Encountering Jesus*

KINGDOM

through

COVENANT

KINGDOM
through
COVENANT

A BIBLICAL-THEOLOGICAL
UNDERSTANDING OF THE COVENANTS

PETER J. GENTRY

STEPHEN J. WELLUM

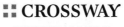

WHEATON, ILLINOIS

Library of Congress Cataloging-in-Publication Data

Gentry, Peter John.
   Kingdom through covenant : a biblical-theological understanding of the covenants / Peter J. Gentry and Stephen J. Wellum.
      p. cm.
   Includes bibliographical references (p.) and indexes.
   ISBN 978-1-4335-1464-7 (hc)
   1. Covenants—Biblical teaching. 2. Covenants—Religious aspects—Christianity. 3. Theology, Doctrinal. I. Wellum, Stephen J., 1964- II. Title.
BS680.C67G46   2012
231.7′6—dc23   2012001514

A Legacy

for
My Children

Stewart John,
Laura and Stephen,
Joseph Daniel and Emma Grace
—Peter Gentry

He established a testimony in Jacob
and appointed a law in Israel,
which he commanded our fathers
to teach to their children,
that the next generation might know them,
the children yet unborn,
and arise and tell them to their children,
so that they should set their hope in God
and not forget the works of God,
but keep his commandments (Ps. 78:5–7, ESV)

With Gratitude to Our Covenant Lord

for
My Parents
Colin and Joan Wellum
—Stephen Wellum

CONTENTS

PART THREE
THEOLOGICAL INTEGRATION

PREFACE

The design for *Kingdom through Covenant* is based on the conviction that biblical theology and systematic theology go hand in hand. To be specific, systematic theology must be based upon biblical theology, and biblical theology in turn must be founded upon exegesis that attends meticulously to the cultural/historical setting, linguistic data, literary devices/techniques, and especially the narrative plot structure, i.e., the larger story which the text as a unitary whole entails and by which it is informed. The converse is also true: exegesis and biblical theology is not an end in itself but a means to the larger end of doing systematic theology which simply attempts to bring all of our thought and life captive to Scripture and thus under the lordship of Christ.

In this work, the disciplines of biblical and systematic theology have joined forces to investigate anew the biblical covenants and the implications of such a study for conclusions in systematic theology. Such a work has demanded a book written by a biblical scholar and a systematic theologian.

Peter Gentry has served as the biblical scholar who has expounded at length the biblical covenants across redemptive-history in Part 2, which is comprised of chapters 4–15. He has also written the appendix on Covenant at the end of the book. In these chapters, a detailed exegesis is undertaken of the crucial covenantal texts *plus* those biblical passages that are essential for putting the biblical covenants into a larger story—a story that comes from the Bible and not from our own imagination or worldviews be they present or past. Care has been taken to let the Scripture speak for itself as the biblical covenants are progressively unfolded in God's plan, reaching their culmination in the new covenant inaugurated by our Lord Jesus Christ.

Stephen Wellum has served as the systematic theologian who has written Part 1, comprised of chapters 1–3, and Part 3, comprised of chapters 16–17. In Part 1, he provides the framework for the discussion of the biblical covenants in terms of covenantal discussion within systematic theology. Specifically he sets the backdrop for Gentry's discussion over against the two dominant theological viewpoints today, i.e., dispensationalism and covenant theology. After discussing how each biblical-theological system understands the biblical covenants, he lays out crucial hermeneutical issues that underlie the entire discussion and the way forward if arbitration between the two viewpoints is to be achieved. In Part 3, he provides a "big picture" summary of our *via media* proposal of *Kingdom through Covenant* and begins to draw out some of the implications of the study for systematic theology especially in the areas of theology proper, Christology, ecclesiology, and eschatology.

After the time of writing and before final publication, a number of major works have appeared on the same topic. Only comments of a limited nature are possible concerning these works. One is by Scott W. Hahn, *Kinship by Covenant: A Canonical Approach to the Fulfillment of God's Saving Purposes* (Yale, 2009). Although Hahn is presently a confessing Roman Catholic, he was trained at Westminster Theological Seminary and was given a good background in biblical theology. His work is focused more on the New Testament, while our work is focused more on the Old Testament and how the New Testament is a direct line from Old Testament thought. Hahn's exegesis dealing with the covenants in the Old Testament follows the ancient Near Eastern categories of royal grant versus suzerain-vassal more rigidly than exegesis of the text of Scripture permits.

Another is by James M. Hamilton, *God's Glory in Salvation through Judgment: A Biblical Theology* (Crossway, 2010). Hamilton correctly emphasizes the unity of the biblical texts and claims a centre for biblical theology, i.e., that the idea or theme of "the glory of God displayed in salvation through judgment" is *the* theme which unites the entirety of Scripture and that the parts or individual texts of Scripture cannot be understood without reference to it. We agree with the former, but we do not argue for the latter. We do not deny that "salvation through judgment" is *a* theme of Scripture, even a major one, but we will not defend the assertion that it is *the* theme to the neglect of other themes. In addition, Hamilton does not give much attention to the biblical covenants, their unfolding, progressive nature, and how the biblical covenants provide the entire substructure to the plot line of Scripture. Yet it is our contention that apart from thinking through the relationships between the biblical covenants, one does not fully grasp the Bible's own intrasystematic categories and thus how the parts are related to the whole in the overall plan of God. Before one argues for *the* overarching *theme* of Scripture, one must first wrestle with the unfolding nature of the biblical covenants and their fulfilment and consummation in Christ.

A third is that of Greg Nichols, *Covenant Theology, A Reformed Baptist Perspective* (Solid Ground Christian Books, 2011). This work assumes much of the standard exegesis found in classic covenant theology and seeks to modify it in a way that is consistent with Baptist theology. Yet research during the last fifty years provides information on culture, language, and literary structures that both makes possible and necessitates exegesis *de novo*.

A fourth is a guide to the Old Testament for lay people by Sandra Richter, entitled *The Epic of Eden: A Christian Entry into the Old Testament* (InterVarsity Press, 2008). She uses Adam, Noah, Abraham, Moses, and David as key figures for both covenants and periods of history. Thus she argues, as we do, that the covenants are the key to the plot structure of the Old Testament. The scope of her work is more limited than ours, and differences in exegesis cannot be defended in her work as they are in ours.

Finally, in November, a magisterial volume entitled *A New Testament Biblical Theology* by G. K. Beale appeared (Baker, 2011). Comparison of Beale's work and ours would require more than we can do in this preface, but one difference between his approach and ours centres on how he unpacks the story line of Scripture. Beale argues that the "thought" and "themes" of Genesis 1–3 and the later patterns based on it form the story line of Scripture. His metanarrative turns out to be essentially creation, judgement, and new creation. He summarises as follows:

> The Old Testament is the story of God, who progressively reestablishes his new-creational kingdom out of chaos over a sinful people by his word and Spirit through promise, covenant, and redemption, resulting in worldwide commission to the faithful to advance this kingdom and judgment (defeat or exile) for the unfaithful, unto his glory (p. 87).

We are the first to acknowledge that there is much that is good and right in Beale's work. It is filled with rich insights and is worth careful reflection. Beale does rightly acknowledge a covenant in Genesis 1–3, and he speaks of the commission of Adam inherited by Noah, Abraham, and Israel. Nonetheless, he does not provide a detailed unpacking of the biblical covenants. Instead he treats creation and new creation as the main themes of Scripture, but in our view, creation and new creation only serve as the bookends of the plot structure and not the structure itself. Beale fails to use the covenants to develop adequately and properly the plot structure *between* creation and new creation. It is not the case that the canon merely provides a repetition of the patterns and themes in Genesis 1–3 as we progress across redemptive-history. Instead, the covenants provide the structure and unfold the developing plot line of Scripture, and a detailed investigation of those covenants is necessary to understand God's eternal plan of salvation centred in Christ. Each covenant must be first placed in its own historical/textual context and then viewed intertextually and canonically if we are truly going to grasp something of the whole counsel of God, especially the glory of the new covenant our Lord has inaugurated. It is for this reason that we are convinced that Beale's otherwise full treatment of subjects goes awry when he comes to the end of his work. Since he does not provide a detailed treatment of the covenantal unfolding which reaches its climax in Christ and the new covenant, he, in our view, wrongly identifies Sunday as a Christian Sabbath when the former is a sign of the new creation and the latter is a sign of the first creation and (now obsolete) old covenant. He also argues for infant baptism, thus confusing the sign of the new covenant with circumcision as the sign for the Abrahamic covenant. These are distinct and separate as covenants and covenant signs. Thus Sabbath and baptism are not sufficiently discussed in their covenantal contexts and fulfilment in Christ. In the end, Beale leaves us with a sophisticated treatment of covenant theology which we are convinced needs to be modified in light of the Bible's own unfolding of the biblical covenants.

In any work of this magnitude we have received help from our colleagues, family, and students. We would like to thank our colleagues, Daniel Block, Stephen Dempster, Stephen Kempf, Tom Schreiner, Charles Halton, Miles van Pelt, and Gregg Allison for their many helpful comments as the entire manuscript or parts of it were read and valuable feedback was given to us. In addition, various family members and students also helped in a variety of ways, and we want to thank specifically, Barbara Gentry, Laura Musick, John Meade, Jason Parry, Brent Parker, Andrew Case, Brian Davidson, Joseph Lumbrix, Chip Hardy, Richard Lucas, Matt Dickie, Uche Anizor, and Andrew McClurg. We would also like to thank Paul Roberts and the library staff at SBTS for help in digging up materials necessary for our research.

One final note in regard to the dedication of this work. Peter dedicates this work to his children and grandchildren. His Göttingen Edition of Ecclesiastes will be dedicated to his parents, Norm and Marg Gentry, who inspired a love for diligent study of the Word of God. In the passage from Psalm 78, "testimony" (*'ēdût*) and "law" (*tôrâ*) are synonyms for covenant in the Old Testament. God has entrusted the transmission of covenant instruction to a covenant community: the family. We have a great heritage that must be passed on.

Stephen dedicates this work to his parents. We all stand on the shoulders of those who have gone before us, men and women who were faithful in their generation and who stood firm on God's Word and who passed it on to the next generation. In my case, I (Stephen) owe much to my parents, Colin and Joan Wellum, who did precisely this in their lives and ministry to their children. It is due to my parents' faithfulness to the Lord, exhibited in their teaching their children to love God's Word; to their sacrificial love in so many ways; to their conviction to place their children under the sound teaching of God's Word in a local church committed to expounding the "whole counsel of God;" and their living out in the home what they taught, that I stand where I stand today. I give our triune covenant God thanks for my parents as ongoing evidence of God's grace in my life.

It is our prayer that this work will not only enable us to think through the biblical covenants better but will also lead us to know, love, and serve our great covenant God as his holy people—those who are completely devoted and faithful to him.

Peter J. Gentry
Stephen J. Wellum
Written on the Cloud between Göttingen, Louisville, and Toronto

LIST OF ABBREVIATIONS

AOAT — Alter Orient und Altes Testament

EV(V) — English version(s)

GKC — *Gesenius' Hebrew Grammar*, ed. E. Kautzsch, rev. A. E. Cowley. 2nd. English ed. (Oxford, 1910)

HALOT — *The Hebrew and Aramaic Lexicon of the Old Testament*, ed. L. Koehler and W. Baumgartner, et al., trans. M. E. J. Richardson, study edition, 2 vols. (Leiden: Brill, 2001)

JETS — *Journal of the Evangelical Theological Society*

JSOT — *Journal for the Study of the Old Testament*

JSOTSup — Journal for the Study of the Old Testament: Supplement Series

MT — Masoretic Text

NDBT — *New Dictionary of Biblical Theology*, ed. T. D. Alexander, Brian S. Rosner, D. A. Carson, and Graeme Goldsworthy (Downers Grove, IL: InterVarsity Press, 2000).

NSBT — New Studies in Biblical Theology

SBJT — *The Southern Baptist Journal of Theology*

s.v. — *sub verbo* (listed alphabetically under that word)

TDOT — *Theological Dictionary of the Old Testament*, edited by G. Johannes Botterweck, Helmer Ringgren, and Heinz-Josef Fabry, 15 vols. (Grand Rapids, MI: Eerdmans, 1986–2006).

WBC — Word Biblical Commentary

* — Asterisk in Hebrew text marks Qere in Masoretic text.

PART ONE:

PROLEGOMENA

Chapter One

THE IMPORTANCE OF COVENANTS IN BIBLICAL AND SYSTEMATIC THEOLOGY

> The idea of covenant is fundamental to the Bible's story. At its most basic, covenant presents God's desire to enter into relationship with men and women created in his image. This is reflected in the repeated covenant refrain, "I will be your God and you will be my people" (Exodus 6:6-8; Leviticus 26:12 etc.). Covenant is all about relationship between the Creator and his creation. The idea may seem simple; however, the implications of covenant and covenant relationship between God and humankind are vast . . .[1]

The purpose of this book is to demonstrate two claims. First, we want to show how central the concept of "covenant" is to the narrative plot structure of the Bible, and secondly, how a number of crucial theological differences within Christian theology, and the resolution of those differences, are directly tied to one's understanding of how the biblical covenants unfold and relate to each other. In terms of the first claim, we are *not* asserting that the covenants are the centre of biblical theology. Instead, we assert that the covenants form the backbone of the metanarrative of Scripture and thus it is essential to "put them together" correctly in order to discern accurately the "whole counsel of God" (Acts 20:27).[2] Michael Horton nicely captures this point when he writes that the biblical covenants are "the architectural structure that we

---

[1] Alistair I. Wilson and Jamie A. Grant, "Introduction," in *The God of Covenant: Biblical, Theological, and Contemporary Perspectives*, ed. Jamie A. Grant and Alistair I. Wilson (Leicester, UK: Apollos, 2005), 12.

[2] We are not going to enter into the thorny issue of the centre of biblical theology. Many proposals have been given, and in the end they all tend toward reductionism. For example, see the discussion in Gerhard F. Hasel, *Old Testament Theology: Basic Issues in the Current Debate*, 2nd ed. (Grand Rapids, MI: Eerdmans, 1991); and the proposals of G. K. Beale, "The Eschatological Conception of New Testament Theology," in *"The Reader Must Understand": Eschatology in Bible and Theology*, ed. K. E. Brower and M. W. Elliott (Leicester, UK: Apollos, 1997), 11–52; and James M. Hamilton, *God's Glory in Salvation through Judgment: A Biblical Theology* (Wheaton, IL: Crossway, 2010). Our claim is much more modest: the biblical covenants form the backbone of the metanarrative of Scripture, and apart from understanding each biblical covenant in its historical context and then in its relation to the fulfilment of all of the covenants in Christ, we will ultimately misunderstand the overall message of the Bible.

believe the Scriptures themselves to yield. . . . It is not simply the concept of the covenant, but the concrete existence of God's covenantal dealings in our history that provides the context within which we recognize the unity of Scripture amid its remarkable variety."[3] If this is the case, which we contend it is, then apart from properly understanding the nature of the biblical covenants and how they relate to each other, one will not correctly discern the message of the Bible and hence God's self-disclosure which centres and culminates in our Lord Jesus Christ.

Obviously this is not a new insight, especially for those in the Reformed tradition who have written at length about the importance of covenants and have structured their theology around the concept of "covenant."[4] In fact, almost every variety of Christian theology admits that the biblical covenants establish a central framework that holds the story of the Bible together. From the coming of Christ and the beginning of the early church, Christians have wrestled with the relationships between the covenants, particularly the old and new covenants. In fact, it is almost impossible to discern many of the early church's struggles apart from covenantal wrestling and debates. For example, think of how important the Jew-Gentile relationship is in the New Testament (Matt. 22:1–14, par.; Acts 10–11; Romans 9–11; Eph. 2:11–22; 3:1–13), the claim of the Judaizers, which centres on covenantal debates (Galatians 2–3), the reason for the calling of the Jerusalem Council (Acts 15), the wrestling with the strong and weak within the church (Romans 14–15), and the implications for the church on how to live vis-à-vis the old covenant now that Christ has come (Matthew 5–7; 15:1–20, par.; Acts 7; Romans 4; Hebrews 7–10). In reality, all of these issues are simply the church wrestling with covenantal shifts—from old covenant to new—and the nature of fulfilment that has occurred in the coming of Christ.

How Christians have understood the relationship between the biblical covenants has differed. This is one of the reasons why we have different theological systems and is probably best exemplified in our contemporary context by dispensationalism and covenant theology, even though it is certainly not limited to these views. Even though they agree on the main issues central to "the faith that was once for all delivered to the saints" (Jude 3), at

---

[3] Michael S. Horton, *God of Promise: Introducing Covenant Theology* (Grand Rapids, MI: Baker, 2006), 13.

[4] As we will discuss in more detail in chapter 2, Reformed theology or "covenant theology" has rightly understood that "covenant" is central to the organisation of Scripture and thus of all theologizing. In fact Horton, *God of Promise*, 11, states it this way: "*Reformed* theology is synonymous with *covenant* theology." However, it is not only Reformed theology that has argued this point. All Christian theology has rightly viewed the covenants as central to how the Scriptures unfold and how we think of what our Lord Jesus has accomplished as our new covenant head.

their heart these two systems differ on many matters which, in the end, are rooted in their different views on the nature of the biblical covenants and how these covenants relate to each other. Thus, beyond our basic agreement that the story of Scripture moves from Adam to Abraham to Sinai, which ultimately issues in a promise of a new covenant whose advent is tied with Jesus' cross work (Luke 22:20; 1 Cor. 11:23–26), there is disagreement on how to "put together" the biblical covenants. This disagreement inevitably spills over to other issues, especially the question of what from the old covenant applies to us today as new covenant believers. It is at this point, on such matters as the Sabbath, the application of the Old Testament law to the state, the application of various moral prohibitions, and many more issues, that we discover significant differences among Christians.[5]

For this reason, correctly "putting together" the biblical covenants is central to the doing of biblical and systematic theology and thus to the theological conclusions we draw from Scripture in many doctrinal areas. If we are going to make progress in resolving disagreements within Christian theology, especially in regard to dispensational and covenant theology, then how we understand the nature of the biblical covenants and their relationship to each other must be faced head on and *not* simply assumed. It is our conviction that the present ways of unpacking the biblical covenants across the Canon, especially as represented by dispensational and covenant theology (and their varieties), are not quite right. That is why we believe it is time to present an alternative reading which seeks to rethink and mediate these two theological traditions in such a way that we learn from both of them but also provide an alternative—a *via media*. We are convinced that there is a more accurate way to understand the relationship of the biblical covenants which makes better sense of the overall presentation of Scripture and which, in the end, will help us resolve some of our theological differences. If, as

---

[5] Differences of viewpoint regarding the relation of the covenants not only distinguishes various Christian theological systems; it also distinguishes how Christians and Jews in the first century differed with one another, especially in regard to how they viewed the relationship between the Mosaic covenant and the coming of Christ. For first-century Judaism, the law was imperishable, immutable, eternal (e.g., *Wisd. Sol.* 18:4; *Ag. Ap.* 2.277; *Mos.* 2.14; *Jub.* 1:27; 3:31; 6:17). But Paul, for example, interprets the law-covenant differently than a Jew: he relativizes the importance of the law-covenant by arguing from the law's placement in the plot line of the Pentateuch (cf. Gal. 3:15–4:7). The promise to Abraham that in his seed all the nations of the earth would be blessed *antedates* Moses and the giving of the law by centuries, and that promise cannot be annulled by the giving of the law (Gal. 3:17), regardless of how much space is given over to the law in the text, or how large a role it played in Israel's history. What, then, was the purpose of the law? Ultimately, the entire New Testament argues, its function was to lead us to Christ (cf. Rom. 3:21). Obviously this Christian interpretation of the law-covenant is radically different from a Jewish one. On this point see D. A. Carson, "Systematic Theology and Biblical Theology," in *NDBT*, 89–104; idem, "Mystery and Fulfillment: Toward a More Comprehensive Paradigm of Paul's Understanding of the Old and the New," in *Justification and Variegated Nomism: Volume 2—The Paradoxes of Paul*, ed. D. A. Carson, P. T. O'Brien, and M. A. Seifrid (Grand Rapids, MI: Baker, 2004), 393–436.

church history warns, that goal is too ambitious, minimally our aim is to help us become more epistemologically self-conscious in how we put our Bible together in relation to the biblical covenants. In so doing, hopefully the discussion among Christians can profitably progress as we compare and contrast our basic theological commitments in a variety of doctrinal areas.

"Kingdom through covenant" is our proposal for what is central to the narrative plot structure of the Bible, which we want to develop in detail in the following chapters. If we were to label our view and to plot it on the map of current evangelical discussion, it would fit broadly under the umbrella of what is called "new covenant theology,"[6] or to coin a better term, "progressive covenantalism."[7] Obviously the problem in attaching a label to any view is that we do not completely agree with all the proposals in the category.

In identifying our proposal as "progressive covenantalism," or a species of "new covenant theology," we are stressing two points. First, it is a *via media* between dispensational and covenant theology. It neither completely fits nor totally disagrees with either system. Second, it stresses the *unity* of God's plan which is discovered as we trace God's redemptive work through the biblical covenants. It is not our desire to focus on the new covenant to the exclusion of the other covenants; rather we are concerned with each and every biblical covenant. Yet, given the fact that God has progressively revealed his eternal plan to us over time and through the covenants, in order to discern God's plan correctly we must understand each biblical covenant in its own redemptive-historical context by locating that covenant in relationship to what precedes it and what comes after it. When we do this, not only do we unpack God's unfolding plan, but we discover how that one plan comes

---

[6] There is a great amount of literature under the umbrella of "new covenant theology." We do not endorse all of it, but a good place to start is with the following literature: Tom Wells and Fred Zaspel, *New Covenant Theology* (Frederick, MD: New Covenant Media, 2002); Thomas R. Schreiner, *New Testament Theology: Magnifying God in Christ* (Grand Rapids, MI: Baker, 2008); Jason C. Meyer, *The End of the Law: Mosaic Covenant in Pauline Theology* (Nashville: B&H Academic, 2009); John G. Reisinger, *Abraham's Four Seeds* (Frederick, MD: New Covenant Media, 1998); Steven Lehrer, ed., *Journal of New Covenant Theology*; A. Blake White, *The Newness of the New Covenant* (Frederick, MD: New Covenant Media, 2007). See also Michael F. Bird, "New Testament Theology Re-Loaded: Integrating Biblical Theology and Christian Origins," *Tyndale Bulletin* 60/2 (2009): 265–291. Even though Bird does not adopt the label "new covenant theology," he presents his own view as "a theology of the New Covenant." He rightly argues that the advent of the new covenant implies "*a continuing and yet transformed relationship between the new epoch of redemptive-history and the Old Covenant economy*" (284, emphasis his). The New Testament authors assume that the story of Israel is continued in the story of the church, but they also stress a strong element of discontinuity due to the superiority of the new covenant to the old because of the person and work of Christ.

[7] "Progressive covenantalism" was a term suggested to us by Richard Lucas, presently a PhD student at The Southern Baptist Theological Seminary, Louisville, Kentucky. Even though it is a new term, it nicely captures our basic proposal. "Progressive" seeks to underscore the progress or the unfolding of God's revelation from old to new, and "covenantalism" emphasises that God's plan across redemptive-history unfolds through covenants as all of these covenants are terminated, culminated, and fulfilled in Christ and the arrival of the promised new covenant age.

to fulfilment and culmination in Christ and the inauguration of the new covenant with all of its theological entailments (see Heb. 1:1–3; 7:1–10:18; cf. Eph. 1:9–10). Furthermore, given the fact that we live in light of the achievement of Christ's glorious work, we must apply the entire Scripture to us, including all of the previous covenants, through the lens of the achievement of our Lord and the new covenant realities he inaugurates. Hence the reason for the label "progressive covenantalism" or "new covenant theology."[8] Yet, regardless of the particular label, our intent is to propose an alternative way of understanding the nature of the biblical covenants and their relationship to the new covenant in Christ. We want to begin to spell out some of the implications of this view for various theological loci since one's understanding of the covenants is so foundational to how one "puts together" the entire Bible. In the end, how one approaches the very doing of biblical and systematic theology is greatly affected by one's comprehension of how the biblical covenants unfold and relate to each other in God's one plan of redemption.

Our procedure is to begin this study by establishing the importance of biblical covenants for biblical and systematic theology. There are numerous ways this point could be demonstrated but we will do so by setting our discussion of the covenants in the context of the two dominant theological systems within evangelical theology. Dispensationalism and covenant theology (along with their varieties) largely frame how evangelicals put their Bibles together. Each view attempts to serve as an interpretive grid for how to understand the metanarrative of Scripture. In this way, both systems function as examples of biblical theologies, i.e., "whole-Bible theologies," which then lead to various systematic theological conclusions. Yet, it is well known that each system draws vastly different conclusions—not so much on primary gospel issues—but on significant theological matters which lead to differences among us. Specifically we notice these differences in the doctrinal areas of ecclesiology and eschatology, but it is not limited to these matters, as we will seek to demonstrate. Thus it is helpful to establish the importance of biblical covenants by doing so through the lens of these two theological systems and discerning where they differ from each other especially in their understanding of these covenants. In this way, our proposal is viewed against the backdrop of current views in the church.

---

[8] This view may also be thought of as a "Baptist theology" since we believe that it best provides the grounding to a Baptist ecclesiology over against other ecclesiologies. However, since our view has more implications than merely that of ecclesiology and since Baptists differ in matters of God's sovereignty, soteriology, and eschatology, "progressive covenantalism" is probably a more appropriate label.

Before we turn to that task, in chapter 1 we will first give a brief discussion on how we conceive of the nature of biblical theology and its relation to systematic theology. Since we are viewing dispensational and covenant theology as examples of biblical *and* systematic theologies it is important to describe our use of these terms, given that there is no unanimous agreement regarding their use.

Chapter 2 will describe the basic views of dispensational and covenant theology, noting variations and debates within each view. As one would expect, each view is not monolithic; however, in our description of these biblical-systematic theologies particular attention will be focused on their respective understanding of the biblical covenants and how it is that each view differs, given their specific way of relating the biblical covenants to each other.

Building on this description of the two theological systems, chapter 3 will conclude the introductory section in two ways. First, we will describe some basic hermeneutical assumptions we will employ in our reading of Scripture and thus describe something of our theological method in doing biblical and systematic theology. Second, we will then resume our discussion of dispensational and covenant theology by outlining some of the hermeneutical similarities and differences between them which need resolution in order to adjudicate these two systems and thus argue for a *via media*.

Chapters 4–15 will serve as the heart of the book. Here our proposal of "kingdom through covenant" is unpacked in detail as each biblical covenant is described in its own redemptive-historical context and then in its relationship to the dawning of the new covenant in the person and work of our Lord Jesus Christ. Finally, chapters 16–17 will conclude the book by tying the loose ends together in a summary of the proposal and then briefly showing some of the theological ramifications of it which highlight how our understanding of "kingdom through covenant" affects the conclusions drawn from systematic theology for the various doctrinal loci, specifically, but not limited to, Christology, soteriology, ecclesiology, and eschatology.

Let us now turn to a brief discussion of our understanding of the nature of biblical theology and its relation to systematic theology. This will allow us to describe how we are using these terms and to explain why we view dispensational and covenant theology as examples of both biblical and systematic theology, even though we disagree with various aspects of each view.

THE NATURE OF BIBLICAL THEOLOGY

We believe this attempt to understand the biblical covenants across redemptive-history and to unpack their relationship to one another and to their ultimate fulfilment in Christ is an exercise in "biblical theology." It is also the first step in drawing legitimate theological conclusions from Scripture and thus applying the "whole counsel of God" to our lives, which is the task of "systematic theology." But given the fact that people mean different things by "biblical" and "systematic" theology, let us explain how we are using these terms and how we conceive of the relationship between them.

At the popular level, for most Christians, when the term "biblical theology" is used it is probably heard as expressing the desire to be "biblical" or "true to the Bible" in our teaching and theology. Obviously, to be "biblical" in this sense is what all Christians ought to desire and strive for, but this is *not* exactly how we are using the term. In fact, in church history, "biblical theology" has been understood in a number of ways.[9]

Generally speaking, before the last two or three centuries, biblical theology was often identified with systematic theology, even though many in church history practised what we currently call "biblical theology," that is, an attempt to unpack the redemptive-historical unfolding of Scripture.[10] One can think of many examples, such as Irenaeus (c. 115–c. 202), John Calvin (1509–1564), and Johannes Cocceius (1603–1669). In this important sense, biblical theology is not entirely new, since the church has always wrestled with how to put the whole Canon together, especially in light of the coming of Christ. Any position, then, that seeks to think through the canon of Scripture is doing "biblical theology" in some sense. Granting this point, it is still accurate to note that, in the past, there was a tendency to treat the Scripture in more logical and atemporal categories rather than to think carefully through the Bible's developing story line as it was forged across time. Even in the post-Reformation era where there was a renewed emphasis on doing a "whole-Bible theology," biblical theology was mostly identified

---

[9] For a helpful overview of the history of biblical theology, see C. H. H. Scobie, "History of Biblical Theology," in *NDBT*, 11–20. See also Schreiner, *New Testament Theology*, 867–888; Robert W. Yarbrough, *The Salvation Historical Fallacy? Reassessing the History of NT Theology* (Leiden, Netherlands: Deo, 2004); H. G. Reventlow, "Theology (Biblical), History of," in *Anchor Bible Dictionary*, ed. David Noel Freedman, 6 vols. (Garden City, NY: Doubleday, 1992), 6:483–505; G. E. Ladd, "Biblical Theology, History of," and "Biblical Theology, Nature of," in *The International Standard Bible Encyclopedia*, rev. ed., ed. Geoffrey W. Bromiley, 4 vols. (Grand Rapids, MI: Eerdmans, 1979), 1:498–509.

[10] For a fine example of this approach to biblical theology see Graeme Goldsworthy, *According to Plan: The Unfolding Revelation of God in the Bible* (Downers Grove, IL: InterVarsity Press, 2002).

with systematic theology, and systematic theology was identified more with "dogmatic" concerns.[11]

With the rise of the Enlightenment, biblical theology begins to emerge as a distinct discipline. Some have argued, and rightly so, that this is tied to the Enlightenment's "historical consciousness."[12] However, one must carefully distinguish the emergence of biblical theology in the Enlightenment era along two different paths, one path serving as an illustration of an illegitimate approach to biblical theology tied to the Enlightenment's *Zeitgeist* and the other path a legitimate one seeking to develop previous insights in church history but now in a more precise, detailed, and historically conscious manner, dependent upon the Bible's own internal presentation. Let us first think briefly about the illegitimate development of biblical theology associated with the Enlightenment and classic liberal theology before we discuss what we believe is the legitimate view of biblical theology.

During the period of the Enlightenment there was a growing tendency to approach Scripture *critically* and thus uncoupled from historic Christian theology.[13] This resulted in approaching the Bible "as any other book,"[14] rooted in history but, unfortunately, also open to historical-critical methods. This meant that the Bible was not approached on its own terms, i.e., as God's Word written. Instead, the idea that Scripture is God-breathed through human authors—a text which authoritatively and accurately unfolds God's redemptive plan centred in Christ—was rejected as the starting point of biblical theology.

The person first associated with this path of biblical theology is Johann Philipp Gabler, often viewed as the father of "biblical theology." In his inaugural lecture at the University of Altdorf on March 30, 1787—"An Oration on the Proper Distinction between Biblical and Dogmatic Theology and the Specific Objectives of Each"—he defined biblical theology as an inductive, historical, and descriptive discipline, in contrast to systematic theology, which he viewed as a deductive, ahistorical, and normative discipline. It

---

[11] See D. A. Carson, "Systematic Theology and Biblical Theology," 89–104, who makes this point. Carson notes that the first occurrence of the expression "biblical theology" is in 1607 by W. J. Christmann, who used it to refer to a compilation of proof texts supporting Protestant systematic theology (90).

[12] See Carson, "Systematic Theology and Biblical Theology," 89–94.

[13] For a brief description of the Enlightenment era see W. Andrew Hoffecker, ed., *Revolutions in Worldview: Understanding the Flow of Western Thought* (Phillipsburg, NJ: P&R, 2007), 240–280; cf. Stanley J. Grenz, *A Primer on Postmodernism* (Grand Rapids, MI: Eerdmans, 1996); cf. D. A. Carson, *The Gagging of God: Christianity Confronts Pluralism* (Grand Rapids, MI: Zondervan, 1996), 13–137.

[14] This is Benjamin Jowett's expression. For a discussion of the Enlightenment's reading of the Bible see Kevin J. Vanhoozer, *Is There a Meaning in This Text? The Bible, the Reader, and the Morality of Literary Knowledge* (Grand Rapids, MI: Zondervan, 1998); cf. idem, "Exegesis and Hermeneutics," in *NDBT*, 52–64.

is crucial to note that Gabler used the term "historical" in a more histor-ical-*critical* sense. He did *not* use the term in the sense that we ought to read Scripture as God's authoritative, trustworthy Word, rooted in history, and along its redemptive-historical axis. In its *critical* use, he meant that we ought to read Scripture in light of Enlightenment rationalist presupposi-tions, which minimally assumed the following points: (1) in doing biblical theology we do *not* need to assume the Scripture's inspiration; (2) biblical theology involves the work of carefully collecting the ideas and concepts of individual biblical writers, and this task is accomplished by means of his-torical, literary, and philosophical criticism (tied to a rationalist epistemol-ogy); and (3) as a historical discipline, biblical theology must distinguish between the several periods of the old and new religion, which, for Gabler, is basically following the "history of religions" approach to Scripture, thus assuming from the outset that Scripture is not authoritatively and accurately given in its totality. In Gabler's understanding of biblical theology, then, his overall goal was to uncouple the study of Scripture from dogmatic or doctri-nal aims and to study Scripture historically-*critically* to determine what was legitimately true and what was not. In so doing, he opened the door to the drift toward the denial of a high view of Scripture and the increasingly atom-istic reading of Scripture, given the fact that he did not believe Scripture was a unified, God-given revelation.[15]

As this path of biblical theology developed in the late eighteenth and early nineteenth centuries, practitioners increasingly made use of the histori-cal-critical method, which for the most part, assumed a *methodological* natu-ralism.[16] Over time the end result of such an approach was the fragmentation

---

[15] For a more detailed treatment of Gabler's significance, along with his approach to biblical theology, see Carson, "Systematic Theology and Biblical Theology," 89–90; Vanhoozer, "Exegesis and Hermeneutics," 53; J. V. Fesko, "On the Antiquity of Biblical Theology," in *Resurrection and Eschatology: Theology in Service of the Church*, ed. L. G. Tipton and J. C. Waddington (Phillipsburg, NJ: P&R, 2008), 443–477. Fesko (447–448) nicely sum-marises Gabler's approach to Scripture in the following steps: (1) He viewed Scripture as "inspired" but we must still decide what is truly divine versus what is not. All of Scripture, then, is not God-given; (2) How do we decide what is God-given? We ask whether the portion of Scripture we are reading is consistent with "eternal universal religion" or whether it merely reflects the opinion, time, and culture of the biblical author; and (3) He denied that Scripture was a unified, organic, historically unfolding divine revelation which in its totality gives us God's authoritative revelation. For a contrary yet not convincing view of Gabler see Michael F. Bird, "Biblical Theol-ogy: An Endangered Species in Need of Defense," http://euangelizomai.blogspot.com/2008/01/biblical-theology-endangered-species-in.html.

[16] "Methodological naturalism" is the view that approaches our study of history (including our study of the Bible) and science without considering God's involvement in the world and divine action as represented by divine revela-tion and miracles. Methodological naturalism does *not* necessarily require a commitment to atheism, even though it is consistent with it. Deism and panentheism (both Enlightenment views) also assume methodological natural-ism, given their denial of divine action in an effectual, supernatural sense. For a helpful discussion and critique of methodological naturalism see Alvin Plantinga, "Methodological Naturalism?" *Origins and Design* 18/1, accessed at http://www.arn.org/docs/odesign/od181/methnat181.htm; and "Methodological Naturalism? Part 2" *Origins and Design* 18/2 accessed at http://www.arn.org/docs/odesign/od182/methnat182.htm.

of Scripture, and biblical theology as a discipline became nothing more than merely a "descriptive" discipline, governed by *critical* methodologies and alien worldview assumptions. As a result, this approach to biblical theology emphasised more "diversity" than "unity" in Scripture, and ultimately, as a discipline which sought to unpack the unified plan of God, it came to an end.[17] In the twentieth century, there were some attempts to overcome the Enlightenment straightjacket on Scripture. In theology, the work of Karl Barth is notable. He is often seen as the forerunner of narrative theology and the post-liberal school, a school which broadly attempts to read Scripture as a unified canon, but which, when all is said and done, does not operate with a traditional view of the authority and accuracy of Scripture. In biblical studies there was also the "Biblical Theology Movement."[18] Its goal was to overcome the more negative results of the historical-critical method and allow the biblical text to come alive for the contemporary church although, sadly, it did not return to the assumptions of historic, orthodox Christianity. In Old Testament theology, for example, Walther Eichrodt, who was part of this movement, wrote an Old Testament biblical theology centred on the notion of the covenant. Others in the movement wrote a biblical theology centred on different corpora or themes. However none of these wrote or attempted to write a "whole Bible theology" because, given their view of Scripture and theological commitments, very few of them believed that there was a unified message in the whole Canon.[19] As a result, just as Geerhardus Vos, the evangelical pioneer of a legitimate approach to biblical theology, had warned at the beginning of the twentieth century, the Biblical Theology Movement failed. Vos had warned that one cannot truly do a biblical theology in the

---

[17] See Hans Frei, *The Eclipse of Biblical Narrative: A Study in Eighteenth and Nineteenth Century Hermeneutics* (New Haven, CT: Yale University Press, 1980). In the nineteenth century, "biblical theology" was eventually identified with "classic liberalism" as represented by various schools of thought associated with such people as F. C. Baur, J. Wellhausen, the history of religions school, and so on. On these people and movements see Stanley J. Grenz and Roger Olson, *20th Century Theology: God and the World in a Transitional Age* (Downers Grove, IL: InterVarsity Press, 1992).

[18] For a survey of this movement see Gerhard F. Hasel, "The Nature of Biblical Theology: Recent Trends and Issues," *Andrews University Seminary Studies* 32:3 (1994); 211–214; and James Barr, "Biblical Theology," in *Interpreter's Dictionary of the Bible: Supplementary Volume*, ed. K. Crim (Nashville: Abingdon, 1976), 104–106.

[19] For this assessment see Carson, "Systematic Theology and Biblical Theology," 90. Carson writes, "With more and more emphasis on close study of individual texts, and with less and less emphasis on serious reflection on the relationship of these findings to historic Christian faith, the tendency was toward atomization. . . . the tendency was away from whole-Bible biblical theology, and toward Old Testament theology and New Testament theology. By the 20th century, these works most commonly divided up their subject matter into smaller corpora (Pauline theology; Matthean theology; Q-theology; theology of the major prophets; *etc.*) or into organizing structures (the covenant for W. Eichrodt; a specialized understanding of salvation history for G. von Rad; a form of existentialism for R. Bultmann; *etc.*)." But what they did not produce were whole-Bible theologies which sought to unpack the unity of God's plan amidst its diversity.

grand scale if one denies the full authority of Scripture and dismisses the historic Christian theology that grounds this view.[20]

Today in non-evangelical theology there are a variety of options that attempt to read Scripture as a unified whole, but most of them are weak on Scripture and do not operate under consistent Christian assumptions.[21] This is why for most non-evangelicals "biblical theology" in the sense of doing a "whole-Bible" theology is viewed as impossible. Given their rejection of the unity of Scripture as a divine revelation and the methodological naturalistic assumptions of the historical-critical method which questions the integrity of the narrative of biblical history, Scripture is viewed, more often than not, simply as an anthology of religious writings put together by the religious communities of Israel and the church.

In our opinion, this is *not* the proper way to *view*, let alone to *do* biblical theology. Already this approach to biblical theology stands in antithesis to historic Christian theological convictions, especially in regard to theology proper and the doctrine of Scripture. In the history of the church, and particularly in the post-Reformation and post-Enlightenment era, there was another path taken which provides a legitimate way to view and do biblical theology. This path also emphasised a renewed attempt to root the Bible in history by stressing the "literal sense" (*sensus literalis*) tied to the intention(s) of the divine and human author(s), and by seeking to discern how God had disclosed himself through the biblical authors across redemptive-history, grounded in a larger Christian theology and worldview. Mention has already been made of Johannes Cocceius, who sought to read Scripture in terms of the focus on "covenant" throughout redemptive-history, and who operated

---

[20] For a more detailed discussion of these movements see the articles by Scobie, "History of Biblical Theology," 11–20; Vanhoozer, "Exegesis and Hermeneutics," 52–64; Carson, "Systematic Theology and Biblical Theology," in *NDBT*, 89–104; also see David L. Baker, *Two Testaments, One Bible: The Theological Relationship between the Old and New Testaments*, 3rd ed. (Downers Grove, IL: InterVarsity Press, 2010), 42–165. On the contribution of Geerhardus Vos, see Fesko, "On the Antiquity of Biblical Theology," 449–453.

[21] One can think of the recent movement known as the "Theological Interpretation of Scripture" (TIS). This movement is fairly diverse and encompasses evangelicals and non-evangelicals alike. For the non-evangelicals, generally speaking, their commitment to the unity of Scripture is not tied to Scripture's own self-attestation as God's Word written but to decisions of the church to choose these texts as Scripture. In this regard, one thinks of the canonical approach of Brevard Childs, who chooses to read texts in their final form and canonical shape. However, as Paul Noble, *The Canonical Approach: A Critical Reconstruction of the Hermeneutics of Brevard S. Childs* (Leiden, Netherlands: Brill Academic, 1995), has astutely argued, unless Childs grounds his preference for final form and canonical shape in the doctrine of inspiration and divine authorship, it is a view hanging in midair. See Vanhoozer, "Exegesis and Hermeneutics," 60–61, who makes this same point. See also a more detailed critique of post-liberalism and their view and use of Scripture in Kevin J. Vanhoozer, *The Drama of Doctrine: A Canonical Linguistic Approach to Christian Doctrine* (Louisville: Westminster John Knox, 2005). For a helpful introduction to the TIS movement see Daniel J. Treier, *Introducing Theological Interpretation of Scripture: Recovering a Christian Practice* (Grand Rapids, MI: Baker, 2008). As helpful as TIS is in its attempt to recapture the voice of Scripture for the church, given that it is comprised of such a diverse number of people with such divergent views of Scripture, one wonders how long it can be sustained without a return to orthodox convictions and theology.

self-consciously within Christian theological presuppositions. However, this was also true of John Calvin before him and the post-Reformation Reformed Protestant scholastics after him.[22]

Probably the best-known twentieth-century pioneer of biblical theology, who sought to follow the path distinct from that of the Enlightenment, was Geerhardus Vos, who developed biblical theology at Princeton Seminary in the early twentieth century.[23] Vos, who was birthed out of the Dutch Calvinistic tradition, along with such figures as Abraham Kuyper and Herman Bavinck, sought to do biblical theology with a firm commitment to the authority of Scripture.[24] Vos defined biblical theology as "that branch of Exegetical Theology which deals with the process of the self-revelation of God deposited in the Bible."[25] In contrast to Gabler, Vos argued that biblical theology, as an exegetical discipline, must not only begin with the biblical text but must also view Scripture as nothing less than God's own self-attesting Word, fully authoritative and reliable. Furthermore, as one exegetes Scripture, Vos argued, biblical theology seeks to trace out the Bible's unity and multiformity and find its consummation in the coming of Christ and the inauguration of the new covenant era. Biblical theology must follow a method that reads the Bible on its own terms, following the Bible's own internal contours and shape, in order to discover God's unified plan as it is disclosed to us over time. The path that Vos blazed was foundational for much of the resurgence of biblical theology within evangelicalism, in the twentieth and now the twenty-first century.[26]

We reject the former view despite its label of "biblical theology." Accordingly, in light of this history, we define "biblical theology" by employing Brian Rosner's helpful definition: "Biblical theology" is "theological interpretation of Scripture in and for the church. It proceeds with

---

[22] For a detailed treatment of the post-Reformation Protestant scholastics see Richard Muller, *Post-Reformation Reformed Dogmatics: The Rise and Development of Reformed Orthodoxy, ca. 1520 to ca. 1725*, 4 vols. (Grand Rapids, MI: Baker, 2003). See also the application of some of the insights of the Protestant scholastics for biblical and systematic theology in Michael S. Horton, *Covenant and Eschatology: The Divine Drama* (Louisville: Westminster John Knox, 2002); and Richard Lints, *The Fabric of Theology: A Prolegomenon to Evangelical Theology* (Grand Rapids, MI: Eerdmans, 1993).

[23] See Geerhardus Vos, *Biblical Theology: Old and New Testaments* (Grand Rapids, MI: Eerdmans, 1948; repr., Carlisle, PA: Banner of Truth, 2004); idem, *Pauline Eschatology* (Phillipsburg, NJ: P&R, 1979); Richard B. Gaffin, Jr., ed. *Redemptive History and Biblical Interpretation: The Shorter Writings of Geerhardus Vos* (Phillipsburg, NJ: P&R, 2001).

[24] See Richard B. Gaffin, Jr., "Systematic Theology and Biblical Theology," *Westminster Theological Journal* 38 (1976): 281–299, especially 286–288 for his discussion of Kuyper, Bavinck, and Vos.

[25] Vos, *Biblical Theology*, 5.

[26] Vos' influence is directly seen at Westminster Theological Seminary in the work of John Murray, Richard Gaffin, Jr., Sinclair Ferguson, Vern Poythress, and so on. But it was also felt in the larger evangelical world in such people as Graeme Goldsworthy, G. K. Beale, D. A. Carson, T. R. Schreiner, and so on.

historical and literary sensitivity and seeks to analyse and synthesize the Bible's teaching about God and his relations to the world on its own terms, maintaining sight of the Bible's overarching narrative and Christocentric focus."[27] In this definition, Rosner emphasises some important points crucial to the nature and task of biblical theology. Biblical theology is concerned with the overall message of the whole Bible. It seeks to understand the parts in relation to the whole. As an exegetical method, it is sensitive to literary, historical, and theological dimensions of various corpora, as well as to the interrelationships between earlier and later texts in Scripture. Furthermore, biblical theology is interested not merely in words and word studies but also in concepts and themes as it traces out the Bible's own story line, on the Bible's own terms, as the plot line reaches its culmination in Christ. In a similar way, D. A. Carson speaks of biblical theology as an inductive, exegetical discipline which works from biblical texts, in all of their literary diversity, to the entire Canon—hence the notion of *intertextual*. In making connections between texts, biblical theology also attempts to let the biblical text set the agenda. This is what we mean by saying that we are to read Scripture *on its own terms*, i.e., *intratextually*. Scripture is to be interpreted in light of its own categories and presentation since Scripture comes to us as divinely given, coherent, and unified.[28] In other words, all theologizing starts with the Bible's own presentation of itself as we seek to live under its authority and teaching and not over it.[29]

With these basic ideas in mind, let us now summarise what we believe biblical theology to be. Simply stated, it is the *hermeneutical* discipline which seeks to do justice to what Scripture claims to be and what it actually is. In terms of its claim, Scripture is nothing less than *God's* Word written, and as such, it is a unified revelation of his gracious plan of redemption. In terms of what Scripture actually is, it is a *progressive* unfolding of God's plan, rooted in history, and unpacked along a specific redemptive-historical

---

[27] Brian Rosner, "Biblical Theology," in *NDBT*, 10 (italics removed from original).

[28] For these points see Carson, "Systematic Theology and Biblical Theology," 89–104.

[29] To start with the Bible's own presentation of itself, or to read the Bible *on its own terms* is at the heart of biblical theology. Even within evangelical biblical theology this point is not always followed. For example, some argue that biblical theology is the approach by which redemptive-history is divided into various historical epochs and then the development between those epochs is traced. Or, others view biblical theology as merely thinking through the large themes of Scripture. Still others approach the discipline by working through the Bible book by book. All of these approaches have their place but, in our view, they fall short. Their fundamental problem is that they do not follow the Bible's own presentation of itself, or, in other words, they do not carefully trace out the Bible's own literary plot structure. If we are going to read the Bible *on its own terms*, we have to ask, how has God given Scripture to us, what are the Bible's own internal structures, and how ought those structures shape our doing of biblical theology? We are convinced that working through the biblical covenants is tracing out the Bible's own internal structures and learning to read Scripture as God intended it to be read.

plot line primarily demarcated by covenants. Biblical theology as a herme-neutical discipline attempts to exegete texts in their own context and then, in light of the entire Canon, to examine the unfolding nature of God's plan and carefully think through the relationship between *before* and *after* in that plan which culminates in Christ.[30] As such, biblical theology provides the basis for understanding how texts in one part of the Bible relate to all other texts, so that they will be read correctly, according to God's intention, which is discovered through the individual human authors but ultimately at the canonical level. In the end, biblical theology is the attempt to unpack the "whole counsel of God" and "to think God's thoughts after him," and it provides the basis and underpinning for all theology and doctrine. With this understanding of biblical theology in place, let us now briefly reflect on what systematic theology is, before we think through the relationship between the two methods.

THE NATURE OF SYSTEMATIC THEOLOGY

As with "biblical theology," there are various understandings of what "sys-tematic theology" is. In this book, it is not necessary to delve into all of these diverse views; rather, we simply want to state how we conceive of the disci-pline of systematic theology.[31] As with biblical theology, generally speaking, one's construal of systematic theology is tied to one's larger theological, worldview commitments, and any differences between various definitions

---

[30] Two words that helpfully describe how biblical theology seeks to interpret texts first in their immediate and then in their canonical context are *synchronic* and *diachronic*. *Synchronic* refers to viewing events occurring at a given time (sometimes referred to as a "cross-cut" approach to interpretation). Hence reading texts synchronically refers to reading them in their immediate context. As we exegete texts we place them in their redemptive-historical context, we interpret them according to the grammatical-historical method, and we inquire about the theology of a particular prophet, book, or corpus. This is called a "cross-cut" approach because it involves our cutting across the progressive revelation and taking a look at what is going on at any given point in time. Biblical exegesis begins at this level as it involves an analytical examination of the "parts." But our interpretation of Scripture does not end here. The unity of Scripture drives us to say more, which introduces the notion of diachronic. *Diachronic* refers to viewing events over time (sometimes referred to as the "long-cut" approach to interpretation). Texts must be read not only in terms of their immediate context but also in terms of the "whole." Scripture is both unified and progres-sive. Thus biblical theology is concerned to read the "parts" in terms of the "whole" and to trace out how God's plan develops *throughout* redemptive-history, leading us to its fulfilment in Christ and ultimately to the consumma-tion. For more on this see Graeme Goldsworthy, *Gospel-Centered Hermeneutics: Foundations and Principles of Evangelical Biblical Interpretation* (Downers Grove, IL: InterVarsity Press, 2006), 268–272; and Lints, *Fabric of Theology*, 293–310, who likewise addresses the relationship between the "parts" and the "whole" in his discussion of how to interpret biblical texts.

[31] For a helpful discussion on the nature of systematic theology and its relation to biblical theology see Gaffin, "Systematic and Biblical Theology," 281–299. See also Gerhard F. Hasel, "The Relationship between Biblical Theology and Systematic Theology," *Trinity Journal* 5 (1984): 113–127. For a current discussion of systematic theology and how it is viewed in the larger theological orbit, see John Webster, "Principles of Systematic Theol-ogy," *International Journal of Systematic Theology* 11/1 (2009): 56–71; idem, "Systematic Theology," in *The Oxford Handbook of Systematic Theology*, ed. John Webster, Kathryn Tanner, and Iain Torrance (Oxford: Oxford University Press, 2007), 1–18.

can be traced back to this. For our purposes, we will employ as our basic definition the one given by John Frame: systematic theology is "the application of God's Word by persons to all areas of life."[32]

In our view, this entails at least two key components. First, in order to *apply* Scripture properly, we must first interpret Scripture correctly, which requires the doing of biblical theology, as described above, namely, unpacking the biblical story line and letting the Bible, on its own terms, describe for us how God's plan unfolds, centred in Christ. This is why we have argued that biblical theology provides the basis and underpinning for all theologizing and doctrine, since we are not doing theology unless we are correctly understanding the entire canon of Scripture and rightly applying it to our lives.[33] Second, systematic theology is more than just the doing of biblical theology since it involves the *application* of Scripture *to all areas of life*. Systematic theology, then, inevitably involves theological construction and doctrinal formulation, grounded in biblical theology and done in light of historical theology, but which also involves interacting with all areas of life—history, science, psychology, ethics, and so on. In so doing, systematic theology leads to worldview formation as we seek to set the biblical-theological framework of Scripture over against all other worldviews and learn "to think God's thoughts after him," even in areas that the Bible does not directly address. In this important way, systematic theology presents a well-thought-out worldview, over against all of its competitors, as it seeks to apply biblical truth to every domain of our existence. As a discipline, systematic theology is also *critical* in seeking to evaluate ideas within and outside of the church. Outside the church, systematic theology takes on an apologetic function as it first sets forth the faith to be believed and defended and then critiques and evaluates views that reject the truth of God's Word. In this sense, apologetics is rightly viewed as a subset of systematic theology. Within the church, theology is *critical* by analysing theological proposals first in terms of their fit with Scripture and secondly in terms of the implications of these proposals for other doctrines. In all these ways, systematic theology is the discipline which attempts "to bring our entire thought captive to Christ" (see 2 Cor. 10:1–5) for our good, for the good of the church, and ultimately for God's glory.

---

[32] John M. Frame, *The Doctrine of the Knowledge of God* (Phillipsburg, NJ: P&R, 1987), 76.

[33] We can also add that unpacking the biblical-theological framework of Scripture, on its own terms, then becomes our interpretive matrix (metanarrative) by which we interpret the world. All of our thought and life is subsumed under Scripture, so that we are continually transformed by the renewing of our minds (Rom. 12:1–2).

With this basic understanding in mind, what is the best way to think of the relationship between biblical and systematic theology? As presented here, obviously we view them as intimately related and central to the *theological* task to conform our thinking and lives to God's Word. As also noted, we think it best to view biblical theology as primarily a *hermeneutical* discipline since it is the discipline which seeks to handle correctly the word of truth (2 Tim. 2:14–15).[34] This is why the conclusions of systematic theology must first be grounded in the exegetical conclusions of biblical theology. But then systematic theology goes further: on the basis of biblical theology it attempts to construct what we ought to believe from Scripture for today, to critique other theological proposals within the church, and also false ideas of alien worldviews outside the church, so that we learn anew to live under the lordship of Christ.[35]

How does all of this discussion apply to what we are doing in this book? Basically we are setting forth a proposal for a better way of understanding the nature of biblical covenants and how those covenants relate to each other. In reality, we are doing systematic theology by first grounding our proposal in biblical theology. Our argument is that the traditional ways of putting together the biblical covenants is not quite right, biblically speaking. In order to make our case, we want to describe how others have put the covenants together, discern the key points of differences between the views, set

---

[34] In a similar way, Carson, "Systematic Theology and Biblical Theology," 95, calls biblical theology a "bridge" discipline since it is the bridge "between the texts of Scripture and the larger synthesis of systematic theology," what he calls the culminating discipline. This is a helpful way of thinking of the relation between the two disciplines. However, Carson, in his "New Testament Theology," in *Dictionary of the Later New Testament and Its Developments*, ed. Ralph P. Martin and Peter H. Davids (Downers Grove, IL: InterVarsity Press, 1997), 808, also tends to think of biblical theology as a discipline which works primarily within a temporal framework, i.e., the redemptive-historical unfolding of Scripture, while systematic theology primarily asks of biblical texts more atemporal and logical questions, "thereby eliciting atemporal answers." We are not completely pleased with this way of stating the relationship between the two disciplines. It is better to think of biblical theology as the hermeneutical discipline which allows us to draw *biblical* conclusions for systematic theology, and that systematic theology as the *application* of Scripture must stay true to the Bible's own framework, structure, and categories as she draws theological conclusions and constructs a Christian worldview. In this way, biblical theology is not only foundational to systematic theology but is also a subset of it, and systematic theology does not necessarily have to organise itself in atemporal categories.

[35] Goldsworthy, *Gospel-Centered Hermeneutics*, 258–272, says something very similar as he speaks of the interrelationship and interdependence between biblical and systematic theology. He rightly argues that we should not view the direction from text to theological formulation in a straight-line, i.e., exegesis → biblical theology → systematic theology. Instead, he views the relationship more in terms of a "hermeneutical spiral." He writes, "From one point of view, biblical theology is what makes dogmatics [systematic theology] necessary. If it were not for the progressive nature of revelation, then all texts would stand in the same general relationship to the believer. Dogmatics is the discipline of saying what the total redemptive and revealing activity of God means for us now. It recognises that all texts do not stand in the same relationship to us now, but that in view of the unity of revelation they do stand in some identifiable relationship to all other texts and therefore to us. Biblical theology examines the diversity within the unity. . . . The dogmatic basis of biblical theology lies in the fact that no empirical datum of exegesis has independent meaning, and no datum of theology or interpretation has independent meaning" (270–271). Systematic theology, then, is rooted in biblical theology but it is different in the sense that it is the final product of what we believe as the church and what we say to the world.

over against those views an alternative theological proposal, and argue that our proposal makes better sense of the entire canon of Scripture. In addition, we want to argue that the theological conclusions drawn from other ways of "putting together" the covenants go awry at a number of points and that ultimately, in order to correct this, we must return anew to Scripture and make sure our understanding of the covenants is true to how Scripture unpacks those covenantal relations across redemptive-history.

Let us now turn to this task by first setting the context for our proposal. We will begin in chapter 2 by describing the two predominant biblical-theological systems within evangelical theology in order to understand the nature of the biblical covenants and their relations to each other, which will be the subject matter of chapter 3.

Chapter Two

COVENANTS IN BIBLICAL-THEOLOGICAL SYSTEMS: DISPENSATIONAL AND COVENANT THEOLOGY

Within evangelical theology, dispensational and covenant theology largely frame how people "put together" their Bible and, as such, function as dominant theological viewpoints. Each "system" serves as an interpretive grid for understanding the story line of Scripture and thus functions as "whole-Bible theologies" (i.e., biblical theologies) which lead to systematic theological conclusions. In this way, both views are similar in their attempt to discern the overall unity of God's revelation, from creation to the new creation. Despite their differences, both views acknowledge some notion of "progressive revelation," redemptive epochs (or "dispensations"), fulfilment in Christ, change in God's plan across redemptive-history, and so on. They differ, however, over the specifics of God's plan, the kind of changes that result, and especially over the role of national Israel in that plan. Obviously, one must be careful *not* to overplay the differences between these views, for when it comes to a basic understanding of the gospel, they agree more than they disagree. At crucial points, however, they differ on how to think through the "whole counsel of God," and much of that disagreement centres on their understanding of the nature of the biblical covenants and their relationships to each other. This is why it is helpful to compare and contrast them in order to discover precisely how they relate the biblical covenants one to another and thus where the two views differ from each other.

Additionally, in order to provide a context to our proposal of "kingdom through covenant" as a better way of unfolding the biblical covenants, it is helpful to set our view over against these two biblical-systematic theologies. If we disagree with each view at various points, we need to know where and why. Thus, in what follows, even though our discussion of each view is brief, we have a twofold goal. First, we want to demonstrate how central one's understanding of biblical covenants is to each view. Second, we want to set the stage for an alternative way of thinking through the relationships of the biblical covenants as they find their *telos* in Christ.

DISPENSATIONALISM AND ITS VARIETIES[4]

Dispensationalism as a movement first took shape in the Brethren movement in early nineteenth-century England.[2] Originally it was associated with such names as John Darby (1800–1882), Benjamin Newton (1807–1899), and George Müller (1805–1898), and in North America with such names as D. L. Moody (1837–1899), J. R. Graves (1820–1893), and C. I. Scofield (1843–1921) and the famous *Scofield Reference Bible*, which provided various notes for its readers on how to interpret Scripture and put the whole Canon together through the lens of dispensational theology. Probably the most extensive systematic theology written from a dispensational viewpoint was Lewis Sperry Chafer's eight-volume *Systematic Theology*.[3]

Over the years, dispensational theology has gone through a number of revisions even though it remains united by a common core, which we will discuss below. As Craig Blaising observes about the movement, "There has been no standard creed freezing its theological development at some arbitrary point in history,"[4] even though it continues to maintain specific doctrinal distinctives.[5] This has made it difficult to classify all the differences among dispensationalists, yet, as Blaising notes, we can classify "three broad forms of

---

[1] For helpful summaries of dispensational theology see Craig A. Blaising and Darrell L. Bock, *Progressive Dispensationalism* (Wheaton, IL: BridgePoint, 1993); Craig A. Blaising and Darrell L. Bock, eds., *Dispensationalism, Israel, and the Church: A Search for Definition* (Grand Rapids, MI: Zondervan, 1992); Robert L. Saucy, *The Case for Progressive Dispensationalism* (Grand Rapids, MI: Zondervan, 1993); Herbert W. Bateman IV, ed., *Three Central Issues in Contemporary Dispensationalism: A Comparison of Traditional and Progressive Views* (Grand Rapids, MI: Kregel, 1999); Wesley R. Willis and John R. Master, eds., *Issues in Dispensationalism* (Chicago: Moody, 1994); John S. Feinberg, ed., *Continuity and Discontinuity: Perspectives on the Relationship between the Old and New Testaments* (Wheaton, IL: Crossway, 1988); Ron J. Bigalke, Jr., ed. *Progressive Dispensationalism: An Analysis of the Movement and Defense of Traditional Dispensationalism* (Lanham, MD: University Press of America, 2005). For a helpful covenantal treatment of dispensationalism see Vern S. Poythress, *Understanding Dispensationalists*, 2nd ed. (Phillipsburg, NJ: P&R, 1994).

[2] On the history and development of dispensationalism see Craig A. Blaising, "The Extent and Varieties of Dispensationalism," in Blaising and Bock, *Progressive Dispensationalism*, 10–13; Charles C. Ryrie, *Dispensationalism*, rev. ed. (Chicago: Moody, 2007), 69–88; Ron J. Bigalke, Jr. and Thomas D. Ice, "History of Dispensationalism," in *Progressive Dispensationalism: An Analysis of the Movement*, xvi–xlii; cf. Michael Williams, *This World Is Not My Home: The Origins and Development of Dispensationalism* (Fearn, Ross-shire, UK: Mentor, 2003).

[3] Lewis Sperry Chafer, *Systematic Theology* (1948; repr., Grand Rapids, MI: Kregel, 1993).

[4] Blaising, "Extent and Varieties of Dispensationalism," 22.

[5] Ibid., 13–21, lists eight common features of dispensationalism which unite it as a theological tradition: the authority of Scripture, dividing up redemptive-history into dispensations, the newness and uniqueness of the church over against Israel, the significance of the universal church, a literal understanding of biblical prophecy, premillennialism, the imminent return of Christ, and a national future for Israel in the land of Israel.

dispensational thought"[6] which are important to distinguish in order to grasp the theological development of the view: "classic" (e.g., John Darby, Lewis S. Chafer, *Scofield Reference Bible*), "revised" (e.g., John Walvoord, Charles Ryrie, J. Dwight Pentecost, revised *Scofield Bible*), and "progressive" (e.g., Craig Blaising, Darrell Bock, John Feinberg, Robert Saucy, Bruce Ware).

The term "dispensationalism," similar to "covenant theology," can rightly argue for biblical support. "Dispensation" is a word derived from *oikonomia* (see Eph. 1:10; 3:2, 9; Col. 1:25), which means "to manage, regulate, administer, and plan the affairs of a household."[7] Behind this term is the idea of God's plan or administration being accomplished in this world and how God arranges and orders his relationship to human beings. "Dispensation," then, as Blaising explains, "refers to a distinctive way in which God manages or arranges the relationship of human beings to Himself."[8] Dispensationalists are probably best known for how they divide redemptive-history into a number of distinct "dispensations" and how, during each of these periods of time, they believe God works out a particular phase of his overall plan. However, as Vern Poythress rightly notes, there is a sense in which the word "dispensation" is *not* completely helpful for distinguishing dispensationalism from other views, since "virtually all ages of the church and all branches of the church have believed that there are distinctive dispensations in God's government of the world, though sometimes the consciousness of such distinctions has grown dim. The recognition of distinctions between different epochs is by no means unique to D-theologians."[9]

Most current dispensationalists also acknowledge this point. For example, John Feinberg agrees that one's defense of the uniqueness of dispensationalism is *not* tied merely to the word "dispensation," or even to the idea behind the word. If this were the case then all Christians would be "dispensationalists" in this broad sense, since everyone recognises that God's salvific plan across redemptive-history involves various "dispensations" and that, as his plan reaches its fulfilment in Christ, there are various changes that have taken place. Feinberg correctly notes, "Since both dispensationalists and nondispensationalists use the term and concept of a dispensation,

---

[6] Ibid., 22.
[7] See Craig A. Blaising, "Dispensations in Biblical Theology," in Blaising and Bock, *Progressive Dispensationalism*, 106–111; John S. Feinberg, "Systems of Discontinuity," in *Continuity and Discontinuity*, 68–69; cf. Poythress, *Understanding Dispensationalists*, 9–13. Technically the word "dispensation" is the anglicized form of *dispensatio*, the Latin Vulgate rendering of *oikonomia*.
[8] Blaising, "Extent and Varieties of Dispensationalism," 11.
[9] Poythress, *Understanding Dispensationalists*, 9–10.

that alone is not distinctive to dispensationalism. It is no more distinctive to dispensationalism than talk of covenants is distinctive to covenant theology. Dispensationalists talk about covenants all the time."[10]

This observation, then, raises the important question: what is unique to dispensational theology, especially given its diversity over the years? What is its *distinctive* feature, or, what is its *sine qua non*? Much discussion and debate has taken place over this question, and people answer it differently.[11] It is our conviction, however, that the *sine qua non* of the view is the Israel-church distinction, which is largely tied to their understanding of the covenantal differences between the ethnic nation of Israel under the old covenant and the church as God's people under the new covenant. For all varieties of dispensationalism, "Israel" refers to a physical, national people and it is *not* the case that the church is the New Testament replacement of historic Israel in God's plan of salvation, as, for example, covenant theology teaches. Thus, for dispensationalists, the salvation of Gentiles in God's plan is not the fulfilment of the promises made to Israel as a nation, particularly those associated with the specific land promise to them. Rather the "church" is distinctively new in God's redemptive purposes and it finds its origin in Christ and particularly in the baptism of the Spirit that Christ has bestowed equally upon all in the church at Pentecost. Thus, what constitutes the church as "new" are these blessings of the Holy Spirit connected to the coming of Christ which are *qualitatively* different from the blessings of the Holy Spirit in the Old Testament. That is why, for dispensational theology, the salvation experience of the person under the new covenant is qualitatively different from the salvation experience of the Israelite under the old covenant.[12]

It is for this reason that dispensational theology, given the Israel-church distinction, sees more *discontinuity* from the old to the new covenant vis-à-vis the nature of the covenant communities. Furthermore, coupled with the Israel-church distinction is God's unchanging promise to Israel of a literal land, ultimately to be fulfilled in the millennial reign of Christ. It is probably at these two points—ecclesiology and eschatology—that we see the greatest differences between dispensational and covenant theology.

---

[10] Feinberg, "Systems of Discontinuity," 69. In addition, Feinberg helpfully notes two other important points: (1) to prove "dispensationalism" requires more than showing the biblical evidence for "dispensations" (68–69), and (2) the number of "dispensations" one holds to is not essential to "dispensationalism" (70).

[11] For example, see the discussions regarding a proper definition of dispensationalism in such works as Ryrie, *Dispensationalism*, 27–55, and Craig A. Blaising, "Dispensationalism: The Search for Definition," in *Dispensationalism, Israel, and the Church*, 13–34.

[12] See Feinberg, "Systems of Discontinuity," 71–85, and Blaising, "Extent and Varieties of Dispensationalism," 13–21, who unpack the unique features of dispensational theology primarily in terms of the Israel-church relation.

With regard to ecclesiology, since the church is distinctively *new* in the divine dispensations due to the coming of Christ and the *newness* of the Spirit's permanent indwelling in the believer, dispensationalists view the nature of the church, along with its structure and ordinances, as distinct from the nation of Israel under the old covenant. For example, in terms of the nature of the church, contra covenant theology, dispensational ecclesiology views the church as comprised of a regenerate community, born of and permanently indwelt by the Spirit, and not as a "mixed" community of believers and unbelievers.[13] Furthermore, it is for this reason that dispensational theology affirms credobaptism, contra paedobaptism, since one cannot equate the sign of the old covenant with the sign of the new, given the fundamental distinction between Israel and the church and what the sign of baptism signifies under the new covenant. In contrast, covenant theology does *not* draw the same Israel-church distinction and instead argues for more of a continuity between Israel and the church, not only in terms of the nature of the covenant community (and thus similarity of salvation experience) but also in regard to the similarity in meaning of the covenant signs of circumcision and baptism. In all of these ways, dispensational ecclesiology differs from covenant theology's ecclesiology.

Regarding eschatology, given the Israel-church distinction and God's unchanging promise to Israel of living out her existence in a physical land ruled by the Davidic King (who we now know is our Lord Jesus Christ), dispensational theology affirms a distinct national future for Israel in a future millennial age. Much of the rationale for this is that the physical land promise given to national Israel under the Abrahamic covenant has not yet been realised, hence the need for a future millennial kingdom where the specific land promise to national Israel will be fulfilled in a manner distinct from the church. It is for this reason, at the popular level, that dispensationalism is often identified with a distinctive eschatology which has been promulgated through books, movies, and other forms of media.[14] By contrast, covenant

---

13 The "mixed" nature of the covenant communities refers to the belief that under both the old and new covenants, the locus of the covenant community and the locus of the elect are distinct. As we will note in chapter 17, on the basis of this "mixed" view of the church, covenant theology maintains the invisible-visible church distinction. In their view, the church is constituted of believers *and* unbelievers or, as covenant theologians like to say, "believers and their children"—children who may or may not be among the elect. Dispensational theology has argued for the unique, new nature of the church as a regenerate community and thus structurally different from Israel of old.
14 One has only to think of such books as Hal Lindsey, *The Late Great Planet Earth* (Grand Rapids, MI: Zondervan, 1973); idem, *There's a New World Coming* (Santa Ana, CA: Vision, 1974); Tim LaHaye and Jerry Jenkins, *Left Behind: A Novel of the Earth's Last Days* (Carol Stream, IL: Tyndale, 1996); and the entire "Left Behind" series of books and movies.

theology rejects a dispensational, premillennial eschatology for a variety of reasons but mainly because they believe that the land promise given to Israel is ultimately fulfilled in the church and the dawning of the new creation.[15] For our purposes, it is important to note that the differences between dispensational and covenant theology on these points is directly related to their different understanding of the Israel-church relationship and thus how they relate the biblical covenants to each other in redemptive-history.

Let us now briefly discuss some of the varieties within dispensational theology as described by the terms classic, revised, and progressive, and note how each one attempts to understand the relationships between the biblical covenants, especially in light of the Israel-church distinction.

CLASSIC DISPENSATIONALISM

At the heart of classic dispensational theology is a dualistic conception of redemption linked to God's pursuit of two different purposes, one related to heaven and one related to earth, and tied to two different groups of people, a heavenly and an earthly humanity.[16] In terms of God's earthly purpose in redemption, it is God's plan to redeem the creation from its curse and to grant immortality to an earthly humanity who will exist on the earth forever. This immortal earthly humanity first appears in the millennial age. It consists of those who are living on the earth when the Lord returns and reaches its completion in the new creation. They will not experience a final resurrection since they will not experience death, but they will continue to live on the earth forever. But alongside God's earthly purpose is his heavenly purpose, which is centred in a heavenly humanity. This heavenly people consist of all the redeemed from all dispensations (a transdispensational people) who have died prior to Christ's millennial return. They still await the final resurrection, and when they are resurrected they will experience a "heavenly" inheritance.[17]

Classic dispensationalists are also famous for dividing redemptive-history into seven different dispensations: Innocence (Eden); Conscience

---

[15] Covenant theology holds to a variety of millennial viewpoints, ranging from historic premillennialism to amillennialism and postmillennialism, but dispensational theology always maintains a distinctive dispensational form of premillennialism tied to their understanding of the Israel-church relationship. For a helpful description of covenant theology's treatment of the land promise, see Anthony A. Hoekema, *The Bible and the Future* (Grand Rapids, MI: Eerdmans, 1994).

[16] See Blaising, "Extent and Varieties of Dispensationalism," 23; cf. Poythress, *Understanding Dispensationalists*, 19–29.

[17] For a more detailed description of this point see Lewis S. Chafer, "Dispensationalism," *Bibliotheca Sacra* 93 (1936): 390–449; cf. Blaising, "Extent and Varieties of Dispensationalism," 23–24.

(fall to flood); Human Government (Noah to Babel); Promise (Abraham to Egypt); Law (Moses to John the Baptist); Grace (church age); and Kingdom (millennium).[18] They viewed these dispensations as *different* arrangements under which human beings are tested. As Blaising notes in regard to these different dispensations, "God arranged the relationship of humankind to Himself to test their obedience to him."[19] In the early dispensations, God gave promises regarding earthly life, but we failed, due to our sin, to obtain these promises. The present dispensation of the church is the first dispensation that clearly presents God's "heavenly" purpose, and as a result, the church, unlike people in previous dispensations, is to know that it is a heavenly people destined for an eternal inheritance in heaven. Given this view of the church, classic dispensationalists argued that the church was a parenthesis in the history of God's earthly purpose of redemption—an earthly purpose which was revealed in the previous dispensations and covenants.[20] In this sense, the primary purpose of the church as a heavenly people was to pursue spiritual and not earthly matters and concerns.

How did classic dispensationalists correlate the biblical covenants? Similar to all forms of dispensational theology, they argued that the foundational covenant of Scripture is the Abrahamic and not the Adamic (or covenant with creation), since they did not recognise such a covenant. In the Abrahamic covenant God's earthly purpose was primarily revealed as involving physical descendants who would become a great nation in a specific land, and Israel, as a nation and as the offspring of Abraham, was given the important role of mediating God's blessing to the Gentile nations. Classic dispensationalists did not deny that one could interpret the Abrahamic covenant *spiritually* (which they argued the New Testament does to reveal God's heavenly purpose), but they strongly asserted that in relation to Israel the Abrahamic covenant was to be interpreted "literally," thus showing God's early purpose for an earthly people.[21] The same point is asserted in relation to the other biblical covenants, which were all interpreted as "earthly" covenants (e.g., the Palestinian, i.e., the land promise to Israel, the Mosaic, and the Davidic covenants). Interestingly, their "literal" hermeneutic, when

---

18 See *Scofield Reference Bible*, note on Genesis 1:28; cf. Poythress, *Understanding Dispensationalists*, 21–22.
19 Blaising, "Extent and Varieties of Dispensationalism," 24.
20 Ibid., 27; cf. Poythress, *Understanding Dispensationalists*, 21–22.
21 Poythress, *Understanding Dispensationalists*, 24, nicely captures classic dispensationalism at this point. He says, "Scofield is a (*sic*) not a pure literalist, but a literalist with respect to what pertains to Israel. The dualism of Israel and the church is, in fact, the deeper dualism determining when and where the hermeneutical dualism of 'literal' and 'spiritual' is applied."

applied to the "new covenant" of Jeremiah 31, led them to affirm that it applied only to Israel and *not* to the church. As their argument went, Jeremiah 31:31 clearly states that the new covenant is made "with the house of Israel and with the house of Judah," and since Israel, as an earthly people, is *not* the church, it cannot apply to the church. What about when the New Testament applies the new covenant to the church (e.g., Hebrews 8–10)? They argued that it must refer to an entirely different covenant, which, as critics rightly pointed out, is a difficult view to maintain given the New Testament teaching at this point.[22] Ultimately, for classic dispensationalists, all of the biblical covenants, including the new covenant, find their fulfilment in an earthly people—first in the millennium and then in the final state—but they do not apply to the church. The new covenant, then, must not be applied to the church other than in a *spiritual* or *allegorical* sense. In this way, the biblical covenants are tied to God's earthly purpose for his earthly people and not to God's heavenly purpose or people.

This understanding of the biblical covenants was also linked to classic dispensationalists' view of the kingdom. Classic dispensationalism famously made a distinction between the "kingdom of heaven" (i.e., the fulfilment of the covenant made to David, in which God promised to establish the kingdom of his Son) and the "kingdom of God" (i.e., the moral rule of God in the hearts of his subjects). The kingdom of "heaven" begins to appear with Christ, but since Israel rejected it initially, the parenthesis age of the church was established. Ultimately the kingdom of "heaven" will culminate in the millennium and the final state, where it merges with the kingdom of "God" in the hearts of his earthly people.[23] Interestingly, this understanding of "kingdom" was the first thing revised by the next generation of dispensationalists.

REVISED DISPENSATIONALISM

Probably the greatest change that occurred within dispensationalism began in the 1950s with the abandonment of the distinction between the "earthly" and "heavenly" peoples of God. As Blaising notes, revised dispensationalists "did not believe that there would be an eternal distinction between one humanity in heaven and another on the new earth."[24] In its place, they argued

---

[22] See Blaising, "Extent and Varieties of Dispensationalism," 28–29. One has only to note how Jesus applies the new covenant to his death and thus to the church (Matt. 26:27–28, par.), let alone the book of Hebrews (Hebrews 7–10).
[23] For a more detailed treatment of the relationship between the kingdom and the covenants in classic dispensationalism, see Blaising, "Extent and Varieties of Dispensationalism," 30–31.
[24] Ibid., 31.

for two peoples of God along more dispensational lines, namely, "Israel" as an ethnic, national entity tied to the covenants of the Old Testament, and the "church" as a distinct international community. In this way, people belonged to either one or the other, but not to both at the same time, and each group was "structured differently, with different dispensational prerogatives and responsibilities."[25] Revised dispensationalists were also quick to point out that the salvation each group ultimately received was the same (thus avoiding the charge of two plans of salvation), namely, eternal life in a glorified, resurrection state, yet they maintained an eternal distinction between the two groups, since "the church is always church, Israel is always Israel."[26]

In addition, revised dispensationalists simplified their understanding of the number of dispensations across time. Even though most retained the classic understanding of seven dispensations, they primarily distinguished between God's purposes in the dispensations prior to grace (i.e., prior to the church), the dispensation of grace (i.e., the church age), and the kingdom viewed as the millennial reign of Christ on earth. In the era prior to grace, God worked through the nation of Israel to the Gentile nations. Through Israel, God achieved political, national, and spiritual purposes, but now in the church age, God's purpose in and through the church is primarily spiritual. Even though Israel's and the church's spiritual experiences are similar, it is not the same; the church experiences the qualitatively *new* reality of the baptism, sealing, and permanent indwelling of the Spirit—something not experienced by Israel under the old dispensation. But it is not only in salvation that we see differences between Israel and the church; it is also in terms of the *nature* of the church as a regenerate community in contrast to the "mixed" composition (i.e., believers and unbelievers) of the people of Israel. In all these ways, revised dispensationalists spoke of the differences between Israel and the church, and thus the discontinuity in God's plan of salvation.[27]

In regard to the biblical covenants there was also another crucial revision that took place, especially in respect to the dispensationalists' understanding of the new covenant and its relationship to the church. As noted above, in classic dispensational thought the new covenant prophesied in Jeremiah 31

---

[25] Ibid., 32.

[26] Ibid. Between revised dispensationalists there was a debate over the precise location of the eternal state. A. McClain, D. Pentecost, and H. Hoyt argued for a resurrected, glorified state on earth, while J. Walvoord and C. Ryrie argued for that state in heaven and not on the earth.

[27] For a more complete view of the Israel-church relation see Ryrie, *Dispensationalism*, 143–157, and S. D. Toussaint, "Israel and the Church of a Traditional Dispensationalist," in *Three Central Issues in Contemporary Dispensationalism*, 227–252.

(and in Isaiah and Ezekiel) was either only for Israel as a national, ethnic people and thus not for the church, or there were two new covenants: one for Israel (e.g., Jeremiah 31) and one for the church (Hebrews 8–10). The problem with this view is that it was virtually impossible to sustain biblically. How does one make sense of our Lord's understanding of his death as a ratification of the new covenant (e.g., Luke 22:20 par.), or the book of Hebrews, which clearly applies Jeremiah 31 to the church? It is at this point that revised dispensationalists rightly rejected the idea that the "new covenant" of Jeremiah was not for the church. No doubt, they continued to maintain, along with their classic colleagues, that the Abrahamic covenant was the foundational covenant and that tied to it were the Mosaic, Palestinian (e.g., land promise), and Davidic covenants, along with the new covenant, as earthly, political, and national covenants. However, they now admitted that the church was to be viewed minimally as the "spiritual" seed of Abraham (Gal. 3:16–29), and that the Abrahamic covenant was fulfilled *spiritually* in the church because the church is related to Messiah Jesus. Yet they strenuously argued that the national, political terms of these Old Testament covenants, particularly associated with the land promise, had to be fulfilled in a "literal" way, i.e., Israel must receive her land once again under the rule of Christ, the Davidic King, in the future millennial age. The Old Testament covenants, then, are all unconditional, and it is God himself, in his Messiah, who would bring them to pass. But, as Elliot Johnson says,

> God does not *replace* Israel in accomplishing her share when Israel rejects Him. . . . Nor does God *reinterpret* Israel's share . . . . Nor does God *expand* those who share in fulfillment of Israel's role temporarily when Israel rejects Him. . . . Rather, God *sets aside* the nation temporarily and incorporates believing Gentiles along with a believing Jewish remnant to continue the ministry of the Servant until He returns as the Son of David and the Son of Abraham for judgment and rule. *That ministry is based on the provisions of the new covenant* received by faith in the provision of Christ. . . . This setting aside of the nation-servant creates the discontinuity in the fulfillment of covenant agreements with Israel.[28]

In a similar fashion, as Blaising summarises, proponents of revised dispensationalism argued that the new covenant "was being fulfilled *spiritually* in the church today" but this did not preclude that "Israel would experience

---

[28] Elliott E. Johnson, "Covenants in Traditional Dispensationalism," in *Three Central Issues in Contemporary Dispensationalism*, 155 (emphasis mine).

the national and political aspects (the earthly features) of the covenant in the future,"[29] which, as we shall note below, distinguishes this view sharply from covenant theology's understanding of the Israel-church relationship.

This revised way of thinking about Israel and the church was an important change which eventually led to the church being viewed as "standing in the line of a *historical* fulfilment of the new covenant promise to Israel"[30] and not merely as a parenthesis in the plan of God. Interestingly, in this change, dispensationalists were moving slightly closer to covenant theology's understanding of the Israel-church relationship except that they maintained that Israel, as a national, ethnic people would still experience God's promises to her in terms of specific land promises that had not yet been realised in their fullness. Thus, in this revised trajectory, dispensationalists were now able to speak of the fulfilment of the promises made to Israel in a "literal" way, while simultaneously applying the Abrahamic and new covenant to the church in a "spiritual" way or fulfilment. It is at this point that we see one of the sharpest disagreements between dispensational and covenant theology. For dispensationalism, God's promise to Israel as an ethnic, national entity involves a "literal" land promise which is fulfilled only by God giving to this nation a specific land in the millennial age and beyond. For covenant theology, given their view that there is much more *continuity* between Israel and the church, i.e., Israel is the church and the church is the new Israel, the promise of land to Israel is also a promise of land to the church, which is now fulfilled either spiritually in terms of our eternal inheritance, or more commonly today, typologically in the new creation, which is now "already" here in Christ, but which still awaits the "not yet."

Finally, it is important to mention how revised dispensationalists modified their understanding of the "kingdom" with respect to their classic colleagues. The classic view had made a sharp distinction between the "kingdom of heaven" (i.e., earthly kingdom) and the "kingdom of God" (i.e., the spiritual, moral rule in God's people). However, due to the influence of George Ladd, the classic distinction was dropped. Even though there were a number of alternative kingdom views proposed, most began to talk in terms of the "universal" kingdom (i.e., God's sovereignty over all things) and the "mediatorial" kingdom (i.e., God's rule over the earth through a God-chosen

---

[29] Blaising, "Extent and Varieties of Dispensationalism," 38.
[30] Ibid. 38.

mediator such as the Davidic kings and ultimately culminating in Christ). In terms of the latter kingdom, most argued that since Christ was not presently on earth, the mediatorial kingdom will appear again only when Christ returns, and after the millennial reign we will see the universal and mediatorial kingdoms become one. However, Charles Ryrie and John Walvoord began to speak of a *spiritual* kingdom in this present dispensation, i.e., the rule of Christ over believers today in the church, even though the political, national, and earthly fulfilment of the Davidic kingdom is not realised until Christ returns.[31] As Blaising notes, this was an important revision, since this allows dispensationalists to now begin to define "Christ's relation to the church as a kingdom,"[32] something not done by previous dispensationalists. It is this last revision which has paved the way for a further revision within the movement, a view to which we now turn.

PROGRESSIVE DISPENSATIONALISM

In contrast to the dualism of "classic" dispensational thought and the sharp separation of the church from Israel of "revised" thought, progressive dispensational theology argues that the church is more organically related to God's one plan of redemption. The appearance of the church, due to the coming of Christ, does not signal a secondary redemption plan, either to be fulfilled in heaven apart from the new earth or in a class of Jews and Gentiles who are forever distinguished from the rest of redeemed humanity.[33] Instead the church today is a revelation of spiritual blessings which all of God's people throughout the ages will share while preserving their distinctive ethnic and national differences.

The term "progressive" is used by its advocates in the progressive revelation sense, i.e., to underscore the unfolding nature of God's plan and the *successive* (not *different*) arrangements of the various dispensations as they ultimately culminate in Christ. In this way, progressive dispensationalists stress the *continuity* of God's plan across redemptive-history, and in this regard, they are much closer to how covenant theology understands the unfolding nature of God's plan, yet with important differences. Blaising describes it this way:

---

[31] For a discussion by Ryrie, see *Dispensationalism*, 182–183, and for Walvoord see John F. Walvoord, "Biblical Kingdoms Compared and Contrasted," in *Issues in Dispensationalism*, 75–91.
[32] Blaising, "Extent and Varieties of Dispensationalism," 41.
[33] See ibid., 46–48. Cf. J. Lanier Burns, "Israel and the Church of a Progressive Dispensationalist," in *Three Central Issues in Contemporary Dispensationalism*, 263–291.

The plan of redemption has different aspects to it. One dispensation may emphasize one aspect more than another, for example the emphasis on divinely directed political affairs in the past dispensation and the emphasis on multi-ethnic spiritual identity in Christ in the present dispensation. But all these dispensations point to a future culmination in which God will *both* politically administer Israel and the Gentile nations *and* indwell all of them equally (without ethnic distinctions) by the Holy Spirit. Consequently, the dispensations *progress* by revealing different aspects of the final unified redemption.[34]

However, progressives are quick to point out, in contrast to much of covenant theology, that as one moves across redemptive-history there is a "*qualitative* progression in the manifestation of grace" which underscores a fundamental *discontinuity* in God's redemptive plan.[35] That is why the dispensations are "not simply different historical expressions of the *same* experience of redemption (as in some forms of covenantalism), although they do lead to and culminate in one redemption plan."[36] This is also why progressives continue to view the church as a *new* entity in God's unfolding plan and hence different from Israel but *not* new as previous dispensationalists thought. Blaising comments,

> Earlier dispensationalists viewed the church as a completely different kind of redemption from that which had been revealed before or would be revealed in the future. The church then had its own future separate from the redemption promised to Jews and Gentiles in the past and future dispensations. Progressive dispensationalists, however, while seeing the church as a new manifestation of grace, believe that this grace is precisely *in keeping with* the promises of the Old Testament, particularly the promises of the new covenant in Isaiah, Jeremiah, and Ezekiel. The fact that these blessings have been inaugurated in the church distinguishes the church from Jews and Gentiles of the past dispensation. But, only *some* of those blessings have been inaugurated. Consequently, the church should be distinguished from the next dispensation in which *all* of the blessings will not just be inaugurated, but completely fulfilled (which fulfillment will be granted to the saints of all dispensations through the resurrection of the dead).[37]

For progressives, then, the church should be viewed in light of its place in redemptive-history. It is *not* the same as Israel prior to Christ; it is

---

34 Blaising, "Extent and Varieties of Dispensationalism," 48.
35 Ibid., 48 (emphasis mine).
36 Ibid.
37 Ibid., 49.

something *new*. It is tied to this dispensation, namely, the coming of Christ, and it is comprised of both redeemed Jews and redeemed Gentiles. Yet even though in this "new man" (Eph. 2:15), the church, there is only one people of God and as such there is no distinction in the salvation blessings they receive, God's specific promises to the nation of Israel centred on the land are *not* nullified. The prophetic promises given to Israel and the Gentiles will be realised according to each person's national identities. So, for example, a Jewish Christian today, who is a member of the church alongside Gentile believers, does not lose his relationship to Israel's future promises. Both Jews and Gentiles, now and in the future, share the same salvation blessings, but "the same redeemed Jews and Gentiles will be directed and governed by Jesus Christ according to their different nationalities,"[38] tied to God's promises to each nationality. In this way, progressives preserve the New Testament emphasis on the one people of God throughout the ages and the one plan of redemption centred in Christ, but also the fulfilment of the "literal" promise of land to the nation of Israel in the future age.

Interestingly, progressives, in order to support these differences from previous dispensationalists, began to argue that typology is more than merely a "spiritual" interpretation.[39] Similar to covenant theology, typology was viewed as that which "refers to patterns of resemblance between persons and events in earlier history to persons and events in latter history."[40] Thus, for example, the Davidic kingdom can serve as a type of the future, eschatological kingdom, or the nation of Israel as a type of the church. By moving in this direction, progressives were able to avoid such a sharp distinction between dispensations and see much more of the progressive, successive, unified unfolding of God's redemptive plan.

How does all of this relate to the biblical covenants? Progressive dispensationalists want to take seriously the unfolding, organic nature of the biblical covenants as they lead to Christ. Similar to earlier dispensationalists, they argue that the Abrahamic covenant, in all of its diverse dimensions, national and spiritual, is foundational to all the biblical covenants.[41]

---

[38] ibid., 50.

[39] See ibid., 52–53. Older dispensationalists equated typology with spiritual interpretation. Blaising gives the example of how oil was thought to be a type of the Holy Spirit in that the "oil" was symbolic of the Spirit. However, older dispensationalists did not view typology as a divine planned and purposed "person, event, or institution" which pointed beyond itself to something greater in God's unfolding plan and which over time came to be recognised as such.

[40] Ibid., 52.

[41] See Craig A. Blaising, "The Structure of Biblical Covenants: The Covenants Prior to Christ," in Blaising and Bock, *Progressive Dispensationalism,*134–135; cf. Eugene H. Merrill, "The Covenant with Abraham: The

It is through the Abrahamic promise that we learn of God's promise to bless all life on earth, including the nations. Following a fairly standard way of thinking about covenants today, based on covenant patterns from the ancient Near East, Blaising interprets the Abrahamic covenant as a "royal grant" or unconditional covenant in contrast to a bilateral or conditional covenant.[42] Even though Abraham is required to obey God and his obedience functions "as *the means* by which he experiences God's blessing"[43] and the commands to Abraham "condition the *how* and the *when* of the blessing,"[44] God's promise is guaranteed ("unconditional") in the sense that God has promised to take the initiative unilaterally to bless the nations by resolving the problem of human sin.

Additionally, given the foundational nature of the Abrahamic covenant, all biblical covenants must be viewed in relation to it. God's blessing and the mediation of that blessing is passed to Abraham's descendants as they are chosen by God to inherit the covenant. In the Mosaic covenant, which Blaising views, along with much of contemporary scholarship, as a "bilateral" or "conditional" covenant, a new dispensation for blessing is established.[45] The descendants of Abraham through Isaac and Jacob are constituted as a nation, a nation which is to function as the means by which the blessing of God is brought to the nations. However, given the bilateral nature of the covenant, it is possible for Israel to break the covenant by their dis-

---

Keystone of Biblical Architecture," *Journal of Dispensational Theology* 12 (2008): 5–17; Darrell L. Bock, "Covenants in Progressive Dispensationalism," in *Three Crucial Issues in Contemporary Dispensationalism*, 169–203. Blaising begins his analysis of the structure of the biblical covenants with the Noahic covenant although recognising the links to the divine intentions in Genesis 1–2 ("Structure of Biblical Covenants," 128–129). However, Merrill does recognise an Adamic covenant in Genesis 1:26–28. See Eugene H. Merrill, *Everlasting Dominion: A Theology of the Old Testament* (Nashville: B&H, 2006), 239–241; and idem, "Covenant and the Kingdom: Genesis 1–3 as Foundation for Biblical Theology," *Criswell Theological Review* 1/2 (1987): 295–308.

[42] A "royal grant" covenant is an "unconditional" or "unilateral" covenant. The king enters into a relationship with his subjects and guarantees a certain gift to his subjects regardless of whether or not they obey. In contrast, a "bilateral" or "conditional covenant" is a covenant similar to the suzerain-vassal treaties of the ancient Near East. In such an arrangement the suzerain or king enters into relationship with his vassals or subjects. The king promises certain things to the subjects and the subjects in return promise to obey the terms of the covenant. They also agree that if they disobey the king, the king has the right to bring punishment upon them, but if they obey, then the king must keep his promises to them. Merrill also identifies the Abrahamic covenant as a royal grant; see *Everlasting Dominion*, 239; idem, "Covenant with Abraham," 8. For a more detailed discussion of these various kinds of covenants see Paul R. Williamson, *Sealed with an Oath: Covenant in God's Unfolding Purpose*, NSBT 23 (Downers Grove, IL: InterVarsity Press, 2007), 17–43; Meredith G. Kline, *The Structure of Biblical Authority* (Grand Rapids, MI: Eerdmans, 1975); cf. George E. Mendenhall, *Law and Covenant in Israel and the Ancient Near East* (Pittsburgh: The Biblical Colloquium, 1955).

[43] Blaising, "Structure of Biblical Covenants," 133. See also Merrill, "Covenant with Abraham," 10–11.

[44] Blaising, "Structure of Biblical Covenants," 134.

[45] A "bilateral" covenant is a covenant similar to the suzerain-vassal treaties of the ancient Near East. In such an arrangement the suzerain or king enters into relationship with his vassals or subjects. The king promises certain things to the subjects, and the subjects in return promise to obey the terms of the covenant. If they disobey, the king will bring punishment upon them, but if they obey, then he promises to keep his side of the bargain and bless them. In contrast, a grant covenant is an unconditional covenant in that the king guarantees a certain gift to his subjects regardless of whether or not they obey.

obedience and thus come under the covenant's curse, which, unfortunately, is what occurred in history and is what led to the exile. Yet, Israel's disobedience did not overturn God's unilateral promise found in the Abrahamic covenant to bless the whole world. As Blaising notes, "The Mosaic covenant is dependent upon it [the Abrahamic covenant]. This means that even though a certain generation (or generations) fails the terms of the Mosaic covenant and experiences the curse instead of the blessing, the opportunity still exists for a renewed offer of blessing to that generation or later descendants of Abraham,"[46] which is precisely what occurs in the later biblical covenants, especially the new covenant.

Under the Davidic covenant, which Blaising interprets, similar to the Abrahamic, as a royal grant covenant, "the role of mediating blessing was politically restructured as a function of the Davidic king. A covenant was made with David to bless him and his son(s) with rulership over Israel and the rest of the nations, an intimate and blessed relationship with God, and the mediation (even priestly mediation) of *blessing* to Israel and to all peoples and nations."[47] But given the failure of the Davidic kings, the prophets looked forward to the coming of a new dispensation in which a new covenant would replace the Mosaic and would bring the Abrahamic blessing to its ultimate consummation.

In this new covenant, then, God would bring about full forgiveness of sin, the giving of the Spirit, and a transformation of the people of God culminating in resurrection life. It is this new covenant which Jesus has inaugurated in his cross work for us. However, not all the promises and blessings of that covenant have been fully realized in Christ's first coming and thus it must be interpreted in terms of the "already–not yet" tension. As Blaising notes, "There are features promised in that covenant whose fulfillment has been delayed until the return of Christ (such as the national and territorial promises in Jer. 31:31, 36 and Ezek. 36:28 and 37:14)."[48] But since these latter features, specifically Israel's land promise, go back to the Abrahamic covenant, they still await their fulfilment when Christ returns. In this sense, the new covenant should be viewed as "*the form* in which the Abrahamic covenant has been inaugurated in this dispensation, and will be fulfilled

---

[46] Blaising, "Structure of Biblical Covenants," 144.

[47] Ibid., 173. For a detailed discussion of the Davidic covenant and kingdom promise, see Darrell L. Bock, "Current Messianic Activity and OT Davidic Promise: Dispensationalism, Hermeneutics, and NT Fulfillment," *Trinity Journal* 15 (1994): 55–87.

[48] Blaising, "Structure of Biblical Covenants," 202.

in full in the future."[49] But the present form of the new covenant does not exhaust the Abrahamic promises which still await their fulfilment in the future, when the specific national promises to Israel are finally realized.[50]

In regard to how progressives understand the kingdom and its relation to the covenants there is a lot of similarity, as we will note below, with covenant theology. For one thing, there is no major distinction between the terms "kingdom of heaven" and "kingdom of God." Further, as Blaising notes, in contrast to earlier forms of dispensationalism, "Instead of dividing up the different features of redemption into self-contained 'kingdoms,' progressive dispensationalists see one promised eschatological kingdom which has both spiritual and political dimensions."[51] For progressives the stress is on the eternal kingdom for understanding all previous forms of it including the millennial kingdom. Yet, unlike most proponents of covenant theology, progressive dispensationalists view the future consummation of the kingdom, i.e., the "not yet" aspect of the kingdom, as bringing about the specific promises to Israel as a nation in regard to her inheritance of the land, first in the millennium and then continuing in the eternal state. It is only when this takes place that the Abrahamic covenant is truly and fully realized and achieved.

SUMMARY OF DISPENSATIONALISM AND ITS VARIETIES

Over the years there has been quite a bit of development within dispensational theology, and in our view, for the better. Any theological view which is willing to correct itself by Scripture should receive our appreciation. But with that said, in order to clarify what is at the heart of these varieties of dispensational theology, we return to where we began. It seems that what is at the heart of all forms of dispensationalism is the "Israel-church" distinction. Hopefully this is evident not only from our description of the varieties of dispensational theology but also when dispensationalists themselves summarise what they believe are the distinctive features of their view. Even

---

[49] Blaising, "Extent and Varieties of Dispensationalism," 53.

[50] As noted above, progressives appeal to the "already–not yet" tension of inaugurated eschatology to explains this. In Christ and the arrival of the new covenant, God's promises "already" are beginning to reach their fulfilment, yet, as Blaising comments, "The fact that the fullness of new covenant blessing awaits the return of Christ is not surprising since the prophecies of the new covenant envisioned Messiah reigning upon the earth over a transformed people. Included in that vision was the political restoration of Israel in peace with all other nations" (Craig A. Blaising, "The Fulfillment of the Biblical Covenants through Jesus Christ," in Blaising and Bock, *Progressive Dispensationalism*, 210). But what is important to note is that progressives are convinced that there is still a future land promise for Israel tied to the Abrahamic covenant—a covenant which is irrevocable and not yet fully realized in all its promises.

[51] Blaising, "Extent and Varieties of Dispensationalism," 54.

though a number of features are listed, dispensationalists eventually return to the crucial Israel-church distinction.

For example, Craig Blaising lists eight distinctive features of dispensational theology and John Feinberg lists six.[52] However when these distinctive or essential features are probed deeper, either they are shown not to be distinctive to dispensational theology alone (e.g., the authority of Scripture, dispensations in redemptive-history, the newness of the church, or even premillennialism), or they reduce to the Israel-church distinction. Given this fact, it seems safe to say that the *sine qua non* of the view (in all of its varieties) is the Israel-church distinction. Furthermore, and intimately related to this distinction, there is the dual conviction that: (1) Israel, as a national, ethnic people, still awaits the "literal" fulfilment of the land promise in the future millennial and eternal age, which has theological implications for eschatology; and (2) "God's relationship to the church differs in some significant ways from the dispensation with Israel"[53] which has theological implications for soteriology and ecclesiology.

At this juncture it is important to ask how dispensationalists hermeneutically ground this crucial Israel-church distinction which is so central to their view. This question is especially vital in light of how covenant theologians will attempt to argue their view. But before we address some of these crucial hermeneutical-theological differences between the two systems we will finish the current discussion by describing the alternative biblical-theological view of covenant theology. We do so not only to set it over against dispensational theology but, more importantly, to set the larger context by which we will argue for a *via media*—"kingdom through covenant."

COVENANT THEOLOGY AND ITS VARIETIES[54]

Covenant theology, as a biblical-theological system, has its roots in the Reformation (e.g., Ulrich Zwingli [1484–1531]; Heinrich Bullinger [1504–1575], John Calvin [1509–1564]) and, in the post-Reformation era,

---

[52] See ibid., 13–21; and Feinberg, "Systems of Discontinuity," 71–85.

[53] Blaising, "Extent and Varieties of Dispensationalism," 15.

[54] For some introductory books on covenant theology see Michael S. Horton, *God of Promise: Introducing Covenant Theology* (Grand Rapids, MI: Baker, 2006); Peter Golding, *Covenant Theology: The Key of Theology in Reformed Thought and Tradition* (Fearn, Ross-shire, UK: Mentor, 2004); Geerhardus Vos, "The Doctrine of the Covenant in Reformed Theology," in Richard B. Gaffin, Jr., ed. *Redemptive History and Biblical Interpretation: The Shorter Writings of Geerhardus Vos* (Phillipsburg, NJ: P&R, 1979); O. Palmer Robertson, *The Christ of the Covenants* (Grand Rapids, MI: Baker, 1980); William J. Dumbrell, *Covenant and Creation: A Theology of the Old Testament Covenants* (Carlisle, UK: Paternoster, 1984); Vern Poythress, *Understanding Dispensationalists*, 39–51; Willem VanGemeren, "Systems of Continuity," in *Continuity and Discontinuity*, 37–62.

was systematized by Herman Witsius (1636–1708) and Johannes Cocceius (1603–1669). It is ably represented in the Westminster Confession of Faith (1643–1649) as well as other Reformed confessions.[55]

As the name suggests, *covenant* theology not only organises the history of the world in terms of covenants, it also contends that what brings together all of the diverse themes of Scripture is the theme of covenant. Michael Horton, in answering the question, "What brings all of the themes of Scripture together?" says it this way: "What unites them is not itself a central dogma but an architectonic structure of biblical faith and practise. That particular architectural structure that we believe the Scriptures themselves to yield is the covenant. It is not simply the concept of the covenant, but the concrete existence of God's covenantal dealings in our history that provides the context within which we recognize the unity of Scripture amid it remarkable variety."[56] Continuing to speak of the importance of covenants for covenant theology, Horton writes, "The covenant is the framework, but it is far from a central dogma. The various covenants are visible and significant, in some 'rooms' (ie., topics) more than others. The covenant of redemption is prominent in discussion of the Trinity, Christ as mediator, and election, while the covenant of creation is more obvious when we talk about God's relationship to the world (especially humanity), and the covenant of grace is most visible when we take up the topics of salvation and the church. However, whenever Reformed theologians attempt to explore and explain the riches of Scripture, they are always thinking *covenantally* about every topic they take up."[57]

Historically, covenant theology has maintained that all of God's relations to human beings are understood in terms of three covenants—the pretemporal "covenant of redemption" (*pactum salutis*) between the persons of the Godhead; the "covenant of works" (*foederus naturae*) made with Adam before the Fall on behalf of the entire human race; and the "covenant of grace" (*foederus gratiae*) made through Christ with all who are to believe, namely, the elect.[58] Covenant theology subsumes all of the subsequent bibli-

---

[55] Of course, no theological viewpoint arises without historical precedents. Thus R. Scott Clark, "Theses on Covenant Theology," in http://www.wscal.edu/clark/covtheses.php is right to argue that although covenant theology arose in the sixteenth and seventeenth centuries, there are elements of it in the Patristic era as well. See also Golding, *Covenant Theology*, 13–45, who discusses some early thinkers who move in the covenantal direction.

[56] Horton, *God of Promise*, 13; cf. idem, *Covenant and Eschatology: The Divine Drama* (Louisville: Westminster John Knox, 2002), for a more extensive development of this idea.

[57] Horton, *God of Promise*, 14.

[58] As we will note below, there is disagreement within covenant theology as to exactly with whom the covenant of grace is made, i.e., whether it is the elect alone or the elect and their children.

cal covenants under the overarching theological category of the "covenant of grace." It views the relationships between the biblical covenants in terms of an overall unity or continuity tied to their conviction that the biblical *covenants* are merely an expression of the *one* covenant of grace. No doubt, they acknowledge that throughout redemptive-history the one covenant of grace is administered differently, but overall it is substantially the same in all eras in history.[59] However, as we will note below, the nature of the continuity in the covenant of grace varies among covenant theologians, and as Vern Poythress correctly acknowledges, "Covenant theology has always allowed for a diversity of administration of the one covenant of grace. This diversity accounted in large part for the diversity of epochs in biblical history. But the emphasis was undeniably on the unity of *one* covenant of grace."[60]

It is for this reason, contra dispensationalism, that covenant theology has always seen much more *continuity* in God's plan across the ages, especially in regard to the "Israel-church" relationship. In fact, it is at this precise point that we see a major difference between these two theological systems which leads to corresponding differences in how each views aspects of ecclesiology and eschatology. For example, covenant theology has always insisted that God has one plan of redemption and one people of God and that the similarities between Israel and the church as covenant communities are significant. Unlike dispensational theology, "Israel" is viewed as "the church" and vice versa.[61] That is why covenant theology has argued that there is continuity between Israel and the church in many ways—e.g., the nature of the covenant communities as comprised of both believers and unbelievers (i.e., a "mixed" community),[62] the continuity in covenant signs (i.e., circumcision spiritually signifies the same realities as baptism), as well as sameness in relationship to the salvation experience of old and new covenant believers, with some modifications made for the final realities that Christ has achieved. In this way, within covenant theology, "Israel-church" are so linked that it

---

[59] See Poythress, *Understanding Dispensationalists*, 40, who makes this point.

[60] Ibid.

[61] If one asks the question, "When did the church begin?" dispensational and covenant theology answer differently. For dispensational thought, the church is new in redemptive-history and thus begins at Pentecost. For covenant theology, the church begins immediately after God's first promise of redemption in Genesis 3:15, acknowledging redemptive-historical difference but basically conceiving of the two communities as the same.

[62] As noted above, the "mixed" nature of the covenant communities refers to the belief that, under both the old and the new covenants, the locus of the covenant community and the locus of the elect are distinct, hence covenant theology's important emphasis on the "visible" versus "invisible" church. Against a believers' view of the church, i.e., that the church is constituted by regenerate people, covenant theology contends that the church is constituted by both believers and unbelievers or, as they like to say, "believers and their children"—children, who may or may not be a part of the elect.

becomes hard not to say that the only major difference between the old and new covenant people of God is that the New Testament "church" is a racially mixed and non-national Israel, and that the "church" is a more knowledgeable version of the old covenant people of God. But the work of the Spirit in terms of regeneration, indwelling, and sealing is basically the same across redemptive-history.

With this general introduction in place, let us now describe the basic contours of covenant theology, especially in regard to their understanding of the biblical covenants. We will focus on three areas: how covenant theology understands the nature and relations among the biblical covenants, the nature of the church in relationship to Israel, and the nature of the covenant signs in the old and new covenants. By focusing on these three areas we will then be in a better position to compare and contrast the differences between dispensational and covenant theology.

COVENANT THEOLOGY AND THE BIBLICAL COVENANTS

For covenant theology the theme of "covenant(s)" is probably the most important unifying theme in Scripture, but what precisely is a covenant? Throughout the ages, "covenant" has been variously defined, but we will use Michael Horton's definition as a place to start: "a covenant is a relationship of 'oaths and bonds' and involves mutual, though not necessarily equal, commitments."[63] For Horton, the emphasis on "not necessarily equal, commitments" is important since he rightly contends that in redemptive-history there is a "substantial variety of covenants in Scripture"[64] and not all of the biblical covenants are exactly the same. How, then, should we think of the relationship between the diverse biblical covenants? As noted above, the answer to that question is that covenant theology views the biblical covenants under two larger theological headings—the covenant of works and the covenant of grace—both of which are grounded in the eternal covenant of redemption.[65]

The Covenant of Redemption

Some theologians have questioned the use of the term "covenant" to refer to the eternal pact between the persons of the Trinity since Scripture is silent

---

[63] Horton, *God of Promise*, 10. See also Paul R. Williamson, *Sealed with an Oath*, 34–43, for a more detailed discussion of how to define covenant biblically.

[64] Horton, *God of Promise*, 10.

[65] For a helpful summary see Horton, *God of Promise*, 77–110; cf. Peter Golding, *Covenant Theology*; Geerhardus Vos, "The Doctrine of the Covenant in Reformed Theology," 234–267; John Murray, "Covenant Theology" in *Collected Works*, vol. 4 (Carlisle, PA: Banner of Truth, 1982), 216–240; and Robertson, *Christ of the Covenants*.

about such an eternal covenant and sometimes covenants are defined too narrowly.[66] However, Horton is correct to argue that, "If we hold simultaneously to the doctrine of the Trinity and unconditional election, it is unclear what objection could be raised in principle to describing this divine decree in terms of the concept of an eternal covenant between the persons of the Godhead."[67] Historically, this is precisely what covenant theology has done. Furthermore, as covenant theology has contended, one cannot deny that the triune God has an eternal plan which is then executed in history (e.g., Eph. 1:4–14)—a plan conceived before the foundation of the world, made known on the stage of human history, and which involves the work of all three persons of the Godhead. Scripture speaks of this plan in terms of the Father giving a people to the Son (e.g., John 6:39; 10:29; 17:2, 6–10; Eph. 1:4–12), the Son accomplishing that plan by his life and death (John 6:37–40; 10:14–18; Heb. 10:5–18), and the Spirit's work to bring those same people to faith union in Christ (Rom. 8:29–30; Eph. 1:11–13; 1 Pet. 1:5). Given this fact and given that Scripture speaks of these kinds of arrangements, plans, and promises under the category of "covenant," it is legitimate to think in terms of an intra-Trinitarian covenant.

When it comes to the covenants *in history*, covenant theology locates all of the biblical covenants under the theological headings of "the covenant of works" and "the covenant of grace."

The Covenant of Works

The covenant of works was made with Adam as the head and representative of the human race. To him and his entire posterity, eternal life was promised upon the condition of perfect obedience to the law of God. However, due to his disobedience, he, along with entire human race, was plunged into a state of sin, death, and condemnation (see Rom. 5:12–21). But God, due to his own free and sovereign grace, was pleased to make another covenant—"the covenant of grace"—with human beings (specifically, the elect) wherein

---

[66] If one defines covenants completely in terms of ancient Near Eastern suzerain-vassal treaties then obviously the eternal plan of God is not covenantal in this sense, since Scripture knows of no suzerain-vassal arrangement between the persons of the Godhead. As Horton, *God of Promise*, 81–82, rightly notes, "After all, each person [of the Trinity] is equally divine: there are no lords and servants in the eternal trinitarian relationship. Furthermore, there is no formal treaty structure to this covenant in Scripture—no historical prologue, stipulations, sanctions, and so forth . . . . Only an overly restrictive definition of covenant would seem to justify the claim that the covenant of redemption is speculative rather than biblical."

[67] Horton, *God of Promise*, 79. Cf. also Charles Hodge, *Systematic Theology*, 3 vols. (1852, repr., Grand Rapids, MI: Eerdmans, 1982), 2:354–373; Louis Berkhof, *Systematic Theology* (1941; repr., Grand Rapids, MI: Eerdmans, 1982), 265–283; Murray, "Covenant Theology," 216–240.

God freely offered to sinners life and salvation through the last Adam, the Lord Jesus Christ.

At this point, it should be noted that within covenant theology there is disagreement over the precise nature of the "covenant of works."[68] Some have sought to avoid the idea of "works" and instead opt for "covenant of creation" or "covenant of nature" to underscore the fact that grace is fundamental to any divine-human relationship including the relationship with Adam in the original situation, even though this is a minority view within covenant theology.[69] More commonly, Reformed theology has referred to this original arrangement as a "covenant of works" with Adam, the head of the human race, who was created in a state of integrity (moral goodness) but not glorification, with the ability to obey God and thus be confirmed in righteousness, yet also able to disobey and thus bring about a state of death and condemnation upon the entire human race, which unfortunately he did. This understanding of Adam's role is not only foundational for Reformed orthodoxy's understanding of the active obedience of Christ, who, as the last Adam, obeys God's commands (the law) and thus wins righteousness for us; it is also foundational in establishing the "law-gospel" pattern of Scripture. "Law" refers to the covenant of works and "gospel" refers to the covenant of grace, and for many within covenant theology, this becomes the means by which various biblical covenants are divided up: "law" associated with Adam and Sinai (i.e., the old covenant, which is viewed as the republication of the original covenant of creation) and "gospel," associated with Abraham, David, and the new covenant in Christ.[70]

It is important that this distinction not be misunderstood. Often the "law-gospel" contrast is understood in terms of a negative-positive relation. But as Horton explains, this is not correct. "In creation (and in the institution of the theocracy at Sinai), law as the basis for the divine-human relationship is wholly positive. In fact, this republication of the law is itself *gracious*, even if the principle of the two covenants (works and grace) fundamentally differs."[71] As this is applied to the Sinai covenant, even though it begins with God's act of liberation of Israel from bondage—a gracious and powerful act indeed—Sinai must still be viewed as primarily a law covenant, following the suzerain-vassal pattern of blessings tied to obedience and curses if the

---

[68] See Horton, *God of Promise*, 83–104, for a helpful discussion of the debate within covenant theology.
[69] See Robertson, *Christ of the Covenants*, 56; cf. Murray, "Covenant Theology."
[70] See Berkhof, *Systematic Theology*, 612; cf. Horton, *God of Promise*, 77–110.
[71] Horton, *God of Promise*, 88.

parties of the covenant disobey. God's way of salvation was always tied to his promises, by grace through faith, but Israel's national status in God's land depended on their obedience to the covenant; apart from that obedience, they came under the curses of the covenant.

The Covenant of Grace

As for the "covenant of grace" (i.e., gospel, promise), it began immediately after the Fall with the promise of grace in Genesis 3:15. This promise was then progressively revealed and fulfilled in history through variously administered covenants with Noah, Abraham, Israel, and David. Ultimately it was brought to fulfilment in the new covenant inaugurated by our Lord in his victorious cross work on our behalf. But it is important to stress that even though there are different covenants described in Scripture, there is, in reality, only *one* overarching covenant of grace. That is why one must view the relationships between the covenants in terms of an overall continuity. Randy Booth underscores this point in his comments on the "newness" of the new covenant. He says, "the new covenant is but a new—though more glorious—administration of the same covenant of grace."[72] Thus, under the old covenant, the covenant of grace was administered through various promises, prophecies, sacrifices, rites, and ordinances (e.g., circumcision) that ultimately typified and foreshadowed the coming of Christ. Now, in light of our Lord's coming and work, the covenant of grace is administered through the preaching of the Word and the administration of the sacraments. But in God's plan there are not two covenants of grace, one in the Old Testament and the other in the New Testament, but one covenant differing in substance but essentially the same across the ages.

At this point it is legitimate to ask, are there any changes in the covenant of grace across time? Covenant theology answers in the affirmative, especially in light of the coming of Christ. However, these changes are only changes that God himself has explicitly revealed to us, and even in these changes there is a basic underlying continuity from age to age. Hermeneutically speaking, unless God has specifically abrogated something from the Old Testament then it is still in force in the New Testament era. Interestingly, this hermeneutic is similar to dispensational theology except that each system employs it in different areas. For example, for dispensationalism the land

---

[72] Robert R. Booth, *Children of the Promise: The Biblical Case for Infant Baptism* (Phillipsburg, NJ: P&R, 1995), 9; cf. Murray, "Covenant Theology," 223–234.

promise to Israel, grounded in the Abrahamic covenant, has not been abrogated in the coming of Christ and is thus still in force, hence the fulfilment of it in the millennial age for national Israel. Covenant theology does *not* argue for the land promise in the same way,[73] yet it does appeal to the circumcision-baptism relationship in a similar way linked to the genealogical principle—"to you and your children." Circumcision, as a covenant sign, was given in the Abrahamic covenant and it carries over, now in baptism, as the new covenant sign, but underneath both signs is the unchanging genealogical principle. In the new covenant the sign of the covenant (baptism) does reflect one of the several administrative changes that have taken place, yet it still carries the same *spiritual* significance as circumcision in the old administration, given the continuity of the covenant of grace and the fact that the genealogical principle is not specifically abrogated in the New Testament. Booth emphasises this point when he writes, "under the old administrations of the covenant of grace, circumcision was the sign and seal of covenant admission. Under the final administration of the covenant of grace (the new covenant), water baptism has replaced circumcision as the sign of covenant admission."[74] Yet, even though the form of the covenant sign has changed, given the underlying unity of the covenant of grace, the meaning and application of the signs remains essentially the same in all eras.

For covenant theology, then, what is *new* about the new covenant, given its stress on continuity in the one covenant of grace? What is the main difference, if any, between the older and newer administrations of the covenant of grace? Within Reformed theology the answer to this question is not monolithic. However, despite various nuances, covenant theology agrees that the main difference is that of "promise-fulfilment," i.e., what the older administration promised through types, ceremonies, and sacrifices, has now come to fulfilment in Jesus Christ. It is with this understanding that most covenant theologians view the "newness" of the new covenant in terms of a *renewal* rather than a replacement or a strong sense of fulfilment that leads to a

---

[73] Covenant theology views the land promise in a twofold way: first it is tied to the Sinai covenant, which was broken by the nation of Israel. Horton, *God of Promise*, 47, states it this way: "It is hardly anti-Semitic to observe that the covenant with Israel as a national entity in league with God was conditional and that the nation had so thoroughly violated that covenant that its theocratic status was revoked. Dispensationalism . . . treat[s] the land promise as eternal and irrevocable, even to the extent that there can be a difference between Israel and the church in God's plan . . . . [This fails] to recognize that the Hebrew Scriptures themselves qualify this national covenant in strictly conditional terms." Second, covenant theology also views the land as typological of the new creation which has now come in Christ. On this point see O. Palmer Robertson, *The Israel of God: Yesterday, Today, and Tomorrow* (Phillipsburg, NJ: P&R, 2000), 3–31.

[74] Booth, *Children of the Promise*, 10.

discontinuity with the previous covenants.[75] That is why most argue that the new covenant administration simply expands the previous era by broadening its extent and application and bringing with it greater blessing, yet leaving intact the fundamental elements of the covenant of grace—hence the assertion of the continuity of the covenant of grace across the ages. Specifically, but not limited to these points, covenant theology views the "newness" of the new covenant in the following ways:[76]

> 1. On the basis of Christ's cross and through the application of it by the Spirit, a greater power of obedience is possible in the new covenant.
> 2. Under the new covenant there is an extension of the knowledge of God to all nations. In the new covenant more people will know more about the Lord, which fulfills the Abrahamic promise of blessings to the nations.
> 3. The promise of redemption is now accomplished in Christ with the full payment of sin. The old Levitical administration, along with the ceremonial law, has now been fulfilled.
> 4. The new covenant is the final manifestation of God's redemptive plan. There are no more covenant administrations to be revealed.

Interesting and very important for highlighting theological differences, especially in the area of ecclesiology, is any discussion of "newness" in the new covenant in terms of the changes which have occurred in the *nature and structure* of the new covenant community. For those who argue that the church is substantially different from Israel, as do many dispensationalists and those in the believers church tradition (including Baptists), what makes the new covenant "new" is that *all* those within the "new covenant community" are, by definition, people who presently have experienced

---

[75] See, for example, Booth, *Children of the Promise*, 51; Jeffrey D. Niell, "The Newness of the New Covenant," in Gregg Strawbridge, ed. *The Case for Covenantal Infant Baptism* (Phillipsburg, NJ: P&R, 2003), 127–155; cf. Walter C. Kaiser, Jr., *Toward Rediscovering the Old Testament* (Grand Rapids, MI: Zondervan, 1987), 25–26. In stating that covenant theology views the new covenant in *renewal* terms, I am highlighting their emphasis on continuity in the covenant of grace. No doubt, as I will discuss below, covenant theologians such as Michael S. Horton do talk about the "newness" of the new covenant in qualitatively different terms, especially when contrasted with the Sinai (old) covenant. As Horton, *God of Promise*, 53, states, "The point could not be clearer [from Jer. 31:31–34]: the new covenant is not a renewal of the old covenant made at Sinai, but an entirely different covenant with an entirely different basis." Yet it is important to acknowledge that Horton views the Sinai covenant more in terms of the covenant of works and not the covenant of grace. When it comes to viewing the new covenant in relation to the Abrahamic and other biblical covenants, which he believes are "gospel" covenants given their unconditional, royal grant nature, he does see much more continuity between the Old Testament covenants and the new covenant.
[76] These points are taken from a variety of sources. See Booth, *Children of the Promise*, 63–66; Douglas Wilson, *To a Thousand Generations: Infant Baptism—Covenant Mercy for the People of God* (Moscow, ID: Canon, 1996), 22–34; Niell, "Newness of the New Covenant," 127–155; Richard L. Pratt, Jr. "Infant Baptism in the New Covenant," in *Case for Covenantal Infant Baptism*, 156–174; Geoffrey W. Bromiley, "The Case for Infant Baptism," *Christianity Today* (October 9, 1964), 7–10; Berkhof, *Systematic Theology*, 299–301; and R. Scott Clark, "A Contemporary Reformed Defense of Infant Baptism," http://public.csusm.edu/public/guests/rsclark/Infant_Baptism.html, 1–29.

regeneration of heart and the full forgiveness of sin. Jeremiah 31:29–34 certainly seems to point in this direction, and it is here that various understandings of the nature of the church begin to part paths. Obviously this latter view of "newness" implies a *discontinuity* at the structural level between the old and new covenants, a view which covenant theology rejects given their understanding of the unity of the covenant of grace. That is why Reformed theology continues to view the church like Israel of old, i.e., as a mixed community which includes within it simultaneously both the elect (covenant keepers) and the non-elect (covenant breakers). Thus how one understands the *nature and structure* of the new covenant in relation to the previous biblical covenants is a crucial matter which needs to be resolved in order to make headway in theological areas that divide us, especially in our understanding of ecclesiology.

At this point, it is necessary to pause for a moment and address two important differences within covenant theology in regard to their understanding of the biblical covenants vis-à-vis the one covenant of grace. Both of these issues have been widely discussed within covenant theology. The first issue deals with the *nature* of the covenant of grace, particularly the issue of whether the covenant of grace is unconditional and/or conditional. The second issue raises the question, with whom does God enter into a covenant relation in the covenant of grace? Let us look at each of these issues in turn in order to highlight not only these different viewpoints within covenant theology but also important points that illustrate its overall position.

First, is the covenant of grace unconditional and/or conditional? For the most part, covenant theology has argued that the covenant is *unconditional*. God acts in a sovereign and unilateral fashion to establish the covenant. Furthermore, he not only sovereignly establishes the covenant relation but he also maintains and fulfills completely the promises that he makes to his people. In the end, everything God demands of his people in terms of repentance, faith, and obedience, he graciously grants them by sovereign grace in Christ and by the power of the Spirit. As Cornelius Venema nicely summarises,

> Not only are the covenant's obligations preceded by God's gracious promise, but these obligations are fulfilled for and in believers by the triune God—Father, Son, and Holy Spirit—in their respective operations. God's demands are born of grace and fulfilled in us by grace. In these respects, the covenant of grace is unconditional, excluding every possible form of

merit, whereby the faith and obedience of God's people would be the basis for their obtaining life and salvation.[77]

With that said, however, within covenant theology, and related to the above discussion on the relation between the covenants of works and grace, some have wanted to distinguish the biblical covenants further in terms of the unconditional/conditional category. For example, Michael Horton following Meredith Kline argues that the old covenant (i.e., Sinaitic or Mosaic) is predominately a law-covenant and republication of the "covenant of works" with Adam and is thus conditional, while the Abrahamic, Davidic, and new covenants are unconditional covenants. He argues this based on the assumption that the Adamic and Sinaitic (old) covenants follow the ancient Near East's suzerain-vassal pattern, while the other biblical covenants are grounded in God's unconditional promise to act unilaterally on behalf of his people. It is for this reason, now that the new covenant has been inaugurated in Christ, that the Sinai covenant is no longer in force, even though the Abrahamic covenant is, given its unconditional nature.[78] It is also for this reason that he argues, contra dispensational thought, that the land promise is tied to the Sinai covenant and is thus conditional. Israel, then, in disobeying the covenant, forfeited the land and as such, "its theocratic status was revoked."[79]

On the other hand, covenant theology has also argued that the covenant of grace (including the new covenant) is *conditional* in at least two senses. The first sense is in terms of the blessings of the covenant being totally dependent on the work of Christ, the last Adam, fulfilling the conditions of obedience first set down in the covenant of works as both the representative and substitute of his people. The second sense of viewing the covenant of grace's conditionality is in terms of the covenant obligations placed on us in order to benefit from the covenant, namely, the requirements of repentance, faith, and obedience. No doubt, these covenant obligations are not viewed as meritorious grounds for our justification; rather they are "necessary

---

[77] Cornelius P. Venema, "Covenant Theology and Baptism," in *Case for Covenantal Infant Baptism*, 211.

[78] For a development of this argument see Horton, *God of Promise*, 23–76. Horton, as did Blaising in his discussion of the covenants, follows a fairly standard way of categorising the covenants today: royal grant and suzerain-vassal. A royal grant covenant, as represented by the Noahic, Abrahamic, Davidic, and new covenants, is unconditional. They all represent a promise of God to fulfill unilaterally the covenant regardless of what the covenant parties do. On the other hand, a suzerain-vassal covenant is conditional and bilateral and thus dependent upon the parties of the covenant keeping its obligations. In this category Horton places Adam and Israel and their respective covenants.

[79] Horton, *God of Promise*, 48.

responses to the covenant's promises" and, as such, are "instrumental to the enjoyment of the covenant's blessings."[80] Even Horton, who strongly argues that the new covenant is an unconditional or a royal grant covenant, contra the bilateral covenant of Sinai, maintains both of these kinds of conditionality within the new covenant.[81]

It is at this place in the discussion that most covenant theologians contend that the covenant of grace always involves a "conditional promise" *"with blessings for those who obey the conditions of the covenant and curses for those who disobey its conditions."*[82] In principle, then, the covenant of grace, which includes the new covenant, is conditional in the second sense described above and is thus *breakable.*[83] It is at this point that most covenant theologians argue for the "mixed" nature of the covenant of grace, that is, the covenant community is comprised of both covenant keepers and covenant breakers. That is why, given the mixed nature of the covenant community, the circle of the covenant community, whether in the old or new era, is wider and larger than the circle of election.[84] For example, Horton insists on this precise point: the covenant of grace, including the new covenant, "in its *administration* involves conditions," since "It is a covenant made with believers and their children."[85] As Horton and all covenant theologians acknowledge, not everyone in the covenant of grace is elect. It is possible, as in the nation of Israel under the old covenant, to have those within the church who are believers as well as those who are unbelievers, with all of them being new covenant members. Appealing to the often-cited parable of the weeds (Matt. 13:24–30, 36–43), Horton and covenant theology argue that "not everyone who belongs to the covenant community will persevere to the end. Some are weeds sown among the wheat, seeds that fell on rocky soil or that is choked by the weeds. . . . Not everyone in the covenant of grace is

---

[80] Venema, "Covenant Theology and Baptism," 211. For a further discussion of this point see Berkhof, *Systematic Theology*, 280–281; and Murray, "Covenant Theology," 223–234.

[81] See Horton, *God of Promise*, 182–186. Horton argues that the new covenant has a vast array of conditions attached to it for final salvation. These conditions involve not only initial repentance and faith, but perseverance in both, as well as holiness of life. However, within the new covenant, since it is a covenant of promise, "everything that God *requires* in this covenant is also *given* by God!" (184).

[82] Booth, *Children of the Promise*, 24 (emphasis his).

[83] For a development of the "conditional" and "breakable" nature of every biblical covenant including the new covenant see Wilson, *To a Thousand Generations*, 81–96; Pratt, "Infant Baptism in the New Covenant," 169–174.

[84] On this point see Venema, "Covenant Theology and Baptism," 214.

[85] Horton, *God of Promise*, 182. Horton's more complete statement is this: "Nevertheless, the covenant of grace in its *administration* involves conditions. It is a covenant made with believers and their children. Not everyone in the covenant of grace is elect: the Israel below is a larger class than the Israel above. Some Israelites heard the gospel in the wilderness and responded in faith, while others did not—and the writer to the Hebrews uses this as a warning also to the New Testament heirs of the same covenant of grace (Heb. 4:1–11)."

elect."[86] In fact, it is due to this understanding of the nature of the "covenant of grace" that covenant theology argues for their "mixed community ecclesiology," which also grounds their argument for paedobaptism. In principle, they argue, there is nothing objectionable in viewing unregenerate people as part of the covenant community and thus to apply to them the covenant sign, contra the believers church tradition (and those in the dispensational tradition) who contend that baptism ought to apply only to believers, i.e., those who profess faith in Christ.[87] At the heart of this difference between these two ecclesiologies is a larger covenantal debate regarding the similarity and difference between the old and new covenant communities.

This understanding of the nature of the covenant flows directly into the second important issue discussed within covenant theology, namely, the question, in the covenant of grace, with whom does God enter into covenant relation? Given the "conditionality" of the covenant of grace, and the fact that not everyone in the covenant of grace is elect, who exactly are the parties of the covenant? Does God covenant with the elect only, or does he covenant with "believers and their children"—children who may or may not be the elect? It would seem that, given their view of "conditionality," the answer would be the latter, given the mixed nature of the community. However, within covenant theology, there has been a significant debate over this question. For example, the Westminster Confession of Faith (7.3) and the Westminster Larger Catechism (question 31) opt for the first option, namely, that God covenants with the elect only in the covenant of grace. Cornelius Venema succinctly summarises the Confession at this point when he writes, "In the strictest sense of the covenant as a saving communion with God, the parties of the covenant of grace are the triune God and his elect people"[88] and the condition of reception into that covenant is repentance and faith. Thus, all those who reject the free offer of the gospel stand *outside* the covenant of grace and, it would also seem to imply, they are also outside the covenant community.

If this is so, however, then why do so many covenant theologians argue that the covenant of grace also embraces "all believers and their children"—children who, we know in reality, are not necessarily brought to saving faith and thus may constitute the non-elect. This is what is referred to as the "dual

---

[86] Horton, *God of Promise*, 185, 182.
[87] See also Pratt, "Infant Baptism in the New Covenant," 170, for an affirmation of this point.
[88] Venema, "Covenant Theology and Baptism," 212.

aspect" of the covenant. As Venema correctly notes, "These theologians, while acknowledging that the life and salvation promised in the covenant of grace are inherited only by the elect, argue that the covenant promise, together with its accompanying obligation, is extended to Abraham and his seed."[89] How do we make sense of this seemingly contradictory answer? This is not a minor point. Theologically speaking, much of the argument for a covenantal view of the church and ordinances, especially its defense of paedobaptism, centres on this very issue. That is why a standard contention of paedobaptists is the following: "the children of believers were always included in the covenant of grace under the older covenant administrations. In deference to this established biblical pattern, *we must assume that, apart from explicit biblical warrant to the contrary*, the children of believers are still included in the covenant of grace."[90] Thus, infants, like their adult believing parents, are to be circumcised and now baptized because they are both members of the covenant community.

Regardless of whether one thinks this "dual aspect" of the covenant is biblical, especially in regard to the nature of the new covenant (an issue we will return to in chapter 17), what is instructive in this debate is how covenant theologians understand the relationship between the biblical *covenants* in relation to the *one* covenant of grace. The only way they can justify the "dual aspect" of the covenant, especially in regard to the new covenant community, is by viewing the "covenant of grace" (an overarching theological category) through the lens of the Abrahamic covenant (a specific historical covenant which includes within it national, typological, and spiritual aspects).[91] That is why the genealogical principle found in the Abrahamic covenant and linked to circumcision—"to you and your children"—continues *unchanged* across redemptive-history, even with the inauguration of the new covenant era. A common complaint against covenant theology at this point is that it tends to reduce the national (physical) and typological aspects of the Abrahamic covenant to the *spiritual* aspects, which, in turn, becomes the grid by which all other biblical covenants are viewed, specifically the

---

[89] Ibid., 214. For a further discussion of this "dual aspect" see Berkhof, *Systematic Theology*, 272–289.

[90] Booth, *Children of the Promise*, 10 (emphasis mine).

[91] Interestingly and a bit ironically, covenant theology appeals to the Abrahamic covenant similarly to the way dispensational theology does but with different conclusions. As noted above, dispensationalism argues that the Abrahamic covenant is foundational to all the other covenants and that, hermeneutically speaking, the specific promises which were given and not explicitly abrogated in the New Testament (particularly the land promise) are now still in force. Covenant theologians do *not* view the land promise in exactly the same way, but they argue in a similar fashion for the "genealogical principle" across the Canon starting with the Abrahamic covenant. We will return to this point in chapters 3 and 17.

new covenant. Thus, to speak of the "covenant of grace" is really to speak of the Abrahamic covenant reduced to its spiritual aspects alone. That is why in the discussion regarding the parties of the "covenant of grace," covenant theologians can speak of the "dual aspect" of the parties of the covenant, even though "believers and their children" is a genealogical formula specifically tied to the Abrahamic covenant (primarily interpreted in physical terms). This genealogical principle is certainly picked up in later covenants, but, as we will contend (along with the dispensational tradition), it is highly questionable whether there is no modification of it now that Christ has come and inaugurated the new covenant. Additionally, it is at this point that covenant theology also displays the tendency to marginalize the national elements of the Abrahamic covenant and to interpret them solely in spiritual terms—another point dispensational thought has criticised repeatedly.

Examples of the equation of the "covenant of grace" with the "Abrahamic covenant" abound in covenant theology. For example, Louis Berkhof admits that, at least in theory, the Abrahamic covenant has both national and spiritual aspects to it,[92] but in reality the national aspects of the covenant fall by the wayside and the *spiritual* aspects are treated as primary. That is why he can say that circumcision is "the initiatory sign and seal of *the covenant of grace*" (when in truth it is the sign of the Abrahamic covenant and not of all of the biblical covenants) and that "this covenant [Abrahamic] is still in force and is *essentially identical* with the 'new covenant' of the present dispensation"[93] with little regard for the redemptive-historical *distinctions* between the biblical covenants. Or, this is why John Murray argues that since "the new covenant is the fulfillment and unfolding of the Abrahamic covenant" and "the covenant made with Abraham included the infant seed, and was signified and sealed by circumcision," and "that circumcision is the sign of the covenant in its deepest spiritual significance,"[94] we are under divine command, derived

---

[92] See Berkhof, *Systematic Theology*, 632.

[93] Berkhof, *Systematic Theology*, 633 (emphasis mine). In fact, Berkhof argues that what is normative for Christians today is not the Mosaic (Sinaitic, old) covenant but the Abrahamic covenant (interpreted in light of its spiritual aspects). The Sinaitic, argues Berkhof, "is an interlude, covering a period in which the real character of the covenant of grace, that is, its free and gracious character, is somewhat eclipsed by all kinds of external ceremonies and forms, which, in connection with the theocratic life of Israel, placed the demands of the law prominently in the foreground, cf. Gal. 3. In the covenant with Abraham, on the other hand, the promise and the faith that responds to the promise are made emphatic" (296–297). In a similar fashion, R. Scott Clark argues that the new covenant is "new" because it is contrasted with Moses (old covenant), but not with Abraham (or Adam), and it is the covenant with the latter that continues in the new covenant ushered in by our Lord Jesus Christ. See "Contemporary Reformed Defense of Infant Baptism," 4. Cf. Horton, *God of Promise*, 40–57, who makes this same point.

[94] See John Murray, "Baptism," in *Collected Writings of John Murray*, 4 vols. (Carlisle, PA: Banner of Truth, 1977), 2:374. See also this same emphasis in Venema, "Covenant Theology and Baptism," 222; and Bryan Chapell, "A Pastoral Overview of Infant Baptism," in *Case for Covenantal Infant Baptism*, 11–18.

from the continuity of the covenant of grace, to baptize our infant children, thus making them full members of the church. In the end, what Berkhof, Murray, and most covenant theologians do is to strip the Abrahamic covenant of some of its aspects, identify it as a pure gospel covenant, and then equate it, almost in a one-to-one fashion, with the new covenant.

The huge question that remains, though, is whether this understanding of the relationship between the biblical covenants and the "covenant of grace" is legitimate. No doubt, within covenant theology, this construction explains why there is continuity across redemptive-history—even a continuity which helps establish their view of the church and her ordinances. But does it do justice to the biblical *distinctions* between the covenants which lead us to affirm some crucial covenantal *discontinuities*—all of which have massive theological implications in many areas, not least ecclesiology. Let us now develop in more detail covenant theology's view of the nature of the church as it pertains to their understanding of the biblical covenants.

COVENANT THEOLOGY AND THE NATURE OF THE CHURCH

We have already stated that covenant theology insists that, in the administration of the covenant of grace across time, there are many who belong to the covenant community, with all of the covenant privileges pertaining thereto, who are not among the elect. That is why covenant theologians have admitted that the circle of the covenant community is wider than the circle of election.[95] What is crucial to note is how this view of the nature of the church is directly linked to their understanding of the covenant of grace.

Intimately related to the unity of the covenant of grace is the unity of the people of God across the ages. Instead of viewing the relationship between "Old Testament Israel" and the "New Testament church" in ways that preserve an emphasis on continuity *and* discontinuity, covenant theology tends to emphasise the element of *continuity* at the expense of discontinuity, even though, it must be admitted, there are fine nuances within the system.[96] Randy Booth, for example, strongly asserts that a covenantal understanding of the people of God entails that "God has had one people throughout all the ages. Although this *one church* has developed through various stages, she is still the *same church*

---

[95] See Venema, "Covenant Theology and Baptism," 214; cf. Horton, *God of Promise*, 182.

[96] See, for example, the very nuanced discussion of the relationship between Old Testament Israel and the New Testament church in Edmund P. Clowney, *The Church: Sacraments, Worship, Ministry, Mission* (Downers Grove, IL: InterVarsity Press, 1995), 27–70; and Robertson, *Christ of the Covenants*, 271–300; and idem, *Israel of God*, 33–51.

from age to age."[97] One of the crucial ecclesiological conclusions drawn from this view is a justification for infant baptism. As covenant theology contends, if God, in the Old Testament, included "believers and their children" into the membership of the covenant community (Israel) then nothing has changed in the New Testament era (in the church). Booth draws this exact conclusion when he says, "*Since God has not changed the terms of church membership, new covenant believers and their children are likewise included in his church.*"[98]

This stress on the *continuity* of the people of God across redemptive-history reminds us of an earlier observation we noted regarding the *nature* of the church: covenant theology not only views the Old Testament covenant people of God (Israel) and the new covenant people of God (church) as one people, they also view the New Testament church, in its very nature, to be like Israel of old, that is, as a "mixed" community comprised of believers and unbelievers simultaneously. Thus, parallel to Old Testament Israel, the circle of the church is wider than the circle of true believers, born of the Spirit of God, united to Christ by faith, justified, and sanctified.

It is at this point in the discussion that covenant theology employs the famous "invisible-visible" distinction so important to their ecclesiology. The *invisible* church refers to the church as God sees it, that is, the elect—those from all times and places whom the Lord knows are his and his alone, perfectly and infallibly. In this sense, the church, whether under the old or the new covenant, is a spiritual entity, invisible to the natural eye—the one people of God throughout the ages. Louis Berkhof states it this way: "The Church is said to be invisible, because she is essentially spiritual and in her spiritual essence cannot be discerned by the physical eye; and because it is impossible to determine infallibly who do and who do not belong to her. The union with Christ is a mystical union; the Spirit that unites them constitutes an invisible tie; and the blessings of salvation, such as regeneration, genuine conversion, true faith, and spiritual communion with Christ, are all invisible to the natural eye—and yet these things constitute the real *forma* (ideal character) of the Church."[99]

However, it must be quickly added that the invisible church manifests itself in history in a *visible*, local form. As John Murray reminds us, "The

---

[97] Booth, *Children of the Promise*, 73 (emphasis mine). For this same point see Hodge, *Systematic Theology*, 3:549–552; Berkhof, *Systematic Theology*, 565–572; Bromiley, "Case for Infant Baptism," 8–9; and John Murray, *Christian Baptism* (Phillipsburg, NJ: P&R, 1980), 31–44.

[98] Booth, *Children of the Promise*, 73 (emphasis his).

[99] Berkhof, *Systematic Theology*, 566. For a similar discussion of the invisible-visible distinction as applied to the church see Booth, *Children of the Promise*, 88–90; and Murray, *Christian Baptism*, 31–33.

church may not be defined as an entity wholly invisible to human perception and observation. The church is the company or society or assembly
or congregation or communion of the faithful."[100] The church is a divinely
created bond between God and his people and between other human beings.
It becomes visible in the ministry of the Word, in the practise of the sacraments, and in external organisation and government.[101] But as a visible entity
it is a "mixed" one, including within it both believers and unbelievers.

How does this understanding of the nature of the church lead covenant
theology to draw the crucial theological entailment of infant baptism? As
the argument goes, since, in the Old Testament, infants of believing households were included in the *visible* church (Israel) by their circumcision and
prior to a personal profession of faith and, additionally, by that act were
considered full members of the covenant community even though they
were not yet regenerate members, the same is true under the new covenant.
Hence the rationale to apply the covenant sign of baptism to the infants of
believing parents even though these infants have not yet exercised faith, and
even though this practise disrupts the biblical order of baptism in the New
Testament, namely, first repentance toward God and faith in Christ, and then,
secondly, a confession of that faith publicly in water baptism.[102]

Obviously, covenant theology's view of the *nature* of the church differs
substantially from that of many in the dispensational tradition, including
Baptists, who identify themselves as part of the believers church tradition.
In a believers church view, at least in the one we will defend, even though
there is only one people of God throughout the ages, there is, at least, a
redemptive-historical difference between Old Testament Israel and the New
Testament church. No doubt there is a significant amount of continuity in the
one people of God, but there is a significant amount of discontinuity as well
by virtue of the our Redeemer's work which has inaugurated the entire new
covenant age, and who has brought to fulfilment all of the promises, types,
and covenants of the Old Testament. That is why, in this view of the church,
what is unique about the nature of the new covenant community is that it is
comprised of a regenerate, believing people, not a mixed people like Israel
of old. That is why Baptists, for example, view those who are true members

---

[100] Murray, *Christian Baptism*, 32.
[101] See Berkhof, *Systematic Theology*, 566.
[102] On the issue of the biblical order of baptism, namely, first conversion then baptism, and the close relationship
between the two, see the excellent treatment in G. R. Beasley-Murray, *Baptism in the New Testament* (Grand
Rapids, MI: Eerdmans, 1962), 93–305; and Robert H. Stein, "Baptism and Becoming a Christian in the New
Testament," *SBJT* 2/1 (1998): 6–17.

of the new covenant community as only those who have actually entered into faith union with Christ by regeneration, repentance, and faith, and as such are partakers of all of the benefits and blessings of the new covenant age. Furthermore, it is for this reason that baptism, which is the covenant sign of the new covenant church, is reserved only for those who have entered into these glorious realities by the sovereign work of God's grace in their lives. However, in contrast to this view, covenant theology argues for a "mixed" nature of the church tied to their understanding of the nature of the covenants. The members of the visible church are all those who "are marked out by baptism and actual membership in a local church"[103]—which, in the end, includes "all believers and their children."

What evidence is typically given for covenant theology's view of the church? For our purposes, there are at least three pieces of biblical and theological evidence often cited.[104]

1. The most foundational evidence is the appeal to the essential continuity of the covenant of grace across redemptive-history. For them, this entails two truths. First, it entails that there is only *one* people of God throughout the ages. Second, it entails that the nature of the covenant community is essentially the same. Hence, what may be said about the nature of the covenant community with Abraham and his children and the nation of Israel is also true of the nature of the new covenant community, the visible church, which includes within it both believers and unbelievers.

2. The corroboratory evidence given to support this claim is an appeal to the warning passages of Scripture, especially those warnings that speak of the possibility of apostasy (e.g., Heb. 6:4–6; 10:28–30). Why are these warning texts cited as corroboratory evidence? For the simple reason that these texts seem to imply that it is possible for a person to be a member of the new covenant community (i.e., the visible church), but then, sadly, to depart from the faith, thus demonstrating that they never were a regenerate, believing person even though they were externally and objectively members of the covenant community. Thus, whether one thinks of the nature of the covenant community in the Old Testament (Israel) or in the New Testament (church), it is essentially the same in both eras. That is why Old Testament Israel and the New Testament church may include within it the elect and non-elect, believers and

---

[103] Booth, *Children of the Promise*, 88.
[104] These three pieces of evidence are fairly standard in covenant theology literature. See, for example, Berkhof, *Systematic Theology*, 632–635; Murray, *Christian Baptism*, 31–68; Booth, *Children of the Promise*, 71–95; and Wilson, *To A Thousand Generations*, 13–96.

unbelievers, that is, those who by receiving the covenant sign (circumcision or baptism) are externally and objectively brought into covenant membership but who may never exercise saving faith. Covenant theology then applies this understanding to infant baptism and contends that there is nothing objectionable in applying the covenant sign of baptism to infants and viewing them as full members of the church apart from explicit faith in Christ.

Obviously, at this point someone could dispute this particular interpretation of the warning and apostasy passages. In fact, one could contend that this line of argument leads to the interpretation that it is possible for true, regenerate Christians to lose their salvation. After all, has not Arminian theology repeatedly argued this exact point from these texts?[105] Needless to say, covenant theologians counter by arguing that the Arminian understanding of these texts is unbiblical *as applied to the elect*.[106] The Bible does not teach that true Christians (elect) can lose their salvation. Ironically, however, they agree with the Arminian exegesis and conclusion *as applied to full covenant members who are not the elect*. Thus, in the hands of most covenant theologians, these texts do not imply that it is possible for the elect to lose their salvation; rather they demonstrate that "unregenerate members of the visible church can be covenant breakers in the new covenant"[107] and that the new covenant is a breakable covenant like the old. In commenting on the implications of the warning texts for understanding the nature of the church, Doug Wilson confidently asserts, "the *elect* and the *covenant members* are not identical sets of people."[108] Hence, accordingly, the warning texts of Scripture are corroboratory evidence supporting their view that the covenant community across the ages is a "mixed" community. Wilson nicely summarises this view when he writes,

> The baptistic assumption [those who reject a mixed view] is that the covenants are *unlike* in this respect. Some Old Covenant members were regenerate, some were not. All New Covenant members are regenerate. The paedobaptist [covenant theology] assumption is that the covenants are *alike* in this respect. Some Old Covenant members were regenerate, some were not. Some New Covenant members are regenerate, some are not. The paedobaptist holds that the *difference* between the covenants is that the promises in the New are much better—meaning that the ratio of believer to

---

[105] For example, see Clark H. Pinnock, ed., *Grace Unlimited* (Minneapolis: Bethany, 1975); and idem, *The Grace of God, the Will of Man* (Grand Rapids, MI: Zondervan, 1989).
[106] See Berkhof, *Systematic Theology*, 545–549; Robert L. Reymond, *A New Systematic Theology of the Christian Faith* (Nashville: Thomas Nelson, 1998), 781–794.
[107] See Gregg Strawbridge, "Introduction," in *Case for Covenantal Infant Baptism*, 4–5.
[108] Wilson, *To a Thousand Generations*, 34.

unbeliever will drastically change. The history of the New Israel will not be dismal like the Old Israel.[109]

3. Further supporting evidence to buttress the data already cited is found in the promise given in Acts 2:39—"for you and your children"—as well as in the household theme across the Canon, and the household baptisms in the New Testament (see Acts 16:15; 32–33; 18:8; 1 Cor. 1:16). Covenant theology is not bothered by the fact that there is no unambiguous example of infant baptism in the New Testament; rather they are convinced that passages such as Acts 2:39, alongside the importance of family relations in Scripture and the recording of household baptisms in the New Testament, provide a strong biblical warrant to ground the practise of infant baptism. Why? Because it is almost unthinkable that infants would not be considered part of the church through the covenantal sign of baptism given the continuity of the covenant of grace and given the importance of households and family solidarity in the Old Testament. Infants, in the church, especially of Jewish-Christian parents, would naturally be regarded as subjects of baptism, just as they were of circumcision in the Old Testament. Since infants of believers were always included in the covenant under older covenant administrations, then we must assume that, apart from explicit biblical warrant to the contrary, infants of believers are still included in the church today. We do not need a specific command to baptize infants nor do we need any unambiguous example of infant baptism in the New Testament. The principle of continuity leads us to assume that infants are included in the church unless we are explicitly told they are not. As noted above, ironically, this is a similar hermeneutical argument that dispensational theology makes, yet in different areas. Dispensational thought makes it in regard to the land promise while covenant theology makes it in regard to the genealogical principle, both of which are tied to the Abrahamic covenant![110]

Given what has been stated, it should not surprise us that this has important implications for how covenant theology views the nature and

---

[109] Ibid., 34–35.

[110] John Murray, *Christian Baptism*, 48–50, makes this precise point. He writes, " . . . are we to believe that infants in this age are excluded from that which was provided by the Abrahamic covenant? In other words, are we to believe that infants now may not properly be given the sign of that blessing which is enshrined in the new covenant? Is the new covenant in this respect less generous than was the Abrahamic? Is there less efficacy, as far as infants are concerned, in the new covenant than there was in the old? . . . If infants are excluded now, it cannot be too strongly emphasized that this change implies a complete reversal of the earlier divinely instituted practice. So we must ask: do we find any hint or intimation of such reversal in either the Old or the New Testament? More pointedly, does the New Testament revoke or does it provide any intimation of revoking so expressly authorized a principle as that of the inclusion of infants in the covenant and their participation in the covenant sign and seal? . . . In the absence of such evidence of repeal we conclude that the administering of the sign and seal of the covenant to the infant seed of believers is still in operation and has perpetual divine warrant."

function of the covenant signs since, given the continuity of the covenant of grace and the covenant community, it is assumed that the covenant signs (circumcision and baptism) signify the same realities. Let us now turn to this last point.

COVENANT THEOLOGY AND COVENANT SIGNS

Given the continuity of the covenant of grace and the covenant community across the ages, covenant theology also contends that the covenant signs carry essentially the same meaning. In fact, it is this understanding which is part of the overall defense of infant baptism since the relationship between circumcision and baptism is viewed in terms of *replacement*. No doubt, in replacing circumcision, baptism signifies that the promised era of the Old Testament has come to fulfilment in Christ. In this sense, the new covenant brings with it change. However, the basic underlying meaning and significance of circumcision and baptism is essentially the same thing.[111]

What, then, is the essential meaning of the two covenantal signs? Primarily the signs signify entrance into the covenant community and all the blessings pertaining thereto. Thus, for example, covenant theology argues that in the Old Testament circumcision was the outward "sign and seal" of entrance into the covenant of grace and the covenant community. It was a "sign" in the sense that it signified something; it was a "seal" in that it confirmed the binding nature of the covenant, grounded in God's promises to his covenant people.[112] Circumcision was administered to all infant male children when they were eight days old. However, circumcision was not effective on its own in any kind of *ex opere operato* fashion; it always had to be combined with faith. If it was not, one showed himself to be covenant breaker instead of a covenant keeper. This explains why many Israelites who were circumcised externally showed themselves in the end to be covenant breakers as they failed to persevere in an obedient faith. Furthermore, it was for this reason that one could legitimately distinguish between the covenant members (those who were externally circumcised) and the spiritual remnant or elect (those who were externally circumcised and internally regenerated) within the covenant community of Israel. What may be said about circumcision, so the argument goes, is also true of baptism. In the New Testament,

---

111 For examples of this assertion see Booth, *Children of the Promise*, 96–119; Murray, *Christian Baptism*, 45–68; Wilson, *To a Thousand Generations*, 39–80; and Bromiley, "Case for Infant Baptism," 8–9.
112 For a helpful discussion of "sign and seal" see Booth, *Children of the Promise*, 98–99.

baptism *replaces* circumcision as the covenant "sign and seal." In baptism, as with circumcision, we are brought into the *visible* church, identified with Christ, and considered full covenant members. But, as with circumcision, baptism does not effect a saving union in and of itself. It is only by God's grace, when God's Spirit makes us alive, grants us faith and repentance, and unites us with Christ that we experience true salvation—the reality to which baptism points. That is why, parallel to the Old Testament, even if infants are baptized under the new covenant and considered covenant members, they are truly the remnant or part of the *invisible* church only if they exercise saving faith in our Lord and persevere in him.

For our purposes, what is important to observe regarding this discussion of circumcision is that most of the argument attempts to demonstrate the *spiritual* meaning and significance of the rite.[113] Why? Because central to the covenantal argument is the *continuity* of the covenantal signs—a continuity that seeks to point to the *spiritual* realities of such things as regeneration, justification, union with Christ, and ultimately the cross work of Christ. Hence, for baptism to *replace* circumcision, it must be shown that both circumcision and baptism signify the same realities. But, to anticipate our argument in chapter 17, no one disputes the fact that baptism signifies *spiritual* realities won by Christ and applied to us as his people. However, the point of contention is whether circumcision, *in its Old Testament covenantal context*, conveys *the exact same realities* as baptism does in the New Testament. Does not circumcision also convey more—e.g., national, typological, and spiritual realities—which minimally demands that circumcision and baptism are similar in meaning but *not* exactly parallel? The only way to resolve this issue is to think through the relationships between the biblical covenants. In so doing, one must be careful of reading new covenant realities into the old without first understanding the Old Testament rite in its own covenantal context and then carefully thinking through the issues of continuity and discontinuity between the covenantal signs.

In covenant theology literature the *spiritual* meaning of Old Testament circumcision is usually understood in at least three ways—ways that

---

[113] Examples of this abound. For example, Louis Berkhof, *Systematic Theology*, 632–633, admits that the covenant made with Abraham has a national aspect to it, but then he turns around and contends that the Abrahamic covenant must be viewed primarily as a *spiritual* covenant, parallel to the new covenant, including the rite of circumcision. Or, as Randy Booth, *Children of Promise*, 99–100, contends, "The argument that circumcision had a purely natural or physical reference cannot stand the test of biblical teaching. Circumcision carried primarily a spiritual significance (i.e., justification by faith), and therefore may not be regarded as simply a physical sign of descent. It represented cleanliness (cf. Deut. 30:6; Isa. 52:1). Circumcision was an outward sign of the fact that God required a 'circumcised' or cleansed heart." Cf. Murray, *Christian Baptism*, 46–47.

ultimately link it to baptism under the new covenant, so that what may be said about circumcision may also be said about baptism.[114]

1. At the heart of the Abrahamic covenant is the covenantal formula— "I will be your God, and you shall be my people"—which speaks to the blessing of union and communion with the Lord. As a sign of the covenant, circumcision signifies and seals this blessing. Objectively, it makes one a member of the covenant community. The same may be said of baptism, which signifies that the recipient has objectively entered into faith union with Christ in his redemptive work.[115] This is not to deny that the recipient must still exercise faith before covenant blessings may be appropriated. Failure to respond in faith to one's baptism brings covenant curses instead of blessings. But note: like circumcision, baptism is viewed as a sign that promises and anticipates gospel realities; it does *not* affirm or testify that these same gospel realities have already taken place in the recipient.

2. Circumcision, as a physical act, signified the removal of the defilement of sin, the cleansing from sin, and it pointed to the need for a spiritual circumcision of the heart (see Ex. 6:12, 30; Lev. 19:23; 26:41; Deut. 10:16; 30:6; Jer. 4:4; 6:10; 9:25). Likewise, baptism is an outward sign of the inward, spiritual need for the grace of God in the heart of the covenant member—"it points to the necessity of spiritual regeneration";[116] it does *not* testify that regeneration has already taken place.

3. Circumcision was the seal of the righteousness Abraham had by faith while he was as yet uncircumcised (Rom. 4:11). As such, in circumcision, "God signified and sealed the fact that he justifies believers by faith and considers us as righteous through faith."[117] Circumcision is not a guarantee that Abraham has faith, nor even that Abraham (or anyone else, for that matter) has righteousness. Instead, "what circumcision guarantees is the word of God's promise: that *righteousness will be given on the basis of faith.*"[118] The same may be said of baptism. This is why both circumcision and baptism testify to God's promise to justify the ungodly by faith. This is also why one can circumcise or baptize an infant before faith is present. The covenant sign is simply a promise that righteousness will be given when a person believes the promises of God.

Thus, when thinking of the significance of circumcision and baptism,

---

[114] For a discussion of these points see Murray, *Christian Baptism*, 45–68; Booth, *Children of the Promise*, 96–119; Mark E. Ross, "Baptism and Circumcision as Signs and Seals," in *Case for Covenantal Infant Baptism*, 85–111.
[115] See Booth, *Children of the Promise*, 107.
[116] See ibid.
[117] Ibid., 102.
[118] Mark Ross, "Baptism and Circumcision as Signs and Seals," 94 (emphasis his).

covenant theology argues that essentially they signify the same gospel realities, namely, regeneration (Col. 2:11–12; Rom. 2:29), union with Christ (Rom. 6:4; Gal. 3:27–29), and all of the blessings related to that union (Acts 2:38). Because the signs are parallel in meaning and application, if it is legitimate in the Old Testament to apply the sign to "believers and their children," then the same is true in the new covenant era. This, however, raises an obvious question: If the covenantal signs are so similar in meaning then why did circumcision disappear as a covenant sign, especially for the Jewish Christian? Most covenant theologians argue that the change was due to the greater blessings that the new covenant has ushered in, especially in terms of extending more blessings to more people than before (e.g., Jew and Gentile). As we have noted above, as we move from old to new covenant, we also move from promise to fulfilment. Now that Christ has come, some of the rites of the Old Testament have been changed to reflect the completed work of Christ. Baptism has replaced the bloody rite of circumcision, just as the Lord's Supper has replaced the bloody Passover lamb.[119]

Here in a nutshell is the basic viewpoint of covenant theology, especially in relation to how it conceives the nature and relationship of the biblical covenants, and the implications of this for its view of the nature of the church and its covenant signs. As with dispensationalism and its varieties, covenant theology is a biblical-theological viewpoint which seeks to "put together" the entire canon of Scripture and thus grasp something of the incredible plan of God. Even though both views agree with each other at a number of key points, at the heart of their differences is their understanding of the nature of the biblical covenants and the relationship of these covenants to each other. In the next chapter, after a brief hermeneutical discussion where we lay out how we go about the task of reading and applying Scripture, we will return to these two theological systems by highlighting some of the key issues that need adjudication and why it is that we are convinced that our *via media*— "kingdom through covenant"—provides a better alternative than the present two biblical-theological systems. In the remaining chapters we will seek to demonstrate this thesis.

---

[119] Within the larger Reformed community there is a growing debate regarding paedocommunion. Some covenant theologians argue that covenant children should be included in communion given the fact that they are full covenant members of the new covenant. In favour of paedocommunion, see the writings of Douglas Wilson, Peter Leithart, and Gregg Strawbridge in Gregg Strawbridge, ed., *The Case for Covenant Communion* (Monroe, LA: Athanasius, 2006). For the case against paedocommunion, see Cornelius P. Venema, *Children at the Lord's Table?* (Grand Rapids, MI: Reformation Heritage, 2009). For a survey of positions and critique from a "progressive covenantal" or "new covenant theology" perspective, see Brent Parker, "Paedocommunion, Paedobaptism, and Covenant Theology: A Baptist Critique and Assessment" (unpublished paper).

Chapter Three

HERMENEUTICAL ISSUES IN "PUTTING TOGETHER" THE COVENANTS

What does it mean to be "biblical?" How do we rightly exegete biblical texts and draw proper theological conclusions? At the heart of Christian theology is the attempt to be biblical, to "take every thought captive to obey Christ" (2 Cor. 10:5, ESV). But how do we do so? In fact, how does one know that one's theological proposals are faithful to Scripture, and thus biblically warranted?[1] Obviously these questions are not new; they have been with us since Scripture was first given and interpreted. And, it must be admitted, these questions are not as easy and straightforward to answer as many often assume. We have all experienced diversity of opinion within the church, even among those of us who affirm the same high view of Scripture. This has apparently led some to treat the Bible like a wax nose, i.e., twisting and shaping it at will to fit a variety of viewpoints, with the conclusion that it is not possible to demonstrate one's interpretation as better or more biblical than another.

It is for this reason that it is necessary to devote a short space to reflect on the hermeneutical task, at least how we are approaching Scripture, interpreting it, and drawing our theological conclusions. Given our proposal of a *via media* on the covenants as more *biblical*, it is incumbent upon us to state clearly our basic hermeneutical approach. How do we approach Scripture? How do we interpret it? How do we draw our theological conclusions? Our goal in discussing these points is twofold: first, to describe our basic hermeneutical commitments; and secondly, to provide a point of entry for discussing why and where we differ from the biblical-theological positions of both dispensational and covenant theology.

---

[1] I was first confronted with this question of what it means to be *biblical* as a student of Kevin J. Vanhoozer during the 1980s at Trinity Evangelical Divinity School. For his response to this question see his *The Drama of Doctrine: A Canonical Linguistic Approach to Christian Doctrine* (Louisville: Westminster John Knox, 2005).

Certainly, the debate between dispensational and covenant theology is a complicated one. As most acknowledge, adjudication of these theological systems is more involved than merely appealing to one or two texts; rather it involves a discussion of how texts are understood in their context, how those texts are interrelated to other texts, and ultimately how the entire canon of Scripture is "put together." We enter this discussion with a particular focus: a careful investigation of the nature of the biblical covenants and their relationships to each other, since we contend that it is the covenantal issue that takes us to the heart of the debate.

Before the biblical covenants are expounded in detail in chapters 4–15, this chapter will focus on two broad areas. First, we will discuss how we are approaching, interpreting, and applying Scripture. Second, building on these hermeneutical points, we will revisit the systems of dispensational and covenant theology and discuss some of the key hermeneutical issues that separate them—issues that need adjudication in order to make headway in evaluating which system is more *biblical*. As we do this, "kingdom through covenant" will be set over and against these two systems as a view which better "puts together" the biblical covenants in light of the whole counsel of God.

HERMENEUTICAL BASICS: BEING "BIBLICAL" IN OUR THEOLOGICAL PROPOSALS

Obviously, in terms of hermeneutical basics much could be said; we can only begin to scratch the surface. In addition, most of what follows is in agreement with a majority of approaches to biblical hermeneutics, so it is not as if anything new is being stated. But with that said, it is important to lay out in a forthright manner how we approach the task of reading and applying Scripture and thus how we move from text to theological formulation. Where we differ with dispensational and covenant theology is not over the larger issues of hermeneutics but more in terms of some of the specific details, and particularly the application of certain points, which we will discuss in due course.[2]

Let us describe our overall hermeneutical approach by unpacking the following statement: In order to be *biblical* in our theology, our interpretation

---

[2] Here are some of the more standard hermeneutical texts that are helpful in discussing a basic evangelical approach to reading and applying Scripture: Graeme Goldsworthy, *Gospel-Centered Hermeneutics: Foundations and Principles of Evangelical Biblical Interpretation* (Downers Grove, IL: InterVarsity Press, 2006); Dan McCartney and Charles Clayton, *Let the Reader Understand: A Guide to Interpreting and Applying the Bible*, 2nd ed. (Phillipsburg, NJ: P&R, 2002); Grant R. Osborne, *The Hermeneutical Spiral: A Comprehensive Introduction to Biblical Interpretation*, 2nd ed. (Downers Grove, IL: InterVarsity Press, 2006).

and application of Scripture must: (1) take seriously what Scripture claims to be; and (2) interpret Scripture in light of what it actually is as God's unfolding revelation across time. Let us look at these two points in turn before we develop some of the hermeneutical implications.

THE SCRIPTURAL CLAIM FOR ITSELF: SCRIPTURE'S SELF-ATTESTATION

In order to be *biblical* in our theology we must take seriously what Scripture claims to be. What, then, does Scripture claim for itself? It is not our aim to give a comprehensive explication and defense of the doctrine of Scripture; many books have undertaken that task and have done it well.[3] Along with dispensational and covenant theology, indeed along with historic Christian orthodoxy, we affirm that Scripture is God's Word written, the product of God's mighty action through the Word and by the Holy Spirit whereby human authors freely wrote exactly what God intended to be written and without error.[4]

Why has the church throughout the ages affirmed this about Scripture? The answer is simple and straightforward: Scripture itself makes this claim about itself. In other words, the church does not confer authority upon this book because we so desire it to be the Word of God; rather, Scripture itself comes to us making claims, testifying to itself that it is God's authoritative Word, written through the agency of human authors. As we read Scripture, it bears witness to itself that it is God-given and is from the sovereign-personal

---

[3] For the most recent explication and defense of the Christian view of Scripture see John M. Frame, *The Doctrine of the Word of God* (Phillipsburg, NJ: P&R, 2010).

[4] Kevin J. Vanhoozer has called this view the "Received View," in contrast to more current views of Scripture, since it was held in the early church and passed on throughout the ages, at least up until recent times. See his article, "God's Mighty Speech-Acts: The Doctrine of Scripture Today," in *A Pathway into the Holy Scriptures*, ed. Philip E. Satterthwaite and David F. Wright (Grand Rapids, MI: Eerdmans, 1994), 143–181. Until fairly recently, evangelicals and non-evangelicals alike have agreed that the witness of church history has favoured a high view of Scripture, including its inerrancy. But in recent years this view has been challenged by a revisionist historiography. A new generation of historians is arguing that the modern conservative position on Scripture is something of an aberration that owes its impetus in part to scholastic theology of the post-Reformation period and in part to the Princetonians, especially Charles Hodge, A. A. Hodge, and B. B. Warfield. Probably the best-known work to espouse this view is that of Jack B. Rogers and Donald K. McKim, *The Authority and Interpretation of the Bible* (San Francisco: Harper & Row, 1979). Rogers and McKim's thesis is that the historic position of the church maintains the Bible's authority only in areas of *faith and practise* (understood in a restrictive sense), *not* its reliable truthfulness in every area on which it chooses to speak. This proposal, however, has been shown to be seriously flawed. For a critique of this viewpoint see John D. Woodbridge, *Biblical Authority* (Grand Rapids, MI: Zondervan, 1982); Paul Kjoss Helseth, *"Right Reason" and the Princeton Mind: An Unorthodox Proposal* (Phillipsburg, NJ: P&R, 2010). See also the historical essays in the following works: D. A. Carson and John D. Woodbridge, eds., *Scripture and Truth* (Grand Rapids, MI: Zondervan, 1983); idem, *Hermeneutics, Authority, and Canon* (Grand Rapids, MI: Zondervan, 1986); Norman L. Geisler, ed., *Inerrancy* (Grand Rapids, MI: Zondervan, 1979); Earl D. Radmacher and Robert D. Preus, eds., *Hermeneutics, Inerrancy, and the Bible* (Grand Rapids, MI: Zondervan, 1984); John D. Hannah, ed., *Inerrancy and the Church* (Chicago: Moody, 1984).

"God who is there," the God who "is not silent."[5] As such, Scripture both attests and bears the marks that it is of divine origin and hence completely authoritative, sufficient, and reliable. It should not surprise us that some biblical scholars and theologians have challenged this claim, i.e., whether Scripture actually makes such a pervasive claim about itself. James Barr, for example, denies this claim.[6] But it has been shown repeatedly that when Scripture is read on its own terms, there is, in the words of Sinclair Ferguson, a "canonical self-consciousness" from Genesis to Revelation that Scripture is God's authoritative Word written.[7] We will leave the reader to the literature in the footnotes for a development of this assertion. At this point, we simply assume this high view of Scripture as we approach and interpret it.

How does this view of Scripture impact our interpretation of it? At least two assertions must be made, both of which historic Christian theology has always affirmed. First, given that Scripture is *God's* Word, from the triune God who is the sovereign-personal, omniscient Lord of the universe, we expect *an overall unity and coherenc*e between the Testaments, despite the diversity of Scripture, that together declares God's unfailing plan and purposes in this fallen world. Kevin Vanhoozer nicely describes Scripture this way: it is "a unified communicative act, that is, as the complex, multilevelled speech act of a single divine author,"[8] which leads us to view and interpret Scripture as a *unified* revelation. As we think through the biblical covenants, given our view of Scripture, we will *not* view the covenants as independent and isolated from each other, but as together, in all of their diversity, unfolding the one plan of God centred in our Lord Jesus Christ (Eph. 1:9–10).

Second, given that Scripture is God's Word through human authors, we discover God's intent by reading what the biblical authors say; hence the expression, "what God says, Scripture says" (i.e., the biblical authors), and

---

[5] The expressions "the God who is there" and "the God who is not silent" are taken from Francis A. Schaeffer's two works, *The God Who Is There*, 30th anniversary edition (Downers Grove, IL: InterVarsity Press, 1998); and *He Is There and He Is Not Silent* (Carol Stream, IL: Tyndale, 1972).

[6] See James Barr, *Fundamentalism* (London: SCM, 1977), 78.

[7] See Sinclair B. Ferguson, "How Does the Bible Look at Itself?" in *Inerrancy and Hermeneutic*, ed. Harvie M. Conn (Grand Rapids, MI: Baker, 1988), 47–66. For more on Scripture's self-attestation and what it claims for itself see E. J. Schnabel, "Scripture," in *NDBT*, 34–43; Wayne Grudem, "Scripture's Self-Attestation and the Problem of Formulating a Doctrine of Scripture," in *Scripture and Truth*, 19–59; John M. Frame, "Scripture Speaks for Itself," in *God's Inerrant Word*, ed. John W. Montgomery (Minneapolis: Bethany, 1974), 178–181; John Wenham, *Christ and the Bible*, 3rd ed. (Grand Rapids, MI: Baker, 1994); Timothy Ward, *Words of Life: Scripture as the Living and Active Word of God* (Downers Grove, IL: InterVarsity Press, 2009). For a brief description of the biblical data grounding this conviction, including a discussion of the doctrines of inspiration and inerrancy, see Stephen J. Wellum, "The Inerrancy of Scripture," in *Beyond the Bounds: Open Theism and the Undermining of Biblical Christianity*, ed. Paul K. Helseth, Justin Taylor, and John Piper (Wheaton, IL: Crossway, 2003), 237–274.

[8] Kevin J. Vanhoozer, "Exegesis and Hermeneutics," in *NDBT*, 61.

vice versa. Ultimately, this point leads us to a canonical reading of Scripture in order to discover how to interpret specific texts and the meaning of those texts. It is not enough to read Scripture in a "thin" manner, i.e., as isolated texts apart from the whole. Instead we must read texts in a "thick" way, i.e., in light of the entire canon of Scripture.[9] We discover God's intent through the writing(s) of the biblical authors, but given the diversity of authors throughout the ages, we must ultimately interpret biblical authors in light of the entire canon of Scripture. It is only by reading Scripture "thickly" that we discover the true meaning of Scripture, i.e., what God's intent is, and how Scripture applies to us today. This observation is simply another way of stating the important Reformation principle for biblical interpretation: "Scripture must interpret Scripture."

It is also another way of speaking about the "fuller meaning" of Scripture or what has been labelled *sensus plenior*.[10] This expression is understood in diverse ways, so it requires careful definition.[11] We agree with Greg Beale's understanding of the term when he argues that, for example, "the Old Testament authors did not exhaustively understand the meaning, implications, and possible applications of all that they wrote."[12] As authors who wrote under divine inspiration, what they wrote was God-given, true, authoritative, and reliable. However, they might not, and probably did not, understand where the entire revelation was going, given the fact that God had not yet disclosed all of the details of his eternal plan. Thus, as more revelation was given over time and through later authors, we discover more of God's plan and where that plan is going. It is for this reason that the New Testament's interpretation of the Old Testament becomes definitive in helping us interpret the details of the Old Testament, since later revelation brings with it greater clarity and understand-

---

[9] For a discussion of a "thin" versus "thick" reading of Scripture, see Vanhoozer, "Exegesis and Hermeneutics," 61–62.

[10] On this expression see D. J. Moo, "The Problem of Sensus Plenior," in *Hermeneutics, Authority, and Canon*, 179–211; G. K. Beale, "Did Jesus and His Followers Preach the Right Doctrine from the Wrong Texts?" in *The Right Doctrine from the Wrong Texts: Essays on the Use of the Old Testament in the New*, ed. G. K. Beale (Grand Rapids, MI: Baker, 1994), 392–393.

[11] For a detailed discussion of *sensus plenior*, see Raymond E. Brown, *The Sensus Plenior of Sacred Scripture* (Baltimore: St. Mary's University, 1955), 88–122; Matthew W. I. Dunn, "Raymond Brown and the *Sensus Plenior* Interpretation of the Bible," *Studies in Religion* 36 (2007): 531–551; Douglas A. Oss, "Canon as Context: The Function of *Sensus Plenior* in Evangelical Hermeneutics," *Grace Theological Journal* 9 (1988): 105–127. For most proponents of *sensus plenior*, the "fuller sense" is a meaning that the human author did not consciously intend and, as such, the meaning of the text cannot be discovered by grammatical-historical exegesis. The problem with this view is that it opens the door to a subjective reading of the text without hermeneutical controls. Instead we argue for a thorough exegetical theology which seeks to uncover the author's intent yet is also sensitive to intertextual development across the Canon. In this way, we discover God's intent through the human authors of Scripture at the canonical level. God says more than the individual authors may have known, yet he does not contravene what the authors wrote and intended.

[12] Beale, "Did Jesus and His Followers Preach the Right Doctrine from the Wrong Texts?" 393.

ing. In other words, we must carefully allow the New Testament to show us how the Old Testament is brought to fulfilment in Christ. In this way, as Beale rightly acknowledges, the New Testament's interpretation of the Old Testament may expand the Old Testament author's meaning in the sense of seeing new implications and applications. However, given that we discover God's intent through the human authors, later texts do *not* contravene the integrity of the earlier texts, "but rather develops them in a way which is consistent with the Old Testament author's understanding of the way in which God interacts with his people"[13] in previous eras of redemptive-history. Thus, Scripture as an entire Canon must interpret Scripture; the later parts must "draw out and explain more clearly the earlier parts,"[14] and theological conclusions must be exegetically derived from the entire Canon.

Even though this point is widely acknowledged in biblical hermeneutics, it is a major point of contention between dispensational and covenant theologians, especially when it comes to the land promise and the genealogical principle of the Abrahamic covenant. For dispensational theology the land promise must be interpreted in the same way across redemptive-history—as an irrevocable promise given to the nation of Israel—and thus requires a future fulfilment in a "literal" way. Conversely, for covenant theology, the New Testament helps us understand that the land promise is that which is fulfilled in the coming of Christ and the dawning of the new creation and, as such, is typological of the new creation. One crucial area needing resolution is how much the New Testament governs our understanding of the meaning of Old Testament texts and how those Old Testament texts find their fulfilment in the new covenant era. Grammatical-historical exegesis needs to be set in the larger context of a canonical reading of Scripture; the parts must be read in terms of the whole. In regard to covenant theology, the same point must be stated in terms of the genealogical principle. In the hands of covenant theologians, the genealogical principle remains unchanged across redemptive-history even though the New Testament does not seem to apply

---

[13] Ibid. Michael D. Williams, *Far as the Curse Is Found: The Covenant Story of Redemption* (Phillipsburg, NJ: P&R, 2005), 81–82, rightly argues that fanciful and allegorical interpretations are preventable "not by denying the reality of the fuller sense but by insisting that the fuller sense be established only as an extension of the original sense and solely on the basis of subsequent biblical revelation." He adds that an acceptable form of *sensus plenior* should be "a fuller sense of what is already present, not an entirely other sense, as one finds in allegorical interpretation. While it is fair to see an oak within an acorn, it is not fair to see a cow within an acorn. But we must not lose sight of the author and his intention" (82).

[14] Beale, "Did Jesus and His Followers Preach the Right Doctrine from the Wrong Texts?" 393. See also Jared M. Compton, "Shared Intentions? Reflections on Inspiration and Interpretation in Light of Scripture's Dual Authorship," *Themelios* 33 (2008): 23–33, especially 30–33.

it in the same way that the Old Testament does. We will return to this point in later chapters. For our purposes now we simply note that how one applies a canonical reading is important in adjudicating differences between dispensational and covenant theology.

Furthermore, it is important to stress that, given what Scripture is, a canonical reading is *not* an optional way to interpret Scripture. In fact, to read the Bible canonically is demanded by the nature of Scripture and its claim regarding itself. Thus, *not* to read Scripture in this way is to fail to interpret it correctly and to be less than "biblical." As we shall discover in due course, how one applies this hermeneutical principle is where the differences arise. At this juncture, we simply state how we approach Scripture in conjunction with its claim regarding itself. Let us now turn to the second point, i.e., in order to be "biblical" we must interpret Scripture in light of what it actually is as God's unfolding revelation across time.

INTERPRETING SCRIPTURE ACCORDING TO WHAT IT IS

What *is* Scripture? Here we are not thinking primarily in terms of what Scripture says about itself, but more in terms of the actual phenomena of Scripture, or better, how God has chosen to give us Scripture and disclose himself to us through human authors. Let us discuss the phenomena of Scripture by focusing on two points: Scripture is a word-act revelation *and* Scripture is a progressive revelation. Then, we'll draw out some of the hermeneutical implications.

Scripture Is a Word-Act Revelation

A helpful way of describing the phenomena of Scripture is by viewing it as a word-act revelation. What does this mean? Simply stated, it means that Scripture is God's own authoritative interpretation of his redemptive acts through the agency of human authors. Let us think about this in three steps.

First, it is important to affirm that all of God's redemptive acts are revelatory of him, his plan, and his purposes. In history, God has disclosed himself in his mighty acts, what we often identify as special revelation in contrast to the revelation of God in the natural world. For example, in the Old Testament, the greatest revelatory redemptive act of God was his deliverance of Israel from their slavery in Egypt (cf. Ex. 6:6–7). In the New Testament, the proclamation of the gospel involves the recitation of God's acts in history (cf. Acts 2:22ff.; 3:13ff.; 10:36ff.; 13:26ff.; 1 Cor. 15:3f.). In fact, supremely the focal point of Scripture centres around what God has done in Jesus Christ. The New Testament continually proclaims that what God had promised in ages past, what the Old Testament prophets anticipated, God has now brought to fulfilment in the life, death, and resurrection of our Lord Jesus—the greatest display of the mighty acts of God. That is why expressions of fulfilment are everywhere in the New Testament (cf. Mark 1:15; Luke 4:21; Gal. 4:4).

Second, as important as it is to affirm that God acts in order to reveal himself and to redeem his people, God's redemptive acts are never left to speak for themselves and they never appear separated from God's verbal communications of truth. In this important way, word *and* act always accompany each other, especially in regard to Scripture. Furthermore, just as redemption is historically successive, so also is revelation, for God's revelatory word interprets God's redemptive acts. For example, Exodus 15:1–18 interprets the events of the Red Sea crossing; events are never left as self-interpreting. As Geerhardus Vos said many years ago, borrowing a phrase from the philosopher Immanuel Kant but employing it differently, "without God's acts the words would be empty, without his words the acts would be blind."[15]

In fact, in terms of word and act, there is a general order Scripture follows: first there is a preparatory word, then the divine act, followed by the interpretive word. For example, in the giving of the old covenant we first see a preparatory word (Exodus 19), then the divine act of giving the law (Exodus 20), followed up by an interpretative explanation of the law (Exodus 21ff.). In many ways, this same order may be observed of the Bible as a whole. The Old Testament reveals the predictive word and anticipates greater realities tied to the coming of our Lord; the Gospels give the account of the redemptive-revelatory fact of the coming of the Son; and the remainder of the New Testament supplies, along with the Gospels, the final interpretation of not only who the Son is but the full implications of what he has achieved in the inauguration of the new covenant era and the fulfilment of the prophetic word.

Third, we affirm that Scripture, as a word-act revelation, is also the product of God's own mighty actions. Scripture not only chronicles the

---

[15] Geerhardus Vos, "The Idea of Biblical Theology," in *Redemptive History and Biblical Interpretation*, ed. Richard B. Gaffin, Jr., 10. See also Ladd, who rightly finds that the "events themselves. . . . are not self-explanatory; there was always a divinely initiated prophetic or apostolic word of interpretation. That Jesus died is an objective fact that even the Pharisees could affirm. That Jesus died *for our sins* is no less an 'objective' fact; but it is a theological event occurring within the historical fact which could be understood only from the prophetic word of interpretation. Revelation, therefore, occurred in the complex of event-Word" (G. E. Ladd, "Biblical Theology, Nature of," in *The International Standard Bible Encyclopedia*, rev. ed., ed. Geoffrey W. Bromiley, 4 vols. [Grand Rapids, MI: Eerdmans, 1979], 1:506).

activities of God's redemption in history; it not only is a word which interprets God's redeeming acts; it, itself, is a product of God's own redemptive
acts for the purpose of teaching, edification, and instruction, and as such is
fully authoritative and sufficient for our thinking and lives. Scripture, then,
as a written text, in its final form, is God's own divine interpretation, through
human authors, of his own redemptive acts that carries with it a true, objective, and authoritative interpretation of his redemptive plan. Though it is not
an exhaustive Word-revelation, nonetheless it is a true, objective, and first-
order text which requires that we read it as a complete canonical text on its
own terms, according to its own structure and categories, in order to discern
correctly God's intent and redemptive plan. Once again, hermeneutically
speaking, this reminds us that Scripture must be read as an entire revelation,
i.e., canonically, in order to discern God's overall plan, what we have called
a "thick" reading of Scripture.[16] This point is further underscored by viewing
Scripture as a progressive revelation.

Scripture Is a Progressive Revelation

Scripture as a word-act revelation also involves historical progression, since,
just as God's plan of redemption and mighty acts did not happen all at once,
so revelation (i.e., the word interpretation of those acts) unfolds over time.[17]
Revelation, alongside redemption, unfolds in a *progressive* manner by
unique twists and turns in separate but related epochs, largely demarcated by
God's acts and redemptive covenants, which ultimately finds its culmination
in the person and work of our Lord Jesus Christ.

Hebrews 1:1–3 beautifully describes this point. "Long ago," the author
reminds us, "God spoke to our fathers by the prophets," and he did so "at
many times and in many ways" (ESV). God's word-act revelation took place
over a period of time, and as it was given it pointed beyond itself to something more to come. In fact, this is the precise point that the author makes by

---

[16] "Intratextual" is another term that nicely describes our interpretation and application of Scripture. While the
term may be used in New Testament studies to refer to how a biblical author alludes to other passages within his
own writing, "intratextual" is employed here to emphasise how the self-description of Scripture should direct and
shape our theology. Over and against an "extratextual" reading of Scripture, which assumes that people approach
Scripture with a prior worldview which then squeezes the Scripture into that grid and interprets it accordingly,
"intratextual" seeks to let Scripture speak *on its own terms*, according to its own presentation, worldview framework, and structures. As we read the biblical text leading to an entire canonical reading, we let Scripture unfold its
own plan along its plot line, which is the only way to "think God's thoughts after him."

[17] "Progressive" is used in the sense of the unfolding plan of God, not in the sense that an earlier era was inferior
and the later era has progressed or has reached a superior stage. The latter idea is associated with classic liberalism
and its evolutionary and Hegelian understanding of religion, including Christianity. Instead, "progressive" emphasises the idea that God's redemptive plan did not occur all at once but was gradually disclosed in redemptive-
history as God entered into covenant relationships with his people and brought his plan to fulfilment in Christ.

his use of "at many times and in many ways" (*polumerōs kai polutropōs*); i.e., not only was the Old Testament revelation repetitive, it was also incomplete. In the progress of revelation, more and more of God's plan was disclosed to us, pointing forward to and culminating in the coming of Christ. As William Lane rightly notes, "The fragmentary and varied character of God's self-disclosure under the old covenant awakened within the fathers an expectation that he would continue to speak to his people. . . . The ministry of the prophets marked the preparatory phase of that history."[18] But now, with the coming of the Son, the last days have dawned—the last days which the Old Testament revelation anticipated. That revelation has now come to fulfilment literally "in Son" (*en huiō*; v. 2), underscoring that in Christ the final, definitive, complete revelation has now come. In this way, the author of Hebrews, along with the entire New Testament, places the Son in a qualitatively different category than the prophets who preceded him. The effect of this is not to downplay the authority of the Old Testament prophetic revelation; rather the point is that the previous revelation was incomplete and by its very nature was intended by God to point beyond itself to God's full self-disclosure in his Son. This is why the Son is more than a mere prophet (though he is the fulfilment of the entire prophetic institution): he is the one about whom the prophets spoke; he is the one who brings to completion the fragmentary revelation of the previous era. Even more: the Son is the one in whom all of God's revelation and redemptive purposes culminate.

All of this is to say that Scripture as a word-act revelation is also a progressive revelation. Hermeneutically speaking, this has important implications for how we read and apply Scripture and thus draw conclusions from Scripture and warrant our theological proposals. Our interpretation of Scripture must do justice to the fact that Scripture has not come all at once. As we read Scripture our task is to trace out how Scripture unfolds God's plan of redemption, which leads us back to our discussion in chapter 1 about the important role "biblical theology" plays in our interpretation of Scripture. Biblical theology seeks to do justice to what the Scripture is, i.e., what it is as a word-act revelation that is progressively given. In this way, biblical theology attempts to give a theological reading of Scripture, grounded in exegesis, which essentially seeks to grasp "the whole counsel of God" in terms of the redemptive-historical progression in Scripture. No doubt, as many have stressed, Scripture consists of many literary forms, all

---

[18] William L. Lane, *Hebrews 1–8*, WBC 47a: (Dallas: Word, 1991), 11.

of which must be interpreted carefully, but underneath all of these literary forms is an underlying story line, beginning in creation and moving to the new creation, which unfolds God's plan centred and culminated in Jesus Christ.[19] And it is crucial that we read Scripture in such a way that we do justice to the Bible's unfolding story line—to the Bible's own presentation and in the Bible's own categories—as it leads us to Christ and all that he has achieved for us. We must, in other words, let Scripture speak for itself in its own structure and categories, i.e., on its own terms.

Michael Horton emphasises these precise points as he draws out their implications for a proper way of doing theology.[20] Given what Scripture is, he contends that the most "biblical" theological method ought to be categorised as "redemptive-historical-eschatological." By these terms he is saying what we have just described. Given the authority of Scripture and how it has come to us, we are to interpret Scripture according to its own presentation and in its own intrasystematic categories, i.e., on its own terms, which he argues are captured by the terms "eschatological" and "redemptive-historical."[21]

By "eschatological" Horton means more than a mere locus of theology. Rather, it is a lens by which we read Scripture and do our theology. Scripture itself comes to us as a redemptive revelation, rooted in history, unfolding God's eternal plan worked out in time, and as such the very "form" and "shape" of Scripture is "eschatological." It is for this reason that Horton is rightly uncomfortable with what George Lindbeck has labelled a "cognitive-propositionalist" approach to theology.[22] Scripture is more than a storehouse of facts or propositions, since Scripture unfolds for us a *plot*, a story line, a divine interpretation of the drama of redemption, which is eschatological at heart and Christological in focus, and as such, our interpretation of Scripture and our drawing of theological conclusions must reflect this. By "redemptive-historical," Horton is referring to Scripture's own presentation of itself as "the organic unfolding of the divine plan in its execution through

---

[19] Kevin Vanhoozer is probably the one who has stressed the most in recent days the importance of literary forms for understanding the intent of the biblical authors and thus the intent of the divine author as well. For a full defense of this, see his *Is There a Meaning in This Text? The Bible, the Reader, and the Morality of Literary Knowledge* (Grand Rapids, MI: Zondervan, 1998). D. A. Carson, agreeing with Vanhoozer in regard to literary forms, rightly stresses the second point, that, as important as literary forms are for our understanding the author's intent, we must also interpret Scripture along its God-given story line. On this point see Carson's *The Gagging of God: Christianity Confronts Pluralism* (Grand Rapids, MI: Zondervan, 1996) 141–278; cf. Michael S. Horton, *Covenant and Eschatology: The Divine Drama* (Louisville: Westminster John Knox, 2002), 147–264.

[20] See Horton, *Covenant and Eschatology*, 1–19, 147–276.

[21] Horton's use of "intrasystematic categories" is basically what we mean by the term "intratextual."

[22] See George A. Lindbeck, *The Nature of Doctrine: Religion and Theology in a Postliberal Age*, 25th anniversary ed. (Louisville: Westminster John Knox, 2009).

word (announcement), act (accomplishment), and word (interpretation)."[23] Given that redemption is progressive and unfolding, so is revelation, as it is God's own interpretation of his action and of the human response in actual historical contexts.

Given this understanding, for Horton there are a number of important implications for our interpretation of Scripture and the doing of theology. We will focus on one of them. Our reading of Scripture and our doing of theology must attend to the historical unfolding of redemptive-history that is *organically* related and ultimately centred on Jesus Christ. The very "form" and "shape" of Scripture reminds us that God did not disclose himself in one exhaustive act but in an organic, progressive manner, and in fact, it is this organic quality of revelation that serves to explain the diversity of Scripture. Theology, as a result, must be very careful not to proof-text without considering the redemptive-historical structure and progression in Scripture and reading Scripture as a canonical text.[24]

"PUTTING TOGETHER" THE CANON: THE THREE HORIZONS OF BIBLICAL INTERPRETATION

What does all of this have to do with understanding the nature and relationships of the biblical covenants? The simple answer is *everything*. As we think through the biblical covenants, since God has not disclosed himself in one exhaustive act but progressively, we must carefully think through every biblical covenant first in its own redemptive-historical context, then ask what has preceded that covenant, and then relate that particular covenant to that which comes after it and how it relates to the inauguration of the new covenant in our Lord Jesus Christ. It is only when we do this that we begin to understand how each covenant relates to previous and later covenants, and how all the biblical covenants relate to what has now come in Christ. We must also be careful as we trace out the historical unfolding of redemptive-history, as demarcated by the biblical covenants and their covenant heads—Adam, Noah, Abraham, Israel, David, and then our Lord—how the entire plan is *organically* related yet at the same time preserving its diversity, thus maintaining a proper balance between the continuity and discontinuity of God's plan as it reaches its culmination and fulfilment in Christ.

In this regard, it is important to reference the helpful work of Richard

---

[23] Horton, *Covenant and Eschatology*, 5.
[24] See ibid., 1–19, 147–276.

Lints. Lints, in laying out an evangelical theological method, stresses the same points emphasised above, at least in terms of how we must interpret any text of Scripture. He rightly contends that the discipline of biblical theology is foundational to the doing of systematic theology and crucial in drawing "biblical" conclusions from Scripture. He also proposes, given that Scripture is a word-act and progressive revelation, that we interpret biblical texts according to three horizons: textual, epochal, and canonical.[25] By emphasising these three horizons, Lints helps us think through how to interpret Scripture properly—in light of what Scripture claims for itself and in terms of what it actually is—while simultaneously enabling us to avoid "proof-texting." He also reminds us that, in biblical interpretation and theological formulation, "context" is king and, in fact, three contexts are crucial in "putting together" the entire Bible, including the biblical covenants.[26] Let us briefly discuss each of these three horizons in turn as we note their importance for a proper biblical-theological interpretation of Scripture.[27]

Context, Context, Context

Our interpretation of Scripture begins with a specific text, what Lints calls the *textual horizon* or the immediate context. This is an obvious point, but it still needs to be said; we cannot read the Bible all at once, so we must start somewhere, and wherever we begin is our first context. In terms of this context, biblical hermeneutics has sought to read texts according to the grammatical-historical method, seeking to discern God's intent through the human author's intent by setting the text in its historical setting, understanding the rules of language the author is using, analysing the syntax, textual variants, word meanings, figures of speech, and the literary structure, including the genre of the text. By paying careful attention to all of these areas,

---

[25] See Richard Lints, *The Fabric of Theology: A Prolegomenon to Evangelical Theology* (Grand Rapids, MI: Eerdmans, 1993), 259–311.

[26] We can borrow from the domain of real estate where the three rules are "location, location, location," and apply it to biblical interpretation. The three rules of biblical-theological interpretation are "context, context, context," i.e., textual horizon context, epochal horizon context, and finally, canonical horizon context.

[27] It is important to note that the proposal of reading Scripture according to three horizons is not new. In truth, it is what all Christians have done, at least implicitly though not consistently, in their reading and application of the biblical text. For others who advocate this approach see Edmund P. Clowney, *Preaching and Biblical Theology* (Grand Rapids, MI: Eerdmans, 1961), 16; Carson, *Gagging of God*, 190, n. 133; Horton, *Covenant and Eschatology*, 147–180; Vanhoozer, "Exegesis and Hermeneutics," 60–62. In his own way, Vanhoozer states the basic thrust of the three horizons: "When describing 'what it meant/means', it is perhaps best to think of a series of expanding interpretative frameworks. There is first the semantic range of what words could possibly have meant in their historical situation, then the historical context of what authors could have meant at a particular point in the history of redemption, then the literary context of what the words could have meant as part of a particular kind of literature, and finally what the words at a certain time in a certain kind of text mean today when read as part of a unified Canon that, taken as a whole, points to Jesus Christ" (62).

a reader discovers what authors are seeking to communicate in their texts. Standard books in hermeneutics work through these areas, and we assume all of this in our exegesis of individual passages of Scripture.[28] However, it is important to note that our interpretation of texts does not terminate here, which leads to the second horizon of biblical interpretation.

The *epochal horizon* is the second context by which we interpret texts. Here we seek to read texts in light of where they are in redemptive-history, or where they are in terms of the unfolding plan of God. Since Scripture is a progressive revelation, texts do not come to us in a vacuum; rather they are embedded in a larger context of what has come *before* them. As God communicates through biblical authors, these same authors write in light of what has preceded them. When Lints labels this context the "epochal horizon" he does not intend to convey, nor do we, that the "epochs" embody different plans of God; rather, they remind us of the fact that God's revelation of redemption develops over time. There is a unity within this development because God's plan and unfolding purposes provide unity across the ages and thus hold the epochs together. But this fundamental unity should not lead us to minimize the differences among epochs, hence the balance between continuity *and* discontinuity in Scripture.

Furthermore, locating texts in their place in God's unfolding plan helps illuminate *intertextual* relationships between early and later revelation. As later authors refer to earlier texts they build upon what is given, not only in terms of greater understanding and knowledge of where God's plan is going, but also they begin to identify God-given patterns between earlier and later events, persons, and institutions within the unfolding of God's plan, what is rightly labelled "typology." It is by this means, but not limited to it, that God's plan moves forward and ultimately reaches its consummation in Christ. As later authors draw out these God-given patterns (types), they do *not* arbitrarily make connections; rather, they develop

---

[28] For example, see Vanhoozer, "Exegesis and Hermeneutics," *NDBT*, 52–64. Vanhoozer (64) describes a text as "an extended piece of discourse—something said by someone to someone else about something—fixed by writing." He views literary texts as "communicative actions performed on a variety of levels for the reader's contemplation." To understand a text properly one needs to do more than parse every verb, Vanhoozer contends; one "needs to know what an author is doing," which entails paying attention to what authors *do* in their sentences, paragraphs, and entire literary works. Interpreting texts properly involves "not only linguistic and historical but also *literary* competence." It is only when we do this that we interpret texts, including the biblical text, "on its own terms" and thus according to what the author is seeking to communicate to his readers. See also Osborne, *The Hermeneutical Spiral*; McCartney and Clayton, *Let the Reader Understand*; Goldsworthy, *Gospel-Centered Hermeneutics*; Walter C. Kaiser and Moisés Silva, *Introduction to Biblical Hermeneutics: The Search for Meaning*, 2nd ed. (Grand Rapids, MI: Zondervan, 2007); cf. Vanhoozer, *Is There a Meaning in This Text?*

these patterns in ways that God intends and which do not contravene earlier texts.[29] It is only by reading texts first in their immediate context and then in relation to where these texts are in God's unfolding plan that we begin to grasp God's overall plan and purposes. Individual texts do not become fragmented, and the road from "text" to "reader" is *not* a matter of one's intuition, preference, or prejudice.

Is it necessary to be precise as to what the epochal differences are in Scripture? Probably not; people may disagree on these differences. The important point is to always read texts in light of what has preceded them in reference to God's redemptive actions and plan.[30] Obviously, most agree that the most significant epochal division is between the Old Testament era and the fulfilment of God's plan in the coming of our Lord. But there are also other divisions that are crucial, and Scripture does divide up redemptive-history in a number of ways. For example, in Romans 5:12–21, Paul divides all

---

[29] For a discussion of this point see Beale, "Did Jesus and His Followers Preach the Right Doctrine from the Wrong Texts?" 391–398. See also D. A. Carson, "Systematic Theology and Biblical Theology," *NDBT*, 98. Carson nicely discusses different senses of "intertextuality" today. One use of the term refers to current ways of thinking through how later texts use early texts in Scripture but also expands this to how contemporary interpreters absorb biblical texts which then affects how they interpret biblical texts. This is *not* what we mean by intertextuality. We are using the term as referring to how later biblical authors legitimately interpret earlier biblical texts and intentionally use an earlier text, identifying textual clues that are legitimately there and which are unpacked as God's revelation is given more definition. In this way, intertextuality, as Carson notes, establishes "the beginnings of a typology that develops across the sweep of redemptive history" (98). Carefully used, this kind of intertextuality allows the reader to understand how God's revelation hangs together, develops, and finds its culmination in Christ. For a further discussion of intertextuality which we find helpful see G. K. Beale, *We Become What We Worship: A Biblical Theology of Idolatry* (Downers Grove, IL: InterVarsity Press, 2008), 22–35. For a broader discussion of intertextuality see Richard B. Hays, *Echoes of Scripture in the Letters of Paul* (New Haven, CT: Yale University Press, 1989); idem, *The Conversion of the Imagination* (Grand Rapids, MI: Eerdmans, 2005). Also see the application of intertextuality to the use of the Old Testament in the New Testament in G. K. Beale and D. A. Carson, eds., *Commentary on the New Testament Use of the Old Testament* (Grand Rapids, MI: Baker, 2007).

[30] Today there is a legitimate and important debate over whether we ought to read Scripture, particularly the Old Testament, in terms of the ordering of the Hebrew Canon. For example, Stephen G. Dempster, *Dominion and Dynasty: A Biblical Theology of the Hebrew Bible*, NSBT 15 (Downers Grove, IL: InterVarsity Press, 2003), 15–51, argues this point. See also idem, "An 'Extraordinary Fact': *Torah* and Temple and the Contours of the Hebrew Canon" (Parts 1 and 2), *Tyndale Bulletin* 48 (1997): 23–53, 191–218; Paul R. House, *Old Testament Theology* (Downers Grove, IL: InterVarsity Press, 1998), 53–57; John H. Sailhamer, *Introduction to Old Testament Theology: A Canonical Approach* (Grand Rapids, MI: Zondervan, 1995); cf. Craig G. Bartholomew, et al., *Canon and Biblical Interpretation* (Scripture and Hermeneutics Series 7: Grand Rapids, MI: Zondervan, 2006). Even though we are very sympathetic with this approach and basically adopt it in our reading of the Old Testament Canon, one potential problem with the approach is the difficulty of establishing *the* official order of the Old Testament Canon since there are a variety of canonical orderings. Regardless of whether *the* official order of the Old Testament Canon can be established (for which we believe a strong case can be made), we minimally maintain that the actual practise of New Testament authors is to interpret Old Testament texts in relation to where they are located in redemptive-history, and thus it is crucial to read texts in light of *earlier* and then *later* texts (hence epochal and canonical horizons). G. K. Beale and D. A. Carson, "Introduction," in *Commentary on the New Testament Use of the Old Testament*, xxvi–xxvii, make this basic point. They state, "one of the distinctive differences one sometimes finds between the way NT writers read the OT and the way their non-Christian Jewish contemporaries read it *is the salvation-historical grid* that is often adopted by the former. Some kind of historical sequence under the providence of a sovereign God is necessary for almost any kind of typological hermeneutic, of course, but there is something more" (emphasis mine). They then go on to illustrate this point, as we do below, by appealing to Galatians 3, Romans 4, and the book of Hebrews to underscore the interpretive significance of reading texts in terms of historical sequence. Given this fact, then, whether one can establish the precise order of the Canon is probably not as significant as seeking to interpret biblical texts in terms of where they are located in the unfolding plan of God.

of human history under two heads: Adam and Christ. Under these two heads, Paul further subdivides redemptive-history by the following epochs: Adam (vv. 12–13), from Adam to Moses (vv. 14–17), from Moses and the giving of the law-covenant to Christ (vv. 18–21). Or, in Acts 7:1–53, Stephen identifies three distinct periods: the age of the patriarchs (vv. 2–16), the Mosaic age, which included within it the time of the exodus and conquest of the Promised Land (vv. 17–45a), and the age of the monarchy (vv. 45b–53). Or, in the genealogy in Matthew 1, Matthew divides up redemptive-history into three distinct periods: Abraham to David (vv. 2–6a); Solomon to the exile (vv. 6b–11); and the exile to the coming of Christ (vv. 12–17).

It is Matthew's structuring of redemptive-history that Graeme Goldsworthy follows. However, in addition to the three epochs from Matthew, Goldsworthy adds the epochal differences between creation (Genesis 1–2), the impact of the historic fall (Genesis 3), and primeval history (Genesis 3–11), thus speaking of the era of Genesis 1–11 prior to Abraham. Concerning the first epoch, i.e., creation, fall, primeval history, Goldsworthy argues that it provides the main theological presuppositions to all of redemptive-history, which are then worked out as God's plan unfolds and ultimately culminates in Christ.[31]

Interesting and important for our purposes is the observation that most of these epochal divisions follow the unfolding of the biblical covenants. In this regard, one of the major weaknesses of Goldsworthy's work is that he discusses in detail the unfolding of the "kingdom" as the major framework, backbone, or, to use Michael Horton's term, "intrasystematic" category of Scripture, yet discusses little how the unfolding of the biblical covenants unite and bind the plot line of Scripture together.[32] No doubt, *kingdom* is a crucial theme as one works across the Canon,[33] but "kingdom through

---

[31] For a discussion of these points see Graeme Goldsworthy, *According to Plan: The Unfolding Revelation of God in the Bible* (Downers Grove, IL: InterVarsity Press, 2002), 80–234; idem, *Preaching the Whole Bible as Christian Scripture: The Application of Biblical Theology to Expository Preaching* (Grand Rapids, MI: Eerdmans, 2000); idem, *Gospel-Centered Hermeneutics*, 70–73, 245–257.

[32] Goldsworthy, *Gospel-Centered Hermeneutics*, 241–245, does speak of the covenants, but it does not serve for him as one of the main ways God's plan unfolds across history. Kingdom is much more of a predominant category, but his failure to link "kingdom" with "covenants" and to argue that it is "kingdom through covenant," in our view, is a weakness of his work and something we are seeking to remedy in this book.

[33] Besides the writings of Goldsworthy cited above, works that highlight the framework of *kingdom* include: G. E. Ladd, *The Presence of the Future: The Eschatology of Biblical Realism*, rev. ed. (Grand Rapids, MI: Eerdmans, 1974); G. R. Beasley-Murray, "The Kingdom of God in the Old and New Testaments," in *Reclaiming the Prophetic Mantle: Preaching the Old Testament Faithfully*, ed. George L. Kline (Nashville: Broadman, 1992), 179–201; Bruce Waltke, "The Kingdom of God in Biblical Theology," in *Looking into the Future: Evangelical Studies in Eschatology*, ed. David W. Baker (Grand Rapids, MI: Baker, 2001), 15–27; Darrell L. Bock, "The Kingdom of God in New Testament Theology," in *Looking into the Future*, 28–60; Dan G. McCartney, "*Ecce Homo*: The Coming of the Kingdom as the Restoration of Human Viceregency," *Westminster Theological Journal* 56 (1994): 1–21.

covenant" is a better way of thinking through the Bible's own *internal* structure and thus grasping the various epochal divisions in God's plan of redemption.[34]

At this point, it is important to ask whether these epochal differences, tied to *before* and *after* categories in Scripture, are really that hermeneutically significant. Or, better, is this how Scripture, on its own terms, "puts itself together?" Does thinking through where various texts are placed in the unfolding revelation of God impact the conclusions we draw from Scripture, especially in regard to how we understand the nature and relations of the biblical covenants? The answer is *yes*. For example, let us think about Paul's argument in Romans 4. In Romans 4, Paul argues that Abraham serves as the paradigm for Jews *and* Gentiles of one who was justified by grace through faith apart from works. Warrant for this assertion is found in Genesis 15:6, where God declares Abraham just on the basis of his believing the promises of God. But in order to demonstrate that God's declaration of justification is for both the Jew and the Gentile, Paul then argues that in the life of Abraham this declaration took place *before* he was circumcised (which took place in Genesis 17, which comes *after* Genesis 15), thus demonstrating that Abraham's justification was *not* tied to circumcision but was solely on the basis of his faith in the promises of God. It is for this reason that Abraham can serve as the paradigm of faith for Jews *and* Gentiles. This is not to say that circumcision is not significant in the Old Testament, for certainly it was, especially as it was given in the context of the Abrahamic covenant and later to Israel in the old covenant. But it is to affirm that one cannot draw the conclusion, which the Judaizers unfortunately did, that, to know God, Gentiles had to first be circumcised in order to enter into covenant relationship with the Lord. In the life of Abraham, not only was this *not* the case, but now that Christ has come, that covenant sign is no longer in force (1 Cor. 7:19), due

---

[34] There is more that can be said in regard to epochal divisions. In this discussion we have sought only to highlight the major ways Scripture distinguishes various epochs of redemptive-history, but this is certainly not exhaustive. In fact, one can even speak of epochal differences in a very short period of time. For example, in the life and ministry of our Lord, the Gospel writers distinguish between pre-cross and resurrection versus post-resurrection, ascension, and Pentecost. Where we are in this time period makes all the difference in many areas—e.g., our knowledge of God and our grasp of what our Lord has achieved and accomplished, our experience of the Spirit, the covenant we are under, and God's expectations of us as the people of God. On this point see John 2:20–22, which demonstrates that it was not until after the resurrection that people began to see the full implications of what our Lord had achieved. Or, John 7:39 makes it clear that our experience of the Spirit is tied to specific events occurring in redemptive-history, that is, all of the events associated with the cross work of Christ, including Pentecost. The same may be said of Acts 2, which speaks of the incredible change that occurred now that the Spirit was given in fulfillment of Old Testament expectation. Prior to Pentecost, the full experience of the Spirit did not occur as it did after these redemptive acts with their epochal significance. This last observation is important in discerning such issues as what is new in the new covenant and especially its implications for soteriology and ecclesiology.

to the fact that, in the plot line of Scripture, God was teaching us that salvation was always by grace through faith. It is important to note, however, that Paul's argument works *only* if you interpret the significance of circumcision by properly locating Genesis 17 *after* Genesis 15. In other words, texts must carefully be interpreted in terms of what comes *before* and *after* them, in order to draw correct "biblical" conclusions.

Galatians 3 is another example of this point and is a very significant text in thinking through covenantal relationships. In Galatians 3, Paul is countering the Judaizers who, like many conservative Jews, "saw in the law given at Sinai not only a body of instruction but a hermeneutical key to the rest of Scripture."[35] In this way these individuals viewed the old covenant as an end in itself and not a means to a larger end found in Christ and the inauguration of the new covenant. That is why, in order for a Gentile to become a Christian, these Judaizers argued that Gentiles had to come under the Mosaic law-covenant. On the other hand, Paul's argument is that, now that Christ has come, Christians are *not* bound by the Mosaic law-covenant; rather, we come to Christ by faith apart from it (vv. 1–6). How does Paul ground his point? He first appeals to Genesis 15:6 to demonstrate that Abraham was justified by grace through faith (vv. 6–9) and then argues that God's declaration of justification in Abraham's life was long *before* the giving of the Mosaic law (vv. 15–29). In light of this he wrestles with the obvious question of why the law was given, but his conclusion is the same: since Abraham is declared just *before* the Mosaic law-covenant was given, it cannot set aside the previous covenant.

Hermeneutically and theologically speaking, then, in order to grasp how God's plan fits together, and, for our purposes, how the biblical covenants fit together, one must locate each covenant in its place in redemptive-history and discern how it relates to what preceded it and what comes after it. Unless we read texts in terms of the "textual" and "epochal" horizons we will misread Scripture and fail to understand how the *parts* of God's plan fit with the *whole*.[36] In this regard, this was one of the key failures of a Jewish

---

[35] Carson, "Systematic Theology and Biblical Theology," in *NDBT*, 98. Cf. Beale and Carson, "Introduction," in *Commentary on the New Testament Use of the Old Testament*, xxvi–xxvii.

[36] There are other examples that illustrate this point, particularly the book of Hebrews. In chapters 7–8, the author makes the same argument that Paul makes in Romans 4 and Galatians 3, namely, that one must read texts following carefully their placement in the story line of Scripture. So, for example, in Hebrews 7, the author concludes that the Old Testament did not view the Levitical priesthood as an end in itself but as something that was temporary, given God's announcement of another priest, in a different order, in Psalm 110, *which came many years later than the establishment of the Levitical priesthood* (Heb. 7:11, 28). Also, in Hebrews 8, building on his argument in chapter 7, the author concludes that, since the promise of the new covenant in Jeremiah 31 comes *after* the

reading of Scripture. Generally speaking, Old Testament Jews, along with the Judaizers, did not interpret the law-covenant in relation to its place in redemptive-history. If they had done so, they would have drawn the same conclusion that the New Testament draws: in God's overall plan the Mosaic law-covenant should be viewed as more of a parenthesis or something temporary, leading us to what that old covenant was ultimately pointing forward to, namely, the dawning of the new covenant in Christ.[37] As we conclude this discussion of the epochal horizon, we must go one step further by emphasising that texts must also be read in terms of what comes *after* them, which leads us to a discussion of the canonical horizon.

The third and last context that must be considered in our interpretation of any biblical text is the *canonical horizon*. Given the fact that Scripture is *God's* Word and thus a *unified* revelation, in the final analysis texts must be understood in relation to the entire Canon. We cannot adequately interpret and apply Scripture if we ignore the canonical level. As Kevin Vanhoozer rightly notes, it is only when we read Scripture in terms of the canonical horizon that we are interpreting it in a truly "biblical" manner—"according to its truest, fullest, *divine* intention."[38] In fact, to read the Bible canonically is not merely a matter of how the church has read Scripture; it best corresponds to what the Bible actually *is*. That is why, "To read the Bible as unified Scripture is not just one interpretative interest among others, but the interpretative strategy that best corresponds to the nature of the text itself, given its divine inspiration."[39] The Canon may then be viewed "as a great hall of witnesses in which different voices all testify to the Lord Jesus Christ. Over and above the laws and promises, the warnings and commands, the stories and the songs, is an all-embracing act, that of witnessing to what God was and is doing in Christ. . . . Thanks to their overarching canonical

---

establishment of the old covenant, this is proof that the old covenant should have been viewed as temporary and as pointing beyond itself to something greater. In all these ways, Scripture is read by tracing out the Bible's story line and interpreting texts in light of where they are on that story line in terms of what comes *before* and what comes *after*. On these points see P. T. O'Brien, *The Letter to the Hebrews*, Pillar New Testament Commentary (Grand Rapids, MI: Eerdmans, 2010), 255–303.

[37] On this point see Carson, "Mystery and Fulfillment," in *Justification and Variegated Nomism: Volume 2—The Paradoxes of Paul*, ed. D. A. Carson, P. T. O'Brien, and M. A. Seifrid (Grand Rapids, MI: Baker, 2004), 410–412. Carson makes the point that Paul understands the significance of the Mosaic covenant by paying strict attention to its place in the story line of the Pentateuch. When Paul does so, Carson contends, Paul almost treats the law-covenant as a parenthesis (Gal. 3:15–4:7). Carson states, "The promise to Abraham that in his seed all the nations of the earth would be blessed antedates Moses and the giving of the law by centuries, and that promise cannot be annulled by the giving of the law (3:17), regardless of how much space is given over to the law in the sacred text, or how large a role it played in the history of Israel" (412).

[38] Vanhoozer, "Exegesis and Hermeneutics," 61.

[39] Ibid. For a more detailed development of this point see Kevin J. Vanhoozer, *First Theology: God, Scripture, and Hermeneutics* (Downers Grove, IL: InterVarsity Press, 2002), 194–203.

context, the smaller communicative acts are caught up and reoriented to the larger purpose of 'making wise unto salvation.'"[40] As texts are placed along the story line of Scripture and ultimately interpreted in light of the culmination of God's plan in Christ, we begin to read Scripture in the way God intended and thus "biblically."

What, then, does it mean to be "biblical?" If we take seriously Scripture's claim for itself and what Scripture actually is, a three horizon reading of the Canon is the place to start—a *theological* reading, which may be summarised as a grammatical/linguistic-historical-canonical method of interpretation. In the final analysis, the best way to read Scripture and to draw theological conclusions is to interpret a given text of Scripture in its linguistic-historical, literary, redemptive-historical, and canonical context. In this way, we are letting Scripture interpret Scripture; we are seeking to unfold how the Bible itself is given to us, in its own intrasystematic categories and presentation, so that in the end, we read, apply, and draw theological conclusions from Scripture "biblically," i.e., as God intended and "on its own terms."[41]

At this point it is legitimate to ask, in what ways does Scripture itself link the Canon together in terms of its own intrasystematic categories? Obviously much could be said here, but Richard Lints is on track when he notes that, in the big scheme of things, "essential to the canonical horizon of biblical interpretation is the continuity between the promises of God and his fulfillment of those promises."[42] That is why one of the important ways that God has glued the diverse epochs of redemptive-history together is by the *promise-fulfilment* motif, which then becomes important in one's reading of Scripture correctly. But note: it is well nigh impossible to think of God's promises apart from unpacking the biblical covenants, since the triune God

---

[40] Vanhoozer, "Exegesis and Hermeneutics," 62.

[41] On this point, Richard Lints, *Fabric of Theology*, 268–289, rightly contends that our reading of Scripture, if it is on the Bible's "own terms," must follow the "interpretive matrix of the Scriptures." "In order to do this, a theological framework cannot simply mine the Scriptures looking for answers to a set of specific questions that arise uniquely in the modern era. It should seek out the questions that the Scriptures are asking, for these remain the questions that are important for understanding the past and present and future" (269). As Lints notes, the attempt to follow the interpretive matrix of Scripture is not searching "for doctrinal models and keys that fit the Bible's complex locks and open them up to the reader" (270). Rather, we must seek to unpack the *Bible's own structure* (what I mean by intratextual) and make sure that "the conceptual categories of the theological framework adequately reflect the phenomena of Scripture" (270) in terms of both its specific content *and* its structure (see 270–274). Our understanding of the interpretive framework may have to be modified in light of exegesis, however. As Lints notes, "the fact that this framework is properly subject to reform should in no way be taken to imply that the Scriptures themselves contain data that may be organized in any number of conflicting fashions or indeed that there are a variety of competing frameworks in the Scriptures themselves" (288). In this work, it is our argument that the biblical covenants serve as the main framework and backbone of the plot line of Scripture, and that to ignore this fact or to misunderstand the relations between the biblical covenants and how Scripture intends for them to be "put together" leads to a misreading of Scripture on its own terms and as God intended.

[42] Lints, *Fabric of Theology*, 303.

who makes promises to his creatures, both in terms of creation and redemption, does so by entering into covenant relations with them. In truth, unpacking the "promise-fulfilment" motif is another way of unfolding the biblical covenants across redemptive-history, and this is why the biblical covenants serve as the framework and backbone to the entire narrative plot structure of Scripture. By unfolding the biblical covenants, the biblical authors are able to grasp both the continuity of God's plan (tied to his promises) and its discontinuity (how fulfilment in Christ brings with it God-intended changes). Lints states it this way: "The biblical authors frame their writings with the assertion that God has been faithful to his promises in times past, and so he shall be faithful in the future. The promise-fulfillment model is a thread that secures the unity of the diverse collection of these writings. It provides meaning in the midst of present circumstances and hope for future deliverance."[43] Thus, as we trace out the story line of Scripture, as we move from promise to fulfilment, and unfold the biblical covenants across the Canon, we are better able to see how all of Scripture hangs together and reaches its consummation in Christ Jesus. We begin to appreciate even more that the diverse stories of Scripture are not randomly thrown together but are part of a larger tapestry that finds its terminus in Christ.

Richard Lints also suggests that intimately associated with the "promise-fulfilment" theme is biblical typology. In fact, one of the crucial means by which God's redemptive-historical plan unfolds, indeed how the "promise-fulfilment" motif is developed in Scripture, is by the use of God-given "typology." No doubt, "typology" is a hotly disputed topic in biblical and theological studies, and it can mean different things to different people. As Paul Hoskins reminds us, "Studies in biblical typology have been complicated by the use of the terms 'typology' and 'type' where no definitions of these terms are given."[44] But regardless of the debate over typology, getting

---

[43] Ibid.

[44] Paul M. Hoskins, *Jesus as the Fulfillment of the Temple in the Gospel of John* (Eugene, OR: Wipf & Stock, 2006), 18. Hoskins goes on to describe two different conceptions of typology within contemporary biblical studies: a traditional view, which believes that the correspondence between type and antitype is God-given, intentional, and predictive, versus a more critical view, which is more skeptical about the predictive and prospective significance of the types (18–36). Our view of typology will argue for the traditional understanding of it. For a defense of such a view see Richard Davidson, *Typology in Scripture: A Study of Hermeneutical TUPOS Structures*, Andrews University Seminary Doctoral Dissertation Series 2 (Berrien Springs, MI: Andrews University, 1981). See also John H. Stek, "Biblical Typology Yesterday and Today," *Calvin Theological Journal* 5 (1970): 133–162; Leonhard Goppelt, *Typos: The Typological Interpretation of the Old Testament in the New*, trans. D. H. Madvig (Grand Rapids, MI: Eerdmans, 1982); Carson, "Mystery and Fulfillment," 404; Moo, "Problem of *Sensus Plenior*," 175–212; Lints, *Fabric of Theology*, 304–310; G. K. Beale, "Did Jesus and His Followers Preach the Right Doctrine from the Wrong Texts?" 387–404; idem, *Gospel-Centered Hermeneutics*, 234–257; David L. Baker, *Two Testaments, One Bible: The Theological Relationship between the Old and New Testaments*, 3rd ed. (Downers Grove, IL: InterVarsity Press, 2010)

at the character of typology is crucial to adjudicating the biblical-theological systems of dispensational and covenant theology. One of the reasons for the differences between these two views, as we will note in more detail below, centres on the issue of the nature of typology and how that typological understanding relates to the biblical covenants. For example, as already mentioned in chapter 2, major disagreements over how dispensational theology understands the land promise, contra covenant theology, is related to typological debates. Furthermore, covenant theology's understanding and use of the genealogical principle, contra dispensational theology, is tied to typological debates as well. And, it must be noted, these typological discrepancies are intimately tied to dispensational and covenant theology's understanding of the biblical covenants. Given the importance of this issue, it is necessary to discuss briefly how we understand typology, since our proposal understands and utilizes typology in a specific way.

The Nature and Importance of Typology

In discussions of typology it is first crucial to distinguish it from "allegory." What is the difference? The major difference is that typology is grounded in *history*, the *text*, and *intertextual* development, where various "persons, events, and institutions" are intended by God to correspond to each other, while allegory assumes none of these things. In addition, since allegories are not grounded in authorial intent which is (inter)textually warranted, "allegorical interpretation" depends on some kind of extratextual grid to warrant its explanation. As Kevin Vanhoozer notes, allegorical interpretation is represented by the interpretive strategy for declaring *"This* (word) means *that* (concept)"[45] with *that* being determined by an extratextual framework. This is not what typology is and how typology functions in Scripture. In fact when one investigates the six explicit New Testament texts that deal with typology (Rom. 5:14; 1 Cor. 10:6, 11; 1 Pet. 3:21; Heb. 8:5; 9:24), a consistent picture emerges which clearly distinguishes it from allegory. What

---

169–189; Clowney, *Preaching and Biblical Theology*; Daniel J. Treier, "Typology," in *Dictionary for Theological Interpretation of the Bible*, ed. Kevin J. Vanhoozer (Grand Rapids, MI: Baker, 2005), 823–827.

[45] Vanhoozer, *Is There a Meaning in This Text?* 119. Galatians 4:24–26 is a difficult text. Many argue that Paul is employing an allegorical interpretation while others explain the passage along the lines of typology. A. B. Caneday has recently argued that *allegory* is present, but not on the basis of Paul's interpretative prowess; rather, the Genesis text itself is allegorical in that the characters in the historical narrative are invested with symbolic representations and significance. For an analysis of this textually warranted form of allegory, see A. B. Caneday, "Covenant Lineage Allegorically Prefigured: 'What Things Are Written Allegorically' (Galatians 4:21–31)," *SBJT* 14/3 (2010): 50–77.

exactly is that pattern? Let us describe it by first starting with a definition of typology and then explaining the key features of it.[46]

We will employ Richard Davidson's definition of typology. Typology as a New Testament hermeneutical endeavour is the study of the Old Testament salvation historical realities or "types" (persons, events, institutions) which God has specifically designed to correspond to, and predictively prefigure, their intensified antitypical fulfilment aspects (inaugurated and consummated) in New Testament salvation history.[47] There are two explanatory points to note from this definition.

First, typology is symbolism rooted in *historical* and *textual* realities. As such, it involves an *organic* relation between "persons, events, and institutions" in one epoch and their counterparts in later epochs. The early "person, event, and institution" is called the "type" while the later one is the "antitype." As Richard Lints reminds us, "The typological relation is a central means by which particular epochal and textual horizons are linked to later horizons in redemptive revelation. It links the present to the future, and it retroactively links the present with the past. It is founded on the organic connection of God's promises with his fulfillment of those promises."[48]

Second, typology is *prophetic* and *predictive* and thus divinely given and intended. In other words, God intended the "type" to point beyond itself to its fulfilment or "antitype" in a later epoch of redemptive-history. It is for this reason that typologies are not mere "analogies" but are recurrent patterns pointing forward to and culminating ultimately in Christ. Typology ought to be viewed as a subset of predictive prophecy, not in the sense of verbal predictions, but in the sense of predictions built on models/patterns that God himself has established, that become known gradually as later texts reinforce those patterns, with the goal of anticipating what comes later in Christ.[49] In

---

[46] Our treatment of typology is heavily indebted to a number of people, but particularly the helpful dissertation of Richard Davidson (see note 44, above), who investigates all of the uses of *typos* in the New Testament and then draws conclusions as to the nature of typology on that basis.

[47] This definition is compiled from the summary discussion in Davidson, *Typology in Scripture*, 397–408. Graham A. Cole, *He Who Gives Life: The Doctrine of the Holy Spirit* (Wheaton, IL: Crossway, 2007), 289, also gives a helpful definition of typology: "The idea that persons (e.g., Moses), events (e.g., the exodus), and institutions (e.g., the temple) can—in the plan of God—prefigure a later stage in that plan and provide the conceptuality necessary for understanding the divine intent (e.g., the coming of Christ to be the new Moses, to effect the new exodus, and to be the new temple)."

[48] Lints, *Fabric of Theology*, 304. The emphasis on history is important since it distinguishes a traditional view of typology from what Davidson (*Typology in Scripture*, 46–75) labels a post-critical neo-typological viewpoint. For the latter view, the historicity of the types is not essential. For a traditional view, the correspondence between type and antitype is not a mere literary phenomena but rather is rooted in historical realities. See Hoskins, *Jesus as Fulfillment of the Temple*, 27; Carson, "Mystery and Fulfillment," 404.

[49] The predictive nature of typology is another distinguishing feature of a traditional view over against the post-critical neo-typology view. For the latter, the discovery of typological patterns is based on analogies and a

this way, typology is more "indirect" prophecy, which corresponds well with the Pauline emphasis on "mystery" (see, e.g., Eph. 1:9–10; 3:1–10).[50] In a number of places, Paul says that the gospel was hidden in the past, but now, in light of the coming of Christ, is made known and disclosed publicly for all to see. Simultaneously, then, Scripture says two things: first, the gospel was *promised* beforehand and was *clearly* revealed through the prophets (e.g., Rom. 3:21), while, secondly, it was *hidden* in ages past and *not* fully known until the coming of Christ (e.g., Rom. 16:25–27). How do we bring these two ideas together? Ultimately the answer will help explain how those who read the Old Testament were indicted for not understanding it correctly *and* why so many failed to "see" and grasp the coming of the Lord of Glory (see, e.g., John 3:10–11; 5:39–40; 1 Cor. 2:7–8). A crucial way to reconcile these two ideas is through typology. Given the *indirect* nature of it, not only does typology require carefully discernment; it also requires the passing of time in order to determine how the "type" is fulfilled in the coming of the Lord Jesus Christ.

At this point, it is important to state a hidden assumption undergirding a predictive, God-given view of typology. Such a view presupposes a strong view of divine providence and knowledge.[51] How so? While the type has significance for its own time, its greater significance is directed toward the future; it testifies to something greater than itself that is still to come. But the future antitype *will* surely come, not only because God completely knows that it will, according to his eternal plan, but also because God sovereignly and providentially will *guarantee* that the prophetic fulfilment of the original type will occur in Christ.[52] In other words, the relationship between type and antitype is *not* arbitrary, a mere analogy, or retroactively constructed by the reader; it is an *organic* relationship ordained by God so that specific types do in fact point beyond themselves to their fulfilment in Christ. Apart from this conception of God, typology in the way we are describing it makes no sense at all. This is *not* to say that everyone associated with the Old Testament type

---

retrospective reading of later persons, events, and institutions on the Old Testament. Typology is not viewed as predictive and prospective and thus it is not exegetically grounded. Interestingly, David Baker, *Two Testaments, One Bible*, 180–189, argues for the neo-typological understanding when he contends that typology is not prophecy, nor is typology exegetically derived since "it [typology] is theological reflection on relationships between events, persons and institutions recorded in biblical texts" (181).

[50] For a helpful article on "mystery" in Paul see Carson, "Mystery and Fulfillment," 393–436.

[51] See Beale, "Did Jesus and His Followers Preach the Right Doctrine from the Wrong Text?" 394–395; and Lints, *Fabric of Theology*, 306–310, who makes this same argument.

[52] See Lints, *Fabric of Theology*, 303–311. Cf. Goldsworthy, *Gospel-Centered Hermeneutics*, 245–257; and Hoskins, *Jesus as the Fulfillment of the Temple*, 21–27.

understood and knew the pattern to be pointing forward. Rather, it is to say that *when* the type is *discovered* to be a type (at some point along the trajectory of its repeated pattern due to intertextual development) it is then viewed as such and rightly as God-given.[53]

Given this basic description of typology, how, then, does it *work* in Scripture? It is best to think of typology exhibiting a twofold character. First, typology involves a *repetition* of the "promise-fulfilment" pattern of redemptive-history so that various types find their fulfilment in later persons, events, or institutions, but ultimately all types find their fulfilment in Christ. So, for example, Scripture presents Adam as a type of Christ (Rom. 5:12–21; 1 Cor. 15:21–49). As redemptive-history unfolds, other "Adams" (the idea of repetition) show up on the stage of human history that take on the role of the first Adam (e.g., Noah, Abraham, Israel, David), but these "other Adams" are *not* the ultimate fulfilment.[54] Instead, it is only in Christ that we have the "last Adam"—the one whom all these other persons point to and anticipate. In this way, God intends the first Adam to point beyond himself to Christ, and we come to know God's intention as the Adamic pattern intertextually develops and ultimately finds it culmination in Christ. This is why types are viewed as both *predictive* and *hidden*. They are *predictive* since God intends for them to anticipate Christ in a variety of ways. They are *hidden* not only due to their indirectness but also due to the fact that we come to know that they are types as God's redemptive plan unfolds and *later* texts pick up the recurring pattern.

Or, for example, think of the nation of Israel. Israel not only is presented in Scripture as "another Adam" who as the son (Ex. 4:22–23) takes on

---

[53] Another way of saying this is that typological patterns are discovered *exegetically*. In the immediate context where the type is first introduced there are clues in the text which speak of its importance. The significance of the type might not be grasped in the first instance, but through intertextual development within the Old Testament (e.g., later authors picking up these persons, institutions, and events, thus underscoring their importance as well as leading us to anticipate something more in the future) and then in terms of the entire Canon, readers begin to grasp the significance of the type and how that type fits in God's overall plan, which points forward to the consummation of that plan in the person and work of Christ, who is always first and foremost the antitype of these typological patterns. The need for textual warrant for typology has rightly been emphasised among theologians. Louis Berkhof, *Principles of Biblical Interpretation: Sacred Hermeneutics*, 2nd ed. (Grand Rapids, MI: Baker, 1952), 145, rightly stressed that the "[a]ccidental similarity between an Old and New Testament person or event does not constitute the one a type of the other. There must be some Scriptural evidence that it was so designed by God." Cf. Geerhardus Vos, *Biblical Theology*, 145–146. For a study of the intertextual development of exodus typology in the Old Testament, see Friedbert Ninow, *Indicators of Typology within the Old Testament: The Exodus Motif* (Berlin: Peter Lang, 2001). For other studies that seek to demonstrate how persons and events are understood as typological within the Old Testament, see Chad L. Bird, "Typological Interpretation *within* the Old Testament: Melchizedekian Typology," *Concordia Journal* 26 (2000): 36–52; and Daniel R. Streett, "As It Was in the Days of Noah: The Prophets' Typological Interpretation of Noah's Flood," *Criswell Theological Review* 5 (2007): 33–51.

[54] As will be argued in subsequent chapters, it is important to notice how the development of Adam as a type of Christ is unpacked by the unfolding of the biblical covenants.

Adam's role in the world; Israel also anticipates the coming of the true Son, the true Israel, the true servant, the true vine, namely, our Lord Jesus Christ (see, e.g., Isa. 5:1–7; Hos. 11:1; Matt. 2:15; John 15:1–17). Furthermore, since types find their fulfilment first in Christ and not in us, we as God's people participate in the typological pattern by virtue of our relationship to Christ. Thus, in the case of Israel as a typological pattern, Christ is first and foremost its fulfilment and we, as the church, are viewed as the "Israel of God" only because of our union with Christ. In other words, we, as the church, are *not* the antitypical fulfilment of Israel in the first sense; Christ alone fills that role. Yet in faith union with Christ, we are the beneficiaries of his work. In relationship to him, the true Son/Israel, we become adopted sons (Gal. 3:26–4:7), the "Israel of God" (Gal. 6:16), Abraham's spiritual offspring (Gal. 3:29), restored to what God created us to be as his image-bearers (Eph. 4:20–24).[55] It is in this way that the new covenant promise given to the "house of Israel" and the "house of Judah" (Jer. 31:31) is applied to the church. Christ, as the antitypical fulfilment of Israel, takes on the role of Israel, and by faith union in him, his work becomes ours as his new covenant people.

A second characteristic of typology is its *a fortiori* (lesser to greater) quality, or the fact that it exhibits *escalation* as the type is fulfilled in the antitype. For example, as one moves from Adam or David, to the prophets, priests, and kings, across redemptive-history, to the last Adam, the true Davidic King, the great High Priest, and so on, the antitype is *always* greater than the previous types/patterns. Yet it is important to note that escalation across time does *not* occur incrementally from the original type to each "little" installment and then to Christ, as if there were a straight line of increase. Rather escalation occurs fully only with the coming of Christ. The previous typological patterns point forward to the greater one to come (Rom. 5:14), but the *greater* aspect is realized only in Christ. So, for example, Adam serves as a type of Christ, and "little Adams" arise across time, yet all of these "other Adams" (e.g., Noah, Abraham, Israel, David) fail in their obedience and faith; there is *not* an increase in them. Yet, all of them anticipate the coming of a greater Adam—the last Adam—who will *not* fail in his obedience and faith. Or, think of David and his sons. Rooted in the

---

[55] As we will later develop in more detail, this observation that we, as the church, are the "Israel of God" only by virtue of our union with Christ, who is the antitypical fulfilment of Israel, is crucial for carving a *via media* between dispensationalism's and covenant theology's views of the church.

Davidic covenant, they serve as types of Christ. As one moves from David to Solomon there is a minimal escalation but it does not last long. Solomon, at the end of his life, as great as he was, horribly fails. In fact, all of the Davidic kings fail, including David, and as such they are not able to usher in God's saving rule and reign (kingdom) and fulfill their God-appointed purpose. It is only in the coming of David's greater Son, our Lord Jesus Christ, that we have escalation as he brings the Davidic pattern to its antitypical fulfillment.

This observation is important for a number of reasons. Not only does the *a fortiori* quality of typology serve as the crucial means by which Scripture unpacks the unique identity of Christ, it is also the way in which Scripture grounds the uniqueness of the entire era of fulfillment associated with the dawning of the new covenant. In other words, it is the means by which a legitimate *discontinuity* between the old and new in God's unified plan is established. When the antitype arrives in history, or better, when it is inaugurated, not only are the previous types brought to their *telos* but the entire era introduced entails massive changes in many areas. This is why, in the unfolding of God's plan, the era of fulfillment inaugurated by Christ (what is often called the "already"), even though it still awaits the consummation (the "not yet"), has introduced greater realities—realities directly linked to the inauguration of the kingdom, the dawning of the new covenant era, and the arrival of the new creation.[56]

Before we leave the discussion of typology, it is important to note how closely typological structures and biblical covenants are related. It is difficult to think of biblical types and patterns that are not associated with the biblical covenants. In other words, to reflect upon typological structures and their development is simultaneously to unpack the biblical covenants across redemptive-history. For example, Adam and the "other Adams" who follow him are all associated with the covenants of creation, Noah, Abraham, Israel, and David. In all these covenant heads, the role of Adam is continued in the world, and each one of them points forward to the coming of the last Adam, who through his obedience accomplishes for us our redemption.[57] Or, think of the promise to Abraham regarding his "seed." As the seed promise unfolds it does so in Isaac, later in the nation of Israel, the Davidic king, and supremely in our Lord Jesus, and then by extension to the

---

[56] For a helpful discussion of inaugurated eschatology see Thomas R. Schreiner, *New Testament Theology: Magnifying God in Christ* (Grand Rapids, MI: Baker, 2008), 41–116.

[57] See texts such as Genesis 1–3; 5:1–2; 9:1–17; 12:1–3; Exodus 4:22–23; 2 Samuel 7:5–16; Psalm 8; Romans 5:12–21; Hebrews 2:5–18.

church as Abraham's spiritual offspring.[58] Or, think of how Moses, who is foundational for the entire institution of prophets and who inaugurates the entire priestly role under the old covenant, is developed in terms of an entire institution of prophets and priests which ultimately culminates in Christ.[59] Many more examples could be given in relation to David and his sons, the entire tabernacle-temple structure, the event of the exodus which eventually anticipates a greater exodus to come, and so on. All of these biblical types are organically related to the biblical covenants. One cannot properly think of them apart from wrestling with how the covenants relate to each other and how the covenants as a whole point forward to the coming of Christ and the new covenant age. In this way, all of biblical history is prophetic, not merely in terms of verbal predictions but in types/patterns associated with the covenants, which anticipate and predict the dawning of the end of the ages in the coming of the Lord of Glory. This is why the entire New Testament is Christological in focus, since Jesus is the one that the covenants and prophets anticipate (e.g., Matt. 5:17–18; 11:11–15; Rom. 3:21, 31). This is another reason why "putting together" the biblical covenants is the means by which we grasp the plan of God and thus understand the Scriptures. Apart from doing so, we fail to discern how the "parts" fit with the "whole" and we are less than "biblical" in our reading of Scripture.

What does it mean to be *biblical*? How do we rightly exegete biblical texts and draw proper theological conclusions? Obviously what we have stated only begins to scratch the surface in terms of a full-orbed answer. What we have sought to describe is how we are approaching the hermeneutical task and the theological interpretation of Scripture. This is especially important since we are attempting to argue for a *via media* position on the covenants. With these basic points in mind, let us now turn to the second portion of this chapter and revisit the biblical-theological systems of dispensationalism and covenant theology by discussing some of the key hermeneutical issues that divide them in order to better adjudicate their overall fit with Scripture. As we do so, we will begin to sketch out how "kingdom through covenant" serves as an alternative position, which we will explain in more detail in the chapters to follow.

---

[58] See texts such as Genesis 1:2–3; 17:1–22; Exodus 1:1–7; 2 Samuel 7:5–16; Galatians 3:16, 29. On the development of this theme see T. D. Alexander, "Seed" in *NDBT*, 769–773.
[59] See Exodus 19–20, 24, 32–34; Leviticus 8–9; Deuteronomy 18:15–22; 34:10–12; John 1:14–18; Hebrews 1:1–3; 3:1–6.

KEY HERMENEUTICAL ISSUES SEPARATING DISPENSATIONAL AND COVENANT THEOLOGY

In terms of basic theological convictions, dispensational and covenant theology agree on more than divides them, so one should not exaggerate their differences. Yet, as described in the previous chapter, on some crucial points, specifically the Israel-church relation and its linkage with each position's view of the biblical covenants, substantial differences remain which affect how these two different biblical-theological systems "put together" their Bible.

What, then, are some of the key hermeneutical differences that separate dispensational and covenant theology? Our answer to this question will draw on the helpful discussion of John Feinberg in the fine work *Continuity and Discontinuity*, which probes these issues in detail.[60] Feinberg, in describing the core hermeneutical distinctives of dispensational theology, or what he labels "systems of discontinuity," perceptively captures some of the differences between dispensational and covenant theology. Specifically, we will focus on three areas of difference from his discussion: the priority of the New Testament over the Old Testament, the nature of the biblical covenants, and the use of typology. These areas will help us grasp better the central core of dispensational theology and enable us to compare and contrast dispensational and covenant theology while we outline our approach to these same issues, which later chapters will develop in more detail.

In discussing these three areas, it is important to observe how interrelated they are and how each point does not stand on its own but requires and assumes the other points. This should not surprise us since these three points take us to the core of each system. Furthermore, all of these points, as noted in chapter 2, are rooted in a specific conception of the Israel-church relationship, which in turn is related to their view of the covenants. Specifically, there is debate over the precise nature of God's unchanging promises to ethnic Israel and how those promises are fulfilled in the church and the new covenant. Since dispensational and covenant theology view this relationship differently, these points help us grasp the essential differences between them in these crucial areas. Let us now turn to these three points incrementally, fully aware that all three of them together are necessary to comprehend the core differences between each view and to grasp better how each system "puts together" the biblical covenants.

---

[60] See John S. Feinberg, "Systems of Discontinuity," in *Continuity and Discontinuity: Perspectives on the Relationship between the Old and New Testaments*, ed. John S. Feinberg (Wheaton, IL: Crossway, 1988), 63–86.

THE PRIORITY OF THE NEW TESTAMENT OVER THE OLD TESTAMENT IN THE PROGRESS OF REVELATION

One of the key hermeneutical differences, Feinberg contends, between dispensational and covenant theology is the priority given to the New Testament over the Old Testament especially in conclusions drawn regarding the role and future of ethnic Israel in God's plan.[61] Feinberg correctly rejects the false claim that only dispensationalists consistently apply a "literal" hermeneutic in their interpretation of Scripture and that covenant theologians interpret the Bible nonliterally or spiritually.[62] This way of distinguishing the views, though often voiced by dispensationalists, is not accurate. It is especially inaccurate given the fact that covenant theologians repeatedly claim that they interpret the Bible "literally," in the *sensus literalis* use of the term.[63] As Feinberg observes, "Both sides claim to interpret literally, and yet they derive different theological systems. This suggests that the difference is not literalism v. non-literalism, but different understandings of what constitutes literal hermeneutics."[64] On this point, Feinberg is correct. But where, then, do the differences lie?

Feinberg proposes that the first area where the differences lie is in how each view understands "the progress of revelation to the priority of one Testament over the other."[65] No doubt, both views take seriously progressive revelation and acknowledge that the New Testament fulfills the Old Testament, but there is a basic disagreement over whether the New Testament can be used to "reinterpret" the Old Testament. For example, as Feinberg contends, dispensational theology often begins with the Old Testament, "but wherever they begin they demand that the OT be taken on its own terms rather

---

[61] For this discussion see Feinberg, "Systems of Discontinuity," 73–79.

[62] Vern S. Poythress, *Understanding Dispensationalists*, 2nd ed. (Phillipsburg, NJ: P&R, 1994), 78–96, nicely discusses the thorny issue of "literal" interpretation. He demonstrates, like Feinberg, that the difference between dispensational and covenant theology is not at this point but over how "literal" is employed in specific areas, particularly the relation of Israel-church. It is not enough, then, to reduce the differences to this point. Furthermore, it is best to understand "literal" in the *sensus literalis* sense, i.e., the meaning of sentences tied to the intention of authors and their employment of various literary forms. Thus, as Kevin Vanhoozer (*Is There a Meaning in This Text?* 312) states it, "Taking the Bible literally means reading for its literary sense, the sense of its communicative act. This entails, first, doing justice to the propositional, poetic, and purposive aspects of each text as a communicative act and, second, relating these to the Bible considered as a unified divine communicative act: the Word of God." For a historical survey of the concept of *sensus literalis*, see Charles J. Scalise, "The 'Sensus Literalis': A Hermeneutical Key to Biblical Exegesis," *Scottish Journal of Theology* 42 (1989): 45–65.

[63] See, e.g., Horton, *Covenant and Eschatology*, 171–175; cf. Berkhof, *Principles of Biblical Interpretation*, 57–60; Poythress, *Understanding Dispensationalists*, 78–129.

[64] Feinberg, "Systems of Discontinuity," 74. See also David L. Turner, "The Continuity of Scripture and Eschatology: Key Hermeneutical Issues," *Grace Theological Journal* 6/2 (1985): 275–287, and his finding that the charge of hyperliteralism or spiritualising will not move the debate forward (esp. 275–278).

[65] Feinberg, "Systems of Discontinuity," 74.

than reinterpreted in light of the NT."[66] On the other hand, Feinberg argues that nondispensationalists (i.e., covenant theologians) begin "with NT teaching as having priority, and then go back to the OT"[67] so that the Old Testament is reinterpreted in light of the New Testament teaching. The reason they do so, Feinberg insists, is because covenant theology views the Old Testament as provisional in God's unfolding plan whereas the New Testament is that which is permanent and final. Hence the rationale to view the New Testament as having priority over the Old Testament and the tendency to argue that whatever the New Testament does not explicitly affirm is no longer in force in the new covenant era.[68]

In stressing this point, it is crucial to note, and perhaps even ironically, that Feinberg does *not* disagree with the application of this hermeneutical rule in most places. For example, he affirms, along with covenant theology, that the sacrificial system, the food laws, the priesthood, and so on, were provisional and temporary in the Old Testament era and that these things now, in light of Christ's coming and the progress of revelation, have reached their terminus. As Feinberg acknowledges, "If the NT explicitly rejects an OT institution, etc., it is cancelled."[69] In this sense, *all* Christians, regardless of whether they are dispensational or covenantal, agree that the New Testament has priority over the Old Testament. However, this is *not* Feinberg's primary concern. After all, he is discussing the core *differences* between the two systems, which, as we have argued in chapter 2, are centred in different understandings of the Israel-church relationship and thus the relationships between the covenants. Hence, Feinberg's real concern is *not* with the priority of the New Testament over the Old Testament per se, but with how covenant theology applies this hermeneutic to *the* specific relationship he is concerned about, namely, that of Israel and the church, including the future role of ethnic Israel in God's plan.

In other words, Feinberg and dispensational theology contend that *at this specific point* it is illegitimate to read New Testament realities back on

---

[66] Ibid., 75.

[67] Ibid.

[68] See Feinberg, "Systems of Discontinuity," 75–76. Feinberg quotes Willem VanGemeren, "Israel as the Hermeneutical Crux in the Interpretation of Prophecy (II)," *Westminster Theological Journal* 46 (1984): 262, to illustrate this basic hermeneutical point from the side of covenant theology. VanGemeren, in noting how covenant theology determines what is still in force from the Old Testament, observes that the basic hermeneutical approach is as follows: "whatever the NT did not explicitly affirm was rejected and OT prophetic language was typologically interpreted" (cited in Feinberg, "Systems of Discontinuity," 76). It must also be admitted that this hermeneutical observation is related to how dispensational and covenant theology employ the use of typology, a point we will return to below.

[69] Feinberg, "Systems of Discontinuity," 76.

the Old Testament and to view ethnic Israel as something provisional and shadowy, or, as merely a type of the church in God's plan. One must first work from the Old Testament to the New Testament before appealing to the New Testament to overturn these Old Testament realities. Even more to the point, Feinberg is concerned that covenant theology appeals to the priority of the New Testament in order to *reinterpret* the land promises to national Israel in a spiritual or typological fashion. How so? Given the fact that the New Testament lacks a detailed treatment of the land promise, covenant theology has argued that the land promise is *not* explicitly affirmed in the New Testament and thus is no longer in force.[70] But, as Feinberg argues, this is the problem with covenant theology: it has wrongly appealed to the priority of the New Testament and has not done justice to the Old Testament teaching in regard to this specific promise. As Feinberg asserts, one must first allow the Old Testament to speak on its own terms, especially in regard to the land promise, before one appeals to the New Testament to determine the issue.

In Feinberg's criticism of covenant theology, he raises an important question which everyone must address: how do we know "whether something in the OT (especially prophecy about Israel's future) is still binding in the NT,"[71] especially if the New Testament does not explicitly deal with the issue or promise? Feinberg responds in a twofold way. First, "If an OT prophecy or promise is made unconditionally to a given people and is still unfilled to them even in the NT era, then the prophecy must still be fulfilled to them. While a prophecy given unconditionally to Israel has a fulfillment for the church if the NT *applies* it to the church, it must also be fulfilled to Israel. Progress of revelation cannot cancel unconditional promises."[72] Second, and related to the first point, the fact that the land promise is not

---

[70] To be fair, the claim of covenant theology at this point is a bit more complicated than simply saying that the New Testament does not explicitly affirm the land promise to Israel and thus it is no longer in force. In addition, covenant theology argues that the land promise is tied to the conditionality of the old covenant, which Israel as a nation broke. As Michael Horton states, "It is hardly anti-Semitic to observe that the covenant with Israel as a national entity in league with God was conditional and that the nation had so thoroughly violated that covenant that its theocratic status was revoked. Dispensationalism . . . treat[s] the land promise as eternal and irrevocable, even to the extent that there can be a difference between Israel and the church in God's plan. . . . [This, however, fails] to recognize that the Hebrew Scriptures themselves qualify this national covenant in strictly conditional terms" (Michael S. Horton, *God of Promise: Introducing Covenant Theology* [Grand Rapids, MI: Baker, 2006], 47). Also cf. Keith A. Mathison, *From Age to Age: The Unfolding of Biblical Eschatology* (Phillipsburg, NJ: P&R, 2009), 83–84. However, it is important to note that dispensationalism responds to covenant theology by arguing that the land promise is tied not merely to the old covenant and its conditionality but also to the unconditional nature of the Abrahamic covenant which has preceded it. What this debate highlights is two points which we will discuss below: first, whether the covenants should be viewed as either unconditional or conditional, and second, whether the land promise is typological in nature.

[71] Feinberg, "Systems of Discontinuity," 76.

[72] Ibid.

repeated in the New Testament does not entail that it is not in force if the New Testament has not explicitly or implicitly overturned it, since it is grounded, dispensational theology insists, in God's unconditional promise.[73] In this response Feinberg raises some important issues regarding the priority given to the New Testament over the Old Testament. Covenant theology, according to dispensationalism, tends to read the Old Testament in terms of the New Testament and does not let the Old Testament speak on its own terms, especially in regard to the unconditional land promise to national Israel. On the other hand, a dispensational hermeneutic wants to let the Old Testament speak on its own terms first, and unless the New Testament explicitly or implicitly abrogates it, what is unconditionally promised in the Old Testament era is still in force today.

What are we to think of this charge? Is Feinberg correct in his observation? What can we learn from this discussion for our purposes? This charge is certainly a common one made by dispensationalists against covenant theologians, yet it requires some deeper reflection. Let us offer two reflections which we hope will advance the discussion and illustrate how we approach this same hermeneutical issue of the priority of the New Testament over the Old Testament. First, we agree that there is much truth in Feinberg's assertion, but, secondly, we do not think that he is completely accurate. In fact, it is our conviction that, ironically, both dispensational and covenant theology follow the *same* hermeneutic in appealing to the Old Testament and drawing theological conclusions, yet they do so in *different* areas central to their theological system. But before we unpack this latter point, let us first focus on what is right about Feinberg's assertion.

As we will argue in chapter 17, we agree that in specific areas central to covenant theology, namely, in the areas of ecclesiology and the ordinances (which, of course, are related to their understanding of the covenants), but not limited to these areas,[74] covenant theology tends to read new covenant

---

[73] Ibid. Feinberg writes, "If the NT explicitly rejects an OT institution, etc., it is canceled. But if God makes a point once (the OT), why must he repeat it in the NT for it still to be true and operative? So long as he neither explicitly or [sic] implicitly rejects the OT teaching, why assume it is canceled just because the NT does not repeat it? . . . Some may respond that the key word here is 'implicit.' While God may not explicitly negate OT promises to Israel in the NT, he surely does implicitly by applying them to the church. My response is that the promises cannot be canceled even implicitly *if they are made unconditionally*!" (emphasis his).

[74] We are also thinking of the area of soteriology. Covenant theology tends to argue that the salvation experience of the Old Testament believer is basically the same as that of the new covenant believer, thus reading new covenant realities such as the indwelling of the Holy Spirit and even union with Christ back into the old covenant. See Sinclair B. Ferguson, *The Holy Spirit* (Downers Grove, IL: InterVarsity Press, 1996), 68; B. B. Warfield, "The Spirit of God in the Old Testament," in *Biblical Doctrines* (New York: Oxford University Press, 1929; repr., Carlisle, PA: Banner of Truth, 1988), 121–128; cf. James M. Hamilton, Jr., *God's Indwelling Presence: The Holy Spirit in the Old and New Testaments* (Nashville: B&H Academic, 2006), 1–24.

realities back into the Old Testament and vice versa. They do so without first unpacking the covenants, the nature of the covenant community, and the covenantal signs in their own redemptive-historical context and then thinking carefully through the issues of continuity and discontinuity now that Christ has come. On this point we agree with Feinberg's basic criticism of covenant theology. However, we do not agree with him in the area that he is most concerned about, i.e., the land promise to national Israel. We are not convinced that dispensational theology has rightly understood the nature of the land promise.[75] Instead, we think that a better example of Feinberg's criticism is found in his own treatment of how Scripture speaks of the multiple senses of the terms "Israel" and the "seed of Abraham."[76]

Feinberg is correct, contrary to most dispensational polemics, that covenant theology does distinguish between Israel and the church, yet their tendency is *not* to recognize the multiple senses of terms such as "Israel" and "the seed of Abraham." For example, covenant theology views the Abrahamic covenant as essentially identical with the new covenant, other than in a few explicit changes. In so doing, they tend to flatten the Abrahamic covenant by reducing it primarily to *spiritual* realities while neglecting its national and typological aspects. This is why covenant theology is able to take the genealogical principle operative in the Abrahamic covenant—"you and your seed" (Gen. 17:7)—and apply it *in exactly the same way* across the Canon without suspension, abrogation, and reinterpretation in the new covenant. In fact, this is why covenant theology argues that baptism is the *replacement* of circumcision and that the covenant sign, regardless of one's covenantal location, is for "you and your seed" (i.e., physical children). Even though the new covenant era is described as the *fulfilment* of the old, given the continuity of "the covenant of grace" interpreted in light of the genealogical principle of the Abrahamic covenant, covenant theology assumes that "believers and their children" are included in the church exactly as they were in Israel of old, which we contend is a mistake.[77]

---

[75] We do agree with covenant theology that the land of Israel is typological. It is a type which looks back to Eden as an archetype and forward in eschatological expectation to its fulfilment in the new creation. For a fine discussion of this point see G. K. Beale, *The Temple and the Church's Mission: A Biblical Theology of the Dwelling Place of God*, NSBT 17 (Downers Grove, IL: InterVarsity Press, 2004).

[76] See Feinberg, "Systems of Discontinuity," 71–73.

[77] As we noted in chapter 2, this identification and equation of the Abrahamic covenant with the new covenant is particularly seen in the discussion of the parties of the covenant. In arguing for the "dual aspect" of the covenant, namely, that in the "visible church" the parties of the covenant are "believers and their children," covenant theology demonstrates that they view new covenant membership through the lens of the Abrahamic covenant, thus identifying the two covenants without acknowledging the redemptive-historical differences between them.

As Feinberg rightly observes, the problem with covenant theology at this point is that they reduce the Abrahamic covenant to its *spiritual* aspects alone, thus neglecting its national and physical aspects. But to do so is to read new covenant realities into the old era *too quickly* and in this way to prioritize the New Testament over the Old Testament without first doing justice to the Old Testament in its own context. We must first understand the Abrahamic covenant in its own immediate context before we relate it to what has now come in Christ. No doubt, everyone agrees that the Abrahamic covenant ultimately leads us to the new covenant, but we must ask: what is the nature of that covenant first in its own setting? As dispensational theology has rightly argued, the Abrahamic covenant is much more diverse than covenant theology often presents it since it encompasses not only spiritual elements but also national and typological elements that result in significant discontinuity as the era of fulfillment is inaugurated. This is best illustrated by the different senses Scripture gives to the "seed of Abraham."[78] Feinberg argues for four distinct senses. First, there is the biological, ethnic, and national sense. Second, there is a political sense that refers to the entire nation. Third, there is a spiritual sense, which can apply to the redeemed, i.e., people who are properly related spiritually to God by faith. Fourth, there is the typological sense, in which Israel can function as a type of the church.[79]

For Feinberg, and for dispensational theology in general, *not* to distinguish these diverse senses of Abraham's seed is illustrative of how covenant theology tends to reduce the Abrahamic covenant merely to its *spiritual* aspects. On the other hand, what is distinctive of dispensational thinking is that all these diverse senses are viewed as operative in the New Testament and "that no sense (spiritual especially) is more important than any other,

---

[78] On this point, in addition to Feinberg, see Alexander, "Seed," 769–773; John G. Reisinger, *Abraham's Four Seeds* (Frederick, MD: New Covenant Media, 1998).

[79] Interestingly, Feinberg discusses the typological nature of the "seed of Abraham" only in terms of the church. He admits that some New Testament passages can draw lessons from Israel for the church (e.g., 1 Cor. 10:1–6) and thus justify this typological relation. However, there are two points missing that we will discuss in more detail below. First, Feinberg follows a specific understanding of typology which we will disagree with, i.e., typology is understood more in terms of analogy than predictive and prospective. Second, he never discusses Christ as the antitype of Israel and hence the "new Israel." In our view, this is a major problem with his discussion of the four senses of Abraham's seed and, as we will develop below and in later chapters, he misses a crucial Christological point. This observation, as we will develop, has important implications for our "kingdom through covenant" view which will distinguish it from both dispensational and covenant theology at this precise point as we think of the Israel-church relationship across the Canon. Feinberg's claim, then, in "Systems of Discontinuity," 73, that the "more one emphasises the distinctness and importance of the various senses [of Abraham's seed], the more dispensational and discontinuity-oriented his system becomes, for the distinct senses necessitate speaking of Israel ethnically, politically, and spiritually, as well as speaking of the church" may be true, generally speaking, but in our proposal, we will emphasise the distinctness and importance of the various senses of Abraham's seed, yet we will also argue that Israel is typological of the new Israel, namely, Christ, and as such, we do not fit in the dispensational category. More on this below.

and that no sense cancels out the meaning and implications of the other senses."[80] In other words, it is Feinberg's contention that covenant theology, by prioritizing the New Testament over the Old Testament *in this area* and by reading new covenant realities back into the Old Testament era, tends to emphasise only a spiritual sense and downplays the national sense of the "seed of Abraham." For Feinberg, this tendency explains why covenant theology fails to distinguish Israel from the church and why they reinterpret the land promises to national Israel in either a spiritual or a typological fashion. As already noted, we will *not* follow Feinberg *on this specific application* for reasons discussed below, but his basic point, we believe, is on track. In our view, his point is better illustrated in explaining why covenant theology can take the sign of the Abrahamic covenant, namely circumcision, marginalize its primary significance of marking out a physical seed, interpret it solely in terms of its spiritual significance, and then argue that circumcision signifies the same reality as baptism signifies under the new covenant.[81]

Regardless of the specific example, in terms of Feinberg's important observation we are in basic agreement that covenant theology tends to read new covenant realities back into the Old Testament era *too quickly* without first letting the Old Testament context and the biblical covenants be understood in their own canonical context—before relating it to what has now come in Christ. That is why we have emphasised the necessity of the three horizons in the theological interpretation of Scripture. Each biblical covenant must first be interpreted in its own immediate context (textual horizon), then in terms of what has preceded it (epochal horizon), and then finally in terms of the entire Canon (canonical horizon). When we follow this procedure, we contend that the New Testament does have priority over the Old Testament. The New Testament's interpretation of the Old Testament is definitive in interpreting the details of the Old Testament but *not* in such a way that contravenes the earlier texts. This is why we must carefully allow the New Testament to show us how the Old Testament is brought to fulfilment in Christ, while simultaneously doing justice to texts in their Old Testament context. In the end, given the progressive nature of Scripture we must carefully unfold the *intertextual* development of biblical

---

[80] Feinberg, "Systems of Discontinuity," 73.
[81] For a development of this point see chapter 17, and Stephen J. Wellum, "Baptism and the Relationship between the Covenants," in *Believer's Baptism: Sign of the New Covenant in Christ*, ed. Thomas R. Schreiner and Shawn D. Wright (Nashville: B&H Academic, 2006), 97–161. Cf. Paul K. Jewett, *Infant Baptism and the Covenant of Grace* (Grand Rapids, MI: Eerdmans, 1978), 89–137.

texts and covenants *within* the Old Testament first and then in terms of an entire canonical theology.[82] Scripture must interpret Scripture.

However, even though we agree with Feinberg's basic observation, we are also convinced that he is not completely accurate in two areas. In fact, we are persuaded that discerning why this is the case is important in setting our view over against both dispensational and covenant theology. Let us look at each of these two areas in turn.

First, Feinberg is not completely accurate in charging covenant theology with prioritizing the New Testament over the Old Testament such that the original Old Testament context is not respected but is instead reinterpreted in light of the New Testament.[83] In fact, we contend, ironically, that dispensational *and* covenant theology actually follow the *same* hermeneutic in appealing to the Old Testament, yet they do so *in different areas* which are central to their theological system. Furthermore, we are also persuaded that both systems, in their own respective areas, fail to grasp the *intertextual* development related to the unfolding covenants that ultimately culminates in Christ and the dawning of the new covenant. Let us focus on two examples which take us to the heart of each theological system.

On the one hand, for dispensational theology the area of contention pertains to the Israel-church relationship. Specifically the issue at debate is regarding the land promise made to national Israel under the *unconditional* Abrahamic covenant. This promise, they contend, given that it is unconditional, remains unchanged across redemptive-history. This is why it must be fulfilled in the future millennial age and beyond. On the other hand, for

---

[82] G. K. Beale, "Did Jesus and His Followers Preach the Right Doctrine from the Wrongs Texts?" 393, has some helpful observations in this regard. Given the progressive nature of Scripture, Beale acknowledges that probably "the Old Testament authors did not exhaustively understand the meaning, implications, and possible applications of all that they wrote." As authors who wrote under divine inspiration, what they wrote was God-given, true, authoritative, and reliable. However, they might not, and probably did not, understand where the entire revelation was going, given the fact that God had not yet disclosed all of the details of his eternal plan. Thus, as more revelation is given across redemptive-history through later authors, God discloses more of his plan along with its implications. That is why, in this important way, the New Testament does have priority over the Old Testament, i.e., the New Testament's interpretation of the Old Testament becomes definitive in helping us interpret the details of the Old Testament. Furthermore, that is why we must carefully allow the New Testament to show us how the Old Testament is brought to fulfilment in Christ while simultaneously doing justice to texts in their original context. In this way, as Beale rightly acknowledges, the New Testament's interpretation of the Old Testament may expand the Old Testament author's meaning in the sense of seeing new implications and applications; however, given that we discover God's intent through the human authors, later texts do *not* contravene the integrity of the earlier texts but rather develop them "in a way which is consistent with the Old Testament author's understanding of the way in which God interacts with his people" in previous eras of redemptive-history. Thus, Scripture as an entire Canon must interpret Scripture; the later parts must "draw out and explain more clearly the earlier parts." Cf. G. K. Beale, *The Erosion of Inerrancy in Evangelicalism* (Wheaton, IL: Crossway, 2008), 223–260.

[83] For this charge see Feinberg, "Systems of Discontinuity," 75. Jewett, *Infant Baptism*, 105, also argues that on the matter of circumcision, covenant theology reads the Old Testament through the New and the New Testament "as though it were the Old."

covenant theology the area of contention also pertains to the Israel-church relationship, but *not* in terms of national, land promises to Israel. Rather they appeal to the *unconditional* Abrahamic covenant in terms of the genealogical principle—"to you and your children." For covenant theology, given the unity of "the covenant of grace," the two covenant communities, Israel and the church, remain structurally the same as "mixed" bodies, and the two covenant signs, circumcision and baptism, remain the same in terms of their *spiritual* meaning across redemptive-history.

However it is important and ironic to observe that at work in both systems is the *same* hermeneutic, only in different places. Both views appeal to understanding the Old Testament on its own terms and *not* letting the New Testament interpret how the specific points of their system are brought to fulfilment. What, then, will *we* argue? We will disagree with both views precisely because they follow the same hermeneutic! Instead, as discussed above, we believe that biblical texts and biblical covenants must be interpreted and theologized in light of the three horizons. We must understand the land promise *and* the genealogical principle first in its Old Testament covenantal context and do justice to the Old Testament on its own terms. Next, we must ask how these two issues intertextually unfold across the covenants with special focus on development *within* the Old Testament itself. Finally, we must let the entire Canon inform how these two issues are brought to fulfilment in the new covenant. In this way we are letting all of Scripture tell us the precise relationships between the covenants including the land promise and genealogical principle as they reach their terminus in Christ.

Second, and related to the above point, we are convinced that Feinberg is not completely accurate in his charge against the hermeneutic of covenant theology, especially in relation to the land promise to ethnic Israel. In our view, his discussion of the entire issue somewhat begs the question, but before we are too hard on him we need to acknowledge that he admits that more needs to be said than merely that covenant theology prioritizes the New Testament over the Old Testament. He also admits that, to make his charge stick, other assumptions about the nature of the covenants and especially the role of typology have to be addressed, a subject to which we now turn.

THE NATURE OF THE BIBLICAL COVENANTS

In arbitrating theological systems, Feinberg is fully aware that more than one issue is involved. As he builds on his previous point he correctly admits that a second issue of disagreement between the two views centres on each one's "understanding of the covenants,"[84] specifically how each view understands promises made to national Israel. Astutely, Feinberg observes that the debate is not "simplistically that OT covenants like the Abrahamic and Davidic are viewed as conditional by nondispensationalists and unconditional by dispensationalists," since that is not true in all cases.[85] Instead, the debate centres on whether *unconditional* land promises were made to ethnic Israel in the Old Testament. If this is the case, Feinberg insists, regardless of how the New Testament applies Old Testament texts concerning Israel to the church,[86] not only must the original meaning of these texts remain the same vis-à-vis the promise of land to Israel, but also we must think in terms of "double fulfilment," i.e., an initial application and fulfilment to the church but an ultimate fulfilment to ethnic Israel in the future.[87] One cannot, Feinberg argues, do what covenant theology often does, namely, treat the New Testament application of these texts to the church as proof that they are now completely being fulfilled spiritually in the church. For dispensationalists, this interpretation not only overturns the unconditional nature of these promises and the meaning of the Old Testament texts, it also illegitimately views Israel and the church as basically the same communities. Instead, as Feinberg and dispensational theology argue, the church must be viewed neither as the replacement nor as the continuation of Israel but as something unique, which requires that we think of ethnic Israel as distinct from the church, "despite the fact that spiritual aspects of the kingdom are now being applied to the church."[88]

For our purposes this discussion highlights two important issues. First, it reminds us that discerning properly the nature of the biblical covenants

---

[84] Feinberg, "Systems of Discontinuity," 79.

[85] Ibid. Within both dispensational and covenant theology there is a legitimate debate over which biblical covenants are conditional versus which are unconditional. See Horton, *God of Promise*, 23–110; Bruce K. Waltke, "The Phenomenon of Conditionality within Unconditional Covenants," in *Israel's Apostasy and Restoration: Essays in Honor of Roland K. Harrison*, ed. Avraham Gileadi (Grand Rapids, MI: Baker, 1988), 123–139; Craig A. Blaising, "The Structure of Biblical Covenants: The Covenants Prior to Christ," in Craig A. Blaising and Darrell L. Bock, *Progressive Dispensationalism* (Wheaton, IL: BridgePoint, 1993), 128–211; Elliott E. Johnson, "Covenants in Traditional Dispensationalism," in *Three Central Issues in Contemporary Dispensationalism: A Comparison of Traditional and Progressive Views*, ed. Herbert W. Bateman IV (Grand Rapids, MI: Kregel, 1999), 121–168; Bock, "Covenants in Progressive Dispensationalism," in *Three Central Issues in Contemporary Dispensationalism*, 169–223.

[86] Feinberg, "Systems of Discontinuity," 77, lists the following examples: Joel 2:28/Acts 2:16–17; Amos 9:11–12/Acts 15:16–18; Hosea 11:1/Matthew 2:15.

[87] See Feinberg, "Systems of Discontinuity," 77–83; cf. Bruce A. Ware, "The New Covenant and the People(s) of God," in *Dispensationalism, Israel, and the Church*, ed. Craig A. Blaising and Darrell L. Bock (Grand Rapids, MI: Zondervan, 1992), 68–97.

[88] Feinberg, "Systems of Discontinuity," 83.

is crucial in adjudicating differences between dispensational and covenant theology. This involves becoming clear as to whether the biblical covenants are unconditional or conditional, and asking to whom these promises were made? Second, we must also think carefully about the Israel-church relationship as united to the biblical covenants. Is it the case that unconditional promises regarding a distinct future for ethnic Israel tied to the land promise were made and thus remain unchanging across redemptive-history? Or, should we view Israel and the promises made to her as conditional and thus forfeited, and now spiritually fulfilled in the church? Furthermore, as covenant theology contends, is the church the continuation of Israel and thus basically the same in nature and structure as Israel of old, or is the church something new and distinct from ethnic Israel? Obviously answering these questions takes us to the heart of the differences between dispensational and covenant theology, but what shall we propose that mediates them?

In regard to these issues, in the following chapters we will argue two points. First, we will argue that dividing up the biblical covenants in terms of unconditional versus conditional is not correct. Instead, the Old Testament covenants blend both aspects and in an unfolding way tell a story of God's incredible promises, his unilateral action to save, and the demand for a covenant mediator who, unlike his Old Testament counterparts, obeys perfectly, even unto death on a cross, and thus accomplishes our redemption. In other words, in the coming of our Lord Jesus, we find God's promise brought to pass by his own sovereign action through an obedient Son, who by his life and glorious cross work achieves and secures our redemption on unshakeable grounds by the inauguration of a new covenant. Second, we will argue that what is missing in the covenantal discussion is a stronger emphasis on Christology. This is *not* to say that dispensational and covenant theology do not focus on Christ; they certainly do. Rather, we contend that in order to grasp the unfolding nature of the biblical covenants we must see that all of the covenants, including the various covenant mediators, find their ultimate *telos* and antitypical fulfilment in Christ and him alone.

So, contra these two biblical-theological systems, the genealogical principle rooted in the Abrahamic covenant (covenant theology) and the promise of land to Abraham and the nation of Israel (dispensational theology), even Israel herself as a people, all function typologically to point us forward to Christ. In this way, as we move across the Canon, the genealogical principle does *not* remain unchanged; rather it must be viewed in relation to the head of the new covenant, our Lord Jesus Christ, and those he represents, namely, people of faith who have been born of the Spirit and united to Christ their covenant head. Furthermore, as we think of Israel, we must also view Israel typologically as not only looking back to Adam and picking up his role but also pointing forward to the coming of the "true Israel," our Lord Jesus Christ, who by his obedient life and death achieves, secures, and inaugurates a new covenant in his blood. In this way, the church is not merely the continuation of Israel of old but something new. However it is *not* new in the dispensational sense; it is new in the redemptive-historical sense that, now that the last Adam and the true Israel have come in the fullness of time, both Jew and Gentile now become the "one new man" in Christ in fulfilment of the Abrahamic promise (Eph. 2:11–22). In a related way, when it comes to the land, like the nation of Israel, it too is typological—looking back to Eden and creation yet also looking forward to that to which it points, namely, its antitypical fulfilment in the new creation—which our Lord Jesus has now inaugurated in the new covenant and which he will consummate when he returns again in glory and power.

Obviously in sketching out our position in this way, we are convinced that a crucial point of division between dispensational and covenant theology is over the nature of typology and how these typological structures are related to the biblical covenants. In fact, this is the third area that Feinberg argues is a point of division between the two biblical-theological systems and, as such, we want to address it briefly as we conclude this section.

THE NATURE OF TYPOLOGY AND ITS USE IN DISPENSATIONAL AND COVENANT THEOLOGY

Another crucial issue which divides dispensational and covenant theology is the nature of typology. For dispensational theology, typology is often employed (although not in a uniform manner), but it is never used in the predictive/prospective sense in relation to the land of Israel *and* the nation of Israel as a type of Christ, the "true Israel." In a similar way, covenant theology utilizes typology repeatedly, but never in terms of the genealogical principle of the Abrahamic covenant. In addition, even though covenant theology speaks of Christ as the "true Israel" it does not do so consistently. In other words, covenant theology often refers to Christ as the "new, true Israel," but it moves *too quickly* from Israel to the church without first thinking how Israel as a "type" leads us to Christ as the "antitype" which then has ecclesiological implications for us. This is why covenant theology can argue that the nature of the covenant communities—Israel and the church—are a similar "mixed" entity and that the covenant signs—circumcision and baptism—signify the same spiritual realities. What is missing is a careful analysis of how Scripture moves across the covenants—from Israel *to* Christ and then *to* the church—which results in some major changes in how we conceive of the nature of the church and the significance of its covenant sign, namely baptism.

To say it another way, it is no doubt true that dispensational and covenant theology employ typology in many places and often with similar results. For example, they agree that such persons as Adam, Moses, David, prophets, priests, and kings point forward to and reach their fulfilment in our Lord Jesus Christ. They agree that the sacrificial system, tabernacle, and temple are fulfilled in the coming of Christ who brings these types to an end, or that the great exodus event anticipates a greater redemption to come in Christ, etc. However, we contend that both views do not employ typology (as defined above) to those areas *which are at the core of their system*, yet this is precisely the issue which must be decided biblically. Let us illustrate this typological point by once again returning to each theological system in turn.

In the case of dispensational theology, if they viewed as typological both the land of Israel and the nation itself, then their view, at its core, would no longer be valid. Why? For the reason that the land promise would not require a future, "literal" fulfilment in the millennial age; the land itself is a type and pattern of Eden and thus the entire creation, which reaches its fulfilment in the dawning of a new creation. Christ, then, as the antitype of Israel, receives the land promise and fulfills it by his inauguration of a new covenant which is organically linked to the new creation. However, it is this precise way of viewing things that Feinberg and dispensational theology reject. This is why Feinberg, in his discussion of typology, not only adopts a different view of typology (as outlined above) but also argues that Israel's land is *not* a typological pattern *and* that Christ is *not* the antitype of Israel. Let us look at each of these areas in turn in order to clarify our point.

First, Feinberg acknowledges that a common way to view typology, such as we maintain, is that the "type is shadow and the antitype is reality" and thus the implication is that "the meaning of the antitype supersedes and cancels the meaning of the type in its own context."[89] Yet, as he admits, he and dispensational theology reject this view. He says dispensationalists "do not think types necessarily are shadows, and they demand that both type and antitype be given their due meanings in their own contexts while maintaining a typological relation to one another."[90] In addition, he endorses the view of David Baker that typology is not grounded in exegesis and thus is not intended to point beyond itself to its antitypical reality; that it rests on analogies between two persons, events, and institutions which is only known retrospectively; that types do not prefigure something in the future, since that future thing would have a meaning different than what was apparent in the original context; and that even if the New Testament interprets the Old Testament typologically, unless the New Testament antitype explicitly cancels the meaning of the Old Testament type, the meaning of the Old Testament text is still in force.[91] As Feinberg summarises, a "proper understanding of typology informs us that even if the NT interprets the OT typologically and even if we are to do so, that does not allow us to ignore or cancel the meaning of the type or substitute the meaning of the antitype for it. . . . [Types] are concrete historical events, persons, promises. They look to the future, but not in a way that makes their meaning equivalent to the antitype. . . . NT antitypes neither explicitly nor implicitly cancel the meaning of OT types."[92] From this discussion it should be obvious that we differ with Feinberg on typology and that we are working with different understandings of it, which leads us to a second observation.

Why does Feinberg argue in this way? The answer is found throughout his entire discussion of what is essential to dispensational theology. He is convinced that the land promise to ethnic Israel and Israel as a nation is *not* typological in a predictive sense of Christ as the new Israel who also brings with him the antitype to the land, namely, the new creation.[93] He is

---

[89] Ibid., 78. Feinberg's treatment of typology begs the question. He assumes that this understanding of typology (1) fails to do justice to the original context; (2) is not predictive and prophetic in the sense that God intended the type to point beyond itself to the antitype; and (3) is not developed intertextually in the Old Testament, so that the New Testament's superseding of the type is precisely what God intended. We strongly agree that types must be given their due meanings in their own context, but we disagree that types are not predictive/prophetic, and that when that to which they point arrives (i.e., antitype), they have reached their terminus. Further, we know God's intention regarding the type by tracing the intertextual development of it, eventually culminating in its fulfilment in Christ.

[90] Feinberg, "Systems of Discontinuity," 78.

[91] See ibid., 77–79. For the discussion of typology in David Baker see, *Two Testaments, One Bible*, 169–189.

[92] Feinberg, "Systems of Discontinuity," 78–79. See also a similar point in Feinberg, "Hermeneutics of Discontinuity," 122–124.

[93] This can be seen in John Feinberg's discussion of the four senses that Scripture uses in reference to the phrase "seed of Abraham" in his article, "Systems of Discontinuity," 71–73. As noted above, he argues that "seed of Abraham" carries a biological/ethnic/national sense, a political sense, a spiritual sense, and a typological sense.

persuaded that, if he were to adopt this way of viewing things, it would go against what he believes is the unconditional promise made to Abraham (and the nation of Israel), which remains unchanged across the covenants. Yet his interpretation of these points begs the question since he must assume, for his view to stand, that Israel and the land is *not* typological of Christ and the new creation. But as we will argue in our exposition of the biblical covenants, the Old Testament text does present the land and the nation as types and patterns of something greater. From the covenant of creation with Adam, Eden is presented as the archetype, which the "land" later on looks back to and forward to in anticipation of the recovery of the new creation. Furthermore, Adam as a covenant head is typological of the "last Adam" to come, and as we move across the covenants, Adam and the land is developed in terms of Noah, Abraham and his seed, the nation of Israel and her land, and ultimately in the Davidic King who will rule the entire creation. In fact, as the covenants unfold there is plenty of biblical evidence of *intertextual* development of all of these patterns, so that when the new covenant era is inaugurated by the last Adam and the true Israel—our Lord Jesus Christ—these types, which point beyond themselves, now find their terminus and fulfilment in Christ and the new covenant age. We contend that this construal of the story line of Scripture is a more "biblical" rendering of how the biblical covenants unfold and find their *telos* in Christ, and it is for this reason that we are convinced that dispensational theology has gone awry at these points.[94]

What about covenant theology? Where do we differ with them in their use of typology and understanding of the relationships between the covenants? Two points will illustrate our differences. First, we are persuaded that their understanding of the genealogical principle is flawed. It is a mistake to think that the genealogical principle of the Abrahamic covenant is not reinterpreted as we move from promise to fulfilment. Under the Old Testament covenants the genealogical principle, that is, the relationship between the covenant mediator and his seed, was *physical* (e.g., Adam, Noah, Abraham, David).

However, in his discussion of typology he argues that Israel can be viewed as a type of the church, but what is absent from his discussion is how Israel is typological of Christ, the new and true Israel.

[94] Feinberg, "Hermeneutics of Discontinuity," 122–124, faces similar problems in regard to typology. We agree with his commitment to "historical-grammatical" hermeneutics in determining the meaning of a text but he fails to do justice to intertextual development *within the Old Testament* for types and patterns. He assumes that the land promise is non-typological and that, since the New Testament does not explicitly abrogate it, the promise is still in force. However, if the land is a type that looks back to Eden and looks forward to the new creation, *and the Old Testament itself develops this point*, then Feinberg's position does not stand. The New Testament is not changing the meaning of the "land," rather it properly shows what the land promise was prophetically anticipating in God's redemptive plan.

However now, in Christ, under his mediation, the relationship between Christ and his seed is no longer physical but is *spiritual*, which entails that the covenant sign must be applied only to those who are in fact the *spiritual* seed of Abraham. As we will argue, is this not precisely what is at the heart of the *promise* of the new covenant in Jeremiah 31, namely, that the Lord will unite himself with a *spiritually* renewed covenant people, *all* of whom will know him, in contrast to the "mixed" nation of Israel who broke the covenant? And that *all* of these new covenant people will be marked by the knowledge of God, the forgiveness of sins, and the reality of a circumcised heart which will allow them to be covenant keepers and not covenant breakers? In other words, covenant theology, in failing to grasp the significant progression in the covenants across redemptive-history, particularly in terms of the relationship between the covenant mediator and his seed, have failed to understand correctly how the genealogical principle has changed from Abraham to Christ—and ultimately the "newness" of the new covenant. Their emphasis on the continuity of the covenant of grace has led them to flatten the covenantal differences and thus misconstrue the nature of the new covenant community.

Second, we are also convinced that at the heart of the problem with covenant theology is not viewing Christ consistently as the antitype of Israel. This criticism is similar to our evaluation of dispensational theology but for different reasons. In the case of covenant theology, contra dispensational theology, it views Christ as the "true Israel," but it moves *too quickly* from Israel to the church without first thinking how Israel as a "type" leads us to Christ as the "antitype," which then has important ecclesiological implications. As noted above, this is why covenant theology tends to flatten the differences between the covenant signs and communities. However, a better way of conceiving of these relationships is by noting how, as we move from type to antitype, from covenant heads such as Adam, Noah, Abraham, Moses/Israel and David to Christ, we must view Israel first in relation to Christ rather than in relation to the church. This is why we will argue, contra covenant theology, that it is *incorrect* to view the church as simply the replacement of Israel or a kind of "renewed" instantiation of it. Instead, the church is something *new* in the redemptive-historical sense. Due to her identification with Christ, the antitype of Israel and the head of the new creation, the church is a "new man" (Eph. 2:11–22) and is by nature and structure different from Israel of old. Moreover, all of this is true because Christ Jesus has fulfilled all of the previous covenants, inaugurated the new covenant, and as such has brought massive covenantal change. And we, as the new covenant people of God, receive the benefits of his work in only one way—through individual repentance toward God and faith in our Lord Jesus Christ—which then, by God's grace and power, transfers us from being "in Adam" to being "in Christ," with all of the benefits of that union. Furthermore, the New Testament is clear: to be "in Christ" and thus to be a member of the new covenant entails that one is a regenerate person, since the New Testament knows nothing of one who is "in Christ" who is not effectually called of the Father, born of the Spirit, justified, holy, and awaiting glorification (see Rom. 8:28–39). It is in all of these areas and their entailments that we part company with covenant theology and argue for a *via media*.

SUMMARY STATEMENT

We must now turn to the detailed exposition of the biblical covenants. In so doing, we will follow the hermeneutical method as outlined above. Each biblical covenant will first be placed in its own immediate context, then understood in terms of what comes *before* it in redemptive-history, and then finally what comes *after* it, ultimately in light of the entire Canon and the coming of Christ. It is only by following this procedure that we take seriously the Old Testament context on its own terms, unpack the intertextual development within the Old Testament, and then discover how all the biblical covenants find their fulfilment in our Lord Jesus Christ. In addition, as each covenant is treated and then related to the whole, we will also note the development of legitimate typological patterns as well, with special focus on crucial points of difference between dispensational and covenant theology. Specifically, attention will be given to the various covenant heads and their relation to Christ; the covenant signs and how they are unfolded across the Canon and related to the new covenant; the promise of the land and what it is typological of and how it is related to the inauguration of the new creation; and the important role of Israel in the biblical covenants and how Israel as a type and pattern finds its fulfilment in Christ, the church, and new covenant realities.

We readily admit that the debate between dispensational and covenant theology is a complicated one, but important in its own right. Even though we stand on the shoulders of giants in both camps, our goal is to propose a mediating biblical-theological system—"kingdom through covenant"—which we believe does better justice to the story line of Scripture and how God has "put together" the biblical covenants. Let us now turn to that task.

PART TWO:

EXPOSITION OF THE BIBLICAL COVENANTS

Chapter Four

THE NOTION OF COVENANT IN THE BIBLE AND IN THE ANCIENT NEAR EAST

INTRODUCTION

Those who have lived during the past forty years have experienced enormous changes and shifts in culture and society. I am certainly no expert in government, politics, or society, and cannot provide a profound study of changes in our culture and the reasons for them. I may, however, be allowed a non-expert opinion based on my own experience, observations, and reading over the years. Two factors appear to be fundamental in the changes in culture and society in North America at least. First, relationships in family and society are no longer characterised by generosity, love, and trust. Instead, everything is measured out precisely. The cost of every little thing is detailed and we must pay for everything. When a person is hired, every minute duty and responsibility of work is detailed in many, many rules so that if anything goes wrong the business knows exactly the situation. Nothing is presumed. For example, about thirty years ago a ministry in Canada called Christian Horizons fired a worker because that worker was having homosexual relations. The employee took the matter to court, and the judge upheld the complaint of the worker because the employer had not specifically spelled out in any document that those employed by this Christian mission could not be homosexual. Homosexuality is not the point of this illustration. The point is that what was formerly sufficient as "understood," now has to be detailed in writing. There is a basic lack of confidence and trust behind almost all business relations. Twenty years ago I bought a house in Toronto. I did not hire an inspector. I checked the house out myself, believed what the former owner related verbally about the condition of the house, and proceeded to purchase it. Some ten years ago, when we moved to Louisville, the people who bought our house in Toronto did not believe the information we provided about the house. They hired an inspector. I had informed them that the basement was dry, but they did not believe me. The inspector measured the humidity. He told them the basement was dry. In Louisville, we had to hire a house inspector and a termite inspector, and had to look at the disclosure agreement signed by the former owner. One can still be cheated after all that.

Second, our country is becoming fragmented by individual and regional interests. What our country is all about, the larger plan, the overall purpose, what draws us together as a nation, is absent. This is partly due to the spirit of our times and the central character of our society today. A major change and shift is taking place. For the last two hundred years, civilisation has been dominated by reason. Reason was king. Everything could be worked out by reason and everything could be conquered by science. Earlier in this period, people were not interested in stories, because stories are not always logical and ordered and scientific. Today, reason is no longer king and people are keenly interested in stories, as we can easily see from the amount of money and time spent on movies or at theatres. But people are not interested in the "Big Story." Why? Because big stories attempt to explain all the little stories, and when you propose an explanation that covers everything, you are bigoted, you are forcing your opinion on someone else. You have committed the unpardonable sin of being intolerant. Alternatively, there is so much information that the task of adducing a big story that encompasses it all seems too daunting or even hubristic.

Both the question of relationships and the question of an overall plan are handled in the Bible by one concept, one word: covenant.

COVENANTS IN THE BIBLE

The idea and notion of covenant *as found in the Bible and in the biblical world*, and likely even the term itself, is foreign to our culture, society, and thought-world today. A brief overview of covenants in the Old Testament and in the ancient Near East along with definitions will begin to adjust our perspective to that of the Bible.

COVENANTS IN THE OLD TESTAMENT

In the Old Testament the Hebrew word for covenant is *bĕrît*. The same word is used in Scripture for a wide diversity of oath-bound commitments in various relationships. It is used to refer to international treaties (Josh. 9:6; 1 Kings 15:19), clan alliances (Gen. 14:13), personal agreements (Gen. 31:44), national agreements (Jer. 34:8–10), and loyalty agreements (1 Sam. 20:14–17), including marriage (Mal. 2:14).

International Treaties

In Joshua 9, when Joshua led Israel into the land of Canaan and attacked the Canaanites who were living in the land at that time, they were deceived and were tricked by the Gibeonites into making a treaty with them. This was a peace treaty between two nations.

In 1 Kings 5:12, Hiram, King of Tyre, a city in ancient Phoenicia, and Solomon, King of Israel, made an international treaty. There were peaceful relations between the two countries and agreements for commerce and trade.

Clan/Tribal Alliances

In Genesis 14:13, powerful nomads of the desert formed an alliance to help each other in case of attack by enemies. This was essentially an alliance between clans or tribes.

Personal Agreements

After years of attempting to best and outwit each other, Laban and his nephew Jacob finally made an agreement not to harm each other (Gen. 31:44). This was a private agreement between two individual persons.

Loyalty Agreements

Jonathan, the son of King Saul, developed a deep friendship with David during the years when Saul sought to get rid of David and kill him. This friendship was formally solemnised twice by agreements of loyalty (1 Sam. 18:3; 23:18).

Marriage

The marriage relationship is a loyalty agreement formally solemnised by a vow before God. This is clearly indicated by Proverbs 2:17 and Malachi 2:14.

National Legal Agreements

In Jeremiah 34:8–10, King Zedekiah made a covenant with the people to proclaim freedom for all the slaves. Although this may seem somewhat similar to a legal agreement or contract, it was different in character from contracts and legal documents of today. Since the covenant was made between king and people, it operated at a national level.

DEFINITION AND ILLUSTRATION

The definition of the term "covenant" (*bĕrît*) is debated, but for heuristic purposes the following may be used as a place to start. Gordon Hugenberger's definition is brief and clear:

> A covenant, in its normal sense, is an elected, as opposed to natural, relationship of obligation under oath.[1]

The following description, adapted from Daniel C. Lane, is similar but fuller:

> A covenant is an enduring agreement which defines a relationship between two parties involving a solemn, binding obligation(s) specified on the part of at least one of the parties toward the other, made by oath under threat of divine curse, and ratified by a visual ritual.[2]

Hugenberger, who produced a thorough and scholarly treatment of marriage as a covenant, notes that in the history of Israel a covenant always entails (1) a relationship (2) with a nonrelative (3) that involves obligations and (4) is established through an oath.[3] Thus a *bĕrît* is a relationship involving an oath-bound commitment.

Scholars debate whether *bĕrît* "can denote a relationship between parties, or simply the obligation one party takes upon himself."[4] This debate seems to be based upon a false dichotomy. Fulfilling an obligation between human parties involves a relationship formalising some understanding between them, and no relationship between human parties is without obligations unless it functions only at a merely animal level.

Extensive studies of the etymology or origin of the word *bĕrît* have not

---

[1] Gordon Hugenberger, *Marriage as a Covenant: A Study of Biblical Law and Ethics Governing Marriage Developed from the Perspective of Malachi*, Supplements to Vetus Testamentum 52 (Leiden, Netherlands: Brill, 1994), 11.

[2] Adapted from Daniel C. Lane, "The Meaning and Use of the Old Testament Term for 'Covenant' (*bᵉrît*): with Some Implications for Dispensationalism and Covenant Theology" (PhD diss., Trinity International University, 2000). Lane's actual wording is as follows: "A *berith* is an enduring agreement which establishes a defined relationship between two parties involving a solemn, binding obligation to specified stipulations on the part of at least one of the parties toward the other, which is taken by oath under threat of divine curse, and ratified by a visual ritual" (314).

[3] Hugenberger, *Marriage as a Covenant*, 11.

[4] John A. Davies, *A Royal Priesthood: Literary and Intertextual Perspectives on an Image of Israel in Exodus 19:6*, JSOTSup 395 (London: T. & T. Clark, 2004), 175–176.

been particularly illuminating as to its meaning.[5] In the branch of the Semitic family to which Hebrew belongs, *běrît* is attested as a loanword in Egyptian texts as early as 1300 B.C.[6] This fact indicates that the use of the word was already well established before that time. Later we will see that examples and usage are better helps than etymology in understanding the term.

Davies helpfully notes that "the fundamental image behind each of the applications of ברית [*běrît*] is the use of familial categories for those who are not bound by ties of natural kinship."[7] Thus, by a ceremony or (quasi-)legal process, people who are not kin are now bound as tightly as any family relationship. Marriage is the best example and illustration of this. A man and a woman, who are not previously related, are now bound closer than any other bond of blood or kinship.

COVENANTS IN THE ANCIENT NEAR EAST

We must not think that the kind of agreements or covenants described in the Bible were entirely unique to the nation of Israel. Covenants or treaties either identical or similar to those mentioned in the Old Testament were common all across the ancient Near East, in lands and regions known today as Egypt, Iraq, Syria, and Turkey. Two types of treaties in the ancient Near East are especially noteworthy: (1) the suzerain-vassal treaty and (2) the royal charter or land grant. The first type is a diplomatic treaty between a great king or suzerain and client kings or vassals. The focus of these treaties was to reinforce the interests of the suzerain by arguments from history and oath-bound affirmations of loyalty on the part of the vassal states, backed up by divine sanctions. The second type of treaty involves a grant of property or even a privileged position of a priestly or royal office given as a favour by a god or king. The focus of these treaties is on honour and the interpersonal relationship.

In an important study, Moshe Weinfeld described the differences between the vassal-treaty and the royal grant in this way:

> While the "treaty" constitutes an obligation of the vassal to his master, the suzerain, the "grant" constitutes an obligation of the master to his servant. In the "grant" the curse is directed towards the one who will violate the

---

[5] A useful summary of positions taken concerning etymology is provided by Paul R. Williamson, *Sealed with an Oath: Covenant in God's Unfolding Purpose*, NSBT 23 (Downers Grove, IL: InterVarsity Press, 2007), 37.
[6] Kenneth A. Kitchen, "Egypt, Ugarit, Qatna and Covenant," *Ugarit-Forschung* 11 (1979): 453–464.
[7] John A. Davies, *Royal Priesthood*, 177.

rights of the king's vassal, while in the treaty the curse is directed towards the vassal who will violate the rights of his king. In other words, the "grant" serves mainly to protect the rights of the servant, while the treaty comes to protect the rights of the master. What is more, while the grant is a reward for loyalty and good deeds already performed, the treaty is an inducement for future loyalty.[8]

In addition to the differences between the two, there are important similarities as well:

> While the grant is mainly a promise by the donor to the recipient, it presupposes the loyalty of the latter. By the same token the treaty, whose principal concern is with the obligation of the vassal, presupposes the sovereign's promise to protect his vassal's country and dynasty.[9]

John Davies nicely summarises the differences between grant and suzerainty treaties as follows:

> If a difference is to be observed, it will be in terms of the fact that a suzerainty treaty places the emphasis on the interstate relationships (expressed in terms of the monarch's personal dealings), while the grant treaty has its focus more on the interpersonal relationships, and the favour of the greater king to the lesser.[10]

Scholars have found it helpful to compare and contrast biblical covenants in form and structure to treaties in the ancient Near East. For example, the book of Deuteronomy is identical in form (but not in content) to the international treaties in the ancient Near East, especially to the suzerain-vassal treaties of the Hittites from the second millennium.[11] Discussion of the biblical covenants in this work will benefit from noting both differences and similarities between the major covenants in the Old Testament and those in the nations surrounding Israel. Two important points have frequently eluded scholars as they have attempted to use models or patterns of treaties in the ancient Near East to analyse and characterise those in the Old Testament. First, it may be that the biblical treaty in question is an adaptation of a genre or literary model in the ancient Near East and not necessarily a consciously

---

[8] M. Weinfeld, "The Covenant of Grant in the Old Testament and in the Ancient Near East," *Journal of the American Oriental Society* 90 (1970): 185.

[9] M. Weinfeld, *Deuteronomy and the Deuteronomic School* (1972; repr., Winona Lake, IN: Eisenbrauns, 1992), 74.

[10] John A. Davies, *Royal Priesthood*, 183.

[11] Many scholars believe that the later neo-Assyrian treaties are also similar to the structure of Deuteronomy. This position is critiqued in the chapter on Deuteronomy.

close imitation of the literary structure in all aspects, so that one need not "discover" every feature of the genre or model in the biblical example. Second, although one may distinguish these two types of treaties, they represent different emphases on a continuum rather than polar opposites.[12] Thus, rather than categorising a treaty as either suzerain-vassal or royal grant, it may be that a covenant in the Old Testament has features of both types and it would diminish the communication of Scripture to represent the covenant solely in terms of one model.

MAJOR COVENANTS IN THE BIBLE

While there are a great number and variety of covenants or treaties described in the Old Testament, certain covenants between God and other parties—be they groups or individuals—stand out in the plot structure of the narrative as determined by the canon of the Old Testament. Table 4.1 concisely lists the major covenants:

Table 4.1: The Major Covenants

Covenant	Main Scripture Texts
1. The Covenant with Creation	Genesis 1–3
2. The Covenant with Noah	Genesis 6–9
3. The Covenant with Abraham	Genesis 12/15/17
4. The Covenant at Sinai	Ex. 19:3b–8/20–24
5. The Covenant with David	2 Samuel 7/Psalm 89
6. The New Covenant	Jeremiah 31–34/Ezek. 33:29–39:29

Some debate exists as to what should or should not be included in a list such as this. Not all are persuaded that the features portrayed in Genesis 1–2 can be labelled a covenant. Some would add to this list covenants such as the covenant with Levi (Num. 25:6–13, cf. Mal. 2:1–9). At least the six covenants in this list, however, need to be discussed and studied.

THE DOCUMENTS OF THE OLD TESTAMENT

At first glance, what we call the Old Testament seems to be an odd assortment of texts of various genres or literary types. Manuscripts that transmit the Hebrew Old Testament demonstrate different arrangements of the individual literary pieces included in the collection as a whole. There are, in fact,

---

[12] John A. Davies, *Royal Priesthood*, 183.

approximately seventy different arrangements in the manuscripts. These arrangements can be classified according to three types: (1) chronological, i.e., in the order in which it is thought they were written, (2) liturgical, i.e., in the order in which passages are read in synagogue services, and (3) literary-rational, i.e., in an arrangement based on literary principles.

The literary-rational order divides the documents into three groups: (1) Torah (instruction or law), (2) Prophets, and (3) other Writings. Table 4.2 shows this arrangement:

Table 4.2: Old Testament Canon: The 24 Books

The Law	1. Genesis
	2. Exodus
	3. Leviticus
	4. Numbers
	5. Deuteronomy
The Prophets	6. Joshua
	7. Judges
	8. Samuel
	9. Kings
	10. Jeremiah
	11. Ezekiel
	12. Isaiah
	13. The Twelve Prophets
The Writings	14. Ruth
	15. Psalms
	16. Job
	17. Proverbs
	18. Ecclesiastes
	19. Song of Songs
	20. Lamentations
	21. Daniel
	22. Esther
	23. Ezra—Nehemiah
	24. Chronicles

Each group or section contains history or narrative plus another genre of texts. The name for each section is derived from the "other genre," so that the Torah consists of history plus "instruction"; the Prophets consists of history plus "prophecy"; and the Writings consists of history plus various other "writings." There is also a guiding principle for the arrangement of the books within each section: the history books are arranged according to the chronology of the events narrated and the non-history books are arranged in order of size. This is what is meant by a literary-rational arrangement.

The chronological and liturgical arrangements are later and secondary, based on minor rearrangements of the literary-rational order. The literary-rational arrangement is the original one. The arrangement of the books in our English versions today is not derived from the Hebrew Canon but from Christian manuscripts of the Greek translation that rearrange the texts according to genre.

Historical evidence shows that the arrangement in the Hebrew Canon certainly dates from the second century B.C. and possibly even earlier, from Ezra and Nehemiah in the late fifth century B.C.[13] This arrangement was accepted and adopted by Jesus and his apostles in the New Testament.[14] The arrangements in Christian manuscripts of the fourth century A.D. show a failure to preserve this tradition.

One can see from the arrangement in the Hebrew Canon that the first nine books and the last four are historical or narrative. Sandwiched in between are non-narrative books that form a commentary on the historical/narrative section.

Important questions arise from observing the collection of documents known as the Old Testament. Is this just an anthology of texts, or is it a single text? Is it a book and not just a library of books? The apostles taught that the Scriptures are not only human in origin, but also divine. Thus although a wide variety of authors are involved from the human standpoint, there is only one author from the divine standpoint. This suggests the collection should be considered a single text.

The focus here is on the Hebrew Canon (i.e., the Old Testament) since this is the part of the Christian Bible where the major texts relating to the covenants are located and also where the literary plot structure of the whole is established. Obviously we consider the documents of the New Testament

---

[13] See Roger Beckwith, *The Old Testament Canon of the New Testament Church and Its Background in Early Judaism* (Grand Rapids, MI: Eerdmans, 1985). His argument is solid in spite of later publications.

[14] Luke 24:44.

to be integral to the canon of the Christian Bible as a whole and essential and vital to this biblical theology.[15]

THE MAJOR COVENANTS AS THE FRAMEWORK OF THE BIBLICAL METANARRATIVE

What, we may well ask, in literary terms, is the plot structure of the Old Testament or even the entire Bible as a single text? The thesis of this work is that the covenants constitute the framework of the larger story. They are the backbone of the biblical narrative.

The biblical story begins with the fact that there is only one God. He has created everything and especially made humankind to rule under him. In this context, God is the centre of the universe and we humans find our purpose in having a right relationship to God and to one another. The first man and woman, however, rejected this way. Now, what happens when God is no longer the centre of our universe? Who steps in to take his place? Why, we do. I want to be at the centre of the universe. Will this work? No, because you want to be there too. And so chaos and evil have reigned since the rebellion of Adam and Eve because we no longer had a right relationship with God and did not treat each other as genuinely human.

God judged the entire human race and made a new start with Noah. This too ended up in chaos and evil, as is clear from the story of the Tower of Babel.

Finally he made a fresh start with Abraham. He would restore a creation and humanity ruined by pride and rebellion by using Abraham and his family as a pilot project. The people of Israel would be an example, a light to the world of what it means to be properly related to God and to treat each other properly according to the dignity of our humanity. We may call this the Mosaic covenant, set forth in Exodus and restated in Deuteronomy.

But the people of Israel did not keep the Mosaic covenant. They were to be blessed for obedience, cursed for disobedience. That is why the biblical story ends up by talking about a new covenant. This time it would be possible to keep this covenant.

---

[15] It is our conviction that the canon of the New Testament was fixed as early as A.D. 125 and that the original order of the documents was as follows: Matthew, Mark, Luke, John, Acts, James, 1 Peter, 2 Peter, 1 John, 2 John, 3 John, Jude, Romans, 1 Corinthians, 2 Corinthians, Galatians, Ephesians, Philippians, Colossians, 1 Thessalonians, 2 Thessalonians, Hebrews, 1 Timothy, 2 Timothy, Titus, Philemon, Revelation. For discussion and defense of this view, see especially David Trobisch, *Paul's Letter Collection* (Minneapolis: Fortress, 1994); and idem, *The First Edition of the New Testament* (Oxford: Oxford University Press, 2000). Also noteworthy is C. E. Hill, "The New Testament Canon: *Deconstructio ad Absurdum*?" *JETS* 52 (2009): 101–120; and idem, *Who Chose the Gospels?* (Oxford: Oxford University Press, 2010).

This summary of the biblical story illustrates that in less than three hundred words—the amount of space allowed for a PhD dissertation abstract—the *covenants* adequately account for the literary or plot structure of the Bible as a text. The Jewish scholar Rabbi Richard Elliott Friedman has recognised this:

> With the Noahic covenant promising the stability of the cosmic structure, the Abrahamic covenant promising people and land, the Davidic covenant promising sovereignty, and the Israelite covenant promising life, security, and prosperity, the biblical authors and editors possessed a platform from which they could portray and reconcile nearly every historical, legendary, didactic, folk, and the like, account in their tradition. If we could delete all references to covenant—which we cannot do, precisely because it is regularly integral to its contexts—we would have an anthology of stories. As it is we have a structure that can house a plot.[16]

The claim here is that the covenants are the key to the larger story of Scripture, the biblical metanarrative. While the claim is based on the idea that the Canon is a single book or text and not just an anthology of texts, it is not the same as discovering a plan to the arrangement of the books, although that is in part related.[17] It is a question of the literary plot structure of the metanarrative as a whole, even though, strictly speaking, not every part is narrative. Even genres that are not narrative have at base a larger story that provides the framework for understanding them.[18] Thus the non-narrative genres are based on the story.

Nor is this claim the same as the goal pursued by the biblical theology movement of the twentieth century, where the aim was to find a "centre" for, e.g., the Old Testament. Walther Eichrodt, for example, in his magisterial *Theology of the Old Testament*, proposed that "covenant" was the central idea or notion upon which a biblical theology could be constructed.[19] The claim here is not that "covenant" is central to a biblical theology of the Old Testament, but rather that the covenants (plural) are at the heart of the metanarrative plot structure.

---

[16] Richard Elliott Friedman, "The Hiding of the Face: An Essay on the Literary Unity of Biblical Narrative," in *Judaic Perspectives on Ancient Israel*, ed. Jacob Neusner, Baruch A. Levine, and Ernest S. Frerichs (Philadelphia: Fortress, 1987), 215.

[17] See, e.g., Stephen G. Dempster, *Dominion and Dynasty: A Biblical Theology of the Hebrew Bible*, NSBT 15 (Downers Grove, IL: InterVarsity Press, 2003).

[18] Scholars have shown that, for Paul's writings in the New Testament, there is a narrative substructure to his thought.

[19] Walther Eichrodt, *Theology of the Old Testament*, trans. J. A. Baker, 2 vols., Old Testament Library (Philadelphia: Westminster, 1961/1967).

A COMPARISON OF CONTRACT AND COVENANT

In our culture in North America, the biblical understanding of a covenant relationship is disappearing and being replaced by the notion of contract. In table 4.3, Elmer Martens provides a comparison and contrast between covenant and contract that clarifies and sharpens our understanding of the biblical idea of a covenant relationship:[20]

Table 4.3: Comparison and Contrast between Covenant and Contract

Category	Contract	Covenant
Form/Literary Structure	1. Date 2. Parties 3. Transaction 4. Investiture 5. Guarantees 6. Scribe 7. List of witnesses	1. Speaker introduced 2. History of relationship 3. General command 4. Detailed stipulations 5. Document statement 6. Witnesses 7. Blessings and curses
Occasion	Expected benefit	Desire for relationship
Initiative	Mutual agreement	Stronger party
Orientation	Negotiation Thing-oriented	Gift Person-oriented
Obligation	Performance	Loyalty
Termination	Specified	Indeterminate
Violation	Yes	Yes

Various categories help to highlight the similarities and differences between contract and covenant and so enable us to appreciate the significance of the loyalty aspect in covenant. The most obvious difference between contract and covenant is the form or literary structure. We have many contracts in Egyptian Aramaic from the fifth century B.C. A consistent format gives the date, lists the parties, describes the transaction, and is followed by guarantees and witnesses. This format differs markedly from that of the covenants or treaties, whether of the second or first millennium B.C. Yet beyond the aspect of form there are other fundamental differences. Martens comments helpfully on these as follows:

> The occasion for contract is largely the benefits that each party expects. Thus for a satisfactory sum one party agrees to supply a specified quantity of some desired product for the other party. The contract is characteristically

---

[20] Elmer A. Martens, *God's Design: A Focus on Old Testament Theology* (Grand Rapids, MI: Baker, 1981), 73. Used by permission.

thing-oriented. The covenant is *person*-oriented and, theologically speaking, arises, not with benefits as the chief barter item, but out of a desire for a measure of intimacy. In a contract negotiation an arrival at a mutually satisfactory agreement is important. In a covenant, negotiation has no place. The greater in grace offers his help; the initiative is his. 'Gift' is descriptive of covenant as 'negotiation' is descriptive of contract. Both covenant and contract have obligations, but with this difference. The conditions set out in a contract require fulfillment of terms; the obligation of a covenant is one of loyalty. A covenant, commonly, is forever; a contract for a specified period. A ticking off of terms in check-list fashion can reveal a broken contract, and the point of brokenness can be clearly identified. A covenant, too, can be broken, but the point at which this transpires is less clear, because here the focus is not on stipulations, one, two, three, but on a quality of intimacy. Of all the differences between covenant and contract, the place in covenant of personal loyalty is the most striking.[21]

At the heart of covenant, then, is a *relationship* between parties characterised by faithfulness and loyalty in love. In the Hebrew of the Old Testament there is a word pair which is consistently used to express this: *ḥesed* and *'ĕmet*. Neither word has a convenient and simple equivalent in English. The first, *ḥesed*, has to do with showing kindness in loyal love. The second, *'ĕmet*, can be translated by either "faithfulness" or "truth." As a word pair, one cannot easily reduce the meaning of the whole to the sum of its constituent parts, just as one cannot explain the meaning of "butterfly" in English by describing "butter" and "fly." This word pair operates, then, within covenant relationships and has to do with demonstrating faithful loyal love within the covenant context.

REFLECTIONS ON COVENANT RELATIONSHIP

An excellent illustration of the word pair *ḥesed* and *'ĕmet* is found in Genesis 47:29–30:

> [29] When the time drew near for Israel to die, he called for his son Joseph and said to him, "If I have found favor in your eyes, put your hand under my thigh and promise that you will show me kindness and faithfulness (*ḥesed* and *'ĕmet*). Do not bury me in Egypt, [30] but when I rest with my fathers, carry me out of Egypt and bury me where they are buried."
> "I will do as you say," he said. (NIV)

---

[21] Ibid., 72–73 (emphasis his). See also George E. Mendenhall, *The Tenth Generation: The Origins of the Biblical Tradition* (Baltimore: Johns Hopkins University Press, 1973), xi-xiii, 16–31, where he discusses the differences between covenant societies and contract societies: in the former the emphasis is on obligations, in the latter, on rights; in the former on the common good, in the latter on the private interest group.

Jacob, also called Israel, is asking his son Joseph to bury him in Canaan and not in Egypt. There is a covenant relationship between father and son, since family relationships are covenantal in the Old Testament. There is an obligation on the part of the stronger party, Joseph, to help the weaker party, Jacob. The fulfilment of this obligation is referred to as showing *ḥesed* and *'ĕmet*, i.e., faithful loyal love:

1. Covenant relationship
2. Obligation to help weaker party
3. Fulfilment of obligation demonstrates faithful loyal love

Concerning *ḥesed*, Leon Morris notes, "In men it is the ideal; in God it is the actual."[22] When Solomon dedicated the temple, he affirmed in his prayer, "there is no God like you, in heaven above or on earth beneath, keeping covenant and showing steadfast love to your servants who walk before you with all their heart" (1 Kings 8:23, ESV). The comment of Francis Andersen is significant:

> Contrary to what some commentators have inferred, this statement does not define *ḥesed* as covenant keeping. Rather "covenant and *ḥesed*" (hendiadys) identify the Lord's covenant as one of *ḥesed* as distinct from say, a political treaty or a commercial contract. Much of the discussion of biblical covenants in recent decades, arising from the observations of G. E. Mendenhall, has inverted the real order of things by placing *ḥesed* in the framework of the formalities of covenant-making instead of placing the biblical covenant on the basis of *ḥesed*. In particular, what is celebrated here is the fact the Lord kept his promise, and to that extent one might say, fulfilled an obligation. But it was self-imposed. The giving of the promise was the foundational act of *ḥesed*. The promise formalized the undertaking. Keeping the promise is not itself a subsequent and dependant act of *ḥesed*, it is simply "keeping" *ḥesed* and in that sense, God is reliable.[23]

The groundbreaking study of *ḥesed* by Nelson Glueck in 1967 has been challenged, and the description of the meaning of *ḥesed* has been refined in a number of significant studies since that time, mainly by K. Sakenfeld, F. Andersen, and G. R. Clark.[24] Andersen reacted to Glueck's study, attempting

---

[22] Leon Morris, *Testaments of Love: A Study of Love in the Bible* (Grand Rapids, MI: Eerdmans, 1981), 81.

[23] Francis I. Andersen, "Yahweh, the Kind and Sensitive God," in *God Who Is Rich in Mercy: Essays Presented to Dr. D. B. Knox*, ed. Peter T. O'Brien and David G. Peterson (Homebush West, NSW, Australia: Lancer, 1986), 65.

[24] Nelson Glueck, *Hesed in the Bible*, trans. Alfred Gottschalk and ed. Elias L. Epstein (Cincinnati: Hebrew Union College Press, 1927, 1967); Katharine D. Sakenfeld, *The Meaning of Hesed in the Hebrew Bible: A New Inquiry* (Harvard Semitic Monographs 17; Missoula, MT: Scholars Press, 1978); and idem, *Faithfulness in Action: Loyalty*

to defend that *ḥesed* means "a quite spontaneous expression of love, evoked by no kind of obligation."[25] In a helpful analysis, John Meade distinguished between ontological and functional *ḥesed* in the being of God.[26] God freely demonstrates *ḥesed* because it is his nature to do so. The key passage in the Old Testament is the revelation given to Moses in Exodus 34:5–7. Stephen Dempster developed the distinction of Meade following the key literary markers in the text.[27]

In the context, Moses asks Yahweh to show him his glory. Yahweh responds in Exodus 33:19ff.:

> [19] And he said, "I will make all my goodness pass before you and will proclaim before you my name 'The LORD.' And I will be gracious to whom I will be gracious, and will show mercy on whom I will show mercy. [20] But," he said, "you cannot see my face, for man shall not see me and live." [21] And the LORD said, "Behold, there is a place by me where you shall stand on the rock, [22] and while my glory passes by I will put you in a cleft of the rock, and I will cover you with my hand until I have passed by. [23] Then I will take away my hand, and you shall see my back, but my face shall not be seen." (ESV)

Then, after Moses cuts another two tablets and ascends the mountain, Yahweh descends in the cloud and proclaims the name of the Lord (Ex. 34:6–7), as shown in tables 4.4a and 4.4b:

Table 4.4a: Yahweh Yahweh

'ēl raḥûm wĕḥannûn	Ontology
'erek appayim wĕrab ḥesed wĕ'emet	
nōṣer ḥesed lā'ălāpîm	Function +
nōśē' 'āwôn wāpeša' wĕḥaṭṭā'â	
wĕnaqqēh lō' yĕnaqqeh	Function –
pōqēd 'āwôn 'ābôt 'al bānîm wĕ'al bĕnē bānîm 'al šillēšîm wĕ'al ribbē'îm	

---

in Biblical Perspective (Philadelphia: Fortress, 1985); Andersen, "Yahweh, the Kind and Sensitive God," 41–87; Gordon R. Clark, *The Word Hesed in the Hebrew Bible*, JSOTSup 157 (Sheffield, UK: JSOT Press, 1993).
25 Andersen, "Yahweh, the Kind and Sensitive God," 42.
26 John D. Meade, "OT *Ḥesed* in the NT," unpublished paper presented to faculty of Southern Baptist Theological Seminary, 2006.
27 Personal communication, March 2, 2011; tables 4.4a and 4.4b used by permission.

Table 4.4b: Yahweh Yahweh

a God merciful and gracious		Ontology
slow to anger, and abounding in steadfast love and faithfulness		
keeping steadfast love for thousands		Function +
forgiving iniquity and transgression and sin		
but who will by no means clear the guilty		Function −
visiting the iniquity of the fathers on the children and the children's children, to the third and the fourth generation		

The revelation begins by repeating the name Yahweh. This is the only instance in the entire Old Testament where the name is repeated twice. The repetition means, "Pay attention!" The number two is also the key to the literary structure. There are three pairs of qualities of the divine nature, and the first pair makes a chiasm with the last revelation of that nature, in Exodus 33:19b, which was a preview for Moses:

$$\text{וְחַנֹּתִי אֶת־אֲשֶׁר אָחֹן וְרִחַמְתִּי אֶת־אֲשֶׁר אֲרַחֵם:}$$

And I will be gracious to whom I will be gracious, and will show mercy on whom I will show mercy. (ESV)

Thus in Exodus 33:19b we have "gracious" and "merciful," whereas in Exodus 34:6 we have "merciful" and "gracious" (A-B::B'-A'). These two qualities stress the incredible grace and compassion—unmerited—in Yahweh. The next two stress his qualities of forbearance (slowness to anger) as well as his overflowing faithful lovingkindness.

These ontological qualities then flow into incredible positive functions that form a chiasm with the negative functions. In "he guards *ḥesed*" the word *nōṣer* ("guard") is chosen because of its assonance with *nōśē'* (forgive) and also because it is more active than "do." The usual expression in the Hebrew Bible is "do *ḥesed*." To guard *ḥesed* is stronger—God earnestly maintains and preserves *ḥesed*. As we can see from Exodus 20:5–6, "thousands" does not mean thousands of people, but specifically stands in contrast to "visiting iniquity to the third and fourth generation" and hence means thousands of generations. This is something that is an outflow of the divine nature. Second, this *ḥesed* issues in a comprehensive forgiveness, but a forgiveness which nonetheless still takes sin very seriously (he does not acquit the guilty)—in other words this is a costly forgiveness. There is a tension here within the divine nature, caused by human sin, but that will be resolved someday.

And this incredible and matchless revelation is what it means to see Yahweh's back! Imagine looking him full in the face!

Another wonderful illustration is Psalm 117:

[1] Praise the LORD, all you nations;
  extol him, all you peoples.
[2] For great is his love [*ḥesed*] toward us,
  and the faithfulness [*'ĕmet*] of the LORD endures forever.
Praise the LORD. (NIV)

This is the briefest and shortest hymn in the whole of Israel's Songbook (Psalms). According to the format standard for a hymn, there is a call to praise Yahweh, followed by the reason for praise. In Psalm 117, verse 1 is the Call to Praise and verse 2 is the Reason for Praise. In the section giving the reason for praise the word pair *ḥesed* and *'ĕmet* is split over parallel lines. Thus the reason for boasting about the Lord is his faithful loyal love in his covenant with his people Israel. In fact, the celebration of this quality summarises the entire Psalter. When a budding scholar completes a doctoral dissertation, the dissertation must be summarised in three hundred words. This is called a dissertation abstract. And Psalm 117 is the dissertation abstract for the entire book of Psalms. It summarises in just a very few words *all* of the Laments, Hymns, and Songs of Thanksgiving in Israel's hymnal, including the enormously long Psalm 119. The Lord is worthy of the worship of his people Israel because he demonstrates faithful loyal love in the covenant relationship.

Chapter Five

THE COVENANT WITH NOAH

INTRODUCTION

The *Toronto Star* is a major newspaper in the largest city in Canada. This newspaper published an article in November 1996 announcing that Mr. Jean Chrétien, the Prime Minister of Canada at that time, had completely fulfilled 78 percent of his election promises. By contrast, the God revealing himself in a progression of covenants has completely fulfilled his promises to Noah and to the entire human race as entailed in the covenant with Noah, 100 percent for several thousand years. The proof is in the alternating progression of seasons experienced up to the present time.

THE CONTEXT OF THE COVENANT WITH NOAH

Whether or not a covenant per se is entailed in Genesis 1–3 is debated. The first occurrence in the Bible of the word "covenant" (*bĕrît*) is in Genesis 6:18 and is in reference to the covenant with Noah. God says to Noah, "But I will establish my covenant (*bĕrît*) with you" (NIV). Consequently Genesis 6–9 and the covenant with Noah will be examined first, and only then, the issues raised by Genesis 1–3 can and will be considered.

First we need to consider the context in which God makes this statement to Noah (in Gen. 6:18) and the meaning of the language used in this text.

In the previous verse, God informs Noah that he is going to destroy all life upon the earth—all human and animal life in the entire world. The means of destruction will be a cataclysmic event—floodwaters covering the entire earth. God instructs Noah, however, to construct a big "box" which will be the means of rescue and deliverance from the destruction of the flood.

The earlier part of chapter 6 explains why God had apparently given up on the human race and decided upon such a cataclysmic course of action. In verse 5 we are told, "The LORD saw how great the wickedness of the human race on the earth had become and that every inclination of the thoughts of their hearts was only evil all the time." A bit further on in verses 11–13 we read,

> Now the earth was corrupt in God's sight and was full of violence. God saw how corrupt the earth had become, for all the people on earth had corrupted their ways. So God said to Noah, "I am going to put an end to all people, for the earth is filled with violence because of them." (NIV)

Verse 5 describes the human situation as "bad," "evil," or "wicked," and traces this to the condition of the human heart, the centre of our being where we feel, reason, and make decisions and plans. In verses 11–13 two terms in particular stand out: "corrupt" and "violence." The first word occurs three times and the second word twice, so that the cumulative effect is pronounced. It is difficult for the reader to miss the message! The term "corrupt" shows that a beautiful and good situation is now ruined, spoiled, and twisted. Frequently, not many hours after opening the presents on Christmas Day, children manage to ruin and spoil beautiful and intricate toys so that they are damaged in appearance and function. The term violence (*ḥāmās*) is a word that refers specifically to social violence and conditions in human society where social justice is lacking.

The evil of the human heart resulting in corruption and social violence brings a response from God, according to verses 6 and 7:

> The LORD was grieved that he had made man on the earth, and his heart was filled with pain. So the LORD said, "I will wipe mankind, whom I have created, from the face of the earth—men and animals, and creatures that move along the ground, and birds of the air—for I am grieved that I have made them." (NIV)

Some translations speak of God "regretting" or "feeling sorry" that he had made man on the earth. The divine response refers to God's consistent opposition to injustice, social violence, and wickedness and does not indicate that he is changeable or capricious. Waltke's comment is helpful:

> we see many cases in Scripture that show that if God plans to do evil and the people repent and do good, the evil will not transpire, and vice versa (e.g., Jer. 18:5–11). God regrets precisely because he is unchangeable. Paul House notes, "God's regret means action must be taken, not that a great cosmic mistake has been made." In other words, God's motives are always good and just.[1]

The flood, then, is a divine judgement in response to the evil of the human heart and the resultant corruption and violence.[2]

---

[1] Bruce K. Waltke with Charles Yu, *An Old Testament Theology* (Grand Rapids, MI: Zondervan, 2007), 286.

[2] The approach here contrasts with that of John Goldingay regarding the cosmic mistake: It almost seems as if at times God is a mad scientist, trying to get things right in the laboratory, trying plan B after plan A fails. See John Goldingay, *Old Testament Theology: Volume One—Israel's Gospel* (Downers Grove, IL: InterVarsity Press, 2003), 161–184.

EXCURSUS

The relationship of Genesis 6:1–4 to the flood story, and the interpretation of these four verses, is extremely problematic. Only a brief comment is possible in the scope of this work. Two main issues are significant: (1) the identity of the "sons of God" who marry the daughters of the human race and have children by them (6:2, 4), and (2) interpretation of the temporal expressions "those days" and "afterwards" in 6:4. Three views predominate on the identity of the sons of God: (1) they represent the godly line of Seth (Gen. 4:25–5:32) intermarrying with the ungodly line of Cain (Gen. 4:17–24); (2) they represent powerful kings/tyrants ruling at the time; (3) they represent angels who married human women. The last view is a problem since one would then have to wonder if the flood was a judgement upon angelic rather than human corruption and violence. This view should be considered seriously, however, since the exact expression "sons of God" refers consistently and exclusively to angelic beings in the Old Testament (Job 1:6, 2:1, 38:7, cf. Ps. 29:1, Dan. 3:25) and is also supported by the New Testament in 2 Peter 2:4 and Jude 6–7.[3] Peter and Jude seek to bolster the faith of their readers by reference to events *well known* from the Old Testament. Their comments are structured in such a way as to refer in particular to two texts in Genesis (Genesis 6–9 and 18–19).[4] They speak of angels who sinned and were cast into a particular prison awaiting further judgement. According to Jude, both examples (i.e., angels and cities of the plain) involved gross immorality.

The temporal expressions "those days" and "afterwards" both occur in verse 4. For purposes of discussion, a literal translation of this verse is useful:

The Nephilim were on the earth in those days and also afterwards when the sons of God had relations with human women

---

[3] Some have argued that intermarriage between angels and humans is impossible, citing Jesus' statement in Mark 12:25: "When the dead rise, they will neither marry nor be given in marriage; they will be like the angels in heaven" (NIV). What Jesus actually says, however, is that the angels *in heaven* do not marry, and Jude specifies that the angels who sinned "did not keep their own position of rule but abandoned their own/proper dwelling place" (Jude 6).

[4] Second Peter 2:4–8 cites *two* examples from the history of the Old Testament, not *three*. The text contains three καί conjunctions (i.e., "ands"). The centre "and" joins the two examples. Then each example has two parts: (1) the angels who sinned *and* the contemporaries of Noah, *and* (2) the cities of Sodom and Gomorrah *and* righteous Lot. Thus the clear literary structure associates the narrative of the angels with the narrative of Noah and must refer to the account in Genesis 6:1–4 rather than some event not narrated in the Old Testament, such as the fall of Satan.

and they bore children for them. They were the heroes who
were from the ancient past, men of reknown.

Two main possibilities exist for interpretation of the temporal expressions. If one interprets "those times" to be the times
described in verses 1–3, then what is distinguished are the times
before the flood from the times after the flood. The relative clause
introduced by "afterwards" would seem to indicate that the cohabitation of angelic and human beings continued after the flood. One
might conclude that the Nephilim were the product of such unions
(cf. Num. 13:22, 28, 33).

Yet a different interpretation is possible. The expression "afterwards" (*'aḥărê-kēn*) usually occurs in the second of two verbal sentences: the first sentence says that event X did or will happen; the
second says that subsequent to the event in the first sentence, event
Y did or will happen.[5] Here we must note that the expression *'aḥărê-
kēn* is modified by a relative sentence which refers specifically to
the event in verse 2.[6] Therefore one could assume that "those days"
means before the cohabitation of divine and human beings. Verse 4
would then comment that the Nephilim were in the earth before the
business of angelic and human beings cohabiting and also afterwards
and therefore had nothing to do with these unions.

This latter interpretation is strengthened by considerations of
discourse grammar. Verse 4 consists of two clauses or sentences,
the first verbal, the second nominal. Both are marked by asyndeton
(i.e., no conjunction or connector at the beginning of the clause/
sentence). In the first, the verb is non-initial. This pattern marks
a commentary or explanatory digression. The fact that the first
sentence is subject-initial indicates a new topic. The relative sentence in verse 4 correlates this new topic with the events of verse 2.
The nominal sentence is a further comment on the Nephilim. They
were the heroes from the distant past. This may mean the distant
past with reference to the writer, or it may indicate a period long
past in reference to the event of 6:2. Therefore the writer would be
demythologizing the Nephilim. These heroes of ancient times were
there before and after the events of 6:2 and were not necessarily

---

[5] Although this pattern is standard or usual, it is not the only kind of construction, as Genesis 41:31
shows.
[6] This is apparently the only occurrence of *'aḥărê-kēn* where it is modified by a relative sentence.
The Oxford Lexicon adduces 2 Chronicles 35:20, but the parallel is not exact or compelling.

related to them at all. Thus, verse 1 describes an increase in female humans, verse 2 describes a cohabitation of angelic and human beings, verse 3 concludes that the result is still human and therefore under God's judgement, and verse 4 states that all this has nothing to do with the well-known Nephilim. Since the word Nephilim is not otherwise explained, they must have been well known to the ancient (first) readers of this text.

What this digression shows, then, is that if one assumes that Genesis 6:1–4 is referring to a union of angelic and human beings, this may not be connected to the causes of the flood. In addition, according to 2 Peter 2:4 and Jude 6, the judgement of the angels was separate from the judgement of the flood.

In contrast to his contemporaries, Noah was righteous in an age of social violence. Verse 8 indicates that Noah was the object of divine favour. This was not an arbitrary result, since the next verse reveals that "Noah was a righteous man, blameless among the people of his time, and he walked with God" (NIV). The expression "Noah . . . walked with God" clearly shows that Noah had a relationship with God long before God "established" his covenant with him. The term "righteous" (Heb. *ṣaddîq*) is a word that speaks of Noah's conduct in his relationship with God. Noah's actions toward God and toward his fellow man were based on faithfulness and loyalty to his relationship with God. Since any relationship with the creator God of the Bible would involve moral standards, "righteous" means that Noah's conduct was based upon conformity to God's way out of his commitment to God. In an important study, J. W. Olley defines righteousness as "to bring about right and harmony for all, for individuals, related in the community and to the physical and spiritual realms."[7] To this definition Bruce Waltke adds, "the righteous (*ṣaddîq*) are willing to disadvantage themselves to advantage the community; the wicked are willing to disadvantage the community to advantage themselves."[8] God decides, then, in this context, to confirm his covenant with Noah.

---

[7] J. W. Olley, "'Righteous' and Wealthy? The Description of the *Ṣaddîq* in Wisdom Literature," *Colloquium* 22 (1990): 38–45.

[8] Bruce K. Waltke, *The Book of Proverbs: Chapters 1–15*, New International Commentary on the Old Testament (Grand Rapids, MI: Eerdmans, 2004), 97.

COVENANT MAKING IN THE OLD TESTAMENT AND ANCIENT NEAR EAST

Before further consideration of God's covenant with Noah, it is necessary to acquire a better grasp and understanding of covenant making in the culture of the biblical world. What is normally involved in initiating a covenant or treaty? The events described in Genesis 21:22–34 provide an excellent example of what is entailed in covenant making in the ancient Near East. The narrative concerns the king of Gerar (a city in the south of Canaan, just west of Beersheba), who makes a covenant/treaty with Abraham. The agreement between the parties resolves a dispute over water rights relating to the well of Beersheba. Four features characterise this treaty and, in fact, are normative of covenants in general:

(1) A covenant does not necessarily begin or initiate a relationship. It can formalise in binding and legal terms an agreement or commitment between parties who have developed and established a relationship before the covenant is made. Abimelech and Abraham have already developed a relationship together. When the covenant is made, Abimelech appeals to this already established understanding between them by speaking of the loving-kindness (*ḥesed*) he has shown Abraham in the past. As we will see, it is true that the covenant does specify a new level to this relationship, but the parties have had dealings in the past.

(2) There is a conventional language for initiating covenants or treaties which is standard in the Old Testament. The standard expression for initiating a covenant is "to cut a covenant" (*kārat běrît*; 21:27, 32). How and why this peculiar expression arose will become clear shortly.

(3) A covenant gives binding and quasi-legal status to a relationship by means of a formal and solemn ceremony. As a general rule, covenants belong to the public sphere rather than the private sphere. This is why, for example, elopement is inappropriate for marriage: no formal or public ceremony is involved.

(4) Covenant making involves a commitment or oath or promise and frequently signs or witnesses. Here the parties of the treaty solemnly swear to the agreement. As W. J. Dumbrell notes, the oath "is obviously an important ingredient in the total arrangement, but it is not the covenant itself."[9]

Although the ceremony is not described in complete detail in Genesis

---

[9] William J. Dumbrell, *Covenant and Creation: A Theology of Old Testament Covenants* (Nashville: Thomas Nelson, 1984), 17.

21, we can put the pieces together from different sources. Animals are slaughtered and sacrificed. Each animal is cut in two and the halves are laid facing or opposite each other. Then the parties of the treaty walk between the halves of the dead animal(s). This action is symbolic. What is being expressed is this: each party is saying, "If I fail to keep my obligation or my promise, may I be cut in two like this dead animal." The oath or promise, then, involves bringing a curse upon oneself for violating the treaty. This is why the expression "to cut a covenant" is the conventional language for initiating a covenant in the Old Testament.

Many other covenants and treaties are recorded in the Bible. As examples, one may mention the covenant between Joshua and the Gibeonites (Joshua 9), between the men of Jabesh Gilead and Nahash the Ammonite (1 Sam. 11:1–3), two covenants between David and Jonathan (1 Sam. 18:3; 23:18), one between David and Abner (2 Sam. 3:12–21), David and Israel (2 Sam. 3:21; 5:1–3), Ahab of Israel and Ben-Hadad of Syria (1 Kings 20:31–34), and between Jehoiada the high priest and King Joash of Judah (2 Kings 11:17). While the components and also the nature and status of the parties differ, and the language varies somewhat, in each case a covenant concluded involves a commitment or promise solemnised by oath in which an agreement and level of relationship between parties is specified.

Although this description of covenant making in the Old Testament is indebted to the pioneering labours of William J. Dumbrell, carefully nuanced differences from his presentation have been expressed here as well. Dumbrell's work has been sharply criticised in recent studies by Paul Williamson[10] and Jeffrey J. Niehaus.[11] Niehaus summarises the definition of Dumbrell as follows: "a covenant does not create a relationship between two parties. Rather it confirms an already existing relationship."[12] He argues that the approach of Dumbrell blurs the distinction between covenant and covenant renewals. Niehaus also critiques Hafemann, who follows Dumbrell. His critique should be noted:

> . . . he [Hafemann] follows in Dumbrell's footsteps by believing that "[l]ike
> a treaty or a marriage, a 'covenant' is a particular kind of political or legal
> arrangement that confirms or formalizes a relationship that already exists

---

[10] Paul R. Williamson, *Sealed with an Oath: Covenant in God's Unfolding Purpose*, NSBT 23 (Downers Grove, IL: InterVarsity Press, 2007).

[11] Jeffrey J. Niehaus, "An Argument against Theologically Constructed Covenants," *JETS* 50/2 (2007): 259–273; idem, "Covenant: An Idea in the Mind of God," *JETS* 52/2 (2009): 225–246.

[12] Niehaus, "Argument against Theologically Constructed Covenants," 265.

between two parties." As in Dumbrell's case, so with Hafemann, it is this mistaken definition of covenant which makes the "one covenantal relationship" view possible. Yet, as we have pointed out above, it was covenant renewals, and not covenants, that served this function in the ancient Near East and in the Bible. The fact that marriage is a covenant is actually a piece of contrary evidence. Marriage does not confirm an existing relationship: it takes an existing relationship (in which a couple is engaged) to an entirely new level—thus transforming it—and establishes a new state of affairs, with new privileges and new responsibilities.[13]

This critique is helpful, but only partially right. A covenant, e.g., marriage, does specify a different and new level of relationship from what has been true in the past, but certainly this is not the beginning of relationship between the two parties. Dumbrell may possibly blur the distinction between covenant and covenant renewals in some instances, but his definition is based firmly on passages like the treaty in Genesis 21. Past relationship between the parties is admitted by Niehaus in some measure:

> A point that appeared for a long time to have been well understood, or at least taken for granted, among scholars who studied ancient Near Eastern covenants is this: a covenant assumes some past history of relationship (however minimal) between two parties, but a covenant, once agreed upon, changes the relationship between the two covenanting parties and takes it to a different level. . . . With regard to these facts, the historical prologues, found in second millennium BC treaties, at least, provide a valuable service. They document the relationship that had existed, or the events of mutual involvement or interest, that had occurred, before the two parties agreed to enter into a covenant relationship. The historical prologue illustrates the fact that some sort of prior relationship, however minimal or even hostile, had obtained in the past. Now, however, the parties enter into a covenant which declares, sanctions, witnesses and ratifies the stipulations that shall govern the new, covenant relationship (be it parity or suzerain-vassal) according to which both parties shall live going forward.[14]

In summary, Craig Bartholomew's adjustment of Dumbrell's definition is helpful:

> Dumbrell neglects the constitutive side of the divine covenants in his understanding of covenants as commitments that normalize existing relationships.

---

[13] Ibid., 270.
[14] Niehaus, "Covenant: An Idea in the Mind of God," 235–236.

The divine covenants do operate within existing relationships, but they shape and give future direction to the relationship, just as does the marriage covenant.[15]

INITIATE VERSUS UPHOLD COVENANT

The first occurrence(s) of the term covenant (*bĕrît*) in the Hebrew Scriptures is significant. The word appears first in the flood narrative (Gen. 6:18; 9:9, 11, 12, 13, 15, 16, 17). In four instances God speaks of "confirming" or "establishing" a covenant with Noah (Gen. 6:18; 9:9, 11, 17). The construction in Hebrew is *hēqîm bĕrît*. The remaining four occurrences have to do with the sign of the covenant and remembering the covenant. Thus, when we consider the covenant God made with Noah and his descendants, we notice right away that the standard expression or language for covenant initiation is lacking. Nowhere do we read of God cutting a covenant (*kārat bĕrît*). Why is the language different here and what does it signify? An exhaustive study of all instances of *bĕrît* in the Hebrew Bible and classification of all constructions and expressions in which this noun occurs reveals a completely consistent usage: the construction "to cut a covenant" (*kārat bĕrît*) refers to covenant initiation while the expression "to establish a covenant" (*hēqîm bĕrît*) refers to a covenant partner fulfilling an obligation or upholding a promise in a covenant initiated previously so that the other partner experiences in historical reality the fulfilling of this promise, i.e., one makes good on one's commitment, obligation, or promise.[16]

The difference in the expressions can be illustrated in the case of the covenant with Abraham. In Genesis 15 God's promises to Abraham of land and seed given earlier in chapter 12 are formalised in a covenant. Notice that in 15:18 we have the standard terminology in the Hebrew text: "cut a covenant" (*kārat bĕrît*). Later in Genesis 17 God *upholds* his covenant promise. Verses 7, 19, and 21 consistently employ the expression *hēqîm bĕrît*, while the expression *kārat bĕrît* is not used. Here God is bringing to personal experience in the life of someone who is already a covenant partner the fulfilment

---

[15] Craig G. Bartholomew, "Covenant and Creation: Covenant Overload or Covenantal Deconstruction, *Calvin Theological Journal* 30 (1995): 25.

[16] The difference between the expressions *kārat bĕrît* and *hēqîm bĕrît* was already recognised by Cassuto. Recently, Paul R. Williamson and Jeffrey J. Niehaus have reacted to the way in which the difference was described by William J. Dumbrell. This is partly due to the inadequate description by Dumbrell and partly to inadequate lexical study on the part of Niehaus and Williamson. See Peter J. Gentry, "Kingdom through Covenant: Humanity as the Divine Image," *SBJT* 12/1 (2008): 16–42. For our exhaustive analysis of the term *bĕrît* and verbal constructions with this noun, see the appendix.

of his promise entailed in the covenant initiated previously in chapter 15. So God upholds his promise and says Sarah will have a baby within the year.

Therefore the construction *hēqîm bĕrît* in Genesis 6 and 9 indicates that God is not initiating a covenant with Noah but rather is upholding for Noah and his descendants a commitment initiated previously. This language clearly indicates a covenant established earlier between God and creation or God and humans at creation. When God says that he is confirming or upholding his covenant with Noah, he is saying that his commitment to his creation, the care of the creator to preserve, provide for, and rule over all that he has made, including the blessings and ordinances that he initiated through and with Adam and Eve and their family, are now to be with Noah and his descendants.

The idea that the covenant with Noah was a kind of reinstatement and upholding of a covenant initiated at creation was advanced by Dumbrell.[17] He based his view in part on the distinction in usage between *kārat bĕrît* and *hēqîm bĕrît*. The claim that these expressions were distinct in usage did not originate with him. Already in 1934, the great Italian scholar Umberto Cassuto had described the usage this way.[18] Subsequent scholarship has corroborated and supported this understanding,[19] but recently it has been challenged by Paul Williamson.[20]

Williamson claims that Dumbrell's discussion is flawed and argues that it is difficult in a number of texts to maintain that key verbs employed with *bĕrît* refer back to a covenant that has already been initiated (Gen. 6:18; 9:9, 11; 17:2, 9, 19; Num. 25:12; Deut. 29:11 (29:12 EV); Ezek. 16:8; 17:13; 2 Chron. 15:12).[21] Yet the texts he lists as evidence either entail begging the question, as in the case of the references in Genesis, or they do not involve the expression *hēqîm bĕrît*.[22] The problem with Williamson's study is two-fold: (1) the basic claim of Dumbrell concerning the distinction between

---

[17] See Dumbrell, *Covenant and Creation*, 15–26.

[18] Umberto Cassuto, *La Questione della Genesi* (Florence: Felice le Monnier, 1934), 112–116. See also idem, *The Documentary Hypothesis: Eight Lectures*, trans. I. Abrahams (Jerusalem: Magnes, 1961), 47–48.

[19] See especially Jacob Milgrom, *Leviticus 23–27*, Anchor Bible 3B (New York: Doubleday, 2001), 2343–2346 and bibliography provided there.

[20] First in his published doctoral dissertation, Paul R. Williamson, *Abraham, Israel, and the Nations: The Patriarchal Promise and Its Covenantal Development in Genesis*, JSOTSup 315 (Sheffield, UK: Sheffield Academic Press, 2000), and later in a general work on the covenants, idem, *Sealed with an Oath: Covenant in God's Unfolding Purpose*, NSBT 23 (Downers Grove, IL: InterVarsity Press, 2007).

[21] Paul R. Williamson, *Abraham, Israel, and the Nations*, 196; and idem, *Sealed with an Oath*, 73.

[22] Ezekiel 17:13 and Deuteronomy 29:11 (29:12 EV) employ *kārat bĕrît* and refer to covenants being initiated. (See below discussion of the relationship of Exodus 19–24 and Deuteronomy.) Ezekiel 16:8 and 2 Chronicles 15:12 use *bô' bĕrît* ("enter a covenant"), an expression equivalent to *kārat bĕrît*. Numbers 25:12 employs the verb *nātan* ("give"). This verb is simply a substitute verb higher in the hierarchical level, like "do," and is dependent on the context as to whether it may refer to covenant initiation or upholding. In general, the only occurrences of

kārat běrît and *hēqîm běrît* was not adequately expressed by Dumbrell and needs to be modified somewhat by a more thorough study of all the texts, and (2) Williamson bases his research on the lexical study of Weinfeld and criticisms of Dumbrell offered by others such as Roger Beckwith.[23] He argues that "Weinfeld offers a more comprehensive list of relevant biblical texts and therefore provides a better basis on which to evaluate Dumbrell's assertion."[24] On the one hand, then, Williamson is reacting to propositions by Dumbrell that could be better described and nuanced. On the other hand, he does not seem to have based his own research on a careful examination of all the primary sources, but rather has relied on secondary studies like that of Weinfeld.

The description given here is based on an examination of all the primary sources[25] and, although indebted to Dumbrell, avoids claims he makes not supported by the evidence and offers a carefully nuanced modification of the usage. While full review of Williamson's critique of Dumbrell cannot be given here, examples from his discussion will be given. In attempting to show that *hēqîm běrît* can mean to initiate a covenant and is equivalent in meaning to *kārat běrît*, he says, "[s]imilarly, in Jeremiah 34:18 a strong case can be made in support of a covenant being instituted and not just renewed (cf. Jer 34:10)."[26] The evidence, however, is otherwise. The expression *kārat běrît* is employed in Jeremiah 34:8, 13, and 15 as well as a similar expression *bô' bibrît* (enter a covenant) in 34:10 for initiating or making a covenant between King Zedekiah and all the people of Jerusalem to proclaim freedom for Hebrew slaves. The people then fulfilled the obligation by freeing the slaves, but later reneged on the covenant and re-enslaved the manumitted slaves. Jeremiah was sent to challenge this covenant violation (see the expression *'ābar běrît* in 34:18) and called upon the people in 34:18 to "uphold the covenant" (*hēqîm běrît*), meaning to bring to pass in the experience of the people the promise entailed in the covenant made earlier to free the slaves. The people must make good on the commitment and promise made in the covenant. A simple straightforward reading of this text, then,

---

the collocation *nātan běrît* are found in contexts which employ the expression *hēqîm běrît* or an equivalent idea (Gen. 9:12, 17:2; Num. 25:12).

[23] See M. Weinfeld, "בְּרִית *běrît*," in *TDOT* 2:253–279; and Roger Beckwith, "The Unity and Diversity of God's Covenants," *Tyndale Bulletin* 38 (1987): 92–118.

[24] Paul R. Williamson, *Abraham, Israel, and the Nations*, 195–196.

[25] I have carefully examined all instances of *běrît* and, in particular, all expressions in which *běrît* is the modifier of a verb in the Hebrew Bible. This research was performed in two independent and separate studies of all the evidence, conducted ten years apart. The evidence is provided in the appendix.

[26] Paul R. Williamson, *Sealed with an Oath*, 73.

shows that a "strong case" can be made *for* the distinction in usage between *kārat bĕrît* and *hēqîm bĕrît* as described herein rather than a "strong case" against. Williamson construed the argument of Dumbrell to mean that *hēqîm bĕrît* meant covenant *renewal* and has misunderstood the usage in Hebrew.

For Exodus 6:4, Williamson appeals to Beckwith as follows:

> As Beckwith observes, the deployment of הקים in Exod. 6.4 illustrates that this verb does not necessarily suggest the confirmation or perpetuation of a pre-existing covenant. This latter text is of particular significance for a number of reasons. Although three patriarchs are alluded to, the covenant is spoken of in the singular. There is only one feasible explanation for this: God did not establish three different covenants, one with each patriarch, but made a singular commitment or covenant (i.e., solemn promise), initially to Abraham, but subsequently to Isaac and Jacob. It would appear from Exod. 6.4 that the commitment or promise in question relates essentially to the question of territory; only the promissory aspect relating to nationhood is picked up here; there is neither mention of nor allusion to the international dimensions of the promise that are reflected in Gen. 12.3; 17 and 22.18. It is reasonable to conclude, therefore, that the covenant referred to in Exod. 6.4 is that solemnly established by divine oath in Gen. 15.18. If this is indeed the case, the fact that the verb הקים should be applied in Exod. 6.4 to the establishment of the 'covenant between the pieces' is most significant; as Beckwith asserts, this would appear to confirm that this verb does not relate exclusively to the confirmation of a pre-existing covenant. While the latter interpretation of הקים could be said to fit in the case of Isaac and Jacob, it is rather strange in the case of Abraham; prior to Genesis 15 there was no pre-existing covenant to be 'confirmed'.[27]

Whether Williamson is appropriately representing Beckwith or not, his reasoning seems to be tortuous. Williamson is correct that there is only one covenant, made with Abraham, the promises of which were later repeated to Isaac and Jacob, so that one could easily speak of a single covenant with all three.[28] Yet at the same time, Williamson considers Genesis 15 and 17 as separate covenants. This leads him to affirm that *hēqîm* in Exodus 6:4 should be applied to Genesis 15 and therefore the expression *hēqîm bĕrît* does not

---

[27] Paul R. Williamson, *Abraham, Israel, and the Nations*, 199.

[28] In Genesis 26 Yahweh communicates to Isaac in a vision after the death of Abraham, and the covenant promises to Abraham are repeated and affirmed for him. Note that the expression in 26:3 in the Hebrew text is *hēqîm 'et-hašševu'āh* (confirm or uphold the oath). This expression is equivalent to *hēqîm bĕrît* and indicates that God will confirm and uphold to Isaac his covenant promises to Abraham. Thus God is not initiating another or a different covenant *de novo* with Isaac, but only affirming that the promises of the one covenant made to the father are valid also for the son.

refer to confirming a preexisting covenant. The point being made in Exodus 6:4, however, is that God will now uphold his covenant promise to give to them the land of Canaan, a promise that *none* of the patriarchs experienced during their lives, as the author to the Hebrews shrewdly noted (Heb. 11:13). This is why the expression *hēqîm běrît* is aptly used in this text. Moreover, the land promise is part of Genesis 17 (see v. 8) as well, so that one could see an allusion to either Genesis 15 or 17, the latter being a confirmation of the former. Either way, the explanation provided by Williamson is difficult to follow since affirming Genesis 15 and 17 as separate covenants seems to contradict the affirmation of one covenant with all patriarchs. His reasoning, moreover, appears to beg the question.

Although the analysis here is based on my own exhaustive firsthand lexical studies, it is interesting to see that a recent check of the lexica some twenty years later fully supports the conclusions reached. For the *hiphil* of קוּם, *HALOT* has eight categories: (1) erect, put up, (2) take out, keep, (3) fulfill, (4) tell to get up, (5) raise, help up, (6) raise someone, nominate, (7) raise, erect, obtain, and (8) particular instances.[29] For the first category, the objects of the verb are "stone," "stones," "siege towers," "ruins," "courtyard," "curtains," "throne of David," "altar," "stela," "tent" or "hut," "pillar," "pillars," etc. The point is that one is causing to stand, i.e., erecting or setting up architectural features, buildings, monuments, etc. For the second category, the English rendering "take out" does not adequately render the original German *ausführen*.[30] In this category the verbal objects are usually "word," "words," "command," "vow," "covenant," and "oath." When one causes a "word" to stand, it means to carry out or keep the promise or word. It is quite natural to put "covenant" in this category since "keeping one's word" and "keeping a covenant" are in the same semantic field along with "oath" and "vow."[31] The same categories are in the first and second editions of Koehler-Baumgartner.[32]

When one turns to the older Oxford Lexicon,[33] the classification is almost the same. Instances of the expression *hēqîm běrît* (6d) are classified with the

---

[29] L. Koehler and W. Baumgartner, et al., *The Hebrew and Aramaic Lexicon of the Old Testament* (*HALOT*), study edition, trans. and ed. under the supervision of M. E. J. Richardson, 2 vols. (Leiden, Netherlands: Brill, 2001), s.v. קוּם.

[30] The original is in L. Koehler and W. Baumgartner, *Hebräisches und Aramäisches Lexikon zum Alten Testament*, 3rd ed., ed. W. Baumgartner, J. J. Stamm, and B. Hartmann (Leiden, Netherlands: Brill, 1967–1995), s.v. קוּם.

[31] The parallel between *hēqîm běrît* and *hēqîm dābār* is further supported by the fact that *kārat* likewise has *dābār* (Hag. 2:5), *'ālâ* (Deut. 29:13 [EV 14]), and *'āmānâ* (Neh. 10:1 [EV 9:38]) as objects with meanings parallel to *běrît*.

[32] L. Koehler and W. Baumgartner, *Lexicon in Veteris Testamenti Libros*, 2nd ed. (Brill, 1958, 1985).

[33] Francis Brown, S. R. Driver, and C. A. Briggs, *A Hebrew and English Lexicon of the Old Testament*, (Oxford: Clarendon, 1907, 1953).

notion of keeping a vow (6e) or one's word (6f). The definition offered, however, is "*establish* (make, ratify) covenant." The English word "establish" is confusing at this point since "establish" a covenant could mean either to initiate something new or to uphold something already in place. The reason for this confusion is not hard to find. The lexicographers who produced this lexicon were committed to the Documentary Hypothesis and believed that the expressions *kārat bĕrît* and *hēqîm bĕrît* were equivalent in meaning and evidence of different sources. Thus they were combining lexicography with literary criticism.[34]

The eighteenth edition of Gesenius, the most recent Hebrew lexicon, and an excellent one at that, separates cases where *hēqîm bĕrît* means to "keep a covenant" from places where they think it means to "initiate a covenant" based on a prior commitment to source theory.[35] The new *Dictionary of Classical Hebrew* has the same classification as *HALOT*, as does the article on קום in the *Theological Dictionary of the Old Testament* in spite of the fondness in the latter work for the "assured results" of source analysis.[36] Conversely, the *Theological Lexicon of the Old Testament* by Jenni and Westermann are influenced by the Documentary Hypothesis in the same way as the authors of the Oxford Lexicon.[37]

What this brief survey shows is that no one is free from presuppositions, but where lexicography is based only on linguistic science (without interference from criticism from source theory) all the lexica support the position taken here.[38]

To view the covenant with Noah as a kind of reinstatement and upholding of a covenant or commitment initiated at creation is not equivalent to saying that this is a covenant renewal. Niehaus is correct to call for a clear demarcation between covenants made for the first time and renewal covenants which confirm or ratify covenants initiated previously.[39] It is

---

[34] See Umberto Cassuto, *The Documentary Hypothesis*, trans. I. Abrahams (Jerusalem: Magnes, 1961), who argued that the different expressions correlated instead with different meanings. His approach was strictly linguistic, without interference from presuppositions about the sources.

[35] R. Meyer and H. Donner, *Wilhelm Gesenius Hebräisches und Aramäisches Handwörterbuch das Alte Testament*, 18th ed. (Berlin: Springer, 2009), Lfg. 5, s.v. קום.

[36] David J. A. Clines, *The Dictionary of Classical Hebrew* (Sheffield, UK: Sheffield Phoenix, 2010), 7:231–235; and J. Gamberoni, "קום *qûm*," in *TDOT* 12:589–612.

[37] Ernst Jenni and Claus Westermann, eds., *Theological Lexicon of the Old Testament*, 3 vols., trans. Mark E. Biddle (Peabody, MA: Hendrickson, 1997), s.v. קום *qûm*.

[38] An interesting question for those who claim *kārat bĕrît* and *hēqîm bĕrît* are essentially synonymous (e.g., M. Weinfeld, "ברית *bĕrît*," in *TDOT* 2:260) is this: what motivates the different usages? The distribution in the Hebrew Bible is difficult to explain merely in terms of sources or stylistic variation: half of the fourteen instances are in the Noah Story and Genesis 17.

[39] Jeffrey J. Niehaus, "An Argument against Theologically Constructed Covenants," 266–267, and idem, "Covenant: An Idea in the Mind of God," 236–237.

interesting, however, to note that the distinction in usage between *kārat bĕrît* and *hēqîm bĕrît* does not correlate with this perfectly valid difference between covenant initiation and covenant renewals or renewal covenants. Frequently *kārat bĕrît* is employed for renewal covenants[40] since they can be viewed as separate covenants even though they entail ratifying a previously existing covenant. So in the covenant with Noah, God "makes good on his commitment to creation." This might be conceived as ratifying a preexisting covenant, but not in the sense in which Niehaus and Williamson have understood Dumbrell.

The claim I am making for the distinction between *kārat bĕrît* and *hēqîm bĕrît* is not something special in relation to the word *bĕrît* but rather is based on the normal meaning of *hēqîm*. Consider the following example from Deuteronomy 27:26:

אָרוּר אֲשֶׁר לֹא־יָקִים אֶת־דִּבְרֵי הַתּוֹרָה־הַזֹּאת לַעֲשׂוֹת אוֹתָם

"Cursed is the man who does not uphold the words of this law by carrying them out" (NIV). The NIV has rendered the Hebrew text quite well: a person upholds the Torah by carrying out the obligations or stipulations that are specified in it.

In summary, based on the expression *hēqîm bĕrît*, linguistic usage alone demonstrates that when God says that he is confirming or establishing his covenant with Noah, he is saying that his commitment initiated previously at creation to care for and preserve, provide for and rule over all that he has made, including the blessings and ordinances that he gave to Adam and Eve and their family, are now to be with Noah and his descendants. This can be substantiated and further supported by noting the parallels between Noah and Adam, and between the covenant terms given to Noah and the ordinances given to Adam and his family.

PARALLELS WITH ADAM/THE CREATION NARRATIVES

In terms of literary techniques, we note that *key words*, *dominant ideas*, *parallel sequences* of actions, and *similar themes* clearly link the Noah narrative of Genesis 6–9 to the creation narratives in Genesis 1 and 2.

---

[40] Joshua 24:25 is an example of a renewal covenant, where Joshua leads the people to renew their commitment to Yahweh which was initiated in the Mosaic covenant.

THE FLOOD STORY AS A NEW CREATION

First, the flood story is presented in the narrative as a new creation. Just as God ordered the original heavens and earth out of the chaotic deep or ocean (Gen. 1:2; Heb. *těhôm*), so here God orders the present heavens and earth out of the chaotic floodwaters. Genesis 8:1 records that God caused a wind (Heb. *rûăh*) to pass over the waters of the flood covering the entire earth, which reminds one of the creation narrative where the Spirit (Heb. *rûăh*) of God hovers over the waters of the original chaotic deep.[41] In the creation narrative, God gathers the waters together, and the dry land emerges; then he commands the earth to bring forth vegetation. After the flood, the dry land emerges as the waters subside and the earth brings forth vegetation, as we see when the dove returns with an olive leaf in her beak. These parallels indicate that after the flood, we have a new beginning like the first beginning.

Bruce Waltke, following Kenneth Mathews, demonstrates that the flood narrative follows seven progressive phases of renewing creation that are modelled on the progression of the creation week in Genesis 1:[42]

> **Phase 1: precreation.** Just as God's Spirit hovered over the abyss (1:2), God sends a wind over the engulfing waters to renew the earth:
>   1:2: "earth," "deep," "Spirit" (*rûah*), "waters"
>   8:1b–2: "wind" (*rûah*), "earth," "waters," "deep"

> **Phase 2: second day.** Just as God initially divided the waters (1:6–7), God regathers the waters, reestablishing the boundaries between sky and earth:
>   1:6–8: "waters," "sky"
>   8:2b: "sky"

> **Phase 3: third day.** Just as God separated the dry, arable ground from the water to sustain vegetation, so again, the dry ground emerges in successive stages:
>   1:9: "water," "dry ground," "appear"
>   8:3–5: "water," "tops of the mountains," "appear"

> **Phase 4: fifth day.** The sky once again houses the winged creatures, as God first proclaimed it so to be:
>   1:20–23: "birds," "above ['al] the ground [NIV, "earth"]"
>   8:6–12: "raven," "dove," "from [mē'al] . . . the ground"

---

[41] This connection is stronger in the original text because the term for "wind" or "spirit" in Hebrew is the same word (*rûăh*).

[42] Taken from Bruce K. Waltke with Cathi J. Fredricks, *Genesis: A Commentary* (Grand Rapids, MI: Zondervan, 2001), 128–129.

Phase 5: sixth day. The living creatures of sky and land are called out from the ark, as in their first creative calling from the voice of God:

> 1:24–25: "creatures," "livestock," "creatures that move along the ground," "wild animals"
>
> 8:17–19: "creature," birds," "animals," "creatures that move along the ground"

Phase 6. The reappearance of the nuclear family, all of whom bear God's image, as the heads and sole representatives of the human race functions as a reprise of the creation of *'ādām*, male and female in God's image:

> 1:26–28: "man," "image of God," "male and female"
>
> 8:16, 18: Noah and his wife
>
> 9:6: "man," "image of God"

Phase 7. The heavenly King graciously grants his blessing on humanity, feeds them with the fruit of the restored earth, and, renewing the cultural mandate, restores them as lords over the creation:

> 1:28: "blessed," "be fruitful," "increase in number," "fill the earth," "rule . . . every living creature"
>
> 9:1–2: "blessed," "be fruitful," "increase in number," "fill the earth," "fear of you . . . upon every creature"

NOAH AS A NEW ADAM

Second, Noah is presented in the narrative as a new Adam. The blessing and commission given to Noah is the same as the one given to Adam (Gen. 9:1 = 1:28a). In this way the narrator portrays Noah as a new Adam. As we look at the terms of the covenant next, we will see that Noah is recommissioned with all of the ordinances given at creation to Adam and Eve and their family.

These literary techniques are important in determining the author's intent in communication. Williamson minimizes them because he does not see a covenant in Genesis 1–3:

> Nevertheless, while the conclusion that Genesis 1–3 must portray an ante-diluvian covenantal relationship is a non sequitur, Dumbrell and others are obviously correct to recognize several clear echoes of the creation narrative in the Noahic covenant. But these echoes suggest merely that God intended, through Noah, to fulfil his original creative intent; they do not presuppose the existence of a covenant between God and inanimate creation or indicate that the material in Genesis 1–3 must be understood covenantally.[43]

---

[43] Paul R. Williamson, *Sealed with an Oath*, 75.

What, in fact, is a non sequitur, is that Williamson clearly states that in the covenant with Noah, God is maintaining his original creative "intent" or "purpose" but denies that the divine-human relationship in Genesis 1–3 is covenantal. This non sequitur should be clear from the subtitle of his work, which links covenant to divine purpose: "Covenant in God's Unfolding Purpose." Furthermore, the flaw lies in exegesis and in an inadequate definition of covenant. The biblical metanarrative constructed by Williamson is one essentially beginning with Noah in which Adam has largely disappeared. This damages the parallels Paul draws between Adam and Christ as well as diminishes understanding of the covenant with Noah. See, at the end of this chapter, table 5.2 from Warren Austin Gage which draws out all the parallels between the first creation and the recreation after the flood.

From the flood narrative in Genesis 6–9, then, both the language used as well as the literary techniques indicate a covenant confirmed which had been initiated previously. This covenant entails a divine-human relationship initiated and specified at creation. Such a covenant could not, by definition, involve a ceremony between both parties, since what was involved was the creation of one of the parties in the relationship. That is a possible reason why the normal or standard language "to cut a covenant" is absent in Genesis 1–5.[44] Another reason is suggested by John H. Stek.[45] He argues as follows:

> . . . biblical covenants do not belong to the fundamentals of the God-creature relationship. . . . Covenants served rather to offer assurances, bolster faith, and reinforce commitments. In a world not invaded by sin, there would be no need for adding oaths to commitments, no need for "covenants"—no more than in such a world would oaths be necessary to establish the truth of one's "yes" or "no" (see Matt. 5:34–37; Jas. 5:12; cf., Heb. 6:16). Biblical covenants were ad hoc emergency measures occasioned by and ministering to human weaknesses—until the kingdom of God has fully come.[46]

This argument is erroneous and flawed. Biblical covenants are not ad hoc emergency measures. The divine-human relationship is *essentially* and *fundamentally* covenantal, because covenant is intrinsic to the being of God himself.[47] Stek may possibly have a point in arguing that, after the fall into

---

[44] See Dumbrell, *Covenant and Creation*, 15–26.

[45] John H. Stek, "'Covenant' Overload in Reformed Theology," *Calvin Theological Journal* 29 (1994): 12–41.

[46] Ibid., 40.

[47] Cf. Niehaus, "Covenant: An Idea in the Mind of God," 225–246. Niehaus critiques attempts to base the origin of covenant in the Old Testament on evolutionary or family models and argues that it comes from the mind of God. Although it might be better to say it comes from the *being* of God, the corrective contribution of Niehaus is cogent and necessary.

sin, oaths added assurances in relationships. Indeed, oaths will be completely unnecessary in the new creation.[48] Yet Craig Bartholomew notes in answer to Stek that marriage is an example of a covenant that is not just a postfall phenomenon.[49] Thus Genesis 1–3 may well be described as a covenant between God and his creation, or at least a commitment on God's part to his creation, including conduct stipulated for his creatures. Let us remember, too, that covenants include oaths, but the oath is not the covenant itself. Part of the problem may be the way in which Stek and Williamson emphasise the role of oaths in their definition of covenant. Waltke's definition is simpler: "*covenant* (Heb. *bᵉrît*) means 'a solemn commitment of oneself to undertake an obligation'."[50]

THE TERMS OF THE COVENANT

In Genesis 9:1–7 God blesses Noah and commissions him as a new Adam, giving him Adam's mandate, modified somewhat to suit the circumstances of a fallen world. Genesis 9:8–17 describes the covenant, its parties, and its sign. The verses in Genesis 9:1–17, then, are an expansion on the statement made to Noah in Genesis 6:18. Let us briefly note the blessing and terms set before Noah in verses 1–7 of chapter 9.

(1) First, Noah is told to "be fruitful," to "increase in number," and to "fill the earth." As already noted, this is the blessing originally given to Adam at creation. This command is repeated in verse 7 with stylistic variation and so provides brackets or bookends, i.e., a framework for the covenant stipulations and terms.

(2) Second, we read in verse 2 that "the fear of you and the dread of you will be upon all the wild animals of the earth and upon all the birds of the sky, upon all the creatures that crawl on the ground, and upon the fish of the sea." In Genesis 1, mankind was commanded to rule over the earth and subdue it. God now assists humans in this task in a fallen world by placing the fear of them upon the animals, birds, fish, and all creatures that move. Fear of humans may also assist them in catching creatures for consumption and nourishment and so relate to the next instruction or stipulation.

---

[48] See D. B. Garlington, "Oath-Taking in the Community of the New Age (Matthew 5:33–37)," *Trinity Journal* n.s. 16/2 (1995): 139–170.

[49] See Craig Bartholomew, "A Time for War and a Time for Peace: Old Testament Wisdom, Creation, and O'Donovan's Theological Ethics," in *A Royal Priesthood? The Use of the Bible Ethically and Politically—A Dialogue with Oliver O'Donovan*, ed. Craig Bartholomew, Jonathan Chaplin, Robert Song, and Al Wolters (Grand Rapids, MI: Zondervan, 2002), 106; and especially idem, "Covenant and Creation: Covenant Overload or Covenantal Deconstruction," 11–33.

[50] Waltke, *Old Testament Theology*, 287.

(3) Third, the animals are given to the human race for food, just as the plants were given at creation for food (Gen. 1:29–30). There are two important restrictions to this provision. First, humans are not to eat flesh or meat with its blood in it. Later, instructions given in the law of Moses clarify this stipulation. Several passages describe properly draining the blood from meat when animals are slaughtered before the meat can be eaten (Lev. 3:17; 7:26–27; 19:26; Deut. 12:16–24; 1 Sam. 14:32–34). So, while God gave the flesh of birds, fish, wild animals, and all creatures that move to sustain human life, he makes a restriction to maintain and preserve respect among humans for all of life. God remains the Lord of Life. Second, human life is set apart. This prevents not only cannibalism but also homicide. Even animals that kill humans are held responsible.

(4) Fourth, human life is special and of priceless value and worth. God specifies two things concerning homicide. First, the human race is one family. We are all related. When a human life is wantonly taken, we are our brother's keeper. This is the first time in the Hebrew text since the story of Cain and Abel that the word "brother" is used (cf. Gen. 4:2, 8, 8, 9, 9, 10, 11, 21). This is frequently obscured in modern translations. Genesis 9:5 can be literally translated, "and surely the blood of your lives I will require; from the hand of every creature I will require it and from the hand of humans, i.e., from the hand of the man's brother, I will require the life of humans." Thus the narrator reminds us of God's ordinance given originally to the family of Adam (Gen. 4:9–10) that he would require an accounting of life from fellow family members. Thus God holds the community responsible. He demands an accounting from society. Second, God requires retributive justice. That is, the penalty for taking a life is paying with a life.

EXCURSUS: GENESIS 9:6

(בְּאָדָם דָּמוֹ יִשָּׁפֵךְ // שֹׁפֵךְ דַּם הָאָדָם)

Interpretation of Genesis 9:6 is debated. The translation in the NIV is as follows: "Whoever sheds the blood of man, by man shall his blood be shed." The expression "by man" is rendering *bā'ādām*, a prepositional phrase consisting of the preposition "*b*" plus the article and the collective generic noun *'ādām* for humans. The preposition is capable of being construed in two different ways: (1) *beth instrumenti*, i.e., the preposition signals an instrumental use: "Whoever sheds the blood of mankind, *by means of* mankind shall his blood be shed;" (2) *beth pretii*, i.e., the preposition signals an economic exchange: "Whoever sheds the blood of mankind, his blood will be shed *in exchange for* the [murdered/slain] man." A thorough treatment is provided in E. Jenni, *Die hebräischen Präpositionen, Band 1: Die Präposition Beth* (Stuttgart: Kolhammer, 1992), 154. According to the first interpretation, the text is authorising the agency of humans in administering the death penalty. This interpretation is popular in many modern English translations. Nonetheless, Jenni, in his magisterial treatment of prepositions in Hebrew, argues that the second interpretation is more probable and fits as well the *lex talionis*, the fundamental principle of retribution in the Torah. If Jenni's exegesis is followed, it is important to note that the text does affirm elsewhere that human agency is authorised to administer the death penalty. Genesis 9:5 states, "And surely I shall demand an accounting of your life-blood, from the hand of every animal I shall demand it, and from the hand of mankind, that is, from the hand of his fellow-man I shall demand an accounting of the life of mankind." Thus God holds the community responsible; he demands an accounting from society.

Thus God holds the community responsible; he demands an accounting from society. It is clear from the text that retribution is in the hands of government, and not left to the anger and vengeance of an individual; nor are blood feuds authorised.

(5) God holds the human family/society responsible to administer retribution when a human life is taken wantonly. This accounting principle is based on the fact that humans, men and women, are made in the image of God. The mention of the image of God is significant. It reasserts the creation standard and the unique status of mankind and explains why human life is specially protected while animal life is not protected to the same extent.[51] Humanity owns the animals and thus can kill them, but humans cannot be killed because they are owned by God—stamped with his seal of ownership. Furthermore, as we shall see, the mention of the divine image is a direct reference to the covenant between God and creation and God and humanity established at creation.

---

[51] One is saddened to live in a country where an eagle's egg has more protection than an unborn human.

Table 5.1 outlines the terms of the covenant with Noah and his family and shows how they correspond to, renew, and repeat the terms of God's covenant at creation with Adam and Eve and their family.

Table 5.1: Comparison of Covenant with Noah and Covenant with Creation

Covenant with Noah	Covenant with Creation
be fruitful and increase in number	Gen. 1:28: be fruitful . . .
fear of you	Gen. 1:28: rule over fish, birds, animals
animals given for food	Gen. 1:29: plants given for food
don't eat meat with blood	
your blood . . . his brother's life	See Gen. 4:8–24
in the image of God	Gen. 1:27: in his own image

Genesis 9:8–17 now describes the covenant promise, its parties, and its sign.

THE PARTIES OF THE COVENANT

In Genesis 6:18 the covenant is made between God and Noah and his family. Here in verses 8–17 of chapter 9 there is an expansion. The partners of the covenant are referred to in six different ways:

> vv. 9–10: "with you and with your seed after you and with every living being which is with you: birds, animals domesticated, animals wild . . ."
> v. 12: "between me and you and every living being which was with you"
> v. 13: "between me and the earth"
> v. 15: "between me and you and every living being among all flesh"
> v. 16: "between God and every living being among all flesh which is on the earth"
> v. 17: "between me and all flesh which is on the earth"

The statements in verses 8–17 are highly repetitive and monotonous to Western ears. This repetition is like a cathedral bell ringing out again and again, reverberating into the future, that God is committing himself to all his living creatures while the earth lasts. There can be no mistaking of the parties specified in the covenant.

THE PROMISE OF THE COVENANT

Genesis 9:11 specifies the obligation that God places upon himself, the promise he makes to Noah and to the entire human race through him: "Never again will all life be cut off by the waters of a flood; never again will there be a flood to destroy the earth" (NIV). God reiterates his promise in verse 15 with stylistic variations. We first learn of this divine decision in 8:21:

> And Yahweh smelled the soothing smell and Yahweh said to himself, "I will never again curse the ground on account of mankind, because the inclination of the heart of mankind is evil from his youth."

Dumbrell aptly comments,

> The reference to the heart of man in Gen. 8:21 which remains unchanged by the experience of the flood refers initially to the eight who have been saved and thus throws into clear relief the nature of Noah's righteousness as something extrinsic to him. Since we are virtually being told that a deluge would be an appropriate response by God to the sin of any age, mankind has been preserved by grace alone. Until the end of time the continued existence of the created order will thus be grounded simply in the gracious nature of the divine character.[52]

The references to the "inclination of the heart of mankind" harks back to the previous instance of these words in Genesis 6:5, where we were informed of the cause of the great judgement: "The LORD saw how great the wickedness of the human race on the earth had become and that every inclination of the thoughts of their hearts was only evil all the time." The condition of humanity after the cataclysmic judgement remains the same as it was before; so the judgement has not altered or changed the condition of the human heart. The implication is that God would be completely justified in wiping out every generation of humanity by means of a great judgement. There is only one reason why he does not do so: because of his own grace and mercy toward us. The earth is maintained and preserved in spite of the human situation. Thus the covenant made with Noah creates a firm stage of history where God can work out his plan for rescuing his fallen world.

Dumbrell draws attention to the fact that four of the eight occurrences of the word "covenant" in this narrative have the possessive pronoun "my" attached to it: "I will confirm/uphold *my* covenant with you" (Gen. 6:18; 9:9, 11, 15).[53] We must pause for a moment and consider the force of the "my" which is involved in the expression "my covenant" in these texts. We

---

[52] Dumbrell, *Covenant and Creation*, 26–27.
[53] Ibid., 28.

have already noted that covenant, on any understanding of the term, has the notion of commitment or obligation built into it. Is this a covenant by which humans are obligated, or does God bind himself and thus make mankind the beneficiary of the obligation so undertaken? Dumbrell rightly suggests that the "my" of "my covenant" indicates that the latter is the correct interpretation. This is a covenant in which God binds himself, God obligates himself, and he will maintain the covenant in spite of human failure.

In Genesis 9:18–29 we have the strange story of the drunkenness of Noah and his curse upon Canaan. Like the first Adam, the second Adam is also a gardener who plants a vineyard. Like the first Adam, the second Adam is also a disobedient *son* whose sin results in shameful nakedness. One of the points this episode is making is that once again the human partner has failed as a covenant keeper, and that the fulfilment of the promise will be due solely to the faithfulness and grace of God, who is always a faithful covenant partner. This is the parallel in the Noah story to the Fall in Genesis 3.

THE SIGN OF THE COVENANT

God gives to Noah and to all of his descendants, to the entire human race, a physical sign of the covenant. The sign of the covenant with Noah is a rainbow in the clouds. There is, in fact, no word in Hebrew for "rainbow." The word that is used here is the ordinary term for an archer's bow. The only other occurrence in the Old Testament where it refers to a rainbow is Ezekiel 1:28, where a circumlocution such as "the bow which will be in the clouds" is required to indicate that a rainbow is in view and not an archer's bow. I like the comment of Warren Austin Gage: "The bow is a weapon of war, an emblem of wrath. God will now set it in the heavens as a token of grace. The Lord who makes his bow of wrath into a seven-colored arch of beauty to ornament the heavens is the one who will finally command the nations to beat their swords into plowshares and spears into pruninghooks (Mic. 4:3) for the Prince of Peace takes pleasure in mercy (Mic. 7:18) and the Righteous Judge delights in grace."[54] The rainbow, then, is a physical picture that God has "laid his weapons down," as indicated in the promise, "never again will there be a flood to destroy the earth." It is interesting that the bow set in the clouds is always aimed or pointed up to the heavens, and never downward at us on the earth.

---

[54] Warren Austin Gage, *The Gospel of Genesis: Studies in Protology and Eschatology* (Winona Lake, IN: Carpenter, 1984), 135.

Although not every covenant has a sign, this is the only covenant sign which can be given only by the divine partner. All of the other covenant signs are given by the human partner.

THE PLACE OF THE COVENANT WITH NOAH IN THE LARGER STORY

The covenant with Noah is in effect today. The promises and future statements made by God employ an emphatic negative "never again" four times (8:21; 9:11 [2x]; 9:15). His commitment is throughout everlasting generations (9:12). And in 9:16 he calls the arrangement an everlasting covenant. Indeed the sign of this covenant, the rainbow, remains as a witness to God to the present time. It is still with us today. There is no evidence anywhere in the completed canon of Scripture as a whole that this covenant has been annulled or superseded.

Earlier the claim was made that the covenants (plural) are at the heart of the metanarrative plot structure. The method that substantiates this claim is twofold: (1) to exegete the main texts for each of the covenants, paying attention to cultural context, linguistic data, literary devices and structures, and larger story; and (2) to exegete key texts that explicate the relationship between one or more covenants, so that the metanarrative is constructed from Scripture and not from an external metanarrative, i.e., philosophy or worldview. We would claim that classic covenant theology on the one hand and dispensational theology on the other (whether classic or so-called progressive) entail too much in the metanarrative that is external to Scripture. Moreover, the exegesis offered by these classic systems involves categories that are not sufficiently accurate in explaining the meaning of the key texts. Someone once shrewdly stated, "she who marries the spirit of the age will be a widow in the next." Francis Schaeffer noted well that the theology of Thomas Aquinas is a good example of combining biblical metanarrative and pagan worldview.[55]

The relationship of the covenant with Noah and the covenant with creation will become clearer once the covenant with creation is explained in detail. Nonetheless, some of the later passages dealing with the covenant with Noah can be considered here.[56]

---

[55] See Colin Duriez, *Francis Schaeffer: An Authentic Life* (Wheaton, IL: Crossway, 2008), 168.

[56] Passages which some scholars have erroneously connected to the covenant with Noah are appropriately eliminated from consideration here; see the evaluation of Dell by Williamson: K. J. Dell, "Covenant and Creation in

ISAIAH 24:3–5

Chapters 13–27 of Isaiah constitute a literary unit consisting of judgement oracles against foreign nations divided into three sets of five. Chapter 24 marks the onset of the third group of five oracles: all nations and peoples of the earth are indicted; this "city of man" will be destroyed because humans have broken the "everlasting covenant" by disobeying the instructions and violating its statutes:

> [3] The earth will be completely laid waste
>   and totally plundered.
>   The LORD has spoken this word.
>
> [4] The earth dries up and withers,
>   the world languishes and withers,
>   the exalted of the earth languish.
> [5] The earth is defiled by its people;
>   they have disobeyed the laws,
>   violated the statutes
>   and broken the everlasting covenant. (NIV)

Since the reference is to all humans breaking the "everlasting covenant," the Mosaic covenant given to Israel at Sinai is hardly in view. The most probable referent is the covenant made with Noah, which in reality reestablished and upheld the covenant with creation in Genesis 1, reaffirming the commitment of the Creator to his creation and the responsibilities placed upon humans at that time. Isaiah's oracle predicts complete desolation upon the earth because its people have violated the instructions and terms of the Noahic covenant.

ISAIAH 54:9–10

> [9] "To me this is like the days of Noah,
>   when I swore that the waters of Noah would never again cover the
>   earth.
>   So now I have sworn not to be angry with you,
>   never to rebuke you again.
> [10] Though the mountains be shaken
>   and the hills be removed,
>   yet my unfailing love for you will not be shaken

Relationship," in *Covenant as Context: Essays in Honour of E. W. Nicholson*, ed. A. D. H. Mayes and R. B. Salters (Oxford: Oxford University Press, 2003), 111–133; and Paul R. Williamson, *Sealed with an Oath*, 65–76.

nor my covenant of peace be removed,"
says the LORD, who has compassion on you. (NIV)

This passage is extremely important for letting the biblical text define in its own terms the relationships between the various covenants; it will be considered at length later. Nonetheless, Isaiah compares here the new covenant with the covenant with Noah. What is precisely similar between both covenants is the undeterred, unswerving commitment of Yahweh to carry out the promises enshrined in them. Just as he promised never again to cover the entire earth with floodwaters as a judgement, so he will never be angry with his people and so withdraw his loyal love in the covenant of peace.

JEREMIAH 33:19–26

In a context where Jeremiah is communicating divine promises to restore the fortunes of Judah and Israel, he also speaks of the fulfilment of the promises of Yahweh to David:

> [19] The word of the LORD came to Jeremiah: [20] "This is what the LORD says: 'If you can break my covenant with the day and my covenant with the night, so that day and night no longer come at their appointed time, [21] then my covenant with David my servant—and my covenant with the Levites who are priests ministering before me—can be broken and David will no longer have a descendant to reign on his throne. [22] I will make the descendants of David my servant and the Levites who minister before me as countless as the stars of the sky and as measureless as the sand on the seashore.'"
>
> [23] The word of the LORD came to Jeremiah: [24] "Have you not noticed that these people are saying, 'The LORD has rejected the two kingdoms he chose'? So they despise my people and no longer regard them as a nation. [25] This is what the LORD says: 'If I have not established my covenant with day and night and the fixed laws of heaven and earth, [26] then I will reject the descendants of Jacob and David my servant and will not choose one of his sons to rule over the descendants of Abraham, Isaac and Jacob. For I will restore their fortunes and have compassion on them.'" (NIV)

The divine oracle affirms that the covenant with David is unbreakable, just as the covenant with the day and the covenant with the night is unbreakable. What is being referred to in the expression "my covenant with the day and my covenant with the night"? Debate exists as to whether these words refer to the covenant with Noah or to what is being called here the covenant with creation (in Genesis 1). Since I have argued that the covenant with Noah "upholds" the covenant with creation in Genesis 1, either way the point is the same, and the debate can be evaluated later.

SUMMARY

Later references to the covenant with Noah pick up on features that are clearly expressed within the text of Genesis 6–9. Two of the texts, Isaiah 54 and Jeremiah 33, note the emphatic "never again" so that God promises never again to employ floodwaters in judgement to destroy all flesh. Nonetheless there are stipulations and terms given to both animals and humans. God demands an accounting. Isaiah 24 picks up on the importance of human responsibility.

Theologians have attempted to classify and describe covenants as either conditional or unconditional. That is, are the commitments bilateral or unilateral and is their fulfilment conditioned (in the case of a divine-human relationship) upon the obedience of the human party? These categories are not helpful or fruitful if one desires to accurately represent the biblical text. The covenant with Noah entails divine promises whose fulfilment cannot be thwarted, yet it also calls the community of animals and humans to answer for their actions and stewardship.

The covenant with Noah "upholds" the divine image. This is to be discussed next. As we shall see, it entails a covenant relationship between God and humans on the one hand and between humans and creation on the other. The human community must express obedient sonship in faithful loyal love to the creator God and rule over the creation with humble servanthood and responsible stewardship. Worship is a priority in achieving these purposes. The narratives of Genesis 6–8 begin by depicting Noah as an obedient son and steward of animal life in the earth. He also offers significant worship in a sacrifice that appeases the anger of the Lord and turns away further judgement. Nonetheless, like the first Adam, he ends up as a disobedient son whose nakedness reveals shame rather than full integrity.

As Bruce Waltke aptly notes, the covenant with Noah is instructive because it shows that being given a fresh start and a clean slate is not a sufficient remedy for the human plight:

> The sin of Noah sheds light on the human plight. At one time or another, most people become disgusted with what is going on in the world—the

intractable problems among people: hatred, prejudice, and greed that lead to cruelty and war. The problems are insoluble because hatred and prejudice are burdens of our depraved nature and our history. Because we cannot change or forget, our nature and memory doom us. In response, the idealistic ones among us ask: "What if we started over? What if we expunged history and wiped the slate clean?" The account of Noah puts the lie to that solution.[57]

The unmerited favour and kindness of God in preserving his world in the covenant with Noah creates a firm stage of history where God can work out his plan for rescuing his fallen world. It also points ahead to the coming deliverance in Jesus Christ. Williamson's summary of the significance of the covenant with Noah is the same:

> The theological significance of the Noahic covenant is at least twofold. First of all, it is the basis for our present confidence in God as sustainer. It is the Noahic covenant that gives us the assurance that God will sustain the creation order, despite the chaos that continually threatens to engulf it. . . . Secondly, given that the Noahic covenant provides the biblical-theological framework within which all subsequent divine-human covenants operate, its universal scope is undoubtedly significant. As suggested by the allusions to Genesis 1 noted above, the universal scope of this covenant implies that the blessing for which humanity had been created and the creation had now been preserved will ultimately encompass not just one people or nation, but rather the whole earth. Accordingly, while the patriarchal narratives reflect an obvious narrowing in focus, the universal emphasis of Genesis 1–11 is not lost entirely in the subsequent chapters of Genesis and beyond.[58]

Warren Austin Gage helpfully draws the parallels between Adam and Noah together into a table (see table 5.2).

---

[57] Waltke, *Old Testament Theology*, 298.
[58] Paul R. Williamson, *Sealed with an Oath*, 67–68.

Table 5.2: The History of the World: The Macrocosm[59]

Genesis 1		The World That Was		Genesis 7
Creation	*Adam*	*Fall*	*Conflict of Seed*	*Judgement*
1. Waters of chaos cover the earth, Gen. 1:1–2	1. Man commissioned in God's image, Gen. 1:26	1. Adam sins in a garden, Gen. 3:6	1. Cain condemned to wander, founds wicked city of Enoch, Gen. 4:17	1. Days of Noah are upon the earth, Gen. 6:13
2. Spirit hovers upon face of the waters, Gen. 1:2	2. Man commanded to fill the earth, Gen. 1:28	2. Adam partakes in fruit of tree of knowledge, Gen. 3:6	2. Seth, with son Enosh, begins to call upon name of Lord, Gen. 4:26	2. God brings cloud upon earth to destroy the wicked with a flood, Gen. 7:23
3. Dry land emerges, vegetation brought forth, Gen. 1:9	3. God brings animals to Adam for naming, Gen. 2:19	3. Adam shamefully naked, Gen. 3:7	3. Daughters of men taken to wife by sons of God, Gen. 6:2	3. Old heavens and earth pass away before the present heavens and earth, 2 Pet. 3:5–7.
4. Old world finished, God rests, Gen. 2:2		4. Adam's nakedness covered by God, Gen. 3:21		
		5. Adam's sin brings curse upon seed, Gen. 3:15		
Genesis 8		**The World That Now Is**		**Revelation 22**
The New Creation	*Noah, The New Adam*	*The Fall Renewed*	*Seed Conflict Renewed*	*The New Judgement*
1. Waters of Noah cover the earth, Gen. 7:18–19	1. Man recommissioned in God's image, Gen. 9:6	1. Noah sins in a vineyard, Gen. 9:20–21	1. Noah's sons, to avoid wandering, found wicked city of Babel, Gen. 11:4	1. "Days of Noah" again upon the earth, Matt. 24:37–39
2. Dove "hovers" upon face of the waters, Gen. 8:9	2. Man commanded to fill the earth again, Gen. 9:7	2. Noah partakes of fruit of vine, Gen. 9:21	2. Shem's descendent Abram begins to call upon name of Lord, Gen. 12:8	2. God comes in clouds to destroy the wicked with a fire, Matt. 24:30; cf. 2 Pet. 3:7
3. Olive leaf betokens emergence of dry land, Gen. 8:11	3. God brings animals to Noah for delivering, Gen. 7:13–15	3. Noah shamefully naked, Gen. 9:21	3. The harlot Babel seduces the sons of Zion throughout the ages, cf. Dan. 1:1; Isa. 47:1–15; Rev. 17–18	3. Present heavens and earth pass away before the new heavens and earth, 2 Pet. 3:12–13
4. Present world finished; God receives sacrifice of rest, Gen. 8:21		4. Noah's nakedness covered by sons, Gen. 9:23		
		5. Noah's sin brings curse upon seed, Gen. 9:25		

---

[59] Adapted with permission from Gage, *Gospel of Genesis*, 16.

Chapter Six

THE COVENANT WITH CREATION IN GENESIS 1–3

INTRODUCTION

Whether or not a covenant is entailed in Genesis 1–3 continues to be debated. In his recent work, *Sealed with an Oath*, for example, Williamson argues that a divine-human covenant is introduced for the first time in the flood narrative in Genesis 6:18. He notes arguments *for* a covenant in Genesis 1–3 by Dumbrell and Robertson. According to Williamson, Dumbrell relies on interpretation of the pronoun in the phrase "my covenant" (Gen. 6:18; 9:9, 11, 15), the difference in meaning between "cut a covenant" (*kārat běrît*) and "uphold a covenant" (*hēqîm běrît*), and a divine commitment to achieve the purpose of creation observed in Genesis 1:1–2:4a. Robertson's main proof is based upon Jeremiah 33:20–26, a passage that can be considered after exegesis of Genesis 1–3. Williamson finds these arguments wanting.

Before our analysis of Genesis 1–3, a few points can be briefly made in response to arguments offered by scholars against a covenant in the creation narrative.

First, Williamson states what for many scholars is apparently a strong argument: "prior to Genesis 6:18 there is not even a hint of any covenant being established—at least between God and humans."[1] The absence of the Hebrew word for "covenant" in Genesis 1–5, however, cannot constitute an argument to demonstrate the absence of any covenant before Genesis 6:18. It is fully possible in biblical literature to speak of a covenant without actually using the word. To illustrate this important principle of interpretation, consider, for example, a recent study of "The King in the Book of Isaiah" by Richard Schultz.[2] Naturally the first step in his investigation is to carefully analyse all contexts in which the Hebrew root *mlk*—the basis of all adjectives, nouns, and verbs in Hebrew having to do with royal rule—occurs in Isaiah. This is only, however, a first step. Wisely, Schultz looks for other

[1] Paul R. Williamson, *Sealed with an Oath: Covenant in God's Unfolding Purpose*, NSBT 23 (Downers Grove, IL: InterVarsity Press, 2007), 72.
[2] Richard Schultz, "The King in the Book of Isaiah," in *The Lord's Anointed: Interpretation of Old Testament Messianic Texts*, ed. Philip E. Satterthwaite, Richard S. Hess, and Gordon J. Wenham (Grand Rapids, MI: Baker, 1995), 141–165.

ways in which the notion of kingship is communicated. A passage in Isaiah that fairly shouts the kingship of Yahweh without actually employing any word based upon the root *mlk* is 66:1:

> This is what the LORD says:
>
>> "Heaven is my throne,
>>   and the earth is my footstool.
>> Where is the house you will build for me?
>> Where will my resting place be?" (NIV)

As one might expect, this verse forms an important part of Schultz's treatment of kingship in Isaiah. And just as one can speak of kingship without the word "king," so one can speak of covenant without using that word. Later we will see that the phrase, "I will be their God and they will be my people" is a frequent method of referring to a divine-human covenant. Furthermore, the word "Torah" implies covenant as its reflex just as faith implies repentance as its reflex. These are just a couple of examples. The absence of the word for "covenant" (*bĕrît*) in Genesis 1–3, then, is no argument at all against the notion that a divine-human covenant is established at creation, if exegesis can demonstrate that the idea is there.

It is legitimate to ask, as Dumbrell indeed does, why the expression "to cut a covenant" does not occur in Genesis 1–3.[3] Probably the answer is simply that the ceremony involving cutting an animal in half to symbolise a self-imprecatory oath would have been anachronistic and unsuitable as a communicative instrument for the covenant at creation established between God and humans on the one hand and humans and the creation on the other. Exegesis of Genesis 1:26–28 will substantiate this.

Second, some have argued (as, for example, John Stek), that covenants are necessary only after the Fall in Genesis 3. Yet marriage is a covenant relationship that existed prior to the Fall, as Bartholomew has observed, and so this, too, is not an argument against a divine-human covenant in Genesis 1.

Third, although the description of the difference in meaning between "cut a covenant" (*kārat bĕrît*) and "uphold a covenant" (*hēqîm bĕrît*) given by Dumbrell must be adjusted and his interpretation of some contexts modified, the difference is nonetheless real and substantiated by exhaustive examination

---

[3] William J. Dumbrell, *Covenant and Creation: A Theology of Old Testament Covenants* (Nashville: Thomas Nelson, 1984), 32.

of all the data. Williamson relied on Weinfeld and did not analyse all the data for himself. From the flood narrative we have seen that the language employed there does indeed point to the upholding of a covenant initiated previously between God and humans as well as between humans and creation in which Noah appears as a new Adam. Williamson's argument that there is no covenant in Genesis 1–3 results in an emasculated biblical metanarrative which essentially begins with Noah and greatly endangers the parallels drawn by Paul between Adam and Christ from the larger story of Scripture.

Fourth, the way in which covenant is defined can prejudice the question of a covenant at creation. Williamson says,

> for Reformed theologians, apparently, any relationship involving God must be covenantal in nature—whether his relationship with creation in general or his relation with human beings in particular. Covenant is seen as framing or establishing any such relationship. This, however, is not in fact what the biblical text suggests. Rather than establishing or framing such a divine-human relationship, a covenant seals or formalizes it.

While no attempt is made here to provide support for classic covenantal theology or classic/progressive dispensational treatments of covenants, the statement by Williamson seems confused. The covenant with Noah which Williamson has just expounded as universal in scope should be sufficient to show that God's relationship to all creatures and humans is covenantal. This is so, as we will see, because covenant is essential to the being of God. Nonetheless, Williamson employs an ill-defined notion of covenant against those who hold that there is a covenant at creation.

Jeffrey J. Niehaus also finds the treatment of Williamson problematic at this point, and his evaluation needs to be cited in full:

> Williamson further uses the understanding that a covenant ratifies or seals an existing relationship as an argument against a creation covenant, and in doing so he notes the background of relationship in the divine-human covenants:
>
> > Leaving aside creation for a moment, just consider the ensuing biblical examples of divine-human relationships that are subsequently sealed by means of a covenant: God was clearly in relationship with Abraham from Genesis 12, yet it is not until Genesis 15 that God formalizes that relationship by means of a covenant. Similarly, God was in relationship with Israel before the covenant

he formally established with them on Mount Sinai. Likewise, God was in relationship with David long before he sealed that relationship by covenant in 2 Samuel 7. And a straightforward reading of Genesis 6 suggests that God was in relationship with Noah before sealing that relationship by covenant immediately after the Flood. Thus the question is not whether or not a relationship existed between God and creation or between God and humanity prior to the fall. Undoubtedly, such a relationship existed. However, to insist on calling this relationship a "covenant relationship" is another matter entirely. There is no indisputable evidence in the text for doing so. This is hardly surprising if, as suggested above, a covenant was primarily a means of sealing or formalizing such a relationship; it did not establish it.[4]

The question is not, however, whether a relationship existed between God and Abraham, God and Israel, God and David, and God and Noah, before God entered into covenants with them. The question is what sort of relationship existed in each case. The answer is: pre-covenantal (and not a covenantal) relationship. That relationship, which existed before the covenant was actually "cut" or made, would become the stuff of the historical prologue of the future covenant. So, Yahweh commanded Abram to leave his homeland (Gen 12:1), and later, when the covenant was made (Genesis 15), identified himself as Yahweh who brought him up out of Ur of the Chaldeans (Gen 15:7). Likewise, Yahweh delivered Israel out of Egypt, and then, when he began to give them the laws of the covenant he was now making with them, identified himself as "Yahweh, who brought you out of Egypt, out of the land of slavery" (Exod 20:2). The pattern is exactly what we typically see in the late second millennium BC international treaties.[5]

Covenants in both the biblical texts and the ancient Near Eastern culture vary widely, and a definition which is narrower than the evidence permits prejudges the situation in Genesis 1–3, as is illustrated by the skewed definition of Williamson. It is interesting to note that Williamson speaks of "God's universal purpose" in creation and that "God intended, through Noah, to fulfil his original creative intent."[6] These are, in essence, backdoor references to the (covenantal) *commitment* of the Creator to his creation, which Williamson cannot escape.

In the end, exegesis must show—an exegesis based not only on the cultural and linguistic data but also attuned to literary structures and techniques

---

[4] Paul R. Williamson, *Sealed with an Oath*, 75–76.

[5] Jeffrey J. Niehaus, "Covenant: An Idea in the Mind of God," *JETS* 52/2 (2009): 237–238.

[6] Paul R. Williamson, *Sealed with an Oath*, 51, 75.

and a canonical metanarrative—whether or not there is a covenant in Genesis 1. It may be that Dumbrell's exegesis is inadequate and so not persuasive for Williamson, but Williamson provides no exegesis of Genesis 1–3 whatsoever.

EXEGESIS OF GENESIS 1–3

A covenant initiated at creation is clearly indicated by the text of Genesis 1:26–28 as well as by elements in 2:4–3:24.

Although centuries of analysis and debate have been focused on interpretation of the divine image in Genesis 1:26–28, a significant contribution can yet be made to our understanding of this text by combining biblical theology on the one hand and recent insights into the cultural setting and language of the text on the other. The biblical-theological framework of Genesis 1:26–28 has been provided first from a consideration of the language used in the flood narratives, so now an exegesis of the text itself with close attention to its cultural setting and linguistic and literary features is a desideratum.

THE DIVINE IMAGE IN GENESIS 1:26–28

HUMANS ARE THE CROWN OF CREATION

The creation narrative, Genesis 1:1–2:3, is divided according to the chronological structure of a week into seven paragraphs. Genesis 1:26–28 describes the creation of humans in a paragraph delimited by Genesis 1:24–31 that is devoted to the events of Day Six. The following considerations may appear to belabor the point unnecessarily, but verses 26–28 are intended to be viewed as the climax and crown of God's creative work.

(1) The clauses describing the creation of humans are marked by a notable change in style. To this point the creation has been achieved by a series of divine words always introduced by third person singular verbs. Surely the first person plural "Let us . . . " catches the attention of the reader and signals something significant. The interpretation of the first person plural will be discussed later, but whatever the interpretation, the main point is that something special is happening in this section.

(2) The paragraph in Genesis 1:24–31 has a different pattern from the other paragraphs. Table 6.1 shows that the paragraphs in the creation narrative follow a standard sequence of (1) announcement, (2) command, (3) action, (4) evaluation or report, and (5) temporal framework, with minor

variations. The pattern of events in paragraph six deviates from the norm considerably and thus informs the reader that the topic is important.[7]

Table 6.1: Sequence of Day Six versus the Other Days of Creation

Day One (1:3–5)

Announcement
Command
Report
Evaluation
Action described
Naming
Temporal framework

Day Four (1:14–19)

Announcement
Command and purpose
Report
Action and purpose
Evaluation

Temporal framework

Day Two (1:6–8)

Announcement
Command
Action described
Report
Naming
Temporal framework

Day Five (1:20–23)

Announcement
Command
Action described
Evaluation
Blessing
Temporal framework

Day Three (1:9–13)

Announcement
Command
Report
Naming
Evaluation
Announcement
Command
Report
Action described
Evaluation
Temporal framework

Day Six (1:24–31)

Announcement
Command
Report
Action described
Evaluation
Announcement
Decision and purpose
Action and purpose
Blessing and purpose
Food provision
Report
Temporal framework

Day Seven (2:1–3)

Completion statement
Divine rest
Blessing of 7th day
Consecration of 7th day
No temporal framework

(3) In terms of the larger literary structure, the work of creation is accomplished in six days. In such a sequence, Day Six is clearly the climax of this creation work.

(4) Figure 6.1 concisely indicates the number of words per paragraph in

---

[7] Note that both Day Three and Day Six entail a doubling of the pattern.

the creation narrative. The number of words in paragraph six is far above the norm—another indication of the significance of the creation of humans.[8]

Words Describing Each Day of Creation

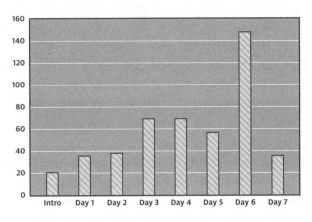

Fig. 6.1

(5) Genesis 2:4–25, the so-called second account of creation, is in fact not evidence of an editor patching together different sources but corresponds well to the normal pattern of Hebrew narrative to consider a topic in a resumptive manner. We cannot critique *ancient, eastern* texts using principles of literary analysis based on *modern, Western* literature. Instead, the approach in ancient Hebrew literature is to take up a topic and develop it from a particular perspective and then to stop and take up the same theme again from another point of view. This pattern is kaleidoscopic and recursive. The first creation story (1:1–2:3) gives a global perspective. The second creation story (2:4–3:24) begins by focusing on the creation of man. Thus the first focuses on the origin of the universe, the second on humanity. Therefore, 2:4–3:24 is, in fact, devoted to further development of the topics broached in the sixth paragraph of the "first account" and so adds to the significance of the creation of mankind.

(6) The clause marking the temporal framework normally has the pattern "and it was evening and it was morning, a ___th day." Thus, it is striking that, for paragraph six, the definite article is used: "*the* sixth day." The

---

[8] The table is derived from my own research, but compare a table similar to this in Stephen G. Dempster, *Dominion and Dynasty: A Biblical Theology of the Hebrew Bible* (Downers Grove, IL: InterVarsity Press, 2003), 57.

function of the article here has yet to be explained satisfactorily, but adds to the significance of the creation of humans.[9]

(7) The use of *bārā'*, the verb "to create" in Hebrew, is interesting. This verb always and only has God as subject and seems to be a special word.[10] It occurs only three times in the creation narrative: in 1:1, which some commentators see as the creation of matter *ex nihilo*; in 1:21 at the creation of organic life; and in 1:26 at the creation of human life.[11] In between, other synonyms are used. Thus this verb seems to mark important points in the creation work.

(8) *'ādām*, a generic term for mankind as both male and female, is created as the image of God. This is another indication of humans as the crown of God's creation.[12]

(9) Humans exercise royal rule. This requires some discussion but points to the significance of mankind within creation as a whole.

(10) Psalm 8, attributed to David, in verses 5–8 constitutes a word-by-word commentary and meditation on Genesis 1:26–28. The psalmist understands that mankind is at the apex of God's creation, however one understands the disputed verse 5.

In sum, a large number of literary techniques point to the significance of the creation of humans. The interpretation of the creation of man as the divine image will unfold this significance.

THE IMAGE OF GOD

Explanations of the divine image during the last two thousand years have been numerous and varied.[13] Since the amount of ink spilled on the subject is enormous, careful exegesis is necessary, as well as humility, in interpre-

---

[9] See David A. Sterchi, "Does Genesis 1 Provide a Chronological Sequence?" *JETS* 39/4 (1996): 529–536. The connection claimed between anarthrous designations in number and chronology claimed by Sterchi remains to be tested, but he is doubtless right that the article signifies something significant.

[10] For recent analysis and research on *bārā'* see John H. Walton, *Genesis*, NIV Application Commentary (Grand Rapids, MI: Zondervan, 2001), 67–70; idem, *The Lost World of Genesis One: Ancient Cosmology and the Origins Debate* (Downers Grove, IL: InterVarsity Press, 2009), 38–46; and idem, *Genesis One as Ancient Cosmology* (Winona Lake, IN: Eisenbrauns, 2011).

[11] See C. I. Scofield, ed., *The New Scofield Reference Bible* (Oxford: Oxford University Press, 1970), 1 n. 4.

[12] Usages of the term *'ādām* in the text of Genesis 1–5 move almost imperceptibly from (1) a generic sense of humankind to (2) Man, i.e., the primal human being, to (3) Adam as a personal name. See especially Richard S. Hess, "Splitting the Adam: The Usage of *'ĀDĀM* in Genesis I-V," in *Studies in the Pentateuch*, ed. J. A. Emerton, Supplements to Vetus Testamentum 41 (Leiden, Netherlands: Brill, 1990), 1–15. Occasionally in this chapter I employ "Man" because of this ambiguity in the original text, although I would argue in the strongest terms that the image of God applies generically to all humans, both male and female.

[13] For an excellent and impressive survey of views in just the last one hundred years, see Gunnlauger A. Jónsson, *The Image of God: Genesis 1:26–28 in a Century of Old Testament Research*, Coniectanea Biblica: Old Testament Series 26 (Lund, Sweden: Almqvist & Wiksell, 1988).

tation. An extremely brief survey of the different views follows, adapted from the commentary by Gordon Wenham.[14] The present writer, however, is ultimately responsible for the evaluation of each view.[15]

Survey of Views

(1) The terms "image" and "likeness" are distinct aspects of man's nature (from Irenaeus, c. A.D. 180 onwards). The "image" denotes the natural qualities in man (personality, reason, etc.) that make him resemble God, while the "likeness" refers to the supernatural (i.e., ethical) graces that make the redeemed godlike. Lexical analysis of "image" and "likeness" according to the cultural setting of the biblical text shows that this distinction is foreign to Genesis.

(2) The divine image refers to the mental and spiritual qualities that man shares with his creator. The fact that commentators cannot agree in identifying these qualities makes this approach suspect.

(3) The image consists of a physical resemblance. In favour of this, the Hebrew term *ṣelem* does refer to a physical image or statue in a majority of its occurrences. Moreover, in Genesis 5:3 Adam is described as fathering Seth "after his image," which most naturally refers to physical appearance. The Old Testament, however, emphasises the incorporeality and invisibility of God (Deut. 4:12). Also, if the terminology is related to Egyptian and Mesopotamian thinking, the image of God there refers to the function of the king and not to his appearance. Furthermore, the Old Testament does not sharply distinguish the material and spiritual realms in the way that we sometimes do. The image of God must characterise the whole man, not simply his mind or spirit on the one hand or his body on the other. Finally, the image of God is what separates man from the animals, and yet the practice of sacrifice must have made the ancient people of Israel well aware of the physiological similarities between humans and animals.

(4) The divine image makes man God's representative on earth. Careful exegesis below indicates that the ruling function is a *result* of being made in the divine image and *not the image itself.*

(5) The image is a capacity to relate to God. The divine image means that God can enter into personal relationships with man, speak to him, and make covenants with him. Karl Barth propounded this view and Claus

---

[14] Gordon J. Wenham, *Genesis 1–15*, WBC 1 (Waco, TX: Word, 1987), 29–32.
[15] Even when material is adapted and borrowed from Wenham.

Westermann further argued that the "image of God" is not part of the human constitution so much as it is a description of the process of creation which made man different. Although this view has something to commend it, in that relationship to God is fundamental to the image of God, nonetheless passages like Genesis 5:3 and Exodus 25:40 suggest that the phrase "in the image" describes the product of creation rather than the process.

Critique of the Traditional View

The majority of Christians have followed the second view, believing that the image refers to mental and spiritual qualities which humans share with the creator God. Since God is invisible (John 4:24), man does not resemble God physically but rather in terms of morality, personality, reason, and spirituality. This interpretation did not originate with the Christian church, but can be traced to Philo of Alexandria, a Jewish philosopher living in the time 30 B.C. to A.D. 45 (*On the Creation* § 69).

The traditional view is inadequate because it is not the result of grammatical and historical interpretation of the text. Rather, it is based largely on a kind of reasoning from systematic theology. It does not come to grips with the fact that "image" normally refers to a physical statue and cannot be exegetically validated as the author's intended meaning or the first audience's natural understanding of the text in terms of the ancient Near Eastern cultural and linguistic setting.

Exegesis of Genesis 1:26–28

An attempt to determine the meaning of this text according to the historical setting and linguistic usage of the time in which it was written begins with the literary structure, consideration of grammatical and lexical issues, and the ancient Near Eastern background.

THE STRUCTURE OF GENESIS 1:24–31

As already noted, the paragraph in the creation narrative devoted to describing events of the sixth day is structured differently from the other paragraphs. The following outline builds upon the work of P. E. Dion as best representing the structure in the text.[16]

---

[16] P. E. Dion, "Ressemblance et Image de Dieu," in *Suppléments aux Dictionnaire de la Bible*, ed. H. Cazelles and A. Feuillet, 55:383.

The Sixth Day—Genesis 1:24–31

A. Creation of the Animals	1:24–25
1. Command for creation of animals	24a
Confirmation	24b
2. Execution of creation of animals	25a
Evaluation	25b
B. Creation of Mankind	1:26–31
1. Decision for creation of man	26
To make man	26a
To give him a certain role	26b
2. Execution of creation of man	27–28
Creation of man	27
Proclamation of his role	28
3. Food regulations	29–30
For man	29
For animals	30
C. Conclusion	1:31
Evaluation	31a
Day notation	31b

For the creation of humans, instead of the normal pattern of giving a command and indicating a result, there is first a divine decision followed by a divine execution of that decision. Note that the decision has two parts and the execution of the decision has the same two corresponding parts. This observation leads to consideration of two separate grammatical issues before looking at the ancient Near Eastern setting.

KEY GRAMMATICAL ISSUES IN GENESIS 1:26–28

The sequence of verbs in verse 26 is inadequately represented in most modern translations. The first verb in the divine speech is נַעֲשֶׂה. Randall Garr's analysis is both adequate and complete:

> Technically, this form is ambiguous; the imperfect and cohortative of final weak roots are usually not distinguished in the morphology but are expressed by the self-same ending ה ֶ . The interpretation of נעשה, however, is clear enough. Not only does the clause-initial position of the verb suggest the cohortative reading, but a comparison with the jussives that engaged other acts of creation reinforces its desiderative sense.[17]

---

[17] W. Randall Garr, *In His Own Image and Likeness: Humanity, Divinity, and Monotheism*, Culture and History of the Ancient Near East 15 (Leiden, Netherlands: Brill, 2003), 85.

The first verb, then, is a command form and is correctly rendered "let us make" in all of the English versions. The second verb in the sequence is וְיִרְדּוּ. This, too, could be construed as either imperfect or jussive. What is important, however, is that grammarians of Hebrew agree that this particular sequence (cohortative followed by imperfect) marks purpose or result.[18] The correct translation, therefore, is "let us make man . . . *so that* they may rule . . ." Here many modern versions fail to represent properly the grammar of the Hebrew text. An important exegetical point is at stake: the ruling is not the essence of the divine image, but rather a result of being made as the divine image.

Another grammatical issue concerns the clause patterns in verse 27. The verse contains three clauses or sentences: (1) and God created man in his image; (2) in the image of God he created him; (3) male and female he created them. The first sentence has a normal clause pattern: verb-subject-object. The conjunction *waw* is used, and the verb is a *waw*-consecutive imperfect—standard in Hebrew narrative. The remaining two sentences have a different clause pattern: modifier-verb-object. Both are also asyndetic, i.e., not connected by the conjunction *waw*; the verbs are both perfects. This is a clear macrosyntactical signal with pragmatic significance: these clauses do not advance the narrative but digress and pause to comment on the first clause in the verse.[19] These two short sentences are grammatically marked as circumstantial information or parenthetical remarks. The author is *digressing from* the narrative in order to stress two particular aspects or features of the creation of man:

a) creation of mankind entails male and female
b) mankind resembles God in some way

By pausing to stress these two things, the author prepares us for the two commands given to man in the very next verse:

a) be fruitful (three imperatives in Hebrew)
b) rule over the other creatures (two imperatives in Hebrew)

The actual literary presentation is chiastic in structure: The word *chiasm* comes from the letter in the Greek alphabet known as *chi* (χ), which is shaped like an X. The top half of the letter has a mirror image in the bottom half.

---

[18] See Paul Joüon, *Grammaire de l'hébreu biblique* (Rome: Biblical Institute Press, 1923), § 116; and Thomas O. Lambdin, *Introduction to Biblical Hebrew* (New York: Charles Scribner's Sons, 1971), § 107.
[19] Stephen G. Dempster, "Linguistic Features of Hebrew Narrative: A Discourse Analysis of Narrative from the Classical Period" (PhD diss., University of Toronto, 1985).

If, for example, a literary piece has four distinct units and the first matches the last while the second matches the third, the result is a mirror image, a chiasm. The following diagram illustrates the chiastic structure:

God created mankind in his image
    according to his likeness:
A   in the image of God he created him
B   male and female he created them

B'   be fruitful and increase in number
        and fill the earth
A'   and subdue it
    and rule over the fish/birds/animals

Thus, duality of gender is the basis for being fruitful, while the divine image is correlated with the command to rule as God's viceroy. These observations from the discourse grammar of the narrative are crucial. They are decisive in showing that the divine image is *not* to be explained by or located in terms of duality of gender in humanity.[20]

THE CLAUSE "LET US MAKE MAN IN OUR IMAGE, ACCORDING TO OUR LIKENESS"

We are now in a position to explain the meaning of the clause in 1:26a, "let us make man in our image, according to our likeness." The exegetical

---

[20] As, for example, in the exposition of M. Smith: "[t]he creation of the human person involves male and female. . . . The imagery of the human in terms of the Divine in Genesis 1 seems to assume a divine couple, male and female, since the human person is created in the image of the Divine, partaking of both maleness and femaleness (M. Smith, "God Male and Female in the Old Testament: Yahweh and His 'Asherah'," *Theological Studies* 48 [1987]: 339). Earlier, Karl Barth promoted an approach to the divine image also based upon the duality of gender (Karl Barth, *Church Dogmatics,* 3/1, authorised trans. J. W. Edwards, O. Bussey, and Harold Knight (Edinburgh: T. & T. Clark, 1958), 186; and idem, *Church Dogmatics,* 3/2, authorised trans. Harold Knight, G. W. Bromiley, J. K. Reid, and R. H. Fuller (Edinburgh: T. & T. Clark, 1960), 203. Note the following description and assessment by Bruce Waltke: "Karl Barth rightly argued from Genesis 1:26–27 that God endowed humanity with the ability to have social interaction with him and each other as male and female, but he went too far when he argued that the image of God is a matter of relationship. The meaning of the phrase elsewhere does not support this notion. Genesis 5:1–3 and 9:6 pertain to the individual, apart from their social relationships, calling Barth's dogma into question. Each man and woman bears the image of God apart from his or her counterpart" (Bruce K. Waltke with Charles Yu, *An Old Testament Theology: An Exegetical, Canonical, and Thematic Approach* [Grand Rapids, MI: Zondervan, 2007], 217). This assessment is confused and only partly true. Waltke is correct to affirm that each man and woman bears the image of God apart from his or her counterpart because the text affirms that *'ādām,* clearly a generic term, bears the image of God. Barth's attempt, however, to base a description of the divine image as relationship upon the duality of gender in humanity constitutes exegetical error, as he did not observe the macrosyntactic signals in the text. Since Waltke infers that the image entails social relationships because "the image is represented as male and female and God is asexual," his claim that Barth has argued rightly is incorrect. Waltke's denial of the divine image as a matter of relationship *as propounded by Barth* is probably right, but as the following exegesis will show, his exposition fails to infer from the data in the text that the image entails a divine-human relationship and a human-world relationship. Thus his comment at this point in an otherwise illuminating exposition is unclear and unhelpful.

microscope will be focused on (1) the ancient Near Eastern background to the text, (2) the meaning of the nouns "image" and "likeness," (3) the exact force of the prepositions "in" and "according to," and (4) the referent of the first person plural pronoun "let us," in that order.

THE ANCIENT NEAR EASTERN BACKGROUND

In biblical revelation, God communicates in the culture and language of the people. Yet, in employing language people understand he also fills the terms with new meaning. The key to correct interpretation, therefore, is to *compare and contrast* the biblical text and the data from the contemporary cultures. One must notice not only the similarities between the Bible and the ancient Near Eastern background but also the differences, which show the new meaning being revealed by God.

This can be illustrated by considering the tabernacle (Exodus 25–40). If we consider the plan of the tabernacle or the plan of Solomon's temple, there is nothing unusual or unique.[21] Its overall plan was just like any other temple in the ancient Near East. They all had an outer courtyard, an altar of sacrifice, and a central building divided into a "Holy Place" and a "Holy of Holies." What made the faith of Israel different from the faith of the pagan religions surrounding her? If one were to enter a pagan temple, passing through the courtyard, and through the Holy Place into the Holy of Holies, what would one find there? An image representing one of the forces of nature. But that is not what one finds at the centre of Israel's worship. What was in the Holy of Holies in the tabernacle? First of all, there was no image or statue there representing God himself, because God is spirit and cannot be properly represented by man-made images.[22] All there is in the Holy of Holies is just a little box. And what is in that box? The Ten Commandments. Thus, what God is saying to the Israelites is that he cannot be manipulated by magic. If they want the good life, they must conform their lifestyle to his revealed standards of right and wrong. Ethics guarantee the good life, not manipulation of the powers that be by magic.[23] The meaning is clear when one both compares and contrasts the biblical text with the ancient Near Eastern cultural setting.

---

[21] See Othmar Keel, *The Symbolism of the Biblical World: Ancient Near Eastern Iconography and the Book of Psalms*, trans. Timothy J. Hallett (New York: Seabury, 1978), 151–163.

[22] The *cherubim* would not be considered "images," but rather guardian figures. In the case of Israel, they are guarding empty space.

[23] The divine image is particularly revealed in the living out of the Ten Commandments. This is why there could be no image at the centre of Israel's worship—God wanted the commands or instructions in the ark to be imaged in one's actions: this was the divine character embodied in human lives!

At the outset, the differences appear to be small and insignificant. Yet in the end, the differences are so radical that only divine revelation can explain the origin of the text.

THE MEANING OF IMAGE AND LIKENESS IN THE BIBLE AND THE ANCIENT NEAR EAST

Paul Dion has produced one of the most careful and thorough studies of the ancient Near Eastern background to the image of God.[24] His work can be consulted for the detailed evidence which the following only briefly summarises. In the ancient Near East we see the flourishing of plastic arts; it was part and parcel of religion. Statues and likenesses of all sorts have been preserved to the present time.

The epithet or descriptive title of the Egyptian king as a "living statue of such and such a god" was common in Egypt from 1630 B.C. onwards and therefore was well known to the Israelites. In Egyptian thinking, the king is the image of god because he is the son of god.[25] The emphasis or stress is not on physical appearance, e.g., a male king could be the image of a female goddess. Rather the behaviour of the king reflects the behaviour of the god. The image reflects the character traits of the god.[26] The image reflects the essential notions of the god.

Commonly associated with the image is the notion of conquest and power. A clear example is an inscription from the Karnak Temple marking the triumph of Thutmoses III at Karnak, c. 1460 B.C. In the following stanza, the god is speaking in the first person and the second person refers to the king:

> I came to let you tread on Djahi's chiefs,
>> I spread them under your feet throughout their lands;
> I let them see your majesty as lord of light,
>> so that you shone before them in my likeness.[27]

The god Amen-Re, in giving victory to Thutmoses III, calls the king his son

---

[24] Dion, "Ressemblance et Image de Dieu," 55:365–403.

[25] On the birth of the king in Egypt as divine son see Keel, *Symbolism of the Biblical World*, 247–256.

[26] Notions concerning the "image of God" in Mesopotamia were similar. M. Stol states, "[i]n Babylonia, being the 'image' of a god does not point to physical resemblance but to abilities (justice, magic) or character ('fierce but merciful'). Most likely, Genesis also transcends the primitive idea of physical resemblance and sees the first human being(s) in terms of their spiritual resemblance to God." See M. Stol, *Birth in Babylonia and the Bible: Its Mediterranean Setting* (Cuneiform Monographs 14; Groningen, Netherlands: Styx, 2000), 151.

[27] Miriam Lichtheim, *Ancient Egyptian Literature: A Book of Readings*, (Berkeley: University of California Press, 1976), 2:36–37.

in the prologue of the poem and in this stanza indicates that the extension of the rule of the king entails him shining before his enemies in the likeness of his god.

In the thirteenth century B.C., Pharaoh Ramesses II had his image hewn out of rock at the mouth of the Kelb River, on the Mediterranean just north of Beirut. His image—displayed like the presidents at Mount Rushmore—meant that he was the ruler of this area. In the ancient Near East, since the king is the living statue of the god, he represents the god on earth. He makes the power of the god a present reality.

To sum up, the term "the image of god" in the culture and language of the ancient Near East in the fifteenth century B.C. would have communicated two main ideas: (1) rulership and (2) sonship. The king is the image of god because he has a relationship to the deity as the son of god and a relationship to the world as ruler for the god. We ought to assume that the meaning in the Bible is identical or at least similar, unless the biblical text clearly distinguishes its meaning from the surrounding culture.

LIKENESS AND IMAGE

Careful and exhaustive lexical studies of the Hebrew terms "likeness" (דמות) and "image" (צלם) indicate the possible range of meaning.[28]

"Likeness" (דמות) may refer to a physical entity, such as the model of the altar King Ahaz sent Uriah the priest (2 Kings 16:10b). It may also refer to a likeness that is real yet referentially unspecific or inexact (Isa. 40:18). It can even be nonreferential to express resemblance or relative similarity (Isa. 13:4). Ezekiel 1:26 is instructive since, opposite to Genesis 1:26, which speaks of humanity created in the likeness of God, Ezekiel's vision speaks of God appearing in the likeness of humanity. As Garr notes, either way, God and humanity are morphologically similar.

"Image" (צלם) frequently refers to an object in the real world that can have size, shape, colour, material composition, and value. The image erected by King Nebuchadnezzar in the plain of Dura is an example (Dan. 3:1). Yet as Psalm 39:6–7 shows, ṣelem can also be abstract and nonconcrete. And like děmût, "image" can simply be an imprint etched on a wall (Ezek. 23:14b, 15b).

---

[28] Numerous studies are available in addition to the lexica. See, e.g., J. Barr, "The Image of God in the Book of Genesis—A Study of Terminology," 11–26; H. D. Preuss, "דָּמָה dāmāh; דְּמוּת," in *TDOT* 3:250–260; F. J. Stendebach, "צֶלֶם ṣelem," in *TDOT* 12:386–396. The brief comments here are indebted to the full lexical treatment in Garr, *In His Own Image and Likeness*, 117–176.

Particularly instructive for Genesis 1:26–28 is the usage of the words "likeness" and "image" in the Tell Fakhariyeh Inscription.[29] Inscribed on a large statue of King Hadduyith'î of Gozan, a city in what is now eastern Syria, is an Akkadian-Aramaic bilingual text from the tenth or ninth century B.C. The text is divided thematically into two sections. The first half focuses on the role of the king as a supplicant and worshipper of his god and is headed in the Aramaic text by דמות, equivalent of the Hebrew דמות. The second half focuses on the majesty and power of the king in his role in relation to his subjects. This is headed in the Aramaic text by the word צלם, equivalent of the Hebrew צלם.[30] While both terms can and do refer to the statue of the king, each has a different nuance.

Akkadian texts containing the cognate for the Hebrew word "image" support the force and meaning of the word in the Tell Fakhariyeh Inscription. Three brief examples will suffice to further clarify the use of the term "image":

LAS 125:14b–19 (K 595; from the time of Esarhaddon, 681–668 B.C.):
What the king, [my lord] wrote to me: "I heard from the mouth of my father that you are a loyal family, but now I know it from my own experience", the father of the king, my lord, was the very image of the god Bēl, and the king, my lord, is likewise the very image of Bēl.[31]

The author of the letter is a loyal subject. He proclaims that the king is the image of the god Bel because he is acknowledging the authority and majesty of the king in the king-subject relationship.[32]

LAS 143 o. 14–r. 6 (K 583; from the time of Esarhaddon, 681–668 B.C.):
Why, today already for the second day, is the table not brought to the king, my lord? Who (now) stays in the dark much longer than the Sun, the king of the gods, stays in the dark a whole day and night, (and) again two days?

---

[29] Although I have read and studied the inscription myself, I am indebted for these observations to W. Randall Garr, "'Image' and 'Likeness' in the Inscription from Tell Fakhariyeh," *Israel Exploration Journal* 50/3–4 (2003): 227–234. Those wishing to read a translation in English may consult T. Muraoka, "The Tell-Fekherye Bilingual Inscription and Early Aramaic," *Abr-Nahrain* 22 (1983–1984): 79–117.

[30] The forms in the Aramaic Tell Fakhariyeh Inscription are actually articulate: דמותא and צלמא.

[31] Simo Parpola, *Letters from Assyrian Scholars to the Kings Esarhaddon and Assurbanipal, Part I: Texts* (Winona Lake, IN: Eisenbrauns, 2007), 98–99 (= LAS).

[32] The editor comments as follows: "the king was likened to Marduk (or Bēl) especially when it was appropriate to extol his *goodness* and *mercifulness*, and it would accordingly seem that these indeed were characteristics most popularly associated with Marduk at the period concerned." See Simo Parpola, *Letters from Assyrian Scholars to the Kings Esarhaddon and Assurbanipal, Part II: Commentary and Appendices* (Neukirchen-Vluyn, Germany, Neukirchener, 1983; repr., Winona Lake, IN: Eisenbrauns, 2007), 112.

The king, the lord of the world, is the very image of the Sun god. He (should) keep in the dark for only half a day![33]

The king is the image of the god Shamash and should be treated as representing his authority and power.

SAA 8:333 (82–5–22,63; from the period 697–665 B.C.):
The wisest, merciful Bel, the warrior Marduk, became angry at night, but relented in the morning. You, O king of the world, are an image of Marduk; when you were angry with your servants, we suffered the anger of the king our lord; and we saw the reconciliation of the king.[34]

The king represents the majesty, authority, and power of god to his subjects.

Evidence from the Nebuchadnezzar Inscription of Brisa also offers an important parallel for the biblical texts. Nebuchadnezzar says,

I let the people in the Lebanon lie in safe pastures; I did not allow an intimidator (against them). So that nobody will oppress them, I installed an eternal image of myself as king to protect (them).[35]

We must now *compare and contrast* the data in Genesis 1:26–28 with these ancient Near Eastern data.

Similarities

As Garr notes, the grammar of the first sentence in Genesis 1:26a is unusual.[36] Following a hortatory predicate (נעשה) and an undetermined direct object (אדם) are two distinct prepositional phrases which are not obligatory either grammatically or semantically. The exact force of each preposition will be discussed shortly. This much is clear: the nonobligatory phrases specify a divine-human relation in the creation of mankind, and the differential marking suggests each phrase has distinct meaning.

Given the normal meanings of "image" and "likeness" in the cultural and linguistic setting of the Old Testament and the ancient Near East, "likeness" specifies a relationship between God and humans such that *'ādām* can be described as the son of God, and "image" describes a relationship

---

[33] Parpola, *Letters from Assyrian Scholars (Part I)*, 112–113.
[34] Hermann Hunger, *Astrological Reports to Assyrian Kings* (State Archives of Assyria [= SAA], vol. 8; Helsinki: Helsinki University Press, 1992), 188–189.
[35] Rocío Da Riva, "A Note to the Nebuchadnezzar Inscription of Brisa," Nouvelles Assyriologiques Brèves et Utilitaires (2009/1): 15–16. I am indebted to Charles Halton for drawing my attention to this text.
[36] Garr, *In His Own Image and Likeness*, 95.

between God and humans such that *'ādām* can be described as a servant king. Although both terms specify the divine-human relationship, the first focuses on the human in relation to God and the second focuses on the human in relation to the world. These would be understood to be relationships characterised by faithfulness and loyal love, obedience and trust— exactly the character of relationships specified by covenants after the Fall. In this sense the divine image entails a covenant relationship between God and humans on the one hand, and between humans and the world on the other. In describing a divine-human relationship, the terms in Genesis 1:26–28 correspond precisely to the usage of the same words in the Tell Fakhariyah Inscription.[37]

Confirmation of this interpretation of "likeness" and "image" comes from both the context of Genesis 1 and interpretation of Genesis 1 found later in the Old Testament.

1) The term "likeness" indicates that *'ādām* has a special relationship to God like that of father and son. This is clearly implied by Genesis 5:1–3:

[1] This is the book of the generations of Adam. When God created man, he made him in the likeness of God.
[2] Male and female he created them, and he blessed them and named them Man when they were created.
[3] When Adam had lived a hundred and thirty years, he became the father of a son in his own likeness, after his image, and named him Seth (RSV).

The comment of Stephen Dempster is both adequate and succinct:

By juxtaposing the divine creation of Adam in the image of God and the subsequent human creation of Seth in the image of Adam, the transmission of the image of God through this genealogical line is implied, as well as the link between sonship and the image of God. As Seth is a son of Adam, so Adam is a son of God. Language is being stretched here as a literal son of God is certainly not in view, but nevertheless the writer is using an analogy to make a point.[38]

This can be further supported from later texts: (1) Luke 3:38 interprets the "likeness of God" in Genesis to indicate that Adam is the son of God;

---

[37] For support of this view, see Stephen G. Dempster, "The Servant of the Lord," in *Central Themes in Biblical Theology: Mapping Unity in Diversity*, ed. Scott J. Hafemann and Paul R. House (Grand Rapids, MI: Baker, 2007), 136ff.
[38] Dempster, *Dominion and Dynasty*, 58–59.

(2) Israel inherits the role of Adam and Eve and is specifically called the son of God (Ex. 4:22, 23). The Song at the Sea pictures Israel as a new Adam entering the Promised Land as a new Eden (Ex. 15:17). Later the divine sonship devolves particularly upon the king in the Davidic covenant (2 Sam. 7:14–15): what was true of the nation will now be fulfilled specifically and solely by her king.

2) The term "image" indicates that *'ādām* has a special position and status as king under God. Humans rule *as a result of* this royal status. The term "to rule" (*rādâ* in Gen. 1:26, 28) is particularly true of kings, as Psalm 72:8 illustrates. Also the term "to subdue" (*kābaš*) especially speaks of the work of a king (e.g., 2 Sam. 8:11).

Further confirmation comes from Psalm 8, in which verses 5–8 constitute a word-by-word commentary and meditation on Genesis 1:26–28. Verse 5, which says, "you have made him a little less than the gods; you have crowned him with glory and honour" is a commentary on 1:26a, "let us make mankind in our image and according to our likeness."[39] Verses 6–8 then detail and unfold the rule of mankind specified in 1:26b. It is clear and obvious that the psalm writer has the text of Genesis 1:26 before his mind word-by-word. Note in particular that the terms in Hebrew for "crowned" (עטר), "glory" (כָּבוֹד), and "honour" (הָדָר) are all royal terms. This shows that the psalm writer understood "image" to speak of royal status. Furthermore, the Hebrew word "rule" (מֹשֵׁל) used in Psalm 8:7 (8:6 EV) is a broad term meaning "have dominion, reign, rule," but generally speaks of a king (examples of royal uses are Ps. 103:19; Mic. 5:1 (5:2 EV); Isa. 14:5; 19:4; 2 Sam. 23:3; Prov. 29:26a). The phrase "place under his feet" (שׁית תחת רגליו) is an image associated with royalty. This is clear from 1 Kings 5:17 (5:3 EV), Egyptian texts like the Poem of Thutmoses III cited above, Phoenician inscriptions (Karatepe A.i.16), and Assyrian Royal Texts.[40]

In verses 7–8 of Psalm 8, humans rule over the animals. Paul Dion appropriately suggested that the word "all" in Psalm 8:6b is restricted to the

---

[39] Debate continues over the meaning of *'ĕlōhîm* in Psalm 8:5—does it refer to gods (i.e., angels) or to God? Instances of *'ĕlōhîm* in Judges 9:9, 13 and Psalm 82:1, 6 show that "gods" is fully possible. This is the interpretation taken by the Jewish Targums, the Septuagint (Greek translation), the Latin Vulgate of Jerome, and the Syriac Peshitta. A valiant effort to support the interpretation of "God" was made by Donald Glenn, "Psalm 8 and Hebrews 2: A Case Study in Biblical Hermeneutics and Biblical Theology," in *Walvoord: A Tribute*, ed. Donald K. Campbell (Chicago: Moody, 1982), 39–51. His approach is flawed because a sentence such as "you (God—second person address) have made him a little lower than God (third person address)" is ungrammatical in Hebrew. He also disengages inner-biblical interpretation by arguing that the context of Genesis 1 is no more determinative for Psalm 8 than for Hebrews 2.

[40] Dion, "Ressemblance et Image de Dieu," 55:369, 398.

earthly sphere in the light of Genesis 1:14–19 and 26–28, where Man rules only the earthly sphere.[41]

Differences

Correct interpretation requires one to contrast as well as compare the biblical text with the contemporary documents.

In Egypt, only the king is the image of god.[42] In the Bible, all humans constitute the image of God. The covenant relationship between God and Man is not restricted to an elite sector within human society.

Precise Meaning of the Prepositions
"in" (bĕ) and "as/according to" (kĕ)

As already noted, the grammar of the first sentence in Genesis 1:26a is unusual. Two distinct prepositional phrases which are not obligatory either grammatically or semantically follow the predicate (*na'ăśeh*) and direct object (*'ādām*): "in our image, according to our likeness." The preposition "in" corresponds to the preposition *bĕ* in Hebrew, while "as" or "according to" corresponds to Hebrew *kĕ*. What is the exact semantic value of each preposition?

The phrase "made in his image" has been construed in two different ways. First, the "in" has been interpreted to indicate the norm or standard. This is normal usage of the preposition "in" following the verb "to make." The statement that man is created "in" the image of God would then mean that man conforms to a representation of God.[43] As Gordon Wenham explains, "man is made '*in* the divine image,' just as the tabernacle was made '*in* the divine pattern.' This suggests that man is a copy of something that had the divine image, not necessarily a copy of God himself."[44] The traditional view, however, does not do full justice to the meaning of the words "image" and "likeness," nor does the explanation of Wenham account for the fact that the prepositions *seem* somewhat interchangeable. The phrase is found in six instances:

---

[41] Ibid., 55:398.

[42] There is only one exception of which I am aware, in the Instruction of Merikare, where there is a description of all humanity as the image(s) of God: "Well directed are men, the cattle of the god. He made heaven and earth according to their desire, and he repelled the water-monster. He made the breath of life for their nostrils. They who have issued from his body are his images" (ll. 131ff.); see James B. Pritchard, ed., *Ancient Near Eastern Texts Relating to the Old Testament*, 3rd ed. with supplement (Princeton, NJ: Princeton University Press, 1969).

[43] In particular, see Barr, "Image of God in the Book of Genesis," 11–26.

[44] Gordon J. Wenham, *Genesis 1–15*, 32 (emphasis his).

Genesis 1:26a   *in* our image, *according to* our likeness
Genesis 1:27aα   *in* his image
Genesis 1:27aβ   *in* the image of God
Genesis 5:1b   *in* the likeness of God
Genesis 5:3a   *in* his likeness, *according to* his image
Genesis 9:6b   *in* the image of God

It is possible to use "in" with "likeness" as well as "image," and Genesis 5:3a has the prepositions exactly the reverse of what we find in Genesis 1:26a. Indeed, in the example of the tabernacle used by Wenham, the expression "made *in* the pattern" in Exodus 25:40 is "made *according to* the pattern" in Exodus 25:9. James Barr has shrewdly observed, "that *bᵉ*, commonly 'in' *when combined with nouns of the semantic function 'likeness'*, is thereby brought to have almost the same effect as the preposition *kᵉ* 'like, as'. It is the semantics of the noun, not those of the preposition alone, which are here decisive."[45] Thus, when the verb "make" is followed by "in" (*bě*), *because it is used with nouns indicating likeness*, the "in" likewise receives by this fact a value almost identical to "as" (*kě*).[46] This makes the expression in Genesis 1:26a differ somewhat from that in Exodus 25:9, where the object of the preposition is "pattern" (*tabnît*).

It is possible, then, that the preposition "in" could be translated "as" in Genesis 1:26a. The usage shows that *bě* = "in" and *kě* = "as" have roughly the same value in these texts. God indeed created man *as* the divine image. Humans do not conform to a representation of God; they are the divine image. This interpretation is supported by the New Testament. In 1 Corinthians 11:7, Paul says that man is the image of God. Why, then, is the statement in Genesis not more forthright in explicitly saying that man *is* the divine image? Why is this expressed in a slightly more indirect manner? I suggest that a more indirect expression is used in the cultural and linguistic setting of the ancient Near East to prevent man from being considered an idol and being worshipped as such.

In spite of the fact that the two prepositions are close in meaning, we must not assume that the meaning is identical. This has been discussed extensively in a recent 300-page monograph on the divine image by Randall Garr.

---

[45] James Barr, "The Image of God in Genesis—Some Linguistic and Historical Considerations," in *Proceedings of the Tenth Meeting (1967) of Die Ou-Testamentiese Werkgemeenskap in Suid-Afrika*, ed. A. H. van Zyl (Pretoria: Craft Press, 1971), 9 (emphasis his). Paul Dion discovered a linguistic phenomenon similar to this in the Elephantine Papyri of the fifth century B.C., cf. Dion, "Ressemblance et Image de Dieu," 55:388–389.

[46] Technically, then, this is not a *beth essentiae*, but "as" is an excellent functional English equivalent. See J. Barr, "Image of God in Genesis," 8.

Garr is correct to affirm that "the differential marking of each nonobligatory phrase suggests that each phrase has distinct meaning, at least in relation to one [an]other."[47] His careful and thorough linguistic analysis reveals that the preposition *bĕ* = "in" emphasises proximity while the preposition *kĕ* = "as" or "according to" emphasises something similar, yet distinct and separate. Garr's linguistic analysis is also supported by the exhaustive research of Ernst Jenni, who has produced an entire monograph on each of the three basic prepositions in Hebrew. One volume analyses all 15,570 instances of the preposition *bĕ*, a second all 3,000 instances of *kĕ*, and a third all 20,000 instances of the preposition *lĕ* ("to" or "for") in the Hebrew Bible. Jenni concludes that, in fundamental meaning, *kĕ* stands between the opposition pair *bĕ* (marking an equating relation) and *lĕ* (marking a non-equating relation) as an expression of partial equation (and so also partial non-equation) of the semantic characteristics of two quantifications.[48] Thus, again, *bĕ* indicates something locative and proximate while *kĕ* indicates something similar but distal and separate.

We have already seen that, although the words "image" and "likeness" share similar meanings, each has a different emphasis. In the Tell Fakhariyeh Inscription the word "likeness" focuses on the king as a suppliant and worshipper of his god and communicates sonship. The word "image" focuses on the majesty and power of the king in relation to his subjects. These ancient Near Eastern data confirm and correspond to the use in the biblical text. The word "likeness" in Genesis is closely associated with the creation of the human race, human genealogy, and sonship. It occurs in Genesis 1:26 in the creation of humans and again in 5:1, when this is recapitulated under the heading "Birth History of Humankind."[49] The third use is in 5:3 with the generation of Seth. The word "image" is consistently used of man representing God in terms of royal rule. Putting the nouns and prepositions together, humans closely represent God in image, i.e., they represent his rule in the world. Humans are also similar to God in performing the action of creating human life, but not in the same way. Thus *bĕ* emphasises a way in which humans are closely like God, *kĕ* a way in which humans are similar, but distinct. This interpretation also explains the reversal of the prepositions in Genesis 5:3. Seth shares precisely in the

---

[47] Garr, *In His Own Image and Likeness*, 95.
[48] Ernst Jenni, *Die hebräischen Präpositionen, Band 1: Die Präposition Beth* (Stuttgart: Kolhammer, 1992), 11–40; idem, *Die hebräischen Präpositionen, Band 2: Die Präposition Kaph* (Stuttgart: Kolhammer, 1994), 11–12.
[49] The Hebrew term *tôlĕdôt* is construed as a heading in the text.

matter of generation and sonship, but is only similar and not identical in the representation of his father's image.

Before considering the difficult first person plural "let us," it may be useful to crystalise, consolidate, and summarise the exegetical results to this point.

SUMMARY

Genesis 1:26 defines a divine-human relationship with two dimensions, one vertical and one horizontal. First, it defines human ontology in terms of a covenant relationship between God and man, and second, it defines a covenant relationship between man and the earth. The relationship between humans and God is best captured by the term sonship. The relationship between humans and the creation may be expressed by the terms kingship and servanthood, or better, servant kingship.

This interpretation best honours the normal meaning of *ṣelem* ("image") according to the cultural and linguistic setting. Hans Walter Wolff expressed the matter well as follows:

> In the ancient East the setting up of the king's statue was the equivalent to the proclamation of his domination over the sphere in which the statue was erected (cf. Dan. 3.1, 5f.). When in the thirteenth century BC the Pharaoh Ramesses II had his image hewn out of rock at the mouth of the *nahr el-kelb*, on the Mediterranean north of Beirut, the image meant that he was the ruler of this area. Accordingly, man is set in the midst of creation as God's statue. He is evidence that God is the Lord of creation; but as God's steward he also exerts his rule, fulfilling his task not in arbitrary despotism but as a responsible agent. His rule and his duty to rule are not autonomous; they are copies.[50]

Thus the image is physical and yet goes far beyond being merely physical. This is an interpretation that allows for the physical aspect of "image" but results in an emphasis such that the character of humans in ruling the world is what represents God.

It is important to note that this definition of the divine image is not a functional but an *ontological* one. As Wenham points out, the phrase "in the image" describes the product rather than the process of creation, as suggested by usage in Genesis 5:3 and Exodus 25:40.[51] The grammar reveals that man rules as a result of being made as the divine image; ruling is not

---

[50] Hans Walter Wolff, *Anthropology of the Old Testament* (Philadelphia: Fortress, 1974), 160–161.
[51] Wenham, *Genesis 1–15*, 31.

the essence of the image itself. Thus those who define the image merely in functional terms are in error both linguistically and theologically.[52]

Man *is* the divine image. As servant king and son of God mankind will mediate God's rule to the creation in the context of a covenant relationship with God on the one hand and the earth on the other. Hence the concept of the kingdom of God is found on the first page of Scripture. Indeed, the theme is kingdom through covenant. No wonder the Mosaic covenant, which seeks to implement this in Abraham's family, can be summarised as providing divine direction concerning (1) a right relationship to God, (2) how to treat each other in genuinely human ways, and (3) how to be good stewards of the earth's resources.

Theologians have debated the extent to which the divine image was marred or even lost by the fall into sin (Genesis 3). Normally it is argued that the divine image was marred but not lost through the Fall (Gen. 9:6; James 3:9). The interpretation given here of the divine image as God establishing his rule in the world through covenant clarifies the matter. The human rebellion described in Genesis 3 violated the love, loyalty, obedience, and trust at the heart of the covenant. God sought to confirm and reestablish this relationship in the covenant with Noah; hence the expression *hēqîm běrît*. The story of the drunkenness of Noah (Gen. 9:20–27) shows once more the inability of the human partner in the covenant relationship. God makes a new start with Abraham and his family in the covenant made with Abraham. The Abrahamic covenant is implemented in the Iron Age, with Israel as Abraham's family through the Mosaic covenant. Israel, or more particularly, Israel's king, as the Davidic covenant later makes plain, will be the instrument for renewing the covenant relationship and establishing the instruction and will of Yahweh (i.e., *tôrâ*) in the hearts and lives of his people and, through them, to the nations. In a long history of apparent failure, Jesus of Nazareth came as Israel's King to renew the relationship by inaugurating a new covenant and bringing about the rule of God in the lives of those who are part of his new creation. Thus Jesus' proclamation of the kingdom is nothing less than the message we already find in Genesis 1:26–27.

When we look at the New Testament and the references there to the renewal of the divine image brought about by the work of Jesus Christ, terms

---

[52] See Eugene H. Merrill, "A Theology of the Pentateuch," in *A Biblical Theology of the Old Testament*, ed. Roy B. Zuck (Chicago: Moody, 1991), 7–87, who says, "[i]t is a functional statement and not one of essence" (14).

are used which emphasise man's *relation* to God. This is clear in the parallel texts in Ephesians and Colossians:

Ephesians 4:24

and put on the new humanity created according to God in righteousness and holiness which derives from the truth

Colossians 3:10

and have put on the new humanity that is being renewed to a true knowledge according to the image of the One who created it

God has planned a new creation—a new heavens and a new earth. Unlike the first creation, where he first made the place and afterwards the people to live there, in the new creation he is first making the people and afterwards the place where they will live. The new creation begins in the midst of the old: when God raised Jesus from the dead, he was the first man in the new creation. And anyone who is joined to Jesus Christ by faith *is* new creation (2 Cor. 5:17; frequently incorrectly translated as "is a new creation"). This happens first in the inner person, and later at the resurrection, in the outer person. The passages in Ephesians 4:24 and Colossians 3:10 call believers to adopt in daily lifestyle all that is entailed in the new creation life within them. The phrase "according to God" in Ephesians 4:24 may be ambiguous by itself, but is clarified by the parallel in Colossians 3:10 and means that the new creation is, like the old, according to the image and likeness of God. The words that Paul uses in connection with this are righteousness and holiness in Ephesians 4 and knowledge in Colossians 3.[53] This has been misconstrued in studies on the divine image in the past. Paul mentions holiness, knowledge, and righteousness, not because one can identify ethical or mental or spiritual qualities as *elements* of the divine image, but because these terms are *covenantal* and describe a covenant relationship. Thus the New Testament supports the explanation of the divine image in Genesis 1:26 advanced here. The divine image indicates man's relationship and spiritual fellowship with God.[54]

---

[53] Holiness in particular is a concept not well understood by the church today. See especially the illuminating study by Claude-Bernard Costecalde, *Aux origines du sacré biblique* (Paris: Letouzey & Ané, 1986).

[54] The exegesis of "image" and "likeness" presented here as well as the interpretation of Adam's role in the garden of Eden supplied below received confirmation from a paper entitled "New Light on Genesis 1–3 and Man as the Image of God," presented by Catherine Beckerleg, at the annual meeting of the Evangelical Theological Society, Providence, RI, November 19, 2008.

THE MEANING OF THE FIRST PERSON PLURAL

The interpretation of the first person plural "let us make" is a difficult problem. The recent commentary by Kenneth A. Mathews provides an excellent summary of the various views and the impasse in scholarship over this issue:

> Among commentators the plural reference is variously understood: (1) a remnant of polytheistic myth; (2) God's address to creation, "heavens and earth"; (3) a plural indicating divine honor and majesty; (4) self-deliberation; (5) divine address to a heavenly court of angels; and (6) divine dialogue within the Godhead. It is unlikely when we consider the elevated theology of 1:1–2:3, that any polytheistic element would be tolerated by the author; therefore, the first option can be ruled out. The second option is flatly contradicted by v. 27, where God alone is identified as the Creator. The plural as used to show special reverence (honorific plural) is flawed since the point of the verse is the unique correspondence between God and man, not the majesty of God. The fourth viewpoint considers "Let us make" a plural of self-deliberation, depicting God anthropomorphically as someone in contemplation. This is supported by the change to the singular ("*his* own image") in v. 27 which indicates that the figure of "deliberation" is completed. In ancient myths divine deliberation prefaces the creation of humans. Self-deliberation is attested in the Old Testament (e.g., Ps 42:5, 11; 43:5), but there is no attestation that the plural form is used in this way.[55]

Mathews finds evidence from the Old Testament and from ancient Near Eastern parallels for the view that God is addressing a heavenly court of angels to be impressive, but rejects this view on theological grounds: how can humans be said to be created in the image of angels? He then develops the interpretation that it refers to divine dialogue within the Godhead, although he admits that this can only be entertained as a possible "canonical" reading of the text. This admission, in fact, shows how unlikely his final proposal is to be right. The Bible is a divine-human book. A reference to the Trinity may possibly have been intended by the divine author, but this cannot be discovered until one comes to the New Testament. D. J. A. Clines argues that the plural refers to a dialogue between God and the spirit of God mentioned in 1:2,[56] but Bruce Waltke shows that this construes "spirit of God" in

---

[55] Kenneth A. Mathews, *Genesis 1–11:26*, New American Commentary 1A (Nashville: Broadman & Holman, 1996), 161.

[56] D. J. A. Clines, "The Image of God in Man," *Tyndale Bulletin* 19 (1968): 69.

a New Testament sense.[57] It is virtually impossible that such a meaning was intended by the human author of Genesis 1 or even understood by the original audience. Interpretation that rides roughshod over the human authorship and audience in the text in this way is highly suspect. Canonical reading of the text is imperative, but this appears more along the lines of special pleading.

Is there a way out of this impasse? Evidence for the view that God is addressing his heavenly court is impressive. Some readers may be unfamiliar with this approach. Texts from ancient Canaan and Mesopotamia depict a pantheon in which the high or supreme god operates in an assembly or community of gods. Yet one need not look to the culture contemporary to the Old Testament since evidence abounds within the Old Testament itself. Psalm 82:1 is a case in point:

> God presides in the divine assembly;
>   He gives judgement in the midst of the gods.

We also glimpse the divine assembly in Job 1 and 2, 1 Kings 22, Isaiah 6, and Jeremiah 23:18. They are variously referred to as "messengers"/"angels" (מלאכים), "gods" (אלהים) or "divinities" (בני האלהים = sons of the gods, i.e., those of the class of gods or divinities). The angels or gods in the Old Testament are subordinate and subservient to God. They bow down to him (Ps. 29:2), obey him (Ps. 103:20–21), praise him (Ps. 148:2–5), and minister to and serve him (1 Kings 22:19).[58]

John Walton has recently shown that the First Commandment, when interpreted in the context of the ancient Near Eastern setting, is directed against falsely construing these "gods" as sharing power with Yahweh or being worthy of worship in any sense. Although the command "you shall have no other gods before me" is normally understood in terms of priorities, this interpretation is contrary to the linguistic data, where every occurrence of the preposition "before" plus personal object in the Hebrew Bible is spatial. Walton argues that the correct interpretation entails a reference to the divine assembly. His argument must be cited in full to avoid misunderstanding:[59]

---

[57] Waltke, *Old Testament Theology*, 213. See also Walton, *Genesis*, 128–129, for further treatment showing that understanding the Trinity in Genesis 1 fails the test of proper interpretation. Walton opts for the plural as referring to the heavenly court, but does not think humans are created in the image of angels.

[58] From Garr, *In His Own Image and Likeness*, 69–70.

[59] The citation includes footnotes from Walton and excludes a table listing occurrences of the preposition לפני plus personal object: John H. Walton, "Interpreting the Bible as an Ancient Near Eastern Document," in *Israel—Ancient Kingdom or Late Invention? Archaeology, Ancient Civilizations, and the Bible*, ed. Daniel I. Block (Nashville: B&H, 2008), 306–309.

In the light of even deeper probing of the practises and beliefs that were current in the ancient Near East, Werner Schmidt has proposed a couple of other alternatives. He begins by suggesting that the first commandment prohibited the setting up of the images of other deities in the temple.[60] However, this does not follow the common logic of ancient Near Eastern practises in which temples were typically made to honor a single deity along with his consort.[61] Schmidt advocates another approach that focuses on God's heavenly rather than His earthly presence. That is, when the first commandment prohibits other gods in the presence of Yahweh, it is ruling out the concept that He operates within a pantheon, a divine assembly, or with a consort. J. Bottéro compares this system to that of a king at the head of the state with his family and functionaries around him operating in a structured hierarchy.[62]

Having this image as background suggests that the Israelites were not to imagine any other gods in the presence of Yahweh. Scholars could have arrived at this meaning by simple lexical study, but without the benefit of the ancient Near Eastern material, the results of the lexical study made no sense to interpreters. Consequently, they devised alternative explanations, even though when the prepositional combination that occurs in the Hebrew text takes a personal object the meaning is consistently spatial. Using comparative cultural information, we have recovered a neglected sense of the text that was there all the time.

In view of the information provided from outside the Bible, this spatial sense gains credibility. In the ancient Near East the gods operated within pantheons and decisions were made in the divine assembly. Furthermore, the principal deities typically had consorts. For the gods life was a community experience. The destinies of the gods were decreed in assembly, as were the destinies of kings, cities, temples and people. The business of the gods was carried out in the presence of other gods. Lowell Handy helpfully summarises this system as a hierarchy of authoritative deities and active deities.

> The highest authority in the pantheon was responsible for ordering and maintaining earth and cosmos but was not actively engaged in the actual work necessary to maintain the universe. The next lower level of deities performed this function. Serving under the authority of those who actually owned the universe, the active gods were expected to perform in a way that would enable the cosmos to operate smoothly. Each of the gods at this level

---

60 Werner Schmidt, *The Faith of the Old Testament* (Philadelphia: Westminster, 1983), 71.

61 Manasseh set up altars in the temple courtyard to offer sacrifices to other deities and put an Asherah pole in the temple. This object functioned either as a cultic object for the worship of Yahweh or as a symbol of Yahweh's consort (2 Kgs 21:5–7; Ezek 8:5).

62 J. Bottéro, "Intelligence and the Technical Function of Power: Enki/Ea," in *Mesopotamia: Writing, Reasoning and the Gods* (Chicago: University of Chicago, 1992), 232–50; the citation is found on 233.

of the pantheon had a specific sphere of authority over which to exert his or her control. Ideally, all the gods were to perform their duties in a way that would keep the universe functioning perfectly in the manner desired by the highest authority. Yet the gods, like human beings, are portrayed as having weaknesses and rivalries that kept the cosmos from operating smoothly.[63]

Accordingly, by a comparative interpretation of the first commandment the Israelites were not to construe Yahweh as operating within a community of gods. Nor were they to imagine Him functioning as the head of a pantheon surrounded by a divine assembly, or having a consort. In short, He works alone. The concept of a pantheon/divine assembly assumed a distribution of power among many divine beings. The first commandment declared simply and unequivocally that Yahweh's authority was absolute. Divine power was not distributed among other deities or limited by the will of the assembly.

The point of the prohibition of the worship of any other gods "besides" Yahweh was to ensure that Israel's perception of divinity was to be distinct from the peoples around them. This text is readily misunderstood if the interpreter is not aware of the notions being rejected. According to this revised interpretation, the purpose of the first commandment was not simply to promote monolatry; it served the monotheistic agenda another way. Although this text does not explicitly deny the existence of other gods, it does remove them from the presence of Yahweh. If Yahweh does not share power, authority, or jurisdiction with them, they are not gods in any meaningful sense of the word.[64] Thus, the first commandment does not insist on the non-existence of other gods; only that they are powerless. In so doing it disenfranchises them, not merely by declaring that they should not be worshiped; it leaves them with no status worthy of worship.[65]

The approach in the Old Testament to the divine assembly is thus twofold. On one hand it acknowledges the existence of beings known as angels or gods who serve God in his presence. On the other hand, it rejects the notion prevalent in the societies around Israel that these gods share authority or power or status worthy of worship with Yahweh.

Evidence that the phrase "let us" refers to the divine assembly is stronger than even Mathews allows as a result of the work of Randall Garr. Garr

---

[63] Lowell Handy, *Among the Host of Heaven* (Winona Lake: Eisenbrauns, 1994), 97.

[64] The significance of this notion may be extended if we attach to it the idea that in the ancient Near East something was not considered to exist if it had not been assigned a name, a place, or a function. See discussion in J. Walton, *Ancient Near Eastern Thought and the Old Testament* (Grand Rapids: Baker, 2006), 87–97.

[65] This is close to the view of Christopher Wright, who says, "The fundamental thrust of the verse is not Yahweh's sole deity, but Yahweh's sole sovereignty over Israel." *Deuteronomy* (Peabody, MA: Hendrickson, 1996), 68.

notes that Genesis 1:26–27 follows the formula or pattern for clauses introduced by *hābâ*. In form, *hābâ* is an extended imperative, *qal* stem, masculine singular from the root *yāhab*, "to give." There are two distinct uses of this verb: literal and nonliteral. In the literal use, the verb actually means to give. In the nonliteral use, the verb functions as a manipulative and suasive particle prefixed asyndetically to commands exactly like "c'mon" in English: "C'mon, let's play together." Unlike לְכָה and קוּמָה, however, the imperative *hābâ* is always connected without a conjunction and need not agree in number and person with the command to which it is prefixed. What is significant is that all clauses beginning with *hābâ* have a fixed pattern as follows:

(1) a directive or assertive utterance (represented by a cohortative or imperfect, respectively)
(2) which proposes an activity (event)
(3) jointly and cooperatively, between the speaker and a referentially distinct addressee;
(4) the speaker's proposal receives the tacit consent of the addressee and
(5) is executed by an agent, whether unidentified or identified and salient (e.g., addressee, leader).

This pattern can be observed in all instances: Genesis 11:3, 4, 7; 38:16; and Exodus 1:10. What is noteworthy is the fact that Genesis 1:26–27 has exactly this formulaic pattern, albeit without the introductory particle *hābâ*. The absence of the particle *hābâ* in Genesis 1:26 is explained by Garr as dialect-specific to a particular source, but this approach is unnecessary. During his exhaustive analysis he also observes that the particle *hābâ* is always used to introduce situations spelling trouble, and there is no sign of trouble in Genesis 1:26. This is a compelling explanation for the absence of the particle *hābâ*. Thus, the formulaic pattern of Genesis 1:26–27 provides a strong argument that God is addressing the heavenly court.

It remains to show what this could possibly mean in context. A proposal is at hand from the discussion of the ancient Near Eastern setting described by John Walton. The ancients believed that the ruling of the world was a community effort on the part of the gods. I propose that Genesis 1:26–27 be understood as a polemic to subvert such an idea. God announces to the heavenly court his decision to share rule with humanity. This entails both a negative and positive result. On the positive side, it elevates humanity to a status almost equal to the angels. Like the angels, humans will in obedience and subservience to Yahweh effect the rule of God in the world. This is exactly the point being made in Psalm 8:5: "you have made him a little less than the gods." There is also, however, a negative side. This decision in effect disenfranchises the gods according to ancient Near Eastern thinking. Yahweh does not share rule with them in the sense understood in ancient Canaan.[66] This is another way of saying, "You shall have no other gods before me," and it strongly makes the point of monotheism.

Clines' objection to this view "that the *elohim* would be said to have shared in man's creation" does not give adequate attention to the details of the text.[67] As Garr notes, citing Gemser,

> in the plural of vs. 26 a plurality of heavenly beings may be understood, but there is not a hint of diversity of will or purpose. God's divine court agrees to his proposal.[68]

Garr also points out the contrast between proposal and execution in the text. In the proposal, God involves his heavenly court. Yet in the execution, the sole use of third person verbs and the significant shift from עשה to ברא shows that the execution is absolutely and exclusively reserved for God.[69] The creation of all, including the creation of humans, is solely the work of God.

Some, no doubt, may not be persuaded by the above argument. It is not necessary for the exegesis given of Genesis 1:26–27, but it is in harmony with it because it fits the interpretation of the divine image as expressing the theme of kingdom through covenant. God has communicated to the divine assembly that his rule in the world will be effected largely through humans, not through "gods" or "angels."

THE GOAL OF THE COVENANT: REST

Day Six is the climax of the creation week, but not the consummation. The conclusion is Day Seven. Thus the account of creation does not conclude with man and his mandate, for humankind is not the consummation of all

---

[66] After arriving at this conclusion independently, I found Garr had already expressed it in print; Garr, *In His Own Image and Likeness*, 222.

[67] Clines, "Image of God in Man," 67. Construing the "us" in the clause "let us make man in our image" to refer to God addressing the heavenly court does not require the interpretation that the angels co-create or join God in making humans. It is the Judge and King of the heavenly court announcing to the angels that their rule of the cosmos will be shared with humans. This is comparable to the chairman and CEO of a corporation announcing to his board of directors/shareholders, "let us make all employees shareholders."

[68] Garr, *In His Own Image and Likeness*, 201.

[69] Ibid., 203–204.

things, even though he is the agent through whom the aims of creation will be realised. Dumbrell aptly says,[70]

> The symmetry of the eight creative acts spread over the preceding six days, and set in what seems to be an inner parallelism and progression between days one to three and four to six, receives its real significance from the addition of the seventh day. By the divine rest on the seventh day the goal of creation is indicated, a goal which will be maintained notwithstanding sustained human attempts to vitiate it. Not only does the seventh day rest note the goal to which creation points, but it is the call to man to begin history holding firmly to the view that the "goal of creation, and at the same time the beginning of all that follows, is the event of God's Sabbath freedom, Sabbath rest and Sabbath joy, in which man, too, has been summoned to participate."[71]

GENESIS 1:26–27 IN THE CONTEXT OF GENESIS 2:8–17

The interpretation advanced here for the creation of humans as the divine image and according to the divine likeness is corroborated by Genesis 2:8–17 and developed further there. Indeed, Genesis 2:4 begins an explanation and exposition of Genesis 1:26–28 in which the creation of man as a species is related and royal rule over the world is conferred upon man.[72] Chapter 2, in effect, tells us how this royal rule which is given to humankind within the covenant structure is to operate. The writer indicates that man was created outside Eden and then placed within the garden. The garden is presented as a centre of blessing in the world. In it arose the world river which divided outside the garden into four systems. The garden also functions as a divine sanctuary, the point where the divine presence was experienced and enjoyed in a close and immediate way. Gordon Wenham, followed by William Dumbrell, has described the garden in Eden as a sanctuary and Adam as a priest worshipping there. This may be briefly summarised and connected to the divine image.[73]

THE GARDEN AS SEPARATE SPACE

The Hebrew word for garden (*gan*) comes from a root meaning to "enclose," "fence," or "protect." The garden envisioned in Genesis 2:8–17 is an

[70] Dumbrell, *Covenant and Creation*, 34–35.
[71] Dumbrell is citing Karl Barth, *Church Dogmatics*, 3/1 (Edinburgh: T. & T. Clark, 1958), 98.
[72] I am dependent here upon Dumbrell, *Covenant and Creation*, 35.
[73] See below.

enclosed or protected space. In the Old Testament, walls surrounded both royal gardens (2 Kings 25:4; Neh. 3:15; Jer. 39:4; 52:7) and vineyards (Prov. 24:30–31; Isa. 5:5). The Septuagint, the Greek translation of the Old Testament, employed a loan word from Persian (παράδεισος) in Genesis 2 that means a pleasure garden surrounded by an earthen or stone wall. In our culture and society today we normally think of "gardener" as a lowly task, a job or vocation for a blue-collar worker or lower on the ladder of success. The culture of the ancient Near East was similar: in addition to royal gardens, temples had gardens owned and worked by entrepreneurs, and people had private gardens. Gardeners could be considered as some of the least valuable members of society. For example, in the substitute king ritual which took place during certain eclipses when Jupiter was not present, the king ritually stepped down from the throne and installed a substitute. After the allotted time the substitute was killed. Substitutes were drawn from the expendable peoples in society: prisoners of war, criminals condemned to death, political enemies of the king, the mentally deficient, and gardeners.[74] Nonetheless, kings in Mesopotamia created and kept extravagant gardens. In fact, "gardener" was a descriptive title or epithet for monarchs in Mesopotamia.[75] This use has a similarity to Louis XIV's gardens in Versailles—it showed that he was able to control nature and form entire trees into topiaries. Thus "gardener" was a royal vocation. The role of Adam as gardener further portrays him as a *royal figure*.

The role of Adam as gardener comes up much later in Scripture. After the crucifixion of Jesus, on that first Easter Sunday, the disciples (Peter and John) ran to the tomb. They found it empty and returned to their homes:

> But Mary stood weeping outside the tomb. . . . She turned around and saw Jesus standing there, but she didn't know that it was Jesus . . . . *Supposing him to be the gardener*, she said to him, 'Sir, if you have carried him somewhere, tell me where you have laid him, and I will take him away.' Jesus said to her, 'Mary!' She turned and said to him in Aramaic, 'Rabbouni!' (which means Teacher). (John 20:11–16)

As N. T. Wright notes, "it wasn't, after all, such a silly mistake for Mary to think that Jesus, the true Adam, *was the gardener*."[76]

---

[74] For the substitute king ritual, see Simo Parpola, *Letters from Assyrian Scholars (Part II)*, xxii-xxxii.

[75] See M. Hutter, "Adam als Gärtner und König (Gen. 2:8, 15)," *Biblische Zeitschrift* 30 (1985): 258–262.

[76] N. T. Wright, *Following Jesus: Biblical Reflections on Discipleship* (Grand Rapids, MI: Eerdmans, 1995), 57–59 (emphasis mine).

THE GARDEN AS SACRED SPACE/SANCTUARY

Creation accounts in the ancient Near East commonly connected creation and temple building. For example, the temple Esagila was built for Marduk in *Enuma Elish*. Genesis 2:8–17 portrays the first man as a kind of priest in a garden sanctuary. In terms of literary structure, 2:8a describes the creation of the garden and 2:8b the placing of the man there. In what follows, 2:9–15 elaborates on 2:8a and 2:16–17 elaborates on 2:8b.

Parallels between the description of the garden in Eden and descriptions of sanctuaries elsewhere in the Old Testament and ancient Near East reveal that the garden is being portrayed as a sanctuary.[77] Some of the evidence is summarised as follows:

1. The garden in Eden is characterised by the presence of God. There God comes to meet man at the cool of the day. The verb *hālak* in the *hithpael* stem ("to walk to and fro," Gen. 3:8) is the same term employed to describe the divine presence in the later tent sanctuaries (Lev. 26:12; Deut. 23:15 (23:14 EV); 2 Sam. 7:6–7).

2. When humans were cast out of the garden in Eden, *kĕrûbîm* ("cherubim," i.e., guardian creatures) were stationed east of the garden to guard the way to the tree of life (Gen. 3:24). This clearly indicates that the entrance to the garden was in the east.[78] Like the garden in Eden, the entrances to the later tabernacle and temple were also in the east and were guarded by *kĕrûbîm* (1 Kings 6:23–28; Ex. 25:18–22; 26:31; 1 Kings 6:29). Two guarded the inner sanctuary of Solomon's temple and two more the mercy seat of the ark in the inner sanctuary. Pictures of *kĕrûbîm* decorated the curtains of the tabernacle and the walls of the temple (Ex. 26:31, 1 Kings 6:29).

3. In the centre of the garden in Eden is the tree of life. Similarly, in the centre of the tabernacle and temple is the menorah (i.e., the branching lampstand), which, as Carol Meyers has shown, is a stylised tree of life.[79] The idea that fullness of life can be found in the sanctuary is basic to the instructions for the sacrifices in the Torah and is a recurrent theme in the Psalms.

4. The responsibility and task given to Adam in the garden is *lĕʿobdāh*

---

[77] See William J. Dumbrell, *The Search for Order* (Grand Rapids, MI: Baker, 1994), 23–26; Gordon J. Wenham, "Sanctuary Symbolism in the Garden of Eden Story," in *I Studied Inscriptions from before the Flood: Ancient Near Eastern, Literary, and Linguistic Approaches to Genesis 1–11*, ed. R. S. Hess and D. T. Tsumura, Sources for Biblical and Theological Study 4 (Winona Lake, IN: Eisenbrauns, 1994), 399–404. I lean heavily on both scholars here.
[78] Umberto Cassuto, *A Commentary on the Book of Genesis I* (Jerusalem: Magnes, 1961), 174. There may at the same time be a literary link to the fact that Israel was exiled to the east.
[79] Carol L. Meyers, *The Tabernacle Menorah: A Synthetic Study of a Symbol from the Biblical Cult*, American Schools of Oriental Research Dissertation Series 2 (Missoula, MT: Scholars Press, 1976).

ûlĕšomrāh (to serve/work it and to keep it). The only other passages in the Torah where the same two verbs occur together are Numbers 3:7–8; 8:26; 18:5–6, which describe the duties of the Levites in guarding and ministering in the sanctuary. These words are also commonly used in the Old Testament for worship. Thus Adam is portrayed as a kind of Levite who fulfills his role or task by maintaining the priority of worship.

5. According to Genesis 2:10, "A river flows out of Eden to water the garden." This river brings fertility and life to the entire world, as we see in verses 11–14. Similarly, in Psalm 46:5 (46:4 EV) we read of "a river whose streams make glad the city of God," and Ezekiel 47 describes a great river flowing out of the temple in the new Jerusalem to sweeten the Dead Sea. Such a source of fertility and life is an indication that the divine presence is there. One of these rivers was called the Gihon, which was also the name for the spring under the Jerusalem temple (1 Kings 1:33, 38, 45).

6. The river giving life to the garden divides into four as it issues from Eden. Since water flows downhill, this fact clearly indicates that Eden was an elevated place.[80] In the ancient Near East, temples were situated on mountains because that is where the heavens meet the earth. In Ezekiel 28:13–14, Eden is also described and portrayed as a mountain sanctuary. Interestingly, there are passages in the Old Testament which portray Canaan, the Promised Land given to Israel, as a new Eden. These texts speak of the "new Eden" as a mountain sanctuary, the dwelling place of God (Ex. 15:17; Psalm 78:54). After divine judgement brings devastation to the land of Israel, God's plan of renewal involves restoring the desert so that it is like Eden (Isa. 51:3; Ezek. 36:35). The future new Jerusalem/Zion is likewise a mountain sanctuary (Isa. 2:2–4; 4:5; 11:9; 25:6–8; 56:7; 57:13; 65:11, 25).

7. The garden is the place of divine decrees. After placing the Man whom he had formed in the garden (Gen. 2:8, 15), God gave commands to the Man there. The Lord daily met the Man there, and as Judge and King he called him to account for his sin in one of these daily meetings. Similarly, the purpose of the tabernacle (and later Solomon's temple) is the place from which God rules as King: "then make for me a sanctuary so that I may dwell among them" (Ex. 25:8). The ark in the centre of the inner

---

[80] If "Eden" stems from Sumerian, the term means "plain, steppe, open country." We should note, however, that the text indicates God planted a garden *in* Eden. Thus Eden was an area larger than the garden. Nonetheless, the term is probably to be derived from another word of similar sound meaning "bliss/luxury." "Not until the inter-testamental literature is there an explicit picture of paradise as a mountain." See http://www.aakkl.helsinki.fi/melammu/database/gen_html/a0001371.php.

room of the sanctuary is a kind of footstool of God's throne: "the LORD sits enthroned above the cherubim" (1 Sam. 4:4; 2 Sam. 6:2 = 1 Chron. 13:6; 2 Kings 19:15; Ps. 99:1).

8. The tree of knowledge in the garden in Eden was recognised as "pleasant to the sight, good for food and to be desired to make one wise" (Gen. 3:6). These characteristics are echoed by Psalm 19, where the covenant/Torah/law is described as "making wise the simple, rejoicing the heart, and enlightening the eyes." Referred to as the "testimony," the covenant/Torah was kept in the ark in the holy of holies, the inner sanctuary (Ex. 25:16; Deut. 31:26). Touching the ark brought death just as eating from the tree of knowledge did (2 Sam. 6:7; Num. 4:20).

9. Genesis 3:21 records that "the LORD God made tunics of skin for them and clothed them." In the accounts of the ordination of the priests, Moses clothed them (Ex. 28:40–41; 29:8; 40:14; Lev. 8:13).

10. The first branch of the river coming forth from Eden goes round the land of Havilah (Gen. 2:11) and perhaps is reminiscent of the gold in the tabernacle and the temple. There were *šōham* (onyx?) stones in the sanctuary (Ex. 25:7; 28:9, 20; 1 Chron. 29:2). Two such stones were engraved with the names of the twelve tribes and worn by the high priest on his ephod (Ex. 28:9–14). The substance called *bĕdōlaḥ* in Hebrew (= bdellium, a kind of special gum or resin from a tree) was also found in the Land of Havilah. The only other occurrence of *bĕdōlaḥ* is Numbers 11:7, where the appearance of manna is compared to this substance. Some manna was kept in the tabernacle (Ex. 16:33–34).[81]

CONNECTIONS BETWEEN THE GARDEN IN EDEN AND THE EXODUS TABERNACLE

Other passages in the Old Testament support the cultic connections between the garden in Eden and the later sanctuaries.[82] Wenham notes the following:

> [Gen.] 1:1-2:3 tells of the creation of the world in six days. The parallels in phraseology between the conclusion of the creation account in 1:1-2:3 and the tabernacle building account in Exodus 25-40 have long been noted.[83]

---

[81] See especially Jon D. Levenson, *Theology of the Program of Restoration of Ezekiel 40–48* (Harvard Semitic Museum 10; Missoula, MT: Scholars Press, 1976), 26–36.

[82] Parallels between the structure and wording of Exodus 25–40, the account of the building of the tabernacle, and Genesis 1–3, the account of creation were first introduced to me by Daniel I. Block, "Introduction to the Old Testament, Part I: Pentateuch and Historiographic Literature 20200," course notes, The Southern Baptist Theological Seminary, 2004.

[83] U. Cassuto, *A Commentary on the Book of Exodus* (Jerusalem: Magnes, 1976), 476.

Kearney[84] argued that the six commands in the instructions for building the tabernacle corresponded to the six days' creation. More recently Weinfeld[85] argued that God's rest on the first sabbath (2:1-3) corresponds to his resting, i.e. dwelling in the tabernacle.[86]

John Davies also notes these parallels between creation and tabernacle accounts:

> A stronger point may be made of the use of the sabbatical structure, the six-days-plus-one cycle, which was used as the structuring device for the account of creation in Gen. 1.1–2.3. The pattern of six days plus a seventh forms an *inclusio* around the entire set of tabernacle instructions. The prelude to the tabernacle instructions is the account of Moses being taken up into the divine cloud on the mountain, where we read, 'For six days the cloud covered the mountain, and on the seventh day Yhwh called to Moses from within the cloud' (Exod. 24.16).
>
> Further, just as the first section of the Genesis creation account concluded with the record of the divine rest (Gen. 2.2-3), so the whole *fiat* section of the tabernacle account (including the directives concerning the priesthood) concludes with a summons to its 'creators' to imitate the divine rest (Exod. 31.13-17). Batto remarks: 'There can be no doubt that the Priestly Writer intends this scene to parallel the opening scene in Genesis with six days of active creation and a seventh day in which God ceased his activity and "rested"'.[87] Kearney likewise draws attention to what he considers to be the framework of the P redactor, though in a somewhat more elaborate manner.[88] He detects in the wider framework of Exodus 25–40 a reflection of the thematic structure of creation (chs. 25–31), the fall (chs. 32–33) and the reconstruction (chs. 34–40). The seven separate divine speeches in the first section (commencing at 25.1; 30.11, 17, 22, 34; 31.1, 12) have a thematic correspondence in sequence to each of the seven creation days of Gen. 1.1–2.3. Not all of Kearney's parallels are equally convincing, though even the fact that there are seven speeches, of which the seventh is a summons to Sabbath rest is instructive. The sabbatical cycle of work and rest is also specifically enjoined on the people in connection with the work to be done in constructing the tabernacle (Exod. 35.2).
>
> Then just as the divine spirit overshadowed the original creative enterprise (Gen. 1.2), so the mountain top is covered by the כבוד ('glory') of

---

[84] P. J. Kearney, "Creation and Liturgy: The P Redaction of Exod 25—40," *ZAW* 89 (1977), 375–87.

[85] M. Weinfeld, "Sabbath, Temple and the Enthronement of the Lord—The Problem of the Sitz im Leben of Gen. 1:1–2:3," in *Melanges bibliques et orientaux en l'honneur de M. Henri Cazelles*, eds. A. Caquot and M. Delcor, 501–512, AOAT 212 (Kevelaer: Butzon and Becker, 1981).

[86] Wenham, "Sanctuary Symbolism in the Garden of Eden Story," 404.

[87] Bernard F. Batto, *Slaying the Dragon: Mythmaking in the Biblical Tradition* (Louisville, KY: Westminster/John Knox, 1992), 120.

[88] Peter J. Kearney, "Creation and Liturgy: The P Redaction of Exod 25—40," *ZAW* 89 (1977), 375–87.

God (Exod. 24.16, 17). The spirit endows gifted craftsmen (31.3; 35.31) for the creative work.[89]

In addition, the sanctuary is described as a place of rest for Yahweh in Psalm 132:14. In Exodus 20:11, we note the same word used to describe the Sabbath—God "rested" on the seventh day. Thus we can see that the planting of the garden on the sixth day is the construction of a sanctuary, and on the seventh day, God rests, i.e., enters his sanctuary.[90]

T. Desmond Alexander also follows the work of Beale and Wenham and notes the garden in Eden pictured as a sanctuary/temple. He draws out the implications as follows:

> (1) Since the garden is a place where divinity and humanity enjoy each other's presence, it is appropriate that it should be a prototype for later Israelite sanctuaries. This explains why many of the decorative features of the tabernacle and temple are arboreal in nature. (2) Because they met God face to face in a holy place, we may assume that Adam and Eve had a holy or priestly status. Only priests were permitted to serve within a sanctuary or temple. (3) Although it is not stated, the opening chapters of Genesis imply that the boundaries of the garden will be extended to fill the whole earth as human beings are fruitful and increase in number.[91]

This is excellent, but it does not explore the implications sufficiently. It reveals the weakness of a biblical theology based on themes instead of one focused on discovering the narrative plot structure through attention to cultural and linguistic data from exegesis and analysis of the literary structures, both macro and micro. We must remember that the pattern of Hebrew literature is recursive, resumptive, and holographic. Genesis 1 goes round the topic of creation, and Genesis 2 goes round the topic again from a different perspective. Put the two together and you have a hologram of the creation.

Genesis 2:8–17 pictures Adam as a kind of king-priest worshipping in a garden sanctuary. This passage explains how the royal rule given to humankind within the covenant structure established in 1:26–27 is to operate. W. J. Dumbrell begins to draw out the implications of this as follows:

---

[89] John A. Davies, *A Royal Priesthood: Literary and Intertextual Perspectives on an Image of Israel in Exodus 19.6*, JSOTSup 395 (London: T. & T. Clark, 2004), 146–147 (emphasis his).

[90] See M. Weinfeld, "Sabbath, Temple and the Enthronement of the Lord—The Problem of the Sitz im Leben of Gen. 1:1–2:3," in *Melanges bibliques et orientaux en l'honneur de M. Henri Cazelles*, ed. A. Caquot and M. Delcor, AOAT 212 (Kevelaer, Germany: Butzon & Becker, 1981), 501–512.

[91] T. Desmond Alexander, *From Eden to the New Jerusalem: An Introduction to Biblical Theology* (Grand Rapids, MI: Kregel, 2008), 25.

In short, created in the world with dominion over it, man is immediately abstracted from the world and placed directly in the divine presence. What is being said in all this is surely how the dominion mandate was to be exercised. . . . Man was to control his world, not primarily by immersing himself in the tasks of ordering it, but by recognizing that there was a system of priorities by which all of life was to be regulated. If he were rightly related to his Creator, then he would rightly respond to creation.[92]

Included in the covenant was an ordering of male/female relationships and family life so that part of responding rightly to creation was true humanness defined in proper ways of treating each other.

The relationship between Genesis 2:8–17 and Genesis 1:26–27 is significant. Genesis 2:8–17 explains the relationship between "likeness" and "image" in the covenant relationship between man and God. Only when the father-son relationship is nurtured through worship, fellowship, and obedient love will humankind appropriately and properly reflect and represent to the world the kind of kingship and rule intrinsic to God himself. Kingship is effected *through* covenant relationship.

THE DEMAND OF THE COVENANT AND ITS BREACH

There was a real and vital element of condition in the covenant relationship in the garden. Eating the fruit of the tree of the knowledge of good and evil was prohibited. We know that the conditions for maintaining love, loyalty, and trust in the covenant relationship were not met. When the fruit of the forbidden tree was eaten, we were all involved somehow, as Romans 5:12–21 makes plain.

A brief comment is necessary to discuss the breaking of the covenant. Just what was involved in this initial transgression? Was the prohibition against eating the fruit of the forbidden tree an arbitrarily imposed means for testing loyalty and obedience? This is surely true, but it does not do justice to what was offered by the snake and confirmed by God after the Fall, that they would be "like gods, knowing good and evil" (see Gen. 3:5, 22).

Some have explained knowing good and evil as reflecting sexual understanding of each other. This is inadequate because it does not make plain how the acquisition of such knowledge would make one like God.

Others have explained good and evil as a way of expressing the totality

---

[92] Dumbrell, *Covenant and Creation*, 35–36.

of knowledge by describing opposite poles. But certainly neither Adam and Eve nor any subsequent humans can claim the totality of knowledge.

The best explanation to date is that of W. M. Clark,[93] who carefully analysed all the occurrences of the phrase in the Hebrew Bible and showed that the "knowledge of good and evil" has to do with the exercise of absolute moral autonomy. That is to say, knowing good and evil means choosing or determining for oneself what is right and wrong independently of God. The decision of Adam to be self-legislating did make him like God in one sense, but also unlike God in that he would not be able to foresee the consequences of his choices long term or always be certain of the issues before him.

SUMMARY

Careful exegesis of Genesis 1–3 has shown that at creation, God made humankind as his image and according to his likeness. In the cultural and linguistic setting of the fifteenth century B.C. and according to the literary techniques embedded in the text and the framework provided by the meta-narrative, this speaks of man's relationship to God as son and his relationship to creation as servant king. In the ancient Near East, both the context of the family and the relationship of king and people is covenantal, requiring loyal love, obedience, and trust.

LATER TEXTS IN THE OLD TESTAMENT

Several texts later in the Old Testament may have a bearing directly on the question of whether there is a covenant at creation.[94]

HOSEA 6:7

Explicit support for a covenant at creation may be found at Hosea 6:7, although the text is disputed. The Masoretic Text has *wĕhēmmâ kĕ'ādām 'ābĕrû bĕrît*, which may be literally translated, "but they, like Adam, have transgressed the[95] covenant." Williamson notes the problem and argues as follows:

---

[93] W. M. Clark, "A Legal Background to the Yahwist's Use of 'Good and Evil' in Genesis 2–3," *Journal of Biblical Literature* 88 (1969): 266–278. See also H. Blocher, *In the Beginning* (Downers Grove, IL: InterVarsity Press, 1984), 126–133.

[94] No attempt is made here to canvas Second Temple Judaism for its understanding of Genesis 1 and 2. Nonetheless, *Sir.* 14:17 is noteworthy, in that this text clearly refers to Genesis 1–3 and clearly employs the term covenant: πᾶσα σὰρξ ὡς ἱμάτιον παλαιοῦται, ἡ γὰρ διαθήκη αἰῶνος Θανάτῳ ἀποθανῇ. While this may not prove a covenant in Genesis 1–3, it indicates the thought of early Judaism on this question.

[95] Although *bĕrît* is unarticulated, it is both common and normal to omit the article in Hebrew poetry. Williamson renders the noun as indefinite, "a covenant," but the reference in context is doubtless to *the* Mosaic Torah.

Although several translations and commentators interpret *kĕ'ādām* in a personal sense, meaning 'like Adam', most interpreters emend the key word to read *bĕ'ādām* (in/at Adam), taking the proper noun in its geographical sense—referring to the first town Israel reached after crossing into the Promised Land (Josh. 3:16). Indeed, arguably, a geographical interpretation may not necessitate a textual emendation at all (cf. the similar syntax *kammidbār* [Lit. 'as in the wilderness'] in Hos. 2:3; MT v. 5). Further support for this geographical understanding is found in the reference to Gilead (Hos. 6:8) and Shechem (Hos. 6:9) in the immediate context, and especially in the deployment of the locative *šām* (there) immediately after *bĕrît* in Hosea 6:7.[96]

The arguments of Williamson appear to be persuasive. Nonetheless, John Davies shows that Hosea 6:7 is probably linked to Hosea 4:4–6:

> [4] Yet let no one contend,
>   and let none accuse,
>   for with you is my contention, O priest.
> [5] You shall stumble by day;
>   the prophet also shall stumble with you by night;
>   and I will destroy your mother.
> [6] My people are destroyed for lack of knowledge;
>   because you have rejected knowledge,
>   I reject you from being a priest to me.
> And since you have forgotten the law of your God,
>   I also will forget your children. (ESV)

Davies argues convincingly that Hosea is alluding directly to Exodus 19:6 and addressing corporate Israel with the words "O priest." Because the people have rejected the Torah, God has rejected them as his royal priesthood. Davies further says,

> This understanding might lend support to the unfashionable reading 'like Adam' (Vulgate, RV, NASB, NIV) for כאדם at 6.7. If Hosea has as part of his shared presupposition pool with his readers the story of Genesis 2, with Adam as the idyllic priest-king (cf. Ezek. 28.12–15; Jub. 4.23–26), together with the notion that Israel at Sinai was constituted as the new humanity, the true successors of Adam (cf. 4 Ezra 3.3–36; 6.53–59; 2 Bar. 14.17–19), then it makes sense to compare the breach of the Sinai covenant (e.g., Hos. 4.1, 2) with the rebellion in the garden (Gen. 3; cf. Ezek. 28.16–17). The LXX ὡς ἄνθρωπος understands the reference to be to a

---

[96] Williamson, *Sealed with an Oath*, 55.

man. An alternative is to read כאדם as a place reference (cf. שׁם, 'there', which seems to call for a place reference), though why the preposition כ should have been chosen (it is usually emended to ב on this understanding), and why the notion of 'covenant' should be introduced in connection with the place Adam (RSV, JB, NRSV) or Admah (NEB) is unclear.[97]

The royal priesthood of Israel is an Adamic role assigned her at the exodus, as indicated by being addressed as the "son of God" (Ex. 4:22), a fact to which Hosea directly refers in 11:1. By violating the Mosaic covenant, Israel has forfeited this role. The connection with Genesis 2 is natural and suitable. Williamson, however, has been less than precise with the linguistic data. It is true that the adverb *šām* (there) follows *běrît* in Hosea 6:7, but it begins a new clause: "there they acted treacherously against me." It is normal that the adverb has a locative and spatial function, as in Hosea 9:15 and 12:4:

> Every evil of theirs is in Gilgal;
>> there I began to hate them (9:15, ESV)

> He met God at Bethel,
>> and there God spoke with us— (12:4, ESV)

Yet the anaphoric referent of the adverb may specify a location more indirectly by referring to circumstances. Consider Hosea 10:9 (below) and compare 9:9:

> From the days of Gibeah, you have sinned, O Israel:
>> there they have continued. (ESV)

The phrase "like Adam" in Hosea 6:7 indicates sin in a place, the garden of Eden. The "there" can refer back to these circumstances. If the Masoretic Text of Hosea 6:7 is taken at face value, it seems to imply that the failure of Israel's role as another Adam was doomed from the garden of Eden because all are somehow involved in Adam's covenant breaking:

> But like Adam they transgressed the covenant;
>> there they dealt faithlessly with me. (ESV)

Admittedly the text is difficult and disputed, but Williamson has not shown

---

[97] John A. Davies, *Royal Priesthood*, 202–203.

that a face value reading of the text is to be rejected. Hosea is a book with many geographical allusions, but nowhere does the Old Testament clearly speak of covenant breaking at the location known as Adam (Jos. 3:16). Such a reference would be more than obscurantist.

JEREMIAH 33:19–26

In Jeremiah 33:19–26 the certainty of Yahweh's covenant with David is correlated with the certainty of his covenant with the arrangement of day and night:

> [19] The word of the LORD came to Jeremiah: [20] "Thus says the LORD: If you can break my covenant with the day and my covenant with the night, so that day and night will not come at their appointed time, [21] then also my covenant with David my servant may be broken, so that he shall not have a son to reign on his throne, and my covenant with the Levitical priests my ministers. [22] As the host of heaven cannot be numbered and the sands of the sea cannot be measured, so I will multiply the offspring of David my servant, and the Levitical priests who minister to me."
>
> [23] The word of the LORD came to Jeremiah: [24] "Have you not observed that these people are saying, 'The LORD has rejected the two clans that he chose'? Thus they have despised my people so that they are no longer a nation in their sight. [25] Thus says the LORD: If I have not established my covenant with day and night and the fixed order of heaven and earth, [26] then I will reject the offspring of Jacob and David my servant and will not choose one of his offspring to rule over the offspring of Abraham, Isaac, and Jacob. For I will restore their fortunes and will have mercy on them." (ESV)

Apparently Williamson wishes to argue that this is a reference to the covenant with Noah (Gen. 8:22) and does not indicate a covenant in Genesis 1. This, however, is specious reasoning. The covenant with Noah is a renewal of the commitment of the Creator to the ordinances established at creation, so the reference in Jeremiah 33 is to both his commitment to Noah and his original commitment at creation. God's commitment to "the fixed order of heaven and earth" was initiated at creation and upheld in the covenant with Noah. Williamson admits as much when he says, "God intended, through Noah, to fulfil his original creative intent."[98] To aver that this is a reference

---

[98] Paul R. Williamson, *Sealed with an Oath*, 51, 75.

to the covenant with Noah but not creation is schizophrenic and is a result of Williamson's misunderstanding and misuse of the phrases "cut a covenant" (*kārat bĕrît*) and "uphold a covenant" (*hēqîm bĕrît*). A parallel reference is Jeremiah 31:35–37, which surely refers to creation and indicates that God's commitment to Israel is as certain as his commitment to creation. The reason for this is that Israel's doctrine of *salvation* is based on her doctrine of *creation*. Williamson has lost sight of this.

Chapter Seven

THE COVENANT WITH ABRAHAM (I)

INTRODUCTION

After the covenant at creation established between God and humans and humans and creation, and the subsequent covenant with Noah upholding the original covenant at creation, next in the grand story comes the covenant with Abraham. Brian Walsh, Christian Reformed Chaplain to the University of Toronto in Canada, wrote some time ago of the importance of this grand story to the challenges facing the church in a postmodern age:

> Postmodern culture is deeply suspicious of all grand stories. Again, The Smashing Pumpkins prove to be insightful in this regard. In their infinitely sad song, "tales of a scorched earth," they sing, "we're all dead yeah we're all dead/inside the future of a shattered past." We live inside the future of a shattered past because that "past" told grand stories of Marxist utopia, technological freedom, or capitalist paradise. Yet we have come to see not only that these stories are unfinished, but that they are also fundamentally unfinishable, for the simple reason that they are fundamentally lies. The postmodern ethos insists that stories such as these that have so shaped our lives are not stories of emancipation and progress after all, but stories of enslavement, oppression and violence. And on such a view, any story, any world view, that makes grand claims about the real course and destiny of history will be perceived as making common cause with such violence and oppression. This characteristic of the postmodern shift is, I think, the most challenging to Christian faith. If there is one thing that Christianity is all about it is a grand story. How else can we interpret the cosmic tale of creation, fall, redemption and consummation that the Scriptures tell? Yet it is precisely this story that we must tell in a postmodern culture. In the face of the dissolution of all grand stories, Christians have the audacity to proclaim, week after week,

the liberating story of God's redemption of all creation. It is, we insist, the one story that actually delivers on what it promises.[1]

ABRAHAM IN THE GENESIS PLOT STRUCTURE

If we are to construct a metanarrative that is, in fact, the metanarrative of Scripture and not a marriage of biblical data and secular worldviews, we must pay attention to the shape of the text and the literary techniques used by the narrator to locate the narratives concerning Abraham within the larger plot structure of Genesis, the Pentateuch, the Old Testament, and the Bible as a whole. Afterwards we can reckon with the internal movement and literary structure within the Abraham narratives.

N. T. Wright, an evangelical scholar in England, describes the story of Abraham this way:

> Abraham emerges within the structure of Genesis as the answer to the plight of all humankind. The line of disaster and of the 'curse', from Adam, through Cain, through the Flood to Babel, begins to be reversed when God calls Abraham and says, 'in you shall all the families of the earth be blessed'.[2]

Here, after Adam and Noah, God is making another new start. Abram and his family constitute another Adam. Notice the parallels in the biblical narrative: Adam and Eve had three sons (besides other children who are not named in the text; Gen. 5:4). Similarly, the genealogy in Genesis 5 ends with a man who also had three sons (Shem, Ham and Japheth). The genealogy in Genesis 11 ends in the same way: with a man who had three sons (Abram, Nahor and Haran). This parallel is a literary technique inviting the reader to compare Abram with Noah and Adam.

There are other parallels between Genesis 1–3 and Genesis 12 which suggest that we should view Abram as a new Adam, and we will now explore some of them.

GENESIS 12 AS A NEW CREATION

According to the apostle Paul, the choosing of Abram by God involved calling into existence that which is nonexistent. Paul says,

---

[1] Brian Walsh, "The Church in a Postmodern Age: Ten Things You Need to Know," in *Good Idea! A Resource Sheet on Evangelism and Church Growth* 3/4 (Toronto: Wycliffe College Institute of Evangelism, 1996), 1–5.
[2] N. T. Wright, *The New Testament and the People of God* (Minneapolis: Fortress, 1992), 262.

[16] That is why it depends on faith, in order that the promise may rest on grace and be guaranteed to all his offspring—not only to the adherent of the law but also to the one who shares the faith of Abraham, who is the father of us all, [17] as it is written, "I have made you the father of many nations"—in the presence of the God in whom he believed, who gives life to the dead and calls into existence the things that do not exist. (Rom. 4:16–17, ESV)

When Paul speaks of Abraham believing in the God who calls into existence the things that do not exist, what does this language which he employs bring to our minds? Paul can have only one passage of Scripture in mind to which he is alluding directly: Genesis 1. Over and over again in the creation narrative we read the words, "And God said, 'Let x be.' And x was." God simply speaks his word and calls into existence things that do not exist. Therefore, according to the New Testament, as we read Genesis 12–25, we are to view the call of Abram as a kind of "new creation." Just as the divine word in Genesis 1:3 brings into being and existence things that are not, so in Genesis 12:3 it is the divine word that brings into existence a new order out of the chaos resulting from the confusion and curse of Babel—the condition of the world just prior to Genesis 12. Note that Genesis 10 and 11 are not presented in chronological order. Genesis 10 constitutes a "Table of Nations," showing the various families and peoples of the world lost and scattered over the face of the earth. Genesis 11 presents the narrative of the "Tower of Babel," which explains how the nations were scattered throughout the world in this way. Just as the first Adam failed as a covenant keeper and his family line through Cain ended up with the corruption and violence displayed by Lamech, a polygamist who murdered a boy and promised severe vengeance for any who would redress his heinous act, so the second Adam, Noah, also failed to produce a covenant community practising social justice, resulting in the humanistic hubris of Babel. The earth returns once more to chaos before God begins anew by calling Abram. As one commentator notes, "in this way the absolutely free and unconditioned nature of the choice of Abram is emphasised, and thus the presence of the divine will as the power which shapes and directs all history is at this point made perfectly clear."[3]

---

[3] William J. Dumbrell, *Covenant and Creation: A Theology of Old Testament Covenants* (Nashville: Thomas Nelson, 1984), 58.

ISRAEL AS LAST ADAM

Other parallels are established by the use of key words. Let us now notice how the language of the commission to Adam is repeated throughout the book of Genesis by following the use of "bless," "be fruitful," and "multiply" in the narratives subsequent to the creation narrative.

1:28: And God *blessed* them, and God said to them, "Be *fruitful* and *multiply*, and fill the earth, and subdue it; and have dominion over the fish of the sea and over the birds of the air, and over every living thing that moves upon the earth."

12:2f.: "And I will make of you a great nation, and I will *bless* you, and make your name great; and be a *blessing*! And I will *bless* those who *bless* you . . ."

17:2, 6, 8: "I will make my covenant between me and you, and will *multiply* you exceedingly. . . . I will make you exceedingly *fruitful*, . . . and I will give to you and to your seed after you, . . . all the land of Canaan, . . ."

22:16ff.: "Because you have done this, . . . I will certainly *bless* you, and I will greatly *multiply* your descendants as the stars of heaven and as the sand which is on the seashore. . . . and in your seed all the nations of the earth shall be *blessed*, because you have obeyed my voice."

26:3f.: [The Lord said to Isaac] "I will be with you and will *bless* you; for to you and to your descendants I will give all these lands, and I will fulfill the oath which I swore to your father Abraham. I will *multiply* your descendants as the stars of heaven, and will give your descendants all these lands; and by your descendants all the nations of the earth shall be *blessed* . . ."

26:24: "Fear not, for I am with you. I will *bless* you, and *multiply* your descendants, for the sake of my servant Abraham."

28:3: [Isaac blessed Jacob and said] "God Almighty *bless* you and make you *fruitful* and *multiply* you, that you may become a company of peoples. May he give you the blessing of Abraham, to you and to your descendants with you, that you may possess the land of your sojournings, which God gave to Abraham."

35:11f.: And God said to [Jacob], "I am God Almighty: be *fruitful* and *multiply*; a nation and company of nations shall come from you, . . . and the land which I gave to Abraham and Isaac I will give to you, and I will give the land to your descendants after you."

47:27: Thus Israel lived in the land of Egypt, . . . and they gained possessions in it, and were *fruitful* and *multiplied* exceedingly.

48:3f. Jacob said to Joseph, "God Almighty appeared to me . . . and said to me, 'Behold, I will make you *fruitful*, and *multiply* you, . . . and will give this land, to your seed after you . . .'"

From tracing this trail of the terms "bless," "be fruitful," and "multiply" through Genesis, N. T. Wright concludes as follows:

Thus at key moments—Abraham's call, his circumcision, the offering of Isaac, the transition from Abraham to Isaac and from Isaac to Jacob, and in the sojourn in Egypt—the narrative quietly makes the point that Abraham and his family inherit, in a measure, the role of Adam and Eve. The differences are not, however, insignificant. Except for 35.11 f., echoed in 48.3 f., the command ('be fruitful . . . ') has turned into a promise ('I will make you fruitful . . . '). The word 'exceedingly' is added in ch. 17. And, most importantly, possession of the land of Canaan, and supremacy over enemies, has taken the place of the dominion over nature given in 1.28. We could sum up this aspect of Genesis by saying: Abraham's children are God's true humanity, and their homeland is the new Eden.[4]

The last point made by Wright is forcefully illustrated by Exodus 15:17. At the end of the song sung by Israel after crossing the Red Sea we read,

You will bring them in and plant them on your own mountain,
    the place, O LORD, which you have made for your abode,
    the sanctuary, O Lord, which your hands have established. (ESV)

In this verse the establishment of Israel in the land of Canaan is pictured as the planting of a tree in a *mountain sanctuary*, exactly the picture of Eden presented in Genesis 2 and Ezekiel 28. The same thought is expressed in Psalm 78:54, which reads as follows:

And he brought them to the border of his sanctuary,
    the mountain which his right hand had acquired.

---

[4] N. T. Wright, *The Climax of the Covenant* (Minneapolis: Fortress, 1991), 21–23.

The verse describes the event of the exodus in which the Lord brought Israel to Canaan, but the terms used to describe the land of promise depict it in Edenic terms as a mountain sanctuary. This depiction is strengthened by two texts in which, after the desolation of the land brought by the divine judgement through the Assyrians and Babylonians, a restoration is promised wherein the land will once more be like Eden:

> The LORD will surely comfort Zion
>> and will look with compassion on all her ruins;
>> he will make her deserts like Eden,
>> her wastelands like the garden of the LORD. (Isa. 51:3, NIV)

> [33] This is what the Sovereign LORD says: On the day I cleanse you from all your sins, I will resettle your towns, and the ruins will be rebuilt. [34] The desolate land will be cultivated instead of lying desolate in the sight of all who pass through it. [35] They will say, "This land that was laid waste has become like the garden of Eden; the cities that were lying in ruins, desolate and destroyed, are now fortified and inhabited." [36] Then the nations around you that remain will know that I the LORD have rebuilt what was destroyed and have replanted what was desolate. I the LORD have spoken, and I will do it. (Ezek. 36:33–36, NIV)

Thus Abraham and his family, later called Israel, is, as it were, a last Adam. God made a major new start with Noah. Now he is making a new start with Abraham. There are no major new beginnings after this in the narrative of Scripture (until we come to the new creation at the end of the story).

When we see that Israel is, according to the Old Testament, the last Adam, and as later Jewish tradition understood it, the one undoing the sin of Adam,[5] we see the background for Paul's understanding of Christ as the last Adam,[6] because as history unfolds, Jesus accomplishes in his person and work what God intended for Israel as a people.

OVERVIEW OF GOD'S DEALINGS WITH ABRAM

It was over a period of forty years that God had dealings with Abram, later called Abraham. During this time there was a call to leave his homeland and journey to a country unknown to him. Initially God made promises to Abram

---

[5] *Genesis Rabbah* 14.6.
[6] See Romans 5:12–21 and 1 Corinthians 15. In 1 Corinthians 15:45–48 Paul contrasts "the first man Adam" with "the last Adam" and "the first man" with "the second man." Jesus Christ is not the second Adam—that was Noah, but rather the *last* Adam. And in terms of contrasting the new creation with the old creation, he is the second Man.

(Genesis 12) that were later enshrined in a covenant (Genesis 15 and 17) and confirmed finally by an oath (Genesis 22). All throughout this period of time, one can perceive development and growth in the character and life of Abram in terms of faith in God's promises and obedience to his instructions revealed to him (frequently by means of visions). The book of Genesis is characterised by a literary structure in which the sections are divided according to "Birth/Family Histories." The narratives concerning Abram fall within the "Family History" of Terah (11:27–25:11), which divides naturally into nineteen sections as follows:

Birth/Family History of Terah	*11:27–25:11*
Terah's family and journey to Haran	11:27–32
Call of Abram and journey to Canaan	12:1–9
Abram and Sarai in Egypt	12:10–20
Abram and Lot separate	13:1–18
Battle with four kings from east	14:1–24
Making of covenant with Abram	15:1–21
Birth of Ishmael by Hagar	16:1–16
Confirming of covenant with Abram	17:1–27
Abraham's hospitality and social justice	18:1–33
Lot rescued from destruction of Sodom	19:1–29
Lot's daughters' incest	19:30–38
Abraham sojourns in Gerar	20:1–18
Birth of Isaac	21:1–21
Covenant with Abimelech	21:22–34
Abraham tested and God's oath	22:1–19
Nahor's family	22:20–24
Death and burial of Sarah	23:1–20
A wife for Isaac	24:1–67
Abraham's remarriage and death	25:1–11

To be sure, these divisions are arranged according to the skill of the narrator in a more artful literary structure than the above outline shows, but the outline indicates simply the flow of the plot in the divine dealings with Abram according to its basic divisions.

As far as the covenant God made with Abraham is concerned, three or four episodes in the Abram narrative are particularly prominent. First, in Genesis 12, God makes incredible promises to Abram involving progeny and land (i.e., a place where his progeny can live and that they can call home). Then, in chapter 15, both of these promises are enshrined in a covenant. Later on, in chapter 17, after Abram and Sarai's attempt to fulfill the promise of progeny through Hagar and Ishmael, God repeats his promises and confirms his covenant, this time adding the rite of circumcision. Some ten to fifteen years afterwards, according to chapter 22, God "tests" Abraham and, upon his obedience, swears by himself in another mighty confirmation of the promises.

> *Key Points in the Abraham Narratives*
> 1. The Giving of the Promise: the Call of Abram (Genesis 12)
> 2. Making the Covenant: the Promise of Descendants and Land (Genesis 15)
> 3. Confirming the Covenant: the Sign of Circumcision (Genesis 17)
> 4. Abraham's Obedience and Confirmation of the Promises by Oath (Genesis 22)

We might compare the relationship between God and Abraham to a marriage. The giving of the promises in chapter 12 would then represent the betrothal or engagement. The covenant making in chapter 15 and confirmation in chapter 17 would correspond to the wedding vows of the marriage covenant. After testing Abraham, God reiterates his promises by a mighty oath.

OUTLINE OF GENESIS 12

Careful consideration of key grammatical issues and the literary structure of Genesis 12 are necessary for a correct interpretation of the promises made by God to Abram and the covenant ensuing from them. In fact, interpretation at this key point affects how one understands the rest of the Bible.

> *The Giving of the Promise: The Call of Abram (Genesis 12)*
>
> **The divine word: command and promise   12:1–3**
>
> *Go (Command)*
>
> | | |
> |---|---|
> | 1. I will make you into a great nation | (Promise) |
> | 2. I will bless you | (Promise) |
> | 3. I will make your name great | (Promise) |
>
> *Be A Blessing (Command)*
>
> | | |
> |---|---|
> | 1. I will bless those who bless you | (Promise) |
> | 2. I will curse him who curses you | (Promise) |
> | 3. In you all nations will be blessed | (Promise) |
>
> **Abram's response: obedience   12:4–9**
>
> | | |
> |---|---|
> | 1. Obedience | (vv. 4–6) |
> | 2. Confirmation | (v. 7) |
> | 3. Obedience | (vv. 8–9) |

The chapter divides into two sections: verses 1–3 constitute the divine word to Abram, and verses 4–9 indicate his response to that word. Noting the literary structure of verses 1–3 is crucial. In the Hebrew text, there are two commands (i.e., verbs marked in the Hebrew verbal system as imperatives): "go" and "be." Each of these two commands is followed by three prefix forms (which could be construed as either cohortatives or imperfects), and normally prefix forms following commands mark purpose or result. Thus three promises flow from each of the two commands.

Since the literary structure is debated, the data must be analysed in detail. The divine speech to Abram in Genesis 12:1–3 contains eight verbs (not including verbs in embedded or relative sentences): לֶךְ, וְאֶעֶשְׂךָ, וְנִבְרְכוּ, אָאֹר, וַאֲבָרְכָה, וְהְיֵה, וַאֲגַדְּלָה, וַאֲבָרֶכְךָ. The first and fourth, לֶךְ and וְהְיֵה, are formally unambiguous and must be analysed as *qal* imperatives, second person singular. The remaining verbs are all first person volitives (i.e., cohortative), determined either from the termination in -*â* or from their clause-initial position.[7] The verb forms with pronominal suffixes (וְאֶעֶשְׂךָ, וַאֲבָרֶכְךָ) naturally cannot have the -*â* termination, but are clause-initial and in a sequence of volitives and so ought to be construed as such. The prefix forms in Genesis 12:1–3 could also be read as simple future indicatives without altering the meaning significantly. אָאֹר in 12:3 is not prefixed by *waw* and is not clause-initial since a clause component is preposed. This clause pattern marks the sentence as part of a matching pair with the preceding clause (i.e., "I will bless the ones blessing you, *but* the one cursing you I will curse" are clauses marked by discourse grammar signals as a matched pair).[8]

The form most troublesome to scholars in this sequence is וְהְיֵה. Many prefer to construe it as an emphatic consequence clause, "so that you will be a blessing." Mathews explains:

> וְהְיֵה בְּרָכָה (lit. "be a blessing," v. 2d) is preceded by the cohortative וַאֲגַדְּלָה ("I will make . . . great"); by this sequence of verbs the imperative expresses expected certainty or intention (GKC § 110i). The use of the imperative instead of an imperfective verbal form heightens the certainty of the promise (*IBHS* § 34.4c).[9]

---

[7] See Peter J. Gentry, "The System of the Finite Verb in Classical Biblical Hebrew," *Hebrew Studies* 39 (1998): 7–39.

[8] See Stephen G. Dempster, "Linguistic Features of Hebrew Narrative: A Discourse Analysis of Narrative from the Classical Period" (PhD diss., University of Toronto, 1985).

[9] Kenneth A. Mathews, *Genesis 11:27–50:26*, New American Commentary 1B (Nashville: B&H, 2005), 107, n. 51.

Mathews appeals to *An Introduction to Biblical Hebrew Syntax*, by Waltke and O'Connor. The relevant section states:

> The imperative, like the jussive, has uses in which its ordinary force is lost. The figure of *heterosis* involves the exchange of one grammatical form for another; with the imperative, *heterosis* creates a promise or prediction to be fulfilled in the future, made more emphatic and vivid than would be the case were the prefix conjugation used.[10]

Certainly the line of demarcation between command and future indicative is fuzzy in many languages; one need not appeal to a figure of speech with a Latin name to substantiate this.[11] The three examples given by Waltke and O'Connor are not particularly convincing (2 Kings 19:29; Ps. 110:2; Isa. 54:14) and can most simply be construed as straightforward commands. Genesis 12:3 is not listed as an example, although elsewhere Waltke appears to agree with the analysis of Mathews.[12] The explanation of Mathews is hardly satisfying. The assumption here is that the choice of every verb form is *motivated*. A consequence clause would be more clearly marked by a prefix form in clause-initial position. If the author intended a consequence, forms such as וְתִהְיֶה or וּתְהִי would have been clearer and more natural than וְהָיֵה.

While one might construe the imperative following the cohortative as a purpose sequence as in GKC §110i, such sequences are common with cohortatives and jussives but extremely rare with imperatives as recent studies on Hebrew volitives have shown.[13] This is what creates the problem. The alert reader, however, would immediately pair וְהָיֵה with לֵךְ since both are not only imperatives but are also *second person* in contrast to the *first person* forms that dominate the divine speech. This is indeed the author's literary signal

---

[10] Bruce K. Waltke and Michael P. O'Connor, *An Introduction to Biblical Hebrew Syntax* (Winona Lake, IN: Eisenbrauns, 1990), 572.

[11] Also discussed in Gentry, "System of the Finite Verb in Classical Biblical Hebrew."

[12] Bruce K. Waltke with Charles Yu, *An Old Testament Theology: An Exegetical, Canonical, and Thematic Approach* (Grand Rapids, MI: Zondervan, 2007), 149. The issue is not addressed in Bruce K. Waltke with Cathi J. Fredericks, *Genesis: A Commentary* (Grand Rapids, MI: Zondervan, 2001).

[13] See Hélène Dallaire, "The Syntax of Volitives in Northwest Semitic Prose" (PhD diss., Hebrew Union College, Cincinnati, OH, 2002); and Ahouva Shulman, "The Use of Modal Verb Forms in Biblical Hebrew Prose" (PhD diss., University of Toronto, 1996). The results of these studies supersede the grammar of Waltke and O'Connor in regard to volitives in Hebrew. Another recent study, Joel S. Baden, "The Morpho-Syntax of Genesis 12:1–3: Translation and Interpretation," *Catholic Biblical Quarterly* 72 (2010): 223–237, provides analysis based on the author's own research on all volitives in the prose of Genesis—Kings, Jeremiah, Jonah, Zechariah, Malachi, Ruth, Esther, Daniel, Ezra, Nehemiah, and Chronicles. Unfortunately, Baden does not seem aware of the excellent work of Shulman and Dallaire and does not further grammatical knowledge or contribute much to interpretation of the text, as he misses key literary cues.

that divides the speech into two sections, so that there are just *two* commands, and each is followed by *three* promises.

Such an analysis does not remove the problem for some scholars, since what could the *command* "be a blessing" mean? What we see here, even before the divine-human relationship is solemnised as a covenant in chapter 15, is that in a relationship with God, there are commands or obligations to be obeyed and fulfilled, but these are always surrounded and supported by the mighty promises of God. Long ago Augustine expressed it this way: What God commands, he also enables. God is promising to do something. But he is doing it in the context of using Abram as an agent of blessing to the world. The three promises that follow begin to explain the command "be a blessing" and unfold how this will work out: "I will bless the ones blessing you but the one cursing you I will curse, and in you all the clans of the world will be blessed." Although God commands Abram, God is still the implied agent who will enable Abram to bring blessing to others.[14]

The exegesis of Williamson ought to be cited as well on this important point of grammar in Genesis 12:3:

> As it stands, the traditional Hebrew text (MT) can be interpreted either as an emphatic consequence clause, 'so that you will indeed be blessed', or as a second command, 'Be a blessing'. While modern English translations clearly favour the former, most recent studies support the latter. Unfortunately, therefore, this is an area over which scholarly opinion is sharply divided. Indeed, some have even suggested removing the problem altogether through textual surgery—by retaining the Hebrew consonants but supplying different vowel points, the text may be emended to read, 'and it [i.e., "your name", v. 2c] shall be a blessing'. However, such an extreme measure is unnecessary, especially since it is possible to make sense of the text as it stands, and the latter is undoubtedly the harder reading.
>
> Support for reading the verb as a second divine command may be found in Genesis 17:1b, in which a similar construction (an imperative verb string involving *hyh* + X) is found, and here the verb undoubtedly retains its imperative force ('Walk before me and *be* blameless' Gen. 17:1 NIV; my italics). Further support for retaining the imperative reading can be adduced from the fact that both imperatives in Genesis 12:1–3 are directly followed by cohortatives—a construction that normally expresses purpose or result. Since the first of these imperative-cohortative clauses expresses a conditional promise, it seems reasonable to conclude that an identical

---

[14] The only direct reference to "be a blessing" elsewhere is Zechariah 8:13. This reference in Zechariah shows that it is possible to construe the form in Genesis 12:2 as a command: "be a blessing!"

construction in the same text-unit should be similarly interpreted (i.e. as a second conditional promise). Thus understood, Abraham's divine commission was twofold: he was to 'Go', and he was to 'Be a blessing!'[15]

Apart from the first statement, the analysis of Williamson is excellent. Those who consider that the form can be construed as an emphatic consequence clause have misconstrued the text and missed important clues to the literary structure. The verb וֶהְיֵה is in sequence with לְךָ and not with וַאֲגַדְּלָה. A Hebrew imperative followed by an imperative merely shows a logical sequence of commands but does not mark emphatic consequence, purpose, or result as do other sequences of volitives.[16] This analysis alleviates the problem in a possibly difficult text. An imperative of the verb "to be" is not in itself problematic or singular in attestation.[17]

As the outline shows, God's six promises to Abram are arranged in two groups of three: (1) the first group of three promises blessing for Abram as an individual—he will develop into a great nation, be blessed, and be given a great name; (2) the second group of three promises blessing (or cursing) for the nations of the world through their relation to Abram. As biblical history unfolds, we will see what this means: the creator God's world has been broken and ruined by human pride and rebellion. God intends to use Abram and his family as the instrument of rescuing and restoring his broken creation.

Bruce Waltke in his magisterial *An Old Testament Theology* describes the call of Abraham this way: "God makes seven promises to Abraham pertaining to the irruption of his kingdom."[18] God's command "accompanied by seven promises, pertains to three expanding horizons that *en nuce* present God's salvific program."[19] The expanding horizons are pictured in concentric circles beginning with Abraham in the first circle (2000 B.C.), the nation of Israel in the second (1400 B.C.), and then all families (present day). The description of a sevenfold promise is an unfortunate mistake. It misses and obscures the literary structure which divides the promises into two foci, an aspect corresponding directly to the later distinct and

---

[15] Paul R. Williamson, *Sealed with an Oath: Covenant in God's Unfolding Purpose*, NSBT 23 (Downers Grove, IL: InterVarsity Press, 2007), 78–79.
[16] On the meaning of different sequences of Hebrew volitives, see Thomas O. Lambdin, *Introduction to Biblical Hebrew* (New York: Charles Scribner's Sons, 1971), § 107; Allen P. Ross, *Introducing Biblical Hebrew* (Grand Rapids, MI: Baker, 2001), § 20.7; Paul Joüon, *Grammaire de l'hébreu biblique* (Rome: Biblical Institute Press, 1923), § 116.
[17] For הְיֵה: Exodus 18:19; 1 Samuel 18:17; Isaiah 33:2; Psalm 30:11; 31:3; 71:3; Ecclesiastes 7:14; for וֶהְיֵה: Genesis 17:1; Exodus 24:12; 34:2; Judges 17:10; 18:19.
[18] Waltke, *Old Testament Theology*, 149.
[19] Ibid., 314.

double foci of chapters 15 and 17. Furthermore, "the expanding horizons" obscure the fact that there is a twofold, not threefold structure. God blesses Abraham, and the nations in relation to Abraham (singular). The picture of concentric circles in three stages is not part of this text.

The promises given to Abram as an individual focus on nationhood, blessing, and a great name. First, Abram will become a great nation. Now, you cannot have a great nation without land, without territory, without a place for a large number of people to live and call home. So the idea of land is implied in this promise, and the Lord makes this explicit in verse 7: "The LORD appeared to Abram and said, 'To your offspring I will give this land.'" The promise of land is also implicit in the first command: "Go from your country!" One cannot become a great nation and inhabit territory without first becoming distinct from the land and nation where one starts out. The confirmation and promise of land or territory for the future nation in verse 7 is in a chiastic structure showing Abram's response to the divine promises. On either side of the confirmation by divine revelation in verse 7 is the obedience and worship of Abraham. Verses 8 and 9 speak of Abram building an altar and calling out in the name of Yahweh and pitching his tent. The altar and the tent characterise Abram's activities in Canaan. Note that the altar is mentioned only in connection with sojourning in Canaan (Gen. 12:7, 8; 13:4, 18; 22:9 [2x]). There is no altar during his sojourns in Egypt or in Gerar; only half-truths, lies, and troubles. We saw above that Canaan is depicted in Edenic language as a mountain sanctuary. Now we see Abram fulfilling *an Adamic role*: he offers sacrifice as a priest and worships God in this mountain sanctuary. The only occurrence of the word "altar" prior to Genesis 12 is in Genesis 8:20 where Noah, the second Adam, offers sacrifice to the Lord after the judgement of the flood. This reinforces the activity of Abraham as last Adam in his role of offering sacrifice in the mountain sanctuary of Canaan. The tent simply emphasises that the fulfilment of the promises and the permanent situation has not yet arrived.[20]

The second promise given to Abram as an individual is blessing. As the

---

[20] After writing this section I came across arguments by Alexander that Abraham functions as a priest. In addition to what I have noted, he states, "Abraham encounters God on various occasions and receives divine communications (Gen. 12:1–3; 13:14–17; 15:1, 4–5, 7, 9, 13–16, 18–21; 17:1–22; 18:1–33; 21:12–13; 22:1, 12, 15–18). His special relationship with God suggests he enjoys a status equivalent to that of a priest, although he is never designated as one" (T. Desmond Alexander, *From Eden to the New Jerusalem* [Grand Rapids, MI: Kregel, 2008], 83). While I agree fully with the last sentence, the fact that Abraham receives communications from God could also be construed to show that he is a prophet (cf. Gen. 20:7).

narrative unfolds, we will see what blessing means and will return again to this topic. The third promise is that God will make Abram's name great. There are possible royal overtones to this promise, as Bill Arnold notes:

> Yahweh will make Abram's name "great," which is more than a promise of renown or acclaim. Rather, in contrast to the tower-builders at Babel, who pathetically strove for permanence themselves by building a name in their own strength (11:4), to have a great name given to one by God in the Hebrew Scriptures is to be viewed as a royal figure (2 Sam 7:9).[21]

Arnold is right. The promise to Abram is similar to the one given to David when God makes a covenant with him: "Now I will make your name great, like the names of the greatest men of the earth" (2 Sam. 7:9).[22] This fits with the clear and direct reference to kings coming from Abraham and Sarah (Gen. 17:6, 16). It also matches the fact that Abram is a royal figure due to his Adamic role. As Alexander notes, Abram is never called a king, but the King of Gerar treats him as an equal, the inhabitants of Hebron designate him a "prince of God" (Gen. 23:6), and his military exploits in Genesis 14 place him on a par with kings.[23]

Genesis 14, in fact, presents a surprising figure, Melchizedek, who is a king-priest, and the narrator describes Abram as identifying with him. The events of Genesis 14 are important to the depiction of Abram and his role as "king-priest." The narrative introduces four major rulers of the east: Amraphel, king of Shinar; Arioch, king of Ellasar; Chedorlaomer, king of Elam; and Tidal, king of Goiim. These kings come to punish Canaanite rulers who have refused to pay the required tribute exacted in conquests fourteen years earlier. They defeat various groups, including five kings ruling cities in the plain south of the Dead Sea: Bera, king of Sodom; Birsha, king of Gomorrah; Shinab, king of Admah; Shemeber, king of Zeboiim, and the unnamed king of Bela, that is, Zoar. The defeat involves the abduction of Lot, who by this time was living in Sodom. Abram stages a dramatic rescue, attacking the four kings at night with only 318 men from his household and his Amorite allies, Mamre, Aner, and Eschol. As Abram returns from his

---

[21] Bill T. Arnold, *Genesis* (Cambridge: Cambridge University Press, 2009), 132.

[22] I am indebted to Stephen Kempf for drawing my attention to this. We may also note that "the men of reknown" (אַנְשֵׁי הַשֵּׁם) in Genesis 6:4 have been considered kings by some scholars (see Waltke with Fredricks, *Genesis: A Commentary*, 115–118.

[23] For further development of this theme in Genesis, see T. Desmond Alexander, "The Regal Dimension of the תּוֹלְדוֹת־יַעֲקֹב: Recovering the Literary Context of Genesis 37–50," in *Reading the Law: Studies in Honour of Gordon J. Wenham*, ed. J. G. McConville and Karl Möller, Library of Hebrew Bible/Old Testament Studies 461 (New York: T. & T. Clark, 2007), 254–266.

victory over the four kings, he is met by two kings: the king of Sodom and the king of Salem (= Jerusalem):

[17] After Abram returned from defeating Kedorlaomer and the kings allied with him, the king of Sodom came out to meet him in the Valley of Shaveh (that is, the King's Valley).
[18] Then Melchizedek king of Salem brought out bread and wine. He was priest of God Most High, [19] and he blessed Abram, saying,

"Blessed be Abram by God Most High,
   Creator of heaven and earth.
[20] And blessed be God Most High,
who delivered your enemies into your hand."

Then Abram gave him a tenth of everything.
[21] The king of Sodom said to Abram, "Give me the people and keep the goods for yourself."
[22] But Abram said to the king of Sodom, "I have raised my hand to the LORD, God Most High, Creator of heaven and earth, and have taken an oath [23] that I will accept nothing belonging to you, not even a thread or the thong of a sandal, so that you will never be able to say, 'I made Abram rich.' [24] I will accept nothing but what my men have eaten and the share that belongs to the men who went with me—to Aner, Eshcol and Mamre. Let them have their share." (Gen. 14:17–24, NIV)

The two kings represent two different types of kingship.[24] The king of Sodom represents the notion that one acquires goods and rules by might: might makes right. It is the normal pattern of kingship in Canaan—an absolute ruler uses his position to aggrandise himself. Melchizedek, king of Salem, represents a different kind of kingship. He acknowledges a supreme God who is Creator/ Possessor of everything. Therefore all rule must acknowledge the sovereignty of the Most High God and must consider that everything one owns is a gift from him. He is a servant of the Most High God; his kingship is based on the *worship* of this God. Abram does three things: (1) he identifies the Most High God as Yahweh, (2) he gives a tenth to Melchizedek, and (3) he refuses to accept from the king of Sodom any of the goods which are his by right as the spoils of war. In other words, he identifies with the kind of king-

---

[24] For this discussion I am indebted to J. Gordon McConville, "Abraham and Melchizedek: Horizons in Genesis 14," in *He Swore an Oath: Biblical Themes from Genesis 12–50*, ed. R. S. Hess, G. J. Wenham, and P. E. Satterthwaite, 2nd ed. (Cambridge: Tyndale House, 1993, 1994), 93–118; and T. Desmond Alexander, *From Eden to the New Jerusalem*, 80–83.

priest rule that Melchizedek represents. Abram is thus adopting a king-priest role originally given to Adam and now given to him.

The second group of three promises offer blessing (or cursing) for the nations of the world through their relation to Abram (and his family). First, God promises to bless those (plural) who bless Abram. Second, the same promise is stated negatively: God will curse the one who slights or treats Abram lightly. Then, in a summary statement, Abram is told that all the clans of the earth would be blessed through him. Blessing both begins the three promises and ends them. Note also that God will bless the ones who bless Abram but will curse the one who treats him lightly. Why the shift from plural to singular? God is hoping that there will be *many* who bless and *few* who curse Abram. The shift from plural to singular emphasises the generosity of God in his plan of rescuing and saving a world that has reverted to chaos and death.

Debate exists concerning the last promise, "in you all the clans of the earth will be blessed." The exact function of the *niphal* form of the verb *brk* ("bless") is in question. Two main options are advanced by scholars. One construes the *niphal* form as passive (i.e., in you all the clans of the earth will be blessed); the other reckons the *niphal* form to be reflexive (i.e., in you all the clans of the earth will bless themselves). Both options are grammatically possible. The *niphal* form of *brk* ("bless") is found elsewhere in the Hebrew Bible only two times (Gen. 18:18; 28:14), both reiterations of the promise in Genesis 12:3. What exacerbates the debate is that two further iterations of the promise in Genesis are constructed with a *hithpael* form of *brk* ("bless"; Gen. 22:18; 26:4) and another two allusions or echoes of Genesis 12:3 elsewhere are also constructed with the *hithpael* form of the verb (Ps. 72:17; Jer. 4:2). Only three instances of the *hithpael* form of *brk* occur in the Hebrew Bible, which are entirely independent of Genesis 12:3 (Deut. 29:19; Isa. 65:16 [2x]).

The *hithpael* form in itself may function to indicate a passive, reflexive, reciprocal, or a middle (involving speech action, it may be rendered "utter a blessing"). The passive function is relatively infrequent. There may be strong temptation to argue from the instances of the *hithpael*, and especially from the occurrences outside Genesis which are not allusions to or reiterations of Genesis 12:3, that the instances in the *niphal* form should be considered reflexive as well, and that the traditional interpretation as passive as reflected by the Septuagint and New Testament (cf. Acts 3:25; Gal. 3:8) be abandoned. Another approach is to argue that the *niphal* forms and *hithpael* forms have distinct meanings.

Williamson argues against interpretation of the *niphal* forms as reflexive, while allowing the *hithpael* forms their primary reflexive force, as follows:

> . . . the fact that the promises are explicitly related to the person of Abraham rather than to his name constitutes a serious problem for those who wish to interpret the verb reflexively. A further difficulty is that the context antici- pates that the nations will participate in Israel's blessing (in v. 3a, what is expected to be the norm is expressed by the plural); thus merely *wishing* for such blessing would be 'decidedly anti-climactic' (Dumbrell 1984: 70). Moreover, an exclusively reflexive interpretation of this text would appear to be exclusively ruled out also by the related texts in which the niphal is employed. This is most transparent in Genesis 18:18, where a statement concerning a mere wish expressed by other nations would hardly explain Abraham's international significance. It seems unlikely, therefore, that these occurrences of the niphal form of *brk* should be interpreted reflex- ively, despite the presence of the hitpael in Genesis 22:18 and Genesis 26:4. But how then are these occurrences of the hitpael to be explained?
>
> One plausible way to account for the latter is by giving the niphal a 'middle' sense (i.e. 'win/find blessing'). This translation has the advantage of incorporating both a passive and reflexive meaning, which may help explain why the compiler of Genesis allowed both forms of the verb to stand unaltered in the final text. Moreover, if a middle rather than a passive sense were intended, this would also explain why the more common pas- sive verb forms (qal passive participle or pual) of *brk* were not employed. Furthermore, as Dumbrell (1984: 71) correctly points out, 'Such a sense would also be more congruent with the general Old Testament position on mission, whereby the nations are consistently presented as seekers, coming in to a reconstituted Israel.'
>
> However, even if the niphal does carry this idea of 'to find blessing', this still leaves unexplained the distribution of the two forms of *brk* in the relevant texts. Why is the niphal used in Genesis 12:3, Genesis 18:18 and Genesis 28:14, but the hitpael in Genesis 22:18 and Genesis 26:4? Rather than assuming that the final editor used these different verb forms arbi- trarily, or was somehow reluctant to impose uniformity on his text because of underlying source material, it is worth examining more closely how the niphal and hitpael are used in these particular texts. A close compari- son suggests that, rather than being used synonymously, each verb form has a distinct nuance (Williamson 2000a; 227–228). Where the niphal is deployed, a less direct situation is implied: the one through whom the nations will acquire blessing is Abraham (or in the case of Gen. 28:14, primarily Jacob). In contrast, in contexts where the hitpael is found, the

channel of blessing is the promised 'seed' through whom the anticipated blessing will be communicated directly (cf. Ps. 72:17; Jer 4:2). Thus the hitpael form of the promise may be understood as action done on one's own behalf (i.e. a 'benefactive reflexive', *IBHS*, §26.2e) and translated as 'in your seed all the nations of the earth will acquire blessing for themselves', whereas the niphal may be understood as middle, 'through you all the families of the earth will experience blessing'.[25]

Williamson's arguments against a reflexive value for the *niphal* forms are cogent and sound. His proposition that the choice of the form of the verb is probably not arbitrary is also valid. Nonetheless, the notion that in the instances of the *niphal* the blessing is communicated less directly than in the instances of the *hithpael* is less than satisfying and flounders on the fact that the "seed" is part of the proposition in Genesis 28:14, despite the caveat of Williamson.

The analysis of Lee is better and moreover is, in general, backed up by the exhaustive and exhausting study by Keith N. Grüneberg on Genesis 12:3 and its reiterations in the Old Testament. Lee says,

> I take the Niphal to be passive ("they shall be blessed") and the Hitpael to be estimative-declarative reflexive ("they shall declare themselves as blessed") for the following reasons. First, although there is definitely a semantic overlap between the pairs of words (התברכו/נברכו, ארץ/אדמה, גוי/משפחה) in Gen 12:3b and its reiterations, it can be established that the variations are intentional and bear a slight difference in nuance. For example, משפחה אדמה [sic] is used in Gen 12:3b as a link to Genesis 1–11, especially to Genesis 10–11. משפחה occurs five times in Genesis 10, of which it occurs four times together with גוי, portraying how each clan of people eventually evolved into a nation. It is also used in Gen 28:14 as an *inclusio* to Gen 12:3b. To show further the continuity of the later reiterations of this blessing with the Table of Nations (Genesis 10), Gen 18:18; 22:18; 26:4 use גויי הארץ instead of משפחת האדמה. As גוי carries strong political overtones, it is therefore natural to use it with ארץ, which has stronger political connotations than אדמה. Second, the patriarchal narrative repeatedly portrays how other people are blessed or cursed by God on account of Abraham and his descendants (examples include Abimelech, Laban, Potiphar, Pharaoh, and Egypt). Furthermore, Laban declared himself as blessed by God due to Jacob (Gen 30:27). Nowhere in the narrative do we see people actively seeking blessing for themselves by their association with Abraham or invoking his name as a formula and paradigm of blessing as a middle or direct reflexive reading

---

would entail. Therefore the passive Niphal and the estimative-declarative Hitpael best fit the context of Genesis. This understanding of the force of the Niphal and the Hitpael is essential to our understanding of how the motif of the blessing for the nations is developed later.[26]

As in the case of Williamson, Lee's arguments against a reflexive *niphal* are also cogent, but his explanation of the motivation for using either *hithpael* or *niphal* better suits the contextual and linguistic data in the text of Genesis. We conclude, then, the *niphal* forms are passive ("they shall be blessed") and the *hithpael* are estimative-declarative reflexive ("they shall consider/ declare themselves as blessed").[27]

BLESSING

In the first three verses of Genesis 12 the word "blessing" occurs five times. As Dumbrell notes, the choice and use of the term is doubtless deliberate, playing upon the notion of the power of the word. His comment is apt:

> In Gen. 12:2a God blesses Abram and here the notion of blessing is bound up with nationhood and fame. As a result Abram is thus to be the embodi- ment of blessing, the example of what blessing should be (v. 2b). God will bless those who rightly recognize the source of Abram's blessing (3a), and then finally in 12:3b Abram becomes the mediator of blessing for mankind.[28]

What is actually meant by "blessing"? Blessing is connected with life, just as cursing brings death. So what would blessing mean in the ancient Near East in Abraham's time? Does "blessing" mean a full, long life, the good life in the sense of having good health, having a big family to look after one as a senior, business success (i.e., having big flocks and herds or crops that are abundant and successful), acquiring land, having power and vic- tory over your enemies? If we convert these ideas into our modern society, what would blessing mean? Does blessing mean health, business success,

---

[26] Chee-Chiew Lee, "גוים in Genesis 35:11 and the Abrahamic Promise of Blessing for the Nations," *JETS* 52/3 (2009): 472.

[27] Moberly interprets the *niphals* in light of the *hithpaels* in Genesis 22:18 and 26:4; see R. W. L. Moberly, *The Bible, Theology, and Faith: Abraham and Jesus* (Cambridge Studies in Christian Doctrine 5; Cambridge: Cam- bridge University Press, 2000). Moberly is followed by Joel N. Lohr, *Chosen and Unchosen: Conceptions of Election in the Pentateuch and Jewish-Christian Interpretation* (Shiphrut 2; Winona Lake, IN: Eisenbrauns, 2009), 113. Moberly's analysis is rejected by his student Keith N. Grüneberg, *Abraham, Blessing, and the Nations: A Philological and Exegetical Study of Genesis 12:3 in Its Narrative Context* (Berlin: Walter de Gruyter, 2003), who distinguishes *niphal* meaning from *hithpael* in these texts. Nonetheless, the analysis of Lee (supra) is superior.

[28] Dumbrell, *Covenant and Creation*, 67–68.

being surrounded by a circle of friends (on *Facebook*?), having influence and power, having a big house and car, having better sex?

Bruce Waltke explains that "the term 'to bless' (*brk*) with God as subject denotes procreative largesse and victory, accompanied with a sense of loyalty to the future generations (Gen. 1:28; 26:24; 27:27–29)."[29] Significantly, however, he adds that "it also connotes redemption, a relationship with God that transforms the beneficiary and provides security."[30] Dumbrell noted this important aspect too. As Abraham's life unfolds, we begin to see what blessing means. Blessing operates in the context of a covenant relationship with God. Blessings are the manifestation of a faithfulness, fidelity, and solidarity in relationships whereby one's natural and personal capacity to fulfill God's intention and purpose is advanced and furthered.[31] God's word to Abram is powerful, enabling the calling to be fulfilled.

CURSE AND BLESSING

In our study of Genesis 12:1–3 we just noted that the word "blessing" occurs five times in that text (Gen. 12:2 [2x], 3 [3x]). What is interesting and noteworthy is that the antonym "curse" (*'ārar*) occurs precisely five times in Genesis 1–11 (3:14; 3:17; 4:11; 5:29; 9:25). H. W. Wolff has pointed out the significance of the curse in Genesis 1–11.[32] The curse in 3:14 brought the loss of freedom and power as well as certain defeat and humiliation (for the serpent). In 3:17 the curse effected an alienation between humans and the soil. Further, in 4:11, Cain was cursed from the land, resulting in estrangement from human society as he became a nomad and wanderer. Noah's curse of Canaan brought further degradation and shame, as Canaan was to be the lowest of slaves. Cumulative deprivation and increasing loss is therefore associated with the word "curse," bringing man from Eden to Babel. The fivefold repetition of the word "blessing" in Genesis 12:1–3 indicates that the call of Abram will change this situation: broken relationships are to be potentially and progressively repaired. The ruptured relationships that had developed between man and God and man and man are to be eventually restored. The new powerful word calling Abram out of Ur is to annul the curse of chapters 1–11.

There is, then, in Genesis 12:1–3 a causal relationship between the first

---

[29] Waltke, *Old Testament Theology*, 316.
[30] Ibid.
[31] See Dumbrell, *Covenant and Creation*, 68.
[32] H. W. Wolff, "The Kerygma of the Yahwist," *Interpretation* 20 (1966): 131–158.

group of three promises and the second group of three promises. God's plan to bless Abram and his family is a means to bring blessing and salvation to all the nations.[33] Paul House comments appropriately on the divine choice of Abram and the decision to bless him and his family: "Election here does not exclude or condemn anyone. Rather it works exclusively as a benefit to a world that has no intention of doing what is right."[34]

ABRAM AND THE CITY OF GOD

The call of Abram in Genesis 12:1–3 consists of two commands ("go" [v. 1] and "be" a blessing [v. 2]). Each command is followed by three promises. The first promise is, "I will make you into a great nation," and the last promise is "all the clans/families of the earth will be blessed in you" (12:1, 3). We need to pay attention to the terms used here to describe both the people of God and the other peoples of the world. God promises to make Abram into a great *nation*; this is the word *gôy* in Hebrew. The other people groups of the world are called *clans* or *families*; here the Hebrew term is *mišpāḥâ*.

First consider the term *gôy* or nation. It is highly unusual for this term to be applied to the people of God. There is in the language of the Old Testament a completely consistent usage: the word *'am* is almost always reserved for Israel. It is a *kinship* term which expresses effectively the closeness of the family/marriage relationship between God and Israel established by the covenant made at Sinai (Exodus 24). On the other hand, the word *gôy* is the standard term for the communities or other societies in the world excluding Israel. So consistent is this use, that when we see something different, we need to ask why. For example, there are instances where the term *gôy* is applied to Israel in a pejorative sense. Sometimes Israel is called "nation" and not "people" because the author may wish to communicate that because of her wickedness she is behaving as if she were *not* the people of God. Her actions and attitudes indicate she is like those communities who have no special status as the chosen people of God (e.g., Judg. 2:20).

Why, then, in Genesis 12 does God speak of Abram becoming a great *gôy* or nation? The basic meaning of *gôy* is an *organised* community of people having *governmental*, *political*, and *social structure*. This contrasts with the fact that the other nations are derogatorily termed *mišpāḥâ* in Genesis 12.

---

[33] One of my professors never understood this, citing the rhyme, "How odd of God to choose the Jews."
[34] Paul R. House, *Old Testament Theology* (Downers Grove, IL: InterVarsity Press, 1998), 73.

This word refers to an amorphous kin group larger than an extended family and smaller than a tribe.

The background of Genesis 12 is chapters 10 and 11. There we have the history of Babel (Genesis 11), where we see a complete confidence and naive optimism about human achievement and effort. Man is at the centre of his world, and he can achieve anything. This philosophy comes under divine judgement in Genesis 11 and results in the nations being lost and scattered over the face of the earth (Gen. 11:9 and chapter 10). By contrast, Genesis 12 presents a political structure brought into being by the word of God, with God at the centre and God as the governmental head and rule of that community. In other words, we have the kingdom of God brought into being by means of the covenant (i.e., the covenant between God and Abram). Hence, we have *kingdom through covenant*.

The promise in Genesis 12:3 is cited or quoted several times in later texts of the Old Testament. In Genesis 28:14 the nations of the world are also called *mišpāḥôt* to form an *inclusio* with Genesis 12:3 and mark off a literary section. In Genesis 18:18, 22:18, 26:4, Jeremiah 4:2, and Psalm 72:17, however, the five other texts directly referring to Genesis 12:3, the nations of the world are called by the more common and normal term, *gôyim*. This shows that the author has a real purpose in Genesis 12:3 in using the term *mišpāḥôt*: he wants to indicate that the kingdoms of this world will never amount to anything; only the kingdom of God will last forever. The author's choice of terms emphasises that the family of Abram is a real kingdom with eternal power and significance while the so-called kingdoms of this world are of no lasting power or significance.

This is backed up by the work of Eberhard Ruprecht, a German scholar, who has detected in the promises that the Lord made to Abram a royal ideology. What Abram is promised in Genesis 12 was the hope of many oriental monarchs (cf. 2 Sam. 7:9; Ps. 72:17).[35]

The word in Hellenistic Greek which best conveys this meaning is the term *polis* or "city." In our modern world we tend to think of cities as great centres of population in contrast to the rural areas which by definition are sparsely populated. In contrast to the modern notion, in the first century the term "city" conveyed the idea of an organised community with

---

[35] See Gordon J. Wenham, *Genesis 1–15*, WBC 1 (Waco, TX: Word, 1987), 275; and Eberhard Ruprecht, "Vorgegebene Tradition und Theologische Gestaltung in Genesis XII 1–3," *Vetus Testamentum* 29 (1979): 171–188; and idem, "Der Traditionsgeschictliche Hintergrund der Einzelnen Elemente von Genesis XII 2–3," *Vetus Testamentum* 29 (1979): 444–464.

governmental headship and appropriate political and social structure—what we normally convey by the English word *state*. Thus the promises of God to Abram really did entail the *city of God*, and the author to the Hebrews is accurately explaining for his readers the author's intended meaning in Genesis 12. Abraham was to go to a country God would indicate to him and reside there—even if as an alien and a stranger: he was awaiting "the city that has foundations, whose architect and builder is God" (Heb. 11:10).

In Genesis 15 and 17 the great promises to Abram will be enshrined in a divine-human covenant between God and Abraham. For now, in chapter 12, we note that although the context, expressions, idioms, and language are completely different from the creation narrative and the image of God in Genesis 1:26–28, the *ideas* are identical. Abram (and the nation that comes from him) constitutes an *Adamic* figure, indeed the last Adam, since there are no major new starts after this. God intends to establish his rule over all his creation through his relationship with Abram and his family: kingdom through covenant. Through blessing Abram and his descendants, the broken relationship between God and all the nations of the world will be reconciled and healed. As we will soon see, the covenant entails not only a relationship with God that can be described as sonship, but also a relationship to the rest of creation that entails kingship in establishing the rule of God.

Chapter Eight

THE COVENANT WITH ABRAHAM (II)

INTRODUCTION: SUMMARY OF THE LARGER STORY TO THIS POINT

The larger story of Scripture begins with a creator God who is the maker of our world and all that is in it. Humans are the crown of his work. There is a difference, moreover, between human creatures and all other creatures: we alone have been made as the image of this creator God, resulting in a covenant relationship with God and with all creation that entails a particular role and special tasks in the world. The first humans, however, rebelled against the creator God. As a result, there is chaos and discord in the creation at every level, bringing destruction and death.

The destructive path chosen by the first humans led continually downward until divine intervention was required. God judged the human race and made a new beginning with Noah and his family. Noah is portrayed as a new Adam. As soon as the dry land appears out of the chaos of waters, Noah is placed there and commanded to be fruitful and multiply (Gen. 9:1); i.e., he is given Adam's commission or mandate. Eventually, however, the family of Noah ends up in the same chaos and corruption as the family of the first Adam.

So God makes another new start, with Abram and his family. Abraham and his family, called Israel, is another Adam, who will be God's true humanity. Israel is, in fact, the last Adam because there will be no major new starts for the human race from this point. Israel will display to the rest of the world within its covenant community the kind of relationships—first to God and then to one another, as well as stewardship of the ecosystem—that God originally intended for all of humanity. In fact, through Abraham's family God plans to bring blessing to all the nations of the world. In this way, through the family of Abraham, through Israel, his last Adam, he will bring about a resolution of the sin and death caused by the first Adam. The fact that the blessing to the nations through Abraham and his family included dealing with the sin and death caused by the first Adam is not *plainly* stated until much later, such as in the passages relating to the Suffering Servant in Isaiah (Isa. 42:1–9; 49:1–13; 50:4–9; 52:13–53:12).

Key Points in the Abraham Narratives
1. The Giving of the Promise: the Call of Abram (Genesis 12)
2. Making the Covenant: the Promise of Descendants and Land (Genesis 15)
3. Confirming the Covenant: the Sign of Circumcision (Genesis 17)
4. Abraham's Obedience and Confirmation of the Promises by Oath (Genesis 22)

We have considered the call of Abram and the promises given to him, recorded in Genesis 12. Now, in Genesis 15, the divine promises are enshrined in a covenant between Yahweh and Abram that is confirmed and upheld in Genesis 17. We need to trace the development of the covenant relationship between God and Abram and the progress of Abram's faithfulness and love in this relationship.

THE MAKING OF THE COVENANT (PROMISE OF DESCENDANTS AND LAND)—GENESIS 15

The literary structure of Genesis 15 is clear. The text is divided in half, and each half has an identical pattern and structure. First, the Lord reveals himself to Abram (by vision) and makes promises. Second, Abram responds in complaint, asking about the fulfilment of God's promises. Third, God expands and extends his revelation a second time, confirming and reiterating his promises. Each half, then, has a (chiastic) tripartite structure in which the first and last parts are matching. The promises in the first half are centred on the gift of descendants; the promises in the second half are centred on the gift of land. The covenant, therefore, enshrines the promises given in Genesis 12, with a focus on fulfilment of the first three promises in Genesis 12:1–3, i.e., a focus on the divine promises particularly to Abram himself.

Outline of Genesis 15

Part 1—Seed/descendants	15:1–6
A God reveals himself and makes promises	1
B Abram's complaint and question	2–3
A' God's revelation and confirmation	4–6

Part 2—Land   15:7–21
A   God reveals himself and makes promises   7
B   Abram's complaint and question   8
A' God's revelation and confirmation   9–21

Genesis 15 begins with the words "after these things," referring to the victory over the four kings from the east recorded in chapter 14. Thus, sometime following the defeat of these kings, Yahweh communicates to Abram by means of a vision. The translation in the King James Version, followed by such newer versions as the NKJV and NIV, can be greatly improved at this point. The KJV rendering is as follows:

> After these things the word of the LORD came unto Abram in a vision, saying, Fear not, Abram: I *am* thy shield, *and* thy exceeding great reward. (Gen. 15:1)

First, the italicised "am" indicates a verbless clause in Hebrew, and the italicised "and" denotes a word not in the original text. The KJV construes as one verbless clause with "I" as subject and "thy shield" and "thy exceeding great reward" as the predicate. This is not a likely or plausible reading of the Hebrew text. The fact that "and" is not in the text signals a new, separate verbless clause in which "your reward" is subject and "very great" is the predicate. The lack of a clause connector (asyndeton) is not unusual in such a sequence of nominal sentences. God commands Abram not to be afraid. This is backed up by two statements: (1) God will protect him, and (2) God will reward him. Both the command and the promises relate directly to the events of chapter 14. Will the "Four Big Bad Guys from the East" be back next year to take their vengeance on Abram? Certainly the fear of reprisal is both real and significant. Yahweh will be Abram's shield. He will protect Abram from possible reprisal. Second, at the end of Genesis 14, Abram took none of the spoils of the victory which were his by right. He wanted his sources of wealth to come from the Lord and not from the king of Sodom. So Yahweh promises Abram that he will reward him. He is not saying that he, Yahweh, is Abram's reward instead of the spoils of victory. He is saying that he will give something to Abram that will compensate for the fact that he took none of these spoils. That this is the correct interpretation is clear from Abram's response. He says, "What will you *give* me?" not "How will you be my reward?" Abram is exasperated: Yahweh has made big promises, but

Abram is anxiously waiting for the beginning of this great nation to reveal itself by the birth of at least *one baby*.

Yahweh responds to Abram's complaint with another night revelation. Asking Abram to count the stars, if he is able, he promises that Abram's descendants will be as numerous as the sand on the seashore or the stars of the night sky. At this point, all the Lord is doing is repeating the promise in grandiose terms. Yet Abram is hanging on to this. Verse six could be rendered, "Now Abram *was believing* in Yahweh and he credited it to him as righteousness." K. A. Mathews correctly describes the discourse grammar involved:

> The syntax of the verb *wĕhe'ĕmin* diverts from the typical pattern found in past tense narrative. The force of the construction conveys an ongoing faith repeated from the past. The author is editorializing on the events reported, not including Abram's faith in the chain of events as a consequence of the theophanic message.[1]

Thus Genesis 15:6 reports that Abram is, as a general rule, still strapped into the roller-coaster and hanging on to his ride of faith.

An alternative view is that the *waw*-consecutive perfect *wĕhe'ĕmin*, due to its imperfective aspect, marks prominence pragmatically and so indicates something such as the climax in the narrative sequence.[2] Following this view, 15:6 would be the climax of the sequence in Genesis 15:1–6. Dumbrell speaks of Abram's act/attitude as a response of further trust.[3]

Verse 7 begins the second half of Genesis 15, and again Yahweh communicates to Abram, repeating the promise of land made clear and explicit in Genesis 12:7. Again, Abram is exasperated: How will he know for sure that this promise will be fulfilled? So far in his experience, there is no evidence of its reality. Again Yahweh repeats his promise, but he does so by enshrining it within a covenant.

The ceremony or ritual described here is somewhat strange. Nonetheless,

[1] Kenneth A. Mathews, *Genesis 11:27–50:26*, New American Commentary 1B (Nashville: B&H, 2005), 166–167.
[2] Cf. Robert E. Longacre, "Analysis of Preverbal Nouns in Biblical Hebrew Narrative," *Journal of Translation and Textlinguistics* 5/3 (1992): 218; and idem, "*Weqatal* Forms in Biblical Hebrew Prose," in *Biblical Hebrew and Discourse Linguistics*, ed. Robert D. Bergen (Dallas: SIL, 1994), 50–98. It is also possible to construe the *weqatal* form as a variant of the preterite *wayyiqtol*; see Rudolf Meyer, "Auffallender Erzählungstil in einem angeblichen Auszug aus der 'Chronik der Könige von Juda'," in *Festschrift Friedrich Baumgärtel zum 70. Geburstag*, ed. J. Herrmann and L. Rost (Erlangen, Germany: Universitätsbund Erlangen, 1959), 115–122; and Stephen G. Dempster, "Linguistic Features of Hebrew Narrative: A Discourse Analysis of Narrative from the Classical Period" (PhD diss., University of Toronto, 1985), 266.
[3] William J. Dumbrell, *Covenant and Creation: A Theology of the Old Testament Covenants* (Carlisle, UK: Paternoster, 1984), 54.

as verse 18 clearly states, this ceremony formalises a covenant between God and Abram. The normal or standard terminology "to cut a covenant" (*kārat bĕrît*) is used. The interpretation of this mysterious rite is much discussed. The ceremony of covenant making involves an oath in which the covenant partners bring the curse of death upon themselves if they are not faithful to the covenant relationship and promises. Walking between the animals cut in half is a way of saying, "May I become like these dead animals if I do not keep my promise(s) and my oath." Scholars describe this as a self-maledictory oath, i.e., an oath where one brings the curse of death upon oneself for violating the covenant commitments. The detail with which covenant making ceremonies are narrated varies from text to text. The covenant making in Jeremiah 34:18–20 is also explicit about walking between the pieces of the animal sacrificed for the rite:

> [18] The men who have violated my covenant and have not fulfilled the terms of the covenant they made before me, I will treat like the calf they cut in two and then walked between its pieces. [19] The leaders of Judah and Jerusalem, the court officials, the priests and all the people of the land who walked between the pieces of the calf, [20] I will hand over to their enemies who seek their lives. Their dead bodies will become food for the birds of the air and the beasts of the earth. (NIV)

In the vision given to Abram, a "smoking firepot and a blazing torch" pass between the dead pieces. What would these represent? When we remember that Genesis was a book given to the Israelite people at the time of entering the land of Canaan, we can see from that perspective, i.e., after the exodus event, that smoke and fire are symbols of God's presence. The angel of the Lord first appeared to Moses in the flames of a burning bush (Ex. 3:2). During the desert journey, God appears as cloud and fire (Ex. 13:21). At Mount Sinai, his presence is manifested by smoke and fire (Ex. 19:18; 20:18). The fact that only God passes between the pieces is quite remarkable and shows that the promise depends upon him and him alone.

There may, however, be more to this mysterious rite than that. One commentator, Gordon Wenham, stirred my thinking with the following questions:

> While this interpretation could explain the phrase, "to cut a covenant," it leaves many features of this rite unexplained. It does not explain the choice of these particular animals. Why are only sacrificial types selected? Why must they be three years old? Why are the birds not cut up? Why

does Abram drive off the birds of prey? Finally it must be asked whether a divine self-imprecation is really likely. Is it compatible with OT theology for God to say "May I die, if I do not keep my word"? Divine oaths generally take the form, "As I live, says the LORD" (cf. Num. 14:21).[4]

Wenham further notes that every kind of clean, sacrificial animal used in Israel's worship was involved. He suggests that the animals represent Israel. The birds of prey represent the attacks of foreign nations. Abram defends his descendants against foreign attackers. Similarly, Gideon sacrificed a seven-year-old bull to represent the seven years of Midianite oppression (Judg. 6:1, 25). Later on, the deliverance of the exodus is explained as God keeping his oath to Abraham (Ex. 2:24; Deut. 9:5). The animals are three years old, representing the three generations spent in Egypt. The fire and smoke passing between the animal halves represents God walking in the midst of his people (Lev. 26:12).[5]

Recent scholarship has backed away from viewing the ceremony as a self-maledictory oath. Correlation of the rite in Genesis 15 with the rite in Jeremiah 34 led some to date the Genesis narrative to Jeremiah's time rather than the period appropriate to the patriarchs (c. 2000 B.C.). Significant articles by G. Hasel and R. Hess have attempted to show that the account in Genesis 15 corresponds better to cultural evidence known from second millennium B.C. texts than the neo-Assyrian and Aramaic treaties of the first millennium.[6] This attempt is only partially fruitful as the data has become somewhat skewed in the ensuing exegesis. Hasel claims, "Jer 34:18–19, however, is definite and clear on one point: Only one covenanting party, namely, 'the princes of Judah, the princes of Jerusalem, the eunuchs, the priests, and all the people of the land' (vs 19) passed between the parts of the cut bull-calf. The similarity between Jer 34:18–19 and Gen 15:17 rests in the fact that in each case one party passed between the pieces." Unfortunately, Hasel is entirely mistaken. The only parties making the treaty in Jeremiah 34:8–22 are the persons listed in verse 19. This was not a covenant made *between* these parties and God. It was a covenant made by these parties *before* God (34:15), and in failing to release their slaves they have violated the Mosaic

---

[4] Gordon J. Wenham, *Genesis 1–15*, WBC 1 (Waco, TX: Word, 1987), 332.

[5] Wenham, *Genesis 1–15*, 333.

[6] See Gerhard F. Hasel, "The Meaning of the Animal Rite in Genesis 15," *JSOT* 19 (1981): 61–78; and Richard S. Hess, "The Slaughter of the Animals in Genesis 15: Genesis 15:8–21 and Its Ancient Near Eastern Context," in *He Swore an Oath: Biblical Themes from Genesis 12–50*, ed. R. S. Hess, G. J. Wenham, and P. E. Satterthwaite, 2nd ed. (Cambridge: Tyndale House, 1993, 1994), 55–65.

covenant. It is the Mosaic covenant that is between the people and God. That is the clear meaning of verse 18. So in Jeremiah 34 all the parties making the treaty pass between the pieces and in Genesis 15 only God passes between the pieces. The slaves may have been beneficiaries of the covenant made by the leaders and the people, but they were not parties to the covenant. Mathews' recent commentary is an excellent example of research that builds on the recent studies by Hasel and Hess, but like them ends up "throwing the baby out with the bathwater."

It is necessary and useful to cite Mathews in full and to critique this confusion of the data in important texts dealing with covenants:

> The word "pieces" (*beter*) appears in the similar ritual described in Jer 34:18–19. Often scholars appropriate the rite of Jeremiah 34 as the template for explaining the practice in Genesis 15. Two wordplays describe the practice in Jeremiah. A calf was "cut" (*kārat*, v. 18) into pieces, formalizing a covenant that was "cut" ("made," NIV, i.e., "to cut a covenant," *kārat běrît*) between God and the leadership of Judah regarding the freeing of Hebrew slaves. Because they acted treacherously, the people are deemed "transgressors" (*hā 'ōběrîm*, NIV "the men who have violated," v. 18) who had "walked between" (*hā 'ōběrîm*, v. 18) the parts signifying acceptance of the sanctions of transgressing the covenant. The threat of death, like the gruesome results of the slaughtered calf, awaited them (v. 18). The Lord threatens that "the birds [*'ôp*] of the air" will feast on the violaters' dead flesh (v. 20). This imprecatory aspect of the symbolic slaying has parallels with Assyrian and Aramaic vassal treaties of the first millennium. For this reason Genesis 15 is usually dated at the time of Jeremiah or later.
>
> There are, however, significant differences between the practices in the patriarchal account and Jeremiah that make doubtful this conclusion. Although the Jeremiah passage involves the slaughter of a calf and mentions birds, the practice in chap. 15 calls for several animals. Also the description of the ritual cleaving in 15:10 uses the term *bātar* (NIV "cut in two") instead of Jeremiah's word *kārat* (NIV "made") occurring in the idiomatic expression "cut a covenant" (34:18). Also importantly, the threat of curse for failure to observe the covenant is not explicit in chap. 15. When read in light of Jeremiah 34's imprecatory character, it may be implied that God submits to his own self-imprecation by passing through the parts. It is difficult, however, to reconcile this idea of God theologically and impossible to explain how the imprecation could be carried out. More promising are the examples of second-millennium texts from Alalakh involving an oath by a superior that is confirmed by slaying a lamb or sheep. If the Abram incident compares to these promissory oaths, Genesis describes

a covenant pledge undertaken by God that is formally ratified by animal slaughter (cp. Exod 24:3–8).

There are still significant features of Genesis 15 that diverge from the oath rituals at Alalakh. The number and sort of animals and the halving procedure of chap. 15 have no parallel yet found in the ancient Near East. Although the rite of chap. 15 ostensibly affirms the covenant oath, the prophecy that follows (vv. 13–16) hints at an emblematic significance attached to the rite's peculiarities. From hindsight we know that the prophecy previews Israel's Egyptian bondage, exodus, and conquest. Most agree that the smoking firepot and burning torch represent the Lord, a picture corresponding to the pillar of cloud and pillar of fire indicating the presence of God in the wilderness (e.g., Exod 13:21–22). The "birds of prey" Abram disperses indicate a threat against the slaughtered animals. "Birds of prey ('*ayiṭ*) differ from the general terms for "birds" (*ṣippôr*, v. 10; '*ôp*, Jer 34:20) by their ravenous character (Isa 18:6; Jer 12:9) and are unclean. In the context of the prophecy (vv. 13–16), the animal portions represent Abram's descendants, and the birds of prey are the nation (Egypt) that enslaves them. The appearance of Abram as defender of the animal portions may refer to his obedient piety that confirmed his loyalty and ensured Israel's future (e.g., 22:16–18) or his intercessory function as prophet (e.g., 18:16–33; 20:7, 17). Since Abram does not walk through the pieces, he is not under obligation to the Lord to realize the promises. By the passing of the firepot through the severed pieces, the Lord's presence with enslaved Israel symbolically ensures the preservation and deliverance of Abram's descendants.[7]

An exhaustive analysis of all texts in the Old Testament dealing with covenants (such as the present study) reveals, first, that certain features of covenant making are constant throughout this period of time (2000–400 B.C.) alongside a changing typology of covenant documents and, second, that alongside the constant and standard features of covenant making, each instance may have its own peculiar variations. In addition, since the details of the rituals were considered by the authors to be background information that was already understood by their audiences, no single passage includes all the features of covenant making. Each narrator relates only what is relevant to his purpose in the context of his story line. A full picture of the constant features of covenant making can be derived only by consideration of all covenant making contexts.

Abram belongs to c. 2000 B.C. and Jeremiah to 600 B.C. Standard features

---

[7] Mathews, *Genesis 11:27–50:26*, 171–172.

are common to both of these covenant making rituals. An animal is cut and covenant making parties pass or walk between the pieces of the dead animal. Both texts employ the standard terminology *kārat běrît*, "to cut a covenant." These commonalties attest to age-old cultural data in the ancient Near East. The Old Testament is part of that cultural data even if no other texts from the Near East specifically mention "halving an animal." Why should the accounts describe what is assumed by the culture and is therefore unnecessary to describe in most instances? The texts from Alalakh discussed by Hess do not provide all the details either. One text mentions cutting the neck of a lamb (rather than halving it and walking between the pieces) but it is clearly a self-maledictory oath. The covenant partner curses himself if he takes back what he is giving in the property grant of the treaty.[8]

In Genesis 21:22–34, Abram and Abimelech make a treaty together, which we have already discussed. The ceremony is not described in detail. We are told, "Abraham took sheep and oxen and gave them to Abimelech, and the two men made a covenant" (v. 27, ESV). Presumably they cut the animals in half and then walked between the pieces just as in Genesis 15 and Jeremiah 34. (Or maybe they cut the necks as in the Alalakh texts? But the ceremony still involved a self-maledictory oath.) Such culturally understood details need not be described in full for the readers. The animals were not gifts to Abimelech, because Abraham set aside seven ewe lambs as a gift (Gen. 21:28–30). This was unusual, and Abimelech called for an explanation. Abraham told him they were a witness that he had dug the disputed well. So here, too, we see features that are constant to covenant making alongside features that suit a peculiar set of circumstances.

Possibly quite similar to the covenant making of Genesis 21 is a document from Mari, c. eighteenth century B.C. This brief text reads as follows: "I had a donkey foal, the young of a she-ass, slaughtered, I (thus) established peace between the Haneans and the Idamaraṣ."[9] Here a suzerain has sent his lieutenant to supervise a covenant ratification ceremony between two of the suzerain's vassals. The ceremony or ritual itself is not described in full.[10]

---

[8] Designated AT 456, this text from the early second millennium B.C. states, "Abba-AN swore an oath of the gods to Yarimlim and he cut the neck of one lamb (saying): (May I be cursed) if I take what I have given to you." See Richard S. Hess, "Slaughter of the Animals in Genesis 15," 57.

[9] Cited from A. Leo Oppenheim et al., eds., *The Assyrian Dictionary*, 1 A:2 (Chicago: Oriental Institute, 1968), 482. See Charles-F. Jean, *Archives Royales de Mari* (Paris: Imprimerie Nationale, 1950), II 37:11.

[10] What is interesting in the text from Mari is that the suzerain's lieutenant takes with him a puppy dog, a bird, and a donkey for the covenant making ritual/sacrifice. The parties would not accept the puppy dog or the bird; only the donkey would do. This confirms the pattern in the Old Testament that bigger animals are employed in covenants or treaties at the level of a large group of people(s) or nation(s).

Why should it be? Mathews' comment, therefore, that "the number and sort of animals and the halving procedure of chap. 15 have no parallel yet found in the ancient Near East" has little value. No details are provided in Genesis 21 either, but they are in Genesis 15 *because the fact that only one party passes between the pieces is remarkable.* The details are important in this text and are therefore given in full.

The differences adduced by Mathews between Jeremiah 34 and Genesis 15 only prevent correct interpretation of Genesis 15. The vocabulary differences that he lists are due to the author's wordplay in Jeremiah 34 on the one hand and the prophetic symbolism Yahweh wished to convey by the ceremony in Genesis 15 on the other. Nonetheless, both texts use the same standard covenant making terminology. A calf in Jeremiah 34 is more suitable to a covenant made at a national level. Similarly, oxen and sheep are used in the ceremony between Abraham and Abimelech in Genesis 21. The animals in Genesis 15, however, are chosen for a specific symbolism, as explained by Wenham and appropriated by Mathews. Thus the evidence does not indicate that we are mistakenly "appropriating the rite of Jeremiah 34 as the template for explaining the practice in Genesis 15."[11]

The fact that the idea of God taking a self-maledictory oath is difficult theologically only shows that we should exercise restraint in imposing upon the text our notions of what is possible and right for God. It is also difficult to reconcile theologically that God asks Abraham to offer Isaac as a sacrifice in Genesis 22. May not a critical approach to the text preclude the narrator's right to build mystery and tension into his story line?

The statement that in Genesis 15 the concept of a self-maledictory oath is not explicit is an argument without any weight. If one can boldly interpret the symbolism of the special features of the ceremony as Mathews does, why not the standard features that are constant in the Old Testament for more than 1,500 years? It seems that a concern to defend a conservative dating for Genesis 15 against interpretation by more critical scholars has resulted in a skewed picture of its meaning.

CONCLUSION

Ray Vander Laan has nicely expressed the powerful communication of the covenant making ritual in Genesis 15:

---

[11] Mathews, *Genesis 11:27–50:26*, 170–172.

What an awesome God we have! What incredible love he has for his creatures!

Imagine! The Creator of the universe, the holy and righteous God, was willing to leave heaven and come down to a nomad's tent in the dusty, hot desert of Negev to express his love for his people.

"Bring me a heifer, a goat and a ram . . . along with a dove and a young pigeon," God told Abraham. Then, when those animals had been sacrificed and laid out on both sides of their shed blood, God made a covenant. To do that, he walked "barefoot," in the form of a blazing torch, through the path of blood between the animals.

Think of it. Almighty God walking barefoot through a pool of blood! The thought of a human being doing that is, to say the least, unpleasant. Yet, God, in all his power and majesty, expressed his love that personally. By participating in that traditional, Near Eastern covenant-making ceremony, he made it unavoidably clear to the people of that time, place and culture what he intended to do.

"I love you so much, Abraham," God was saying, "and I promise that this covenant will come true for you and your children. I will never break My covenant with you. I'm willing to put My own life on the line to make you understand."

Picturing God passing through that gory path between the carcasses of animals, imagining the blood splashing as he walked, helps us recognize the faithfulness of God's commitment. He was willing to express, in terms his chosen people could understand, that he would never fail to do what he promised. And he ultimately fulfilled his promise by giving his own life, his own blood, on the cross.

Because we look at God's dealings with Abraham as some remote piece of history in a far-off land, we often fail to realize that we, too, are part of the long line of people with whom God made a covenant on that rocky plain near Hebron. And like those who came before us, we have broken that covenant.

When he walked in the dust of the desert and through the blood of the animals Abraham had slaughtered, God was making a promise to *all* the descendants of Abraham—to everyone in the household of faith. When God splashed through the blood, he did it for *us*.

We're not simply individuals in relationship to God, we're part of a long line of people marching back through history, from our famous Jewish ancestors David, Hezekiah, and Peter to the millions of unknown believers; from the ancient Israelites and the Jewish people of Jesus' day to the Christian community dating from the early church. We're part of a community of people with whom God established relationship in the dust and sand of the Negev.

But there's more. When God made covenant with his people, he did something no human being would have even considered doing. In the usual blood covenant, each party was responsible for keeping only his side of the promise. When God made covenant with Abraham, however, he promised to keep *both* sides of the agreement.

"If this covenant is broken, Abraham, for whatever reason—for My unfaithfulness or yours—I will pay the price," said God. "If you or your descendants, for whom you are making this covenant, fail to keep it, I will pay the price in blood."

And at that moment, Almighty God pronounced the death sentence on his Son Jesus.[12]

CONFIRMING THE COVENANT: THE SIGN OF CIRCUMCISION–GENESIS 17

The covenant between God and Abraham made in Genesis 15 is confirmed and upheld in Genesis 17. The precise relationship between Genesis 15 and 17 is debated. Before this relationship can be adequately articulated, however, we must consider the literary structure of this text, the exegetical details of the text, and its context in the flow of the narratives dealing with Abraham.

As in the case of Genesis 15, the literary structure of Genesis 17 is clear. Again, the text is divided in half and each half has an identical pattern and structure. Again the Lord communicates to Abram, presumably in a vision, although this is not explicit in the text as it is in Genesis 15. Yahweh begins by expressing his intention to confirm his covenant promise concerning descendants. Abram responds by falling on his face. God speaks further about his promises of both descendants and land. He prescribes circumcision to Abram as a covenant sign. Then the pattern is repeated. Yahweh expresses his intention to bless Sarah with progeny. Again Abram falls on his face. God speaks further and announces in particular the birth of a son to Sarah in about a year's time. The section ends with Abraham obeying the instructions concerning circumcision for himself, Ishmael, and his entire household.

Outline of Genesis 17

A. Yahweh's intention to confirm his oath about progeny	1–2
B. Abram falls on his face	3
C. God promises descendants and the gift of land	4–8
D. The sign of circumcision given	9–14

---

[12] Ray Vander Laan with Judith Markham, *Echoes of His Presence: Stories of the Messiah from the People of His Day* (Colorado Springs: Focus on the Family, 1996), 8–9.

A'. Yahweh's intention to bless Sarah with progeny	15–16
B'. Abram falls on his face	17–18
C'. God promises a son from Sarah	19–22
D'. The sign of circumcision practised	23–27

Just as the covenant making in chapter 15 came in response to the events preceding in chapter 14, so the covenant confirmation in chapter 17 comes in response to the events in chapter 16, where Sarai and Abram seek descendants through Hagar.

Our attention is focused on several things in this text. Yahweh appears to Abraham and says, "I am God Almighty; walk before me and be blameless" (Gen. 17:1, ESV, NIV).

First, Yahweh reveals himself as El Shaddai (God Almighty). This is the first occurrence of this divine name in the Scriptures. In an attempt to determine the meaning of the Hebrew term "Shaddai," scholars have argued over the origin of the word and have come to a stalemate. Its meaning, however, can be determined quite well from the usage of the word. This name for God is associated especially and particularly in the Old Testament with the lives of the patriarchs, Abraham, Isaac, and Jacob. It seems that this name was given to encourage faith because of the disparity between the covenant promises and the reality of the situation in which they found themselves at that time. Thus, in this context, Yahweh is the God who intervenes powerfully. It is customary in the Greek Old Testament to translate El Shaddai by "almighty" (παντοκράτωρ),[13] and this expresses the meaning very well. As noted previously, the Abram narratives are presented as a new creation. Out of the post-Babel chaos portrayed by the nations and peoples of the world lost and scattered in the earth, and by the deadness and infertility of Abram and Sarai's bodies, the word of God to Abram is a powerful word bringing something out of nothing.

Second, El Shaddai commands Abram, saying, "Walk before me!" (התהלך לפני). What does it mean to walk before someone? John Walton carefully analyses the use of this expression throughout the Old Testament:[14]

> The Qal (G) stem and Hithpael (HtD) stem occurrences may be considered together because there are related contexts that express the same meaning

---

[13] In the Septuagint, the rendering παντοκράτωρ is not employed by the Genesis translator, but is popularised rather by the Job translator.

[14] John H. Walton, *Covenant: God's Purpose, God's Plan* (Grand Rapids, MI: Zondervan, 1994), 72–73. Table used by permission.

by using the variant form (cf. Qal usage in 1 Kings 9:4 and Hithpael usage in 2 Kings 20:3). The collocation of verb and preposition occurs nearly thirty times in a wide variety of contexts. These occurrences may be classified as follows:

1. People as Object of the Preposition
1. God as pillar of cloud *going before* Israel (Ex. 13:21; etc.) [G]
2. God *going before* Israel into the land (Deut. 1:30; 31:8) [G]
3. The Army *going before* the priests and the priests before the ark around Jericho (Josh. 6:9, 13) [G]
4. Used parallel to "rear guard" (Isa. 52:12; 58:8) [G]
5. The purpose of Jacob's gifts to Esau (Gen. 32:21) [G]
6. Actual role-conduct of Samuel (1 Sam. 12:2) [HtD]
7. Expected role-conduct of new priestly line ("before my anointed" (1 Sam. 2:35) [HtD]

2. God as Object of the Preposition
1. Expected role-conduct of Davidic kings (1 Kings 2:4; 8:23, 25; 9:4; 2 Chron. 6:16; 7:17) [G]
2. Actual role-conduct of Hezekiah (2 Kings 20:3; Isa. 38:3) [HtD]
3. Expected-actual role-conduct of the Patriarchs (Gen. 17:1; 24:40; 48:15) [HtD]
4. Expected role-conduct of priests (1 Sam. 2:30) [HtD]
5. Anticipated role-conduct of psalmist who has been delivered (Ps. 56:13 [14]; 116:9) [HtD]

The results of Walton's careful study may be summarised as follows. When God walks before someone, this expression means to give guidance and protection. Conversely, when people walk before God, it means that they serve as his emissary or diplomatic representative. In Genesis 17:1 God commands Abram to walk before him. Thus, Abram is to be God's agent or diplomatic messenger and representative in the world. When the world looks at Abram they will see what it is like to have a right relationship to God and to be what God intended for humanity. To see the significance of the geographical location of the land promised to Abraham and grasp its importance for the promises given to Abram in Genesis 12, consider a map of the ancient Near East, showing travel routes (fig. 8.1). Canaan, the land promised to Abram, is a minuscule piece of property about 30 miles wide and 100 miles long. The superpowers of the ancient world were on either side: Egypt to the west and Mesopotamia (Assyria and Babylon) to the east. Most of the area between Canaan and Mesopotamia is desert. The only functional route for commerce and travel between the great superpowers of the ancient world is the tiny country given to Abram. In modern terms, Abram and his family are to be settled along the *central spine of the Internet* in the ancient world. All of the communication, commerce, and trade back and forth between Egypt and Mesopotamia will pass through Canaan. And when it does, what are they supposed to see? They are supposed to see a group of people who demonstrate a right relationship to the one and only true God, a human way of treating each other, and a proper stewardship of the earth's resources.[15] God calls Abram to be a light to the nations. This is the beginning of his method and plan to bless all the nations through Abram and his family. Thus the command "walk before me" correlates directly with the command in 12:3 to be a blessing to the nations.

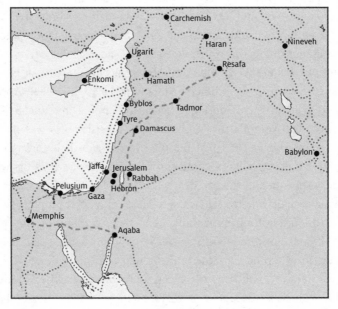

Fig. 8.1

The divine command to Abram in Genesis 17:1 is actually twofold: (1) walk before me and (2) be blameless. The Hebrew word rendered "blameless" is *tāmîm*. This adjective comes from a root meaning "complete," "entire"

---

[15] Little space is given in this work to the way in which the Abrahamic narratives address the issue of proper stewardship of the land and the earth's resources. This is developed in great detail in Byron L. Wheaton, "Abraham, Land, and Stewardship: Reading the Abraham Narratives for Their Contribution to Israel's Land Ethic" (PhD diss., Westminster Theological Seminary, 2001). The comments made herein are dependent upon his work.

or "whole" and denotes a "totality without any diminution."[16] Although the adjective *tāmîm* and the closely related adjective *tām* are not infrequent terms in the Old Testament (*tāmîm* occurs approximately 91 times and *tām* 15 times), use in reference to humans is uncommon since most of the instances concern animals for cultic use. In fact, in all of Genesis, *tāmîm* is found only here (17:1) in reference to Abram and in 6:9, in reference to Noah, both Adamic figures according to the literary techniques of the narrator:

> Noah was a righteous man. He was blameless (*tāmîm*) in his contemporary circles. (Gen 6:9)

The adjective *tāmîm* is also collocated with "righteous" (צַדִּיק) in Job 12:4, where Job protests that he, a completely righteous man, has become a laughingstock (cf. Prov. 11:5). Moreover, *tāmîm* is collocated with יָשָׁר ("upright") in Deuteronomy 32:4 and Job 12:4. Thus, God is calling Abram to be morally blameless and impeccable, honest and sincere in the covenant relationship.

As a matter of fact, however, when we consider the narratives concerning Abram to this point, we note that Abram has been less than honest and sincere in his dealings with others. Already in 12:17–20, when Abram and Sarai sojourned in Egypt during a period of famine in Canaan, Pharaoh complained that Abram's ruse calling Sarai his sister was less than truthful. Again, in chapter 16, when the plan to have an heir through Sarai's maidservant Hagar results in contempt for Sarai, Abram tells his wife that this is her problem, and she can deal with Hagar however she wants. Hagar and Ishmael are driven away into the wilderness with scant provision. This conduct, too, is far from impeccable. And the command of God given in chapter 17 does not remove this trait from Abram's subsequent behaviour. In chapter 20, when he sojourns in the country of the Philistines, again he represents Sarah in public as his sister, and Abimelech, the king, charges Abraham with being deceptive in this matter. In chapter 21 Abraham and Abimelech make a treaty. Abraham complains that he has been mistreated by Abimelech's people over the matter of a well he had dug, but Abimelech counters that this is the first he has heard of it. This, too, is not impeccable behaviour among the nations. God must have been embarrassed to own Abraham as his emissary and prophet (Gen. 20:7), the one who would intercede for Abimelech so that he would not die as a penalty for his adultery. The

---

[16] B. Kedar-Kopfstein, "תָּמַם *tāmam*; תָּם *tām*; תָּמִים *tāmîm*; תֹּם (תֻּם) *tōm* (*tom-*); תֻּמָּה *tummâ*; תֻּמִּים *tummîm*," in *TDOT* 15:72.

author of Genesis is at pains to show that, in the course of time and in the passing of generations, little things become big things. So later, in Genesis 26:6–11, Isaac also represents his wife Rebekah as his sister; only this time what was a "white lie" or half-truth in the mouth of his father (Sarah was in fact a half sister of Abram) becomes a black lie in his mouth. In the third generation, Isaac's son, Jacob, in turn is a complete deceiver and shyster. And Jacob, who deceived his father by means of a coat and a goat, was in turn deceived by his sons by means of a coat and a goat. To be sure, Abram has had an altar in Canaan and has called out (i.e., proclaimed) in the name of Yahweh. He has been an ambassador for his god; but he has not represented his god with complete integrity.

The circumstances of chapter 16 are important motivation for the covenant confirmation in chapter 17. Genesis 17:2 begins with the verb *wĕ'ettĕnâ*, a form almost certainly to be identified as a first person singular modal, which in direct sequence with the commands of the previous verse marks a purpose or result clause: "Walk before me and be blameless so that I may make my covenant between me and you." Obedience is expected of Abram in the covenant relationship. Already in Genesis 12, when Yahweh called Abram and gave him such great promises, there were commands: "Go" . . . and "Be a blessing!" Chapter 15 reiterated the great promises and enshrined them in a covenant. Abram has not demonstrated full integrity, and so, in chapter 17, God comes to confirm/uphold his covenant and emphasise, among other things, the need for an obedient son in Abram's Adamic role.

An exegetical question that cannot be ignored is the sense of the verb נתן when ברית is the direct object. The analysis of Williamson must be cited in full since he challenges the view adopted here:

> If one understands Genesis 17 in terms of a reaffirmation of the covenant formally ratified in Genesis 15, the deployment in Gen. 17.2 of the imperfect inflection of the verb נתן is rather puzzling. As Wenham tellingly admits, 'it is not immediately obvious in what sense God needs to give a covenant to Abraham, as it has already been inaugurated (כרת "cut") in 15.18. Wenham resolves this difficulty by resorting to the most popular synchronic interpretation, suggesting that here (Gen. 17) the concern is the confirmation or ratification of the covenant with stress on the human response (summed up in the phrase "walk before me and be blameless," and explicated in the demand to circumcise every male) rather than merely on the divine initiative. The difficulty of the long delay (c. 14 years) between the covenant's establishment by God and the stress on its inherent obligations on man has

already been underlined. The reason why the obligatory aspects were not clarified much earlier is somewhat obscure; if these two passages simply describe two aspects/stages of the one covenant, why did God wait so long to elaborate upon the human partner's responsibilities? Surely the theological effect would have been the same had Genesis 15 already alluded to the intrinsic responsibilities on Abraham's part? If, on the other hand, a redactor is blamed for this literary enigma, the rationale for separating two such intimately related passages has not been adequately explained. Surely the redactor could have incorporated the Hagar episode into the narrative at a more suitable place—for example, before the latter half of ch. 15—and amalgamated the J and P accounts of the covenant's institution. Thus the anticipated 'giving' of the covenant in Genesis 17 does not sit easily with either the standard synchronic or diachronic explanations; the former offers no rationale for the unnecessary delay in revealing the covenant's obligatory aspects, whereas the latter challenges the literary competence of the redactor(s).

Dumbrell understands the sense of נתן (in 17.2) to be 'setting the covenant in operation'. By this he means the realization of the covenant of Genesis 15 in the form of activated promises. Thus Gen. 17.2 should presumably be understood: ' . . . so that I may set in motion my covenant between me and you and greatly increase your numbers'. Such a translation is certainly supported by Labuschagne's lexical study of נתן; he contends that the basic connotation of the verb is the act through which an object or matter is set in motion. Further support for this interpretation is found in the fact that נתן, when used in association with promised covenant blessings, heralds their realization or fulfilment. Fulfilment of the gift of 'land' is heralded in 12.7; 13.15, 17; 15.7, 18; 17.8, and implicitly in 15.2. In 17.5, 6 and 20 the verb relates to the promise of international (or in Ishmael's case, national) significance. The focus in 17.16 is the promised son. This leaves 17.2, which in the context seems to relate to the promise of Abraham's phenomenal expansion (17.2b; cf. 12.2; 13.16; 15.5); this, as we have seen, is undoubtedly a major theme in Genesis 17. Thus נתן in Gen. 17.2 may suggest the setting in motion of the covenant promise(s) in question: viz. Abraham's phenomenal expansion (as the latter half of the verse seems to imply).

However, even if it is correct to interpret the verb נתן as heralding the implementation of fulfilment of covenant promises, the legitimacy of identifying the covenant announced in Genesis 17 with the covenant already inaugurated in ch. 15 cannot simply be assumed. This still fails to take adequate cognisance of the different promissory emphases of the two chapters. The promissory focus of the covenant established in ch. 15 is the inheritance of the land by Abraham's innumerable offspring—an aspect of the promissory programme which, though reiterated in the context of ch. 17 (v. 8), was certainly not implemented until very much later (and after at least one additional divine-human covenant; viz. the Sinaitic). However, the *primary* focus of the covenant 'set in motion' in Genesis 17 does not appear to be Abraham's national inheritance, but rather his international significance. Thus the fact that the prospect of nationhood appears to assume a rather subsidiary position in ch. 17 seriously weakens the case for understanding the 'covenant of circumcision' as *merely* another step towards the implementation of the covenant promises recorded in ch. 15. At the very least there is a difference in emphasis in these two chapters which any attempt to correlate the two records must take into account and seek to explain.

However, it is possible that, though overstating his case, Dumbrell is correct to see a continuum between Genesis 15 and 17; the emphasis in ch. 17 on Abraham's descendants clearly provides a literary and theological lynchpin. This pericope leaves the reader in no doubt that Abraham's international significance must not be isolated entirely from the prospect of his national inheritance. Both expectations are related in some way; indeed, given the order both here and elsewhere, Abraham's international significance appears to be somehow contingent upon the prospect of nationhood having first been realized.[17]

To determine the sense of *nātan bĕrît* Williamson rightly wrestles with the relationship of Genesis 15 and 17. Much in his discussion is helpful. He contributes to the discussion by noting the emphasis in chapter 17 on the nations. He correctly notes the prominence in this text; the focus on "becoming nations" is, in fact, in both halves of the chapter, in relation to both Abraham and Sarah:

> [4] As for me, this is my covenant with you: You will be the father of many nations. [5] No longer will you be called Abram; your name will be Abraham, for I have made you a father of many nations. [6] I will make you very fruitful; I will make nations of you, and kings will come from you. (Gen. 17:4–6, NIV)

> I will bless her and will surely give you a son by her. I will bless her so that she will be the mother of nations; kings of peoples will come from her. (Gen 17:16, NIV)

Ishmael is promised both nationhood and royalty:

> And as for Ishmael, I have heard you: I will surely bless him; I will make him fruitful and will greatly increase his numbers. He will be the father of twelve rulers, and I will make him into a great nation (Gen. 17:20, NIV).

---

[17] Paul R. Williamson, *Abraham, Israel, and the Nations: The Patriarchal Promise and Its Covenantal Development in Genesis*, JSOTSup 315 (Sheffield, UK: Sheffield Academic Press, 2000), 203–205 (emphasis his).

In Genesis 17 the royal ideology of the promises in Genesis 12:1–3 comes to the fore and it seems that, not only will Abraham be a blessing to the nations, but he will become more than one nation, in fact a *multitude* of nations. No wonder Paul speaks of "the promise to Abraham and to his seed that he would be the inheritor of the *world*" (Rom. 4:13). He would inherit more than the land of Canaan; he would inherit the world.

Nonetheless, the exegesis of Williamson is faulty because of inadequate attention to linguistic matters, reliance on secondary sources for lexical studies of strategic words, overreaction to the faults of Dumbrell's interpretation, and his own skewed definition of covenant making.[18] Thus he argues in the end that chapters 15 and 17 are two separate but related covenants.

Apart from Genesis 17:2, the expression *nātan běrît* is found elsewhere only in Genesis 9:12 and Numbers 25:12.[19] The context in Numbers 25:12 appears to require the sense "give" whereas the contexts of Genesis 9:12 and 17:2 call for the meaning "set up." According to semantic field theory, in most languages, nouns and verbs not only have a specific field of meaning but operate in a hierarchy of related words in semantic domains. A verb higher up the hierarchy can usually be used as a substitute for one lower down. Thus *nātan* is employed as a substitute for *hēqîm* in both Genesis 9:12 and 17:2. This substitution is a natural stylistic variant since both the flood narrative and Genesis 17 are dominated exclusively by the expression *hēqîm běrît* rather than *kārat běrît*. The expression *hēqîm běrît* is found in Genesis 6:18, 9:9, 11, 17 and 17:7, 19, 21 whereas *kārat běrît* is not found at all in these contexts. Thus Dumbrell's proposal for *nātan* (acceded to by Williamson in the main) is not far off the mark at all, and linguistic principles can account appropriately for both the sense and the usage.

The first person pronominal suffix on ברית is also part of the discussion on the relationship of Genesis 17 to 15. Note again Williamson's assessment of the claims of Dumbrell:

> In over half of its occurrences in ch. 17 (including its first occurrence in the pericope) ברית has a first person singular possessive pronoun attached (vv. 2, 4, 7, 10, 13, 19 and 21). It has been inferred, on the basis that the covenant is so introduced in this chapter, that 'my covenant' is to be identified with the covenant previously mentioned in ch. 15. This inference,

---

[18] Discussed earlier.

[19] Williamson lists only Genesis 9:12 and 17:2 (*Abraham, Israel, and the Nations*, 204, n. 63) although elsewhere he criticises Wenham for missing Genesis 9:12 (*Abraham, Israel, and the Nations*, 201, n. 52) and discusses Numbers 25:12 without mentioning the verb *nātan* (*Abraham, Israel, and the Nations*, 200).

however, does not bear up under close scrutiny. A number of telling criticisms can be levelled against it.

The fact that the Noahic covenant (cf. Gen. 6.18; 9:8–17) is also enigmatically (so McEvenue) introduced in the same manner (i.e. בריתי) seriously undermines the suggestion that the pronominal suffix points to an already established covenant. By analogy the 'covenant' referred to in Gen. 6.18 must also be a reaffirmation of an already established covenant. However, prior to this there is not even a hint of a covenant being established in the book of Genesis. The reference to ברית in Gen. 6.18 reflects not just the first occurrence of the noun in the flood narrative, but the first explicit reference to covenant in the Pentateuch as a whole. Thus to what pre-existing covenant could Gen. 6.18 possibly allude?

Dumbrell's conjecture, that the allusion in Gen. 6.18 is to an original covenant with creation, allegedly reflected in the opening chapters of Genesis, lacks firm exegetical support and therefore remains unconvincing. While Dumbrell is undoubtedly correct in recognizing several clear echoes of the creation narrative in the Noahic covenant, his conclusion—that Genesis 1–3 must accordingly portray an antedeluvian covenantal relationship—is a *non sequitur*.[20]

These arguments are, apparently, Williamson's strongest. We have already seen that his analysis of the expressions *kārat bĕrît* and *hēqîm bĕrît* is flawed and moreover based on data from Weinfeld rather than from exhaustive examination of the primary sources himself. We have also seen—and will see again shortly in considering chapter 17—that there are fundamental ways of describing covenants in the narratives of Scripture without actually using the term ברית. Furthermore Williamson provides no exegesis of Genesis 1–3 to substantiate the claim that no covenant is found there. Nor does he provide an adequate explanation for the variant expressions and terms used in Genesis 6–9 and 17. Therefore his claims constitute begging the question.

Dumbrell's proposal that the instances of the pronominal suffix on ברית in Genesis 17 point to an already established covenant is noteworthy. The noun ברית has a first person singular pronominal suffix in 47 instances in the Old Testament. It is remarkable that 13 of these, i.e., more than one-quarter, occur in two texts: Genesis 6–9 and 17.[21] Linguistically, a pronominal suffix makes the noun definite and the grammatical function may be anaphoric (i.e., a backward pointing) reference. Careful examination of all instances in the

---

[20] Paul R. Williamson, *Abraham, Israel, and the Nations*, 190–191.
[21] Williamson's list, cited above, is missing Genesis 17:9.

Old Testament shows that in every case but one the reference is anaphoric and refers to an already established covenant.[22] It seems that Dumbrell's proposal is on solid ground and that the thesis of Williamson flies in the face of the linguistic data.

We may be confident, then, that just as Genesis 6–9 is a confirmation of God's covenant with creation in Genesis 1–3, so Genesis 17 is a confirmation of God's covenant with Abraham initiated in Genesis 15. Genesis 15 and Genesis 17 correlate respectively with the first three promises and the second three promises of 12:1–3. Abraham has shown a great deal of interest in God's promises to bless him personally with fame and nationhood, but these promises are foundational to the second three promises to bless all the nations through Abram, and Abraham has not shown any interest in being a blessing to the nations. So Williamson is quite right to note the international emphasis in Genesis 17. Abraham's response to the revelation in Genesis 17 is clear:

> [17] Then Abraham fell on his face and laughed and said to himself, "Shall a child be born to a man who is a hundred years old? Shall Sarah, who is ninety years old, bear a child?" [18] And Abraham said to God, "Oh that Ishmael might live before you!" (Gen. 17:17–18, ESV)

Abraham is quite skeptical about the divine plan and urges God to consider his own attempt to implement God's plan in Genesis 16: "If only Ishmael might live under your blessing!" There is room, indeed, in the blessings promised for Abraham's son Ishmael to develop into a nation that entails great chieftains, but the covenant will be upheld with a son born only to Abraham and Sarah in about a year's time. Abraham laughs at this. He can see how the divine plan would work through Ishmael, but how would life come out of a couple whose bodies are both dead. Yet this is precisely the theme of chapter 17—"I am God *Almighty*. Walk before me and be blameless." The reason for the fourteen-year lapse between chapter 15 and chapter 17 is that Yahweh wants a covenant relationship in which Abraham really knows and understands who God is, and is faithful and loyal in precisely that level of understanding. Not until Abraham has

---

[22] The 47 instances are as follows: Gen. 6:18; 9:9, 11, 15; 17:2, 4, 7, 9, 10, 13, 14, 19, 21; Ex. 6:4, 5; 19:5; Lev. 26:9, 15, 42 (3x), 44; Num. 25:12; Deut. 31:16, 20; Jos 7:11; Judg. 2:1, 20; 1 Kings 11:11; Ps. 50:5, 16; 89:35; 132:12; Isa. 59:21; Jer. 11:10; 31:32; 33:20 (2x), 21, 25; Ezek. 16:60, 62; 44:7; Hos. 8:1; Zech. 11:10; Mal. 2:4, 5. In Psalm 50:5, the first person pronominal suffix means "the covenant with me," and the occurrence in Ezekiel 16:62 may possibly be of a covenant cataphoric or proleptic.

tried everything in his own strength and is completely powerless will he know God as El Shaddai.

In the course of discussing the relationship of Genesis 15 and 17, Williamson notes from T. D. Alexander parallels between Genesis 9 and 17, as seen in table 8.1:[23]

Table 8.1: Parallels between Genesis 9 and 17

Expression	Noahic Covenant	Abrahamic Covenant
הקים ברית	9:9, 11, 17	17:7, 19, 21
נתן ברית	9:12	17:2
אתה וזרעך אחריך	9:9	17:7, 8, 9, 10, 19
במאד מאד	7:19	17:2, 6, 20
לדרתם	6:9; 9:12	17:7, 9, 12
ונכרתה הנפש ההוא	9:11	17:14
פרה ורבה	8:17; 9:1, 7	17:20
הוליד	6:10	17:20
בעצם היום הזה	7:13	17:23, 26
כל־זכר	6:19; 7:3, 9, 16	17:10, 12, 23

What these parallels show, rather than aiding and abetting the Documentary Hypothesis, is that the narrator is at pains to portray both Noah and Abraham as Adamic figures. The command to Adam to "be fruitful and multiply" is passed on to Noah and becomes for Abraham a promise with the adverb "exceedingly" added to it.

In chapter 17, God renames both Abram and Sarai. Abraham's name is changed from Abram ("exalted father") to Abraham, father of a multitude (of nations). Sarai's name is changed to Sarah. Although both are dialectical variants meaning "princess," as Waltke notes, "Sarai, her birth-name, probably looks back on her noble descent, whereas Sarah, her covenantal name, looks ahead to her noble descendants."[24] Williamson believes this is cause for distinguishing 15 and 17 as separate covenants:

> One of the most obvious aspects distinguishing the two covenant chapters
> is the introduction of new names for both Abraham and Sarah in ch. 17. It is
> significant that not only are these name-changes unmentioned in Genesis 15,

---

[23] Adapted from Paul R. Williamson, *Abraham, Israel, and the Nations*, 86, who cites it from T. D. Alexander, "A Literary Analysis of the Abraham Narrative in Genesis," (PhD diss; The Queen's University of Belfast, 1982), 179. Used by permission.

[24] Bruce K. Waltke with Cathi J. Fredricks, *Genesis: A Commentary* (Grand Rapids, MI: Zondervan, 2001), 262.

but also that their non-usage prior to Genesis 17 is perfectly matched by the consistency of their usage after their introduction in the latter chapter

In that these new names are given covenantal significance in ch. 17, their non-introduction in ch. 15 would imply that the covenant recorded there served a different purpose—or at least had a distinct emphasis. Again, this inference is confirmed by a careful analysis of each chapter. Genesis 15 stresses Abraham's role as the progenitor of a single nation who would inherit the Promised Land, whereas Genesis 17 stresses Abraham's role as the 'father' of a multitude of nations who would inherit the promised blessing (cf. 17.4–6, 16). Thus the name-changes in ch. 17 subtly alert the reader to the fact that the scope of the two covenant passages in the Abrahamic narrative is not the same.[25]

The scope of chapter 17 is bigger than chapter 15 because it is characteristic of the Abraham narrative as a whole for God to answer every question with bigger promises. God also uses cultural means to communicate to his people who he is and what he wants in the relationship, such as a covenantal name-change. But this need not be seen as any reason to consider 15 and 17 different covenants.

Third, in verses 7b and 8b of chapter 17, note that the covenant is with Abraham and his descendants:

[7] And I will establish my covenant between me and you and your offspring after you throughout their generations for an everlasting covenant, *to be God to you and to your offspring after you.* [8] And I will give to you and to your offspring after you the land of your sojournings, all the land of Canaan, for an everlasting possession, *and I will be their God.* (ESV)

Yahweh will be the God of Abraham and the God of his descendants. He will be their God. The italicised words constitute the first instance in Scripture of the Covenant Formula (at least the first half of it). We find the full formula in Exodus 6:7:

I will take you as my own people, and I will be your God. Then you will know that I am the LORD your God, who brought you out from under the yoke of the Egyptians. (NIV)

Attention was first drawn to the formula by Rudolf Smend.[26] Elmer Martens' book *God's Design: A Focus on Old Testament Theology* is a

---

[25] Paul R. Williamson, *Abraham, Israel, and the Nations*, 106.
[26] Rudolf Smend, *Die Bundesformel* (Theologische Studien 68; Zürich: EVZ-Verlag, 1963).

wonderful exposition of this phrase in the Scriptures.[27] As the scholarly study of Rendtorff has shown, sometimes only the first half of the formula is found (A), sometimes only the second half (B), and sometimes the entire formula (C).[28]

Formula A: I will be your God
Formula B: You will be my people
Formula C: I will be your God and you will be my people = A + B

Rendtorff concludes his analysis of the Covenant Formula as follows:

> It therefore emerges under the most diverse aspect that in important sectors of the Hebrew Bible the covenant formula is an element of theological language which is introduced in a *highly conscious manner*. It expresses in an extremely pregnant way God's relationship to Israel and Israel's to God. At the same time, it combines with other terms, above all 'covenant' and 'choose', as well as other elements of theological language. . . . In many cases it binds these elements together and interprets them afresh, or creates new theological coherences through their association.[29]

Thus, at the heart of the covenant is this relationship: "I will be their God and they will be my people." Although this phrase occurs here in Genesis 17 where the term ברית abounds, in many passages of the Bible the identical phrase or words occur where the term "covenant" is not found, and it always signals covenant as the subject and topic of discussion. Significant examples are 2 Corinthians 6:16 and Revelation 21:3:

> What agreement is there between the temple of God and idols? For we are the temple of the living God. As God has said: "I will live with them and walk among them, and I will be their God, and they will be my people." (2 Cor. 6:16, NIV)

> And I heard a loud voice from the throne saying, "Behold, the dwelling place of God is with man. He will dwell with them, and they will be his people, and God himself will be with them as their God. (Rev. 21:3, ESV)

Neither Paul nor John employ the word "covenant," but the Covenant

---

[27] Elmer Martens, *God's Design: A Focus on Old Testament Theology* (Grand Rapids, MI: Baker, 1981).
[28] Rolf Rendtorff, *Die "Bundesformel": eine exegetisch-theologische Untersuchung* (Stuttgart: Katholisches Bibelwerk, 1995).
[29] Rolf Rendtorff, *The Covenant Formula: An Exegetical and Theological Investigation*, trans. Margaret Kohl, Old Testament Studies (Edinburgh: T. & T. Clark, 1998), 92 (emphasis mine).

Formula communicates this idea powerfully as they describe and discuss the new covenant in these texts.

Fourth, Abram is given a covenant sign. In the Old Testament, it is common for a covenant to be accompanied by a physical sign, although by no means is a physical sign a necessary or obligatory part of covenant making. We saw that the rainbow was the sign of the covenant with Noah, and later the Sabbath is the sign of the covenant with Israel at Sinai. Abraham is commanded to practise circumcision as the physical sign of the covenant God was confirming between him and his descendants (Gen. 17:9–14).

The central question here is, what does circumcision indicate or signify? According to Genesis 17:14, this sign defines membership in the covenant community:

> Any uncircumcised male, who has not been circumcised in the flesh, will be cut off from his people; he has broken my covenant. (NIV)

The question remains, however: how does circumcision signify or symbolise belonging to the covenant community? Unfortunately the Christian church has had largely mistaken ideas and understandings of the rite of circumcision, mainly because the proper background to the meaning of this rite was not adequately researched. O. Palmer Robertson, for example, in his otherwise helpful work on the covenants, proposes that circumcision means cleansing. This is based on the gratuitous assumption that for the people in question, "the hygienic act of the removal of the foreskin symbolized the purification necessary for the establishment of a covenant relation between a holy God and an unholy people."[30] Other cultures circumcised children at puberty as a rite of passage from childhood to manhood. Abraham and his descendants are to circumcise children at eight days old. Correct understanding must be illuminated by the background of the ancient Near East and, in particular—in view of the connection between Abraham and Egypt, and Israel and Egypt—the Egyptian background. The best research to date on this topic has been advanced and summarised by John D. Meade.[31] After demonstrating that the most plausible background—the common milieu criterion—for

---

[30] O. Palmer Robertson, *The Christ of the Covenants* (Phillipsburg, NJ: Presbyterian & Reformed, 1980), 150.
[31] John Meade, "The Meaning of Circumcision in Israel: A Proposal for a Transfer of Rite from Egypt to Israel," *Adorare Mente* 1 (2008): 14–29 (http://adoraremente.sbts.edu/). David A. Bernat, *Sign of the Covenant: Circumcision in the Priestly Tradition* (Atlanta: Society of Biblical Literature, 2009) is a new book-length study devoted to the topic of circumcision. The author's commitment to source theory and his lack of attention to ancient Near Eastern cultural setting provide results that are not illuminating.

understanding both Abraham's and Israel's circumcision is Egypt, he draws his conclusion, which should be cited in full:

> First, and most importantly, God adds the rite of circumcision to an already existing covenant relationship (cf. Gen. 15:18, where the Hebrew verb כרת means to initiate a covenant). What does circumcision contribute to this covenantal relationship? The answers to this question have ranged between viewing Abraham's circumcision as a reminder to God to keep his promise of posterity to a multi-valent meaning including malediction and consecration. This study accedes with the latter of these conclusions. . . . Egyptian circumcision was an initiation rite for priests.
>
> Second, just as the king-priest was the son of the god in Egypt, and was consecrated to him through circumcision, Israel as the first born son of Yahweh (Ex. 4:22–23) has undergone and will undergo circumcision (Josh. 5:2–9) in order to be consecrated to his service. We cannot delve into the biblical language of sonship and image in this paper, but it is interesting to note that the Egyptian background would reveal to Israel that they indeed belonged to Yahweh as his first born Son, since they had undergone circumcision just as the Pharaoh.
>
> Third, only the priests were obligated to be circumcised in Egypt, but in Israel *every* male was to be circumcised on the eighth day (Gen. 17:12), signifying that Abraham's family consists of priests. Later in the story Israel is called a *kingdom of priests* and a holy nation (Ex. 19:6). The phrase "holy nation" also means consecrated to God or belonging to God and would complement the meaning of kingdom of priests. As a kingdom of priests, circumcision is the appropriate sign for the people of Israel, for it will remind every male Israelite that he is a priest, specially consecrated to Yahweh and his service.
>
> [Thus] circumcision in Egypt means affiliation or identification with the deity and consecration to his service. The rite was obligatory for all priests to the deity, while the evidence suggests that circumcision was not forced upon the laity. . . . although formal differences existed between the Egyptian rite and the Israelite rite, these differences actually functioned as the grounds for significant theologizing in Israel. In Israel every male baby is consecrated or devoted to God at eight days old. The family of Abraham and Sarah were to be signified as the priesthood of Yahweh from birth.[32]

The comment of Henry Morris is also helpful:

> Furthermore, it was primarily a sign only to the individual concerned, his parents, and his wife. It was not a sign to be shown to people in general, but

---

[32] Meade, "Meaning of Circumcision in Israel," 27–29.

was uniquely personal. To his parents it would confirm that they had been faithful in transmitting the seed to the son with whom God had blessed their union, and that they were trying to follow God's will in training him. To his wife, it would give assurance that he indeed was a descendant of Abraham, to whom she could joyfully submit in the marriage relation, in faith that God would bless their home and their children. To the man himself, it would be a daily testimony that he and his family were consecrated to the God of Abraham and that they shared in his calling and ministry to the world.[33]

Contrary to the culture in the ancient Near East where males were circumcised as adults or at puberty, males in Abraham's family were to be circumcised just after birth, at eight days old. Mathews connects this with the day of atonement:

> In the cult seven days of uncleanness were counted for the new mother, followed by the infant's circumcision on the eighth day and the thirty-three days of purification of the mother (Lev 12:2–4). The eighth held special meaning as the day of atonement or dedication to the Lord (e.g., Exod 22:30; Lev 9:1; 14:10, 23; 15:14, 29; 22:27; 23:39; Num 6:10; Ezek 43:27).[34]

This explanation is inadequate. The eighth day derives its significance from the account of creation, where God made the world in six days and rested on the seventh. Since the seventh day is indefinite, the eighth day is the beginning of the new creation, and this fits with the new creation imagery connected with Abraham as a new Adam.

Meredith G. Kline has proposed a negative meaning for this rite. Like the dismembering ritual in Genesis 15:7–18 (cf. Jer. 34:17–20), circumcision graphically portrayed the covenant curse of excision and threatened the cutting off of descendants (Gen. 17:14). Although other nations besides Israel practised circumcision, the Israelites were the only nation to completely cut off and remove the foreskin. Thus the negative meaning is that circumcision symbolises being cut off from the covenant community for disloyalty to the covenant demand to "walk before me and be blameless" (Gen. 17:1).[35] This negative aspect of circumcision is clearly supported in the text by verse 14, already cited.

Thus circumcision was a ritual required by Abraham and his family

---

[33] Henry M. Morris, *The Genesis Record: A Scientific and Devotional Commentary on the Book of Beginnings* (Grand Rapids, MI: Baker, 1976), 334.

[34] Mathews, *Genesis 11:27–50:26*, 204.

[35] See Jason S. DeRouchie, "Circumcision in the Hebrew Bible and Targums: Theology, Rhetoric, and the Handling of Metaphor," *Bulletin for Biblical Research* 14/2 (2004): 175–203.

signifying membership in the covenant community. Negatively, the person who remained uncircumcised would be cut off from the covenant community. Positively, circumcision symbolised complete devotion to the service of God as a priesthood. The covenant sign underlines Abraham's Adamic role as a priest in his calling to bring blessing to the nations. Paul in Romans 4:11 rightly sees the obedience of Abraham described in 17:23–27 as an expression of the righteousness of faith which according to Genesis 15:6 characterised his relation to Yahweh. And Robert D. Bergen rightly notes, "with the sign of the covenant now on his body, Abraham was qualified to father the covenant child."[36]

ONE COVENANT OR TWO?

The *NIV Study Bible* has a table on page 19 entitled, "Major Covenants in the Old Testament," which lists the divine dealings with Abraham as two covenants, described as Abrahamic A and Abrahamic B. Abrahamic A corresponds to Genesis 15 and is characterised as a royal grant; Abrahamic B corresponds to Genesis 17 and is characterised as a suzerain-vassal treaty. Recent support for this view has been provided by the doctoral dissertation of Paul R. Williamson.[37] Williamson has also written a more general work on all the biblical covenants,[38] where he summarises the technical treatment given of the Abrahamic covenant in his doctoral thesis. Williamson summarises previous analyses of Genesis 15 and 17 as follows:

> Scholars operating from a diachronic perspective generally consider the 'stages' of the Abrahamic covenant to be a literary construct as opposed to chronologically distinct events. This literary construct, it is suggested, has developed from the amalgamation of different sources or traditions that allegedly lie behind the final form of the Abraham narrative. Thus understood, Genesis 15 and 17 are simply variant accounts, from different periods, of what is essentially a single event or episode in the Abraham saga. The idea of distinct or chronologically separate stages in the establishment of the Abrahamic covenant has been introduced artificially by the editorial process that took place during the compilation of the Abraham cycle. Thus what originally were two separate accounts of a single Abrahamic

---

[36] Robert D. Bergen, in *HCSB Study Bible*, ed. Edwin A. Blum and Jeremy Royal Howard (Nashville: Holman, 2010), 40.

[37] Now published as Paul R. Williamson, *Abraham, Israel, and the Nations: The Patriarchal Promise and Its Covenantal Development in Genesis*, JSOTSup 315 (Sheffield, UK: Sheffield Academic Press, 2000).

[38] Paul R. Williamson, *Sealed with an Oath: Covenant in God's Unfolding Purpose*, NSBT 23 (Downers Grove, IL: InterVarsity Press, 2007).

covenant now appear as two chronologically distinct stages in the covenant relationship.

However, as well as involving several unwarranted presuppositions with respect to the literary and theological differences between Genesis 15 and 17 (see Williamson 2000a: 81–95), such diachronic analyses fail to explain the inclusion of these two covenant pericopes in the final form of the Abraham narrative. The latter must be addressed, for—unless one uncritically assumes a somewhat piece-meal and incoherent process of final redaction—each of these chapters makes its own distinct theological contribution to the narrative as a whole.

From a synchronic perspective, those who hold to a single Abrahamic covenant typically understand its staged revelation in terms of Abraham's developing relationship with Yahweh. Opinion is divided over when the covenant is initially established (i.e. whether in Gen. 12 or Gen. 15), but it is agreed that subsequent chapters focusing on God's promises to Abraham simply confirm and amplify the same covenant. Thus understood, Genesis 17 is not an alternative account of the establishment of the Abrahamic covenant, but is either a renewal of the previously established covenant, or the next phase of its development, in which its promissory aspects are supplemented with important, but previously undisclosed, obligatory dimensions.

However, the problem with these suggestions is that they fail to explain the long time lapse between these two 'stages' of covenant-making, or to account adequately for the significant differences between Genesis 15 and 17—both in terms of their covenantal framework and their promissory emphases.[39]

Two approaches are described: (1) diachronic and (2) synchronic. Those who follow a diachronic approach are critical scholars whose methodology includes form, redaction, and source criticism. Those who follow a synchronic approach accept the text in its canonical form. Williamson's description (although not the precise terms diachronic and synchronic) is indebted to John Barton, *Reading the Old Testament: Method in Biblical Study*,[40] but his use of "diachronic" and "synchronic" as technical terms may be confusing. As a technical term, diachronic study is a purely genetic study of the compilation of sources. In literal, ordinary usage, diachronic means "development through time" while synchronic means "at the same time." Thus, in the nontechnical use of the term, the idea of God responding to Abraham's developing faith and understanding of the divine revelations given to him would better be described as diachronic. Williamson's problem with the

---

[39] Ibid., 85–86.
[40] John Barton, *Reading the Old Testament: Method in Biblical Study* (Philadelphia: Westminster, 1984).

long lapse between these two "stages" of covenant making or the differences between Genesis 15 and 17 will be addressed shortly.

After discussing Genesis 15 and 17 separately Williamson concludes in the following summation:

> It is clear from the above analysis that the covenants mentioned in Genesis 15 and Genesis 17 are manifestly different in both nature (temporal/eternal; unilateral/bilateral) and primary emphases (national/international). The suggestion that they are simply two stages of the one covenant is seriously undermined by the inexplicable gap of some thirteen years between them, and by the consistent projection of the covenant in Genesis 17 into the future (lit. 'I will give my covenant' [Gen. 17:2]; 'I will establish my covenant' [Gen. 17:7 my trans.]). Both these anomalies, as well as the significant differences between the two covenant chapters, suggest a more plausible synchronic explanation: these chapters focus on two distinct, but related covenants (Williamson 2000a: 212–214).
>
> Such a conclusion is further suggested by the fact that the different emphases in Genesis 15 and 17 mirror the two separate strands set out in the programmatic agenda of Genesis 12:1–3. Genesis 15 concentrates on the divine promise to make Abraham a 'great nation' (Gen 12:2), whereas Genesis 17 focuses more on the divine promise that through Abraham 'all the families of the ground will experience blessing' (Gen. 12:3 my trans.). Thus understood, two distinct covenants were established between God and Abraham. The first (established in Gen. 15) solemnly guaranteed God's promise to make Abraham into a 'great nation'. The second covenant (anticipated in Gen. 17, but not yet established) similarly guaranteed God's promise to bless the nations through Abraham and his 'seed'.[41]

Williamson's arguments that Genesis 15 and 17 constitute separate covenants appear to be more weighty than they actually are.

The reading of the Abraham narratives that we have just presented (Genesis 12 = the giving of the promise; Genesis 15 = the making of the covenant; and Genesis 17 = the confirming of the covenant) is not possible for Williamson for a number of reasons. One is that he does not allow the expressions "cut a covenant" (*kārat bĕrît*) versus "confirm/uphold a covenant" (*hēqîm bĕrît*) distinct meanings as explained here and also substantiated in usage. His analysis is based on data from Weinfeld (instead of his own analysis of primary sources) in reaction to Dumbrell's interpretation, which does require modification. This is a fundamental linguistic point which

---

[41] Paul R. Williamson, *Sealed with an Oath*, 89.

affects one's interpretation. Williamson offers no satisfactory explanation of why the phrase "to confirm a covenant" occurs consistently in chapter 17 as opposed to the more usual expression elsewhere in the Hebrew Bible. In fact, frequently Williamson's arguments work against him:

> It may be argued that the allusion in Exod 6.4 (in the case of Abraham) is actually to Gen. 17.8, an explicit confirmation of the covenant/prom-ise ratified formally in Gen. 15.18. However, this patently fails to take adequate account of the particularly striking allusions to Genesis 15 in the sixth chapter of Exodus.[42]

It is strange that Williamson does not see that, if 15 and 17 are one covenant, his counter-argument has just been removed.

Second, in both of Williamson's works his analysis is focused on exege-sis of chapters 15 and 17, and he does not adequately discuss the flow of the plot line in the Abraham narratives as a whole. The different divine revela-tions to Abraham are given in direct response to Abraham's developing and growing faith, obedience, and understanding over the years of God's com-mands, promises, and revelations. This is a genuine diachronic approach and should not be confused with Williamson's use of the term "diachronic approach" for critical reconstructions of the editorial history of the text.

There is a chronological growth and progression in Abraham's faith and obedience and understanding of God's dealings with him. The argument that Genesis 15 concentrates on the divine promise to make Abraham a "great nation" (national), whereas Genesis 17 focuses more on the divine promise that through Abraham "all the families of the ground will experience bless-ing" (international) is part of a real contribution made by Williamson, but the differences may be overstressed. Both chapter 15 and chapter 17 speak of "land" and "seed."[43] It is interesting to note that chapter 17 speaks in a number of places about giving the land to Abraham and giving him a son (vv. 8, 16), which belong to the blessing to Abram and not to the blessings through him to the nations.

Since the promises made by God in chapter 12 focus first on blessings to Abraham and then on blessings through him to the nations, it is logical

---

[42] Paul R. Williamson, *Abraham, Israel, and the Nations*, 199–200.
[43] Bruce Waltke's outline of Genesis 12–50 entitles 15:1–16:16 as "Land covenant with Abraham and annunciation of Ishmael" and 17:1–18:15 as "Seed covenant with Abraham and annunciation of Isaac" (see Bruce K. Waltke with Charles Yu, *An Old Testament Theology: An Exegetical, Canonical, and Thematic Approach* [Grand Rapids, MI: Zondervan, 2007], 311). This does not square with the facts in the text, as both "land" and "seed" are in focus in both 15 and 17. Later, on p. 318, an outline of Genesis 15 acknowledges as much.

that in Abraham's own life he would be interested in seeing how the first part would be fulfilled before he would demonstrate interest in knowing how the second part would be fulfilled. Thus chapters 15 and 17 develop the promises in chapter 12 in the same order in which they were given to Abraham.

Williamson argues that "the suggestion that [chapters 15 and 17] are simply two stages of the one covenant is seriously undermined by the inexplicable gap of some thirteen years between them."[44] This is an astonishing statement. The thirteen-year gap between Genesis 15 and 17 is supplied by chapter 16, the narrative of the attempt by Abraham and Sarah to achieve the fulfilment of God's promise through human efforts and machinations. The story of Hagar is an adequate reason for a delay in confirming and bringing into Abraham and Sarah's experience the historical reality of what was promised. It also shows the need to broaden Abraham's horizons beyond himself and his family to his calling to bring blessing to the nations. Abraham's failure in this respect is characteristic of the rest of the history of Israel right down to the time of Jesus' own disciples.

The argument that chapter 15 is a temporal covenant and chapter 17 is an eternal covenant is based on an argument from silence. Chapter 17 says that the covenant is eternal (17:7, 13, 19), but no such thing is said in chapter 15. This is also begging the question because if chapters 15 and 17 are referring to the same thing, then the statement in 17 about the covenant being eternal would also apply to 15. Note that in chapter 15 the covenant grants "land" to Abraham (15:18–21) and in chapter 17 this is referred to as an "eternal possession" (17:8). God's promises get bigger and better all the way through the Abraham narratives, but this is no reason to argue for separate covenants.

The argument that the covenant in chapter 15 is unilateral and the one in chapter 17 is bilateral is based upon a misunderstanding. The traditional language describing covenants as being either unconditional or conditional is inadequate. We would argue that God guarantees the faithfulness of both partners in the Abrahamic covenant, but still requires faithful obedience on the part of Abraham to bring the blessing to the nations promised in the covenant. The biblical metanarrative is about God seeking in Adam an obedient son from beginning to end. Chapters 15 and 17 are one and the same covenant, and together these texts present a full-orbed holographic image of the one covenant.

---

44 Ibid.

There are also difficulties in reading chapter 17 from the perspective Williamson suggests. If the covenant there is not the one in chapter 15, then the occurrences of the word *covenant* are referring to the covenant God is about to establish. In 17:9 God asks Abraham to keep his covenant. In verse 10 he explains that the covenant involves circumcision. Then in verse 11 he says that this is for a covenant sign. This seems to reduce the covenant keeping to a covenant sign. If chapter 17 is confirming the covenant in chapter 15, then a sign is supplied for the Abrahamic covenant in general. If, however, chapter 17 is instituting a separate covenant, then the human obligation is reduced to being a covenant sign. This reading does not provide a satisfactory understanding.

Williamson's approach is flawed because later texts in both Old and New Testaments never refer to God's dealings with Abraham as "covenants"—*in the plural*. Never in all the historical summaries in the Old Testament (e.g., Nehemiah 9) is there a reference to two Abrahamic covenants. There is only one covenant with Abraham, confirmed to Isaac and Jacob.

ABRAHAM'S OBEDIENCE AND GOD'S MIGHTY OATH

GENESIS 18–19

A short time—no more than two to four months—after the covenant confirmation in Genesis 17, Abraham is visited by three men at Hebron.[45] Turns out the mysterious strangers are Yahweh and two of his agents or messengers; the text describes this visitation in the same way that we find in earlier communications from God ("the LORD appeared to Abram"). In Genesis 15 the communication came by way of a vision. In Genesis 12:1, 7 and 17:1 the manner of divine revelation is left unspecified. Here God appears to Abraham as a human.

Abraham urges the strangers to accept hospitality, and they accede to his request. While the men are eating and Abraham is serving them, they ask him where Sarah his wife is at that moment. Abraham answers curtly, "Here in the tent." No doubt cultural protocol in the ancient Near East would not allow men to address a man's wife directly. A conversation of sorts can be arranged with her behind the door of the tent. Suddenly the verb of speaking switches from third person plural to third person singular and the speaker

---

[45] In Genesis 17, Yahweh promised that Sarah would bear a son within a year. In chapter 18, she is not yet aware of any pregnancy, so this visit must be within a period of just two to four months after the revelation of Genesis 17.

repeats the promise (of becoming [a] great nation[s]) made particular and specific in Genesis 17 of a *son* given *through Sarah* within a year. Sarah laughs at this. The narrator informs us that she is not only menopausal but is no longer enjoying physical relations with her husband: they are just that *old*.[46] Yahweh asks Abraham why Sarah laughed, since nothing is impossible for him, and again he repeats his promise of a son born through her. Although the question is directed to Abraham, it is really intended for Sarah, who, out of fear, denies that she laughed. Thus, here, Sarah lies out of fear just as her husband Abraham lied out of fear when he entered Egypt and falsely declared that Sarai was only his sister.

The interchange between the Lord and Sarah is important background to the next scene in this episode. The visitors depart, heading for an "overlook" of Sodom with a Scots send-off by Abraham (i.e., he walks with them part way). Again Yahweh opens the conversation, this time with these words:

> [17] The LORD said, "Shall I hide from Abraham what I am about to do,
> [18] seeing that Abraham shall surely become a great and mighty nation, and
> all the nations of the earth shall be blessed in him?" (Gen. 18:17–18, ESV)

Yahweh opens with a rhetorical question—should he hide (lit. cover) his plan (of judging the cities of the plain) from Abraham? Of course not! Verse 18 expresses the motivation or reasons why Yahweh needs to be open and transparent. First, the statement that Abraham will become a great nation corresponds to the first set of promises in Genesis 12:1–3; and second, the statement that all the nations of the earth shall be blessed in him corresponds to the second set of promises in Genesis 12:1–3. The first set of promises were enshrined and solemnised in the covenant made in Genesis 15, while the second set were emphasised in the covenant confirmation of Genesis 17. Thus these two statements circumscribe the fact that God has a covenant relationship with Abram, and this type of relationship especially requires integrity, i.e., openness and transparency in the context of faithfulness and loyal love. These are precisely characteristics that Abraham and his wife Sarah have not shown in relationship with fellow humans or God, as is evidenced by the call to be blameless in Genesis 17:1 and by the lie of Sarah in Genesis 18:15. The rhetorical question, then, shows that Yahweh is modelling for Abraham and Sarah the kind of covenant relationship he

---

[46] Mathews, *Genesis 11:27–50:26*, 218.

would like to have with them. This is clear as Yahweh goes on to explain his motivation for revealing to Abraham his plan (still veiled, as far as the reader is concerned):

> [19] "For I have chosen him, that he may command his children and his household after him to keep the way of the LORD by doing righteousness and justice, so that the LORD may bring to Abraham what he has promised him." [20] Then the LORD said, "Because the outcry against Sodom and Gomorrah is great and their sin is very grave, [21] I will go down to see whether they have done altogether according to the outcry that has come to me. And if not, I will know." (Gen. 18:19–21, ESV)

Several points in these verses must be either clarified or stressed. Normally in prose, when the words "justice" and "righteousness" are coordinated, they form a single concept or idea: social justice. This is a figure of speech known as a hendiadys, one concept expressed through two words. The word pair becomes an idiom expressing a single thought that is both different from and greater than just putting the two words together. Just as one cannot analyse "butterfly" in English by studying "butter" and "fly," so one cannot determine the meaning of this expression by analysing "justice" and "righteousness" individually. Later on in the Old Testament, this word pair becomes a way of summarising the requirements and stipulations of the Mosaic covenant, which in turn are an expression of the character of Yahweh. This defines the content of what is meant here by social justice in contrast to how the term might commonly be used today.

According to the syntax of the clause in Genesis 18:19, "practising social justice" is the manner in which Abraham and his family are "to keep the way of Yahweh." And this "way of Yahweh" has already been clearly shown to Abraham. Yahweh began by modelling for Abraham the openness and transparency that is necessary in a covenant relationship, i.e., what it means to be blameless ("Shall I hide from Abraham what I am about to do?").

It seems in the flow of the narrative plot structure that as Abraham begins to plead with Yahweh not to destroy the righteous with the wicked in an attempt to avert destruction of the cities of the plain—and save Lot—he is taking his very first steps in practising social justice, and this is also the beginning of being a blessing to the nations. Thus the instruction of Genesis 17 is effective in shifting his focus from the first three promises of Genesis 12:1–3 to also give attention to the second three: "in you all the nations of the earth will be blessed."

The reader is invited to compare and contrast Genesis 14 and 18, since in both of these events Abraham is seeking to rescue his nephew Lot, who is in trouble. Genesis 18, however, differs significantly from Genesis 14, where Abraham with his 318 household servants rescue Lot from the marauding kings. Here Abraham faces not the big bad boys from the east, but Yahweh himself, God Almighty. It is God who is determined to judge the wicked cities. To rescue Lot this time Abraham must abandon his own shrewd schemes of subterfuge (surprise attack by night; Gen. 14:15). Instead he must buy into the "way of Yahweh," i.e., the character of Yahweh himself, in the covenant relationship. He must embrace "the way of Yahweh" and practise social justice. He cannot call for mercy upon Lot solely on the basis that he is a relative. He must plead for "the righteous" as a group and call upon God as a just judge who would not destroy the righteous along with the wicked. Thus he intercedes *as a priest for the nations* on the basis of God's own character. Yahweh is patient as he intercedes and gradually reduces the required number of righteous people in the city six times from 50 to just 10. Apparently, there were only six people who might deserve to be called righteous: Lot, his wife, and his two daughters and their fiancés (for the divine agents of judgement sought to extract them from the city before the destruction). As the sorry story of Lot at the end of Genesis 19 shows, Abraham succeeded in saving two entire (future) nations: Moab and Ammon. Abraham is beginning to be a blessing to the (other) nations.

GENESIS 22

Another episode emphasising the connection between Abraham's obedience and the fulfilment of the covenant promises is Genesis 22:15–18. After the destruction of Sodom and Gomorrah in Genesis 19, Abraham sojourns for a time in Gerar, a Philistine territory, and the events recorded in Genesis 20 are almost identical to his sojourn in Egypt in Genesis 12:10–20. Finally, in Genesis 21, a son is born to Sarah, named Isaac in memory of the fact that both parents laughed at the promises of God. Abraham also makes a covenant or treaty with Abimelech concerning ownership of wells in Genesis 21 (which was discussed earlier).

Then in Genesis 22, Abraham is tested by God and asked to offer Isaac, the son of promise, now an adolescent or young man,[47] as a sacrifice. This is

---

[47] We do not know the age of Isaac precisely, since the narrator does not tell us. Nonetheless, the boy was old enough to carry wood and ask questions, as Grüneberg notes (Keith N. Grüneberg, *Abraham, Blessing, and the*

a difficult request to understand whether for Abraham or for the reader of the narrative. Isaac is now the centre of his father's affections and love. Timothy Keller considers Genesis 22 "the second call of Abraham" (in relation to Genesis 12 as the first call):[48]

> . . . Abraham got another call from God. And it could not have been more shocking.

> *Take your son, your only son, Isaac, whom you love, and go to the region of Moriah. Sacrifice him there as a burnt offering on one of the mountains I will tell you about. . . .*

> This was the ultimate test. Isaac was now *everything* to Abraham, as God's call makes clear. He does not refer to the boy as "Isaac," but as "your son, your only son, whom you love." Abraham's affection had become adoration. Previously, Abraham's meaning in life had been dependent on God's word. Now it was becoming dependent on Isaac's love and well-being. The center of Abraham's life was shifting. God was not saying you cannot love your son, but that you must not turn a loved one into a counterfeit god.[49]

Keller hits the nail on the head. Abraham is blessed by God, but his covenant relationship with God must be more important than the blessings of God, i.e., he must desire God himself and not simply desire God for his gifts or promises. He must seek God as a greater treasure than what he gives or promises.

In the course of the Abraham narratives the narrator is redefining what blessing means. The narrative plot structure invites us to compare and contrast Abraham and Lot in the matter of blessing. By the cultural standards of their time, both men are blessed. They have children and families. Abraham was satisfied, in fact, with just Ishmael as the beginning of becoming a great nation (Gen. 17:18). They have flocks and herds and camels. Lot becomes an alderman on the Town Council of Sodom, the leading city of the five in the plain. Abraham, and vicariously Lot, have victory over their enemies. Yet the narrator makes plain that Lot's path is spiraling downwards: (1) Lot lifted up

---

Nations: A Philological and Exegetical Study of Genesis 12:3 in Its Narrative Context [Berlin: Walter de Gruyter, 2003], 228).

[48] A connection between the call of Abram in Genesis 12:1–3 and the call in Genesis 22:1–18 is established by clear literary markers. Grüneberg notes, "First, the phrase לְךָ־לְךָ is found only in these two places in the Hebrew Bible. Second, on each occasion Abraham is told to go to a place not yet completely specified." See Grüneberg, *Abraham, Blessing, and the Nations*, 222. This justifies Keller's perception of Genesis 22 as a "second call."

[49] Timothy Keller, *Counterfeit Gods: The Empty Promises of Money, Sex, and Power, and the Only Hope that Matters* (New York: Dutton, 2009), 7 (emphasis his).

his eyes (13:10); (2) Lot chose for himself (13:11); (3) Lot moved his tent toward Sodom (13:12); (4) Lot was dwelling in Sodom (14:12); (5) Lot sat in the gate of Sodom, i.e., he was an alderman on the Town Council (19:1). Lot is successful by the standards of the time, but he is unaware that by his choices he is destined for destruction. Such "blessings" are empty without a covenant relationship with God.

When Abraham is prepared to sacrifice Isaac, at the moment he is ready to slay his son, Yahweh's messenger stops him in the act. Then Abraham notices a ram caught in the bushes and offers it instead.

> [15] And the angel of the LORD called to Abraham a second time from heaven [16] and said, "By myself I have sworn, declares the LORD, because you have done this and have not withheld your son, your only son, [17] I will surely bless you, and I will surely multiply your offspring as the stars of heaven and as the sand that is on the seashore. And your offspring shall possess the gate of his enemies, [18] and in your offspring [seed] shall all the nations of the earth be blessed, because you have obeyed my voice" (Gen. 22:15–18, ESV).

As Grüneberg notes, "Gen 22:16–18 is the only promise to Abraham explicitly containing a divine oath."[50] In addition, the verbs in the promises are both emphasised by free infinitives, rendered in English by "surely." God affirms his promises given in Genesis 12, solemnised by covenant in Genesis 15, given in covenant confirmation in Genesis 17 and also mentioned in Genesis 18:19, by a mighty oath. If anything, this is the strongest statement of a guarantee by God. Yet the fulfilment of these promises is clearly connected to the obedience of Abraham. Again, the comments of Grüneberg are apt concerning the obedience of Abraham:

> Only evidence that Abraham will give up what is most precious in response to God's call when there seems no advantage to him in so doing will establish that he has pure motives in his response to God. . . . Abraham's obedience is not blind, a matter merely of outward performance or of submission to arbitrary divine whims. It rather stems from his relationship with a God who does provide (v14) and remain faithful to his promises (vv16–18), who is working for good even when demanding something painful or puzzling.
>
> Human obedience does not enable something other than can come from God's promise; rather Abraham's actions become a further grounding for the promise alongside God's free decision.[51]

---

[50] Grüneberg, *Abraham, Blessing, and the Nations*, 228.
[51] Ibid., 223, 224, 226.

Abraham's obedience is the obedience of faith, i.e., obedience as faithful loyal love in the context of a covenant relationship. God has made commitments, obligations, and promises, but these are not to be fulfilled without an obedient son in the covenant relationship.

Genesis 22:17 deals a decisive blow to Williamson's proposal that Genesis 15 and 17 represent distinct and separate covenants, the former unilateral and the latter bilateral, since this verse specifically connects the promise that Abraham's seed will be as myriad as the stars of the sky and the sand on the seashore with Abraham's obedience. Grüneberg notes, "the promise that Abraham's offspring will be as numerous as the stars is found at 15:5 and 26:4 (and also Ex. 32:13); comparison with the sand of the shore is found at 32:13[12]. The double comparison in 22:17 is unique."[52] The focus on seed in Genesis 22:16–18 is similar to Genesis 17, but the promise of seed as numerous as the stars connects specifically with Genesis 15. Thus there is only one covenant, and one cannot simplistically say that this covenant is unilateral. The traditional terminology of conditional versus unconditional covenants needs to be overhauled. One must pay attention to the flow of the plot in the Abraham narratives. In Abraham's roller-coaster of faith, just as the events of Genesis 16 motivate the covenant confirmation in Genesis 17, so the abysmal sell-out of his wife Sarah in Genesis 20 precipitates the need for the test and the affirmation by mighty oath in Genesis 22.

Included in the mighty oath is a reiteration of the last promise of Genesis 12:1–3, "and in your offspring shall all the nations of the earth be blessed, because you have obeyed my voice," this time tying it to Abraham's obedience. Three grammatical issues in the Hebrew text require attention:

$$\text{וְהִתְבָּרֲכוּ בְזַרְעֲךָ כֹּל גּוֹיֵי הָאָרֶץ}$$

wĕhitbārăkû bĕzar'ăkā kōl gôyê hā'āreṣ

all the nations of the earth will be blessed through your seed (Gen. 22:18)[53]

First, what is the semantic value of the *hithpael* of *bārak*? There is an ancient tradition—as old as the Septuagint—that construes the form as passive. Recent scholarship, however, such as one finds in the exhaustive study of Grüneberg, argues for a "speech action hithpael" meaning "utter blessing." Nonetheless,

---

[52] Ibid., 229.
[53] This is just a literal working translation for purposes of discussion.

Benjamin Noonan has demonstrated that the linguistic foundation of the research by Grüneberg is unsound.[54] There is no evidence from other languages related to Hebrew to support Grüneberg's contention that the *hithpael* of *bārak* functions as a speech action middle. The clear meaning of the *hithpael* would be a reflexive of the declarative-estimative function found in the base form, the *piel*. Thus the *hithpael* of *bārak* should mean, "to consider or declare oneself blessed," and this semantic value works well in this context.

Also significant is determining the exact function of the *beth* preposition on the suffixed noun "your seed." Ernst Jenni has a magisterial work analysing all 15,570 instances of *beth* according to linguistic principles.[55] Fundamentally, "the *beth* preposition indicates two correlates, x and y, such that x refers to y."[56] The first correlate x is related to the second correlate y; therefore y is the point or standard of reference. The particular function of *beth* in this text is what Jenni calls a *beth communicationis*, a sub-category of the *beth realisation*.[57] What this jargon means in simple terms is that y is a person, animal, or thing (*beth realisation*), and that y speaks indirectly for x (*beth communicationis*). Thus the "seed" of Abraham will speak indirectly for the nations, i.e., the nations will utter blessing through, or better, "in the name of" the "seed" of Abraham. This analysis appears to assume a speech action middle. With the analysis of the *hithpael* given by Noonan, the *beth* is simply instrumental: the nations consider/declare themselves blessed by or through Abraham's seed. In this way, the passive and "declarative-estimative hithpael" are virtually the same thing. The overall thrust of Genesis 22:16–18 is nicely summed up by Grüneberg:

> 22:18 does not deny that the nations will gain blessing: by implication it affirms it. But its main thrust is to stress Israel's own prosperity. This prosperity, it suggests, is grounded in three things: the divine promise, Abraham's faithful obedience, and Israel's own ongoing commitment to Yhwh—maintaining his law, worshipping at Jerusalem, and acknowledging herself entirely dependent on him for her life.[58]

His conclusion is also based on the focus on Moriah (= Jerusalem) in Genesis 22 and the mention of *tôrâ* in Genesis 26:5.

---

[54] Benjamin J. Noonan, "Abraham, Blessing, and the Nations: A Reexamination of the Niphal and Hitpael of ברך in the Patriarchal Narratives," *Hebrew Studies* 51 (2010): 73–93.

[55] E. Jenni, *Die hebräischen Präpositionen, Band 1: Die Präposition Beth* (Stuttgart: Kolhammer, 1992).

[56] See E. Jenni, *Die hebräischen Präpositionen, Band 1: Die Präposition Beth*, 64.

[57] Ibid., 164.

[58] Grüneberg, *Abraham, Blessing, and the Nations*, 235.

Third, what is the referent of "your seed" in verses 17 and 18? The problem arises from the fact that, like the noun in English, the noun "seed" in Hebrew can be construed either a collective singular (a bag of seed) or a unitary singular (seed as opposed to seeds). Jack Collins made a complete and exhaustive analysis of all the data and discovered the following principles regarding whether the intended meaning is collective or unitary singular: (1) when זֶרַע serves as a collective for "offspring or posterity" in general, the verbs are commonly singular although the plural is found a number of times; (2) when זֶרַע denotes "posterity," the pronouns (independent pronouns, object pronouns and suffixes) are always plural; (3) when זֶרַע indicates a specific (individual) descendant, it appears with singular verb inflections, adjectives, and pronouns.[59]

According to these grammatical principles, the final clause of Genesis 22:17 appears to be set apart from what proceeds. T. D. Alexander comments as follows:

> A striking feature of the final clause is the way in which it does not begin with a *vav*-consecutive; rather it is introduced by the imperfect verb יִרַשׁ preceded by a non-converting וֹ. This syntactical arrangement leaves open the possibility that the זֶרַע referred to in the final clause differs from that mentioned in the first part of the verse. Whereas the first זֶרַע obviously refers to a very large number of descendants, the second would, following Collins' approach, denote a single individual who is victorious over his enemies.
>
> This latter reading of 22:17 has implications also for 22:18a which states: וְהִתְבָּרֲכוּ בְזַרְעֲךָ כֹּל גּוֹיֵי הָאָרֶץ ('and all the nations of the earth will be blessed through your offspring'). If the immediately preceding reference to 'seed' in 22:17 denotes an individual, this must also be the case in 22:18a, for there is nothing here to indicate a change in number. The blessing of 'all the nations of the earth' is thus associated with a particular descendant of Abraham, rather than with all those descended from him.[60]

The same syntactical arrangement can be noted in Genesis 24:60. There is also an allusion to Genesis 22:17b–18a in Psalm 72:17: "may all nations be blessed through him." According to the context of the psalm, the individual mentioned here through whom all nations shall be blessed is a royal figure. Alexander explains:

---

[59] Jack Collins, "A Syntactical Note (Genesis 3.15): Is the Woman's Seed Singular or Plural?" *Tyndale Bulletin* 48/1 (1997): 142–144.

[60] T. Desmond Alexander, "Further Observations of the Term 'Seed' in Genesis," *Tyndale Bulletin* 48/1 (1997): 365. See also idem, "Genesis 22 and the Covenant of Circumcision," *JSOT* 25 (1983): 17–22.

While the psalm's title associates it with Solomon, its contents clearly envisages a king whose reign surpasses by far that of Solomon. Indeed, this future monarch is described as ruling the entire earth, bringing deliverance to the oppressed by defeating their enemies (*cf.* Ps 72:4–14).[61]

So Paul's argument in Galatians 3:16 that the text speaks of "seed" and not "seeds" appears to be based upon solid exegesis of the Hebrew Scriptures.[62]

GENESIS 26

The last of the six promises of Genesis 12:1–3 is again repeated in Genesis 26:1–5 and here, too, as in Genesis 22:18, it is connected with Abraham's obedience:

> [1] Now there was a famine in the land—besides the earlier famine of Abraham's time—and Isaac went to Abimelech king of the Philistines in Gerar. [2] The LORD appeared to Isaac and said, "Do not go down to Egypt; live in the land where I tell you to live. [3] Stay in this land for a while, and I will be with you and will bless you. For to you and your descendants I will give all these lands and will confirm the oath I swore to your father Abraham. [4] I will make your descendants as numerous as the stars in the sky and will give them all these lands, and through your offspring all nations on earth will be blessed, [5] because Abraham obeyed me and kept my requirements, my commands, my decrees and my laws." (Gen. 26:1–5, NIV)

When Isaac has obtained land, wealth, and water, verse 24 repeats the connection with Abraham:

> [23] From there he went up to Beersheba. [24] That night the LORD appeared to him and said, "I am the God of your father Abraham. Do not be afraid, for I am with you; I will bless you and will increase the number of your descendants for the sake of my servant Abraham."
> [25] Isaac built an altar there and called on the name of the LORD. There he pitched his tent, and there his servants dug a well. (Gen 26:23–25, NIV)

In Genesis 26 the narrator depicts Isaac following in his father's footsteps.[63] While he does not go down to Egypt, he does—like his father—sojourn in Gerar (Philistine territory), lie about his wife, gain victory in the matter of

---

61 Alexander, "Further Observations of the Term 'Seed' in Genesis," 365.
62 See C. John Collins, "Galatians 3:16: What Kind of Exegete Was Paul?" *Tyndale Bulletin* 54:1 (2003), 75–86.
63 Grüneberg, *Abraham, Blessing, and the Nations*, 235.

wells, and conclude a treaty with Abimelech at Beersheba. As Janzen notes, "the compact rehearsal of Isaac's life in this chapter shows his vocation to be largely one of consolidating the trail Abraham has blazed by retracing many of its episodes."[64] Four times Yahweh links the promises to Abraham (vv. 3, 5, 24 [2x]).

In the divine revelation in Genesis 26:2–5 Yahweh promises to "be with Isaac," i.e., protect him and give him success in his undertakings. This is the first time this is promised to a patriarch, although Abimelech observed this of Abraham in 21:22 and (another?) Abimelech observes it of Isaac in 26:28. The promises of blessing, descendants, and land made to Abraham are given to Isaac. Note that the promise of lands chiastically surrounds the promise of descendants in an A-B-A pattern.

Yahweh promises to "confirm the oath" which he swore to Abraham. The expression is *hēqîm šĕvu'â* and is directly equivalent to *hēqîm bĕrît*, only the object is "oath" and not "covenant." The use of "oath" is probably a direct reference to the oath in 22:16–18, which confirms in a mighty way the covenant established in 15 and upheld in 17. The "oath" therefore stands for the covenant but refers especially to Genesis 22:16–18. The reference to descendants as numerous as the stars is a direct reference also to Genesis 15:5, although this is taken up in Genesis 22:17, and the promise that "through your offspring all nations on earth will be blessed" connects with the emphasis of Genesis 17 and its modification in 22:18.

This last of the six promises of Genesis 12:1–3 is given five times in the narratives of Genesis: 12:3; 18:18; 22:18; 26:4; 28:14. In 12:3 the prepositional phrase is "in you"; in 18:18 the prepositional phrase is "in him." Both pronouns refer directly to Abraham. In 22:18 and 26:4 the prepositional phrase is changed to "in/through your offspring." Abraham has been faithful loyal, and obedient in the covenant relationship. Henceforth, the blessing of the nations depends upon the prosperity of Israel. In 28:14, God is speaking to Jacob and says "in you and in your offspring." Genesis 28:14 is the only other place apart from 12:3 that speaks of the peoples of the world as *mišpāḥôt* ("clans"); all other reiterations use the term *gôyîm* ("nations"). This is because 28:14 forms a kind of *inclusio* with 12:3 in the narrative structure.[65] Conversely, Lee says, "to show further the continuity of the later

[64] J. G. Janzen, *Genesis 12–50: Abraham and All the Families of the Earth*, International Theological Commentary (Grand Rapids/Edinburgh: Eerdmans/Handsel, 1993), 103.

[65] See Chee-Chiew Lee, "גוים in Genesis 35:11 and the Abrahamic Promise of Blessings for the Nations," *JETS* 52/3 (2009): 472.

reiterations of this blessing with the Table of Nations (Genesis 10), Genesis 18:18; 22:18; 26:4 use גויי הארץ instead of משפחת האדמה."[66] Genesis 28:14 is also the only place in which we have "in you and in your offspring"—both the pronoun referring to the patriarch and the term "offspring" or "descendants" because, as a patriarch, Jacob is the last person to whom the promise can be both through him and also through his family. After the patriarchs, the blessing comes through the nation descended from them, i.e., Israel.

The repetition of the promises to Isaac is concluded by connecting their fulfilment to the obedience of Abraham in 26:5, as we also see in 26:24. This text is clear: "through your offspring all nations on earth will be blessed, *because* Abraham obeyed me and kept my charge (i.e., his obligations to me), my commands, my decrees and my laws." The four terms *mišmartî, miṣwōtay, ḥuqqôtay,* and *tôrôtay* are all characteristic of the Mosaic covenant *because this narrative was written* (by Moses) *to instruct Israel*: blessing for the nations depends upon their obedience.

GENESIS 35

Before concluding our discussion on the connection between fulfilment of the promises and Abraham's obedience, we may observe how a remarkable twist is added when the promises are later repeated to Jacob. After his exile with Laban he returned to the land of Canaan and lived at Beersheba, where Abraham and Isaac had lived. From there God called him to go north toward Haran to revisit Bethel, where God had first revealed himself to him in the dream of the ladder to heaven. As Gordon Wenham comments,

> Just as Abraham's three-day pilgrimage to sacrifice on Mount Moriah climaxed in the most categorical reaffirmation of the promises in his career, so, too, Jacob's sacred journey is crowned with the strongest statement of the promises that he ever heard. And it is to this revelation that Jacob looked back at the end of his life when he blessed Ephraim and Manasseh in 48:3–4.[67]

The content of the revelation is expressed in verses 9–13:

> [9] After Jacob returned from Paddan Aram, God appeared to him again and blessed him. [10] God said to him, "Your name is Jacob, but you

---

66 Ibid.
67 Gordon J. Wenham, *Genesis 16–50*, WBC 2 (Waco, TX: Word, 1994), 325.

will no longer be called Jacob; your name will be Israel." So he named him Israel.

[11] And God said to him, "I am God Almighty; be fruitful and increase in number. A nation and a community of nations will come from you, and kings will come from your body. [12] The land I gave to Abraham and Isaac I also give to you, and I will give this land to your descendants after you." [13] Then God went up from him at the place where he had talked with him. (NIV)

The command to be fruitful and increase shows that Jacob, like Abraham and Isaac, inherits the role of a new Adam and that Canaan is a new Eden. Then, the promises of descendants and land are specifically and strongly vouchsafed to him. There is an interesting twist, however, to the promises. Jacob is told that a nation and an "assembly" or "congregation" of nations will come from him. We already know that a nation will come from him. But what could it mean that "a company of nations" will come from him? This cannot refer to the "tribes" of Israel, for this would not satisfy the Hebrew term *gôyîm*, which refers to the groups of peoples in the world as politically and socially structured entities with government. Nor could it be a reference to the later development when Israel was split into two kingdoms. Two kingdoms are not exactly a company of nations. In the context of the later narrative, it can only portend the inclusion of the Gentiles in the community under the blessing promised through Abraham. As Chee-Chiew Lee notes in a careful exegetical study of this text,

> Paul Williamson argues that the metaphorical usage of אב "father" to portray the idea of counselor, protector, or benefactor in the Hebrew Bible suggests that Abraham's fatherhood here goes beyond genealogical linkage and implies that Abraham shall be a spiritual benefactor of many nations, "the mediator of God's blessing to them."[68] The nuance between the promise made to Abraham in Gen 17:4–5 and its reiteration to Jacob in 35:10–12 is as follows: while Abraham becoming "the father of many nations" may still be fulfilled through other physical descendants of Abraham, Jacob becoming "a nation and a company of nations" can only be fulfilled beyond his physical descendants.[69]

It could be reasonably argued that the promise of Abraham becoming the "father of many nations" is fulfilled by the nation of Israel, the descendants

---

[68] Paul R. Williamson, *Abraham, Israel and the Nations*, 158–160.
[69] See Chee-Chiew Lee, "גוים in Genesis 35:11 and the Abrahamic Promise of Blessings for the Nations," 473–474.

of Ishmael (Gen. 25:12–18), the descendants of Abraham's second wife Keturah (Gen. 25:1–5), the descendants of Esau (Gen. 36:1–19, 31–43), Moab (Gen. 19:37), and Ammon (Gen. 19:38). This is a common understanding, as Lee points out,[70] but the statement in Genesis 35:11 does not permit this. What we can observe is that there appears to be a pattern in God's dealings with the patriarchs. God makes big promises. He promises that Abraham will become a great nation and have Canaan as his possession—this much already in chapter 12. Abraham would have been happy to begin the great nation with Ishmael, fathered through Hagar, and wait for future descendants to gain possession of the land. Yet God had to make plain to him in Genesis 17 that the nation would come from his union with his wife Sarah. The pattern, then, is that the human perception of God's promises, great as they are, almost always forms a stunted vision of what God really has in mind and in store for his people.

It should also be noted in passing that Genesis 35:11 repeats the promise of Genesis 17:6 that kings as well as nations will come from Abraham and now Jacob. This thread will be picked up later, but it is the divine intention for Abraham and his family, and only human perception will stunt this vision for the future as well.

Two further texts in the Old Testament may possibly be considered either citations of or allusions to the last promise of Genesis 12:3—Jeremiah 4:2 and Psalm 72:17. If they are genuine allusions, they connect the Abrahamic covenant to the Davidic covenant and the new covenant respectively. Thus they will be discussed later when the Davidic and new covenants are considered.

TENSIONS IN THE METANARRATIVE

Significant tensions have been introduced into the plot structure of the metanarrative in the course of the unfolding of the story of Abraham. The larger story began with creation and the first man in covenant with the Lord God as obedient son and royal vicegerent over the world. Human disobedience brought chaos and death. God made a new start after the flood with a brand new world and a second Adam. Here, too, we saw that the human partner was not faithful in the covenant relationship. Divine grace alone preserves the world.

So out of the chaos leading to Babel, God begins another new creation

---

[70] Ibid.

with another new Adam, Abraham and his family. Abraham is depicted in the narratives as a new Adam placed in Canaan, a new Eden. From the meta-narrative to this point, we now know that the human partner not only will not but cannot be faithful in the covenant relationship. We also now know that a fresh, new start is a non-solution to the original problem of human disloyalty and disobedience that resulted in the arrival of death in the creation.

Nevertheless, God calls Abram and makes huge promises concerning blessing in his life and salvation for the entire world through him. Later in Genesis 15, these big promises are strengthened by a covenant, although Abram still has nothing to show from God's word. Although this covenant is patterned in general after ancient Near Eastern treaties, strangely God undertakes the self-maledictory oath for both partners in the covenant. This is completely unheard of in Abraham's world and introduces another tension. Since we know that the human partner will not demonstrate complete devotion and full obedience within the covenant relationship, God seems to be guaranteeing only his own death at this point. How can God die? We understand how this works from the end of the story, but at this stage, we must allow this tension in the narrative.

Yet as Genesis 17:2 shows (as well as subsequent texts such as Gen. 18:19; 22:18; and 26:5, where God upholds his covenant [later confirmed by a mighty oath]), God still requires an obedient son in the covenant relationship and bases fulfilment of the promises not only upon himself but also upon Abraham's obedience and, indeed, upon the future obedience of Abraham's family, Israel. In sum, Abraham was not a perfect covenant partner and badly represented Yahweh to the world of that time in a number of ways. His lack of complete devotion and obedience points to the fact that another is coming who will be obedient in every respect.

There are theological tensions as well as tensions in the narrative plot structure. We wonder how another divine-human covenant relationship can survive, given that disloyalty is *endemic* in the human partner, i.e., the human partner is unfaithful *by nature*. The narrative assures the reader that this covenant is undergirded by the mighty promises of the Almighty. God guarantees the covenant promises and yet he also requires an obedient son in the covenant relationship.

All of these tensions are important to the later plot structure of the meta-narrative, and we must not attempt to remove them through eisegesis. They must be allowed to stand. We must let the text stand over us; we must not stand over the text to judge what can and cannot be allowed in the story.

THE PURPOSE OF THE ABRAHAMIC COVENANT—HOW THE GRAND STORY UNFOLDS

Why did God make a covenant with Abraham? And how is this covenant, made so long ago, relevant to us today? Exegesis of the relevant texts has shown that although the cultural-historical setting and language differ from Genesis 1–3 or Genesis 6–9, the main idea is still that God is establishing his rule in the context of a covenant relationship. Abraham and his descendants will be a light to the nations in this matter.

Looking backward and forward in the canon of Scripture, two things must be said about the covenant with Abraham. First, the covenant with Abraham is the basis for all of God's dealings with the human race from this point on, and the basis of all his later plans and purposes in history. Thus the covenants (with creation, with Noah, with Abraham) are the backbone of the metanarrative plot structure. A quick overview of the Old Testament demonstrates this.

The book of Genesis ends with Israel, the family of Abraham, becoming a great and numerous people. The promise of descendants and posterity is being fulfilled.

The point of the book of Exodus will be to add, by way of redemption from slavery, the gift of the land. So the covenant with Abraham is the basis for delivering Israel from slavery in Egypt. Israel becomes a great nation, and God makes a covenant with the nation at Sinai (Deut. 7:7–9).

The Mosaic covenant at Sinai is, in turn, the basis for God's covenant with David. The king of Israel is the administrator and mediator of the Mosaic covenant, representing God's rule to the people and representing the people as a whole (2 Sam. 7:22–24).

As the story unfolds, however, it is marked by divine faithfulness on the one hand and human unfaithfulness on the other. At every point along the way, it seems that God's plan is doomed to failure. Israel is a major bottleneck in the plan of God to bless the nations. How can blessing flow through her to the world when she is just as riddled with sin? Paul explains this in Galatians 3:

[8] The Scripture foresaw that God would justify the Gentiles by faith, and announced the gospel in advance to Abraham: "All nations will be blessed

through you." [9] So those who have faith are blessed along with Abraham, the man of faith.

[10] All who rely on observing the law are under a curse, for it is written: "Cursed is everyone who does not continue to do everything written in the Book of the Law." [11] Clearly no one is justified before God by the law, because, "The righteous will live by faith." [12] The law is not based on faith; on the contrary, "The man who does these things will live by them." [13] Christ redeemed us from the curse of the law by becoming a curse for us, for it is written: "Cursed is everyone who is hung on a tree." [14] He redeemed us in order that the blessing given to Abraham might come to the Gentiles through Christ Jesus, so that by faith we might receive the promise of the Spirit. (Gal. 3:8–14, NIV)

When we come to the time of Jesus, Israel is under a curse because they have been unfaithful to the Israelite covenant. Do they want to be an instrument of blessing to the nations? No, they want to raise an army of guerrillas who will conquer and smash the might of Rome, drive the nations away, and bring glory to Israel by setting her over the world. And so God sent Jesus to fulfill his promises. First, Jesus had to deliver Israel from the curse and put her back into a right relationship with God. Then as King of Israel, he had to do what the nation as a whole had failed to do: bring blessing to the nations. He accomplished both by dying on the cross. Several texts in the New Testament specifically connect the coming of Jesus Christ with the Abrahamic covenant. First, Luke 1:54–55:

[54] He has helped his servant Israel,
    remembering to be merciful
[55] to Abraham and his descendants forever,
    even as he said to our fathers. (NIV)

Mary's Song of Praise in Luke 1 describes the birth of her son as God "remembering mercy." Behind the Greek word that is rendered "mercy" is the Hebrew term *hesed*, which has to do with fulfilling covenant obligations. The covenant promises being fulfilled are the ones made to Abraham, according to Mary.

Then, in verses 69–75:

[69] He has raised up a horn of salvation for us
    in the house of his servant David
[70] (as he said through his holy prophets of long ago),
[71] salvation from our enemies

and from the hand of all who hate us—
[72] to show mercy to our fathers
and to remember his holy covenant,
[73] the oath he swore to our father Abraham:
[74] to rescue us from the hand of our enemies,
and to enable us to serve him without fear
[75] in holiness and righteousness before him all our days.
(Luke 1:69–75, NIV)

At the birth of John the Baptist, Zechariah, the father, regains speech and opens his mouth in a prophecy. He speaks here of God fulfilling his promises to Abraham in bringing help to Israel.

Then, in Acts 3:24–26:

[24] Indeed, all the prophets from Samuel on, as many as have spoken, have foretold these days. [25] And you are heirs of the prophets and of the covenant God made with your fathers. He said to Abraham, "Through your offspring all peoples on earth will be blessed." [26] When God raised up his servant, he sent him first to you to bless you by turning each of you from your wicked ways. (NIV)

After the beggar is healed in the Porch of Solomon, Peter preaches at the temple and announces good news through God's servant Jesus, crucified and risen from the dead. The good news is that God has fulfilled his promises to Abraham and sent Jesus "to bless you by turning each of you from your wicked ways." Thus it is clear, from even a few texts in the New Testament, that the covenant with Abraham is the basis and foundation for the gospel message announcing forgiveness of sins and justification through Jesus Christ.

No doubt the claim that the covenants, and in particular the Abrahamic covenant, form(s) the backbone of the metanarrative will be criticised. One problem faced by many biblical theologies is that they comprehend the history and the prophets, but where do the Psalms and Wisdom texts fit in the picture? Yet books like the Psalms are founded on the Abrahamic covenant and the Mosaic and Davidic covenants flowing from it. Two examples may suffice at this point.

Psalm 47 is a brief psalm inviting the nations to rejoice because Yahweh is supreme sovereign over all peoples and has subdued them under Israel. At the end, the lyrics read as follows:

[8] God reigns over the nations;
   God sits on his holy throne.
[9] The princes of the peoples gather
   as the people of the God of Abraham.
For the shields of the earth belong to God;
   he is highly exalted! (Ps. 47:8–9, ESV)

Note how "the princes of the peoples [plural] gather as the people [singular] of the God of Abraham." Non-Israelite nations are included in the one people of God. The mention of the "God of Abraham" is sufficient to remind those singing this psalm that the inclusion of the Gentiles into the one people of God can be possible only through Abraham becoming father in a spiritual sense, i.e., the model of faith, for a company of nations, as Genesis 35:11 intends.

Psalm 117, although the shortest in the entire Psalter, the Hymnal of ancient Israel, is perhaps the most profound because it functions like a dissertation abstract, encapsulating in as few words as possible the burden of the entire book of Psalms:

[1] Praise the LORD, all nations!
   Extol him, all peoples!
[2] For great is his steadfast love toward us,
   and the faithfulness of the LORD endures forever.
Praise the LORD! (ESV)

The word pair steadfast love (*ḥesed*) and faithfulness (*'ĕmet*) is actually a summary of the behaviour required by both parties in the Mosaic covenant/Torah. This, the shortest hymn in Israel's Hymnal, sums up the whole Psalter: Yahweh is to be praised by the nations for his covenantal faithfulness and love. The key exegetical issue is identifying the referent of the pronoun "us" in verse 2. Lohfink and Zenger express themselves strongly on this in a footnote:

Ps 117:2 is meant to be inclusive: YHWH's steadfast love and faithfulness hold sway powerfully "over us," that is over Israel and the nations. That is to be maintained against the majority of interpreters, also against Mathys, *Dichter*, 292–97. That Psalm 117 was created for the Hallel, Psalms 113–118, precisely with a "theology of the nations" in mind is shown by the Münster dissertation of Jutta Schröten, *Entstehung, Komposition und Wirkungsgeschichte des 118. Psalms*, BBB 95 (Weinheim: Beltz Athenaeum, 1995).[71]

Lohfink and Zenger demonstrate in their work the importance of interpreting a psalm not as a stand-alone text but in the context of the editorial work of Israel's Hymnal—Psalms. If, however, the standard view is taken, the command to the nations to praise the Lord is given by Israel. The "us" would then be taken to refer to Israel. Faithfulness and loyal love is what Israel has experienced in covenant relationship with God. But then, due to God's faithful loyal love, the blessing flows to the nations by virtue of the Abrahamic covenant. This indeed seems to be Paul's point in Romans 15:11.[72] Thus, in the end, there hardly seems to be much difference between the two positions.

Second, the purpose of the covenants is for God to reveal himself. After the covenant with Noah we know that everything depends on divine favour. Humans will not and cannot demonstrate faithfulness in the covenant relationship with God that is fundamental to life in this world. So, one of my friends, Don Wood, asked, "If everything depends on God's grace, then why such a long story?" Why doesn't God just zap us with his grace in Genesis 12? We know for sure by this point in the metanarrative that chaos and death will be overcome only by divine grace. The answer to this question is that God wants to reveal himself. John Walton explains:

> God has a plan in history that he is sovereignly executing. The goal of that plan is for him to be in relationship with the people whom he has created. It would be difficult for people to enter into a relationship with a God whom they do not know. If his nature were concealed, obscured, or distorted, an honest relationship would be impossible. In order to clear the way for this relationship, then, God has undertaken as a primary objective a program of self-revelation. He wants people to know him. The mechanism that drives this program is the covenant, and the instrument is Israel. The purpose of the covenant is to reveal God.[73]

---

[71] Norbert Lohfink and Erich Zenger, *The God of Israel and the Nations: Studies in Isaiah and the Psalms* (Collegeville, MN: Liturgical Press, 1994), 182, n. 44.

[72] I am indebted to Stephen G. Dempster for drawing my attention to Paul's use of Psalm 117.

[73] Walton, *Covenant: God's Purpose, God's Plan*, 24.

Chapter Nine

THE ISRAELITE (MOSAIC) COVENANT: EXODUS

Central to the book of Exodus—and indeed to the entire Pentateuch—is the covenant made between Yahweh and Israel at Sinai, comprised in chapters 19–24. The eighteen chapters preceding describe the release of Israel from bondage and slavery in Egypt and the journey through the wilderness to Sinai. Chapters 25–40 are devoted to the construction of a place of worship as the appropriate recognition of the divine kingship established through the covenant.

A much bigger claim, however, can be made for Exodus 19–24. This unit is entitled the "Book of the Covenant" by Moses himself (Ex. 24:7). The Book of the Covenant, along with the book of Deuteronomy as an addition or supplement to it (cf. Deut. 28:69 MT [29:1 EV]), forms the heart of the old covenant. And it is the interpretation of the relation of the old covenant to the new that is the basis of all the major divisions among Christians, i.e., all denominational differences derive ultimately from different understandings of the relation of the covenant at Sinai to us today.

This brief treatment of Exodus 19–24 seeks to base accurate exposition of this text on (1) closer attention to the larger literary structure, (2) exegesis based on the cultural, historical, and linguistic setting of the text, and (3) consideration of the larger story of Scripture (metanarrative) and explicit indications of how this text fits within this larger story.

Where and how Exodus 19–24 fits into the larger story of Scripture will be briefly detailed at both the beginning and the end of the section—framing all analysis of the covenant at Sinai as bookends.[1] In between, attention will be given to the literary structure of Exodus 19–24, and afterwards exegesis will be focused on the divine purpose of the covenant in Exodus 19:5–6, the

---

[1] The covenant in Genesis 1–2 and the covenant with Noah in Genesis 6–9 have been discussed in greater detail in Peter J. Gentry, "Kingdom through Covenant: Humanity as the Divine Image," *SBJT* 12/1 (2008): 16–42.

first four of the Ten Commandments, and the ceremony of covenant ratification in Exodus 24:1–11.

EXODUS 19–24 WITHIN THE LARGER STORY OF SCRIPTURE

The biblical narrative begins with a creator God who is the maker of our world and, indeed, of the entire universe. We humans are the crowning achievement of his creative work. There is a difference, moreover, between humans and animals, in fact, between us and all other creatures: we alone have been made as the image of this creator God and have been given special tasks to perform on behalf of the Creator.

According to Genesis 1:26–28, the divine image defines human life (ontologically—not just functionally) in terms of a covenant relationship with the creator God on the one hand, and with the creation on the other. The former may be captured by the term sonship and is implied by Genesis 5:1–3. The latter relationship, i.e., between humans and the creation, may be reflected in the terms kingship and servanthood. We noted previously that in the ninth-century Aramaic Tell Fakheriyeh Inscription, ṣalmā' ("image") refers to the king's majestic power and rule in relation to his subjects, while děmûthā' ("likeness") refers to the king's petitionary role and relation to the deity.[2] Thus the ancient Near Eastern data confirm, correspond to, and illustrate precisely the terms used in the biblical text.

Furthermore, as Genesis 2:4–25 shows, the Adamic son is like a priest in a garden sanctuary. He must first learn the ways of God in order to exercise the rule of God as God himself would.[3]

The biblical narrative, then, is focused at the start on establishing the rule of God through covenant relationship: *kingdom through covenant*.

The first humans, however, rebelled against the creator God. As a result, there is chaos, discord, and death in the creation at every level.

The destructive path chosen by the first humans led to a downward spiral of corruption and violence until divine intervention was required. God judged the human race by a flood and made a new beginning with Noah

---

[2] W. Randall Garr, "'Image' and 'Likeness' in the Inscription from Tell Fakhariyeh," *Israel Exploration Journal* 50/3–4 (2003): 227–234.

[3] See Gordon J. Wenham, "Sanctuary Symbolism in the Garden of Eden Story," in *I Studied Inscriptions from before the Flood: Ancient Near Eastern, Literary, and Linguistic Approaches to Genesis 1–11*, ed. R. S. Hess and D. T. Tsumura, Sources for Biblical and Theological Study 4 (Winona Lake, IN: Eisenbrauns, 1994), 399–404; William J. Dumbrell, *The Search for Order: Biblical Eschatology in Focus* (Grand Rapids, MI: Baker, 1994), 24–25; and M. Hutter, "Adam als Gärtner und König (Gen. 2:8, 15)," *Biblische Zeitschrift* 30 (1985): 258–262.

and his family. Noah is presented in the narrative as a new Adam. As soon as the dry land appears out of the chaos of the floodwaters, Noah is placed there and commanded to be fruitful and multiply (Gen. 9:1); i.e., he is given Adam's commission or mandate. The correspondence to Genesis 1 is striking. Eventually, however, the family of Noah ends up in the same chaos and corruption as the family of the first Adam. With the Tower of Babel, the nations are lost and scattered over the face of the earth.

So, God made another new start, this time with Abraham. Abraham and his family, called Israel, is another Adam, who will be God's true humanity. God makes great promises to Abraham in Genesis 12. These promises are enshrined eventually in a covenant made with him and his descendants in chapters 15 and 17 and confirmed by a mighty oath in chapter 22.

The first of God's promises to Abram, "I will make you into a great nation," employs the term *gôy* in Hebrew, while the last of God's six promises, "all the clans/families of the earth will be blessed in you," employs instead the term *mišpāḥâ*. This contrast in terms carries forward the focus on kingdom through covenant.

Thus, Abraham, and Israel, have inherited an Adamic role.[4] Yahweh refers to the nation as his *son* in Exodus 4:22–23. The divine purpose in the covenant established between God and Israel at Sinai is unfolded in Exodus 19:3–6. As a kingdom of priests, they will function to make the ways of God known to the nations and also to bring the nations into a right relationship to God. Israel will display to the rest of the world within its covenant community the kind of relationships first to God and then to one another and to the physical world, that God intended originally for all of humanity. In fact, through Abraham's family, God purposes and plans to bring blessing to all the nations of the world. In this way, through the family of Abraham, through Israel, his last Adam, he will bring about a resolution of the sin and death caused by the first Adam. Since Israel is located geographically on the one and only communications link between the great superpowers of the ancient world (Egypt and Mesopotamia), in this position she will show the nations how to have a right relationship to God, how to treat each other in a truly human way, and how to faithfully steward the earth's resources. This is the meaning of Israel's sonship.

The promises of God to Abraham focused on two things: descendants and land. When we come to the books of Exodus to Deuteronomy, which

---

[4] Exodus 15:17 shows that Canaan becomes for Israel what the garden sanctuary was for Adam.

constitute the Mosaic covenant or covenant with Israel, we have the fulfilment of these promises. First, God has greatly increased the descendants of
Abraham so that they are innumerable, like the sand upon the seashore or the
stars of the night sky. Second, he has given them the land of Canaan.

God's plan and purpose, however, has not changed. He wants to bless
the descendants of Abraham and, through them, all the nations. In fact, his
plan is to restore his broken and ruined creation through Israel. As they
come out of Egypt and before they enter the land, God makes an agreement
with Israel. The purpose of this agreement or covenant is to enable them to
enjoy the blessings he wants to give them and to be the blessing to the other
nations. This covenant will show them how to be his true humanity. It will
direct, guide, and lead them to have a right relationship with God and a right
relationship with everyone else in the covenant community. It will also teach
them how to have a right relationship to all the creation, to be good stewards of the earth's resources. We might say, then, that the Mosaic covenant
is given at this time to administer the fulfilment of the divine promises to
Abraham and to the nation as a whole, and through them to the entire world.

LABELLING COVENANTS

Frequently this covenant is entitled "the covenant at Sinai," but what is
the biblical terminology? From the point of view of the New Testament,
i.e., latinized English for "new covenant," it is called the "old covenant" in
2 Corinthians 3:14 (and compare v. 15).[5] Hebrews 8–9 also uses the term
"first" for this covenant. In the Old Testament, however, it is commonly
called the Torah (law) or the Torah (law) of Moses (Ex. 24:12).

In Scripture, covenants are normally named according to the human
partner. The covenant in Genesis 6–9 is between God and Noah. This is
expanded to include his family and, through them, all of humanity. It is fair
to call this "the covenant with Noah." The covenant in Genesis 15 and 17
is called the "covenant with Abram" in Genesis 15:18. Since it is passed
directly on to Isaac and Jacob, it is called the covenant with Isaac and also
the covenant with Jacob in Leviticus 26:42. Later we find the term "the covenant with the fathers" (Deut. 4:31) referring to Abraham, Isaac, and Jacob.
Note that the term covenant is always singular. It is never "the covenants
with the fathers." We can conveniently and legitimately call it the "covenant

---

[5] The term "New Testament" is derived from the Latin *Novum Testamentum*, in which *novum* means "new" and
testamentum means covenant.

with Abram/Abraham." The covenant made at Sinai is simply called "the Book of the Covenant" in Exodus 24:7. In Exodus 34:27 this same covenant is with Moses and with Israel. Hence some scholars have called it the Mosaic covenant. It could just as well be called the Israelite covenant or covenant with Israel. In any case, it is never called the Sinai covenant in Scripture, and it is more in accordance with the pattern of Scripture to name it according to the human partner. Later, when God makes a covenant with David, it is called just that, his "covenant with David" (2 Chron. 13:5, 21:7, Ps. 89:3, Jer. 33:21). Finally, God makes what is called a "new covenant" in Jeremiah 31:31.

THE LITERARY STRUCTURE OF EXODUS 19–24

One of the reasons why both popular and scholarly discussions of the relation between the Old Testament and the New have resulted in futile debates over false dichotomies and issues is directly due to a failure to consider properly the literary shape of this text. Instead what is foisted upon the text is a framework or structure it does not clearly indicate itself or possess.

Outline of Exodus 19–40

1. The background	19
2. The Ten Words	20
3. The Judgements	21–23
4. The ceremony of covenant ratification	24
5. Worship—the recognition of divine kingship	25–40

The broad outline and shape of the text is indicated by headings and the use of specific terms. At the heart of the text are two sections: (1) the "Ten Words" in chapter 20 and (2) the "Judgements" (or "laws"/"ordinances") in chapters 21–23. *These are the actual headings in the text.* Exodus 20:1 introduces the matter simply: "And God spoke all these words." While Christians commonly refer to this section as the "Ten Commandments," the commands which form the basis of the covenant are simply referred to as the "Ten Words" in Exodus 34:28 and Deuteronomy 4:13; 10:4. The precise expression, "the Ten Commandments" occurs nowhere in the Old Testament, although in a general way the Ten Words are included when reference is made to the commands of Yahweh. They are frequently referred to as commandments in the New Testament (Matt. 19:17; Mark 10:19; Luke 18:20; Rom. 13:9; 7:7–8; Matt. 5; 1 Tim. 1:9–10), and that is why the preferred

term today is the Ten Commandments. So first we have just "the Words."
Then in chapters 21–23 we have the "Judgements": 21:1 is clearly a heading
for this entire section.

Not only the headings but also the contents clearly distinguish the two
sections. The Ten Words are presented as absolute commands or prohibitions, usually in the second person singular. They are general injunctions
not related to a specific social situation. They could be described as prescriptive law since no fines or punishments are specified. As an example,
"You (singular) shall not steal!" The construction *lô'* + imperfect in Hebrew
is durative and nonspecific. You shall not steal today, not tomorrow, not this
week, not this month, not this year—as a general rule, never! By contrast,
the Judgements are presented as case laws. These are presented as if they
were court decisions functioning as precedents. They are normally in the
format of conditional sentences. Here the fundamental principles embodied
in the Ten Words are applied in particular to specific social contexts. They
could be described as descriptive law since they impose fines and punishments. As an example, Exodus 21:28–32 addresses the case where a bull
gores a human and looks at whether or not this was the animal's habit. More
will be said about these case laws later. So chapter 20 and chapters 21–23
constitute specific sections of the covenant, simply labelled "the Words"
and "the Judgements":

Commandments: The Ten Words (Ex. 20:1; 34:28; Deut. 4:13)
- absolute commands, usually second person singular prohibition
- general injunctions not related to a specific social situation
- prescriptive law—no fines or punishments mentioned

Ordinances (Judgements, KJV; Laws, NIV)
- case decisions, case laws, judicial precedents
- the fundamental principles embodied in the Ten Commandments as applied
  in particular to a specific social context
- descriptive law imposing fines and punishments (usually in the form of "if . . .
  then" statements or conditional sentences)

These two distinct sections to the covenant are clearly referred to in
chapter 24, where the covenant ratification ceremony is described. Note
carefully the particular terms used in verses 1–8 of chapter 24 as follows.
Chapter 24:1, according to the clause pattern in the Hebrew text as well
as the topic, connects and directly follows 20:21–22. In verses 21–26 of

chapter 20 and verses 1–2 of chapter 24 Yahweh speaks to Moses from the cloud on Mount Sinai and gives instructions concerning altars and who will ascend the mountain for the covenant ratification meal. In 24:3 Moses comes and gives a report to the people: "And Moses came and reported to the people all the words and all the judgements, and all the people responded with one voice, 'All the words which Yahweh has spoken we will do.'" Note that Moses reported "all the words" and "all the judgements." These two terms clearly refer to the "Ten Words" in chapter 20:2–17 and the "Judgements" in chapters 21–23. When the people say, "All the words which Yahweh has spoken we will do," the term "the words" is an abbreviated form of the expression "all the words and all the judgements" occurring earlier in the verse. Similarly in the next verse, 24:4, we read, "And Moses wrote all the words of Yahweh."[6] Here, again, "the words of Yahweh" is a short way of saying, "the words and the judgements." The shortening of long titles is typical in this culture. Much later, the Hebrew Canon, whose full title is "the Law and the Prophets and the Writings," may be simply shortened to "the Law." For example, Paul says that he is quoting from "the Law" and then cites a passage from Isaiah (1 Cor. 14:21). So "Law" must be short for "Law and Prophets." Alternatively, since "the judgements" are simply unfolding "the ten words" in practical situations, the expression "the words" in 24:3 and 4 may refer to the whole (words and judgements) by specifying just "the words." So the two parts or sections of the covenant are written down by Moses. And this is called "the Book of the Covenant" in 24:7.

Chapters 19 and 24 form the bookends to this "Book of the Covenant." At the beginning, chapter 19 provides the setting in space and time, the divine purpose of the covenant, and the preparation of the people for the revelation of Yahweh at Mount Sinai. At the end, chapter 24 describes the ceremony of covenant ratification. Following this, chapters 25–40 describe the construction of a place of worship, showing the proper response to the divine kingship established among the people by means of the covenant. Just as Genesis 1 establishes divine rule via covenant, followed by the priority of worship in sanctuary in Genesis 2, so the book of Exodus establishes God as

---

[6] William M. Schniedewind claims, "Writing has no role in the so-called Covenant Code in Exod 21–23." See William M. Schniedewind, *How the Bible Became a Book: The Textualization of Ancient Israel* (Cambridge: Cambridge University Press, 2004), 131. The claim has been thoroughly refuted by Alan Millard, "The Tablets in the Ark," in *Reading the Law: Studies in Honour of Gordon J. Wenham*, ed. J. G. McConville and Karl Möller (Library of Hebrew Bible/Old Testament Studies 461; New York: T. & T. Clark, 2007), 254–266.

king in the midst of Israel, followed by the priority of worship for the nation as God's Adamic son.

The shape and structure of Exodus 19–24, then, is clearly marked in the text. Chapters 20–23 constitute "the Book of the Covenant" consisting of "the Words" (chapter 20) and "the Judgements" (chapters 21–23). Chapters 19 and 24 frame the Book of the Covenant as bookends, with chapter 19 providing the background and setting and chapter 24 describing the ceremony of covenant ratification.

As has been noted by scholars for some time, the structure of this text is parallel in broad outline to the form and structure of international treaties in the Near Eastern culture of the fifteenth–thirteenth centuries B.C. Parallels between the book of Deuteronomy and the Hittite suzerain-vassal treaties are more striking than between the Book of the Covenant in Exodus and the Hittite treaties, but the parallels are noteworthy nonetheless. International treaties followed a specific form: (1) preamble (author identification), (2) history of past relationship between the parties, (3) basic stipulation, (4) detailed stipulations, (5) document clause, (6) witnesses, (7) blessings and curses. Table 9.1 portrays how "the Book of the Covenant" conforms broadly to this pattern:

Table 9.1: Structure of the Covenant in Exodus

1. Preamble	20:1
2. Historical Prologue	20:2

3. Stipulations
    a. Basic
    b. Detailed
	
	20:3–17
	21–23

4. Document Clause	24

Unlike in Deuteronomy, the "blessings and curses" section is absent here. Nonetheless, the commands are enshrined in what would have been clearly recognised at the time as a covenant or treaty form. The implications of this form for proper theological understanding will be developed later. This much is clear: the covenant is formulated as a suzerain-vassal treaty in order to define God as Father and King, and Israel as obedient son in a relationship of loyal love, obedience, and trust. This is confirmed by the fact that the epiphany on Mount Sinai is heralded by the blowing of a trumpet (Ex. 19:16, 19; 20:18), a clear signal in Israel for the accession and coming of a king (2 Sam. 15:10; 1 Kings 1:34, 39, 41; 2 Kings 9:13).[7] Space permits now only a brief analysis of the divine purpose of the covenant as given in Exodus 19, a summary treatment of the Ten Words, and a consideration of the ceremony of covenant ratification and its significance, before the implications for Christian theology are spelled out.

THE DIVINE PURPOSE OF THE COVENANT (EXODUS 19:5–6)

As already stated, chapter 19 provides the background to the Book of the Covenant (Exodus 19–24) and acts as a bookend on the opening side of the covenant document. Israel arrives at Mount Sinai in her travels through the desert to the Promised Land. Central to the chapter is the flurry of movement by Moses going up and down the mountain. Three sequences of up and down dominate the section: (1) up (19:3) and down (19:7); (2) up (19:8) and down (19:14); and (3) up (19:20) and down (19:25). These three sequences form the boundaries of three sections within the chapter delimiting (1) the divine purpose of the covenant, (2) the preparation of the people to meet Yahweh and receive his revelation and Torah,[8] and (3) the actual epiphany of God on the mountain. The literary structure of the chapter, then, is as follows:

Literary Structure of Exodus 19

1. The setting in time and space	19:1–2
2. The divine purpose in the covenant	19:3–8
3. The human preparation for the covenant	19:9–15
4. The revelation of Yahweh at Sinai	19:16–25

The constant ascending and descending provides a vivid portrayal of the distance between the people and God and the need for a mediator. It then emphasises the miracle of a covenant relationship of love, loyalty, and trust between parties such as these.[9]

[3] Then Moses went up to God, and the LORD called to him from the mountain and said, "This is what you are to say to the house of Jacob and what you are to tell the people of Israel: [4] 'You yourselves have seen what I did to Egypt, and how I carried you on eagles' wings and brought you to

---

[7] H. Ringgren, "שׁוֹפָר *šôpār*," in *TDOT* 14:541–542. So also John A. Davies, *A Royal Priesthood: Literary and Intertextual Perspectives on an Image of Israel in Exodus 19.6*, JSOTSup 395 (London: T. & T. Clark, 2004), 109.

[8] The Hebrew word *tôrâ* simply means "direction" or "instruction."

[9] There is a contrast here between the covenant at Sinai and the covenant at creation. In Eden, the man dwells on the mountain and walks with God without a mediator. I am indebted to John Meade for this insight.

myself. [5] Now if you obey me fully and keep my covenant, then out of all nations you will be my treasured possession, for the whole earth is mine.[10] [6] You will be for me a kingdom of priests and a holy nation.' These are the words you are to speak to the Israelites." [7] So Moses went back and summoned the elders of the people and set before them all the words the LORD had commanded him to speak. [8] The people all responded together, "We will do everything the LORD has said." So Moses brought their answer back to the LORD (Ex. 19:3–8, NIV).

By paying attention to the number of the verbs, John Davies demonstrates a chiastic structure to this text as follows:[11]

A People of Israel camp at the mountain (3rd plur. verbs) (vv. 1–2).
  B Moses' ascent and Yhwh's summons (3rd plur. verbs) (v. 3a).
    C Divine instruction regarding delivery of message to Israel
      (2nd sing. verbs) (v. 3b).
      D Divine declaration concerning Israel (2nd plur. verbs)
        (vv. 4–6a).
    C' Divine instruction regarding delivery of message to Israel
      (2nd sing. verbs) (v. 6b).
  B' Moses' descent and summons to the elders (3rd sing. verbs) (v. 7).
A' People of Israel respond (3rd plur. verbs) (v. 8a).

This chiastic structure aids by clearly delineating verses 3–8 as a self-contained unit. Chiastic structures usually focus on the centre. The structure shows that the central theme is the divine purpose in the covenant between God and Israel.

Thus, after verses 1–2 specify the place and time in history, verses 3–8 detail the purpose of the covenant from God's point of view. What we have in these verses is a proposal of the covenant in a nutshell: (1) verse 4 describes the past history of relationship between the two covenant partners; (2) verses 5 and 6 propose a relationship of complete loyalty and obedience of Israel as a vassal to Yahweh as the great king, and promise certain blessings; and (3) in verses 7 and 8 the people agree to the proposal. Thus, even in this covenant proposal in verses 3–8 the form and structure corresponds to the formulae of ancient Near Eastern covenants and treaties.

Verse 4 is a marvellous encapsulation of the past relationship between

---

[10] This citation follows the text of the footnote in the NIV rather than the main text, which has " . . . possession. Although the whole earth is mine, [6] you." The grammar clearly signals the adverbial clause as dependent on the preceding and not the following and therefore a causal rather than a concessive clause is signalled.
[11] Adapted from John A. Davies, *Royal Priesthood*, 35.

the people and the Lord, using the imagery of being carried out of trouble on the wings of an eagle: "You yourselves have seen what I did to Egypt, and how I carried you on eagles' wings and brought you to myself." This brief statement summarises the abject condition of the people in slavery in Egypt and the signs and wonders performed by Yahweh in both the ten plagues and the crossing of the Red Sea that delivered and freed them from slavery. It also speaks of the way in which God had directed them through the mazes and mirages of the desert using a pillar of cloud by day and of fire by night. This form of leadership also protected them from extreme heat by day and cold by night. Every day, bread rained from heaven for their nourishment and water gushed from the rock to satisfy their thirst. Our culture today can picture this from the movie world in the miraculous rescue of Gandalf by the eagles in the *Lord of the Rings*. God had protected the people and provided for them during the difficult desert journey, bearing them on eagles' wings, so to speak, and had so arranged their itinerary as to bring them to himself, that is, to the place already prepared as a meeting place between God and men, to Sinai, the mountain of God (Ex. 3:1).

As John Davies notes, the phrase "I brought you to myself" is without parallel in the Hebrew Bible. His comment is worth citing in full:

> . . . the 'bringing to myself' expresses the underlying motivation of the preceding divine actions and focuses on relationship rather than location. For a moment the mountain and all terrestrial indicators fade from view, such that we are not sure where God is to be located. Is it in the heights of the mountain, where eagles have their nests (Job 39.27–30; Obad. 1.4; Jer. 49.16)? Or is it in heaven, or among the stars, where eagles venture (Prov. 23.5; 30:19; Lam. 4.19)? If an answer is felt to be needed, possible support for the latter alternative is to be found at Exod. 20.22 where again we have a recitation of divine acts which employs a closely parallel introductory formula: 'Yhwh said to Moses, "This is what you are to say to the house of Israel, 'You yourselves saw that it was from heaven that I spoke with you.'"' . . . in this central summary declaration giving, as it purports, a divine perspective on the exodus experience with its climax at Sinai, it is the resulting heightened *proximity* of Israel to God which is paramount, a proximity which is the result of divine initiative and accomplishment.[12]

---

[12] John A. Davies, *Royal Priesthood*, 40–41.

Verses 5–6 are constructed in the form of a conditional sentence: "If you do this . . . then you will be . . . and you will be. . . . " The "if clause" or protasis specifies absolute obedience to the covenant stipulations. The "then clause" or apodosis defines the result in terms of relationship to Yahweh: they will belong to him in two ways, (1) as a king's treasure, and (2) as a kingdom of priests and a holy nation.

Before explaining the meaning of the terms defining the divine goal in the covenant relationship, the relation of verses 5–6 to verse 4 must be stressed. Perhaps a diagram may be used to picture this:

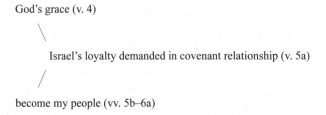

God's grace (v. 4)

Israel's loyalty demanded in covenant relationship (v. 5a)

become my people (vv. 5b–6a)

Verse 4 shows that the motivation for concluding and keeping a covenant with Yahweh is sovereign grace. The creator God has chosen to display favour and kindness to Israel and has acted in history to redeem them and make them his people. A lot of misunderstanding has been caused by comparing the old covenant to the new in terms of "law" and "grace." This text is clear: the old covenant is based upon grace, and grace motivates the keeping of the covenant, just as we find in the new covenant. God had protected the people and provided for them during the difficult desert journey, bearing them on eagles' wings, so to speak, and had so arranged their itinerary as to bring them to himself, that is, to Sinai, the mountain of God. This teaches, then, that the basis for the covenant from the point of view of the human partner was confidence and trust in as well as gratitude to Yahweh as established by the events of the exodus. (What is unlike the new covenant is that covenant keeping depends on Israel's promise to obey.)

Verses 5 and 6, then, describe the purpose, from God's point of view, for which the covenant was given to the people, and the nature of the relationship between God and Israel that will result from ratifying the covenant proposed by Yahweh.

Scholars have debated the logic of the conditional sentence in verses 5–6. Some, like Muilenburg, have considered the situation similar to biblical passages that offer a reward conditional on obedience.[13] Others, like Patrick, argue that the protasis or "if clause" does not so much lay down a precondition for benefits as define the content and nature of the status in the apodoses or "then clauses."[14] Davies illustrates these options by comparing two sentences:

> 'If you accept my offer to teach you, and you devote yourself to learning Hebrew and other cognate languages, you will get a well-paid university position and a rewarding superannuation package,' and 'If you accept my offer to teach you and you devote yourself to learning Hebrew and other cognate languages, you will have the satisfaction of being a Semitics scholar.'[15]

The second sentence is a conditional definition where the "then clause" spells out what is inherent in the "if clause." Strong support for this latter understanding may be found on the grammatical level from the linguistic research of Dancygier and Sweetser. Standard classification of conditional sentences by grammarians as either real or unreal is inadequate.[16] Dancygier and Sweetser classify conditions according to three major types: (1) *content conditionals*, where the speaker makes a prediction about the external socio-physical world—so the protasis postulates a situation (the prototypical "real" conditional); (2) *epistemic conditionals*, where the speaker draws an inference (abductive, internal) in the apodosis—so the protasis provides the basis for the inference; (3) *speech-act conditionals*, where the speaker performs a speech act conditionally in the apodosis—thus the protasis makes the speech act "relevant."[17] The conditional sentence in Exodus 19:5–6 clearly belongs to the last category.[18] Thus the conditional sentence is proclaiming the privileged status of Israel inherent in the covenant relationship. Important parallels in Deuteronomy such as 7:6–11, 14:2, and especially 26:18–19 also substantiate this view.[19] After evaluating both interpretations Davies concludes as follows:

---

[13] James Muilenburg, "The Form and Structure of the Covenantal Formulations," *Vetus Testamentum* 9 (1959): 347–365.

[14] Dale Patrick, "The Covenant Code Source," *Vetus Testamentum* 27 (1977): 145–157.

[15] John A. Davies, *Royal Priesthood*, 43–44.

[16] Traditionally, אם introduces the protasis of a *real* as opposed to *irreal* conditional; see, e.g., Bruce K. Waltke and M. O'Connor, *An Introduction to Biblical Hebrew Syntax* (Winona Lake, IN: Eisenbrauns, 1990), § 38.2.

[17] See Bill Bivin, "Translating IM," paper presented at 2010 Genesis Workshop, SIL International, Dallas, TX, October 20, 2010; and Barbara Dancygier and Eve Sweetser, *Mental Spaces in Grammar: Conditional Constructions* (Cambridge Studies in Linguistics 108; Cambridge: Cambridge University Press, 2005). I am grateful to Bill Bivin for alerting me to the work of Dancygier and Sweetser.

[18] Confirmed by personal communication with B. Dancygier at the annual meeting of the Society of Biblical Literature, November 19–23, 2010.

[19] Deuteronomy 26:18–19 is discussed in our next chapter, "The Israelite (Mosaic) Covenant: Deuteronomy."

> Perhaps in the end not too much weight should be placed on the distinction between a reward based on the condition of faithful service (as Muilenburg), and a favour which entails elevation to a position calling for honoured and faithful service (as Patrick). . . . There would be no significant weakening of the case being presented [below] for the meaning and function of the honorific designations of Israel in vv. 5–6a if one were to read some form of conditional reward at v. 5, provided this is understood to be within the framework of an already established relationship.[20]

As we have seen already, the categories of conditional and unconditional often used in characterising covenants are not helpful or fruitful because they result in failing to hear the different emphases in the biblical text.[21] We will return to this topic later when dealing with the relationship of the old covenant to the new.

A grammatical question directly related to the logic of the conditional sentence is the discourse-grammar pragmatic value of the free infinitive/ infinitive absolute שָׁמוֹעַ in verse 5: וְעַתָּה אִם־שָׁמוֹעַ תִּשְׁמְעוּ בְּקֹלִי. This is a difficult matter to treat. The analysis of Davies is exhaustive and thorough, but as he admits, not conclusive or greatly illuminating. Nonetheless, more recent study of this aspect of grammar in Hebrew may be of help.[22] It is interesting to note that the root שמע is found in free infinitive plus finite verb in eight instances in the Hebrew Bible: Exodus 15:26; 19:5; 22:22; 23:22, Deuteronomy 11:13; 15:5; 28:1; and 1 Samuel 23:10. In six of the occurrences, the meaning has specifically to do with obedience as indicated by a complement such as בקול; thus Exodus 22:22 and 1 Samuel 23:10 are excluded.[23] The research of Kim shows that the infinitive absolute functions not as a manner adverb modifying the predicate but rather modifying the sentence as a whole and, in fact, as a discourse grammar or macrosyntactic signal far beyond the level of the sentence. In each of the six occurrences the infinitive absolute is preposed to the verb, a position marking focus or topic in Hebrew as well as in many languages. The brief but seminal study of Lynell Zogbo explores further the macrosyntactic functions. Not only does

---

[20] John A. Davies, *Royal Priesthood*, 46.

[21] On the categories of conditional and unconditional being inadequate to describe, e.g., the Abrahamic covenant, see John A. Davies, *Royal Priesthood*, 180–181.

[22] Scott N. Callaham, *Modality and the Biblical Hebrew Infinitive Absolute* (Wiesbaden: Harrassowitz, 2010); Yoo-Ki Kim, *The Function of the Tautological Infinitive in Classical Biblical Hebrew*, Harvard Semitic Studies 60 (Winona Lake, IN: Eisenbrauns, 2009); Lynell Zogbo, "Interface entre l'exégèse et la traduction de la Bible: le cas de l'infinitif absolu en hébreu," paper presented at 2010 International Symposium, May 25–26, Montréal.

[23] In Deuteronomy 11:13 the verbal complement is אל־מצותי; elsewhere בקול or בקול is used. Both specify the hearing of obedience.

the infinitive absolute mark asseverative or contrastive focus and relevance, it also foreshadows events in the future or marks a major theme. Moreover, the infinitive absolute often occurs in "zones of turbulence" marking climactic peaks and pivotal points in the narrative.[24] Here the introductory "and now" (וְעַתָּה) along with the figurative language ("I bore you on eagles' wings") help to signal a zone of turbulence. Davies recognises this much:

> The macrosyntactic introductory particle ועתה ('now') has the rhetorical effect of drawing attention to the change of subject from the first person clauses of v. 4 (recounting divine activity) to the second person clauses (referring to Israel), as well as marking a temporal shift from the narration of past events to the setting forth of present and future consequences, particularly, as Kalluveetil notes, in covenant settings (Deut. 4.1; 10.12; Josh 24.14; 1 Sam 12.13; 1 Chron. 22.11).[25]

The free infinitive also comes in the middle of the speech. Lynell Zogbo concludes from her study,

> the Infinitive Absolute has a discourse function, global role, that is, it is *marking a very crucial part of this text*. As a verbal repetition, it is itself linguistically MARKED. It is also accompanied by signs which highlight it: middle placement, figurative language, repetition, listen-listen, I-I, all ... all. Also significantly for exegesis this line is parallel to *KEEP MY COVENANT*. To me this is what the infinitive absolute is about here! It is there to highlight COVENANT, the THEME of the book.[26]

It is interesting that the instances in Exodus 15:26 and 23:22 corroborate this and function in tandem to help highlight Exodus 19:5–6 as a climax and to underline the covenant. Noteworthy is the fact that the only other occurrences are in Deuteronomy, also at key junctures in the text highlighting the covenant.

1. PERSONAL TREASURE (1 CHRONICLES 29:3, ECCLESIASTES 2:8)

The meaning of the terms defining the divine plan for the role and status of Israel in the covenant relationship may now be explained. It is crucial to note

---

[24] For the expression "zones of turbulence" see Robert E. Longacre, "The Grammar of Discourse," in *Topics in Language and Linguistics*, ed. Thomas A. Seboek and Albert Valdman (New York: Plenum, 1983).

[25] John A. Davies, *Royal Priesthood*, 42.

[26] Personal communication, Lynell Zogbo, July 17, 2010 (emphasis hers).

the literary structure of Exodus 19:5–6 in explaining the terms, "personal treasure," "kingdom of priests," and "holy nation." Two clauses joined by the conjunction *waw* ("and") constitute the content of the declaration by Yahweh. The first is, "you will be my treasured possession more than/out of all the nations, for the whole earth is mine." The second is, "and you will be for me a kingdom of priests and a holy nation." The relationship of these two statements is best understood by recalling the description given earlier of the approach in ancient Hebrew literature of taking up a topic and developing it from a particular perspective and then stopping and taking up the same theme again from another point of view. This pattern is holographic and is pursued recursively at both the macro and micro levels. One begins a conversation on a topic and then closes that conversation down and begins another. Taken together, both conversations are like the left and right speakers of a stereo sound system: each differs slightly, and together they produce Dolby Surround Sound or a 3D holographic image. In other words, both statements are saying the same thing, but each does it in a different way and looks at the topic from a different perspective. Once the terms are explicated it will become clear that "royal priesthood" and "holy nation" taken together is another way of saying, "God's personal treasure." In other words, the terms "royal priesthood" and "holy nation" constitute the right and left speakers of stereo sound, and then, together, they form the left speaker for which the term "personal treasure" is the right speaker.

The first purpose of the covenant is that these chosen, redeemed people might become God's own possession and private treasure. The word *sĕgullâ* in Hebrew that is translated "possession" is the same word used in 1 Chronicles 29:3 for King David's own private cache or vault of gold and silver, his personal store of all things precious and valuable.[27] If we were to travel back in time to the ancient Near East, we would find at capital cities such as Hattusa (Boğazkale, Turkey) and Ugarit (Syria) the rich treasure-vaults of the kings. It is difficult for us to imagine, since we have no monarchy such as the monarchs of Europe in the nineteenth century. Perhaps something comparable today would be the Crown Jewels in London. The use in Ecclesiastes 2:8 is also of a king's personal treasure. These two are the only non-metaphorical occurrences of the word in the Old Testament.

---

[27] Hebrew *sĕgullâ* occurs only in Exodus 19:5; Deuteronomy 7:6; 14:2; 26:18; 1 Chronicles 29:3; Malachi 3:17; Psalm 135:4; and Ecclesiastes 2:8. All occurrences refer back to Exodus 19:5 except 1 Chronicles 29:3 and Ecclesiastes 2:8, which are valuable to show the concrete, ordinary use of the word.

John Davies' discussion of the meaning of *segullâ* is most illuminating. Although the word is not common in Biblical Hebrew, it is common in the postbiblical literature of the Mishna as a commercial-legal term, where it refers to the personal property of a social inferior (such as a wife or slave). Davies notes that a connection between the Hebrew word and Akkadian *sikiltu* has been posited by Greenberg.[28] Found in Old, Middle, and Standard Babylonian, at Nuzi, and also in Middle Assyrian texts, the Akkadian word refers to "acquisition" or "possession," first of illegally acquired goods, then of private possessions in distinction from those possessions which form part of an estate.

In the Old Babylonian period, there is a metaphorical usage that casts light on the passage in Exodus. It is used no later than the fifteenth century B.C. by a god to refer to an honoured king. Davies cites the following designation of King Abban: "Abban, the mighty king, son of Šarran, the servant of the god . . . the beloved of the god . . . the treasure of the god."[29] Thus a royal figure is seen as a devoted servant of the god. A similar usage is found in Ugaritic, as Davies explains:

> Text 60 (18.38) of *PRU* 5 dates from the early twelfth century BCE and is a copy of a letter (no doubt a translation of the original Akkadian) from the Hittite suzerain to Ammurapi, the last king of Ugarit. It describes the vassal king in relation to the suzerain as both his 'servant ([']*bdh*) and *sglth'*. This spelling out of the relationship between the two kings is a preface to a reproach by the suzerain for the failure of the Ugaritic vassal king to pay the customary visits of homage.[30]

Note that the use of the Ugaritic word for "personal treasure" is paired with the notion of servant as in the above example in Akkadian from Alalakh. "Personal treasure" is used in the context of devoted service in a relationship defined by a treaty. The same pairing of service and personal treasure is found in the Bible, in Malachi 3:17, as noted by Dahood.[31]

> "They shall be mine," says the LORD of hosts, "in the day when I make up my treasured possession (סגלה), and I will spare them as a man spares his son (בן) who serves (עבד) him." (ESV)

[28] Moshe Greenberg, "Hebrew *segulla*: Akkadian *sikiltu*," *Journal of the American Oriental Society* 71 (1951): 172–174.

[29] John A. Davies, *Royal Priesthood*, 53.

[30] Ibid.

[31] Mitchell Dahood, "Ugaritic Hebrew Parallel Pairs," in *Ras Shamra Parallels: The Texts from Ugarit and the Hebrew Bible*, ed. Loren R Fisher, 3 vols., Analecta Orientalia, 49–51 (Rome: Pontifical Biblical Institute Press, 1975), 2:1–33.

What is parallel here to "personal treasure" is "son," qualified by the concept of devoted *service*. This biblical passage, corroborated by the Akkadian and Ugaritic parallels, casts enormous light on Exodus 19:5. When Yahweh calls Israel to be his personal treasure, he is speaking of the kind of devoted service given by a son.[32] We are back, here, to the divine image in Genesis 1:26–28. Israel has inherited an Adamic role, giving the devoted service of a son and honoured king in a covenant relationship.[33]

A causal-explanatory כי clause[34] explains that the whole world belongs to Yahweh. In one sense, the King is owner or possessor of the entire country, but in addition to this, he may also have a personal/private treasure. The whole world is like a ring on God's hand, and his chosen people are the jewel in that ring.

2. KINGDOM OF PRIESTS

Although some expositions consider the meaning of "kingdom of priests" and "holy nation" separately, in a real sense they should be taken together. The text clearly divides the goal of the covenant relationship into two statements. The first is supported by an explanation or reason. A second statement combines the phrases "kingdom of priests" and "holy nation" either as a hendiadys or at least as an expression similar to Hebrew poetry, where a pair of parallel lines allows one to consider a topic from two slightly variant but similar viewpoints to create a full-orbed perspective on some proposition. These phrases will be explained here, each in turn, but with the meaning of the other phrase kept in mind. In turn, we should keep in mind that both phrases together are unpacking the full meaning of "personal treasure."

First consider the phrase "kingdom of priests" found in this text. The full sentence is, "You will belong to me as a kingdom of priests" (*tihyû lî mamleket kōhănîm*). The *lamed* preposition in the phrase *lî* clearly indicates

---

[32] In modern German, the term *Schatz* ("treasure") is employed in *family settings* as a term of endearment, particularly of a man referring to his wife.

[33] Priests are given the honourific epithet "servants of Yahweh" (עבדי יהוה) in Psalm 134:1 and 135:1. Similarly, the participial form in the *piel* of שרת (i.e., "servant") is also used to describe priests as the servants of Yahweh (Jer. 33:21; Ezek. 45:4; Joel 1:9; 1:13; 2:17; Neh. 10:37 [EV 10:36]; 2 Chron. 13:10). In Psalm 103:21, משרתיו is parallel to צבאיו, i.e., the heavenly army or host who attend upon God, and in Isaiah 61:6 the priests who are designated as the servants of Yahweh are corporate Israel, i.e., the calling of Exodus 19:5–6, once defiled by covenant violation, is now renewed in the new covenant. See John A. Davies, *Royal Priesthood*, 154–155.

[34] Some would employ the term "explanatory" or "evidential," as the use is not strictly causal. See A. Aejmelaeus, "Function and Interpretation of כי in Biblical Hebrew," *Journal of Biblical Literature* 105/2 (1986): 193–209. For a detailed analysis and evaluation see John A. Davies, *Royal Priesthood*, 55–60. Scholars have proposed that the כי is (1) causal, (2) concessive, (3) asseverative, and (4) explanatory. Causal and concessive are not logically satisfying, for what motive does it offer the reason, or why would a concession to Yahweh's universal ownership be needed? As Aejmelaeus has shown, the asseverative use is unlikely.

possession.[35] The Hebrew word for "kingdom" may refer to the domain or realm which is ruled, or to the exercise of kingly rule and sovereignty.[36] According to the main options, then, the phrase "kingdom of priests" could mean a domain of priests whom God rules or, alternatively, the exercise of royal office by those who are in fact priests, i.e., a royal priesthood. It is difficult to decide between the two main options since the *lamed* preposition suggests the former reading while the term "priests" modifying "kingdom" suggests the latter. Yet in the latter option, understanding *kōhănîm* as a genitive of apposition after the collective *mamleket* ("royalty, royal body, royal house") would be a more natural reading than to construe it as an attributive genitive.[37] Thus we may view in "priests" a collective reference to all Israel as being in some sense "priests" rather than as being a "priestly kingship" or "priestly royalty." Perhaps both meanings are intended, so that both the relationship between God and Israel and the relationship between Israel and the world is indicated. This ambiguity would serve the theme "kingdom through covenant."

What is the function of a priest? This is also important in the interpretation. Some readings focus on the priest as an intermediary, so that the function of a priest is to bring others into the presence of God by offering sacrifices on their behalf. Dumbrell, who follows this track, sees the intermediary role as passive rather than active and missionary. Davies comments,

> Dumbrell is on surer ground, then, with a moderate 'service to the nations' position, seeing the service as somewhat passive in character. That is, it is by being who they are in relation to God that Israel serves the nations. Dumbrell ties this notion to the role of Abraham as the one through whom the nations would find blessing (Gen. 12.2–3; 18.18; 22.18; 26.4). Dumbrell, however, regards any notion of status in v. 6 as being anticlimactic because status has already been dealt with in the word סגלה. Yet if my understanding of the syntax is correct, the expressions ממלכת כהנים and גוי קדוש are epexegetic of סגלה, and spell out further dimensions for

---

[35] See the magisterial treatment by E. Jenni, *Die hebräischen Präpositionen, Band 3: Die Präposition Lamed* (Stuttgart: Kolhammer, 2000), 23–25, 54–57, 77.

[36] See F. Brown, S. R. Driver, and C. Briggs, eds., *A Hebrew and English Lexicon of the Old Testament* (Oxford: Clarendon, 1907; repr., 1953), s.v. Davies debates at length the merits of what he terms the "active" and the "passive" interpretations. This is not an accurate approach. In Hebrew noun formations, a prefix *mem* normally marks (1) instrumentality, (2) location, or (3) a verbal abstract. This would yield (1) a means of ruling, (2) a place of ruling, or (3) just the act of ruling. This is the correct analysis of the data in linguistic terms and yields, according to the lexica, precisely these meanings for the word in question (see John A. Davies, *Royal Priesthood*, 70–86). In the end, the ambivalent meaning argued above is reached in the argumentation of Davies.

[37] See John A. Davies, *Royal Priesthood*, 94.

the reader's understanding of the extent of the privilege it is to be Yhwh's 'special treasure'.[38]

Alternatively, Davies' reading focuses on priesthood as access to the divine presence. He argues that Exodus 19 itself provides an all-important clue to the significance of priesthood in verse 22:

> Also let the priests who come near to the LORD consecrate themselves, lest the LORD break out against them. (ESV)

This passage offers a virtual definition of what it is to be a priest: priests are those who approach or come near to Yahweh and who are consecrated and devoted to him. Davies notes further,

> central to any understanding of what a priest is, is the notion of his fitness to approach the deity and 'minister' in his presence like an attendant in the court of a king. The tabernacle cult depicted in Exodus 25–31 and 35–40 is a stylized replica of what, in the widespread ideology of the ancient world, took place within the divine realm of the heavenly temple.[39]

Another argument supporting the emphasis Davies sees is found in the verb "consecrate" in Exodus 19:22, from the root קדש. Indeed, this verb and the related adjective קדוש are employed frequently in all things dealing with the activity of priests. Moreover we should note that here in Exodus 19:5–6 the parallel term to the expression ממלכת כהנים is גוי קדוש. If "kingdom" is parallel to "nation," then "holy" is parallel to "priests" in these two expressions. Although the common understanding of "holy" in North America has to do with separation, as we will see shortly, Davies rightly asserts that the primary meaning has rather to do with the divine sphere to which the person or object relates, not the sphere from which it has thereby been separated:

> Persons or objects are holy to Yhwh, or in one case to Baal (2 Kgs 10.20). They are fit to be associated with the one who is inherently קדוש, particularly when he is pictured as enthroned in his sanctuary (Isa. 6.3; Ps. 99.5, 9). It is no light matter to stand in the presence of Yhwh, the holy God, as the men of Beth Shemesh were aware (1 Sam 6.20). The 'entrance liturgies' of

---

[38] John A. Davies, *Royal Priesthood*, 97. See William J. Dumbrell, *Covenant and Creation: A Theology of the Old Testament Covenants* (Carlisle, UK: Paternoster, 1984), 89–90.
[39] John A. Davies, *Royal Priesthood*, 98.

Psalms 15 and 24 reinforce this demand for holiness on the part of the one
who would approach God's dwelling place.

If we regard קדוש as being a guide to the understanding of כהנים,
the character of Israel as כהנים will relate to their consecration or readi-
ness to encounter Yhwh. This is the point of the preparations outlined
in Exod. 19.14–15, including the washing of clothes, and the abstinence
from sexual relations.[40]

Finally, Davies notes that the Sinai pericope simply contains no direct reference to Israel's responsibilities toward the nations, and he believes we ought
not to be looking for a *functional* definition of priesthood, but an *ontological*
one.[41] What priests *are* in their relation to God and in the eyes of the community is the issue.

The emphasis and focus for which Davies argues is correct because the
arguments are based solidly on the text. Nonetheless, the focus on Israel's
priesthood as access to the divine presence and a priority in the worship of
Yahweh alone as God does not exclude the perspective of Dumbrell, who has
rightly kept his eye on the metanarrative as the context for Exodus 19:5–6.
Just as in Genesis 1–2 God establishes his rule through a covenant relationship between himself and man and between man and the creation (wherein
Adam's priority according to Genesis 2 is to spend time in the divine presence to order his perspectives and role in the world), so through the covenant with Abraham (Genesis 12–22), promising blessing to the nations in
relationship to Abraham and now through the covenant with his family Israel
(Ex. 19–24) as a royal priesthood (with a priority on worship that results in
being a light to nations), God is extending his rule. Since Israel is settled at
the navel of the world, the nations of the world will see displayed a right
relationship to God, social justice in human interaction, and good stewardship of the earth's resources. Apparently it is appropriate and convenient
for Davies to expound the duties of priests at a later point in his exposition,
and he demonstrates from the biblical text that this includes the function of
the priest as intermediary between God and people, so why exclude it from
purview here?[42]

We see, then, that Israel, the last Adam, will belong to God as a people
under his rule, and will exercise royal rule by spending time in the worship of God so necessary for display of the divine rule in one's thoughts,

---

[40] Ibid., 99–100.
[41] Ibid., 97–98.
[42] Ibid., 162–164.

words, and ways. Davies notes that the tabernacle, the construction of which is the topic of the literary unit following Exodus 19–24, is in form a miniaturized and portable reproduction of God's heavenly sanctuary, of which Israel has caught a glimpse in the covenant ratification ceremony in Exodus 24:9–11.[43] The cloud denoting the divine presence on Mount Sinai settles on the tabernacle in Exodus 40. Thus Israel carries the divine presence with them. Moreover, the tabernacle is also a replica of the garden of Eden and a representation of the universe, so just as Adam was to fulfill his mandate by devoting himself to worship as a priest in the garden sanctuary, so Israel as a new Adam is to fulfill her mandate by devoting herself to worship as a priest in the tabernacle and later the temple. Since in the Bible and the ancient Near East, kings are the ones who build temples,[44] Israel as a nation building the tabernacle in Exodus 25–40 also depicts her royal status. She is a king-priest. And as we noted earlier, this is the point in Hosea 6:7: "but they [i.e., Israel], like Adam, have transgressed the covenant." Israel's covenant violation was in her role as king-priest.

Israel is also a vehicle for bringing the nations to the divine presence and rule. Israel would be a people completely devoted to the service of God. The rite of circumcision as practised in Israel is an excellent illustration of this. Probably the background for understanding circumcision is Egypt, where only the aristocracy, the highest order of priests, and the noblest elite warriors along with the Pharaoh and his family were circumcised, because only they were completely devoted to the service of the gods.[45] In Deuteronomy 10:16 the command to Israel, "Circumcise your hearts," is an exposition of the earlier command "to fear the LORD your God, to walk in all his ways, to love him, to serve the LORD your God with all your heart and with all your soul, and to observe the LORD's commands and decrees that I am giving you today for your own good" (Deut. 10:12–13, NIV). Thus circumcision is an apt expression for the idea: be completely devoted to Yahweh.

Again, the summary provided by Davies is apt and deserves a hearing:

> Israel's cult shares some common features with the sanctuary ideology of the ancient world. The tabernacle is a representation of an ideal or restored cosmos, where God and man meet in an environment which transcends the limitations of the mundane world. The priest, granted access to the sacred

---

[43] Ibid., 139.
[44] Ibid., 144.
[45] See John Meade, "The Meaning of Circumcision in Israel: A Proposal for a Transfer of Rite from Egypt to Israel," *Adorare Mente* 1 (2008): 14–29 = http://adoraremente.sbts.edu/.

space, is a model of the ideal held out to Israel of the meaning of its collective priesthood and the access to the presence of God of which it speaks. The priests are the chosen and privileged ones who are granted a royal dignity and the right of access to this realm, even, in the case of the high priest, to that sacred space which is regarded as the throne-room of heaven, the innermost sanctum of an ideal cosmos.

Priests share characteristics of royalty in the prevailing ideology of priesthood in the ancient Near East. Israel had a collective memory of ancient priest-kings, and the descriptions of the garb of the Israelite priests preserve something of these royal associations. In their priests, the Israelites had a perpetual reminder of their own royal-priestly standing and privilege. The detailed literary portrayal of the priesthood of Aaron and his sons serves to flesh out for the reader something of what is meant by the image of Israel's corporate royal priesthood.

In keeping with the expectation that sanctuary-building is the work of a chosen king, acting on instructions of a god and according to a divinely revealed pattern, it is suggested that Israel corporately functions as the royal sanctuary builder, according to Exodus, in keeping with the designation of Israel as a 'royal priesthood'.[46]

In a work on biblical theology entitled *Dominion and Dynasty*, Stephen Dempster analyses the phrase "kingdom of priests" in a way similar to the exposition given here:

The final phrase designates Israel as a particular type of kingdom. Instead of being a kingdom of a particular king, it will be a kingdom marked by priesthood; that is service of God on behalf of people and *vice versa*. It will be 'a kingdom run not by politicians depending upon strength and connivance but by priests depending upon faith in Yahweh, a servant nation instead of a ruling nation' (Durham 263). Israel will thus redefine the meaning of dominion—service. This will be its distinctive task, its distinguishing characteristic among the world of nations.[47]

In sum, the call of Israel to be a royal priesthood connects the Israelite covenant to the Abrahamic. Psalm 67 draws this out very well:

[1] May God be gracious to us and bless us
    and make his face to shine upon us,   *Selah*
[2] that your way may be known on earth,

---

[46] John A. Davies, *Royal Priesthood*, 169.
[47] Stephen G. Dempster, *Dominion and Dynasty: A Biblical Theology of the Hebrew Bible*, NSBT 15 (Downers Grove, IL: InterVarsity Press, 2003), 101–102.

your saving power among all nations.
[3] Let the peoples praise you, O God;
     let all the peoples praise you! (ESV)

In verse 1 we see Israel praying as a priest, since the nation as a whole is invoking the Aaronic blessing of Numbers 6. The goal or purpose of invoking this blessing is so that salvation may come to the nations. This is none other than the goal of the Abrahamic covenant.

3. HOLY NATION

The parallel phrase to "kingdom of priests" is "holy nation" (gôy qādôš in Hebrew). As already mentioned, this phrase is not necessarily identical in meaning to "kingdom of priests" but both phrases function as a pair, like parallel lines in Hebrew poetry, to paint a three-dimensional picture in one's mind.

The term gôy or "nation" is the parallel term to kingdom. It is an economic, political, and social structure in which a final governmental headship operates.[48] It therefore clearly reminds us of Genesis 12:2, as explained earlier. This is the city of God, the kingdom of God. In fulfilment of the promises to Abraham, Israel, by virtue of the Mosaic covenant, will provide under the direct rule of God a model of God's rule over human life, which is the divine aim for the entire world.

"Nation" is modified by the adjective "holy." What is a "holy" nation? Unfortunately the term holy is one that is not very well understood by the church today. Definitions commonly given are "pure" or "set apart." Such definitions are erroneous because the meaning is being determined by etymology rather than usage, and the etymology is completely speculative. The idea that "holy" means set apart can be traced to the influence of W. W. Baudissin, who proposed in 1878 that the root of "holy" in Hebrew, i.e., qdš, is derived from qd-, "to cut."[49] Recently, exhaustive research by a French evangelical scholar, Claude-Bernard Costecalde, has cast better light on the meaning of this term since his analysis was based on the way the word is used rather than on hypothetical origins.[50] Costecalde's study examined all occurrences in the Old Testament and in ancient Near Eastern literature of

---

[48] In addition to the discussion given previously on "nation" in Genesis 12:2, in chapter 6, see the authoritative study by Daniel I. Block, "The Foundations of National Identity: A Study in Ancient Northwest Semitic Perceptions" (PhD diss., University of Liverpool, 1981).

[49] W. W. Baudissin, "Der Begriff der Heiligkeit im Alten Testament," in Studien zu semitischen Religionsgeschichte (Leipzig, Germany: Grunow, 1878), 2:1–142.

[50] Claude-Bernard Costecalde, Aux origines du sacré biblique (Paris: Letouzey et Ané, 1986). Unfortunately for North America, this work is in French and therefore not widely known in the evangelical world.

the same time (e.g., Akkadian and Ugaritic). Not surprisingly, he discovered that the biblical meaning was similar to that in the languages of the cultures surrounding Israel. The basic meaning is not "separated" but rather "consecrated to" or "devoted to." This is also the basic meaning of ἅγιος, the counterpart in Greek.[51]

Noteworthy is the passage in Exodus 3 where Moses encounters Yahweh in the burning bush and is asked to remove his sandals because he is standing on "holy ground." This is the first instance in the Old Testament of the root *qdš* in either an adjectival or a noun form. In the narrative, Moses is commanded to stay away from the bush, that is, from the place from which God speaks, but he is not commanded to stay away from the holy ground. There is nothing inaccessible or set apart about the holy ground. Moreover, his fright and shock come from a revelation of God, not from the holiness of the place. The "holy ground" (Ex. 3:5) encompasses a larger space than just the bush from which God speaks and is equivalent to "the mountain of God" in 3:1. The act of removing one's sandals, like the act of the nearest relative in Ruth 4:7, is a ceremony or rite of de-possession well known in the culture of that time. Moses must acknowledge that this ground belongs to God and must enter into an attitude of consecration. Thus, rather than marking an item as set apart, "holy" ground is ground prepared, consecrated, or devoted to the meeting of God and man.

A holy nation, then, is one prepared and consecrated for fellowship with God and one completely devoted to him. Instructions in the Pentateuch are often supported by the statement from Yahweh, "for I am holy." Such statements show that complete devotion to God on the part of Israel would show itself in two ways: (1) identifying with his ethics and morality, and (2) sharing his concern for the broken in the community. The commands and instructions in Leviticus 19 and 20 are bounded by the claim that Yahweh is holy (19:2; 20:26) and include concern against mistreating the alien and the poor, the blind and the deaf. In the "Judgements" of the Book of the Covenant (Exodus 19–24), some instructions relate to the oppression of orphans and widows (Ex. 22:23). God was concerned about the rights of the slave (e.g., Ex. 21:2–11) and the disenfranchised in society. Over the past thirty years we have heard the strident voice of the feminist, of the anti-nuclear protest, and of the gay rights movement. But God hears the voice of those who are

---

[51] See H. G. Liddell, R. Scott, and H. S. Jones, *A Greek-English Lexicon*, 9th ed. with revised supplement (Oxford: Oxford University Press, 1996), s.v. ἅγιος who give as the fundamental meaning, "devoted to the gods."

broken in body, in economy, and in spirit. If we are in covenant relationship with him, we must, like him, hear the voice that is too weak to cry out.

God also jealously protects what is devoted to him. His anger flares when his holiness is violated, as in the case of Uzzah (2 Sam. 6:7), who extended his hand to touch the ark of the covenant. Also in Psalm 2, when the kings and princes of the earth gather to touch the Anointed of the Lord, he flares out in anger to protect his King. Also in the case of Paul, in the New Testament, who in persecuting the church was reaching up to heaven, as it were, to shake his rebellious fist at Jesus, the Anointed One (= the Christ), and slap him in the face, and it resulted in his calling himself the chief of sinners (1 Tim. 1:15).

Explanation of the terms "personal treasure," "kingdom of priests," and "holy nation," then, shows the goal and purpose of the Sinai covenant for Israel. Although the language is different from that of Genesis 1:26–28 and Genesis 12:1–3, we can clearly see that the covenant at Sinai achieves and administers in the Iron Age, through the nation as a whole, the purposes of the promises given to Abraham. God is establishing his kingdom through covenant. The covenant entails relationship with God on the one hand and relationship with the world on the other hand. Israel will model to the world what it means to have a relationship with God, what it means to treat each other in a genuinely human way, and what it means to be good stewards of the earth's resources. As priests, they will mediate the blessings of God to the world and will be used to bring the rest of the world to know God.

Christopher J. H. Wright observes that Exodus 19:5–6 has a chiastic structure as follows:

> Now then, if you really obey my voice and keep my covenant,
> A   you will be for me a special personal possession
> B   among all the peoples;
> B'   for indeed to me belongs the whole earth
> A'   but you, you will be for me a priestly kingdom and a holy nation.[52]

Wright says, "After the initial conditional clause (the first line), there is a chiastic structure of four phrases, in which the two central lines portray God's universal ownership of the world and its nations, while the two outer lines express his particular role for Israel. This structure also makes clear that the double phrase 'priestly kingdom and holy nation' stands in apposition to

---

[52] Translation by Christopher J. H. Wright (see below).

'personal possession.' . . . The *status* is to be a special treasured possession. The *role* is to be a priestly and holy community in the midst of the nations."[53] The literary structure as explained by Wright reinforces the exposition here of Israel's covenant relationship with God and with the world that takes up the sonship and kingship of the divine image in Genesis 1.

The new covenant succeeds where the old covenant failed. The purposes of the Mosaic covenant are now being fulfilled in the church. The apostle Peter calls the church God's special treasure, a kingdom of priests and a holy nation (1 Pet. 2:9–10). God has forged both Jews and non-Jews into his new [Man, i.e., Adam] humanity, according to Ephesians 2:15. And as we shall see later on, this cannot be called "replacement theology."

THE TEN WORDS (EXODUS 20)

A brief explanation of the Ten Words will make plain the claim made repeatedly that the Mosaic covenant entails a right relationship to God and social justice in human relationships.

Some general observations on the Ten Words are fundamental to a proper understanding of this covenant.

The Ten Words form the heart of the covenant between God and Israel at Sinai. The Book of the Covenant, as we have seen, consists of the Ten Words and the Judgements. The former constitute the basic and fundamental requirements of the covenant. The latter are detailed stipulations based on the Ten Words, which apply them in practical ways to specific social situations and draw out and nuance their meaning in various contingencies and circumstances.

Attention has already been drawn to the fact that the earliest tradition in the biblical text refers to these requirements as the "Ten Words" (Ex. 34:28, Deut. 4:13, 10:4) and not, e.g., as the "Ten Commandments" as we now know them. There is, in fact, a particular reason for this and for why there are precisely ten instructions. A connection is being made between the covenant at Sinai and the creation. In the creation narrative, God creates the universe by simply speaking, i.e., by his word. In the Hebrew text, the verb *wayyō'mer*, "and he [= God] said" occurs ten times. In a very real way, entire creation depends or hangs upon the word of God. Here, the Book of the Covenant is what forges Israel into a nation. It is her national

---

[53] Christopher J. H. Wright, *The Mission of God: Unlocking the Bible's Grand Narrative* (Downers Grove, IL: InterVarsity Press, 2006), 255–256 (emphasis his).

constitution, so to speak. And it is also Ten Words that brings about the birth of the nation. Like the creation, Israel as a nation hangs upon the Ten Words for her very being.

Although the biblical text explicitly tells us that there are *ten* words, the Jewish, Catholic, and Protestant traditions have differed in enumerating them. Differences in itemisation are focused on commands one, two, and ten, and debate is based on issues of cantillation in the Masoretic Text and on issues of form, meaning, and style as well as on the fact that the repetition of the Ten Words in Deuteronomy 5 entails some slight variations from the text in Exodus. Since the discussion here of the first "four" commands is indebted to the treatment of John Walton, it follows the Protestant or Reformed Tradition. Then a brief argument will be given for the arrangement in the Catholic-Lutheran tradition and some alternate interpretations made possible from this point of view.

The Protestant tradition divides the Ten Words into four commands defining Israel's relationship to Yahweh and six commands dealing with human interpersonal relationships within the covenant community. They define a genuinely human way to treat each other.

Note in particular that a reason or rationale is given for keeping the first four commands, introduced by *kî* = "because" or "for" (20:5, 6, 11). One reason is supplied after commands 1 and 2, and one each after the third and fourth commands. This is a hint, structurally, to consider the first four commands in pairs.

No reason or rationale is given for keeping the last six commands. These entail the basic and inalienable rights of every human and have been recognised by the customs and laws of every society.[54] These "laws" can be paralleled in law codes from other societies in the ancient Near East:

Legal Treatises of the Ancient Near East[55]

The Laws of Ur-Nammu	21st century B.C.
The Laws of Lipit-Ishtar	19th century B.C.
The Laws of Eshnunna	18th century B.C.
The Code of Hammurabi	18th century B.C.
The Old Hittite Laws	17th century B.C.
The Middle Assyrian Laws	12th century B.C.

---

[54] See C. S. Lewis, *The Abolition of Man* (London: Geoffrey Bles, 1943, 1946).

[55] John H. Walton, *Ancient Near Eastern Thought and the Old Testament: Introducing the Conceptual World of the Hebrew Bible* (Grand Rapids, MI: Baker, 2006), 69–71.

Although the Ten Words expresses these laws negatively, they could also be expressed positively in terms of the inalienable rights of every human person:

Thou shalt not murder	= the right of every person to their own life
Thou shalt not commit adultery	= the right of every person to their own home
Thou shalt not steal	= the right of every person to their own property
Thou shalt not bear false witness	= the right of every person to their own reputation

No society can endure that does not respect the basic inalienable rights of every human person. Since the last six commands can be paralleled in the law codes of other societies in the ancient Near East and were well known to the Israelites, no rationale for keeping them need be supplied in the text. The first four commands, however, as Professors Andrew and Stamm have argued, are unparalleled in the ancient Near East.[56] Certainly the command to worship only one God, the command not to manufacture or worship idols, and the command to observe the Sabbath are absolutely unique. In fact, the seventh day in Mesopotamia was considered unlucky. These commands constitute a new revelation, and God graciously supplies a rationale for keeping them, so that Israel may grasp an adequate motivation for following a practise that was unprecedented.

The question must also be raised as to why the commands are given as prohibitions and why they are formulated in the second person singular. Why not express them positively as inalienable rights? Why not indicate by a second person plural that they are addressed to all? The reason for this is simple. God wants each and every individual person to think first of the inalienable rights of the other person and not first about their own inalienable rights. This explains both the negative formulation and the second person singular.

From the start and right throughout the entire history of Israel, attempts were made to boil down, digest, and summarise the instructions of the covenant—both the many Judgements that elaborate the Ten Words in practical situations as well as the Ten Words themselves. For example, Leviticus 18–20 contains a collection of instructions that develop further in particular

---

[56] Johann J. Stamm and Maurice E. Andrew, *The Ten Commandments in Recent Research*, Studies in Biblical Theology, Second Series 2 (Naperville, IL: Alec R. Allenson, 1967). I have not carefully researched whether the command concerning misuse of the divine name is found in other ancient Near Eastern societies.

the last six of the Ten Words. It is interesting to note that at the mid- and end-points of Leviticus 19 we find the instruction, "You shall love your neighbour as yourself" (vv. 18, 34).[57] Jesus and other rabbis of the first century demonstrated exegetical insight to observe that this was a summary statement of the various instructions in this section of Leviticus and indeed of the last portion of the Ten Words that they elaborate. Later on, the prophets and poets used two pairs of words as summaries of the Torah. One is the pair "lovingkindness and truth" and the other is "justice and righteousness." Each pair of words is a hendiadys—communicating a single idea through two words. The first pair speaks of faithful loyal love and the second speaks of social justice. These are attempts to boil down the covenant stipulations into a single "sound bite." They are important because they show that the instructions represent faithful love as well as social justice in human interrelationships.

Space permits in this brief treatment of the Mosaic covenant a short explanation of each of the first four of the Ten Words, as these have been more troublesome for Christians to understand than the last six.

FIRST COMMAND: NO OTHER GODS BEFORE ME

Some scholars and traditions have construed the first of the Ten Words as Exodus 20:2–3. Yet the fact that the covenant is broadly structured according to a Hittite treaty demonstrates plainly that verse 2, in which Yahweh says, "I am the LORD your God who brought you out from the land of Egypt, from the house of slaves," is, in fact, the historical prologue of the treaty, so that the first command is just verse 3: "You shall have no other gods before me." In both Roman Catholic and Lutheran interpretive traditions, the command in verse 3 and the command in verse 4 ("You shall not make for yourself an idol") are counted as one command while the command against coveting is separated into two: "you shall not covet your neighbour's wife" and "you shall not covet your neighbour's house." As Bruce Waltke notes, "according to the latter construction, the first commandment condemns false worship and the tenth commandment distinguishes wife from property."[58]

---

[57] The command means "to provide assistance" or "be useful" to one's neighbour. See A. Malamat, "'You Shall Love Your Neighbour as Yourself': A Case of Misinterpretation," in *Die Hebräische Bibel und ihre zweifache Nachgeschichte: Festschrift für Rolf Rendtorff zum 65. Geburtstag*, ed. E. Blum, C. Macholz, and E. W. Stegemann (Neukirchen-Vluyn, Germany: Neukirchner, 1990), 111–115.

[58] Bruce K. Waltke with Charles Yu, *An Old Testament Theology: An Exegetical, Canonical, and Thematic Approach* (Grand Rapids, MI: Zondervan, 2007), 411. The exposition here shows clearly the difference between "having no other gods before Yahweh" and "not making an idolatrous image," whereas "coveting a neighbour's wife" and "coveting a neighbour's house" are not as distinct notions. Therefore the Jewish and Reformed division is followed here.

The interpretation of the Reformers and the creeds following in this tradition construe the text to mean we should not have any other gods before the Lord, i.e., in preference to the Lord. Thus the prohibition is understood in terms of priorities. According to the Westminster Confession, God must be the highest priority in our attitudes, thoughts, words, and ways. Others have interpreted the prohibition philosophically and argued that the main point is to establish absolute monotheism and rule out the existence of other deities.

The command, however, does appear to acknowledge the existence of other gods. In courses taught in the history of religion at universities in the Western world, the suggestion is frequently made that, at an earlier stage of the history of Israel, the people were henotheists—that is, they believed in the existence of many gods but consciously chose to worship only one. At a later point in the development of Israel's religion, henotheism gave way to monotheism, i.e., the belief that there *is* only one god.

Bruce Waltke alleviates this problem by distinguishing between religious command and theological statements:

> For theological statements of whether other gods exist, we turn to Deuteronomy 4:39: "Acknowledge and take to heart this day that the LORD is God in heaven above and on the earth below. There is no other." Furthermore, Deuteronomy 32:17–21 identifies idol worship as bowing down to demons. Verse 17 reads, "They sacrificed to demons, which are not God [*lō'-'elōhîm*, "no-God"]." These declarative sentences serve as foundations for theological beliefs and doctrines.
>
> On the other hand, religious commands deal with subjective reality. The truth is, regardless of the existence of other gods, human beings create and worship what is "no-God" (1 Cor. 8:4–8). As stated above, Calvin noted that the human heart is a perpetual idol factory. Thus, rather than tacitly assuming the existence of other gods, the commandment assumes the depravity of the human race to create and worship their own gods. The religious command reflects the reality of the human situation but does not serve as a theological statement. Other passages teach monotheism.[59]

This distinction is extremely helpful but nonetheless assumes that the exegesis in terms of priorities is correct. Yet this exegesis is difficult to maintain. As John Walton notes, "the focus on God as the highest priority is as far back as the LXX, which translated the Hebrew *'l pny* ('before me') with the Greek preposition *plēn*, 'except.' However, if Hebrew meant to say 'except' there

---

[59] Waltke, *Old Testament Theology*, 415–416.

were several ways to do this (e.g., *'ak* or *raq*). Similarly, if the Hebrew had intended to express priority, it could have used language such as that found in Deut 4:12 or Isa 45:21."[60] In an exhaustive study of the use of the preposition *'l pny-* ("before") plus personal object in the Hebrew Bible, Walton shows that the meaning is consistently spatial.[61] The linguistic data, then, demand that a spatial sense be considered as the main option.

In the past, students of the text have avoided this interpretation because they could not understand how it could make any sense. Data from the ancient Near Eastern culture now illuminate how a spatial sense is eminently suitable. In the culture of the ancient Near East at this time the gods operated within a pantheon, a divine assembly. John Walton argues that the first commandment is distinguishing Yahweh from this common understanding of deity in the ancient world, and his analysis is worth citing in full:[62]

> . . . when the first commandment prohibits other gods in the presence of Yahweh, it is ruling out the concept that He operates within a pantheon, a divine assembly, or with a consort. J. Bottéro compares this system to that of a king at the head of the state with his family and functionaries around him operating in a structured hierarchy.[63]
>
> Having this image as background suggests that the Israelites were not to imagine any other gods in the presence of Yahweh. Scholars could have arrived at this meaning by simple lexical study, but without the benefit of the ancient Near Eastern material, the results of the lexical study made no sense to interpreters. Consequently, they devised alternative explanations, even though when the prepositional combination that occurs in the Hebrew text takes a personal object the meaning is consistently spatial. Using comparative cultural information, we have recovered a neglected sense of the text that was there all the time.
>
> In view of the information provided from outside the Bible, this spatial sense gains credibility. In the ancient Near East the gods operated within pantheons and decisions were made in the divine assembly. Furthermore, the principal deities typically had consorts. For the gods life was a community experience. The destinies of the gods were decreed in assembly, as were the destinies of kings, cities, temples and people. The business of the gods

---

[60] John H. Walton, "Interpreting the Bible as an Ancient Near Eastern Document," in *Israel—Ancient Kingdom or Late Invention? Archaeology, Ancient Civilizations, and the Bible*, ed. Daniel I. Block (Nashville: B&H, 2008), 306.

[61] Ibid., 307.

[62] The citation includes footnotes from Walton and excludes a chart listing occurrences of the preposition לפני plus personal object: John H. Walton, "Interpreting the Bible as an Ancient Near Eastern Document," in *Israel—Ancient Kingdom or Late Invention? Archaeology, Ancient Civilizations, and the Bible*, ed. Daniel I. Block (Nashville: B&H, 2008), 306–309.

[63] J. Bottéro, "Intelligence and the Technical Function of Power: Enki/Ea," in *Mesopotamia: Writing, Reasoning and the Gods* (Chicago: University of Chicago, 1992), 232–50; the citation is found on p. 233.

was carried out in the presence of other gods. Lowell Handy helpfully summarises this system as a hierarchy of authoritative deities and active deities.

> The highest authority in the pantheon was responsible for ordering and maintaining earth and cosmos but was not actively engaged in the actual work necessary to maintain the universe. The next lower level of deities performed this function. Serving under the authority of those who actually owned the universe, the active gods were expected to perform in a way that would enable the cosmos to operate smoothly. Each of the gods at this level of the pantheon had a specific sphere of authority over which to exert his or her control. Ideally, all the gods were to perform their duties in a way that would keep the universe functioning perfectly in the manner desired by the highest authority. Yet the gods, like human beings, are portrayed as having weaknesses and rivalries that kept the cosmos from operating smoothly.[64]

Accordingly, by a comparative interpretation of the first commandment the Israelites were not to construe Yahweh as operating within a community of gods. Nor were they to imagine Him functioning as the head of a pantheon surrounded by a divine assembly, or having a consort. In short, He works alone. The concept of a pantheon/divine assembly assumed a distribution of power among many divine beings. The first commandment declared simply and unequivocally that Yahweh's authority was absolute. Divine power was not distributed among other deities or limited by the will of the assembly.

The point of the prohibition of the worship of any other gods "besides" Yahweh was to ensure that Israel's perception of divinity was to be distinct from the peoples around them. This text is readily misunderstood if the interpreter is not aware of the notions being rejected. According to this revised interpretation, the purpose of the first commandment was not simply to promote monolatry; it served the monotheistic agenda another way. Although this text does not explicitly deny the existence of other gods, it does remove them from the presence of Yahweh. If Yahweh does not share power, authority, or jurisdiction with them, they are not gods in any meaningful sense of the word.[65] Thus, the first commandment does not insist on the non-existence of other gods; only that they are powerless. In so doing it disenfranchises them, not merely by declaring that they should not be worshiped; it leaves them with no status worthy of worship.[66]

---

[64] Lowell Handy, *Among the Host of Heaven* (Winona Lake: Eisenbrauns, 1994), 97.

[65] The significance of this notion may be extended if we attach to it the idea that in the ancient Near East something was not considered to exist if it had not been assigned a name, a place, or a function. See discussion in Walton, *Ancient Near Eastern Thought and the Old Testament*, 87–97.

[66] This is close to the view of Christopher Wright, who says, "The fundamental thrust of the verse is not Yahweh's sole deity, but Yahweh's sole sovereignty over Israel." *Deuteronomy* (Peabody, MA: Hendrickson, 1996), 68. For the entire quote, see Walton, "Interpreting the Bible as an Ancient Near Eastern Document," 306–309.

In the progressive revealing and unfolding of God in history and Scripture, the completed Canon shows that God has revealed himself completely and fully in Jesus Christ. Jesus said, "All authority in heaven and on earth has been given to me." Our lives, our service and work, our worship must recognise his authority alone. This disenfranchises all gods and idols worshipped in our culture. There is no one else I am living my life for than Jesus Christ.

SECOND COMMAND: NO IMAGES/IDOLS

The second of the Ten Words is as follows: "You shall not make for yourself an image and form which is in the heaven above and which is in the earth below and which is in the waters under the earth" (Ex. 20:4). As John Walton notes, popular prohibition of images has been influenced significantly by four factors: (1) Jewish interpretation, (2) controversies over icons in the Eastern Orthodox tradition, (3) statues of saints in the Roman Catholic tradition, and (4) debate over what constitutes art from a Christian perspective.[67] In classical Jewish and Muslim traditions the second command led to a prohibition of the representation of any living creature. Christian interpretation up to the nineteenth century was dominated by the idea that since God was invisible and transcendent he could not be contained in an image. Others have spiritualised the text, reducing idols to anything to which we devote our energy, money, and worth as deity.

Such misunderstandings of the second command are due to a couple of factors. First is ignorance of the ancient Near Eastern ideas concerning the nature and role of idols. Walton classifies ancient Near Eastern thinking about idols into three categories.

One category is the manufacture of images. In the ancient Near Eastern mindset, only the god could approve and initiate the manufacturing process. At the end of the process, special ceremonies and rituals, in particular the mouth-opening ritual, allowed the god to inhabit the image and permitted the image to drink, eat food, and smell incense.

A second category concerns the use of the image. Walton notes that, "in the ancient world all formal and public worship revolved around the image."[68] Thus the image involved mediation. It mediated revelation from the deity to the people and also mediated worship by the people to the deity as they brought clothes, drink and food to honour it.

---

[67] Walton, "Interpreting the Bible as an Ancient Near Eastern Document," 309–313.
[68] Ibid., 311.

A third category has to do with ancient Near Eastern perceptions concerning the function and nature of images. According to Walton, "as a result of the induction ritual the material image was animated by the divine essence. Therefore, from now on it did not simply represent the deity but also manifested its presence. However, this does not mean that the image had thereby been deified. The deity was the reality that was embodied in the image."[69]

Misunderstanding of the second command is due not only to ignorance of the ancient Near Eastern culture and worldview but also to faulty analysis of the grammar of this text. Let us consider closely the exact text of the second of the Ten Words in both Exodus and Deuteronomy. Below, the Hebrew text is provided as well as the translations of the KJV and NIV.

Exodus 20:4: לֹא תַעֲשֶׂה־לְךָ פֶסֶל וְכָל־תְּמוּנָה

KJV: Thou shalt not make unto thee any graven image, or any likeness of any thing . . .

NIV: You shall not make for yourself an idol in the form of anything . . .

Deuteronomy 5:8: לֹא־תַעֲשֶׂה־לְךָ פֶסֶל כָּל־תְּמוּנָה

KJV: Thou shalt not make thee any graven image, or any likeness of any thing . . .

NIV: You shall not make for yourself an idol in the form of anything . . .

The translation of the KJV represents early Jewish rabbinic understanding, no doubt mediated through the Latin Vulgate of Jerome. This is the way orthodox Jews today understand the text and also the way in which Muslims have consistently understood the text.

The original text in Hebrew actually conjoins the objects of the verb with *waw*, a copulative coordinating conjunction that always means "and." A series of alternative clauses may be joined by *waw*, but this does not mean that *waw* has the same value as "or" in English.[70] Hebrew does have a conjunction "or," i.e., *'ô*, and it could have been used here to designate the alternative possibility. The text in Exodus 20:4 is difficult, but the early rabbinic understanding does not follow the norms of grammar in Hebrew. Note that the parallel text in Deuteronomy does not have the conjunction *waw* but employs instead a Construct Phrase, "a carved image/idol *of* any form . . . ." Certainly the rendering by "or" is contrary to the syntax here. It seems that

---

[69] Ibid., 312.
[70] See Brown, Driver, and Briggs, *Hebrew and English Lexicon of the Old Testament*, s.v. ו § 1d.

interpretive traditions have molded Deuteronomy 5:8 to suit their understanding of Exodus 20:4

If we believe in the analogy of Scripture, however, where we interpret the unclear by the clear, the Jewish understanding cannot be the correct meaning of this text. Consider, for example, the art in the tabernacle and also in Solomon's temple. Artwork in the construction of Solomon's temple had representation of the creation with images of bulls, cherubim, lion, palm trees, and pomegranates (1 Kings 7:18, 25, 36). Since the grammar of the text in Deuteronomy 5:8 is clear, a better approach is to use the clear text there to interpret the unclear in Exodus 20:4. The construction in Exodus 20:4 could be understood as a hendiadys, a common figure of speech in Hebrew literature where one idea is communicated by two nouns or verbs joined by "and." The first notable example in the Bible is Genesis 3:16. The Hebrew text has, "I will greatly increase your pain and your pregnancy." This does not mean an increase of pain on the one hand and pregnancy on the other. The next sentence goes on to explain, "In pain you will bring forth children." So the earlier expression must mean "pain in pregnancy"—an example of a hendiadys. In Exodus 20:4, "a carved image and any form" must therefore in the light of Deuteronomy 5:8 mean "a carved image/idol in any form." This is the approach taken by the NIV and is one that accurately follows the grammar of the Hebrew language and uses the clear meaning of one text to assist the interpretation of the other rather than impose the faulty interpretation of Exodus on the clear text in Deuteronomy.

Accurate exegesis of the second command, then, shows that this text has nothing to do with art or the representation of aspects of the created order with images. Rather the command has to do with images used as mediators of the presence or revelation of deity from god to human, or mediation of the worship of people to the deity. As Walton observes, "the prohibition of images excluded in particular that sort of worship that understood cultic rituals to meet the needs of the deity through the image."[71]

THIRD COMMAND: DO NOT MISUSE THE NAME OF GOD

Popular misunderstanding also exists concerning the third of the Ten Words: "You shall not lift up the name of Yahweh your God worthlessly (*laššāw'*)"

---

[71] Walton, "Interpreting the Bible as an Ancient Near Eastern Document," 313.

(Ex. 20:7). Once again, better knowledge of both cultural setting and linguistic data can improve our understanding of this text.

First, the basic import of this instruction is not related to the use of God's name idly in blasphemy, minced oaths, or profanity. This is certainly inappropriate, and respect and reverence for the divine name is enjoined in Deuteronomy 28:58.

Second, the traditional view has focused on false oaths. As Bruce Waltke notes,

> . . . the operative word is *šāw'* (KJV, "in vain"; cf. Lev. 24:15). . . . *Šāw'* is used in biblical Hebrew in several ways: to denote to be false or deceitful with respect to speaking (Deut. 5:20 in reference to being a false witness against a neighbor; Exod 23:1 in reference to a false report or rumor); with respect to being false in worship (Isa. 1:13, which discusses a false tribute to God where the people hold to a form of worship, but their heart is not there); and with respect to being false in prophecy (Ezek. 13:3–7, which refers to false prophets who claim to have seen a vision, but there is no reality to what they have seen). Herbert Huffmon argues from both biblical and extrabiblical evidence that the commandment prohibits false or frivolous swearing. "The focus is on not making God an accomplice, as it were to one's falseness, whether of intent or of performance."[72]

Thus, according to analysis of the linguistic data, the command has to do with lifting up the name of God falsely or worthlessly. But this does not provide a full picture.

Third, in order to get a valid understanding, the results from the study of the linguistic data must be set within the context of the ancient Near Eastern culture. As Walton points out, this depends upon a careful definition of magic, the world in which the false or proper use of names occurs.[73] In the ancient Near East and also in the Greco-Roman world there was no demarcating line between religion and magic. Later, influence from the Medieval church and the Enlightenment resulted in distinguishing the two. In the past, however, interpreters have not appreciated how names were used in the framework of magic and power.

G. Frantz-Szabó offers a comprehensive and helpful definition of magic in the context of invoking supernatural powers:

---

[72] Waltke, *Old Testament Theology*, 419.
[73] See Walton, "Interpreting the Bible as an Ancient Near Eastern Document," 316.

> [Magic] is a reasoned system of techniques for influencing the gods and other supernatural powers that can be taught and learned. . . . Magic is a praxis, indeed a science, that through established and for the most part empirical means seeks to alter or maintain earthly circumstances, or even call them forth anew. Magic not only manipulates occult forces but also endeavors to master the higher supernatural power with which religion is concerned.[74]

The name of God represents and sums up his entire character and person. To use that name brings his person and his power into a particular situation. As C. Seitz helpfully points out, God truly responds to "Moses' request in [Exodus 3] to know his name, but in a way that neither the reader nor Moses is prepared for. . . . God's name is the most personal revelation of God's own character, and as such is not a proper name in the strict sense (like Jim or Sally) but a name appropriate to God's character as God."[75] When we use his name for something that is contrary to who he is, contrary to his character, we lift it up to a lie. Walton observes that "the name is equivalent to the identity of the deity, and the divine identity can be commandeered for illicit use. The problem of identity theft is widely recognized today."[76] In Psalm 139:19ff. David disassociates himself in the strongest of terms from fellow Israelites who want him to join them in a scheme to murder someone and are doing this using the name of Yahweh. Misusing the name of God occurs among Christians today when someone says, "the Lord led me to do such and such a thing," when we know from Scripture that this is not according to the revealed will of God.

FOURTH COMMAND: KEEP THE SABBATH

The fourth of the Ten Words is a positive injunction to observe the Sabbath (Ex. 20:8–11). The importance of this injunction is indicated by its length—it is the longest of the Ten Words.

For several decades in the twentieth century, scholars attempted to find precursors to the Israelite Sabbath in the nations surrounding ancient Israel. This effort was entirely unsuccessful. The Hebrew *šabbāt* is not connected to the Babylonian *šabbatu*, which is the fifteenth day of the month. Moreover

---

[74] G. Frantz-Szabó, "Hittite Witchcraft and Divination," in *Civilizations of the Ancient Near East*, ed. Jack M. Sasson, 4 vols. (New York: Charles Scribner's Sons, 1995), 3:2007.

[75] Christopher Seitz, "The Call of Moses and the 'Revelation' of the Divine Name: Source-Critical Logic and Its Legacy," in *Theological Exegesis: Essays in Honor of Brevard S. Childs*, ed. Christopher Seitz and Kathryn Greene-McCreight (Grand Rapids, MI: Eerdmans, 1991), 154.

[76] Walton, "Interpreting the Bible as an Ancient Near Eastern Document," 318.

the 7th, 14th, 21st, and 28th days of certain months in the Babylonian calendar were considered unlucky. Nonetheless, the concept of divine rest is well attested in ancient Near Eastern texts, and the cultural context can cast great light on interpretation of the fourth command.

Six aspects of the notion of divine rest in the ancient Near East, drawn mainly from the great epics such as the Babylonian *Enuma Elish*, are delineated by Walton.[77] These can be briefly summarised as follows: (1) in the ancient epics, the divine rest was disturbed by rebellion; (2) divine rest was achieved after conflict; (3) divine rest was achieved after acts of creation, establishing order; (4) divine rest was achieved in the temple; (5) divine rest was characterised by ongoing rule and stability; and (6) divine rest was achieved by the gods by creating people to do their work.

There are both similarities and differences between the biblical command to observe the Sabbath and the cultural context of the ancient Near East. We need to attend carefully to the linguistic data in the relevant texts. In Exodus 20:8–11, the Israelites are commanded to remember the Sabbath Day to consecrate it. In the Old Testament, the notion of remembering is not merely mental recall; it entails acts in space and time based on keeping something at the front of one's mind. Israel is to consecrate the Sabbath; it is a commemorative event that belongs to Yahweh and is to be devoted to him. Both humans—free or slaves, citizens or resident aliens—and animals are to cease from the business and labour ordinarily undertaken to provide for our own life and sustenance. It is an act of faith acknowledging Yahweh as the creator and giver of life and as the one who rules our lives.

The biblical viewpoint is fundamentally different from the ancient Near Eastern perspectives, in spite of many parallels on the surface. Walton says, "in the Old Testament people work for their own benefit and provision, rather than to meet the needs of God or to do his work for him. When commanded to share the rest of God on the Sabbath, it is not to participate in it per se, but to recognize His work of bringing and maintaining order. God's rest symbolizes His control over the cosmos, which His people recognize whenever they yield to Him the day they could have used to provide for themselves."[78]

On the other hand, the parallel between the ancient Near Eastern building of temples for divine rest and the biblical creation narrative culminating

---

[77] Ibid., 319–322.
[78] Ibid., 322.

in divine rest is valid. The framework of the account of creation in the Bible strongly suggests that the cosmos is constructed as a sanctuary/temple in which God may take up his rest.

Discussion of this command brings us right into the middle of the problem of the relationship between the old covenant and the new, a matter which cannot be adequately discussed in this chapter. Nonetheless, a few comments on the Sabbath are in order.

First, we must note that the Sabbath was the sign between Yahweh and Israel of the old covenant, as is clearly stated in Exodus 31:12–18. Covenants often have a physical sign associated with them. The rainbow was given as a physical sign of God's promise in his covenant with Noah. Circumcision was commanded as a physical sign in the body of every male in Israel as a sign of God's covenant with Abraham. Similarly, the Sabbath is stipulated as a permanent sign between Yahweh and Israel that the God who created the world in six days and then rested has consecrated them to himself.

Second, as we compare the old covenant and the new covenant, we see that the self-identity of the people of the Lord in the old covenant was that of children, while the self-identity of the people of the Lord in the new covenant is that of mature adults (Gal. 3:24–25). The external forms and shadows of the old covenant have been done away now that the reality has come in Christ (Col. 2:16–17).

Now of what does the Sabbath speak? Let us notice at once that, in the two texts in the Old Testament where we have the Ten Words, the reason given for the Sabbath in one text is different from the reason given in the other text. In Exodus, the reason is given in 20:11. God's work of creation was complete, it was finished; the people could add nothing to it. They were invited to enter his rest and enjoy his work. Hebrews applies this notion to the work of Christ (Heb. 3:7–4:11). We cannot do anything to add to the work of Jesus Christ. We are simply to enjoy it.

In Deuteronomy 5:15, a different reason is given for the Sabbath. The people of Israel must remember that they were slaves in Egypt and God brought them out of slavery, so they should give their slaves a chance to rest as they do on the Sabbath. Paul, in Colossians 1:12–14, speaks as do many authors of the New Testament of the work of the Lord Jesus as a new exodus. Egypt is a picture or symbol of the world; Pharaoh is a symbol of Satan, and the slavery is a symbol of our enslavement to our passion and pride from which Christ has redeemed us in his death on the cross. Jesus is the new

Joshua, who will lead those people connected to him by the new covenant to enter and enjoy God's Sabbath rest.

SUMMARY

The first four commands in the Ten Words can be construed as two pairs. John Walton's summary is helpful in grasping their function and intent:[79]

Commandments 1 and 2

Yahweh's mode of operating in the two realms (divine and human):
- Commandment 1 concerns how Yahweh was *not* to be perceived as operating in the divine realm—no distribution of authority to other divinities.
- Commandment 2 concerns how Yahweh was *not* to be perceived as operating in the human realm—no iconographic mediator of his presence, revelation, or worship should be offered to him.

Commandments 3 and 4

Yahweh's exercise of power:
- Commandment 3 concerns how Yahweh's power/authority was *not* to be perceived—people were to recognise it by refraining from attempts to control it.
- Commandment 4 concerns how Yahweh's power/authority *was* to be perceived—people were to recognise it by refraining from attempts to control their own lives on the Sabbath.

ALTERNATIVE INTERPRETATIONS

Several alternate possibilities for interpretation of the Ten Words deserve serious consideration and, in one or two of them, further research.

First, recent research on the enumeration of the Ten Words by Jason S. DeRouchie supports the Catholic-Lutheran analysis as follows:[80]

(1) No other gods
(2) No use of name deceitfully
(3) Sabbath
(4) Honour parents
(5) No murder

---

[79] Adapted from ibid., 323.
[80] See Jason S. DeRouchie, *A Call to Covenant Love: Text Grammar and Literary Structure in Deuteronomy 5–11*, Gorgias Dissertations 30 (Piscataway, NJ: Gorgias, 2007), 115–117, 127–132; and idem, "Numbering the Decalogue: A Textlinguistic Reappraisal," paper presented at the Upper Midwest Regional Meeting of the Society of Biblical Literature, April 2007. This analysis is also supported by Daniel I. Block, "Reading the Decalogue Right to Left: The Ten Principles of Covenant Relationship in the Hebrew Bible," in *How I Love Your Torah, O LORD! Studies in the Book of Deuteronomy* (Eugene, OR: Cascade, 2011), 56–60; and idem, *Deuteronomy*, NIV Application Commentary (Grand Rapids, MI: Zondervan, 2012).

(6) No adultery
(7) No theft
(8) No false witness
(9) No coveting wife
(10) No desiring household members/objects

DeRouchie's analysis is convincing because it is based on discourse grammar/macrosyntax/textlinguistic analysis. This area of linguistic study pays close attention to features in the language that are grammatical markers above or beyond the boundary of individual sentences in the text as a whole. In particular, in the version of the Ten Words in Deuteronomy 5:6–21, the enumeration is clarified because commands 5–10 are joined by the conjunction *waw* ("and"), while commands 1–4 are set off from the last six by asyndeton (absence of the conjunction).[81] Moreover, the fact that only one reason in both Exodus 20:3–6 and Deuteronomy 5:7–10 supports commands 1 and 2—according to the enumeration of the Protestant tradition—provides further corroboration that they should be considered a single command.

Second, then, in the light of a correct enumeration of the Ten Words, the command "You shall have no other gods before me" and the command "You shall not make for yourself images/idols" taken together constitute the first command and "You shall not bear/lift up the name of the Lord your God in vain" is now the second command.

D. I. Block proposes a different interpretation for this second command, "You shall not take the name of the LORD your God in vain."[82] The traditional interpretations and translations in the English versions may "miss the central issue, namely, that of wearing the name of Yahweh as a badge or brand of ownership."[83] The key to this injunction is the verb נָשָׂא, which does not mean "to misuse," or "to pronounce," or "to take" in this text, since all of these translations would require different idioms. Instead, here the normal sense "to bear, carry" is most suitable. The collocation of this verb with "name" occurs elsewhere only in Exodus 28:12 and 29, where it refers to Aaron, the high priest, bearing the names of the sons of Israel since they were inscribed on two onyx stones on the shoulder pieces of his ephod. In addition, Block notes,

---

[81] For description and evidence of asyndeton versus use of the conjunction *waw* as a macrosyntactic signal, see Stephen G. Dempster, "Linguistic Features of Hebrew Narrative: A Discourse Analysis of Narrative from the Classical Period" (PhD diss., University of Toronto, 1985).

[82] Daniel I. Block, "Bearing the Name of the Lord with Honor," in *How I Love Your Torah, O LORD!* 61–72 (originally published in *Bibliotheca Sacra* 168 [2011]: 20-31).

[83] Ibid., 63.

According to Numbers 6:27 in the future the Aaronic priests would "put" Yahweh's name on the Israelites by declaring for them what came to be known as "the Aaronic blessing." And because they bore the stamp of His name they were objects of His blessing. In Deuteronomy the expression קָדֹשׁ לַיהוה, "holy belonging to Yahweh," is applied to Israel as a whole (Deut. 26:19; cf. 7:6; 14:2, 21). Like the Shema', which was to be inscribed on houses and gates and on phylacteries on the forehead, to bear the name of God means to have His name branded on one's person as a mark of divine ownership.

Several other passages may be briefly mentioned to support this view. The notion of branding (e.g., cattle) used metaphorically may underlie Isaiah 44:5b:

> This one will say, "I am the LORD's,"
>> another will call on the name of Jacob,
> and another will write on his hand, "The LORD's,"
>> and claim as honorific title the name of Israel.

Further, Deuteronomy 28:9–10 clearly connects belonging to the Lord (i.e., holy to Yahweh) and bearing the name of the Lord:

> [9] The LORD will establish you as a people holy to himself, as he has sworn to you, if you keep the commandments of the LORD your God and walk in his ways. [10] And all the peoples of the earth shall see that you are called by the name of the LORD, and they shall be afraid of you. (ESV)

Finally, observe that when God judged his people in exile, he scattered them among the nations because they had *desecrated his holy name* (Ezek. 36:17–23). Conversely, in Daniel's famous prayer for the end of exile and judgement, he asks God to act for his own sake, *because your city and your people bear your name* (Dan. 9:16–19).

What then would the clause "bear the name" mean when modified by the adverbial phrase *laššāw'* (KJV, "in vain"). The comments cited earlier by Bruce Waltke are apt in spite of the fact that he is arguing for a traditional Jewish interpretation of this text. Although the noun can mean "empty" or "worthless," as Waltke points out, it frequently has to do with what is deceitful or false. Isaiah 59:3, "your lips have spoken deceitfully," is a good example (cf. Isa. 5:18). Psalm 139:20 actually alludes to the second of the Ten Words, and the context clarifies the issue:

> They speak against you with malicious intent;
> your enemies take your name in vain! (ESV)

Here David (according to the title of the Psalm) is confronting men who plan to murder someone and want David to join them in this. This is bearing the name of Yahweh deceitfully, and David identifies them instead as the enemies of God because the act they intend under the umbrella of his name is contrary to who he is and what he represents.

Third, on the basis of the analysis of the second command given by D. I. Block, a further insight is possible concerning commands one and two. According to the numbering scheme of the Catholic-Lutheran tradition, the first command, "no other gods," is identical to the claim "I am your God," and the second command, "no wearing his name deceitfully/worthlessly," is identical to the claim "You are my people," since bearing the name indicated belonging to Yahweh, i.e., wearing his brand mark as a badge of honour. In this way, as shown in table 9.2, the first two of the Ten Words may be seen as an exposition of the Covenant Formula (I will be your God, and you shall be my people).

Table 9.2: The First Two of the Ten Words as an Exposition of the Covenant Formula

No other gods before me	→	I will be your God
No bearing my name dishonourably	→	You will be my people

The mention of *'ēl qannā'* [KJV, "a jealous God"] in the first command adds support for this view since the Hebrew word *qannā'* refers to acting to protect one's property and the next command indicates that Israel belongs to Yahweh.

Fourth, a proposal made recently by Stephen Dempster could be further explored.[84] He suggests that the Ten Words are a further explication of the divine name, especially in light of the revelation of the divine name in Exodus 34:5–7. He notes that "I am Yahweh your God" (Ex. 20:2) is the first use of this formulation of divine identification in the Bible and is followed by what he understands as an explanatory gloss on the divine name—"who brought you out of servitude to Egypt."[85] He observes that the first command

---

[84] Personal communication, February 4, 2011.
[85] It may be that "I am the LORD your God who brought you out of the land of Egypt" is the first use of this formulation of the divine name, but it is, in another sense, a reworking of part of the Covenant Formula occurring as early as Genesis 17:7–8.

stresses Yahweh's uniqueness and therefore Israel's exclusive worship—Yahweh is One. The second command [according to the enumeration in the Protestant tradition] stresses his incomparability in the material realm—so much so that there cannot be any material duplicate. In particular, the motivation for keeping the command—*'ēl qanna'* [KJV, "a jealous God"]—is clearly related to the divine identity (cf. Ex. 34:14). In the Ten Words there is punishment down to the third and fourth generation of "those who hate me" versus *hesed* for the thousands of generations of "those who love me." In the revelation of the divine name in Exodus 34:5–7, this punishment is omitted. In the third command [according to the enumeration in the Protestant tradition], the divine name cannot be profaned because it is incomparable—note that the guilty party will not be acquitted and compare this to the revelation of the divine name in 34:6–7: "He will not acquit the guilty." This approach makes sense in the rest of the Ten Words as well, but explicit indications of it given there are lacking. Note as well that Exodus 22:25–26 is the first reference to חַנּוּן ("gracious," as in the revelation of the divine name in Ex. 34:6) in the Bible in the context of motivation for keeping a law. At any rate, central to the exodus is the revelation of the divine name (Exodus 3, 6, and now 20–24). Seitz has explained that God's name is the most personal revelation of God's own character. Therefore the Ten Words as a revelation of the divine name is at the same time a revelation of the character of Yahweh. No doubt the structure of the Ten Words is arranged with such skill that different analyses are possible at the same time.

THE JUDGEMENTS (EXODUS 20:22–23:33)

Following the "Ten Words" is a section entitled the "Judgements." This section is an expansion on the Ten Words. Although parts of the section are in the form of apodictic or prescriptive statements (You shall/shall not; e.g., 22:18–23:10), large parts are in the form of conditional sentences, i.e., case decisions or descriptive law or judicial precedents (e.g., 21:2–22:17). Like the Ten Words, provisions for cultic issues (i.e., festivals; 23:10–19) are mixed together with moral matters and issues of restitution and social justice.

Davies observes that this section begins and ends with a warning of the dangers of worshipping other gods, and this inclusio characterises the function of the section.[86]

---

[86] John A. Davies, *Royal Priesthood*, 112.

John Walton has devoted significant study to comparing and contrasting these materials with counterparts in ancient Near Eastern culture and society.[87] Earlier, a table listed similar texts as follows:

Legal Treatises of the Ancient Near East

The Laws of Ur-Nammu	21st century B.C.
The Laws of Lipit-Ishtar	19th century B.C.
The Laws of Eshnunna	18th century B.C.
The Code of Hammurabi	18th century B.C.
The Old Hittite Laws	17th century B.C.
The Middle Assyrian Laws	12th century B.C.

Walton draws upon scholars who have devoted a lifetime to the study of such texts in Egypt and Mesopotamia, Israel's neighbours. The consensus is that the texts are not law codes as we who have a Graeco-Roman heritage think of them, because they are neither *comprehensive* nor *prescriptive*. The ancients loved to compile lists, and these are anthologies of examples that model judicial wisdom. J. Bottéro, an expert in ancient Near Eastern legal material says:

> In the eyes of its author the "Code" [of Hammurabi] was not at all intended to exercise by itself a univocal normative value in the legislative order. But it did have value as a model; it was instructive and educative in the judicial order. A law applies to details; a model inspires—which is entirely different. In conclusion, we have here not a law code, nor the charter of a legal reform, but above all, in its own way, a treatise, with examples, on the exercise of judicial power.[88]

Bottéro compares legal treatises to treatises for divination and medicine. They are similar in form and function. All three contain conditional statements and are intended to assist practitioners through cases that serve as models or paradigms. As Walton says,

> The medical treatises teach medical practitioners about diagnosis, the divinatory treatises teach the practitioners about prognostication through omens, and the legal treatises teach practitioners (whether future kings or

---

[87] John H. Walton, *Ancient Near Eastern Thought and the Old Testament: Introducing the Conceptual World of the Hebrew Bible* (Grand Rapids, MI: Baker, 2006).
[88] J. Bottéro, "The 'Code' of Hammurabi," in *Mesopotamia: Writing, Reasoning and the Gods* (Chicago: University of Chicago Press, 1992), 156–184.

court personnel) about judicial wisdom, all through multiplying examples through patterns.[89]

Again, Bottéro concludes,

The cuneiform treatises are nothing else but types of paradigms or tables. It was by repetition and the variation of particular cases, of models to be considered in a spirit of analogy, that the substance of the discipline in question was assimilated, that the habit of scientific judgment was formed, that the sense of correct reasoning was acquired at the same time as the capacity to extend these same judgments and reasoning to all the material objects of the science in question, according to their eventual presentation.[90]

Thus the ancient legal treatises were not law codes in the sense in which we think of them in the Western world, but they give instruction in model justice through exemplary verdicts.

Hammurabi compiled his list of exemplary verdicts as a legitimization of his reign and rule, showing that his skill in administrative justice was derived from the sun god Shamash. In this sense, there is a similarity between such legal texts and wisdom literature.

It is also important to note that Hammurabi's legal treatise was not considered the "law of the land," and it imposed no obligations on the courts or society. In extensive research and study of court cases from the ancient Near East, never is there any direct reference or appeal to the six major legal treatises that have been frequently listed as "law codes."

The covenant at Sinai (Exodus 19–24) must be not only compared to the culture of the ancient Near East, but contrasted as well. Walton provides a table (table 9.3) that helps to see some of the differences.[91] Since the covenant in Exodus 20–23 entails covenant stipulations embodying the guidelines and Torah (i.e., instruction) of Yahweh for life in the land, the prescriptive statements were certainly intended to be obeyed. Nonetheless, the case laws illustrate the righteousness of God in an Iron-Age cultural setting and are bound by the psychology of that time. This aspect shows that the "law" is not eternal.

---

[89] Walton, *Ancient Near Eastern Thought and the Old Testament*, 289.
[90] Bottéro, "'Code' of Hammurabi," 178.
[91] Adapted with permission from Walton, *Ancient Near Eastern Thought and the Old* Testament, 293.

Table 9.3: Literary Context of the Law in the Pentateuch and Ancient Near East

Exodus 19–24/Deuteronomy	Ancient Near Eastern Treatises
Essentially a self-revelation of deity	Essentially a self-glorification of the king
Covenant charter that synthesizes an entire detailed and organised vision of the "right" exercise of what it means to be a holy nation (Ex. 19:5–6; Deut. 26:19)	Political charter that synthesizes an entire detailed and organised vision of the "right" exercise of justice
Stipulations of the covenant	Treatise on jurisprudence
Portrays the ideal covenant keeper	Portrays the ideal king
The prime purpose of the biblical compilation is sanctification	The prime purpose of the Mesopotamian compilations is justice

Jeffrey Niehaus objects to the treatment of legal material provided by Walton. His lengthy objections can be cited in summary:

> . . . the treatise hypothesis seems to fall short in light of the highly detailed nature of most of the laws contained in the ancient codes. A familiar example is the Code of Hammurapi [hereafter *CH*]. Hammurapi's laws address many different cases with a high degree of specificity and are laws in their own right, not just paradigms in a treatise (although, of course, they often provide models of judgment, just as the Mosaic laws, or for that matter, any secular laws can do, since we understand that no law code can anticipate all the details of every case that will arise). Furthermore, Hammurapi refers to himself as "the king of righteousness, to whom Shamash has given law/justice/truth (Akkadian *kīnātum*)" (*CH* xxvb.95–98)—a claim that hardly seems refuted by the casuistic and lists forms of the codex's contents (cf. Walton, *Ancient Near Eastern Thought*, 288–91). Even if we understand *kīnātum* as "justice/truth" rather than "law," its historical usage indicates a state of being in alignment with divinely given standards of what is right (cf. *The Assyrian Dictionary of the Oriental Institute of the University of Chicago*, 8:383–84), and, again, it is given to the king by Shamash, the Mesopotamian god of laws and covenants. Moreover, this statement and statements by the king that he has given the land its law/judgments (*CH* xxvb.60–74; cf. *CH* xxvb.80–84, "The procedure, the administration, and the law of the land, which I have given") stand in direct contradiction to Walton's statement, "In the ancient Near East we found that neither Shamash (the deity) nor Hammurabi (the king) could be considered a lawgiver" (297).[92]

---

[92] Jeffrey J. Niehaus, *Ancient Near Eastern Themes in Biblical Theology* (Grand Rapids, MI: Kregel, 2008), 56–57.

Unfortunately, Niehaus seems to miss the point made in the hypothesis that the legal materials are treatises. Two main issues are at stake. First, Niehaus confuses covenant and law. He says, "All covenants involve law, that is, stipulations that must be obeyed by one or both parties."[93] This is a major confusion of categories. Covenant stipulations are not the same as laws in a legal code. Laws in a legal code are closer to requirements in a contract, not covenant stipulations. Second, Niehaus attempts to counter Walton by saying that the laws in the "law codes" are real precedents or precedents from real life. This completely misses the point of Walton's strong claim that the precedents in the "legal treatises" are never once appealed to in actual court cases in the many court records from Assyria and Babylonia. They may be real precedents in origin, but their purpose is to illustrate the justice and wisdom of the king, not to provide actual laws to be used in court (however real they may seem). Of course the cases are specific; this is fundamental and natural for a model or paradigm. Moreover Niehaus misrepresents Walton since he says that neither Shamash nor Hammurabi could be considered lawgivers. In an identical statement earlier, on page 295,[94] Walton put "lawgivers" in quotes to show that he does not mean lawgivers in the sense that we use the word in our Western society based on its Graeco-Roman heritage. At the end of our next chapter, on Deuteronomy, the issue of implications of the form of covenants and legal treatises will be carefully examined. Niehaus does not reflect on the fact that Exodus 19–24 and Deuteronomy may look like "law codes" in content, but in fact are not in form, and may look like a covenant in form but, they differ somewhat in content. Finally, Niehaus bolsters his point of view by employing "law" as an equivalent for Akkadian *kīnātum*, but the *Chicago Assyrian Dictionary* to which he appeals gives only "correct measure, justice, truth" and never "law" as an equivalent. Even if in the genre of literature of which we are speaking the king gives justice as divinely given, this does not mean we have a law code as opposed to a treatise of the judicial wisdom of the king. Thus his appeal to the *Chicago Assyrian Dictionary* is weak.

THE CEREMONY OF COVENANT RATIFICATION (EXODUS 24:1–11)

Exodus 24 picks up the narrative after the Ten Words and the Judgements are recounted. Davies notes the close connection between chapters 24 and 19:

---

[93] Ibid., 56.
[94] Walton, *Ancient Near Eastern Thought and the Old Testament*, 295.

in many ways Exod. 24.1–11 relates closely to the narrative of ch. 19, which it resumes after the suspension of movement by the recounting of the laws in chs. 20–23. Sarna has drawn attention to the perhaps deliberate use of דבר seven times in both chapters, and the sevenfold use of ירד ('descend') in ch. 19, matched by a sevenfold use of עלה ('ascend') in ch. 24. This is an extraordinary *inclusio* which would serve to bind the two chapters as anticipation and realization. In particular a close link is sometimes observed between the units 19.3b–8 and 24.3–8, units where the covenant is first proposed, then consummated.[95]

Two episodes dominate Exodus 24. The ceremony of covenant ratification is described in verses 1–11. In verses 12–18 Moses ascends Mount Sinai to receive instructions on how Israel is to worship God.

The ceremony of covenant ratification is significant for our understanding of the Sinai covenant. First, Moses reports the Ten Words and the Judgements to the people who, as in Exodus 19:7–8, agree to the covenant. Then Moses commits the Words and the Judgements to writing, in a document referred to in Exodus 24:7 as "the Book of the Covenant." Early in the morning he builds an altar and erects twelve pillars. Presumably the altar represents Yahweh, for we are clearly told that the twelve stone stelae represent the people, i.e., the twelve tribes of Israel. Moses has assistants from the twelve tribes offer burnt offerings and fellowship/peace offerings. Moses collects the blood from the bulls sacrificed and pours half on the altar. Next he reads the Book of the Covenant and the people vow to obey and practise the covenant stipulations. Then he scatters/tosses the other half of the blood on the people. In reality he may have actually sprinkled the blood on the pillars that represented the people.

Concerning the blood tossed on the people, Bruce Waltke says, "The latter is called the 'blood of the covenant' because it effects the covenant relationship by cleansing the recipients from sin."[96] This interpretation may appear plausible, but in this instance it is not sustained by the evidence from the text. Fellowship offerings can be for an expression of thanksgiving or can be offered as the result of a vow, according to Leviticus 7:12–18. The latter is appropriate, since covenant making entails vows. The offering in Exodus 24 is not specified as a sin or reparation sacrifice, nor is the verb "sprinkled" used, as is normal for offerings for sin. The blood is applied to

---

[95] John A. Davies, *Royal Priesthood*, 116.
[96] Waltke, *Old Testament Theology*, 435.

the altar representing Yahweh as well as to the people, and certainly Yahweh does not need to be cleansed from sin. Instead, the ceremony indicates the meaning. Half of the blood is put on Yahweh and half of the blood is put on the people. In between these two symbolic acts are the reading of the Book of the Covenant and the vow of the people to keep its stipulations. The symbolism is that the one blood joins the two parties.[97] What is most similar to the ceremony of Exodus 24 is a wedding. Two people who are not related by blood are now, by virtue of the covenant of marriage, closer than any other kin relation. It is by virtue of the covenant at Sinai that Yahweh becomes the *gō'ēl*, i.e., the nearest relative, and that Israel becomes not just a nation but a "people" (עַם), i.e., a kinship term specifying relationship to the Lord.

This interpretation is confirmed by the fact that a party representing the people ascends the mountain and eats a meal. Examples of eating a communal meal to conclude a covenant are numerous.[98] This ancient Near Eastern and biblical practice is the basis for banquets at weddings today.

Davies proposes an alternative interpretation to the covenant ratification ceremony. He sees the rituals as a service for the ordination of Israel as a priest to God. At the conclusion, seventy elders who represent Israel have direct access to the divine presence. A chiasm is identified as support:

A Expectation of nearness (19.1–19).
    B Unexpected warning to keep distance for fear of reprisal
        (19.20–25).
        C Revelation of the character expected of the people, their fear
           and plea for mediation (ch. 20).
    B' Expectation of distance (24.1–2).
A' Unexpected nearness without reprisal (24.9–11).[99]

Since access to the divine presence is at the heart of being a priest, the literary structure supports the concept of arriving at this goal in the covenant ratification ceremony.

Davies further supports his view by noting parallels between the covenant ratification ceremony and the description of the service for ordaining the priests in Leviticus 8 as follows:

---

[97] Walther Eichrodt, *Theology of the Old Testament*, trans. J. A. Baker, 2 vols. (Philadelphia: Westminster, 1961), 1:43, 156–157.
[98] Examples of a communal meal as covenant ratification: Genesis 31:44–46, 54; 2 Samuel 3:12–13, 20. The accession of a king involved a covenant (2 Sam. 3:21; 5:3 = 1 Chron. 11:3; Jer. 34:8–18) and communal meal as ratification (1 Sam. 11:15; 1 Kings 1:9, 25; 3:15).
[99] John A. Davies, *Royal Priesthood*, 119.

There is a ritual washing and donning of clothing (Lev. 8.6–9; cf. Exod. 19.10), sacrifices (Lev. 8.14–23; cf. Exod. 24.5), the application of blood to the altar (Lev. 8.15, 19, 24; cf. Exod. 24.6), the application of blood to the 'ordinands' (Lev. 8.23, 24, 30; cf. Exod. 24.8), followed by a meal before Yhwh (Lev. 8.31; cf. Exod. 24.11) and a period of time spent at the entrance to the tabernacle, that is, at the threshold of the replica of the heavenly sanctuary (Lev. 8.33, 35; cf. Exod. 24.10). There is the injunction [Hebrew] ושמרתם את־משמרת יהוה ולא תמותו ('You are to keep Yhwh's charge, that you do not die', Lev. 8.35), and the chapter concludes with the note that 'Aaron and his sons observed (ויעשׂ) all that Yhwh commanded through Moses' (Lev. 8.36; cf. Exod. 24.3, 7).[100]

Davies' proposal that the ceremony in Exodus 24 "ordains" Israel as a royal priest is confirmed in general terms by the movement from denial of access to the divine presence to unbelievable access to the divine presence. The parallels noted with Leviticus 8, however, are not persuasive. What is significant is that the sacrifices in Leviticus 8 differ notably from those in Exodus 24. The ceremony in Leviticus 8 entails three sacrifices: (1) a bull for a sin offering (חטאת), (2) a ram for a burnt offering (עלה), and (3) a second ram of ordination (מלאים). The sacrifices in Exodus 24 are only two: (1) burnt offerings (עלה) and (2) peace or fellowship offerings (זבח שלמים), both of bulls (number of sacrifices unspecified). The two kinds of sacrifices in Exodus 24, "taken together," says Davies, "have the characteristics of a rite for the removal of sin, that is, the movement from a state of unholiness to a state of holiness, the characteristic of God. They speak of reconciliation (atonement, Lev. 1:4), or the establishment of a communion with the deity, perhaps even a royal dignity, which would not otherwise be possible."[101]

Davies' explanation confuses the issue. The best brief and simple explanation of the meaning of Israel's sacrifices as described in Leviticus 1–7 can be found in the book *A House for My Name*, by Peter J. Leithart.[102] Naturally, *all* of the sacrifices have to do with humans who are defiled and sinful approaching God and being accepted by him. The burnt offering, however, communicates the idea of consecration and devotion, and the fellowship or peace offerings focus on communion with God. The purification or sin offering is notably absent at the covenant ratification ceremony in Exodus 24.

---

[100] Ibid., 122–123.
[101] Ibid., 120.
[102] Peter J. Leithart, *A House for My Name: A Survey of the Old Testament* (Moscow, ID: Canon, 2000), 87–97.

Holiness has to do with being consecrated or devoted, but the focus here is not specifically on atonement or removal of sin.

Davies explores different options in an attempt to understand the significance of the meal in Exodus 24:

> Little is to be gained by insisting that the meal of Exod. 24.11 in and of itself be taken as constituting the definitive act of formal ratification of a covenant. In its literary setting, however, we cannot escape the observation that the meal follows close behind the references to 'covenant' (vv. 7, 8) and more generally brings to a certain climax the whole section (from ch. 19) which has had this relationship with Yhwh as its undergirding theme. While the word ברית may be lacking in the text right at this point, this fact of course is not determinative, as it is entirely lacking from 2 Samuel 7 as well, yet it is clear from such passages as Psalms 89 and 132 that the ברית or covenant of grant to David forms the substance of this chapter. Nicholson acknowledges that at a redactional level at least, the meal does function as closure to a covenant pericope. Some of the difficulty has been with some ill-founded assumptions about the nature of a covenant, and we must be wary of assuming that we have here something closely analogous to a suzerainty treaty (which is popularly regarded as the only viable covenant paradigm for the Sinai covenant). We must allow the text to speak for itself as to the nature of the 'covenant' with which this meal is associated, at least in the final form of the text.
>
> In line with the understanding presented here of the entire Sinai event as a recognition and affirmation of Israel's royal-priestly character, and hence favoured access to the presence of God, the meal may be regarded as a further demonstration of the substance of the declaration already made regarding Israel. That is, whatever else the meal may suggest, it is above all a clear indication of the unconstrained access enjoyed by Israel to the domain of God as his royal attendants, or priests.[103]

Certainly Davies is on firm ground to assert that the meal represents favoured access to God. But he misses much by not paying attention to the offerings and the one blood sprinkled on the two parties. Note Leithart's comments on Israel's offerings:

> At the tabernacle, Israel worships God mainly through bringing animals, killing them, and burning them on the altar. This kind of worship is often called "sacrifice," but this word is not exactly right. In the Bible, a

---

[103] John A. Davies, *Royal Priesthood*, 134.

"sacrifice" is an offering that is followed by a meal. When there is no meal, the offering should not be called a "sacrifice."

To understand Israel's worship, we need to understand two words that are used for all the animal offerings. The first word is the Hebrew word *qorbān* (see Leviticus 1:2, 2:1; 3:1–2; 4:23; 5:11; 7:38). This word means a "gift" or "something brought near." For Israel, a gift is a very important thing. It is not just a "present," like we might give on a birthday. When two people exchange gifts, they are forming a friendship or continuing a friendship. Exchanging gifts is one way of making a "covenant" with someone, like a man and a woman who exchange rings at a wedding. At Sinai, God makes a covenant with Israel, so that Israel becomes His "bride." Yahweh as the Husband of Israel promises many gifts, and to continue in the "marriage" covenant, Israel is supposed to bring gifts.[104]

Note that the ordination in Leviticus 8 has no sacrifices, i.e., no meal is involved in the ceremony. Leithart is on target to describe the covenant making at Sinai in terms of a marriage or wedding. Certainly later prophets like Ezekiel and Hosea see it this way. And as Leithart goes on to point out, we eat to enjoy time with family and friends as well as to celebrate important events like birthdays, holidays, and weddings.[105] The seventy elders, representing Israel, eat a meal with God because they are *family* and are *celebrating* a friendship, i.e., *marriage* with God. Davies' interpretation, while not incorrect, is too narrow and restrictive, not considering the larger context of culture and the metanarrative of Scripture. The *one* blood is placed upon the *two* parties to portray that their relationship is now as close as a blood or kin relationship. As the message of Hosea so loudly proclaims, it is the covenant at Sinai that makes Israel a people, i.e., a kinship term showing that they are kin to Yahweh. Adultery, a violation of the marriage covenant, makes them "not my *people*" (Hos. 1:9).

THE COVENANT AT SINAI WITHIN THE LARGER STORY: THE SIGNIFICANCE OF THE FORM

Observing the form of the covenant as given in Exodus and Deuteronomy is important for a proper understanding of the Mosaic covenant and foundational for correlating the old covenant with the new. The form and literary structure in both Exodus and Deuteronomy shows the following points:

---

[104] Leithart, *House for My Name*, 87.
[105] Ibid., 88.

(1) The Ten Commandments are foundational to the ordinances and, conversely, the ordinances or case laws apply and extend the Ten Commandments in a practical way to all areas of life. Nonetheless, one cannot take the Ten Commandments as "eternal" and the ordinances as "temporal," for both sections together constitute the agreement or covenant made between God and Israel.

(2) It is common to categorise and classify the laws as (a) moral, (b) civil, and (c) ceremonial, but this classification is foreign to the material and imposed upon it from the outside rather than arising from the material and being clearly marked by the literary structure of the text. In fact, the ceremonial, civil, and moral laws are all mixed together, not only in the Judgements or ordinances but in the Ten Words as well (the Sabbath may be properly classified as ceremonial). Those who claim the distinction between ceremonial, civil, and moral law do so because they want to affirm that the ceremonial (and in some cases, civil) laws no longer apply but the moral laws are eternal. Unfortunately John Frame in his new and magisterial work on *The Doctrine of the Christian Life* and Bruce Waltke in his equally magisterial *An Old Testament Theology* perpetuate this tradition.[106] This is an inaccurate representation of Scripture at this point. Exodus 24 clearly indicates that the Book of the Covenant consists of the Ten Words and the Judgements, and this is the covenant (both Ten Words and Judgements) that Jesus declares he has completely fulfilled[107] and Hebrews declares is now made obsolete by the new covenant.[108] What we can say to represent accurately the teaching of Scripture is that the righteousness of God codified, enshrined, and encapsulated in the old covenant has not changed, and that this same righteousness is now codified and enshrined in the new.[109]

(3) When one compares Exodus and Deuteronomy with contemporary documents from the ancient Near East in both content and form, two features are without parallel:

---

[106] John M. Frame, *The Doctrine of the Christian Life* (Phillipsburg, NJ: P&R, 2008), 213–217. Frame says, "the distinction [moral, ceremonial and civil law in the Westminster Confession] is a good one, in a rough-and-ready way" (213). Later he admits that "the laws of the Pentateuch are not clearly labelled as moral, civil, or ceremonial" (214). In the end, he struggles to provide clear criteria to show what is and what is not applicable for Christians today from the old covenant. See also Waltke, *Old Testament Theology*, 434, 436.

[107] Matthew 5:17.

[108] Hebrews 8:13.

[109] Waltke does say that the Ten Words are an expression of the character and heart of God, but his approach does not provide a biblical criterion for determining how the old covenant applies to us today (see Waltke, *Old Testament Theology*, 413). *As a code*, including the Ten Words, it does not apply. The righteousness enshrined in this code, however, is the same that is now enshrined for us in the new covenant.

a) in content, the biblical documents are identical to ancient Near Eastern law codes, but do not have the form of a law code;

b) in form, the biblical documents are identical to ancient Near Eastern covenants or international treaties, but not in content.

This is extremely instructive. God desires to rule in the midst of his people as king. He wants to direct, guide, and instruct their lives and lifestyle. Yet he wants to do this in the context of a relationship of love, loyalty, and trust. This is completely different from Greek and Roman law codes or ancient Near Eastern law codes. They represent an impersonal code of conduct binding on all citizens and enforced by penalties from a controlling authority. We should always remember that Torah, by contrast, means personal "instruction" from God as Father and King of his people rather than just "law"; thus a term like "covenantal instruction" might be more useful.[110]

Our view of the old covenant is enhanced by accurate exegesis which not only properly attends to the cultural context and language of the text but also allows the text to inform us of its own literary structure and considers the place of the text in the larger story. The biblical-theological framework is especially important because there we come to see the Ten Commandments not merely as fundamental requirements determining divine-human and human-human relationships as moral principles, but as the foundation of true social justice and the basis of what it means to be a son or daughter of God, an Adamic figure, i.e., truly and genuinely human.

---

[110] This extremely important point is forcefully made by Waltke in an extended footnote in *An Old Testament Theology* (Grand Rapids, MI: Zondervan, 2007), 405. Nonetheless, it is not properly integrated into his discussion of the relationship between the old and new covenants.

Chapter Ten

THE ISRAELITE (MOSAIC) COVENANT: DEUTERONOMY

INTRODUCTION: THE HEART OF THE MATTER AND THE MATTER OF THE HEART

The book of Deuteronomy brings us to the heart of the matter and also to the matter of the heart in relation to the Israelite (or Mosaic) covenant. In particular, Deuteronomy 6:4ff. is arguably the key text of the Old Testament. This is not stated for rhetorical effect or to register my opinion as a scholar. Our Lord Jesus himself said so in his earthly instruction and teaching (Matt. 22:34–40). We must learn from Jesus and his apostles how to interpret the Old Testament as they did and discover how/why they came to this conclusion.

In John Bunyan's classic *Pilgrim's Progress*, "Christian" is living in the City of Destruction until he is instructed by "Evangelist" to flee the coming wrath and pursue the road to the Celestial City. Away over the bogs and fields he is pointed to a little wicket gate. When he passes through this gate he will begin his journey to the Celestial City. We can say that Deuteronomy 6:4–9 is the Wicket Gate to the Spiritual High Road (i.e., metanarrative) of the Old Testament.

1. THE DATE OF DEUTERONOMY

The consensus among scholars of the Old Testament is that the book of Deuteronomy was given its final form in the fifth century B.C.[1] This is unfortunate. The literary form/structure of the text may be analysed according to different perspectives (i.e., homilies/sermons vs. treaty) which are *not* mutually exclusive. According to markers in the text, the book can be divided into three homilies or speeches given by Moses: (1) 1:1–4:43; (2) 4:44–26:19; (3) 27:1–30:20. Alternatively, and not necessarily as a competing structure,

---

[1] See M. Weinfeld, *Deuteronomy 1–11: A New Translation with Introduction and Commentary*, Anchor Bible 5 (New York: Doubleday, 1991), 12–13; and idem, "Book of Deuteronomy," in *The Anchor Bible Dictionary*, ed. David N. Freedman (New York: Doubleday, 1992) 2:168–183; Duane L. Christensen, *Deuteronomy 1:1–21:9*, rev. ed., WBC 6A (Nashville: Thomas Nelson, 2001), lxviii; and Gordon J. Wenham, *Exploring the Old Testament: A Guide to the Pentateuch* (Downers Grove, IL: InterVarsity Press, 2003), 1:187–195.

the book may be analysed as having the form of a suzerain-vassal treaty of the type common among the Hittites in the fourteenth century B.C. An example of scholars interpreting the literary structure this way is the work of K. A. Kitchen (table 10.1a).[2]

Table 10.1a: Deuteronomy as a Suzerain-Vassal Treaty (Kitchen)

1. Title	1:1–5
2. Historical Prologue	1:6–3:29
3. Stipulations 　　a. Basic 　　b. Detailed	 4–11 12–26
4a. Deposit of Text	31:9, 24–26
4b. Public Reading	31:10–13
5. Witnesses	31:16–30, esp. 26; 32:1–47
6. Blessings and Curses 　　a. Blessings 　　b. Curses	 28:1–14 28:15–68

My own analysis of the text, however, led me to recognise chapter 27 as corresponding to the Deposition of Text and Public Reading and to conclude that the Appeal to Witnesses section was absent. From a formal point of view, then, the pattern of the treaty structure would end at Deuteronomy 28:68. This analysis can be displayed in table 10.1b.

Table 10.1b: Deuteronomy as Suzerain-Vassal Treaty (Gentry)

1. Title	1:1–5
2. Historical Prologue	1:6–4:43
3. Stipulations 　　a. Basic 　　b. Detailed	 4:44–11:32 12–26
4a. Deposition	27:1–8
4b. Public Reading	27:9–26
(Witnesses	30:19)
Blessings and Curses 　　a. Blessings 　　b. Curses	 28:1–14 28:15–68

---

[2] See K. A. Kitchen, *Ancient Orient and Old Testament* (Downers Grove, IL: InterVarsity Press, 1966), 96–98; idem, *The Bible in Its World: The Bible and Archaeology Today* (Downers Grove, IL: InterVarsity Press, 1977), 82; and idem, *On the Reliability of the Old Testament* (Grand Rapids, MI: Eerdmans, 2003), 283–289. Although Kitchen actually dates the exodus to the thirteenth century B.C., he nonetheless argues that the form does not allow a composition date later in time. Table used with permission.

As a fundamental point, it must be noted that since no gods exist besides Yahweh, no appeal can be made to them, and this section by definition could not be part of a covenant or treaty between Yahweh and Israel. This explanation may provide a reason for the absence of the Witnesses section in Deuteronomy.

The most recent in-depth study of the literary structure in the light of the ancient Near Eastern treaties is that of Steven Guest, whose analysis is quite similar to my own (table 10.1c).[3]

Table 10.1c: Deuteronomy as Suzerain-Vassal Treaty (Guest)

1. Preamble	1:1–5
2. Historical Prologue	1:6–4:44

3. Stipulations
    a. General
    b. Specific
	
	4:45–11:32
	12:1–26:19

4. Document Clause	27:1–10
5. Appeal to Witness	27:11–26
6. Blessings and Curses	28:1–69 (EV 29:1)
7. Solemn Oath Ceremony	29:1 (EV 29:2)–30:20

Guest argues that 27:11–26 constitutes the Appeal to Witness section and that the appeal is to Yahweh himself, since there is no other possibility:

> Instruction is given as to the division of the tribes for this ceremony. Half are to stand on Mount Gerizim to bless the people and half are to stand on Mount Ebal to pronounce the curses. And although the recitation of the blessings by the Levites is not recorded in Deuteronomy 27, there is no reason (except from silence) to argue that these blessings were not pronounced. The repeated call can be understood as a plea from the community to Yahweh for the separation from its midst those who are acting in violation of the stipulations of the covenant. In other words, the community is entreating Yahweh to act as the enforcer of the covenant.[4]

With either my own analysis or that of Guest, the literary structure of the book of Deuteronomy is demonstrated to be virtually identical to that

---

[3] Steven W. Guest, "Deuteronomy 26:16–19 as the Central Focus of the Covenantal Framework of Deuteronomy" (PhD diss., The Southern Baptist Theological Seminary, 2009), 55. Used by permission.
[4] Ibid., 62–63.

of a suzerain-vassal treaty common among the Hittites in the fourteenth century B.C.

The analysis of chapter 27 provided by either myself or Guest is not entirely satisfactory, although the questions one might raise do not affect the main point concerning the date of Deuteronomy. The following issues were raised in communication with D. I. Block:

> But if this [i.e., Deuteronomy 27] is the equivalent of the document clause in the Hittite treaties, the transcription of the Torah on the stones certainly performs a different function. We have no hint that after this one-off event (Joshua 8) the Israelites were ever supposed to return there for covenant renewal or recommitment ceremonies. . . . I actually think Moses depends on the document produced at Sinai (cf. 10:1–6). Indeed what he does with the Decalogue here is what Hittite vassals were supposed to do with their documents—remind themselves of their obligations to the suzerain. Since the original document governs this covenant renewal event there is no specific need for a document clause—unless of course this role is played by 31:9–13. In the end, while the book has the broad structures and features of ANE treaties, homiletical and rhetorical concerns trump the legal style.[5]

If, then, chapter 27 is the document clause, further research on the function of the document clause is required.

Extensive analysis of the form of treaties has been made by K. A. Kitchen. What is interesting is that the literary form of the ancient Near Eastern treaties changes over time. This can be demonstrated quickly through tables. First, table 10.2 provides a comprehensive list of covenants/treaties and legal treatises over three millennia in the ancient Near East.[6]

Table 10.2: Ancient Near East Covenants/Treaties and Legal Treatises

Phase	Date	List of Documents
I. *Archaic:* Treaties	ca. 2500–2300	A. East: Eannatum/Umma; Naram-Sin/Elam B. West: Ebla and Abarsal
II. *Early:* Laws	ca. 2100–1700	Late 3rd: Ur-Nammu Early 2nd: Lipit-Ishtar; Hammurabi

---

[5] Personal communication from Daniel I. Block, January 21, 2011.

[6] Adapted with permission from Kitchen, *On the Reliability of the Old Testament,* 285.

III. *Early:* Treaties	ca. 1800–1700	Several Mari and Tell Leilan treaties 2 Old Babylonian treaties
IV. *Intermediate:* Treaties	ca. 1600–1400	2 North Syrian (Alalakh) 4 Hittite (Anatolia; Cilicia)
V. *Middle:* Treaties	ca. 1400–1200	31+ Hittite treaties, Anatolia, Egypt, Syria
VI. *Late:* Treaties	ca. 900–650	A. East: 10 Mesopotamian treaties B. West: 3 Sefiré Aramaic treaties

The literary structure of the early legal treatises can be displayed as shown in table 10.3.[7]

Table 10.3: Literary Structure of the Early Legal Treatises

Ur-Nammu	Lipit-Ishtar	Hammurabi
[1. Preamble (lost)]	1. Preamble	1. Preamble

2. Prologue:
    Theological
    Historical
    Ethical
	2. Prologue:
	    Theological
		2. Prologue:
		    Theological

3. Laws	3. Laws	3. Laws
(lost)	9. Epilogue	9. Epilogue
(lost)	6b. Blessings	6b. Blessings
(lost)	6c. Curses	6c. Curses

Finally, tables 10.4a and 10.4b present the form and literary structure of the treaties of Phases III through VI:[8]

Table 10.4a: Phases III and IV

Phase III		Phase IV	
Mari/Leilan		North Syria	Hittites
5. Witness	7. Oaths	1. Title	1. Title
			5. Witnesses
3. Stipulations		3. Stipulations	3. Stipulations
6c. Curses		6c. Curses	7. Oath 6c. Curses

---

[7] Adapted with permission from ibid., 287.
[8] Adapted with permission from ibid., 287–288.

Table 10.4b: Phases V and VI

Phase V	Israelite Covenant	Phase VI: West	Phase VI: East
Hittite Treaties	Exodus 20 Deuteronomy	Sefiré	Assyria
1. Title	1. Title	1. Title	1. Title
2. Hist. Prologue	2. Hist. Prologue	5. Witnesses	5. Witnesses
3. Stipulations	3. Stipulations	6c. Curses	3. Stipulations
4. Dep./Reading	4. Dep./Reading	3. Stipulations	6c. Curses
5. Witnesses	5. Witnesses		
6c. Curses	6b. Blessings		
6b. Blessings	6c. Curses		

Two major observations are obvious by considering the hard data. First, the form and literary structure of the treaties changes over the centuries, and the form of Deuteronomy best matches only those of the late fourteenth century B.C. It does not match the forms of the earlier or later treaties.

Second, while the form of Deuteronomy clearly follows that of the Hittite suzerain-vassal treaties of the late fourteenth century, in actuality it represents an amalgam or confluence of the legal treatises and political treaties of its time, since the order of the blessings and curses matches that of the legal treatises, although the fact that there are few blessings and many curses corresponds to the suzerain-vassal treaties. K. A. Kitchen expresses it this way:

> Sinai is neither just law nor properly a treaty. It represents a *confluence* of these two, producing a further facet in group relationships, namely, social-political-religious covenant. Law, treaty, and covenant in this context are three parts of a triptych. Law regulates relations between members of a group within the group. Treaty regulates relations between members of two groups politically distinct (or, with vassals, originally so). Covenant in our context regulates relations between a group and its ruling deity. It is thus "religious" in serving its deity through worship; social in that the mandatory content of the covenant is rules for practical living (law); and political in that the deity has the role of exclusive sovereign over the group. The confluence shows up in three details in particular. First the *overall* framework format and main range of contents is drawn from the treaty format of the fourteenth/thirteenth centuries; second the law content of the stipulations derives from law, not treaty, and the Sinai covenant's use of short blessings plus longer curses (not the roughly equal curses and blessings of the Hittites) goes back to the older law collections' usage; third, use

of the interim epilogues before these final sanctions likewise goes back to the older law collections, not treaty.[9]

More will be said about this later, but the evidence from the ancient Near East strongly supports the book of Deuteronomy as coming from the time which the internal evidence of the text indicates: the era of Moses.

2. DEUTERONOMY—THE CENTRE OF THE OLD TESTAMENT

The book of Deuteronomy is the centre of the entire Old Testament, in terms of both metanarrative and theology.

First, Deuteronomy brings to a climax and conclusion the Pentateuch or first five books of the Bible. According to the book of Genesis, God called Abraham to give him a land from which would emanate his blessing and salvation to the ends of the earth. In Deuteronomy, Abraham's family are now poised at the entrance to that land and they are given instructions on how to live in the land, so that they might be a blessing and bring salvation to the ends of the earth.

The book of Exodus narrates how God redeemed Israel out of Egypt so that they might come to a mountain and worship him and begin to live their lives in conformity with his word as a holy nation and royal priesthood. Further instructions for their worship of God and detailed guidelines on what devotion to the covenant Lord entails are given in the book of Leviticus. The book of Deuteronomy supplements the covenant thus given in Exodus and Leviticus; it completes it (Deut. 28:69 [29:1 EV]). Moreover, the wanderings through the wilderness that are the subject of the book of Numbers bring them to this very point. Thus, Deuteronomy is the climax of the Pentateuch.

The historical books Joshua, Judges, Samuel, and Kings (known in the Hebrew Canon as the Former Prophets) present a history of Israel based on and evaluated from the point of view of the Israelite covenant, particularly as given in Deuteronomy. For example, Israel and Judah are evaluated on the basis of the command for the centralisation of worship in Deuteronomy 12— Israel for the centres established by Jeroboam, and Judah for her high places. The history of the monarchy is evaluated according to chapter 17 of Deuteronomy. The efficacy of the prophetic word is evaluated on the basis

---

[9] Kitchen, *On the Reliability of the Old Testament*, 289 (emphasis his).

of Deuteronomy 18 (e.g., 2 Kings 24:2). It is commonplace among scholars today to refer to Joshua through Kings as "the Deuteronomistic History" since the perspective of the book of Deuteronomy provides the "historio-graphic method/philosophy" of the authors. Where scholars are entirely askew, however, is in dating the book of Deuteronomy to the sixth or fifth century B.C. Deuteronomy was written first, and *afterwards*, the history of Israel was written from the perspective of this central document in the canon of the Old Testament.

The Israelite covenant, especially the expression or form of the cov-enant as it is constituted in Deuteronomy, is also the basis and foundation for the Latter Prophets Isaiah, Jeremiah, Ezekiel, and the Twelve Prophets. The central concern of the prophets was to call the people back to the cov-enant. The people constantly violated the covenant by following idols and failing to fulfill the covenant stipulations. As demonstrated so ably by Claus Westermann in his book *Basic Forms of Prophetic Speech*, both their prom-ises and their threats, as well as even their sentences, are all based upon the book of Deuteronomy.[10] Just one example is the expression "the stubborn-ness of their (evil) heart"—an absolute favourite of the prophet Jeremiah. He uses it eight times (Jer. 3:17; 7:24; 9:14; 11:8; 13:10; 16:12; 18:12; 23:17). This expression is derived from Deuteronomy 29:18, and it occurs elsewhere in the Old Testament only in Ps. 81:13 (81:12 EV).[11]

When Psalms speaks of the Torah of Yahweh—"on his law he medi-tates day and night" (Ps. 1:2)—the psalmist is referring to the book of Deuteronomy. It is also what is celebrated in the longest Psalm—Psalm 119.

Professor Bruce Waltke has shown that the book most closely con-nected to the theology of the book of Proverbs is the book of Deuteronomy.[12] Proverbs contains the instruction the king and queen together gave their son to raise him in the ways of the Lord. The Torah or instruction of the cov-enant (Deuteronomy) is presented as a beautiful woman to attract the son to follow this way. Failure to follow this way is not so much sin against the Lord as just plain folly and stupidity, bringing loss in every way in one's life. Similarly, Song of Songs presents the skillful way in marriage. And as far as Job is concerned, without the covenant and the related notion of the

---

[10] Claus Westermann, *Basic Forms of Prophetic Speech*, trans. Hugh Clayton White (Louisville: Westminster/John Knox, 1991).

[11] For a list of deuteronomic phrases in Jeremiah, see Louis Stulman, *The Prose Sermons of the Book of Jer-emiah: A Redescription of the Correspondences with the Deuteronomistic Literature in the Light of Recent Textual Research*, SBL Dissertation Series 83 (Atlanta: Scholars Press, 1986), 31–44.

[12] Bruce K. Waltke, "The Book of Proverbs and Old Testament Theology," *Bibliotheca Sacra* 136 (1979): 302–317.

goel (kinsman redeemer), its instruction on suffering would be emasculated. Precisely because Israel is married to Yahweh by virtue of the covenant making at Sinai and she becomes "his people," he is now their nearest relative who will step in to lift them out of debt and suffering.

The centrality of Deuteronomy to the rest of the Old Testament may perhaps be diagrammed as follows:

Deuteronomy and Genesis (land promised, land entered)
Deuteronomy and Exodus—Leviticus (addition to covenant)
Deuteronomy and Numbers (completes wanderings)
Deuteronomy basis of Joshua—Kings (Deuteronomistic history)
Deuteronomy basis of Prophets
Deuteronomy basis of Wisdom texts

3. DEUTERONOMY 6:4–5—THE CENTRE OF THE BOOK OF DEUTERONOMY

When the book of Deuteronomy is considered from the perspective of the form of the suzerain-vassal treaty, the command in 6:5 ("you shall love the LORD your God with all your heart and with all your soul, and with all your strength") is placed *immediately after* the Preamble and Historical Prologue in the section providing the General Stipulation of the covenant. Within this section, it is, in fact, the *first* command given after material *repeated* from Exodus 19–24 and it is also the *greatest* command among all the covenant stipulations: to be completely devoted and loyal to Yahweh. This command is the foundation to all the requirements and stipulations of the covenant.[13] In the section Deuteronomy 4:45–11:32, Moses is concerned to expound *this one requirement* as fully as possible.

Viktor Korošec, who pioneered analysis of the suzerain-vassal treaties,[14] makes the following statement concerning this section of the treaty:

What the description amounts to is this: that the vassal is obligated to perpetual gratitude toward the great king because of the benevolence,

---

[13] Some scholars have argued that the section containing the Specific Stipulations (chapters 12–26) is arranged according to the Ten Words/Commandments. See Stephen A. Kaufman, "The Structure of the Deuteronomic Law," *Maarav* 1/2 (1978–1979): 105–158; John H. Walton, "Deuteronomy: An Exposition of the Spirit of the Law," *Grace Theological Journal* 8/2 (1987): 213–225; and more recently John D. Currid, *Deuteronomy* (Darlington, UK: Evangelical Press, 2006). Daniel I. Block, however, does not find this persuasive. See Block, *Deuteronomy*, NIV Application Commentary (Grand Rapids, MI: Zondervan, 2012), 301–302. Cf. also Jeffrey H. Tigay, *Deuteronomy = [Devarim]: The Traditional Hebrew Text with the New JPS Translation* (Philadelphia: Jewish Publication Society, 1996), ad loc.

[14] Viktor Korošec, *Hethitische Staatsverträge: Ein Beitrag zu ihrer juristischen Wertung* (Leipzig, Germany: T. Weicher, 1931).

consideration, and favor which he has already received. Immediately following this, the devotion of the vassal to the great king is expressed as a logical consequence.[15]

Placing Deuteronomy 6:5 within the context of the literary structure demonstrates, as one might expect, that Jesus was right: this is both the first and the greatest command in the covenant: wholehearted devotion to the great king.[16] From what has been said so far, it is therefore the key text of the Old Testament.

4. WHAT IT MEANS TO LOVE GOD

The central command to love God is modified by three prepositional phrases: (1) with all your heart, (2), with all your soul, and (3) with all your strength. Each will be considered in turn.

In Hebrew, the word "heart" refers to the core of who you are, the centre of each person. It refers, in particular, to the place where we feel, where we think, and where we make decisions and plans, i.e., emotions, mind, and will. This can be easily seen from the following illustrative passages:

A. FEELINGS:

A glad heart makes a cheerful face,
　　but by sorrow of heart the spirit is crushed. (Prov. 15:13, ESV)

A joyful heart is good medicine,
　　but a crushed spirit dries up the bones. (Prov. 17:22, ESV)

When these proverbs refer to a "glad heart" or a "joyful heart" they are clearly referring to one's emotions and feelings in terms of a healthy psyche.

B. REASONING:

But to this day the LORD has not given you a heart to understand or eyes to see or ears to hear. (Deut. 29:4, ESV)

---

[15] George E. Mendenhall, "Covenant Forms in Israelite Tradition," in *The Biblical Archaeologist Reader*, ed. Edward F. Campbell and David N. Freedman, 3 vols. (New York: Doubleday, 1970), 3:33.

[16] *Pace* R. Frankena ("The Vassal-Treaties of Esarhaddon," *Oudtestamentische Studiën* 25 (1965): 122–154), who sees the notion of wholehearted devotion as influence from the later neo-Assyrian treaties, this idea of loyalty is clearly stated, sometimes in exactly these words (wholehearted) in the earlier second millennium B.C. treaties. See, e.g., Gary Beckman, *Hittite Diplomatic Texts*, 2nd ed. (Atlanta: Scholars Press, 1995, 1999), 27–28, 55–56, 105. For a view similar to that of Frankena, see M. Weinfeld, *Deuteronomy 1–11*, Anchor Bible 5 (New York: Doubleday, 1991), 7. I am indebted to John D. Meade for these references.

> Make the heart of this people dull,
>> and their ears heavy,
>> and blind their eyes;
> lest they see with their eyes,
>> and hear with their ears,
>> and understand with their hearts,
> and turn and be healed. (Isa. 6:10, ESV)

In both Deuteronomy 29:4 and Isaiah 6:10, one *understands* with the heart; surely then what is being referred to is what we normally call the mind. This is the place where we reason and think and understand.

C. WILL:

> The heart of man plans his way,
>> but the LORD establishes his steps. (Prov. 16:9, ESV)

> May he grant you your heart's desire
>> and fulfill all your plans! (Ps. 20:4, ESV)

Proverbs 16:9 and Psalm 20:4 show that the "heart" makes plans and has desires; it is the place where we make decisions. Concerning the Hebrew word "heart," H. W. Wolff says:

> In by far the greatest number of cases it is intellectual, rational functions that are ascribed to the heart—i.e. precisely what we ascribe to the head and, more exactly, to the brain; cf. I Sam. 25.37. . . . We must guard against the false impression that biblical man is determined more by feeling than by reason.[17]

According to Wolff, the Hebrew word "heart" refers to the mind in approximately 400 out of 814 passages speaking of the human heart. This supports his warning that "we must guard against the false impression that biblical man is determined more by feeling than by reason."

We should note, then, that the biblical language differs markedly from our own in the Western world. For us, the heart is associated with emotions, feelings, love, and Valentine's Day. Conversely, for the Bible, the heart is where we reason and think and make decisions and plans. We can frequently speak of people who cannot bridge the eighteen-inch gap between the head

---

[17] Hans W. Wolff, *Anthropology of the Old Testament*, trans. Margaret Kohl (Philadelphia: Fortress, 1974), 46–47.

and the heart.[18] The ancient Hebrews knew no such gap. The heart is the centre of one's being and the place where emotions, mind, and will operate in harmony and union.

Notice how the text of Deuteronomy 6:5 is quoted in the Gospels:

[34] Hearing that Jesus had silenced the Sadducees, the Pharisees got together. [35] One of them, an expert in the law, tested him with this question: [36] "Teacher, which is the greatest commandment in the Law?" [37] Jesus replied: "'Love the Lord your God with all your heart and with all your soul and with all your mind.' [38] This is the first and greatest commandment. [39] And the second is like it: 'Love your neighbor as yourself.' [40] All the Law and the Prophets hang on these two commandments." (Matt. 22:34–40, NIV)

[28] One of the teachers of the law came and heard them debating. Noticing that Jesus had given them a good answer, he asked him, "Of all the commandments, which is the most important?"

[29] "The most important one," answered Jesus, "is this: 'Hear, O Israel, the Lord our God, the Lord is one. [30] Love the Lord your God with all your heart and with all your soul and with all your mind and with all your strength.' [31] The second is this: 'Love your neighbor as yourself.' There is no commandment greater than these."

[32] "Well said, teacher," the man replied. "You are right in saying that God is one and there is no other but him. [33] To love him with all your heart, with all your understanding and with all your strength, and to love your neighbor as yourself is more important than all burnt offerings and sacrifices." [34] When Jesus saw that he had answered wisely, he said to him, "You are not far from the kingdom of God." And from then on no one dared ask him any more questions. (Mark 12:28–34, NIV)

He answered: "'Love the Lord your God with all your heart and with all your soul and with all your strength and with all your mind'; and, 'Love your neighbor as yourself.'" (Luke 10:27, NIV)

In the Gospel of Matthew, the command is cited as loving God with all your heart (καρδία), soul (ψυχή), and mind (διανοία). In the Gospel of Mark the command is cited as loving God with all your heart (καρδία), soul (ψυχή), mind (διανοία), and strength (ἰσχύς), which the response of the scribe shortens to with all your heart (καρδία), understanding (σύνεσις), and strength (ἰσχύς). And in the Gospel of Luke the command is cited as

---

18 Note Anne Murray's old album, "Heart over Mind."

loving God with all your heart (καρδία), soul (ψυχή), strength (ἰσχύς), and mind (διανοία). In Matthew "strength" is omitted while "mind" is added; in Mark and in Luke "mind" is added and nothing is omitted—four things are mentioned. In the shortened version of the scribe, "soul" is omitted and "understanding" is added. Central to all citations in the Gospels is the addition of mind or understanding. The reason for this is that the Greek word καρδία (heart) does not sufficiently convey to the audience of the first century the fact that reasoning and thinking are included in the functions of the heart in Hebrew.

We should not think that merely intellectual pursuits are equivalent to loving God. According to the context, loving God has to do with fearing him, obeying his commands, and passing on his instructions to another generation.

Second in the command in Deuteronomy 6:5 is to love the Lord "with all your soul." "Soul" renders the Hebrew word *nepesh* (נֶפֶשׁ). One of the best discussions of this term is by H. W. Wolff.[19] The original meaning is "throat" and hence by extension it can refer to our "desire" or "longing." The soul thus designates the organ of "desire" or of "vital needs" which have to be satisfied if man is to go on living. In this way the term comes to mean soul or life. Our entire life in terms of our desires and needs is to be devoted to the Lord.

Third, we are to love the Lord with all our "strength." This renders the Hebrew word מְאֹד, normally an adverb meaning "exceedingly" or "greatly." The lexicons give the meaning "power" or "strength" for מְאֹד as a noun only for Deuteronomy 6:5 and 2 Kings 23:25 in the approximately 300 instances in the Hebrew Bible.[20] Possibly the word ought to be construed as functioning as an adverb here as well. The meaning would be, "you shall love the Lord your God with all your heart and with all your soul—and that to the fullest extent."

5. THE COVENANT FORMULA IN DEUTERONOMY

In our analysis of Genesis 17, we noted the first instance of the Covenant Formula ("I will be their God" 17:8; cf. v. 7). Rendtorff, in a major study, identified three variants of this formula. He designates them "Formula A," "I will be God for you, להיות לך לאלהים" (occurring 16 times); "Formula B," "You

---

19 Wolff, *Anthropology of the Old Testament*, 11–25.
20 Second Kings 23:25 is a direct allusion to Deuteronomy 6:5. Thus the evidence for מְאֹד as a noun is based only on interpretation of Deuteronomy 6:5.

shall be a people for him לעם לו להיות" (occurring 10 times); and "Formula C," which is a combination of the two formulae (occurring 12 times).[21]

Recently, Steven Guest completed a doctoral dissertation devoted to the study of the Covenant Formula in Deuteronomy.[22] The main points of his research are summarised as follows. He notes that the Covenant Formula is found precisely seven times in the book of Deuteronomy as a whole (Deut. 26:17–18 is counted as one instance):[23]

1. Deuteronomy 4:20

וְאֶתְכֶם לָקַח יְהוָה וַיּוֹצִא אֶתְכֶם מִכּוּר הַבַּרְזֶל מִמִּצְרָיִם
לִהְיוֹת לוֹ לְעַם נַחֲלָה כַּיּוֹם הַזֶּה:

But as for you, the LORD took you and brought you out of the iron-smelting furnace, out of Egypt, to be the people of his inheritance, as you now are (NIV).

....

2. Deuteronomy 7:6

כִּי עַם קָדוֹשׁ אַתָּה לַיהוָה אֱלֹהֶיךָ בְּךָ בָּחַר יְהוָה אֱלֹהֶיךָ
לִהְיוֹת לוֹ לְעַם סְגֻלָּה מִכֹּל הָעַמִּים אֲשֶׁר עַל־פְּנֵי הָאֲדָמָה:

For you are a people holy to the LORD your God. The LORD your God has chosen you out of all the peoples on the face of the earth to be his people, his treasured possession (NIV).

....

3. Deuteronomy 14:2

כִּי עַם קָדוֹשׁ אַתָּה לַיהוָה אֱלֹהֶיךָ וּבְךָ בָּחַר יְהוָה
לִהְיוֹת לוֹ לְעַם סְגֻלָּה מִכֹּל הָעַמִּים אֲשֶׁר עַל־פְּנֵי הָאֲדָמָה:

For you are a people holy to the LORD your God. Out of all the peoples on the face of the earth, the LORD has chosen you to be his treasured possession (NIV).

---

[21] Rolf Rendtorff, *The Covenant Formula: An Exegetical and Theological Investigation*, trans. Margaret Kohl, Old Testament Studies (Edinburgh: T. & T. Clark, 1998), 13–32.

[22] Steven Ward Guest, "Deuteronomy 26:16–19 as the Central Focus of the Covenantal Framework of Deuteronomy" (PhD diss., The Southern Baptist Theological Seminary, 2009).

[23] Ibid., 155–156.

4a. Deuteronomy 26:17

אֶת־יְהוָה הֶאֱמַרְתָּ הַיּוֹם לִהְיוֹת לְךָ לֵאלֹהִים

You have declared this day that the LORD is your God (NIV).

....

4b. Deuteronomy 26:18

וַיהוָה הֶאֱמִירְךָ הַיּוֹם לִהְיוֹת לוֹ לְעַם סְגֻלָּה כַּאֲשֶׁר דִּבֶּר־לָךְ

And the LORD has declared this day that you are his people, his treasured possession as he promised (NIV).

....

5. Deuteronomy 27:9

הַיּוֹם הַזֶּה נִהְיֵיתָ לְעָם לַיהוָה אֱלֹהֶיךָ:

You have now become the people of the LORD your God (NIV).

....

6. Deuteronomy 28:9

יְקִימְךָ יְהוָה לוֹ לְעַם קָדוֹשׁ כַּאֲשֶׁר נִשְׁבַּע־לָךְ

The LORD will establish you as his holy people, as he promised you on oath (NIV).

....

7. Deuteronomy 29:13 (29:12 MT)

לְמַעַן הָקִים־אֹתְךָ הַיּוֹם לוֹ לְעָם וְהוּא יִהְיֶה־לְךָ לֵאלֹהִים
כַּאֲשֶׁר דִּבֶּר־לָךְ

to confirm you this day as his people, that he may be your God as he promised you (NIV).

Not only is the Covenant Formula found seven times in Deuteronomy, however; the Covenant Formula occurs just once in each of the seven sections of the book divided according to the literary structure of Hittite treaties from the fourteenth century B.C.

Table 10.5: The Covenant Relationship Formula (CRF) in the Literary Sections of Deuteronomy[24]

Hittite Treaty Formulary	Represented in Deuteronomy	CRF used (reference)
1) Preamble	1:1–5	None
2) Historical Prologue	1:6–4:44	Formula B (4:20)
3a) General Stipulation	4:45–11:32	Formula B (7:6)
3b) Specific Stipulations	12:1–26:15	Formula B (14:2)
	26:16–19	Formula C (26:17–19)
4) Document Clause	27:1–8	None
	27:9–10	Formula B (27:9)
5) Appeal to Witness	27:11–26	None
6) Blessings and Curses	28:1–69 [Eng 29:1]	Formula B (28:9)
7) Solemn Oath Ceremony	29:1 [Eng 29:2]–30:20	Formula C (29:12)

Not only is the Covenant Formula found just once in each of the major sections, it occurs at a key point in the literary structure of each section. Two examples may suffice.

The literary structure of 4:15–24 may be represented by the following chiasm:[25]

A Watch yourselves (v. 15)
    B Don't act corruptly (vv. 16–19)
        X Covenant relationship formula (v. 20)
    B' I acted corruptly (vv. 21–22)
A' Watch yourselves (vv. 23–24)

Note how the Covenant Formula appears at the centre of the section according to its chiastic structure.

---

[24] Ibid., 158. Used by permission.
[25] Ibid., 164–165. Used by permission.

The blessings in 28:7–14 are also arranged in a chiastic pattern:[26]

A Blessing against enemies (v. 7)
    B Blessing in the land (v. 8)
        X Blessing in relationship (vv. 9–10)
    B' Blessing on the land (vv. 11–12)
A' Blessing over all (vv. 13–14)

Once again, the covenantal formula occurs in verse 9, at the centre of this literary structure.

Guest likens the double version of the Covenant Formula in Deuteronomy 26:17–19 to the keystone of a bridge (made of stone) and provides support for this claim by demonstrating the centrality of 26:17–19 in the chiastic macrostructure of the book as a whole:[27]

A Blessing and curse in a covenant renewal under Moses (11:26–28)
    B Blessing and curse in a covenant renewal at Shechem (11:29–32)
        X Mutual commitments made between YHWH and Israel
          (26:16–19)
    B' Blessing and curse in a covenant renewal at Shechem (27:1–16)
A' Blessing and curse in a covenant renewal under Moses (28:1–69)

The text of Deuteronomy 26:16–19 is difficult because of the *hiphil* forms of the verb אמר ("to say") found only here in the Hebrew Bible. A literal translation could read:

> You have caused the LORD to say today to be your God, to walk in his ways, and to keep his statutes and his commandments and his ordinances, and to obey his voice. And the LORD has caused you to say today to be to him a people of special treasure, just as he promised you, and to keep all his commandments, and to set you high above all the nations which he has made for praise and for fame and for honor, and to be a holy people to the LORD your God, just as he promised.[28]

Each partner is "caused to say" four phrases (expressed in infinitives in Hebrew). The partner obligations are as shown in table 10.6:[29]

---

[26] Ibid., 210.

[27] Ibid., 152.

[28] Our own translation; for Guest's, see ibid., 126.

[29] Ibid., 126. Used by permission.

Table 10.6: Treaty Obligations in Their Infinitival Forms

Speaker	Speaker Obligation	Partner Obligation
Yahweh (v. 17)	לִהְיוֹת לְךָ לֵאלֹהִים	וְלָלֶכֶת בִּדְרָכָיו וְלִשְׁמֹר חֻקָּיו וּמִצְוֹתָיו וּמִשְׁפָּטָיו וְלִשְׁמֹעַ בְּקֹלוֹ
Israel (vv. 18–19)	וְלִשְׁמֹר כָּל־מִצְוֹתָיו	לִהְיוֹת לוֹ לְעַם סְגֻלָּה כַּאֲשֶׁר דִּבֶּר־לָךְ וּלְתִתְּךָ עֶלְיוֹן עַל כָּל־הַגּוֹיִם אֲשֶׁר עָשָׂה לִתְהִלָּה וּלְשֵׁם וּלְתִפְאָרֶת וְלִהְיֹתְךָ עַם־קָדֹשׁ לַיהוָה אֱלֹהֶיךָ כַּאֲשֶׁר דִּבֵּר

The first phrase in the first set of four is the commitment of Yahweh and the last three are Israel's; the second phrase in the second set of four is the commitment of Israel and the first one and last two phrases are Yahweh's. Guest diagrams the commitments as follows (table 10.7):[30]

Table 10.7: Mutual Covenant Commitments (Deuteronomy 26:16–19)

Yahweh Speaks		Israel Speaks
Commitment	לִהְיוֹת לְךָ לֵאלֹהִים	
	וְלִשְׁמֹר כָּל־מִצְוֹתָיו	Commitment
The Terms	וְלָלֶכֶת בִּדְרָכָיו	
	וְלִשְׁמֹר חֻקָּיו וּמִצְוֹתָיו וּמִשְׁפָּטָיו	
	וְלִשְׁמֹעַ בְּקֹלוֹ	
	לִהְיוֹת לוֹ לְעַם סְגֻלָּה כַּאֲשֶׁר דִּבֶּר־לָךְ	
	וּלְתִתְּךָ עֶלְיוֹן עַל כָּל־הַגּוֹיִם אֲשֶׁר עָשָׂה	The Benefits
	לִתְהִלָּה וּלְשֵׁם וּלְתִפְאָרֶת	
	וְלִהְיֹתְךָ עַם־קָדֹשׁ לַיהוָה אֱלֹהֶיךָ כַּאֲשֶׁר דִּבֵּר	

Thus the subjects of the infinitives could be filled out as follows:[31]

> A *I shall be your God*
> > B You shall walk in my ways
> > > You shall keep my statutes and my commandments and my ordinances
> > > You shall listen to my voice
> > B' *We shall keep all your commandments*
> A' You shall make us your people of special possession
> > You shall set us high above all the nations you have made
> > You shall make us a holy people

In this diagram the first four phrases (A and B lines) are spoken by Yahweh and the final four phrases (B' and A' lines) are spoken by Israel. Nonetheless, the arrangement is given an interlocking structure for rhetorical effect.

Guest comments on the difficulty of the *hiphil* forms as follows:[32]

> The difficulty arises, as noted above, that the English language does not have a functional equivalent to "X caused Y to say" that can capture the juridical nature of the exchange. It may be that the best one can offer is a periphrastic translation that maintains the integrity of the identities of the corresponding partners and their statements of the obligations accepted upon themselves and the corollary stipulations expected from the other. The relational component of the covenant must be fronted in both expressions to highlight the priority given to the relationship by Yahweh.

Guest then supplies an idiomatic rendering:[33]

> Today, you have ratified the declaration of the LORD: that he would be your God, that you will walk in his ways, and that you will keep his statutes, his commandments, and his ordinances, and that you will listen to his voice. Today, the LORD has ratified your declaration: that you would be to him a people of special possession, just as he promised you, and that you will keep all his commandments, and that he will set you high above all the nations which he has made for praise and for fame and for honor, and that you will be a holy people to the LORD your God, just as he promised.

The narrative that undergirds these verses is the covenant oath exchanged between Yahweh and Israel on the plains of Moab, articulated in relational terms. The statements of mutual obligation and stipulations are declared and ratified by both partners. As Guest puts it,

> It is at this moment that the suzerain Yahweh steps forward, and—as anticipated by and as required by this solemn and sacred ceremony—makes his gracious and awesome offer: "I will be your God." But his declaration does not stop there. He continues by asserting fully the stipulations commensurate with the obligation which he has assumed: "You will walk in my

---

[32] Ibid., 126.
[33] Ibid.

ways, you will keep my statutes, my commandments, and my ordinances, and you will listen to (obey) my voice."

In response—recognizing the incredible privilege of having Yahweh as their God—vassal Israel acknowledges its unique relationship that is the result of Yahweh's ancient oath to the patriarchs and states, "We are your people of special possession, *just as you promised us*; we will keep all your commandments. You will set us on high above all the nations you have made—for your praise and fame and honor; and we will be a people holy to Yahweh our God, *just as you promised*.

Thus this text reveals that Yahweh initiates the covenant by committing himself to be Israel's God and by reiterating the attending stipulations of that covenant.[34]

Deuteronomy 26, in which the double Covenant Formula is found, is devoted to three ceremonies: (1) ceremony of confession for First-Fruits Tithe (vv. 1–11), (2) ceremony of confession for Triennial Tithe (vv. 12–15), and (3) ceremony of confession of covenant ratification (vv. 16–19). Guest observes interesting parallels hitherto unnoticed in form, offering, confession, and grace between all three of these ceremonies:[35]

Yahweh—instead of giving gifts of land, produce, or even deliverance from slavery, as in the first two ceremonies—offers *himself* to Israel to be their God. And in a strikingly parallel manner, Israel *responds* to Yahweh's gracious gift by offering themselves back to Yahweh to be his people of special possession and a people holy to Yahweh. In this instance, the "token" of Israel's grateful response and pledge of continual faithfulness is neither a first fruit nor a tithe but rather a commitment to covenant loyalty as expressed in the wholehearted keeping of all his commandments (וְלִשְׁמֹר כָּל־מִצְוֹתָיו).[36]

As Guest claims, the Covenant Formula is central to tying the literary structure together:

Once the alternative schema for the covenantal framework of Deuteronomy was established, the observation that the covenant relationship formula was employed a single time in each of the components of the covenantal framework reinforced the notion that there was a literary, if not theological, significance to the formula. The utilization of that formula in its two individual constituents in 26:17 and 26:18–19 occurs as

---

[34] Ibid., 122.
[35] See chart, ibid., 133.
[36] Ibid., 142.

the covenant formulary in Deuteronomy crescendos from the Historical Prologue (1:6–4:44), the General Stipulation (4:45–11:32), the Specific Stipulation (12:1–26:15), to the climactic point whereat the ratifying oath between the covenantal partners would take place as the transaction is brought to its completion with the recording of the Document Clause (27:1–10) and Appeal to Witness (27:11–26), the recitation of the Blessings and Curses (28:1–69), concluding in a Solemn Oath Ceremony (29:1–30:20).[37]

Guest concludes, then, by noting that the Covenant Formula in 26:16–19, "like the keystone in the old stone bridge, serves as the focal point which defines, unifies, and bears the weight of the covenantal framework of Deuteronomy. In turn this affirms Rendtorff's observation that the 'covenant formula is an element of theological language which is introduced in a *highly conscious manner.*'"[38]

6. THE RELATIONSHIP OF DEUTERONOMY TO EARLIER COVENANTS

An important question is the relationship between the book of Deuteronomy and Exodus 19–24, designated in Exodus 24:7 as "the Book of the Covenant." Later we can consider the relationship of Deuteronomy to the Abrahamic covenant.

Within the book of Deuteronomy itself there are clear references to the earlier covenant made at Sinai. Five instances are found using the standard terminology, *kārat bĕrît*, i.e., cut a covenant: 4:23; 5:2; 5:3; 9:9; 28:69 (29:1 EV).[39] Deuteronomy 9:9 may be cited by way of illustration:

> When I went up the mountain to receive the tablets of stone, the tablets of the covenant that the LORD made with you, I remained on the mountain forty days and forty nights. I neither ate bread nor drank water.

The expression "the covenant that the LORD made with you" is described as going up the mountain to receive the tablets. This obviously refers to the events at Sinai.

There are also passages in Deuteronomy where the same standard

---

[37] Ibid., 228.

[38] Ibid., 230 (emphasis his).

[39] In Deuteronomy 7:2, the expression *kārat bĕrît* refers to making treaties with the Canaanites.

terminology (*kārat bĕrît*) is employed with direct and specific reference to the book of Deuteronomy itself as a covenant, e.g., 28:69 (29:1 EV):

אֵלֶּה דִבְרֵי הַבְּרִית אֲשֶׁר־צִוָּה יְהוָה אֶת־מֹשֶׁה
לִכְרֹת אֶת־בְּנֵי יִשְׂרָאֵל בְּאֶרֶץ מוֹאָב מִלְּבַד הַבְּרִית אֲשֶׁר־כָּרַת אִתָּם בְּחֹרֵב

> These are the words of the covenant that the LORD commanded Moses to make with the people of Israel in the land of Moab, besides the covenant that he had made with them at Horeb.

Deuteronomy 28:69 (29:1 EV) is the beginning of a new section, since the curses concluded in 28:68 end the covenant according to the form and struc-ture in terms of a suzerain-vassal treaty. The clause "these are the words" with the demonstrative pronoun "these" then refers directly to Deuteronomy 1:1–28:68, the bulk of the book of Deuteronomy. This text constitutes a cov-enant made (i.e., cut) with the people in the land of Moab before they enter Canaan. The preposition "beside" (מִלְּבַד) is crucial in this text. The mean-ing of this preposition is "beside," "besides," or "in addition to."[40] This text clearly states that the book of Deuteronomy is a covenant in its own right, made with the people, *besides* the Book of the Covenant in Exodus 19–24 with expansions in Leviticus and Numbers. Deuteronomy is thus a *supple-ment* to—and not a replacement for—the covenant at Sinai. It is a bit like a codicil added to a will (though here the codicil is larger than the will itself).

A passage of some significance in the relationship of Deuteronomy to the Israelite covenant at Sinai is Deuteronomy 5:1–6:

> [1] And Moses summoned all Israel and said to them, "Hear, O Israel, the statutes and the rules that I speak in your hearing today, and you shall learn them and be careful to do them. [2] The LORD our God made a covenant with us in Horeb. [3] Not with our fathers did the LORD make this covenant, but with us, who are all of us here alive today. [4] The LORD spoke with you face to face at the mountain, out of the midst of the fire, [5] while I stood between the LORD and you at that time, to declare to you the word of the LORD. For you were afraid because of the fire, and you did not go up into the mountain. [6] He said: 'I am the LORD your God, who brought you out of the land of Egypt, out of the house of slavery.'" (ESV)

---

[40] See F. Brown, S. R. Driver, and C. Briggs, eds., *A Hebrew and English Lexicon of the Old Testament* (Oxford: Clarendon, 1907; repr., 1953), s.v. בַּד; and see, e.g., L. Koehler and W. Baumgartner, *Hebräisches und Aramäisches Lexikon zum Alten Testament*, 3rd ed., ed. W. Baumgartner, J. J. Stamm, and B. Hartmann (Leiden, Netherlands: Brill, 1967–1995), s.v. בַּד.

This passage reviews the covenant material from Exodus 19–24 before presenting the main stipulation of the covenant (Deut. 6:5) followed by the detailed stipulations. Verse 2 of Deuteronomy 5 says, "the LORD our God made a covenant with us in Horeb" (ESV) and employs the standard terminology, *kārat berît*, i.e., cut a covenant. This is a clear reference to the Israelite covenant made at Sinai, i.e., Exodus 19–24. Then Moses says, "Not with our fathers did the LORD make this covenant, but with us, who are all of us here alive today." The question arises here, what does he mean by "our fathers"? Does this refer to the generation at Sinai that have now passed away, or is it a specific reference to Abraham, Isaac, and Jacob—a normal referent for "fathers" in Deuteronomy. Part of the problem is also the referent of "this covenant" in the same sentence, which has been construed to refer to the book of Deuteronomy. Jerry Hwang, in a major study of this term in Deuteronomy, concluded that the author of Deuteronomy has fused the Book of the Covenant at Sinai and the book of Deuteronomy as one.[41] If this is the case, then "fathers" could be both the patriarchs and the previous generation. In any case, the previous generation violated the covenant and died in the wilderness, and now the covenant needs to be renewed with a new Israel. This is clearly understood by Peter Leithart:

> The Pentateuch ends with Israel camped in the plains of Moab, east of Canaan. They are still "east of Eden," but they are now preparing to cross the Jordan to receive their land. While they are camped in Moab, Moses preaches to them, and his sermons make up the book of Deuteronomy. Since this is a new Israel, the covenant that God made at Sinai is renewed.[42]

In fact, Deuteronomy, rather than Exodus 34, should be viewed and understood as the covenant renewal.[43] Editorial headings in modern English versions frequently label Exodus 34:10–27 as "the Covenant Renewal." There is, however, no real basis for such a description in the text itself. Granted, the chronological sequence of events in Exodus 19–40 is not always abundantly clear. Nonetheless, the rehearsal of these events in Deuteronomy 9:9–29 aids in clarifying the narrative in Exodus. It seems that after the covenant ratifica-

---

[41] Jerry Hwang, "The Rhetoric of Remembrance: An Exegetical and Theological Investigation into the 'Fathers' in Deuteronomy" (PhD diss., Wheaton College, 2009).

[42] Peter J. Leithart, *A House for My Name: A Survey of the Old Testmament* (Moscow, ID: Canon, 2000), 106.

[43] Indeed, apparently all of the covenants to this point are double: (1) the covenant with creation is reaffirmed in the cosmic covenant with Noah; (2) the covenant with Abraham in Genesis 15 is reaffirmed in Genesis 17; and (3) the covenant with Israel at Sinai (Ex. 19–24) is reaffirmed in the covenant with Israel on the plains of Moab in Deuteronomy. For this observation I am indebted to Georges-Émile Durand of Montréal, Québec.

tion in Exodus 24 Moses is called to ascend further up the mountain. We read in Exodus 24:12:

> The LORD said to Moses, "Come up to me on the mountain and wait there, that I may give you the tablets of stone, with the law and the commandment, which I have written for their instruction." (ESV)

While Moses has written the Book of the Covenant (Ten Words and Judgements) given orally, God will give him the stone tablets and the Instruction (Torah) and the Commandment which he has personally written to instruct them. So when Moses went up the mountain, the cloud, i.e., the glory of Yahweh, covered the mountain for six days, and on the seventh, Moses was summoned and enveloped by the cloud and was on the mountain forty days and forty nights (Ex. 24:15–18). At the end of this time, Moses descended the mountain in anger because the people had broken the first (and second) of the Ten Words and thus violated the covenant (Ex. 32:15–20). No doubt Moses' breaking of the tablets symbolised the broken covenant. Then Moses interceded for the people and was on the mountain another forty days and forty nights (Ex. 34:27–28). During this time God revealed himself to Moses as compassionate and forgiving. Moses appealed immediately to the character of God newly revealed. It is in this context that God makes the following statement:

> And he said, "Behold, I am making a covenant. Before all your people I will do marvels, such as have not been created in all the earth or in any nation. And all the people among whom you are shall see the work of the LORD, for it is an awesome thing that I will do with you. (Ex. 34:10, ESV)

Note particularly in verse 10 the use of the active participle, "I am making a covenant" (אָנֹכִי כֹּרֵת). Whether the action is construed as imminent or as non-perfective, the context indicates that God *is in the midst of* covenant making.[44] First the Ten Words were given verbally; then they were written. The covenant was violated before the stone tablets were given to the people. God forgave Israel at Moses' request and carried on with his covenant making in writing another set of stone tablets to give to the people. There is no indication that Exodus 34 entails a "covenant renewal" apart from the

---

[44] On the function and meaning of the participle in Hebrew see Ronald J. Williams, *Williams' Hebrew Syntax*, 3rd ed., rev. and expanded by John C. Beckman (Toronto: University of Toronto Press, 2007), 88; Christo H. J. van der Merwe, Jackie A. Naudé, and Jan H. Kroeze, *A Biblical Hebrew Reference Grammar*, Biblical Languages: Hebrew 3 (Sheffield, UK: Sheffield Academic Press, 1999), § 20.3; and Peter T. Nash, "The Hebrew Qal Active Participle: A Non-Aspectual Narrative Backgrounding Element" (PhD diss., University of Chicago, 1992).

people being given a rewritten set of stone tablets. In the end, the generation entering the covenant at Sinai died in the wilderness, and another generation arose.[45] Deuteronomy is a renewal of the covenant with them as well as a covenant made for the first time as a supplement to the covenant at Sinai. There are only three other constructions in the Hebrew Bible where the participle is employed in the standard terminology (*kārat bĕrît*): Deuteronomy 29:11, 13 and analogously, Nehemiah 10:1. In each case the participle corresponds to the present tense in English and refers to something in the making that is in the process of being completed.

The remaining instances where the expression *kārat bĕrît* is used could be construed to refer to Exodus 19–24 and Deuteronomy fused as one: Deuteronomy 29:11, 13 (29:12, 14 EV); 29:24 (29:25 EV); 31:16:

> [10] "You are standing today all of you before the LORD your God: the heads of your tribes, your elders, and your officers, all the men of Israel, [11] your little ones, your wives, and the sojourner who is in your camp, from the one who chops your wood to the one who draws your water, [12] so that you may enter into the sworn covenant of the LORD your God, which the LORD your God is making with you today, [13] that he may establish you today as his people, and that he may be your God, as he promised you, and as he swore to your fathers, to Abraham, to Isaac, and to Jacob. [14] It is not with you alone that I am making this sworn covenant, [15] but with whoever is standing here with us today before the LORD our God, and with whoever is not here with us today." (Deut. 29:10–15, ESV)

> Then people will say, 'It is because they abandoned the covenant of the LORD, the God of their fathers, which he made with them when he brought them out of the land of Egypt, . . . '" (Deut. 29:25, ESV)

> And the LORD said to Moses, "Behold, you are about to lie down with your fathers. Then this people will rise and whore after the foreign gods among them in the land that they are entering, and they will forsake me and break my covenant that I have made with them." (Deut. 31:16, ESV)

To sum up the discussion to this point, according to 29:1, the book of Deuteronomy is a covenant in its own right, separate from the covenant

---

[45] According to the covenant stipulations, God "[visits] the iniquity of the fathers on the children to the third and fourth generation of those who hate me, but [shows] steadfast love to a thousand generations of those who love me" (Deut. 5:9–10; cf. Ex. 20:5–6). Nonetheless, when Israel broke the covenant, only one generation was destroyed in the desert. What a demonstration of Yahweh's name as compassionate and gracious (Ex. 34:5–7)! I owe this insight to Stephen G. Dempster.

at Sinai/Horeb. In essence this covenant is a supplement to the covenant at Sinai. The covenant making on the plains of Moab is also a covenant renewal of the broken Sinai/Horeb-covenant with the subsequent generation. Thus, although the book of Deuteronomy is a separate covenant, at the same time it is part and parcel of the covenant at Sinai and therefore the two are fused together as one in many passages in Deuteronomy.

John H. Sailhamer, however, sees Deuteronomy 29 as a separate covenant—without stipulations—related to the covenant promised in the prophets and not related to any part of the book of Deuteronomy preceding chapter 29.[46] His main argument is as follows:

> The covenant identified by Deuteronomy 29:1 cannot be the Sinai (Horeb) covenant, since it is a "covenant that God commanded Moses to make [*likrōt*] with Israel in Moab besides [*millĕbad*] the covenant [*habbĕrît*] which [God] had made with [Israel] at Horeb" (Deut. 29:1 28:69 MT]). If it is a covenant that is distinguished from the Sinai covenant, it must therefore not refer to any covenant that precedes Deuteronomy 29, since all such references to a covenant prior to Deuteronomy 29 are clearly identified in the narrative with the Sinai (Horeb) covenant. No one disputes that.[47]

He is right to insist that the text clearly states that Deuteronomy is a covenant in its own right separate from that of Sinai. Nonetheless, his claim that all references prior to Deuteronomy 29 are clearly identified with Sinai is false: he did not have the benefit of the study by Jerry Hwang. Deuteronomy clearly fuses Moab and Sinai together. Thus, the division in MT is correct and the covenant is to be construed as referring to the book of Deuteronomy to this point.

Finally, brief comments on Deuteronomy 4:29–31 and 8:18 are necessary:

DEUTERONOMY 4:29–31

When Moses reviews the history of past relationship with Yahweh in the Historical Prologue section of the covenant/treaty, covenant breaking and faithlessness are duly noted. In 4:1–14 Moses commands obedience and in verses 15–31 he warns them of the danger of covenant violation and idolatry in the future, leading to curse, exile, and death. Nonetheless, when they are

---

[46] John H. Sailhamer, *The Meaning of the Pentateuch: Revelation, Composition, and Interpretation* (Downers Grove, IL: InterVarsity Press, 2009), 399–404.
[47] Ibid., 400.

exiled, even then the Lord will not destroy his people or forget the covenant with "your fathers":

> [29] But from there you will seek the LORD your God and you will find him, if you search after him with all your heart and with all your soul. [30] When you are in tribulation, and all these things come upon you in the latter days, you will return to the LORD your God and obey his voice. [31] For the LORD your God is a merciful God. He will not leave you or destroy you or forget the covenant with your fathers that he swore to them. (ESV)

The long shadow of Sinai looms over the people. Dempster details how events before and after Sinai are similar, but those after are judged more severely.[48] The possibility of a faithful human partner to this point in the narrative plot structure is not great. Thus, this factor explains the need for chapter 30 after chapters 28 and 29 and also 32:34–43 of the Song of Moses—though the word *bĕrît* does not occur here.[49] Both Deuteronomy 30 and 32:34–43 foresee the faithlessness and future judgement of Israel. Deuteronomy 4:29–31 also under-scores the relationship between the Israelite covenant and the Abrahamic: because of the Abrahamic covenant, violation of the Israelite covenant by Israel does not mean the end of God's purposes for the family of Abraham.

DEUTERONOMY 8:18

וְזָכַרְתָּ אֶת־יְהוָה אֱלֹהֶיךָ כִּי הוּא הַנֹּתֵן לְךָ כֹּחַ לַעֲשׂוֹת חָיִל
לְמַעַן הָקִים אֶת־בְּרִיתוֹ אֲשֶׁר־נִשְׁבַּע לַאֲבֹתֶיךָ כַּיּוֹם הַזֶּה

> You shall remember the LORD your God, for it is he who gives you power to get wealth, that he may confirm his covenant that he swore to your fathers, as it is this day. (ESV)

In the context, Moses is warning the people with all his rhetorical skill of the danger of forgetting the Lord. Hebrew has two words for "forget," and the one used here entails a moral lapse, not a mental lapse. It is the situation of arriving at a place where one enjoys a family, house, fruitful farm, and deliverance from enemies and concludes, "Who needs the Lord?" This is forgetting the Lord.

By contrast, to "remember Yahweh" according to this verse is to love

---

[48] Stephen G. Dempster, *Dominion and Dynasty: A Biblical Theology of the Hebrew Bible*, NSBT 15 (Downers Grove, IL: InterVarsity Press, 2003), 113.

[49] I am indebted to Daniel Block for his helpful review of this chapter, pointing out areas that needed inclusion.

him by obeying the covenant stipulations. When they do this, Yahweh will bring the blessings he promised, i.e., wealth, and will thus "fulfill" or "keep" his covenant which he swore to their fathers. The mention of "fathers" along with the verb "swore" would most likely recall the mighty oath made to Abraham in Genesis 22 and later confirmed to Isaac and Jacob. Oaths do not seem to be mentioned in Exodus 19–24. Thus, the gift of the land and the ability to make wealth in it comes about as the Lord gives strength to make that wealth and so uphold his oath to the fathers. If, however, we interpret "fathers" to refer to the previous generation, obedience to the covenant stipulations given in Exodus 19–24 would result in the wealth and the fulfilment of the promises to the fathers. Either way, obedience to the Lord is the means for fulfilling his promises, and this entails divinely given strength.

The comment of Daniel I. Block on this difficult verse is also helpful:[50]

> The NIV's rendering of אֲבֹתֶיךָ as "your forefathers" follows a longstanding tradition of understanding the covenant in question to be that which Yahweh made with the patriarchs.[51] Although this is probably the correct interpretation of the word in verse 1, within the context of this chapter, particularly in light of verses 3 and 16, it seems more likely that Moses has the exodus generation in mind. This interpretation is reinforced by the fact that, although Yahweh promised to bless Abraham and his descendants in general (Gen. 12:2; cf. 17:20), this is not a prominent theme in the references to the covenant/promises. The narratives do indeed speak of Yahweh blessing Abraham (24:1 ["in every way"], 35) and Isaac (25:11; 26:12–14, 29), but the profusion of material blessings at the disposal of the Israelites in verses 7–9 (cf. 7:12–16) are most appropriately understood as the fulfillment of the blessings promised within the terms of the covenant made with Israel at Horeb/Sinai (Lev. 26:1–13; cf. Deut. 28:1–14). This understanding is strengthened by Moses' addition of כַּיּוֹם הַזֶּה, "as this day," an expression that recurs often in the book to stress the significance of an event for Moses' present audience, often in contrast to the experience of the exodus generation.[52]

Jerry Hwang observes the progression in chapter 8. Since verse 18 assumes a future date, after the people have eaten and are satisfied and become arrogant, the ancestors could even be the present generation involved in this

---

[50] I am quoting Block from a prepublication version of his recently released commentary on Deuteronomy, cited above in note 14.

[51] This interpretation goes back as far as the Samaritan Pentateuch and the LXX[L], which insert the names of Abraham, Isaac, and Jacob at this point. Cf. BHS, s.v.

[52] Deuteronomy 2:22, 30; 3:14; 4:20, 38; 6:24; 8:18; 10:8, 15; 11:4; 29:28; 34:6. Cf. also 26:16; 27:9; 29:4.

ceremony in Moab. He suggests again that there is an intentional blurring of the boundaries of the covenants.[53]

7. THE SIGNIFICANCE OF THE FORM

Earlier we discussed the significance of the form of the Book of the Covenant and included Deuteronomy in that discussion. Analysis of the book of Deuteronomy requires reinforcement of one or two things.

Just as in Exodus 19–24 the Ten Words are foundational to the Judgements and, conversely, the Judgements applied and extended the Ten Words in a practical way to all areas of life, so in Deuteronomy, the Specific Stipulations in chapters 12–26 illustrate application and extension of the basic requirement of loyalty and the review of the Ten Words to various areas of life (in an Iron Age culture).

Once again, the classification of the laws as (a) moral, (b) civil, and (c) ceremonial is foreign to the literary structure of the text. In fact, the ceremonial, civil, and moral laws are all mixed together.

Comparison of Deuteronomy with contemporary documents from the ancient Near East in both content and form reveals that the book belongs to the fourteenth century B.C. in relation to other treaties (see figure 10.1, where columns 1 and 2 belong to the fourteenth century B.C., while columns 3 and 4 belong to the seventh century B.C.).

Comparison of Ancient Near Eastern Treaty Forms

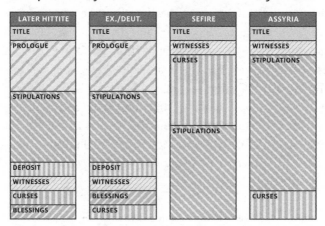

Fig. 10.1

---

53 Hwang, "Rhetoric of Remembrance."

The Israelite covenant, as found in the book of Deuteronomy, is without parallel in the ancient Near East in terms of content and form taken together: (1) in content, Deuteronomy is most similar to ancient Near Eastern legal treatises, but it does not have the form of a law treatise; (2) in form, Deuteronomy is most similar to ancient Near Eastern treaties, but not in content. This is obvious from figure 10.2:

Comparison of Ancient Near Eastern Laws/Treaties and Deuteronomy

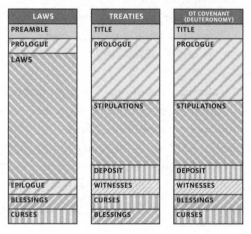

Fig. 10.2

God desires to direct and instruct the lives/lifestyle of his people; yet he wants to do this in the context of a family relationship characterised by love, loyalty, and trust. This is completely different from Greek and Roman law codes or ancient Near Eastern legal treaties. We should always remember that Torah means "instruction" rather than "law." It might be better for Christians to simply speak of the "instruction" in the covenant.

Also instructive is the comparison of covenant and law by George E. Mendenhall (table 10.8),[54] which was followed by John Walton in his helpful book, *Ancient Near Eastern Thought and the Old Testament.*[55]

---

[54] George E. Mendenhall, "The Conflict between Value Systems and Social Control," in *Unity and Diversity: Essays in the History, Literature, and Religion of the Ancient Near East*, ed. Hans Goedicke and J. J. M. Roberts (Baltimore: Johns Hopkins University Press, 1975), 169–180. Table © 1975 The Johns Hopkins University Press. Reprinted with permission of The Johns Hopkins University Press.

[55] See John H. Walton, *Ancient Near Eastern Thought and the Old Testament: Introducing the Conceptual World of the Hebrew Bible* (Grand Rapids, MI: Baker, 2006), 299–301.

Table 10.8: Mendenhall's Table Comparing Covenant and Law

	Covenant	Law
Purpose	Creates a community where none existed before, by establishing a common relationship to a common lord.	Presupposes a social order in which it serves as an instrument for maintaining an orderly freedom and security.
Basis	Gratitude: response to benefits already received = grace.	Social fear: attempts to protect society from disruption and attack by threat of force.
Enactment	By voluntary act in which each individual willingly accepts the obligations presented.	By competent social authority. It is binding upon each individual by virtue of his status as a member of the social organization, usually by birth.
Validity	Binding upon each person without regard to social context. It is as universal as God himself and is, therefore, the real basis for the concept of the "omnipresence of God."	Entirely dependent upon social boundary lines. Completely irrelevant to one who has crossed the boundary of the social order.
Sanctions	Not under control of social organizations, unpredictable in specific cases, but connected with cause-and-effect concepts in human history. Both positive and negative sanctions are included.	Enforced by social organization through its chosen authorities. Sanctions are largely negative, though nonpolitical organizations use economic and prestige motivations to obtain conformity.
Norms	Typically presented as verbal abstractions, the definition of which is an obligation of persons in concrete circumstances and the "fear of God" = conscience.	Defined by social authority in advance, usually with specific sanctions defined for specific violations. Arbitrary and formal in nature, since only forms of actions can be witnessed to in a court of law.
Orientation	Toward the future: makes individual behavior reliable and therefore a basis for both private and public security. Prediction of consequences extends to four generations in case of violation.	Toward the past: attempts to punish violations of the public order in order to make that public order more secure. It is oriented toward the future only in the sense that it gives warning in advance of the penalties that the society has power to impose upon the violator. Very short attention span (statute of limitations).
Social Aspect	Obligations individual, but consequences (blessings and curses) are of necessity social, since they are "acts of God"— drought, epidemic, defeat in war, etc. Powerfully reinforces individual responsibility to society, and social responsibility to refrain from protection of the guilty.	Obligations defined by society are binding upon all members, but sanctions are imposed only upon guilty individual, in adversary procedure and rite. Is a form of warfare pitting society against the guilty person.
Evolution	Forms basis for social custom especially in early stages. As social control takes over, may degenerate into mere ritual reinforcement of a social solidarity.	Presupposes a customary morality that it attempts to protect, but cannot create. Tends to become increasingly rigid in formal definition, and increasingly devoid of real ethical content.
Continuity	Since it is not produced by society, it cannot be guaranteed by society. Essentially private, individual, independent of roles. Prophets, the Christ, apostles. Destruction of a particular social control system, therefore, does not mean the end of the value system.	Cannot exist apart from social institutions— king, priest, political officers, legislative, executive, judicial. Ceases to exist when political structure falls.

8. THE RELATIONSHIP OF THE ISRAELITE COVENANT TO THE ABRAHAMIC COVENANT

In order to construct a metanarrative that is true to the biblical text, we must not only accurately determine the meaning of the foundational texts, we must also listen to what the text says about interrelationships between two or more covenants.

Two main points are made in the text concerning the relationship of the Israelite covenant to the Abrahamic covenant. First, the exodus from Egypt is a fulfilment of the covenant with Abraham (Ex. 2:24; Deut. 7:7–9; 9:5; Jer. 11:2–4). In Genesis 15, when God made the covenant with Abraham, he predicted that Abraham's descendants would be enslaved and mistreated in a country not their own for four hundred years, but afterwards would come out with great possessions. Among the several texts that refer to this, we can cite Deuteronomy 7:7–9 as an example:

> [7] The LORD did not set his affection on you and choose you because you were more numerous than other peoples, for you were the fewest of all peoples. [8] But it was because the LORD loved you and kept the oath he swore to your forefathers that he brought you out with a mighty hand and redeemed you from the land of slavery, from the power of Pharaoh king of Egypt. [9] Know therefore that the LORD your God is God; he is the faithful God, keeping his covenant of love to a thousand generations of those who love him and keep his commands. (NIV)

Here, deliverance from enslavement in Egypt is attributed to the Lord keeping his covenant of love. This is a clear reference to his promise to Abraham in Genesis 15.

Second, Exodus 19:5–6 shows that by means of the Israelite covenant, God intends for the nation to fulfill the Adamic role reassigned to Abraham. Through covenant, God will bring his blessing and establish his rule in the lives of his people and, through them, to the rest of the world.

Chapter Eleven

THE DAVIDIC COVENANT[1]

INTRODUCTION

Another key point in the narrative plot structure of Scripture is the agreement or covenant which God initiated with David, king of Israel. As a convenient and short title we shall call this agreement the Davidic covenant, observing the language of the biblical text.

As we shall see, the Davidic covenant functions in the larger story in a number of significant ways. In the history of the people of Israel, it inaugurates a divinely designed model of kingship for the nation. Furthermore, it implements the kingship of Yahweh among his people at a deeper and higher level. In addition to addressing concerns and problems of the developing nation of Israel, the Davidic covenant carries forward in specific ways the intentions and purposes of God expressed in the Israelite covenant and, even further back, in the covenant with Abraham.

First we shall look at the context and historical situation in which kingship was inaugurated. Then we shall examine the main passages on the covenant with David and also look at how this was appropriated and understood by later texts of the Old Testament, particularly Isaiah 55. Finally, we shall briefly describe the connections and relations between the Davidic covenant and the Israelite covenant and the covenant with Abraham.

JOSHUA

Joshua was a leader like Moses. He led the people into the land of Canaan, the land promised to the patriarchs in the covenant with Abraham. The book of Joshua is divided into two parts: the first half describes the conquest of the land; the second half describes the division of the land among the twelve tribes of Israel according to their *clans* (מִשְׁפָּחוֹת). This result was a clear fulfilment of the Israelite covenant, but also led Israel to a higher level of

---

[1] Much of the material presented here on the Davidic covenant was published earlier as Peter J. Gentry, "Rethinking the 'Sure Mercies of David' in Isaiah 55:3," *Westminster Theological Journal* 69 (2007): 279–304.

commitment, as we see when the book ends with a ceremony of covenant renewal (Josh. 24:25). The expression employed there is *kārat běrît*, i.e., to cut a covenant. Some scholars have incorrectly assumed from such texts that the expression *kārat běrît* does not always refer to covenant initiation, but can be used for covenant renewal. This is an erroneous conclusion. What in fact happened is that Joshua *made a covenant* with the people *to keep the covenant*—the Israelite covenant inaugurated through Moses at Sinai and Moab. So technically, from a linguistic point of view, *kārat běrît* only refers to covenant initiation.[2] Another example, precisely similar to Joshua 24, is 2 Kings 23:2–3:

> [2] And the king went up to the house of the LORD, and with him all the men of Judah and all the inhabitants of Jerusalem and the priests and the prophets, all the people, both small and great. And he read in their hearing all the words of the Book of the Covenant that had been found in the house of the LORD. [3] And the king stood by the pillar and made a covenant before the LORD, to walk after the LORD and to keep his commandments and his testimonies and his statutes with all his heart and all his soul, to perform the words of this covenant that were written in this book. And all the people joined in the covenant. (ESV)

Here King Josiah makes a covenant (*kārat běrît*) to keep a covenant, i.e., "to perform the words of this covenant" (*lěhāqîm 'eth dibrê habběrît hazzō't*).

JUDGES

The next period is dark in every way. The nation of Israel is constantly breaking the covenant at this time. The writer of the book of Judges portrays recurring cycles in which (1) the people break the covenant and sin against Yahweh, (2) Yahweh disciplines them by allowing aggression against Israel by foreign nations, (3) there is a call to repentance and a cry for help, and (4) Yahweh raises up a hero or deliverer, called a judge, who rescues the people from their enemies and rules them for a time. At the end of this book, the author comments, "In those days there was no king in Israel; everyone did what was right in his own eyes" (Judg. 21:25). Here the author is really referring to the condition of the people and how the covenant would be preserved. He is saying that, despite the lack of human support which might

---

[2] It is common today for couples to renew their marriage vows on their silver wedding anniversary in what is essentially a covenant making ceremony. This is a modern-day example of "making a covenant to keep a covenant." It does not mean that the expression "make a covenant" in and of itself now refers to covenant renewal.

have preserved a political or religious ideal, in spite of the fact that there was no king and each person followed his own standard, Yahweh, by direct intervention through a series of saviour figures, preserved the covenant with Israel at this time. The book of Judges, then, suggests that, in any age, the people of Israel would not owe their existence to political constitutions devised by themselves, such as the monarchy. Israel would owe its survival to the faithfulness of its covenant partner, who would never defect from his obligations to which he was bound by oath and promise.[3]

SAMUEL AND THE BEGINNING OF THE MONARCHY

When the book of Samuel opens, the worship of God is debased among the people of Israel. Eli, the high priest, is primarily responsible because he was not able to discipline his sons, Hophni and Phinehas. God prepared Samuel as the man to rescue his people from this crisis.

In 1 Samuel 8, the elders of Israel ask Samuel to appoint a king to lead them, like the nations surrounding them. This request reveals a number of issues confused in the minds of the people. First, Samuel was a judge. Normally Yahweh appointed the judges by his Spirit. It was not an office which was passed to one's natural sons as in a dynasty. Second, they wanted a king like the nations surrounding them. Here the problem was not in wanting a king per se. As Merrill says, God had planned for this from the start. "Man was created as the divine image in order to 'rule over the fish of the sea and the birds of the sky and over every living creature that moves on the ground' (Gen. 1:26–28). He was placed in the garden of Eden to exercise sovereignty over it and over all things."[4] Later, when God made his last new start, he told Abraham and Sarah that kings would come from them (Gen. 17:6, 16), and this promise was reaffirmed to Jacob (Gen. 35:11). Jacob's blessing on the tribes, given at the time of his death, announced that "the scepter will not depart from Judah,/nor the ruler's staff from between his feet,/until he comes to whom it belongs/and the obedience of the nations is his" (Gen. 49:10). Even Balaam, in his second oracle, says, "the shout of a king is among them" (Num. 23:21), and in his fourth oracle, "a star shall come out of Jacob and a scepter shall rise out of Israel" (Num. 24:17). Finally, Moses in Deuteronomy

---

[3] See William J. Dumbrell, *Covenant and Creation: A Theology of the Old Testament Covenants* (Carlisle, UK: Paternoster, 1984), 132.

[4] Eugene H. Merrill, *Kingdom of Priests: A History of Old Testament Israel*, 2nd ed. (Grand Rapids, MI: Baker, 1987, 2008), 208.

17:14–20 lays down provisions and regulations for a monarchy brought about according to God's choice and God's timing. The king must be the man of Yahweh's choice (v. 15) and must govern the people according to the principles of the Israelite covenant (vv. 18–20).[5] The problem was not, then, in wanting a king. It was in wanting one like the nations. Kingship in Canaan at this time was centralised, absolute, and contained the potential abuse of power. In addition, there was a danger that through alliances, compacts, and treaties the Israelites would depend on others and not on the Lord. Moreover, since kings would come to the throne by dynasty and not by direct intervention from the Lord, God's direct rule of the people could be thwarted.

SAUL: 2 SAMUEL 6

The book of Samuel relates that, because of the degeneration of worship and disobedience of the people, God allowed the Philistines to capture the ark. Symbolically, this indicated that Yahweh, who was enthroned upon the ark, had departed from his people and gone into a self-imposed exile. The return of the ark in 2 Samuel 6 indicates that Yahweh is returning to live in the midst of his people as king. The fact that 2 Samuel 6 precedes 7 shows that only when the kingship of Yahweh among his people is firmly established can the issue of kingship in Israel be discussed. A sanctuary for the Lord comes before the monarchy.[6]

Another significant factor is the emergence of the office of prophet in Israel at this time. Samuel is the beginning of the prophets. The office of prophet also comes directly from the Israelite covenant (Num. 12:6–9; Deut. 18:15–22). And it arises at this time because it provides a check against the absolute rule of the king and makes sure that Yahweh—that God—is ruling the people through the king of Israel. For every David there must also be a Nathan who can come directly into the king's presence and confront his decisions and actions by the authority of the word of God.

DAVID: 2 SAMUEL 7

The main passages in the Old Testament dealing with the Davidic covenant are 2 Samuel 7 with its parallel text in 1 Chronicles 17 and Psalm 89 (esp. vv. 3–4 and 19–37). While 2 Samuel 7 does not specifically call the arrangement a covenant, the term בְּרִית is in fact used in 2 Samuel 23:5; Jeremiah 33:21;

---

[5] Expanded and adapted from Merrill, *Kingdom of Priests*, 208.
[6] See John H. Walton, *Covenant: God's Purpose, God's Plan* (Grand Rapids, MI: Zondervan, 1994), 65–73.

Psalm 89:3, 28, 34, 39; 132:12; and 2 Chronicles 13:5. Moreover, חֶסֶד, the term used of the Davidic covenant in Isaiah 55:3, *is used* in 2 Samuel 7:15.

Let us begin by carefully determining the literary structure of the text so that we can observe how this communication is shaped.

2 Samuel 7—Outline

I. God's promise to David	1–17
A. David's plan	1–3
(David proposes to build a house for Yahweh)	
B. God's promise	4–17
1. Will you build a house for me?	4–7
2. I will build a house for you!	8–16
a. Promises to be realized during David's lifetime	8–11a
b. Promises to be realized after David's death	11b–16

i. The covenant promises–Yahweh's part
          seed
          kingdom
          throne (eternal)
	11b–13

ii. The covenant relationship—the king's part (Obedience in a father-son relationship)	14–15

iii. Summary of the covenant promises
          an eternal seed
          an eternal kingdom
          an eternal throne
	16

II. David's prayer to God	18–29
A. David's praise and worship	18–24
1. Wonder	18–20
2. Praise	21–24
B. David's requests	25–29
1. David asks God to confirm his word	25–27
2. David expresses trust in God's word	28
3. David asks God to bless his house	29

The passage is divided in half, with the first half narrating the revelation of divine promises given to David and the second half recording David's response in worship. When it says in verse 18 that "King David went in and sat before the LORD" it means that he entered the sanctuary to reflect, worship, and pray.[7]

---

[7] David's prayer is remarkable in that this passage is *unique* in the entire Deuteronomistic history (Joshua—Kings) for the sheer repetition and variety of names for God. Divine names in 2 Samuel 7:18–29 are as follows: יהוה 18, 24; אדני יהוה 18, 19, 19, 20, 22, 28, 29; אלהים 22, 23, 24, 28; יהוה אלהים 25; יהוה צבאות 26, 27; אלהים על ישראל 26; אלהי ישראל 27. I owe this insight to Florence White, a former student of Stephen G. Dempster.

Again, the first half is divided into two parts: in the first part David proposes to build a grander sanctuary of cedar panelling than the present temporary tent. In response, God promises to build a house for David. There is a play on the word "house" (בַּיִת). The "house" that David wants to build for Yahweh is a sanctuary or temple. The "house" that Yahweh will build for David is a dynasty or royal family line. This play on words is taken up again and again in the Old Testament. For example, in Amos 9 the prophet predicts a future time when the sorry state of the Davidic dynasty, a "fallen hut," will be rebuilt. Since the context also refers to bringing down the temple, which had become devoted to corrupt worship, both dynasty and temple are involved in the reference to the "fallen hut" of David (Amos 9:11).

David's initial plan is approved by the prophet Nathan and then revoked when Nathan is given a divine revelation by dream or vision in the night. This is significant because it is part of a theme in 2 Samuel that kingship in Israel must be subservient to Yahweh, the Great King.[8]

In verses 8–16, the section detailing the divine gift and promises to David, several key markers of the literary structure need to be observed. First, the shift from perfect and waw-consecutive imperfect verb forms in verses 8 and 9a to waw-consecutive perfect forms marking future time in the middle of verse 9 clearly marks the break between past blessings and future promises. Second, the messenger formula which opens verse 8 (כה אמר יהוה צבאות) is repeated in verse 11b, albeit in a different form (והגיד לך יהוה). This is a clear marker in the text, along with the temporal clause beginning verse 12, which refers to a time after David's death, to separate the promises to be fulfilled during David's life from the promises to be fulfilled after David's death.

The covenant clearly demarcates both divine and human obligations. The divine obligations or promises are divided by the literary structure into promises to be fulfilled during David's lifetime and promises to be fulfilled after David's death. The former are listed in verses 8–11a: (1) a great name, (2) a firm place for Israel as the people of God and, (3) rest for David from his enemies. The latter are listed in verses 11b–13 and 16. Here what Yahweh promises David is a lasting dynasty, kingdom, and throne. The promises are given initially in verses 11b–13 and are repeated in verse 16. At the centre of this A-B-A' chiastic structure is the covenant between Yahweh and David,

---

[8] See Donald F. Murray, *Divine Prerogative and Royal Pretension: Pragmatics, Poetics, and Polemics in a Narrative Sequence about David (2 Samuel 5.17–7.29)*, JSOTSup 264 (Sheffield, UK: Sheffield Academic Press, 1998), 281–301.

defined as a father-son relationship. This stresses the need for obedience to Yahweh on the part of the king. Traditionally, theologians have viewed the Davidic covenant as unconditional. It is true that the content of the covenant consists in the mighty promises made by Yahweh. Nonetheless, as verses 14–15 show, faithfulness is expected of the king, and these verses foreshadow the possibility of disloyalty on the part of the king, which will require discipline by Yahweh. In effect, verses 14–15 are saying that the covenant will be fulfilled not only by a faithful father alone (i.e., Yahweh keeping his promises), but also by a faithful son (i.e., the obedience of the king to Yahweh's Torah). The chiastic literary structure actually portrays in a visual manner the nature of the covenant: faithfulness and obedience in the father-son relationship is crucial, but it is supported on both sides by the faithfulness and sure promises of Yahweh to David of descendants, kingdom, and throne (the order is the same before and after the chiastic centre). This same chiastic literary structure is observed in Psalm 132:11b–12, a later commentary on the Davidic covenant. Verses 11a and 12b emphasise the promises of God and verse 12a speaks of the need for an obedient son. Thus once more, the promises of God undergird and support on both sides the need for a faithful, obedient son.

The consideration given by later texts to both divine and human obligations in the covenant will be noted shortly. First, however, the meaning of describing the relationship between Yahweh and the Davidic King as "father" and "son" must be fully explained. Factors involved in this include the use of the word בֵּן in Hebrew, the cultural context of kingship in Canaan and in the ancient Near East, the use of familial language in treaties, and the canonical context of the passage.[9]

---

[9] In the following literature consulted, the most useful article was that of Hoffmeier: John Day, "The Canaanite Inheritance of the Israelite Monarchy," in *King and Messiah in Israel and the Ancient Near East*, ed. John Day, JSOTSup 270 (Sheffield, UK: Sheffield Academic Press, 1998), 72–90; H. Frankfort, *Kingship and the Gods* (Chicago: University of Chicago Press, 1948), 300–301; Ivan Engnell, *Studies in Divine Kingship in the Ancient Near East*, 2nd ed. (Oxford: Blackwell, 1967); J. K. Hoffmeier, "The King as God's Son in Egypt and Israel," *Journal of the Society for the Study of Egyptian Antiquities* 24 (1994): 28–38; T. Jacobsen, "The Concept of Divine Parentage of the Ruler in the Stela of the Vultures," *Journal of Near Eastern Studies* 2 (1943): 119–121; T. Kleven, "Kingship in Ugarit (= *KTU* 1.16 I 1–23)," in *Ascribe to the Lord: Biblical and Other Studies in Memory of Peter C. Craigie*, ed. L. Eslinger and G. Taylor, JSOTSup 67 (Sheffield, UK: Sheffield Academic Press, 1988), 29–53; Marjo C. A. Korpel, *A Rift in the Clouds: Ugaritic and Hebrew Descriptions of the Divine* (Münster, Germany: Ugarit-Verlag, 1990), 252–261; A. Latto, "Second Samuel 7 and Ancient Near Eastern Royal Ideology," *Catholic Biblical Quarterly* 59 (1997): 244–269; T. N. D. Mettinger, *King and Messiah: The Civil and Sacral Legitimation of the Israelite Kings* (Lund, Sweden: Gleerup, 1976), 259–274; J. Tigay, *The Evolution of the Gilgamesh Epic* (Philadelphia: University of Pennsylvania Press, 1982), 152–156; Juan-Pablo Vita, "The Society of Ugarit," in *Handbook of Ugaritic Studies*, ed. W. G. E. Watson and N. Wyatt (Handbook of Oriental Studies I: The Near and Middle East 39; Leiden, Netherlands: Brill, 1999), 455–498; K. W. Whitelam, "Israelite Kingship: The Royal Ideology and Opponents," in *The World of Ancient Israel*, ed. R. E. Clements (Cambridge: Cambridge University Press, 1989), 119–140. I am grateful to John Walton for assistance in locating literature on this topic.

A literal, physical family relationship is clearly contrary to the context. Nonetheless, בֵּן, the term for "son" in Hebrew, has a much broader field of meaning than "son" in English. In an agrarian, preindustrial economy and society, trades were normally transmitted within a family setting. In this way, sons customarily did what their fathers did in addition to displaying common characteristics passed on from family setting, upbringing, and genetics. Thus the term "son" can be used to mean "possessing the characteristics" of something. In the Parable of the Vineyard in Isaiah 5:1, the beloved has a vineyard בְּקֶרֶן בֶּן־שָׁמֶן. The horn, i.e., a hillside or terrace on a mountain spur or slope, is "a son of fatness," i.e., characterised by abundant produce. An idiomatic English translation would be "a fertile hillside."

The ancient Near Eastern and Canaanite cultural context is significant. In Egypt, from at least 1650 B.C. onwards, people perceived the king as the image of god because he was the son of god. The emphasis was not on physical appearance. For example, a male king could be the image of a female goddess. What is stressed is that the behaviour of the king reflects the behaviour of the god. The king as the image of god reflects the characteristics and essential notions of the god.[10]

From Ugarit we have the story of King Keret, who is described as the son of El.[11] His excellent health must indicate his divine origin.[12]

The Old Testament records an Aramean king of Damascus known as Ben-Hadad.[13] By his name, he is the son of his god. The prosopography of the Amarna Correspondence and also at Ugarit shows a number of people from various levels of society whose names are of the format "son of Divine Name."[14] Thus we do not know if the name Ben-Hadad proves that he considered himself as the representative of Ba'al to his people. It might depend upon whether the name was a birth name from his parents or a name taken upon accession to the throne.[15]

---

[10] See P. E. Dion, "Ressemblance et image du Dieu," *Suppléments aux Dictionnaire de la Bible* X, ed. H. Cazelles and A. Feuillet, 55:365–403.

[11] See Gregorio del Olmo Lete and Joaquín Sanmartín, *A Dictionary of the Ugaritic Language in the Alphabetic Tradition*, trans. W. G. E. Watson, 2 vols. (Handbook of Oriental Studies I: The Near and Middle East 67; Leiden, Netherlands: Brill, 2003), 226. Also noteworthy: K. A. Kitchen, "The King List of Ugarit," *Ugarit Forschungen* 9 (1977): 131–142; T. Kleven, "Kingship in Ugarit (*KTU* 1.16 I 1–23)," in *Ascribe to the Lord: Biblical and Other Studies in Memory of Peter C. Craigie*, ed. L. Eslinger and G. Taylor, JSOTSup 67 (Sheffield, UK: Sheffield Academic Press, 1988), 29–53.

[12] Cf. also P. Kyle McCarter, Jr., "Two Bronze Arrowheads with Archaic Alphabetic Inscriptions," *Eretz-Israel* 26 (1999): 124*–128*.

[13] 1 Kings 15:18, 20; 2 Chronicles 16:2, 4. See M. Cogan, *1 Kings*, Anchor Bible 10 (New York: Doubleday, 2000), 399–400.

[14] See appendix to this chapter for a listing of all names in texts from Amarna and Ugarit of the type, "son of DN."

[15] Some argue that this is a dynastic name, but there is no clear evidence to support this. See K. Lawson Younger, Jr., "Shalmaneser III and Israel," in *Israel—Ancient Kingdom or Late Invention? Archaeology, Ancient Civilizations,*

The Canaanite and ancient Near Eastern culture shows that the notion of the king as a son of god was well established.[16] The meaning may have differed in Egypt, Canaan, and Mesopotamia, but the common denominator is the idea that the king represents the character of the god in some way to the people.

Also in the ancient Near East, those bound by suzerain-vassal treaties may refer to each other as father and son.[17] This has a significant bearing on 2 Samuel 7. Earlier theologians discussed covenants in terms of unconditional or conditional promises. More recently, covenants have been classified according to suzerain-vassal models on the one hand or royal grant models on the other. The former emphasises the obligations of the vassal king to the suzerain, the latter the obligations of the great king to his noble or vassal. The Davidic covenant has frequently been identified as a royal grant, yet it does not fit neatly either the unconditional-conditional categories or the more recent suzerain-vassal versus royal grant models.[18] Verses 14–15 clearly emphasise the need for obedience on the part of the son, yet the literary structure shows that this is undergirded primarily by the promises of the father.[19]

Second Samuel 7 must also be read according to the arrangement of the books in the Hebrew Canon.[20] A canonical reading indicates that the Davidic king is inheriting the role of both Adam as son of God and Israel as son of

---

and the Bible, ed. Daniel I. Block (Nashville: B&H, 2008), 225–256.

[16] See especially Engnell, *Studies in Divine Kingship in the Ancient Near East*, 80.

[17] For Mesopotamia, see, e.g., W. Heimpel, *Letters to the King of Mari: A New Translation, with Historical Introduction, Notes, and Commentary* (Winona Lake, IN: Eisenbrauns, 2003), p. 48, and note texts such as 26:347 (p. 311) and 26:372 (p. 326), where "father" is used to refer to the suzerain. For Egypt and Canaan, "father" and "son" are terms used in the Amarna Letters (EA) of parties in suzerain-vassal treaties, e.g., EA 44, 73, 82 in William L. Moran, ed. and trans., *The Amarna Letters* (Baltimore/London: John Hopkins University Press, 1987, 1992, 2002). Similar language comes from Phoenicia, as in the Kilamuwa and Karatepe inscriptions; see J. C. L. Gibson, *Textbook of Syrian Semitic Inscriptions: Phoenician Inscriptions*, 3 vols. (Oxford: Clarendon, 1982), 3:47–48, 130–131. I am indebted to Gregory Smith and Jim Harriman for helping me locate these texts.

[18] Anderson believes 2 Samuel 7 involves three overlapping concepts: adoption, covenant, and royal grant; A. A. Anderson, *2 Samuel*, WBC 11 (Waco, TX: Word, 1989), 122. A main proponent of the Davidic covenant as a royal grant is M. Weinfeld, "The Covenant of Grant in the Old Testament and in the Ancient Near East," *Journal of the American Oriental Society* 90/2 (1970): 184–203; and idem, "בְּרִית *bᵉrîth*," in *TDOT* 2:253–279. Yet evidence to demonstrate that 2 Samuel 7 lacks essential elements of the royal grant and may better fit a suzerain-vassal treaty model was provided by Paul Kalluveettil, *Declaration and Covenant*, Analecta Biblica 88 (Rome: Biblical Institute Press, 1982), 181. See also the critique of Weinfeld by Gary N. Knoppers, "Ancient Near Eastern Royal Grants and the Davidic Covenant: A Parallel?" *Journal of the American Oriental Society* 116/4 (1996): 670–697. Thus Anderson is more to the point. Recently Gordon Johnston has demonstrated that Weinfeld's dichotomy between royal grant and suzerain-vassal treaties is too rigid and not supported by a re-examination of the evidence. See Gordon Johnston, "A Critical Evaluation of Moshe Weinfeld's Approach to the Davidic Covenant in the Light of Ancient Near Eastern Royal Grants: What Did He Get Right & What Did He Get Wrong?" Unpublished paper presented at the Annual Meeting of the Evangelical Theological Society, November, 2011, San Francisco, CA.

[19] Note in particular the connection between servant and sonship in the context of covenant in 2 Kings 16:7; and see Stephen G. Dempster, "The Servant of the Lord," in *Central Themes in Biblical Theology: Mapping Unity in Diversity*, ed. Scott J. Hafemann and Paul R. House (Grand Rapids, MI: Baker, 2007), 136f.

[20] For the approach, see especially Stephen G. Dempster, *Dominion and Dynasty: A Biblical Theology of the Hebrew Bible*, NSBT 15 (Downers Grove, IL: InterVarsity Press, 2003).

God according to the instructions of Deuteronomy 17. This can be briefly reviewed and summarised at this point.

First to be considered is the fact that humans are created as the divine image according to Genesis 1:26–28. The divine image defines human ontology in terms of a covenant relationship with the creator God on the one hand and with the creation on the other hand. The former may be captured by the term "sonship" and is implied by Genesis 5:1–3:

> By juxtaposing the divine creation of Adam in the image of God and the subsequent human creation of Seth in the image of Adam, the transmission of the image of God through this genealogical line is implied, as well as the link between sonship and the image of God. As Seth is a son of Adam, so Adam is a son of God. Language is being stretched here, as a literal son of God is certainly not in view, but nevertheless the writer uses an analogy to make a point.[21]

The latter relationship, i.e., between humans and the creation, may be reflected in the terms kingship and servanthood. Earlier we noted that in the ninth-century Tell Fakhariyeh Inscription, צלמא ("image") refers to the king's majestic self and power in relation to his subjects, while דמותא ("likeness") refers to the king's petitionary role and relation to the deity.[22] The ancient Near Eastern data confirm and correspond exactly to this exegesis of the biblical text.

As Genesis 2:4–25 shows, the Adamic son is like a priest in a garden sanctuary. He must first learn the ways of God in order to exercise the rule of God as God himself would.[23]

Second, Israel inherited this Adamic role.[24] Yahweh refers to the nation as his son in Exodus 4:22–23. The divine purpose in the covenant established between God and Israel at Sinai is unfolded in Exodus 19:3–6. As a kingdom of priests, they will function to make the ways of God known to the nations and also to bring the nations into a right relationship to God. Since Israel is located geographically on the one and only communications link

---

[21] Ibid., 58–59.

[22] W. Randall Garr, "'Image' and 'Likeness' in the Inscription from Tell Fakhariyeh," *Israel Exploration Journal* 50/3–4 (2003): 227–234.

[23] See Gordon J. Wenham, "Sanctuary Symbolism in the Garden of Eden Story," in *I Studied Inscriptions from before the Flood: Ancient Near Eastern, Literary, and Linguistic Approaches to Genesis 1–11*, ed. R. S. Hess and D. T. Tsumura, Sources for Biblical and Theological Study 4 (Winona Lake, IN: Eisenbrauns: 1994), 399–404; William J. Dumbrell, *The Search for Order: Biblical Eschatology in Focus* (Grand Rapids, MI: Baker, 1994), 24–25; and M. Hutter, "Adam als Gärtner und König (Gen. 2:8, 15)," *Biblische Zeitschrift* 30 (1985): 258–262.

[24] Exodus 15:17 shows that Canaan becomes for Israel what the garden sanctuary was for Adam.

between the great superpowers of the ancient world, in this position she will show the nations how to have a right relationship to God, how to treat each other in a truly human way, and how to be faithful stewards of the earth's resources. This is the meaning of Israel's sonship.

Third, Deuteronomy 17 intimates that the king will be the leader in this role. Verses 16–20 describe the manner in which the future king is to exercise his responsibilities. After three negative commands in verses 16–17, verses 18–20 specify three positive commands, all relating to Torah: (1) the king shall copy the Torah; (2) the king shall have the Torah with him; and (3) the king shall read the Torah.[25] In other words, the only positive requirement is that the king embody Torah as a model citizen.[26] This is exactly the point of the father-son relationship set out in 2 Samuel 7.

The response of David to this revelation through the prophet Nathan in verses 18–29 reveals David's own understanding of the covenant. In this regard, the problematic verse 19 is critical. In verse 18 David expresses the fact that he and his house have been highly exalted. Now in verse 19, however, he says that this honour is dwarfed by the promises concerning the distant future: *zō 't tôrat hā'ādām*. This clause has been enigmatic for scholars. The NIV rendering, "Is this your usual way of dealing with man?" represents a standard interpretation. However this interpretation is problematic. First, reading the clause as an affirmative, declarative statement is far more normal when no contextual or grammatical signals exist to indicate a question.[27] Second, although "manner" is suggested as the possible meaning of *tôrâ* by the Oxford Lexicon,[28] "instruction" or "law" is by far the first meaning that comes to mind. In the bound phrase, the free member may be subjective or objective. When the free member is a person, it is frequently a subjective genitive, but construing it as an objective genitive gives good sense here.[29] Thus we should translate, "This is the instruction for humanity." Dumbrell

---

[25] I am indebted to Daniel I. Block for the privilege of consulting a preliminary version of his new commentary, *Deuteronomy*, NIV Application Commentary (Grand Rapids, MI: Zondervan, 2012).

[26] See Daniel I. Block, "The Burden of Leadership: The Mosaic Paradigm of Kingship (Deuteronomy 17:14–20)," in *How I Love Your Torah, O Lord! Studies in the Book of Deuteronomy* (Eugene, OR: Cascade, 2011), 118–139 (originally published in *Bibliotheca Sacra* 162 [2005]: 259–278).

[27] Walter C. Kaiser, Jr., "The Blessing of David: The Charter for Humanity" in *The Law and the Prophets: Old Testament Studies Prepared in Honor of Oswald Thompson Allis*, ed. John H. Skilton, Milton C. Fisher, and Leslie W. Sloat (Philadelphia: Presbyterian & Reformed, 1974), 311–312.

[28] So F. Brown, S. R. Driver, and C. Briggs, eds., *A Hebrew and English Lexicon of the Old Testament* (Oxford: Clarendon, 1907; repr., 1953), s.v. Yet 2 Samuel 7:19 is the only instance provided for this meaning of *tôrâ*.

[29] Fokkelman follows the JPS translation in construing the clause as precative, but nonetheless views *hā'ādām* as objective: "May that be the law for the people." See J. P. Fokkelman, *Narrative Art and Poetry in the Books of Samuel: A Full Interpretation Based on Stylistic and Structural Analyses: Vol. III: Throne and City (II Sam. 2–8 & 21–24)* (Assen, Netherlands: Van Gorcum, 1990), 240 n. 67, 242.

and Kaiser note that the expression "law of man" has been shown to have parallels in the similar Akkadian phrase, *tērīt nīshē*, which has the sense of a "charter for humanity."[30]

What could David mean when he says that the covenant revealed through Nathan is Yahweh's instruction for humanity? In verses 14–15 the human obligations in the relationship between Yahweh and the Davidic king are indicated by establishing a father-son relationship. We saw that, in the ancient Near East, a country or region was thought to be ruled by the god of that territory, and the king was considered the representative of the local god. This explains how the king could be called the son of God. Therefore, as the divine son, the Davidic king was to effect the divine instruction or torah in the nation as a whole and was, as a result, a mediator of the Mosaic Torah. However, since the god whom the Davidic king represented was not limited to a local region or territory, but was the creator God and Sovereign of the whole world, the rule of the Davidic king would have repercussions for *all* the nations, not just for Israel. This is developed in Psalm 2 and many other psalms, but is *already* suggested in 2 Samuel 7. Thus, faithfulness on the part of the Davidic Son would effect the divine rule in the entire world, much as God intended for humanity in the covenant of creation as indicated by the divine image in Genesis 1:26ff. This, I submit, is the logic behind David's response in verse 19, and this is why he claims that a covenant that makes the Davidic king son of God is the instrument of bringing Yahweh's Torah to all the nations. David's own understanding of divine sonship is clearly indicated by his statement in 7:19 that the covenant is God's charter or instruction for humankind.

The parallel text in 1 Chronicles 17:17 is problematic textually, but instructive. The clause corresponding to *zō't tôrat hā'ādām* is *ûrĕ'îtanî kĕtôr hā'ādām hamma'ălāh*. The most thorough treatment of the problem and the best proposal for the meaning of *tôr* (not an error for *tôrâ*) is in *Critique Textuelle de l'Ancien Testament*: "you see me according to the rank of the man placed high."[31] This is equivalent to the last words of David in

---

[30] Dumbrell, *Covenant and Creation*, 151–152; and Walter C. Kaiser, Jr., "Blessing of David: The Charter for Humanity," 314–315.

[31] Dominique Barthélemy, *Critique Textuelle de l'Ancien Testament*, 1. Josué, Juges, Ruth, Samuel, Rois, Chroniques, Esdras, Néhémie, Esther, Rapport final du Comité pour l'analyse textuelle de l'Ancien Testament hébreu institué par l'Alliance Biblique Universelle, établi en coopération avec Alexander R. Hulst, Norbert Lohfink, William D. McHardy, H. Peter Rüger, coéditeur, James A. Sanders, coéditeur. Orbis Biblicus et Orientalis 50/1 (Göttingen, Germany: Vandenhoeck & Ruprecht, 1982), 457–458.

2 Samuel 23:1–7, where he refers to Nathan's oracle as a בְּרִית (v. 5) and calls himself "the man set on high" (הַגֶּבֶר הֻקַם עָל) in verse 1. The statement in Psalm 89:28 (89:27 EV) is similar:

> I will also appoint him my firstborn,
> the most exalted of the kings of the earth. (NIV)

The second line explicates the meaning of the Davidic sonship as being "the most exalted of the kings of the earth." All of these texts represent interpretations of verse 19 of 2 Samuel 7, and show that since the god who is represented by the Davidic king is both supreme and universal, the Davidic king has the highest rank among human beings. Despite critical textual problems,[32] 2 Samuel 7:19 is the key to the universalisation of the messianic vision in the psalms and prophets.[33]

In the response section, 2 Samuel 7:18–29, note how the word "good" can be used to refer to the covenant. The comment of Höver-Johag is apt:

> In 2 S. 7:28, *ṭôḇâ* refers to the covenant of Yahweh with the house of David (cf. v. 29; 1 S. 25:30; 2 Ch. 24:16; Akk. *dabābu ṭābūta* = Heb. *dabbēr ṭôḇ*).[34]

This demonstrates that the term *běrît* need not occur in a text for the author to be speaking about a covenant.

LATER INTERPRETATIONS OF 2 SAMUEL 7

Brief observations are now in order on the consideration given by later texts to both divine and human obligations in the covenant between Yahweh and

---

[32] On which see P. Kyle McCarter, *II Samuel*, Anchor Bible 9 (New York: Doubleday, 1984), 233; and Hans J. Stoebe, *Das zweite Buch Samuelis* (Kommentar zum Alten Testament VIII 2; Gutersloh, Germany: Gutersloher, 1994), 231.

[33] I owe this precise wording to Daniel I. Block. William M. Schniedewind, *Society and the Promise to David: The Reception History of 2 Samuel 7:1–17* (Oxford: Oxford University Press, 1999) is a major contribution made recently to the study of 2 Samuel 7. His approach focuses on diachronic and synchronic aspects of interpretation as well as the function of the literature in the society at the time and yields important insights. While he is to be commended for dating the texts earlier than previous scholars, his analysis of editorial layers in the history of the text is seriously flawed because he does not consider the linguistic science of discourse grammar/text linguistics (See, e.g., S. G. Dempster, "Linguistic Features of Hebrew Narrative: A Discourse Analysis of Narrative from the Classical Period" [PhD diss., University of Toronto, 1985]). It is also strange that, in a work dedicated to reception history, his analysis is limited to verses 1–17 of 2 Samuel 7, and he does not consider the first step in the reception history: the response of King David himself to the promise in verses 18–29. His brief comments on the connection between the promise to David and Isaiah 55 follow the standard view and do not illuminate the problems under discussion here.

[34] I. Höver-Johag, "טוֹב *ṭôḇ*," in *TDOT* 5:296–317, esp. 312. For discussion of the cognate Akkadian phrases, see idem, "טוֹב *ṭôḇ*," in *TDOT* 5: 296–317, esp. 301–302. In addition, note in the Sefire Treaty from the eighth century B.C. that one may break the treaty by overturning "good" and by establishing "evil" (KAI 222 [Sefire I] C. 16–23). I am indebted to Chip Hardy for help on this point.

David.[35] These are also crucial in a correct interpretation of Isaiah 55:3, and frequently scholars have depended heavily on intertextual links particularly with Psalm 89. In one of the most enlightened treatments of intertextual links between Psalm 89 and Isaiah 55:3, K. Heim addresses concerns of scholars who hold that Nathan's oracle has been reinterpreted or altered in different directions based on current political realities in Israel and Judah. Heim responds to M. Fishbane as follows:

> Fishbane's notion that the psalm's developments or changes were intro-duced mainly to protect the validity of the original oracle loses convic-tion when we note that more effective changes to this effect could have been introduced. Yet Psalm 89 still maintains that the Davidic promise-covenant is unconditional, although changing the unconditional nature of the psalm into a conditional one would have brought the covenant more in line with political reality and resolved the theological problem. Such a transformation would have been part of the psalmist's toolbox, for many other texts employed exactly this type of change (e.g., Ps. 132.12; 1 Kgs 2.3–4, 6.12, 8.25).[36]

Heim's main point is well taken. Yet what has not been noted sufficiently in recent scholarship is that, while later writers do adapt and apply Nathan's oracle to their present context and theological tensions, their exegesis is more firmly rooted in the original oracle than is frequently allowed.[37] This is because the oracle itself has elements that are both conditional and uncondi-tional. Later writers may focus more on the unconditional aspects found in verses 11b–13 and 16 (e.g., 2 Sam. 22:51=Ps. 18:51 [18:50 EV]), or on the conditional aspects found in verses 14–15 (Ps. 132:12; 1 Kings 2:3–4; 6:12; 8:25; 2 Chron. 6:16; 7:17–18; Jer. 22:1–5, 24). Indeed in Psalm 89, which is so focused on the unconditional aspect, the conditional side does surface. Two verses in particular should be highlighted:

PSALM 89:31–34 (89:30–33 EV)

[31] אִם־יַעַזְבוּ בָנָיו תּוֹרָתִי   וּבְמִשְׁפָּטַי לֹא יֵלֵכוּן׃
[32] אִם־חֻקֹּתַי יְחַלֵּלוּ   וּמִצְוֹתַי לֹא יִשְׁמֹרוּ׃

---

[35] For a recent study of texts related to 2 Samuel 7 governed by the methodology of redaction criticism, see Petri Kasari, *Nathan's Promise in 2 Samuel 7 and Related Texts* (Helsinki: Finnish Exegetical Society, 2009).

[36] Knut M. Heim, "The (God-)forsaken King of Psalm 89: A Historical and Intertextual Enquiry," in *King and Messiah in Israel and the Ancient Near East: Proceedings of the Oxford Old Testament Seminar*, ed. John Day, JSOTSup 270 (Sheffield, UK: Sheffield Academic Press, 1998), 296–322.

[37] It is not uncommon in recent studies to set the different texts addressing the covenant with David as disparate traditions at odds with one another, e.g., Steven L. McKenzie, *Covenant* (St. Louis: Chalice, 2000).

וּבִנְגָעִים עֲוֹנָם: [33] וּפָקַדְתִּי בְשֵׁבֶט פִּשְׁעָם

וְלֹא־אֲשַׁקֵּר בֶּאֱמוּנָתִי: [34] וְחַסְדִּי לֹא־אָפִיר מֵעִמּוֹ

[30] if his sons abandon my Torah
   and do not walk in my ordinances
[31] if they profane my statutes
   and do not keep my commands
[32] I will punish their transgression with a rod
   and their offence with strokes
[33] but my covenant loyalty I will not cancel from him
   and I will not prove false in my faithfulness

Verse 31 relates directly to Deuteronomy 17 and emphasises that the Davidic king must know and keep Torah in order for this to be the basis of his rule of the nation (as in Isaiah 11:3a). While the emphasis is on the faithfulness of Yahweh, the need for Torah-keeping on the part of the king is duly noted.

PSALM 89:50 (89:49 EV)

נִשְׁבַּעְתָּ לְדָוִד בֶּאֱמוּנָתֶךָ:   אַיֵּה חֲסָדֶיךָ הָרִאשֹׁנִים אֲדֹנָי

Where are your former *ḥăsādîm*, O Lord,
   which you swore to David in your faithfulness?

This text appeals to the acts of *ḥesed* promised by Yahweh in the Davidic covenant and performed by the Lord for at least some of the descendants of David, although apparently not in the life situation of the psalmist. Williamson proposed that when the referent is God, it is normal to think of him as demonstrating *ḥesed* and so the subjective genitive is standard. He argued that in the first instance where the referent is certainly postulated of a human, the meaning is spelled out to avoid misunderstanding.[38] I would argue that the pronominal referent is normally subjective, regardless of whether God or a human is the referent. Here, the pronominal suffix on Hebrew *ḥăsādêkā* must be read as subjective genitive, as Williamson acknowledges.[39] But in order for the psalmist to clarify that the acts of covenant kindness performed by Yahweh are previous in time and promised in the Davidic covenant, the modifiers "former" and a relative clause are added to the bound phrase. Thus

---

[38] See above for analysis of his discussion of Nehemiah 13:14.
[39] H. G. M. Williamson, "'Sure Mercies of David,'" 36.

clarifying modifiers can be added regardless of whether the referent is divine or human.

First Kings 3:6 and parallel 2 Chronicles 1:8 are illuminating in revealing Solomon's understanding of the role of David's faithfulness in the fulfilment of Yahweh's promise:

וַיֹּאמֶר שְׁלֹמֹה אַתָּה עָשִׂיתָ עִם־עַבְדְּךָ דָוִד אָבִי חֶסֶד גָּדוֹל
כַּאֲשֶׁר הָלַךְ לְפָנֶיךָ בֶּאֱמֶת וּבִצְדָקָה וּבְיִשְׁרַת לֵבָב עִמָּךְ
וַתִּשְׁמָר־לוֹ אֶת־הַחֶסֶד הַגָּדוֹל הַזֶּה
וַתִּתֶּן־לוֹ בֵן יֹשֵׁב עַל־כִּסְאוֹ כַּיּוֹם הַזֶּה:

> Solomon answered, "You have shown great kindness to your servant, my father David, because he was faithful to you and righteous and upright in heart. You have continued this great kindness to him and have given him a son to sit on his throne this very day." (NIV)

Here Yahweh performs his covenant obligation, but David performs his as well, and thus the promise is fulfilled.

Lastly, before considering the exegetical issues in Isaiah 55, 2 Chronicles 6:42 must be treated as the only other place where the bound phrase *ḥasdê dāwīd* occurs. Without repeating the excellent observations of Beuken,[40] we may note here the emphasis is not only on Yahweh fulfilling his covenant obligations, but also on the Davidic son fulfilling his.

The first section of 2 Chronicles 6 entails the blessing of Solomon in verses 1–11. Verse 4 contains references to Yahweh's promises to David. Two promises are mentioned in verse 5: (1) choosing a city for the temple, and (2) choosing a leader over Israel. Then verse 6 observes the fulfilment of these two promises: (1) Yahweh chose Jerusalem for the temple and (2) he chose David to rule his people Israel. Verses 7–11 go on to explain why it would be David's son and not David who would build the temple that stores the documents of the Mosaic Torah or Israelite covenant. The explanation appeals directly to Nathan's oracle. The two themes, choice of Jerusalem for temple and choice of David for leader established in verses 1–11, are important for understanding the Chronicler at the end of the prayer.

The second section records the prayer of Solomon in verses 12–42. In verse 14 Solomon begins by praising Yahweh as the God who keeps

---

[40] W. A. M. Beuken, "Isa. 55,3–5: The Reinterpretation of David," *Bijdragen* 35 (1975): 49–64.

covenant and *hesed* to those who walk before him in complete devotion. This is central. Certainly the covenant with David entails promises that Yahweh must keep to be faithful. But the oracle through Nathan makes clear that Yahweh will keep them only to and through a faithful son. Therefore, from the Chronicler's point of view, the promises of Yahweh will be fulfilled only when the throne is occupied by an obedient son. What the subsequent course of history shows is that Yahweh must not only keep the promises but also provide the obedient son, if the covenant is to be maintained.

Verse 15 emphasises that Yahweh spoke with his mouth and fulfilled with his hands the commitments he made in regard to Solomon's father, David.

In verse 16 Solomon asks Yahweh to fulfill his promises to David concerning David's sons only if the sons faithfully follow Torah, *as David did*. Verse 17 repeats the request for Yahweh to fulfill his promise.

To this point Solomon is calling upon Yahweh to be faithful to his promises to David, but he has underlined (1) the obedience of David and (2) the necessity of the obedience of the sons for the promises to work.

Verses 18–40 constitute a request that God hear prayers made in and toward this temple. The various situations are all based on the Mosaic covenant (Exodus and Deuteronomy).

At the end of the prayer something interesting happens in the Chronicler's account, which is different from the prayer in 1 Kings 8. First, 2 Chronicles 6:39b and 40 quickly summarise verses 50–53 in 1 Kings 8. Then in 2 Chronicles 6:41–42, the Chronicler quotes, almost verbatim, Psalm 132:8–10. Beuken's comments on this use of Psalm 132 need not be repeated here. His point may be strengthened, however, by a few significant observations. When we recall that the book of Psalms was Israel's Hymnal, the reader of Chronicles immediately picks up Psalm 132 as part of the context in 2 Chronicles 6. This is because Psalm 132 addresses the concerns raised at the beginning of 2 Chronicles 6: (1) the choice of Zion for the temple and (2) the choice of David and his sons as leaders of Israel. From the historical point of view of the Chronicler, both of these have been in grave jeopardy. Yet Psalm 132 is a *prayer* for Yahweh to keep his oath to David based upon a faithful David. This is the clear meaning of verse 12 and especially of the phrase in verse 10, "on account of David your servant." The Hebrew for "on account of" is the preposition *ba'ăbûr*, employed in 49 instances in the Hebrew Bible: in 18 instances *ba'ăbûr* is bound to an infinitive or prefixed verb form and means "in order that." In the 31 remaining instances the preposition is bound to a proper noun/pronoun or suffixed verb form[41] and means "on account of" or "for the sake of."[42] In every case where the preposition is bound to a proper noun the prepositional phrase means "on account of what a person did" and not "on account of doing something on behalf of a person." An interesting confirmation of the use of *ba'ăbûr* is found in Genesis 26:24, where *ba'ăbûr 'abrāhām* is a shorthand equivalent of *'ēqeb 'ăšer šāma' 'abrāhām bĕqōlî* (because Abraham obeyed my voice) in Genesis 26:5.[43] In 2 Chronicles 6:42 the phrase *ḥasdê dāwîd* substitutes for *ba'ăbûr dāwîd* in the citation of Psalm 132:10 and therefore probably intended the same thing.[44] In this way the Chronicler has Solomon praying for Yahweh to keep his promises on account of the faithfulness of David. It would work well in the context that Solomon is appealing for Yahweh to be faithful because of the obedience of his father.[45] However, in the context of Chronicles, with its messianic focus, this is more likely a hope in a future king who will at last be an obedient son, so that the promises may be fulfilled by Yahweh.

In sum, some of the later texts emphasise the part of the son (1 Kings 2:2–4; 6:12; 8:25; 9:4–9; 2 Chron. 6:42; 7:17; Ps. 132:11–12) while others stress the faithfulness of the father (2 Sam. 22:51; 1 Kings 3:6; 8:15, 24–26; 1 Chron. 17:13; 2 Chron. 1:8, 6:4, 10, 14–15, 16; 7:10; Ps. 89:28–37; Jer. 33:19–26) in the covenant relationship.

INTERPRETATION OF ISAIAH 55:3

> [3] Incline your ear, and come to me;
>   hear, that your soul may live;
> and I will make with you an everlasting covenant,
>   my steadfast, sure love for David.
> [4] Behold, I made him a witness to the peoples,
>   a leader and commander for the peoples.
> [5] Behold, you shall call a nation that you do not know,
>   and a nation that did not know you shall run to you,
> because of the LORD your God, and of the Holy One of Israel,
>   for he has glorified you. (Isa. 55:3–5, ESV)

---

[41] The only occurrence of *ba'ăbûr* bound to a suffixed verb in MT is Micah 2:10.

[42] Analysis based on A. Even-Shoshan, *A New Concordance of the Bible*, 3 vols. (Jerusalem: Kiryat-Sefer, 1982). About five years after analysing all instances, I had forgotten my work and asked Stephen Dempster about the use of *ba'ăbûr*. He analysed all instances and came up with the same analysis independently. He noted Exodus 9:16 as an excellent example of a minimal pair showing the two uses of *ba'ăbûr*. Personal communication, January 27, 2010.

[43] This insight I owe to Stephen Dempster.

[44] This was noted by Beuken, but the point is strengthened by the above considerations on the use of *ba'ăbûr*.

[45] So recently (*pace* Williamson) G. Gakuru, *An Inner-Biblical Exegetical Study of the Davidic Covenant and the Dynastic Oracle* (Lewiston, NY: Edwin Mellen, 2000), 222.

Isaiah 55:3–5 is an extremely important text in relation to understanding both the Davidic covenant and the new covenant in Scripture. Debate has raged for some time over the interpretation of the phrase *ḥasdê dāwīd* in verse 3, a phrase rendered in the King James Version by "the sure mercies of David." We will engage the major players in the debate and challenge the standard view by rethinking the evidence from the grammar of the Hebrew language and from the versions. We will argue, contrary to the consensus of scholarship, that the "sure mercies" are *by David* rather than *for David*. Moreover, by properly relating the text in a canonical and theological trajectory from Genesis 1 through Deuteronomy 17 and 2 Samuel 7 to Isaiah 55:3, the passage in Isaiah can be interpreted as applying 2 Samuel 7:19 to the future Davidic servant king who brings about the everlasting covenant in Isaiah 53–54. The citation in Acts 13 is seen as providing strong support for this interpretation.

THE CONSTRUCT PHRASE IN SCHOLARLY DEBATE

In 1965 Caquot challenged the standard view[46] that *dāwīd* is to be construed as object in the bound noun phrase *ḥasdê dāwīd* in Isaiah 55:3 and argued instead that David is to be understood as the subject of the acts of covenant kindness and love.[47] His analysis was adopted and developed further by Beuken in 1974,[48] but was rejected in 1978 by Hugh Williamson[49] and by Walter Kaiser in 1989.[50] Recent commentators follow Williamson directly or simply maintain the standard view.[51]

---

[46] For the standard view, cf. "H.-J. Zobel, "חֶסֶד *ḥesed*," in *TDOT* 5:44–64; and H. J. Stoebe, "חֶסֶד *ḥesed*," in *Theological Lexicon of the Old Testament*, ed. Ernst Jenni and Claus Westermann, trans. Mark E. Biddle, 3 vols. (Peabody, MA: Hendrickson, 1997), 2:449–464. For the meaning of *ḥesed*, a plethora of studies have appeared in the last fifty years. Still fundamental is Nelson Glueck, *Hesed in the Bible*, trans. Alfred Gottschalk and ed. Elias L. Epstein (Cincinnati: Hebrew Union College Press, 1927, 1967). For a recent study, see Sung-Hun Lee, "Lament and the Joy of Salvation in the Lament Psalms," in *The Book of Psalms: Composition and Reception*, ed. Peter W. Flint and Patrick D. Miller, Jr., Supplements to Vetus Testamentum 94 (Leiden, Netherlands: Brill, 2005).

[47] A. Caquot, "Les «Graces de David». A Propos d'Isaie 55/3b," *Semitica* 15 (1965): 45–59.

[48] W. A. M. Beuken, "Isa. 55,3–5: The Reinterpretation of David," *Bijdragen* 35 (1975): 49–64.

[49] H. G. M. Williamson, "'The Sure Mercies of David': Subjective or Objective Genitive?" *Journal of Semitic Studies* 23 (1978): 31–49. Williamson's interpretation of Isaiah 55:3–5 is essentially unaltered in more recent statements; see H. G. M. Williamson, *Variations on a Theme: King, Messiah and Servant in the Book of Isaiah* (Carlisle, UK: Paternoster, 1998), 113–131.

[50] Walter C. Kaiser, Jr., "The Unfailing Kindnesses Promised to David: Isaiah 55.3," *JSOT* 45 (1989): 91–98.

[51] E.g., John N. Oswalt, *The Book of Isaiah: Chapters 40–66* (Grand Rapids, MI: Eerdmans, 1998), 438. Also maintaining the standard view are Klaus Baltzer, *Deutero-Isaiah*, Hermeneia (Minneapolis: Fortress, 2001), 470; Joseph Blenkinsopp, *Isaiah 40–55*, Anchor Bible 19 (New York: Doubleday, 2000), 367, 370; Walter Brueggemann, *Isaiah 40–66* (Louisville: Westminster John Knox, 1998), 158–159; Gakuru, *Inner-Biblical Exegetical Study of the Davidic Covenant and the Dynastic Oracle*, 205–207, 229; John Goldingay, *Isaiah*, New International Biblical Commentary (Peabody, MA: Hendrickson, 2001), 313–314; J. Alec Motyer, *The Prophecy of Isaiah: An Introduction and Commentary* (Downers Grove, IL: InterVarsity Press, 1993), 121; Christopher Seitz, *Word Without End: The Old Testament as Abiding Theological Witness* (Grand Rapids, MI: Eerdmans, 1998), 160.

First, Williamson scrutinises the ancient versions and concludes that the Septuagint, contrary to claims by Caquot, in fact supports construing David as objective genitive (in the phrase *ḥasdê dāwīd*). He further maintains that not only the Vulgate, as Caquot admits, but also the Targum preserves the ambiguity of the Hebrew. Only the Peshitta supports the subjective genitive. Later we shall return to the ancient versions, and in particular, to the Septuagint of Isaiah 55:3 and the citation of it in Acts 13:34.

Second, Williamson considers the claim from grammatical observations that when *ḥesed* is bound to a noun or pronominal suffix, virtually everywhere the free member or pronominal suffix indicates the subject or agent of the kindness. With Caquot he notes that the plural of *ḥesed* occurs eighteen times in the Hebrew Bible. Apart from Genesis 32:11, the noun is always in a bound phrase and the free member is always subjective—aside from the disputed passages, Isaiah 55:3 and 2 Chronicles 6:42. But do these facts, he argues, necessarily require that we read Isaiah 55:3 as subjective?

As an alternative approach, Williamson claims that in every text that precedes Isaiah 55:3 chronologically, the one who exercises *ḥăsādîm* is God. Thus, the readers of Isaiah would have construed the phrase in 55:3 as referring to the covenant loyalty of God rather than of David. He bolsters this by asserting that in the first instance where *ḥăsādîm* is certainly postulated of a human, the meaning is spelled out to avoid misunderstanding: *ḥăsāday 'ăšer 'āśîtî* (Neh. 13:14). Williamson then turns attention to the far more common singular use of *ḥesed* and argues that in Psalm 5:8 (5:7 EV), Ezra 7:28, 9:9, Nehemiah 13:22b, and especially in Psalm 144:2 and Jonah 2:9 (2:8 EV) we have examples where the objective use is possible, probable, or even certain.

Lastly, Williamson considers the context of Isaiah 55:3. He argues that the use of *ḥesed* and *ne'ĕmān* link the passage strongly to 2 Samuel 7 and critiques the proposals of Beuken and Caquot to demonstrate that the context emphasises the faithfulness of God to David and not the reverse. Evidence is brought forward to show that *ḥasdê dāwīd hanne'ĕmānîm* must be read in apposition to *bĕrît 'ôlām*, and that construing the text this way is not only the most natural reading but also requires the interpretation that David is objective rather than subjective.

In responding to Williamson we must begin by affirming that both Beuken and Caquot are correct in observing that the normal way to construe

---

Occasionally one encounters interpreters influenced by postmodernism who think they can have it both ways (objective and subjective).

the bound phrase is to interpret David as agent or subject. Out of eighteen instances in the plural in the Old Testament, only two are considered objective, and after Williamson thoroughly scoured the materials, out of 228 occurrences of the singular, only six can be found that may possibly or probably be read as objective.[52] There is no point in debating the interpretation of these six texts. The extreme paucity and debatable interpretation of these texts only supports the contention of Beuken and Caquot and strongly suggests that arguments to the contrary constitute special pleading. Linguistic usage demands, then, that the first notion to enter the mind of the native reader is to construe the free member as subject. That the free member in Isaiah 55:3 and 2 Chronicles 6:42 is human and not divine is an interesting point that does not necessarily support construing the free member as objective.[53] Williamson's argument that in the first case where *ḥăsādîm* is certainly postulated of a man, the meaning is spelled out to avoid misunderstanding, *ḥăsāday 'ăšer 'āśîtî* (Neh. 13:14), fails to observe that the construction in Nehemiah 13:14 is basically the same as in Genesis 32:11 (32:10 EV), where God is agent of the acts of loyal love. The addition of the relative sentence in Nehemiah 13:14 is motivated only by the fact that it emphasises the agent and does not function to avoid misunderstanding over whether the pronominal suffix is objective or subjective. In Genesis 32:11, however, Williamson fails to note that the speaker is the recipient of the acts of loyal love, and this may be the reason why here, and only here, *ḥesed* (in the plural) is not and perhaps, according to usage, cannot be used in a construct phrase.

The use of *ḥesed* in bound phrases, however, is only one factor in the correct interpretation of Isaiah 55:3. Other important contextual, grammatical, and lexical considerations are as follows. The most natural reading of the bound phrase in relation to the whole is to construe it in apposition to the *bĕrît 'ôlām* of verse 3a. This Williamson has defended well, as have many scholars before him. For דָּוִד, one normally thinks of the historical person who was king over Israel after Saul and who began the only lasting dynasty in Israelite monarchy. Here, then, is the *crux* of the matter. We know of a covenant relationship established between Yahweh, God of Israel, on the one hand and David and his descendants on the other (2 Samuel 7). Yet what *ḥăsādîm*, i.e.,

---

[52] 129 of the 228 singular instances of *ḥesed* occur in a bound phrase where the free member is a person (see A. Even-Shoshan, *A New Concordance of the Bible*, [Jerusalem: Kiryat-Sefer, 1982], s.v. חֶסֶד).

[53] In 4QMMT e.25 David is called איש חסדים (see E. Qimron and J. Strugnell, *Miqṣat Ma'aṣe Ha-Torah*, Qumran Cave 4, vol. 5; Discoveries in the Judean Desert, 10 (Oxford: Clarendon, 1994), 62–63, 91). The editors correctly render this "a man of righteous deeds." The text shows an exegesis of Isaiah 55:3 at Qumran which construed the free member of the bound phrase as subjective. I am indebted to Simon Gathercole for drawing my attention to this text.

what acts of covenant kindness on the part of David or his sons, what acts fulfilling the human obligations in this covenant, could possibly constitute an everlasting covenant and so satisfy the context of Isaiah 55? Here is where scholars are driven to consider other possibilities, and the conventional interpretation has for the most part opted for construing דָּוִד in the bound phrase as objective. At this point rebuttals of and rejoinders to Beuken and Caquot by Williamson and Kaiser are persuasive. Acts of grace and kindness by King David do not satisfy the context in Isaiah 55. Yet neither is the conventional interpretation free of problems. Williamson understands the phrase to mean God's covenant faithfulness to David,[54] "giving rise to such translations as 'my steadfast, sure love for David' (RSV)."[55] The NIV renders "my faithful love promised to David." Kaiser's translation is similar: "the unfailing kindnesses promised to David."[56] The fact of the matter, however, is that reading David as objective genitive does not yield a translation such as that of Kaiser or the NIV. The term *ḥasdê* in the bound phrase means the acts performed either by David (subjective) or for David (objective). *Ḥasdê dāwīd* cannot, therefore, mean "blessings" or "faithfulness promised" to David. It can only mean actions that fulfill covenant obligations/stipulations.

EXEGESIS OF ISAIAH 55:3

We may now turn directly to the exegesis of Isaiah 55:3. At once the major problem for Williamson, who readily admits that *ḥesed* nearly always governs a subjective genitive, is to understand how acts of *ḥesed* performed by David can possibly satisfy the context of Isaiah 55:3. Here one can sympathise with objections raised by Williamson and others to the proposals of Beuken and Caquot. Nonetheless, there is a third option, and that is to construe "David" as a rubric for the future king who will arise from the Davidic dynasty and not as the founder of the line.[57] Clear evidence exists for this in the context in that Isaiah 55:3b is expressed in the future tense. In 55:4, however, although נְתַתִּיו is a perfect tense, it refers to the fact that Yahweh *has planned* a *future* role for the Davidic king to play. This interpretation fully preserves standard usage for the Hebrew perfect and shows how the future orientation is maintained.

---

54 H. G. M. Williamson, "'Sure Mercies of David,'" 44.
55 Ibid., 31.
56 Kaiser, "Unfailing Kindness Promised to David," 91.
57 George Adam Smith seems to favour this view; see George Adam Smith, *The Book of Isaiah*, 2 vols. (New York: Doubleday, 1927), 2:430–431 and n. 1.

This option was considered—and rejected—previously by F. Delitzsch and more recently by Walter Kaiser following Delitzsch.[58] Delitzsch says, "the directly Messianic application of the name 'David' is to be objected to, on the ground that the Messiah is never so called without further remark."[59] This objection is not serious. It wrongly assumes that the manner of reference in Isaiah must match that in other prophets and fails to note the patterns of reference in Isaiah itself. The name David in Isaiah refers elsewhere to the historical personage in the expression, "the city of David" (22:9; 29:1). In addressing Hezekiah, Isaiah calls Yahweh the "God of David your father" (38:5). However, the phrases "house/tent of David" (7:2; 7:13; 16:5; 22:22) and "throne of David" (9:7) are expressions used to refer to descendants of David, whether in the author's present or future. Thus the use of the name David in Isaiah shows that a future descendant is uppermost in the author's thought. D. I. Block's recent study "My Servant David: Ancient Israel's Vision of the Messiah" provides strong evidence that need not be repeated here that the figure of the servant of Yahweh in Isaiah is both Davidic and royal.[60] The figurative language in which the Davidic king and kingdom are portrayed as a majestic tree cut down (Isa. 6:13) and the reference to the shoot and root in Isaiah 53:2 clearly connect this text to the vision of the future king who is the shoot and root of Jesse in Isaiah 11:1, 10. As Motyer notes, "the reference to *Jesse* indicates that the *shoot* is not just another king in David's line but rather another David."[61] The connection between the future king of Isaiah 9 and 11 and the servant of Yahweh in Isaiah 53 in the history of interpretation is as old as the Septuagint. The rendering of *yônēq* in 53:2 by παιδίον shows a clear connection with 9:5 (9:6 EV) in the mind of the Greek translator.[62] Key to the identity of the servant of Yahweh is Isaiah 49:3 and 6 in the Second Servant Song.[63] One text says the servant is Israel; another affirms that the servant will restore the tribes of Jacob (= Israel). The servant is Israel, yet restores Israel. How can we resolve this enigmatic and apparently contradictory situation?

---

[58] F. Delitzsch, *Biblical Commentary on the Prophecies of Isaiah*, trans. J. Martin, 2 vols. (Grand Rapids, MI: Eerdmans, 1950), 2:355. The English translation was based on the fourth edition (1875) of the German original. See also Kaiser, "Unfailing Kindnesses Promised to David," 95.

[59] Ibid.

[60] Daniel I. Block, "My Servant David: Ancient Israel's Vision of the Messiah," in *Israel's Messiah in the Bible and the Dead Sea Scrolls*, ed. Richard S. Hess and M. Daniel Carroll (Grand Rapids, MI: Baker, 2003), 17–56. See also Ivan Engnell, "The 'Ebed Yahweh Songs and the Suffering Servant Messiah in 'Deutero-Isaiah'," *Bulletin of the John Rylands Library* 31 (1948): 93; and E. J. Kissane, *The Book of Isaiah: Translated from a Critically Revised Hebrew Text with Commentary*, 2 vols. (Dublin: Browne & Nolan, 1943), 2:179–180.

[61] Motyer, *Prophecy of Isaiah*, 121 (emphasis his).

[62] This insight I owe to Stephen Dempster.

[63] I am painfully aware of the brevity of my statement concerning the identity of the servant in contrast to the difficulties in interpretation and the voluminous literature on this topic.

When the servant is seen as a royal figure, we can propose a solution. There is a sense in which the king *is the nation in himself*, and yet can also be the deliverer of the nation. If "David" refers to the future king in 55:3, a precedent would already be set by Hosea 3:5, a usage more similar than those in Jeremiah (30:8–9) and Ezekiel (34:23; 34:24; 37:24; 37:25).

With the above exposition of "sonship" in the Davidic covenant of 2 Samuel 7 and the understanding that Isaiah 55:3 refers to a future David, the pieces of the text can now be put together. This approach best suits the flow of thought in Isaiah and best explains what the phrases "witness of the peoples" and "leader and commander of the peoples" mean in context; it best explains the apposition of "faithful acts of loyal love by David" to "eternal covenant" and why "faithful" is used as a modifier. These arguments can be unpacked as follows.

The first vision of a future restored Zion is found in Isaiah 2, where Mount Zion becomes the highest mountain in the new world and all the nations stream to it to receive instruction (*tôrâ*) and the word of the Lord. This vision, along with the one in chapter 4, shows that the future Mount Zion has inherited the role of both Eden and Sinai and that the city, once a whore (1:21), is now characterised by social justice (1:26), as the term holy (4:3) indicates.

The vision in 9:5–6 (9:6–7 EV) and 11:1–10 brings a new twist. A future king, a new David, will arise. He will delight in the fear of the Lord, here a synonym for Torah as in Psalm 19. Thus he will fulfill the command of Deuteronomy 17:18–20 and as a result will implement the social justice of the Torah (Isa. 11:3b–5). According to verse 10, the King himself will become a banner for the nations. Here we see that the nations who stream to Zion in 2:1–4 will receive the Torah of Yahweh *through* the Davidic King. The servant of Yahweh—already connected to this future king—will bring justice to the nations in 42:1, 3–4; 49:3, 6. Also in the context of a Servant Song, the fact that a banner is raised to the nations is repeated in 49:22. In short, as the son of God, a future David will bring God's instruction and rule to all the nations, as indicated in 2 Samuel 7.

Scholars have emphasised that *ḥasdê dāwīd hanne'ĕmānîm* in Isaiah 55:3b functions in apposition to *bĕrît 'ôlām* in 3a. What acts of *ḥesed* on the part of the future David can constitute an eternal covenant? The arm of Yahweh is part of the new exodus theme that permeates all of Isaiah. The occurrence in 50:2 initiates a focus on the arm that reaches a climax in the

Fourth Servant Song 53:1 (51:5; 51:9; 52:10). Nevertheless when Yahweh rolls up his sleeves and bares his arm to deliver his people, the result is unexpected. The future king does not crush his enemies and rid the land of evil (11:3–5) by military force, prowess, and strategies, but simply by his word (11:4; 49:2; 50:4) and by offering himself as an *'āšām* (53:10).[64] Thus the means and manner in which Yahweh's Torah is brought to the nations and in which his kingship is effected among them (through a "leader and commander of the peoples"; Isa. 55:4) is detailed by the four Servant Songs, and in particular by the Fourth Song in 52:13–53:12. It is the acts of *ḥesed* on the part of the servant that establish and initiate the discussion on the eternal covenant in chapter 54, of which 55:3 continues the thread.[65] It is because the servant is the "covenant of the people" in himself (42:6; 49:8) that the apposition of *ḥasdê dāwīd* and *běrît 'ôlām* in verse 3 makes sense.

Isaiah 55:4–5 speaks of the future David being a witness to the nations and a leader and commander of the peoples. This speaks far more of fulfilling the human obligations in the Davidic covenant than of fulfilling the divine obligations. In explaining the phrase עֵד לְאוּמִּים Beuken concludes that "David's witness had consisted neither of his lot in itself nor of the trustworthiness of the connection between proclamation and fulfillment of rescue. More properly it consisted of the outspoken praise of God among the nations."[66] Williamson counters by appealing to John Eaton: "Eaton here finds three aspects to this royal role, each of which fits the context, namely, of the king as one who exhorts and admonishes, as one who is able out of his own experience to testify to God's revelation and salvation, and thirdly as one who, by his very existence, is an 'evidential sign' to the nations."[67] Eaton argues that the second is the most significant. This fails to consider the central function of the king to effect the instruction of Yahweh in the lives of the people and even among the nations: "this is the instruction for humankind" (2 Sam. 7:19). This is what is prominent in Isaiah. The servant of Yahweh brings Yahweh's Torah to the distant islands.

---

[64] Kaiser seems to be moving in this direction. Concerning Isaiah 55:3 he states, "What the Servant of the Lord has provided for and accomplished by his great act of suffering in Isaiah 52:13–53:12 is now offered in 55:1–13" (Walter C. Kaiser, Jr., *The Messiah in the Old Testament* [Grand Rapids, MI: Zondervan, 1995], 182). Yet in spite of this he interprets the *ḥasdê dāwīd* as objective genitive.

[65] Similarly Ivan Engnell, in a statement that begs further elaboration: "the passage liv: 1 ff forms a hymnic conclusion of the 'Ebed Yahweh song. . . . Here the consequences of the Servant's resurrection and exaltation are depicted: the restoration of Zion and the erection of the new Jerusalem on the basis of the Davidic covenant, fulfilled in 'Ebed Yahweh" (I. Engnell, "The 'Ebed Yahweh Songs and the Suffering Servant Messiah in 'Deutero-Isaiah'," *Bulletin of the John Rylands Library* 31 (1948): 89).

[66] W. A. M. Beuken, "Isa. 55,3–5: The Reinterpretation of David," *Bijdragen* 35 (1975): 60.

[67] Williamson, "'Sure Mercies of David,'" 47–48.

A false start was made in trying to connect David as witness in Isaiah 55:4 and Psalm 89:38 (89:37 EV). The idea that David or his seed is the witness in Psalm 89:38 is suggested by Eaton and found "attractive" by Williamson.[68] As Timo Veijola has shown, *ne'ĕmān* in Psalm 89:38 is a predicate adjective,[69] not attributive, and verses 37ab–38a form a tricolon so that verse 38b is not parallel to 38a.[70] Consequently we cannot translate, "the faithful witness in the sky," as does the NIV. Williamson's rendering, "and he is established to be witness in the clouds"[71] does recognise the grammatical problem in construing *ne'ĕmān* as attributive, but this is not a natural reading of what is a simple nominal sentence. In Psalm 89:38, therefore, Veijola suggests that Yahweh, not the Davidic Seed, is the Witness: "the Witness in the sky is faithful."

A careful examination of all instances of *'ēd* in the Hebrew Bible points in a different direction from earlier proposals for Isaiah 55:4 and better suits the interpretation proposed. The role of the Davidic king in fulfilling his covenant obligations is defined by divine sonship based on 2 Samuel 7:14–15 and Deuteronomy 17:18–20. The king's rule is to exhibit the justice and righteousness of Yahweh himself. Foundational to this is the Torah that the king must copy for himself and keep with him. Then the divine justice and righteousness in the Torah will shine through every aspect of the king's decisions and government. The logic of being a son of a universal deity and the statement of 2 Samuel 7:19 shows that this instruction is not only for Israel but for all the nations. This explains how and why the Davidic king is a witness and is more to the point than that given by Eaton and Williamson.

Nonetheless, there is much more. A lexical study of *'ēd* shows that a witness functions in *covenant* relationships, especially with a view to restoring broken relationships. When Laban and Jacob make a covenant, a heap of stones functions as a witness. As Timo Veijola explains, "When a treaty is violated, it is the duty of the witness to stand forth and accuse the partner who transgressed the treaty (cf. Gen 31:50)."[72] This is what the Davidic King is for the nations. Note that in the Servant Songs, twice the servant of Yahweh is informed that he will become in his person a covenant with the people (Isa. 42:6; 49:8). Just as the term "witness" can sometimes replace "covenant," so that the "ark of the covenant" becomes the "ark of witness," so here: to say

---

[68] John Eaton, "The King as God's Witness," *Annual of the Swedish Theological Institute* 7 (1970): 25–40; and H. G. M. Williamson, "'Sure Mercies of David,'" 48.
[69] C. Brockelmann, *Hebräische Syntax* (Neukirchen-Vluyn, Germany: Neukirchener, 1956), § 58.
[70] Timo Veijola, "The Witness in the Clouds: Ps 89:38," *Journal of Biblical Literature* 107/3 (1988): 413–417.
[71] Williamson, "'Sure Mercies of David,'" 48.
[72] Veijola, "Witness in the Clouds: Ps 89:38," 417.

that David is a witness to the peoples is correlative to the statements in the Servant Songs that he is a covenant to the people. Moreover, the background of Isaiah 19 is significant. *David* is to the *nations* what the *altar* is to *Egypt* in Isaiah 19:20.[73] He speaks to the nations of their covenant disloyalty, of their broken obligations to the creator God, and he brings about the restoration of the covenant relationship between Yahweh and the nations. As stated earlier, the means and manner in which Yahweh's Torah is brought to the nations and in which his kingship is effected among them is detailed by the four Servant Songs, and in particular by the Fourth Song in 52:13–53:12. And this is why a nation that does not know Israel and also one that Israel does not know comes running to her (55:5) through the work of her king as witness.

The king is also a leader and commander of peoples (*nāgîd ûmĕṣawwēh lĕ'ummîm*). The most recent and thorough treatment of *nāgîd*, particularly in the context of 2 Samuel 5:17–7:29, is that of Donald F. Murray. His conclusion is worth citing:

> In our texts the *melek* is one who sees his power from Yahweh as susceptible to his own arbitrary manipulation, who obtrudes himself inappropriately and disproportionately between Yahweh and Israel, and who treats Israel as little more than the subjects of his monarchic power. The *nāgîd*, on the other hand, is positively portrayed as one who sees his power as a sovereign and inviolable devolvement from Yahweh, who acts strictly under the orders of Yahweh for the benefit of Yahweh's people, and holds himself as no more than the willing subject of the divine monarch.[74]

No description better fits the role of the future King in Isaiah 1–39 and the role of the servant of the Lord in Isaiah 40–66 in implementing Yahweh's kingship. Thus Isaiah employs *nāgîd* because the future David fulfills the role of obedient son in the framework of the Davidic covenant.

Finally, one must adequately explain the description of *ḥasdê dāwīd* as *hanne'ĕmānîm* (55:3). Williamson finds that Caquot "merely suggests an

---

[73] Isaiah 19 is a judgement oracle against Egypt. The judgement involves civil strife and war and government by a harsh king. The rivers and streams will dry up, affecting the agrarian and fishing economy. Conventional Egyptian wisdom and religion will fail them. They will be in fear of Judah and of Yahweh. At that time an altar to Yahweh will be in the centre of Egypt and a monument to Yahweh at the border. "It will be a sign and a witness to Yahweh of Armies in the land of Egypt." The Egyptians will cry out to the Lord because of their oppressors and he will send a saviour to them. Thus Yahweh will make himself known to the Egyptians and they will become worshippers of Yahweh. There are some similarities between this text and Joshua 22:34. There the witness reminds the two and a half tribes that they belong to Yahweh. In a similar way, this altar functions to bring those outside the border of Israel into a relationship with the Lord. Only in Joshua 22, those outside are Israelites, whereas here they are Egyptians. The altar functions to restore relationship to the Lord.

[74] Donald F. Murray, *Divine Prerogative and Royal Pretension: Pragmatics, Poetics, and Polemics in a Narrative Sequence about David (2 Samuel 5.17–7.29)*, JSOTSup 264 (Sheffield, UK: Sheffield Academic Press, 1998), 299.

interpretation that suits his view" while Beuken "sees the problem posed by *hanne'ĕmānîm* more clearly." [75] Williamson then seeks to show that *ne'ĕmān* in association with *ḥesed*, *dāwīd*, and *bĕrît* must surely point to Nathan's oracle. If we grant this, it may support interpreting *dāwīd* as subjective genitive as much or more than objective genitive, since the oracle is just as concerned with the faithfulness of an obedient son as it is with the faithfulness of Yahweh to his promises. Even here, Williamson is somewhat unfair in his treatment of the evidence:

> . . . in Ps. lxxviii. 37 we find that the Israelites "were not true to his covenant". However, since this unique explicit application of *n'mn* to the human partner in a covenant with God is cast in the negative, it would be precarious indeed to seek to use it in any way to elucidate the quite different atmosphere of Isa. lv. 3 (*contra* Beuken, p. 53). Finally, in Neh. ix. 8 it is said that God found Abraham's heart faithful (*n'mn*), so that he made his covenant with him. However, whilst this is certainly the closest parallel to Isa. lv. 3 which could suggest a subjective genitive, it should be pointed out against this conclusion that whereas in Neh. ix. 8 *n'mn* qualifies Abraham's heart (and hence Abraham himself), in Isa. lv. 3 the plural *hanne'ᵉmānîm* must be construed with *ḥasdê*, and not with the singular *dwd*.[76]

This can only be classified as specious linguistic reasoning. Whether the person or the person's deeds are counted faithful does not affect whether one is speaking of God or of human beings. And whether the actions are negative in one place and positive in another does not change the fact that the term can be applied to humans. What Williamson has missed is the atmosphere of Isaiah, where in both the section concerning bad King Ahaz (7–9) and the section concerning good King Hezekiah (36–39) the history of the monarchy shows that we are still awaiting desperately for an obedient Davidic son. While the faithfulness of Yahweh may be questioned in Psalm 89, it is not an issue in Isaiah.

Williamson summarises his approach to the problem as follows:

> Thus far we have sought to show, first, that the versions cannot legitimately be invoked to settle the issue of how to construe *ḥsdy dwd*, and, secondly, that, although it is true that *ḥsd* nearly always governs a subjective genitive,

---

there are indications that this need not necessarily be so in every case, but that the context should be the deciding factor.[77]

This is largely sound. The ancient versions do hold weight in the history of interpretation, but they cannot settle the issue. The pattern of constructions used with *hesed*, however, carries great weight. While I am not persuaded that Williamson has succeeded in showing that genuine cases of objective genitive exist, the first datum in the context is the predilection of the native speaker to construe *hasdê dāwīd* as subjective. So the burden of proof lies in showing that the context requires a meaning other than the subjective genitive. The main reasons interpreters have sought to interpret the text from the point of view of an objective genitive are a failure to see that a future, not historical David is in view and a failure to observe properly the trajectory of the covenants in the Old Testament and the flow of thought both in the book of Isaiah as whole and in the near context of chapter 55. The fact that some interpreters use such renderings in English as "the promises of grace to David"[78] or "the unfailing kindnesses promised to David,"[79] paraphrases which actually go beyond linguistic parameters for a literal translation as objective genitive, really show how awkward it is to construe it this way. A proper rendering would be something like "the faithful kindnesses of David." The blessings do come to the nations, not because Yahweh's promises to David are democratised in the way some think,[80] but because a new David who is an obedient son succeeds in bringing Yahweh's Torah to all humans. If we follow through on the subjective genitive, the kindnesses of David could involve sharing the victory of the one with the many (see Isa. 53:10–12)[81] so that all are now sons and daughters of God, just as all are now servants. This might be a way in which the future David democratises the covenant.

---

[77] Ibid., 41.

[78] So Otto Eissfeldt, "The Promises of Grace to David in Isaiah 55:1–5," in *Israel's Prophetic Heritage: Essays in Honor of James Muilenburg*, ed. Bernhard W. Anderson and Walter Harrelson (New York: Harper, 1962), 196–207.

[79] So Kaiser, "Unfailing Kindnesses Promised to David," 91–98.

[80] E.g., Claus Westermann, *Das Buch Jesaia: Kapitel 40–66*, 2nd ed. (Göttingen, Germany: Vandenhoeck & Ruprecht, 1970), 227–230. No doubt a significant work on this topic is Benjamin D. Sommer, *A Prophet Reads Scripture: Allusion in Isaiah 40–66* (Stanford, CA: Stanford University Press, 1998). The discussion of methodological principles distinguishing allusion, influence, and echo is most incisive and illuminating. Sommer completely fails, however, to provide convincing evidence of allusion to Psalms 89 and 132 in Isaiah 55. Obviously all three texts are dealing with the covenant with David and so share common vocabulary and themes. But the foundational role of 2 Samuel 7 is ignored by Sommer and the connections between Isaiah 55 and the Psalms were not worked out rigorously according to the principles initially set forth. Sommer's exegesis of Isaiah 55:1–3 is based on that of Eichrodt (see Sommer, *Prophet Reads Scripture*, 265, n. 25) and does not advance beyond the traditional view.

[81] See Peter J. Gentry, "The Atonement in Isaiah's Fourth Servant Song (Isaiah 52:13–53:12)," *SBJT* 11/2 (2007): 20–47.

THE CITATION OF ISAIAH 55:3 IN ACTS 13:34

The question remains, does the LXX of Isaiah 55:3 and the citation in Acts 13:34 support an objective genitive as Williamson claims? He notes that the neuter plural ὅσια occurs only [sic] in Deuteronomy 29:18 (29:19 EV) where šālôm yihyeh-lî is rendered idiomatically by ὅσιά μοι γένοιτο. Then he appeals to independent studies by Dupont[82] and Lövestam,[83] who argued that ὅσια signifies "a general expression for blessings and good gifts which may be expected from the deity."[84] Finally, he argues that according to the majority of commentators, this meaning best suits the citation in Acts 13:34.

First, one should begin by considering the normal meaning of ὅσιος and the translation technique used for ḥesed in Isaiah. As our standard Greek lexica show, ὅσιος has two basic meanings: (1) it refers to what is divinely permitted or sanctioned, and (2) it describes persons or their deeds as devout, holy, pious, etc. There are actually two parallel passages where the neuter plural is found: Deuteronomy 29:18 and Wisdom of Solomon 6:10. In both passages, the first meaning, "sanctioned by divine law" fits well. Thus ὅσιά μοι γένοιτο in Deuteronomy 29:18 may be rendered "may I be allowed to . . . ."[85] and οἱ γὰρ φυλάξοντες ὁσίως τὰ ὅσια (in Wisdom 6:10) may be translated "those who have kept the holy ordinances in holiness."[86] Whether these parallels assist in interpreting Isaiah 55:3 remains to be seen.

The term ḥesed was encountered in eight instances by the Greek translator of Isaiah, and normally he employed ἔλεος, a standard equivalent among LXX translators (Isa. 16:5; 54:8; 54:10; 63:7 [2x]). The rendering of 'anšê ḥesed in 57:1 by ἄνδρες δίκαιοι and the use of δόξα in 40:6 for the charm or grace of a blossom illustrate well that the translator is sensitive to context and capable of fully idiomatic renderings. Since the rendering τὰ ὅσια Δαυιδ in 55:3 deviates from the norm, it is likely a contextually motivated idiomatic rendering. If divine sanctions are in view, it could mean "the divine decrees of David." This seems an odd way to refer to the divine promises made to David in 2 Samuel 7. An objective genitive is possible, but such English renderings as "divine blessings/promises to David" stretch the field of meaning permitted for ὅσιος beyond the

---

[82] J. Dupont, "ΤΑ ΄ΟΣΙΑ ΔΑΥΙΔ ΤΑ ΠΙΣΤΑ (Ac XIII 34 = Is LV 3)," *Revue Biblique* 68 (1961): 91–114.

[83] E. Lövestam, *Son and Saviour: a Study of Acts 13, 32–37*, Coniectanea Neotestamentica XVIII (Lund, Sweden: Gleerup, 1961).

[84] Lövestam, *Son and Saviour: a Study of Acts 13, 32–37*, 75, cited by Williamson, "'Sure Mercies of David,'" 32.

[85] This is, in fact, the interpretation and rendering of T. Muraoka, *A Greek-English Lexicon of the Septuagint, Chiefly of the Pentateuch and the Twelve Prophets* (Leuven, Belgium: Peeters, 2009), s.v. ὅσιος.

[86] Translation from David Winston, *The Wisdom of Solomon*, Anchor Bible 43 (New York: Doubleday, 1979), 151.

norm.[87] The phrase may also mean the divine duties or holy deeds/things of David. Again, an objective genitive is also possible, but a subjective genitive seems less awkward. Honesty, however, compels one to admit that either subjective or objective genitive is possible and that the meaning of the LXX translator is not readily transparent. Nonetheless, one might argue that he avoided the usual ἔλεος to show that God's kindnesses were not in view. Williamson does not explain why the Isaiah translator deviated from a more straightforward way of expressing that God's mercies were in view and used instead a unique expression.

Lastly, we note the citation of Isaiah 55:3 in Acts 13:34. Although this text has been discussed extensively and the majority view favours an objective genitive, an alternative interpretation is briefly argued here.

According to the context, in Acts 13 Paul is attending a meeting of the synagogue in Pisidian Antioch, where he speaks to an audience consisting of Jews and god-fearing Gentiles (vv. 16, 26). His address is a retelling of the story of Israel, so one must pay attention to what is included and what is omitted. Doubtless what we have recorded in Acts constitutes only the main points. Nonetheless the election of the fathers, the exodus, and the period of the judges get only the barest mention as he hurries to the time when Israel requests a king. After Saul is given and also removed, he comes to David. Only one comment is made about David, but it is important: he will do everything that God wants. This is the faithful king of 2 Samuel 7. Next Paul attempts to show that Jesus is the Saviour whom God promised to bring to Israel from the line of David (v. 23). Finally, Jesus' death and resurrection fulfill the words of the prophets (v. 27). In verse 32 Paul offers good news to "you" (second person plural), i.e., his audience. What God promised to the fathers is now fulfilled for us, their descendants, when he raised Jesus from the dead. Paul cites Psalm 2:7 and then affirms that God raised Jesus, no longer to return to corruption. That the resurrection of the Davidic son of Psalm 2 is to an incorruptible life is demonstrated by two further texts: Isaiah 55:3 and Psalm 16:10. In Isaiah 55:3 he (i.e., God) said, "I will give to you the faithful ὅσια of David." (Note that the "you" is second person plural. The recipients, according to Paul, are his audience in Pisidian Antioch, the

---

[87] The Hellenistic inscriptions in pagan temples which Dupont and Lövestam adduce actually belong to the regular use meaning "things divinely sanctioned" and hardly support a rendering such as "divine blessings." While Williamson accepts this, Bauer's lexicon does not seem to acknowledge the research of Dupont or Lövestam. See Walter Bauer, *A Greek-English Lexicon of the New Testament and Other Early Christian Literature*, trans. and rev. by W. F. Arndt and F. W. Gingrich, 2nd ed. rev. by F. W. Gingrich and F. W. Danker (Chicago: University of Chicago Press, 1979), s.v. ὅσιος.

descendants of the people first promised "the faithful ὅσια of David." This makes perfect sense in view of Isaiah's doctrine of a remnant.) Now if Paul meant τὰ ὅσια Δαυιδ τὰ πιστά to be subjective genitive and understood "David" not as the historical David, but as a rubric for the Messiah, his argument in context becomes plain. The explanation that David served his *own* generation is a clear statement that the historical David is not in view in verse 34. Instead, Isaiah refers to the Messiah. Since the pious deeds of David in the context of Isaiah 55:3 are the sufferings and death of the servant in 53, the reference to resurrection becomes clear. Isaiah 53:11 affirms that "after the suffering of his soul, he will see the light *of life* and be satisfied (NIV)." Isaiah 53:12 shows the servant sharing his victory with the many. And it is natural for Paul to cite 55:3 and not a verse or two in 53 because 55 is the text that applies the work of the servant to the nations. Once again, perhaps the reason why scholars have laboured so hard to find an appropriate meaning for τὰ ὅσια in Acts 13:34 is that they are thinking of the wrong David.[88] This interpretation, then, for Acts 13:34 is plausible and also matches the proposal for Isaiah 55:3.

Finally, not only seasoned scholars but even beginners should cast a doubtful eye at an entry in the lexicon which allocates a meaning for ὅσια in one instance that is apparently so disconnected in meaning from standard usage. The new third edition by Danker removes Acts 13:34 from the section on "things divinely sanctioned" and gives it a numbered paragraph of its own. The explanation, however, is almost identical to that in the previous edition:

> The ref. to ὅσ. in δώσω ὑμῖν τὰ ὅς. Δαυιδ τὰ πιστά *I will grant to you* (pl.) *the unfailing divine assurances* or *decrees relating to David* **Ac 13:34** is of special interest (for τὰ ὅσ. in the sense of divine decrees or ordinances s. Wsd 6:10; Jos., Ant. 8,115—). This quot. fr. Is 55:3 is evidently meant to show that the quot. fr. Ps 15:10, which follows immediately, could not refer to the Psalmist David, but to Christ alone (cp. a sim. line of argument relating to a referent Hb 2:6–9). The promises to David have solemnly been transferred to 'you'. But David himself served not you, but his own generation (vs. 36). So the promises of God refer not to him, but to his Messianic descendant.[89]

---

[88] Stephen G. Dempster has reminded me that the same distinction between the historical David and future David is made in Acts 2:22–32 (private communication).

[89] Walter Bauer, *A Greek-English Lexicon of the New Testament and Other Early Christian Literature*, 3rd ed., rev. and ed. F. W. Danker (Chicago: University of Chicago Press, 1957, 1979, 2000), 728.

The movement from "assurances" or "decrees" to "promises" is an unwarranted jump linguistically. If we supply from regular usage a meaning like "the pious deeds of David," the comment in the lexicon would make good sense.

CONCLUSION

In conclusion, "the faithful kindnesses of David" mentioned in Isaiah 55:3 are kindnesses performed by David—a rubric for the future king in this text. The faithful or obedient acts of loyal love are those of the servant king in Isaiah 53, whose offering of himself as an *'āšām* and whose resurrection enables him to bring to fulfilment the promises of Yahweh in the Davidic covenant and who is at the same time the basis for the new or everlasting covenant. This future King then fulfills the roles required for the king in Deuteronomy 17 and 2 Samuel 7 by bringing the divine instruction or Torah to Israel (Deuteronomy 17) and, indeed, to all the nations (2 Sam. 7:19). He is therefore a leader and commander of the peoples and becomes a covenant witness in himself to the nations. This is exactly how Acts 13:34 interprets Isaiah 55.

THE FULFILMENT OF PROMISES TO DAVID

The promises entailed in the covenant with David are divided by the text into two: (1) those to be fulfilled during his lifetime and (2) those to be fulfilled after his death. Second Samuel 7:8–11a gives the promises to be fulfilled during David's lifetime: (1) a great name, (2) a firm place for Israel as the people of God, and (3) rest for David from his enemies. Second Samuel 8 gives a list of David's victories and is placed by the author strategically after chapter 7 to show the fulfilment of these three promises. According to 8:13, "David made a name for himself when he returned from striking down 18,000 Edomites in the Valley of Salt." The defeat of the enemies listed in chapter 8 shows that God made a firm place for his people Israel through these victories. In 1 Kings 5:4 Solomon attests to the fact that he has rest on every side—a legacy received from his father David.

The promises to be fulfilled after the death of David are also three: (1) an eternal house, (2) kingdom, and (3) throne. There are two ways in which God could give David an eternal house. It could be that every descendant would be successful in producing a male heir—something which has always created problems for every human royal house. Or it could be that someday, a descendant would be born who would never die. According to the New Testament, this is what happened: the eternal house/

seed is fulfilled in Jesus Christ, a descendant of David who according to his resurrection is an eternal person. And through the coming, person, and work of Jesus Christ, an eternal kingdom has been already begun (2 Pet. 1:11). When Jesus ascended to the right hand of the Father after his resurrection, the authors of the New Testament make plain that he is ruling from an eternal heavenly throne (Acts 2:29–36, Heb. 12:22–24).

RELATIONSHIP OF THE DAVIDIC COVENANT TO THE ISRAELITE COVENANT

As we have seen in the exposition of 2 Samuel 7, the king of Israel was to be the administrator of the Israelite covenant.[90] By depending on Yahweh for military victories, the king would point the people to the kingship of Yahweh. In his rule of the people he would represent God's social justice and also embody in his person the obedience of the people. Thus kingship in Israel was to be a means of accomplishing Exodus 19:3b–6: the king would be a devoted servant and son of God and would also function as a priest, instructing the nations in the righteousness of God and inviting them to come under the rule of Yahweh.

We see the priestly role of David in that he wears an ephod. The description of David in 2 Samuel 6:14 is identical in the Hebrew text to that of Samuel in 1 Samuel 2:18. We further see the priestly role of the Davidic king in Psalm 110:4. All of this indicates that the king will accomplish in his person the purpose that God had for the nation of Israel as a whole, to be a kingdom of priests. The king will embody the nation in himself.

Above, in the discussion of the Fourth Servant Song (Isa. 52:13–53:12), we saw that there is a sense in which the king *is the nation in himself,* and yet can also be the deliverer of the nation. Genesis 20:4 is an excellent illustration of the corporate solidarity between king and people that was part and parcel of the culture of the ancient Near East:

[1] Now Abraham moved on from there into the region of the Negev and lived between Kadesh and Shur. For a while he stayed in Gerar, [2] and there Abraham said of his wife Sarah, "She is my sister." Then Abimelech king of Gerar sent for Sarah and took her. [3] But God came to Abimelech in a dream one night and said to him, "You are as good as dead because of the woman you have taken; she is a married woman." [4] Now Abimelech had not gone near her, so he said, "Lord, will you destroy an innocent

---

90 See further Walton, *Covenant: God's Purpose, God's Plan,* 68–69.

nation? [5] Did he not say to me, 'She is my sister,' and didn't she also say, 'He is my brother'? I have done this with a clear conscience and clean hands." (Gen. 20:1–5, NIV)

Notice in this text that God communicates to Abimelech that he is a dead man because he has taken a married woman. Abimelech responds, "Lord, will you destroy an innocent nation?" Therefore the culture assumes that to kill the *king* is to destroy the *nation* (גּוֹי). This is a clear illustration of federal headship: the king *is* the nation *in himself*. Thus it is natural in the plan of God for the king of Israel, as Israel, to accomplish for the nation as a whole what the group of individuals have failed to do.[91]

RELATIONSHIP OF THE DAVIDIC COVENANT TO THE ABRAHAMIC COVENANT

First, God will use David to bring rest to his people and give to them a place. Compare for a moment Genesis 15:18–21, Deuteronomy 11:24, and 1 Kings 4:20–21 (4:20–5:1 MT):

> [18] On that day the LORD made a covenant with Abram, saying, "To your offspring I give this land, from the river of Egypt to the great river, the river Euphrates, [19] the land of the Kenites, the Kenizzites, the Kadmonites, [20] the Hittites, the Perizzites, the Rephaim, [21] the Amorites, the Canaanites, the Girgashites and the Jebusites." (Gen. 15:18–21, ESV)

> Every place on which the sole of your foot treads shall be yours. Your territory shall be from the wilderness to the Lebanon and from the River, the river Euphrates, to the western sea. (Deut. 11:24, ESV)

> [20] Judah and Israel were as many as the sand by the sea. They ate and drank and were happy. [21] Solomon ruled over all the kingdoms from the Euphrates to the land of the Philistines and to the border of Egypt. They brought tribute and served Solomon all the days of his life. (1 Kings 4:20–21, ESV)

The borders of the land as envisioned in Genesis 15:18–21 are defined in Deuteronomy 11:24 as Israel's "place." First Kings 4:20–21 indicates that this geographical "place" belonged to Israel during the time of Solomon,

[91] For a detailed discussion of the corporate solidarity between king and people in the Fourth Servant Song see Gentry, "Atonement in Isaiah's Fourth Servant Song (Isaiah 52:13–53:12)," 20–47.

David's son. So the covenant with David was a means to fulfill the promises in the Abrahamic covenant.

Second, God will use David to bring blessing to the nations as promised in the covenant with Abraham. The covenant with David is the charter or instruction for mankind. Isaiah 55 shows how the future king will by his acts of lovingkindness be a witness and a commander and leader of the peoples as he brings the divine instruction or Torah to all the nations.

The relation of the Davidic king to the Abrahamic covenant is described precisely by Psalm 72:17:

יְהִי שְׁמוֹ לְעוֹלָם
לִפְנֵי־שֶׁמֶשׁ יָנִין *יִנּוֹן שְׁמוֹ
וְיִתְבָּרְכוּ בוֹ
כָּל־גּוֹיִם יְאַשְּׁרוּהוּ:

May his name endure forever,
  his fame continue as long as the sun!
May people be blessed in him,
  all nations call him blessed! (ESV)

Verse 17b begins with another instance of the *hithpael* form of *bārak*. The rendering "may people be blessed in him" in the ESV is passive, as is common in the English versions. Grüneberg argues that a speech action *hithpael* is more suitable:

> . . . the verse begins with a request that the king's name endure. This would neatly introduce a statement that his fame will be such that other nations will use it in their blessings. . . . Gen 48:20 provides a clear example of how a person's name might be thus used. More importantly, יתברכו is parallel to יְאַשְּׁרוּהוּ, "call him happy"; this parallelism is close if the "blessing" is an utterance on the part of the nations.[92]

Benjamin Noonan, however, has shown that the analysis of Grüneberg makes several questionable assumptions concerning the relationship of Genesis 48:20 and the general usage of the *hithpael* of *bārak*. The use of the *beth* preposition there may not necessarily be the same as in the uses with the *hithpael*.[93]

Although the word which the ESV translates as "continue" in verse

---

[92] Keith N. Grüneberg, *Abraham, Blessing, and the Nations: A Philological and Exegetical Study of Genesis 12:3 in Its Narrative Context* (Berlin: Walter de Gruyter, 2003), 213.

[93] Benjamin J. Noonan, "Abraham, Blessing, and the Nations: A Reexamination of the Niphal and Hitpael of ברך in the Patriarchal Narratives," *Hebrew Studies* 51 (2010): 80.

17aβ is a bit obscure, it seems to belong to the plant/tree imagery employed for kings and kingdoms. We could render the verse thus:

> May his name endure forever,
>> his name make shoots as long as the sun endures!
> May they consider themselves blessed by him,
>> all nations call him happy!

The flow of thought in the psalm is simple. Either "by" or "for" Solomon, it begins in verse 1 as a prayer to God to give his judgements and righteousness to the king. In verse 2 the result is that the king will judge with social justice.[94] In such a kingdom the cause of the needy and weak are given justice. His rule is extended to universal space and time. In verse 10, kings from the ends of the world pay tribute and in verse 11, all nations serve him. So far we have an excellent exposition of 2 Samuel 7:19. In verses 12–17, the same theme is developed in another "round of discourse" on the same topic. The needy and weak receive help. The psalmist prays that many will offer prayer all day long for this king so that his name and the prosperity of his rule continue. Verse 17 fits appropriately into this flow of thought, praying that his fame endure and individuals of all nations declare themselves blessed by him and call him happy. Noonan's analysis is similar:

> Recent analysis of Psalm 72 has focused on its structure and content vis-à-vis ancient Near Eastern ideologies of Kingship, in which the king is portrayed as a mediator of prosperity and blessing. While the specific structure of this psalm is debated, many scholars acknowledge that verses 8–11 constitute a distinct unit portraying the king's international domination. These verses, which describe the world's nations as ingratiating themselves to the king in terms of submission, service, and tribute, are structurally and thematically linked to verse 17b. In light of this, the parallelism of וְיִתְבָּרְכוּ with יְאַשְּׁרוּהוּ should be understood in terms of ingratiation. . . . The preposition בְ signifies the instrument of blessing since the king is the one whom the people rely upon for blessing and favor. . . . Thus, the point of this verse is not the uttering of blessings, but the nations' acts of ingratiation as a response to the king's role as mediator of blessing.[95]

Grüneberg notes, as many have observed, that the wording of verse

---

[94] Note the split word pair "righteousness" and "justice."

[95] Benjamin J. Noonan, "Abraham, Blessing, and the Nations: A Reexamination of the Niphal and Hitpael of ברך in the Patriarchal Narratives," *Hebrew Studies* 51 (2010): 81.

17bα is identical to the promises to Abraham: we have the same verb in the *hithpael*, the preposition *beth*, and the subject "all nations." Nonetheless, he is not inclined to see an allusion to Genesis:

> Some commentators propose that Psalm 72:17 alludes to the patriarchal promises, the Psalmist suggesting that those promises are fulfilled in or through the Davidic monarch. While this is hard to disprove, the Psalm seems perfectly comprehensible without seeing any allusion, and little else in the context suggests dependence on patriarchal traditions.[96]

Nonetheless, the idea that all nations are elated with the rule of the Davidic King could be expressed otherwise. In Psalm 2, the kings of the nations are invited to "kiss the Son" and develop an appropriate relation to him. Yet the wording in Psalm 72:17 is identical to the patriarchal promises. According to Genesis 28:14, the blessing of the nations comes through the nation of Israel. While the ideas in Psalm 72 are developed logically from the covenant promises to David in 2 Samuel 7, we see that the blessing of the nations comes through the king of Israel. It is hard to avoid the thought that here in Psalm 72 Solomon sees, as did David, that the Davidic covenant narrows the mediator of blessing to the nations from the nation of Israel as a whole to the king, who represents and stands for the nation.

The Septuagint translation of Psalm 72:17 is significant, because there the connections between this verse and the promises to Abraham are absolutely clear:

καὶ εὐλογηθήσονται ἐν αὐτῷ πᾶσαι αἱ φυλαὶ τῆς γῆς, πάντα τὰ ἔθνη μακαριοῦσιν αὐτόν. (Ps. 71:17b [72:17b EV])

The phrase πᾶσαι αἱ φυλαὶ τῆς γῆς clearly recalls כֹּל מִשְׁפְּחֹת הָאֲדָמָה in Genesis 12:3 and the *inclusio* verse Genesis 28:14. While we need not pause to declare whether the parent text of LXX is inferior or superior to MT, one may certainly say it is possible that the text in MT is possibly due to omission of text resulting from the eye of a scribe skipping over phrases beginning with the same letters (כל). The poetic line verse 17bα also seems short and lacks an explicit subject. On the other hand, the text in the LXX may be due to the interpretation of the translator. Either way, the text in the LXX,

---

[96] Grüneberg, *Abraham, Blessing, and the Nations*, 216.

probably from 200 B.C., clearly connects Psalm 72:17 to the Abrahamic covenant and its witness cannot lightly be set aside.

These considerations of Psalm 72 are strengthened by the arrangement in the final redaction of the Hebrew Psalter. David Mitchell, in his classic work on the eschatological programme in the book of Psalms, notes the placement of Psalms 2 and 72 at the beginning of the First Book and the ending of the Second Book in the Psalter respectively.[97] The former announces a victory for Yahweh's King and the latter speaks of the kingdom established. These connections indicate that the blessing to the nations promised to Abraham is coming through the Davidic King/kingdom.

---

[97] David C. Mitchell, *The Message of the Psalter: An Eschatological Programme in the Book of Psalms*, JSOTSup 252 (Sheffield, UK: Sheffield Academic Press, 1997), 243–253.

APPENDIX TO CHAPTER 11: SON OF DN IN AMARNA/ UGARITIC TEXTS

What follows is an analysis of all personal names in the Amarna and Ugaritic Texts of the type "son of DN" (Divine Name).

1. Amarna Texts[1]

Name	Meaning	Comments	Reference(s)
Bin-Ana	son of Ana	detained with Aziru in Egypt[2]	EA 170:37
Ben-Elima	son of Elu	(honorific plural?) identity unknown[3]	EA 256:15
Šum-Adda	child of Adda	son of Balume[4]	EA 8:8, 13, 35; 224:3 (GAGI, 222)
Šumu-Haddi	child of Haddu	mayor(?), detained in Egypt[5]	EA 97:1 (GAGI, 222)

2. Texts from Ugarit[6]

Name	Text Reference	Comments
bnil	PRU 3:253	(van Soldt 32 n. 259, 139, 163)
	PRU 4:201 (RS 18:2):18	= 4.623:6 (van Soldt 11)
	Ug 5 2 rev. 12'	
	Ug 5 3 rev. 6'	
	3.10:17	

---

[1] Analysis based on the following sources: Richard S. Hess, "Amarna Proper Names" (PhD diss., Hebrew Union College, 1984); idem, *Amarna Personal Names*, American Schools of Oriental Research Dissertation Series 9 (Winona Lake, IN: Eisenbrauns, 1993); William L. Moran, ed. and trans., *The Amarna Letters* (Baltimore/London: John Hopkins University Press, 1987, 1992, 2002) = EA; and Daniel Sivan, *Grammatical Analysis and Glossary of the Northwest Semitic Vocables in Akkadian Texts of the 15th–13th C.B.C. from Canaan and Syria*, AOAT 214 (Neukirchen-Vluyn, Germany: Neukirchener, 1984) = GAGI.

[2] Hess, *Amarna Personal Names*, 381.

[3] Ibid.

[4] Ibid, 384.

[5] Ibid.

[6] Analysis based on the following sources: Frauke Gröndahl, *Die Personennamen der Texte aus Ugarit* (Studia Pohl 1; Rome: Pontifical Biblical Institute, 1967); Gregorio del Olmo Lete and Joaquín Sanmartín, *A Dictionary of the Ugaritic Language in the Alphabetic Tradition*, trans. W. G. E. Watson, 2 vols. (Handbook of Oriental Studies I: The Near and Middle East 67; Leiden, Netherlands: Brill, 2003) = DULA. References given according to abbreviations and format in DULA. All references were carefully checked in best editions using M. Dietrich, O.

Name	Text Reference	Comments
	4.86:12	
	4.297:3	
	4.377:19	
	4.609:8, 19	
	4:616:10	
	4.623:6	list of maryannus[7]
	4.723:1	
	4.791:13	
bn'myn	4.69 III 5	
	4.75 IV 8	
	4.77:11	
	4.280:12	(van Soldt 17, 139)
	4.290:11	of high rank? (van Soldt 37)
	4.356:5	of high rank? (van Soldt 37)
	4.357:25?	of high rank? (van Soldt 37)
	4.677:5	
	4.755:9?	
	4.785:19	
bn'n	4.33.32	royal guard from Rqd
	4.35 II 19	persons grouped by profession[8]
	4.232:47	buyer from Rqd
	4.753:14	
	9.423:8 (RS Ou 14 46)	
bn'nt	PRU 3:194 (RS 11.839:12)	
	PRU 3:194 (RS 11.839:16)	? ('Ilî-'abu also possible[9])
	4.307:6	serf on royal farm at village of Yny
	4.320:4	
bin-ba'alana	PRU 3:193 (RS 12.34:15)[10]	From village of Bekani

Loretz, and J. Sanmartín, *The Cuneiform Alphabetic Texts from Ugarit, Rab Ibn Hani and Other Places* (= *KTU*, 2nd, enlarged ed.) (Münster, Germany: Ugarit-Verlag, 1995); AT WO5 = Alalah Tablets, *Die Welt des Orients* 5; PRU = F.-A. Claude Schaeffer, ed., *Le Palais Royal d'Ugarit* (Mission de Ras Shamra 6–9; Paris: Klincksieck, 1955–); RSOu = P. Bordreuil, ed., *Ras Shamra-Ougarit* (Publications de la Mission Française Archéologique de Ras Shamra-Ougarit; Paris: Éditions Recherche sur les Civilisations, 1991–); Ug = F.-A. Claude Schaeffer, ed., *Ugaritica* (Paris: P. Guethner, 1939–). Additional information is provided from R. Hess, "The Onomastics of Ugarit," in *Handbook of Ugaritic Studies*, ed. W. G. E. Watson and N. Wyatt (Handbook of Oriental Studies I: The Near and Middle East 39, Leiden, Netherlands: Brill, 1999), 499–528; Wilfred H. van Soldt, *Studies in the Akkadian of Ugarit: Dating and Grammar*, AOAT 40 (Neukirchen-Vluyn, Germany: Neukirchener, 1991); and W. G. E. Watson, "Ugaritic Onomastics (1)," Aula Orientalis 7 (1990): 113–127.

[7] Member of social group (< titular of war chariot), DULA, 580.

[8] Should be read "son of Annu"; *bn* is not part of name. Profession = *ṯnn* (archer?), cf. van Soldt 38.

[9] So John Huehnergard, *The Akkadian of Ugarit*, Harvard Semitic Monographs (Atlanta: Scholars Press, 1989), 400, n. 85.

[10] Cf. also DULA, 226.

Name	Text Reference	Comments
bnhd(d)	see below	
bnpdr	4.655:8	
bn rpiyn	4.232 (I) 8	From village of Rqd
bnršp	4.33:12	guard from Ary
	4.155:15	
	4.170:9	
bnršpy	4.69. I 22	titular of war-chariot
	4.93 II 17	cf. PRU 3:20 (RS 15.63:11, 12, 19)
bin-šapši	PRU 3:195 (RS 15.09 B I 17)	
	PRU 6:79 (RS 19.42:5)	
	RSOu 7 3:7 =	
	dumu-ᵈutu dumu ͫdingir-silim	= Bin-šapši mār ilī-šalim?[11]
bnšpš	4.63 IV 6	
	4.194:18	
	4.227 I 11	
	4.628:5	
	4.666:4	
	4.422:43 broken context	
btšpš?	RSOu 14 44:6 or bnšpš?	
bnymn	4.64 IV 9	
	4.69 II 3	
	4.123:4	
	4.617 (I) 19	
	4.785:9	
DUMU ad-dá	AT WO5 p. 63 (136,4)	(cf. GAGI, 222)
šùm-adì	PRU 3:59 (RS 16.133:6)	son of Giše (Akkadian Text)
šu-um-ᵈaddu	PRU 3:151 (RS 16.197:14)	(Akkadian Text)

---

[11] So Pierre Bordreuil, *Une bibliothèque au sud de la ville: Ras Shamra-Ougarit VII* (Paris: Éditions Recherche sur les Civilisations, 1991), 20. See also F. Gröndahl, *Die Personennamen der Texte aus Ugarit*, 326, 354.

Chapter Twelve

THE NEW COVENANT:
INTRODUCTION/
ISAIAH/EZEKIEL

INTRODUCTION: WHO WERE THE PROPHETS AND WHY DID THEY SPEAK OF A NEW COVENANT?

The metanarrative begins with a creator God who made our world, our universe. As Creator, he is committed to caring for and sustaining all of his creation. He governs and rules over all his creatures and works wisely. The apex and crown of his creative work is humankind. He has entrusted to the human race the administration and stewardship of his world. This covenantal arrangement was violated by human disloyalty and rebellion. The first man decided to act and manage things independently of the Creator. Everything is now riddled with chaos and evil.

God responds to human rebellion in various ways as the story unfolds. At the centre of a plan to restore his ruined world and bring it to serve his original intentions are a series of agreements called covenants. First, the covenant with Noah reestablishes the commitment of the Creator to his creation as a whole. Then God begins to work through one individual, Abraham, and through his family, to model a new humanity in right relationship with the creator God and with one another. The Israelite covenant at Sinai (supplemented by Deuteronomy) forges the nation into the people of God and governs life in the land. The covenant with David institutes a kingship where the rule of God is established among his people since the king is to function as covenant administrator. What God planned for the nation as a whole will now be implemented through the king and his leadership.

Later on, between 750 and 550 B.C., a group of men who functioned as spokesmen for God were raised up to call attention to the failure of the people to be covenant keepers. These were the prophets, servants of God who spoke for him. They confronted the people of God and exposed the clever and

433

devious ways by which they had gradually slipped away from a proper relationship with God and with one another as defined by the Israelite covenant. The prophets were given visions from God and announced coming events. Some events would happen fairly soon; others would not happen for some time. They announced various ways in which God would act to deal with his faithless people and bring his overall plan of restoring his broken creation to fulfilment. Because the people had broken and violated the Israelite covenant, the prophets announced that God would put in place a new covenant in which not only would he be faithful, but his people would be faithful too.

REFERENCES TO THE NEW COVENANT

The prophets spoke of the new covenant in different places at different times in a variety of ways. Six times they refer to the everlasting covenant, three times to a covenant of peace, three times to a promise that God will give his people a new heart and a new spirit, and only once is the phrase "new covenant" actually used. But they are all referring to the same thing.

> *Major Texts Dealing with a New Covenant*
> 1. Everlasting covenant: Jeremiah 32:36–41; 50:2–5; Ezekiel 16:59–63; 37:15–28 (esp. v. 26); Isaiah 55:1–5; 61:8–9.
> 2. Covenant of peace: Isaiah 54:1–10 (esp. vv. 9–10); Ezekiel 34:20–31 (esp. v. 25); 37:15–28 (esp. v. 26).
> 3. Promise of a new heart and a new spirit: Ezekiel 11:18–21; 18:30–32; 36:24–32 (esp. v. 26) [cf. Isa. 59:21].
> 4. New covenant: Jeremiah 31:31–34.

It is interesting to note that, when we look at the New Testament, we find that the same covenant is referred to as the new covenant six times (Luke 22:20; 1 Cor. 11:25; 2 Cor. 3:6; Heb. 8:8; 9:15; 12:24) and only once as the everlasting covenant (Heb. 13: 20). Therefore the title for this covenant most used in the Old Testament is employed only once in the New Testament, and the title employed only once in the Old Testament is the one commonly used in the New Testament.

THE NEW COVENANT IN ISAIAH

Previous works on the covenants in the Old Testament have tended to deal with the topic of the new covenant by discussing a number of passages selected from the prophets presented *together*. Here, the contribution of each of the major prophets (Isaiah, Jeremiah, and Ezekiel) will be considered *separately*. The prophets do not have a monolithic presentation on how God will restore things, although variation does not mean contradiction. The contribution of each prophet needs to be considered in the context of his ministry and, especially, within the flow and literary structure of his work. When the contribution of each prophet has been heard *separately*, then the multifaceted presentation can be put together into a *whole*. In addition to discussing passages that treat the topic of the new covenant, it is important to analyse passages in which a prophet deals with the relationships of the new covenant to any of the previous major covenants. In this way, the assembling of the biblical teaching on the covenants from the fundamental passages will be put together into a superstructure that is derived from Scripture and not from our own imagination or human philosophy.

ISAIAH 54:1–55:13

Isaiah 54:1–55:13 is a major text dealing with the new covenant. We see the terms "covenant of peace" in 54:10 and "everlasting covenant" in 55:3. First we need to situate this text within the larger literary structure of the book as a whole. Although recent studies of Isaiah have focused more on the canonical shape of the text rather than on fragmentary sources adduced by critical scholarship, few have laboured to discover the larger literary structure inherent to the work as a whole.[1] Prophetic preaching and writing certainly does not follow the patterns of Aristotelian rectilinear logic so fundamental to our discourse in the Western world. Instead, the approach in ancient Hebrew literature is to take up a topic and develop it from a particular perspective and then to stop and take up the same theme again from another point of view. This pattern is kaleidoscopic and recursive. When one discourse is heard against the background of another, they function like the left and right speakers of a stereo and we have an idea that is like Dolby Surround Sound or a holographic image. The book of Isaiah is no exception to this technique. The main theme is the development from corrupt Zion in the old creation to restored Zion in the new creation. After the topic is presented in approximately seven major sections, the reader ends up with a full-orbed mental picture.[2] The major recursive sections of Isaiah may be roughly delineated as follows:

---

[1] A notable exception is the commentary by Motyer, cited below.

[2] This outline is indebted in part to J. Alec Motyer. Discourse grammar markers demand a major break between 37:38 and 38:1, which considerations of space do not permit to be set forth here.

The Book of Isaiah: From Zion in the Old Creation to Zion in the New

Isaiah makes the first round of his theme in 1:2–2:5, beginning with the broken covenant between God and Israel—excoriating the people for their sins—and concluding with the vision of a future transformed Zion. From 2:6 to 4:6 Isaiah makes the second round of his theme, moving again in a short treatment from sin and judgement in the present corrupt Zion to the vision of a future transformed Zion.

Chapters 5 through 37 comprise at least three sub-units which treat in detail the issues of failure to keep the covenant/Torah and the threat of judgement. Isaiah focuses on the failure of the people to practise social justice in spite of many, many acts of divine discipline. The covenant is broken and irreparably violated. Everything is in order in their services of worship, but the people have failed to demonstrate the lifestyle required of them as God's new humanity. The instruction in the covenant can properly be summarised by the term "social justice."[3] As a community in covenant relationship to Yahweh, they are called to mirror to the world the character of Yahweh in terms of social justice and to be a vehicle of divine blessing and salvation to the nations. But the way that the people of God have treated each other is characterised by social injustice. The City of Truth has become a whore (Isa. 1:21). The Lord has no choice now but to fulfill the gravest curses and threats entailed in the covenant in Deuteronomy 28. The final threat is exile, and this theme is taken up in chapters 5–37.

The sixth section of thematic treatment (covering chapters 38–55) is focused in particular on comfort and redemption for both Zion and the world. The following outline, adapted from the commentaries by Motyer,[4]

---

[3] See Thomas L. Leclerc, *Yahweh Is Exalted in Justice: Solidarity and Conflict in Isaiah* (Minneapolis: Fortress, 2001); and especially Peter J. Gentry, "Speaking the Truth in Love (Eph 4:15): Life in the New Covenant Community," *SBJT* 10/2 (2006): 70–87, an adaptation of which is included here as chapter 15.

[4] See J. Alec Motyer, *The Prophecy of Isaiah: An Introduction and Commentary* (Downers Grove, IL: InterVarsity Press, 1993); and idem, *Isaiah: An Introduction and Commentary*, Tyndale Old Testament Commentaries (Downers Grove, IL: InterVarsity Press, 1999).

is effective in clarifying the movement of thought in this cycle, dealing with the transformation of Zion in the old creation to Zion in the new creation:

Isaiah 38–55: The Book of the Servant

A. Historical Prologue—Hezekiah's fatal choice	38:1–39:8
B¹. Universal consolation	40:1–42:17
1. The consolation of Israel	40:1–41:20
2. The consolation of the Gentiles	41:21–42:17
C¹. Promises of redemption	42:18–44:23
1. Release	42:18–43:21
2. Forgiveness	43:22–44:23
C². Agents of redemption	44:24–53:12
1. Cyrus: liberation	44:24–48:22
2. Servant: atonement	49:1–53:12
B². Universal proclamation	54:1–55:13
1. The call to Zion	54:1–17
2. The call to the world	55:1–13

First, the outline of the literary structure of Isaiah 38–55 shows that the return from exile involves two distinct issues and stages. As already noted, Isaiah 38–55 looks farther into the future, beyond the judgement of exile, to the comfort and consolation of Israel, i.e., bringing them back from exile. Then the Lord will establish Zion as the people/place where all nations will seek his instruction for social justice. This is described in the language of the exodus, so that the return from the Babylonian exile will be nothing less than a new exodus—indeed a greater exodus![5] This new exodus is also described by the term "redeem" (*gāʾal*), which refers to the duties of the nearest relative. Since by virtue of the Israelite covenant Yahweh is Israel's nearest relative, he will "buy back" his people from exile as he once delivered them from bondage and slavery in Egypt. The return from exile, however, is not a chronologically single task. The promises of redemption are divided into two distinct events: release (42:18–43:21) and forgiveness (43:22–44:23). Release refers to bringing the people physically out of exile in Babylon and back to their own land; forgiveness entails dealing fully and finally with their sin and the broken covenant. It has been neatly expressed that you can take the people out of Babylon, but how do you get Babylon

---

[5] For a discussion of exodus language and themes in Isaiah see Bernhard W. Anderson, "Exodus Typology in Second Isaiah," in *Israel's Prophetic Heritage: Essays in Honor of James Muilenburg*, ed. Bernhard W. Anderson and Walter Harrelson (New York: Harper, 1962), 177–195.

out of the people?[6] The books of Ezra and Nehemiah show that the people have returned from exile but have not changed at all in terms of their relationship to God: the failure to practise social justice remains a central problem. That is why for a postexilic prophet like Zechariah the return from exile is both a present reality and a future hope. The exile will be over only when God deals with the people's sin and renews the covenant, the temple is rebuilt, and the Lord returns to dwell in their midst as King.

Zechariah 3:9 and 5:5–11 show that the forgiveness/removal of sins is still future. Indeed, the major point of Daniel's vision of seventy weeks is that the exile will not be over in seventy years, but rather in seventy weeks of years: "seventy sevens are decreed for your people and your holy city to finish transgression, to put an end to sin, to atone for wickedness, to bring in everlasting righteousness, to seal up vision and prophecy and to anoint the Holy of Holies" (Dan. 9:24). So there are two issues in the return from exile: physical return from Babylon and spiritual deliverance from bondage and slavery to sin. And corresponding to these two issues there are two distinct agents of redemption: Cyrus and the servant. The former will bring about the first task: physical return to the land of Israel (44:24–48:22); the latter will bring about the second task: the forgiveness of sins (49:1–53:12).

Second, the larger literary structure clarifies why there is a gap in the text between the first of the Servant Songs (42:1–9) and the last three (49:1–13; 50:4–9; 52:13–53:12). The First Servant Song belongs to the introductory opening section, which is devoted to the theme of the consolation of Israel and of the nations (40:1–42:17). The Abrahamic covenant undergirds this introductory section. At the heart of the covenant with Abraham is the promise that blessing will come to the entire world through Abraham and his family, Israel. The arrangement in this section is important. The consolation of Israel comes first because at this time Israel is under a curse; she is part of the problem and not part of the solution. First God must console and restore Israel and only then can he use Israel to be an instrument of consolation and restoration for all the nations. After consolation is defined in terms of redemption (1) from exile and (2) from sin in 42:18–44:23, Isaiah describes in 44:24–53:12 the work of Cyrus to accomplish the former before proceeding to develop the work of the servant of the Lord to accomplish the latter. At this point three passages on the servant of the Lord are placed together to

---

[6] The vision in Zechariah 5:5–11 of the woman in a basket carried by flying women back to Babylon seems to symbolise the task of removing Babylon from the people.

focus on redemption from sin. Each passage consists of a first presentation of the topic, a comment as a second presentation of the topic, except for the third section (per outline below), and a response section:[7]

Outline of Isaiah 49:1–55:13

A[1]. The servant's double mission: Israel and the world	49:1–6	
B[1]. Comment: mission to world and Israel confirmed	49:7–13	
C[1]. Response: Zion despondent and unresponsive	49:14–50:3	
A[2]. The servant obedient and responsive in suffering	50:4–9	
B[2]. Comment: the obedient and the self-willed	50:10–11	
C[2]. Zion summoned to respond	51:1–52:12	
A[3]. The servant successful, sin-bearing, and triumphant	52:13–53:12	
B[3]. Response: invitation to Israel and the world	54:1–55:13	

Third, the literary structure sheds light on the identity of the servant. Debate over the identity of the servant has raged for centuries and continues to the present time unabated.[8] One good reason for this debate is in the text itself: it is characteristic of Isaianic style to begin discussing a topic in an ambiguous and mysterious manner and to add critical information bit by bit until the matter is plain.[9] For example, in the oracle against Babylon in 21:1–9, Isaiah begins by talking about the Wilderness by the Sea. Only at the end, in v. 9, does one realise that the prophet is speaking about Babylon. Isaiah's presentation of the servant of Yahweh is similar. At the start, in 41:8, the servant is Israel, who in the biblical-theological scheme of the larger story has inherited the Adamic roles of son of God and servant king, and who in the covenant at Sinai in Exodus 19:5–6 was called to be a holy nation and a kingdom of priests. The servant, however, seems to be deaf and disobedient in 42:18–19. This contradicts the picture of the servant in 42:1–9 and especially in 50:4–11. Israel as a servant is in dire need herself, not just of rescue from exile and all that entails, but also of a full resolution of the problem of a broken covenant relationship (e.g., 43:22–28). Idolatry and social injustice are endemic in Israel. This is the dilemma: how can God keep his promises to Abraham when Israel has completely failed as the servant of the Lord?

---

[7] Once again I have adapted my outline from Motyer, *Prophecy of Isaiah*, 383.

[8] See Murray Rae, "Texts in Context: Scripture in the Divine Economy," *Journal of Theological Interpretation* 1/1 (2007): 1–21, for documentation of recent discussion. His concern for a canonical interpretation is commendable, but his postmodern solution to keep both Christians and Jews happy is implausible. Even during the last year, discussion on the Internet between Christians and Jews was considerable.

[9] Goldingay has noted this as well in his study of Isaiah: "As is often the case, the prophet begins by hinting at something that will receive further explication" (John Goldingay, *The Message of Isaiah 40–55: A Literary-Theological Commentary* [London: T. & T. Clark, 2005], 492).

Israel was to model three things to the rest of the nations: (1) faithfulness and loyalty in their relationship to God, (2) social justice in their human relationships, and (3) responsible stewardship of the creation/environment.

The answer to this question, developed at length elsewhere, is addressed immediately in the Second Servant Song, which begins the detailed response to this question (49:1–13). At the beginning of this second Song we hear again in 49:3 the affirmation that Israel is the servant, as in 41:8. So the servant is the nation. Yet in verses 5–6, the servant's task is to bring the nation back. This is a return from exile, both physically and spiritually, as described earlier. How can the servant be both the nation and the deliverer of the nation? There is only one possible solution that resolves this conundrum fairly, and Isaiah has prepared us for this in the first part of his work: the servant must be the future king described earlier (e.g., 11:1–10). As an individual, the king can say, "I am Israel." The king can represent the nation as a whole, yet he can be distinguished from Israel. This is difficult for Americans to grasp because we have no monarchy. In monarchies, both ancient and modern, there is a sense in which the king *is* the nation. At the same time, the king is the deliverer of the nation and fights her battles for her. Many Christians move too quickly to identify Jesus of Nazareth as the servant of Yahweh without following carefully the progression in the text. The main problem with the standard Jewish interpretation of identifying the servant as the nation is that the nation of Israel is, neither in the text nor in history, able to rescue itself, let alone atone for its own sins.[10]

For each of the latter three Servant Songs there is a pattern repeated in the text. First Isaiah presents the topic, then there is a comment which further develops the ideas, and finally there is a response section. The fourth song, in chapter 53, contains four stanzas in two pairs: two stanzas providing details and describing events (53:1–3, 7–9), each followed by a stanza explaining the meaning of the events (53:4–6, 10–12). We could consider the first pair the basic topic and the second pair of stanzas the comment. Chapter 54 begins the section inviting Israel to respond. She is called to burst out in a ringing cry/shout/song of joy. She is to sing because her family, her marriage, and her city of righteousness are restored. This is essentially a discussion of the new covenant.

The theme of chapter 54 is bringing back the exiles, bringing about

---

[10] What clinches the argument for the servant being an individual is the fact that in Isaiah 49:6 the servant delivers the nation and in Isaiah 53 the detail is so rich that it could not be anyone but an individual. See Peter J. Gentry, "The Atonement in Isaiah's Fourth Servant Song (Isaiah 52:13–53:12)," *SBJT* 11/2 (2007): 20–47.

reconciliation between God and his people, restoring the covenant relationship, and rebuilding Zion, since the city of God in terms of people has been so decimated. What ties together the diverse paragraphs and sections is a metaphor in which the people of God are represented as a woman. In verses 1–3 the people of God are pictured as a barren woman who now has more children than the married woman. In verses 4–10 the people of God are portrayed as a forsaken wife (i.e., divorced woman), someone who has long borne the reproach of widowhood, but who is now reconciled and married to her creator God. Included in this section is a comparison of the promise of the new covenant to the promise of the Noah covenant; just as God promised that never again would he judge by a flood, so now he promises never again to be angry with his people. Finally, in verses 11–17, the woman is the city of Zion, lashed by storms but now fortified by redoubtable foundations and battlements and rebuilt with stunning precious jewels and stones. Thus, in the brief span of 17 verses, the new covenant is in some way either compared or correlated and linked to all of the previous major covenants in the Bible.

Chapter 54, then, discusses the new covenant, which is based on the death and resurrection of the servant king in 53. Certain key words join the Servant Song in chapter 53 to this chapter. The "many" in 53:11–12 are the many in the miracle family in 54:1—the exact same word in Hebrew. The seed or offspring of the servant, seemingly cut off in 53:8, but appearing after his resurrection, are now the descendants who possess the nations in 54:3. The just one justifies the many in 53:11. He makes them righteous. The city is established in righteousness in 54:14, which is almost equivalent to vindication from accusing opponents in 54:17. And the servant in the singular becomes the servants of the Lord in the plural in 54:17.

Outline of Isaiah 54:1–17

A. Sarah: the barren woman	54:1–3
B. Israel: the deserted wife	54:4–10
C. Zion: the afflicted woman	54:11–17
1. The city rebuilt	11–14a
2. The city secure	14b–17

The Miracle Family (54:1–3)

God's people are called to burst out in ringing shouts of joy. They need to prepare for a massive expansion in the family. Why? Isaiah 54:3 says that their descendants will inherit/occupy/possess the nations. This statement is somewhat vague in itself. It might be interpreted to mean that Israel will at last conquer the nations surrounding and troubling them. But verse 1 will not permit this interpretation. It talks about the children of the desolate woman far outstripping those of the married woman. What does this mean? The married woman is Israel during the days of the old covenant. The desolate woman is the decimated Israel who comes back from the destruction of exile. The family restored after the exile is far more numerous than before. From the point of view of the New Testament, it becomes clear: Israel inherits the nations because they become part of the family.

The barren woman in the history of Israel is Sarah. The allusion to the times of Abraham and Sarah is also clear from the allusion to the tent and the mention of seed/descendants. Thus the reference to the barren woman is a way of referring to the Abrahamic covenant and so recalls the promise to Abraham of descendants as numerous as the sand on the seashore and as the stars of the sky. But the covenant with Abraham also promised blessing to the nations through Israel. Thus Israel dispossesses the nations not as a destructive military conquest but as the blessing brings them into the family. Simply bringing the exiles back to the land to grow and prosper as a nation does not explain sufficiently the need for a massive enlargement of the family tent.

The Reconstituted Marriage (54:4–10)

The next section, verses 4–10, speaks of God as Husband, Maker, and Redeemer. This is a clear reference to the Israelite/Mosaic covenant, the covenant made between God and Israel at Sinai. This marriage relationship was broken by Israel's unfaithfulness, and God brought the curse of exile upon Israel, and so he forsook (i.e., divorced) his unfaithful wife. This display of wrath was only for a moment, so to speak. The marriage relationship was broken, the wife forsaken/widowed, but now reconciliation brings about renewing of the marriage.

Verse 4 begins with commands which call the woman out of disgrace, humiliation, and shame. She must forget the shame of her youth. This represents the four hundred years of bondage and slavery in Egypt, when Israel was at the beginning of her life as a nation. She must no longer remember the reproach of her widowhood. This represents the seventy years of exile in Babylon. She had been married to the Lord, but she was an unfaithful wife and ended up deserted and alone like a widow; all her lovers (i.e., idols/alliances with foreign nations) and even her husband turned their backs upon her.

Verse 5 speaks of the Lord as her husband and maker. God is not only the creator God, the God of all the earth, but he is the creator and maker of Israel as a nation. Through the covenant at Sinai he married Israel and so is her husband, and now the redeemer, i.e., the nearest relative, who has the duty to buy her back from exile and slavery.

According to verse 6, Israel may feel like a woman who was married as a high school sweetheart and then rejected. This, however, is only a momentary turning away. God will now show her compassion, mercy, and covenant loyal love forever. The marriage relationship will be restored. There will be a new covenant, called a covenant of peace in verse 10 to emphasise the fact of reconciliation. God's anger has been appeased and finished. Israel may now benefit from the healing of a broken relationship in a new covenant. The new covenant renews and restores the broken old covenant. But it is more than that. It is a new covenant, different from the old one and superior to it, because it depends not upon God's people but instead upon the everlasting kindness of God. Momentary wrath is contrasted with everlasting love and mercy.

This is illustrated by a comparison between the new covenant and the covenant God made with Noah. Just as he promised there that never again would he judge the entire world by a flood, so now he is promising never again to be angry with his people. The mountains will give way and the hills will totter, but his *ḥesed*, his covenant faithfulness and love will never be taken away in the new covenant. That is why it is called a covenant of peace.

The City of Righteousness (54:11–17)

1. THE CITY REESTABLISHED/REBUILT (VV. 11–14A)

Verses 11–17 speak of the woman as a city, the city of Zion. She has been afflicted and lashed by storms but will be rebuilt and reestablished. Her new foundation will be with a solid construction of mortar and stone. She will be adorned by precious jewels and fiery, sparkling stones. This construction represents the fact that all will know the Lord.

The city of Zion brings to mind the Davidic covenant and the place where Yahweh rules in the midst of his people as King and where his Son, always a descendant of David, represents his rule to the people and to the nations beyond.

In verse 13 we read that "all your sons will be taught by the LORD." This correlates perfectly with Jeremiah 31:33–34. What is new about the new covenant is that in the covenant community all are believers. In the Israelite/Mosaic covenant—indeed in the Abrahamic covenant which the Israelite covenant seeks to implement in Iron Age Israel for the nation as a whole—one is born into the covenant community. This results in a situation where one may be a member of the covenant community but not a believer. In the new covenant community, the believing community and the covenant community will be perfectly coextensive. This is what Isaiah means when he says "all your sons will be taught by the LORD," and this is the explanation of the statement that the restored city will be built with beautiful and lasting materials. It is comparable to Peter's picture of believers in the new covenant as living stones in the new temple (1 Pet. 2:5). Since every covenant member knows the Lord, every member or "piece" of the city will constitute beautiful and lasting materials, i.e., jewels. The proof that this is the correct interpretation lies in the fact that the Hebrew word translated as "taught" is לִמּוּד and means "disciple." The same word is used of the servant of Yahweh in 50:4 and applies to the people of the Lord here because, according to 54:17, they too are servants of the Lord.

2. THE CITY SECURE (VV. 14B–17)

The city is established in righteousness. This is part of her foundation and will characterise this community. This righteousness will also protect and save her in the end. The same Hebrew word for "righteousness" is used in verse 17 almost in the sense of vindication against those who accuse her in court.

The Lord does not promise that the renewed city will have no enemies, will experience no attacks. But she is not to be afraid. There is no need for terror. In terms of destroying weapons, Yahweh is in charge of the manufacturer, the product, and the intent of the user. Nothing will harm the city of God. Any weapon forged against her will not prosper or succeed. Any accusing tongue will in fact be pronounced guilty by the city of God, and God's people will triumph in court. Peace between God and his people results in peace and wholeness for them.

This city is the final resting-place of the servants of the Lord, the reward and vindication for all that they have suffered because of their faithfulness to God (v. 17). Subtly and quietly, but also unmistakably, Isaiah links them to the greatest servant of all. As he was a disciple, taught by the Lord (50:4), so are they (v. 13). They have suffered affliction (v. 11) as did he (53:4). And as he will surely be vindicated (50:8), so will they be (v. 17). They are called servants of the Lord because they follow in the footsteps of the perfect servant. They share his sufferings and will also share in his glory. They are "his offspring," the fruit of his sacrifice (53:10), and the city of God will be their home.

The new covenant therefore brings to fruition God's promises and purposes in all the others: (1) it brings the numerous seed promised in the Abrahamic covenant, (2) it brings the righteousness between God and humans and among humans aimed at in the Israelite covenant, and (3) it establishes the city of God ruled by the Davidic King. All of this is as certain as the promises to Noah.

ISAIAH 55:1–5

In Isaiah 55:3 God announces that he is initiating an everlasting covenant. This covenant is described as the acts of loyal love performed by David, i.e., the atoning death of the servant king in chapter 53. Here Isaiah is connecting the Davidic covenant and the new. The new covenant will accomplish what was promised in God's covenant with David. Second Samuel 7:19 reveals that the covenant with David is God's instruction for all mankind. Isaiah follows this up by speaking of the Gentiles being called by Israel, who then look to Israel's king as their commander and leader who, as witness, brings the instruction (Torah) of the Lord to them. This is exactly what happened when Peter and Paul began proclaiming the good news to the nations in the book of Acts.

ISAIAH 56:1–8

Chapter 56 begins the last section of the book, where the prophet develops his themes from yet another perspective. His ideas follow the pattern at the beginning of the book. First the people are accused of idolatry and injustice and are condemned. Next comes a vision of the future restored and transformed city of Zion. This is followed by descriptions of the coming anointed conqueror and his work in bringing about this transformation as an act of deliverance and salvation. Finally, the book closes with prayers and promises for the future.

Although Isaiah 56 begins a new major section in the book, it nonetheless is also directly linked to the preceding and shows the next step in the divine programme of salvation for Israel and the world. Those being gathered as the new Zion are to practise social justice and keep Sabbath.

Outline of Isaiah 56:1–8

1. The renewed Zion to practise righteousness   56:1–2
   and keep Sabbath
2. Membership in the community worshipping Yahweh   56:3–8
   A. The foreigner's complaint   56:3a
   B. The eunuch's complaint   56:3b
   B'. The eunuch's place in the temple   56:4–5
   A'. The foreigner's place in the temple   56:6–8

The Renewed Zion to Practise Righteousness and Keep Sabbath (56:1–2)

Isaiah 56:1–8 forms an introduction to the last section of the book, and many of the main themes of this final section are expressed here in broad outline. The first half of verse 1 is a call and command to keep or observe justice and to do righteousness. Right away we can see the pair of words "justice-righteousness" distributed over a poetic couplet in parallelism, which forms the idiomatic phrase for social justice. The second half of verse 1 gives a motive or reason for the command: "because my salvation is about to happen and my righteousness is about to be revealed." So the first half of verse 1 is a command to practise social justice and the second half of verse 1 bases the command on the sovereign work of God, who provides his righteousness as an act of deliverance and salvation.

Before proceeding any further, it is important to see that this final section of the book of Isaiah is interlocked and interwoven with the first two sections by the first verse. The word pair "justice-righteousness," frequently split across lines by poetic parallelism, has occurred so far only in the first section of Isaiah, chapters 1–37: 1:21; 1:27; 5:7; 5:16; 9:6 (9:7 EV); 11:4; 16:5; 26:9; 28:17; 32:1; 32:16; 33:5. This word pair is also found six times in the third section: 56:1; 58:2 [2x]; 59:4; 59:9; 59:14.[11] The word pair "righteousness-salvation" or "salvation-righteousness" in the second half of verse 1 speaks of righteousness as an attribute or characteristic of God; it is the way he works in all his relationships, and since humans do not possess this characteristic in their relationships it must come from God as an act of deliverance and salvation, i.e., as a gift. And this word pair is found only in the

---

[11] Leclerc, *Yahweh Is Exalted in Justice*, especially 10–13, 88, 157.

second section of the book of Isaiah, constituted by chapters 38–55 (45:8; 45:21; 46:13; 51:5; 51:6; 51:8). This first verse, then, of the third section of Isaiah combines phrases that are found only in the first and second sections respectively. This is a testimony to the unity of the book and also to the fact that this third section will now build programmatically on these two ideas.

The second verse pronounces a blessing on the person who keeps the Sabbath and who keeps his hand from doing any evil. Two things about this statement cry out for our attention. First, the blessing, expressed just like the beatitudes of Jesus in Matthew 5, is not directed specifically to Jews or Israelites. Instead, it is general. The first line uses the word "man" (אֱנוֹשׁ) as a generic term, and the line matching it uses the expression "son of man" (בֶּן־אָדָם), the normal Hebrew way of saying "a human being." Thus the invitation is not specifically for Israelites but for all who belong to the human race. This will be made absolutely clear in verses 3–8, but for now we can note that chapter 55 summons all alike to the free banquet; 56:1–8 portrays the gathering people in which all are one, all are equal, and all are welcome in the house of prayer. The second thing that cries out for our attention is that, unlike the first section of Isaiah, no specifics are given about practising social justice. There is only a general statement about keeping one's hand from doing any evil. He does not mention the orphan and the widow. He does not address specific issues of injustice. Instead, there is a call to keep the Sabbath. There is a focus on worshipping the Lord. What does all this mean? Verses 3–8 clarify and expand upon these two ideas.

Membership in the Community Worshiping Yahweh (56:3–8)

First, instead of focusing on the orphan and the widow, this section focuses on the foreigner and the eunuch. The foreigner was excluded from the people of God. The eunuch was also excluded from the worship of God according to Deuteronomy 23:1 (23:2 MT). In addition, the eunuch had no descendants or posterity to carry on his name and leave a memorial for him. And yet these verses explicitly show the foreigner joined to the Lord and the eunuch keeping the Sabbath, and that both are included in the one people of God. Many passages have, to this point, been somewhat vague. They could be interpreted to mean that Israel conquers the nations and takes over their lands. But not these verses. We shall look at them closely.

First we see the foreigner and the eunuch cut off from the people of God. In verse 3 the foreigner is complaining that the Lord will surely separate him from his people. The eunuch is complaining that he is a dry tree. Instead of being a tree that bears fruit and produces seeds that result in reproducing itself, he is a dry tree.

Second, according to verse 3 and verse 6, we see foreigners joining themselves to the Lord. According to verse 6 they are ministering to the Lord and loving his name. The verb "to minister or serve" (שרת) is most commonly used in the Old Testament of the work of the Levites and priests in the temple. So these foreigners are not just permitted in the temple, they are involved like the Levites and priests. At the end of verse 6 they become the servants (עֲבָדִים) of the Lord (cf. Isa. 54:17; 56:6; 63:17; 65:8, 9, 13, 15; 66:14). We were shocked to discover in 54:17 that those who are included in the new covenant community are called the servants of the Lord. The sins of the many have been born by the servant, and the victory of the one servant is shared by the many and in the end they become servants too. Now, we are further shocked because it is foreigners who are called the servants of the Lord. The end of verse 6 shows them as Sabbath keepers and firmly grasping and laying hold of the covenant. At the beginning of the book of Isaiah, Israel, those who were born into the covenant community, the nation, physical Israel, were not Sabbath keepers. They were Sabbath breakers. And now, it is the foreigners who are Sabbath keepers. The same sort of things are said about the eunuch. In verse 4 he is choosing what pleases the Lord and laying hold of his covenant. As a result, God gives to him a memorial and a name in his house (i.e., temple) and within his walls, which is better than sons and daughters. His name is carried on for eternity and will never be cut off. We see, then, that those who were formerly outside of the people of God and excluded from worshipping in the temple are now joined to the Lord and characterised as true worshippers.

Third, not only are individuals who are extreme examples of excluded people now characterised as true worshippers of the Lord, they are considered to be included in the covenant community. Notice the expressions in verses 7 and 8: God will bring them to his holy mountain; he will give them joy in his house of prayer, and they will offer acceptable burnt offerings and sacrifices. There is a progression in these statements of belonging and being included. First, they are brought to God's holy mountain as the place where the Lord is to be found. Second, they are welcomed into his presence and into his family, as indicated by bringing them to celebrate in his house of prayer. Third, they participate in those ordinances which guarantee acceptance and fellowship—they bring offerings (עוֹלוֹת) and sacrifices (זְבָחִים) that are accepted at his altar.[12] Nothing could be clearer on just how far in the in-group are these foreigners! Verse 8 makes it even clearer. The first line speaks about gathering the exiles of Israel. Then the second line says that God will gather others in addition to his gathered ones. We have here clearly specified what was also indicated in 49:6. First God will gather his own people. Then the servant(s) will be a light to the nations.

PSALM 87

While we are considering passages in the prophets that speak of foreign nations being included in the one people of God, we should note the conversation between Isaiah and the Psalms noted by Norbert Lohfink and Erich Zenger.[13] An excellent example is Psalm 87, which deserves to be heard and briefly discussed (see table 12.1):

Table 12.1: Text of Psalm 87

1a. Of the Korahites. A Psalm. A Song.

1b. His foundation in the holy mountains Yahweh loves;
2. the gates of Zion more than all the dwellings of Jacob.

3a. Glorious things are said about you
3b. City of God.   [*Selah*]

4a. I mention Rahab and Babylon among those who know me
4b. See—Philistia and Tyre along with Cush
4c. "This one was born there."
5a. Yes, of Zion it will be said:
5b. "Every single one was born in it."
5c. Yes, he will establish it—the Most High.
6a. Yahweh counts them
6b. When he registers the nations:
6c. "This one was born there."   [*Selah*]

7a. They sing when they dance:
7b. "All my springs are in you."

---

[12] According to the authors of the New Testament (Rom. 12:1; Phil. 4:18; Heb. 13:15–16; 1 Pet. 2:5) these prophecies are fulfilled by the gifts, hymns, and prayers of Christians (whether Jew or Gentile) engaged in the worship of the church.

[13] Norbert Lohfink and Erich Zenger, *The God of Israel and the Nations: Studies in Isaiah and the Psalms*, trans. Everett R. Kalin (Collegeville, MN: Liturgical Press, 2000). The discussion of Psalm 87 here is dependent upon and directly taken from the chapter by Erich Zenger. The translation of Psalm 87 differs slightly.

Literary Structure of Psalm 87

The poem consists of four short sections or stanzas arranged in concentric circles. The first stanza (vv. 1–2) constitutes a heading for the entire poem and is separate from the concentric structure. It declares that Yahweh loves Zion. The second stanza (v. 3) announces that grand things are being said (by the nations) about Zion and is matched by the fourth stanza (v. 7), expressing the same thing. In stanza three (vv. 4–6) Yahweh is speaking, and he recounts the birth registry of the nations. It is arranged in three sections according to the scheme ABA:

> A. This one   was born there (v. 4)
> B. Every single one   was born in it (v. 5)
> A. This one   was born there (v. 6)

The repeated statement in verses 4 and 6 forms a frame (*inclusio*) for which the background is the image of Yahweh registering the nations. The expression at the centre is emphatic and thematic.

Around this middle section lie the second and fourth stanzas, which are connected by the prepositional phrase "in/about you" (3a, 7b), and which also through these phrases are interwoven with the centre which has the prepositional phrase "in it." It may be that the first and second stanza could be considered a unit and thus the concentric pattern is perfect. The poetic structure is confirmed and supported by the fact that verses 3 and 6 end with the term *Selah*.

Message of Psalm 87

The two outer sections/stanzas of the poem (vv. 1–3 and v. 7) agree in presenting a coherent and unified picture of Zion typical in the Old Testament. Zion is the city of God situated on the "holy mountain," which is both the cosmic mountain of the world and the mountain of paradise, where Yahweh is enthroned and dwells as king of the world and God of all-encompassing *shalom*. In the centre of the city of God, or better, in the midst of the palace/temple of the God who dwells within it, the "springs of life" gush forth. The "springs" are integral to this picture, derived from the garden of Eden. It is noteworthy that Gihon is a name applied only to one of the four rivers just outside the garden of Eden (Gen. 2:13) and to the spring just outside the city wall of Jerusalem (1 Kings 1:33, 38, 45; 2 Chron. 32:30, 33:14). Zion is like Eden in possessing the same source of water.

The "gates of Zion" mentioned in verse 2b may possibly connote a number of things. City gates are peculiar to a city, which in contrast to a village is characterised by a wall with its gate or gates. The gates of the city in ancient Israel correspond to the town hall of cities in the Western world. This was the place where important business transactions and court judgements took place. Therefore, it was key to the justice and righteousness of the city. By metonymy, the "gates of Zion" might also refer to the gates of the temple. The ordering of justice and life established by Yahweh is connected with "the gates" of the temple (cf. Psalm 15, 24, Isa. 33:14–16). Just as in the vision of future Zion proclaimed by Isaiah 2, where the nations are streaming to Zion to receive instruction from Yahweh, so here, too, the two outer sections proclaim Zion as a source of universal social justice and righteousness for the nations.

The middle section (vv. 4–6) is thoroughly stamped by the image that Yahweh confers citizenship in the city of God on the members of the many nations, in that Yahweh enters them in the "citizenship rolls." With artistic skill this idea is repeated three times. The background may be the heavenly book of destiny and life attested elsewhere in the ancient Near East. Within the Old Testament itself we find the institution of membership in the temple-congregation (Isa. 4:3; Ezek. 13:9; Ps. 69:28 [29 MT] Ex. 32:32) and this is a better proposal as to the background of the text in Psalm 87. The first statement is the most shocking and significant: Yahweh has accorded to the two great traditional enemy powers Egypt (Rahab) and Babylon, as well as to the lands of Philistia, Phoenicia, and Cush, in a legally binding way (with rights and obligations), a connection to Zion.

The enumeration of the five names is not intended to be exclusive. Rather, the whole world is in view, with Zion proclaimed as the centre or navel of the earth.[14] The four names that are mentioned correspond to and mark the four compass points, West (Egypt), East (Babylon), North (Philistia and Tyre) and South (Cush). In this geographical and spatial perspective, Zion is a location, a place. But in Hebrew, "city" is feminine, and the image of birth and registration in Zion gives the idea that Zion is the mother of the nations. In the Greek translation an error in the copying and transmission of the text resulted in the city actually being called "Mother Zion." This error in the textual transmission conveys the meaning of the passage quite well.

---

[14] On Jerusalem as the centre of the earth, see Thomas Renz, "The Use of the Zion Tradition in the Book of Ezekiel," in *Zion, City of Our God*, ed. Richard S. Hess and Gordon J. Wenham (Grand Rapids, MI: Eerdmans, 1999), 86–87.

Isaiah 66:7–14 also pictures Zion as a woman giving birth to her children, those who are citizens in Israel. In Psalm 87, Zion becomes the mother of the nations, not through natural birth but through Yahweh's own determination and election. If one connects the middle section in verses 4–6 to the statement of themes in verses 1–2, Yahweh gives the nations to Zion as "children" because Yahweh loves Zion.

The pattern of thought in Psalm 87 is similar to the eschatological vision of Zechariah 2:10–12 [14–16 MT], although the order of thematic elements in the two texts is opposite to each other:

Zechariah 2:10–12 [14–16 MT]		Psalm 87
v. 10 [14]	Sing and rejoice, O daughter Zion! For see, I will come and dwell in your midst, declares the LORD.	v. 7
v. 11 [15]	Many nations shall join themselves to the LORD in that day, and shall be my people; and I will dwell in your midst . . .	vv. 4–6
v. 12 [16]	The LORD will inherit Judah as his portion in the holy land, and will again choose Jerusalem.	vv. 1–2

Two exegetical difficulties remain: (1) how do we interpret Psalm 87:5c and (2) how do we interpret the nations mentioned in Psalm 87? Some interpreters avoid the idea that the nations are incorporated as citizens of Zion by saying that the mention of these nations refers to the Jews in the Diaspora. The correct interpretation of Psalm 87:5c is provided by considering the relationship of Psalm 87 to the Korah Psalms. The correct interpretation of the nations is resolved by noting the relationship between Psalm 87 and the Asaph Psalms, in particular Psalm 83.

Zenger discusses the editorial *arrangement* of the hymns in the Psalter in detail. Psalm 87 belongs to the Psalms of Korah (42–49; 84–85; 87–89) and is preceded by the Psalms of Asaph (50; 73–83).

In Psalm 87 Yahweh establishes Zion in verse 1 and equips Zion as a beneficent force in the world in verse 5c. Verse 5c is in fact a citation of Psalm 48:8 (9 MT); the psalms of the sons of Korah share a common linguistic and theological profile and also develop an argument in the collection as a whole. Concerning the connections between Psalm 87 and the Korah Psalms, Zenger says,

> It is possible that in 87:5c there is also a reminder of the manner in which YHWH "equips" Zion to be the source of life for the nations. In Ps 48:9–11

[10–12] the equipping of Zion spoken of in 48:8 [9] is explicitly seen in the saving gifts of "righteousness and justice" that are present there or go forth from there; with these YHWH as king of the world "deprives" the enemy nations "of their power." This legal aspect is also found in Psalm 87: from the seat of power YHWH, the king of the world, takes the nations into YHWH's realm in a legal and binding way and obligates them from that time on to follow the laws of this realm. That YHWH declares in 87:4a that Rahab and Babylon are among "those who (ac)know(ledge) me," from the perspective of Ps 46:10 [11] ("Be still, and know that I am YHWH") means precisely this: the nations are prepared to take instructions from YHWH in his ordering of world peace. On the level of the book of Psalms, 87:4a has to be read from the perspective of Ps 25:14: Egypt and Babylon belong to those who acknowledge YHWH—because YHWH has given them knowledge about himself and the covenant.[15]

Psalm 87 is connected to Psalm 83, the concluding Psalm of the Asaph group, and by several key words:

(1) The geographical designations "Philistia and Tyre" occur in 83:7 [8 MT] and 87:4.

(2) Psalm 83 culminates with a statement that Yahweh should show himself and demonstrate in a dramatic way that he alone is the Most High (83:18) [19 MT]). According to Psalm 87:5, Yahweh is shown to be the Most High by "equipping" Zion as the "centre" and "source of life" for the nations.

(3) The goal of Yahweh's intervention against the assault of the nations intent on annihilating Israel is, according to 83:18 [19 MT], that the nations (ac)know(ledge) Yahweh and Yahweh's name; in Psalm 87:4 Yahweh lists the great powers as those "who (ac)know(ledge) me."

Psalm 86 is the prayer of a poor and persecuted person, whom the superscription identifies as David, making an urgent appeal that Yahweh let the vision laid out in Psalm 87—of the universal liberation of the nations by the actualization of Yahweh's royal reign (Ps. 86:8–10)—at long last become reality. Psalm 86 also anticipates eagerly the decisive eschatological turning when the God of the Sinai covenant is revealed, as it affirms with a citation of Exodus 34, which is the basis for extending the covenant to the nations in Psalm 25.

Thus the context of Psalm 87 decisively requires that we interpret the nations in Psalm 87 as the foreign nations and not as Diasporic Jews. Psalm 87 clearly teaches that the Lord will take the foreign nations, the enemies of

---

[15] Lohfink and Zenger, *God of Israel and the Nations*, 145.

Israel, and make them citizens of Zion. This teaching echoes the remarkable statement in Isaiah 19:24–25:

> [24] In that day Israel will be the third with Egypt and Assyria, a blessing in the midst of the earth, [25] whom the LORD of hosts has blessed, saying, "Blessed be Egypt my people, and Assyria the work of my hands, and Israel my inheritance."

Here Isaiah predicts that the renewed and restored Zion will involve taking the worst enemies of Israel and incorporating them into the one people of God.[16]

ISAIAH 59:21

Another significant text is 59:21:

> "As for me, this is my covenant with them," says the LORD. "My Spirit, who is on you, and my words that I have put in your mouth will not depart from your mouth, or from the mouths of your children, or from the mouths of their descendants from this time on and forever," says the LORD. (NIV)

The comment of John Davies is both apt and concise:

> After a description of the lamentable situation of Zion in Isa. 59.1–15, the result of separation from God through the people's sins and offences (59.2), a turning point is reached at v. 16, where the arm of Yhwh intervenes on his people's behalf. There follows a sustained depiction of a glorious restoration of Zion, once again to be graced with the divine presence and glory. This depiction continues without interruption through to the end of ch. 62.
>
> The key to the restoration is Yhwh's return to Zion in zealous pursuit of the interests of his people and his glorious presence there (59.17–20), together with his declared 'covenant' (v. 21) or commitment to remain forever with his people through his spirit and his words. Chapters 60–62 then draw on a rich store of imagery to portray the implications of this restoration of Zion (the remnant of Israel) to an exalted status.[17]

ISAIAH 61:1–11

Many Christians are familiar with the first three verses of Isaiah 61, since Jesus cited them in the synagogue service recorded in Luke 4:16–21.

---

[16] The Septuagint translator could not stomach the literal meaning of verses 24–25!

[17] John A. Davies, *A Royal Priesthood: Literary and Intertextual Perspectives on an Image of Israel in Exodus 19:6*, JSOTSup 395 (London: T. & T. Clark, 2004), 212.

Nonetheless, Christians in general are not so well versed in what the rest of Isaiah 61 has to say about the new covenant.

[1] The Spirit of the Sovereign LORD is on me,
   because the LORD has anointed me
   to proclaim good news to the poor.
He has sent me to bind up the brokenhearted,
   to proclaim freedom for the captives
   and release for the prisoners,
[2] to proclaim the year of the LORD's favor
   and the day of vengeance of our God,
to comfort all who mourn,
[3] and provide for those who grieve in Zion—
to bestow on them a crown of beauty
   instead of ashes,
the oil of joy
   instead of mourning,
and a garment of praise
   instead of a spirit of despair.
They will be called oaks of righteousness,
   a planting of the LORD
   for the display of his splendor.
[4] They will rebuild the ancient ruins
   and restore the places long devastated;
they will renew the ruined cities
   that have been devastated for generations.
[5] Strangers will shepherd your flocks;
   foreigners will work your fields and vineyards.
[6] And you will be called priests of the LORD,
   you will be named ministers of our God.
You will feed on the wealth of nations,
   and in their riches you will boast.
[7] Instead of your shame
   you will receive a double portion,
and instead of disgrace
   you will rejoice in your inheritance.
And so you will inherit a double portion in your land,
   and everlasting joy will be yours.
[8] "For I, the LORD, love justice;
   I hate robbery in a burnt offering.
In my faithfulness I will reward my people
   and make an everlasting covenant with them.
[9] Their descendants will be known among the nations

and their offspring among the peoples.
All who see them will acknowledge
   that they are a people the LORD has blessed."

A coming king, anointed by Yahweh and filled by his Spirit, will bring about a great jubilee—no doubt the word דְּרוֹר in 61:1 is a direct allusion to Leviticus 25:10. The king anointed by the Spirit is also doubtless the same one described in Isaiah 11. As a result of his leadership, mourners in Zion are restored, and the long-standing ruins are rebuilt. Foreigners will care for the fields and the orchards, but Israel will be called priests of Yahweh (61:6). This simple statement is examined extensively by Davies,[18] who is surely right to see here an allusion to Exodus 19:6. Israel's role as a royal priesthood, lost through violation of the Israelite covenant, is restored by the new covenant. Significantly, the text expressly states in verse 8 that in the new covenant it is the faithfulness of Yahweh that brings about or causes the giving of this reward: "in my faithfulness I will reward my people and make an everlasting covenant with them." This is a clear reference to the new covenant, which is brought about by the faithfulness of Yahweh and entails a reward: the status (as priests) and the wealth mentioned in the context. It is also noteworthy that in verse 6, which specifies the restored status as priests, they are called "ministers of God," exactly the same term applied to foreigners in 56:6. The double portion was the inheritance of the firstborn son—another connection to the role given to Israel in Exodus (4:22).

ISAIAH 62:12

They will be called the Holy People,
   the Redeemed of the LORD;
and you will be called Sought After,
   the City No Longer Deserted. (NIV)

The designation "holy people" here in 62:12 confirms the interpretation of 61:6: the renewed people of God are given in the new covenant what Israel lost in violating the Israelite covenant—the status as holy nation and royal priesthood.[19] This, as we saw earlier, is an Adamic role—functioning as king-priest.

---

[18] Ibid., 212–217.
[19] Ibid., 215.

ISAIAH 66:18–24

Many passages relating to the role of the nations in the new covenant could be examined with profit. Isaiah 66:18–24 is one of the more important texts:

> [18] "For I know their works and their thoughts, and the time is coming to gather all nations and tongues. And they shall come and shall see my glory, [19] and I will set a sign among them. And from them I will send survivors to the nations, to Tarshish, Pul, and Lud, who draw the bow, to Tubal and Javan, to the coastlands far away, that have not heard my fame or seen my glory. And they shall declare my glory among the nations. [20] And they shall bring all your brothers from all the nations as an offering to the LORD, on horses and in chariots and in litters and on mules and on dromedaries, to my holy mountain Jerusalem, says the LORD, just as the Israelites bring their grain offering in a clean vessel to the house of the LORD. [21] And some of them also I will take for priests and for Levites, says the LORD.
>
> [22] "For as the new heavens and the new earth that I make shall remain before me, says the LORD, so shall your offspring and your name remain. [23] From new moon to new moon, and from Sabbath to Sabbath, all flesh shall come to worship before me, declares the LORD.
>
> [24] "And they shall go out and look on the dead bodies of the men who have rebelled against me. For their worm shall not die, their fire shall not be quenched, and they shall be an abhorrence to all flesh." (ESV)

Outline of Isaiah 66:1–24

A¹. Where is the temple of Yahweh and its worship?   66:1–4
    B¹. Assurance for those who tremble at God's word   66:5–14
    B². Divine judgement upon the false worshippers   66:15–17
A². Worldwide pilgrimage to the temple of Yahweh   66:18–24

Four paragraphs are arranged in chapter 66 in chiastic fashion. The last paragraph is verses 18–24. Here Isaiah speaks of a worldwide pilgrimage bringing a pure offering to the Lord's house (vv. 18–21), and then in verses 22–23 we see that all humanity is keeping Sabbath. This section returns to the themes raised in the important questions at the beginning of chapter 66: Where is the true temple of the Lord, and who are the people worshipping there? The answer is that God is not worshipped at a particular geographical location but by a certain type of people: the humble and lowly, who tremble at his word. At the same time this section also returns to the theme at the beginning of chapter 65 of the nations playing a role in the future Zion and people of God. The issues of true Sabbath keepers and true worshippers raised in chapters 56 and 58 are brought to a conclusion as well.

There is also a way in which the end of the book of Isaiah matches its beginning. In chapter 1 Isaiah lambasts the people for corrupt forms of worship, and here at the end of his work he returns to this theme, showing how the problem has at last been resolved.

Verse 18 is difficult because apparently some words are missing from the text in Hebrew. It begins with the words "and I." Then follow the words "their deeds and their intentions." After that the verb "is coming" is feminine, which rules out the translation of the NIV that it is the Lord who is coming. The best proposal is to translate, "And as for me, in view of their deeds and intentions, the time is coming to gather all the nations and tongues, and they will come and see my glory." In Ezekiel 21:12 (21:7 EV) and 39:8 we have the verb "coming" as a feminine form and the omitted subject is the word "time," so this is a possible way to interpret this text as well. The question is whether this gathering of nations is negative or positive, i.e., will God gather them for judgement or for salvation? According to the context, both are possible. But in verses 18–24 the emphasis is on gathering from the nations those who will become true worshippers of the Lord. So the emphasis here is a positive one. This passage reminds us of Isaiah 2:2–4, where the nations are streaming to Mount Zion to receive Instruction or Torah from the Lord for daily living. It also reminds us of 11:10, where the Root of Jesse will stand as a banner for the peoples, who will then rally to him. A parallel passage is Zechariah 2:15 (2:11 EV), which speaks of many nations being joined to the Lord in a future day. Another parallel is Psalm 22:27 (28 MT): "All the ends of the earth will remember and turn to the LORD, and all the families of the nations will bow down before him" (NIV). The end of this verse (Isa. 66:18) says that the nations will see the glory of Yahweh. The glory of the Lord in the Old Testament was a bright cloud, indicating that God was dwelling in the midst of the people. This seems to be the thought here. When the tabernacle was constructed, Israel saw the glory of the Lord as a bright cloud descending upon it, showing that the creator God was coming to dwell with them and rule in their midst as king. Here, the nations will see the glory of the Lord.

How will the nations recognise that God is gathering them to see his glory? Verse 19 speaks of God placing a sign among the nations. Since this passage refers to the gathering of the nations into the new Jerusalem, we can see and understand from our vantage point that the sign probably refers to the cross. Isaiah, however, knows and speaks only in a general way of some sign that will be a common cause to bring the nations to see the glory of the Lord.

Next, survivors are dispatched and sent to distant nations. Some interpret the survivors to be from Israel, but Isaiah 45:20 speaks specifically of survivors from the nations. These will be sent to distant countries. It is difficult to identify the countries listed here. Tarshish may be in Spain. The Hebrew text mentions Pul and Lud. According to Genesis 10:13 there is a Lud in Africa and, according to 10:22, a Lud associated with the Semites, possibly in Asia Minor. It could be that the NIV is right in speaking of Libya and Lydia as places in Africa and then Tubal and Greece as places in eastern and western Turkey. The Greeks known to Israel were the Ionians who lived in southwestern Turkey. At any rate, all of these places represent those countries on the edge of the map as far as geography in Isaiah's time is concerned. And the amazing thing is that survivors are sent out to these distant nations because they have not heard about Yahweh or seen his glory. This is a hint in the Old Testament of the missionary enterprise in the New Testament. Normally in the Old Testament, all the nations come to Israel to learn about her God and the right way to treat each other. In the New Testament, Jesus sends his disciples out to the far ends of the earth. This text in Isaiah comes close to the Great Commission in Matthew 28.

Verse 20 of Isaiah 66 states, "'and they will bring all your brothers from all the nations as an offering to the LORD, on horses, in chariots and wagons, on mules and camels, to my holy mountain, Jerusalem,' says the LORD." There are different interpretations of this verse. Some think that because the term "brothers" is used, Isaiah is speaking about gathering Israelites from the nations. But it is more probable that he uses the term "brother" to show that converts from the nations will become part of the one people of God.

Several considerations support the interpretation of "brothers" as referring to Gentiles. Every word in the text of Isaiah is carefully chosen and motivated. Note, for example, Isaiah 58:7, where true fasting is defined: "Is it not to share your food with the hungry and to provide the poor wanderer with shelter—when you see the naked, to clothe him, and not to turn away from your own flesh and blood?" (NIV). Here Isaiah employs the term בָּשָׂר ("flesh") to show that the "poor" are *family*. They are not other people; they are our own, and we must feed them with the same responsibility with which we would feed our own family. Likewise in Isaiah 56:6 the text speaks of the foreigners as "ministers" and "servants" to show that they have the same status as priests. The same technique is employed in Isaiah 66:20, where אָח (brother) is used to show that those drawn from the nations are *family* as well.

Admittedly "brother" is rare in Isaiah (3:6; 9:19 [18 MT]; 19:2; 41:6; 66:5; 66:20) and refers to Israelites in 66:5. Nonetheless, if "brothers" were fellow-Israelites, the point would be anti-climactic and the comparison between offering the brothers as an offering just as the Israelites offer an offering would be completely tautologous and meaningless. Romans 15:16 is directly dependent upon this verse in Isaiah, and Paul is interpreting the text to refer to Gentiles, non-Jews, being joined to the people of God. This also agrees with the vision in Isaiah 2 of the nations streaming to Mount Zion. John 11:49–52 would confirm this:

> Caiaphas, who was high priest that year, said to them, "You know nothing at all. [50] Nor do you understand that it is better for you that one man should die for the people, not that the whole nation should perish." [51] He did not say this of his own accord, but being high priest that year he prophesied that Jesus would die for the nation, [52] *and not for the nation only, but also to gather into one the children of God who are scattered abroad* (ESV, emphasis mine).

Verse 21 of Isaiah 66 goes one step further. Not only will people from the nations come to worship the Lord just as Israel used to bring a pure offering, some of them will be chosen for priests, for Levites, i.e., to be leaders in the worshipping community (61:6). Again, the term "priest" is employed sparingly in the book of Isaiah: 8:2; 24:2; 28:7; 37:2; 61:6; 66:21. In 61:6 we saw that the renewed people of God are once more assigned the status proclaimed earlier in the Israelite covenant. Now Israel as a royal priesthood includes Gentiles; the context puts an emphasis on honour, privilege, absorbing the riches of the nations, and nearness to Yahweh.

To sum up where we have come in Isaiah 66:18–21: God will gather the nations and put a sign among them. He will dispatch survivors (of judgement) to distant lands to bring the peoples there to know and see the glory of the Lord. These messengers will bring non-Jews as a kind of offering to the Lord, and the nations will worship in Jerusalem with some of them even being chosen as priests.[20]

Verse 22 now offers a guarantee: "just as the new heavens and new earth are before the LORD [i.e., so certain that he can already see them], so are your offspring and your name." This is a clear reference to God's promises to Abraham. His name and his offspring are preserved because now God

---

[20] See Romans 15:16.

has joined Jews and non-Jews into one family. The new world involves two things: a new place and a new people. Verse 22 shows that both of these are certain because they are in God's mind; he can actually see them before him. Verse 23 then refers to all the nations coming every New Moon and every Sabbath to worship the Lord.

The last verse of Isaiah (66:24) indicates that those rescued will observe the final judgement of those who have responded negatively to Isaiah's message of salvation.

ISAIAH 65:1–25

The transformation of Zion reaches consummation and conclusion with the announcement of a new creation/Jerusalem. Motyer demonstrates that Isaiah chapters 65 and 66 form one chiastically structured unit. This important text deserves to be heard in full:

> [1] "I revealed myself to those who did not ask for me;
> I was found by those who did not seek me.
> To a nation that did not call on my name,
> I said, 'Here am I, here am I.'
> [2] All day long I have held out my hands
> to an obstinate people,
> who walk in ways not good,
> pursuing their own imaginations—
> [3] a people who continually provoke me
> to my very face,
> offering sacrifices in gardens
> and burning incense on altars of brick;
> [4] who sit among the graves
> and spend their nights keeping secret vigil;
> who eat the flesh of pigs,
> and whose pots hold broth of unclean meat;
> [5] who say, 'Keep away; don't come near me,
> for I am too sacred for you!'
> Such people are smoke in my nostrils,
> a fire that keeps burning all day.
> [6] "See, it stands written before me:
> I will not keep silent but will pay back in full;
> I will pay it back into their laps—
> [7] both your sins and the sins of your fathers,"
>   says the LORD.
> "Because they burned sacrifices on the mountains

and defied me on the hills,
I will measure into their laps
the full payment for their former deeds."

[8] This is what the LORD says:

"As when juice is still found in a cluster of grapes
and men say, 'Don't destroy it,
there is yet some good in it,'
so will I do in behalf of my servants;
I will not destroy them all.
[9] I will bring forth descendants from Jacob,
and from Judah those who will possess my mountains;
my chosen people will inherit them,
and there will my servants live.
[10] Sharon will become a pasture for flocks,
and the Valley of Achor a resting place for herds,
for my people who seek me.
[11] "But as for you who forsake the LORD
and forget my holy mountain,
who spread a table for Fortune
and fill bowls of mixed wine for Destiny,
[12] I will destine you for the sword,
and you will all bend down for the slaughter;
for I called but you did not answer,
I spoke but you did not listen.
You did evil in my sight
and chose what displeases me."

[13] Therefore this is what the Sovereign LORD says:

"My servants will eat,
but you will go hungry;
my servants will drink,
but you will go thirsty;
my servants will rejoice,
but you will be put to shame.
[14] My servants will sing
out of the joy of their hearts,
but you will cry out
from anguish of heart
and wail in brokenness of spirit.
[15] You will leave your name

to my chosen ones as a curse;
the Sovereign LORD will put you to death,
    but to his servants he will give another name.
[16] Whoever invokes a blessing in the land
    will do so by the God of truth;
he who takes an oath in the land
    will swear by the God of truth.
For the past troubles will be forgotten
    and hidden from my eyes.

[17] "Behold, I will create
    new heavens and a new earth.
The former things will not be remembered,
    nor will they come to mind.
[18] But be glad and rejoice forever
    in what I will create,
for I will create Jerusalem to be a delight
    and its people a joy.
[19] I will rejoice over Jerusalem
    and take delight in my people;
the sound of weeping and of crying
    will be heard in it no more.

[20] "Never again will there be in it
    an infant who lives but a few days,
    or an old man who does not live out his years;
he who dies at a hundred
    will be thought a mere youth;
he who fails to reach a hundred
    will be considered accursed.
[21] They will build houses and dwell in them;
    they will plant vineyards and eat their fruit.
[22] No longer will they build houses and others live in them,
    or plant and others eat.
For as the days of a tree,
    so will be the days of my people;
my chosen ones will long enjoy
    the works of their hands.
[23] They will not toil in vain
    or bear children doomed to misfortune;
for they will be a people blessed by the LORD,
    they and their descendants with them.
[24] Before they call I will answer;

while they are still speaking I will hear.
[25] The wolf and the lamb will feed together,
and the lion will eat straw like the ox,
but dust will be the serpent's food.
They will neither harm nor destroy
on all my holy mountain,"

says the LORD. (NIV)

Outline of Isaiah 65:1–66:21[21]
(Chiastic Structure of the Lord's Promises)

A¹. The Lord's call to those who had not sought him	65:1
B¹. God's repayment to a rebellious people	2–7
C¹. Promise of a preserved remnant	8–10
D¹. Those who forsake the Lord destined for slaughter	11–12
E. Joys of the Lord's servants in the new creation	13–25
D². Those who forsake the Lord destined for slaughter	66:1–4
C². Promise of a preserved remnant	5–14
B². God's repayment to a rebellious people	15–17
A². The Lord's call to those who had not sought him	18–21

The purpose of the chiastic literary structure here is twofold. The first purpose is to rivet our attention on the centre section: the promise of a new creation, with a new Zion at its centre. The second purpose is to show the conditions and steps to the fulfilment of this vision and, on the other side of the central section, to develop these truths in greater detail. While we might expect more space to be devoted to a description of the final state, Isaiah devotes more space to the process by which we get there.

We may begin by focusing on Isaiah 65:13. It starts with the word "therefore" and so summarises the contrasting destinies outlined in the paragraphs of verses 2–12. The section comprising verses 13–18 brings together three streams of thought: the worldwide stream of verse 1, the judgement streams of verses 2–7 and 11–12, and the remnant stream of verses 8–10.

The remnant are referred to as the servants of God. They will eat, but the rebels will go hungry. They will drink, but the rebels will go thirsty. They will know celebration and joy, while the rebels will know shame. They will be so filled with cheerfulness within that they will burst out with a cry of

---

[21] Adapted from Motyer, *Prophecy of Isaiah*, 522–523.

joy so loud that it echoes and rings while the rebels will be filled with pain inside and will howl with broken spirits. These terms speak of both physical and spiritual well-being. Every external need is met and, internally, they are fully satisfied.

Both this paragraph (vv. 13–25) and the paragraph in verses 8–10, which refers to the remnant, are amazing in speaking of them as the Lord's servants. Already in chapter 54, where the sacrificial death and suffering of the Servant King results in a new and everlasting covenant, we see in verse 17 that those who are joined to the servant as the new covenant community are also referred to as servants. More astonishing is 56:6, which makes plain that individuals from the nations are included as the servants of the Lord. Then in 63:17, in the prayer of the watchman, the person praying asks for God to show mercy on his servants. And now this prayer is answered as we see the blessings to be poured out on the servants of the Lord.

Isaiah 65:15–16 shows that the promises to Abraham and the covenant with Abraham find fulfilment in the new covenant community, who are referred to as "the servants of the Lord." In an ironic reversal, the name of unbelieving Israel becomes a curse to God's chosen ones, and the Lord puts them to death. The new covenant community is given a new name, which is left unspecified. And the one being blessed or uttering a blessing in the land will be blessed or will utter a blessing by a "God of Amen," and the one swearing in the land will swear by a God of Amen. The epithet "God of truth" (so most English versions) is actually "a God of Amen" in the Hebrew text. The English word "amen" is a transliteration of an adverb, אָמֵן, that means something like "surely" and is employed by someone who is acknowledging an oath or promise. In contrast to rebellious Israelites who have uttered a blessing by false gods who cannot back it up, members of the new community will utter blessings by a God who will acknowledge and back up blessings uttered in his name.[22]

There is a clear connection between this paragraph (vv. 13–25, esp. 15–16) and the covenant made with Abraham. First, note that it was in the covenant with Abraham in Genesis 17 that Abram was given a new name, i.e., Abraham (Gen. 17:5). Second, note that the covenant promised blessing for those

---

[22] The relative particle אֲשֶׁר begins verse 16. Motyer assumes that "name" in verse 15 is the antecedent, but no resumptive pronoun within the clause supports such a reading. It may mark result, "so that," or we may have a null head relative identified by another null head relative (i.e., a relative article on the participle). The effect of this is that the one being blessed in the land is necessarily restricted to the class of entities who are characterised as blessed by a God of Amen. I am grateful to Robert Holmstedt of the University of Toronto for his assistance in analysing this text.

blessing Abram and his family. Third, note that there is a curse for the one—and it is specified in the singular—who rejects Abram's family. The blessing and cursing in Isaiah 65:15–16 clearly recall the promises of Genesis 12:2–3, but they redefine them according to the new covenant community and its "God of Amen." The name "God of Amen" is found only here in the Old Testament, and it is explained in 2 Corinthians 1:20.[23] As Paul explains, it is in the new covenant community that all of the promises of God receive a resounding "yes."

Grüneberg argues that the *hithpael* of *bārak* means "utter an oath" since it is parallel to "swear" in verse 16b.[24] Nonetheless, the A line of the poetry need not be identical to the B line in meaning, and it seems as if Paul construes the form as passive, for those who hear a "yes" to God's promises are being blessed. Thus we can translate "whoever is blessed in the land will be blessed by a God of Amen."

Verse 17 begins with the conjunction "for" to introduce an explanation for the particular and worldwide blessings of the preceding section. This section ended by promising blessings for the one who is related to the God of "Amen" or truth. This experience is so radical that the former distresses and troubles are forgotten—not just by humans, but by God himself. Verse 17 picks up the thought of the former things and shows why the former things will not be remembered: God is making all things new.

The promise of a new creation—a new heavens and a new earth—shows that the divine plan of salvation is no halfway job. God has something bigger in mind. Yes, it involves return from exile and deliverance from the nations that have been oppressing God's people. Even more than that, it entails the forgiveness of sins and reconciliation so that the covenant is renewed, the temple is rebuilt, and Yahweh returns to Zion. God is dwelling once more in the midst of his people as king. Not only, then, do God's people have a right relationship to him, but they treat one another in genuinely human ways with faithfulness and truth, with justice and righteousness—social justice. And astonishing as it may seem, these blessings flow to the nations who are included now in the one people of God. But the creation itself has been subject to futility and destruction on account of human sin, and God is not finished until this is rectified. He will make a completely brand new universe: a new heavens and a new earth. We see, then, that the plan of

---

[23] Note that in the New Testament, Jesus uniquely begins his statements with "Amen Amen."

[24] Keith N. Grüneberg, *Abraham, Blessing, and the Nations: A Philological and Exegetical Study of Genesis 12:3 in Its Narrative Context* (Berlin: Walter de Gruyter, 2003), 211.

salvation is no halfway fix-it job. God's plan of restoration brings us back to the pristine state of Eden—in a world now much better and much greater. Augustine once said that he feared to entrust his soul to the great physician lest he be more thoroughly cured than he cared to be. God's plan of salvation is absolutely thorough, and he is not going to be satisfied with some half job of reformation and renewal in our lives.

God's forgetting of the old things results in our forgetting of the old creation. And we are commanded to delight and rejoice in the new just as God finds his delight and joy in the new.

It must be emphasised that the final state is not heaven, but rather life in a new creation. The gospel I heard as a child was one where I was warned of eternal judgement in hell and of heaven offered through faith in Jesus Christ. It is true to the Scriptures that, when a believer dies, he or she goes to "be with the Lord." And in Hebrews 12 we are given a glimpse of the heavenly Zion, where the spirits of just men made perfect are kept safe in the Lord's presence. But this is not our final goal. The final goal is not to get away from this world, full of evil and completely ruined by our poor stewardship, but to live in a new creation where we have a brand new start.

Isaiah 65:18b describes creating Jerusalem a delight and God's people a joy. It seems that Jerusalem is the new creation. As T. Desmond Alexander notes, "Significantly, in verses 17–18 the creation of the 'new heavens and a new earth' parallels the creation of Jerusalem (cf. Isa. 24:23). The repeated use of the Hebrew verb *bārā'*, 'to create', suggests that Jerusalem is *deliberately equated* here with the new heavens and the new earth. They are one and the same."[25] Possibly this is not the only way to understand the text, but in Revelation 21 we see that it is the correct interpretation. Jerusalem is not only at the centre of the new world, but in fact is coextensive with it. The new creation is the new Jerusalem and vice versa. This conclusion is clear from Isaiah 65:25, where the new creation is described as God's holy mountain—Mount Zion has become the new Eden!

The order in producing the new creation is reversed from that in producing the old creation. In the old creation, first God made the place where we live, and then he made the creatures to live there.[26] In the new creation,

---

[25] T. Desmond Alexander, *From Eden to the New Jerusalem: An Introduction to Biblical Theology* (Grand Rapids, MI: Kregel, 2008), 53–54. Cf. Jon D. Levenson, *Creation and the Persistence of Evil: The Jewish Drama of Divine Omnipotence* (San Francisco: Harper & Row, 1988), 89–90.

[26] See Craig G. Bartholomew, "The Theology of Place in Genesis 1–3," in *Reading the Law: Studies in Honour of Gordon J. Wenham*, ed. J. G. McConville and Karl Möller, Library of Hebrew Bible/Old Testament Studies 461 (New York: T. & T. Clark, 2007), 173–195.

however, first God will make his new people, and then he will make the home where they will live. This order is first observed in Genesis 12, where God makes his last new start with Abram and his family. The promises in verses 1–3 begin by announcing that God will make Abram into a great nation. Nothing is said about land, but surely this is implied. A great nation cannot exist apart from a place to call home. This is actually made explicit later on in verse 7, where God promises to Abram the land of Canaan. Nonetheless, as the history of the divine dealings with Abram show, God's priority is to create a covenant people first rather than settle the issue of the land where they will dwell. As we saw in the Davidic covenant, the land as defined in the covenant with Abram in Genesis 15:18–21 and described in Deuteronomy 11:24–25 as Israel's place becomes Israel's possession in the time of Solomon (1 Kings 4:24–25 [5:4–5 MT]). Yet the Israelite covenant curses brought the loss of the land: first the area of Galilee, then the northern kingdom, then Judah, and last, Jerusalem itself. Yet in his treatment of the new covenant Isaiah announces that the people of the new Zion will be far more numerous than those of the old (barren woman, Isa. 54:1–3) because the nations will be drawn in to the new Zion. Implicit in this is the fact that more land will be required than just the real estate entailed in historical Israel. How can the new Zion find enough space in the new Jerusalem/Israel? Isaiah 65 solves the puzzle: new Jerusalem and the new creation will be coextensive. As Paul says, Abram believed he would inherit the world (Rom. 4:13).

Some may find this discussion of the promises concerning the future of the city of Jerusalem and the land of Israel troublesome. It is extremely important to observe the *development* within the book of Isaiah in regard to the transformation of Zion. At the outset we noted that the main theme of Isaiah's prophecy is the change or movement from corrupt Zion in the old creation to restored Zion in the new creation, and that this topic is presented in seven major recursive sections. Five of these seven sections end with a vision of the future Zion (2:1–4; 4:2–6; 11:1–10; 25:6–12; 65:17–25). The first (2:1–4) pictures the Temple Mountain higher than all others, with the nations streaming to it to receive instruction (Torah). The second (4:2–6) combines images of a fruitful land, a city devoted to the Lord, and a place of worship overshadowed by a canopy of glory as in the exodus. The third (11:1–10) portrays the future as an Edenic paradise (recall that Eden was on a mountain). The fourth (25:6–12) paints the scene of a mountain banquet with aged wine where death is swallowed up forever. The last (65:17–25) combines the new creation and the new Jerusalem together in one tableau. We must put all of these pictures together holographically to see Isaiah's vision of future Zion. This is much better than a two- or even four-speaker audio system!

Let us note in particular the first and second visions in chapters 2 and 4 of Isaiah. In the vision of 2:1–4, the Mountain of the Temple of Yahweh becomes higher than all other hills and mountains. In the ancient Near East, mountains were viewed as a meeting place between heaven and earth and hence a place where humans could meet God. Consequently it is no surprise that sanctuaries and temples and places of worship were all constructed on mountaintops. In the Tigris-Euphrates river valley, where the country was as flat as a pancake, the temples were built *as* mountains, the ziggurats. Here in Isaiah 2, the Mountain of the Temple of the Lord is a high and lofty mountain; all other places are mere hills by comparison. This is to say that the oracles in all other religions have been found wanting and are silenced. Zion has been restored as a place from which Yahweh speaks and his Word is supreme in and for the entire world.

This Mountain Temple City calls to mind other mountains in the past. First of all, the garden of Eden was on a high mountain. How else could one river divide into four and water the whole world? Although the word "mountain" does not occur in Genesis 2, it does occur in the description of Eden in Ezekiel 28:13–14. The garden of Eden was not only a mountain, it was also a sanctuary, a place of worship. It was characterised by the presence of the Lord God. There he gave his decrees to rule the lives of his creatures.

Second, Mount Zion as the source of the Torah reminds us of Sinai, called the "mountain of God" (Ex. 3:1), the place from which he issued the Ten Words or Commands, his instructions to rule and regulate the daily lives of his people. In Isaiah 2 we see that it is no longer from Sinai that Yahweh gives his word, but from Mount Zion. Moreover, the Torah is not simply the law, a code of laws and regulations for just and righteous living which pleases God. At the same time it constitutes a covenant, the formalising of a relationship of love, loyalty, and trust between God and his people. Torah is, in a way, the flip side of the word covenant.

We have a picture of the nations travelling up Mount Zion to worship there, and there they are given the Torah of Yahweh, instruction on daily living that involves not only giving God his proper place in their lives but also treating other people in a truly human way. Isaiah's use of the word "Torah" as the flip side of covenant subtly suggests that all the nations will be in a covenant relationship with God. In Isaiah 2:3 Torah and the Word of Yahweh are in parallel lines. This occurs elsewhere in Isaiah only in 1:10. There, Zion has rejected Yahweh's instruction and word; here, his instruction and word are restored to their rightful place. Thus, in the vision of future Zion in 2:1–4, the future Zion has assumed roles earlier played by Eden and Sinai.

In the vision in 4:2–6, the picture is of a fruitful land *and* a holy city (Israel and Jerusalem). Moreover, there is a canopy of glory over the whole site of Mount Zion and over all its assemblies. In the exodus desert wanderings, the canopy of glory was over the tabernacle. Thus it is as if the entire city of Zion is now the tabernacle or the temple (a precursor to Revelation 21–22). The future Zion, then, takes up the imagery of Eden and Sinai. It is not just the old city of Jerusalem or the land of Israel. It is that and more—it is a changed and transformed Zion: the whole new creation as the place where God's people dwell and where God is worshipped (temple). Thus earlier sections of Isaiah prepare us to recognise in the vision in Isaiah 65 that the new Jerusalem and the new creation are coextensive.

THE NEW COVENANT IN EZEKIEL

At the heart of establishing God's kingship in the world is worship. We saw this indicated by Genesis 2, which depicts Adam and Eve placed in a garden sanctuary. Only as they spend time in the presence of God will they be equipped to implement his rule in the world in the way in which God himself would relate to his creation. Israel inherited the Adamic role of son of God at the exodus (Ex. 4:22), and the priority of worship becomes evident right away with the instructions to build the tabernacle. When the construction of this portable tent for worship was complete, a bright cloud symbolic of the divine presence settled on the tent to show that the creator God was dwelling in the midst of his people as king (Ex. 25:8; 40:34).

This is where prophets like Isaiah, Jeremiah, and Ezekiel fit into the story. The people of God had repeatedly violated the terms of the Israelite covenant. Love of God and love of one's neighbour had been replaced by idolatry and the corruption of social justice in every way. As a result, Israel's worship had become hollow and hypocritical. Jeremiah is the first of the latter prophets in the Hebrew Canon. In Jeremiah 7–10 we have his famous "Temple Sermon": "Do not trust in deceptive words and say, 'This is the temple of the LORD, the temple of the LORD, the temple of the LORD!'" (Jer. 7:4, NIV). The threefold repetition is the strongest form of emphasis possible. Jeremiah is saying, "You can't live as you please and then treat the temple like a good luck charm or rabbit's foot." The people thought they would always be protected as long as God was dwelling among them. Jeremiah's message was that covenant violation meant that God would be true to his threats and bring upon his people the curse of exile (Deuteronomy 28). Most importantly, he could no longer live among them, since their behaviour and lifestyle contradicted his own character as expressed in the Torah.

Ezekiel carries the "Temple Sermon" of Jeremiah one step further. The opening vision shows the bright cloud, the glory of the Lord, in motion, and the divine throne has wheels. *Why?* Because God is getting ready to move out! God is surrounded by social injustice and idolatry, and the temple has lost its five-star hotel status—he can no longer live there. This message must have come as an awful shock to the people of Judah. In Ezekiel 8–11 the opening vision is developed further and the bright cloud—the glory of the Lord—actually begins to move from the temple to the Eastern Gate. Finally, the glory of the Lord departs from the city of God. I express it in these terms to show that the city of God can no longer be the city of God when God is no longer there.[27] A brief consideration of the structure and shape of Ezekiel's book shows the development and resolution of this problem.

THE STRUCTURE AND SHAPE OF EZEKIEL'S BOOK

Outline of Ezekiel

1. Opening vision and call of Ezekiel	1:1–3:15
2. Ezekiel's role and message	3:16–7:27
3. The glory of the Lord leaves the temple	8–11
4. The exile symbolised	12–24
5. Oracles against the foreign nations	25–32
6. Divine leadership and restoration	33–36
7. The valley of dry bones	37–39
8. The new temple	40–48

As already noted, the "opening vision" portrays the glory of the Lord in motion because God is getting ready to move out. The second section (3:16–7:27) presents Ezekiel's role and message. Like all the prophets, he

---

[27] The departure of God from Jerusalem is not entirely negative. It has a positive side in that God will be a sanctuary for his people in exile (11:16).

employs every means and method of communication to get through to the people: because of idolatry in relation to God and social injustice in relation to others, they have broken the covenant, and the curse of exile is upon them. This is communicated through preaching, but also through symbolic dramas. In 4:1–3 Ezekiel is commanded to draw a diagram of Jerusalem on a brick as a prop to act out the coming attack of the Babylonians. He holds an iron pan between himself and the city to show that the prayers of the people will not get through to God. Again, in 4:4–8 he is commanded to lie on one side for 390 days for the sin of Israel and on the other side for 40 days for the sin of Judah. The sum is 430 days, which represents the period of bondage in Egypt. Just as prophets like Isaiah had foretold a future salvation, describing it as a new exodus, so Ezekiel indicates another "Egyptian bondage" *before* the new exodus occurs. This is similar to Daniel's vision of seventy weeks (Dan. 9:24). The exile may be over in seventy years according to the prophecy of Jeremiah (25:1–11), but it will take a lot longer to deal effectively with sin and to restore the broken covenant relationship with God. Unfortunately, the people did not heed Ezekiel's message. According to 33:32 the prophet was viewed only as an entertainer singing songs with a beautiful voice.

Chapters 8–11 constitute a second vision, in which the glory of the Lord departs from the temple. This is followed by further messages to Judah in chapters 12–24, largely through symbolic dramas, to communicate the coming judgement and exile.

Chapters 25–32 constitute oracles against foreign nations. Such oracles are included in all the major prophets because of the programme laid out in Deuteronomy 32. The covenant violation of Israel will bring the curse of exile. At first God plans to completely erase his people (Deut. 32:26). But he fears the taunt of the foreign nations (32:27). The foreign nations will conclude that they have defeated Israel by their own gods and prowess instead of realising that God allowed them to conquer Israel only because of her sins. So the nations must be punished for their arrogance and idolatrous worldview and for their harsh treatment of the people of God.

Then in Ezekiel 33–36 Israel will be given new leadership in the form of a new David—the Messiah. The messianic theme is summarised well by Stephen Dempster:

> Even the divided kingdom of exiles is reunited under a new leader, who is said to be 'my servant David' (Ezek. 37:24–25; cf. 34:23–24). But he is

also described as one who will come to power through relative obscurity. In a remarkable allegorical passage, a Davidic descendant is compared to a tender shoot (*yōneqet*) plucked from a tall tree, taken to Mount Zion and planted there to grow into a huge tree, bearing fruit and providing shade for all the birds of the forest (17:22–24). Thus all the trees of the forest (peoples of the world) will know that 'I the LORD lower the tall tree and raise the low tree. I dry up the green tree and make the dry tree flourish' (17:24). Later, this 'David' who will come to power is remembered for his humble origins as a shepherd (34:23); he will provide true leadership, as opposed to past leaders, who are symbolized as corrupt and destructive shepherds. Both these motifs of Davidic rule (a tender shoot and a shepherd) echo Jeremiah's prediction of a 'plant growth' from the line of David, which will bring good shepherds—justice for the nation (Jer. 23:1–8).[28]

Then there will be a new covenant to renew the relationship with God and his people, a covenant that will deal effectively with hearts stubbornly bent on sin (36:24–32). This is followed by an announcement of return from exile described in terms of resurrection from the dead. The vision of the Valley of Dry Bones shows the people of God miraculously restored to life and given victory over enemies (37:1–14).

The book concludes in chapters 40–48 with a vision of a renewed temple and God dwelling in the midst of his people once more in a healed land. The conclusion of the book is extremely powerful: THE LORD IS THERE. The glory of the Lord has returned to the temple. God is once more dwelling in the midst of his people as king. Thus restoration involves the rebuilding of the Davidic house in both of its meanings in 2 Samuel 7—the dynasty of David and the temple.

EZEKIEL 11:16–21

The first important text is Ezekiel 11:16–21:

[16] "Therefore say: 'This is what the Sovereign LORD says: Although I sent them far away among the nations and scattered them among the countries, yet for a little while I have been a sanctuary for them in the countries where they have gone.'

---

28 Stephen G. Dempster, *Dominion and Dynasty: A Biblical Theology of the Hebrew Bible*, NSBT 15 (Downers Grove, IL: InterVarsity Press, 2003), 170–171.

[17] "Therefore say: 'This is what the Sovereign LORD says: I will gather you from the nations and bring you back from the countries where you have been scattered, and I will give you back the land of Israel again.' [18] "They will return to it and remove all its vile images and detestable idols. [19] I will give them an undivided heart and put a new spirit in them; I will remove from them their heart of stone and give them a heart of flesh. [20] Then they will follow my decrees and be careful to keep my laws. They will be my people, and I will be their God. [21] But as for those whose hearts are devoted to their vile images and detestable idols, I will bring down on their own heads what they have done, declares the Sovereign LORD." (NIV)

This prophetic text is direct and straightforward. Israel has been scattered among the nations. God will gather his people from the nations and give them the land once more. The exiles who return will be given by God "one heart and a new spirit"—according to a literal translation of the Hebrew. Yet those who are devoted to idolatry will be judged—so not all exiles are restored. We can see in Ezekiel, just as we saw in Isaiah, that the return from exile is both physical and spiritual. Verse 20 contains the Covenant Formula, so although the word "covenant" is not in this passage, the text is speaking clearly about a new covenant.

The statement, "I will give them one heart and put a new spirit in them" is similar to the "new heart and new spirit" in Ezekiel 36:26 and to the "one heart and one way" mentioned in Jeremiah 32:39. Paul's admonitions to the new covenant community in the New Testament to "mind the one thing/same thing" (normally rendered "be in harmony") may well be based on passages such as these:

Acts 4:32	καρδία καὶ ψυχὴ μία
Romans 12:16	φρονεῖν τὸ αὐτό
Romans 15:5	φρονεῖν τὸ αὐτό
2 Corinthians 13:11	φρονεῖν τὸ αὐτό
Philippians 2:2	φρονεῖν τὸ αὐτό
	φρονεῖν τὸ ἕν
Philippians 4:2	φρονεῖν τὸ αὐτό

Indeed, perhaps when Paul speaks of one spirit in Ephesians 4:4, he is thinking of the one heart and new spirit in Ezekiel, and perhaps his one baptism (4:5) refers to the instruction (i.e., Torah, i.e., the entire complex of repentance, faith, conversion) of the new covenant written on the heart.

EZEKIEL 16:59–63

[59] This is what the Sovereign LORD says: "I will deal with you as you deserve, because you have despised my oath by breaking the covenant. [60] Yet I will remember the covenant I made with you in the days of your youth, and I will establish an everlasting covenant with you. [61] Then you will remember your ways and be ashamed when you receive your sisters, both those who are older than you and those who are younger. I will give them to you as daughters, but not on the basis of my covenant with you. [62] So I will establish my covenant with you, and you will know that I am the LORD. [63] Then, when I make atonement for you for all you have done, you will remember and be ashamed and never again open your mouth because of your humiliation," declares the Sovereign LORD. (NIV)

This passage concludes a long parable in which Jerusalem is depicted as a bride cheating on her husband on many occasions with many lovers. Her crimes are compared to those of the kingdom of Israel to the north and the city of Sodom to the south.

As a result of her many acts of unfaithfulness, Jerusalem will experience the curses of the Israelite covenant, according to verse 59. Verse 60 speaks of Israel breaking the covenant, and then it speaks of God confirming (*hēqîm běrît*) an everlasting covenant with them. Normally the expression *kārat běrît* (to cut a covenant) is used to describe covenant making. The expression *kārat běrît* indicates a covenant that did not exist previously and is being initiated now between partners for the first time. Excellent examples are Isaiah 55:3, Jeremiah 31:31, and Ezekiel 34:25 and 37:26. Conversely, *hēqîm běrît* usually indicates upholding a commitment or promise already in place. Yet Ezekiel 16:60, 62 employs *hēqîm běrît* for the new covenant. How are we to interpret and understand the language of Ezekiel at this point? Two possibilities present themselves.

One possibility is that Ezekiel's language may indicate that there is a link between the Israelite covenant and the new. He may be using the expression "affirm or uphold a covenant" to show that the new covenant establishes effectively what God intended in the Israelite covenant. It is interesting to note that the term "everlasting covenant" occurs sixteen times in the Old Testament: two times of the covenant with Noah (Gen. 9:16; Isa. 24:5), four times of the covenant with Abraham (Gen. 17:7, 19; Ps. 105:10; 1 Chron. 16:17), once of the covenant with David (2 Sam. 23:5; cf. 2 Chron. 13:5), six times of the new covenant (Isa. 55:3; 61:8; Jer. 32:40; 50:5; Ezek. 16:60; 37:26), and three times of covenant signs (Gen. 17:13; Ex. 31:16; Lev. 24:8).

Nowhere in the Old Testament is the Israelite covenant at Sinai called an everlasting or permanent covenant.

It is important to note that there are different perspectives in the prophets on the new covenant. Their contributions are *not monolithic*, but view the faceted gem of God's future covenant renewal from many different angles. Perhaps we should not assume here, against the linguistic use in general, that the expression is now equivalent to *kārat běrît*, but rather that it looks at the making of the new covenant from a different point of view. Ezekiel 16:60 speaks of Israel breaking the covenant of Sinai and of God subsequently upholding an everlasting covenant with them. Ezekiel's language indicates that there is a link between the Sinai covenant and the new. He employs the expression "confirm or uphold a covenant" to show that the new covenant establishes effectively what God intended in the Sinai covenant. The point is supported by the fact that the new covenant is called here an everlasting covenant, whereas the term "everlasting" is never used of the Sinai covenant.

Another possibility is that the distinction between *kārat běrît* and *hēqîm běrît* found in earlier texts does not hold in later texts. Scholarship has shown that Ezekiel's language represents a transition between Classical Biblical Hebrew and Late Biblical Hebrew, with many changes and developments occurring in the language.[29] Both instances of *hēqîm běrît* in this text certainly seem to mean "to initiate a covenant." We could translate literally, "I will cause to stand an everlasting covenant for you" = I will put an everlasting covenant in place for you. It seems clear from the context that the everlasting covenant is something that did not exist before but will be initiated for the first time at an unknown point in the future. This second possibility seems far more probable. Thus the double occurrence of *hēqîm běrît* in this one passage would be the only place in the entire Old Testament where this expression seems to mean "initiate a covenant." In any case, what was not permanent will now be lasting and enduring.

Jerusalem will be given both Samaria and Sodom, but not on the basis of the Israelite covenant (16:61). This statement hints at the fact that in the new covenant, the old divisions in Israel are healed and the Gentiles are included.

---

[29] See Mark F. Rooker, *Biblical Hebrew in Transition: The Language of Ezekiel*, JSOTSup 90 (Sheffield: JSOT Press, 1990).

EZEKIEL 18:1–4, 30–32

[1] The word of the Lord came to me: [2] "What do you people mean by quoting this proverb about the land of Israel:

"'The fathers eat sour grapes,
   and the children's teeth are set on edge'?

[3] "As surely as I live, declares the Sovereign Lord, you will no longer quote this proverb in Israel. [4] For every living soul belongs to me, the father as well as the son—both alike belong to me. The soul who sins is the one who will die. . . ."

[30] "Therefore, O house of Israel, I will judge you, each one according to his ways, declares the Sovereign Lord. Repent! Turn away from all your offenses; then sin will not be your downfall. [31] Rid yourselves of all the offenses you have committed, and get a new heart and a new spirit. Why will you die, O house of Israel? [32] For I take no pleasure in the death of anyone, declares the Sovereign Lord. Repent and live!" (NIV)

Verses 1–4 of Ezekiel 18 set forth the thesis of a message sent through the prophet, while verses 30–32 provide the conclusion. This important text deals with how the relationship between God and his people is structured under the old covenant and the difference promised in the new covenant. Jeremiah sets his passage on the new covenant (Jer. 31:31–34) in the context of the same proverb and problem (Jer. 31:29–30). The important comment of D. A. Carson relevant to the proverb cited by Ezekiel along with a detailed discussion and evaluation will be provided in the next section, in the analysis of Jeremiah 31:29–34. For now, we can see that the mention of a "new heart and a new spirit" in Ezekiel 18:31 clearly demonstrates that the prophet is describing changes brought about by new covenant realities. Under the old covenant, the corporate solidarity between the people and their fallible human leaders meant that they could suffer for the sins of another, but this will not be true under the new covenant.

EZEKIEL 34:17–31

[17] "'As for you, my flock, this is what the Sovereign Lord says: I will judge between one sheep and another, and between rams and goats. [18] Is it not enough for you to feed on the good pasture? Must you also trample the rest of your pasture with your feet? Is it not enough for you to drink clear water? Must you also muddy the rest with your feet? [19] Must my

flock feed on what you have trampled and drink what you have muddied with your feet?

[20] "'Therefore this is what the Sovereign LORD says to them: See, I myself will judge between the fat sheep and the lean sheep.[21] Because you shove with flank and shoulder, butting all the weak sheep with your horns until you have driven them away, [22] I will save my flock, and they will no longer be plundered. I will judge between one sheep and another. [23] I will place over them one shepherd, my servant David, and he will tend them; he will tend them and be their shepherd. [24] I the LORD will be their God, and my servant David will be prince among them. I the LORD have spoken.'" (NIV)

Since this passage is in the section of Ezekiel dealing with leaders in Israel who have aggrandised themselves and have not served the people nor the interests of the divine king above and over them, it is natural for Ezekiel to speak of the divine restoration of all things in terms of a coming king who will be a good shepherd of the sheep, caring for the interests of the people and serving at the same time the interests of the divine overlord. The coming king is referred to as "my servant David," similar to the manner in which the coming king is referred to in Isaiah 55:3 and Hosea 3:5, Isaiah's contemporary.

EZEKIEL 36:22–36

[22] "Therefore say to the house of Israel, 'This is what the Sovereign LORD says: It is not for your sake, O house of Israel, that I am going to do these things, but for the sake of my holy name, which you have profaned among the nations where you have gone. [23] I will show the holiness of my great name, which has been profaned among the nations, the name you have profaned among them. Then the nations will know that I am the LORD, declares the Sovereign LORD, when I show myself holy through you before their eyes.

[24] "'For I will take you out of the nations; I will gather you from all the countries and bring you back into your own land. [25] I will sprinkle clean water on you, and you will be clean; I will cleanse you from all your impurities and from all your idols. [26] I will give you a new heart and put a new spirit in you; I will remove from you your heart of stone and give you a heart of flesh. [27] And I will put my Spirit in you and move you to follow my decrees and be careful to keep my laws. [28] You will live in the land I gave your forefathers; you will be my people, and I will be your God. [29] I will save you from all your uncleanness. I will call for the grain and make it plentiful and will not bring famine upon you. [30] I will increase the fruit of the trees and the crops of the field, so that you will no longer suffer disgrace among the nations because of famine. [31] Then you

will remember your evil ways and wicked deeds, and you will loathe yourselves for your sins and detestable practices. [32] I want you to know that I
am not doing this for your sake, declares the Sovereign LORD. Be ashamed
and disgraced for your conduct, O house of Israel!'" (NIV)

This famous passage on the new covenant in Ezekiel, a text to which
Jesus alludes directly in John 3, speaks of God restoring his people to covenant relationship by dealing with their sin—their impurities and idols. The
intractable stubbornness and unfaithfulness of the human partner will be
changed by giving them a new heart and a new spirit, as in Ezekiel 11 and
18. The divine spirit will enable and motivate the human partners to follow
the divine instructions. Fertility and fruitfulness in the land will result. God
will do this not for the sake of his people but for his own sake—to demonstrate that he is holy, i.e., completely committed and devoted to his character,
plans, and purposes—as laid out in the Song of Moses in Deuteronomy 32.

EZEKIEL 37:15–28

The sixth section of the book, on "Divine Leadership and Restoration,"
moves naturally into the seventh section, containing the vision of the "Valley
of Dry Bones," which foresees Israel's restoration as a resurrection from
the dead. As part of this vision, Ezekiel communicates divine revelation by
means of a mini-drama or one-act play:

> [15] The word of the LORD came to me: [16] "Son of man, take a stick of
> wood and write on it, 'Belonging to Judah and the Israelites associated
> with him.' Then take another stick of wood, and write on it, 'Ephraim's
> stick, belonging to Joseph and all the house of Israel associated with him.'
> [17] Join them together into one stick so that they will become one in
> your hand.
> [18] "When your countrymen ask you, 'Won't you tell us what you
> mean by this?' [19] say to them, 'This is what the Sovereign LORD says: I
> am going to take the stick of Joseph—which is in Ephraim's hand—and of
> the Israelite tribes associated with him, and join it to Judah's stick, mak-
> ing them a single stick of wood, and they will become one in my hand.'
> [20] Hold before their eyes the sticks you have written on [21] and say to
> them, 'This is what the Sovereign LORD says: I will take the Israelites out
> of the nations where they have gone. I will gather them from all around
> and bring them back into their own land. [22] I will make them one nation
> in the land, on the mountains of Israel. There will be one king over all
> of them and they will never again be two nations or be divided into two

kingdoms. [23] They will no longer defile themselves with their idols and vile images or with any of their offenses, for I will save them from all their sinful backsliding, and I will cleanse them. They will be my people, and I will be their God.

[24] "'My servant David will be king over them, and they will all have one shepherd. They will follow my laws and be careful to keep my decrees. [25] They will live in the land I gave to my servant Jacob, the land where your fathers lived. They and their children and their children's children will live there forever, and David my servant will be their prince forever. [26] I will make a covenant of peace with them; it will be an everlasting covenant. I will establish them and increase their numbers, and I will put my sanctuary among them forever. [27] My dwelling place will be with them; I will be their God, and they will be my people. [28] Then the nations will know that I the LORD make Israel holy, when my sanctuary is among them forever.'" (NIV)

Ezekiel's dramatic action of joining two sticks of wood represents the divided kingdoms of Judah and Israel being gathered from exile and joined together as one nation.

God will deal with their sin and their sinfulness. Note the Covenant Formula occurring twice: "They will be my people, and I will be their God" (v. 23); and again, "I will be their God, and they will be my people" (v. 27). The two-part formula is used in both orders.

The covenant relationship will be restored once they are cleansed from sin. Ezekiel uses both the term "covenant of peace" and the term "everlasting covenant," showing that these are two ways of referring to the same covenant. The former term is employed especially in contexts emphasising reconciliation between Yahweh and his people, so necessary because of their disloyalty through idolatry and violation of his covenant instructions. The latter term is employed to stress that the problem in the Israelite covenant (and indeed in earlier covenants) of the faithless human partner will be permanently addressed: Israel will be truly holy, i.e., committed, devoted, and faithful to the Lord.

A Davidic king will be established as ruler over the renewed Israel and, as a result, the people will carefully keep the instructions in the covenant.

As a result, the temple will be restored: "my sanctuary is among them forever" (v. 28).

Verse 25 is a powerful statement drawing together several significant strands in the Old Testament: "They will live in the land I gave to my servant Jacob, the land where your ancestors lived. They and their children and their children's children will live there forever, and David my servant will be their prince forever." Readers who have been carefully following the development and progression of thought in Ezekiel—and indeed in Isaiah and Jeremiah as well—will realise that the promise concerning the renewed Israel living in the land is fulfilled in that the new Jerusalem and the new creation are coextensive. Indeed the apostle John in Revelation 21–22 recognises the new creation in Ezekiel's description of the new temple in chapters 40–48. Careful readers will also draw the conclusion from what has preceded in Ezekiel 16 that the renewed Israel is no longer based on ethnic parameters but is defined as those who are reconciled to the Lord and believing in him: "Jerusalem will be given both Samaria and Sodom, but not on the basis of the Israelite Covenant" (see 16:61). In the new covenant, the old divisions in Israel are healed and the Gentiles are included. Only faithful human partners (i.e., believers) constitute the covenant community. And the Davidic Messiah is ruler over all.

This passage, then, draws together all the different strands dealing with the new covenant that are treated separately in earlier passages in Ezekiel.

Chapter Thirteen

THE NEW COVENANT: JEREMIAH

Jeremiah's basic message can be summarised in a very few words: "the Babylonians are coming." He ministered from 627 B.C. to just a few years after the destruction of Jerusalem in 587 B.C. During this time he witnessed the fall of the Neo-Assyrian empire and the rapid rise of the Babylonian empire led by Nabopolassar and his famous son, Nebuchadnezzar. He knew that the attempts of kings like Josiah to reform the nation were inadequate, and in his famous "Temple Sermon" he warned the people about hypocritical worship, just like Isaiah before him and Ezekiel after him.

Serious differences between the Masoretic Text and the Septuagint (that have not been resolved) plague our study of the text. In spite of this, Dumbrell rightly notes that the prophecy is intended to relate Judah to the world. His defense of the arrangement in the Masoretic Text is noteworthy:

> It is not insignificant that oracles against foreign nations conclude the prophecy in the Hebrew text. Admittedly, these oracles are placed between Jer 25:13a and 15 in the Greek OT, but this seems to have risen from a desire for a more consistent historical structure, as well as from the purpose of ending the book with the account of the fall of Jerusalem and what immediately preceded the fall. But the Hebrew placement of these oracles at the conclusion of the book, viewed together with the nature of the prophet's call, draws into obvious focus the internationalism of the prophecy. This broader political perspective recognized that all the organized world as Jeremiah knew it was involved in a new societal structure under the leadership of Babylon.
>
> Moreover, from a formal structural perspective, Jer 51:64 forms an inclusion with 1:1. In chapters 46–51 the oracles against the foreign nations are arranged geographically (Egypt, Philistia, Moab, Ammon, Edom, Damascus, Arabs, Elam and finally Babylon) and have the common theme of failure to submit to Babylon. Finally, Babylon herself is punished for *hubris*. These oracles underscore the tenor of Jeremiah's constant

prophecy of Judah's need to recognize Babylonian hegemony as the new factor in the world situation.[1]

THE STRUCTURE AND SHAPE OF JEREMIAH

A brief outline of this longest of the prophetic works will assist us as we consider key texts within the work dealing with the new covenant and matters that relate to it.

Outline of Jeremiah

Superscription	1:1–3
1. Call of Jeremiah and visions	1:4–19
2. Judgement on Judah and Jerusalem	2–25
A. Israel's guilt and punishment	2–6
B. Jeremiah's Temple Sermon	7–10
C. Warnings and Judgement	11:11–15:9
D. Confessions, symbolic acts, and preaching	15:10–25:38
3. Jeremiah's controversy with false prophets	26–29
4. The Book of Consolation	30–31
5. The days of Jehoiakim and Zedekiah	32–39
6. Jeremiah's experiences after the fall of Jerusalem	40–45
7. Oracles against the foreign nations	46–51
8. Appendix: fall of Jerusalem	52

JEREMIAH 4:2

Our attention is drawn, first of all, to Jeremiah 4:2, a passage early in the book of Jeremiah that focuses on Israel's relationship to Yahweh and its impact and significance for all the nations:

> [1] "If you return, O Israel,
> > declares the LORD,
> > to me you should return.
> If you remove your detestable things from my presence,
> > and do not waver,
> [2] and if you swear, 'As the LORD lives,'
> > in truth, in justice, and in righteousness,
> then nations shall bless themselves in him,
> > and in him shall they glory." (ESV)

---

[1] William J. Dumbrell, *The End of the Beginning: Revelation 21–22 and the Old Testament* (Homebush West, NSW, Australia: Lancer, 1985), 83.

To aid the discussion, the Hebrew text for verse 2 is as follows:

וְנִשְׁבַּעְתָּ חַי־יְהוָה בֶּאֱמֶת בְּמִשְׁפָּט וּבִצְדָקָה
וְהִתְבָּרְכוּ בוֹ גּוֹיִם וּבוֹ יִתְהַלָּלוּ:

Four issues require discussion in the interpretation of Jeremiah 4:1–2. First, the Hebrew verb rendered "waver" in the ESV is נוד and has as its fundamental meaning "go back and forth/swing to and fro/flutter/oscillate/shake/wave" (e.g., 1 Kings 14:15). Some secondary meanings are "be aimless, wander" (e.g., Gen. 4:12, 14) or "flee" (e.g., Jer. 49:30; 50:3, 8). John Bright renders "nor stray from my presence,"[2] and similarly the NIV. Yet the ESV is good here because the meaning is metaphorical of Israel's fickle vacillation between loyalty and disloyalty in the covenant relationship with Yahweh. Israel's covenant disloyalty and fickleness is a major theme in Jeremiah; he speaks frequently of the "stubbornness of their evil hearts" and of their incurable wound. Indeed, the entire section from 3:1–4:4 is a call to return to devoted, faithful loyalty in covenant love to Yahweh.

Second, once again we have the *hithpael* of the verb *bārak*, and a number of different interpretations are possible. The analysis of Grüneberg is one of the most thorough and deserves to be cited in full:

The hithpael here is commonly judged a reflexive (NASB, NKJV, JB, RSV), though passive translation is not unknown (e.g. NIV, NRSV, Bright). Yet once again passive force appears unlikely. For התברכו stands parallel to יתהללו, probably used passively in Proverbs 31:30 (above pp 200–201) but elsewhere regularly meaning "glory", "boast in": the context makes clear that the subject is doing the praising in e.g. Jer 49:4 (where it is linked to "trusting in her treasures", הבטחה באצרתיה); Psalm 34:3[2] (where the Psalmist is praising God); Psalm 105:3 (bidding people to give thanks, make known, sing and rejoice); Isa 41:16 (parallel to √גיל). Elsewhere it is more difficult conclusively to exclude passive sense, but non-passive sense seems more plausible (e.g. Jer 9:22–23; 1 Kings 20:11; Psalm 52:3[1]). Hence it seems overwhelmingly likely that in Jer 4:2 the meaning of בו יתהללו is "they will boast in him [i.e. by speaking in praise of him]", and hence of והתברכו בו that "they will bless by him [i.e. in his name]". For once passive force has been excluded, the analysis will repeat that given to יתברכו in Ps 72:17 (pp 213–14 above, which see for detailed arguments): the primary situation described is probably that of individuals uttering blessings on other individuals, which does not obviously fit either reflexive

[2] John Bright, *Jeremiah*, 2nd ed., Anchor Bible 21 (New York: Double days, 1965), 21.

or reciprocal semantics; however the main point is not precisely who is blessed (or who blesses), but the use of God's name when blessings are uttered. Thus again we most plausibly have a speech action hithpael.[3]

Note that this analysis matches that of Lee cited earlier in the discussion of the form in Genesis 12:3 and its later reiterations. We concluded that the *niphal* forms are passive ("they shall be blessed") and the *hithpael* are declarative-estimative reflexive ("they shall declare themselves as blessed"). Nonetheless, as Noonan has shown in his discussion of the *hithpael* of *bārak*, the declarative-estimative reflexive is the meaning of the *hithpael*, not a "speech action hithpael":

> If the nations pride themselves in God, placing their trust in him and finding their happiness in him, the parallelism indicates that the nations likewise seek out blessing from him. Once again, the point is not that blessings or statements of praise are being uttered, even though this may occur. Rather, the point is that the nations are placing their trust in God and seeking his blessing. This understanding is coherent within the larger context of this literary unit, in which Jer 3:17 refers to the inclusion of the nations within God's blessing. Jeremiah thus expresses the view Israel will provoke the nations to jealousy (cf. Isa 19:24–25): when Israel repents, the nations will see how Israel benefits from its covenant relationship and seek to enter into that relationship in order to also obtain blessing from God.[4]

Third, in "the nations [*gôyīm*] will consider themselves blessed in him," to whom does the third person pronoun *him* refer? According to the principle of proximity in the context, it must refer to Yahweh.[5] If there is an allusion to the promise in Genesis 12:3 and its reiterations,[6] then this text does present the reader with a variant: rather than being blessed by Abraham or the family of Abraham, the nations declare themselves blessed by Yahweh.[7]

Fourth, Jeremiah 4:1–2 is an extended conditional sentence, and interpreters differ over where the protasis or "if" clause ends and the apodosis or "then" clause begins. While many English versions of verse 2a render

---

[3] Keith N. Grüneberg, *Abraham, Blessing, and the Nations: A Philological and Exegetical Study of Genesis 12:3 in Its Narrative Context* (Berlin: Walter de Gruyter, 2003), 217. Bright actually renders the *hithpael* by a reflexive, not a passive (see Bright, *Jeremiah*, 21).

[4] Benjamin J. Noonan, "Abraham, Blessing, and the Nations: A Reexamination of the Niphal and Hitpael of ברך in the Patriarchal Narratives," *Hebrew Studies 51* (2010): 83.

[5] For a lengthier treatment of the pronominal referent, see Grüneberg, *Abraham, Blessing, and the Nations*, 217–218.

[6] The question of whether or not Jeremiah 4:2 entails allusion or use of Genesis 12:3 and repetitions will be discussed shortly.

[7] See J. A. Thompson, *The Book of Jeremiah*, New International Commentary on the Old Testament (Grand Rapids, MI: Eerdmans, 1980), 213, for affirmation that the text in Jeremiah 4:2 entails a variant of Genesis 12:3, etc.

as does the above citation from the ESV, John Bright, by contrast, sees the "then" clause beginning at verse 2a instead of verse 2b, as follows:

> If you return, O Israel—Yahweh's word—
>   To *me* return,
> If you put your vile things aside,
>   Nor stray from my presence,
> Then might you swear, "As Yahweh lives,"
>   Truthfully, justly, and rightly;
> And the nations by him would bless themselves,
>   And in him exult.[8]

Bright's rendering makes better sense of the Hebrew text. Both verse 2a and verse 2b begin with *waw*-consecutive perfect verbs. Moreover the "if" which is repeated in 1b from 1a is no longer repeated in verse 2a. This is a clear sign that we are shifting from the protasis to apodosis, but no clear sign can distinguish 2b as the beginning of the apodosis. Bright also makes better sense of the flow of thought. If Israel returns to an unadulterated devotion and loyalty to Yahweh in the covenant relationship, then her use of the name Yahweh will demonstrate faithfulness and justice. This *in turn* would impact the nations to turn to Israel's God—this is the plot structure of the Old Testament from Genesis 12 onwards.

Grüneberg doubts that Jeremiah 4:2 entails an allusion to Genesis, mainly because few identical lexemes are used.[9] But allusion is not always a matter of reusing lexemes or phrases from earlier texts. Previously we saw that Genesis 12 is describing God establishing his rule in the hearts and lives of humans through covenant relationship, exactly as described by Genesis 1:26–27. The ideas are precisely the same. The lexemes and language, however, are not remotely similar. The idea expressed in Jeremiah 4:2, that when Israel is faithful in her relationship to Yahweh, blessing will flow to the nations, is based squarely on the Israelite covenant as an outworking of the promises to Abraham.

JEREMIAH 12:14–17

The interpretation of Jeremiah 4:1–2 just provided is confirmed and strengthened by the oracle of Jeremiah 12:14–17, which reads as follows:

---

[8] Bright, *Jeremiah*, 21.
[9] Grüneberg, *Abraham, Blessing, and the Nations*, 218–219.

[14] This is what the LORD says: "As for all my wicked neighbors who seize the inheritance I gave my people Israel, I will uproot them from their lands and I will uproot the house of Judah from among them. [15] But after I uproot them, I will again have compassion and will bring each of them back to his own inheritance and his own country. [16] And if they learn well the ways of my people and swear by my name, saying, 'As surely as the LORD lives'—even as they once taught my people to swear by Baal— then they will be established among my people. [17] But if any nation does not listen, I will completely uproot and destroy it," declares the LORD. (NIV)

Yahweh speaks of "all my wicked neighbours who harm the inheritance which I gave to my people Israel." Historically speaking, this would refer to the lands and peoples surrounding Israel who have brought harm to its land and people down through the years: the Arameans, the Edomites, the Moabites, the Philistines, and wider afield, the Assyrians, Babylonians, and Egyptians, just to name a few of them.

Verse 14 speaks of an exile, not just for Judah but also for each of these lands and peoples. The verb "uproot" may have a double meaning: uprooting a land would mean sending the people into exile; uprooting Judah from among them would mean bringing Judah back from exile. What is astonishing, however, is that according to verse 15, *each land* and *people* will have a return from exile. And when all the exiles are brought home, if the nations learn from Israel to swear by the God of Israel, then they will be "built up" or established in the midst of the restored Israel. If they do not, each will be permanently eradicated as a nation.

What is precisely parallel in this text to Jeremiah 4:1–2 is the idea that, through a renewed and restored Israel (who is faithful and loyal to the Lord by faithfulness and social justice), the nations may become worshippers of this same Lord and will be established *in the midst* of the renewed people of God.

What is additional and new in this text is that the notion of a return from exile applies to the nations as well as to Judah and Israel. This idea is developed further in our next text, Jeremiah 16:14–18.

JEREMIAH 16:14–18

[14] "However, the days are coming," declares the LORD, "when men will no longer say, 'As surely as the LORD lives, who brought the Israelites up out of Egypt,' [15] but they will say, 'As surely as the LORD lives, who brought the Israelites up out of the land of the north and out of all the

countries where he had banished them.' For I will restore them to the land I gave their forefathers.

[16] "But now I will send for many fishermen," declares the LORD, "and they will catch them. After that I will send for many hunters, and they will hunt them down on every mountain and hill and from the crevices of the rocks. [17] My eyes are on all their ways; they are not hidden from me, nor is their sin concealed from my eyes. [18] I will repay them double for their wickedness and their sin, because they have defiled my land with the lifeless forms of their vile images and have filled my inheritance with their detestable idols." (NIV)

As already stated, Jeremiah has a consistent message: "the Babylonians are coming! Judah will be carried away into exile." This, however, is not the whole message. There is also a message of consolation: "God will bring his people back from exile." This message of return from banishment and exile is expressed first in plain speech in verses 14 and 15 and then repeated in figures of speech in verse 16.[10]

In verses 14–15, the return from exile is described as a new exodus. The exodus from Egypt was the big event in the history of Israel. Nonetheless, in terms of magnitude and significance, the exodus will be overshadowed by the future return from exile. In the future, the renewed people of the Lord will be defined and determined not by the exodus from Egypt, but rather by a "new exodus" event in which all the exiles are brought home. In the new exodus, the Israelites are brought back from the land of the north, according to verse 15, because the normal routes of travel from Assyria and Babylon enter Israel from the north and not from the east.

Verse 16 employs some unusual figures of speech to depict and portray the effort and length to which the Lord goes to bring back all the exiles. A comparison is drawn between fishing and hunting and bringing back the exiles. Those who fish and hunt require patience, strategy, and time to catch their prey. In a similar way, God will expend considerable patience, strategy, and time to catch his "prey," i.e., the exiles.

It is instructive to pause and follow the interpretation of Jesus and the apostles in the fulfilment of this prophecy. There is a clear and unmistakable allusion to Jeremiah 16:16 in Matthew 4 as Jesus is in the process of choosing twelve men whom he would train as his special agents:

---

[10] Cf. Jeremiah 23:8 and 31:8 for a repetition of these thoughts and words.

[18] While walking by the Sea of Galilee, he saw two brothers, Simon (who is called Peter) and Andrew his brother, casting a net into the sea, for they were fishermen. [19] And he said to them, "Follow me, and I will make you fishers of men." (Matt. 4:18–19, ESV)

When Jesus says to Peter and Andrew that he will make them "fishers of men," he is referring directly to Jeremiah 16:16, and he is saying that he will use his followers to bring the exiles home. We saw earlier that the return from exile entails two stages: (1) (physical) release from Babylon and (2) (spiritual) release from sin, condemnation, and death. The second stage of return from exile is inaugurated with the coming of Jesus and his ministry. This is substantiated from the many passages in the Gospels that indicate that the new exodus has begun in the person and work of Jesus Christ.

The work of bringing the exiles home is, in fact, begun by the first coming of the Lord Jesus and concluded with his second coming. This is made plain by Paul's clear allusion to Isaiah 27:12–13 in 1 Thessalonians 4:13–18:

[13] But we do not want you to be uninformed, brothers, about those who are asleep, that you may not grieve as others do who have no hope. [14] For since we believe that Jesus died and rose again, even so, through Jesus, God will bring with him those who have fallen asleep. [15] For this we declare to you by a word from the Lord, that we who are alive, who are left until the coming of the Lord, will not precede those who have fallen asleep. [16] For the Lord himself will descend from heaven with a command by the voice of an archangel and the sound of the trumpet of God. And the dead in Christ will rise first. [17] Then we who are alive, who are left, will be caught up together with them in the clouds to meet the Lord in the air, and so we will always be with the Lord. [18] Therefore encourage one another with these words.[11]

The descent of the Lord is heralded by an archangel blowing the trumpet of God. The trumpet of which Paul speaks is not something he was told about by direct revelation, but rather it is something he learned from his own Bible, the Old Testament, in Isaiah 27:

[12] In that day from the river Euphrates to the Brook of Egypt the LORD will thresh out the grain, and you will be gleaned one by one, O people of Israel. [13] And in that day a great trumpet will be blown, and those who were lost in the land of Assyria and those who were driven out to the

---

[11] ESV modified according to author's own translation.

land of Egypt will come and worship the LORD on the holy mountain at Jerusalem. (Isa. 27:12–13, ESV)

Isaiah is referring here to the final gathering of the exiles, which is compared to gathering a grain harvest. A great trumpet is sounded, and the exiles in Assyria and Egypt will be brought home. The great trumpet, then, blown to announce the descent of the Lord for his own in 1 Thessalonians 4, is the signal for the final phase of bringing the exiles home.

According to Jesus and the apostles, then, the gathering of the exiles is what is inaugurated by the first coming of Christ and completed by his second coming.

Returning to Jeremiah 16, note that verses 17 and 18 conclude the paragraph by reminding readers of the reason for the banishment and exile that requires a new exodus: the idolatry of the Israelites is not hidden from the Lord, and he will repay them for their violation of the covenant in Exodus 19–24, made at Sinai and supplemented by Deuteronomy on Mount Gerizim and Mount Ebal. The rendering of the NIV in verse 18 (as well as that of most versions), "I will repay them double for their wickedness and their sin," does not adequately bring out the meaning of the original text. A literal rendering of the Hebrew would be, "I shall at first repay the double of their iniquity and sin." This does not mean that the divine punishment is two times the value of the wrongdoing, but rather that the penalty matches precisely the wrongdoing. It is the *lex talionis*, the principle of retribution which is the foundation of the justice in the covenant: life for life, eye for eye, tooth for tooth, hand for hand, foot for foot, burn for burn, wound for wound, stripe for stripe (Ex. 21:24–25). For every crime there is a repayment which must be precisely as much as, but not more than, the damage or harm caused.[12]

JEREMIAH 31:27–40

We come now to Jeremiah 31:27–40—not only the main passage in Jeremiah on the new covenant but the only place in the Old Testament where the term "new covenant" is actually employed. The passage on the new covenant appears in a well-defined section commonly called the "Book of Consolation" (30–31) that follows the bulk of the messages given by Jeremiah and his controversy with false prophets, and precedes his description of the last days

---

[12] I came to this interpretation on my own, but later found it substantiated in Meredith G. Kline, "Double Trouble," *JETS* 32/2 (1989): 171–179.

of Jerusalem and the oracles against foreign nations. Fortunately, Jeremiah's message is not all bad news: in the midst of prophesying destruction and judgement comes a marvellous message of future restoration for the people of God.

It is important to consider the context before examining Jeremiah 31:27–40 in some detail.

OVERVIEW OF JEREMIAH 30–31:
THE BOOK OF CONSOLATION

Introduction: promise of restoration and return of God's people	30:1–3
A coming time of distress, yet Jacob will be rescued	30:4–7
Discipline and rescue for Israel; destruction for the nations	30:8–11
The incurable wound: the discipline of Israel	30:12–17
The restoration of Israel	30:18–24
The Lord (Yahweh) will be God of one united people	31:1
Because of his love, the Lord will rebuild Israel	31:2–6
Regathering the north: images of restoration	31:7–22
Restoring the south: Judah regathered	31:23–26
Once again God's people will be fruitful	31:27–30
The new covenant	31:31–34
The permanence of the new covenant: as permanent as creation	31:35–37
The new Jerusalem	31:38–40

The outline helps to situate our text in its immediate context and to see the flow of thought in the larger context. Jeremiah 30:1–3 forms a kind of general introduction and headline for the section as a whole and 30:4–11 summarises the thought of the whole: destruction for the nations but restoration for Israel. Then the restoration is described in detail, beginning with the northern kingdom of Israel and concluding with the southern kingdom of Judah. As the flow of thought arrives at the place where we have a regathered and restored people, we are presented with an announcement of a new covenant. This is followed by comments on the permanence of the new covenant and a brief glimpse of the new Jerusalem.

The full text is cited here without apology; the author of Hebrews does the same thing and hence is responsible for the longest citation of the Old Testament in the New. Once again, this reveals the importance of this text.

JEREMIAH 31:26–40

[26] At this I awoke and looked, and my sleep was pleasant to me.

[27] "Behold, the days are coming, declares the LORD, when I will sow the house of Israel and the house of Judah with the seed of man and the seed of beast. [28] And it shall come to pass that as I have watched over them to pluck up and break down, to overthrow, destroy, and bring harm, so I will watch over them to build and to plant, declares the LORD. [29] In those days they shall no longer say:

"'The fathers have eaten sour grapes,
    and the children's teeth are set on edge.'

[30] But everyone shall die for his own iniquity. Each man who eats sour grapes, his teeth shall be set on edge.

[The New Covenant]

[31] "Behold, the days are coming, declares the LORD, when I will make a new covenant with the house of Israel and the house of Judah, [32] not like the covenant that I made with their fathers on the day when I took them by the hand to bring them out of the land of Egypt, my covenant that they broke, though I was their husband, declares the LORD. [33] For this is the covenant that I will make with the house of Israel after those days, declares the LORD: I will put my law within them, and I will write it on their hearts. And I will be their God, and they shall be my people. [34] And no longer shall each one teach his neighbor and each his brother, saying, 'Know the LORD,' for they shall all know me, from the least of them to the greatest, declares the LORD. For I will forgive their iniquity, and I will remember their sin no more."

[35] Thus says the LORD,
who gives the sun for light by day
    and the fixed order of the moon and the stars for light by night,
    who stirs up the sea so that its waves roar—
    the LORD of hosts is his name:
[36] "If this fixed order departs
    from before me, declares the LORD,
then shall the offspring of Israel cease
    from being a nation before me forever."

[37] Thus says the LORD:
"If the heavens above can be measured,
    and the foundations of the earth below can be explored,

> then I will cast off all the offspring of Israel
>   for all that they have done,
>   declares the LORD."

[38] "Behold, the days are coming, declares the LORD, when the city shall be rebuilt for the LORD from the Tower of Hananel to the Corner Gate. [39] And the measuring line shall go out farther, straight to the hill Gareb, and shall then turn to Goah. [40] The whole valley of the dead bodies and the ashes, and all the fields as far as the brook Kidron, to the corner of the Horse Gate toward the east, shall be sacred to the LORD. It shall not be plucked up or overthrown anymore forever." (ESV)

Many discussions of this passage delimit the text as verses 31–34. Note the editorial heading "The New Covenant" in the ESV which sets off verses 31ff. Certainly the phrase "Behold, the days are coming" (v. 31) probably marks the beginning of an oracle or unit; verses 27 and 38 begin with the same phrase. Note, however, that verse 26 says that Jeremiah awoke and his sleep was pleasant to him. This indicates that the normal means of communicating to the prophet was in dreams and visions (see Num. 12:6) and that as the content of the Book of Consolation represented good news rather than the usual bad news, Jeremiah found his sleep sweet to him this time. At the same time, the statement that Jeremiah awoke is a clear indication of the end of the divine communication at verse 25, so that what we have attached at the end of the Book of Consolation are several prophetic oracles in definite sections appended to it. As we will see, verses 27–30 are integral to verses 31–34 and important for the interpretation of the new covenant. It is for this reason that I have delimited the unit as 27–40, subdivided by the recurring introductory phrase into three sections. The messenger formula at the onset of verse 35 also marks a new paragraph. In all, then, the section contains four paragraphs (vv. 27–30, 31–34, 35–37, 38–40). Discussions of the new covenant do not, in general, consider the flow of thought integral to these four paragraphs, but instead, they isolate verses 31–34 unnecessarily and focus attention on that one paragraph.

Explanation of this text will be focused around four questions: (1) When did Jeremiah predict the new covenant would be initiated? (2) With whom would God make this covenant? One of the parties is obviously God, but how should we define and delimit the other (human) party? (3) How is this covenant like the old (Israelite) covenant and how is it unlike it? In other words, precisely what is *new* about the new covenant? and (4) What is the power or promise of the new covenant? I.e., is this renewed covenant any better than the former one made at Sinai and supplemented by Deuteronomy on the plains of Moab?

Time

Verses 27, 31, and 38 of chapter 31 all begin with the phrase "Behold, days are coming." This phrase also occurs at 30:3, the general introduction to the Book of Consolation:

> [1] The word that came to Jeremiah from the LORD: [2] "Thus says the LORD, the God of Israel: Write in a book all the words that I have spoken to you. [3] For behold, days are coming, declares the LORD, when I will restore the fortunes of my people, Israel and Judah, says the LORD, and I will bring them back to the land that I gave to their fathers, and they shall take possession of it." (ESV)

The general introduction to the Book of Consolation announces, "Behold, days are coming" (הִנֵּה יָמִים בָּאִים). The next occurrence(s) of this phrase are the three instances in verses 27–40 (in v. 38, בָּאִים is supplied as a Qere in MT). Indeed, this is a familiar phrase in Jeremiah (occurring some fourteen or fifteen times),[13] but it is found only rarely elsewhere in the Old Testament (six times).[14] Note carefully that the word "days" is unarticulated or anarthrous. The translation "*the* days are coming" is not accurate. The text simply says, "days are coming." The days are indefinite. We must not take this as a technical term in the eschatology of the Old Testament or in the writings of the prophets.[15] It simply refers to an *indefinite* future. Whether this indefinite time in the future is near or remote is left entirely unspecified in the prophecy.

Parties

According to the text, Yahweh makes the new covenant "with the house of Israel and the house of Judah" (Jer. 31:31). The human partner is specified in this way because, in Jeremiah, this is the party that has broken the covenant made at Sinai:

> For the *house of Israel* and the *house of Judah*
> have been utterly treacherous to me, declares the LORD. (Jer. 5:11, ESV)

---

[13] Jeremiah 7:32; 9:25 (24 MT); 16:14; 19:6; 23:5; 23:7; 30:3; 31:27; 31:31; 33:14; 48:12; 49:2; 51:47; 51:52. Also Jeremiah 31:38Q.

[14] 1 Samuel 2:31; 2 Kings 20:17; Isaiah 39:6; Amos 4:2; 8:11; 9:13.

[15] Cf. Peter Andreas Munch, *The Expression Bajjôm Hāhū: Is It an Eschatological Terminus Technicus?* (Oslo: I Kommisjon hos Jacob Dybwad, 1936).

> The *house of Israel* and the *house of Judah* have broken my covenant that
> I made with their fathers. (Jer. 11:10, ESV)

The new covenant will bring return from exile and reunification of a divided
kingdom promised earlier:

> In those days the *house of Judah* shall join the *house of Israel*, and together
> they shall come from the land of the north to the land that I gave your
> fathers for a heritage. (Jer. 3:18, ESV)

So "the house of Israel and the house of Judah" are expressly mentioned in
31:31 to show that the previously divided kingdom(s) according to the context of chapters 30–31 will be united. The regathered and restored North and
the regathered and restored South of Jeremiah 30:1–31:26 will be reunited as
one. Jeremiah 31:1 emphasises, as do a number of passages, that there will
be one united people of God.

We have already seen, however, from earlier passages in Jeremiah, that
the Gentiles or non-Jewish nations will be established in the midst of Israel
in this restored people of God. They too are the exiles who will be brought
home by the fishers of men.

Let us now follow this through and see how it is interpreted in the New
Testament by Jesus and the apostles.

First note the clear reference to Jeremiah's new covenant by Jesus during his last Passover meal—which was at the same time his institution of the
Lord's Supper. The text of Matthew 26:26–29 reads as follows:

> [26] Now as they were eating, Jesus took bread, and after blessing it
> broke it and gave it to the disciples, and said, "Take, eat; this is my body."
> [27] And he took a cup, and when he had given thanks he gave it to them,
> saying, "Drink of it, all of you, [28] for *this is my blood of the covenant*,
> which is poured out for many for the forgiveness of sins. [29] I tell you I
> will not drink again of this fruit of the vine until that day when I drink it
> new with you in my Father's kingdom." (ESV)

Jesus redefines the Jewish Passover meal as a drama portraying his atoning
death on the cross. This drama then interprets his crucifixion in precisely
those terms: a new exodus that brings about forgiveness and reconciliation
on the basis of the sacrifice of himself as a "Passover lamb." In this drama,
the cup represents "my blood of the covenant which is poured out for many

for the forgiveness of sins." Although the exact phrase "new covenant" is not recorded in Matthew's account, it is in the account given in Luke 22:20:

> [14] And when the hour came, he reclined at table, and the apostles with him. [15] And he said to them, "I have earnestly desired to eat this Passover with you before I suffer. [16] For I tell you I will not eat it until it is fulfilled in the kingdom of God." [17] And he took a cup, and when he had given thanks he said, "Take this, and divide it among yourselves. [18] For I tell you that from now on I will not drink of the fruit of the vine until the kingdom of God comes." [19] And he took bread, and when he had given thanks, he broke it and gave it to them, saying, "This is my body, which is given for you. Do this in remembrance of me." [20] And likewise the cup after they had eaten, saying, "This cup that is poured out for you is *the new covenant* in my blood. [21] But behold, the hand of him who betrays me is with me on the table. [22] For the Son of Man goes as it has been determined, but woe to that man by whom he is betrayed!" [23] And they began to question one another, which of them it could be who was going to do this. (ESV)

The reference in Matthew to blood "poured out for many" seems to be a clear allusion to Isaiah 53:10–12, where the servant of the Lord is a "Passover lamb" whose atoning death brings about forgiveness for "the many."[16] The reference to Jeremiah's new covenant is explicit, at least in Luke, and the allusion is also clear in Matthew. Jesus' last Passover Meal, then, is converted into a new ceremonial tradition in which the cup represents his life (as Passover lamb) sacrificed to bring about the forgiveness of sins in the new exodus defined by Isaiah and Jeremiah.

Once the connection between the institution of the Lord's Supper in the Gospels and Isaiah 53 and Jeremiah 31 is established, it is interesting to note that Jesus gives this meal to *his disciples*. That is to say, the new covenant is not made with the house of Israel and the house of Judah interpreted as all of Judaism indiscriminately in the first century, but rather it is interpreted specifically as those *who are followers of Jesus*, regardless of ethnicity, Jew first and, later on, also non-Jew.

Another key passage which addresses the question of "how do we define the human party in the new covenant" is Romans 11:13–24:

> [13] Now I am speaking to you Gentiles. Inasmuch then as I am an apostle to the Gentiles, I magnify my ministry [14] in order somehow to make my

---

16 The expression "the many" or "the numerous" occurs four times in Isaiah 53:11–12. See Peter J. Gentry, "The Atonement in Isaiah's Fourth Servant Song (Isaiah 52:13–53:12)," *SBJT* 11/2 (2007): 20–47.

fellow Jews jealous, and thus save some of them. [15] For if their rejection means the reconciliation of the world, what will their acceptance mean but life from the dead? [16] If the dough offered as firstfruits is holy, so is the whole lump, and if the root is holy, so are the branches.

[17] But if some of the branches were broken off, and you, although a wild olive shoot, were grafted in among the others and now share in the nourishing root of the olive tree, [18] do not be arrogant toward the branches. If you are, remember it is not you who support the root, but the root that supports you. [19] Then you will say, "Branches were broken off so that I might be grafted in." [20] That is true. They were broken off because of their unbelief, but you stand fast through faith. So do not become proud, but fear. [21] For if God did not spare the natural branches, neither will he spare you. [22] Note then the kindness and the severity of God: severity toward those who have fallen, but God's kindness to you, provided you continue in his kindness. Otherwise you too will be cut off. [23] And even they, if they do not continue in their unbelief, will be grafted in, for God has the power to graft them in again. [24] For if you were cut from what is by nature a wild olive tree, and grafted, contrary to nature, into a cultivated olive tree, how much more will these, the natural branches, be grafted back into their own olive tree. (ESV)

Paul is explaining in this passage the benefits of the new covenant and, in particular, how they relate to those who are genetically Israelites, since for the most part during Paul's ministry they rejected Jesus as Messiah and his death as the basis for the final stage of the return from exile. Paul's main mission has been to take the Good News to the Gentiles, and this has met with great success. What are we to make of the fact that, during and since Paul's ministry, few Jews but many Gentiles are believing in Jesus and being added to the church? This is the painful problem addressed in Romans 9–11. Paul explains that the acceptance of the person and work of Jesus by the Gentiles, the nations, will arouse jealousy among those of the historical race of Israel and will motivate them to come to faith in Jesus Christ.

As is well known, Paul employs the metaphor of an olive tree to represent Israel. Natural branches have been removed, and non-native branches have been grafted into the one tree. It is common in the Old Testament to represent kings and kingdoms by stately tall trees and fruitful plants. The dream of Nebuchadnezzar in Daniel 4 is an obvious example. Ezekiel 17 pictures the king of Israel this way, and again the kings of Assyria and Egypt in Ezekiel 31. The most common type of "tree" used to represent Israel is the vine (Deut. 32:32; Isa. 3:14; 5:1–7; 27:1–6; Jer. 2:21; 5:10; 12:10–13;

Ezek. 15; 17; 19:10–14; Hos. 10:1–2; Ps. 80:8–19). Psalm 80 is particularly eloquent, for it develops the theme of the extension of the kingdom of God by describing how the vine (i.e., Israel) grew and spread, and it also speaks of Israel's Adamic sonship (v. 15). Only rarely is Israel represented by an olive tree (Jer. 11:16; Hos. 14:6 [7 MT]). Jeremiah is the one who speaks of burning the *olive tree* and breaking its branches (see also the vine described in this way in Jer. 5:10). So the olive tree for Paul represents Israel, and the Jeremiah passage is fundamental for his comments in Romans 11. Unbelieving and rebellious Israelites have been removed, and individuals from other nations have been joined to this one people of God, the new and transformed Zion. As we saw earlier, this theme was already adumbrated in Jeremiah, though it was not stated there as clearly as in the New Testament.

The passages in Ephesians 2 and 3 are among the clearest in the New Testament:

[11] Therefore remember that at one time you Gentiles in the flesh, called "the uncircumcision" by what is called the circumcision, which is made in the flesh by hands—[12] remember that you were at that time separated from Christ, alienated from the commonwealth of Israel and strangers to the covenants of promise, having no hope and without God in the world. [13] But now in Christ Jesus you who once were far off have been brought near by the blood of Christ. [14] For he himself is our peace, who has made us both one and has broken down in his flesh the dividing wall of hostility [15] by abolishing the law of commandments expressed in ordinances, that he might create in himself one new man in place of the two, so making peace, [16] and might reconcile us both to God in one body through the cross, thereby killing the hostility. [17] And he came and preached peace to you who were far off and peace to those who were near. [18] For through him we both have access in one Spirit to the Father. [19] So then you are no longer strangers and aliens, but you are fellow citizens with the saints and members of the household of God, [20] built on the foundation of the apostles and prophets, Christ Jesus himself being the cornerstone, [21] in whom the whole structure, being joined together, grows into a holy temple in the Lord. [22] In him you also are being built together into a dwelling place for God by the Spirit. (Eph. 2:11–22, ESV)

[1] For this reason I, Paul, a prisoner for Christ Jesus on behalf of you Gentiles—[2] assuming that you have heard of the stewardship of God's grace that was given to me for you, [3] how the mystery was made known to me by revelation, as I have written briefly. [4] When you read this, you can perceive my insight into the mystery of Christ, [5] which was not made

known to the sons of men in other generations as it has now been revealed
to his holy apostles and prophets by the Spirit. [6] This mystery is that the
Gentiles are fellow heirs, members of the same body, and partakers of the
promise in Christ Jesus through the gospel. (Eph. 3:1–6, ESV)

When Paul speaks in Ephesians 2:15 of "one new *man*" he is obviously thinking of a new *Adam* and is saying that the *church*—by virtue of
the new creation resulting from the resurrection of Jesus Christ, and by
virtue of the union of head (Christ) and body (church)—constitutes this
new Adam—a renewal of the Adamic role initiated with Abraham and his
family.

The Gentiles—members of nations and peoples in the earth apart from
or outside of the nation of Israel, who were alienated from the commonwealth of Israel—have been forged together with believers from Israel into
one new humanity. Verse 14 says that "he made both groups/the two groups
one." And again verse 15 says that "he created in him the two (groups) into
one new man/humanity." There is no future for either Israelite or non-Israelite apart from the church, and there is no separate future for either Israelite
or non-Israelite—both will be part of the church. This is the body of humans
who will survive the destruction of this creation and will be placed within
the creation of a new heavens and a new earth.

Ephesians 3:5 says that this truth was not made known earlier *as it
has now been revealed* to the apostles and prophets of the church of Jesus
Christ. The word "as" indicates *chronology* and *degree* rather than *kind*.[17]
Paul is not saying that this truth was not revealed at all before this. This
truth was made known by the prophets of the Old Testament, but was not
taught as clearly as it is now taught by the apostles and prophets of the New
Testament Era.

[25] I do not want you to be ignorant of this mystery, brothers, so that
you may not be conceited: Israel has experienced a hardening in part until
the full number of the Gentiles has come in. [26] And so all Israel will be
saved, as it is written:

"The deliverer will come from Zion;
    he will turn godlessness away from Jacob.

---

[17] Harriet Michael, in our Sunday school class at Franklin Street Church, Louisville, helped me to see the element
of time as well as of degree.

> [27] And this is my covenant with them
>   when I take away their sins." (Rom. 11:25–27, NIV)

Romans 11:25–27 is a debated passage among Christians, especially in classic covenant theology versus dispensationalism. Some have taught that the "fullness of the Gentiles" refers to the so-called church age, and that when it is over, then the geopolitical kingdom will be restored to Israel and physical Israel will be saved. They may also appeal to the book of Daniel, which describes four Gentile kingdoms followed by the kingdom of God. Unfortunately, everyone may be blinded by the assumptions they have and the way they put the metanarrative of Scripture together. We all bring this to the reading of any particular text.

In Romans 11, Paul has just portrayed Israel in terms of an olive tree, some of whose natural branches have been removed and some of whose branches are now non-Jewish branches grafted into the one root and tree. What this means is that the new humanity and restored Israel is based on faith and covenant relationship to the Lord rather than on ethnicity. During the period in which the exiles are brought home, a large number of "Gentile exiles" (to use Jeremiah's own imagery) will be brought home first, and this will motivate a large number of Jewish exiles to be brought home toward the end. But the Jewish exiles will be *brought back* to the one olive tree. We must interpret "all Israel" within the context of Paul's teaching in Romans 11. There is no separate future for physical Israel outside of the church—the only humanity to inhabit the new creation. And this is not so-called replacement theology. It is what the prophets teach about the renovated and restored Zion. This is further made clear by Revelation 21:

> [1] Then I saw a new heaven and a new earth, for the first heaven and the first earth had passed away, and there was no longer any sea. [2] I saw the Holy City, the new Jerusalem, coming down out of heaven from God, prepared as a bride beautifully dressed for her husband. [3] And I heard a loud voice from the throne saying, "Now the dwelling of God is with men, and he will live with them. They will be his people, and God himself will be with them and be their God. [4] He will wipe every tear from their eyes. There will be no more death or mourning or crying or pain, for the old order of things has passed away." (NIV)

The community of the new exodus, the new Zion, is defined in Hebrews

12:18–24. This community is presently being gathered before the throne of God in heaven. When the new creation is ready, i.e., the place where they will live, this community comes down out of heaven to the new earth. In Revelation 21:2 it is called "the Holy City," "the new Jerusalem" and "a bride." In the New Testament the bride is a metaphor for the church, and here it is identified as the new Jerusalem. Later on, in verses 10–16, the same community, identified by the same names, i.e., the Holy City, the new Jerusalem, is described as a cube. There are twelve gates, and the names of the twelve tribes of Israel are upon the gates. In addition, there are twelve foundations, and the names of the twelve apostles of the Lamb are on them.

Normally, foundations are underneath. How may we imagine twelve foundations under a cube? Probably one foundation under each corner and two in between each corner. This is fitting, since twelve gates divided by four sides would give three gates per side, i.e., one gate between each foundation.[18] Thus the Israel of the Old Testament and the apostolic community of the New Testament are completely and fully integrated in the new Jerusalem. This is the same as Paul's picture in Ephesians of Jew and non-Jew, forged into one united new humanity and covenant community—note the Covenant Formula in Revelation 21:3.

The New Covenant and the Old: Continuity and Discontinuity

How is this covenant like the old (Israelite) covenant and how is it unlike it? In other words, precisely what is *new* about the new covenant? Jeremiah 31:31–34 describes the new covenant. Scholars have debated extensively the meaning of the word "new" (חָדָשׁ) in Hebrew. Does it mean a renewed covenant, or a covenant that did not exist previously? Is it a new development, or is it a bringing out of something yet again, e.g., a new day. Moon rightly argues that we should let the statements in Jeremiah 31:31–34 define what is meant by a new covenant.[19]

It is important to pay attention to the grammatical and literary structures in the text. Scott J. Hafemann has helpfully diagrammed the text to aid in clarifying the flow of thought.[20] The argument of Jeremiah 31:31–34, according to its constituent propositions, is as follows:

---

[18] See Michael Wilcock, *I Saw Heaven Opened: The Message of Revelation*, The Bible Speaks Today (Downers Grove, IL: InterVarsity Press, 1975), 208.

[19] Joshua N. Moon, *Jeremiah's New Covenant: An Augustinian Reading*, Journal of Theological Interpretation Supplement 3 (Winona Lake, IN: Eisenbrauns, 2011), 168ff.

[20] Adapted from Scott J. Hafemann, "The Covenant Relationship," in *Central Themes in Biblical Theology: Mapping Unity in Diversity*, ed. Scott J. Hafemann and Paul R. House (Grand Rapids, MI: Baker, 2007), 49.

v. 31 "Behold, days are coming," declares the LORD, "when I will make a new covenant with the house of Israel and with the house of Judah.

v. 32a *Specifically–*negatively: I will not make it like the covenant which I made with their fathers . . .

v. 32b because they broke my covenant (at Sinai)

v. 32c although I was a husband to them," declares the LORD.

v. 33a *Specifically–*positively: "But this is the covenant which I will make with the house of Israel after those days," declares the LORD. "I will put my law within them and I will write it upon their heart."

v. 33b *Immediate Result*: "I will be their God and they will be my people."

v. 34a *Ultimate Result*: "They will no longer teach each other saying, 'Know the LORD,'

v. 34b because they will all know me, from the least of them to the greatest of them," declares the LORD.

v. 34c *Basis for this Result*: "I shall forgive their iniquity, and I shall remember their sin no more."

Several points in Jeremiah's announcement of the new covenant must be noted.

First, the new covenant is the divinely promised answer to the perennial problem of Israel's hard-hearted rebellion against the Lord. The Hebrew expression "the stubbornness of his/their heart" (Deut. 29:19 [18 MT]; Jer. 3:17; 7:24; 9:14 [13 MT]; 11:8; 13:10; 16:12; 18:12; 23:17; Ps. 81:12 [13 MT]) occurs ten times in the Old Testament: the one instance in Deuteronomy is picked up by Jeremiah, who uses the phrase a total of eight times. Thus nearly all the occurrences are in Jeremiah. This, along with other phrases used by Jeremiah such as "the incurable wound" in chapter 30, demonstrates his emphasis on the fact that Israel's rebellion is intractable: she cannot avert the coming anger and wrath of God. Judgement is absolutely certain. The new covenant looks beyond judgement to a future in which God will provide a solution to the stubbornness of his partner in the old covenant. The direction and instruction of God for righteous relationships will be internalised and written upon the heart. Since the heart of the people will be transformed, they will be a faithful covenant partner. The new covenant will not be like the Israelite covenant, because the people broke that covenant. Now the people of the Lord will be completely faithful and loyal; they will be covenant keepers. Thus the new covenant in Jeremiah must be interpreted against the background of the

faithless and stubborn heart of Israel in the old covenant. That the human partner in the new covenant will be faithful is nicely stated by Walther Eichrodt:

> The purport of Jer. 31.31ff., even though it does not speak of the spirit, is in
> effect no different from that of Isa. 32.15ff.; 11.9 or Ezek. 36.26ff., namely
> a new possibility, created by God himself, of realizing the will of God in
> human life.[21]

Joshua Moon draws attention to the fact that the new covenant in
Jeremiah 31:31 is not contrasted with a "first" or "old" covenant, but with
the *broken* covenant:

> Our first firm point for reading 31:31–34 can now be established: the refer-
> ence to 'the day when I brought them up out of Egypt' (whether at 31:32
> or 11:4 and 7) is not used to identify which covenant is made the point of
> contrast (e.g., Mosaic or Josianic). Nor does the phrase give justification
> for our leaping out of Jeremiah into a state of affairs described in the book
> of Exodus or Deuteronomy. Rather the phrase points us to the start of the
> relationship between Yhwh and his people, the great act by which Yhwh
> claimed them as his own. In other words, from ch. 11 we learn that the
> infidelity of the people to Yhwh—the broken covenant—has been broken
> from the very start, from the time in which Yhwh acted to call and bring
> them to himself.[22]

Moon is correct to emphasise that what is contrasted with the new covenant
is the infidelity of the people. This clearly defines the new covenant as one
in which all covenant members are faithful, i.e., believers. Nonetheless, just
because scholars debate whether the broken covenant is Josianic or Mosaic
does not mean we need to be agnostic on this issue. As we have demonstrated
earlier, the Josianic covenant according to 2 Kings 23:3–5 was a covenant
initiated to establish or keep the Israelite covenant made at Sinai and renewed
in Deuteronomy. The phrase "the day when I brought them up out of Egypt"
most certainly refers to the events of Sinai and not to those of Josiah's time.

Jeremiah employs a wide variety of expressions to refer to the infidelity
of Israel as a covenant partner. Three in particular ought to be mentioned in
passing:

---

[21] Walther Eichrodt, *Theology of the Old Testament*, 2 vols., trans. J. A. Baker, Old Testament Library (Philadelphia: Westminster, 1961), 2:58, n. 5.
[22] Moon, *Jeremiah's New Covenant*, 194.

[1] Run to and fro through the streets of Jerusalem,
  look and take note!
Search her squares to see
  if you can find a man,
one who does justice
  and seeks truth,
that I may pardon her.
[2] Though they say, "As the Lord lives,"
  yet they swear falsely.
[3] O Lord, do not your eyes look for truth?
You have struck them down,
  but they felt no anguish;
you have consumed them,
  but they refused to take correction.
They have made their faces harder than rock;
  they have refused to repent.

[4] Then I said, "These are only the poor;
  they have no sense;
for they do not know the way of the Lord,
  the justice of their God.
[5] I will go to the great
  and will speak to them,
for they know the way of the Lord,
  the justice of their God."
But they all alike had broken the yoke;
  they had burst the bonds. (Jer. 5:1–5, ESV)

[22] For in the day that I brought them out of the land of Egypt, I did not speak to your fathers or command them concerning burnt offerings and sacrifices. [23] But this command I gave them: 'Obey my voice, and I will be your God, and you shall be my people. And walk in all the way that I command you, that it may be well with you.' [24] But they did not hear or incline their ear . . . (Jer. 7:22–24, ESV)

For long ago I broke your yoke
  and burst your bonds;
  but you said, "I will not serve." (Jer. 2:20, ESV)

Jeremiah 5:1–5, in describing a search for one person who is righteous, so that the city may be saved, recalls Abraham pleading for Sodom and Gomorrah. The phrase "the way of the Lord" refers directly to Genesis 18:19, where Abram is to direct his family to keep the way of the Lord by practising social justice. For Jeremiah to assert that the people do not know the way of the Lord is an accusation of *covenant* infidelity. In Jeremiah 7:23 the command "Obey my voice" is a direct reference to Exodus 15:26 and 19:5, and therefore the refusal to hear or obey is Jeremiah's accusation of *covenant* infidelity. In Jeremiah 2:20 the prophet describes the exodus as breaking the yoke (of serving Pharaoh) so that Israel could give the service of a devoted and obedient son to Yahweh, but Israel would not serve. This is yet another way of referring to Exodus 19:5–6 and describing *covenant* infidelity. Moon is right in stressing that the new covenant reverses this infidelity. Nonetheless, when he contrasts the exegesis of Jerome (the new covenant is a new era) and the exegesis of Augustine (the new covenant is what is characteristic of the faithful believer in any era), he oversimplifies. The new covenant entails a new era in which all covenant members are faithful.

Second, in the new covenant, the תּוֹרָה ("instruction") of God will be internalised and written upon the heart, the centre of one's life, i.e., the inner person where one reasons, feels, and makes decisions and plans.[23] The term תּוֹרָה (inappropriately translated "law") shows that God's direction and instruction for appropriate relationships (divine-human, human-human, human-creation relationships) will not change. The new covenant does not mean a change in God's standards of righteousness, of right and wrong, of what is appropriate in a covenant relationship. No, what is new about the new covenant is the ability of both partners to keep the covenant.

The writing of the divine instruction upon the heart corresponds to the promise made earlier in Jeremiah that the ark of the covenant would become obsolete:

> [16] And when you have multiplied and been fruitful in the land, in those days, declares the LORD, they shall no more say, "The ark of the covenant of the LORD." It shall not come to mind or be remembered or missed; it shall not be made again. [17] At that time Jerusalem shall be called the throne of the LORD, and all nations shall gather to it, to the presence of the LORD in

---

[23] Normally the first statement in Jeremiah 31:33 is rendered as a future tense: "I will place my law in their inward parts." Adrian Schenker argues that because the form in the Hebrew text is a perfect, it ought to be rendered as a past. The word "midst" (קֶרֶב) is construed as "among them" (see Adrian Schenker, *Das Neue am neuen Bund und das Alte am alten: Jer 31 in der hebräischen und griechischen Bibel* (Forschungen zur Religion und Literatur des Alten und Neuen Testaments 212; Göttingen, Germany: Vandenhoeck & Ruprecht, 2006), 30, n. 29). I note that a prophetic perfect followed by a *waw*-consecutive perfect or imperfect (if non-clause-initial) is the normal pattern for beginning a prophecy in the future tense (e.g., Num. 24:17), and that when "midst" (קֶרֶב) is paired with "heart" (לֵב), the meaning must be inward parts of a person. So also Joshua N. Moon, *Jeremiah's New Covenant: An Augustinian Reading*, Journal of Theological Interpretation Supplement 3 (Winona Lake, IN: Eisenbrauns, 2011), 234–238.

Jerusalem, and they shall no more stubbornly follow their own evil heart. [18] In those days the house of Judah shall join the house of Israel, and together they shall come from the land of the north to the land that I gave your fathers for a heritage. (Jer. 3:16–18, ESV)

As Kevin J. Youngblood has noted, hints of a new covenant begin as early as Jeremiah 3:11–22, where Yahweh offers forgiveness to the northern kingdom of Israel if they would only acknowledge their guilt. In this context, Yahweh states that the ark of the covenant will no longer be necessary. Youngblood aptly comments,

> Since this was the box that housed the copy of the covenant document, the implications of its loss should be catastrophic as it was in DtH (1 Sam 4–6). Instead, YHWH says, no ark will be necessary in the future. Why not? Because Jer 31:31ff indicates that the new covenant document will be stored, not in a piece of cultic furniture but in the very hearts of YHWH's people.[24]

Thus the people of God will faithfully keep the new covenant. God's instruction will be internalised, it will be ingrained in their thinking, feeling, and planning. Paul picks this up in 2 Corinthians 3:3 when he speaks of the evidence for the new covenant in the Corinthian Christians:

> You show that you are a letter from Christ, the result of our ministry, written not with ink but with the Spirit of the living God, not on tablets of stone but on tablets of human hearts. (NIV)

Third, the covenant relationship with God is the immediate result of God's "writing" the divine direction for living and the instruction of the new covenant upon the hearts of believers. This is clear from the Covenant Formula, "I will be their God and they shall be my people." Notice, again, how Paul applies the Covenant Formula to the Corinthian Christians in 2 Corinthians 6:14–18:

> [14] Do not be yoked together with unbelievers. For what do righteousness and wickedness have in common? Or what fellowship can light have with darkness? [15] What harmony is there between Christ and Belial? What does a believer have in common with an unbeliever? [16] What agreement

---

[24] Kevin J. Youngblood, "Beyond Deuteronomism: Jeremiah's Unique Theological Contribution," paper presented at Lipscomb University, 2009.

is there between the temple of God and idols? For we are the temple of the living God. As God has said: "I will live with them and walk among them, *and I will be their God, and they will be my people.*"

[17] "Therefore come out from them
    and be separate,
                        says the Lord.
Touch no unclean thing,
    and I will receive you."
[18] "I will be a Father to you,
    and you will be my sons and daughters,
                  says the Lord Almighty." (NIV)

Paul backs up his command not to be "yoked together with unbelievers" by a pastiche of citations from the Old Testament. First, from Leviticus 26:11–12 comes the Covenant Formula.[25] Then, from Isaiah 52:11 is a call to the exiles to leave Babylon and join the community of the new exodus with the promise "I will receive you" added from Ezekiel 20:41, where another paragraph on the same topic can be found. Finally, verse 18 seems to apply the father-son relationship of the covenant with David in 2 Samuel 7:14 to all the members of the new covenant community.

Fourth, the result of inaugurating the new covenant will be that a community will be created in which, "They will no longer teach each other, saying, 'Know the LORD,' because they will all know me, from the least of them to the greatest of them, declares the LORD" (Jer. 31:34). This is a most significant statement, whose import has not been well understood. To begin to grasp the meaning, it must be understood that this verse is a statement that stands in contrast to verses 29–30 and answers the problem posed by these words:

[29] In those days people will no longer say,

    "The fathers have eaten sour grapes,
        and the children's teeth are set on edge."

[30] Instead, everyone will die for his own sin; whoever eats sour grapes— his own teeth will be set on edge. (NIV)

---

[25] The recent work by Stanley E. Porter, "The Concept of Covenant in Paul," in *The Concept of the Covenant in the Second Temple Period*, ed. Stanley E. Porter and Jacqueline C. R. de Roo, Supplements to the Journal for the Study of Judaism 71 (Leiden, Netherlands: Brill, 2003), 269–285, does not mention 2 Corinthians 6:16–18 although he extends his study beyond the term "covenant" to covenant language. The concept of covenant is far more prevalent than many New Testament scholars are aware.

Verse 29 recites a proverb going around among the exiles in Babylon. Normally when a person eats sour grapes, their own lips pucker up. To claim that the parents ate sour grapes and the lips of the children puckered up is a way of saying that the children have been judged (i.e., exiled) for their parents' sins. One of the most illuminating comments on this text is that of D. A. Carson, which we must cite in this context:

> In the sixth century B.C. the prophet Jeremiah, speaking for the LORD, foresees a time when people will no longer repeat the proverb, "The fathers have eaten sour grapes, and the children's teeth are set on edge" (Jer. 31:30). The history of Israel under the Mosaic covenant has been characterized by the outworking of this proverb. The covenant structure was profoundly racial and tribal. Designated leaders—prophets, priests, king, and occasionally other leaders such as the seventy elders or Bezaleel—were endued with the Spirit, and spoke for God to the people and for the people of God (cf. Exod. 20:19). Thus when the leaders sinned, the entire nation was contaminated, and ultimately faced divine wrath. But the time is coming, Jeremiah says, when this proverb will be abandoned. "Instead," God promises, "everyone will die for his own sin; whoever eats sour grapes— his own teeth will be set on edge" (Jer. 31:30). This could be true only if the entire covenantal structure associated with Moses' name is replaced by another. That is precisely what the LORD promises: he will make "a new covenant with the house of Israel and with the house of Judah" that "will not be like the covenant" he made with their forefathers at the time of the Exodus. The nature of the promised new covenant is carefully recorded: God will put his law in the hearts and on the minds of his people. Instead of having a mediated knowledge of God, "they will all know me, from the least of them to the greatest," and therefore "no longer will a man teach his neighbor, or a man his brother, saying, 'Know the LORD'" (31:31ff.). This does not foresee a time of no teachers; in the context, it foresees a time of no mediators, because the entire covenant community under this new covenant will have a personal knowledge of God, a knowledge characterized by the forgiveness of sin (31:34) and by the law of God written on the heart (31:33). "I will give them singleness of heart and action, so that they will always fear me for their own good and the good of their children after them. I will make an everlasting covenant with them: I will never stop doing good to them, and I will inspire them to fear me, so that they will never turn away from me" (Jer. 32:39–40).[26]

We would agree with Carson's analysis, although the fundamental point

---

[26] D. A. Carson, "Evangelicals, Ecumenism, and the Church," in *Evangelical Affirmations*, ed. Kenneth S. Kantzer and Carl F. H. Henry (Grand Rapids, MI: Zondervan, 1990), 359–360.

might be more clearly stated. He claims that the difference between the old covenant community and the new covenant community is that the latter will have no mediators. This is not quite true. It will indeed have a (human) covenant mediator, namely Jesus Christ, who is prophet, priest, and king in one person. In the old covenant community, these covenant mediators sinned and the community suffered because of *faulty mediators*. In the new covenant, however, our covenant mediator is without sin and as a result, the community will never suffer because of a faulty mediator.

What verse 34 is saying, however, in contrast to verses 29–30, is that in the old covenant, people became members of the covenant community simply by being born into that community. As they grew up, some became believers in Yahweh and others did not. This resulted in a situation within the covenant community where some *members* could urge other *members* to know the Lord. In the new covenant community, however, one does not become a member by physical birth but rather by the new birth, which requires faith on the part of every person. Thus only believers are members of the new community: all *members* are *believers*, and *only* believers are members. Therefore in the new covenant community there will no longer be a situation where some members urge other members to know the Lord. There will be no such thing as an unregenerate member of the new covenant community. All are believers, all know the Lord, because all have experienced the forgiveness of sins.

What Jeremiah is teaching in 31:33–34 is identical to what Isaiah is teaching in Isaiah 54:13: "all your children shall be taught by the LORD, and great shall be the peace of your children" (ESV). Everyone in the covenant community will experience reconciliation (peace) with God, and so everyone will have a living relationship with the Lord, and so the divine instruction for living will be written upon the heart.

As the last part of verse 34 indicates, the basis for these characteristics of the new covenant community is the divine forgiveness of sins brought about by the establishment of the new covenant.

Jeremiah 31:34 is important since it shows that the Presbyterian understanding is flawed. There are no covenant members who are not believers. This challenge to the Presbyterians must be given in humility since, by and large, they have had a much better grasp of the meaning and role of the covenants than Baptists.

In *An Old Testament Theology*, Bruce K. Waltke claims that Jesus' parables in Matthew 13 show that the new covenant administration includes both regenerate and unregenerate members:

> The first parable, the parable of the sower (Matt. 13:1–23), reveals that only a fraction of those who outwardly accept Jesus Christ as Messiah persevere and bear good fruit (i.e., love of God and of others). The second parable, the parable of the weeds (vv. 24–30), reveals that at present good seed (the people of God's kingdom) and weeds (the people of Satan's kingdom) co-exist in the world, growing together until the final judgment at the end of the age, when the weeds will be burned and the wheat will be saved. The Lord's final parable, the parable of the net (vv. 47–50), climactically clarifies that the visible kingdom of God consists of good and bad fish that are caught in the same net and not separated from one another until the end of the age.
>
> Consequently, the new covenant administration includes both true (regenerate) and nominal (unregenerate) followers of Jesus Christ. The latter fall away because they lack the root of regeneration and the eternal life that perseveres and prevails over temptation. The apostles confront this reality in their letters to the churches (cf. 1 Cor. 15:2; Gal. 1:6–9; Heb. 6:4–6; 10:26–39; 1 John 2:3–6, 19; Rev. 2:14, 20–23; 3:1–5; 16). In other words, true believers and nominal believers can be found in both the old and new covenant administrations. The former receive covenant blessing; the latter, covenant curses.[27]

Unfortunately, what is claimed in the second paragraph does not follow from the exegesis in the first, i.e., the problem is with the word "consequently." This is due to a larger problem in classic covenant theology: the metanarrative of this system is not true to the Bible because it does not pay adequate attention to what the biblical texts say in defining the relationship(s) of one covenant to another. First, we cannot speak of "the covenant" in the way the theologians of classic covenant theology do, because this language is never found in the Bible. Instead, we can speak only of the covenants (plural), i.e., the covenant with creation, the covenant with Abraham, the Israelite covenant, the Davidic covenant, and the new covenant. Furthermore, we must let the biblical texts define the relationships between them.

In the Abrahamic covenant, God promises blessing for Israel and for the nations through Israel. The Israelite covenant is inaugurated to implement the promises to Abraham. The Davidic covenant reveals that the blessing will come through the King of Israel (rather than through the nation as a

---

[27] Bruce K. Waltke with Charles Yu, *An Old Testament Theology: An Exegetical, Canonical, and Thematic Approach* (Grand Rapids, MI: Zondervan, 2007), 442.

whole) as he administers justice to Israel and to the nations. Israel's idolatry and sin is covenant violation and thus the plan of salvation for the world appears doomed. The new covenant restores the broken relationship between God and Israel by bringing about the forgiveness of sins. Redemption is the achievement and victory of a Davidic king who then administers righteousness to a restored Israel, in which Jew and Gentile are created to be the new humanity. The community of the new covenant is the only humanity to inherit a new creation—a new heavens and earth.

In the present time, when there is overlap between the old creation and the new, God rescues believers in Jesus Christ from "the authority of darkness" and "transfers them to the kingdom of his beloved son" according to Colossians 1:13. In the church, believers experience the blessings of the new covenant. In what way, however, does the new covenant "administer" the unregenerate? The only blessings the unregenerate receive are the blessings given in the covenant with creation to all humans alike.

In the first parable the field is the world, where the sons of the kingdom and the sons of the Evil One are not clearly separated. Nonetheless, the church and the world are not the same thing. This is why, in church discipline, putting people out of the church is to hand them over to Satan, i.e., remove them from the protection administered by the new covenant and expose them to the dangers of Satan's kingdom (1 Tim. 1:20). This is the opposite of the transferral in Colossians 1:13.

In the second parable, the netted fish represent all those who appear to become members of the new covenant by outward acceptance of the gospel, but the actual, regenerate members of the new covenant are sorted out at the end of the age. The purpose of church discipline is to begin that sorting process now (Matt. 18:17; 1 Cor 5:13) in order to keep the visible church aligned to actual new covenant membership as much as possible, recognising that this will be accomplished perfectly *only* at the end of the age. Consequently, the net does not represent actual membership in the new covenant, only apparent.

Fifth, the expression "I will cut a new covenant" (*kārat běrît*) shows that God is not simply confirming or reestablishing or upholding the Sinai covenant in a covenant renewal; he is initiating or inaugurating a new covenant. Therefore the new covenant is not the old covenant. It is a *new* covenant. This automatically renders the Israelite covenant obsolete as a code or formalised agreement. Recall that the Israelite covenant is both a law treatise and a covenant or vassal treaty. A new arrangement or code will be put into place between God and his people; but the instruction in that code will be the same. As a result, when we compare and contrast the old and new covenants, we can say that we are not bound to the old covenant as a code, but that the righteousness of God demonstrated in the old covenant has been enshrined and incorporated into the new.

This is something that in general is poorly grasped in many discussions of the Christian life. As a Christian, I am not bound by the Ten Commandments, because they are part of an agreement between God and Israel that does not apply to me. My relationship to God is based upon and defined by the new covenant. Nonetheless, within the new covenant the divine instruction calls me to love my neighbour so that adultery, murder, stealing, etc., are still covenant violations. The righteousness of God has not changed. Thus those like the theonomists who want to put the Christian under the old covenant are false teachers.

Some of the similarities and differences between the old and new covenants can be diagrammed simply:

Similarity of the New Covenant to the Old Covenant
1. Basis is the same (the grace of God)
2. Purpose is the same (cf. 1 Pet. 2:9–10)
3. Initiated by blood (Heb. 9:6–10:18)
4. Character of divine instruction is the same (Rom. 13:8; Gal. 5:14)

Dissimilarity of the New Covenant to the Old Covenant
1. Better mediator (without sin) (Heb. 8:6; 9:15; 12:24)
2. Better sacrifice (Heb. 9:6–10:18; Isa. 42:6; 52:13–53:12)
3. Better provision (the Spirit of God; Ezek. 36:24–28)
4. Better promise (impartation of a new heart; Ezek. 36:24–28)

The Power of the New Covenant: Daring to Draw Near

Hidden and tucked away in the Book of Consolation, separate from the paragraphs on the new covenant, are some amazing statements concerning the power and promise of the coming new situation. Let us consider the amazing prediction of Jeremiah 30:21–22:

[21] Their prince shall be one of their own,
   their ruler shall come from their midst;
I will bring him near, and he shall approach me,

> for who would otherwise dare to approach me?
>   says the LORD.
> [22] And you shall be my people,
>   and I will be your God. (NRSV)

The import of these words for the new covenant can be developed under three headings.

1. No One Can Approach God on His or Her Own Initiative

Jeremiah employs a bold figure of speech in this text. This figure of speech is usually not translated in most of the English versions. Verse 21c might be rendered, "For who would mortgage his heart to draw near to me." This is a metaphor in which a comparison is drawn between a person using property as collateral for a loan and a person giving away his life for something. Just as mortgaging a house or property for money due to one's desperate financial straits is an extreme and radical step, even more so is it an act of desperation to give away one's heart, i.e., one's life. The inner person is one's most precious possession. Here Jeremiah portrays a man selling his soul as it were to have an audience with God. Could one's most valuable possession be used as collateral to gain an audience with God? Absolutely *no*! The metaphor expresses the fact that there is no initiative on the part of a human that can bring him close to God; the initiative must come from God and God alone.

2. God Has Brought the King-Priest of His People Near

Although no human initiative can bring a person into the awesome presence of the divine King of kings and Lord of lords, God has brought the King of his people near. This is of greater moment than that of Esther coming before the great king of the Persian empire. J. A. Thompson comments,

> To enter the divine presence unbidden was to risk death. The ruler thus appears to be undertaking a sacral or priestly function rather than one that is specifically political. The picture is of a ruler-priest performing both political and priestly duties. Such a concept was well known in the Middle East.[28]

We should carefully note the language used in verse 21. The text speaks of a prince (אַדִּיר) or ruler (מֹשֵׁל). The first word is literally a "mighty one" and

---

[28] See Thompson, *Book of Jeremiah*, 562. Bright notes that "the ruler here (the word 'king' is avoided) discharges a sacral or priestly function, rather than one that is specifically political" (Bright, *Jeremiah*, 280. Also, cf. *HALOT*, s.v. נגשׁ).

the second is a participle from a generic verb "to rule." Bright is right to note that the normal term for "king" (מֶלֶךְ) is avoided for the same reasons that the author of Samuel prefers נָגִיד. Furthermore, the verb "to draw near" (נגשׁ) and the verb "to bring near" (קרב) belong primarily to the description of priestly service and work.[29] The language of this text, then, portrays a coming figure who is both priest and king. The combination of priest and king is extremely rare in the messianic texts of the Old Testament (cf. Psalm 110) but indicates that the coming figure fulfills an Adamic role planned by God from the beginning for a man over his creation. The text also speaks of the coming ruler emerging from the midst of Israel. This is exactly the language used in Deuteronomy 18:15 for God raising up a prophet and perhaps also in Deuteronomy 17:15 for God choosing a king for Israel.

3. WE CAN DRAW NEAR THROUGH HIM

The implication is that those who are joined to this ruler, his people, can draw near to God through him. And this is made explicit in Hebrews 10:19–22:

> [19] Therefore, brothers, since we have confidence to enter the Most Holy Place by the blood of Jesus, [20] by a new and living way opened for us through the curtain, that is, his body, [21] and since we have a great priest over the house of God, [22] let us draw near to God with a sincere heart in full assurance of faith, having our hearts sprinkled to cleanse us from a guilty conscience and having our bodies washed with pure water. (NIV)

Verses 35–36 of Jeremiah 31 speak of the new covenant as enduring, as lasting, as permanent, by affirming that it is as enduring as the divine arrangement that gave the sun to light up the day and the moon and stars to light up the night. Williamson argues that this is probably a reference to the covenant with Noah rather than to creation:

> While some scholars have pointed to Jeremiah 33:20–26 for further support [of a covenant at creation in Genesis 1–2], the references here to a covenant with inanimate created things seem to allude more to dimensions of the Noahic covenant reflected in Genesis 8:22–9:13 (esp. Gen. 8:22) than to an implicit 'covenant with creation' in Genesis 1–3. Admittedly, the somewhat similar analogy drawn in Jeremiah 31:35–37 may indeed allude

---

[29] See, e.g., L. Koehler and W. Baumgartner, *Hebräisches und Aramäisches Lexikon zum Alten Testament*, 3rd ed., ed. W. Baumgartner, J. J. Stamm, and B. Hartmann (Leiden, Netherlands: Brill, 1967–1995), s.v. נגשׁ and קרב.

to the fixed order established at creation, although this appears to build an argument from silence.[30]

The text of Jeremiah 31:35–36 mentions specifically the sun as a light for the day and the stars as a light for the night. This is more obviously a reference to Genesis 1:14–16 than to Genesis 8:22. If one allows for a covenant with creation that is reaffirmed and upheld in Genesis 6–9, then one can have it both ways. Nonetheless, Williamson's argument appears to be special pleading, especially when he feels the force of the connection between Jeremiah 31:35–37 and the fixed order of creation. How is this an argument from silence when Genesis 1:14–16 speaks of this fixed order?

Finally, Jeremiah 31:38–40 describes the dimensions of the renovated and restored Jerusalem and claims that even the areas formerly used for refuse will be devoted to the Lord. Not all of the locations mentioned in the text are known, but Jeremiah appears to move from the northeast to northwest, then to southwest and around to southeast. It seems that the geography of the new Jerusalem will be different, and that the Valley of Hinnom defiled by corpses and garbage will become holy to the Lord. The new Jerusalem will be both different and expanded from the old.

---

[30] Paul R. Williamson, *Sealed with an Oath: Covenant in God's Unfolding Purpose*, NSBT 23 (Downers Grove, IL: InterVarsity Press, 2007), 74.

EXCURSUS

The book of Jeremiah is notorious for problems in the history of the transmission of the text. Many differences exist between the Hebrew Masoretic Text and the Septuagint. Scholars attribute some of the differences to copyists' errors, some to the process of translation, and some to a different parent text. Frequently the argument is made that the parent text behind the Greek translation is older than and superior to what we have in the Masoretic Text.

One of the most recent treatments on Jeremiah 31 in the Hebrew and Greek Bible is by Adrian Schenker.[31] Schenker argues that the differences in the Greek translation, particularly those in verse 32,

---

[31] Adrian Schenker, *Das Neue am neuen Bund und das Alte am alten: Jer 31 in der hebräischen und griecischen Bibel* (Forschungen zur Religion und Literatur des Alten und Neuen Testaments 212; Göttingen, Germany: Vandenhoeck & Ruprecht, 2006).

are due largely to a different parent text which represents a different understanding. The parent text behind the Greek translation may even be older and superior.

Here we may briefly provide an English translation of the Greek (Septuagint) version of Jeremiah 31 and consider claims made by Schenker relevant to the discussion of the new covenant.

First, a rendering of verses 27–34 of the Greek version is useful:

> [27] "Behold, days are coming," says the LORD, "and I will sow Israel and Judah with human seed and animal seed. [28] And it will be, just as I was watching over them to tear down and bring evil, so I will watch over them to build and plant," says the LORD. [29] "In those days, they will no longer say, 'The fathers ate unripe grapes and the teeth of the children are set on edge,' [30] but each will die for his own sin, and the one eating unripe grapes, his teeth will be set on edge."
>
> [31] "Behold days are coming," says the LORD, "and I will make with the house of Israel and with the house of Judah a new covenant, [32] not like the covenant which I made with their fathers when I took them by their hand to bring them out of the land of Egypt, because they did not remain in my covenant and I was not concerned about them," says the LORD. [33] "For this is the covenant which I will make with the house of Israel after those days," says the LORD. "Giving I will give my laws in their mind and I will write them on their hearts. And I will become a god to them and they will become a people to me. [34] And they will never again teach each his fellow citizen and each his brother, saying, 'Know the LORD.' For they will all know me, from their small even to their great, because I will be propitious regarding their wrongdoings, and their sins I will never again remember."

A brief comparison of Greek and Hebrew texts yields the following differences. In verse 27, διὰ τοῦτο is a plus in the LXX in relation to MT. Yet in verse 31a, where the wording in MT is identical to verse 27a in MT, the LXX corresponds quantitatively to MT. The Greek translator does not render אֶת־בֵּית יִשְׂרָאֵל וְאֶת־בֵּית יְהוּדָה in בֵּית by οἶκος in verse 27 as he does for the identical phrase in MT in verse 31. Hence a minus in the LXX in relation to MT. If the putative parent text of LXX is identical to MT, then this represents an attempt to provide stylistic variation. In verse 28 MT has five bound infinitives describing negative "watching over" God's people in the past and two bound infinitives describing positive "watching over" God's people in the future. The LXX has two infinitives in both cases. It is possible that the parent text of LXX differs from MT, but it looks more like the Greek translator made the negative and positive dependent clauses match in length. In verse 29a, 34a, and 34b MT employs a negative + imperfect + עוֹד. This construction is rendered by οὐ μή + aorist subjunctive (i.e., emphatic future denial) in verses 29a and 34a, but more quantitatively by οὐ μή + aorist subjunctive + ἔτι in 34b. Again, apparently the Greek translator exercised freedom in his task. In verse 30b, MT employs a cleft sentence while the LXX omits כָּל־הָאָדָם and has the participle directly dependent on the subject rather than employing extraposition. The possessive pronoun αὐτοῦ at the end, although corresponding quantitatively to MT, is redundant in Greek. For verse 32, בְּיוֹם הֶחֱזִיקִי בְיָדָם is rendered by ἐν ἡμέρᾳ ἐπιλαβομένου μου τῆς χειρὸς αὐτῶν. Thus the Greek translator employs a genitive absolute and demonstrates concern for the demands of the target language. As a result, a *beth* preposition in MT has no formal equivalent in LXX. Moreover, the dependent clause ὅτι αὐτοὶ οὐκ ἐνέμειναν ἐν τῇ διαθήκῃ μου does not correspond formally to the relative clause אֲשֶׁר־הֵמָּה הֵפֵרוּ אֶת־בְּרִיתִי in MT nor does καὶ ἐγὼ ἠμέλησα αὐτῶν correspond to וְאָנֹכִי בָּעַלְתִּי בָם in MT, although the καὶ ἐγώ for וְאָנֹכִי is a wooden rendering and may suggest a parent text not greatly different. In verse 33, διδοὺς δώσω does not match נָתַתִּי in MT but suggests a parent text like נתון אתן. [Note that the citation in Hebrews 8 lacks δώσω]. The phrase εἰς τὴν διάνοιαν αὐτῶν for בְּקִרְבָּם shows concern for the demands of the culture of the target language while καὶ ἐπὶ καρδίας αὐτῶν for וְעַל־לִבָּם does not, except that the "hearts" are pluralised according to the demands of Greek. Nonetheless, לֵב is frequently literally translated in the LXX. The direct object אֶת־תּוֹרָתִי in MT, although singular, is rendered in Greek by the plural νόμους and the third feminine singular suffix on אֶכְתֳּבֶנָּה is rendered by αὐτούς to match in number. For verse 34, the direct objects with third masculine plural pronominal suffixes are translated as plurals in Greek: ταῖς ἀδικίαις αὐτῶν καὶ τῶν ἁμαρτιῶν αὐτῶν.

When one considers the character of the translation *as a whole*— data that are not in general considered by Schenker—we get a more holistic perspective of the work of the translator and see that the Greek translator varies considerably from formal correspondence to functional correspondence to his parent text. Moreover, the biographical notes in the book of Jeremiah clearly indicate that the work was rewritten several times. The book was sent to the exiles in Babylon, but Jeremiah himself migrated to Egypt. This history in itself suggests that perhaps the version in Egypt is not the canonical version in the library authorised by Ezra and Nehemiah.[32] It could also be that the

---

[32] Recent essays by Emanuel Tov, "The Nature of the Large-Scale Differences between the LXX and MT S T V, Compared with Similar Evidence in Other Sources," in *The Earliest Text of the Hebrew Bible: The Relationship between the Masoretic Text and the Hebrew Base of the Septuagint Reconsidered*, ed. Adrian Schenker (Septuagint and Cognate Studies 52; Atlanta: Scholars Press, 2003), 121–144; and idem, "The Septuagint as a Source for the Literary Analysis of Hebrew Scripture," in *Exploring the Origins of the Bible: Canon Formation in Historical, Literary, and Theological Perspective*, ed. Craig A. Evans and Emanuel Tov (Grand Rapids, MI: Baker, 2008), 31–56, only attempt to provide a brief overview and summary. Nonetheless he presents as established fact the view that the shorter LXX Jeremiah is an earlier edition, while that of MT is a later edition which "added various new ideas" (126). Tov discussed this problem in detail in his doctoral dissertation; see E. Tov, *The Septuagint Translation of Jeremiah and Baruch—A Discussion of an Early Revision of the LXX of Jeremiah 29–52 and Baruch 1:1–3:8*, Harvard Semitic Monographs 8 (Missoula, MT: Scholars Press, 1976); idem, "The Characterization of the Additional Layer of the Masoretic Text of Jeremiah," *Eretz-Israel* 26 (1999): 55–63; idem, "Exegetical Notes on the Hebrew *Vorlage* of the Septuagint of Jeremiah 27 (34)," in *The Greek and Hebrew Bible: Collected Essays on the Septuagint*, ed. E. Tov (Leiden, Netherlands: Brill, 1999), 315–332; and idem, "The Literary History of the Book of Jeremiah in Light of Its Textual History," in *Greek and Hebrew Bible*, 363–384. See also Young-Jin Min, "The Minuses and Pluses of the LXX Translation of Jeremiah as Compared with the Masoretic Text: Their Classification and Possible Origins" (PhD diss., Hebrew University of Jerusalem, 1977). Support for Tov's view is found, for example, in studies by P.-M. Bogaert, "La *vetus latina* de Jérémie: texte très court, témoin de la plus ancienne Septante et d'une forme plus ancienne de l'hébreu (Jer 39 et 52)," in *The Earliest Text of the Hebrew Bible: The Relationship between the Masoretic Text and the Hebrew Base of the Septuagint Reconsidered*, ed. Adrian Schenker, Septuagint and Cognate Studies 52 (Atlanta: Scholars Press, 2003), 51–82; and Adrian Schenker, "Est-ce que le livre de Jérémie fut publié dans une édition refondue au 2ᵉ siècle? La multiplicité textuelle peut-elle coexister avec l'édition unique d'un livre biblique?" in *Un Carrefour dans l'histoire de la Bible: Du texte à la théologie au IIᵉ siècle avant J.-C.*, ed. Innocent Himbaza and Adrian Schenker, Orbis biblicus et orientalis 233 (Fribourg, Switzerland: Academic Press, 2008), 58–74. Schenker argues that the Teacher of Righteousness could authorise a revision of Jeremiah = MT while the previous version (= LXX) still circulated. Yet recent studies on LXX Jeremiah reveal the complexity of the textual transmission of Jeremiah and show that this knotty problem is far from solved: Sven Soderlund, *The Greek Text of Jeremiah. A Revised Hypothesis*, JSOTSup 47 (Sheffield, UK: JSOT Press, 1985); Louis Stulman, *The Other Text of Jeremiah: A Reconstruction of the Hebrew Text Underlying the Greek Version of the Prose Sections of Jeremiah With English Translation* (Lanham, MD: University Press of America, 1985), H.-J. Stipp, *Das masoretische und alexandrinische Sondergut des Jeremiabuches—Textgeschichtlicher Rang, Eigenarten, Triebkräfte*, Orbis biblicus et orientalis 136 (Fribourg, Switzerland: Éditions Universitaires/Göttingen, Germany: Vandenhoeck & Ruprecht, 1994). J. Lundbom has also done extensive research and claims that 1,700 of the 2,700 words by which LXX Jeremiah is shorter than MT could be explained by haplography—a problem to be expected in the transmission of a text whose chief literary feature is repetition; see J. Lundbom, "Haplography in the Hebrew *Vorlage* of Septuagint Jeremiah" (paper presented at the annual meeting of the Society of Biblical Literature, San Antonio, November 22, 2004; and David Noel Freedman and Jack R. Lundbom, "Haplography in Jeremiah 1–20," *Eretz-Israel* 26 (1999): 28*–38*. Two doctoral students working under A. Pietersma at the University of Toronto did further research: Marc Saunders and Tony S. L. Michael. Michael suggested from his studies that the LXX Jeremiah belongs more to the classification of a resignified text (private communication). A. Pietersma, "Greek Jeremiah and the Land of Azazel," in *Studies in the Hebrew Bible, Qumran, and the Septuagint, Presented to Eugene Ulrich*, ed. Peter W. Flint, Emanuel Tov, and James C. VanderKam, Supplements to Vetus Testamentum 101 (Leiden, Netherlands: Brill, 2006), 403–413, offers good evidence that differences between LXX and MT may be translational rather than textual. See also A. Pietersma, "Of Translation and Revision: From

parent text behind the LXX was updated from archaic Hebrew to the demands of contemporary forms of the language at the time of translation. All of these factors make it difficult to be certain in the claim that we should consider the text of the Greek translation superior at any point, especially when, as Schenker admits, the precise wording of the parent text is impossible to reconstruct.[33] Even if the long citation in Hebrews 8:7–13 generally follows the LXX, this does not mean that the different wording in verse 32 is somehow a better text, when the author of Hebrews draws no specific argument based on it.

Perhaps what Schenker has not considered sufficiently is the possibility that the Greek translation in verse 32 actually represents an interpretation of a Hebrew parent text identical to that transmitted in MT. The clause ὅτι αὐτοὶ οὐκ ἐνέμειναν ἐν τῇ διαθήκῃ μου could be construed as a dynamic rendering of אֲשֶׁר־הֵמָּה הֵפֵרוּ אֶת־בְּרִיתִי in MT. How ἠμέλησα in the clause following might be a dynamic rendering of בָּעַלְתִּי has yet to be adequately explored. Could the translator have thought that the people did not remain in the covenant and God said, "Never mind! [I have another plan]." The apparatus of *Biblia Hebraica Stuttgartensia* at least considers the possibility that the LXX = MT here.

Greek Isaiah to Greek Jeremiah," in *Isaiah in Context: Studies in Honour of Arie van der Kooij on the Occasion of His Sixty-Fifth Birthday*, eds. Michaël N. van der Meer, Percy van Keulen, Wido van Peursen, Bas ter Haar Romeny, Supplements to Vetus Testamentum 138 (Leiden, Netherlands: Brill, 2010), 359–387, where Tov's hypothesis of revision in Greek Jeremiah 29–52 has been falsified and which, in fact, may point to a new hypothesis of contextual accommodation and exegesis.
[33] Schenker, *Das Neue am neuen Bund und das Alte am alten*, 23.

JEREMIAH 32:36–41

It is normal and standard in Hebrew literature for a speaker to go around the topic at least twice. The second time, the speaker will usually approach the topic from a different perspective. When the two conversations are heard at the same time, a holographic idea can be mentally viewed. In Jeremiah 32:36–41, Jeremiah goes around the topic of the new covenant a second time:

> [36] You are saying about this city, "By the sword, famine and plague it will be handed over to the king of Babylon"; but this is what the LORD, the God of Israel, says: [37] I will surely gather them from all the lands where I banish them in my furious anger and great wrath; I will bring them back to this place and let them live in safety. [38] They will be my people, and

I will be their God. [39] I will give them singleness of heart and action, so that they will always fear me for their own good and the good of their children after them. [40] I will make an everlasting covenant with them: I will never stop doing good to them, and I will inspire them to fear me, so that they will never turn away from me. [41] I will rejoice in doing them good and will assuredly plant them in this land with all my heart and soul. (NIV)

Here the oracle of the prophet describes gathering of the people from exile and bringing them back to the land of Israel. Note the Covenant Formula in verse 38: "they will be my people, and I will be their God." Verse 40 builds upon this by announcing "an everlasting covenant." The people will have "one heart" (v. 39) and will be inspired to fear the Lord (v. 40).

Williamson compares and contrasts Jeremiah 31:31–34 and 32:37–41 by means of a table (table 13.1).[34] These are like the left and right speakers of a stereo system. Note how the titles "new covenant" and "everlasting covenant" are interchangeable. The fact that the Israelite covenant was broken is contrasted with the faithfulness of the human partner in the new covenant. Verse 39 in the Hebrew text literally reads, "and I will give to them one[35] heart and one way to fear me all the days for good to them and for their sons after them." As Georg Fischer helpfully points out, this verse is based on Deuteronomy 5:29 and is closely connected to Ezekiel 11:19.[36] Having the divine instruction in the heart will give the people undivided emotions, mind, and will focused on the Lord and his *way*. Again, knowing God and fearing the Lord are also looking at the same thing from different perspectives. Finally, the positive side of forgiveness is equivalent to "the good things" God has planned and will do for his people.

Table 13.1: Comparing and Contrasting Jeremiah 31:31–34 and 32:37–41

Jeremiah 31:31–34	**Jeremiah 32:37–41**
v. 31 I will make a new covenant with the house of Israel and with the house of Judah	v. 40a I will make an everlasting covenant with them [i.e., the people of Israel and Judah cf. v. 30]
v. 32 It will not be like the covenant . . . they broke	v. 40c they will never turn away from me

---

34 Paul R. Williamson, *Sealed with an Oath*, 165. Table used with permission.

35 The LXX has "another way and another heart" (ὁδὸν ἑτέραν καὶ καρδίαν ἑτέραν). This is based on confusion of *daleth* as *resh* (reading אחד as אחר) and is an inferior and secondary textual tradition for this word. Note that the LXX also transposes the noun phrases in relation to MT and that the LXX of Ezekiel 11:19 also reads "another heart" instead of "one heart" in MT. The confusion of *daleth* and *resh* is common.

36 Georg Fischer, *Jeremia 26–52*, Herders Theologischer Kommentar zum Alten Testament (Freiburg, Germany: Herder, 2005), 212.

v. 33a I will put my law in their minds and write it on their hearts	v. 39 I will give them singleness of heart and action
	v. 40b I will inspire them to fear me
v. 33b I will be their God and they will be my people	v. 38 They will be my people, and I will be their God
v. 34a they will all know me	v. 39b they will always fear me
v. 34b I will forgive their wickedness	vv. 40b, 41 I will never stop doing good to them
And will remember their sins no more (NIV)	and will assuredly plant them in this land with all my heart and soul (NIV)

JEREMIAH 33:12–26

Jeremiah 33:12–26 is pretty well Jeremiah's final discourse on the new covenant (apart from a brief mention in 50:4–5). And just as Ezekiel draws together a lot of different strands in his last conversation on the new covenant, Jeremiah does the same thing. Return from exile and the new covenant are connected with the covenant with David, the covenant with Levi, and the covenant with creation:

> [12] "This is what the LORD Almighty says: 'In this place, desolate and without men or animals—in all its towns there will again be pastures for shepherds to rest their flocks. [13] In the towns of the hill country, of the western foothills and of the Negev, in the territory of Benjamin, in the villages around Jerusalem and in the towns of Judah, flocks will again pass under the hand of the one who counts them,' says the LORD.
> [14] "'The days are coming,' declares the LORD, 'when I will fulfill the gracious promise I made to the house of Israel and to the house of Judah.
>
> [15] "'In those days and at that time
>   I will make a righteous Branch sprout from David's line;
>   he will do what is just and right in the land.
> [16] In those days Judah will be saved
>   and Jerusalem will live in safety.
> This is the name by which it will be called:
>   The LORD Our Righteousness.'
>
> [17] For this is what the LORD says: 'David will never fail to have a man to sit on the throne of the house of Israel, [18] nor will the priests, who are Levites, ever fail to have a man to stand before me continually to offer burnt offerings, to burn grain offerings and to present sacrifices.'"

[19] The word of the LORD came to Jeremiah: [20] "This is what the LORD says: 'If you can break my covenant with the day and my covenant with the night, so that day and night no longer come at their appointed time, [21] then my covenant with David my servant—and my covenant with the Levites who are priests ministering before me—can be broken and David will no longer have a descendant to reign on his throne. [22] I will make the descendants of David my servant and the Levites who minister before me as countless as the stars of the sky and as measureless as the sand on the seashore.'"

[23] The word of the LORD came to Jeremiah: [24] "Have you not noticed that these people are saying, 'The LORD has rejected the two kingdoms he chose'? So they despise my people and no longer regard them as a nation. [25] This is what the LORD says: 'If I have not established my covenant with day and night and the fixed laws of heaven and earth, [26] then I will reject the descendants of Jacob and David my servant and will not choose one of his sons to rule over the descendants of Abraham, Isaac and Jacob. For I will restore their fortunes and have compassion on them.'" (NIV)

THE NEW COVENANT AND THE COVENANT WITH DAVID

Jeremiah continues the announcement of restoration for Israel that flows from the return from exile. As part of this rebuilding, renewal, and restoration, he will uphold his good word concerning a Davidic King. The rendering of the NIV is, "I will fulfill the gracious promise I made to the house of Israel and to the house of Judah." In the Hebrew text the verb that is used is *hēqîm*. Similar to the expression *hēqîm běrît*, we have the expression *hēqîm 'eth-haddābār haṭṭôb*, which means "he will cause to stand," i.e., confirm, establish, uphold the good word which he gave to the house of Israel and to the house of Judah. The good word or gracious promise to which Jeremiah refers is a prophetic word given by earlier prophets (e.g., Isaiah 11) that ultimately goes all the way back to Nathan in 2 Samuel 7. It is the promise of someone from the lineage of David as king and ruler over the descendants of Abraham, Isaac, and Jacob, as Jeremiah 33:26 puts it. Isaiah had used the term "Branch" for this, as had Jeremiah earlier, in 23:5–6:

[1] A shoot will come up from the stump of Jesse;
　　from his roots a Branch will bear fruit.
[2] The Spirit of the LORD will rest on him—
　　the Spirit of wisdom and of understanding,
　　the Spirit of counsel and of power,
　　the Spirit of knowledge and of the fear of the LORD—

[3] and he will delight in the fear of the LORD. (Isa. 11:1–3a, NIV)

[5] "The days are coming," declares the LORD,
  "when I will raise up to David a righteous Branch,
a King who will reign wisely
  and do what is just and right in the land.
[6] In his days Judah will be saved
  and Israel will live in safety.
This is the name by which he will be called:
  The LORD Our Righteousness." (Jer. 23:5–6, NIV)

In order to adequately grasp the meaning of these texts in Isaiah and Jeremiah and to see the relationship between them, we have to discuss the meaning of the word commonly rendered "Branch" in the English versions. We have discussed earlier that plants or stately tall trees are used as a common metaphor for kings and kingdoms in the Old Testament. Wolter Rose's study of "Branch" is superior and is the basis for the comments here.[37] For the Hebrew word צֶמַח there are two options: either (1) it refers to a part of a plant/tree and means "branch" or "sprout" or (2) it is used for the plant or plants as a whole and means "vegetation." Rose gives a table showing all the terms in Hebrew for parts of plants and plants in general, i.e., vegetation (table 13.2):[38]

Table 13.2: Possible Meanings of צֶמַח *and Corresponding Lexical Fields*

branch	shoot/sprout	plant(s)/vegetation
בַּד	יוֹנֶקֶת	דֶּשֶׁא
דָּלִית	נֵצֶר	חָצִיר
חֹטֶר	[פֶּרַח]	עֵץ
עָנָף		עֵשֶׂב
פֹּארָה		שִׂיחַ
קָצִיר		
שָׂרִיג		

What is interesting in the analysis of these terms is that those in the last column can be used in the expression "the [plants] of the field" whereas those in the first two columns cannot. Therefore, צֶמַח is not a plant part but rather

---

[37] Wolter H. Rose, *Zemah and Zerubbabel: Messianic Expectations in the Early Postexilic Period*, JSOTSup 304 (Sheffield, Sheffield Academic Press, 2000).
[38] Rose, *Zemah and Zerubbabel*, 94.

a generic term for vegetation meaning something like "growth" and should be assigned to column three in the table (Gen. 19:25; Ezek. 16:7).

With the correct meaning of צֶמַח in mind, let us note that Isaiah uses the terms חֹטֶר and נֵצֶר in 11:1 whereas Jeremiah employs צֶמַח in 23:5 and 33:15.[39] The emphasis in each prophet is different, just as the words are different. In Isaiah, the divine judgement means that the tree which represents the Davidic King and kingdom is cut down. Nonetheless, in the gracious restoration brought by God, the remaining stump will bring forth a shoot and grow again.

Jeremiah 23 comes in the context of a curse brought upon Coniah, so that this particular Davidic king will have no one from his line as future king in Israel. Ultimately this means that the king will have to come from another part of the lineage of David. Note what Jeremiah says in 23:5, "I will raise up for David righteous growth." We should pay attention to the little preposition "to" or "for" in this text. Things will be so far gone in destruction that *God* will have to bring about restoration for the line of David; it will not be able to send out a shoot on its own. Rose summarises well the difference between Isaiah's and Jeremiah's prophecies:

> The difference in terminology between Isa. 11.1 and the צמח oracles (those in Jeremiah and in Zechariah) implies that the overall thrust of these passages is substantially different. The imagery in Isa. 11.1 of 'a shoot from the stump of Jesse' and 'a branch . . . out of his roots' leaves room for the Davidic dynasty to make a contribution to its own future. The צמח imagery in Jer. 23.5 suggests that only a divine intervention can safeguard the future of the Davidic dynasty.[40]

In other words, we have to get to the place as in Abraham's experience where only the divine gift of life from dead bodies will bring about fulfilment of the promises.

In Jeremiah 33:15, the growth is given the adjective "righteous," because as the next clause clearly states, "he will do what is just and right in the land." "Just" and "right" constitute a word pair communicating not only the notion of social justice, but the social justice of the Israelite covenant. Thus it is a way of summarising the entire Torah. The king is the administrator of the Israelite covenant. Never again will the family of David fail to have a

---

[39] The only other occurrences in the Old Testament where צֶמַח is employed metaphorically are Zechariah 3:8 and 6:12.
[40] Rose, *Zemah and Zerubbabel*, 120.

man on the throne, and a hint of the coming king is found in the name of the new Jerusalem: "The LORD Our Righteousness" (33:16).

THE NEW COVENANT AND THE COVENANT WITH LEVI

Not only will the future restoration involve no further failure in the continued rule of a Davidic King, administering the divine righteousness, "nor will the priests, who are Levites, ever fail to have a man to stand before me continually to offer burnt offerings, to burn grain offerings and to present sacrifices" (33:18).

A covenant that we have not discussed to this point is one made by God with the Levites. All of the (few) relevant texts in the Old Testament are cited here:

> Whatever is set aside from the holy offerings the Israelites present to the LORD I give to you and your sons and daughters as your regular share. It is an everlasting covenant of salt before the LORD for both you and your offspring. (Num. 18:19, NIV)

> [6] Then an Israelite man brought to his family a Midianite woman right before the eyes of Moses and the whole assembly of Israel while they were weeping at the entrance to the Tent of Meeting. [7] When Phinehas son of Eleazar, the son of Aaron, the priest, saw this, he left the assembly, took a spear in his hand [8] and followed the Israelite into the tent. He drove the spear through both of them—through the Israelite and into the woman's body. Then the plague against the Israelites was stopped; [9] but those who died in the plague numbered 24,000.
>
> [10] The LORD said to Moses, [11] "Phinehas son of Eleazar, the son of Aaron, the priest, has turned my anger away from the Israelites; for he was as zealous as I am for my honor among them, so that in my zeal I did not put an end to them. [12] Therefore tell him I am making my covenant of peace with him. [13] He and his descendants will have a covenant of a lasting priesthood, because he was zealous for the honor of his God and made atonement for the Israelites." (Num. 25:6–13, NIV)

> [1] "And now this admonition is for you, O priests. [2] If you do not listen, and if you do not set your heart to honor my name," says the LORD Almighty, "I will send a curse upon you, and I will curse your blessings. Yes, I have already cursed them, because you have not set your heart to honor me.

[3] "Because of you I will rebuke your descendants; I will spread on your faces the offal from your festival sacrifices, and you will be carried off with it. [4] And you will know that I have sent you this admonition so that my covenant with Levi may continue," says the LORD Almighty. [5] "My covenant was with him, a covenant of life and peace, and I gave them to him; this called for reverence and he revered me and stood in awe of my name. [6] True instruction was in his mouth and nothing false was found on his lips. He walked with me in peace and uprightness, and turned many from sin.

[7] "For the lips of a priest ought to preserve knowledge, and from his mouth men should seek instruction—because he is the messenger of the LORD Almighty. [8] But you have turned from the way and by your teaching have caused many to stumble; you have violated the covenant with Levi," says the LORD Almighty. [9] "So I have caused you to be despised and humiliated before all the people, because you have not followed my ways but have shown partiality in matters of the law." (Mal. 2:1–9, NIV)

Remember them, O my God, because they defiled the priestly office and the covenant of the priesthood and of the Levites. (Neh. 13:29, NIV)

We can quickly summarise the import of these texts. As early as Numbers 18, the Israelite offerings are given to the Levites for their sustenance as a "covenant of salt" (cf. 2 Chron. 13:5). Since salt was used in the ancient world to preserve things, a covenant of salt means one that is enduring and lasting, a permanent agreement.

Then in Numbers 25 Phinehas showed great zeal for the honour of Yahweh, and his actions atoned for the sin of the people, so God rewarded his actions by giving a covenant of peace to him and his tribe. Malachi excoriates the priests in his time for failing to live up to this covenant. The text in Malachi gives us a fuller appreciation for the covenantal role to be played by the Levites—how they were to bring peace. It also demonstrates that the physical return from exile did not bring about a restoration of the priesthood.

John Davies notes how Moses' final blessing in Deuteronomy 33:8–13 "also presents Levi's position as priest in relation to a 'covenant' (v. 9). While other Pentateuchal references to Levi emphasise his zeal for purity and honour (Gen. 34; Exod. 32.25-29), Deut. 33.8-13 moves from singular to plural forms in a manner designed to identify the patriarch Levi with the tribe to which the priestly office was entrusted, and thus to depict the patriarch himself in priestly terms."[41]

---

[41] John A. Davies, *A Royal Priesthood: Literary and Intertextual Perspectives on an Image of Israel in Exodus 19.6*, JSOTSup 395 (London: T. & T. Clark, 2004), 186.

Williamson also comments helpfully on the covenant with Levi:

> In any case, these priestly covenants seem to have served the same general purpose as the Mosaic covenant with which they are so closely related; namely the priests facilitated the maintenance of the divine-human relationship between Yahweh and Abraham's descendants. Significantly, it was when they failed to do their part in this latter respect that they were accused by Malachi of having 'corrupted the covenant of Levi' (Mal. 2:8 ESV). Thus the Priestly and Mosaic covenants, while remaining distinct, run in parallel with one another, and are closely related in purpose; namely, maintaining the relationship between God and Israel.[42]

Williamson rightly sees the covenant with Levi as a mechanism to administer the Israelite covenant especially before the inauguration of kingship in Israel.

Yet in the text under discussion, Jeremiah foresees countless Levites offering sacrifices (33:22). He does not describe in detail how this will work out, but Isaiah does. We have already seen how Gentiles, those from the nations, symbolised by eunuchs and foreigners in Isaiah 56, will become priests in the new temple. The New Testament speaks of their sacrifices as prayers and songs of worship in the gatherings of the church (Heb. 13:15–16, 1 Pet. 2:5, Phil. 4:18).

There is an emphasis in Jeremiah 33:12–26 on the notion of servanthood, indicated by the Hebrew terms עֶבֶד ("servant") and מְשָׁרֵת ("minister"). David is called the servant of Yahweh in verses 21 and 22, and the Levites are described by the parallel term, ministers of God. In a way reminiscent of the servant, singular, becoming the servants, plural, in the last part of Isaiah, verse 22 says that the "seed," i.e., descendants, of David and the Levites, will be countless, and the language used is that of the Abrahamic covenant—the stars of the sky and the sand on the seashore. Thus the new covenant brings the promises of these other covenants to fulfilment.

THE NEW COVENANT AND THE COVENANT WITH CREATION

The last paragraph of Jeremiah 33, verses 23–26, shows that the people no longer believed that God had chosen them and as a result they despised the people (*'am*) of God as a nation (*gôy*); i.e., they no longer recognised the kingdom of God. This goes back to Genesis 12:1–3, where in the Abrahamic

---

[42] Paul R. Williamson, *Sealed with an Oath*, 105–106.

covenant God considers the different groups in the world as amorphous kin groups, and only the family of Abraham will be a real and lasting *kingdom*, i.e., an entity with political and social structure with governmental headship. In verses 19 and 25 the permanence and lasting quality of the situation brought about by the new covenant is compared to the covenant with day and night, the fixed decrees or statutes of heaven and earth—a clear reference to the covenant with creation (in spite of Williamson's protest).

JEREMIAH 50:4–5

There is a final reference to the new covenant in Jeremiah 50:4–5 in the context of an oracle against Babylon. In the end, Babylon, a nation used as an instrument to discipline the Lord's people, will be judged in turn:

[2] "Announce and proclaim among the nations,
   lift up a banner and proclaim it;
   keep nothing back, but say,
'Babylon will be captured;
   Bel will be put to shame,
   Marduk filled with terror.
Her images will be put to shame
   and her idols filled with terror.'
[3] A nation from the north will attack her
   and lay waste her land.
No one will live in it;
   both men and animals will flee away.

[4] "In those days, at that time,"
   declares the Lord,
"the people of Israel and the people of Judah together
   will go in tears to seek the Lord their God.
[5] They will ask the way to Zion
   and turn their faces toward it.
They will come and bind themselves to the Lord
   in an everlasting covenant
   that will not be forgotten." (NIV)

When Babylon is judged, a process of return from exile will begin for the people of Israel and Judah. The process of a physical return and a spiritual return is not spelled out here as separate stages. But the picture presented by Jeremiah is that the people will turn toward Zion and bind themselves to the

Lord in an everlasting covenant. This is a brief summary statement, looking back to the earlier and fuller expositions in the book of Jeremiah.

TWELVE PROPHETS

Explicit references to the new covenant are rare in the Twelve (Minor) Prophets. Our next chapter is devoted to the book of Daniel. Here we may briefly consider a passage in Hosea:

> [16] "When that day comes," says the LORD,
>   "you will call me 'my husband'
>   instead of 'my master.'
> [17] O Israel, I will wipe the many names of Baal from your lips,
>   and you will never mention them again.
> [18] On that day I will make a covenant
>   with all the wild animals and the birds of the sky
>   and the animals that scurry along the ground
>   so they will not harm you.
> I will remove all weapons of war from the land,
>   all swords and bows,
>   so you can live unafraid
>   in peace and safety.
> [19] I will make you my wife forever,
>   showing you righteousness and justice,
>   unfailing love and compassion.
> [20] I will be faithful to you and make you mine,
>   and you will finally know me as the LORD."
>   (Hos. 2:18–22 [2:16–20 EV], NLT)

Hosea's language is somewhat different from the others. Nonetheless, the day when God removes the many names of Baal from the lips of his people and makes Israel his wife forever is the time of the new covenant. The removal of the names of Baal is the end of idolatry and sin, i.e., all that is accomplished between the first and second coming of the Messiah, ending in the Marriage Supper of the Lamb.

The covenant with animals and birds so that they no longer bring harm shows the reversal of the curse, something that is eventually brought about by the new covenant. Therefore, this prophecy must speak of the new covenant.

Chapter Fourteen

THE NEW COVENANT IN DANIEL'S SEVENTY WEEKS[1]

INTRODUCTION

Daniel 9 is famous for the vision of the "seventy weeks." Unfortunately, interpretation of this text has been difficult not only for average readers but for scholars as well. We must not only pay attention to (1) the cultural and historical setting, and (2) the linguistic and textual data, but also carefully analyse and consider (3) the literary structures, (4) the apocalyptic genre of the text, (5) the relation of Daniel 9 to other texts in the Old Testament, and above all (6) the metanarrative or biblical-theological framework crucial for making sense of any individual text. Lack of understanding as to how apocalyptic and prophetic literature communicates has hindered the church, especially in the last hundred years. In addition, a failure to grasp the larger story that alone makes sense of the details in this text has resulted in imposing on it a framework of understanding foreign to it.

OVERVIEW OF DANIEL

The Stories and Visions of Daniel[2]

Part 1: Six stories (chapters 1–6)

1. Daniel and friends in the court of Babylon
2. King's dream: a huge statue/small stone
3. Daniel's friends rescued from the furnace
4. King's dream: a huge tree
5. Belshazzar and the writing on the wall
6. Daniel rescued from the lion's den

---

[1] An earlier version of chapter 14 was published as Peter J. Gentry, "Daniel's Seventy Weeks and the New Exodus," *SBJT* 14/1 (2010): 26–45.

[2] The sections "Overview of Daniel" and "Grasping the Literary Structure" are adapted and summarised from Peter J. Gentry, "The Son of Man in Daniel 7: Individual or Corporate?" in *Acorns to Oaks: The Primacy and Practice of Biblical Theology*, ed. Michael A. G. Haykin (Toronto: Joshua, 2003), 59–75.

Part 2: Four visions (chapters 7–12)
    7. A vision of Daniel: awful beasts/son of man
    8. A vision of Daniel: the ram and the goat
    9. A prayer of Daniel and vision of seventy weeks
    10–12. A vision of Daniel: the writing of truth

The book of Daniel consists of twelve chapters which divide equally into six narrative (1–6) and six visionary chapters (7–12). In the Hebrew Canon, Daniel follows the poetic section which ends with Lamentations—a book focused on the theme of exile. The narratives of chapters 1–6 of Daniel take up this theme of exile and describe how faith in the God of Israel, the one true and living God, is to be maintained in the face of defilement, idolatry, and prohibitions of prayer backed up by wild beasts and fire and great persecution. The dreams and visions of chapters 7–12, apocalyptic in nature, give hope to the people of God by showing God in control of history through four periods of domination by foreign nations until a decisive end is made to rebellion and sin, with a renewal of the broken covenant and restoration of the temple and establishment of God's kingdom as eternal and final.

GRASPING THE LITERARY STRUCTURE

Grasping the literary structures of Daniel is crucial for a proper understanding of chapter 9. Literary structures also aid in dating the work to the sixth century B.C. and seeing it as a unity. Part of the literary artistry of Daniel can be seen in chiastic structures that are parallel, yet complementary. The literary structure of Daniel is complex and rich and only partly revealed in the two tables that follow.[3]

Chiastic Structures in Daniel: Table 1

Prologue	1
Image of four metals: triumph of God's kingdom	2
Persecution of Daniel's friends	3
Humbling of Nebuchadnezzar before God	4
Humbling of Belshazzar before God	5
Persecution of Daniel	6
Vision of four beasts: triumph of God's kingdom	7

---

[3] The first table is adapted from course notes produced for "Introduction to the Old Testament: Part II, 2003" at The Southern Baptist Theological Seminary by Daniel I. Block. The second is adapted with permission from David W. Gooding, "The Literary Structure of the Book of Daniel and Its Implications," *Tyndale Bulletin* 32 (1981): 43–79. The literary structure of a text is related to the author's aim and intention. If one posits parallel literary structures, one might ask which better fits the text. In the case of Daniel, however, the parallel literary structures are complementary and move toward the same communication goal.

Vision of future history	8
Daniel's prayer and God's response	9
Daniel's grief and God's response	10
Vision of future history	11:1–12:4
Epilogue	12:5–13

Note that chiastic structures mark chapters 2–7 and 8:1–12:4 as main sub-units.[4] Thus chiasm firmly links the visions to the stories.

Chiastic Structures in Daniel: Table 2

Daniel's Faithfulness	Daniel's Faithfulness
Ch 1 Refusal to eat the king's food. Daniel is vindicated.	Ch 6 Refusal to obey king's command. Daniel is vindicated.
Two Images	**Two Visions Of Beasts**
Ch 2 Nebuchadnezzar's dream-image Ch 3 Nebuchadnezzar's golden image	Ch 7 The four beasts Ch 8 The two beasts
Two Kings Disciplined	**Two Writings Explained**
Ch 4 Discipline of Nebuchadnezzar Ch 5 Writing on the wall and destruction of Belshazzar	Ch 9 The prophecy in the book of Jeremiah Chs 10–12 The writing of truth and destruction of the king

Again, note that parallel literary structures mark chapters 1–5 and 6–12 as main sub-units. Thus literary parallelism firmly links the visions to the stories. The chiasms and parallel structures may be simultaneously valid.

In summary, the parallel structures divide the book into halves both between chapters 5 and 6 on the one hand and between chapters 7 and 8 on the other, linking chapters 2 and 7 as dreams referring to the same thing. This interlocks the two halves of the book as determined by stories and visions. What is the significance of this unity? It is just this: the first half of the book establishes and proves that Daniel has a gift of interpreting dreams and visions of events which could be independently verified by Daniel's contemporaries. Therefore, we must believe and trust the interpretation of the visions in the second half of the book, which deal with the distant future and hence were not open to verification by the audience of Daniel's time.

---

[4] Instead of Daniel I. Block's four-part chiastic structure in chapters 8:1–12:4, the analysis of A. Kuen offers an A –B –A' structure with A = chapter 8, B = chapter 9 and A' = chapters 10–12. Thus A and A' are the "Expansion Visions" on the Basic Vision of Chapter 7 with the different "Vision of the Seventy Weeks" sandwiched in between. This is more persuasive and may well give chapter 9 greater prominence. See Alfred Kuen, *Soixante-six en un: Introduction aux 66 livres de la Bible* (St-Légier: Editions Emmaüs, 2005), 121. I am indebted to Stephen Kempf for drawing my attention to this.

The literary structures are the key to interpretation. We need a clear view of the whole in order to understand the parts and their relationship to each other.

The dream of chapter 2 and the vision of chapter 7 are at the centre of the book and communicate in different ways the same thing.

In chapter 2 a gigantic image of a man is front and centre in the Babylonian king's dream. Its head consists of gold, its chest and arms of silver, its belly and thighs of bronze, its legs of iron and feet of iron and clay. It is struck down by a rock—cut without hands from a mountain—which then grows to fill the entire earth. This dream foretells four successive human kingdoms succeeded by the kingdom of God, which will endure forever.

Chapter 7 begins the second half of the book, in which the Babylonian king's dream is expanded in a series of visions presented like maps provided with blowup inserts. Each successive vision is an enlargement of part of the previous vision, and each provides greater and greater detail of the same scene. Daniel replaces the king as dreamer and sees four beasts coming out of the chaotic sea. Then, in a picture of the court of heaven, one like a Son of Man is given the kingdom. This vision again foretells four successive human kingdoms succeeded by the kingdom of God. The vision of chapter 8 expands upon the second and third kingdoms; the vision of chapters 10–12 provides an expanded view of events in the third and fourth kingdoms.[5] We now have a detailed road map through the maze of forces arrayed against the people of God throughout successive human kingdoms.

DETAILED OVERVIEW OF CHAPTER 9

Outline of Daniel 9

1. The motivation for prayer	9:1–4a
2. Daniel's prayer for favour	9:4b–19
A. Invocation and confession	9:4b–14
B. Appeal for favour and mercy	9:15–19
3. Revelation through divine messenger	9:20–27
A. Occasion for angelic message	9:20–23
B. Vision of the seventy weeks	9:24–27

---

[5] To be more specific, 11:1–2 provides new details on the second kingdom and 12:1–3 provides new details on the kingdom of God. Thus the vision of 10–12 technically spans all of the still-future kingdoms. Nonetheless, the focus is largely on the Greek kingdom (11:3–35) with some space devoted to the Roman kingdom (11:36–45).

SETTING OF THE VISION OF THE SEVENTY WEEKS (9:1)

Chapter 9 begins in the typical way by giving a chronological notice. The date is the first year of Darius, "who was made ruler over the Babylonian kingdom" (v. 1). This is significant, for this was the year in which the Persians conquered the Babylonians, whose empire, under Nebuchadnezzar, had defeated and exiled Judah some decades earlier. This was also the first year of Cyrus the Great, who gave the decree which permitted the exiles of Judah to return to their homeland.

Nonetheless, chapter 9 is different in many ways. It begins with an extensive prayer by Daniel—the only major prayer recorded by him in the book (aside from 2:20–23). And although the section includes a vision like chapters 7, 8, and 10–12, this vision is obviously not part of these other "roadmap" visions that proclaim a sequence of four human kingdoms followed by the kingdom of God. So interpretation of the vision of seventy weeks must show how it is related to the other visions.

PRAYER MOTIVATED BY SCRIPTURE (9:2–4A)

Daniel's prayer is motivated by Scripture and based upon Scripture. In verses 2 and 3 Daniel indicates that he understood by the word of the Lord given through the prophet Jeremiah that the length of time to complete and end the divine judgement of the exile is seventy years. Although Daniel could not give a particular reference as to the passage(s) he had in mind as we would do today, clearly he is thinking of Jeremiah 25:1–15 and 29:1–23.

His prayer is also based upon 1 Kings 8:33–34, 46–51, where Solomon outlines the necessity and possibility of praying toward the temple when the people sin, whereupon God will hear and forgive and bring the people back to the land.

The prayer of Solomon is based in turn upon Deuteronomy 30:1–10, where Moses promises a restoration after the application of the covenant curse of exile, a restoration contingent upon repentance for sin.

ADDRESSING GOD (9:4B)

Daniel's prayer does not begin by requesting something. It begins by addressing God properly and by acknowledging his character and person. Daniel speaks of God as "the great and awesome God, who keeps the covenant and loyal love (*ḥesed*)" for those who obey the requirements and terms of the covenant. The focus here is on God's loyal love within the covenant relationship. He does not quickly punish his people, and he stands ready to bless them when they obey his laws.

CONFESSING SIN (9:5–10)

The next part of the prayer is devoted to confession of sin. Daniel is not concerned to demonstrate his own personal innocence and piety. Instead, he completely and fully identifies with his people and acknowledges their sin. He confesses that God's people have not obeyed his commands but have rebelled against him instead. They have not listened to the warnings of the prophets who were sent to get them to change their attitudes and behaviour to conform to the directions and instructions for their lifestyle given by God in the covenant. The prophets are like the lawyers of the covenant. When the covenant is broken, they appear in order to accuse the people with the ultimate intention of restoring their love and faithfulness to God. Isaiah, Jeremiah, Ezekiel, and many others were used by God to carry the message of warning and repentance, but they went largely unheeded.

The prophets were sent, according to Daniel, to all strata of society— from kings to common people. None of them, however, responded. Rather, they persisted in their foolish and dangerous rebellion.

Next Daniel marks a contrast between the sin of the people and the mercy of God: God is faithful; his people are rebellious. The prophet is brutally honest in his acknowledgement of the responsibility of God's people for their present dire condition. They are in exile because they have rebelled against the covenant God made with them through Moses.

GOD'S PUNISHMENT (9:11–14)

Then, in verses 11–14 of his prayer, Daniel draws a direct connection between the sin of the people and their present suffering (cf. Lam. 2:2–5). The present suffering is due to the curses promised to those who violated the covenant (Deut. 28:15–68).

APPEALING FOR COMPASSION AND MERCY (9:15–19)

Finally, Daniel calls upon God, as the one who delivered his people out of Egypt, to lift the covenantal curse and to restore the city of Jerusalem and its sanctuary. The exodus was a pivotal event in the life of God's people. It defined them as a nation. Through it, God freed them from slavery and brought them into the Promised Land. The prophets before Daniel saw an analogy between the exodus and the future deliverance that would free them from the shackles of the exile (cf. Isa. 11:11–16; 40:3–5; Hos. 2:14–15 [2:16–17 MT]). In essence, the return from the exile would be a second exodus, a new exodus.

GOD'S RESPONSE: THE VISION OF SEVENTY WEEKS (9:20–27)

As verses 20–23 show, the brief message supplied by vision in verses 24–27 constitute a direct divine response by way of an angelic messenger to the appeal and request raised by Daniel on the basis of Jeremiah's prophecy. What follows is a fairly literal translation of the Hebrew text to show how the numerous problems in the text have been understood. Space does not allow all of the exegetical issues to be given full treatment.

Literal Translation of Daniel 9:20–27

[20] And I was still speaking and interceding in prayer and confessing my sin and the sin of my people Israel, and making my pleading before the LORD my God fall upon the Holy Mountain of my God.

[21] I was still speaking in the petition, when the man Gabriel whom I had seen in the vision at the beginning—while I was made weary by fatigue—was touching me about the time of the evening offering.

[22] And he explained and spoke with me and said, "Daniel, I have now come to give you clear insight.

[23] At the beginning of your supplications a word went out and I came to declare [it], for you are beloved. So pay attention to the word and consider the vision:

[24] Seventy sevens are determined for your people and your holy city, to end the rebellion, and to finish with sin, and to atone for guilt/iniquity, and to bring in eternal righteousness, and to seal up prophetic vision, and to anoint a most holy place/person,

[25] so you must know and understand, from the issuing of a word to rebuild Jerusalem until an Anointed One, a Leader, are seven sevens and sixty-two sevens. It will be rebuilt with plaza and trench and in distressing times.

[26] And after the sixty-two sevens, an Anointed One will be cut off, but not for himself, and the people of the coming Leader will ruin/spoil the city and the sanctuary, and its end will come with the flood. And until the end war—desolations are what is decided.

[27] And he will uphold a covenant with the many for one seven, and at the half of the seven he will cause sacrifice and offering to cease, and upon a wing of abominations is one bringing desolation and until an end and what is decided gushes out on the one being desolated."

Among many difficulties encountered in lexical and syntactic issues facing the translator, the most problematic is the clause division in verse 25. According to the accents in the Masoretic Text, "seven sevens" belongs to the first sentence, while "sixty-two sevens" along with the conjunction preceding this noun phrase (i.e., "*and* sixty-two sevens") begins a new clause. One could argue that beginning a new sentence with the conjunction and noun phrase before the imperfect verb *tāšûb* (from the hendiadys for "it will be rebuilt") is a natural reading according to the rules of syntax in Hebrew. Moreover, if the author desired to delineate sixty-nine weeks, why not just say so specifically? Why divide the period into seven and sixty-two weeks? On the other hand, according to the rules of macrosyntax, beginning a clause by *tāšûb* without a conjunction (asyndeton) would signal a comment or explanation on the previous sentence rather than supply new information.[6] An explanation for dividing the period into 7 and 62 can be given (see below), but the problems of interpretation arising from following the accents in the Masoretic Text are insurmountable. Who is to be identified as the Anointed One after seven weeks? Further, the most natural reading is to identify "Anointed One" and "Leader" in verse 25 with the same terms in verse 26, but this identification is not possible according to the division in the Masoretic Text. In a detailed historical study, Roger Beckwith has demonstrated that the clause division represented by the Masoretic Text represents a reaction against messianic interpretation of the text, while the clause division accepted in the translation above follows the Septuagint, Theodotion, Symmachus, and the Syriac Peshitta.[7] Thus the clause division adopted here is both strongly and widely supported early in the text tradition.

UNDERSTANDING THE END OF EXILE

In order to grasp properly the request as raised by Daniel and the answer as provided through the vision of the seventy weeks, we need to understand the prophetic teaching concerning the end of the exile.

According to the context, Daniel is concerned about the end of the exile. God's people had broken the Israelite covenant (Exodus 19–24/Deuteronomy), and as a result, the covenant curses had fallen upon them.

---

[6] Stephen G. Dempster, "Linguistic Features of Hebrew Narrative: A Discourse Analysis of Narrative from the Classical Period" (PhD diss., University of Toronto, 1985). As an example, see Genesis 1:27, where the second and third clauses are asyndetic because they are epexegetical to the first.

[7] Roger T. Beckwith, "Daniel 9 and the Date of Messiah's Coming in Essene, Hellenistic, Pharisaic, Zealot, and Early Christian Computation," *Revue de Qumrân* 40 (1981): 521–542.

The final curse or judgement was exile (Deut. 28:63–68). Nonetheless, exile was not the last word; God had a plan *from the start* for his people to return (Deut. 30:1–10). Isaiah indicates that the return from exile entails two separate stages: (1) return from Babylon to the land of Israel, and (2) return from covenant violation to a right relationship to God so that the covenant relationship is renewed and restored (see Isa. 42:18–43:21 and 43:22–44:23, respectively). The first stage is the physical return from exile. But as previously noted, "You can get the people out of Babylon, but how do you get Babylon out of the people?" The physical return from exile gets the people out of Babylon, but the problem of getting Babylon out of the people must be dealt with by a second stage. The second stage is the spiritual return from exile: it deals with the problem of sin and brings about forgiveness and reconciliation in a renewed covenant between Yahweh and his people. According to the structure of Isaiah's message, Cyrus is the agent for the return from Babylon, and the servant of the Lord is the agent for the return from sin. Thus there are two distinct agents, and they correspond to the two distinct parts of the redemption that brings about the end of the exile. This can be clearly seen in the structure of Isaiah 38–55, as outlined previously:[8]

Overview of Isaiah 38–55: The Book of the Servant

A. Historical prologue— Hezekiah's fatal choice	38:1–39:8
B[1]. Universal consolation	40:1–42:17
1. The consolation of Israel	40:1–41:20
2. The consolation of the Gentiles	41:21–42:17
C[1]. Promises of redemption	42:18–44:23
1. Release	42:18–43:21
2. Forgiveness	43:22–44:23
C[2]. Agents of redemption	44:24–53:12
1. Cyrus: liberation	44:24–48:22
2. Servant: atonement	49:1–53:12
B[2]. Universal proclamation	54:1–55:13
1. The call to Zion	54:1–17
2. The call to the world	55:1–13

Daniel's prayer is focused upon the physical return from Babylon—the first stage in redemption, but the angelic message and vision of the seventy

---

[8] Adapted from J. Alec Motyer, *The Prophecy of Isaiah: An Introduction and Commentary* (Downers Grove, IL: InterVarsity Press, 1993), 289.

weeks is focused upon the forgiveness of sins and renewal of covenant and righteousness—the second stage in return from exile. Note the six purposes of the message and vision in verse 24:

Three Negative Purposes
1. to end the rebellion
2. to do away with sin
3. to atone for guilt/iniquity

Three Positive Purposes
4. to bring in everlasting righteousness
5. to seal up prophetic vision
6. to anoint a most holy place/person

When one considers the plan of redemption as outlined by Isaiah, clearly the angelic message is concerned principally not with the first stage but especially with the second stage of return: the forgiveness of sins and renewal of a right relationship to God.

The end of the exile is frequently portrayed in terms of the exodus. Just as God brought his people out of Egypt in that great event known as the exodus, so he will now bring about a new exodus in bringing his people back from exile. In fact, many aspects of the return from exile parallel the original exodus. In Ezekiel 4:4–6, for example, the prophet is instructed to lie on one side for 390 days for the sin of Israel and on the other side for 40 days for the sin of Judah: in each case a day for each year. The sum of 390 and 40 is 430—exactly the length of the period of bondage in Egypt. What is being portrayed by the drama of Ezekiel is that just as there was a period of bondage in Egypt before God brought about the exodus, so now there will be a long period of foreign overlords before he brings about the new exodus. Outside of Daniel 9, this longer period of subjugation before the new exodus is referred to in Daniel 8:19 as the "time of wrath" (NIV).[9]

The vision of Daniel 9 communicates the same truth. From the prophecy of Jeremiah, Daniel expects a literal period of seventy years for the exile to be completed. This seventy-year period apparently begins with the death of Josiah in 608 B.C. and extends to the fall of Babylon to Cyrus the Great in 539 B.C. When Daniel brings this issue to God in prayer, the answer is that this seventy-year period deals only with the first stage of the return from exile.

---

[9] Cf. Zechariah 1:12, where the seventy years under Babylonian rule is described as a time of wrath.

Before the new exodus, there will be a longer period of exile. Thus the real return from exile, a return including the forgiveness of sins, renewal of the covenant, and consecration of the temple, will not take just seventy years, but rather seventy "sevens," i.e., a much longer time. This *fundamental point* of the vision has unfortunately escaped the attention of proponents of both dispensational and nondispensational treatments in the last hundred years.

Although the focus of the message is on the city and the people (Jerusalem and Israel), there are broader implications for the nations. This passage must be seen in the light of the Abrahamic and Israelite covenants. The Abrahamic covenant promised blessings for the nations through the family of Abraham (Gen. 12:1–3). The Israelite covenant directed and instructed the family of Abraham as to how to live in a right relationship with God, a right relationship with one another in covenant community, and a right relationship to the earth (as stewards of the creation), so that they could be the blessing to the nations (Exodus 19–24). With the Israelite covenant broken, Israel now needs the forgiveness of sins so that the covenant can be renewed and the blessings can flow to the nations. Thus, the final and real return from exile is achieved by dealing effectively with Israel's rebellion: the first objective in the list of six is to end "the rebellion," i.e., of Israel. Then the blessing can flow to the nations, and this blessing finds fulfilment in the apostolic preaching of the cross and resurrection of Jesus Christ, when each one turns from their wicked ways (Acts 3:26). In this way, the second stage of return from exile has implications specifically for Israel but also universally, for the nations.

THE ROLE OF THE DAVIDIC KING IN ENDING THE EXILE

The angelic message of Daniel 9 mentions an "anointed one" (*māšîaḥ*) and a "leader or ruler" (*nāgîd*). Various proposals have been made for the identification of this person or persons. The grammar of the apposition in verse 25 requires that both terms refer to one and the same person. And without any grammatical or literary signals to indicate otherwise, the simplest solution is that the same two terms in verse 26 also refer to one and the same person—the same individual referred to in verse 25. Although many scholars identify the "anointed one" as the high priest Onias III, whose murder in 171 B.C. is reported in 2 Maccabees 4:33–38, Daniel I. Block provides four cogent reasons to reject this identification:[10] (1) It depends upon dating the composition of the book of Daniel to the second century B.C., a position that is not tenable (I have argued[11]) according to the chronological, linguistic, and literary data. (2) The arrival of this person is associated with the rebuilding and restoration of Jerusalem, so that one naturally thinks of a Davidic figure. (3) Although *nāgîd*, "leader, ruler," is used elsewhere of cultic officials, *nāgîd* and the root *mšḥ* are conjoined elsewhere only with reference to an anointed king (1 Sam. 9:16; 10:1; 1 Chron. 29:22). (4) While the Old Testament speaks of a coming king who will function as a priest, it never speaks of a coming priest in royal terms. In this way the Old Testament consistently distinguishes the Aaronic/Zadokite priesthood from Davidic royalty. As John Oswalt notes, the reference in Daniel 9 is the only unambiguous reference to *māšîaḥ* (the Messiah) as the eschatological Anointed One, in the entire Old Testament.[12]

There is a good reason why the future king is referred to in verses 25 and 26 by the term *nāgîd*, "ruler," rather than by the term *melek*, the standard word in Hebrew for "king." This is revealed by Donald F. Murray, who has provided the most recent and thorough treatment of *nāgîd*, particularly in the context of 2 Samuel 5:17–7:29. His conclusion is worth citing:

> In our texts the *melek* is one who sees his power from Yahweh as susceptible to his own arbitrary manipulation, who obtrudes himself inappropriately and disproportionately between Yahweh and Israel, and who treats Israel as little more than the subjects of his monarchic power. The *nāgîd*, on the other hand, is positively portrayed as one who sees his power as a sovereign and inviolable devolvement from Yahweh, who acts strictly under the orders of Yahweh for the benefit of Yahweh's people, and holds himself as no more than the willing subject of the divine monarch.[13]

In short, *nāgîd* communicates kingship according to God's plan and standards whereas *melek* communicates kingship according to the Canaanite model of absolute despotism and self-aggrandisement. That is why the term *nāgîd* dominates in the passage on the Davidic covenant (2 Samuel 7) and is also the term used here.

---

[10] Adapted in part and cited in part from Daniel I. Block, "Preaching Old Testament Apocalyptic to a New Testament Church," *Calvin Theological Journal* 41 (2006): 17–52.

[11] See Gentry, "Son of Man in Daniel 7: Individual or Corporate?"

[12] J. Oswalt, "משׁח," in *New International Dictionary of Old Testament Theology and Exegesis*, ed. Willem A. VanGemeren, 5 vols. (Grand Rapids, MI: Zondervan, 1997), 2:1126.

[13] Donald F. Murray, *Divine Prerogative and Royal Pretension: Pragmatics, Poetics, and Polemics in a Narrative Sequence about David (2 Samuel 5.17–7.29)*, JSOTSup 264 (Sheffield, UK: Sheffield Academic Press, 1998), 299.

The Davidic king ruling in Jerusalem was removed from the throne by the exile in 586 B.C. Yet according to the eternal and irrevocable promises of Yahweh to David, the prophets spoke of a coming king from David's line. The message and vision given to Daniel associates the king's return with the end of exile and the climactic purposes for Israel and Jerusalem, but with great personal tragedy: he will be cut off, *but not for himself.* The coming king will give his life to deliver his people.

THE INTERPRETATION OF THE SEVENTY WEEKS

The Hebrew word for "week" here is *šāvûa'*. It may refer to a period of seven days, like the English word for week (Gen. 29:27, 28 [cf. Judg. 14:12, Tob 11:19 (18 EV)]; Deut. 16:9 [2x]; Lev. 12:5; Jer. 5:24; Dan. 10:2, 3; Ezek. 45:21[14]). Still referring to a period of seven days, it occurs in the phrase "Feast of Weeks" (Ex. 34:22; Deut. 16:10, 16; 2 Chron. 8:13; and without the head-word "feast," Num. 28:26). It also occurs in Daniel 9:24, 25 [2x], 26, 27 [2x], apparently referring to a period of seven, but not seven days. This is clear from the occurrences in Daniel 10:2, 3 where we find the phrase "week of days" because the author wants to signal a return to the literal and normal use of the word "week." Daniel 10:2 and 3 are the only instances of the phrase "week of days" in the Old Testament, a phrase required by the context in proximity to chapter 9 where the word has a different sense.

The number seventy is clearly connected by the context (9:2) to Jeremiah's prophecy concerning the end of exile (Jer. 25:1–15 and 29:1–23). Chronicles explains the fulfilment of Jeremiah's prophecy of seventy years as lasting "until the land had enjoyed its Sabbaths" (2 Chron. 36:20–22, ESV). Chronicles explicitly connects the seventy years of exile to the principle of sabbatical years, although this is not spelled out by Jeremiah. The explanation given in Chronicles is based squarely on Leviticus 26:34–35: "Then the land shall enjoy its Sabbaths as long as it lies desolate, while you are in your enemies' land; then the land shall rest, and enjoy its Sabbaths. As long as it lies desolate it shall have rest, the rest that it did not have on your Sabbaths when you were dwelling in it" (ESV; cf. Lev. 26:40–45).

Paul Williamson is therefore right on target when he correlates the "seventy sevens" with sabbatical years and the jubilee:

---

[14] There is a problem in the text at Ezekiel 45:21.

The 'seventy sevens' chronography is probably best understood against the background of Jewish sabbatical years, and the Jubilee year in particular (cf. Lev. 24:8; 25:1–4; 26:43; cf. 2 Chr. 36:21). Thus understood, the seventy sevens constitutes ten jubilee years, the last (the seventieth seven) signifying the ultimate Jubilee (cf. Isa. 61:2). Given the Jeremianic context that prompted this revelation (Dan. 9:2; cf. Jer. 25:11–12; 29:10), some explicit association between this climactic Jubilee and the anticipated new covenant is not unexpected.[15]

Thus the "sevens" or "weeks" are periods or units of seven years, i.e., sabbaticals. Understood this way, the "seventy sevens" constitutes ten jubilees, the last (the seventieth seven) signifying the ultimate jubilee. In Luke 4:14–21, when Jesus reads from the scroll of Isaiah, he sees the ultimate jubilee in Isaiah 61:2 as being fulfilled in his own life and ministry.

Retributive justice, the foundation of divine righteousness in the Mosaic covenant, requires a symmetry to the experience and history of the nation of Israel. The period of time from the beginning of the Israelite kingdom to the fall of Jerusalem is essentially seventy sabbaticals. Then come seventy years of exile, a period when the land enjoyed its Sabbath rests. This is followed by seventy sabbaticals before the exile is finally over:[16]

Table 14.1: A Symmetry of Sabbaticals in Israelite History

Seventy Sabbaticals	Seventy Years of Exile	Seventy Sabbaticals
= Causes of Exile	= Sabbaths for the Land	= Solution to Exile

Thus the time required to resolve the problem of Israel's sin is precisely the same time it took to create the problem in the first place.

THE DIVISION OF THE WEEKS AND THE STARTING POINT

A chronology of seventy sabbaticals is required that answers appropriately to the divisions of the seventy "weeks" specified in the text and also allows the details concerning the events and persons predicted for these times to be easily identified. According to Daniel 9:25–27, the period of seventy sabbaticals is divided into three parts: seven sabbaticals in which the city of Jerusalem is rebuilt (v. 25), sixty-two sabbaticals in which nothing noteworthy or remarkable happens in relation to the purposes specified in this vision,

---

[15] Paul R. Williamson, *Sealed with an Oath: Covenant in God's Unfolding Purpose*, NSBT (Downers Grove, IL: InterVarsity Press, 2007), 174–175.

[16] Adapted from Block, "Preaching Old Testament Apocalyptic to a New Testament Church," 49.

and the climactic seventieth sabbatical when a covenant is upheld and offerings and sacrifices are ended, somehow in connection with extreme sacrilege to the temple and someone who causes desolation (v. 27). As Daniel Block similarly notes,

> Despite the textual problems raised by these verses, the focus of attention in this seventieth week of years is on an Anointed One, who is "cut off, but not for himself." Ironically, within the very week that the root problem of Israel's exile (sin) is solved through the death of the Messiah, the city of Jerusalem is destroyed.[17]

In the history of interpretation, four possible dates for the beginning of the period of seventy weeks have been proposed:[18]

586 B.C. = God's word at the fall of Jerusalem (Jer. 25:11–12; 29:10)
537 B.C. = Cyrus' word allowing the return from exile (2 Chron. 36:23; Ezra 1:1–4)
457 B.C. = Artaxerxes' commission to Ezra (Ezra 7:11–26)[19]
444 B.C. = Artaxerxes' commission to Nehemiah (Neh. 2:1–6)[20]

The first proposal is the least likely. The "word" coming from Jeremiah is actually dated by 25:1 to the fourth year of Jehoiakim, i.e., 605 B.C. and predicts the fall of Jerusalem in 586 B.C. Beginning the seventy sabbaticals at either date does not yield a satisfactory solution for the three periods of time or the events occurring in them and the identity of the Anointed One.

Many scholars opt for the fourth proposal because Artaxerxes' commission to Nehemiah specifically entails building the walls and this accounts for the word to rebuild Jerusalem. Yet this proposal faces many problems. It requires that the Messiah be cut off *in* the sixty-ninth sabbatical and leaves the seventieth sabbatical in verse 27 unexplained. This option also simply does not work if we are counting sabbaticals and years in a literal sense. To make this proposal work, Harold Hoehner, one of its most able proponents,

---

[17] Ibid.
[18] Robert C. Newman, John A. Bloom, and Hugh G. Gauch, Jr., "Public Theology and Prophecy Data: Factual Evidence that Counts for the Biblical World View," *JETS* 46/1 (2003): 79–110, especially 104.
[19] Newman, Bloom, and Gauch employ the conventional date of 458 B.C. The fall of 457 B.C. is adopted here based on the chronological work of Bob Pickle, "An Examination of Anderson's Chronological Errors Regarding Daniel 9's First 69 Weeks," www.pickle-publishing.com, accessed November 30, 2009. Newman, Bloom, and Gauch also erroneously provide Ezra 4:11–12 and 23 as references to Artaxerxes' commission to Ezra.
[20] Newman, Bloom, and Gauch employ the conventional date of 445 B.C. Again, the date adopted here is based on the work of Bob Pickle, "An Examination of Anderson's Chronological Errors Regarding Daniel 9's First 69 Weeks," www.pickle-publishing.com, accessed November 30, 2009.

uses so-called "prophetic years" of 360 days, but with scant support for such a calendrical definition or evidence that this is typical in prophetic predictions.[21] Scholars who argue that the death of the Messiah occurs in the sixty-ninth sabbatical explain that "*after* sixty-nine weeks" really means "*in* the sixty-ninth week" in ordinary language or reckoning of the time.[22] Such an argument constitutes special pleading.

According to Ezra 1:1–4 and 2 Chronicles 36:23, the "word" of Cyrus in 537 is focused on building a house for the Lord at Jerusalem. This word matches perfectly the prophecies of Isaiah 44:28 and 45:13, which predict Cyrus giving leadership to rebuild the city and temple of Jerusalem. Cyrus' divinely appointed purpose (Ezra 1:2) led him to allow the people to return to accomplish this task (Ezra 1:3). After the altar was rebuilt and foundations were laid for the new temple, opposition brought the work to a halt. A decree of Darius allowed it to be finished (Ezra 6), spurred on by the ministries of Haggai and Zechariah. In Ezra 7, the "word" of Artaxerxes (c. 457) is focused on support for the new temple. Yet Ezra 6:14 speaks of Cyrus, Darius, and Artaxerxes as though they issued a single decree. Darius' decree (Ezra 6) was based upon the fact that Cyrus had *already* issued the decree to permit the return and rebuilding of Jerusalem (see Ezra 5:17–6:7). Darius' decree was therefore a renewal (6:6–7) and an expansion (6:8–12) of Cyrus' original decree (6:3–5). Ezra 6:14 shows that Artaxerxes' decree to Ezra (in Ezra 7) is also an extension of Cyrus' original decree. So the decree which Cyrus drafted in 537 to restore the temple is not completed until 457 B.C. under Artaxerxes, which is therefore the date of the "word to rebuild Jerusalem" starting with its sanctuary. Artaxerxes' commission to Nehemiah in 444 B.C. is not connected to Cyrus' decree in Ezra 6:14 because the decree of 6:14 has to do specifically with rebuilding the temple, not the walls of Jerusalem. No doubt the rebuilding of the city was not complete until Nehemiah restored the walls, but rebuilding the city and rebuilding the temple were one and the same thing to the Jewish people (cf. Isaiah 44:28).[23]

457 B.C., then, is the correct date to begin marking off the seventy sabbaticals because this "word" to rebuild the city is associated with the return of Ezra and the reestablishing of the judiciary, central to the concept of a city (Ezra 7:25, 26). Ezra is a central figure in the return. (As already noted, the

---

[21] Harold W. Hoehner, *Chronological Aspects of the Life of Christ* (Grand Rapids, MI: Zondervan, 1977).

[22] Robert C. Newman, John A. Bloom, and Hugh G. Gauch, Jr., "Public Theology and Prophecy Data: Factual Evidence that Counts for the Biblical World View," 104.

[23] I acknowledge help from Jason Parry for the argument at this point (personal communication, November 2009).

commission of Artaxerxes to Ezra connects with the earlier contributions of Cyrus and Darius.) In addition, the book of Nehemiah (not separate from Ezra in the Hebrew Canon) is about rebuilding and restoring the city of God. While chapters 1–6 focus on restoring the city in physical terms, chapters 7–13 focus on restoring the city as a group of people devoted to the service and worship of their God. So rebuilding the city for Nehemiah is not merely about bricks and mortar. Daniel had computed the first year of Cyrus (537) as the end of the exile, according to 9:1–2. Ezra 1:1–4 acknowledges Cyrus as the fulfilment of Jeremiah's prophecy. But it seems that the point of the vision of seventy weeks is to mark a beginning *after* the word of Cyrus in 537. Thus Ezra's return commissioned by Artaxerxes is the next possible point. More importantly, the command in 457 is actually at the beginning of a sabbatical cycle.[24] When one begins the computation from this point, the three periods of the seventy weeks and the events and personae associated with them fit both precisely and simply. First, the literary structure of the text must be observed; then the explanation of the chronology and events is straightforward.

THE LITERARY STRUCTURE OF VERSES 25–27

Daniel 9:25–27 is not to be read in a linear manner according to the logic of prose in the Western world based on a Greek and Roman heritage. Instead, the approach in ancient Hebrew literature is to take up a topic and develop it from a particular perspective and then to stop and start anew, taking up the same theme again from another point of view. This approach is kaleidoscopic and recursive. It is like hearing music from stereo speakers sequentially instead of simultaneously. First comes the music of the right speaker; then comes the music of the left speaker. Then the person hearing (i.e., reading) puts the two together into a three-dimensional stereo whole.

First, verse 25 introduces the first period of seven weeks and the gap of sixty-two weeks to the climactic seventieth week. This last week is described twice in verses 26 and 27. Verses 26a and 27a describe the work of the Messiah in dying vicariously to uphold a covenant with many and to deal decisively with sin, thus ending the sacrificial system. Verses 26b and 27b show that, ironically, supreme sacrilege against the temple at this time will result in the destruction of the city of Jerusalem. Thus verses 26–27 have an

---

[24] For the calculation of sabbatical years I follow Benedict Zuckermann rather than Ben Zion Wacholder (see below).

A-B-A'-B' structure.[25] This fits the normal patterns in Hebrew literature to deal with a topic recursively. The literary structure can be diagrammed as follows:

> A   26a   the beneficial work of the Messiah
> > B   26b   ruin/spoliation of the city by his people and its desolation by war
>
> A'   27a   the beneficial work of the Messiah
> > B'   27b   abominations resulting in destruction of the city by one causing desolation

Observing this literary structure is crucial because one can explain difficulties in one section using the parallel section. For example, "the people of the coming leader" in verse 26b bring ruin to the reconstructed Jerusalem. Verse 27b provides further details showing that the "one causing desolation" does so in association with abominations. Below we will see how this makes perfect sense of the role played by both Jewish and Roman people in the fall of the temple. The literary structure also clarifies how the terms *māšîaḥ* and *nāgîd* in 25 and 26 refer to one and the same individual and moreover makes perfect sense of the "strengthening of a covenant" in verse 27a.

THE FULFILMENT OF THE PROPHECY

Verse 25 speaks of the issuing of a word to restore and build Jerusalem until Messiah, the Ruler, as seven and sixty-two sevens. During the seven sabbaticals, the city is rebuilt fully with plaza and town moat. The sentence "It will be rebuilt with plaza and trench and in distressing times" has no sentence-connector (asyndeton) and, according to discourse grammar, indicates a comment on the previous statement that specifies the time. This clause adds the comment that the city will be fully restored and the restoration will occur during distressing times. The seven sabbaticals cover the period roughly 457–407 B.C. and include the efforts of Ezra, Nehemiah, Haggai, Zechariah, and Malachi. If one uses the command of either Cyrus in 537 or Artaxerxes in 444 as a beginning point, the period of approximately fifty years does not correspond well to our records of the history of Israel and the rebuilding of Jerusalem.

Then for sixty-two sevens, there is nothing significant to record as far as

---

[25] Williamson acknowledges this A-B-A'-B' structure although he interprets "leader" or "prince" differently; see Paul R. Williamson, *Sealed with an Oath*, 175.

God's plan is concerned. There is a *good* reason, then, for dividing the sixty-nine weeks into seven and sixty-two weeks: in the sixty-nine weeks to the time of the Messiah, active reconstruction of the city and temple occupies only the first seven weeks.

When the "word to restore Jerusalem" is understood to refer to the decree of Artaxerxes in 457 B.C., sixty-nine sabbaticals or weeks of years bring the time to A.D. 27. The calculation of sabbatical years in Israel for antiquity is based upon evidence from Maccabees, Josephus, inscriptions, the Talmud, and Maimonides. The standard treatment derives from Benedict Zuckermann in 1866.[26] More recently, Ben Zion Wacholder has analysed the data differently and provided a table of sabbatical years from 519 B.C. to A.D. 441[27] Here I follow the standard view of Zuckermann (based on the critique of Ben Zion Wacholder by Bob Pickle), although the difference between the chronologies reconstructed by these two scholars is only one year.[28] Thus, the seventieth sabbatical is from A.D. 27–34 following Zuckermann or A.D. 28–35 following Ben Zion Wacholder.

Halfway through this time, i.e., A.D. 31, the Messiah is cut off, but not for himself. Astonishingly he dies, but his death is vicarious. The phrase ואין לו, commonly rendered "and he will have nothing," is better translated "but not for himself." The quasi-verbal אין in Late Biblical Hebrew can function precisely as the Standard Biblical Hebrew negative לא.[29] The point in the vision is that the coming king dies vicariously for his people.

Serious students of Scripture have not always agreed on the date of the crucifixion. Newman, Bloom, and Gauch have an excellent response for this issue:

> In any case, if the traditional scheme for the location of the sabbatical cycles is followed instead of Wacholder's, the 69th cycle shifts by only one year, to AD 27–34, which still fits equally well. Likewise an error by a year or two on either end—for Artaxerxes's 20th year or the date of the

---

[26] Benedict Zuckermann, *Über Sabbathjahrcyclus und Jubelperiode* (Breslau, Germany: W. G. Korn, 1866).

[27] Ben Zion Wacholder, "The Calendar of Sabbatical Cycles during the Second Temple and the Early Rabbinic Period," *Hebrew Union College Annual* 44 (1973): 153–196.

[28] For the calculation of sabbatical years I follow Benedict Zuckermann rather than Ben Zion Wacholder. See Bob Pickle, "Daniel 9's Seventy Weeks and the Sabbatical Cycle: When Were the Sabbatical Years," www.pickle-publishing.com, accessed November 9, 2008. Pickle offers a critical evaluation of all the evidence employed by Wacholder in setting up the table of sabbatical years. In any case, the seventieth sabbatical is from A.D. 27–34 (Zuckermann) or 28–35 (Wacholder), and one can find satisfaction in either A.D. 31 or 33 for a crucifixion date.

[29] See Stephen G. Dempster, *Dominion and Dynasty: A Biblical Theology of the Hebrew Bible*, NSBT 15 (Downers Grove, IL: InterVarsity Press, 2003), 218. On the use of *'ên* functioning as a simple negation, see *HALOT*, s.v. אין. If expressed by the normal negative, possible aural confusion could and would have resulted: *lō 'lô*.

crucifixion—would not change the result. The prediction fits Jesus even allowing for the largest possible uncertainties in chronology.[30]

Thus, by employing sabbaticals, the prophecy remains an astounding prediction finding fulfilment in Jesus of Nazareth and yet allows for differences as well in calculating the crucifixion. The crucifixion is almost always dated between A.D. 27 and 34.

If we put verses 26a and 27a together, the vicarious death of the coming king brings about a confirming/strengthening/upholding of a covenant with "the many," almost certainly "the many" referred to in Isaiah 53:10–12.[31] Without doubt, Isaiah 53, describing a future Davidic servant of the Lord, who is also both priest and sacrifice, laying down his life for the many, is the background to the brief comment in Daniel's vision. His death will bring an end to the sacrificial system because it is a final solution to the problem of sin. The expression "he will strengthen a covenant" occurs only here in the entire Old Testament. Of all the constructions involving the term "covenant," the expression closest semantically to "*higbîr bĕrît*" in Daniel 9:27 would seem to be "*hēqîm bĕrît*," i.e., to confirm or uphold a covenant. As we have seen, this is an expression which normally refers to a covenant partner fulfilling or upholding an obligation or promise previously enshrined in a covenant so that the other partner experiences in historical reality the fulfilling of this promise, i.e., one makes good on one's promise.[32] In Genesis 15, God's promises to Abraham of land and seed are formalised in a covenant. The expression used is *kārat bĕrît* (15:18). Later, in Genesis 17, God upholds his promise and says Sarah will have a baby within a year. The expression consistently used there is *hēqîm bĕrît* (17:7, 19, 21). Nonetheless, what are we to make of the expression "*higbîr bĕrît*" in Daniel 9:27?

If *higbîr bĕrît* is an alternative for *hēqîm bĕrit*, it seems that the statement "he will uphold a covenant with the many" refers to the work of the Anointed King in effecting the new covenant described by the prophets at

[30] Robert C. Newman, John A. Bloom, and Hugh G. Gauch, Jr., "Public Theology and Prophecy Data: Factual Evidence that Counts for the Biblical World View," 105.

[31] Meredith G. Kline, "The Covenant of the Seventieth Week," in *The Law and the Prophets: Old Testament Studies in Honor of Oswald T. Allis*, ed. J. H. Skilton (Nutley, NJ: Presbyterian & Reformed, 1974), 452–469.

[32] The difference between the expressions *kārat bĕrît* and *hēqîm bĕrît* was already recognised by Cassuto; see U. Cassuto, *The Documentary Hypothesis and the Composition of the Pentateuch* (Jerusalem: Magnes, 1941 [Hebrew], 1961 [English]); and idem, *La Questione della Genesi* (Pubblicazioni della R. Università degli Studi di Firenze, Facoltà di Lettere e Filosofica, 3 Serie, vol. 1, Florence, 1934). Recently, Paul R. Williamson and Jeffrey J. Niehaus have reacted to the way in which the difference was described by William J. Dumbrell. This is partly due to the inadequate description of Dumbrell and partly to inadequate lexical study on the part of Niehaus and Williamson. Exhaustive analysis of constructions with *bĕrît* is provided in the appendix.

different times and in a variety of ways. It could be that this is conceived as a kind of renewal of the broken Israelite covenant.

An alternative explanation proposed by Jason Parry may be more satisfactory.[33] He notes that the construction *higbîr bĕrît* in 9:27 is "similar to the Aramaic expression *tqp* (*pa"el* = "strengthen") plus *'ĕsār* ("injunction or prohibition"), i.e., "to put in force an injunction." This Aramaic expression occurs in Daniel 6:7 (6:8 MT) when the enemies of Daniel want the king to create a new law that they wish to use to trap Daniel and is parallel to the expression "enact a statute." Moreover, a cognate adjective of *tqp* in Imperial Aramaic and Nabataean has the meaning "lawful" or "legitimate." Thus, though the basic meaning of *tqp* in the *pa"el* is "strengthen," a meaning like "make lawful" is appropriate, especially when the object is "injunction." The Hebrew expression *higbîr bĕrît* in 9:27 could be viewed, therefore, as a calque of the Aramaic expression in Daniel 6:7 and, as a result, would be equivalent in meaning to *kārat bĕrît*, i.e., initiating a covenant rather than upholding an existing commitment or promise. A further possibility is that *higbîr bĕrît* in 9:27 reflects linguistic usage similar to Ezekiel 16:60, 62, where the expression *heqîm bĕrît* seems to be an example of linguistic change/development in Late Biblical Hebrew and could mean "to initiate a covenant." Whichever explanation of *higbîr bĕrît* is adopted, there is no doubt that the covenant of 9:27 is the new covenant which was effected by the sacrificial death of the Messiah in order to restore the broken covenantal relationship between God and his people.

Strangely, at the same time that the Messiah comes and effects a final solution for sin, verse 26b says that the people of the coming ruler will destroy the city and the sanctuary. There is no grammatical issue in identifying object and subject in this sentence. The meaning of the sentence is also straightforward. The coming ruler must be the Messiah of verse 25 according to the context and normal rules of reading literature, since no other coming ruler has been introduced. Therefore "the people of the coming ruler" are the Jewish people.[34] The statement is telling us that it is the Jewish people who will ruin/spoil the restored city and temple at the arrival of their coming

---

[33] Personal communication, November 2009.

[34] In the bound phrase עַם נָגִיד הַבָּא, the attributive relative participle הבא modifies נגיד. Normally, the attributive participle and noun would agree in definiteness, but exceptions are found. See Bruce K. Waltke and Michael P. O'Connor, *Introduction to Biblical Hebrew Syntax* (Winona Lake, IN: Eisenbrauns, 1990), 621–622. The participle "who is to come" does not indicate, then, that another person is intended. The phrase means "the people of the ruler who is to come" and the subject of the verb in the sentence in verse 26b is the leader's own kin; the leader is the Anointed One of verse 26a.

king. Historical records confirm that this is precisely right. We have firsthand accounts of the fall of Jerusalem from the first century in *The Wars of the Jews* by Josephus. Anyone who has read and studied these texts will understand the author's point. Although the Roman army actually put the torch to Jerusalem, the destruction of the city was blamed squarely on the Jewish people themselves. Josephus wrote his work to try to exonerate the *masses* by blaming the *few*, i.e., the Zealots. Thus, he wanted people to believe that the fall of Jerusalem was not the fault of the people as a whole, but rather was due to a few extreme rebels who brought down the wrath of Rome upon them. So Josephus is adequate historical proof that the destruction of Jerusalem was entirely the fault of the Jewish people, just as Daniel 9:26b predicts. Since few interpreters find it possible to accept the straightforward statement of the text, ingenious alternative proposals are multiplied. These cannot be detailed here except to say that many of them assume rather unnaturally that the "ruler" in verse 26 is different from the one in verse 25, when verse 25 clearly connects the "ruler" with the "anointed one" and no contextual clues exist that this is a different person.

Moreover, the literary structure of verses 26–27 helps to explain the cryptic phrase in verse 26b, since verse 27b returns to the topic of the ruin of the restored Jerusalem and elaborates, providing further details and information. The "people of the coming ruler" who ruin the city and sanctuary (26b) are responsible for the "abominations" (27b), and the "one causing desolation" (27b) is responsible for the "war" in 26b since there it is the war which brings about "desolations," and "desolations" in Daniel's prayer (9:17–18) are the result of a foreign nation brought against Israel for breaking the covenant (e.g., Lev. 26:31–35). The "abominations," then, refer to the sacrilege which resulted from the struggle between John, Simon, and Eleazar ("people of the coming ruler") for control of Jerusalem, and the "war" refers to the destruction of Jerusalem and the temple by Vespasian/Titus (the "one causing desolation"). The "one causing desolation" (Titus acting on behalf of Vespasian) comes "on the wing of," i.e., in connection with, "abominations" caused by the Jews. The one being desolated by war is the city with its sanctuary. Jesus' mention of the "abomination of desolation" in the Olivet Discourse supports this understanding since he is probably speaking of the sacrilege of John of Gischala as the "abomination," which forewarns of the impending "desolation" of Jerusalem and the temple by the Romans."[35]

---

[35] I acknowledge here the helpful analysis of Jason Parry (personal communication, November 2009).

Verse 27b speaks of the "one causing desolation on the wing of abominations." The term "wing" can mean "edge" or "extremity." The phrase refers to one causing desolation in association with extreme abominations. A similar expression, but not exactly the same, is used to predict the act of Antiochus Epiphanes in Daniel 11:31 and 12:11 in desecrating the temple. Here in 9:27b, however, the agent of the abominations is the Jewish people, not a foreign ruler. The Gospels present Jesus as both genuine Messiah and true Temple. The paralytic lowered through the roof by four friends, for example, was not only healed but was forgiven of his sins.[36] This angered the leaders because Jesus was claiming to do something that could happen only at the temple; thus he was claiming to be the true Temple (John 2:18–22). So when the Jewish people rejected Jesus as Anointed One/Messiah and the high priest blasphemed Jesus, the true Temple, the Herodian temple supported by the Jewish people had to fall and the city had to be destroyed.

According to verse 26b this destruction is something that would happen *after* the sixty-ninth sabbatical. In verse 27b, there is nothing stated that actually requires the desolation of Jerusalem to happen precisely *in* the seventieth week, although this event is associated with the events happening at that time. Thus, the fall of Jerusalem some time after the crucifixion does fit suitably because it is the final working out of the Jewish response to Jesus in the seventieth week. This situation is similar to God telling Adam that in the day he ate of the forbidden fruit, he would die. In one sense this did happen on the very day, but it took time to be worked out. Just so, when the Jewish people rejected the Messiah and the high priest blasphemed Jesus, the true Temple, the Herodian temple had to fall and the city had to be destroyed. The coming destruction, symbolised by the curtain protecting the Holy of Holies being torn in two at the crucifixion, finally came to pass in A.D. 70, i.e., within the time of the generation that committed this sacrilege.

The notion of a person who is both King and true Temple is hinted at by the last of the six purposes in Daniel 9:24: "to anoint a Holy of Holies." The verb "to anoint" is normally used of consecrating persons for offices, e.g., priest (Lev. 4:3), prophet (Ps. 105:15), and most often king (1 Sam. 2:35). It can also be used to refer to the consecration of the Mosaic tabernacle and its holy objects (Ex. 29:36; 30:26; 40:9, 10, 11; Lev. 8:10, 11). Only in Daniel 9:24 do we have a "Holy of Holies" being anointed. This phrase could be

---

[36] For more examples, see N. T. Wright, *Jesus and the Victory of God*, Christian Origins and the Question of God 2 (Minneapolis: Fortress, 1996), 432–437.

construed as "the most holy place" or "the most holy person." The latter meaning would be most unusual. Thus we have a verb that is normally used of a person and an object normally used of the temple. It may suggest that future king and temple are one and the same. It finds fulfilment in Jesus of Nazareth as both Messiah and true Temple.

Some interpreters have opted for a proposal that views *nāgîd* in verse 26b as referring to an evil prince,[37] perhaps even the Antichrist, and different from verse 25 where the *nāgîd* refers to the Messiah. This is bolstered by interpreting verse 27a as referring to this evil ruler making a false covenant which disrupts sacrifice in a way similar to the abomination causing desolation in 8:12–14, 11:31, and 12:11. A supporting connection may even be drawn between the fact that several texts in Daniel appear to speak of a three-and-one-half-year period (7:25; 12:7, 11, 12; cf. 8:14, 26). All of these texts are fraught with interpretive problems, and associated with them is the identification of the four kingdoms portrayed symbolically in the dream of chapter 2 and the vision of chapter 7, followed by the expansions on these themes in chapters 8 and 10–12.

Space does not permit addressing all the difficult exegetical issues pertaining to the connections just outlined. Substantial reasons, however, can be provided to show in a general way that these connections are superficial and lead to faulty interpretation.

Let us focus, first, on the terms "anointed one" (*māšîaḥ*) and "leader or ruler" (*nāgîd*) in verse 25 *before* considering the occurrences in verse 26. Verse 25 has the two terms together, *māšîaḥ nāgîd*, so that the second term is clearly in apposition to the first and both refer to the same individual.

In the case of *nāgîd*, etymology and noun formation are useful. The verbal root has the meaning "be in front," or "be in full sight of everyone." The noun formation is the same as *māšîaḥ*.[38] Nouns formed in this way have either an active or a passive sense. For *māšîaḥ*, the sense is passive, i.e., one anointed. For *nāgîd*, the sense is active. Thus, the word means "a person who is out in front," i.e., a leader. The Oxford Lexicon gives "leader" as the first equivalent and afterwards also lists "ruler" or "prince," since most of the "leaders" indicated by *nāgîd* are kings. All kings are leaders, but not all leaders are kings.

---

37 Cf. Stephen R. Miller, *Daniel*, New American Commentary 18 (Nashville: Broadman & Holman, 1994), 271; and Paul R. Williamson, *Sealed with an Oath*, 175.

38 See H. Bauer and P. Leander, *Historische Grammatik der hebräischen Sprache des Alten Testaments* (Halle, Germany: Max Niemeyer, 1922; repr. Hildesheim, Germany: Georg Olms, 1991), § 470 n.

Some may question our preference for rendering *nāgîd* as "leader" in the translation of 9:20–27 and favour the rendering "prince" due to its royal connotations in some contexts. Yet since *nāgîd* does not always refer to royal figures, and since the root *ngd* does not have specifically royal connotations, probably *nāgîd* is higher in the hierarchy of semantic domains than "prince," so that "leader" would be a more accurate rendering than "prince," although a prince could be one type of *nāgîd*.

Further consideration of the term *nāgîd* is useful. The term is found in 44 instances in the Hebrew Bible, which can be classified as follows: (1) king of Israel (Saul: 1 Sam. 9:16; 10:1; David: 1 Sam. 13:14; 25:30; 2 Sam. 5:2; 6:21; 7:8 = 1 Chron. 11:2; 1 Chron. 5:2; 17:7; 28:4; 2 Chron. 6:5; Solomon: 1 Kings 1:35; 1 Chron. 29:22; Abijah: 2 Chron. 11:22; Jeroboam: 1 Kings 14:7; Jehu: 1 Kings 16:2; Hezekiah: 2 Kings 20:5; unnamed awaited future king = "messiah": Isa. 55:4; Dan. 9:25; 9:26?), (2) Zadokite priest over house of God (1 Chron. 9:11; 9:20; 26:24; 2 Chron. 28:7; 31:12, 31:13; 35:8; Neh. 11:11; Jer. 20:1), (3) military leaders (1 Chron. 12:28 [12:27 EV]; 13:1; 2 Chron. 11:11; 19:11; 32:21), (4) tribal leader (1 Chron. 27:4; 27:16), (5) generic leader (Ps. 76:13 [76:12 EV]; Job 29:10; 31:37; Prov. 8:6; 28:16), (6) foreign leader (Ezek. 28:2; Dan. 11:22).

Several things should be clear concerning the usage of *nāgîd* from the data. The word *nāgîd* is really a generic term for leader. The leader can be high in the hierarchy of society or much lower down. So he can be a king or priest, or military or tribal leader, or just someone in any kind of leadership position.[39]

Second, in itself, *nāgîd* is a neutral term. A *nāgîd* can be a good or a bad leader. Pashhur in Jeremiah 20:1 is a bad leader. The *nāgîd* of Tyre in Ezekiel 28 is a bad leader as well and receives divine censure. It is interesting to note that the ruler of Tyre is called a *nāgîd* in 28:2 and a *melek* in 28:12, which is the second section of this unit of text according to its own literary structure. Since the king of Tyre is presented in Adamic terms in the first section, this explains the use of *nāgîd* following the description of usage by Murray. That is, he had a responsibility *under God* to which he was unfaithful. So even when an evil person is called a *nāgîd*, it may be to emphasise a responsibility or stewardship gone awry.

In addition, the *nāgîd* of Daniel 11:22 is probably an evil person, although precise identification is difficult. This instance, since it is found

---

[39] Whether the latter uses are late is a moot point since the generic usage is found in Job, whose date is uncertain.

in Daniel, may potentially constitute an important datum for the traditional view of 9:26 as an evil leader. The fact that the word "covenant" occurs in both passages must also be considered.

Collins says that the *nāgîd* in 11:22 was identified by Theodoret as a reference to the murder of the high priest Onias III and that "this is universally accepted by modern scholars, although the reference anticipates a slightly later point in Antiochus's reign."[40] This would explain the position represented in the Oxford Lexicon.

Steinmann also takes the *nāgîd* in 11:22 as a reference to "the Jewish high priest," but he acknowledges that "the text leaves ambiguous which high priest is being described."[41] He notes that Onias III and Jason were both high priests deposed by Antiochus IV. Next Steinmann cites Miller as holding to the view that the "leader of a covenant" in 11:22 refers to Ptolemy VI instead; Steinmann rejects this interpretation because he does not see how the "small nation" (which he takes to be Jerusalem and Judea) in 11:23 makes sense if the *nāgîd* in 11:22 is Ptolemy VI.

In order to consider the possibility suggested by Miller a little more fully, the *ESV Study Bible* note on these verses, which also identifies the leader in 11:2 as Ptolemy VI, may provide a helpful summary of this view:

> **11:21–23 In his place shall arise a contemptible person**, Antiochus IV Epiphanes (reigned 175–164 B.C.), who is also the "little horn" of ch. 8 (8:9–12, 23–25). He took the name Antiochus "Epiphanes" ("Manifest One"; see note on 8:25), but others called him "Epimanes" ("madman"). Seleucus IV Philopater's son, Demetrius I Soter, was the rightful heir to the throne, but because he was imprisoned in Rome, Antiochus IV Epiphanes took the throne, even though **royal majesty** had **not been given** to him. He paid off important people for supporting him, which is what the phrase to **obtain the kingdom by flatteries** refers to. Ptolemy VI Philometer (181–145 B.C.) of Egypt came against Antiochus IV but was defeated and held as a hostage. Later Ptolemy VI (**the prince of the covenant**) made an **alliance** (a covenant) with Antiochus IV to regain his throne because his brother (Ptolemy VIII Euergetes II Physcon) had taken it while he was imprisoned in Syria. This worked, and he received his throne back, but later he broke this covenant and joined with his brother Ptolemy VIII, to force Antiochus IV out of Pelusium, one of Egypt's fortress cities.

---

[40] John J. Collins, *Daniel: A Commentary on the Book of Daniel*, Hermeneia (Minneapolis: Fortress, 1993), 382.
[41] Andrew E. Steinmann, *Daniel*, Concordia Commentary (Saint Louis: Concordia, 2008), 526.

On the basis of this description, the following identifications may be inserted into the NASB translation of Daniel 11:21–23:

> [21] "In his [Seleucus IV's] place a despicable person [Antiochus IV Epiphanes (175–164 B.C.)] will arise, on whom the honor of kingship has not been conferred [he took the throne since the rightful heir, Demetrius I Soter, was imprisoned in Rome], but he [Antiochus IV] will come in a time of tranquility and seize the kingdom by intrigue [he paid off important people for supporting him]. [22] "The overflowing forces [of Ptolemy VI Philometer (181–145 B.C.)] will be flooded away before him [Antiochus IV] and shattered, and also the prince of the covenant [Ptolemy VI]. [23] "After an alliance is made with him [Ptolemy VI] he [Ptolemy VI] will practice deception, and he [Ptolemy VI] will go up and gain power with a small force of people [joining his brother Ptolemy VIII to force Antiochus IV out of the Egyptian city of Pelusium].

More work in the original sources is needed to verify whether this interpretation is the best option. If this identification is correct, however, then Ptolemy VI is said to be "flooded away" and shattered in verse 22, even though verse 23 further describes him. It seems that Ptolemy VI's downfall is finally reported in verse 26, according to the interpretation proposed in the notes of the *ESV Study Bible.*

The "*nāgîd* of a covenant" in Daniel 11:22, then, is either a high priest such as Onias III, or the Hellenistic king Ptolemy VI. The covenant in the former possibility would be the Israelite covenant, which legitimates the leadership role of priests in the covenant community (e.g., Deut. 17:8–13). The covenant in the latter possibility would be the alliance between Ptolemy VI and Antiochus IV by which Ptolemy VI reclaimed the throne. In either interpretation, the phrase "leader of a covenant" in 11:22 denotes someone who is made a leader *by means of* that covenant and consequently rules subject to the terms of that covenant. In contrast, the *nāgîd* of 9:26–27 makes or upholds a covenant with "the many." Those who interpret the *nāgîd* in 9:26 as an evil prince typically understand the covenant in 9:27 to be a covenant by which the evil prince guarantees peace for the nation of Israel, whereas those who interpret the *nāgîd* in 9:26 as the Messiah understand the covenant in 9:27 to be the new covenant. In both interpretations, the *nāgîd* of 9:26–27 makes a covenant to guarantee something to "the many," but he is a *nāgîd* apart from the covenant itself. Consequently, even though the terms *nāgîd* and "covenant" appear in both 9:26–27 and 11:22, the nature of the relationship between the *nāgîd* and the covenant associated with him is completely different in each passage, even when the various interpretative options are considered. Therefore, the phrase "leader of a covenant" in 11:22 does not indicate that the author intends to bring to memory specifically the *nāgîd* who makes or upholds a covenant with the many in 9:26–27. For this reason, the instance of *nāgîd* in 11:22 should not be used as support for interpreting the *nāgîd* in 9:26 as an evil prince. The similar vocabulary in 9:26–27 and 11:22 reflects the similar milieu and theme of the two visions in which these verses are found, not similar referents.[42]

Furthermore, the observation that Saul is called a *nāgîd* and he was a bad leader is irrelevant to the argument that the author of Samuel employs the term *nāgîd* and avoids the term *melek* in order to avoid Canaanite notions of kingship and promote *what is expected* of the person God chose to rule his people under him. The authors of Samuel and Kings use *nāgîd* of both bad and good rulers, all the while emphasing the kind of king God is seeking. Indeed, throughout the entire history of Israel, each generation is thinking, "Maybe the next king is the promised scion of David, but not this one." As an illustration, Isaiah 1–39 shows that the future king who fulfills God's intentions is neither bad king Ahaz nor even good king Hezekiah.

Nonetheless, whatever the range of usage, it is context that determines the meaning of a specific instance of a word. Moreover the nearby context is, as a rule, more important than the less proximate context. So before we can discuss Daniel 9:26, let us focus on verse 25. Why do we interpret this passage to refer to the so-called Messiah? After all, wouldn't this be the only place in the Old Testament where the term *māšîaḥ* is used of the coming king? So how do we know this is a prediction of Jesus? On what basis do we interpret this text in this way?

Once again, the term *māšîaḥ* has a broader range of usage, but the majority of uses refer to the person anointed as king of Israel. Moreover, the collocation of *māšîaḥ* with *nāgîd* in 9:25 indicates that *nāgîd* refers to the type of *nāgîd* found in the particular use of the term as defined by Samuel and continued throughout Kings and parallels in Chronicles. Many instances of *nāgîd* in Samuel are found in connection with the anointing of a king, and so the collocation of *māšîaḥ* and *nāgîd* most probably connotes a future anointed king over Israel and refers to the same Davidic figure symbolised by the stone in Daniel 2 and by the "son of man" in Daniel 7. Many who

---

[42] I acknowledge the help of Jason Parry at this point in the argument (personal communication, March 2012).

hold to the "evil prince" view of 9:26 would agree with this analysis. They would construe *māšîaḥ nāgîd* in 9:25 as referring to a coming king over Israel and would contend that these terms connect most probably with the biblical tradition in Samuel and Kings. Again it is noteworthy that the term *melek* is avoided in the vision given to Daniel, probably for the same reasons it is avoided in Samuel.

If *nāgîd* in 9:25 refers to a coming Davidic king, then the author would have to give some clear indication to his readers that a different referent for *nāgîd* is intended in 9:26. Those who hold to the "evil prince" view have not articulated satisfactorily how the author has indicated to his reader that both the positive connotation and the messianic referent of *nāgîd* in 9:25 have suddenly changed to a negative connotation and adversarial referent in 9:26. An adversarial connotation of *nāgîd* in 9:26 cannot legitimately be inferred from the actions of the "people of the *nāgîd*" against the city and sanctuary, since the actions of a king's subjects are not necessarily endorsed by the king.

We should consider next the function of the article on *habbā'*. Verse 26 may be literally rendered, "And after the sixty-two heptads, 'anointed' is cut off, but not for himself, and 'people of leader, the coming one (*habbā'*), will ruin the city and the sanctuary." Both grammatically and rhetorically, the articular participle *habbā'*, i.e., the coming one, is anaphoric. It refers backwards in the text to something that is already mentioned. It is clear that the participle *habbā'* is attributive to the *nomen rectum* of the bound phrase "(the) people of (the) *nagid*," so that the function of *habbā'* is to specify which *nāgîd* is intended, i.e., the previously mentioned *nāgîd* who is to come after 69 heptads. Perhaps the whole phrase could be more accurately rendered in English, "the people of the leader, i.e., the one who is coming." For the "evil prince" view to be clear, the text would have to say, "the people of *another* leader who is to come." As it is, the proponents of this view have not provided any acceptable grammatical reason to explain the article or why *habbā'* is even in the text. If *habbā'* is announcing that an(other adversarial) *nāgîd* will come after the text has already stated that the people of that *nāgîd* will ruin the city and sanctuary, the construction would be rather awkward. This somewhat tedious analysis is necessary to reveal the *assumptions* behind the interpretation of the traditional view. The proponents assume what the text does not explicitly state, that after the messianic king is cut off, (*another*) (*evil*) leader comes on the scene. The text does not say this. It says that the people of the leader, the one who is coming (i.e., anaphoric use) will destroy city and temple. The "evil prince" view seems to deserve the accusation of begging the question. Let us be as clear as possible here: in Daniel 9:26b the text only says that the people of the leader, the one coming, will ruin the city and sanctuary. So it does not say that another leader comes on the scene. It says that the people of the coming leader bring destruction.

Also noteworthy is the fact that 9:26 is like a couplet in poetry, with the word pair *māšîaḥ nāgîd* from 9:25 now split over parallel lines. After verse 25 says that *māšîaḥ nāgîd* is coming, verse 26a says that the *māšîaḥ* is cut off and 26b says that the people of the coming *nāgîd* ruin city and sanctuary. The separation of the words in 9:26 may be significant, but not in the way normally suggested. The fact that the *māšîaḥ* is cut off does not indicate that another *nāgîd* comes on the scene. According to the text it is the people of the *nāgîd* who come on the scene after the *māšîaḥ* is cut off, not the *nāgîd* himself. In general we should not drive a wedge between the king and his people,[43] but the text does drive a wedge between them in this case when it indicates that the coming king is cut off on the one hand and his people ruin the city and sanctuary on the other hand. The two sentences do seem like contrasting statements in an antonymic couplet. And this is exactly what happened: Jesus came and was cut off, and his people ruined the city and the sanctuary. It was Caiaphas' rejection of Jesus' testimony at the trial that meant that that temple had to fall.

In addition, the next statement, "and its end will be in a flood," does not show that "the coming one" is another evil leader. To be sure, the expression does appear to refer to enemy armies, which are sometimes compared to a flood (e.g., Isaiah 8). It could be that the Messiah's people bring down the city and temple and its end entails foreign armies aiding and abetting this destruction. Once again, we should not *assume* what is not necessarily explicit in the text.

It may be natural for one to expect destruction from outsiders, but it is also natural for destruction to come from within. What happened in the exile is both destruction from without and destruction from within. Judah and Jerusalem brought judgement upon themselves; armies from other nations

---

[43] In Daniel 7:27 there is a close connection between king and people. There is, however, a major difference between 9:26 and 7:27. In 7:27 we have several sentences, and what is affirmed for the people is also affirmed for the third masculine singular referent. In 9:26 there is only one sentence, and the subject is "the people of the leader, i.e., the one who is coming." So the parallel between 7:27 and 9:26 falls apart at that point.

aided and abetted this destruction as divine instruments (Assyria = the rod of Yahweh).

One may appeal to the broader context of Daniel to argue for an evil *nāgîd* in 9:26 different from that of 9:25. The theme of persecution from outsiders is in the book of Daniel. However, this theme is not the only theme in the book. There is an additional theme in Daniel: the continued sin of Israel even after their physical return to the land (see 8:12, 23; 11:36 = persecution due to Israel's sin and note also the consciousness of deserved judgement in 2 Maccabees). Note "the time of wrath" in 8:19 (cf. Zech. 1:12). We can argue that the cutting off of the Messiah and the ruination of the city and sanctuary by the people of the Messiah are the culmination of this continued transgression of Israel after the physical return, rather than the culmination of the persecution of the outsiders as some suggest. This interpretation, moreover, better suits the controlling purpose of the paragraph as stated in 9:24. The culmination of the persecution of the outsiders is indeed found in the next part of 9:26: "and its end will come with a flood, and until the end will be war—desolations are determined." This second part refers to the final destruction of Jerusalem at the hands of the Romans in A.D. 70, i.e., the culmination of the persecution of outsiders. In sum, the Jews cut off their Messiah and ruined the city as the culmination of their continued transgression, and the Romans destroyed the city "in a flood" as a culmination of the persecution from outsiders, at the end of the extended "exile" after returning physically to the land. Consequently, 9:26 describes the culmination of two important themes in Daniel: (1) Israel's continued transgression after the physical return from exile, and (2) the persecution of outsiders. Thus the broader context is not necessarily against the understanding of the passage proposed here.

Nor can the interpretation proposed here be accused of being contrary to texts in the New Testament. What may be at stake is *our interpretation* of texts in the New Testament to which we want to make Daniel 9 fit somehow. The approach to Daniel 9 advanced here may fit with various views of texts such as Matthew 24 and Mark 13 or 2 Thessalonians 2:3–13 and Revelation 13 and 17. We have not appealed to Josephus over against these texts; rather, we have used Josephus as a source of historical information in the same way that we use 1—2 Maccabees to demonstrate that certain predictions in Daniel were fulfilled by Antiochus IV.

A problematic passage is Jesus' reference to "the abomination of desolation" in Mark 13:14, which cannot be considered in depth at this point. Cross-referencing Bibles normally supply Daniel 9:27, 11:31, and 12:11 as references. These three texts in Daniel are not at all identical, although they are levelled somewhat in both LXX and Theodotion Daniel. They may well be referring to different events. In any case, is it impossible that rebellious Israel is a type of the Antichrist, since they rejected the Christ in his earthly ministry? Paul himself, like Jesus, uses role reversal and employs terms for the Judaizers that were normally used by Jews of the Gentiles, e.g., "dogs."

By way of summary, the context strongly suggests that *nāgîd* in verses 25 and 26 refers to the same individual. Second, the A-B-A'-B' literary structure of verses 26–27 does not suggest connecting verse 27a to verse 26b. Third, the larger literary structure of Daniel as a whole is against the "evil prince" view. Chapter 7 entails a vision of four successive kingdoms that is followed by the kingdom of God. In the fourth kingdom there is a ruler who is boastful against God (7:8) and oppresses the saints (7:25). In the "blowup maps" of chapters 8 and 10–12 that expand upon the basic vision of chapter 7, there is a ruler who sets himself against the Prince of the Host (8:12–14). This ruler is clearly in the Greek kingdom, according to 8:21. The last vision of chapters 10–12 expands further upon 8:12–14 and speaks of the abomination causing desolation (11:31 and 12:11), ultimately fulfilled in Antiochus Epiphanes, a ruler within the Greek kingdom. Since I would identify the fourth kingdom as Roman and the third as Greek, it is problematic to relate 7:8, which belongs to the fourth empire, to 11:31 and 12:11 which belong to the third.[44] We can see from the literary structure of the book that the vision of the seventy weeks is by virtue of its content directly related to the three visions portraying the sequence of foreign overlords in chapters 7, 8, and 10–12.[45] The seventieth week corresponds to the inauguration of the kingdom of God in the other visions, when atonement is made for sin and righteousness is brought forth (9:24). Thus the referents of 9:26b–27a should be sought in the fourth kingdom, not the third. This is a powerful

---

[44] This does not preclude a typical/ antitypical relationship between the two. A typology between Antiochus Epiphanes and the oppressive ruler of 7:8, 25, however, does not necessarily imply that the *nāgîd* of 9:26b refers to the same individual as described in 7:8, 25.

[45] See Jason Parry, "Desolation of the Temple and Messianic Enthronement in Daniel 11:36–12:3" *JETS* 54/3 (2011): 485–526. He argues that there are allusions in 11:36–45 to 9:26–27 showing that 11:36–45 is the fulfilment of verse 26b and verse 27b, and he shows how 11:36–45 can be understood as a reference to the events of A.D. 67–70. His analysis reveals that 9:26b and 9:27a are to be linked to the descriptions of the fourth kingdom in the other visions, so that Daniel 7:8, 25; 9:26b; 9:27b; and 11:36–45 all refer to Vespasian's invasion of Galilee and Judea, which culminated with the desolation of the city and temple in A.D. 70.

reason against connecting 9:26b and 9:27a with 8:12–14, 11:31, and 12:11. The literary structure of the book prevents the reader from connecting them in spite of some superficial similarities.

THE PLACE OF DANIEL 9 WITHIN CHAPTERS 7–12

The question may be raised, quite legitimately: what *is* the relationship of the vision of seventy weeks to the other visions? How does it fit into the larger literary structure of the book as a whole? This question urgently needs to be addressed.

As already noted, the visions in chapters 7, 8, and 10–12 focus on a series of four Gentile/human kingdoms succeeded finally by the kingdom of God. I attempted to show in an earlier examination of the issue of the "son of man" in Daniel 7 that the "son of man" represents at the same time a divine figure, a human king, and the constituent people of his kingdom: in the end, the saints of the Most High receive the kingdom of God (7:18, 22, 27).[46] These three visions, then, focus on the question, what is happening to God's kingdom now that Israel is in exile, without an earthly king, and subject to foreign powers? Chapter 9, nicely sandwiched between the second and third of the three visions, deals with a different but closely related issue: how long will Israel be in exile? How long will the kingdom of God suffer at the hands of the foreign nations? The final or real return from exile, equivalent to the forgiveness of sins, is *prerequisite* to the saints receiving a kingdom, and so the vision of the seventy weeks reveals how and when the ultimate jubilee is ushered in.

CONCLUSION

The vision of Daniel's seventy weeks, then, can be explained simply. It refers to a period of seventy sabbaticals or periods of seven years required to bring in the ultimate jubilee: release from sin, the establishment of everlasting righteousness, and consecration of the temple. During the first seven sabbaticals the city of Jerusalem is restored. Then for sixty-two sabbaticals there is nothing to report. In the climactic seventieth week, Israel's King arrives and dies vicariously for his people. Strangely, desecration of the temple similar to that by Antiochus Epiphanes in the Greek empire is perpetrated by the Jewish people themselves, resulting in the destruction of

---

[46] See Gentry, "Son of Man in Daniel 7: Individual or Corporate?"

Jerusalem. These events are fulfilled in the person of Jesus of Nazareth. He is the coming King. His crucifixion is the sacrifice to end all sacrifices and the basis of the new covenant with the many. His death is "not for himself," but rather vicarious. The rejection of Jesus as Messiah and the desecration of him as the true Temple at his trial by the high priest result in judgement upon the Herodian temple, carried out eventually in A.D. 70. The notion of a gap between the sixty-ninth and seventieth week is contrary to a vision of chronological sequence. The prophecy is remarkable for its precision as it fits the events concerning Jesus of Nazareth.

Chapter Fifteen

SPEAKING THE TRUTH IN LOVE (EPHESIANS 4:15): LIFE IN THE NEW COVENANT COMMUNITY[1]

INTRODUCTION AND OVERVIEW

In the first half of Paul's letter to the church in Ephesus, all of his readers, the ancient Ephesians as well as us today, are called by the triune God to a destiny beyond our imagination. This destiny is revealed in the Father's love for us before he made the world; in the death and resurrection of his son, Jesus Christ, to free us from the destructive broken relationship between Creator and creation caused by human rebellion; and in the gift of the Spirit as his guarantee that he has not only started but will finish his work in us. He has begun a new creation through the resurrection of Jesus Christ. When Jesus burst from the tomb on that first Easter, he was the first man in the new creation. By believing in Jesus, we are joined to him. We become part of the new creation. We form the new humanity (2:15) which God is creating. Unlike the first creation, where God began by making the world and afterwards made creatures to live in his world, in the new creation he has begun by creating the new humanity and afterwards he will make the new world in which they are to live. The cross has brought not only peace in our relationship to God, but also reconciliation in ruptured human relations (2:11–18). Thus both Jew and Gentile are forged together into the new humanity, which is called the church. The doxology which begins the Ephesian letter (1:3) shows that Paul understands all this to be the blessing of God to the nations through Abraham.

Paul then explains in the second half of his letter (chapters 4–6) how we who are called by God are to fulfill his plan and purpose in practical

[1] I acknowledge with gratitude Daniel I. Block, Chip Hardy, and John Meade for constructive criticism of an earlier form of chapter 15 published as "Speaking the Truth in Love (Eph 4:15): Life in the New Covenant Community," *SBJT* 10/2 (2006): 70–87. They not only rescued me from many mistakes but stimulated my thinking in significant ways. I have especially treasured conversations with Dan Block.

terms of day-to-day living while we are still in the old world that has not yet been given final judgement. How do we live up to this destiny? First he focuses on the unity intrinsic to the covenant community of the new humanity (4:1–6), and second, he shows how the diversity within the community is in fact the gift of the risen Christ to enable us to grow up and mature (4:7–16). The goal for the new humanity is to become like Christ, the first man in the new creation.[2]

Just as Jewish rabbis discussed behaviour required by the Torah, so Paul describes next, from 4:17 to 6:20, the conduct or Christian *halakah*[3] stipulated in the new Torah,[4] the Instruction or Word of Christ.[5] He delineates the behaviour, the conduct and lifestyle, required in the new creation community. The broad outlines of this section are well known. He begins in 4:17–24 by commanding his readers to lay aside the old humanity and adopt the new humanity, and ends in 5:6–14 by talking about moving from darkness to light. These paragraphs form bookends for a well-defined unit. In between, we have specific commands and instructions about life for each member of the new covenant community. Next, Paul describes different relationships inside and outside the covenant community that are now altered and transformed by our new calling and destiny: in 5:15–33 the relationships in marriage between husband and wife, in 6:1–4 the relationships between parents and children, in 6:5–9 the relationships between masters and slaves, and in 6:10–20 our relationship to the enemy and spiritual warfare.

THE SHAPE OF THE TEXT IN EPHESIANS 4:1–6:20

While the general outline of Ephesians 4:1–6:20 is well understood, the covenantal framework intrinsic to the literary structure and the role of speaking the truth in love within the text as a whole needs to be detailed further in order to fully grasp the apostle's message.

---

[2] Combining Ephesians 4:13 and Colossians 1:18b.

[3] Note how six of the eight occurrences of the term *peripateo*, i.e., conduct, lifestyle, *halakah*, employed in Ephesians by Paul (2:2, 10; 4:1, 17 [2x]; 5:2, 8, 15) are concentrated in this section.

[4] Many Christians think of Torah mainly as law, i.e., the law of Moses. Two important facts should shape our thinking about Torah. First, the Hebrew word *tôrâ* means "direction" or "instruction." See L. Koehler and W. Baumgartner, *Hebräisches und Aramäisches Lexikon zum Alten Testament*, 3rd ed., ed. W. Baumgartner, J. J. Stamm, and B. Hartmann (Leiden, Netherlands: Brill, 1967–1995), s.v. Second, these "instructions" are given in the form of a covenant. The Torah, then, is unlike any law code in the ancient Near East. It is a set of directions for living in the framework of a covenant relationship. Here "instruction" and "Torah" are employed interchangeably to try and keep these truths in focus.

[5] Paul refers directly to the Instruction/Teaching/Torah of Christ in Ephesians 4:20. This is also equivalent to "the Word of Christ" in Colossians 3:16.

OVERVIEW OF 4:1–6:20: WHAT THE CHRISTIAN CALLING MEANS IN PRACTICAL TERMS

1. Unity, diversity, and maturity in the body of Christ	4:1–16
2. Life according to the new creation community	4:17–5:14
A. From old humanity to new	4:17–24
B. Specific instructions	4:25–5:5
A'. From darkness to light	5:6–14
3. Relationships within the new creation community	5:15–6:9
4. Relationships without: dark powers and spiritual warfare	6:10–20

The section from 4:1–6:20 is arranged in four parts: (1) 4:1–16 forms an introduction to the section as a whole, (2) 4:17–5:14 represents the general instructions or stipulations of the new covenant for each individual member of the new humanity, (3) 5:15–6:9 explicates how patience and humble submission urged at the outset in 4:2 is exhibited in particular in different relationships within the community, and (4) 6:10–20 fulfills a double role in (a) dealing with the dark powers that oppose the new humanity and (b) recapitulating and summarising the section (and letter) as a whole.

There is, in a way, a parallel structure between this text and Exodus 19:1–23:33. Exodus 19 forms an introduction to the covenant/instructions given to the people of God, Exodus 20 constitutes the Ten Commandments (literally the Ten Words),[6] the heart of the covenant and of Yahweh's instruction to his people, and Exodus 21–23 details how the Ten Words work out in practical terms in different life situations. After the introduction in Ephesians 4:1–16, the section 4:17–5:14 is the Teaching of Christ for his people and, as such, is the new covenant and Torah or Instruction in a nutshell. Thus 5:15–6:20 details the outworking of this teaching in different life situations. Contrary to the ideals of American heritage in which we focus on the individual, Paul begins by focusing on community and on our corporate life together (4:1–16). Then, and only then, from 4:17 onwards, does he deal with day-to-day life as individuals. Even then, he is concerned largely with relationships. Individualism runs strong in Western culture and in the American dream. We exalt the individual who can rise from circumstances of great deprivation or poverty and excel in sports, education, or acting, to become a national idol or even the president. There is, however, a strong

---

[6] Called the "ten words" in Exodus 34:28; Deuteronomy 4:13; and 10:4. They are referred to as commandments in the New Testament (Matthew 5; 19:17–19; Mark 10:19; Luke 18:20; Rom. 13:9; 7:7–8; Eph. 6:2; cf. 1 Tim. 1:9, 10).

emphasis in this text, as well as elsewhere in the Scriptures, on our belonging to a community and on our corporate role and responsibilities before considering our role as individuals.

The *key part* of the section, then, is 4:17–5:14, which details the covenant and its requirements for the renewed people of God. This part is further divided into three units. The units at the beginning and at the end are both general and motivational. The middle unit, sandwiched between these bookends, contains the practical and specific instructions. How Paul presents his teaching can be very instructive pedagogically. He devotes more space to encouragement and motivation than to hammering people with commands.

BEHAVIOURAL REQUIREMENTS OF THE NEW CREATION/COVENANT COMMUNITY

The middle unit is 4:25–5:5. These verses are clearly marked as a unit because Paul delivers six instructions. Each instruction is structured in the same way. First the command is expressed negatively, second the command is given positively, and thirdly, the command is supported by a motivation clause. Slight variation from this pattern is entailed in the second and sixth instruction. Thus the beginning of each of these instructions is marked off formally as seen in table 15.1 (5:1–2 constitutes an interlude, which will be explained shortly):

Table 15.1: Behavioural Requirements of the New Creation/Covenant Community

(1) Do not use falsehood but speak truth	4:25
(2) Do use anger but do not sin	4:26–27
(3) Do not steal but work to give to the needy	4:28
(4) Do not use corrupt words but edify	4:29–30
(5) Do not have a mean spirit but be kind	4:31–32
Love One Another	**5:1–2**
(6) No impure actions/words or greed	5:3–5

The beginning and ending of this middle part (4:25–5:5) are also clearly marked. The conjunction "therefore" (*dio*) in verse 25 identifies implications from the preceding unit and the asyndeton (lack of clause connector) between 5:5 and 6 is a strong signal to mark the end of the second part and beginning of the third.

As already observed, the first and third parts, 4:17–24 and 5:6–14 respectively, form bookends to the central unit. They are the prologue and epilogue and are communicating essentially the same thing. Paul opens with a general appeal and exhortation to lay aside the old humanity and its lifestyle and adopt the new. The appeal is communicated metaphorically in terms of taking off old clothes and putting on new. Paul closes the section with motivation based upon images of darkness and light. Negatively, Christians must avoid greed and immorality because this behaviour will be judged. Positive motivation arises from the change which occurred when they were joined to Christ. This change is not a matter of being in an environment or surroundings of darkness and moving to a context of light. Rather, they themselves *were* darkness. When they were converted, it was their lives, not their surroundings, that were transformed. They are now recreated as light.

The major section which follows, from 5:15 to 6:9, is frequently designated the "household code,"[7] an expression which may obscure important connections between it and the preceding section in 4:17–5:14. The introduction to 5:15–6:9 and bridge between it and the preceding section are verses 15–21 of chapter 5. Here, getting drunk with wine as the doorway to all the corrupt practises of the old humanity is contrasted with being filled by the Spirit as the divine means for fulfilling Christ's instructions to those connected to him as the new humanity. Recently, commentators and exegetes have clarified considerably the meaning of "being filled with the Spirit." This does not refer to the Holy Spirit as the content filling us. As Hoehner notes in his magisterial work, "nowhere in the NT does πληρόω followed by ἐν plus the dative indicate content."[8] Instead, it indicates the means provided by God the Spirit for letting the teaching of our King (i.e., the Torah of Christ) shape our thinking and conduct, as the parallel to this verse in Colossians 3:16 makes plain. The participles in Ephesians 5:19–21 spell this out. When we incorporate Christ's teaching in songs, both horizontally (to one another) and vertically (to the Lord), constantly give thanks for all things, and demonstrate the appropriate submission of certain groups to others in various relationships specified within the community, we are enabled to extend the instructions of 4:17–5:14 in practical ways to all of life in the new covenant community. Paul had spoken specifically of the instruction of the Messiah in 4:20–21. This instruction is listed in specific stipulations in 4:25–5:5. Now the introduction to the next major section, 5:15–21, shows the divine means by which these instructions,

---

[7] See, e.g., Peter T. O'Brien, *The Letter to the Ephesians*, Pillar New Testament Commentary (Grand Rapids, MI: Eerdmans, 1999), 405–409.

[8] Harold W. Hoehner, *Ephesians: An Exegetical Commentary* (Grand Rapids, MI: Baker, 2002), 703.

i.e., "the word of Christ," are to be lived out in the new humanity. Thus the section 5:15–6:9 is linked to 4:17–5:14 in exactly the same way as Exodus 21–23 is linked to the Ten Words in Exodus 20 or as the Specific Stipulations in Deuteronomy 12–26 flow from the basic instruction in 4:44–11:32.

Before the covenantal framework of this literary structure can be adequately appreciated, however, first the centrality of speaking the truth in love to the larger whole must be noted, and also what Paul means by "speaking the truth in love."

THE CENTRALITY OF SPEAKING THE TRUTH IN LOVE

If there is any way to summarise in just a few words the instructions for behaviour and conduct in the new creation community, it is "speaking the truth in love." This expression is central to the structure of the text and forms as well a complete and perfect summary of the instructions of the new covenant, at least on the horizontal level.

The introduction to the second half of the letter is Ephesians 4:1–16, which deals with integral unity, diversity, and maturity in the new humanity. Here Paul describes how the risen and reigning Christ has given gifts to the church. The gifts are leaders who equip the people to serve and build up the community. Negatively, the church must not be like children who are easily deceived. Positively, the church must grow up and mature. Verse 15 explains that this comes about by speaking the truth in love. We can see, then, that this is the key statement in this introductory section, and the key to the whole, because this section introduces the practical part of the letter.

The citation from Psalm 68 in Ephesians 4:8 reveals that Paul sees the incarnation, death, resurrection, and ascension of Jesus as parallel to the deliverance and reign of Yahweh through the giving of the covenant/law at Sinai.[9] Psalm 68 recalls the triumphs of the Lord in the history of Israel as he revealed himself in an earth-shattering way at Sinai, as he led his people through the wilderness, as he defeated the Canaanites, and as he chose to set his sanctuary on Mount Zion. When he entered his sanctuary, he acquired captives and received gifts among men. The psalmist then looks to a future when not only is Israel united in the worship of the Lord, but all nations acknowledge the rule of Yahweh. This is fulfilled by Jesus, the Davidic Son

---

[9] Justin Martyr eloquently connected Jesus' crucifixion and his reign: "the Lord has reigned from the tree" (ὁ κύριος ἐβασίλευσεν ἀπὸ τοῦ ξύλου, *First Apology* 41.4).

who is now on the throne. By his death on the cross, Christ has met the big enemies of sin, Satan, and death and has utterly routed them. He has ransomed us from our sin, defeated the dark powers, and conquered death. His resurrection is not a coming back to life but the beginning of an entirely new creation, a new world. And after his resurrection, Jesus ascended to the highest heaven. This is none other than the one who is both Davidic King and Yahweh himself, entering the heavenly sanctuary/Zion. Just as Yahweh gave his covenant and Torah (instruction) at Sinai and began to reign among his people from the sanctuary, so Paul pictures Jesus as Lord giving his new covenant and instruction and beginning to rule among his people from heaven.

The centre of the second half of the letter is 4:25–5:5 (bounded on either side with 4:17–24 and 5:6–14 as bookends). Here Paul details, as the instruction or Torah of Christ (see esp. 4:20), the requirements of the new covenant in six commands. It is noteworthy that the first of these six commands is about speaking truth with one another and that sandwiched between the fifth and sixth instructions at the end is a summary statement showing that all six commands are about conduct characterised by love (5:1–2) and in imitation of God our Father. According to the structure of the text, then, speaking the truth in love is both at the heart of the new covenant stipulations and is also a short summary of them.

This central notion of speaking the truth in love was expressed in 4:15 by the Greek verb *alētheuō* (ἀληθεύω), whereas here in 4:25 the verb "speak" plus the noun "truth" is used as its object. For the former word, *alētheuō*, Bauer's lexicon gives the meaning "be truthful, speak the truth."[10] Neither the *Greek-English Lexicon* of Liddell-Scott-Jones nor the newer *Diccionario Griego-Español* by Adrados casts further light on the meaning.[11] The exhaustive *Repertorio Bibliográfico de la Lexicografía Griega* lists research by only two scholars.[12] One of them is Père Spicq, whose *Notes de lexicographie néo-testamentaire* offers far more than R. Bultmann in Kittel's *Theological Dictionary of the New Testament*.[13] Spicq cites the *New Jerusalem Bible*

---

[10] "wahrhaftig sein, die Wahrheit reden"; Walter Bauer, *Griechisch-deutsches Wörterbuch zu den Schriften des Neuen Testaments und der frühchristlichen Literatur*, 6th ed., rev. and ed. K. Aland and B. Aland (Berlin: Walter de Gruyter, 1988), 70.

[11] See H. G. Liddell, R. Scott, and H. S. Jones, *A Greek-English Lexicon*, 9th ed. with revised supplement (Oxford: Oxford University Press, 1996), s.v. ἀληθεύω; and Francisco R. Adrados, *Diccionario Griego-Español*, vol. 1 (Madrid: Consejo Superior de Investigaciones Científicas, 1989), ἀληθεύω.

[12] Pilar Boned Colera and Juan Rodríguez Somolinos, *Repertorio Bibliográfico de la Lexicografía Griega, Diccionario Griego-Español Anejo 3* (Madrid: Consejo Superior de Investagaciones Científicas, 1998).

[13] See Ceslas P. Spicq, *Theological Lexicon of the New Testament*, trans. and ed. James D. Ernest (Peabody, MA: Hendrickson, 1994), 1:81–82; and Gerhard Kittel, ed., *Theological Dictionary of the New Testament*, trans. and ed. Geoffrey W. Bromiley (Grand Rapids, MI: Eerdmans, 1964), 1:251.

approvingly, "live by the truth and in love." Morphologically, Greek verbs ending in -euō have the meaning "to act in a certain capacity or role."[14] The verb alētheuō, then, means "to act truthfully." Since this kind of action frequently involves our speech, a common meaning is "to speak truthfully." While the first of the six commands given by Paul is specifically about speaking, and indeed four or five of the six instructions either may or necessarily involve speech, "acting or being truthful" does sum up all of them. This is as far as linguistics and lexicography can take us.

And this acting or being truthful must be expressed in love, as the paragraph in 5:1–2 inserted between the fifth and sixth command indicates. This paragraph is a summary of all the commands and instructions. First, it condenses everything to one command or instruction. Second, it explains why this behaviour, this conduct, this lifestyle is required of us: our actions and our words come from who we are. 5:1–2 is directly related to 4:24, where we see that we have become part of the new creation in which the divine image is restored. The conduct of the new humanity must reflect the character and conduct of God himself. Third, since the cross is at the heart of who God is, it is also at the heart of who we are as his children. We can therefore define love as a *covenant commitment* to the other person, demonstrated in actions that seek the well-being of the other person.

Parallels between this communication of the new covenant and the Ten Words at the heart of the old covenant are hard to miss. The first four of the Ten Commands have to do with loving God and the last six have to do with loving our neighbour. In the new covenant, loving God has been replaced by loving Jesus, and loving our neighbour has been replaced by the one command of the Lord Jesus to love one another (see John 14:15 and 15:12). Since Paul is dealing with life in the covenant community, he focuses here on the horizontal part of the new Torah. Remarkably, this is set forth in six instructions just as in the old covenant and can also be summarised by loving our neighbour (Lev. 19:18; Matt. 22:39). In discussing the meaning of the expression in Leviticus 19:18, Malamat concludes that it means "to provide assistance" or "be useful" to our neighbour[15]—a definition harmonious with the greater revelation at the cross. In the middle section, then, the importance of speaking truth as a way

---

[14] J. H. Moulton and W. F. Howard, *A Grammar of New Testament Greek, Vol. II: Accidence and Word-Formation* (Edinburgh: T. & T. Clark, 1929), 398–400.

[15] A. Malamat, "'You Shall Love Your Neighbour as Yourself': A Case of Misinterpretation," in *Die Hebräische Bibel und ihre zweifache Nachgeschichte: Festschrift für Rolf Rendtorff zum 65. Geburtstag*, ed. E. Blum, C. Macholz, and E. W. Stegemann (Neukirchen-Vluyn, Germany: Neukirchner, 1990), 111–115.

of showing love is clear because it is the first command. Ephesians 5:15–6:9 shows how this is worked out in particular relationships.

The final section at the end of the letter, 6:10–20, as already noted, fulfills a dual role. Here Paul deals with the dark powers that oppose the new humanity and at the same time recapitulates and summarises the section (and letter) as a whole.[16] Drawing from Isaiah 11:4–5 and 59:17, Paul exhorts the church to adopt and use Yahweh's own armour for warfare.[17] What is fitting for the head is also fitting for the body in the new creation. And what is the first piece of the armour to be mentioned? It is the belt of *truth*!

We can see, then, at the beginning, in the middle, and at the end, the prominence given to speaking the truth in the arrangement and structure of the text. If there is any way to summarise in just a few words the instructions for behaviour and lifestyle in the new creation community, it is "speaking the truth in love."

THE OLD TESTAMENT ROOTS OF "SPEAKING THE TRUTH IN LOVE"

It is clear that the expression "speaking the truth in love" is central to the message and structure of this text as a whole. But precisely what is being communicated by this expression must be explored further. Is it simply being honest and telling the truth, yet at the same time doing it in a kindly way? Is this the way for the church to grow and mature until it measures up to Christ himself? There is an even deeper issue. If the expression "speaking the truth in love" summarises living up to the standards of the new humanity, what, beyond mere obedience to the commands of Christ, is the motivation for living this way? An illustration may help at this point. In your church, you find a person who claims to be a Christian but whose actions evince the sexual immorality forbidden in the last of Paul's six commands. You might think, "Well, I have to go to this person and in a loving way tell them the truth. I must tell them this is sin in the eyes of God and they must abandon this relationship." Is this what Christ's instruction for the new humanity through Paul about speaking the truth in love really means?

Notice that the command to speak the truth, the first of the six instructions in 4:25–5:5, is actually a citation from the Old Testament. Paul is

---

16 See, e.g., O'Brien, *Letter to the Ephesians*, 459.

17 The expression "man of war" is applied to Yahweh both in the exodus (Ex. 15:3) and in descriptions of the new exodus (Isaiah 42:13), which is fulfilled in Jesus Christ.

directly quoting Zechariah 8:16, and this citation opens a window into the frame of reference for his thinking. When Jesus and the apostles quote from the Old Testament, they expect you to know the context, because the part that is quoted is usually just the tip of the iceberg. Unfortunately, readers today are not so well versed in the Old Testament and so some discussion of the background is necessary.

The prophet Zechariah wrote to the Jewish people who were returning to their homeland after years of exile in Babylon. The book begins with a call to repent and a promise that if the people turn away from their sins and return to the Lord, he will return to them (Zech. 1:3). A series of apocalyptic night visions from chapters 1–6 unfold the details of the return to Yahweh. Through these visions the prophet announces a return from exile far greater than just leaving Babylon and returning to Jerusalem. Their sins will be forgiven, the broken covenant will be renewed, the city of God will be restored, the temple will be rebuilt, and God the Lord will return to live once more in the midst of his people as King. Table 15.2 outlines the development of these themes in the night visions:

Table 15.2: Summary of Zechariah's Apocalyptic Night Visions

1:7–17	A. Yahweh is omniscient King: he knows the problem of the exiles
1:18–21	B. Four horns and craftsmen: punishing nations who exiled Judah
2:1–13	The return to Jerusalem and restoration of Zion (i.e., the exiles)
3:1–10	C. Office of high priest restored—symbol of future removal of sin
4:1–14	C'. Power and presence of Yahweh through leaders to rebuild temple
5:1–4	B'. Israelite covenant and curses effective in restoration community
5:5–11	The sin/wickedness of the returned exiles removed to Babylon
6:1–8	A'. Yahweh is omnipotent king: punishing Babylon who mistreated Zion

The programme of restoration and return outlined in the night visions is crowned by chapters 7–8, a climactic section which moves from fasting to feasting, i.e., a question about fasting now that the exile is over, is answered with a proclamation that fasts become feasts in the restored Zion. Mike Butterworth has demonstrated that the entire section is a chiastically structured unit—the first paragraph matches the last paragraph, the second matches the second-to-last, and so on, as illustrated in table 15.3.[18]

Table 15.3: Chiastic Structure of Zechariah 7–8

A 2 Bethel sends men to entreat the favour of Yahweh

  B 3 Question about fasting

    5–7 Off-putting response: What was behind the fasting?

    Remember the words of the former prophets

      when the land was settled and prosperous

    C 9–10 Give court decisions that are just

    Show compassion and loyalty in relationships

    Do not devise evil and harm against one another

      D 11–14 They refused the words of the former prophets

      Therefore came great WRATH from the Lord

      The people were exiled among the nations

      The land became desolate

        E 2–8a I was jealous with great jealousy and wrath

        I will . . . *dwell in the midst of Jerusalem*

        Promise of blessing for a **remnant of this people**

        I will **save** from . . . east and west . . .

        They will *dwell in the midst of Jerusalem*

          F 8b They will be my people and I will be

          their God

        E' 9–13 Let your hands be strong

        Promise of blessing for a **remnant of this people**

        You were a curse among the nations

        I will **save** you

        You will be a blessing

        Fear not. Let your hands be strong

      D' 14–15 As I purposed evil when . . . provoked me to

      WRATH

      So now I purpose to do good. *Fear not.*

    C' 16–17 Give court decisions that are just and bring

    well-being

    Speak truth with one another

    Do not devise evil and harm against one another

  B' 18–19 Fasts will become feasts, so love shalom and truth

A' 20–23 Many will come to entreat the favour of Yahweh

Blessing will flow to the nations through Jews[19]

---

[18] Mike Butterworth, *Structure and the Book of Zechariah*, JSOTSup 130 (Sheffield, UK: Sheffield Academic Press, 1992), 149–165.

[19] Adapted from Butterworth, *Structure and the Book of Zechariah*, 163.

Chiastic literary structures function to emphasise what is at the centre. At the centre here is 8:8b, which employs the Covenant Formula, "They will be my people and I will be their God in faithfulness and righteousness." Just a few lines earlier, in 8:3, we have the remarkable words, "I will return to Zion and I will settle in the midst of Jerusalem. And Jerusalem will be called the City of Truth and the mountain of the LORD of Heaven's Armies will be called the Holy Mountain." This is a text, then, that focuses on the covenant between God and his people being renewed and the return of Yahweh to Zion. As a result, Jerusalem will be called the city of truth. This is exactly the topic and theme of Ephesians 4:1–6:20. Paul is describing the new covenant and showing that "speaking the truth" results in the covenant community life. Appropriately, he cites Zechariah 8:16, since this verse describes in practical terms what it means for Jerusalem to regain its title as City of Truth: "But this is what you must do: Tell the truth to each other. Render verdicts in your courts that are just and that lead to peace" (NLT).[20] Clearly, speaking the truth, in Zechariah, is operating in the context of social justice within the community.

Now if we are discerning readers of Zechariah 8, we will quickly realize that Zechariah is reacting and responding to the earlier message of Isaiah. The book of Zechariah is, in fact, dense in allusions to earlier portions of Scripture, particularly Isaiah. And he uses earlier passages of Scripture in much the same way as Jesus and the apostles did—or better, apostolic interpretation of Scripture follows models already found in the Old Testament. We must pursue the trail of the City of Truth back to Isaiah.

Isaiah commences his preaching like a thunderstorm. His opening sermon is full of lightning and thunder. God is so upset with the behaviour of his covenant people that the prophet exclaims, "the faithful city has become a whore, a prostitute" (1:21). The Hebrew word for faithful here comes from the same root as the word for truth in Zechariah 8:3 and 16.

The messages of the prophets are sometimes quite shocking. Prophets functioned as spokesmen for God, raised up to call attention to the failure of the people of God to be covenant keepers. They confronted the people of God and exposed the clever and devious ways by which they had gradually slipped away from the standards defined by the covenant at Sinai for a proper relationship with God and proper treatment of each other. The prophets were

---

[20] Zechariah 8:17 reinforces this teaching negatively, just as verse 16 expresses it positively: "Now do not devise evil in your heart against each other and do not love false oaths."

giants in the art and skill of communication, employing every conceivable method possible, yet all their sentences, their promises and threats, are based on the covenant God made with Israel, especially as found in its fullest form in the book of Deuteronomy.[21]

As Isaiah and other prophets sought to apply the covenant with Moses and Israel to their situation and times, they found new ways to condense and summarise in a single sentence or even phrase the apparently unwieldy mass of commands and instructions in the Torah. Even the Ten Words/ Commandments upon which some six hundred or so instructions are based could be further condensed and summarised.[22]

The heart of Isaiah's message is that the covenant between God and Israel given by Moses at Sinai is broken. He summarises this covenant, the Ten Commandments, using expressions or idioms for social justice and faithful loyal love, or being truthful in love. His expression for social justice can be described and illustrated first. Note Isaiah's prophecy in 16:5:

> In love a throne will be established;
> > in faithfulness a man will sit on it—
> > one from the house of David—
> > one who in judging seeks justice
> > and speeds the cause of righteousness. (NIV)

In contrast to the regime of the kings of Isaiah's time, a future king is promised who will rule in justice and righteousness. Now, according to the Hebrew poetry—which is based upon lines in parallel pairs—justice is matched in the first line by righteousness in the second. Normally in prose when the words "justice" and "righteousness" are coordinated, they form a single concept or idea: social justice. This is a figure of speech known as a hendiadys, one concept expressed through two words. The word pair becomes an idiom expressing a single thought that is both different from and greater than just putting the two words together. Just as one cannot analyse "butterfly" in English by studying "butter" and "fly," so one cannot determine the meaning of this expression by analysing "justice" and "righteousness" individually. Hebrew poetry, however, allows such a word pair to be split so that half is in one line of the couplet and half in the parallel line.

---

[21] See especially Claus Westermann, *Basic Forms of Prophetic Speech*, trans. Hugh Clayton White (Louisville: Westminster/John Knox, 1991).
[22] See Matthew 22:36–40.

Now, Isaiah's promise in 16:5 is based upon Deuteronomy 17. Verses 16–20 of Deuteronomy 17 describe the manner in which the future king of Israel is to exercise his responsibilities. Following three negative commands in verses 16–17 come three positive commands in verses 18–20—all relating to Torah: (1) the king shall copy the Torah; (2) the king shall have the Torah with him; and (3) the king shall read the Torah.[23] In other words, the only positive requirement is that the king embody Torah as a model citizen. This is exactly what Isaiah is saying in 16:5, only he employs the concept "social justice," expressed by the broken word pair "justice-righteousness" as a *summary* for the Torah.[24] Deuteronomy calls for a king who implements the Torah in his regime, and Isaiah predicts a king who will deliver social justice in his rule. They are saying the same thing.

The meaning of the word pair "justice-righteousness" both as an *expression* for social justice and as a *summary* of the covenant/Torah is also clearly illustrated, in particular in Isaiah 5, a damning indictment of the "City of Truth," constructed as a series of six woes. Another instance of the broken word pair "justice-righteousness" is embedded in 5:7, the headline for the section, showing that the violation of social justice is at the heart of all six woes. In the first woe the prophet thunders about land-grabbing: "Woe to those who add house to house and field to field" (5:8). The second woe (5:11) condemns the partying of the nouveaux riches, whose money came from mistreating the poor and vulnerable. The final four woes are all ways of elaborating the original charge of perverting social justice. The last woe is the climax and summarises by combining the two original charges of gaining wealth by social injustice and living a life of pleasure to spend that wealth. Between the two groups of woes Isaiah announces punishments based upon the retributive justice of the covenant/Torah. Of major import in this judgement unit is the broken word pair "justice-righteousness" (5:16) attributed to the Lord in contrast to the Judean nobility: he is completely devoted to

---

[23] I am indebted to Daniel I. Block for the privilege of consulting a preliminary version of his new commentary, *Deuteronomy*, NIV Application Commentary (Grand Rapids, MI: Zondervan, 2012). Part of his research is available in Daniel I. Block, "The Burden of Leadership: The Mosaic Paradigm of Kingship (Deut. 17:14–20)," in *How I Love Your Torah, O Lord! Studies in the Book of Deuteronomy* (Eugene, OR: Cascade, 2011), 118–139 (originally published in *Bibliotheca Sacra* 162 [2005]: 259–278).

[24] Some 21 or 22 instances of the word pair "justice-righteousness," frequently split over poetic parallelism, occur in Isaiah: 1:21; 1:27; 5:7; 5:16; 9:6(7 EV); 11:4; 16:5; 26:9; 28:17; 32:1; 32:16; 33:5; 43:26; 50:8; 51:5; 56:1; 54:17; 58:2 (2x); 59:4; 59:9; 59:14. In 11:4, 51:5, and 59:4, verbal forms of the root *šāphat* are employed instead of the noun *mišpat*; the instance in 51:5 is not listed in the rather exhaustive and excellent study of Leclerc, although it appears as valid as the instance in 11:4. See Thomas L. Leclerc, *Yahweh Is Exalted in Justice: Solidarity and Conflict in Isaiah* (Minneapolis: Fortress, 2001), especially 10–13, 88, 157.

(i.e., holy) and exalted in demonstrating social justice; indeed, the covenant/ Torah is an expression of his own character.

The economic and social situation addressed by Isaiah in chapter 5 signals the breakdown of conventions governing ownership of property.[25] Prior to the monarchic period, Israelite economy was based on farming and shepherding. Property was inherited and preserved within *clans*—a kin group between the extended family and the tribe. Diverse instructions in the Mosaic covenant were given to preserve economic equilibrium in ownership of property and to protect the poor and powerless, e.g., laws concerning boundary markers,[26] the inheritance rights of females,[27] levirate marriage,[28] *gō 'ēl* responsibilities,[29] and jubilee/sabbatical years.[30] Two factors brought changes to this social system: monarchy and urbanization. With the advent of kingship, land could be acquired by the crown: sometimes corruptly as in the case of Naboth's vineyard (1 Kings 21) and sometimes legally through the confiscation of the estates of criminals and traitors. Thus, a family inheritance could be enlarged by a royal grant. Samuel warned about this in 1 Samuel 8:14–15. Recipients of such royal largesse would live in the capital city and eat every day at the king's table, all the while enjoying the revenue of their holdings. In this way, important nobles and officials, especially those who ingratiated themselves to the king and his henchmen, were in a position to acquire by legal and illegal means the property of those vulnerable to oppression.

On the other hand, the development and growth of cities created new ties between peasant farmers and a new class of merchants who usually lived in the towns and influenced public affairs. When a farmer suffered economic setbacks from crop failure due to drought or locusts, for example, he would turn to a merchant or moneylender in town. He would either be charged interest for a loan or be forced to cultivate land belonging to others on a share-cropping or tenant basis. We have documents from the Jewish community in Elephantine, Egypt, from the fifth century B.C. that tell of Jews who had to pay interest rates of 5 percent per month. When unpaid interest is added to the capital, the average annual rate is 60 percent.[31]

---

[25] This description of the background to the social situation in Isaiah 5 is adapted from and based on Leclerc, *Yahweh Is Exalted in Justice*, 59–60, who brings together many seminal studies on the topic.

[26] Deuteronomy 19:14; 27:17.

[27] Numbers 26:33; 27:1–11; 36:1–13.

[28] Deuteronomy 25:5–10; Ruth 4:5, 10.

[29] Redemption of property (Lev. 25:23–28), of persons (25:47–55), of blood (Numbers 35), levirate marriage (Ruth 4:5, 10) by the nearest relative.

[30] Leviticus 25.

[31] If one considers compounded (or unpaid) interest, the rate would be higher.

As agricultural plots become the property of a single owner (perhaps an absentee landlord who is a city dweller), as peasants become indentured serfs or even slaves, and as their goods and services are received as payments on loans, the gap between the rich and poor widens. Since land ownership translates into economic and political power, issues of property rights and taxes, as well as laws concerning bankruptcy, foreclosures, and loans, play into the hands of the rich, thus aiding and abetting a gap in power as well.

The situation which Isaiah condemns is graphically portrayed: large estates amassed by adding field to field on which sit "large and beautiful homes" (5:9b). The acquisition of land comes as debts are foreclosed and the property is expropriated. Since all of this is done according to the laws of the marketplace and by statute, it is all strictly legal—but it is also utterly immoral and violates the social justice of the Torah. This is a powerful demonstration of the parable of the vineyard at work: everything looks legal and proper on the outside, but a closer inspection shows the grapes are rotten and stinking and stunted. The image of a landowner dwelling all alone in the midst of the country is a picture of great horror. While American society idolises and praises rugged individualism, ancient Israel valued the community over the individual. The interests of the group were more important than those of a single individual, no matter how clever or skilled and talented the entrepreneur. It is difficult, therefore, for us to feel the horror of ending up as a society of one.

Readers may well wonder if discussion of Isaiah 5 is not a digression from the topic at hand, i.e., of discovering the meaning of "speaking the truth" in Ephesians. Yet, as already noted, in the last section of Ephesians when Paul exhorts the church to adopt and use Yahweh's own armour for warfare, he draws specifically from Isaiah 11:4–5 and 59:17. The first passage brings to a climax promises of a coming scion of David, indeed a new David, whose rule will be characterised by social justice. Isaiah 11:3b–5 says,

> He will not judge by what he sees with his eyes,
>   or decide by what he hears with his ears;
> but with righteousness he will judge the needy,
>   with justice he will give decisions for the poor of the earth.
> He will strike the earth with the rod of his mouth;
>   with the breath of his lips he will slay the wicked.
> Righteousness will be his belt
>   and faithfulness the sash around his waist. (NIV)

Paul's "belt of truth" comes from the last part of verse 5: "faithfulness [will be] the sash around his waist." The word "faithfulness" translates *'ĕmûnâ* and is related to *'ĕmet*, the usual word for truth. Both are derived from a root meaning to be firm or faithful. The NIV speaks of the belt and the sash of the king. The Hebrew word actually means girdle or loincloth. This is the most basic garment of all our clothing. Even today underclothes are called foundation garments. The foundation of this kingdom is righteousness and faithfulness. Verse 4 combines justice and righteousness to communicate the idea of social justice. The future king will be a true son of God as required by 2 Samuel 7:14–15 because he will exhibit in his rule the social justice of the Torah (Deut. 17:16–20), which is an expression of the character of Yahweh himself. Chapter 59, the other Isaianic text from which Paul draws his depiction of the armour of the Lord, contains three occurrences of the broken word pair "justice-righteousness." It is significant, then, that in citing from Isaiah 11 and 59, almost one-quarter of the occurrences of this word pair in Isaiah are alluded to by Paul in his description of the armour of God.[32]

Discussion of the Isaianic background to Ephesians can be concluded by returning to Isaiah 16:5. The first part of the verse contains another word pair split over lines in poetic parallelism: lovingkindness and truth (Hebrew: *ḥesed* and *'ĕmet*).

This word pair is also a *summary* of the relationship entailed in the covenant/Torah. It is difficult to find an equivalent for *ḥesed* in English that adequately encompasses all it means (usually "lovingkindness" in NASB), and this term has occasioned numerous studies during the last hundred years. It is normally used in a covenant relationship between two parties—a stronger party and a weaker party. It refers to the obligation of the stronger party to help the weaker party. An excellent example is Genesis 47:29:

> When the time for Israel to die drew near, he called his son Joseph and said to him, "Please, if I have found favor in your sight, place now your hand under my thigh and deal with me in kindness and faithfulness. Please do not bury me in Egypt." (NASB)

Here we have a family relationship, a father and a son. In this context the son is stronger and the dying father is weaker. The son must show covenant

---

[32] Isaiah 11:4; 59:4, 9, 14.

kindness and loyalty by fulfilling the father's wish to be buried in Canaan. Genesis 47:29 employs the same word pair as in Isaiah 16:5.

The function of the word pair lovingkindness and truth (*ḥesed* and *'ĕmet*) as a summary of the covenant/Torah is illustrated nicely by Psalm 117. Although this is the shortest hymn in the Israel's Hymnal, it functions like a dissertation abstract, summing up the whole: Yahweh is to be praised for his covenantal faithfulness and love. This, in sum, is what Israel has experienced in covenant relationship with God.

THE COVENANT AS SOCIAL JUSTICE AND TRUE HUMANITY

We have considered the word pairs "justice-righteousness" and "loving-kindness-truth" as summaries of the covenant/Torah. Both social justice and faithful loyal love are expressions of the character of Yahweh and of conduct expected in the covenant community where Yahweh is King. Although Paul's expression "speaking the truth in love" is closer linguistically to the word pair "lovingkindness-truth," both his direct and indirect use of Isaiah and Zechariah show his thinking is also based upon the word pair "justice-righteousness."

Before returning to Ephesians 4–6, a brief sketch of the prehistory of the Mosaic covenant/Torah can cast further light on both the covenantal framework of Paul's teaching and the meaning of "speaking the truth in love." Without consideration of how the communication in Ephesians fits into the larger story, our understanding will be flat and one-dimensional.

The concepts of faithful love and social justice are actually found on the opening pages of Scripture. According to Genesis 1:26–28, humans are created as the divine image. Although gallons of ink have been spilled in the interpretation of the divine image, space permits here only a brief explanation summing up detailed study of this text. The creation of humans as the divine image involves a covenant relationship between humans and the creator God on the one hand and a covenant relationship between humans and the creation on the other hand. It is important to note that the divine image describes who we are as humans, how we are "hard-wired," our ontology. An understanding of the divine image in merely functional or relational terms is false.

The covenantal relationship with the creator God may be captured by the term "sonship" and is implied by Genesis 5:1–3. The covenantal relationship between humans and the creation can be summed up by the terms kingship and servanthood. Earlier we saw how the ninth-century-B.C. Tell Fakhariyeh Inscription uses the same words found in Genesis 1:26: *ṣalmā'* ("image") refers to the king's majestic self and power in relation to his subjects, while *dĕmûtā'* ("likeness") refers to the king's petitionary role and relation to the deity.[33] Thus the ancient Near Eastern data confirm and correspond exactly to this exegesis of the biblical text.

Genesis 2:4–25 casts further light on the divine image, showing that the Adamic son is like a priest in a garden sanctuary. He must first learn the ways of God in order to exercise the rule of God as God himself would.[34] Adam is the precursor to the king of Deuteronomy 17, whose life and rule are drenched in the Torah of Yahweh. What is implied is that the faithful loyal love and social justice in the character of God himself will define both the God-human covenantal relationship and the human-world covenantal relationship.

The larger story of Scripture moves rapidly to show that Israel inherited this Adamic role.[35] Yahweh refers to the nation as his son in Exodus 4:22–23. The divine purpose in the covenant established between God and Israel at Sinai is unfolded in Exodus 19:3–6. As a kingdom of priests, they will function to make the ways of God known to the nations and also bring the nations into a right relationship to God. Since Israel is located geographically on the one and only communications link between the great superpowers of the ancient world, in this position she will show the nations how to have a right relationship to God, how to treat each other in a truly human way, and how to be faithful stewards of the earth's resources. This is the meaning of Israel's sonship.

Within the Mosaic covenant, Deuteronomy 17 intimates that the king will be the leader in this role. Earlier we noted that the key and only requirement is that Israel's king model in his own behaviour and conduct and hence implement in his rule the faithful loyal love and social justice of the Lord himself as enshrined in the covenant/Torah.[36]

---

[33] W. Randall Garr, "'Image' and 'Likeness' in the Inscription from Tell Fakhariyeh," *Israel Exploration Journal* 50/3–4 (2003): 227–234.

[34] See Gordon J. Wenham, "Sanctuary Symbolism in the Garden of Eden Story," in *I Studied Inscriptions from before the Flood: Ancient Near Eastern, Literary, and Linguistic Approaches to Genesis 1–11*, ed. R. S. Hess and D. T. Tsumura, Sources for Biblical and Theological Study 4 (Winona Lake, IN: Eisenbrauns: 1994), 399–404; William J. Dumbrell, *The Search for Order: Biblical Eschatology in Focus* (Grand Rapids, MI: Baker, 1994), 24–25; and M. Hutter, "Adam als Gärtner und König (Gen. 2:8, 15)," *Biblische Zeitschrift* 30 (1985): 258–262.

[35] Exodus 15:17 shows that Canaan becomes for Israel what the garden sanctuary was for Adam. See also N. T. Wright, *The Climax of the Covenant* (Minneapolis: Fortress, 1991), 21–23.

[36] See Block, "Burden of Leadership."

At the heart of the divine image is a right relationship to God on the one hand and a right relationship to the world on the other. It can be summarised by social justice or by lovingkindness and truth, i.e., being truthful in love. Adam and Eve rebelled against God, and chaos and death resulted. God made a new start with Noah, but this, too, ended in chaos and destruction. Finally, he made another new start with Abraham and his descendants. The covenant at Sinai shows Abraham's seed how to have a right relationship to God and also how to treat each other in a truly human way, how to be God's true Adamic son and servant king in the world.

In both Exodus and Deuteronomy, the Mosaic covenant/Torah is divided into two sections: (1) the Ten Commands (literally Ten Words) and (2) the Judgements. All the Judgements in Exodus 21–23 and the Detailed Stipulations in Deuteronomy 12–26 flow from the Ten Commandments and express further how they work out in practical terms. The Ten Words also have a bipartite structure.[37] The first four commands show how to have a right relationship to God and the last six how to have a right relationship to each other as humans. Although these instructions are given negatively, as prohibitions, they could be restated in positive terms as the basic rights of every human: (1) "You must not murder" is the right of every person to his own life, (2) "You must not commit adultery" is the right of every person to his own home, (3) "You must not steal" is the right of every person to his own property, (4) "You must not testify falsely against your neighbour" is the right of every person to his own reputation. No society can endure that does not respect the basic inalienable rights of every person. Thus the last six commands can be paralleled in the law codes of other societies in the ancient Near East: the Laws of Ur-Nammu (2064–2046 B.C.), the Laws of Lipit-Ishtar (1875–1864 B.C.), the Laws of Eshnunna (19th century B.C.), the Code of Hammurabi (18th century B.C.), the Middle Assyrian Laws (12th century B.C.) and the Old Hittite Laws (17th–15th centuries B.C.). But in the Mosaic covenant/Torah, why are these commands given negatively instead of positively? And why are they expressed in the second person singular instead of plural? Because when you say "You must not murder" it means that each and every individual in the community must think first about the right of his neighbour to his life, not first about one's own rights.[38] In other words, all

---

[37] As we have seen, there are different approaches to numbering the Ten Commandments in Catholic, Jewish and Protestant traditions. This does not affect the general observations offered in this paragraph.

[38] I owe this insight to Daniel I. Block, professor of Old Testament, Wheaton College. See Block, "Reading the Decalogue Left to Right," in *How I Love Your Torah, O Lord!* 31–42; idem, "You shall not covet your neighbor's

of these commands are about social justice, about being faithful to love my neighbour as myself, and—in terms of the larger story, about being fully and truly human, i.e., fulfilling the covenant obligations of the divine image.

THE COVENANTAL FRAMEWORK OF PAUL'S TEACHING

The Mosaic covenant/Torah and the larger story that informs it are clearly the background to Paul's statements in Ephesians. Just as the old covenant at Sinai has six commands describing lovingkindness and truth which Jesus encapsulated by saying "love your neighbour as yourself," so Paul's instruction/torah to the new covenant community has six commands which can also be summarised by "speaking the truth in love." When Paul talks about speaking the truth in love, then, he means the same thing as faithfulness and lovingkindness in the Old Testament. The same social justice that underlies the old covenant underlies the new.

These connections both to the old covenant and also to the larger story beginning in Genesis 1 are *consciously* made by Paul. It is no accident that the first command in his list is about speaking the truth, and the grand summary in Ephesians 5:1–2, inserted before the last command, is about acting in love, so that love and truth form both parentheses and a summary of his instructions, just as it does in the old covenant. It is also no accident when Paul says in 5:1–2 that when we love one another we imitate God—a clear reference to the divine image. There is further direct reference to the divine image in the bookend sections in 4:17–24 and 5:6–14. In 4:24 Paul commands us to put on the new humanity that is "created according to God in righteousness and holiness which derives from the truth"—a direct reference to renewing the divine image, as the parallel in Colossians 3:10 shows. Righteousness and holiness are mentioned here, not as elements of the divine image but as facets of being truthful in love in a covenant relationship, for this is what defines the divine image. Likewise, in 5:9, in the closing bookend section, Paul speaks of the fruit of light as goodness, righteousness, and truth, summaries of the divine image as a covenant relationship. And in 4:21, at the outset, he says that truth is in Jesus, because just as the old covenant is an expression of the character of Yahweh, so

---

wife": A Study in Deuteronomic Domestic Ideology," in *The Gospel according to Moses: Theological and Ethical Reflections on the Book of Deuteronomy* (Eugene, OR: Cascade, 2012), 137–168. This is also the thrust of Zechariah 8:16.

the new covenant is an expression of the character of Jesus, whose self-sacrifice in 5:2 lifts matters to a new level. Even the verb *marturomai* ("solemnly testify") in 4:17 is reminiscent of calling the old covenant the "testimony" and so establishes a covenantal context.[39] The motivation for being truthful in 4:25 is that we are members of one another, i.e., we are a covenant community. Finally, the first command is about laying aside "falsehood" (4:25; ψεῦδος) and the nations are characterised as walking in the "futility" of their minds (4:17; ματαιότης). In Psalm 4, which Paul cites in Ephesians 4:26, the king challenges his nobles not to resort to idolatry in the crisis caused by lack of rain. In this way, the terms "futility" and "falsehood" express covenant violation in Ephesians because of their background in Psalm 4.[40]

THE MEANING OF SPEAKING THE TRUTH IN LOVE

The meaning of the phrase "speaking the truth in love" cannot be uncovered by simply consulting a Greek lexicon or even by performing an exhaustive lexical study. The biblical-theological background and framework must first be understood. In the new covenant community, loyalty to Jesus has replaced the old covenant command to love God,[41] and speaking the truth in love sums up the social justice of our relationships in the new humanity.[42]

Earlier a question was raised: "What do I say to a person who claims to know Christ but is following a lifestyle that entails sexual immorality as defined by Christ and the apostles?" What does speaking the truth in love mean in such situations? According to a biblical-theological understanding of Ephesians 4–6, such a lifestyle is not only morally wrong, it is a form of social injustice and leads to being less than fully human. We must address violations of the covenant requirements not simply as offenses against God

---

[39] Cf. "the tablets of testimony" (Ex. 31:18; 32:15; 34:29) and the "ark of the testimony" (Ex. 25:22; 26:33–34; 30:6, 26; 39:35; 40:3, 5, 21).

[40] I owe this insight to John Meade.

[41] Hence John 14:15.

[42] The claim that social justice sums up the requirements of the stipulations for the new creation/covenant community must be considered in context. These instructions are given to a people who are *already justified and forgiven* so that they may know how to live and treat *each other* in the community, which models for the rest of the world life in the new creation. In Ephesians 1:13–14, Paul equates "the word of truth" with "the gospel of your salvation." Nonetheless, the gospel that Paul preached included justification, daily growth in holiness both individually and in relationships in the covenant community, and final redemption. Thus there is no conflict between "speaking the truth" as social justice and "the word of truth" in terms of believing the gospel and being saved. In addition, since the character and righteousness of God expressed in the old covenant is not different from that expressed in the new covenant—although doubtless brought to fuller light in the new covenant—there is continuity between the social justice we see in the Old Testament and the teaching of Paul in the New.

but as a destructive path that constitutes social injustice and inhuman behaviour. This must be part and parcel of both our speech and our actions in the covenant community.

And it is only this humanity that will survive divine judgement and enter the new heavens and the new earth. Do we treat each other with faithful loyal love? We must obey these instructions, because only in this way can we attain social justice, and only in this way can we become truly human. Any other path will lead us to lose what it means to be truly human.

PART THREE:

THEOLOGICAL INTEGRATION

Chapter Sixteen

"KINGDOM THROUGH COVENANT": A BIBLICAL-THEOLOGICAL SUMMARY

A lot of territory has been covered in the previous chapters. It is now our task in the remaining two chapters to summarise what has been covered and to ask the famous question: "So what?" How does our understanding of the relationships between the biblical covenants help make sense of the metanarrative of Scripture? And what are some of the implications of our proposal for biblical and systematic theology? In this chapter, we want to provide an overall summary of our view in order to tie together any loose ends and to highlight the key points of our proposal, especially points which distinguish our view from other positions. In the final chapter we will sketch out the implications of this proposal for some areas of systematic theology, especially on issues pertaining to the differences between dispensational and covenant theology as highlighted in chapters 2–3.

We have sought to capture the essence of our proposal by the phrase "kingdom through covenant." Let us now unpack this expression in two steps. First, we will focus on the term *kingdom* and how we understand the idea of the *kingdom of God* across the Canon. Second, we will summarise our understanding of the relationship between kingdom and covenant and how it is *through the biblical covenants* that God's kingdom comes to this world centred in the person and work of our Lord Jesus Christ.

KINGDOM THROUGH COVENANT

The idea of the *kingdom* has already been highlighted and discussed in previous chapters, but now we want to summarise it biblically and theologically. It is certainly right to affirm with Thomas Schreiner that the *kingdom* or the *kingdom of God* "is of prime importance in NT theology,"[1] and, we would

---

[1] Thomas R. Schreiner, *New Testament Theology: Magnifying God in Christ* (Grand Rapids, MI: Baker, 2008), 41.

add, for the entire Bible. In this regard, Graeme Goldsworthy is correct to assert that, "The idea of the rule of God over creation, over all creatures, over the kingdoms of the world, and in a unique and special way, over his chosen and redeemed people, is the very heart of the message of the Hebrew scriptures."[2] Five points succinctly capture what we affirm about the *kingdom* and how we understand the term and idea.

1. Scripture begins with the declaration that God, as Creator and triune Lord, is the sovereign ruler and King of the universe. In this important sense, the entire universe is God's kingdom since he is presently Lord and King. From the opening verses of Genesis, God is introduced and identified as the all-powerful Lord who created the universe by his word, while he himself is uncreated, independent, self-existent, self-sufficient, and in need of nothing outside himself (Ps. 50:12–14; 93:2; Acts 17:24–25). That is why the God of the Bible is the only true God, utterly unique, and unwilling to share his glory with any created thing (Isa. 42:8). This is also why God alone is to be worshipped, trusted, and obeyed; he is the King, and the entire universe is his kingdom. This truth is illustrated by Psalm 103:19: "The Lord has established his throne in heaven, and his kingdom rules over all" (NIV; cf. Ps. 47:8; Dan. 4:34–35).

In addition, God's kingly work in creation is never presented as an end in itself; rather it is the beginning of God's eternal plan (Eph. 1:11; Rev. 4:11) in time, which he now directs and governs toward a specific *telos*. In this way, creation leads to providence, and both creation and providence establish the eschatological direction of God's plan, particularly worked out in terms of specific covenantal relationships God enters into with his creation, which, in the end, all leads to a specific goal centred in Christ (cf. Col. 1:15–20). In light of such teaching, even though the specific *wording*, "kingdom of God," is not found until much later in Scripture, the *idea* is taught in the opening pages of the Bible. As Graeme Goldsworthy rightly points out,

> The *kingdom of God* is a name that is not used in the Bible until much later, but the idea of it immediately comes to mind as we think of creation. . . .
>
> How may we describe the kingdom of God as it has been revealed up to this point in Scripture? God's rule involves the relationships that he has set up between himself and everything in creation. In other words, God makes the rules for all existence. Both accounts of creation show mankind as the center of God's attention and the recipient of a unique relationship

---

[2] Graeme Goldsworthy, "Kingdom of God," in *NDBT*, 618.

with him. Thus the focus of the kingdom of God is on the relationship between God and his people. Man is subject to God, while the rest of creation is subject to man and exists for his benefit. The kingdom means God ruling over his people in the material universe.[3]

2. Even though the triune God is universal King and Lord, given the Fall, everything changes. Before the Fall, God as Creator and King creates a world that is beautifully summarised by the phrase, "it was very good" (Gen. 1:4, 10, 12, 18, 21, 25, 31). Even though the nature of this goodness is disputed, in light of Genesis 3, it must minimally convey moral goodness and purity.[4] Yet, now in light of human rebellion, God's rightful rule over the entire creation is foolishly rejected by the human race. Sin is essentially rebellion against the claims of the King—moral autonomy—and so, as a result of our sin, we now stand under God's judicial sentence of condemnation, guilt, and death (Gen. 2:16–17; Rom. 3:23; 6:23). It is in light of the Fall that the Old Testament makes an important distinction between the sovereignty and rule of God over the entire creation and the coming of his *saving reign* in the context of a rebellious creation to make all things right. The creation, which was originally created good, now through sin has gone wrong. If God chooses to make things right, he as the Lord and King must act savingly, which of course sets the stage for the development of the redemptive story line of Scripture for the coming of a Redeemer to set creation right—to usher in the *saving reign* of God to this world. As D. A. Carson reminds us, "Ultimately that plot-line anticipates the restoration of goodness, even the transformation to a greater glory, of the universe gone wrong (Rom. 8:21), and arrives finally at the dawning of a new heaven and a new earth (Rev. 21–22; cf. Isa. 65:17), the home of righteousness (2 Peter 3:13)."[5] On the

---

[3] Graeme Goldsworthy, *According to Plan: The Unfolding Revelation of God in the Bible* (Downers Grove, IL: InterVarsity Press, 2002), 94–95. Goldsworthy, "Kingdom of God," 618, states it even more strongly: "The idea of the rule of God over creation, over all creatures, over the kingdoms of the world, and in a unique and special way, over his chosen and redeemed people, is the very heart of the message of the Hebrew scriptures."

[4] Some argue that "goodness" is merely the complete correspondence between divine intention and the universe, which was suitable to fulfill the purpose for which it was brought into being. However, this view does not necessitate an absolutely "perfect" world and thus can allow for the notion of death before the Fall. Thus, on this view, Adam and Eve were created mortal (like animals), and the penalty for their sin was a new kind of death, in anguish and pain. The tree of life, then, would have given them immortality, but this was not part of their existence prior to the Fall. See William J. Dumbrell, *The Search for Order: Biblical Eschatology in Focus* (Grand Rapids, MI: Baker, 1994), 20–22; and Hugh Ross, *Creation and Time: A Biblical and Scientific Perspective on the Creation-Date Controversy* (Colorado Springs: NavPress, 1994), 62ff. A better option is to see "goodness" tied to moral realities, thus arguing that death, pain, and suffering did not exist prior to the Fall and that these realities are a result of Adam's sin and the curse placed upon the world (see Gen. 2:17; 3:19; Rom. 5:12; 6:23). For this view, see, e.g., Andrew S. Kulikovsky, *Creation, Fall, Restoration: A Biblical Theology of Creation* (Fearn, Ross-shire, UK: Mentor, 2009), 204–220.

[5] D. A. Carson, *The Gagging of God: Christianity Confronts Pluralism* (Grand Rapids, MI: Zondervan, 1996), 202.

one hand, then, the kingdom of God will exclude all sin and rebellion. On the other hand, it will include all that is redeemed according to God's gracious will and action. Eventually, when all sin and evil is put down, we will see the fullness of God's kingdom, which Scripture describes in new creation categories, in contrast to that which was lost in the old creation due to Adam's sin and rebellion, acting as our representative head.

3. How does God's kingdom come, in this saving sense? As the Old Testament unfolds, God's kingdom is revealed and comes most clearly *through* the biblical covenants. It is important to note that we are using the preposition *through* in a twofold way. First, as previous chapters have shown, it refers to the fact that the triune God has graciously chosen to create the human race as his image-bearers, literally his priest-kings, to be in covenant relationship with him. Our covenant Lord has given us the supreme privilege of knowing him, and as we give our life to his worship as his servant-kings and are completely devoted and fully obedient to him in every domain of life, God's rule is extended throughout the life of the covenant community *and* to the entire creation. Even though God, who is completely self-sufficient, does not need us to achieve his purposes, incredibly he has chosen us to realize his sovereign rule in this world in the context of a covenant relationship of loyal love (*ḥesed*) and faithfulness (*'ĕmet*) where we are to receive his instructions with obedience and trust. Thus, it is *through* this covenant relationship that we are to fulfill the very purpose of our existence in relationship to our covenant Lord. Yet, as already noted, we have failed in our calling, which leads to a second use of the preposition *through*.

In this second use of *through*, we are emphasising a diachronic perspective. It is *through* the biblical covenants, across time, that God chooses to reverse the disastrous effects of sin and usher in his saving reign to this world. Following the loss of Eden, redemption is linked to the election of a people—Noah and his family, the descendants of Abraham, and uniquely through the Davidic king. These people, particularly tied to the nation of Israel, are promised a land to dwell in; they will be the means of blessing to the nations. *Through* the biblical covenants these covenant promises, which ultimately stretch back to God's initial promise in Genesis 3:15, are realized. In the exodus, which becomes a type and pattern of redemption, God reveals his redemptive plan. At Sinai, the people of God are constituted as a theocratic nation—a *kingdom* of priests called to serve the Lord, reveal God to the nations, and *through* them to usher in God's saving reign to this world.

Though rebellion leads to delay, the nation is eventually given possession of the land. Here the structures of government develop toward kingship under the dynasty of David in Jerusalem. Solomon builds the temple as the place where reconciliation and fellowship with God are established, a temple which stretches back to the garden-sanctuary of Eden itself. The rule of the Davidic kings is representative of the rule of God over his kingdom. But the kings and Israel fail; the kingdom divides and judgement falls. God's saving reign through these people and covenant mediators is not fully realized; it is only typified, foreshadowed, and anticipated. Ultimately it awaits the coming of the great antitype of Adam, Noah, Abraham, Moses, Israel, and David and his sons: our Lord Jesus Christ. It is only through this obedient Son, God the Son incarnate, that we have God's long-awaited kingdom inaugurated in this world (through the new covenant).

4. In the Old Testament, these promises, hopes, and expectations, are picked up, proclaimed, and announced by the prophets. Through the prophets, God announces hope for the nation of Israel and for this poor, lost world. The prophets who proclaim an overall pattern of renewal do so by recapitulating the past history of redemption and projecting it into the future, when the Lord comes to save his people through a new exodus, a new Jerusalem, a new Davidic king to rule in a glorious and eternal kingdom—all of which is tied to the dawning of the new covenant age. In this way, the prophets anticipate the coming of YHWH and Messiah, particularly associated with the Davidic king, who will usher in God's kingdom, making all things right and reversing the effects of sin and death. But what is crucial to note is that this coming of the saving reign of God—God's kingdom—will occur with the coming of the Messiah and the inauguration of a new covenant which will bring to fulfilment all the previous covenants.

5. As the New Testament begins, it is this Old Testament background which serves as the basis for its teaching on the kingdom. In the Gospels, and the entire New Testament, the "kingdom of God" refers primarily to God's *kingly* and *sovereign rule*, and it is especially tied to God's *saving reign* that has broken into this world in the coming, life, death, and resurrection of Jesus the Messiah.[6] It does *not* primarily refer to a certain

---

[6] In the Gospels, the expression "kingdom of God" occurs four times in Matthew, fourteen in Mark, thirty-two in Luke, and four in John. Matthew also uses the expression "kingdom of heaven" thirty-two times (see Schreiner, *New Testament Theology*, 45–49). There is no evidence, contra classic dispensational thought, that there is a major theological distinction between "kingdom of heaven" and "kingdom of God," as discussed in chapter 2. Instead, in Matthew, the two expressions are basically synonymous, except, as Jonathan Pennington, *Heaven and Earth in the Gospel of Matthew*, Novum Testamentum Supplements 126 (Leiden, Netherlands: Brill, 2007), 67–76, has

geographical location, rather the phrase tells us more about *God* (the fact that he reigns) than about anything else. The New Testament announces that, in Jesus, the long awaited kingdom has come and the rule of sin and death has been destroyed. Thus, through Jesus' obedient life and cross work, he has *inaugurated* the kingdom of God over which he now rules and reigns—it is *already* here. And as the ascended King, he commands all people to repent and to enter that kingdom of life. A generation ago, William Manson stated it this way:

> When we turn to the New Testament, we pass from the climate of predic-
> tion to that of fulfillment. The things which God had foreshadowed by the
> lips of His holy prophets He has now, in part at least, brought to accom-
> plishment. The *Eschaton*, described from afar . . . , has in Jesus registered
> its advent. . . . The supreme sign of the *Eschaton* is the Resurrection of
> Jesus and the descent of the Holy Spirit on the Church. The Resurrection
> of Jesus is not simply a sign which God has granted in favour of His Son,
> but is the inauguration, the entrance into history, of *the times of the End*.
>
> Christians, therefore, have entered through the Christ into the New
> Age. Church, Spirit, life in Christ are eschatological magnitudes. Those
> who gather in Jerusalem in the numinous first days of the Church know that
> it is so; they are already conscious of tasting the powers of the World to
> Come. What has been predicted in Holy Scripture as to happen to Israel or
> to man in the *Eschaton* has happened to and in Jesus. The foundation-stone
> of the New Creation has come into position.[7]

However, the New Testament also stresses that even though, in Jesus, the kingdom is here, there is still a *not yet* aspect to it since it awaits its con-summation in Christ's second coming. This crucial "already–not yet" ten-sion, which characterises New Testament eschatology, is famously known as "inaugurated eschatology," i.e., the "last days" that the Old Testament anticipated and predicted have actually arrived in the coming of our Lord Jesus, yet they still await their full consummation.[8] In this sense, there is still more to come even though in principle the promised new age that the Old Testament anticipated and predicted is now here.

---

shown, "kingdom of *heaven*" stresses that God's kingdom is from above and that his kingdom represents his rule over all earthly kingdoms.

[7] W. Manson, "Eschatology in the New Testament," in *Eschatology*, Scottish Journal of Theology Occasional Papers 2 (Edinburgh: Oliver & Boyd, 1953), 6; cited in Anthony A. Hoekema, *The Bible and the Future* (Grand Rapids, MI: Eerdmans, 1994), 14.

[8] See Schreiner, *New Testament Theology*, 41–116, for a more in-depth treatment of inaugurated eschatology. See also Herman Ridderbos, *Paul: An Outline of His Theology*, trans. John Richard de Witt (Grand Rapids, MI: Eerdmans, 1975), 44–90; and K. E. Brower, "Eschatology," in *NDBT*, 459–464.

This tension is presented in a number of ways. For example, in regard to the kingdom of God, the New Testament teaches that the covenant Lord who rules over all (e.g., Ps. 93:1; 97:1; 99:1; 103:19; Dan. 4:34–35) has now brought his saving reign and rule to this fallen world in Jesus Christ as evidenced, for example, by the coming of the Spirit (Matt. 12:28; Luke 11:20) and the miraculous signs and preaching (Luke 4:16–30; cf. Isa. 61:1–2; 58:6; 29:18). Truly in Jesus, as he himself announces, God's sovereign saving rule has broken into this world (Matt. 4:17; Mark 1:14–15). However, even though the kingdom is now here, Jesus still teaches us to pray, "Your kingdom come" (Matt. 6:10) and he speaks to his disciples of a future day when he will come "in his kingdom" (Matt. 16:28; Luke 23:51), "which clearly refers to the future fulfillment of the kingdom promise."[9] The same can be said about the coming of the Spirit. Because Jesus has come and has won victory in his cross, resurrection, and ascension, he has poured out the *promised* Spirit (Acts 2; cf. John 14–16; Eph. 1:13–14). However, the gift of the Spirit is the *arrabōn,* the deposit and guarantee of our promised inheritance awaiting us in the consummation.[10] Thus, the reception of the Spirit means that one has become a participant in the new mode of existence associated with the future age and now partakes of the powers of the "age to come." Yet, the New Testament insists that what the Spirit gives is only a foretaste of far greater blessings to come. As Anthony Hoekema summarises, " . . . we may say that in the possession of the Spirit we who are in Christ have a foretaste of the blessings of the age to come, and a pledge and guarantee of the resurrection of the body. Yet we have only the firstfruits. We look forward to the final consummation of the kingdom of God, when we shall enjoy these blessings to the full."[11] In these ways and many more, the New Testament teaches that in Christ the "last days" have arrived, but they are not yet consummated in all of their fullness.

---

[9] Schreiner, *New Testament Theology,* 51. The "not yet" reality of the kingdom is also seen in such texts as Matt. 5:3–12; 8:11–12; 13:24–30, 36–43; 22:1–14; 25:1–13, 31–46; 26:29; etc.). See Schreiner, *New Testament Theology,* 50–68.

[10] In fact, the "already–not yet" tension vis-à-vis the Spirit's relation to the believer is worked out in five ways in the New Testament. First, the Spirit testifies of our "sonship" (Gal. 4:4–5; Rom. 8:14–27). The Spirit bears witness that we are the children of God now, even though we still await our full rights associated with sonship. Second, the role of the Spirit is that of "firstfruits" (*aparchē;* 1 Cor. 15:20, 23; Rom. 8:23), which speaks both of what we have now and of what we still await in the future. Third, the Spirit is our "pledge" or "deposit" (*arrabōn;* 2 Cor. 1:22; 5:5; Eph. 1:14) guaranteeing our future inheritance. Fourth, the Holy Spirit is also called a "seal" (2 Cor. 1:22; Eph. 4:30; 1:13), which signifies that believers are nothing less than God's possession. Fifth, the Spirit is related to the resurrection of our bodies (Rom. 1:3–4; 8:11; 1 Cor. 15:42–44). The Spirit is said to be active not only in relation to Christ's resurrection but in ours as well, which signifies that someday our bodies shall be raised from the dead, just as Christ was risen from the dead, the last Adam, so that we may share in the glorious existence of the final, consummated state. For a further discussion of these points see Hoekema, *Bible and the Future,* 55–67.

[11] Hoekema, *Bible and the Future,* 67.

It is for this reason that the New Testament stresses that, in the coming of Jesus Christ, the *fulfilment* of all of the predictions, hopes, and expectations of God's promised plan of redemption has now taken place.[12] Moreover, precisely because Jesus has fulfilled the Old Testament, there is also massive change or discontinuity from what has preceded, which entails that in Christ an incredible epochal shift in redemptive-history has occurred, unlike any other time in history. This is why, even though the New Testament continues the basic story line of the Old Testament, once Christ comes and inaugurates the entire new covenant age, many of the themes that were basic to the Old Testament have now been transposed and transformed. In light of the epochal shift Christ has inaugurated, D. A. Carson notes a few examples of the kind of transposition which has taken place:

> "Kingdom" no longer primarily conjures up a theocratic state in which God rules by his human vassal in the Davidic dynasty. It conjures up the immediate transforming reign of God, dawning now in the ministry, death, resurrection, ascension, and session of Jesus, the promised Messiah, and consummated at his return. Eschatology is thereby transformed. The locus of the people of God is no longer national and tribal; it is international, transracial, transcultural. If the Old Testament prophets constantly look forward to the day when God will act decisively, the New Testament writers announce that God has acted decisively, and that this is "good news," gospel, of universal, eternal significance and stellar importance. Thus kingdom, Christology, eschatology, church, gospel, become dominant terms or themes. Temple, priest, sacrifice, law, and much more are transposed; national and tribal outlooks gradually fade from view.[13]

In addition to various Old Testament themes being transposed and transformed due to Christ's coming, the structure of the redemptive-historical time line has also changed. From an Old Testament perspective there is a distinction between "this present age"—an age characterised by sin, death, and opposition to God as represented by earthy *kingdoms*—and "the age to come"—an age in which the covenant Lord will come to rescue his people through his Messiah and to usher in his *kingdom*, i.e., his saving rule and

---

[12] I am using the word "fulfilment" in its broadest prophetic sense, i.e., Jesus "fulfills" the Old Testament in that it points to him and, now that he has come, it is fulfilled. In the New Testament, "fulfilment" can be direct in the sense of prophetic prediction (e.g., Mic. 5:2; Matt. 2:1–12), but it is not limited to this alone. It can also be prophetic in a more indirect sense tied to typological patterns or models that are fulfilled in Christ. Both senses are prophetic, but not in exactly the same way. For a helpful discussion of these points see D. A. Carson, "Matthew," in *Matthew, Mark, Luke*, The Expositor's Bible Commentary 8, ed. Frank E. Gaebelein (Grand Rapids, MI: Zondervan, 1984), 27–29; and Schreiner, *New Testament Theology*, 70–79.

[13] Carson, *Gagging of God*, 254.

reign. But how are these two ages related to each other? David Wells nicely describes the relation: "These two ages were related to one another in a chronological sequence. This αἰών ended with the coming to earth of the Messiah, and with his arrival there began the heavenly αἰών"[14] In other words, from an Old Testament perspective, there would be only one coming of Lord and Messiah in power and might (see figure 16.1). And when the Lord and Messiah will finally come and literally usher in the "last days" and the "age to come," it will be an age characterised by the eschatological hope and expectation spoken of by the prophets. For example, when the "age to come" arrives it will bring with it the coming of God's saving rule and reign—his kingdom—evidenced by the arrival of the new covenant and all that it entails, the dawning of the new creation, judgement upon all of God's enemies, and salvation for the people of God associated with the Day of the Lord. All of these great realities will come at once.

Old Testament

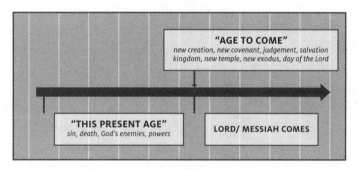

Fig. 16.1

However, the New Testament modifies this basic time-line due to the fullness of revelation in Christ, and as such, it speaks of the two comings of the Messiah, not just one, as well as an overlap of the ages. In the first coming—all that is associated with the Son's incarnation, life and ministry, death, resurrection, ascension, and Pentecost—the "age to come" is now here, just as the prophets anticipated. But, even though the future age is in principle here, it is not fully here until Christ returns in glory and power. As such, "this present age" continues until the second coming even though

---

[14] David F. Wells, *The Person of Christ* (Wheaton, IL: Crossway, 1984), 29.

the "age to come" has been inaugurated in Christ. In this sense, there is an overlap of the ages.

Sometimes this overlap is illustrated by a World War II analogy between D-day and V-day.[15] In World War II, D-day brought about an incredible victory for the allied troops. As a result of that day, the enemy was decisively defeated and it was only a matter of time before final victory would be achieved even though the war was not yet over. D-day is then compared to the first coming of Christ which, in principle, has ushered in the "age to come" but not yet in its fullness. Thus, in Christ's first coming God's promise of redemption has now been realized. God's sovereign saving reign—his kingdom—has broken into this world and along with it the new covenant and the new creation. Sin, death, and the power of the Evil One have been destroyed. It is only a matter of time before final victory is won; in principle the victory has been won and it is now guaranteed. Yet, our D-day still awaits our V-day, i.e., our final victory when Christ comes again and consummates what he began. Thus, in this overlap of the ages, this in-between the times, even though we as the people of God are no longer associated with "this present age" since we are no longer "in Adam" but are now "in Christ"; even though we are participants in the future age and now have eternal life, justification before God, and the Spirit who indwells us (all realities associated with the "age to come"); we still await the fullness of Christ's victory and the arrival of his kingdom in consummated glory. But what Christ has won in his first advent is now our guarantee and pledge that the consummated age is not a vain hope, but a certainty. In light of this, we can draw the New Testament restructuring of the Old Testament time-line as follows (see figure 16.2).

It is within this overall teaching that the New Testament announces the arrival and inauguration of the *kingdom of God* in Jesus Christ our Lord. It is not an overstatement to say that the New Testament's teaching of inaugurated eschatology and its relation to consummated eschatology, whether it is found in the Gospels, Paul, or other New Testament books, forms the entire context within which the New Testament expounds the kingdom, eternal life, the gift of the Spirit, the church, salvation, eschatology, and, most importantly, Christology.[16] To say that Christ has *fulfilled*

---

[15] Oscar Cullmann, *Christ and Time*, trans. Floyd V. Filson (Philadelphia: Westminster, 1950), used this famous way of describing the different results achieved by Christ in his two advents. See also Hoekema, *Bible and the Future*, 21.

[16] See David F. Wells, *God the Evangelist* (Grand Rapids, MI: Eerdmans, 1987), 9–10; Schreiner, *New Testament Theology*, 41–116.

all of God's plans and purposes, that he has inaugurated *God's kingdom* and thus literally has ushered in the "age to come" and all that is associated with that "age," is a staggering affirmation, pregnant with Christological import. But it is also important to note that the New Testament's eschatological perspective centred in its teaching on the *kingdom* cannot be understood apart from the biblical covenants, a point to which we now turn.

New Testament

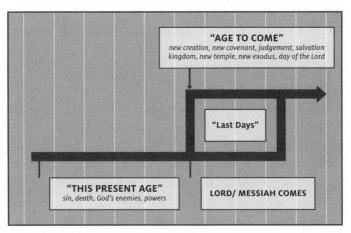

Fig. 16.2

KINGDOM *THROUGH* COVENANT

From what has been stated, it should be fairly evident how we think *kingdom* and *covenant* are conjoined. It is primarily through the biblical covenants viewed diachronically that we learn how the saving reign of God comes to this world.[17] In other words, the relationship between the kingdom of God and the biblical covenants is a tight one, and it is for this reason that grasping the unfolding nature of the biblical covenants is at the heart of understanding how God's kingdom dawns in Jesus; how God's redemptive promise is realized; and how the entire metanarrative of the Bible hangs together, since

---

[17] Even though the diachronic use of *through* is primarily stressed here, there is a twofold use of the preposition, as discussed above. It is *through* the covenant relationship that God has chosen to reveal himself, to enter into relationship with his image-bearers and priest-kings, and to extend his rule to the whole creation. Incredibly, the triune covenant Lord created us for a covenant relationship with him where we would live out our existence, in every domain of life, for his glory, in complete devotion and obedience to and love and worship of him.

the biblical covenants constitute the framework and backbone for the entire story line of Scripture.

No doubt, as already noted, the relationship between the covenants has been and is today disputed in theology.[18] However, minimally Christians throughout the ages have affirmed that God has one plan of salvation and that history is the working out of that plan centred in the coming and cross work of our Lord Jesus Christ. In addition, most evangelicals also agree that the story line of Scripture moves clearly from creation to fall, from Abraham to David, and finally to Christ.[19] Yet, contrary to "covenant theology," which has the tendency to speak of God's one plan of salvation in terms of *the* "covenant of grace," or "dispensational theology," which tends to partition history in terms of dispensations, it is more accurate to think in terms of a *plurality* of covenants (e.g., Gal. 4:24; Eph. 2:12; Heb. 8:7–13), which are part of the progressive revelation of the *one* plan of God that is fulfilled in the new covenant. This allows us to speak properly of the *continuity* of God's plan across the ages now culminated in the new covenant, and it also helps us avoid flattening the relationships between the biblical covenants and downplaying the significant amount of progression between them. This, in turn, allows us to see specific covenantal *discontinuities* in God's unfolding plan which has import for a variety of theological issues. Before we summarise how we think the biblical covenants fit together, let us briefly highlight five key hermeneutical/methodological points central to our proposal—points which not only provide a summary to our approach but which also begin to highlight similarities and differences between dispensational and covenant theology.

A SUMMARY OF SOME KEY HERMENEUTICAL
AND METHODOLOGICAL POINTS

1. *The significance of progressive revelation for the unfolding of the biblical covenants.* Everyone agrees that Scripture, as God's word-act revelation, does not come to us all at once but over time. Revelation, alongside redemption, unfolds in a progressive manner by unique twists and turns in separate but related epochs, largely demarcated by God's acts and redemptive covenants. In this way, God's eternal plan, what Paul refers to as the "mystery" of

---

[18] As discussed in chapters 2–3, within Christian theology, particularly evangelical theology, the relationship between the covenants has been largely disputed between the theological camps of covenant and dispensational theology, and their varieties. As chapters 4–15 have shown, there is dispute over the nature of the covenants in biblical studies and biblical theology as well.

[19] See Matthew 1. See also Goldsworthy, *According to Plan*, who divides up redemptive-history this way.

God, unfolds step-by-step, ultimately finding its culmination in Christ. The biblical covenants are the primary means by which God's one eternal plan is made known, as we move across the Canon from promise to fulfilment, from type/shadow to reality in Christ. The covenants are not independent and unrelated to each other, rather they build on each other, disclosing to us God's plan which encompasses many things. For example, they reveal who our covenant Lord is—the God of *ḥesed* and *'ĕmet*—his character and way.[20] They also reveal the purpose of our creation, the nature of the covenant relationship, and how we are to live in relation to God and to one another.[21] Most importantly, in light of human sin and rebellion, the covenants not only teach us how God chooses to redeem a fallen people for himself and set everything right, but they also reveal a tension in the covenant relationship between God and his image-bearers. We discover how God is always faithful and true to his promises and obligations while we are not, even though he demands our perfect obedience to his will as his responsible creatures. As the covenants unfold, we discover how God's promises to restore his elect to covenant relationship with him from every tribe, nation, people, and tongue, is ultimately achieved through the obedient work of his Son, which was his plan from all eternity (see, e.g., Eph. 1:4, 9–10).

2. *The three horizons of biblical interpretation and their importance for the covenants.* Intimately related to a diachronic reading of the biblical covenants and the story line of Scripture are the three horizons of biblical interpretation as discussed in chapter 3. In chapters 5 through 13, each covenant was placed within three expanding contexts. First, the covenant in question was interpreted within its own immediate, redemptive-historical context (i.e., textual horizon). Second, to understand properly how that covenant fits in God's unfolding plan, it was placed in relation to what preceded it (i.e., epochal horizon) and *intertextual* connections were developed so that we could understand better the interrelations between earlier and later revelation. Third, the covenant was then placed in relation to later covenants and ultimately to the coming of Jesus and the inauguration of the new covenant. By tracing out the biblical covenants in this fashion we are then able to see

---

[20] See John H. Walton, *Covenant: God's Purpose, God's Plan* (Grand Rapids, MI: Zondervan, 1994), 20, who rightly contends that the biblical covenants are the primary means by which God's plan and self-revelation are made known to us. See also the important discussion of how it is *through* the biblical covenants that the character (*shem*) and way (*derek*) of YHWH is revealed. For a full discussion of these point see chapters 4, 8, and 13.

[21] John M. Frame, *The Doctrine of God* (Phillipsburg, NJ: P&R, 2002), 13–15, rightly points out that the way we come to know God is first through his acts, which allows us to reflect on his attributes. As God discloses himself over time though the biblical covenants we grasp who he is, in terms of both his character (ethical qualities) and his nature (metaphysical qualities).

how the entire plan of God is *organically* related yet at the same time reaches its culmination and fulfilment in Christ. Furthermore, it is only when we do this that we rightly see how the *parts* of God's plan ultimately fit with the *whole*, and that the theological conclusions we then draw are truly *biblical* and thus warranted.

3. *The new covenant supersedes all the previous covenants in redemptive-history.* We have sought to demonstrate that the biblical covenants are the framework and backbone to the overall metanarrative of Scripture. As each covenant is introduced in history, God's unfolding plan and promises take on greater clarity, definition, and expansion. No biblical covenant is unrelated to what has preceded it since each covenant contributes to the entire revelation of God centred in Christ. Yet it is important to ask, where is God's plan going? What is the end of that plan? Our conviction is that in the sweep of redemptive-history the end of the road, so to speak, is the coming of Christ and the arrival of the new covenant age. Obviously we are not denying the truth that what Jesus has inaugurated must still be consummated, as captured by our discussion of inaugurated eschatology. Instead, what we are arguing is that when the new covenant arrives, all the previous covenants find their *telos* in him.

In this important way, then, we view the new covenant as *superseding* the previous covenants. How? By *fulfilling* them, i.e., by bringing to pass what those previous covenants revealed, anticipated, and even predicted through various patterns, types, and instruction.[22] That is why our Lord is presented as the new covenant head, who in his person and work is greater than Adam by undoing[23] what Adam did and thus winning for us the new creation; as the true seed and offspring of Abraham, who brings blessings to the nations by his cross work; as the true Israel, fulfilling all that she failed to be; and as David's greater son, who rules the nations and the entire creation as King of kings and Lord of lords. The new covenant's *superseding* the previous covenants does not entail that the earlier covenants have no value for us today or that we can jettison the Old Testament from our Bibles. After all, not only did the previous covenants serve their role in redemptive-history as part of

---

[22] See Carson, *Matthew*, 90–97, 140–147, for this understanding of fulfilment. See also Vern S. Poythress, *The Shadow of Christ in the Law of Moses* (Phillipsburg, NJ: P&R, 1995), 251–288.

[23] We are using the word "undoing" in two ways. Christ, as the last Adam, not only "undoes" the Fall by offering himself as a substitutionary sacrifice on our behalf and thus paying for our sin. He also "does" what Adam failed to do, namely, as the true Son, he acts in complete devotion, worship, and obedience to his Father. These two ways correspond to what Reformed theologians have referred to as the "active and passive obedience" of Christ as our covenant head, acting on behalf of his people.

God's redemptive plan and revelation of himself, which is crucial for us, but they are also forever part of Scripture, which Paul reminds us is God-breathed and useful for our instruction, growth, and ministry (see 2 Tim. 3:16–17). Yet, now that Christ has come, it is important to stress that we are no longer under those previous covenants *as covenants*, since they have reached their fulfilment in Christ. Instead we are under the new covenant and all that that entails.

A crucial implication of this point is that we, as new covenant believers, must view and apply the previous biblical covenants to ourselves in light of Christ, to whom each of the previous covenants pointed and who fulfills every aspect of them completely. This is consistent with the New Testament's presentation of our Lord who, as D. A. Carson rightly notes in his discussion of Matthew 5:17–20, "presents himself as the eschatological goal of the OT, and thereby its sole authoritative interpreter, the one through whom alone the OT finds its valid continuity and significance."[24] This observation is important in discerning how the previous covenants "carry over" to Christians in the new covenant era, especially in matters where there are theological differences among us on these very points.

For example, in regard to covenant theology, debate regarding the continuing validity of the genealogical principle in the church and its application to the ordinance of baptism centres on this very issue. In order to make headway in this debate we have to decide what features of the Abrahamic covenant, if any, are still in force today. What was the role of the Abrahamic covenant in God's overall plan and how is it brought to fulfilment in the new covenant, and are there any changes which have taken place now that Christ has come? Or, in relation to dispensational theology, does the land promise given in the Abrahamic covenant remain unchanged and unchanging across the covenants? Does it remain in force in the same way as given to Abraham, or is it part of an entire pattern rooted in creation which is now fulfilled in the new covenant inaugurated by Jesus? Other examples could be given, some of which we will highlight in the next chapter, but viewing the new covenant in the flow of redemptive-history as that which *supersedes* the previous covenants and brings them to their God-intended end does have implications for how we "put together" the canon of Scripture and understand the "whole counsel of God." In contrast to other theological views, our proposal of "kingdom through covenant" wants consistently to view and apply the previous covenants through the lens of Jesus' person and work

---

[24] Carson, *Matthew*, 144.

and the arrival of the new covenant age. It is only when we do so that our theological proposals and conclusions will be *biblical* in the full sense of that word—according to God's intention and letting Scripture interpret Scripture at the canonical level.

4. *The typological structures of Scripture are developed primarily through the covenants.* In chapter 3 we highlighted the importance of the "promise-fulfilment" theme and the typological patterns of Scripture for an overall biblical and systematic theology. We also noted how central the biblical covenants are to both of these areas. By grasping the unfolding nature of the covenants, one better understands the "promise-fulfilment" motif of Scripture and how all of God's promises are "yes and amen" in Christ (2 Cor. 1:20). Intimately related to this motif is typology, which is also developed diachronically through the covenants. In fact, it is hard to think of legitimate typological patterns which are not related, either directly or indirectly, to the biblical covenants.

For example, Adam, as the covenant head of the old creation, anticipates and looks forward to the coming of the "last Adam," our Lord Jesus, who is the head of the new covenant. In the meantime, as the biblical covenants are introduced and then progressively unpacked, "little Adams" show up on the stage of human history that take on the role of the first Adam (e.g., Noah, Abraham, Israel, David). Yet none of these "little Adams" are the ultimate fulfilment even though they point beyond themselves in prophetic expectation of the "last Adam" to come. In this way, through the diachronic and intertextual unfolding of the covenants, these typological patterns take on greater definition and clarity until that to which they point finally arrives. What is true of Adam is also true of other typological patterns, whether they be various persons (e.g., Moses, Israel, David, prophets, priests, and kings), events (e.g., the exodus), or institutions (e.g., sacrificial system, tabernacle/temple).

Why is this point important? For the reason that it helps illuminate some of the similarities and differences between our proposal and those of dispensational and covenant theology. When we combine points (3) and (4) the significance is this: in order to discern properly how Old Testament types/patterns are brought to fulfilment in God's plan, we must first observe not only how those types are *intertextually* developed *within* the Old Testament but also how they are applied and developed under the new covenant. In other words, Jesus and the new covenant becomes the hermeneutical lens by which we interpret the fulfilment of the types/patterns of the Old Testament.

This may not sound earth-shaking, but it is our conviction that it is *not* consistently applied in the biblical-theological systems of dispensational and covenant theology. As discussed in chapter 3, this is how we believe the priority of the New Testament should function over the Old Testament. There we made the point that to be *biblical* we must first do justice to the Old Testament context, and in the case of typology we must discern whether something is a legitimate type/pattern. Then we must think through that pattern's intertextual development across the biblical covenants, and then finally ask how it is brought to fulfilment in Christ and the arrival of the new covenant age.

In contrast to dispensational thought, as noted previously and to which we will return in the next chapter, we argue that the "land" functions as a type/pattern in the Old Testament context. Thus the "land promise" associated with the Abrahamic covenant cannot be understood apart from a backward and forward look: backward to the archetype reality of Eden and the entire creation, and forward, through the covenants, to its antitypical fulfilment in the new creation that Jesus has inaugurated in the new covenant. In the New Testament, it is our contention that the land promise does not find its fulfilment in the future in terms of a specific piece of real estate given to the ethnic nation of Israel; rather it is fulfilled in Jesus, who is the true Israel and the last Adam, who by his triumphant work wins for us the new creation. That new creation has "already" arrived in the dawning of the new covenant in individual Christians (2 Cor. 5:17; Eph. 2:8–10) and the church (Eph. 2:11–21) and it will be consummated when Christ returns and ushers in the new creation in its fullness (Revelation 21–22). We come to this conclusion for two reasons: first because the land associated with Eden and creation is typological.[25] Second, as we move across the covenants from Adam to Christ, the old creation gives way to the new creation, and the land, which is a type of creation, points forward, even within the Old Testament, to the dawning of the new creation bound up with the new covenant age inaugurated by Jesus.

In a similar fashion, in contrast to covenant theology, the genealogical principle of the Abrahamic covenant does *not* remain unchanged and unchanging as the biblical covenants unfold. Rather, it functions typologically

---

[25] On this point refer to chapter 12, where we saw that, in Isaiah 65, the new Jerusalem and the new creation are treated as coextensive. See also how Revelation 21–22 makes the same point. Cf. G. K. Beale, *The Temple and the Church's Mission: A Biblical Theology of the Dwelling Place of God*, NSBT 17 (Downers Grove, IL: InterVarsity Press, 2004), 313–334.

to point us forward to Christ, and that is why, in the new covenant, as we think of the relation of the covenant head, namely Christ, to his people, it is never Christ, then you as a believer, and then your children, but it is Christ as the head of all those he represents, namely, people of faith who have been born of the Spirit and united to Christ, their covenant head. The physical genealogical link from the Abrahamic covenant is transformed, as the Old Testament itself anticipates, in the dawning of a regenerate people from every nation who become the "one new man" in Christ Jesus our Lord (Eph. 2:11–21). This *new* people is not new in the dispensational sense of new; it is new in the redemptive-historical sense that, now that the last Adam and the true Israel have come, namely our Lord Jesus, both Jew and Gentile are joined together in fulfilment of the Abrahamic promise. More examples could be given but the point is that, in order to discern properly how Old Testament types/patterns are brought to fulfilment in God's plan, Jesus and the new covenant must become the hermeneutical lens by which we interpret the fulfilment of the types of the Old Testament.

5. *Viewing the biblical covenants as either unconditional or conditional is not quite right.* A common way to distinguish the biblical covenants is to employ the unconditional-unilateral (royal grant) versus conditional-bilateral (suzerain-vassal) distinction.[26] It is on this basis that the Abrahamic, Davidic, and new covenants are often characterised as royal grant covenants (unconditional), while the covenant with creation and the covenant with Israel are described as suzerain-vassal covenants (conditional). From here a variety of theological conclusions are drawn depending on the issue. For example, as chapter 8 discussed, on the basis of this distinction Paul Williamson argues that there are two Abrahamic covenants: an unconditional one made in Genesis 15 and a conditional one made in Genesis 17. Or, this distinction is often utilized as part of the larger law-gospel contrast (which is linked to the larger faith-works contrast) so that the covenant with creation and the Sinai covenant are viewed as "law" or examples of the covenant of works, while the Abrahamic, the Davidic, and the new covenant are viewed as "gospel" or a covenant of grace. Or, from another theological issue, dispensational theology argues that the land promise to Israel, which was given

---

[26] See, e.g., Craig A. Blaising, "The Structure of Biblical Covenants: The Covenants Prior to Christ," in Craig A. Blaising and Darrell L. Bock, *Progressive Dispensationalism* (Wheaton, IL: BridgePoint, 1993), 128–211; Paul R. Williamson, *Sealed with an Oath: Covenant in God's Unfolding Purpose*, NSBT 23 (Downers Grove, IL: InterVarsity Press, 2007), 17–43; Michael S. Horton, *God of Promise: Introducing Covenant Theology* (Grand Rapids, MI: Baker, 2006), 23–110.

in the Abrahamic covenant, was an unconditional promise since it was part of an unconditional covenant. It is for this reason that this promise must still be fulfilled in the future millennial age, since not all aspects of it, so dispensationalists claim, have been realized, e.g., the ruling of the Davidic king in the land of Israel over the nations. On the other hand, covenant theology not only views the "land" more typologically but will often argue, as Michael Horton does, that the promises made to Israel, especially in relation to the land, were conditional and were in fact forfeited and are now spiritually fulfilled in the church. Or, in relation to the genealogical principle, covenant theology argues that this principle is given in the unconditional Abrahamic covenant so that it continues unchanged and unchanging even in the new covenant, since the new covenant is basically a continuation and renewal of the Abrahamic covenant, with allowances made for obvious differences due to Christ's work.

However, as discussed in the previous chapters, we dissent from this common way of distinguishing the biblical covenants. As the exposition has demonstrated, we believe it is too reductionistic to view the Old Testament covenants in this way. Instead, the Old Testament covenants consist of unconditional (unilateral) and conditional (bilateral) elements blended together. In fact, it is precisely due to this blend that there is a deliberate *tension* within the covenants—a tension which is heightened as the story line of Scripture and the biblical covenants progress toward their fulfilment in Christ.

On the one hand, what the covenants and story line of Scripture reveal is the sovereign promise making and covenant keeping God who never fails. He is the covenant Lord who supremely reveals himself as the God of *ḥesed* and *'ĕmet* or, in New Testament terms, "grace and truth." As Creator and Lord, he chooses to enter into relationships with his creatures, and in those relationships he always shows himself to be the faithful partner. He always remains true to himself, his own character, and his promises, and it is on this basis alone that we can hope, trust, and find all our confidence in him. Does not the author of Hebrews capture this point well when he reflects on the certainty of God's covenant promises, especially as those promises are brought to fulfilment in Christ? The author states, "So when God desired to show more convincingly to the heirs of the promise the unchangeable character of his purpose, he guaranteed it with an oath, so that by two unchangeable things, in which it is impossible for God to lie, we who have fled for refuge might have strong encouragement to hold fast to the hope set before us" (Heb. 6:17–18, ESV). The covenants, then, reveal first and foremost the incredible sovereign-personal triune God of Scripture who is our covenant Lord, who makes and keeps his promises—and as such they can never be thwarted. It is for this reason that all of the biblical covenants are unconditional or unilaterally guaranteed by the power and grace of God. Whether it is with Adam in the garden or with other covenant heads, God's commitment to his image-bearers and creation, tied to his promise in Genesis 3:15, will never fail. That same promise runs across the entire Canon, and it is developed through the biblical covenants until it comes to its most profound fulfilment in the coming of God's own dear Son. It continues in the Noahic covenant; it is given more definition and expansion in the Abrahamic; it undergirds the old covenant and the Davidic, and, as noted, it reaches its crescendo in the person and work of Christ.

On the other hand, all the biblical covenants also demand an obedient partner. God as our Creator and Lord demands from his image-bearers, who were made to know him, complete devotion and obedience. In this sense, there is a conditional or bilateral element to the covenants. This is certainly evident with Adam as he is given commands and responsibilities to fulfill, with the expectation that he will do so perfectly. Even though we do not agree with all aspects of covenant theology's "covenant of works," at this point we do think they are on the right track. Furthermore, in the Noahic covenant, obedience is also demanded, which is also true of Abraham, the nation of Israel, David and his sons, and in the greatest way imaginable in the coming of the Son, who obeys perfectly and completely, in every aspect of his life and especially even unto death on a cross (Phil. 2:6–11).

Yet, as the biblical covenants progress through redemptive-history, this *tension* grows, since it becomes evident that it is only the Lord himself who remains the faithful covenant partner. From his initial promise in Genesis 3:15 to reverse the effects of sin and death; from his increasingly greater promises made through the covenants; from the beautiful picture of covenant initiation in Genesis 15, which demonstrates that he takes the covenant obligations solely upon himself; from the provision of a sacrificial system to atone for sin (Lev. 17:11); from repeatedly keeping his promises to a rebellious and hardhearted people, God shows himself, time and time again, to be the faithful covenant partner. By contrast, all the human covenant mediators—Adam, Noah, Abraham, Israel, David and his sons—show themselves to be unfaithful, disobedient covenant breakers—some to a greater extent than others. As a result, there is no faithful, obedient son who fully obeys the demands of the covenant. Obedience *must* be rendered, but there is no obedient image-bearer/son to do so. How, then, can God remain the holy and just God that he is and continue to be present with us in covenant relation? How can he remain in relation with us unless our disobedience is removed and our sin is paid for in full? As one works across the covenants and the *tension* increases, there is only one answer to these questions: it is only if God himself, as the covenant maker and keeper, unilaterally acts to keep his own promise through the provision of a faithful covenant partner that a new and better covenant can be established. It is only in the giving of his Son and through the Son's obedient life and death for us as God the Son *incarnate* that our redemption is secured, our sin is paid for, and the inauguration of an unshakeable new covenant is established.

It is only by maintaining the dual emphasis of unconditional/conditional in the biblical covenants, leading us to their fulfilment in the unbreakable new covenant grounded in God's obedient Son, that we appreciate Scripture's incredible Christological focus. The story line of Scripture as told by the covenants leads us to him. He is the one, as our great prophet, priest, and king, who accomplishes our salvation. It is in Christ alone, God the Son incarnate, that the covenants find their fulfilment and this built-in *tension* finds its resolution.

With these five summary hermeneutical/methodological points in mind—points that highlight similarities and differences between other ways of "putting together" the biblical covenants—let us now sketch out a biblical-theological summary of how we understand the relationship between the covenants and their fulfilment in Christ and the inauguration of the new covenant age. Obviously, in what follows, only the most salient points of the previous chapters will be stressed in order to give the "big picture" of our proposal.

A BIBLICAL-THEOLOGICAL SUMMARY OF THE BIBLICAL COVENANTS

Adam and the Covenant with Creation

Covenant theology has primarily spoken of the covenant in Genesis 1–2 as the "covenant of works" and dispensational theology rarely speaks of a covenant with creation.[27] For covenant theology, the "covenant of works" was

---

[27] See chapter 2 for a further discussion of this point.

made with Adam as the head and representative of the entire human race. To him and his entire posterity, eternal life was promised upon the condition of perfect obedience to the law of God. However, due to his disobedience, Adam, along with the entire human race, was plunged into a state of sin, death, and condemnation. However God, by his own sovereign grace and initiative, did not leave the human race in this condition but instead gave a saving promise which is identified with the "covenant of grace"—a covenant made with the elect[28]—wherein God graciously offered to sinners life and salvation through the last Adam, the covenantal head of his people, the Lord Jesus Christ.

Even though this formulation is standard for covenant theology, numerous people have questioned the validity of a "covenant of works" or any covenant in Genesis 1–2. We will not rehearse all the arguments for a rejection of such a covenant since those arguments were covered in detail in chapter 6. Instead, we will focus on the most central objections. First, exegetically, since the word "covenant" (*bĕrît*) is *not* found in the text and it is not used until Genesis 6:18, some have concluded that we should not speak of a covenant prior to Noah.[29] Second, theologically, some have questioned the notion of a covenant *of works*. Is Adam attempting to earn his salvation? Does he not already stand in a right relationship with God? And, though he obviously has everything to lose if he disobeys, should we think of it in a "works" sense?

Why, then, do we argue that there is a "covenant with creation," with Adam serving as the covenant mediator? Five points summarise our overall argument, and by highlighting these points we also want to stress the foundational role Adam plays in the development of the covenants.

1. The absence of the word "covenant" in Genesis 1–2 does *not* entail that there is no covenant. Exegetically, as argued in chapters 5–6, William Dumbrell is correct to note the crucial distinction between the two words "cut" and "establish" the covenant. In Genesis 6:17–18 and 9:8–17 the covenant with Noah is "established" and not "cut."[30] Generally the word "cut" refers to the initiation or origination of a covenant while "established" assumes that a covenant relationship is already in place, or it refers

---

[28] In chapter 2 we noted that within covenant theology there is a dispute over the identification of the parties of the covenant of grace. Does God covenant only with the elect or does he covenant with believers and their children? Both answers are found within covenant theology.

[29] See Paul R. Williamson, *Sealed with an Oath*, 44–58.

[30] See William J. Dumbrell, *Covenant and Creation: A Theology of the Old Testament Covenants* (Carlisle, UK: Paternoster, 1984), 11–26, 31–39.

to a covenant partner fulfilling an obligation or upholding a promise in a covenant previously initiated so that the other partner experiences in history the fulfilling of this promise, i.e., one makes good on his promise (cf. Gen. 17:7, 19, 21; Ex. 6:4; Lev. 26:9; Deut. 8:18; 2 Kings 23:3; Jer. 34:18). It is legitimate, then, to conclude that the phrase "establish my covenant" in Genesis 6:18 (and in Gen. 9:9, 11, 17) refers to the maintenance of a preexisting *covenant* relationship which can only be found in Adam and rooted in creation.[31]

2. Contextually, when we turn to Genesis 2, it is *not* improper to see a "covenantal context." Though the word "covenant" is not used, all of the elements of a Lord/vassal agreement are in the context, including conditions of obedience with sanctions for disobedience.[32] Instead of viewing it as a "covenant of works," it is probably best to view it as a "covenant with creation," i.e., an original and unique situation which involved, especially in light of the rest of Scripture, Adam in a representative role on behalf of the human race (cf. Rom. 5:12–21; 1 Cor. 15:20–21).[33]

This point is buttressed by the incredible truth that Adam, and the entire human race, are created as God's image-bearers and by the link between image and sonship.[34] Even though there is dispute over the exact meaning of the *imago dei*—the terms "image" (*ṣelem*) and "likeness" (*dĕmut*) are rare in the Old Testament as applied to human beings,[35] and the terms are not used in a technical sense "with firm semantic borders"[36]—there is a clear

---

[31] Contra Williamson, *Sealed with an Oath*, 44–58; Jeffrey J. Niehaus, "An Argument against Theologically Constructed Covenants," *JETS* 50/2 (2007): 259–273. For a full treatment of this point see chapters 5–6 of this work. One can also appeal to Hosea 6:7 (see chapter 6 for a discussion of this important text) as further evidence for a covenant with creation. See also Jeremiah 33:19–26, as discussed in chapter 6.

[32] God's demand upon Adam is clearly stated in Genesis 2:16–17. In Hebrew the infinite absolute is used to add great force—"eating you shall eat" and "dying you shall die." In the first case the tone is that of fullness of permission. God is presented as the God of superabundance. God even *commands* this permission. On the other hand, disobedience to the command brings with it the threat of death. The use of the language brings out the importance of humanity's responsibility before God and the juridical aspect of the covenant. On the one hand, there is enjoyment of the Lord's gifts, but on the other hand is the condition, that the free creature shall freely approve of his creaturely status in order to continue in his state of happiness. In light of the entire Canon, most people see that the relationship established in Genesis 2 was temporary. If Adam obeyed God, he would then pass from a state of probation to one of confirmation in righteousness. But the text is silent on these kinds of details and conclusions.

[33] See Horton, *God of Promise*, 83–104, who argues the same point.

[34] For the full discussion of this point see chapter 6.

[35] In terms of biblical data, five texts designate human beings as created as the "image of God" (Gen. 1:27; 9:6; 1 Cor. 11:7) or according to his "likeness" (Gen. 5:1; James 3:9). A couple of other texts refer to the renewal of humanity to the "image" or "likeness" of God through redemption (Col. 3:10; Rom. 8:29; cf. Eph. 4:24; 2 Cor. 3:18). In addition, we also have important Christological texts which present the Son, our Lord Jesus Christ, as the true "image" of God, thus the archetype of our being created as God's image (Col. 1:15; cf. Heb. 1:3).

[36] Carson, *Gagging of God*, 204. In systematic theology, there have been three main views seeking to understand the nature of the "image of God." (1) Substantival (Ontological). This view argues that the *imago Dei* is a particular *quality* found in us (e.g., reason, morality, etc.). And it is due to this "quality" that we continue to have the "image" of God in us, even after the Fall. See, e.g., Aquinas, Luther, and Calvin, who hold to this view. (2) Functional (Ontic). This is the view that human beings image God by what we do, particularly in relation to having

understanding of the concept, given its ancient Near East background. In the ancient world, the concept of the "image of the god" conveys the idea of a physical representation of the "god," which underscores how Adam, and the entire human race, are viewed as vice-regents who are to rule and function in the place of God, as God's representatives, as God's servant kings. However, unlike the ancient Near East, where this concept is applied only to the king, Scripture teaches that the entire human race, under the headship of Adam, was created to be "king" over all creation, thus emphasising the dual relationship of Adam and the human race to God and to the created order.[37] This is borne out in Genesis 1:26c, where it is best translated as a purpose clause: ". . . in order that they [human beings] may have dominion," i.e., function in a kingly and royal way. This does not entail that dominion is the definition of the image, as some have sought to argue, but instead, as Graeme Goldsworthy rightly argues, dominion is best viewed as "a consequence of" the image.[38] A crucial text which buttresses this point is Psalm 8, which describes human beings in royal terms. In an important way, this text is developed in Hebrews 2:5–18 where it is applied to Christ, who is not only the true "image of God" as the divine Son (see Col. 1:15; cf. Heb. 1:3) but also the one who is the "image of God" in that he takes upon himself our humanity, identifies with us, and fulfills the role of Adam by winning for us our salvation as the obedient Son.

In all these ways, "image" is a term that signifies our uniqueness, our dignity before God, and the representative role we play for the entire creation so that God deals with creation on the basis of how he deals with human beings, which certainly seems to imply a unique, covenantal relation as mediated through Adam as our representative and covenantal head. Goldsworthy states this well when he writes,

---

"dominion" over the earth. As proof, this position notes the proximity of the creation mandate to the creation account (see Gen. 1:26–28; Ps. 8:5–6). Gerhard Von Rad is a representative of this perspective. (3) Relational. This view stresses that the "image" is found in our ability to have a relation with God and others. This has been a common view among more neo-orthodox theologians, e.g., Emil Brunner, Karl Barth; cf. G. C. Berkouwer. It is probably best to argue that there is some truth in all of these approaches. For a fine treatment of the issue theologically, see Anthony A. Hoekema, *Created in God's Image* (Grand Rapids, MI: Eerdmans, 1986).

[37] This *dual* relationship of Adam and the human race to God and to the world is important. We cannot rehearse the entire argument regarding "image" and "likeness" from chapter 6. We refer the reader back to the detailed discussion there, which established how the two words, in the ancient Near East, specify both kingship and covenant. "Likeness" specifies a covenantal relation between the king and God, while "image" specifies a covenantal relation between the king and his world.

[38] Goldsworthy, *According to Plan*, 96. Among those who argue that image is primarily functional and focused on the role of dominion, see Eugene H. Merrill, *Everlasting Dominion: A Theology of the Old Testament* (Nashville: B&H, 2006), 169–172; and D. J. A. Clines, "The Image of God in Man," *Tyndale Bulletin* 19 (1968): 53–103. Clines concludes that the "Image is to be understood not so much ontologically as existentially: it comes to expression not in the nature of man so much as in his activity and function. This function is to represent God's lordship to the lower orders of creation. The dominion of man over creation can hardly be excluded from the content of the image itself" (101).

Although God commits himself to the whole of his creation for its good order and preservation, humanity is the special focus of this care. Creation is there for our benefit. Humanity is the representative of the whole creation so that God deals with creation on the basis of how he deals with humans. Only man is addressed as one who knows God and who is created to live purposefully for God. When man falls because of sin the creation is made to fall with him. In order to restore the whole creation, God works through his Son who becomes a man to restore man. The whole creation waits eagerly for the redeemed people of God to be finally revealed as God's perfected children, because at that point the creation will be released from its own bondage (Rom 8:19-23). This overview of man as the object of God's covenant love and redemption confirms the central significance given to man in Genesis 1–2.[39]

In addition, it is also important to link the concept of "image" to "sonship" and then "sonship" to the biblical covenants. Just as "image" carries a strong functional and representational meaning, so does "son."[40] As Stephen Dempster points out, "By juxtaposing the divine creation of Adam in the image of God and the subsequent human creation of Seth in the image of Adam, the transmission of the image of God through this genealogical line is implied, as well as the link between sonship and the image of God. As Seth is a son of Adam, so Adam is a son of God. Language is being stretched here, as a literal son of God is certainly not in view, but nevertheless the writer uses an analogy to make a point."[41] In fact, the New Testament draws this same connection as Adam is called the "son" of God in Luke 3:38. This is possible to do because "sonship" carries a strong representational/functional meaning. Adam is the "image" and "son" because he is the representative of God, as is the entire human race. He is to act and function in a way similar to God, under his sovereign rule, as a creature of God. Later in the Old Testament covenants this same notion of "son" is applied to Israel (Ex. 4:22; cf. Hos. 11:1) as well as to the Davidic king(s) tied to the Davidic covenant (2 Sam. 7:14ff.; Psalm 2). In every instance Israel as a nation and David and his sons are to stand as representatives of the Lord and to carry out God's rule in this world, as Adam did before them. In light of this, it is very difficult not to think in covenantal terms when we see this emphasis on "image"

---

[39] Goldsworthy, *According to Plan*, 96.
[40] On this point see Dan G. McCartney, *"Ecce Homo*: The Coming of the Kingdom as the Restoration of Human Viceregency," *Westminster Theological Journal* 56 (1994): 3–7. See chapter 6 for a full development of this point.
[41] Stephen G. Dempster, *Dominion and Dynasty: A Biblical Theology of the Hebrew Bible*, NSBT 15 (Downers Grove, IL: InterVarsity Press, 2003), 58–59.

and "son." Furthermore, this emphasis is also foundational in making sense of New Testament Christology and Christ as the head of the new covenant, since Scripture applies to the eternal Son the expressions "image" and "Son" (though greater) and then describes him as precisely the antitypical fulfilment of Adam, Israel, and David.

3. Theologically, the entire story line of Scripture is centred on two foundational individuals—Adam and Christ. Canonically, it seems difficult to think of Christ as the head of the new covenant without Adam being the head of some kind of covenant in the original situation. We contend that what best explains this relationship is a "covenant with creation" where Adam stands in a unique and singular situation as head of the human race. As God's image-bearer (and son), Adam and Eve are given the mandate to rule over God's creation, to put all things under their feet (cf. Psalm 8) for God's glory, and to establish the pattern of God's kingdom in this world where everything that God has made stands in right relationship to him as God intended.[42] But sadly, Adam did not obey and thus fulfill the purpose of his existence. Rather, he rebelled against God and as the covenantal head of the human race plunged us down with him, bringing into God's good world the reality and power of sin and death. In Adam, unless God acts in grace and power, the original creation will stand completely under divine judgement. However, thankfully, God chooses to act on our behalf. He promises that his purposes for creation and the human race will continue through his provision of the seed of the woman (Gen. 3:15), which in this context has to be understood as ultimately bringing about the reversal of the disastrous effects of the Fall.

Biblically and theologically, it is difficult to overestimate the importance of the Adam-Christ typological relationship for understanding the story line of Scripture (see Rom. 5:12–21; 1 Cor. 15:20–23; cf. Heb. 2:5–18). Scripture is clear that all human beings fall under the representative headship of two people: Adam and Christ. Adam represents all that is tied to the "old creation" and "this present age," characterised by sin, death, and judgement. Christ represents all that is associated with the "new creation" and the "new covenant," and from the perspective of the Old Testament prophets, "the age to come," characterised by salvation, life, and restoration of what was lost in the Fall.[43] This is why Scripture ultimately subsumes Jew and Gentile under

---

[42] See Goldsworthy, *According to Plan*, 99.
[43] See Henri Blocher, *Original Sin: Illuminating the Riddle*, NSBT 5 (Downers Grove, IL: InterVarsity Press, 2001); Ridderbos, *Paul*, 44–90; Schreiner, *New Testament Theology*, 41–116.

Adam, so that anyone who is "in Adam," given Adam's disobedience, now comes into this world dead in their sins and under the judicial sentence of God (see Eph. 2:1–3). In this way, Adam's headship has the deeper privilege of more than ordinary fatherhood. It also includes the dignity of defining what it means to be human, for he stands not merely as our physical or seminal head but also as our covenantal head.[44] Being human, then, is equivalent to bearing Adam's image (1 Cor. 15:49). Now, in light of the Fall, being "in Adam" is equivalent to being part of the "old creation" and an age associated with and characterised by sin, death, and judgement, while being "in Christ" is equivalent to being part of the "new creation" and an age associated with salvation and life. As Doug Moo says, "All people, Paul teaches, stand in relationship to one of two men, whose actions determine the eternal destiny of all who belong to them. Either one 'belongs to' Adam and is under sentence of death because of his sin, or disobedience, or one belongs to Christ and is assured of eternal life because of his 'righteous' act, or obedience. The actions of Adam and Christ then are similar in having 'epochal' significance,"[45] even though, as Moo rightly notes, there is massive discontinuity between these two men in terms of their identity and actions. The two men are not equal in power, since "Christ's act is able completely to overcome the effects of Adam's."[46]

What is the importance of this point for our view? Much could be said, but the main point is this: the "covenant with creation" and Adam's representative role in that covenant is foundational to *all* the biblical covenants. In other words, whether we think of later covenants with Noah, Abraham, Israel, or David, all of these subsequent relations are a subset of Adam and this covenant.[47] This is why later covenant mediators pick up the role of Adam and function as "little Adams," and this is why the new covenant, mediated by the "last Adam," our Lord Jesus Christ, is that which recovers the original situation, though of course in a greater or *a fortiori* manner. Even though the amount of space devoted to Adam is not large in Scripture, his role as the representative head of creation defines what comes after him. We have sought to capture this emphasis in figure 16.3 ("Time versus Scope

---

[44] See below for a development of this point.

[45] Douglas J. Moo, *The Epistle to the Romans*, New International Commentary on the New Testament (Grand Rapids, MI: Eerdmans, 1996), 315.

[46] Moo, *Epistle to the Romans*, 315.

[47] Contra Williamson, whose story line seems to start with Noah and not Adam. Interestingly, dispensational theology privileges the Abrahamic covenant especially in regard to the land promise. Even covenant theology, which begins with Adam, often fixes on the Abrahamic covenant in their theological construction of the church and baptism.

of Covenant Membership"), where the first covenant's scope is as universal as creation, even though in subsequent covenants it is narrowed. Yet, as the story line of Scripture progresses, the narrowing focus of subsequent covenants is restored in Christ, who comes as the new covenant head and who through his obedience brings about the inauguration of a new creation (see figure 16.4, "Time versus Covenant Partners/Roles").[48]

4. Given the foundational role of the creation covenant for all subsequent covenants, it should not surprise us that foundational typological patterns are established in creation which eventually reach their terminus and *telos* in Christ and the new covenant. For example, think of the creation week, which culminates in the *rest* of God on the seventh day after he declared everything "very good" (Gen. 1:31). This not only speaks of God's entering into covenantal enjoyment of his creation and our enjoyment of God as we carry out our creation mandate as servant kings. It also establishes a structure or pattern which serves to ground the Sabbath law in the time of Moses (Ex. 20:8–11) and ultimately and typologically points forward to a greater "rest" to come (Heb. 3:7–4:13), which is associated with the great salvation rest of the new creation and the new covenant inaugurated by Jesus himself.[49] Or, think of the close connection between Eden as a temple sanctuary, the emphasis on the land tied to creation, and how these structures eventually find their fulfilment in our Lord Jesus, who replaces the temple and brings with him the land, although this land is now understood in terms of the new creation.[50] Or, think of the establishment of marriage in Genesis 2:24–25 and how through the biblical covenants marriage pictures a greater reality, namely, God's relation to his people and Christ's relation to the church, and points forward to the ultimate consummation of the new creation and the end of all things.[51] In these ways, the creation covenant establishes in seed form structures and patterns which, as the covenants unfold, take on full bloom in Christ and the new covenant age.

5. We cannot speak of the "covenant with creation" without mentioning the twofold emphasis on the entrance of sin into the world and God's initial promise of redemption—a promise that takes on greater clarity, definition,

---

[48] Figures 16.3 and 16.4 were designed by Jason T. Parry; used by permission. (Figure 16.3 was adapted from a diagram by Peter Gentry.)

[49] For a development of these ideas see Carson, *Gagging of God*, 202; D. A. Carson, ed., *From Sabbath to Lord's Day: A Biblical, Historical, and Theological Investigation* (Grand Rapids, MI: Zondervan, 1982; repr.; Eugene, OR: Wipf & Stock, 2000).

[50] See Beale, *Temple and the Church's Mission*.

[51] Raymond C. Ortlund, Jr., *God's Unfaithful Wife*, NSBT 2 (Downers Grove, IL: InterVarsity Press, 2003).

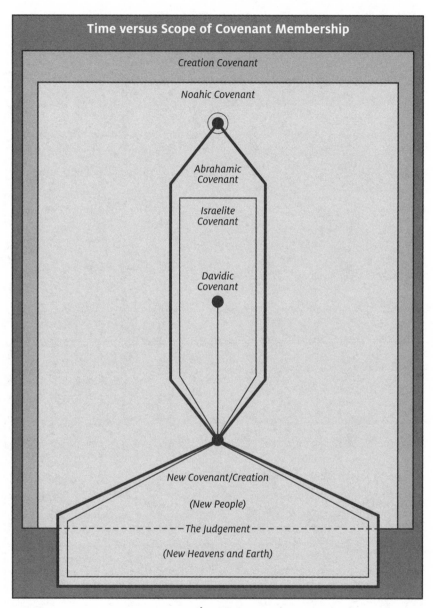

Fig. 16.3

Notes: The line corresponding to the Abrahamic covenant is bold to show that both the Israelite and new covenants are the means of fulfilling the Abrahamic covenant. The Davidic covenant is a single line because, formally, the Davidic covenant is between God and David. The Abrahamic covenant promises blessing to the nations, the Israelite covenant locates Israel in the land bridge between Mesopotamia and Egypt, and the Davidic covenant is a charter for humanity, so they all have worldwide implications in principle, but the diagram is specifically about the scope of covenant membership. The New Creation eventually replaces the Old Creation completely. In the Old Testament God makes the people first (Israel) and then the land (Palestine), and in the New Testament God makes the people first (Christians) and then the land (new heavens and earth).

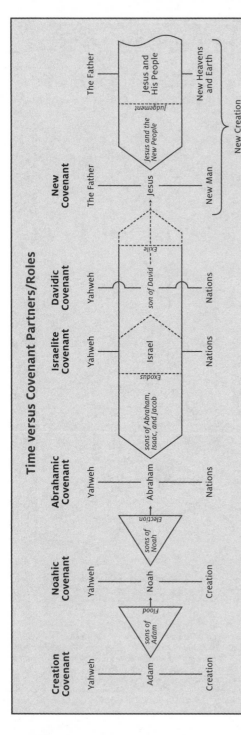

Time versus Covenant Partners/Roles

The middle section (horizontally) identifies the servant king(s)/"son(s) of God" who is/are set up over creation/nations by the corresponding covenant. The New Creation section is provisional and attempts to account for:

- 1 Cor. 15:23–24: "But each in his own order: Christ the first fruits, after that those who are Christ's at His coming, [24] then comes the end, when He hands over the kingdom to the God and Father, when He has abolished all rule and all authority and power" (NASB). The final scene is difficult to portray, since on the one hand Christ "hands over the kingdom" to the Father, but on the other hand, God and the Lamb

share a throne in the New Heavens and Earth (Rev. 22:1, 3), just as they do after Jesus' resurrection (Acts 2:33). I take "handing over the kingdom" to the Father therefore to mean that Jesus has fulfilled both his first-advent role of creating a New People and his second-advent role of purging the nations of the non-elect, so that he "hands over" a regenerate kingdom to the Father, having completed his assigned roles as priest and judge. Then the Father and the Lamb co-rule this New Heavens and Earth; Christ's "handing over the kingdom" to the Father apparently does not mean laying aside his role as a king over the New Creation.

- Rev. 20:4: Christ and those "made alive" in Christ reign during the millennium (= inter-advent period).
- Rev. 21:1: The New Heaven and Earth.
- Rev. 21:3 "And I heard a loud voice from the throne, saying, "Behold, the tabernacle of God is among men, and He will dwell among them, and they shall be His people, and God Himself will be among them" (NASB).
- Rev. 21:7: "He who overcomes will inherit these things, and I will be his God and He will be My son" (NASB).
- Rev. 22:5: The servants of God will reign forever in the New Heaven and Earth.

Fig. 16.4

and expansion in the subsequent biblical covenants. Let us briefly highlight both of these emphases since they are foundational to the entire story line of Scripture and God's progressive revelation through the covenants.

First, Genesis 3 is crucial in describing how, in history, sin and evil came into the human race—and thus the desperate nature of human depravity, which God alone can remedy.[52] Scripture, from beginning to end, takes the reality of sin and evil seriously. In moving from Genesis 1–2, we see how quickly human beings move from a "very good" world (Gen. 1:31) to an abnormal and "cursed" one (Gen. 3:14–24), one now under God's judgement and under the sentence of death. Adam, after having received every blessing imaginable from God as well as the direct command not to eat of the tree of the knowledge of good and evil, and with the warning still ringing in his years—"for in the day that you eat of it you shall surely die" (Gen. 2:17, ESV)—acts in willful, autonomous rebellion against God and thus, tragically, turns the created order upside down. The first temptation and subsequent act of rebellion is stated matter-of-factly in the text, but behind the statement, "So when the woman saw that the tree was good for food, and that it was a delight to the eyes, and that the tree was to be desired to make one wise, she took of its fruit and ate, and she also gave some to her husband who was with her, and he ate" (Gen. 3:6, ESV), is the awful reality that human beings preferred their own will and choice to that of the glorious God of creation. In the words of Paul, human beings chose to worship and serve "the creature rather than the Creator, who is blessed forever!" (Rom. 1:25, ESV). The punishment, sadly, fits the crime: death. The human race is now under a death sentence, described in a variety of ways in Scripture—bondage to sin, dead in our trespasses, under the power of sin, death, the Evil One, and so on (Jer. 17:9; Rom. 6:23; Eph. 2:1–3). But worse than all of these terrible results is that human beings, who were made to know, love, and serve God, are now enemies of God, living under his judgement and wrath, and no longer in a

---

[52] At this point I am not focusing on the entrance of sin into the angelic realm. Not much is said in Scripture about the time or the nature of the fall of the angels. It must have occurred before the fall of man, considering the arrival of the serpent in Genesis 3:1. The passages that come closest to describing this event are probably Jude 6 (cf. 1 Tim. 3:6; 2 Pet. 2:4) and Revelation 12. Furthermore, it is important to stress the *historicity* of Adam and the Fall, for without this affirmation we could not affirm what Scripture teaches. Ultimately, only a historical (and thus responsible) sin and evil may be vanquished and perfectly eliminated. Anything else makes sin intrinsic to what it means to be human, i.e., structurally flawed. But to make sin structural destroys the biblical position in a twofold way: first, by ultimately tracing the responsibility for sin and evil back to our Creator who made us "flawed" from the outset; and secondly, by undercutting the basis for the hope that our fallen condition can be reversed. Ultimately, the hope of a solution to our problem can be found only if our "abnormality" is tied to history and is thus reversible and God, if he so chooses, takes the initiative to reverse what has occurred. On this point see Blocher, *Original Sin*.

living relationship with him—spiritually dead unto God (Rom. 8:7; Eph. 2:1–3; 4:17–19). This in the end is death—physically and spiritually—for to live in relationship and fellowship with God as image-bearers for his glory is life, but to live apart from him is death.

As the text unfolds, the punishment of our sin is described in terms of initial and immediate consequences and then in terms of more explicit and prolonged consequences. Initially, we are told, the act of rebellion "opens" the eyes of Adam and Eve, an opening which is viewed negatively, unlike what the serpent had promised (Gen. 3:7). They depart from God's presence in flight and shame, blaming each other and God for what has happened (3:8–13). Explicitly, God acts judicially by bringing judgement on the serpent, on Eve, and then on Adam, which culminates in the Lord taking two steps that initiate the execution of the punishment announced in Genesis 2. First, God drives the human beings from the garden. Second, God blocks the way to the tree of life, signifying that we are no longer in life-giving fellowship with the Lord, living in his presence in terms of blessing, privilege, and relationship. In order to forbid access to the tree of life, God places the cherubim (cf. Ezek. 1:5ff.; 10:15; Rev. 4:6ff.) and adds "a flaming sword that turned every way to guard the way to the tree of life" (Gen. 3:24, ESV). The flaming sword represents the justice and holiness of God at work in his judgements (cf. Jer. 47:6; Ezekiel 21). By all of this description, Scripture makes it clear that as we move across redemptive-history, the only way back to the presence of God is through God's way and God's provision, which eventually is seen through the biblical covenants and through the provision of the tabernacle, the temple, and ultimately the coming of the one who is the replacement of the temple, our Lord Jesus Christ (see John 2:19–21; cf. Revelation 21–22).

There is no doubt regarding the question of whether Adam's sin is passed on to subsequent generations. Immediately on the heels of Genesis 3 we discover that sin has affected Adam's children to such an extent that there is murder among brothers (Genesis 4). In the genealogical list in Genesis 5 we discover the common refrain, "and he died . . . " (5:5, 8, 11, 14, 17, 20, 27, 31), signifying the effects of Adam's sin upon his progeny. In Genesis 6–9, we see that the spread of sin is so great that it results in God's judgement in the form of a flood upon the human race so that everyone is wiped out except one man and his family. On and on, throughout the Canon, whether it is the Tower of Babel (Genesis 11), or even the people of God as represented by Abraham, Moses, and David, we find that sin has spread to all of them without exception. Eventually, we have Paul's summary statement in Romans 3:23—"for all have sinned and fall short of the glory of God"— and the reason why he can make such a statement is that the problem of sin is universal in the human race. From Genesis 3 on, the story line of Scripture underscores the fact that all of us, not just a few of us, are under the condemnation of sin, and that the only hope for our desperate condition is found in God's provision.[53] Ultimately, the only hope for Adam's helpless race is found in another Adam, the last Adam, who, unlike the first Adam and the entire human race, does not fail, and who accomplishes in his life, death, and resurrection our redemption, salvation, and justification—literally a "new creation." However, before we come to Christ many years later, the biblical covenants in a step-by-step fashion reveal and anticipate in instruction, type, and shadow the coming of our Lord.

Second, Genesis 3 is also crucial in establishing God's initial promise of redemption—a promise which drives the entire story line of Scripture, including the biblical covenants, leading us to Christ. Genesis 3 is situated in the Canon not only to establish the nature of the human problem but also to prepare for God's gracious redemption in and through the covenants. The effects of sin on the world are described in terms of a horrible twofold alienation/separation rooted in the breakdown of the covenantal relationship: (1) alienation between God and humans, and (2) alienation between humans and creation (which results in further alienation with others, ourselves, our inheritance in the garden, and the entire created order). After describing the awful effects of sin on God's good creation, wonderfully the narrative unfolds God's word of promise (Gen. 3:15), which leads us ultimately to the incarnation of God's Son and his redemptive work on our behalf to reverse the alienating effects of sin in all of its depth and dimensions.[54] In this regard, it is important once again to note the first Adam–last

---

[53] Carson, *Gagging of God*, 212–221, says something similar. In commenting on how Genesis 3 and the entire story line of Scripture leads to the doctrinal affirmation of "original sin" and "total depravity," he warns that such categories must be understood carefully, and even then "they do not entirely capture the subtlety, the texture, the variegation of the Bible's depiction of sin, a depiction that is multi-faceted precisely because it comes across in so many genres, with such rich vocabulary and form that it cannot be encapsulated in a doctrinal slogan or two" (215). However, this does not mean that such categories are not legitimate. As Carson rightly notes, "For there is ample biblical evidence, for example, that we are 'totally depraved'—that is, that the impact of sin on human beings reaches to every facet of our existence, our will, our bodies, our emotions, our imagination, our reason, our relationships. Doubtless the Bible says much more than this; it certainly does not say less. And though it is true that not all of this is explicitly laid out in Genesis 3, that is the chapter that begins this downward spiral, and many of the features of sin that will be unpacked in sordid detail in later canonical writings are already there depicted *in nuce*" (215–216).

[54] For a development of this five-fold alienation see Kulikovsky, *Creation, Fall, Restoration*, 201–204.

Adam typological relation. In the biblical story line, it is precisely because the first Adam sinned in history that the last Adam had to come.

Scripture is clear: our greatest problem as human beings is our sin before God. This may seem like an obvious point to many, but in today's world such an understanding is not something we can take for granted. We have lost not only the biblical conception of God but also the biblical conception of human beings and sin.[55] Whether we are talking about the fallout of "modernism" or "postmodernism," the end result is the same: sin and evil are not viewed primarily in relation to God but are reduced to the things of this world. Yet, without viewing sin and evil in relation to God, it begins to be misunderstood and radically removed from a biblical conception of it, which will make it more difficult to grasp correctly how the biblical covenants become redemptive and lead us to the full forgiveness of sin achieved by the work of Christ and the establishment of the new covenant (see Jer. 31:34; cf. Hebrews 8–10).

In many ways, since Genesis 3, given who God is and who we are as fallen creatures, there is increased *tension* in covenantal relations between God and humans. Covenants allow for intimacy with God. God, as our covenant Lord, is present with his people, and his people enjoy rest and relationship with him as we carry out our responsibilities before him. However, given sin, how can the holy, just, and righteous God dwell with us, or better, how can we dwell in his presence? How can God declare us right before him? Since God is, *a se*, holy and personal, he requires nothing less than punishment of our sin; we cannot dwell in his presence apart from our sin being vanquished. That is why Scripture repeatedly emphasises that our sin and God's holiness are incompatible. God's holiness exposes our sin, and it must ultimately be dealt with. Sin cannot approach God, and God cannot tolerate it.[56] Furthermore, closely related to God's holiness is his wrath, i.e., his holy reaction to evil. Scripture speaks of the wrath of God in high-intensity

---

[55] See David F. Wells, *Losing Our Virtue* (Grand Rapids, MI: Eerdmans, 1999). Wells argues that today "sin" has been transformed from being viewed in relation to God and has been replaced with the term "evil." But if removed from the biblical framework, the term "evil" does not express the moral repugnance that it has in Scripture. This is a major problem of postmodern thought: it cannot explain evil because it has no standard to judge it by, so it leaves people eventually speechless before life's brutalities and atrocities. As Wells notes, the difference between the cultural use of *evil* and the Christian use of *sin* is that, while both words may be used to describe the same phenomenon, *sin* deliberately understands it in relationship to God. In our culture, the use of *evil* simply expresses our abhorrence of something; in the Bible, the word *sin* expresses God's abhorrence of it. But in the absence of God and his moral law, these things really cannot *be* evil; they can only be *called* evil. As the significance of the biblical God disappears from our culture, the realm of sin has correspondingly become contracted, which greatly impacts our understanding of the solution to the problem as well.

[56] For a helpful development of this point see John Stott, *The Cross of Christ* (Downers Grove, IL: InterVarsity Press, 1986), 87–110.

language, and it is important to note that a substantial part of the Bible's story line turns on God's wrath. No doubt, God is forbearing, gracious, and longsuffering, but he is also a God of holiness, wrath, and judgement.[57] The *wrath* of God, unlike the love or holiness of God, should not be thought of as an *intrinsic* perfection of God; rather it is a function or expression of God's holiness against sin. Where there is no sin, there is no wrath, but there will always be love and holiness. Where God in his holiness confronts his image-bearers in their rebellion, there *must* be wrath, otherwise God is not the jealous and self-sufficient God he claims to be, and his holiness is impugned.[58]

Now it is precisely this *necessity* of God to judge human sin which creates a severe *tension* in the covenantal relationship, what John Stott labels the "problem of forgiveness." He nicely explains it this way:

> The problem of forgiveness is constituted by the inevitable collision between divine perfection and human rebellion, between God as he is and us as we are. The obstacle to forgiveness is neither our sin alone, nor our guilt alone, but also the divine reaction in love and wrath towards guilty sinners. For, although indeed 'God is love', yet we have to remember that his love is 'holy love', love which yearns over sinners while at the same time refusing to condone their sin. How, then, could God express his holy love?—his love in forgiving sinners without compromising his holiness, and his holiness in judging sinners without frustrating his love? Confronted by human evil, how could God be true to himself as holy love? In Isaiah's words, how could he be simultaneously 'a righteous God and a Saviour' (45:21)?[59]

In a nutshell, here is the "problem of forgiveness." It is an *internal* problem for God in the sense that it arises due to tensions in God's own moral nature. As holy, righteous, and just, God in order to forgive us cannot also deny himself; he cannot arbitrarily forgive without full satisfaction of his own moral character and nature, for he himself is the moral standard of the universe. But as Stott asks, "How can he save *us* and satisfy *himself* simultaneously?"[60] How can God express his holiness without consuming us, and his love without condoning our sins? How can he satisfy his

---

[57] See Carson, *Gagging of God*, 232–234; D. A. Carson, *The Difficult Doctrine of the Love of God* (Wheaton, IL: Crossway, 2000).

[58] See Carson, *Gagging of God*, 232–234; Richard Muller, *Post-Reformation Reformed Dogmatics*, vol. 3, 476–503.

[59] Stott, *Cross of Christ*, 88–89. What Stott describes is also evidenced in Exodus 34. See our chapter 4 for a discussion of this important text and a detailed treatment of the "problem of forgiveness" in the collision between God and his covenant breakers in the golden calf incident.

[60] Stott, *Cross of Christ*, 132. See also the discussion in Garry Williams, "The Cross and the Punishment of Sin," in *Where Wrath and Mercy Meet: Proclaiming the Atonement Today*, ed. David Peterson (Carlisle, UK: Paternoster, 2001), 68–99.

holy love? Or, in the words of Paul, "How can God be *just and justifier* of the ungodly"? (Rom. 3:25–26). How can he be both subject and object in salvation, i.e., take the initiative yet satisfy his own righteous requirements? Scripture's answer to this problem is that *God himself* must solve the problem. God himself—the Creator of the universe and the covenant making God—will have to take upon himself the initiative to save; he will have to act in perfect justice consistent with his own righteous requirements, yet at the same time he will choose to manifest his amazing, sovereign grace. If there is going to be a solution at all, he must act.

Now it is in this context that we should understand God's initial promise of redemption in Genesis 3:15. In addition, as Graeme Goldsworthy rightly observes, "the background to God's work of rescuing sinners is his commitment to his creation."[61] Given the fact that God's plan for the universe is eternal, comprehensive, and unchangeable—a plan which includes and ordains all things including the free, responsible choice of his creatures to sin—there is no hint that God's creation of the universe was "on a trial basis, or with a view to scrapping it after a period of time."[62] Rather, the Genesis narrative, especially with the pronouncement that everything was very good (Gen. 1:31), is best understood as acknowledging not only God's approval of all that he had made but also his commitment to it. In this regard, Goldsworthy is right to argue, "The strength of God's commitment becomes clearer as the narrative progresses. Mankind's rebellion brings judgement but not instant destruction. God preserves order in the universe and in human society, and at the same time begins to reveal his purposes to overcome the effects of human sin."[63] And it is precisely these purposes to reverse the effects of sin in all of its diverse dimensions, to destroy the powers of "this present age," and ultimately to usher in a "new creation" that the story line of Scripture unpacks in terms of the triune God's great plan of redemption unfolded through the biblical covenants.

In terms of the promise itself, God promises to put enmity between the "seed"[64] of the woman and the seed of the serpent; the woman's seed will

---

[61] Goldsworthy, *According to Plan*, 112.

[62] Ibid.

[63] Ibid.

[64] "Seed" (*zera'*) is a key word in Genesis. It occurs 59 times there compared to 170 times in the rest of the Old Testament (see T. D. Alexander, "Seed," in *NDBT*, 769–773). Although the noun does not have distinctive singular and plural forms, one can make a strong case that it is singular, especially given the fact that the rest of Genesis focuses on a single line of seed, descended from Eve, to Noah, through Abram, and so on. See further, C. John Collins, "A Syntactical Note (Genesis 3:15): Is the Woman's Seed Singular or Plural?" *Tyndale Bulletin* 48 (1997): 139–148; T. D. Alexander, "Further Observations on the Term 'Seed' in Genesis," *Tyndale Bulletin* 48 (1997): 363–367.

strike the serpent on the head, signifying defeat, while the serpent's seed will strike a blow to the woman's seed on the heel, signifying some kind of battle and conflict. In the textual horizon, i.e., the immediate context, Stephen Dempster is surely right to argue that the promise would entail that "the triumph of the woman's seed would suggest a return to the Edenic state, before the serpent had wrought its damage, and a wresting of the dominion of the world from the serpent."[65] In other words, it is through the seed of the woman that the Adamic role in creation will be restored, that the curses will be removed, and that the serpent will be destroyed. In addition, it is important to observe, the promise entails that the one to bring about this triumphant work will come from the human race. As Dempster notes, "Just as the woman was built from the man to complete the old creation, so a seed will be built from the woman with the task of restoring the lost dominion of the old creation to its rightful heirs."[66]

This fits with what we have seen about the role of human beings in creation as God's image-bearers. Humanity is the representative of the whole creation, and specifically Adam is the representative head of the human race. It should not surprise us, then, that God deals with creation on the basis of how he deals with humans. When Adam falls because of sin and the creation is cursed as a result, in order to restore the whole creation God promises to provide and work through the seed of a woman, another man, in order to restore what was lost. In many ways, what is at stake in this context is who will have dominion over the created order—human beings or the serpent. The man and the woman in Genesis 1–2 were already told to be fruitful and multiply and to have dominion over the earth. But in light of the "fall," their dominion over the earth is thwarted. The hope for the human race, then, is now found in the seed of the woman who will restore the lost glory. In truth, as Dempster rightly notes, in the seed of the woman, "human—and therefore divine—dominion will be established over the world. The realization of the kingdom of God is linked to the future of the human race."[67]

As the text unfolds there is evidence that Adam lays claim on the promise. For example, Adam names his wife "Eve"—as the mother of all living (Gen. 3:20), which seems to imply more than a mere embracing of life.

---

[65] Dempster, *Dominion and Dynasty*, 68.
[66] Ibid.
[67] Ibid., 69.

Rather, in this context, it is evidence that Adam is reclaiming dominion in faith "through *naming* his wife *the mother*, which cannot help but allude to the more specific role she will have as the one who will provide a seed who will strike the serpent."[68] In addition, God provides clothes to cover the shame and nakedness of Adam and Eve (3:21), which signifies that God will not let his creation project be lost. However, at this point in the story line, it is no doubt the case that this promise is given in "seed-form," and it is truly an enigmatic prediction, which will be fleshed out in far more detail as more of God's unfolding plan is disclosed through the covenants.

In this light, the church was correct to conclude that Genesis 3:15 is rightly called the *protoeuangelion*, i.e., the first gospel proclamation.[69] God is clearly stating that "someone out of the human race itself ("the woman's offspring"), although himself fatally "wounded" in the conflict, would destroy the serpent (Satan)."[70] In fact, it is this promise—*protoeuangelion*—which the entire story line of Scripture unfolds through various twists and turns, with greater clarity and definition, and through the biblical covenants, which ultimately culminates in the person and work of Jesus Christ (Gal. 3:16; cf. Rom. 16:20, 25–27). It is here also that we see the beginning of the important truth, which will be unpacked in greater detail in the biblical covenants, that in every covenant relationship God requires an obedient covenant partner. Yet, as noted above, this is precisely the problem: God remains faithful to his promises, but we do not. It is only if God himself provides an obedient son—his Son—that the covenant relationship will be what it was intended to be from the beginning.

The Noahic Covenant

The word "covenant" first appears in Scripture in relation to Noah (Gen. 6:18; cf. 9:9–11), but as chapter 5 has demonstrated, it is a continuation of a prior covenant relationship established with Adam. God's covenant with Noah is best viewed as a reinstatement and upholding of God's commitment to creation, i.e., his commitment to care for, preserve, provide for, and rule over all that he has made, and in light of sin, to not let the creation project fail. In this sense, the Noahic covenant is a "creation covenant."

---

[68] Ibid., 68–69; cf. Gerhard von Rad, *Genesis: A Commentary*, trans. J. Marks (Philadelphia: Fortress, 1976), 96.

[69] For a discussion of this point see T. D. Alexander, *The Servant King* (Leicester, UK: Inter-Varsity Press, 1998), 16–19; Geerhardus Vos, *Biblical Theology* (Grand Rapids, MI: Eerdmans, 1948), 41–44.

[70] Robert L. Reymond, *Jesus, Divine Messiah* (Fearn, Ross-shire, UK: Mentor, 2003), 69. See also Paul R. House, *Old Testament Theology* (Downers Grove, IL: InterVarsity Press, 1998), 65; John H. Sailhamer, *The Pentateuch as Narrative: A Biblical-Theological Commentary* (Grand Rapids, MI: Zondervan, 1992), 106–109.

However, the difference with the original situation is that creation is now fallen, as evidenced by God's judgement upon the human race in the flood (Genesis 6–8). It would seem that God's commitment to human beings and creation is threatened in light of human sin and depravity, but given God's promise in Genesis 3:15 and the description of the Noahic covenant as "everlasting" and lasting as long as "the earth remains" (8:22), this covenant reinforces God's intention that creation will not be finally lost and that human beings will continue to fulfill their role as God's image-bearers. The "seed of the woman," then, will now come through Noah, the covenant mediator, and his family, and it is this seed who will reverse the effects of sin and usher in a restored situation—a "new creation"—where God's rule and reign is brought to this world.[71]

In this important way, Noah, as the covenant mediator, functions as "another Adam." He stands as the new head of the human race; he is given the same creational mandate (Gen. 9:1–7; cf. 1:26–30); and the scope of this covenant is universal as it was in Adam, since the covenant encompasses not just one people or nation but the entire human race and earth. The universal emphasis of creation which is stressed in Genesis 1–11 is not lost entirely in the subsequent chapters of Genesis (or beyond), despite their narrowing focus in additional covenants (see figure 16.3, which pictures the scope of the Noahic covenant as being as wide as the creation covenant).

In addition, obedience is demanded from Noah as it is demanded from the entire human race. However with Noah, as with Adam, there is incredible failure (Gen. 9:18–28). In fact, by the time we reach Genesis 11, we have Genesis 3 all over again. Even though the entire human race is wiped out except for Noah and his family, and God makes a new start with them, the problem of the human heart remains (see Gen. 6:5–7 with 8:21–22). What is needed is such heart transformation tied to the forgiveness of our sin, literally being born of God's Spirit, so that human beings will fulfill the purpose of their creation, namely, obediently living in relation to their covenant Lord and to each other. Yet, at this point in the story line, that is still future, and what we see is the contrast between the rebellious human attempt to make a name for themselves apart from God and over against his gracious calling, and the election of Abraham, where God graciously makes a name for him (see Gen. 11:4 with 12:1–3).

---

[71] See chapter 5 for a detailed discussion of all the parallels with creation.

The Abrahamic Covenant

It is beyond question that the Abrahamic covenant plays a crucial role in Scripture. In the New Testament, for example, Paul argues that the singular use of "seed" in Genesis 12:7 is ultimately fulfilled in the Lord Jesus Christ (Gal. 3:16).[72] Here Paul is picking up the promise theme from Genesis 3:15, traced through a distinctive line of seed, beginning with Adam, running through Noah, Abraham, Isaac, Israel, and David, and eventually culminating in Christ. In Christ, we have the promised seed, the mediator of God's people, the one who fulfills all God's promises, not least the Abrahamic promises. In addition, Paul's argument in Galatians 3:1–25 is that the Abrahamic covenant *preceded* the law-covenant in redemptive-history, thus demonstrating that the latter covenant does not set aside the former and that the former is in one sense foundational to the latter.

It is also significant that the Abrahamic covenant plays a distinctive role in the biblical-theological systems of dispensational and covenant theology. As discussed in chapter 3, both systems appeal to the Abrahamic covenant to justify their core beliefs. Dispensational theology appeals to the unconditional land promise given to Israel starting with Abraham, while covenant theology appeals to the genealogical principle first given in Genesis 17, which remains unchanged and unchanging throughout the biblical covenants including the new covenant. In light of this, how do we view the nature of the Abrahamic covenant and its relation to the other biblical covenants? Four points will summarise our view.

1. The Abrahamic covenant is one covenant, not two.[73] It starts with God's election and calling of Abraham, God's giving of promises to him (Genesis 12), and the cutting or inauguration of the covenant (Genesis 15), with a further expansion of the initial promises throughout his life as greater definition and clarity of the covenant is given (see Genesis 17, 22).

2. In regard to biblical theology, it is important to note the location of the Abrahamic covenant in the story line of Scripture, coming after Genesis 1–11. Similar to the Noahic covenant, the Abrahamic covenant stands in contrast to the judgements of God on human sin and presents anew the plan of creation. This can be seen in the way that important elements in the creation of human beings are repeated in the blessing to Abraham: God's promise of

---

[72] See Alexander, "Seed," in *NDBT*, 769–773; Thomas R. Schreiner, *Paul: Apostle of God's Glory in Christ* (Downers Grove, IL: InterVarsity Press, 2001), 73–85.

[73] Contra Paul R. Williamson, *Sealed with an Oath: Covenant in God's Unfolding Purpose*, NSBT 23 (Downers Grove, IL: InterVarsity Press, 2007), 77–93. See chapter 7 for a detailed discussion of this point.

a great name and seed, the multiplication of human beings, the provision of the land, a peaceful relationship between God and humanity, the restoration of the nations (Gen. 12:1–3; cf. 15:4–5; 17:1–8; 18:18–19; 22:16–18).[74]

However, unlike the situation with Noah, where God destroyed everyone except Noah and his family, God does not destroy the human race as in the flood. Instead, God allows the nations to exist and then calls Abraham out of the nations. Ultimately, God's intent is to work through the covenant mediator, Abraham, and his seed, to bring blessing to the nations by making him a great nation. See figure 16.3, which emphasises this narrowing feature of the Abrahamic covenant, which ultimately has a universal *telos*.

In this context, then, one must view the Abrahamic covenant as the means by which God will fulfill his promises for humanity (universal, creation focus, which drives us forward to the new covenant), especially in light of the promise given in Genesis 3:15, through his family and offspring (a narrow focus). In this important way, Abraham and his family constitute "another Adam," a calling into existence of something new, parallel to creation of old, but in this case a "new creation" (see Rom. 4:17). The Abrahamic covenant functions rightly as a subset of the "covenant with creation," yet narrowed now through one family and nation. In Abraham and his seed, particularly through Isaac (and then through Israel and the Davidic king), all of God's promises for the human race will be realized—promises that God unilaterally takes upon himself to accomplish, as beautifully portrayed in the covenant inauguration ceremony in Genesis 15. N. T. Wright is correct to summarise the importance of the Abrahamic covenant in the story line of Scripture with these words: "Abraham emerges within the structure of Genesis as the answer to the plight of all humankind. The line of disaster and of the 'curse', from Adam, through Cain, through the Flood to Babel, begins to be reversed when God calls Abraham and says, 'in you shall all the families of the earth be blessed.'"[75]

In this light it should not surprise us that God promises to make Abraham's offspring a great nation (*gôy*), i.e., a world community, a political entity, a *kingdom* in the proper sense of the word. In this way, we have a contrast between two kinds of kingdoms that are part of this world, especially since the Fall. On the one hand, we have the kingdom that is associated with Babel and all that stands in opposition to God (Genesis 11). On the other

---

[74] See Blaising, "Structure of Biblical Covenants," 130–140.
[75] N. T. Wright, *The New Testament and the People of God* (Minneapolis: Fortress, 1992), 262.

hand, we have another kingdom, associated with God's saving initiative and sovereign grace, which will fulfill the role of Adam, bring salvation to the nations, and display to the world the kind of relationships that God originally intended for all humanity. Throughout Scripture these two kingdoms will be contrasted, but it is only through Abraham and his family that God's saving rule will break into this world and the resolution to sin and death will take place. It is only through Abraham and his seed that we will have a recovery of the divine goal for creation and humans, that is, the establishment of God's kingdom and divine rule over this world through this redeemed human society. Ultimately this is fulfilled in the arrival of the new covenant and the new creation as presented in Revelation 21–22.

3. The nature of the Abrahamic covenant is multifaceted and diverse. In other words, in its historical context, it not only encompasses spiritual elements that link us ultimately to the new covenant, it also consists of national/physical and typological elements which must be carefully unpacked as the biblical covenants unfold and which results in a significant amount of discontinuity in the new covenant. This is best illustrated by thinking through how Scripture speaks of Abraham and his seed. First, the "seed of Abraham" refers to a *natural* (physical) seed, namely, every person who was in any way physically descended from Abraham, such as Ishmael, Isaac, the sons of Keturah, and by extension Esau, Jacob, etc. In each case, all of these children received the sign of the Abrahamic covenant, i.e., circumcision, even though many of them were unbelievers, and even though it was only through Isaac that God's promises and covenant were realized (Gen. 17:20–21; cf. Rom. 9:6–9). Second, the "seed of Abraham" refers to a *natural (physical), yet special* seed tied to God's elective purposes, namely Isaac, and by extension Jacob and the entire nation of Israel. Yet even within this chosen nation, under the old covenant, it was a "mixed" people, i.e., it was comprised of believers and unbelievers simultaneously. Not everyone in the nation of Israel were the elect, salvifically speaking, even though they, unlike the mere natural seed (e.g., Ishmael), had the supreme privilege of bringing God's blessing to all nations through the coming of the Messiah. Third, ultimately the "seed of Abraham" refers to the *true/unique* seed, namely Christ (Gal. 3:16), in a typological way. In Christ, then, we have the fulfilment of the promise to Abraham, rooted in Genesis 3:15, so that in the truest sense he is the seed of Abraham, the true Israel, and David's greater Son. In this way, Jesus is the unique seed of Abraham both as a physical seed through a

specific genealogical line and as the antitype of all the covenant mediators of the Old Testament. Fourth, the New Testament teaches that all believers are the *spiritual* "seed of Abraham" now that Christ has come. This includes all believing Jews and Gentiles in the church (Eph. 2:11–22), thus fulfilling the Abrahamic promises of blessings to the nations. In this last sense, only those who have experienced regeneration by the Spirit and faith union with Christ are Abraham's *spiritual* seed (Gal. 3:26–29). Being a member of Abraham's family now does *not* involve being tied to a specific physical lineage, or circumcision, or any kind of physical links to other believers.

Why is it important to stress the multifaceted and diverse nature of the Abrahamic covenant? For at least two reasons: it does justice to the Abrahamic covenant in its historical context, and it is a crucial point of difference between dispensational and covenant theology as discussed in chapter 3. Let us first focus on covenant theology.

The reader will remember that dispensational theology has often criticised covenant theology for their tendency of flattening the Abrahamic covenant by reducing it primarily to *spiritual* realities while neglecting its national and typological aspects. On this point we agree with the dispensational critique. This is why, in the Israel-church relationship, covenant theology so easily views the church as the "new Israel" with the entailment that just as Israel was a "mixed" entity so is the church; and, they say, just as the genealogical principle operative in the Abrahamic covenant—"you and your seed" (Gen. 17:7)—applies to Israel, so also it applies to the church in exactly the same way; and just as the covenant sign of circumcision functioned in Israel, so paedobaptism functions the same way in the church. The problem with this view, however, is that it fails to do justice to the diverse nature of the Abrahamic covenant, and it reads many of the legitimate *spiritual* realities of the new covenant back into it *too quickly*. It does not treat the Abrahamic covenant first in its own immediate context and then think through how it is picked up in later biblical covenants and then ultimately in the new covenant.

However, it is important to note that dispensational theology also criticises covenant theology at this point because dispensationalists are convinced that this is the reason why covenantalists do not view the land promises given to Israel as physical/national promises yet awaiting their fulfilment in the millennial age. This is a fair criticism as long as one can demonstrate that the land promise, in the Abrahamic covenant and throughout the biblical covenants, is not better viewed as typological of the creation, something we contend that dispensationalism cannot demonstrate.

4. The Abrahamic covenant consists of unconditional/unilateral and conditional/bilateral elements and it is not reducible to one of those features alone. As discussed in previous chapters, it is common to argue that the Abrahamic covenant is primarily an unconditional covenant (patterned after the ancient "royal grant" treaties) given the unique covenant initiation in Genesis 15, or, as Williamson argues, that there are two Abrahamic covenants, given the unconditional nature of Genesis 15 and the conditional demands of Genesis 17 (patterned after the suzerain-vassal treaties). Both of these approaches, for the reasons given in chapter 8, we believe are wrong. Instead, it is better to think of one covenant and to view Genesis 17 as a confirmation of God's covenant with Abraham initiated in Genesis 15, tied back to the promises of Genesis 12. No doubt, as promises are given to Abraham and his seed, and then God inaugurates the covenant by the dread symbol of a divine dismemberment (Gen. 15:12–21; cf. Jer. 34:18–20), there is an incredibly strong unilateral emphasis. God will keep his promise regardless of what Abraham does, and Abraham receives God's promises by faith and it is counted to him as righteousness (Gen. 15:6). Craig Blaising captures this point well:

> The way in which Abraham received the covenant also supports the covenant's unconditionality. In Genesis 15, the Lord repeats His promise to Abraham, and Scripture tells us that in spite of circumstances that made the promise seem impossible, "Abraham believed in the Lord; and He reckoned it to him as righteousness" (15:6). . . .
>
> In Romans 4 and Galatians 3, Paul argues that Genesis 15 is foundational for understanding the promissory nature of the Abrahamic covenant. The blessing was not given to Abraham because he performed certain works. Rather, he received it through faith. God gave Abraham a promise. Abraham believed God. God counted him righteous and formalized the promise to him as a grant covenant.[76]

However, even though the strong unilateral emphasis is found throughout, there is also an emphasis on God's demand for obedience (Gen. 17:1; 18:19; 22:16–18).[77] It is right to conclude that these demands for obedience do not nullify God's promises and turn the covenant into a strictly bilateral covenant. Further, it is also true that "Abraham's obedience to God's

---

[76] Blaising, "Structure of Biblical Covenants," 132.
[77] See Paul R. Williamson, *Sealed with an Oath*, 84–91.

commandments does function as *the means* by which he experiences God's blessing on a day to day basis. . . . But these obligations do not condition the fundamental intention to bless Abraham. They condition the *how* and the *when* of the blessing."[78] God's promise, then, is given in such a way that it will be realized regardless of our disobedience because it is rooted in his intention to restore creation and to bring about redemption. Yet, this does not nullify the fact that, tied to the larger story line of Scripture, God demands an obedient son and Abraham does not fully meet that demand, similar to Adam and Noah before him. The tension, then, created in the relationship is that God guarantees the covenant promises and yet, he also requires an obedient son in the covenant relationship. That demand, however, is only met, finally and fully, in the true seed of Abraham, our Lord Jesus Christ.

The "Old Covenant" or the Covenant with Israel[79]
In the Old Testament, the amount of space devoted to the "old covenant" is vast, yet Scripture teaches that it is not an end in itself but rather a means to a larger end which culminates in a greater and better new covenant. This is why Scripture views the "old covenant" as temporary in God's plan, or better, as a crucial part in God's redemptive purposes, yet when that to which it points arrives, the covenant with Israel *as a whole covenant package* comes to its end and Christians are no longer under it *as a covenant*. Unlike first-century Judaism, which viewed the law-covenant as imperishable, immutable, and eternal, Paul, for example, places the "old covenant" in its proper redemptive-historical sequence, arguing, as D. A. Carson points out, that it is almost "a parenthesis (Gal 3:15–4:7)" in God's plan and as such, that which precedes it, namely, the promise to Abraham (which cannot be understood apart from the covenant with creation), "cannot be annulled by the giving of the law (3:17), regardless of how much space is given over to the law in the sacred text, or how large a role it played in the history of Israel."[80] As Carson also notes, this inevitably leads to the question of Galatians 3:19: "What, then, was the pur-

---

[78] Blaising, "Structure of Biblical Covenants," 133–134.

[79] The covenant with Israel has been called a number of things. Sometimes it is referred to as the Mosaic covenant since Moses, in many ways, serves as its mediator. Moses functions in the role of prophet, priest, and king before those offices were separated in the life of Israel. It is also called the Sinai covenant, given its location. Predominately in Scripture it is identified as the "old covenant" set over against the "new covenant." See chapter 9 for further discussion of the terminology.

[80] D. A. Carson, "Mystery and Fulfillment: Toward a More Comprehensive Paradigm of Paul's Understanding of the Old and the New," in *Justification and Variegated Nomism: Volume 2—The Paradoxes of Paul*, ed. D. A. Carson, P. T. O'Brien, and M. A. Seifrid (Grand Rapids, MI: Baker, 2004), 412. See also Douglas J. Moo, "The Law of Christ as the Fulfillment of the Law of Moses," in *The Law, the Gospel, and the Modern Christian: Five Views*, ed. Wayne G. Strickland (Grand Rapids, MI: Zondervan, 1993), 319–324.

pose of the law?" No doubt the answer is complex, but central to the answer is not only showing us what sin is, but also "its function in preparation for the coming of Christ 'when the set time had fully come' (Gal. 4:4), which is itself the fulfillment of the promise."[81] In other words, to understand properly the role of the old covenant in God's progressive plan, one has to think through how it is *organically* related to what has preceded it, how it advances the promise of God given in Genesis 3:15, and how it points forward, anticipates, and prophesies, in diverse ways, the coming of Christ and the consummation of the ages. Four points will summarise the nature of the old covenant and its overall relationship to the biblical covenants.

1. Placing the old covenant in its textual and epochal horizon, it is evident that God's calling and establishing his covenant with Israel is in fulfilment of the promises made to Abraham, which were then confirmed and passed to his sons Isaac and Jacob (Gen. 26:3–5; 28:13–15; 35:9–12). As the God of Abraham, Isaac, and Jacob, God calls Moses to deliver his people from Egypt (Ex. 3:6; cf. 2:24–25; Deut. 4:36–38; 2 Kings 13:22–23; 1 Chron. 16:15–19). God did not set his love on Israel because they were better or more numerous than the nations (Deut. 7:7). Neither was it for their righteousness that they were given the land of Canaan. The basis for God's calling of Israel was not to be found in them, but instead in God's sovereign choice and his covenant loyalty to Abraham (Ex. 19:4; Deut. 7:8). The old covenant, then, cannot be understood apart from the Abrahamic covenant, since it is *organically* related to it, which in turn must be understood in light of the covenant with creation. Moreover, in setting the old covenant in relation to the previous covenants in God's plan, we now see with greater clarity how the "seed" of Abraham is narrowed to the nation of Israel through Isaac and Jacob (see figure 16.3, which presents the old covenant's scope as broad as the Abrahamic, particularly through Isaac, since it is now through the nation of Israel that God will bring blessings to all nations).

In addition, building on the promise given to Abraham, Israel as a nation (*gôy*, Ex. 19:5–6) serves as "another Adam" and fulfills that role to the nations. Given the placement of the covenant with Israel in Scripture, this can only mean that it is through Israel that God will fulfill his promise begun in Genesis 3:15, namely, to bring about a resolution of the sin and death caused by the first Adam, ultimately culminating in the dawning of a

---

[81] Carson, "Mystery and Fulfillment," 412.

new creation. Further evidence for this assertion is seen in how Israel as a nation is described as God's "son" (Ex. 4:22–23). In Exodus 4, God threatens judgement on Pharaoh's son unless Pharaoh releases Israel, God's son, since as God's son Israel was to serve the Lord in complete devotion and obedience, something Pharaoh was not allowing. This relationship between the Lord and Israel, described as a "Father-son" relationship, not only hearkens back to Adam; it is also picked up later in the Davidic covenant, where the Davidic kings are viewed in this same relationship with the Lord, thus linking all of these covenants together in one overall plan and ultimately grounding them in Adam. Thus Israel as a nation served as God's representatives—servant kings, sons—on the earth. They were to demonstrate what it looked like to be God's image-bearers and people. It was through them that the Abrahamic blessing was to be realized and thus God's redemptive promise brought to pass.

2. It is best to view the old covenant as an entire package. As an entire package, one of its primary purposes is to reveal who God is and how we are to live before him (see Lev. 11:45), i.e., God's character (*shem*) and way (*derek*). Further, as the revelation of God's character and ways, the law-covenant also demands our conformity to it. In this regard it is important to stress that the entire covenant is revelatory of God—not just what some identify as the moral law or the Ten Commandments. In fact, as discussed in chapter 9, scripturally speaking, the law-covenant is never partitioned into the later theological tradition of moral, civil, and ceremonial laws. Even though this is a common way of dividing up the law-covenant and then thinking of its fulfilment in Christ—namely, the moral law continues, while the civil and ceremonial are fulfilled—there is no justification for this in Scripture.[82] The old covenant is an entire package: and as an entire unit it governs the life of Israel, and as an entire covenant it is brought to fulfilment in Christ and the new covenant.[83]

3. Building on the previous point, namely, that the old covenant is an entire package, within the law-covenant many typological structures are developed which ultimately find their antitypical fulfilment in Christ and the new covenant. For example, it is in the law-covenant that we see the

---

[82] Those within this tradition differ on exactly what remains in force from the old covenant. Some say that only the moral law comes over, while others argue for moral and civil, with some qualifications. For a fine discussion of this issue see Wayne G. Strickland, ed., *The Law, the Gospel, and the Modern Christian: Five Views* (Grand Rapids, MI: Zondervan, 1993).

[83] See the discussion in Moo, "Law of Christ as the Fulfillment of the Law of Moses," 335–337.

establishment of the priesthood, which in truth is foundational to the entire covenantal relationship (see Heb. 7:11). This makes sense, given the fact of sin, since one cannot have a covenant relationship with the holy and righteous covenant Lord without atonement for sin and a means by which we may enjoy the covenantal presence of God. Of course, related to the institution of the priesthood is the entire tabernacle-temple-sacrificial system. All of these institutions not only serve as a means by which Israel may dwell in the land and know God's covenantal presence among a sinful people, but also point beyond themselves to God's greater provision of atonement in the servant of the Lord (see Isaiah 52–53) who will fulfill and eclipse the role of the Levitical priest (Heb. 5:1–10; 7–10), bring the tabernacle-temple to its terminus in himself (see, e.g., John 2:19–22), and by his new covenant work achieve full atonement for sin (see Jer. 31:34; Heb. 10:1–18). What is said about priest is also true of prophet and king, two other offices which take on typological significance and which reach their fulfilment in Christ (e.g., Prophet: Deut. 18:15–18; 34:10–12; Acts 3:22–26; Heb. 1:1–3; King: Gen. 17:6, 16; 49:8–12; Num. 24:17–19; cf. 24:7; Deut. 17:14–20; 2 Sam. 7:8–16; Matt. 1:1–17; Rom. 1:3–4; Heb. 1:5, 13; 5:4–6). Or, think of the foundational event which first establishes Israel in covenant relationship with God, namely, the exodus and all the events surrounding it such as the Passover. As we work through redemptive-history, the Passover and the great act of redemption as viewed through the exodus becomes a pattern of a greater, new exodus/redemption to come, all of which is associated with the dawning of the new covenant era (see Ex. 15:14–17; cf. Isa. 11:15–16; 40:3–5; 41:17–20; 42:14–16; 43:1–3, 14–21; 48:20–21; 49:8–12; 51:9–11; 52:3–6, 11–12; 55:12–13; Jer. 16:14–15; 23:4–8; 31:32; Hos. 2:14–15; 11:1; 12:9, 13; 13:4–5).

4. Even though the old covenant is predominantly conditional/bilateral in orientation and rightly demands obedience of the people, it is too simple to view it merely in this category. In other words, as with the previous covenants, one cannot understand the old covenant without also grounding it in God's ultimate promise to bring about redemption—something which the covenant Lord must initiate and accomplish unilaterally. In fact, this is what grounds our hope and confidence that God's plan of salvation will actually come about, regardless of our sin and rebellious hearts. Yet with that said, it is no doubt the case that the old covenant takes on characteristics of the ancient Near Eastern form of the suzerain-vassal treaty with all

of its accompanying blessings and curses and God's demand for obedience of the nation.[84]

Israel is called to be an obedient son, as was Adam and the entire human race, yet they fail. Through them, the lost dominion of humanity is to be reclaimed, but they show themselves to be unfaithful sons. The law-covenant holds out the promise of life (Lev. 18:5), yet due to sin they break the law and come under God's curse, as a microcosm of what is true of the entire human race. The law is "holy, righteous, and good" (Rom. 7:12), yet because of sin it cannot save (Deut. 27:26; cf. Gal. 3:10–12); even though the law-covenant as a whole, especially in its typological structures/patterns (e.g., sacrificial system, tabernacle/temple, priesthood, etc.) allows for forgiveness, it was never intended by God to provide ultimate forgiveness and justification.[85] In this way, the law-covenant as a whole pointed forward to God's provision of redemption, but in the end that righteousness comes apart from the law-covenant (Rom. 3:21), tied to God's promise and provision in our Lord Jesus Christ and the new covenant. That is why Scripture can view the law-covenant as prophetic, in many ways, as it anticipates a greater redemption to come in God's own giving of his obedient Son (Matt. 11:13; cf. Rom. 3:21–31; cf. Heb. 2:5–18; 7–10).

As noted above, the old covenant has a built-in *tension*. God demands obedience from Israel, yet they disobey. The law holds out life, but due to sin it cannot ultimately save. There is nothing in the law-covenant that changes the human heart, which is what the people desperately need. In fact, as the history of Israel unfolds, the law-covenant brings greater condemnation because it reveals more and more of Israel's sin; it increases sin quantitatively by defining explicitly what is contrary to God's character and demands (Rom. 5:20); and it imprisons Israel under sin's power and condemnation (Rom. 3:19–20; Gal. 3:10, 13; Col. 2:14). Even God's provision of a sacrificial system, because it was only typological and provisional, functioned as a "reminder of sins" (Heb. 10:3), pointing forward to the need for a new covenant which would bring transformation of heart and the full forgiveness of sin. Yet the old covenant, as part of God's unfolding plan, is the means by which God's initial promise of redemption will take place. Throughout the entire Canon, God's promises are rooted in his sovereign initiative to save,

---

[84] For a discussion of suzerain-vassal treaties, see chapter 10.

[85] For a helpful summary of the purpose of the law-covenant see Moo, "Law of Christ as the Fulfillment of the Law of Moses," 324–343.

for without his unilaterally acting, we, as the entire human race, are without hope. God must act and God alone; but ultimately that action requires the provision of a faithful son through whom all of God's promises are brought to pass. This theme is particularly picked up in the Davidic covenant, to which we now turn.

The Davidic Covenant

In summarising the significance of the Davidic covenant in God's unfolding plan, two points are especially important. First, we must think carefully about the placement of the Davidic covenant in the story line of Scripture in order to grasp its *organic* relationship to what has preceded it and how it anticipates the arrival of the new covenant. Second, we must unpack the unconditional-conditional *tension* within the covenant and show how that tension, as with the previous covenants, contributes to the overall plot line of Scripture.

1. There are two main parts to the Davidic covenant: (1) the promises of God concerning the establishment of David's house forever (2 Sam. 7:12–16; 1 Chron. 17:11–14), and (2) the promises concerning the intimate relationship between God and David's descendant, namely, the Davidic king as a "son" in relation to the Lord (2 Sam. 7:14; 1 Chron. 17:13; cf. Ps. 2; 89:26–27). In this way, the Davidic king(s) is (are) the administrator and mediator of the covenant, and as such, the Davidic sons function as the Lord's representative to Israel.

In relation to the story line of Scripture and the biblical covenants, the significance of this "sonship" is twofold. First, it inextricably ties the Davidic covenant to the previous covenants, and secondly, it anticipates in type and shadow the greater Sonship of the new covenant mediator to come. For example, in terms of the former, the sonship applied to Israel as a nation (Ex. 4:22–23; cf. Hos. 11:1) is now applied to David and his sons. In other words, the Davidic king, as an individual, takes on the representative role of Israel as a nation. He becomes the administrator and mediator of the covenant, thus representing God's rule to the people and representing the people as a whole (2 Sam. 7:22–24). As developed in detail in chapter 11, in the Davidic covenant, kingship becomes the means of accomplishing Exodus 19:3b–6. The king is called to be a devoted servant and son, even functioning sometimes in priestly terms, instructing the nations in the righteousness of God and inviting them to come under the rule of YHWH. Figure 16.3

captures this point by first picturing the Davidic covenant as a subset of the old covenant (for the Davidic king was under Torah as a covenant), and secondly, by showing that the representative, sonship role of Israel is now supremely narrowed in the king as the corporate representative of the people.

It is also important to see that the Davidic covenant is organically related to the Abrahamic covenant and the covenant with creation as mediated through Adam. In regard to the Abrahamic, the great name promise is passed to the Davidic king (2 Sam. 7:9; 1 Chron. 17:8) as well as the promise of a great nation (cf. Gen. 12:2). In this way, the Davidic covenant serves to identify the promised line of "seed" that will mediate blessings to all nations.[86] But there is more: the Davidic king also inherits the role of Adam and Israel as "son of God" to humanity as a whole. As Walter Kaiser has rightly argued, the expression in 2 Samuel 7:19b should read, "This is the charter by which humanity will be directed," indicating David's own understanding of the implications of the Davidic covenant for the entire human race, namely, that his role as covenant mediator would effect the divine rule in the entire world as God intended it for humanity in the original situation.[87] David's understanding of the implications of the Davidic covenant for the entire world not only becomes the basis for messianic expectation in Scripture but also, as noted above, links the Davidic covenant to the Abrahamic, which in turn is linked to God's earlier promises. Thus, under the Davidic king, the Abrahamic promise of the great nation and great name come together. In this sense, the ultimate fulfilment of the Abrahamic covenant coincides with the ultimate fulfilment of the Davidic covenant. The Abrahamic blessings, linked back to Adam and creation, will be ultimately realized only through the Davidic son. Indeed, the final fulfilment of the Abrahamic promise of blessing in a Promised Land will take place under the rulership of the Davidic king. In this important sense, the Davidic king becomes the mediator of covenant blessing, tied back to Abraham, ultimately tied back to Adam as the covenant head of the human race.

This should not surprise us, because at the heart of God's plan of redemption is the restoration of humanity's vice-regent role in creation through the seed of the woman. By the time we get to David, we know that the seed of

---

[86] For a fine discussion of the Davidic covenant, see William J. Dumbrell, *Covenant and Creation: A Theology of the Old Testament Covenants* (Carlisle, UK: Paternoster, 1984), 127–163; and Blaising, "Structure of Biblical Covenants," 159–173.

[87] For a development of this point see chapter 11. See also Walter C. Kaiser, Jr., "The Blessing of David: The Charter for Humanity," in *The Law and the Prophets*, ed. John H. Skilton (Nutley, NJ: P&R, 1974), 311–314; cf. Dumbrell, *Covenant and Creation*, 151–152.

the woman, who will restore the lost fortunes of creation, will come through David's line and will ultimately be fulfilled by the Davidic son. Many places in the Old Testament, particularly the Psalms, carry through this vision of the Davidic son bringing about this kind of rule—psalms, importantly, which are applied to Jesus in the New Testament (e.g., Ps. 2; 8; 45; 72; etc.) and the entire dawning of the new covenant age. When David's greater Son finally comes, all of God's promises will be realized and all of the previous covenant mediator's roles will be fulfilled. In this King, the role of Israel, tied to the role of Adam, will take place, and ultimately, God's promise to reverse the effects of sin and death and to usher in a new creation will come to pass. However, there is a major problem in this regard. As with previous covenant mediators—whether that is Adam, Noah, Abraham, or Israel as a nation—God demands obedience, yet none of those mediators were truly obedient. The same is true of David and his sons, which brings us to the larger discussion of the unconditional-conditional *tension* built within the covenant.

2. As noted above and throughout the previous chapters, God demands perfect obedience from his image-bearers, which is evident for the covenant mediators as well. Yet none of these mediators, including David and his sons, were truly obedient and thus they did not fulfill their role and bring about God's promises. All of the previous mediators could only typify and anticipate another one to come, a Davidic son who would fulfill their role specifically through perfect obedience as the true Son. Yet it is also important to stress the strong unilateral emphasis of the biblical covenants, including the Davidic covenant, alongside the conditional.

Most biblical theologians rightly emphasise the royal grant style of the Davidic covenant; the issue is whether it is solely this kind of covenant.[88] As chapter 11 details, in the establishment of the Davidic covenant God promises many things, to be fulfilled not only during David's lifetime but also after his death—promises which cannot fail. The former are listed in 2 Samuel 7:8–11a: (1) a great name, (2) a place for Israel as God's people, and (3) rest for David from his enemies. The latter are listed in verses 11b–13, and include promises for a lasting dynasty, kingdom, and throne. God's intention, then, is to fulfill his promises despite the many acts of disloyalty on the part of this people (see 1 Kings 11:11–13, 34–36; 15:4–5; 2 Kings 8:19; 2 Chron. 21:7; 23:3), and if God promises it, it will surely take place.

However, as 2 Samuel 7:14–15 makes clear: God demands faithfulness

---

[88] See, e.g., Blaising, "Structure of Biblical Covenants," 159–165; Horton, *God of Promise*, 43–50.

and obedience on the king's part—a faithfulness and obedience which, David understands, will effect nothing less than the divine rule in the entire world as God intended it for humanity in the covenant of creation (vv. 18–19). As noted in chapter 11, in effect, what verses 14–15 are saying is that the covenant will be fulfilled not by a faithful Father alone (i.e., Yahweh keeping his promises), but also by a faithful son (i.e., the obedience of the king to Yahweh's Torah). This is one of the reasons why it is difficult to classify the Davidic covenant as either a royal grant or a suzerain-vassal covenant: it includes elements of both.

Further evidence for this unilateral-bilateral tension within the Davidic covenant is found in Isaiah's prophecy in Isaiah 55:3. As discussed in chapter 11, over the years there has been a debate over the interpretation of the phrase *ḥasdê dāwîd*, often translated the "sure mercies for David." Yet, as argued in chapter 11, this rendering is not correct. The better way to translate the text in normal linguistic usage of this phrase is to interpret David as the agent or subject, not the object, hence, "sure mercies or faithfulness performed by David." This is significant given the importance of Isaiah 55 in Isaiah's prophecy of the Messiah and coming Davidic King. We cannot rehearse all the arguments to demonstrate that the "servant of the Lord" in Isaiah is both Davidic and royal, but this has been repeatedly shown.[89] For example, the figurative language in which the Davidic king and kingdom are portrayed as a great tree cut down (Isa. 6:13) and the reference to the shoot and root in Isaiah 53:2 link the servant of the Lord texts to the vision of a future king who is nothing less than another David (Isa. 11:1, 10). In fact, the ongoing debate regarding the identification of Israel as the servant of the Lord and an individual as the servant who delivers the nation is resolved if we realize that the Davidic king is a representative figure for the entire nation. All of this is to say that Isaiah presents us with a unified vision of a coming Davidic king who is identified as the "servant of the Lord," who as a result of his victorious work will restore Zion (Isa. 2:1–5), who will delight in the fear of the Lord (11:1–10), who will perfectly represent the Lord by implementing social justice (11:3–5), who will become a banner to the nations (11:10) and through his instruction will teach and rule the nations (42:1, 3–4; 49:1, 6), and so on. Then in Isaiah 55, we have a link made between the Davidic covenant and the new covenant, where it is announced

---

[89] For example, see Daniel I. Block, "My Servant David: Ancient Israel's Vision of the Messiah," in *Israel's Messiah in the Bible and the Dead Sea Scrolls*, ed. Richard S. Hess and M. Daniel Carroll (Grand Rapids, MI: Baker, 2003), 17–56; J. Alec Motyer, *The Prophecy of Isaiah: An Introduction and Commentary* (Downers Grove, IL: InterVarsity Press, 1993); cf. our chapter 11 for this discussion.

that, on the basis of the work accomplished by the servant of the Lord, God will make an "everlasting covenant" on the basis of the "faithfulness performed by David" (55:3). In this way, the Lord performs his covenant obligation, but David performs his too, and thus the new covenant is inaugurated and the promise is fulfilled. Not only does this demonstrate the demand within the Davidic covenant for faithful obedience on the part of the king, but it also drives us forward in anticipation for such a Davidic son and king to arise. For in the history of the nation of Israel the Davidic kings were not obedient. At almost every turn they violated the covenant, but Isaiah holds out hope that there will come "another David," i.e., the antitype of David and his sons, David's greater Son who will perfectly obey in his life and death (52:13–53:12) and will inaugurate a new covenant and thus ultimately fulfill the *protoeuangelion*, restoring what was lost in Adam.

It is in this way, as the story line of Scripture unfolds, that God's saving reign and kingdom comes through the biblical covenants culminating in Christ. In other words, the progressive revelation of the covenants tells us a story. They teach us who God is as the covenant Lord and what he expects of his creatures; we come to know the triune God, the God of *ḥesed* and *'ĕmet*, through his covenantal actions. In addition, the covenants reveal to us how we are to live before God and each other and rule over the creation as God's image-bearers and servant-kings. Supremely, in terms of Christ, the covenants unfold the "mystery" of God's eternal plan as God teaches us to expect one who will fulfill the roles of the previous covenantal mediators and bring about the promise stretching back to Genesis 3:15. The covenants, then, anticipate the coming of the perfect, obedient Son who will not fail in his role as the image-bearer of God. They anticipate in many ways that in the coming and work of this Son—this one who is utterly unique—God's saving rule and reign will come to this world and, literally, a "new creation" will result through the inauguration of a new and better covenant. Let us now turn to a brief discussion of that new covenant as it is presented in its Old Testament context and then brought to New Testament fulfilment in Christ Jesus our Lord.

The New Covenant

As one biblical covenant leads to the next, revealing who the triune, covenant God is and his plan for his creation, ultimately all of the covenants find their fulfilment, terminus, and *telos* in the new covenant (see Jer. 31:29–34; cf. Luke 22:20; 2 Corinthians 3; Hebrews 8, 10). It is the new covenant which all of the previous covenants anticipate and typify, and it is in this way that the new covenant *supersedes* all the previous covenants. When the new covenant arrives, we are no longer under the previous covenants in exactly the same way that the people of God were in the past. We are now in Christ and under his covenant headship and all that it entails for our lives as Christians.

In the Old Testament, probably the most famous text in regard to the new covenant is Jeremiah 31. However, as chapters 12–14 of our book demonstrate, the new covenant is not limited to this text alone. It is also found throughout the prophets and especially in the language of "everlasting covenant" and the prophetic anticipation of the coming of the new creation, the Spirit, and God's saving rule and reign among the nations, and so on. For example, as the previous chapters demonstrated at length, among the postexilic prophets there is an expectation that the new covenant will have a purpose similar to the "old covenant," that is, to bring the blessing of the Abrahamic covenant back into the present experience of Israel, and even more than this, to the nations. The new covenant, then, will bring about the Abrahamic blessing in that it will benefit both Israel and the nations and thus have universal implications, as figure 16.3 illustrates. Within the Old Testament, the new covenant is viewed as both national (Jer. 31:36–40; 33:6–16; Ezek. 36:24–38; 37:11–28) and international (Jer. 33:9; Ezek. 36:36; 37:28). In fact, its scope is viewed as universal, especially in Isaiah (42:6; 49:6; 55:3–5; 56:4–8; 66:18–24). These Isaiah texts project the ultimate fulfilment of the divine promises in the new covenant onto an "ideal Israel," i.e., a community tied to the servant of the Lord, located in a rejuvenated new heavens and new earth (Isa. 65:17; 66:22). This "ideal Israel" picks up the promises to Abraham and is presented as the climactic and ultimate fulfilment of the covenants that God established with the patriarchs, the nation of Israel, and David's son (Isa. 9:6–7; 11:1–10; Jer. 23:5–6; 33:14–26; Ezek. 34:23–24; 37:24–28). Furthermore, in the story line of Scripture it is not enough to say that the new covenant merely brings about the Abrahamic blessing to Israel and the nations. One cannot understand the Abrahamic covenant apart from the "covenant with creation," so, in truth, when the new covenant arrives we have the ultimate fulfilment of all of God's promises, the reversal of the effects of sin and death brought about by Adam, and the establishment of the new creation.

In the New Testament, it is clear that the new covenant texts are applied to Christ and the church (cf. Luke 22:20; 2 Corinthians 3; Hebrews 8, 10). Even though the new covenant is made with the "house of Israel and with the house of Judah" (Jer. 31:31), contra classic dispensational teaching the New Testament applies it to the church through the mediatorial work of Jesus Christ, David's greater Son, the true Israel, and the last Adam.[90] Minimally, whatever complex relations exist between Israel and the church, which dispensational and covenant theology dispute, Israel is related to the church in a typological relation through Christ. One cannot separate Israel and the church too much, i.e., ontologically, as much of dispensational thought does. Yet, contra covenant theology, one cannot equate the two either, as if Israel is the church and vice versa, without any distinction between the two in terms of their redemptive-historical and covenantal differences. Israel as a people serves a number of purposes in God's plan. It is a physical nation that is the means by which God brings about his promises; it is typological of a greater Son, our Lord Jesus Christ; and within it the true people of God are found (the elect or the remnant, i.e., people of faith), yet it also anticipates, through Christ, the church. However it is a mistake, which covenant theology often makes, to think that Israel and the church are the same kind of covenant communities.

Probably the most distinguishing difference between the two communities is that Israel is a *mixed* community (i.e., comprised of believers and unbelievers) while the church is a *regenerate* community (i.e., comprised of believers who have been born of the Spirit and have professed faith in Christ). It is important to stress that, not only is this difference taught in the New Testament, it is also anticipated in the Old Testament, particularly in Jeremiah 31. For our purposes, we want to summarise the nature of the new covenant specifically in contrast with the old covenant, by focusing on three major differences—which the Old Testament itself anticipates—that highlight not only the culminating nature of the new covenant but also why it is so much more intimately related to the greater work of Christ, our new covenant head. Let us unpack these three differences by asking this question: what is *new* about the "new covenant"?[91]

1. In contrast with the old covenant, there are *structural* differences in the new covenant. Under the old covenant, as D. A. Carson has noted,

---

[90] It is not enough to say that the New Testament applies the new covenant texts to the church, since as chapters 12–13 demonstrate, the Old Testament itself views the new covenant as applying to the nations, who are included in the renewed and restored Israel as a result of Messiah's work.

[91] There is debate over the meaning of the word "new" (Heb., *hadas*; LXX, *kainos*) in "new covenant." Some argue that the word only means "renewed" (e.g., Lam. 3:22–23) and others argue that it means "new" in a qualitatively different sense (Ex. 1:8; Deut. 32:17; 1 Sam. 6:7; Eccles. 1:10). Ultimately the "newness" of the new covenant must be contextually determined. On this debate see Dumbrell, *Covenant and Creation*, 175; James R. White, "The Newness of the New Covenant: Part 1" *Reformed Baptist Theological Review* 1:2 (2004), 144–152; and Carl B. Hoch, Jr., *All Things New* (Grand Rapids, MI: Baker, 1995), 105–107.

God dealt with his people in a mediated or "tribal" fashion.[92] Despite remnant themes and an emphasis on individual believers, the Old Testament pictures God working with his people as a tribal grouping whose knowledge of God and whose relations with God were uniquely dependent on specially endowed leaders—thus the strong emphasis on the Spirit of God being poured out, not on each believer, but distinctively on prophets, priests, kings, and a few designated special leaders (e.g., Bezalel). Given this hierarchical structure of the covenant community, when these leaders did what was right, the entire nation benefited. However, when they did not, the entire nation suffered from their actions. But what Jeremiah anticipates is that this tribal structure is going to change—"In those days they shall no longer say: 'The fathers have eaten sour grapes, and the children's teeth are set on edge.' But everyone shall die for his own sin. Each man who eats sour grapes, his teeth shall be set on edge" (Jer. 31:29–30). As Carson observes,

> In short, Jeremiah understood that the new covenant would bring some dramatic changes. The tribal nature of the people of God would end, and the new covenant would bring with it a new emphasis on the distribution of the knowledge of God down to the level of each member of the covenant community. Knowledge of God would no longer be mediated through specially endowed leaders, for *all* of God's covenant people would know him, from the least to the greatest. Jeremiah is not concerned to say there would be no teachers under the new covenant, but to remove from leaders that distinctive mediatorial role that made the knowledge of God among the people at large a secondary knowledge, a mediated knowledge.[93]

This is *not* to say that the new covenant is not a mediated covenant; it *is* mediated, in and through our Lord Jesus Christ, the antitype of all the previous covenant mediators. In Christ, we have the promised one, the mediator of God's people, David's greater Son, the true Israel, the true seed of Abraham, and the last Adam. Yet, the covenant community that he mediates is not structurally the same as the previous covenant communities. Those who come under his mediatorial rule and reign include both believing Jews and believing Gentiles, and one enters this relationship, not by physical birth, circumcision, or the Torah, but through spiritual rebirth and faith. Only those

---

[92] See D. A. Carson, *Showing the Spirit: A Theological Exposition of 1 Corinthians 12–14* (Grand Rapids, MI: Baker, 1987), 150–158; cf. D. A. Carson, "Evangelicals, Ecumenism, and the Church," in *Evangelical Affirmations*, ed. Kenneth S. Kantzer and Carl F. H. Henry (Grand Rapids, MI: Zondervan, 1990), 347–385.

[93] Carson, *Showing the Spirit*, 152. It is clear from the context that the knowledge spoken of here is a salvific knowledge. See Dumbrell, *Covenant and Creation*, 177–178; Paul R. House, *Old Testament Theology*, 317–321.

who are in faith union with their covenant head are his family, and *all* of his family know God and have access to God through Christ. Another way of stating this is that under previous covenants the genealogical principle, that is, the relationship between the covenant mediator and his seed, was *physical* (e.g., Adam, Noah, Abraham, Israel, David), but now, in Christ, under his mediation, the relationship between Christ and his people is *spiritual*. This is why *all* those within the covenant community know the Lord in contrast to the "mixed" nation of Israel.

Related to this point is the prophetic anticipation that, in the dawning of the new covenant age associated with the coming of the Messiah, the Holy Spirit would be uniquely poured out first upon Messiah (see Isa. 11:1–3; 49:1–2, 61:1ff.) and then on Messiah's people and the entire new covenant era (see Ezek. 11:19–20; 36:25–27; Joel 2:28–32; cf. Num. 11:27–29).[94] Under the old covenant, the "tribal" structure of the covenant community also meant that the Spirit was uniquely poured out on leaders. But what the prophets anticipate is a crucial change: the coming of the new covenant era would witness a *universal* distribution of the Spirit (see Joel 2:28–32; Acts 2). God would pour out his Spirit on *all* flesh, namely, *all* those within the covenant community. Thus, *all* those "under the new covenant" enjoy the promised gift of the eschatological Holy Spirit (see Eph. 1:13–14). In the New Testament, the Spirit is presented as the agent who not only gives us life but also enables us to follow God's decrees and keep God's laws, thus making us covenant keepers and *not* breakers. The role which Israel was supposed to play is now fulfilled in us, the church, by the Spirit.[95] And it is precisely the dawning of this new age that John the Baptist announces first in Christ (Matt. 3:11), which is signalled at Pentecost in Messiah's people, and which is grounded in the person and work of Christ (see John 7:39; 16:7; Acts 2:33)—a work which is associated with the inauguration of the new covenant era. That is why it came to be understood that the new covenant era, the messianic age, would also be the age of the Spirit. In this age, Christ sends the Spirit to *all* believers and the Spirit becomes the precious seal, down payment, and guarantee of the promised inheritance of the last day. To be "in Christ" is to have the Spirit, for, as Paul reminds us, "if anyone does

---

[94] On this point see Max Turner, "Holy Spirit," in *NDBT*, 551–558; Wells, *God the Evangelist*, 1–4; Geerhardus Vos, "The Eschatological Aspect of the Pauline Conception of the Spirit," in *Redemptive History and Biblical Interpretation: The Shorter Writings of Geerhardus Vos*, ed. Richard B. Gaffin, Jr. (Phillipsburg, NJ: P&R, 2001), 91–125; Hoekema, *Bible and the Future*, 55–67.

[95] On this point see Thomas R. Schreiner, *Romans*, Baker Exegetical Commentary on the New Testament (Grand Rapids, MI: Baker, 1998), 395–468.

not have the Spirit of Christ, he does not belong to Christ" (Rom. 8:9). What is the point of all of this? It is simply this: one cannot understand the *new* covenant without acknowledging the massive *structural* changes that have taken place, all tied to the coming of the Christ, who inaugurates this era along with the massive changes this era brings.

2. The *nature* of the new covenant community is different than the old. Jeremiah signals this in two ways. First, he contrasts the new covenant with the old—"not like the covenant that I made with their fathers on the day ... my covenant that they broke ... " (Jer. 31:32, ESV). Second, he tells us why this covenant will *not* be like the old, due to a change in the very *nature* of the covenant community. Under the new covenant *all* will know the Lord, not in a mediate but in an immediate fashion, and *all* will have the law written on their hearts and will experience the full forgiveness of sin. In fact, it is these last two aspects of the new covenant which high-light the incredible change that is anticipated and that is now a reality in the church. Certainly the expression "law written on the heart" is very close to the language of "circumcision of heart" (cf. Deut. 30:6; cf. Deut. 10:16; Jer. 4:4; 9:25), which refers to regeneration. This does *not* mean that no one in the Old Testament ever experienced a "circumcision of the heart"; rather it signals the change that is taking place in the nature of the *entire* covenant community. Instead of the people being a "mixed" entity, now the entire community will experience a "circumcision of the heart," i.e., it will be a *regenerate* people.[96] Jeremiah 31:32 is clear: this is in direct contrast to the Old Testament people of God. No doubt within national Israel there were many believers. But as an entire community, not "all Israel was Israel" (Rom. 9:6). Within the national community, there was a distinction between the physical and spiritual seed of Abraham. Under the old covenant both "seeds" received the covenant sign of circumcision and both were viewed as full covenant members in the national sense. However, it was only the believers—the remnant—who were the spiritual seed of Abraham, the "true Israel" in a salvific sense. As James White reminds us, built within the very nature of the old covenant community, "... for every David there were a dozen Ahabs; for every Josiah a legion of Manassehs. Unfaithfulness, the

---

[96] See Paul R. House, *Old Testament Theology*, 317–321. House rightly observes that, "Yahweh's assertion that all the covenant people will know the Lord provides a profound shift in the definition of the elect. From Abraham onward the chosen nation has consisted of those who believe and nonfaithful persons, a situation that creates the notion of a remnant. Now, in effect, the whole covenant group will be believers, or what has been called the rem-nant up to now. All will receive the future blessings because none will fail to have had God place the covenant on their hearts. The unbelieving majority will no longer exist" (318).

flaunting of God's law, the rejection of the role of truly being God's people, the rejection of His knowledge, and the experience of His wrath, were the *normative* experiences seen in the Old Covenant."[97] However, this is *not* what is anticipated of those under the new covenant.

3. Related to the previous two points, the newness of the new covenant, at its heart, is found in the promise of *complete forgiveness of sin*. In the Old Testament, particularly under the old covenant, the forgiveness of sins is normally granted through the sacrificial system; however, the Old Testament believer, if spiritually perceptive, knew that this was not enough, as evidenced in the repetitive nature of the system. But now we are told that in the new covenant, sin will be remembered no more (Jer. 31:34). The concept of "remembering" in the Old Testament is not simple recall (cf. Gen. 8:1; 1 Sam. 1:19). In the context of verse 34, for God "not to remember" means that no action will need to be taken in the new age against sin. In the end, to be under the terms of *this* covenant entails that one experiences a full and complete forgiveness of sin.[98] Ultimately, when other texts are considered, Jeremiah anticipates a perfect, unfettered fellowship of God's people with the Lord, a harmony restored between creation and God—a new creation and a new Jerusalem—where the dwelling of God is with men and they will be his people and he will be their God (see Ezek. 37:1–23; cf. Dan. 12:2; Isa. 25:6–9; Rev. 21:3–4). In truth, with the arrival of the new covenant age we have the fulfilment of the *protoeuangelion* and the reversal of what took place under Adam, the head and mediator of the covenant with creation.

In these three areas, the Old Testament anticipates and predicts something *new* in the arrival of the new covenant. For the Old Testament prophets it is still a future reality, but when it dawns, God's redemptive plan will be brought to its intended *telos* and his saving rule and reign, i.e., his kingdom, will be ushered in and everything will be made right. The biblical covenants become the means by which God's incredible plan and promise are brought to pass, and all of the covenants find their fulfilment in Christ. Through the biblical covenants we learn how God and God alone must initiate, act, and provide in order for redemption to occur, otherwise there is no hope for us. We discover that, in order to undo the disobedience of Adam and destroy sin, death, and the serpent, an obedient covenant mediator must come. This obedient one will come through Adam, then Noah, and then be narrowed

---

[97] James R. White, "The Newness of the New Covenant: Part 2," *Reformed Baptist Theological Review* 2/1 (2005): 88.
[98] See Dumbrell, *Covenant and Creation*, 181–185.

through Abraham, the nation of Israel, and David's line. He will faithfully discharge his role and thus bring about God's saving rule, i.e., kingdom, to this world as Adam was to do many years ago as image-bearer and son.

As we move forward in redemptive-history to the coming of Jesus the Messiah, think how the New Testament presents him: Jesus is the obedient Son, the second or last Adam, the true, unique seed of Abraham, and David's greater Son. In Christ, all the promises of God, begun in Genesis 3, are yes and amen (2 Cor. 1:20). As the antitype of all the previous covenant mediators, he is far greater; in fact, he eclipses them in every way. The previous covenantal mediators may have anticipated him in type and shadow, but Jesus far surpasses them as the head of the new covenant because he is both Messiah and Lord. For in him alone, we have accomplished the new covenant reality of the full and complete forgiveness of sin and all that that entails.

This is no small feat in light of the problem of forgiveness discussed earlier. In fact, one of the crucial tensions the biblical covenants bring to the forefront is how human beings can be found acceptable to God, given who God is in relationship to our sin. In creation we see how the entire created order was made for God, especially human beings. This is beautifully described in terms of the theme of "rest" (Gen. 2:3). When God finishes his work of creation not only does he pronounce it "very good" but he then rests, signifying his enjoyment of it and relationship with it. Everything is in its proper place and order. However, with the entrance of sin into the world, human beings are cast out of the presence of God and removed from covenantal relationship with him. The God of holiness and righteousness cannot tolerate sin in his presence; it must be punished and dealt with. But how, then, are human beings going to be brought back into right relationship with God, and indeed, the entire created order, without God in his holiness consuming us? This question is given new form in the biblical covenants because at the heart of the covenant is "intimacy" with God. Think of it in terms of the nation of Israel. The nation is the apple of the Lord's eye; they are graven on his hands (Deut. 32:10; Isa. 49:16). God's devotion to them is crystallized in the famous term *ḥesed*, i.e., a love of devotion in which God binds himself to those who cannot demand or deserve such commitment. But how can there be such intimacy? How can the Lord claim Israel as his own? How can he walk and live among them without destroying them by the flame of his holiness? The very nature of the covenant and covenant relationship raises to new heights the problem of forgiveness.

Ultimately the only solution is found in the new covenant. In the old covenant God provided a sacrificial system which allowed for forgiveness of sin (Lev. 17:11) and thus "intimacy" between the holy covenant Lord and his rebellious creatures. But as the Old Testament makes clear and the new covenant promise anticipates, it was never enough. God must provide in a more definitive way. He himself must come and resolve the problem of sin through the provision of a greater priest and mediator, his own beloved Son. It is only in the coming of Christ and the new covenant that the Spirit of God in his fullness is poured out, hearts of the covenant community are transformed, and ultimately the fortunes of a lost creation are restored.

The New Testament is clear: what the Old Testament anticipated and promised has now arrived in Christ. In some sense it began with his conception, yet most definitively it began in his sacrificial death (Luke 22:20; cf. 1 Cor. 11:25; 2 Corinthians 3; Hebrews 8–10). The benefits of his work are now applied to the church—a new international community—joined to him by faith by the work of the Spirit. The promised age is now here—the last days have arrived—even though it awaits its consummation when Christ comes again. In Jesus the Messiah, God the Son incarnate, God has laid bare his mighty arm to save his people in power and grace. In his obedient life and death, the desperate plight begun in Eden now finds solution and the new creation is won. In Jesus Christ and him alone, the prophetic anticipation of God's coming to save in and through David's greater Son is fulfilled. Indeed, as D. A. Carson reminds us, "the promise that through Abraham's seed all the nations of the earth will be blessed, gradually expanded into a major theme in the Old Testament, now bursts into the Great Commission, the mushrooming growth of the Jewish church into the Gentile world, the spreading flame reaching across the Roman Empire and beyond, in anticipation of the climactic consummation of God's promises in the new heaven and new earth."[99]

In a summary fashion, here is our understanding of the relations between the biblical covenants and the basic backbone and framework of the entire metanarrative of Scripture. "Kingdom through covenant" nicely captures what we are seeking to communicate. In the last chapter, we will briefly highlight a number of implications of our view for selected areas of systematic theology, especially areas of contention between dispensational and covenant theology, thus showing how our view seeks a *via media*.

---

[99] Carson, *Gagging of God*, 263.

Chapter Seventeen

"KINGDOM THROUGH COVENANT": SOME THEOLOGICAL IMPLICATIONS

We now turn to the famous question: "So what?" Given our proposal of *kingdom through covenant* for "putting together" the metanarrative of Scripture, what are some of the implications for systematic theology? Obviously in one chapter we can only sketch *some* of the implications. In truth, every loci[1] of theology is affected by one's understanding of the relationships between the biblical covenants, given the fact that the covenants form the backbone of Scripture's story line. Perennial polemics within theology, such as the law-gospel divide, the application of the old covenant and especially the Ten Commandments to Christians today, the issue of creation ordinances related to Sabbath regulation, church-state issues that have implications for how Christians engage politically in society, etc., are directly related to one's view of the covenants.

In addition, in order to do justice to all of the theological implications, minimally, full book-length treatments are required for each topic, with alternative views described and critiqued in terms of their overall fit with Scripture. Given this reality, our goal is simply to hint at the direction our proposal would take in a few areas, especially in areas related to some of the differences between dispensational and covenant theology. A full treatment of further areas will require future writing projects to flesh out the implications in more detail. Our focus will be on four main loci: theology proper, Christology, ecclesiology, and eschatology.

---

[1] Historically, systematic theology as a discipline has been arranged in terms of various loci (plural of Latin *locus*, for place or location). After an initial discussion of "first things" (prolegomena), discussion then moves to various topics and doctrinal areas: theology proper (doctrine of God), theological anthropology (doctrine of humans and sin), Christology (doctrine of the person and work of Christ), soteriology (doctrine of salvation), ecclesiology (doctrine of the church), and eschatology (doctrine of last things). In order to *do* systematic theology, it is not necessary to arrange it in this way. Any application of the Scripture to all areas of life is *doing* systematic theology, but given that systematic theology has been arranged in this way, we will discuss the implications of our view in terms of various loci of theology.

THEOLOGY PROPER

It is almost a truism to say that the most important doctrine in theology is theology proper. From Genesis to Revelation, the God of the Bible is the primary actor, the Lord of all. Scripture confronts us with the sovereign, supernatural God; the One who is personal yet transcendent—the triune God—who demands all of our attention, love, obedience, and devotion. The God of Scripture is central to everything. This universe is his, not ours, and we have the privilege of knowing him and being his servant kings. He alone is to be our greatest delight and satisfaction, so that in the memorable words of the Westminster Shorter Catechism, "What is the chief end of man? . . . To glorify God and enjoy him forever."[2]

We have seen that the covenants are the key to the narrative plot structure of Old and New Testaments as one text. Why is this? What does it mean? Already by Genesis 9, in the Noahic covenant, the metanarrative has powerfully portrayed the faithfulness of the divine partner and the fickleness of the human partner. At this early stage the plot is filled with tension as we wonder how this can ever be resolved. We asked the question at that time, "Well, if a creation ruined by human disloyalty and faithlessness can be rescued only by divine grace, why doesn't God just zap us with his grace in Genesis 10, before we take the incredibly long road that leads to Calvary and the new creation (an "already" and "not yet" of at least two thousand years)?" One of the answers—provided by John Walton—was that a covenant relationship requires a genuine and honest knowledge of the other partner. The covenants, then, constitute a programme that reveals God. Only if we genuinely know him can we have a *covenant* relationship with him.

We saw in the Abrahamic covenant and in the Israelite covenant at Sinai (Exodus) and Moab (Deuteronomy) that the covenant stipulations expound and unfold the glorious character (*shem*) of the Lord (*Yahweh/kurios*) and his lifestyle or way (*derek*)—a character stamped by *ḥesed* and *'ĕmet* (Ex. 34:5–7). Hence the priority of worship for the human partner as the key to relaying the same *shem* and *derek* in representation of the divine love and rule to the creation. In other words, implementing God's kingdom entails constant covenant communion.

But all of this is only the tip of the proverbial iceberg. Why are covenants central to the metanarrative? And why is it that on the first page of

---

[2] See R. C. Sproul, *Grace Unknown: The Heart of Reformed Theology* (Grand Rapids, MI: Baker, 1997), 23–40, for a fine discussion of the centrality of God to all biblical revelation, grounded in him as the covenant God.

Scripture, God is portrayed as a *father* and Adam as a *son*—called to be both devoted/loyal as well as obedient? The answer is that this is who God is in himself, in the essence of his own being. Father and son constitute covenant language in the ancient Near East, and it is no accident that this covenant relationship is communicated by the terms "image" and "likeness," because such terms are intended to tell us as much about who God is as about our own ontology. By the time we get to the New Testament, we clearly see that the one and only true God exists as a triunity. Within the being of the one God we can speak of a Father who initiates and a devoted, loyal, and obedient Son whose relations in the fellowship of a Holy Spirit are covenantal, i.e., always characterised by *ḥesed* and *'ĕmet*—faithful love and loyal obedience. Michael Horton captures this truth well when he writes, "We were not just created and then *given* a covenant; we were created *as* covenant creatures . . . " because "God's very existence is covenantal: Father, Son, and Holy Spirit live in unceasing devotion to each other, reaching outward beyond the Godhead to create a community of creatures serving as a giant analogy of the Godhead's relationship."[3] It is *through* the biblical covenants that we learn more fully these incredible truths of who God is as the triune God and something about his glorious character (*shem*) and way (*derek*).

Moreover, since this is who God is in himself, it is not surprising that these are the kind of relationships he wants to have with all his creation, especially those who are stamped with his own image and likeness.

John Frame nicely summarises the sweep of biblical data by the expression "God, the covenant Lord." His warrant for doing so is twofold. First, God is the *Lord* (*Yahweh, kurios*). Even though the name "Lord" is not the only name of God in Scripture, it is uniquely the name by which God identifies himself (Ex. 3:13–15; 34:6–7). This identification is at the beginning of the old covenant; it is also the name given to Jesus Christ as the head of the new covenant (Ex. 6:1–8; 20:1ff.; John 8:58; Phil. 2:11). In fact, repeatedly in Scripture, in both the Old Testament and New Testament, God performs his mighty acts and discloses himself so that we may know that he is the sovereign Lord and that there is no other (Ex. 7:5; 14:4, 18; Ps. 83:18; Isa. 43:3; Acts 2:36). Second, God is the *covenant* Lord. He is the God who not only talks the universe into existence but is also active in it. Furthermore, as previous chapters have demonstrated, God's revelation of himself and his action in the world is uniquely seen in covenantal relations, starting with Adam and

---

[3] Michael S. Horton, *God of Promise: Introducing Covenant Theology* (Grand Rapids, MI: Baker, 2006), 10.

finding its culmination in Jesus the Lord.[4] The all-glorious God of Scripture, then, is the one who knows, wills, plans, speaks, loves, becomes angry, asks questions, gives commands, listens to praise and prayer, and interacts with his creatures, and all of these descriptions of him are worked out in the biblical covenants. Indeed, as we progress through the covenants, God discloses himself more fully, not merely as a uni-personal but as a tri-personal being, a being-in-relation, a unity of three persons—Father, Son, and Holy Spirit.

Reformed theology has rightly sought to capture the truth of these covenantal relationships within the Godhead by speaking of the "covenant of redemption" (*pactum salutis*) or God's eternal plan between Father, Son, and Holy Spirit. No doubt, while Scripture does not specify a formal agreement within the one being of God, given the Bible's teaching on God's plan before the foundation of the world, election, and salvation, there is ample reason to think that the relations between the persons of the Godhead are legitimately described as covenantal. Moreover, as Horton reminds us, due to these triune relations, our salvation arises out of the joint solidarity of the divine persons. He rightly says, "The joy of giving and receiving experienced by the Father, Son, and Holy Spirit spills over, as it were, into the Creator-creature relationship" so that the love of the Father and the Spirit for the Son is demonstrated "in the gift of a people who will have him as their living head" while "at the same time, the Son's love for the Father and the Spirit is demonstrated in his pledge to redeem that family at the greatest personal cost."[5] It is out of the fullness of these intra-Trinitarian personal relations that God plans, initiates, and achieves our eternal redemption. Reflecting on the biblical covenants is the way we come to know God in all of his beauty and glory. Theology proper, then, cannot be undertaken correctly without first starting with the biblical covenants and learning "to think God's thoughts after him" by tracing out God's self-disclosure, his character and way, across the Canon and ultimately in the face of our great Lord and Savior, Jesus Christ.

CHRISTOLOGY

In what ways does a proper understanding of biblical covenants affect Christology? We will focus on two related areas: one pertaining to the

---

[4] See John M. Frame, *The Doctrine of God* (Phillipsburg, NJ: P&R, 2002), 11–61.

[5] Horton, *God of Promise*, 79. For a fine discussion of the importance of the doctrine of the Trinity and its relationship to God as the covenant God, see Robert Letham, *The Holy Trinity: In Scripture, History, Theology, and Worship* (Phillipsburg, NJ: P&R, 2004), 377–478.

person of Christ and the other to his *work*. In regard to the *person* of Christ, we are using the term "person" to address the question, "Who is the Jesus of the Bible?" or, in today's terminology, "What is the *identity* of Jesus the Christ?"[6] In terms of the *work* of Christ our focus will turn to the debated issues of the active obedience of Christ and the extent of the atonement.

KINGDOM THROUGH COVENANT AND THE IDENTITY OF JESUS

Who is the Jesus of the Bible? Scripture presents a straightforward answer which the church has confessed throughout the ages: Jesus is *God the Son incarnate*. As God the Son he has existed from all eternity, coequal with the Father and Spirit and thus fully God. Yet, at a specific point in time he took to himself our human nature and became incarnate in order to save us from our sin by his glorious life, death, resurrection, and ascension. Or, as summarised by the later Chalcedonian Creed, Jesus is fully God and fully man, one person existing in two natures now and forevermore.

How does Scripture teach this about Jesus? How did the church draw this theological conclusion from the diverse biblical data? For the most part, the church appealed to individual texts which not only establish Jesus' unique relation to the Father but also demonstrate his unique divine status and prerogatives, his divine work and acts, and his divine name and titles.[7] However, an often neglected way of establishing Jesus' identity is by tracing out the story line of Scripture. As God's redemptive plan is progressively disclosed *through* the biblical covenants (viewed diachronically) the identity of the coming Son (Messiah) becomes more defined.[8] By the time

---

[6] The term "person" of Christ can be misleading because it is used in two ways in theology. The first way is in a more technical sense vis-à-vis the Trinitarian relations (three *persons* who share in one nature) and the Chalcedonian Christological formulation, which wrestles with the "who" or the "subject" of the incarnation. With regards to the second way, which we are using in this context, *person* refers to one's "identity," i.e., who an individual is and his significance for us. For the latter use of the term, see Richard Bauckham, *Jesus and the God of Israel:* God Crucified *and Other Studies on the New Testament's Christology of Divine Identity* (Grand Rapids, MI: Eerdmans, 2008).
[7] See, e.g., Christopher W. Morgan and Robert A. Peterson, eds. *The Deity of Christ* (Wheaton, IL: Crossway, 2011); Robert M. Bowman, Jr., and J. Ed. Komoszewski, *Putting Jesus in His Place: The Case for the Deity of Christ* (Grand Rapids, MI: Kregel, 2007); Simon J. Gathercole, *The Preexistent Son: Recovering the Christologies of Matthew, Mark, and Luke* (Grand Rapids, MI: Eerdmans, 2006); Robert L. Reymond, *Jesus, Divine Messiah: The New and Old Testament Witness* (Fearn, Ross-shire, UK: Mentor, 2003); Murray J. Harris, *3 Crucial Questions about Jesus* (Grand Rapids, MI: Baker, 1994); Murray J. Harris, *Jesus as God: The New Testament Use of* Theos *in Reference to Jesus* (Grand Rapids, MI: Baker, 1992).
[8] In this chapter we will not address the historical-critical issue of whether messianism is prevalent or even exists in the Old Testament; we assume that it does, given our theological and hermeneutical commitments. On this issue, see Stanley Porter, ed., *The Messiah in the Old and New Testaments* (Grand Rapids, MI: Eerdmans, 2007); J. H. Charlesworth et al., eds. *The Messiah: Developments in Earliest Judaism and Christianity* (Minneapolis: Fortress, 1992); John J. Collins, *King and Messiah as Son of God: Divine, Human, and Angelic Messianic Figures in Biblical and Related Literature* (Grand Rapids, MI: Eerdmans, 2008); Walter C. Kaiser, Jr., *The Messiah in the Old Testament* (Grand Rapids, MI: Zondervan, 1995); Robert Reymond, *Jesus: Divine Messiah*.

the curtain of the New Testament opens, Old Testament expectation of a Messiah to come who will inaugurate God's saving reign and usher in the new covenant age is revealed and anticipated in the prophetic testimony. From the Old Testament teaching, the Messiah is viewed as both the obedient son, the antitype of all the previous covenant mediators, and the one who is also uniquely *the* Son who is identified with YHWH, hence God the Son incarnate. Four steps will sketch out how Scripture identifies the Jesus of the Bible by unpacking *kingdom through covenant.*

1. Scripture begins with the declaration that God, as Creator and triune Lord, is the sovereign ruler and King of the universe. From the opening verses of Genesis, God is introduced and identified as the all-powerful Lord who created the universe by his work, while he himself is uncreated, self-sufficient, and in need of nothing outside himself (Ps. 50:12–14; 93:2; Acts 17:24–25). As the Lord, he chooses to enter into covenant relations with his creatures through the first man, Adam. But sadly, Adam willfully and foolishly rebels against God's sovereign rule and, by his act of disobedience, sin and all of its disastrous effects are brought into this world. Instead of God leaving us to ourselves and swiftly bringing full judgement upon us, he acts in grace, choosing to save a people for himself and to reverse the manifold effects of sin.[9] This choice to save is evident in the *protoeuangelion* (Gen. 3:15), given immediately after the Fall to reverse the disastrous effects of sin upon the world through a coming deliverer. This promise, in embryonic form, anticipates the coming of a Redeemer, the "seed of the woman," who, though wounded himself in conflict, will destroy the works of Satan and restore goodness to this world. This promise creates the expectation that when it is finally realized, all sin and death will be defeated and the fullness of God's saving reign will come to this world as God's rightful rule is acknowledged and embraced.

2. God's promise receives greater definition and clarity *through* the biblical covenants. As God's plan unfolds in redemptive-history and as God enters into covenant relations with Noah, Abraham, Israel, and David, step-by-step, God, by his mighty acts and words, prepares his people to anticipate the coming of the "seed of the woman," the deliverer, the Messiah—a Messiah who, when he comes, will *fulfill* all of God's promises by ushering in God's saving

---

[9] In truth, God's plan is an eternal plan and not one that originates in time. Stating it as we have done merely seeks to reflect the drama of the story; it is not meant to deny that God's plan is from before the foundations of the world (see, e.g., Ps. 139:16; Prov. 16:4; 19:21; Isa. 14:24–27; 22:11; 37:26; 46:10–11; Acts 2:23; cf. 4:27–28; 17:26; Rom. 8:28–29; 9–11; Gal. 4:4–5; Eph. 1:4, 11–12; 2:10).

rule to this world.[10] This point is important for establishing the identity of the Messiah, especially the truth that he is God the Son incarnate. On the one hand, Scripture teaches that the fulfilment of God's promises will be accomplished *through a man*, as developed by various typological persons such as Adam, Noah, Moses, Israel, and David, all seen in terms of the covenants. On the other hand, Scripture also teaches that this Messiah is more than a mere man, since he is *identified with God*. How so? Because in fulfilling God's promises he literally inaugurates *God's* saving rule (kingdom) and shares the very throne of God—something no mere human can do—which entails that his identity is intimately tied to the one true and living God.[11] This observation is further underscored by the next point, which brings together the establishment of God's kingdom through the inauguration of the new covenant.

3. How does God's kingdom come in its *saving/redemptive/new creation* sense? As the Old Testament unfolds, God's saving kingdom is revealed and comes to this world, at least in anticipatory form, through the biblical covenants and covenant mediators—Adam, Noah, Abraham, and his seed centred in the nation of Israel, and most significantly through David and his sons. Yet, in the Old Testament, it is clear that all of the covenant mediators (sons) fail and do not fulfill God's promises. This is specifically evident in the Davidic kings, who are "sons" to YHWH, the representatives of Israel, and thus "little Adams," but who fail in their task. It is only when a true, obedient son comes, a son whom God himself provides, that God's rule finally and completely is established and his promises are realized. This is why, in Old Testament expectation, ultimately the arrival of God's kingdom is organically linked to the dawning of the new covenant. This is also why, when one begins to read the Gospels, one is struck by the fact that the kingdom of God is so central to Jesus' life and teaching; he cannot be understood apart from it.[12] But note: in biblical thought, one cannot think of the inauguration of the kingdom apart from the arrival of the new covenant.

---

[10] For a development of these points see the previous chapters, as well as the cited work of Graeme Goldsworthy, *According to Plan: The Unfolding Revelation of God in the Bible* (Downers Grove, IL: InterVarsity Press, 2002); and Stephen G. Dempster, *Dominion and Dynasty: A Biblical Theology of the Hebrew Bible*, NSBT 15 (Downers Grove, IL: InterVarsity Press, 2003).

[11] For a development of these points, see David F. Wells, *The Person of Christ* (Wheaton, IL: Crossway, 1984), 21–81; and Richard Bauckham, *Jesus and the God of Israel*. Some specific texts we have in mind are Psalms 2; 45; 110; Isaiah 7:14; 9:6–7; Ezekiel 34, Daniel 7; etc.

[12] In the Gospels, the kingdom is mentioned directly thirteen times in Mark, nine times in sayings common to Matthew and Luke, twenty-seven additional instances in Matthew, twelve additional instances in Luke, and twice in John (Mark 1:15; 4:11, 26, 30; 9:1, 47; 10:14, 15, 23, 24, 25; 12:34; 14:25; Matt. 5:3 [Luke 6:20]; 6:10 [Luke 11:2]; 6:33 [Luke 12:31]; 8:11 [Luke 13:29]; 10:7 [Luke 10:9]; 11:11 [Luke 7:28]; 11:12 [Luke 16:16]; 12:28 [Luke 11:20]; 13:33 [Luke 13:20]; 5:10, 19, 20; 7:21; 8:12; 13:19, 24, 38, 43, 44, 45, 47, 52; 16:19; 18:1, 3, 4, 23; 19:12; 20:1; 21:31; 22:2; 23:13; 24:14; 25:1; Luke 4:43; 9:60, 62, 10:11; 12:32; 13:28; 17:20, 21; 18:29;

In this regard, Jeremiah 31 is probably the best-known new covenant text in the Old Testament, but, as previous chapters have demonstrated, teaching on the new covenant is not limited to it. New covenant teaching is also found in the language of "everlasting covenant" or "covenant of peace" and in the anticipation of the coming of the new creation, the Spirit, and God's saving work among the nations found through all the prophets. In fact, among the postexilic prophets there is an expectation that the new covenant will have a purpose similar to the Mosaic covenant, i.e., to bring the blessing of the Abrahamic covenant back into the present experience of Israel and the nations,[13] yet there is also an expectation of some massive differences from the old, all of which are outlined in Jeremiah 31. Probably what is most *new* about the new covenant is the promise of complete forgiveness of sin (Jer. 31:34). In the Old Testament, forgiveness of sin is normally granted through the sacrificial system. However, the Old Testament believer, if spiritually perceptive, knew that this was never enough, as evidenced by the repetitive nature of the system. But now in verse 34, Jeremiah announces that sin will be "remembered no more," which certainly entails that sin finally will be dealt with in full.[14] Ultimately, especially when other texts are considered, the Old Testament anticipates a perfect, unfettered fellowship of God's people with the Lord, a harmony restored between creation and God—a new creation and a new Jerusalem—where the dwelling of God is with men (see Ezek. 37:1–23; cf. Dan. 12:2; Isa. 25:6–9; Rev. 21:3–4). That is why

---

21:31; 22:16, 18; John 3:3). Even though John's Gospel does not use kingdom terminology as often, John refers to these same realities in the language of "eternal life" (see I. Howard Marshall, *New Testament Theology* [Downers Grove, IL: InterVarsity Press, 2004], 498; D. A. Carson, *The Gospel according to John*, Pillar New Testament Commentary [Grand Rapids, MI: Eerdmans, 1991], 187–190). For John, eternal life belongs to the "age to come," which is, importantly, identified with Jesus (John 1:4; 5:26; 1 John 5:11–12) since Jesus himself is the "life" (John 11:25; 14:6). In this way, John ties eternal life to Jesus, just as the Synoptics link the kingdom with Jesus in his coming and cross work. We are not to view the Synoptic Gospels' emphasis on the fulfilment of God's promises by speaking of God's kingdom and John's focus on the fulfilment of God's promises by speaking of eternal life as if they are opposed to each other. See Andreas J. Köstenberger, *John*, Baker Exegetical Commentary on the New Testament (Grand Rapids, MI: Baker, 2004), 123, who argues this point.

[13] The "new covenant" will bring about the Abrahamic blessing in that it will benefit both Israel and the nations. Within the Old Testament, the new covenant is viewed as both national (Jer. 31:36–40; 33:6–16; Ezek. 36:24–38; 37:11–28) and international (Jer. 33:9; Ezek. 36:36; 37:28). In fact, its scope is viewed as universal, especially in Isaiah (42:6; 49:6; 55:3–5; 56:4–8; 66:18–24). These Isaiah texts project the ultimate fulfilment of the divine promises in the new covenant onto an "ideal Israel," i.e., a community tied to the servant of the Lord located in a rejuvenated new creation (Isa. 65:17; 66:22). This "ideal Israel" picks up the promises to Abraham and is presented as the climactic and ultimate fulfilment of the covenants that God established with the patriarchs, the nation of Israel, and David's son (Isa. 9:6–7; 11:1–10; Jer. 23:5–6; 33:14–26; Ezek. 34:23–24; 37:24–28). As the new covenant texts are picked up in the New Testament, they are viewed as fulfilled in Christ and then by extension in the church.

[14] The concept of "remembering" in the Old Testament is not simple recall (cf. Gen. 8:1; 1 Sam. 1:19). That is why, in the context of Jeremiah 31:34, for God "not to remember" means that no action will need to be taken in the new age against sin. In the end, to be under the terms of *this* covenant entails that one experiences a full and complete forgiveness of sin. See William J. Dumbrell, *Covenant and Creation: A Theology of the Old Testament Covenants* (Carlisle, UK: Paternoster, 1984), 181–185, for a development of this point.

it is with the arrival of the new covenant age that we also have God's saving kingdom brought to this world, which is precisely the fulfilment of the *protoeuangelion*.

4. Let us now take this basic story line of Scripture and explain how it answers the crucial question: Who is Jesus? If we step back for a moment and ask—*Who* is able, or what kind of person is able to fulfill all of God's promises, inaugurate his saving rule in this world, and establish all that is associated with the new covenant including the full forgiveness of sin?— in biblical thought the answer is clear: it is *God alone* who can do it, and no one else.[15] Is this not the message of the Old Testament? Is this not the message of the covenants? As the centuries trace the history of Israel, it becomes evident that the Lord alone must act to accomplish his promises; he must initiate in order to save; he must *unilaterally* act if there is going to be redemption at all. After all, who ultimately can achieve the forgiveness of sin other than God alone? Who can usher in the new creation, final judgement, and salvation? Certainly none of these great realities will ever come through the previous covenant mediators for they have all, in different ways, failed. Nor will it come through Israel as a nation, for her sin has brought about her exile and judgement. If there is to be salvation at all, God *himself* must come and usher in salvation and execute judgement; the arm of the Lord must be revealed (Isa. 51:9; 52:10; 53:1; 59:16–17; cf. Ezekiel 34). Just as he once led Israel through the desert, so he must come again, bringing about a new exodus in order to bring salvation to his people (Isa. 40:3–5).[16]

However, as the biblical covenants establish, alongside the emphasis that God *himself* must come and accomplish these great realities, the Old Testament also stresses that the Lord will do so *through* another David, a human figure, but a human figure who is also closely identified with the Lord himself. Isaiah pictures this well. This king to come will sit on David's throne (Isa. 9:7) but he will also bear the very titles and names of God (Isa. 9:6). This King, though another David (Isa. 11:1), is also David's Lord who

---

[15] See Bauckham, *Jesus and the God of Israel*, 184, who argues this point. Bauckham labels this teaching of the Old Testament "eschatological monotheism." By this expression he stresses not only God's unique lordship but also that, as sole Creator and Lord, there is the expectation that, "in the future when YHWH fulfills his promises to his people Israel, YHWH will also demonstrate his deity to the nations, establishing his universal kingdom, making his name known universally, becoming known to all as the God Israel has known." On this same point see N. T. Wright, "Jesus," in *New Dictionary of Theology*, ed. Sinclair B. Ferguson, et al. (Downers Grove, IL: InterVarsity Press, 1988), 349, who describes three features of first-century Judaism as: "a. belief in the one creator God who had entered into covenant with Israel; b. hope that this God would step into history to establish his covenant by vindicating Israel against her enemies . . . ; c. the determination to hasten this day by remaining loyal to the covenantal obligations enshrined in the law (Torah)."

[16] See R. E. Watts, "Exodus," in *NDBT*, 478–487.

shares in the divine rule (Ps. 110:1; cf. Matt. 22:41–46). He will be the mediator of a new covenant; he will perfectly obey and act like the Lord (Isa. 11:1–5), yet he will suffer for our sin in order to justify many (Isa. 53:11). It is through him that forgiveness will come, for he is "The LORD our righteousness" (Jer. 23:5–6). In this way, Old Testament hope and expectation, which is all grounded in the coming of the Lord to save, is joined together with the coming of the Messiah, one who is fully human yet also one who bears the divine name (Isa. 9:6–7; Ezekiel 34).

It is this basic story line of Scripture that serves as the framework and background to the New Testament's presentation of Jesus. Who is Jesus? He is the one who inaugurates *God's* kingdom and new covenant age. In him, the full forgiveness of sin is achieved; in him, the eschatological Spirit is poured out, the new creation dawns, and all of God's promises are fulfilled. But, in light of the Old Testament teaching, who can do such a thing? Only one who is both the Lord *and* the obedient Son, which is precisely how the New Testament presents Jesus. The New Testament unambiguously teaches that this *human* Jesus is also the Lord since he alone ushers in *God's* kingdom. He is the eternal Son in relation to his Father (see Matt. 11:1–15; 12:41–42; 13:16–17; Luke 7:18–22; 10:23–24; cf. John 1:1–3; 17:3), yet the one who has taken on our flesh and lived and died among us in order to win for us our salvation (John 1:14–18). In him, as fully human, the glory and radiance of God is completely expressed, since he is the exact image and representation of the Father (Heb. 1–3; cf. Col. 1:15–17; 2:9). In him, all the biblical covenants have reached their *telos*, and by his cross work, he has inaugurated the new covenant and all of its entailments. But it is crucial to point out: to say that Jesus has done all of this is to identify him *as God the Son incarnate*, fully God and fully man.[17]

It is for this reason that the New Testament presents Jesus in an entirely different category from any created thing. In fact, Scripture so identifies him with the Lord in all of his actions, character, and work that he is viewed, as David Wells reminds us, as "the agent, the instrument, and the personifier of

---

[17] David Wells, *Person of Christ*, 38, captures this point well when he unpacks the significance of Jesus inaugurating the kingdom and the new covenant age which, in biblical thought, *only God can do*. He writes, "This 'age,' we have seen was supernatural, could only be established by God himself, would bring blessings and benefits which only God could give, would achieve the overthrow of sin, death, and the devil (which only God could accomplish), and was identified so closely with God himself that no human effort could bring it about and no human resistance turn it back. If Jesus saw himself as the one in whom this kind of Kingdom was being inaugurated, then such a perception is a Christological claim which would be fraudulent and deceptive if Jesus was ignorant of his Godness." For a similar view, see Reymond, *Jesus, Divine Messiah*, 239–241; and G. E. Ladd, "Kingdom of Christ, God, Heaven," in *Evangelical Dictionary of Theology*, ed. W. A. Elwell (Grand Rapids, MI: Baker, 1984), 609.

God's sovereign, eternal, saving rule."[18] In Jesus Christ, we see all of God's plans and purposes fulfilled; we see the resolution of God to take upon himself our guilt and sin in order to reverse the horrible effects of the Fall and to satisfy his own righteous requirements, to make this world right, and to inaugurate a new covenant in his blood. In Jesus Christ, we see the perfectly obedient Son who is also the Lord, taking the initiative to keep his covenant promises by taking upon himself our human flesh, veiling his glory, and winning for us our redemption. In him we see two major Old Testament eschatological expectations unite: he is the sovereign Lord who comes to rescue and save his people, who is, simultaneously, David's greater Son. In this way, our Lord Jesus Christ fulfills all the types and shadows of the Old Testament and is also presented as the eternal Son, identified with the covenant Lord and thus God—equal to the Father in every way. *Kingdom through covenant* teaches us who Jesus is, and he cannot be understood apart from it.

KINGDOM THROUGH COVENANT AND THE WORK OF CHRIST

In regard to the work of Christ, there are at least two places where properly grasping the biblical covenants helps illuminate this important doctrinal area, even though this discussion can only "scratch the surface" in light of the depth and breadth of the subject matter.

The Obedient Son: The Active Obedience of Christ

Historically and in contemporary theological discussions, people have disputed the biblical and theological basis for what has been called the active obedience of Christ.[19] In Reformed theology (but not limited to it), the discussion of Christ's active obedience is part of the larger discussion of the nature of Christ's cross work and how his work is applied to us in salvation. Often the distinction is made between Christ's *active* and *passive* obedience.

---

[18] Wells, *Person of Christ*, 172. Gerald Bray, "Christology," in *New Dictionary of Theology*, 137, makes the same point when he writes, "The NT claims that Jesus, the son of David and inheritor of the kingly tradition of Israel, became the high priest and victim of the atoning sacrifice, made once for all upon the cross in order to save men from their sins. Only God had the authority to overturn the established order of Israelite society in this way, and establish a 'new way.' That this took place is consistent with the first Christians' claim that Jesus was God in human flesh, and this is in fact implicit in the frequent discussions of his authority which occur in the gospels."

[19] For example, see Robert Gundry, "Why I Didn't Endorse 'The Gospel of Jesus Christ: An Evangelical Celebration' . . . Even though I Wasn't Asked To," *Books and Culture* 7:1 (2001); 6–9; cf. the various essays both pro and con in Mark Husbands and Daniel J. Treier, eds., *Justification: What's at Stake in the Current Debates?* (Downers Grove, IL: InterVarsity Press, 2005); J. R. Daniel Kirk, "The Sufficiency of the Cross (I): The Crucifixion as Jesus' Act of Obedience," *The Scottish Bulletin of Evangelical Theology* 24/1 (2006): 36–64; idem, "The Sufficiency of the Cross (II): The Law, the Cross, and Justification," *The Scottish Bulletin of Evangelical Theology* 24/2 (2006): 133–154.

Active obedience, on the one hand, as Wayne Grudem explains, means that, "Christ had to live a life of perfect obedience to God in order to earn righteousness for us. He had to obey the law for his whole life on our behalf so that the positive merits of his perfect obedience would be counted for us."[20] As that active obedience is applied to us, it is viewed in terms of the *imputation* of Christ's righteousness to us, tied to the larger discussion of justification by grace through faith. In other words, our Lord, in his life and death, acts as the obedient Son in our place so that his righteousness is legally reckoned to us by faith union in him. On the other hand, *passive* obedience refers to Christ, as our substitute, bearing our sin in our place and paying the penalty we rightly deserve. Together they emphasise that for our Lord Jesus to act as our Savior, his whole life and death is one act of obedience to the Father on our behalf. Salvation requires that our Lord not only had to pay for our sin as our substitute (passive obedience); he also had to live a life of perfect, devoted obedience before God, as our representative (active obedience). In so doing, as the obedient Son, he fulfilled God's righteous demands for us in regard to both penal sanctions and positive demands.

Why have some disputed the biblical basis for the doctrine of the active obedience of Christ? A number of reasons could be given, all the way from a misunderstanding of the terms, to thinking that the doctrine can be maintained only as it is linked to a specific understanding of the "covenant of works," and to a rejection of the notion that God demands perfect obedience for salvation.[21] Yet, such a dismissal, or even worse, rejection, greatly affects how we think of Christ's cross and its application to us. As Greg Van Court reminds us, the active/passive distinction is not just an attempt to describe the judicial character of justification:

> It is also a means of articulating the holiness and infinite worth of God's character and the positive and negative aspect that is inherently and inseparably bound up in all true obedience to his perfect will. For example, it is not enough to have no other gods before him; if one is to be acceptable before holy god, he must love him with all his heart, mind, and soul. It is not enough to refrain from committing adultery; if a husband is to be

---

[20] Wayne Grudem, *Systematic Theology* (Grand Rapids, MI: Zondervan, 2000), 270. See also Francis Turretin, *Institutes of Elenctic Theology*, ed., James T. Dennison, Jr., trans. George Musgrave Giger, 3 vols. (Phillipsburg, NJ: P&R, 1994), 2:445–455; Herman Bavinck, *Reformed Dogmatics*, ed. John Bolt, trans. John Vriend (Grand Rapids, MI: Baker, 2006), 3:394–395.

[21] For an extensive and excellent discussion of reasons why the doctrine of the active obedience of Christ is disputed or rejected, see Micah J. McCormick, "The Active Obedience of Jesus Christ" (PhD diss., The Southern Baptist Theological Seminary, 2010), 1–93. See also Brian Vickers, *Jesus' Blood and Righteousness: Paul's Theology of Imputation* (Wheaton, IL: Crossway, 2006).

obedient to God, he must love his wife as Christ loved the church and gave his life for her. It is not enough to put off filthiness; one must also put on righteousness. Righteousness is not merely the negative lack of what is bad but also the positive fulfillment of what is good. It is this positive aspect of Christ's obedience to the will of the Father even unto and especially unto death that Reformed theologians have termed *active*.[22]

Or, as John Murray nicely states,

We must not view this obedience in any artificial or mechanical sense. When we speak of Christ's obedience we must not think of it as consisting simply in formal fulfillment of the commandments of God. What the obedience of Christ involved for him is perhaps nowhere more strikingly expressed than in Hebrews 2:10–18; 5:8–10 where we are told that Jesus "learned obedience from the things which he suffered," that he was made perfect through sufferings, and that "being made perfect he became to all who obey him the author of eternal salvation." . . . It was requisite that he should have been made perfect through sufferings and become the author of salvation through this perfecting. It was not, of course, a perfecting that required the sanctification from sin to holiness. He was always holy, harmless, undefiled, and separate from sinners. But there was the perfecting of development and growth in the course and path of his obedience—he *learned* obedience. The heart and mind and will of our Lord had been moulded—shall we not say forged?—in the furnace of temptation and suffering. And it was in virtue of what he had learned in that experience of temptation and suffering that he was able, at the climactic point fixed by the arrangements of infallible wisdom and everlasting love, to be obedient unto death, even the death of the cross.[23]

Given the importance of the active obedience of Christ for understanding Christ's work and its application to us, how is it best demonstrated? As in the discussion of the identity of Christ, one must establish its biblical basis text by text. But it is also important to remember that individual texts are embedded in an overall story line which provides the categories, structures, and framework to make sense of individual texts. In the case of the active obedience of Christ, one's grasp of the biblical covenants is crucial in establishing its grounding. Let us develop this point in three steps.

1. The active obedience of Christ is intimately related to the larger question of the unconditional-conditional nature of the biblical covenants. As

---

[22] Gregory A. Van Court, *The Obedience of Christ* (Frederick, MD: New Covenant Media, 2005), 6.
[23] John Murray, *Redemption Accomplished and Applied* (Grand Rapids, MI: Eerdmans, 1955), 22–23.

previous chapters have discussed, a common way to distinguish the biblical covenants is to employ the unconditional-unilateral (royal grant) versus conditional-bilateral (suzerain-vassal) distinction. We dissent from this thinking, since elements of both are blended together throughout the covenants. In fact, we contend that it is precisely due to this blend that there is a deliberate *tension* within the covenants—a tension that is heightened as the covenants progress toward their fulfilment in Christ *and* a tension that is important in grounding Christ's active obedience.

On the one hand, what the covenants and story line of Scripture reveal is the sovereign promise making and covenant keeping God who never fails. He is the covenant Lord who supremely reveals himself as the God of *ḥesed* and *'ĕmet*. As Creator and Lord, he chooses to enter into relationships with his creatures where he demonstrates that he is always faithful. He always remains true to himself, his own character, and his promises, and it is on this basis alone that we can hope, trust, and rest in him. It is for this reason that all of the biblical covenants are unconditional or, better, are unilaterally guaranteed by God's power and grace. Starting with Adam in the garden and throughout the biblical covenants we discover God's commitment to his image-bearers and creation, tied to his promises which never fail because he never fails. God remains true to his promises across the entire Canon, which reaches its most profound fulfilment in Christ.

On the other hand, all the biblical covenants also demand an obedient partner (son). This is evident with Adam as commands and responsibilities are given to him and the expectation is that he will respond perfectly. Furthermore, as the covenants unfold, the same emphasis is in all of them. Complete obedience and devotion are demanded from the covenant mediators and the people; God demands and deserves nothing less. In this sense, there is a conditional/bilateral element to all the covenants. It is this latter emphasis on God's demand of complete obedience from his creatures which is crucial in establishing the grounding to the active obedience of Christ. This is consistent with who God is as the standard of righteousness and justice. To demand anything less than full devotion from his creatures would be a denial of himself. In addition, in creating us, our triune God made us for himself, to know him, to worship him as servant-kings, to obey him, as we fulfill our task to extend his rule to the entire creation.

2. In the covenant of creation, it is best to think of God's initial arrangement with Adam as holding forth a conditional promise of everlasting life.

Even though this point is often disputed, there are good reasons to maintain it.[24] In this regard, God's specific command and warning to Adam in Genesis 2:16–17 and the emphasis on the tree of life (Gen. 2:9) is important. Admittedly, in the text, no reward is explicitly given, yet in light of the entire Canon, this conclusion is warranted. First, think of the command *not* to eat of the tree of the knowledge of good and evil. It is best to view this command as a test of Adam's obedience to the Lord. He was created to love God and his neighbour. The specific prohibition was a test to discern whether Adam would be what he was created to be: an obedient son. Sadly, Adam failed, and the consequence of his action was no private affair. As the first man and representative head of the human race, his choice brought death into this world—spiritually and physically—for the entire human race.

Second, think of the tree of life. It is best to see it as an implied promise of life, especially in light of Genesis 3:22, where God expels man from Eden so that he will not take of the tree and live forever.[25] The expulsion from Eden not only speaks of God's judgement upon Adam (and the entire human race), it also gives a glimmer of hope that eternal life is still possible, especially set in the context of the Genesis 3:15 promise of a coming deliverer. Together the two trees present two choices in Eden: life or death. As Micah McCormick rightly notes, "If the tree of the knowledge of good and evil loomed over Eden with the threat of death, so too did the tree of life course with the expectation of everlasting life."[26] Canonically, it is significant that the tree of life appears again in the new creation.[27] Not only are believers told that they will eat of the tree of life if they persevere until the end (Rev. 2:7), but all who dwell in the new creation are sons of God who enjoy the tree of life (Rev. 22:1–5). Greg Beale captures the significance of this when he writes, "To 'eat of the tree of life, which is in the paradise of God' is a picture of forgiveness and consequent experience of God's intimate presence (22:2–4). . . . The 'tree' refers to the redemptive effects of the cross, which bring about the restoration of God's presence."[28] In this light, it is legitimate

---

[24] For a detailed defense of this view, see McCormick, "Active Obedience of Jesus Christ," 108–118.

[25] See Gordon J. Wenham, *Genesis 1–15*, WBC 1 (Waco, TX: Word, 1987), 62, who argues that, "Trees as a symbol of life are well-known in the Bible. . . . In Scripture, trees, because they remain green throughout summer drought, are seen as symbolic of the life of God (e.g., Ps 1:3; Jer. 17:8). . . . Furthermore, it seems likely that the golden candlestick kept in the tabernacle was a stylized tree of life; the falling of its light on the twelve loaves of the presence symbolized God's life sustaining the twelve tribes of Israel" (Ex. 25:31–35; Lev. 24:1–9).

[26] McCormick, *Active Obedience of Jesus Christ*, 112.

[27] There are many intertextual links in the Canon to the tree of life as well. See Proverbs 3:18; 11:30; 13:12; 15:4; Ezekiel. 47:12; etc.

[28] G. K. Beale, *The Book of Revelation: A Commentary on the Greek Text*, New International Greek Testament Commentary (Grand Rapids, MI: Eerdmans, 1999), 234–235.

to conclude that the tree of life symbolises eternal life—held out to Adam in the beginning and won by our Lord Jesus Christ.

Putting together these pieces, especially in light of the larger Adam-Christ typological relationship (Rom. 5:12–21; 1 Cor. 15:22, 45–49; cf. Heb. 2:5–18), where Adam failed, Christ succeeded in gaining eternal life for his people. Death (physical and spiritual) was the result of Adam's disobedience; eternal life (spiritual and physical) was the result of Christ's act of obedience—an obedience that characterised his entire life including the supreme act of obedience in his death (Phil. 2:8). Adam acted as our covenantal head yet failed the test. God demanded from him covenant loyalty, devotion, and obedience, but he did not fulfill the purpose of his creation. As Horton rightly notes, "Adam is created in a state of integrity with the ability to render God complete obedience, thus qualifying as a suitable human partner,"[29] yet he failed. Our Lord, as the second Adam, lived a life of complete love, devotion, and obedience to his heavenly Father for us—showing us what an obedient son looks like—and in the greatest act of obedience possible, he went to the cross for us to pay for our sin and to satisfy God's own righteous requirements which we violated in our sin, rebellion, and disobedience.

3. Building on the previous point, it is important to observe how *tension* grows as we progress *through* the biblical covenants in regard to God's demand for obedient covenant partners. To be sure, the Lord himself always remains the faithful covenant partner as the promise maker and promise keeper. By contrast, all the human covenant mediators—Adam, Noah, Abraham, Israel, and David and his sons—show themselves to be unfaithful, disobedient covenant breakers—some to a greater extent than others. As a result, there is no faithful, obedient son who fully obeys the demands of the covenant. Obedience *must* be rendered but there is no obedient son to do so. How, then, can God remain the holy and just God that he is and continue to be present with us in covenant relation? How can he remain in relation with us unless our disobedience is removed and our sin is paid for in full? The only answer is this: God himself, as the covenant maker and keeper, must unilaterally act to keep his own promise *through the provision of a faithful, obedient Son*. It is only through his obedience—in life and in death—that our redemption is secured, our sin is paid for, and the inauguration of an unshakeable new covenant is established.

In this regard, it is important to note how much the New Testament

---

[29] Horton, *God of Promise*, 89.

stresses the obedience of Christ.[30] John Calvin is correct when he says, "Now someone asks, how has Christ abolished sin, banished the separation between us and God, and acquired righteousness to render God favorably and kindly toward us? To this we can in general reply that he has achieved this for us by the whole course of his obedience."[31] It is a "whole course" of obedience that refers not only to Christ's obedient death on our behalf but also to his entire obedient life, lived out for us as our representative head. In the context of the covenant of creation, God's demands must be perfectly satisfied, either personally or representatively. "To reflect God as his image-bearer is therefore to be righteous, holy, obedient—a covenant servant, defined as such by the covenant charter (Hos. 6:7, with Isa. 24:5; Jer. 31:35–37; 33:20–22, 25–26)."[32] Christ fulfills Adam's role; he recapitulates Adam's testing in the garden, yet he does not fail. In his obedient life he fulfills the covenant of creation representatively, and by his obedient death he acts as our substitute, paying the debt we could never repay. And all of his work as the head of the new covenant becomes ours, not by physical birth or anything in us, but solely by God's sovereign grace as the Father chooses us in him, the Spirit unites us to him by new birth, and his righteous standing becomes ours as a result.

It is in this covenantal context that we must think of the imputation of Christ's righteousness to the believer and how it is that his active obedience becomes ours. It is by Christ acting as our covenant head as we, by God's grace and through repentance and faith, come under his covenant headship. As John Murray rightly states, "Christ's obedience was vicarious in the bearing of the full judgment of God upon sin, and it was vicarious in the full discharge of the demands of righteousness. His obedience becomes the ground of the remission of sin and of actual justification."[33] God reckons or counts our entire sin to be Christ's, and Christ's entire righteousness to be ours. This great exchange provides the basis for the forgiveness of sins and the gift of eternal life. In this way, Scripture speaks of three great imputations. "The first great imputation is Adam's entire guilt from the Fall to all people (Rom. 5:12, 18a,

---

[30] The New Testament explicitly speaks of the obedience of Christ in three texts (Rom. 5:19; Phil. 2:8; Heb. 5:8–9; cf. 2:5–18). In addition, the concept or theme of obedience is found in numerous places. For example: the servant theme underscores Christ's obedience (Mark 10:45; Phil. 2:7; cf. Isa. 42:1; 52:13–53:12); the purpose of Jesus' coming is to do his Father's will as the Son (John 5:19–30; 8:28–29; 10:18; 12:49; 14:31; Heb. 10:5–10); he submits to the law (Matt. 3:15; Gal. 4:1–4); and he is perfected through suffering (Heb. 2:10–18; 5:8–10; 7:28).

[31] John Calvin, *Institutes of the Christian Religion*, ed. John T. McNeil, trans. Ford Lewis Battles, 2 vols. (Philadelphia: Westminster, 1960), 2:16.5.

[32] Horton, *God of Promise*, 93.

[33] Murray, *Redemption Accomplished and Applied*, 22.

19a; Ps. 51:5). The second is the elect's entire sin to Christ (Isa. 53:4–6; Rom. 8:3–4; 1 Cor. 5:21a; [sic] Gal. 3:13). The third is Christ's entire righteousness to his elect (Rom. 3:21–22; 5:18a, 19b; 1 Cor. 5:21b; [sic] Phil. 3:9)."[34]

Viewing Christ's active obedience, imputation, and justification within the context of *kingdom through covenant* is nothing new. Yet, in light of today's debates, it helps illuminate and underscore the great gospel truth of salvation by grace alone, by faith alone, and by Christ alone. In a recent article wrestling with the "new perspective on Paul," Kevin Vanhoozer rightly suggests that viewing Christ's work and how it becomes ours in the context of Christ's covenant representation of his people and our faith union with our covenant head, is a more biblical way of thinking. When we do so, it now makes sense to say that,

> God reckons Christ's "right covenantal relatedness" ours .... [since] "Christ does everything that Israel (and Adam) was supposed to do. He suffers the covenant sanction and fulfills the covenant law, including its summary command "to love God and your neighbor as oneself." In counting us righteous, then, God both pardons us ("there is therefore now no condemnation" [Rom 8:1]) and gives us the positive *status* of rectitude, a down payment, as it were, sealed with the Spirit, on our eventually achieving an actual righteous *state* (i.e., sanctification). ...
>
> Christians become members of God's covenant family by receiving the Son's status: *righteous sonship*. Jesus Christ was the righteous Son the Father always wanted Israel, and Adam, to be. ... Sons and daughters in Christ, we have Christ's righteousness (sic) standing before God *and* unity with one another as members of Christ's one body.[35]

Without a metanarrative in which the covenants are key, and especially the Davidic covenant where the king represents the nation, the doctrine of imputation is difficult to properly sustain.

The Extent of the Atonement[36]

Does one's understanding of the biblical covenants have anything to do with the perennial polemics over the extent of the atonement? It is our conviction

---

[34] Van Court, *Obedience of Christ*, 15. The references to 1 Corinthians should cite 2 Corinthians.

[35] Kevin J. Vanhoozer, "Wrighting the Wrongs of the Reformation? The State of the Union with Christ in St. Paul and Protestant Soteriology," in *Jesus, Paul, and the People of God: A Theological Dialogue with N. T. Wright*, ed. Nicholas Perrin and Richard B. Hays (Downers Grove, IL: InterVarsity Press, 2011), 251, 256.

[36] For a more detailed development of this argument see Stephen J. Wellum, "The New Covenant Work of Christ: Priesthood, Atonement, and Intercession" in *From Heaven He Came and Sought Her: Definite Atonement in, Biblical, Theological, and Pastoral Perspective*, ed. David Gibson and Jonathan Gibson (Wheaton, IL: Crossway, forthcoming).

that it does. In this debate, the question asked is, what is the purpose, design, and intent of the Father in sending his Son, and the Son in offering himself for the salvation of humanity? Was the intent of Christ's death merely to make the salvation of all people *possible* though all without exception will not be saved (the Arminian, general atonement view)? Or, was the intent *multiple* in the sense that one intent of the cross was for Christ to secure the certain salvation of his elect, while another intent was for Christ to pay the penalty for the sin of all people universally thus making *possible* for all who believe to be saved (the modified Calvinist, general atonement view)? Or, was the intent of the atonement specially to render *certain* the salvation of the elect, in terms not only of putting away the sins of the elect but also of ensuring "that they would be brought to faith through regeneration, and kept in faith for glory, and that this is what it was intended to achieve" (the Calvinist, particular redemption view)?[37] It is our conviction that the latter view is correct. Christ died for the purpose of saving only those to whom he actually applies the benefits of his work. As such, the *intention* and *outcome* of the cross are in harmony, and the cross work of Christ serves as the sole ground for our salvation in achieving it and securing everything necessary to apply it to our lives by the Spirit.

How does one argue for such a position? Particular or definite redemption must be argued on a number of fronts. As most acknowledge, it is not demonstrated by one text alone but by a whole set of texts and interrelated issues, both exegetical and theological.[38] However, one neglected theological aspect of this debate is viewing Christ's work as a priestly work in light of the new covenant. Most affirm with John Murray that our Lord's work is presented in Scripture as a priestly work: "The atonement must more broadly be subsumed under the mediatorial work of Christ, and more specifically under the priestly office. But there is one Mediator, and Christ alone was called a High Priest after the order of Melchizedek."[39] Yet, many who affirm that Christ's work is a priestly work, including general atonement advocates, divorce Christ's priestly work from its covenantal context, and miss the power of the argument for definite atonement. What is the argument? Christ's work as the great high priest of the new covenant entails a particular

---

[37] J. I. Packer, *Concise Theology: A Guide to Historic Christian Beliefs* (Carol Stream, IL: Tyndale, 1993), 137.
[38] For example, "extent" debates wrestle with the nature of the atonement in terms of penal substitution, the relation of the decree of God, election, and the Spirit's work to the cross, as well as one's understanding of "world/all" texts.
[39] John Murray, "The Atonement," in *Collected Writings of John Murray*, 4 vols. (Carlisle, PA: Banner of Truth, 1977), 2:148. Cf. Hugh Martin, *The Atonement: In Its Relations to the Covenant, the Priesthood, the Intercession of Our Lord* (Edinburgh: James Gemmell, 1882).

redemption. Two steps will sketch out the basic contours of this argument: (1) Christ's work as our great high priest is a *unified* work; (2) Christ's work as the mediator of the new covenant entails a particular and not general representation. Let us look at each of these points in turn.

1. CHRIST'S WORK AS OUR GREAT HIGH PRIEST IS A UNIFIED WORK.

Here is the basic argument in a nutshell. Our Lord, as the great high priest of the new covenant, willingly and gladly offered himself as our substitute in deliberate obedience to his Father's will. In so doing, his intent was not only to achieve the redemption of a particular people but also to secure everything necessary to bring those same people to the end for which his death was designed, namely, the full forgiveness of sin and all the blessings of the new covenant including the gift of the Spirit, who effectively applies his work to those whom the Son represents. Furthermore, due to his powerful resurrection and ascension, our Lord's work as our great high priest continues as he now rules at the Father's right hand as our priest-king and intercedes for his people, thus guaranteeing an eternal salvation for them. However, the problem with all general atonement views is that they must divide Christ's unified priestly work, redefine Christ's relation as priest to his people, and ultimately make ineffective his work as the head of the new covenant—all points that Scripture will not allow.[40]

The priestly argument for definite atonement is nothing new. Almost every defense of particular redemption includes it.[41] Yet it is rarely dealt with by its critics, or if it is discussed at all, only aspects of it are mentioned—aspects which are usually divorced from its full biblical-theological presentation.[42] The New Testament is clear that our Lord is the antitypical fulfilment

---

[40] Robert Letham, *The Work of Christ* (Downers Grove, IL: InterVarsity Press, 1993), 236–237, states the argument this way: "Christ's role as high priest is a whole. It is one unified movement of grace toward humanity whereby he takes our place in obeying the Father, in atoning for our sins and bringing us to God. He makes very clear that he prays for us besides dying for us. This is a dominant theme in his high-priestly prayer to the Father in John chapter 17. In that prayer he says to the Father that he does not pray for the world but for those whom the Father had given him. . . . His intercession is limited. He prays for his own and not for the world. It follows that his atoning death is intended for those the Father had given him and not for all in an indiscriminate fashion. If we see the intercession as particular and the cross as universal, we are positing a disruption in the heart of Christ's high-priestly work."

[41] See John Owen, *The Death of Death in the Death of Christ* (1648; repr., Carlisle, PA: Banner of Truth, 1983). One could make the case that Owen's entire treatise is an unpacking of this argument. See also Turretin, *Institutes of Elenctic Theology*, 2:403–486; Bavinck, *Reformed Dogmatics*, 3:455–475; Louis Berkhof, *Systematic Theology* (Grand Rapids, MI: Eerdmans, 1941), 361–405; Gary D. Long, *Definite Atonement* (Phillipsburg, NJ: P&R, 1977); Tom Barnes, *Atonement Matters* (Darlington, UK: Evangelical Press, 2008); Michael S. Horton, *The Christian Faith* (Grand Rapids, MI: Zondervan, 2011), 486–520.

[42] See, e.g., Donald Lake, "He Died for All," in *Grace Unlimited*, ed. Clark H. Pinnock (Minneapolis: Bethany, 1975), 31–50; Terry Miethe, "The Universal Power of the Atonement," in *The Grace of God, the Will of Man,*

of the Old Testament priest. Uniquely, the book of Hebrews unpacks this glorious truth by comparing and contrasting the qualifications of the Levitical priest with Christ, thus establishing the fact that Jesus meets every qualification for that office, yet he is supremely greater (Heb. 5:1–10; 8:1–10:18). Five points of similarity and contrast will make this point.

1. Just as the Old Testament priest had to meet certain qualifications and be *selected* for this role, so Christ did not take upon himself the glory of becoming a high priest. He too was *divinely called* by the Father and *appointed* to this office and work (Heb. 5:4–6; cf. Psalm 2; 110).

2. Just as the Old Testament priest *represented* a *particular* people before God (namely the nation of Israel), so Christ as the head and mediator of the new covenant represents all those under that covenant, and does so effectively.[43] We will return to this observation below in our discussion of Christ as the great high priest of the new covenant.

3. Just as the Old Testament priest offered sacrifices for sins (Heb. 5:1; 8:3), including his own, which could never (and which God never intended to) take away sins (Heb. 10:4), so Christ offered himself, thus accomplishing a definitive, once-for-all-time atonement (Heb. 7:27; 9:12; 10:15–18). Unlike the Old Testament priests, who never secured perfection, our Lord's priesthood did, so that "he is able to save completely those who come to God through him" (Heb. 7:25).

4. Patterned after the Old Testament priest, yet greater, Christ's work never involves the separation between the provision of atonement and its application to the people.[44] There are two ways to illustrate this point. First,

---

ed. Clark H. Pinnock (Grand Rapids, MI: Zondervan, 1989), 71–96; Bruce Demarest, *The Cross and Salvation* (Wheaton, IL: Crossway, 1997), 189–193.

[43] Under the old covenant, the priest represented a particular people. The Old Testament priests performed their work in a particular place (tabernacle, temple) and for a particular people (Num. 3:7–8). Nowhere in the Old Testament does the priest make atonement for all the nations or function as a universal mediator. This representative, particular work is beautifully portrayed in the clothing of the high priest. From head to toe, the priest's garments were designed to teach Israel something of the priest's work as representative of the people as he bore on his breastplate the twelve gemstones representing the twelve tribes of Israel (Ex. 28:17–21). Each time he went into the presence of God, "he would carry these gems with him (Ex. 28:29), indicating that he was there on behalf of the people with whom Yahweh had entered into covenant" (Letham, *Work of Christ*, 106). Never did the priest ever represent or mediate for a people other than the covenant people of God. The particular representative role of the priests is further reinforced in Numbers, where the Levites serve as representatives for the firstborn Israelites (Num. 3:11–13). In fact, the Lord instructs Moses to count the Levites (Num. 3:14–39) and all the firstborn males in Israel (3:40–43) for the purpose of substituting the Levites for the firstborn males. This highlights not only the substitutionary nature of the priests' work but also its scope: the Old Testament understands representation and substitution in particular terms.

[44] It is important to note that as the priests offered sacrifices for sins before God, there was no separation between the provision of atonement and its application to the people. As the atonement is first applied to the altar in order to propitiate God, the sacrifice did not merely remove a barrier, it also effected something in the very dwelling place of God (see the discussion of this point in Richard Nelson, *Raising Up a Faithful Priest* [Louisville: Westminster John Knox, 1993], 76–78). Nelson describes the priests' work in terms of a twofold obligation: (1) to purify the people who approach or dwell near the Lord; (2) to purify the sanctuary itself. One can also see this in Exodus

as Jesus enters the heavenly sanctuary (Heb. 8:4–5; 9:24) he applies his blood to the altar and inaugurates a new covenant, which is complete and effectual. Given these Old Testament patterns, it is highly unlikely that he is doing this for the non-elect. Instead, our Lord enters God's throne room as the representative of his new covenant people. Second, the link between our Lord's accomplishment and its effects upon his people is underscored in Hebrews 9:11–15. As William Lane notes, the introductory clause in verse 15, "For this reason" (*kai dia touto*), establishes a strong causal relationship between the achievement of Christ's priestly work (vv. 11–14) and the effects of that work in his new covenant people (v. 15).[45] In other words, Jesus' priestly work achieves *and* applies new covenant realities to *all* those in that covenant, which requires a particular redemption. The other alternatives are either universalism or the conclusion that Christ failed in his priestly office, both of which are unbiblical options.[46]

5. Whereas the Old Testament priests' work was a unified yet imperfect work, Christ's work is unified and perfect in provision, instruction, guardianship, and intercession.[47] In regard to intercession, our Lord, as priest, effectively prays for his people *before* the cross (Luke 22:31–32; John 17:6ff.) and *after* his ascension (Rom. 8:32–34; Heb. 7:24–25; 1 John 2:1–2), guaranteeing that all the new covenant blessings are applied to them. There is no evidence that he intercedes salvifically for the non-elect. Three texts buttress this claim.

In John 17:6–19, our Lord effectively prays for his disciples, those whom the Father has given him, but *not* for the world (vv. 9–10). In verses 20–26, Jesus then prays for all future believers, once again given to him by the Father (v. 24; cf. 6:37–44). This intercession is consistent with Jesus'

24:6–8, where Moses places the blood on the altar and the people (cf. Lev. 8:15, 22–24). By this action the priest made the people acceptable to God by applying the sacrificial blood to the altar. This is also seen on the Day of Atonement, where the high priest not only atoned for the people in order to cleanse them but also applied the same blood to the altar in order to cleanse the sanctuary from any defilement before God (Lev. 16:15–19). In this way, there was no division between the provision of atonement and its application to the people. No priest, under the old covenant, offered a sacrifice in which he did not simultaneously apply its blood to the altar. As this is brought to fulfilment in Christ, and as Hebrews so ably proclaims, the ineffectual nature of the old covenant, which God himself intended, was due not to the bifurcation between provision and application but to the inferior nature of those sacrifices. However, in Christ, we have the perfect priest and sacrifice. His death achieves a complete salvation and a complete application of it to his new covenant people.

[45] William L. Lane, *Hebrews 9–13*, WBC 47b (Dallas: Word, 1991), 241.

[46] See Owen, *Death of Death*, 110–124, who makes this argument very strongly.

[47] Space prohibits the development of how Christ is instructor and guardian of his people, yet John develops these points. Those whom the Father has given the Son he dies for and effectively saves (6:37–40; 10:11, 14); those same people hear his voice and receive his instruction (10:16, 26–30; 17:17); but those who are not his people do not hear his voice, and they reject his word (5:46–47; 8:42–47; 10:26–27). As priest and guardian, Jesus lays down his life for the sheep yet stands in judgement upon those who are not his sheep (John 10:11ff.; cf. Isa. 53:6).

teaching previously: he is the good shepherd who dies for the sheep (10:11, 15); his sheep are given to him by his Father (10:29); his sheep receive eternal life due to his death; but *not* all people are his sheep (10:26–27). All of this is consistent with his office as a priest who offers himself for a particular people and intercedes for those same people.

The same truth is taught in Romans 8:28–39. Here the unified work of Christ as priest is developed with the intent of grounding our confidence in the God of sovereign grace. Those whom God has chosen, effectively called, justified, and who will be glorified (vv. 28–30) are confident because in the Son's death for us "all," the Father gives us *all* things, which, in this context, includes the entire application of new covenant realities to us. No one, then, can bring a charge against God's elect, because it is Jesus who has died *and* who intercedes *for us*. In his priestly office, Jesus offers himself and intercedes for us with a certain result: an effective redemption.

Hebrews 7:23–28 makes the same point. The reason why Jesus is so much better than the Old Testament priest is because of who he is as God the Son incarnate. In his offering of himself and in his glorious resurrection he achieves a permanent priesthood which secures a better covenant (see Hebrews 8–10). As a result, Jesus completely saves those who come to him *because* he always lives to intercede for them. As Lane comments, "The perfection and eternity of the salvation he mediates is guaranteed by the unassailable character of his priesthood. . . . The direct result of his intercessory activity is the sustaining of the people and the securing of all that is necessary to the eschatological salvation. . . . "[48]

However, the problem with all general atonement views is that they fragment Christ's priestly work of offering *and* intercession. Either they must view Christ's work apart from these typological patterns and not discuss the atonement within the constraints of these biblical categories, or they must separate Christ's intercession from his death, thus dividing his priestly work. For example, Robert Lightner rightly acknowledges that Christ's intercession is savingly effective for the elect only but then contends that this does not take place until the elect believe, thus limiting Christ's intercession to his heavenly intercession.[49] This argument fails on at least three counts. First, it fails to view Christ's priestly work as unified—those he represents, he also intercedes for effectively. Second, it fails to acknowledge that Christ

---

[48] Lane, *Hebrews*, 189–190.
[49] See Robert Lightner, *The Death Christ Died*, 2nd ed. (Grand Rapids, MI: Kregel, 1998), 102–104.

intercedes for his own, including those who would later believe, during his earthly ministry—an intercession which does not fail since Christ loses none of his people (John 6:39; 10:14–18, 26–30; 17:20–24). Third, it divorces Christ's unified priestly work from its new covenant context and thus has Christ dying for people who cannot be described as new covenant members.

On the other hand, Gary Schultz argues that Christ's intercession may be viewed as salvific for the non-elect. His strongest appeal is to Luke 23:34, where Jesus prays for the forgiveness of his crucifiers.[50] On the basis of this text, Schultz contends that "intercession unto salvation is something that is available to all but only effectual for those who are in Christ."[51] However, he can sustain this argument only by removing Christ's intercession from *biblical* categories. All we know of priests is that they intercede for those they represent covenantally. What about Luke 23:34? Is it proof that Christ intercedes salvifically for the non-elect? No, and for four reasons. First, such an interpretation goes against the entire scriptural presentation of the intercession of the priest. Second, as Owen rightly observed, one cannot conclude from a specific prayer for a handful of people that this is a prayer "for all and every man that ever were, are, or shall be."[52] Third, as the obedient son, Jesus not only fulfills the law by praying for his persecutors, he effectively requests the delay of judgement or the decrease in punishment based *on the people's ignorance.*[53] The act of crucifixion demanded God's judgement (Acts 2:23–24), but Christ prays for a delay of judgement thus allowing history to continue and God's ultimate purposes to save his people to be realized.[54] Tied to this is God's common grace upon the non-elect who crucified him and, by a delay in judgement, the salvation of the elect as evidenced in the thief on the cross and many people on the Day of Pentecost (Acts 2:37–41). This prayer does *not* serve as evidence that Jesus intercedes salvifically for the non-elect. Fourth, for sake of argument, if Schultz is right, does it not entail that Christ failed in his priestly work, i.e., those for whom he died and interceded for salvifically have not been redeemed? But this

---

[50] It should be noted that in some of the earliest manuscripts verse 34 is omitted. We will assume it to be original even though it is a contested point. See Bruce M. Metzger, *A Textual Commentary on the Greek New Testament,* 2nd ed. (Peabody, MA: Hendrickson, 2005).

[51] Gary Schultz, "A Biblical and Theological Defense of a Multi-Intentional View of the Extent of the Atonement" (PhD diss., Southern Baptist Theological Seminary, 2008), 155, fn. 195.

[52] Owen, *Death of Death,* 83.

[53] Note a number of important points. First, the entire setting of the event is apocalyptic signifying divine judgement (see vv. 29–30, 44–46; cf. Matt. 27:45–54). Second, the context is also reminiscent of Jer. 4:18–31 where God judges Israel yet not completely (v. 27). Third, Luke 12:47–48 is also instructive since Jesus teaches that there are distinctions in punishment related to one's knowledge or lack of it.

[54] See Klaas Schilder, *Christ Crucified* (Grand Rapids, MI: Eerdmans, 1940), 129–147.

conclusion goes against everything Scripture teaches about the priestly work of Christ as perfect and effective.

In light of these five points, how do general atonement advocates respond? At least in two ways. First, in terms of representation, they admit, it is true that the Old Testament priest represented a particular people, but now in Christ this representation is expanded to the entire human race, tied to Christ's incarnation.[55] Second, some appeal to the fact that the Old Testament priest offered sacrifices for Israel as a "mixed" group (i.e., believers and nonbelievers), hence warrant for a general atonement.[56] We offer three points in response. First, if we think of priests in biblical categories, we have to affirm that the Old Testament priest represented only the covenant people. Nowhere in the Old Testament does the priest make atonement for the nations or function as a universal mediator. Covenantal blessings of atonement and forgiveness are given to God's people, and the entire law-covenant separated and distinguished Israel from the nations.

Second, what about the appeal to the incarnation? Hebrews 2:5–18 is crucial here. In this text the Son is presented as greater than the angels because he does a work that no angel can do, namely, take on our humanity, undo the work of Adam, and restore us to the purpose of our creation by his atoning work. On the surface it seems like this text supports a general atonement view—Jesus "tastes death for everyone" (2:9). But as the argument unfolds, it becomes clear that his cross work cannot be divorced from his role as the priest and mediator of the new covenant (2:17–18; cf. Hebrews 5–10). Furthermore, as the covenant head, his death does not fail in "bringing many sons to glory," who are then identified "with the people of God (v. 17), who are spoken of as *Abraham's descendants* (v. 16)."[57] The result of Christ's cross, then, has an effective, particular focus with expansion to those who are not merely Abraham's ethnic seed but Abraham's spiritual children, which includes Jew and Gentile, but not all without exception.[58]

---

[55] See A. H. Strong, *Outlines of Systematic Theology* (Valley Forge, PA: Judson, 1907), 771–776; Norman Douty, *Did Christ Die Only for the Elect?* (Eugene, OR: Wipf & Stock, 1998), 21–29.

[56] See Mark Driscoll and Gerry Breshears, *Death by Love* (Wheaton, IL: Crossway, 2008), 179; cf. David Nelson, "The Design, Nature, and Extent of the Atonement," in *Calvinism: A Southern Baptist Dialogue*, ed. E. Ray Clendenen and Brad Waggoner (Nashville: B&H, 2008), 129–130.

[57] Peter T. O'Brien, *The Letter to the Hebrews*, Pillar New Testament Commentary (Grand Rapids, MI: Eerdmans, 2010), 105.

[58] See Barnes, *Atonement Matters*, 214–217. The notion of Christ as covenantal head is intimately associated with union with Christ. However, our union with Christ is *not* due to his incarnation. Even though Christ shares a common nature with us, he does *not* share new covenant blessings of forgiveness of sins through his flesh. This comes only by rebirth by the Spirit and through faith. In contrast to Adam, those whom Christ represents are believers, born of the Spirit.

Otherwise the entire priestly work and Christ's representative headship would not achieve what it was intended to achieve, namely, the reversal of sin and death and the ushering in of a new creation, the defeat of the Evil One, and the guaranteed bringing of many sons to glory.

One cannot conclude from Christ's incarnation and death that he comes as the last Adam to provide salvation for all without exception. Instead, Scripture teaches that our Lord takes on our humanity to win for us a new creation and to redeem the offspring of Abraham, sons and daughters of faith from every tribe, nation, and tongue. Furthermore, individuals are savingly united to Christ as their covenant head, and Jesus serves as their covenantal mediator, only by "covenant-election-calling-faith-repentance-sealing,"[59] which is all grounded in Christ's atoning work. When thinking of Christ as our new covenant head, we have no grounds to say that he acts for all without exception unless we want to rend asunder his priestly work and make the cross ineffective in bringing those he represents to salvation.

Third, what about the Old Testament priest offering sacrifices for a "mixed" people? Does this warrant a general atonement? No, and for three reasons. First, under the old covenant, the priest atoned for the sins of the covenant people alone, which moves in a particular direction, not a universal one. Second, the work of the priest was only typological; it was *ultimately* ineffectual by design (see Heb. 10:4). No doubt, under the old covenant, priest and sacrifice served a number of purposes, rooted in God's purposes for Israel as a physical nation set apart to bring forth the Messiah and to serve as a tutor for later generations (1 Cor. 10:6, 11), but one must carefully move from type to antitype, especially vis-à-vis the question of the atonement's extent. As Tom Barnes rightly notes, "The breadth of this typological work with the entire nation was never meant to define the extent of the atonement through Jesus Christ. As Paul clarifies in Romans 4 and 9 the purpose of God when it comes to his sovereign gracious salvation of individuals was always more particular than the typological purpose accomplished throughout all Israel."[60] Third, this argument fails to see the *discontinuity* between the old and new covenants and thus how much *better* (i.e., more effective) the new covenant is. In other words, for sake of argument, let us grant that the general atonement view is correct, i.e., as we shift from old to new, that, just as the Old Testament priests

---

[59] Donald Macleod, *The Person of Christ* (Downers Grove, IL: InterVarsity Press, 1998), 203.
[60] Barnes, *Atonement Matters*, 82.

atoned for "mixed" Israel, so now Christ atones for *all* humanity without exception. However the problem with this argument is twofold. On the one hand, it makes the new covenant no more effectual than the old was to Israel. If the promise of forgiveness, which is at the heart of the new covenant (Jer. 31:34), is given to all humanity but not all are saved, then how is the new covenant more effectual? Parallel to the old, there are covenant members within it who fail to receive what the covenant was intended to achieve, namely eternal salvation. Yet, this is contrary to the entire argument of Hebrews regarding the effectual work of the new covenant; for, all those for whom Christ died, he successfully leads to God's eternal rest, unlike the covenant mediators before him. That is why the new covenant is better! On the other hand, the general atonement view fails to acknowledge that the new covenant is not the same as the old in terms of the subjects of the covenant, a point to which we now turn.

2. CHRIST'S WORK AS MEDIATOR OF THE NEW COVENANT ENTAILS A PARTICULAR REDEMPTION.

One cannot think of Christ's priestly work, including its design, apart from the biblical covenants, especially the old covenant. What is the significance of this point? In order to understand the nature of Christ's priestly work, including its design, it must be viewed in light of the new covenant. As Sam Waldron and Richard Barcellos rightly note, "The new covenant is clearly the context or framework of the work of Jesus Christ. The work of Jesus Christ has no saving power divorced from the new covenant. . . . Jesus' whole work was a covenant work; His blood covenant blood, His priesthood covenant priesthood, His office as Mediator a covenant office. The question about the scope, extent, or design of the death of Christ ought not to be answered, therefore, without reference to this covenant."[61] The question, then, is this: "What is the scope, extent, and design of the new covenant? Is it a general covenant made with everybody, making salvation possible for everyone, if they will take it? Or, is it a limited covenant made only with certain men and assuring their eternal salvation?"[62] Whom does our Lord, as the high priest of the new covenant, represent in his death and apply the fruits of that covenant to? Does he represent all people universally, or does

---

[61] Samuel Waldron with Richard Barcellos, *A Reformed Baptist Manifesto* (Palmdale, CA: Reformed Baptist Academic Press, 2004), 59–60.
[62] Waldron with Barcellos, *Reformed Baptist Manifesto*, 60.

he represent a particular people who are effectively brought to salvation and receive all the benefits of the new covenant?

From our exposition of the new covenant, we affirm the latter. To answer in any other way is to remove the work of Christ from its new covenant context, which is precisely the problem with general atonement views. Christ's atoning work cannot be extended to all people without also extending the new covenant benefits and privileges to them, which minimally includes regeneration, forgiveness of sins, the gift of the Spirit, and so on. General atonement views must either redefine the nature of the new covenant or argue that Christ dies as the covenantal head of another covenant, whatever that is, which is unsustainable. What is noteworthy to observe is how often general atonement advocates divorce their view from these covenantal categories. There is much discussion of the "world" and "all" texts, the universal call of the gospel, and so on, but there is little discussion of the design of the cross in the Bible's own categories of "priest" and "covenant." For example, Paige Patterson charges defenders of definite atonement as following "a logical system"[63] rather than Scripture, but his view discusses nothing of Christ's priestly death in its new covenant context. Or, David Nelson begins well by saying that he wants "to set the doctrine of the atonement in the grand redemptive narrative of Scripture. This includes the trajectory set with the Abrahamic, Davidic, and new covenants, and the continual calls to trust Yahweh that form the basis for justification before a righteous God (Gen. 15:6; Hab. 2:4)."[64] However, he does none of this when he discusses the intent of the atonement.[65] In Bruce Demarest's discussion he covers familiar territory, nevertheless he concludes by saying, "in terms of the Atonement's *provision* Christ died not merely for the elect but for all sinners in all times and places,"[66] without ever wrestling with the new covenant context of that death.

Who are the subjects of the new covenant? Under the old covenant, its subjects were primarily the nation of Israel as a "mixed" entity, but what

---

[63] Paige Patterson, "The Work of Christ," in *A Theology for the Church*, ed. Daniel Akin (Nashville: B&H, 2007), 585–586. Cf. I. Howard Marshall, "Universal Grace and Atonement in the Pastoral Epistles," in *Grace of God, Will of Man*, 52, who says something similar yet fails to wrestle with these biblical categories.

[64] Nelson, "Design, Nature, and Extent of the Atonement," 127.

[65] The list could be multiplied. When Millard Erickson, *Christian Theology*, 2nd ed. (Grand Rapids, MI: Baker, 1998), 829, discusses the extent issue he does not place it within the context of the priest and new covenant. Nor does David Allen, "The Atonement: Limited or Universal?" in *Whosoever Will* (Nashville: B&H, 2010), 68–109. Lightner, *Death Christ Died*, 118–123, discusses covenants but more in a dismissive way. See also Schultz, "Biblical and Theological Defense of a Multi-Intentional View of the Extent of the Atonement," who does not do so either.

[66] Demarest, *Cross and Salvation*, 191.

about the new? Does Christ, as the new covenant head, represent all people without exception (a "mixed" group) and thus make salvation possible for them, or does he represent a particular people who are effectively brought to salvation and receive all the benefits of that covenant including the application work of the Spirit? Once again, Scripture affirms the latter. Three points will remind the reader of this truth. First, the New Testament is clear that Christ's priestly work is a new covenant work (Luke 22:20; 1 Cor. 11:25; Hebrews 5–10). He is the mediator of this covenant alone and no other.

Second, one of the crucial ways the "newness" of the new covenant may be described is that *all* those in the covenant know God (Jer. 31:34a), *all* are born of the Spirit and have new hearts (Jer. 31:33; cf. Ezek. 11:19–20; 36:25–27; Joel 2:28–32), and *all* experience the full justification for their sins (Jer. 31:34b; Rom. 8:1). This is precisely what the Old Testament prophets anticipated. In the future, the Spirit would be poured out on *all* flesh, namely, *all* those within the covenant community. This is why the New Testament says that *all* those in the new covenant enjoy the promised gift of the eschatological Spirit (Eph. 1:13–14). And the New Testament is also clear: the work of the Spirit is grounded in the cross work of Christ (John 7:39; 16:7; Acts 2:33). As a result of Christ's new covenant work, the Spirit is sent to *all* those in the covenant since the Spirit is one of the blessed gifts of the new covenant purchased for us by the atoning death of Christ. He is the precious seal, down payment, and guarantee of the promised inheritance. To be "in Christ" is to have the Spirit, for, as Paul reminds us, "if anyone does not have the Spirit of Christ, he does not belong to Christ" (Rom. 8:9, NIV). Why is this important to emphasise? Given that Jesus is the mediator of the new covenant and it is a completely effective covenant in terms of both provision and application, it is difficult to deny, unless we want to affirm universalism, that Christ's priestly work is particular and effective. In other words, *all* those in the new covenant, for whom Jesus acted as the covenant mediator, are, in time, regenerated, justified, and brought to glory. Not one of them will be lost, since our Lord Jesus, as the *greater* priest and mediator of a *greater* covenant, does not fail. For those for whom Jesus died as their covenant head, his work is effectively applied by the Spirit—the same Spirit who cannot be divorced from the new covenant, since he is one of the central blessings Jesus has secured by his atoning death.

Third, given this analysis there are at least two problems for general atonement advocates. The first problem is, for whom do they think Christ is the covenant mediator? Biblically they have to affirm that Jesus is the priest of the new covenant, but if so, then, contrary to Scripture, their "new covenant" is no more effective than the old, since many people in that covenant never have new covenant blessings applied to them—e.g., regeneration, justification, the giving of the Spirit, and so on. But Scripture not only denies this "mixed" understanding of the subjects of the new covenant, it also strongly affirms that our Lord, as the *greater* priest, does not fail to apply his work to *all* those in that covenant. In the end, general atonement advocates have to redefine the people of the new covenant and place faith and repentance (tied to the work of the Spirit) outside of the priestly work of our Lord Jesus Christ.[67] Second, general atonement advocates respond by sharply dividing the provision of salvation from its application.[68] No doubt, everyone distinguishes between the objective work of Christ and its subjective application; it is simply not true that definite atonement advocates collapse the distinction. The real issue is that general atonement defenders fail to acknowledge that provision and application are central to the new covenant work of Christ. As the priest and mediator of the new covenant, our Lord dies for all those who belong to the new covenant. He also, as the head of the new covenant, secures all the benefits of the new covenant, which include the Spirit's work of application.[69] In this way, our Lord both provides and applies, which is why it is certain that his *greater* work will not fail. Yes, that application work by the Spirit takes place throughout history as the elect are brought to saving faith, but the certainty of that work is rooted in the plan of the triune God of sovereign grace: the Father's election of a people; the Son's achieving and securing everything necessary for the elect's salvation; and the work of the Spirit, sent by the Father and Son, to apply the benefits of the Son's work to *every* subject of the new covenant.

It is our contention that a proper understanding of the biblical covenants

---

[67] The general atonement advocate who discusses the covenantal context the most is Douty, *Did Christ Die Only for the Elect?* 19–38. However his discussion fails to wrestle with Christ's covenantal representation in new covenant terms, that is, as the head of a particular people for whom he effectively achieves salvation and secures every new covenant blessing, including the work of the Spirit. Douty does what all general atonement advocates do: extend the new covenant blessing of forgiveness to all humanity but then rob the new covenant of its particularity, perfection, permanency, and security.

[68] See Strong, *Outlines of Systematic Theology*, 773; Demarest, *Cross and Salvation*, 189–193; Douty, *Did Christ Die Only for the Elect?* 58–60; Lightner, *Death Christ Died*, 124–135; Nelson, "Design, Nature, and Extent of Atonement," 132–133.

[69] Lightner, *Death Christ Died*, 130–135, argues that the Spirit is given to all people universally, yet, biblically, the Spirit's work is organically linked to the new covenant. General atonement advocates, then, must affirm two kinds of new covenant people: (1) those whose sins are paid for and who receive the Spirit; (2) those whose sins are paid for but who do not have the Spirit. But this not only reduces the new covenant to a "mixed" company like the old, it also does not explain why some subjects of the new covenant receive the Spirit and others do not, especially since Scripture presents the Spirit as the effective gift of the new covenant.

has massive implications for the debate over the extent of the atonement. A major problem with general atonement advocates, whether they are Arminian or modified Calvinists, is that they fail to locate the priestly work of our Lord in its *covenantal* context. If they did, they would defend a particular view of the cross. They would not break the crucial link between Christ and his people. They would rightly see that Christ, as the *great* high priest of the *new covenant*, acts as representative, substitute, instructor, guardian, and intercessor of and for his people, not only paying for their sins but securing everything necessary, including the work of the Spirit, to apply his work to them and to bring them to their eternal rest.

ECCLESIOLOGY

A major difference between dispensational and covenant theology involves their view of the nature of the church. This difference in turn is rooted in each view's conception of the Israel-church relationship, particularly the relationship between the old and new covenants. How does our view of the covenants shed light on some of these old debates? We will answer this question by focusing on two organically related issues: (1) What is the nature of the church? Is it a "mixed" community similar to Israel of old or, is it by nature different from Israel in that it is a regenerate, believing community? (2) How does our understanding of the covenants illumine the age-old divide between credo- and paedobaptism?

KINGDOM THROUGH COVENANT AND THE NATURE OF THE CHURCH

Dispensational theology has a distinct view of the Israel-church relationship. For them, Israel refers to a national, ethnic people with a specific genealogical heritage and distinct privileges and promises. The church, on the other hand, is *not* the continuation or replacement of Israel in God's plan of salvation. Instead, the church is a uniquely *new* people in God's redemptive purposes. She finds her origin in Christ and specifically in the regenerative and indwelling work of the Spirit that Christ has bestowed equally upon the entire church at Pentecost. In this sense, the church is a *spiritual* people comprised of an international community and not tied to ethnicity or national origin. Given this understanding, dispensational theology sees more *discontinuity* between the two covenant communities. Often this discontinuity is described by the difference between a "mixed" versus a "regenerate" community. Israel, as the former, is constituted of believers and unbelievers, while the church, as the latter, is comprised of all those who have been born of the Spirit and united to Christ, and who profess this to be the case. This is one of the major reasons why dispensational theology affirms credo- versus paedobaptism. The covenant sign of baptism must be applied only to those who have been born of the Spirit and profess faith union in Christ.

Covenant theology does not draw the same Israel-church distinction. Even though there are differences between the two communities, they are basically the same in the following ways: they are both the one people of God; they experience a similar salvation experience including regeneration and the indwelling of the Spirit; their covenant signs (circumcision and baptism), though different, basically convey the same meaning; and by nature they are a "mixed" community versus a regenerate community, so that the locus of the covenant community and the locus of the elect are distinct. This latter emphasis has led to the "visible" versus "invisible" distinction, with the former referring to the "mixed" nature of the church and the latter referring to the elect throughout all ages. It is not an accident that, given this view of the church, covenant theology has strongly endorsed paedobaptism as being parallel to the covenant sign of circumcision.

Where does our analysis differ, especially in regard to the *nature* of the church? Given that we are presenting our view of the covenants as a *via media*, it is not surprising that we agree and disagree with both views at various points. For example, in agreement with progressive dispensationalism and covenant theology we believe that there is only *one* people of God (the elect) throughout the ages and *one* plan of redemption centred in Christ. However, in contrast to covenant theology, we believe that the church is different from Israel in at least two ways. First, the church is *new* in redemptive-history precisely because she is the community of the new covenant. With the coming of our Lord Jesus Christ, all of the previous covenants have reached their fulfilment, so that the salvation realities that Jesus achieves and applies to his people are *not* exactly the same as under the old covenant.[70] This is *not* to say, contra dispensational theology, that

---

[70] In particular, we are thinking of salvation experience differences between old and new covenant believers. We affirm that old covenant believers were regenerated and that they were saved by grace through faith in the promises of God. We also believe that old covenant believers knew the Lord and experienced forgiveness of sins under the old covenant structures in anticipation of the fulfilment of those types and shadows in Christ. But we deny that these salvation experiences were true of the entire old covenant community *and* that the Old Testament saint experienced the same access to God, the indwelling of the Spirit, and other experiences unique to the coming and work of our Lord.

Israel is ontologically different than the church and thus still has privileges distinct from Christ and the church.[71] Rather, the *newness* of the church is a redemptive-historical newness, rooted in the coming of Christ and the inauguration of the new covenant. In him, all of the previous covenants, which in type, shadow and prophetic announcement anticipated and foreshadowed him, have now come to their *telos*. In his life and cross work, our Lord has achieved our eternal redemption, secured the new covenant promise and gift of the Spirit, and given birth to a new community—a people in faith union with him. Second, the church, unlike Israel, is *new* because she is comprised of a *regenerate, believing* people rather than a "mixed" group. The true members of the new covenant community are only those who have professed that they have entered into union with Christ by repentance and faith and are partakers of all the benefits and blessings of the new covenant age. This is one of the primary reasons why we argue that baptism, which is the covenant sign of the new covenant church, is reserved for only those who have entered into these glorious realities by the sovereign work of God's grace in their lives.

In our exposition of the biblical covenants we have sought to give reasons for our view. What follows is simply a summary and sketch of the arguments, given here in three points.

1. There is only *one* people of God (elect) across time. Much data could be given at this point but most today do not dispute this fact.[72] In the Old Testament era, people were saved by grace through faith in the promises of God and the same is true in the coming of Christ, except that the promises of God are now Christologically defined with greater clarity due to the progression of revelation across the biblical covenants (see Gen. 15:6; Rom. 4:9–12; Gal. 3:6–9; Heb. 11:8–19). Promise has given way to fulfilment so that one now cannot know God, salvifically, apart from faith in Christ (John 5:23; Acts 4:12; cf. 1 John 2:23; 4:2–3). Furthermore, Scripture assumes a genuine continuity between Old Testament and New Testament saints (see Rom. 1:1–2; 11; Phil. 3:3, 7, 9), and language applied to Israel as God's covenant people is also applied to the church. For example, most people agree that when the language of "assembly" (*qāhāl* and *ekklēsia*) is applied to Israel and the church (e.g., Deut. 4:10; Josh. 24:1, 25; Isa. 2:2–4; Matt. 16:18; 1 Cor. 11:18; Heb.

---

[71] Specifically, we are thinking of the promise of the land of Palestine, which dispensational theology still thinks is a future blessing for Israel in a millennial age distinct from the church.

[72] On this point progressive dispensationalism, in contrast to its earlier forms, and covenant theology agree.

10:25), or when Old Testament language describing Israel (e.g., Ex. 19:6; Isa. 43:20–21; Hos. 1:6, 9; 2:1) or Old Testament texts that were applied to Israel (e.g., Jer. 31:31–34; Hos. 1:10–11) are now applied to the church (e.g., Rom. 9:24–26; Heb. 8:6–13; 1 Pet. 2:9–10), this is strong evidence in favour of the claim that there is only one people of God throughout the ages.

However, affirming this point does *not* entail that Israel and the church are basically the same kind of community. Rather, the church is *new* both redemptive-historically *and* in regard to its *nature* and *structure*. The church, in other words, is *not* a "mixed" entity like Israel of old but is best viewed as a *regenerate, believing* community. The evidence for this assertion is first found *within the Old Testament* as the prophets anticipated the coming of Christ and a new community which would differ from the previous one. This observation leads to the second point.

2. The Old Testament itself anticipates a change in the *structure* and *nature* of the new covenant community. The best place to demonstrate this point is the famous new covenant text of Jeremiah 31. As argued in previous chapters, this text anticipates some massive changes with the arrival of the new covenant community. Let us think first in terms of *structural* changes, which become the basis for understanding the church as the "priesthood of all believers." Under the old covenant, as Carson has noted, God dealt with his people in a mediated or "tribal" fashion.[73] Despite remnant themes and an emphasis on individual believers, the Old Testament pictures God working with his people as a "tribal" grouping whose knowledge of God and whose relations with God were uniquely dependent on specially endowed leaders—thus the strong emphasis on God's Spirit being poured out, not on each believer, but distinctively on prophets, priests, kings, and other designated leaders. Given this hierarchical structure of the covenant community, when these leaders did what was right, the entire nation benefited. However, when they did not, the entire nation suffered for their actions. But what Jeremiah anticipates is that this tribal structure is going to change, hence the statement in Jeremiah 31:29–30.[74]

---

[73] See D. A. Carson, *Showing the Spirit: A Theological Exposition of 1 Corinthians 12–14* (Grand Rapids, MI: Baker, 1987), 150–158; cf. idem, "Evangelicals, Ecumenism, and the Church," in *Evangelical Affirmations*, ed. Kenneth S. Kantzer and Carl F. H. Henry (Grand Rapids, MI: Zondervan, 1990), 347–385.

[74] As noted in chapter 16, Jeremiah anticipates that the tribal nature of the people of God would end and the new covenant would bring with it a new emphasis on the distribution of the knowledge of God to each member of the covenant community, since *all* of God's covenant people would know him. This is *not* to say that there are no teachers or leaders under the new covenant. Instead, Jeremiah anticipates that their distinctive mediatorial role will end since *all* the covenant people will know God directly through the one mediator, our Lord Jesus Christ. Furthermore, it is important to establish that the *knowledge* spoken of here is a salvific knowledge. See Dumbrell,

Intimately related to this anticipated structural change is the Old Testament promise of the Spirit and his empowering work in the new covenant era, first upon the Messiah (Isa. 11:1–3; 49:1–2; 61:1ff.) and then upon Messiah's people (see Ezek. 11:19–20; 36:25–27; Joel 2:28–32; cf. Num. 11:27–29). In terms of the latter, no longer will the Spirit merely empower leaders but instead there will be a *universal* distribution of the Spirit (Joel 2:28–32; Acts 2). God will pour out his Spirit on *all* within the covenant community, which is precisely what occurs (Acts 2; Eph. 1:13–14). In fact, the New Testament presents the Spirit as the agent who not only gives us life but also enables us to follow God's decrees and keep God's laws, thus making us covenant keepers and *not* breakers. The role which Israel was supposed to play is now fulfilled in us, the church, by the Spirit.[75] In the New Testament, John the Baptist announces this coming age (Matt. 3:11), the cross work of Christ procures and secures it (John 7:39; 16:7; Acts 2:33), and Pentecost proclaims that it is now finally inaugurated. This is why the new covenant era is intimately associated with the Spirit—because *all* within the new covenant community are given the Spirit as the seal, down payment, and guarantee of their promised inheritance. To be united to Christ is to have the Spirit; to *not* have the Spirit is to *not* have Christ or be his people (Rom. 8:9).

In addition, these structural changes signal a change in the *nature* of the covenant people. Jeremiah announces that the new covenant will *not* be like the old covenant (Jer. 31:32) because, due to the work of Christ, our representative head and substitute, what Israel could only foreshadow will now become reality. Under the new covenant, in light of Christ's work and through him, *all* will know the Lord directly; *all* will have the law written on their hearts (which is another way of saying "circumcision of the heart" or *regeneration* [cf. Deut. 10:16; 30:6; Jer. 4:4; 9:25]); and *all* will know the full forgiveness of sin (Jer. 31:33–34).

We are *not* to conclude from this that no Old Testament saint knew God, was regenerated, or was forgiven of his or her sins. Instead, under the old covenant these realities were true for the remnant (elect) within the nation in a typological, shadowy, and anticipatory way. Old Testament believers had access to God only mediately, *through* the priesthood and tabernacle/temple

---

Covenant and Creation, 177–178; Richard L. Pratt, Jr., "Infant Baptism in the New Covenant," in Gregg Strawbridge, ed. *The Case for Covenantal Infant Baptism* (Phillipsburg, NJ: P&R, 2003), 159–161; Paul R. House, *Old Testament Theology* (Downers Grove, IL: InterVarsity Press, 1998), 317–321.

[75] See Thomas R. Schreiner, *Romans*, Baker Exegetical Commentary on the New Testament (Grand Rapids, MI: Baker, 1998), 395–468.

structures; their access was not immediate. In the same way, the elect under the old covenant were regenerate, but this was not true of the entire community, and even the elect did not experience the full new covenant realities of the Spirit's work. Their sins were also forgiven (see Gen. 15:6), yet this was not based solely on the sacrificial system but came about as they also believed God's promises and looked forward to God's provision of a greater sacrifice to come (see Rom. 3:21–26; Hebrews 9–10). However, the main point to stress is that Jeremiah is signalling that, under the new covenant, what was true of the remnant (elect) within Israel will now be true of the *entire* covenant community *and* in greater ways. Instead of Israel of old, which *in its very makeup and nature* was a "mixed" group, the anticipation is that the *entire* people will be characterised by: (1) the saving knowledge of God; (2) regeneration; and (3) the declaration of justification. Furthermore, we will be characterised by these realities in a *greater* way since now we will have direct access to God, we will be empowered and indwelt by the Spirit, and the verdict of justification is definitive due to the once-for-all-time nature of Christ's work.

It is hard *not* to conclude that the Old Testament itself anticipates that the *nature* of the new covenant community, which is clearly identified with the church, is both a *new* community and a *believing, regenerate* people in contrast to Israel as a "mixed" people.[76] Under the old covenant, within national Israel, there was a distinction between the physical/biological (not necessarily true) believer and the spiritual/true believer seed of Abraham. Both of these "seeds" received the covenant sign of circumcision and both were viewed as full covenant members in the national sense. Yet, it was only the believers—the remnant—who were "true Israel" in a salvific sense. This simply is *not* what is anticipated for the church.

3. What the Old Testament promises and anticipates in regard to the *newness* of the *nature* of the church is what the New Testament announces is fulfilled in Christ. Contra older forms of dispensational theology, the new covenant is inaugurated and ratified by the sacrificial death of Christ (Luke 22:20; cf. 1 Cor. 11:25; 2 Cor. 3:7–18) and the author of Hebrews unambiguously applies Jeremiah 31 to the church (Hebrews 8–10). This fact entails,

---

[76] See Paul R. House, *Old Testament Theology*, 317–321, who rightly observes that Jeremiah 31 provides a profound shift in the definition of the elect. One can think of the nation of Israel as consisting of both those who believe and nonfaithful persons, a situation that creates the notion of a remnant. However, in the new covenant, the idea of the remnant or the elect within the community is not what Jeremiah anticipates. See also James R. White, "The Newness of the New Covenant: Part 2," *Reformed Baptist Theological Review* 2/1 (2005): 88, who makes this same point.

as Carson notes, that whatever complex relationships obtain between Israel and the church, it is at least a typological connection since the promise of the new covenant in Jeremiah is made to "the house of Israel and with the house of Judah" (Jer. 31:31).[77] The church is *new* but not ontologically so. But note, contra some covenant theology argumentation, Hebrews establishes the reality of the new covenant in the church without any hint that the full establishment of a regenerate community is yet future.[78] No doubt, we still await the "not yet" aspects of our redemption, but this does *not* entail that the community is not "already" a regenerate people. The perfect passive use of the verb in Hebrews 8:6—he "has enacted"—emphasises the completed action even though the full ramifications may be future.[79] Unlike Israel of old, by definition, the locus of the covenant community and the locus of the redeemed are one.

One cannot understand the argument of Hebrews (let alone the New Testament) without seeing that what Jeremiah anticipated has now come to pass in the church. In Christ's coming, the new age is here; the Spirit has been poured out on the entire community (Acts 2); we *all* know God in a direct and immediate fashion (Eph. 2:18; Heb. 10:19–25); we are now experiencing our adoption as sons; and we are declared just before God (Rom. 8:1)—even though we still long for the consummated realities of what has already begun. The massive changes the Old Testament anticipated are now here in the church.

What has brought about these incredible changes? The answer lies in Christology. Given who the new covenant head is and what he has done, fulfilment realities have come. Is this not what the story line of the biblical covenants reveals? As we progress across the Canon we move from type to antitype, from covenant heads such as Adam, Noah, Abraham, Moses/Israel, and David to Christ, and with Christ there is change. This is *the* reason why it is *not* correct to view the church, as covenant theology does, as simply the replacement of Israel—a kind of "renewed" instantiation of it. Rather, the church is *new*. Due to her identification with Christ, the head of the

---

[77] Carson, "Evangelicals, Ecumenism, and the Church," 361.

[78] See Pratt, "Infant Baptism in the New Covenant," who makes this argument. For a detailed and helpful critique of Pratt, see White, "Newness of the New Covenant: Part 2," 97–103.

[79] James R. White, "The Newness of the New Covenant: Part 1" *Reformed Baptist Theological Review* 1:2 (2004), 157, captures this point well when he argues, "There is nothing in the text that would lead us to believe that the full establishment of this covenant is yet future, for such would destroy the present apologetic concern of the author; likewise, he will complete his citation of Jer. 31 by asserting the obsolete nature of the first covenant, which leaves one to have to theorize, without textual basis, about some kind of intermediate covenantal state if one does not accept the full establishment of the new covenant as seen in the term νενομοθέτηται."

new creation, she is a "new man" (Eph. 2:11–22). This is why the church is identified with the "age to come" and not with the structures of the old era, or with what has been labelled "this present age." This is why the church is viewed as the community empowered by the Spirit in which *all* have been born of the Spirit, unlike Israel of old. Furthermore, it is also why dispensational theology goes awry. Instead of making an ontological distinction between Israel and the church, we must view the relationship between the two communities in light of Christ.

The biblical covenants teach us that Jesus is the last Adam *and* the true Israel, the antitypical fulfilment of both. In Christ, God's purposes for creation are realized, including his purposes for Israel. All of God's promises, tied to creation and the biblical covenants, including the promises to Israel, are brought to fulfilment in Christ. This is why the term "new covenant" can be applied to the church in the New Testament even though in Jeremiah it is applied to the "house of Israel." In Christ, the antitype of Israel, all of God's promises are yes and amen. We, as the church, the people of Christ, receive all the benefits of his glorious, effective, and triumphant work *by virtue of our faith union with him*. He, as our covenant head, wins for us our redemption, and all that he has achieved becomes ours due to that union. Once again, this is why the New Testament views the church as a *regenerate* community, since it is only those who actually are in faith union with Christ, born of his Spirit, and declared just, who are his people. The New Testament does *not* view the church as consisting of some who are in faith union with Christ and others who are not—unless one alters the New Testament teaching on what it means to be in union with him.

These points are further buttressed by how the church is described in the New Testament. For example, the church is viewed as an eschatological and "gathered" (*ekklēsia*) community.[80] In this regard, the church as identified with the "age to come" is an illustration of the running tension between the "already–not yet." It is the "gathered" people of God in a singular sense—"*the* church" (see Col. 1:18; cf. Heb. 12:22–24)—because even *now* Christians participate in the heavenly, eschatological church of Christ as the beginnings of the new creation. As Carson reminds us, what this entails for our understanding of the church is that,

---

[80] See Carson, "Evangelicals, Ecumenism, and the Church," 363–367, as well as the helpful discussion in Edmund P. Clowney, *The Church: Sacraments, Worship, Ministry, Mission* (Downers Grove, IL: InterVarsity Press, 1995), 27–33.

> . . . each local church is not seen primarily as one member parallel to a lot of other member churches, together constituting one body, one church; nor is each local church seen as the body of Christ parallel to other earthly churches that are also the body of Christ—as if Christ had many bodies. Rather, each church is the full manifestation in space and time of the one, true, heavenly, eschatological, new covenant church. Local churches should see themselves as outcroppings of heaven, analogies of "the Jerusalem that is above," indeed colonies of the new Jerusalem, providing on earth a corporate and visible expression of "the glorious freedom of the children of God."[81]

However, if this is so, then it is crucial to note that *this* understanding of the church presupposes that it is a *regenerate* community—a community in faith union with Christ, born of his Spirit, those who have been raised and seated with Christ in the heavenly realms (see Eph. 2:5–6; Col. 2:12–13; 3:3). It is difficult to think of the church as a mixed entity. As Carson rightly notes, if this biblical and theological understanding of the church is basically right, "then the ancient contrast between the church visible and the church invisible, a contrast that has nurtured not a little ecclesiology, is either fundamentally mistaken, or at best of marginal importance."[82] Why? Because the New Testament views the church as a *heavenly* community (i.e., tied to the "age to come" and the new creation, not "in Adam" but "in Christ") and a *spiritual* community (i.e., born of and empowered by the Spirit in faith union with Christ), living her life out now while she awaits the consummation, literally "the outcropping of the heavenly assembly gathered in the Jerusalem that is above."[83]

All of this understanding of the church is basic New Testament ecclesiology.[84] And all of it is true because Christ Jesus has come and through his cross work has inaugurated the new covenant age. He, as the fulfilment of Adam, Abraham, Israel, and David has brought covenantal and epochal change. And we, as the new covenant people of God, receive the benefits of his work in only one way—through individual repentance toward God and faith in our Lord Jesus Christ—which then, by God's grace and power, transfers us from being "in Adam" to being "in Christ," with all the benefits of that union. And the New Testament is clear: to be "in Christ" and thus in

---

81 Carson, "Evangelicals, Ecumenism, and the Church," 366. See also P. T. O'Brien, "Church," in *Dictionary of Paul and His Letters*, ed. Gerald F. Hawthorne, et al. (Downers Grove, IL: InterVarsity Press, 1993), 123–131.
82 Carson, "Evangelicals, Ecumenism, and the Church," 367.
83 Ibid., 371.
84 See Clowney, *Church*, 27–70; D. J. Tidball, "Church," *NDBT*, 407–411; Thomas R. Schreiner, *Paul: Apostle of God's Glory in Christ* (Downers Grove, IL: InterVarsity Press, 2001), 331–344. Cf. S. Motyer, "Israel (nation)," *NDBT*, 581–587.

the new covenant, a member of his gathered people (church), means that one is a regenerate believer. The New Testament knows nothing of one who is "in Christ" who is not regenerate, effectually called of the Father, born of the Spirit, justified, holy, and awaiting glorification.[85]

How does covenant theology respond to this analysis, since they continue to affirm the "mixed" nature of both Israel and the church? Probably the most significant response is an appeal to the warning/apostasy passages of Scripture in order to demonstrate that the *visible* church is a "mixed" community, just like Israel of old (see, e.g., Heb. 6:4–6; 10:26–39). Do not these texts demonstrate that it is possible for some people to be members of the new covenant community but then, sadly, to depart from the faith, thus demonstrating that they were never regenerate, believing people even though they were externally members of the church?[86] We can give only a brief reply to this assertion as we note three problems with this response.

First, the "mixed" community interpretation of the warning passages assumes that the nature of Israel and the church is basically the same, but this begs the question. In order for their argument to carry any weight, they must first prove that the nature of the covenant communities is essentially the same, but we have already given reasons to think that this is not correct. As one thinks through the biblical covenants, it is difficult to sustain that Israel and the church are structurally and by nature the same. This assumption does not do justice to what each covenant is in its context and in light of the entire canonical presentation.

Second, this interpretation contradicts the biblical teaching regarding the nature of the new covenant church. It is common to find the assertion that, since the New Testament speaks of the possibility of apostasy and, sadly, we witness it in our daily experience, this demonstrates that the church is a mixed community like Israel of old. The problem is that this goes against what the Old Testament anticipates regarding the *nature* of the new covenant community and what the New Testament confirms. One must carefully distinguish between the *fact* of apostasy taking place and the *status* of the one who commits it. No one disputes the *fact* that apostasy takes place in the new covenant age. What is at dispute is the *status* of those

---

[85] See Sinclair B. Ferguson, *The Holy Spirit* (Downers Grove, IL: InterVarsity Press, 1996); and Grudem, *Systematic Theology*, 840–850, for a development of the biblical and theological data regarding union with Christ.

[86] See, e.g., Douglas Wilson, *To a Thousand Generations: Infant Baptism—Covenant Mercy for the People of God* (Moscow, ID: Canon, 1996), 34; Gregg Strawbridge, "Introduction," in *The Case for Covenantal Infant Baptism*, ed. Gregg Strawbridge (Phillipsburg, NJ: P&R, 2003), 4–5; idem, "Baptism and the Relationship between the Covenants: A Review," at www.paedobaptism.com/Wellum/pdf, 1–7.

apostates. Should they be viewed as "new covenant breakers" (assuming they were once full covenant members) or, as those who *professed* faith, who identified with the church, but who, by their rejection of the gospel, demonstrated that *they were never one with us* (see 1 John 2:19)? For a variety of reasons tied to our overall "putting together" of the covenants, we are convinced that the New Testament teaches the latter. When apostasy takes place, we reevaluate the person's former profession and thus their covenant status. However, this situation is unlike that of unbelievers in the old covenant. The old covenant by its very nature allowed for a mixed group. R. Fowler White hits the mark when he asserts, "Unlike apostates from the Mosaic covenant (Heb. 3:7–11, 16–19) who had heard God say of them that he had (fore)known them in their mediatorial forebears (cf. Deut. 4:37; 7:6–8; 10:15), apostates from the Messianic covenant will hear the Lord of the covenant say to them, 'I never knew you' (see Matt 7:23; cf. 2 Tim 2:17–19)."[87] Other than a few exceptions, one was under the old covenant due to physical/biological relationships which did not assume regeneration and saving faith. But new covenant members, by definition, are those who are "in Christ" and all that that entails.

In addition, often the charge brought against a *regenerate* view of the church is that it would require us to have infallible knowledge regarding someone's regeneration.[88] This is not correct. No doubt, the church has made many mistakes in this regard. However, we receive people into the church *on the basis of their profession that they have come to faith in Christ*. This is quite different from the situation under the old covenant, where many within that covenant did not profess faith toward God. The truth of the matter is this: trying to discern true saving faith is merely a human epistemological problem, and we do our best to discern whether one's *profession* of faith is genuine. But this is a far cry from thinking that people who do *not* profess faith, particularly infants who are baptized, are full new covenant members in faith union with Christ.

Third, even though the "mixed" community interpretation of these texts is a *possible* reading of these texts, in light of a better way to understand the relations between the biblical covenants, the nature of the new covenant community, and what it means for someone to be in union with Christ, there

---

[87] R. F. White, "The Last Adam and His Seed: An Exercise in Theological Preemption," *Trinity Journal* n.s. 6/1 (1985): 72, fn. 19.
[88] See Strawbridge, "Baptism and the Relationship between the Covenants: A Review," 1–7.

are other legitimate ways of reading these texts which, in our view, does better justice to *all* of the scriptural data.[89] Ultimately, in the end, this is the true test for anyone's theology: Does it do justice to *all* of the biblical data? At point after point, we have sought to argue why we think our position makes better sense of the data.

KINGDOM THROUGH COVENANT AND THE BAPTISMAL DIVIDE[90]

The perennial and raging debate over the meaning and subjects of baptism is best viewed in light of the larger polemics regarding the relationships between the biblical covenants. Different views on baptism reflect different ways of "putting together" Scripture in regard to covenants. Covenant theologians and their advocacy and defense of paedobaptism have certainly acknowledged this point. They have repeatedly argued that their view is an implication drawn from their overall understanding of the "covenant of grace." In many ways, all other arguments for infant baptism are secondary to this overall line of reasoning. In their mind, if one establishes the basic continuity of the "covenant of grace" across the Canon, then their view has been demonstrated. It does not bother them that in the New Testament there is no express command to baptize infants and/or no record of any clear case of infant baptism.[91] Rather, as John Murray admits, "the evidence for infant baptism falls into the category of good and necessary inference,"[92] and ultimately this inference is rooted and grounded in a specific covenantal argument. Covenant theology, therefore, according to the paedobaptist, *requires* infant baptism. To make headway in the debate, then, one has to wrestle with the relationships between the biblical covenants, especially in regard to the nature of the covenant communities and the covenant signs and how the covenants come to fulfilment in Christ.

In chapter 2, we highlighted the basic argument for infant baptism. Given the unity of the covenant of grace (with some modifications), the continuity

---

[89] In our view, for the best treatment of the warnings passages in Scripture and how they function in the Christian life, which does *not* conclude that they entail that the church is a "mixed community," see Thomas R. Schreiner and A. B. Caneday, *The Race Set before Us* (Downers Grove, IL: InterVarsity Press, 2001). See also Thomas R. Schreiner, *Run to Win the Prize: Perseverance in the New Testament* (Wheaton, IL: Crossway, 2010)

[90] For a more detailed discussion of this point, which can only be summarised here, see Stephen J. Wellum, "Baptism and the Relationship between the Covenants," in *Believer's Baptism: Sign of the New Covenant in Christ*, ed. Thomas R. Schreiner and Shawn D. Wright (Nashville: B&H Academic, 2006), 97–161.

[91] Most paedobaptists acknowledge this point. See, for example, John Murray, *Christian Baptism* (Phillipsburg, NJ: P&R, 1980), 69; Berkhof, *Systematic Theology*, 632; Robert L. Reymond, *A New Systematic Theology of the Christian Faith* (Nashville: Thomas Nelson, 1998), 936.

[92] Murray, *Christian Baptism*, 69.

of the covenant communities and the covenant signs, plus the fact that the genealogical principle of the Abrahamic covenant remains unchanged in the new covenant, baptism is to be applied to infants in the church. In chapter 3, the hermeneutic at work was discussed. Paedobaptists appeal to the unconditional nature of the Abrahamic covenant and its genealogical principle, so that it remains unchanged across time. Unless God specifically abrogates it, it is still in force even though there is not one New Testament example of infant baptism or the command to do so.[93]

Why do we reject the covenantal argument for infant baptism? Five points will summarise our overall problem with their view, given their understanding of the covenants.

1. Our *overall* criticism is that covenant theology reads new covenant realities back into the Old Testament *too quickly* without first understanding the covenants, the nature of the covenant community, and the covenantal signs in their own redemptive-historical context and then thinking carefully through the issues of continuity and discontinuity now that Christ has come.

2. An excellent illustration of this criticism is how covenant theology treats the Abrahamic covenant. Essentially they view it in direct continuity with the new covenant other than a few explicit changes. By doing so, they "flatten" the Abrahamic covenant by reducing it primarily to *spiritual* realities while neglecting its national and typological aspects.[94] This is why the genealogical principle, operative in the unconditional Abrahamic covenant (Gen. 17:7), is applied in exactly the same way across the Canon without suspension, abrogation, and reinterpretation in the new covenant. This is

---

[93] Bill Smith, "Infant Baptism, the New Man, and the New Creation: A Response to Stephen J. Wellum," 28–29, at http://www.communitypca.org/wp-content/uploads/2007/11/infant-baptism-new-man-new-creation1.pdf charges me with the "explicit references" fallacy. He thinks that since I argue in terms of the New Testament pattern of baptism (repentance, faith, and baptism) and the lack of any specific New Testament command to baptize infants, I have dismissed paedobaptism by assuming that unless the New Testament *explicitly* commands it then it is not justified. He then maintains that such a hermeneutic would undermine allowing women to participate in the Lord's Supper and would undermine the rejection of bestiality, since both of these are not explicitly mentioned in the New Testament. This is not correct. My point is that the hermeneutic of covenant theology *in reference to the genealogical principle* is that it assumes it is unchanging due to their understanding of the continuity between the Abrahamic and new covenant. My overall argument against this view is much more detailed than this point. Not only do I seek to show that their understanding of the relationships between the covenants is flawed, but also that their assumption that the covenant communities remain the same over time is wrong, that the covenant signs do not signify different realities related to their respective covenants, *and* that the New Testament meaning of baptism is not what they think it is.

[94] Bill Smith, "Infant Baptism, the New Man, and the New Creation," 4–6, fundamentally misunderstands what I mean by "spiritual" by thinking I am pitting "physical" against "spiritual." By "physical" I am referring to the biological link between covenant mediators and those they represent. In Adam, Noah, Abraham, David, there is a *physical* relationship in that they represent those who genetically descend from them, while in Christ, the relationship between Christ and his people is *spiritual*, i.e., it is brought about by the sovereign work of the Spirit in new birth (not physical birth) and it is by faith and not national origin or privilege, as in the previous covenants. This does not deny that there were true believers in the previous covenants, hence *spiritual* relationships, but it affirms that the mediation of the covenant head has changed in the new covenant from the previous covenants.

also why they argue that baptism is the replacement for circumcision and that the covenant sign, regardless of one's covenantal location, is for "you and your seed" (i.e., physical children).

As previous chapters have shown, we disagree with how covenant theology understands the relationship between the Abrahamic and new covenants. As we have argued, we do believe that the Abrahamic covenant is crucial in God's plan, as are all the covenants. Abraham and his seed are the means God has chosen to bring blessing to all the nations and to fulfill God's promises to the entire creation in light of the covenant with creation. Abraham and his seed are the answer to the plight of the human race; they are to help bring about the recovery of the divine goal for creation and humanity and the establishment of God's kingdom through a redeemed society. However, we must do justice to the multifaceted and diverse nature of that covenant in its immediate context before we bring it too quickly into the new covenant. This point is best illustrated in reference to the seed of Abraham and the genealogical principle (which has direct implications for the baptismal debate).

The covenantal argument for infant baptism requires us to view the genealogical principle of the Abrahamic covenant (Gen. 17:7) in physical/biological terms as it is applied in the church. However there are two problems with this approach. First, it fails to distinguish the different senses of the "seed of Abraham" both within the Abrahamic covenant and throughout the Canon. So, for example, Abraham's seed is certainly biological (e.g., Ishmael, Isaac, sons of Keturah), but it is also biological/special (e.g., Isaac, Israel), typological (e.g., Christ; Gal. 3:16), and as applied to all believers, spiritual (Gal. 3:26–29). In the first two cases, all of Abraham's seed was marked by the covenant sign of circumcision but it did not necessarily signify anything more than that they were biologically related to Abraham, hence the basis for the "mixed" community of Israel. In the Old Testament era, Israel was both a nation and the people of God; they had a special relationship to God; they were a redeemed people, but not necessarily in the same way that the church (*spiritual* seed of Abraham) is redeemed (since not all of them were redeemed salvifically). As the covenants unfold, the typological nature of Abraham's seed reaches its fulfilment in Christ, which brings with it significant changes in how we understand the relationship between Christ and his people. Christ's people are viewed as Abraham's *spiritual* seed, but this is not dependent on circumcision, Torah, or even ethnic lineage, but is through regeneration and faith union with Christ. All this is to say that we must not equate too quickly the Abrahamic covenant with the new covenant without noting its diverse aspects in its immediate context and how those aspects find their fulfilment in Christ.

Second, the covenantal argument for infant baptism also fails to see that the genealogical principle is transformed across the covenants; it does not remain unchanged. Under the previous covenants the relationship between the covenant mediator and his seed was primarily *physical-biological* (e.g., Adam, Noah, Abraham, Israel, David). But now, in Christ, under his mediation, the relationship between Christ and his seed is no longer physical but *spiritual*, i.e., it is brought about by the work of the Spirit, which entails that the covenant sign must be applied only to those who in fact profess that they are the *spiritual* seed of Abraham. Given the significant progression in the covenants across redemptive-history, particularly in terms of the relationship between the covenant mediator and his seed, covenant theology fails to discern correctly how the genealogical principle has changed from Abraham to Christ—and therefore it ultimately fails to understand the "newness" of the new covenant. Their emphasis on continuity of the covenant of grace has led them to flatten the covenantal differences and thus misconstrue the nature of the new covenant community.

3. As discussed above, this tendency to reduce the covenantal differences, especially in relationship to Israel and the church, is another problem that covenant theology makes. The new covenant community (the church) in its *structure* and *nature* is different from Israel of old. Many things characterise this new community, but as a people identified with the new creation and the "age to come" (Eph. 2:11–22), born of the Spirit, "in Christ" instead of "in Adam," the church must be viewed as a *regenerate, believing* community and not a "mixed" group. The New Testament knows nothing of one who is "in Christ" who is not effectually called by the Father, born of the Spirit, justified, holy, and awaiting glorification. All these blessings of the new covenant are ours given our relationship to our covenantal head, our Lord Jesus Christ. This is why the New Testament does not apply baptism, the sign of the new covenant, to one who has not professed faith in Christ and testified that they have repented of their sins and believed in Christ.

4. The most fundamental *meaning* of baptism is that it signifies a believer's union with Christ, by grace through faith, and all the benefits that are entailed by that union. It testifies that one has entered into the realities of the new covenant and, as such, has experienced regeneration, the gift and down

payment of the Spirit, and the forgiveness of sin. It graphically signifies that a believer is now a member of the body of Christ (Eph. 4:22–25). It is our defining mark of belonging as well as a demarcation from the world (cf. Acts 2:40–41). It is an entry into the eschatological order of the new creation— that which our Lord has ushered in. Through baptism, we are united with Jesus Christ, by faith, and sealed with the Holy Spirit for the day of redemption (Eph. 4:30).[95] Interestingly, J. I. Packer, a paedobaptist, captures the significance of baptism well:

> Christian baptism . . . is a sign from God that signifies inward cleansing and remission of sins (Acts 22:16; 1 Cor 6:11; Eph 5:25–27), Spirit-wrought regeneration and new life (Titus 3:5), and the abiding presence of the Holy Spirit as God's seal testifying and guaranteeing that one will be kept safe in Christ forever (1 Cor 12:13; Eph 1:13–14). Baptism carries these meanings because first and fundamentally it signifies union with Christ in his death, burial, and resurrection (Rom 6:3–7; Col 2:11–12); and this union with Christ is the source of every element in our salvation (1 John 5:11–12). Receiving the sign in faith assures the persons baptized that God's gift of new life in Christ is freely given to them.[96]

In fact, so close is the association between baptism and new covenant blessings in Christ that many have argued that, in the New Testament, baptism "functions as shorthand for the conversion experience as a whole."[97] Evidence for this is quite apparent. For example, in Galatians 3:26–27, Paul can say: "You are all sons of God through faith in Christ Jesus, for all of you who were baptized into Christ have been clothed with Christ." The language of being "clothed" with Christ most certainly refers to the fact of our union with him.[98] But what is interesting about Paul's statement is how Paul can ascribe union with Christ both to faith (v. 26) and to baptism (v. 27). How can Paul do this? Does he have in mind an *ex opere operato* view of

---

[95] For a theological summary of Christian baptism see G. R. Beasley-Murray, *Baptism in the New Testament* (Grand Rapids, MI: Eerdmans, 1962), 263–305.

[96] Packer, *Concise Theology*, 212.

[97] Douglas J. Moo, *The Epistle to the Romans*, New International Commentary on the New Testament (Grand Rapids, MI: Eerdmans, 1996), 355. Moo picks up the suggestion of James Dunn that the early church conceived of faith, the gift of the Spirit, and water baptism as components of one unified experience, what Dunn calls "conversion-initiation." This is an important observation and it is crucial to maintain against the *ex opere operato* view of Roman Catholicism. It is not as if baptism effects regeneration, but it is assumed that faith leads to baptism, and baptism always assumes faith for its validity. This observation underscores the importance the New Testament places on baptism without denying the priority of salvation by grace through faith. See James Dunn, *Baptism in the Holy Spirit* (London: SCM, 1970), 139–146; Moo, *Epistle to the Romans*, 366.

[98] See Ronald Y. K. Fung, *The Epistle to the Galatians*, New International Commentary on the New Testament (Grand Rapids, MI: Eerdmans, 1988), 170–175; Beasley-Murray, *Baptism in the New Testament*, 146–151; Clowney, *Church*, 280.

baptism? No. Paul is not referring to those who have been baptized but have not believed; that would go against the clear statement of verse 26. Rather, he is referring to those who have been converted: all such have clothed themselves with Christ and have been united with him through faith. Thus, baptism, by metonymy, can stand for conversion and can signify, as an outward sign, that a believer has entered into the realities of the new covenant as a result of his union with Christ through faith.[99]

We find something similar in Romans 6:1–4, where Paul sees the initiation rite of baptism as uniting the believer to Jesus Christ in his redemptive acts—his death, burial, and resurrection. No doubt, in this text, Paul is not primarily giving a theological explanation of the nature of baptism, but rather is unpacking its meaning for life. Paul is deeply concerned to rebut the charge that the believer should "remain in sin" in order to underscore grace. Accordingly he uses the language of "realm transfer"[100] to show how inconceivable this suggestion really is. We Christians, Paul affirms, have "died to sin" (v. 2b). We have been transferred from the realm of Adam (sin) to the realm of Christ (life, resurrection, grace), and as such, it is quite impossible for us to still live in sin; its power in us has been decisively broken due to our union with Christ in his death. When did this realm transfer take place, this "death to sin"? It is interesting that in verses 3–4 Paul connects "death to sin" with our baptism—when we were "baptized into Christ Jesus" we were "baptized into his death" (v. 3). We have died to sin because we have become one with the Lord, who died and rose for the conquest of sin and death. Furthermore, "we were buried with him through baptism into death in order that, just as Christ was raised from the dead . . . we too may live a new life" (v. 4). In this sense, then, baptism serves as the instrument by which we are united with Christ in his death, burial, and resurrection.[101] Once again, it is important to stress that it is *not* Paul's point to say that the very practise of baptism unites us to Christ. Rather, as in Galatians 3:26–27, baptism functions as shorthand for the whole conversion experience. Thus, Doug Moo is right in concluding that, "just as faith is always assumed to lead to baptism,

---

[99] See Fung, *Epistle to the Galatians*, 173–174. Beasley-Murray, "Baptism," in *Dictionary of Paul and His Letters*, ed. Gerald F. Hawthorne, et al. (Downers Grove, IL: InterVarsity Press, 1993), 62, states it this way: "The two statements in Galatians 3:26 and 27 are complementary: verse 26 declares that believers are God's children 'through faith,' and verse 27 associates entry into God's family upon union with Christ, and Christ sharing his sonship with the baptized. It is an example of Paul's linking faith and baptism in such a way that the theological understanding of faith that turns to the Lord for salvation, and of baptism wherein faith is declared, is one and the same." On this same point also see Richard N. Longenecker, *Galatians*, WBC 41 (Dallas: Word, 1990), 41:154–156.

[100] Moo, *Epistle to the Romans*, 354.

[101] Ibid., 353–367.

so baptism always assumes faith for its validity. In verses 3–4, then, we can assume that baptism stands for the whole conversion-initiation experience, presupposing faith and the gift of the Spirit."[102] In truth, if we understand Paul's argument, it is *not* baptism that is the primary focus at all; rather it is the redemptive events themselves that Paul is stressing. Baptism is *only* introduced to demonstrate that we were united with Christ in his redemptive work, and now all the new covenant blessings that our Lord has secured for us are ours by virtue of our relationship with him.

Other texts could be multiplied to make this same point[103] but suffice it to say that, in the New Testament, baptism is organically linked with the gospel itself, and all of the realities of the new covenant age and the benefits that come to us are because of our faith union in Christ. Who, then, should receive the covenant sign of baptism? Only those who profess to have experienced the realities it actually signifies—people who have repented of their sins and believed in Christ and him alone.

5. Circumcision, as the covenant sign of the Abrahamic covenant, does *not* carry essentially the same meaning as baptism does in the new covenant era. The argument of covenant theology is that circumcision and baptism carry essentially the same *spiritual* meaning and that is why baptism is the *replacement* of circumcision in the new covenant. What is that meaning? Basically the covenant signs are objective entry markers signifying that one is part of the covenant community, at least in the external sense, and they promise and anticipate the gospel, i.e., pointing forward to the need for a "circumcision of the heart," testifying to God's promise that righteousness will be given by faith, and somehow signifying union with Christ and all the blessings related to that union without necessarily implying that one is a regenerate person in the full salvation sense of the word.[104]

The problem with this view is that it fails to do justice to the covenant signs in their own covenantal context. No doubt they are parallel in

---

[102] Ibid., 366.

[103] For example, see 1 Peter 3:21. On this text see Thomas R. Schreiner, *1, 2 Peter, Jude*, New American Commentary 37 (Nashville: B&H, 2003), 193–197; and Wayne Grudem, *1 Peter*, Tyndale New Testament Commentaries (Grand Rapids, MI: Eerdmans, 1988), 164–165.

[104] There seems to be an equivocation of terms in the covenant position. What does it mean for one to be united to Christ apart from faith, or to affirm that one has entered into new covenant realities apart from faith, regeneration, and forgiveness of sin? In fact, what does infant baptism effect apart from faith? Covenant theology is not clear at this point, even though they attempt to provide some kind of explanation. See the helpful discussion of this problem in David F. Wright, "Recovering Baptism for a New Age of Mission," in *Doing Theology for the People of God: Studies in Honor of J. I. Packer*, ed. Donald Lewis and Alister McGrath (Downers Grove, IL: InterVarsity Press, 1996), 51–66. For an example of a confusing use of the word "regeneration" as it relates to what infant baptism effects, see Rich Lusk, "Do I Believe in Baptismal Regeneration?" http://www.auburnavenue.org/articles/do%20i%20believe%20in%20baptismal%20regeneration.htm.

a number of ways, but circumcision is an Old Testament ordinance established in a specific redemptive-historical context, and the same is true of baptism in the New Testament. It is not correct to equate the two in a one-to-one fashion.[105] In fact, circumcision in light of the entire Canon ought to be viewed as signifying at least two truths. First and foremost it marks out a physical, national people. Second, it serves as a type anticipating New Testament realities which have now come to fulfilment in Christ. We may view circumcision as a type in two ways. First, circumcision is a type in that it anticipates Christ. As noted above, the "seed of Abraham" has a number of nuances including its reference to Christ (Gal. 3:16). In a typological way, then, every male offspring of Abraham—specifically through the line of Isaac, Judah, David—was a type of Christ and thus anticipated his ultimate coming. In this regard, Luke 2:21 is important. Jesus' circumcision is not a minor event; it marks the fulfilment of circumcision in its purpose of preserving a line of descent from Abraham to Christ and marking out the one in whom all of the promises of God have reached their fulfilment. In Christ, Abraham's true seed is now here, and as such, circumcision is no longer necessary, and it was soon to be abrogated. In this sense, Jesus' circumcision is the last significant covenantal circumcision recorded in Scripture. All other circumcisions, such as Timothy's (Acts 16:3), were done only for principled pragmatic concerns in order to win Jews to the gospel.[106] Second, circumcision is a type in that it anticipates the need for a "circumcision of the heart"—a reality that all new covenant people have experienced. In us, the spiritual meaning of circumcision is fulfilled (Rom. 2:25–29; Phil. 3:3). That is why true believers, regardless of whether they have been physically circumcised, are called "the true circumcision." Due to Christ's cross work and the Spirit's work within us, we have now received a circumcision without hands that gives us our new covenant status as God's people and thus makes us heirs and co-heirs with Christ.

In fact, this is the point of Colossians 2:11–13, the only text in the New Testament that brings together circumcision and baptism. But as it has repeatedly been shown, the connection in these verses is *not* between

---

[105] For a development of this argument in greater detail, see Wellum, "Baptism and the Relationship between the Covenants," 153–160.

[106] Contra Doug Wilson, *To a Thousand Generations*, 59–80, in the New Testament there is no covenantal significance in circumcision after the cross work of Christ. The fact that Paul circumcised Timothy or that other Jewish believers circumcised their children (Acts 21:21–26) does not mean that circumcision continued to have covenantal efficacy. Paul circumcised Timothy only for mission purposes, what I have called "principled pragmatic concerns." For a helpful treatment of this issue see D. A. Carson, "Pauline Inconsistency: Reflections on 1 Corinthians 9.19–23 and Galatians 2.11–14," *Churchman* 100:1 (1986), 6–45.

physical circumcision and baptism, as if the latter replaces the former, but *spiritual circumcision* is tied to union with Christ and *baptism*.[107] As Paul reminds these believers, they are complete in Christ not because they were physically circumcised but because they were circumcised in "the circumcision of Christ"—which refers either to "a Christian circumcision of the heart"[108] or to Christ's death on the cross, which entails that the only circumcision believers need is that which has been done by our being united into Christ's death on the cross.[109] Either way, circumcision finds its fulfilment in being joined to Christ and experiencing the promises associated with the inauguration of the new covenant age. But note how the text says even more: verse 12 makes it clear that we participate by baptism in the burial of Christ, and through it "a real death has occurred and the old life is now a thing of the past. Those who have been buried with Christ 'through baptism into death' (Rom. 6:4) can no longer go on living as slaves to sin."[110] It is clear that Paul does not view baptism in an *ex opere operato* fashion, for he clearly stresses the instrumentality of faith. But he does argue that, in baptism, the objective realities of having died to sin and being made alive in Christ have actually taken place—something which cannot be applied to infants unless one affirms some kind of baptismal regeneration.

All of this is to say that circumcision, as a type, *pointed to* a spiritual regeneration and anticipated new covenant realities. Baptism, in contrast to circumcision, is a new covenant sign, commanded by our Lord (Matt. 28:18–20), which communicates the grace of God *to those who have faith*, something which could not be said of circumcision of old. Baptism is a public testimony that one has entered into faith union with Christ, and it marks and defines the children of God, those who believe in Messiah Jesus. That is why we baptize only those who have confessed Jesus as Lord, who have experienced his power, who are, by faith and spiritual rebirth, Abraham's true spiritual seed. Baptism is a new rite for the new covenant people of God; it is not the replacement of circumcision. To argue in a contrary fashion is fundamentally to misunderstand the relations

---

[107] For example, see Herman Ridderbos, *Paul: An Outline of His Theology*, trans. John Richard de Witt (Grand Rapids, MI: Eerdmans, 1975), 404–405, fn. 38. See also Martin Salter, "Does Baptism Replace Circumcision? An Examination of the Relationship between Circumcision and Baptism in Colossians 2:11–12," *Themelios* 35/1 (2010): 15–29.

[108] See Murray J. Harris, *Colossians and Philemon*, Exegetical Guide to the Greek New Testament (Grand Rapids, MI: Eerdmans, 1991), 101–105.

[109] See O'Brien, *Colossians and Philemon*, WBC 44 (Dallas: Word, 1982), 114–121.

[110] O'Brien, *Colossians and Philemon*, 118; cf. Beasley-Murray, *Baptism in the New Testament*, 152–160.

between the biblical covenants and to confuse promise with fulfilment and type with antitype.

ESCHATOLOGY

How does a proper understanding of the biblical covenants affect eschatology? Given the fact that the subject of eschatology encompasses many topics which we cannot even begin adequately to address here, our answer to this question will focus on only one area: the land promise to Israel and how that promise is fulfilled in the inauguration of the new covenant era.

In biblical and theological studies, few doubt that the theme of "land" is important. Walter Brueggemann is probably too strong in his contention that land is one of *the* central themes of biblical faith.[111] J. G. Millar is more on track when he affirms that the land theme is *a* crucial biblical topic and thus functions as "an important theological category in the Bible."[112] Furthermore, as noted in chapters 2–3, the issue of land is also a major dividing point between dispensational and covenant theology. At the heart of dispensationalism is the Israel-church distinction, and intimately related to this distinction is the conviction that Israel, as a national people, still awaits the "literal" fulfilment of the land promise in the future millennial age. A significant amount of discussion in eschatology centres on this issue, and much of the rationale for dispensational premillennialism is centred on how one thinks the land promise, first promised to Abraham and then to Israel, is brought to fulfilment in light of Christ's redemptive work. In fact, how one answers this question also has implications for how Christians think through present geopolitical discussions, particularly the role of Israel in the world, her right to the land of Israel, and other pressing matters that are constantly in the daily news and that fuel much eschatological speculation.

Before we discuss how *kingdom through covenant* impacts the important land question, let us summarise the basic argument of dispensational

---

[111] Walter Brueggemann, *The Land: Place as Gift, Promise, and Challenge in Biblical Faith* (London: SPCK, 1978), 3.

[112] J. G. Millar, "Land," in *NDBT*, 623. For some helpful discussions of "land" in biblical and systematic theology, see Philip Johnston and Peter W. L. Walker, eds., *The Land of Promise: Biblical, Theological, and Contemporary Perspectives* (Downers Grove, IL: InterVarsity Press, 2000); Bruce K. Waltke with Charles Yu, *An Old Testament Theology: An Exegetical, Canonical, and Thematic Approach* (Grand Rapids, MI: Zondervan, 2007), 512–587; C. J. H. Wright, *God's People in God's Land: Family, Land, and Property* (Grand Rapids, MI: Eerdmans, 1994); Moshe Weinfeld, *The Promise of the Land: The Inheritance of the Land of Canaan by the Israelites* (Berkeley: University of California Press, 1993); W. D. Davies, *The Gospel and the Land: Early Christianity and Jewish Territorial Doctrine* (Berkeley: University of California Press, 1974).

theology in order to provide a larger context in which our discussion will proceed. There are at least three interlocking reasons that undergird the dispensational argument.[113] First, dispensationalists believe that the land promise to national Israel still awaits its fulfilment in the millennial age because God promised it *unconditionally* to Israel in the Abrahamic covenant. Since God cannot go back on his promise and since the promise has not yet been fully realized in Christ, it still awaits its fulfilment in the future.[114] Second, and building on the first reason, is a hermeneutical point: unless the New Testament explicitly or implicitly overturns Old Testament teaching then it is still in force, even if the New Testament does not repeat the promise.[115] This is especially the case given the unconditional nature of the promise. The third reason given is often not argued but assumed. For dispensational theology, the "land" must *not* be viewed as a type or pattern of something greater, as we contend it is. Instead, it is a straightforward ("literal") promise that reaches its fulfilment only with Christ ruling and reigning in the millennium in the land of Israel. To view the land as a divinely given pattern which looks back to the creation and forward to the greater reality of the new creation is rejected.[116]

---

113 See, e.g., John S. Feinberg, "Systems of Discontinuity," in *Continuity and Discontinuity: Perspectives on the Relationship between the Old and New Testaments*, ed. John S. Feinberg (Wheaton, IL: Crossway, 1988), 73–83; H. Wayne House, ed., *Israel: The Land and the People* (Grand Rapids, MI: Kregel, 1998), especially 80–83.

114 Walter C. Kaiser, Jr., "Israel and Its Land in Biblical Perspective," in *The Old Testament in the Life of God's People: Essays in Honor of Elmer A. Martens*, ed. Jon Isaak (Winona Lake, IN: Eisenbrauns, 2009), 249–250, stresses this point. Kaiser contends that if we think that the church, not national Israel, is the inheritor of the land promise, two options are available to us, both of which he rejects. Either we view the Abrahamic covenant as conditional or we conclude that the land promise possesses a meaning that is "not the plain or natural meaning of what is said" (249). In terms of the former, he admits that there are conditional elements in the covenants with Abraham and David but contends that God's overall promise makes the covenants irrevocable. In regard to the latter, Kaiser thinks that the promise has to be fulfilled in a "literal" or direct manner, hence its future fulfilment in the millennium. In addition, Kaiser argues that "God never made a covenant with the Church as such!" (252) since it was made with the "house of Israel and the house of Judah" (Jer. 31:31b). No doubt the church shares in the new covenant, but that is only by virtue of its relation to Israel. As noted in the ecclesiology section, Kaiser does not seem to view the new covenant first in relation to Christ, the last Adam and true Israel, but only in terms of national Israel, which then has spillover effects for the church. He also does not view the land promise typologically, which is the reason why he limits one's understanding of the fulfilment of the land promise to only the two options.

115 As noted above, ironically this is the same hermeneutical point that covenant theology adopts in its argument for the continuation of the genealogical principle across the covenants in an unchanged manner. Our response to both systems is to unpack the genealogical principle and land promise according to the three horizons (i.e., textual, epochal, and canonical) and in light of the covenantal progression before we conclude whether they are still in force in exactly the same way as they were in previous eras of redemptive-history.

116 Bruce Ware, "The New Covenant and the People(s) of God," in *Dispensationalism, Israel, and the Church*, ed. Craig A. Blaising and Darrell L. Bock (Grand Rapids, MI: Zondervan, 1992), 92–96, is a fine example of a progressive dispensationalist who does not view the land promise typologically. Instead he bifurcates the spiritual aspects of the new covenant from the territorial/political (i.e., land promise) and appeals to the "already–not yet" tension of inaugurated eschatology to argue that the spiritual aspects of the new covenant are now applied to the church while the territorial/political aspects await future fulfilment in the millennium to national Israel. This argument works only if you interpret the land promise as non-typological of the new creation and thus not already here due to the cross work of Christ and inauguration of the new covenant age. For a similar treatment of the land, see Craig

How, then, does our view differ from the dispensational view?[117] The only way to answer this question is to trace carefully the land theme through the biblical covenants. As already noted in our discussion of theology proper, Christology, and ecclesiology, our construal of the relationships between the biblical covenants does impact how we "put together" these important doctrinal issues. Let us briefly summarise in five steps our understanding of how the land promise is progressively developed across the Canon as the covenants reach their fulfilment in Christ.

1. An appeal to the unconditional nature of the Abrahamic covenant does not settle the issue.

Dispensational theology argues strongly that the land promise is irrevocable. It is unconditionally given and, as such, to deny that it is fulfilled to national Israel in the future millennial age is to say either that God has failed or that he has gone back on his promises, which, of course, are both impossibilities. The problem is that appeal to the unconditional nature of the promise as given in the Abrahamic covenant does not settle the issue, for at least two reasons.

The first reason is that it is *not* accurate to distinguish the biblical covenants into the either/or categories of unconditional (royal grant) or conditional (suzerain-vassal). Instead, the covenants exhibit a blend of unconditional-unilateral and conditional-bilateral elements. In terms of the former, it is only because of God, as the covenant making and keeping Lord, that the promises of the covenants are unilaterally guaranteed. God's commitment first and foremost to himself, his creation, and his image-bearers is what grounds our confidence that the covenant relationship will not fail. Yet, in terms of the latter, God demands an obedient, devoted covenant partner. This is why, as one progresses through the biblical covenants, there is a deliberate *tension* created since God is always the faithful one, and the various covenant mediators are not. It is only in the provision of our Lord Jesus Christ, God's own obedient, devoted Son who does not fail, that the new covenant is established on better grounds; indeed, unbreakable grounds. To

---

A. Blaising, "The Fulfillment of the Biblical Covenants through Jesus Christ," in Craig A. Blaising and Darrell L. Bock, *Progressive Dispensationalism* (Wheaton, IL: BridgePoint, 1993), 174–211.

[117] Our view of "land" is much more in line with recent covenant theology, even though our reasons may differ at points. See, e.g., Anthony A. Hoekema, *The Bible and the Future* (Grand Rapids, MI: Eerdmans, 1994), 274–287; Vern S. Poythress, *Understanding Dispensationalists*, 2nd ed. (Phillipsburg, NJ: P&R, 1994), 97–129; Dumbrell, *Covenant and Creation*; O. Palmer Robertson, *The Israel of God: Yesterday, Today, and Tomorrow* (Phillipsburg, NJ: P&R, 2000), 3–31; and the essays in Johnston and Walker, *Land of Promise*, particularly 15–50, 81–141.

simply distinguish the covenants in the way dispensational theology does (including other views as well) misses the overall story line of the biblical covenants and their incredible Christological focus. There is a sense in which we agree with Michael Horton that Israel forfeited the promise of the land because of her disobedience, hence the reason for the exile.[118] However, as the biblical covenants unfold it becomes clear that God must provide a greater than Israel, an obedient Son, who will keep the provisions of the covenant, who will not fail, and who will bring all of God's promises to pass, *including the land promise*.

This last observation brings us to the second reason why appeal to the Abrahamic covenant alone does not settle the issue. Dispensational theology assumes (almost without argument) that the "land" promised in the Abrahamic covenant refers only to a specific piece of real estate with well-defined geographical borders which remain unchanged across the Canon. They reject the view that the "land" functions as a microcosm, a pattern, or a type of something greater, namely creation. Walter Kaiser is a good example of this approach. He contends that the land promise must possess a meaning that is "plain or natural"[119]—hence the conclusion that it must be fulfilled in terms of a specific land in the millennium. To argue otherwise is to find a "deeper meaning" not discovered by grammatical-historical exegesis and thus not to interpret the biblical authors (including God as the divine author) according to their intention.[120] We reject this conclusion. Instead, we argue that there are exegetical grounds both in the immediate context and across the entire Canon to argue that the "land" was never intended by the biblical authors to be understood *merely* within the limited confines of specific geographical boundaries. In other words, "land," when placed within the biblical covenants and viewed diachronically, was intended by God to function as a "type" or "pattern" of something greater, i.e., creation, which is precisely how it is understood in light of the coming of Christ and the inauguration of the new covenant. In the remaining four points we list some of the reasons for viewing "land" typologically and not merely in a "plain or natural" manner without change and development across the covenants.[121]

---

[118] Horton, *God of Promise*, 47.
[119] Kaiser, "Israel and Its Land in Biblical Perspective," 249.
[120] Ibid.
[121] The reader will remember that our argument here is similar to our argument against covenant theology's understanding of the genealogical principle. In contrast to both dispensational and covenant theology we contend that the "land" *and* the "genealogical principle" are typological and that they must be carefully unpacked through the

2. *"Land," as first understood within the immediate context of the Abrahamic covenant, provides textual clues that it is functioning as a type of something greater.*

No doubt, the land promise is incredibly important in the Abrahamic covenant and as it continues in the Sinai covenant (see, e.g., Gen. 12:1–3; 13:14–16; 15:18–21; 17:8; 26:3, 4, 24; 28:3–4, 13–15; 35:9–12). Not many dispute that the "land" in question refers to a specific land, with well-defined geographical boundaries, i.e., the land of Canaan. However, the more important question is this: are there textual clues that the "land" within the immediate context of the Abrahamic covenant is *merely* referring to a piece of real estate with limited geographical boundaries, or is it pointing to something greater? Two pieces of evidence lead us to affirm the latter conclusion.

First, few dispute that the Abrahamic covenant has both national and international implications. As noted in previous chapters, the Abrahamic covenant has diverse dimensions to it, as illustrated by our discussion of Abraham's "seed." In its national sense tied to Isaac and then eventually to the nation of Israel, the land takes on a specific territorial promise of a comparatively small geographical area whose borders are explicitly delimited. Yet, one cannot forget the international purpose of the covenant. In fact, in terms of the latter, the main reason for the covenant is that through Abraham's "seed" blessing will come to the nations (Gen. 12:1–3; cf. Gen. 17:5–8; 22:15–19). The climax of God's plan through Abraham is not merely the establishment of the nation of Israel but rather that, through Israel, the nations will be blessed, which ultimately is fulfilled in Christ (Gal. 3:16). In light of Christ's work, then, blessing now comes to the nations, i.e., Abraham's *spiritual* seed by new birth and faith union with Christ, who then in turn, whether Jew or Gentile, inherit the promises (Eph. 2:11–22).

However, if this is so, there are important implications for how we view the land promise, even in its immediate context. As Paul Williamson notes, "The promise of land must be understood within this broader context of God's programmatic agenda, an agenda that culminates in the blessing of all the nations of the world through Abraham's seed (cf. Gal. 3:6ff.; Rev. 7:9). Since the latter aspect of the divine plan is patently non-territorial (in the

---

covenants as they reach their fulfilment in Christ. Here are two examples of how *kingdom through covenant* differs from the two dominant biblical-theological systems and provides a *via media*.

sense that it is not restricted to any one geographical location), the national dimension of the territorial promise should probably be understood as a transitional stage in the outworking of God's ultimate plan."[122] In other words, when the international focus on the Abrahamic covenant is considered, it is not enough to say that it is only Abraham's "seed," equated with the nation of Israel, who will inherit the promise. Rather, the ultimate inheritors of the patriarchal promises are an international community. Thus understood, as Williamson rightly contends, "It is certainly difficult to envisage the necessity of a strictly localized fulfillment of the territorial promise *after* the climactic element in the programmatic agenda has begun to materialize. Surely Abraham's multitudinous and international descendants require a much larger, indeed a global, inheritance."[123]

Second, it is also important to note that in the immediate context even the specific texts which lay out the geographical borders of the land are *not* consistent and precise (Gen. 15:18–21; Ex. 23:31ff.; Deut. 1:7; 11:24; Josh. 1:2–4). The extent of the land of promise is not identical in each. What are we to make of this? Some scholars have interpreted this as evidence of redaction, but as Williamson notes, "the fact that no steps were taken to impose uniformity suggests an element of flexibility difficult to harmonize with rigidly defined territorial borders."[124] He offers a better explanation: within the Abrahamic covenant these are textual clues that the Promised Land "was never seen as permanently fixed, but was subject to at least some degree of expansion and redefinition"[125] In other words, this textual ambiguity regarding the land provides clues that the land promise cannot be reduced *merely* to a particular piece of land but rather hints at a more ideal land which will be far greater, and that this promise will not be fulfilled until Abraham's seed fills and occupies the world. If this is the case, it provides a partial basis for Paul's statement regarding Abraham in Romans 4:13a—"For the promise to Abraham and his offspring *that he would be heir of the world . . .*" Paul seems to be saying that Abraham did *not* understand the land promise as referring only to a specific geographical location; rather he viewed the promise as that which ultimately would encompass the entire created order.[126]

---

[122] Paul R. Williamson, "Promise and Fulfillment: The Territorial Inheritance," in Johnston and Walker, *Land of Promise*, 18.

[123] Ibid.

[124] Ibid., 20–21.

[125] Ibid., 21. He further strengthens his point by appealing to texts which seem to indicate the possibility of expansion of the land beyond the geographical parameters indicated elsewhere (Gen. 26:3–4; Ex. 34:24; Num. 24:17–18; Deut. 19:8–9).

[126] See Schreiner, *Romans*, 227–228; Moo, *Epistle to the Romans*, 274, who make this same point.

On the basis of this evidence, Williamson is warranted to assert that, within the Abrahamic covenant, "Canaan was simply the preliminary stage in the ultimate unfolding of God's programmatic agenda—an agenda which not only involves all peoples of the earth but also encompasses all regions of the earth."[127] Within the immediate context there are textual clues to suggest that the promise of land points forward to something greater.

3. The "land" promise of the Abrahamic covenant must also be understood in terms of what preceded it, namely, the covenant of creation. When this is done, there is further biblical warrant to view the "land" as a type or pattern of the entire creation.

As argued in previous chapters, one cannot adequately understand any biblical covenant without thinking through *before* and *after* in God's progressive revelation. The same is true of the "land" embedded in the biblical covenants. If we place the Abrahamic covenant (and the land promise) in light of what *preceded* it, namely, the covenant of creation, land must be linked to Eden and thus the created order. In other words, land did *not* become theologically significant first with Abraham. Instead, Abraham's hope of possessing a land arose out of the concept of restoration to the original state from which Adam had fallen—in truth, an outworking of the *protoeuangelion*.[128] J. G. Millar is correct to note that in this way, "The promise of land guarantees the restoration of intimacy with God in terms which recall the description of Eden."[129] This is significant, as Millar observes, since "the theology of land in the early part of the OT anticipates the final chapters of the Bible, where the apostle John describes the new heaven and earth in language taken from Genesis 1–3."[130]

Furthermore, once we place "land" in the larger context of the covenant of creation, at least two other interrelated truths arise which are all intimately associated with land throughout Scripture: the theme of God's rest; and Eden as a temple sanctuary, with the mandate for God's priest-kings

---

[127] Paul R. Williamson, "Promise and Fulfillment: The Territorial Inheritance," 22.

[128] See Robertson, *Israel of God*, 4. Paul R. Williamson, "Promise and Fulfillment: The Territorial Inheritance," 25, rightly contends that the juxtaposition of Genesis 1–11 and Genesis 12 suggests that the land promise is a reversal of the pattern of expulsion that dominates Genesis 3–11. In addition, God's promise to make Abraham numerous not only continues the creation mandate (Gen. 1:28; 9:1) but is also God's answer to humanity's plight. This is why one must understand land in light of creation if one places the Abrahamic covenant in the context of what preceded it. This also provides the exegetical basis for the author of Hebrews to claim that Abraham was anticipating something more permanent than a temporary piece of land (see Heb. 11:8–16).

[129] Millar, "Land," *NDBT*, 623.

[130] Ibid.

and image-bearers to expand the borders of Eden to the uttermost parts of the world.

First, think of the theme of God's rest. It serves as the climax of the creation week, where God rests on the seventh day after he declares everything "very good" (Gen. 1:31). This speaks of God's entering into covenantal enjoyment of his creation and of our enjoyment of God as we carry out our creation mandate as his servant kings. It also establishes a pattern that runs through the entire Canon, grounding the Sabbath law in the time of Moses (Ex. 20:8–11) and ultimately pointing forward to a greater "rest" to come (Heb. 3:7–4:13), which is associated with the great salvation rest of the new covenant era inaugurated by Jesus himself. But what is also crucial to note is how the theme of "rest" is organically associated with "land."[131] This is evident later in Scripture when the land of promise is clearly associated with rest (Deut. 3:20; 12:9–10; 25:19; cf. Josh. 1:13–15; 21:43–44; 22:4; cf. Psalm 95; Heb. 3:7–4:13). Linked together, this entails that securing possession of the land typifies entering God's eternal rest, of which the land of Canaan is only a type or pattern. As Williamson notes, "God intended humankind to share such a rest with him from the beginning (as reflected in the Edenic Paradise described in Gen. 2). The territorial promise thus anticipated the full restoration of the Edenic conditions that had been lost initially and jeopardized persistently through human disobedience. It is reasonable to conclude, therefore, that anything less than a permanent restoration of the conditions that pertained in Eden stops short of a comprehensive fulfillment of the territorial promise."[132]

Second, think of the theme of the garden of Eden as a temple sanctuary.[133] The most extensive development of this rich biblical theme to date is Greg Beale's excellent work on the temple.[134] Beale convincingly demonstrates that the land of Eden is presented as the archetypal temple, the place where God uniquely dwelt with Adam and Eve as they served as God's priest-kings and sons in obedient devotion and worship of God.[135] Adam and Eve's task

---

[131] See, e.g., T. D. Alexander, "Beyond Borders: The Wider Dimensions of Land," in Johnston and Walker, *Land of Promise*, 36–39, who emphasises this point. For a further development of this point see T. D. Alexander, *From Eden to the New Jerusalem* (Nottingham, UK: Inter-Varsity Press, 2008).

[132] Paul R. Williamson, "Promise and Fulfillment: The Territorial Inheritance," 27. See Alexander, "Beyond Borders," 39, who draws the same conclusion. Rest in the land "represents a return to the idyllic conditions which existed prior to the expulsion of Adam and Eve from the Garden of Eden."

[133] This point is well recognised today, as developed in the previous chapters. Also cf. Alexander, "Beyond Borders," 39–41; Dumbrell, *Covenant and Creation*, 119–123.

[134] G. K. Beale, *The Temple and the Church's Mission: A Biblical Theology of the Dwelling Place of God*, NSBT 17 (Downers Grove, IL: InterVarsity Press, 2004).

[135] Ibid., 66–80.

was to subdue and rule over the entire earth, which suggests that they were "to extend the geographical boundaries of the garden until Eden covered the whole earth,"[136] which, as Psalm 8 makes clear, was a role that the entire human race was to carry out. Adam, however, failed in his task, and because of his disobedience, instead of extending the divine presence of Eden, he was expelled from it. Yet, what is significant for our purposes is the close connection between land and temple, and how Eden serves as the archetype which both the land of Israel and the later tabernacle/temple are patterned after.

When we combine all of these points and set the land promise in the context of creation, we have the biblical warrant to view the "land" as a type and pattern of creation. In this reading, the archetype is the land of Eden, whose borders are to be extended to the entire creation. With the fall of Adam and the removal from the "land" (Eden), God's promise is to restore what was lost and to reverse the disastrous effects of sin and death. Through the "seed of the woman" (Gen. 3:15), as worked out through the biblical covenants (Noah, Abraham, Israel, David and his sons), God's rest, covenantal presence in tabernacle/temple—all associated with the land—is restored in type and shadow but not in ultimate reality. Israel as God's son is to function like another Adam and experience God's presence in the land, but they fail. They were to act as God's priest-kings, as a holy nation, in order to bring God's blessing to the nations. Their land, then, becomes a pattern or a microcosm of the entire world. Through them the nations are to see what God intends for the entire world as they are to live as God's holy people. Just as "Adam and Eve had known God's blessing in Eden, so God would bless his people in a new land."[137] But, sadly, given their failure, they fail to do what God intended for them to do. In order for God's purposes to be finally realized, God will have to provide his Son, who is not only the true Israel but also the last Adam, who in himself replaces the temple, inaugurates a new covenant by his blood, and begins to usher in the new creation.

4. Within the Old Testament and especially in prophetic anticipation, the "land" of Israel is identified with the new creation associated with the inauguration of the new covenant age.

Is there any textual warrant to think that, as we work through the biblical covenants, the "land" is not merely viewed as a specific piece of property

---

[136] Ibid., 81–82.
[137] Robertson, *Israel of God*, 7.

associated with the land of Canaan, but its borders are expanded to encompass the entire creation? We believe the answer is yes. As the biblical covenants unfold, there are two main fulfilments of the land promise. It is first fulfilled in the days of Joshua (Josh. 21:43–45) and secondly in the reign of Solomon (1 Kings 4:20–21), but in each case, the fulfilment of the land promise falls short due to the failure of the nation and the Davidic kings.[138] In addition, it is important to note that the idea of *multiple* fulfilments is also instructive. As Williamson notes, "The fact that the promise of land was fulfilled more than once leaves open the possibility of multiple fulfillments and also raises the question of its ultimate fulfillment."[139] We take this as evidence that in some sense the rest of Eden is partially restored, but not in its ultimate, consummated form. Given the failure of Israel and the Davidic kings, it should not surprise us that, in the Old Testament, the land promise is fulfilled in Israel's history in some sense, but "it nowhere suggests that this dimension of the divine plan has been fulfilled in its most comprehensive sense."[140]

As the prophets anticipate the exile, which is traumatic, to say the least, given the theological significance of the land, they also hold out hope for a return from exile to the land.[141] Yet, the prophets are clear that a return to the land will include incredible realities; literally, it will result in the dawning of a new creation. The prophets painted a picture of land restoration so glorious that it could not be contained within the boundaries of the old covenant forms. The historic city of Jerusalem takes on overtones of a city that is larger than life and ultimately identified with the people of God. It will be one without walls, where God's glory will dwell (Zech. 2:1–5; Hag. 2:9), and into which the Gentile nations will stream, fulfilling the Abrahamic promises (Isa. 56:3–7; Ezek. 47:22). In addition, this new Jerusalem will take on the very borders of the entire creation (Isa. 65:1–66:21).[142] In other words, the prophets anticipate a future day when the "land" will be God's temple sanctuary and its borders, like the rule of the king, will extend to

---

[138] See Paul R. Williamson, "Promise and Fulfillment: The Territorial Inheritance," 28–32, for a discussion of this point.

[139] Ibid., 28.

[140] Ibid., 31.

[141] Millar, "Land," *NDBT*, 626, comments that the exile involved more than being reduced to a homeless status; it raised the idea of being disinherited and questioned God's relationship to his people. The Father (Yahweh)–son (Israel) relationship established by God with his people seemed inviolable, but now the exile brought this into question. It also brought into question God's ultimate salvation purposes for the entire world, since if Israel failed then how would the Abrahamic blessing be brought to pass?

[142] This point is clearly developed in chapter 12.

the entire creation (Ps. 72:8–11, 17–19). It is this Old Testament prophetic vision that is picked up in Revelation 21–22 in light of the coming of Christ.

5. The New Testament announces that the inheritance of the "land" is fulfilled in our Lord Jesus Christ, who brings to completion all of the previous covenants (along with their types and shadows), and who in his cross work inaugurates the new creation.

It is often remarked that there are not many explicit references to the land in the New Testament.[143] However, for a couple of reasons, it is a mistake to think that the New Testament does not say anything about the "land." First, as argued in chapter 12, the order in producing the new creation is reversed from that used in producing the old creation. In the old creation, God first made the place where we live, and then he made the creatures to live there. In the new creation, however, God first will make his new people, and then he will make the home where they will live. The priority of the New Testament is on how God is making a new people, and the land theme is secondary to this, even though it is clearly taught, especially in Revelation 21–22. Second, once the subject of land is placed within the larger discussion of the covenants, the New Testament has much more to say about the land than some think. As discussed above, our Lord is presented as the antitype of both Adam (Rom. 5:12–21; 1 Cor. 15:21–28) and Israel (Matt. 2:13–15; 4:1–11; John 15:1–17). As such, he is the one who brings God's rest to this world through his work (Matt. 11:28–30), and who also receives the land promise and fulfills it by his inauguration of a new creation. By his obedient life and death, he fulfills Adam's role, including the role of all the covenant mediators. In him God's unique presence is found, as the true Temple (John 1:1, 14–18; 2:13–22), and by virtue of our faith union in him, we now are temples that God is building by his Spirit both individually and corporately (1 Cor. 6:19; Eph. 2:19–22). In Christ, we now receive the promised *inheritance* as Abraham's spiritual seed (Rom. 8:17; Gal. 4:7; Eph. 1:14). In fact, as many have noted, Paul develops the Old Testament emphasis on the land in terms of our *inheritance* (Col. 1:13–14) and our adoption, viewed salvifically and cosmically.[144] As Millar notes, "it was as God's sons that

---

[143] Peter W. L. Walker, "The Land in the Apostles' Writings," in Johnston and Walker, *Land of Promise*, 82–83, makes this point. In the New Testament there are fewer than fifty references to land and only a small number of these that refer to the land of Israel rather than the world in general.

[144] It is difficult to think of Paul's understanding of inheritance apart from the Old Testament background of land. For a discussion of these important issues, see James D. Hester, *Paul's Concept of Inheritance: A Contribution to*

the people of Israel received their inheritance. The link is most explicit in Romans 8:14–25, which also links the theology of the land with the theology of creation. Both the creation mandate to 'fill the earth and subdue it' (Gen. 1:28), and the theology of the land in the OT find their ultimate fulfillment in the new creation brought together under Christ."[145]

It is important to note that in this entire discussion of what Christ has accomplished in his new covenant work, there is little evidence that the land promise finds its Christological fulfilment in terms of a specific piece of land given to national Israel. The story line of Scripture simply does not move back in this direction.[146] Rather, the entire New Testament instead announces that in Jesus, the last Adam and true Israel, our inheritance is nothing less than the new creation, which has already arrived in the dawning of the new covenant in individual Christians (2 Cor. 5:17; Eph. 2:8–10) and in the church (Eph. 2:11–21) and will yet be consummated when Christ returns and ushers in the new creation in its fullness (Revelation 21–22). This makes perfect sense if we place the entire land discussion in the flow of redemptive-history as viewed through the biblical covenants. Christ, who is Lord over the whole world, inherits as a result of his work the entire world. "He is the Messiah of Israel, but his rule also extends far beyond the borders of the original promised land (e.g., Phil. 2:10; cf. 1 Cor. 3:22–23; Eph. 1:10)."[147]

This way of thinking of the fulfilment of the land promise in Christ is confirmed by other important New Testament texts (Rom. 4:13; Eph. 6:3; and Heb. 3:1–4:13; 11:8–22). For example, in Romans 4:13, Paul is clear that Abraham did not view the land promise as referring merely to a small piece of Palestinian territory but ultimately saw it as a type and pattern of the entire world. Or, in Ephesians 6:3, Paul can quote the fifth commandment (which clearly pertains to the land of Canaan in its Old Testament context) and now expand it to the entire earth. "God's rule over the promised land is now extended through Christ to the whole world, and his true 'people' are a worldwide community, not an ethnic group associated with a particular

---

the *Understanding of Heilsgeschichte*, Scottish Journal of Theology Occasional Papers 14 (Edinburgh: Oliver & Boyd, 1968), 77–78.

[145] Millar, "Land," *NDBT*, 627.

[146] This is an important point. The flow of redemptive-history as traced through the biblical covenants reaches its *telos* in Christ. What our Lord has inaugurated does *not* go back to the types and patterns of old; it transforms and fulfills them. This is especially crucial to note in regard to the land. When it comes to the future, dispensational theology, at least on the land issue, tends to go backward in redemptive-history instead of forward. But as Robertson, *Israel of God*, states well, in the new creation "the old covenant's promise of land finds its new covenant realization" (26). On this point see also Beale, *Temple in the Church's Mission*, 372–375.

[147] Walker, "Land in the Apostles' Writings," 87.

land."[148] The author of Hebrews makes the same point. In Hebrews 3:1–4:13, on the basis of Psalm 95:11, he argues that the divine rest (associated with Gen. 2:1–3) was not exhausted in the Old Testament by entrance into the Promised Land. Instead, what happened under Joshua pointed forward to a greater rest to come, which has now dawned in Christ and the new covenant age. We now enter God's rest by entering into salvation rest in Christ and enjoying what he has accomplished on our behalf. We enter the "land," so to speak, but now enjoying what the land pointed forward to: participating in new creation realities now as the people of God. Later in the book, the author also develops the themes of Christ as the fulfilment of the tabernacle-temple and the one who brings with him the new Jerusalem, identified with the people of God. All of these themes are intimately associated with the land, and all of them are viewed as fulfilled typologically in Christ. Another crucial text which also makes this same point, similar to what Paul says in Romans 4:13, is Hebrews 11:8–22. There the author contends that Abraham's inheritance ultimately was not the land of Canaan but a heavenly inheritance linked to the new Jerusalem and the new creation.[149]

Given how the biblical covenants unpack the theme of "land," it should not surprise us how the entire story line ends in Revelation 21–22. In the final chapters of Scripture the consummated state is pictured as rest in terms that recall Eden of old, yet far greater. In this new creation, we have the geographical boundaries of Eden ("the land") expanded to the entire creation, which is also beautifully described in the dimensions of the Holy of Holies, signifying God's unique covenantal presence throughout the entire creation, not just in the limited dimensions of the Old Testament tabernacle/temple. In this vision of the new heavens and new earth, God's people take up residence in God's presence, a residence described as the antitypical fulfilment of the Old Testament land. In fact, in this final vision we discover our final inheritance—what Abraham is said to have looked for—namely, a city whose builder and maker is God and a creation that is full of God's glory. And most important, at the centre of this new creation is our covenant Lord, whose presence does not require a temple since the Lord and the Lamb are the temple. In his presence we will dwell for all eternity, not on the clouds of heaven but in a gloriously renewed universe where we will carry out our

---

[148] Ibid. Cf. Peter T. O'Brien, *The Letter to the Ephesians*, Pillar New Testament Commentary (Grand Rapids, MI: Eerdmans, 1999), 442–445.
[149] On these points, see Lane, *Hebrews 1–8*, 70–105; idem, *Hebrews 9–13*, 347–366; O'Brien, *Letter to the Hebrews*, 138–173; 409–427.

calling as God's sons for his glory and honour. In this final vision, as the curtain closes, we now see what the eschatological goal of God's creation was in the first place. Eden as the temple sanctuary now reaches its *telos* in the new creation. The land, which functioned as a type of this greater reality, now reaches its terminus. And the covenant relationship which God created us for in the first place is now realized in its fullness as we enjoy the presence of our great and glorious triune covenant God, and serve him in worship, adoration, devotion, and obedience forevermore.[150]

SUMMARY REFLECTION

We have only scratched the surface in terms of the theological implications of *kingdom through covenant*. Much more needs to be said at every point and even in areas not discussed. In the future it is our goal to flesh out some of these areas in more detail as we attempt to demonstrate how a slightly different way of "putting together" the biblical covenants should inform and even transform our theological conclusions. We stand on the shoulders of those who have come before us; we learn from those who have read and applied Scripture well; but we also desire to follow the Reformation principle of *semper reformanda* ("always reforming") in light of God's most holy Word so that we learn afresh "to think God's thoughts after him" and "to bring every thought captive to Christ." May it also be said of us that we desire above all else not merely to be hearers of God's Word but doers. May we begin to live out what it means to know, enjoy, and glorify our glorious covenant God as his covenant people. May our triune God receive all glory, honour, and praise as we await the glorious return of our Lord and enjoy in fullness the incredible, gracious, and glorious realities of all that Jesus our Lord has won as our new covenant head.

---

[150] See Alexander, *From Eden to the New Jerusalem*, 171–187; Beale, *Temple and the Church's Mission*, 313–334.

Appendix

LEXICAL ANALYSIS
OF *bĕrît* (בְּרִית)

RESOURCES:

BibleWorks 6.0, LLC. Norfolk, VA, 2008.

Clines, David J. A., ed. *The Dictionary of Classical Hebrew*. Vol. 2:ב-ו. Sheffield, UK: Sheffield Academic Press, 1995.

Even-Shoshan, Abraham. *A New Concordance to the Old Testament*. Jerusalem: Sivan, 1982.

Lisowsky, Gerhard. *Konkordanz zum Hebräischen Alten Testament*. 2nd ed. Stuttgart: Württembergische Bibelanstalt, 1958.

Weinfeld, Moshe. "בְּרִית, *bᵉrîth*." In *Theological Dictionary of the Old Testament*. Edited by G. Johannes Botterweck and Helmer Ringgren. 15 vols. 2:253–279. Grand Rapids, MI: Eerdmans, 2003.

Williamson, Paul R. *Sealed with an Oath: Covenant in God's Unfolding Purpose*. New Studies in Biblical Theology 23. Downers Grove, IL: InterVarsity Press, 2007).

NUMBER OF OCCURRENCES:

Concordances and studies vary in the number of instances in the Old Testament: 283x (Even-Shoshan), 284x (Bible Works 6.0), 285x (*Dictionary of Classical Hebrew*), 286x (Williamson, p. 36), 287x (Lisowsky). This analysis lists 288 instances.

LEGEND:

Only references counting as instances of בְּרִית employ a colon; elsewhere a period (.) is used in duplicated references instead of a colon. (N.B.: xxx denotes a relative clause)

EXPRESSIONS WITH ברית
AS OBJECT OF THE VERB
1. כרת ברית

Gen. 15:18

ביום ההוא כרת יהוה את־אברם ברית לאמר
לזרעך נתתי את־הארץ הזאת
מנהר מצרים עד־הנהר הגדל נהר־פרת

Comment   Covenant with Abraham.

....

Gen. 21:27

ויקח אברהם צאן ובקר ויתן לאבימלך
ויכרתו שניהם ברית

Comment   Abraham and Abimelech make a treaty.

....

Gen. 21:32

[31] על־כן קרא למקום ההוא באר שבע כי שם נשבעו שניהם
[32] ויכרתו ברית בבאר שבע
ויקם אבימלך ופיכל שׂר־צבאו וישבו אל־ארץ פלשתים

Comment   Abraham and Abimelech make a treaty.

....

Gen. 26:28

ויאמרו ראו ראינו כי־היה יהוה עמך
ונאמר תהי נא אלה בינותינו בינינו ובינך ונכרתה ברית עמך

Comment   Isaac and Abimelech make a treaty.

Gen. 31:44

וְעַתָּה לְכָה נִכְרְתָה בְרִית אֲנִי וְאָתָּה
וְהָיָה לְעֵד בֵּינִי וּבֵינֶךָ

Comment   Laban and Jacob make an agreement as a witness between them.

....

Ex. 23:32

[31] וְשַׁתִּי אֶת־גְּבֻלְךָ מִיָּם־סוּף וְעַד־יָם פְּלִשְׁתִּים וּמִמִּדְבָּר עַד־הַנָּהָר
כִּי אֶתֵּן בְּיֶדְכֶם אֵת יֹשְׁבֵי הָאָרֶץ וְגֵרַשְׁתָּמוֹ מִפָּנֶיךָ
[32] לֹא־תִכְרֹת לָהֶם וְלֵאלֹהֵיהֶם בְּרִית

Comment   God commands the Israelites not to make treaties with the Canaanites.

....

Ex. 24.8
xxx

וַיִּקַּח מֹשֶׁה אֶת־הַדָּם וַיִּזְרֹק עַל־הָעָם
וַיֹּאמֶר הִנֵּה דַם־הַבְּרִית אֲשֶׁר כָּרַת יְהוָה עִמָּכֶם עַל כָּל־הַדְּבָרִים הָאֵלֶּה

Comment   A relative sentence modifies covenant in the verbless clause "Here is the blood of
the covenant." The relative sentence indicates that the covenant was made on the
basis of the words (i.e., Ten Words and Judgements) given at Sinai.

....

Ex. 34:10

וַיֹּאמֶר הִנֵּה אָנֹכִי כֹּרֵת בְּרִית נֶגֶד כָּל־עַמְּךָ
אֶעֱשֶׂה נִפְלָאֹת אֲשֶׁר לֹא־נִבְרְאוּ בְכָל־הָאָרֶץ וּבְכָל־הַגּוֹיִם
וְרָאָה כָל־הָעָם אֲשֶׁר־אַתָּה בְקִרְבּוֹ אֶת־מַעֲשֵׂה יְהוָה
כִּי־נוֹרָא הוּא אֲשֶׁר אֲנִי עֹשֶׂה עִמָּךְ

Comment   Yahweh makes a covenant with Israel. This is the Sinai covenant, concluded
afresh after it was broken.

Ex. 34:12

השמר לך פן־תכרת ברית ליושב הארץ אשר
אתה בא עליה פן־יהיה למוקש בקרבך

Comment   God commands the Israelites not to make treaties with the Canaanites.

....

Ex. 34:15

פן־תכרת ברית ליושב הארץ
וזנו אחרי אלהיהם וזבחו לאלהיהם וקרא לך ואכלת מזבחו

Comment   God commands the Israelites not to make treaties with the Canaanites.

....

Ex. 34:27

ויאמר יהוה אל־משה כתב־לך את־הדברים האלה
כי על־פי הדברים האלה כרתי אתך ברית ואת־ישראל

Comment   Yahweh makes a covenant with Israel. This is the Sinai covenant, concluded afresh after it was broken.

....

Deut. 4.23
xxx

השמרו לכם פן־תשכחו את־ברית יהוה אלהיכם אשר כרת עמכם
ועשיתם לכם פסל תמונת כל אשר צוך יהוה אלהיך

Comment   Israel is called to be on guard lest they forget the covenant God made with them and make an idol. Probably a reference to the covenant at Sinai.

....

Deut. 5:2

יהוה אלהינו כרת עמנו ברית בחרב

Comment   Yahweh made a covenant with Israel. This is the Sinai covenant.

Deut. 5:3

לא את־אבתינו כרת יהוה את־הברית הזאת
כי אתנו אנחנו אלה פה היום כלנו חיים

Comment   Yahweh made a covenant with Israel. This is the Sinai covenant.

....

Deut. 7:2

ונתנם יהוה אלהיך לפניך והכיתם
החרם תחרים אתם לא־תכרת להם ברית ולא תחנם

Comment   God commands the Israelites not to make treaties with the Canaanites.

....

Deut. 9.9

בעלתי ההרה לקחת לוחת האבנים לוחת הברית
אשר־כרת יהוה עמכם
ואשב בהר ארבעים יום וארבעים לילה
לחם לא אכלתי ומים לא שתיתי

Comment   Reference is made to "the tablets of the covenant which Yahweh cut with you."
This indicates the Ten Words written on the two stone tablets.

....

Deut. 28:69
Deut. 28:69

אלה דברי הברית אשר־צוה יהוה את־משה
לכרת את־בני ישראל בארץ מואב מלבד הברית אשר־כרת אתם בחרב

Comment   The book of Deuteronomy is a covenant Yahweh made with his people Israel, as
an addendum or codicil to the Sinai covenant.

....

Deut. 29:13

ולא אתכם לבדכם אנכי כרת את־הברית הזאת ואת־האלה הזאת

Comment   The book of Deuteronomy is an addition to the Sinai covenant.

Deut. 29:24

ואמרו על אשר עזבו את־ברית יהוה אלהי אבתם

אשר כרת עמם בהוציאו אתם מארץ מצרים

Comment   The book of Deuteronomy is "this book of the torah" which constitutes the covenant made between God and Israel when he brought them out of Egypt.

....

Deut. 31.16

xxx

ויאמר יהוה אל־משה הנך שכב עם־אבתיך

וקם העם הזה וזנה אחרי אלהי נכר־הארץ אשר הוא בא־שמה בקרבו

ועזבני והפר את־בריתי אשר כרתי אתו

Comment   The people will violate the covenant (i.e., Deuteronomy) which God made with them.

....

Josh. 9:6

וילכו אל־יהושע אל־המחנה הגלגל ויאמרו אליו

ואל־איש ישראל מארץ רחוקה באנו ועתה כרתו־לנו ברית

Comment   The Israelites make a treaty with the Gibeonites.

....

Josh. 9:7

ויאמרו *ויאמר איש־ישראל אל־החוי

אולי בקרבי אתה יושב ואיך אכרות *אכרת־לך ברית

Comment   The Israelites make a treaty with the Gibeonites.

....

Josh. 9:11

ויאמרו אלינו זקינינו וכל־ישבי ארצנו לאמר

קחו בידכם צידה לדרך ולכו לקראתם ואמרתם אליהם

עבדיכם אנחנו ועתה כרתו־לנו ברית

Comment   The Israelites make a treaty with the Gibeonites.

Josh. 9:15

ויעש להם יהושע שלום ויכרת להם
ברית לחיותם וישבעו להם נשיאי העדה

Comment   The Israelites make a treaty with the Gibeonites. NB שלום עשה as a parallel to
כרת ברית.

....

Josh. 9:16

ויהי מקצה שלשת ימים אחרי אשר־כרתו להם ברית
וישמעו כי־קרבים הם אליו ובקרבו הם ישבים

Comment   The Israelites make a treaty with the Gibeonites.

....

Josh. 24:25

ויכרת יהושע ברית לעם ביום ההוא וישם לו חק ומשפט בשכם

Comment   Joshua makes a covenant with the people of Israel at Shechem. This covenant is a
commitment to serve Yahweh and obey him.

....

Judg. 2:2

ואתם לא־תכרתו ברית ליושבי הארץ הזאת מזבחותיהם
תתצון ולא־שמעתם בקלי מה־זאת עשיתם

Comment   God commands the Israelites not to make treaties with the Canaanites.

....

1 Sam. 11:1

ויעל נחש העמוני ויחן על־יבש גלעד
ויאמרו כל־אנשי יביש אל־נחש כרת־לנו ברית ונעבדך

Comment   The men of Jabesh Gilead ask the Ammonite king to make a treaty with them in
which they would be a vassal kingdom or a slave kingdom of the Ammonites.

1 Sam. 18:3

ויכרת יהונתן ודוד ברית באהבתו אתו כנפשו

Comment   Jonathan and David make a covenant.

....

1 Sam. 23:18

ויכרתו שניהם ברית לפני יהוה
וישב דוד בחרשה ויהונתן הלך לביתו

Comment   Jonathan and David make a covenant (second time).

....

2 Sam. 3:12

וישלח אבנר מלאכים אל־דוד תחתו *תחתיו לאמר למי־ארץ
לאמר כרתה בריתך אתי והנה ידי עמך להסב אליך את־כל־ישראל

Comment   Abner invites David to make an agreement with him so that he can bring all Israel under David's rule.

....

2 Sam. 3:13

ויאמר טוב אני אכרת אתך ברית
אך דבר אחד אנכי שאל מאתך לאמר
לא־תראה את־פני כי אם־לפני הביאך
את מיכל בת־שאול בבאך לראות את־פני

Comment   Abner invites David to make an agreement with him so that he can bring all Israel under David's rule.

....

2 Sam. 3:21

ויאמר אבנר אל־דוד אקומה ואלכה ואקבצה אל־אדני המלך
את־כל־ישראל ויכרתו אתך ברית ומלכת בכל אשר־תאוה נפשך
וישלח דוד את־אבנר וילך בשלום

Comment   David and Israel make a covenant so that he may rule over them.

2 Sam. 5:3

ויבאו כל־זקני ישראל אל־המלך חברונה
ויכרת להם המלך דוד ברית בחברון לפני יהוה
וימשחו את־דוד למלך על־ישראל

Comment   David and Israel make a covenant so that he may rule over them.

....

1 Kings 5:26 (5:12 EV)

ויהוה נתן חכמה לשלמה כאשר דבר־לו
ויהי שלם בין חירם ובין שלמה ויכרתו ברית שניהם

Comment   Hiram and Solomon make a treaty.

....

1 Kings 8.21
1 Kings 20:34

[20:34] ויאמר אליו הערים אשר־לקח־אבי מאת אביך אשיב
וחוצות תשים לך בדמשק כאשר־שם אבי בשמרון
ואני בברית אשלחך ויכרת־לו ברית וישלחהו

Comment   Ahab and Ben-Hadad make a treaty.

....

2 Kings 11:4

ובשנה השביעית שלח יהוידע
ויקח את־שרי המאיות *המאות לכרי ולרצים
ויבא אתם אליו בית יהוה
ויכרת להם ברית וישבע אתם בבית יהוה
וירא אתם את־בן־המלך

Comment   Jehoiada makes an agreement with certain military units to make Joash king.

2 Kings 11:17

ויכרת יהוידע את־הברית בין יהוה ובין
המלך ובין העם להיות לעם ליהוה ובין המלך ובין העם

Comment   Jehoiada makes a covenant between the Lord and the king and the people and (a covenant) between the king and the people.

....

2 Kings 17.15
2 Kings 17:35

[35] ויכרת יהוה אתם ברית ויצום לאמר לא תיראו אלהים
אחרים ולא־תשתחוו להם ולא תעבדום ולא תזבחו להם

Comment   A back reference to the covenant made at Sinai.

....

2 Kings 17:38

והברית אשר־כרתי אתכם לא תשכחו
ולא תיראו אלהים אחרים

Comment   A back reference to the covenant made at Sinai.

....

2 Kings 23:3

ויעמד המלך על־העמוד ויכרת את־הברית לפני יהוה ללכת
אחר יהוה ולשמר מצותיו ואת־עדותיו ואת־חקתיו בכל־לב
ובכל־נפש להקים את־דברי הברית הזאת הכתבים על־הספר הזה
ויעמד כל־העם בברית

Comment   Josiah makes a covenant to keep the Sinai covenant/Deuteronomic covenant.

Isa. 28:15

כי אמרתם כרתנו ברית את־מות
ועם־שאול עשינו חזה
שיט *שוט שוטף כי־עבר *יעבר לא יבואנו
כי שמנו כזב מחסנו ובשקר נסתרנו

Comment   Scoffers boast they have made a covenant with death. This may be Isaiah's mock-
ing of idolaters. See Isa. 28.18

Isa. 55:3

הטו אזנכם ולכו אלי שמעו ותחי נפשכם
ואכרתה לכם ברית עולם חסדי דוד הנאמנים

Comment   Isaiah announces God will initiate a new covenant, called here an everlasting
covenant.

Isa. 61:8

כי אני יהוה אהב משפט שנא גזל בעולה
ונתתי פעלתם באמת וברית עולם אכרות להם

Comment   God will make a new covenant with his people, called here an everlasting
covenant.

Jer. 31:31

הנה ימים באים נאם־יהוה
וכרתי את־בית ישראל ואת־בית יהודה ברית חדשה

Comment   Jeremiah announces God will initiate a new covenant.

Jer. 31:32

לא כברית אשר כרתי את־אבותם ביום
החזיקי בידם להוציאם מארץ מצרים
אשר־המה הפרו את־בריתי
ואנכי בעלתי בם נאם־יהוה

Comment A back reference to the covenant made at Sinai.

....

Jer. 31:33

כי זאת הברית אשר אכרת את־בית ישראל
אחרי הימים ההם נאם־יהוה נתתי את־תורתי בקרבם
ועל־לבם אכתבנה והייתי להם לאלהים והמה יהיו־לי לעם

Comment Jeremiah announces God will initiate a new covenant.

....

Jer. 32:40

וכרתי להם ברית עולם אשר לא־אשוב מאחריהם להיטיבי אותם
ואת־יראתי אתן בלבבם לבלתי סור מעלי

Comment Jeremiah announces God will initiate a new covenant, called here an everlasting
covenant.

....

Jer. 34:8

הדבר אשר־היה אל־ירמיהו מאת יהוה אחרי כרת המל
צדקיהו ברית את־כל־העם אשר בירושלם לקרא להם דרור

Comment King Zedekiah made a covenant with all the people to proclaim freedom for the
slaves.

....

Jer. 34:13

כה־אמר יהוה אלהי ישראל אנכי כרתי ברית
את־אבותיכם ביום הוצאי אותם מארץ מצרים מבית עבדים לאמר

Comment A back reference to the covenant made at Sinai.

Jer. 34:15

וַתָּשֻׁבוּ אַתֶּם הַיּוֹם וַתַּעֲשׂוּ אֶת־הַיָּשָׁר בְּעֵינַי לִקְרֹא דְרוֹר אִישׁ
לְרֵעֵהוּ וַתִּכְרְתוּ בְרִית לְפָנַי בַּבַּיִת אֲשֶׁר־נִקְרָא שְׁמִי עָלָיו

Comment   King Zedekiah made a covenant with all the people to proclaim freedom for the
            slaves.

....

Ezek. 17:13

וַיִּקַּח מִזֶּרַע הַמְּלוּכָה וַיִּכְרֹת אִתּוֹ בְּרִית
וַיָּבֵא אֹתוֹ בְּאָלָה וְאֶת־אֵילֵי הָאָרֶץ לָקָח

Comment   The king of Babylon made a covenant with a member of the royal family of Judah.
            NB parallel expression "to bring him into the oath."

....

Ezek. 34:25

וְכָרַתִּי לָהֶם בְּרִית שָׁלוֹם וְהִשְׁבַּתִּי חַיָּה־רָעָה מִן־הָאָרֶץ
וְיָשְׁבוּ בַמִּדְבָּר לָבֶטַח וְיָשְׁנוּ בַּיְּעָרִים

Comment   Ezekiel announces a covenant of peace = new covenant.

....

Ezek. 37:26

וְכָרַתִּי לָהֶם בְּרִית שָׁלוֹם בְּרִית עוֹלָם יִהְיֶה אוֹתָם
וּנְתַתִּים וְהִרְבֵּיתִי אוֹתָם וְנָתַתִּי אֶת־מִקְדָּשִׁי בְּתוֹכָם לְעוֹלָם

Comment   Ezekiel announces a covenant of peace = new covenant.

....

Hos. 2:20

וְכָרַתִּי לָהֶם בְּרִית בַּיּוֹם הַהוּא
עִם־חַיַּת הַשָּׂדֶה וְעִם־עוֹף הַשָּׁמַיִם וְרֶמֶשׂ הָאֲדָמָה
וְקֶשֶׁת וְחֶרֶב וּמִלְחָמָה אֶשְׁבּוֹר מִן־הָאָרֶץ וְהִשְׁכַּבְתִּים לָבֶטַח

Comment   Hosea lived and worked in the middle of the eighth century B.C. He announces a
            covenant which Yahweh will make in the future with the animals so that they will
            no longer be instruments of destruction. There will be safety and security in the
            land. Further, see Hos. 6.7 and 8.1.

Hos. 10:4

דברו דברים אלות שוא כרת ברית
ופרח כראש משפט על תלמי שדי

Comment   Hosea here speaks of false treaties initiated by the last monarchs of the northern kingdom of Israel.

Hos. 12:2

אפרים רעה רוח ורדף קדים כל־היום כזב ושד ירבה
וברית עם־אשור יכרתו ושמן למצרים יובל

Comment   Hosea here speaks of false treaties initiated by the last monarchs of the northern kingdom of Israel.

Ps. 50:5

אספו־לי חסידי כרתי בריתי עלי־זבח

Comment   A reference to the Sinai covenant (see Exodus 24.4–8). The passage refers to those in the covenant community as חסידים, i.e., covenant partners, and speaks of a covenant made on the basis of a sacrifice.

Ps. 83:6

כי נועצו לב יחדו עליך ברית יכרתו

Comment   Asaph describes a covenant or alliance formed by a large number of nations against Israel.

Ps. 89:4

כרתי ברית לבחירי נשבעתי לדוד עבדי

Comment   A reference to the Davidic covenant (see 2 Samuel 7).

Job 31:1

ברית כרתי לעיני ומה אתבונן על־בתולה

Comment   Job's declaration of innocence: he had a covenant with his eyes not to look lustfully upon a young woman.

Job 40:28

היכרת ברית עמך תקחנו לעבד עולם

Comment   Yahweh's speech: he challenges Job to control Leviathan. Can Job make an agreement with the monster so that he is Job's slave forever?

Ezra 10:3

ועתה נכרת־ברית לאלהינו להוציא כל־נשים והנולד
מהם בעצת אדני והחרדים במצות אלהינו וכתורה יעשה

Comment   Ezra advises the people to make a covenant with God to divorce their non-Jewish wives.

Neh. 9:8

ומצאת את־לבבו נאמן לפניך וכרות עמו הברית
לתת את־ארץ הכנעני החתי האמרי
והפרזי והיבוסי והגרגשי לתת לזרעו
ותקם את־דבריך כי צדיק אתה

Comment   A reference to the covenant with Abraham (particularly to Gen. 15.18–21). Note that הקים is employed here of God fulfilling his words, i.e., bringing to pass the promises in the covenant initiated previously.

1 Chron. 11:3

ויבאו כל־זקני ישראל אל־המלך חברונה
ויכרת להם דויד ברית בחברון לפני יהוה
וימשחו את־דויד למלך על־ישראל כדבר יהוה ביד־שמואל

Comment   Parallel to 2 Sam. 5.1–3.

....

2 Chron. 21:7

ולא־אבה יהוה להשחית את־בית דויד למען הברית אשר כרת לדויד
וכאשר אמר לתת לו ניר ולבניו כל־הימים

Comment   A reference to the covenant Yahweh had made with David. Jehoram was an evil
king but Yahweh did not destroy him, because of his covenant with David.

....

2 Chron. 23:3

ויכרת כל־הקהל ברית בבית האלהים עם־המלך
ויאמר להם הנה בן־המלך ימלך כאשר דבר יהוה על־בני דויד

Comment   Parallel to 2 Kings 11.4?

....

2 Chron. 23:16

ויכרת יהוידע ברית בינו ובין
כל־העם ובין המלך להיות לעם ליהוה

Comment   Parallel to 2 Kings 11.17.

....

2 Chron. 29:10

עתה עם־לבבי לכרות ברית ליהוה
אלהי ישראל וישב ממנו חרון אפו

Comment   Hezekiah announces his intentions to make a covenant with Yahweh so that his
anger will be turned away from the people. He calls the Levites together so that
they may purify the temple.

2 Chron. 34:31

ויעמד המלך על־עמדו ויכרת את־הברית לפני יהוה
ללכת אחרי יהוה ולשמור את־מצותיו ועדותיו וחקיו בכל־לבבו
ובכל־נפשו לעשות את־דברי הברית הכתובים על־הספר הזה

Comment   Parallel to 2 Kings 23.3.

....

2. הקים ברית

Gen. 6:18

[17] ואני הנני מביא את־המבול מים על־הארץ
לשחת כל־בשר אשר־בו רוח חיים מתחת השמים
כל אשר־בארץ יגוע
[18] והקמתי את־בריתי אתך
ובאת אל־התבה אתה ובניך ואשתך ונשי־בניך אתך

Comment   Covenant with Noah.

....

Gen. 9:9

ואני הנני מקים את־בריתי אתכם ואת־זרעכם אחריכם

Comment   Covenant with Noah.

....

Gen. 9:11

והקמתי את־בריתי אתכם
ולא־יכרת כל־בשר עוד ממי המבול
ולא־יהיה עוד מבול לשחת הארץ

....

Gen. 9.17

XXX
Comment   Covenant with Noah.

Gen. 17:7

[6] והפרתי אתך במאד מאד ונתתיך לגוים
ומלכים ממך יצאו
[7] והקמתי את־בריתי ביני ובינך ובין זרעך אחריך לדרתם
לברית עולם להיות לך לאלהים ולזרעך אחריך

Comment   Covenant with Abraham.

....

Gen. 17:19

ויאמר אלהים אבל שרה אשתך ילדת לך בן וקראת את־שמו
יצחק והקמתי את־בריתי אתו לברית עולם לזרעו אחריו

Comment   Covenant with Abraham.

....

Gen. 17:21

[20] ולישמעאל שמעתיך הנה ברכתי אתו והפריתי אתו
והרביתי אתו במאד מאד שנים־עשר נשׂיאם יוליד ונתתיו לגוי גדול
[21] ואת־בריתי אקים את־יצחק
אשר תלד לך שרה למועד הזה בשנה האחרת

Comment   Covenant with Abraham.

....

Ex. 6:4

[3] וארא אל־אברהם אל־יצחק ואל־יעקב באל שדי
ושמי יהוה לא נודעתי להם
[4] וגם הקמתי את־בריתי אתם לתת להם את־ארץ כנען
את ארץ מגריהם אשר־גרו בה

Comment   Is this a case where הקים ברית means "to establish" or "to institute" rather than
"to confirm" or "to fulfill"? Not necessarily so, for Yahweh says he has confirmed
the covenant to give the land to them. So once again, to confirm or establish a
covenant is not to make a relationship formal by means of an oath or vow but to
affirm the validity of a commitment.

Lev. 26:9

ופניתי אליכם והפריתי אתכם והרביתי אתכם
והקימתי את־בריתי אתכם

Comment This is a section promising blessings for obedience and curses for disobedience. If they obey, Yahweh will "keep" his covenant with them, i.e., bring the blessings he promised.

....

Deut. 8:18

וזכרת את־יהוה אלהיך כי הוא הנתן לך כח לעשות חיל
למען הקים את־בריתו אשר־נשבע לאבתיך כיום הזה

Comment To remember Yahweh is to love him by obeying the covenant stipulations. When they do this, Yahweh will bring the blessings he promised, i.e., wealth, and thus "fulfill" or "keep" his covenant.

....

2 Kings 23:3

ויעמד המלך על־העמוד ויכרת את־הברית לפני יהוה ללכת
אחר יהוה ולשמר מצותיו ואת־עדותיו ואת־חקתיו בכל־לב
ובכל־נפש להקים את־דברי הברית הזאת הכתבים על־הספר הזה
ויעמד כל־העם בברית

Comment Here, Josiah concludes a covenant to follow the Lord and keep his commands. Thus he will "fulfill" or "keep" the words of the covenant.

....

Jer. 34:18

ונתתי את־האנשים העברים את־ברתי
אשר לא־הקימו את־דברי הברית אשר כרתו לפני
העגל אשר כרתו לשנים ויעברו בין בתריו

Comment The expression "to establish the words of the covenant" refers to fulfilling the obligations of a covenant ("cut") made previously.

Ezek. 16:60
Ezek. 16:62

[60] וזכרתי אני את־בריתי אותך
בימי נעוריך והקמותי לך ברית עולם
[61] וזכרת את־דרכיך ונכלמת בקחתך את־אחותיך הגדלות
ממך אל־הקטנות ממך ונתתי אתהן לך לבנות ולא מבריתך
[62] והקימוLתי אני את־בריתי אתך וידעת כי־אני יהוה

Comment   God will deal with Jerusalem as she deserves. Nonetheless, he will remember his covenant with her and "establish" a permanent covenant with her. Here הקים appears to mean "institute." Alternatively, it may have the sense "fulfill" i.e., keep. The first covenant was not kept, but this one will be kept.

....

3. הגביר בברית
Dan. 9:27

והגביר ברית לרבים שבוע אחד
וחצי השבוע ישבית זבח ומנחה
ועל כנף שקוצים משמם
ועד־כלה ונחרצה תתך על־שמם

Comment   Interpretation of this verse is hotly debated and disputed. A central issue is iden- tification of the subject of the verb. Williamson has argued recently in his study, *Sealed with An Oath*, that vv. 26 and 27 follow an identical pattern in which the first half of the verse speaks of the coming king and the second speaks of the destroyer. According to this approach, it is the Messiah who will make strong a covenant with the many and bring an end to sacrifice. The expression is unique, but similar to the expression הקים ברית.

....

4. נתן ברית
Gen. 9.12
Gen. 17:2

[17:2] ואתנה בריתי ביני ובינך
וארבה אותך במאד מאד

Comment   God commands Abram "to walk before him and be perfect so that he may give/ grant his covenant between them and multiply him." The only occurrences of this collocation are found in contexts which employ the expression הקים ברית.

Num. 25:12

לכן אמר הנני נתן לו את־בריתי שלום

5. צִוָּה ברית

Josh. 7.11
Josh. 23.16
Judg. 2.20
Ps. 111:9

[111:9] פדות שלח לעמו צוה־לעולם בריתו
קדוש ונורא שמו

Comment   God's provision of redemption for his people is equivalent to appointing or commanding his covenant forever. This is likely the Abrahamic covenant.

....

6. הגד ברית

Deut. 4:13

ויגד לכם את־בריתו אשר צוה אתכם לעשות עשרת הדברים
ויכתבם על־שני לחות אבנים

Comment   Moses recounts how at Sinai, "God declared his covenant to you, i.e., the Ten
Words." Refers to the Mosaic covenant.

....

7. שִׂים ברית

2 Sam. 23:5

כי־לא־כן ביתי עם־אל
כי ברית עולם שם לי ערוכה בכל ושמרה
כי־כל־ישעי וכל־חפץ כי־לא יצמיח

Comment   David says, "Yahweh placed/set a covenant for me [or with me]." The expression
is perhaps equivalent to נתן ברית. Note also that the text implies the expressions
ערך ברית and שמר ברית (see #15 below). The expressions נתן ברית and ערך ברית
indicate instituting a covenant while שמר ברית indicates fulfilling it.

Jer. 33:25

כה אמר יהוה אם־לא בריתי יומם ולילה
חקות שמים וארץ לא־שמתי

Comment   If God has not ordained his covenant with creation then he will reject the descendants of Abraham and not have one of them rule over Abraham's descendants.

....

8. העמיד ברית

1 Chron. 16:17

ויעמידה ליעקב לחק לישראל ברית עולם

Comment   David moves the ark to Jerusalem, sets up the tent there, and appoints and
arranges men to lead the worship. Then there is a psalm of thanksgiving in which
the people are called to remember the everlasting covenant, "the word directed to
a thousand generations." The next verse identifies this as the Abrahamic covenant,
and the language is reminiscent of Ps. 105.10. Verse 17 explains that Yahweh
caused either the oath to stand as a statute for Jacob, or he caused it to stand as an
everlasting covenant for Israel.

....

Ps. 105:10

[8] זכר לעולם בריתו
דבר צוה לאלף דור
[9] אשר כרת את־אברהם
ושבועתו לישחק
[10] ויעמידה ליעקב לחק
לישראל ברית עולם

Comment   The context clearly identifies the covenant as the covenant with Abraham. This
covenant is a "word" to a thousand generations and also an "oath" to Isaac. It was
caused to stand as a "statute" for Jacob and an "everlasting covenant" for Israel.
The 3 f.s. suffix on ויעמידה has ברית as referent. The covenant with Abraham was
confirmed to Jacob. Thus this expression is similar to הקים ברית.

9. עמד בברית

2 Kings 23:3

ויעמד המלך על־העמוד ויכרת את־הברית לפני יהוה ללכת
אחר יהוה ולשמר מצותיו ואת־עדותיו ואת־חקתיו בכל־לב
ובכל־נפש להקים את־דברי הברית הזאת הכתבים על־הספר הזה
ויעמד כל־העם בברית

Comment   Josiah makes a covenant to keep the Sinai covenant/Deuteronomic covenant (cf. 2 Kings 22.8).

....

2 Chron. 34:32

ויעמד את כל־הנמצא בירושלם ובנימן
ויעשו ישבי ירושלם כברית אלהים אלהי אבותיהם

Comment   The noun phrase "covenant of God" is a clear reference to the Sinai covenant. Josiah, the king, is bringing his people back to the covenant stipulations and back to the God worshipped by their forefathers.

....

10. בוא בברית

1 Sam. 20:8

ועשית חסד על־עבדך כי בברית יהוה הבאת את־עבדך עמך
ואם־יש־בי עון המיתני אתה ועד־אביך למה־זה תביאני

Comment   Jonathan brought David into a "covenant of Yahweh" with him. Probably the thought is that the covenant between David and Jonathan was an oath sworn before the Lord. This is clear in 1 Sam. 23.18 although not in 18.3.

....

Jer. 34:10

וישמעו כל־השרים וכל־העם אשר־באו בברית
לשלח איש את־עבדו ואיש את־שפחתו חפשים
לבלתי עבד־בם עוד וישמעו וישלחו

Comment   This instance demonstrates that the expression בוא בברית is equivalent to the expression כרת ברית: cf. 34.8 and 34.10.

Ezek. 16:8

> ואעבר עליך ואראך והנה עתך עת דדים
> ואפרש כנפי עליך ואכסה ערותך
> ואשבע לך ואבוא בברית אתך נאם אדני יהוה ותהיי לי

Comment   The note in the *NIV Study Bible* is as follows: "*spread the corner of my garment.* Symbolic of entering a marriage relationship (see notes on Deut. 22.30; Ruth 3.9). Since the maiden symbolises Jerusalem, this does not refer to the Sinai covenant but to marriage as a covenant (see Mal. 2.14)." This discards the baby with the bathwater. In Ezek. 16.8 the maiden symbolises the people of God and the covenant of marriage symbolises the Sinai covenant. In fact, Exodus 24 pictures the covenant between Yahweh and his people as a marriage covenant/relationship.

Ezek. 20:37

> והעברתי אתכם תחת השבט
> והבאתי אתכם במסרת הברית

Comment   In a kind of New Exodus, Yahweh will collect the exiles, bring them into the desert of the nations, judge them, and bring them into the bond of the covenant. In the context of Ezekiel, this must refer to the new covenant which in some senses is a renewal of the Mosaic covenant.

2 Chron. 15:12

> ויבאו בברית לדרוש את־יהוה אלהי אבותיהם
> בכל־לבבם ובכל־נפשם

Comment   Asa of Judah's reform entailed assembling the people and offering sacrifices. Then they entered into a covenant to seek the Lord. This is a renewal of commitment to follow Yahweh similar to the one at the end of Joshua.

11. עבר בברית
Deut. 29:11

> לעברך בברית יהוה אלהיך ובאלתו
> אשר יהוה אלהיך כרת עמך היום

Comment   Those hearing Moses' sermon are entering into the covenant, i.e., the agreement between God and Israel defined by the book of Deuteronomy.

12. לקח עם X בברית

2 Chron. 23:1

ובשנה השביעית התחזק יהוידע ויקח את־שרי המאות
לעזריהו בן־ירחם ולישמעאל בן־יהוחנן ולעזריהו בן־עובד
ואת־מעשיהו בן־עדיהו ואת־אלישפט בן־זכרי עמו בברית

Comment   See 2 Chron. 23.3.

....

13. זכר ברית

Gen. 9:15

וזכרתי את־בריתי אשר ביני וביניכם ובין כל־נפש חיה בכל־בשׂר
ולא־יהיה עוד המים למבול לשחת כל־בשׂר

Comment   When God sees the bow he will "remember" his covenant with all living things.

....

Gen. 9:16

והיתה הקשׁת בענן וראיתיה לזכר ברית עולם
בין אלהים ובין כל־נפש חיה בכל־בשׂר אשר על־הארץ

Comment   When God sees the bow he will "remember" his covenant with all living things.

....

Ex. 2:24

וישמע אלהים את־נאקתם
ויזכר אלהים את־בריתו את־אברהם את־יצחק ואת־יעקב

Comment   God remembered his covenant with Abraham, Isaac, and Jacob and acted to deliver his people from oppression in Egypt.

....

Ex. 6:5

וגם אני שמעתי את־נאקת בני ישראל אשר מצרים מעבדים אתם
ואזכר את־בריתי

Comment   God remembered his covenant with Abraham, Isaac, and Jacob and acted to deliver his people from oppression in Egypt.

Lev. 26:42
Lev. 26:42
Lev. 26:42

וזכרתי את־בריתי יעקוב
ואף את־בריתי יצחק ואף את־בריתי אברהם אזכר והארץ אזכר

Comment   If the exiled people confess their sins, God will remember his covenant with them,
i.e., he will act upon his commitments.

....

Lev. 26:45

וזכרתי להם ברית ראשנים אשר הוצאתי־אתם מארץ מצרים
לעיני הגוים להית להם לאלהים אני יהוה

Comment   If Israel is disobedient, they will be duly punished. Yet they will not be completely
destroyed. The bound phrase, "covenant of former persons = ancestors" seems to
refer to the Sinai covenant because that is the covenant whereby Yahweh became
God of Israel and Israel became his people. Yahweh will not completely destroy
his disobedient people because of his covenant commitment to those he brought
out of Egypt on the basis of his promises to Abraham, Isaac, and Jacob.

....

Ezek. 16:60

וזכרתי אני את־בריתי אותך
בימי נעוריך והקמותי לך ברית עולם

Comment   God will deal with Jerusalem as she deserves. Nonetheless, he will remember his
covenant with her and "establish" a permanent covenant with her.

....

Amos 1:9

כה אמר יהוה על־שלשה פשעי־צר ועל־ארבעה לא אשיבנו
על־הסגירם גלות שלמה לאדום ולא זכרו ברית אחים

Comment   The Phoenicians and Israelites had good international relations in the time of King
David. They concluded an international treaty in the time of King Solomon and
also King Ahab (1 Kings 5.15, 26; 16.30–31). Amos denounces actions which
disregarded this "treaty of brotherhood."

Ps. 105:8
Ps. 105:10

[8] זכר לעולם בריתו
דבר צוה לאלף דור
[9] אשר כרת את־אברהם
ושבועתו לישחק
[10] ויעמידה ליעקב לחק
לישראל ברית עולם

Comment   The context clearly identifies the covenant as the covenant with Abraham. This covenant is a "word" to a thousand generations and also an "oath" to Isaac. It was caused to stand as a "statute" for Jacob and an "everlasting covenant" for Israel.

....

Ps. 106:45

ויזכר להם בריתו
וינחם כרב חסדו *חסדיו

Comment   The context refers to the fact that Yahweh handed his people to foreign nations to be subjugated by them as punishment for persistent rebellion. Nonetheless, many times he delivered them because he "remembered his covenant." The covenant is otherwise unspecified; one might argue for the Abrahamic or Mosaic covenant, although the former is probable. Ps. 111.9 also connects the redemption of his people with establishing his covenant forever.

....

Ps. 111:5

טרף נתן ליראיו
יזכר לעולם בריתו

Comment   God's provision of food to those who fear him is attributed to his fulfilling his covenant obligations. Is this the covenant with creation or with Abraham? It seems similar to Ps. 105.8, i.e., the covenant with Abraham.

1 Chron. 16:15

[15] זכרו לעולם בריתו דבר צוה לאלף דור
[16] אשר כרת את־אברהם ושבועתו ליצחק

Comment   David moves the ark to Jerusalem, sets up the tent there, and appoints and
arranges men to lead the worship. Then there is a psalm of thanksgiving in which
the people are called to remember the everlasting covenant, "the word directed to
a thousand generations." The next verse identifies this as the Abrahamic covenant,
and the language is reminiscent of Ps. 105.10.

....

14. נבט לברית

Ps. 74:20

הבט לברית
כי מלאו מחשכי־ארץ נאות חמס

Comment   The author appeals to God as his king and asks him to bring deliverance because
of his covenant. This is probably an appeal to the Mosaic covenant and also to the
Abrahamic covenant which stands behind it.

....

15. שמר ברית

Gen. 17:9

ויאמר אלהים אל־אברהם ואתה את־בריתי תשמר
אתה וזרעך אחריך לדרתם

Comment   Abram is commanded to observe the covenant, both he and his descendants.

....

Gen. 17:10

זאת בריתי אשר תשמרו ביני וביניכם ובין זרעך אחריך
המול לכם כל־זכר

Comment   Abram is commanded to observe the covenant, both he and his descendants.

Ex. 19:5

ועתה אם־שמוע תשמעו בקלי ושמרתם את־בריתי
והייתם לי סגלה מכל־העמים כי־לי כל־הארץ

Comment   This sentence is conditional, and the apodosis refers to "keeping" the Sinai
covenant.

....

Deut. 7:9

וידעת כי־יהוה אלהיך הוא האלהים האל הנאמן
שמר הברית והחסד לאהביו ולשמרי מצותו *מצותיו לאלף דור

Comment   Moses refers to God keeping his covenant. This is both a general statement and a
reference to the book of Deuteronomy since Moses refers to commands "that he
is giving today."

....

Deut. 7:12

והיה עקב תשמעון את המשפטים האלה ושמרתם ועשיתם אתם
ושמר יהוה אלהיך לך את־הברית ואת־החסד אשר נשבע לאבתיך

Comment   Moses refers to God keeping his covenant. This is conditioned upon the people
hearing the Judgements and keeping and practising them.

....

1 Kings 8:23

ויאמר יהוה אלהי ישראל
אין־כמוך אלהים בשמים ממעל ועל־הארץ מתחת
שמר הברית והחסד לעבדיך ההלכים לפניך בכל־לבם

....

2 Chron. 6:14

ויאמר יהוה אלהי ישראל אין־כמוך אלהים בשמים ובארץ
שמר הברית והחסד לעבדיך ההלכים לפניך בכל־לבם

Comment   Solomon opens his prayer of dedication by acknowledging the God of Israel as
the "one who keeps covenant and החסד to those who walk before him in complete commitment." This pattern of prayer is followed by Daniel (9.4) and also
Nehemiah (1.5 and 9.32).

1 Kings 11:11

ויאמר יהוה לשלמה יען אשר היתה־זאת עמך
ולא שמרת בריתי וחקתי אשר צויתי עליך
קרע אקרע את־הממלכה מעליך ונתתיה לעבדך

Comment   God announces to Solomon that the kingdom will be torn from him because he
did not keep the covenant of the Lord, further specified in terms of the decrees
commanded him.

Ezek. 17:14

להיות ממלכה שפלה לבלתי התנשא
לשמר את־בריתו לעמדה

Comment   The king of Babylon defeated Judah and forced her royal offspring into a treaty
to maintain loyalty to himself. This passage explains that the purpose of the treaty
is to keep the kingdom of Judah as an ineffective power able to survive only in
dependence upon Babylon (cf. Ezek. 17.13, 15, 16, 18).

Ps. 78:10

לא שמרו ברית אלהים
ובתורתו מאנו ללכת

Comment   The noun phrase "covenant of God" is a clear reference to the Sinai covenant, as
the parallel line (78.10b) shows.

Ps. 103:18

לשמרי בריתו
ולזכרי פקדיו לעשותם

Comment   The חסד and צדקה of Yahweh are to those who keep his covenant and remember
to practise his statutes. This no doubt refers to the Mosaic covenant.

Ps. 132:12

אם־ישמרו בניך בריתי ועדתי זו אלמדם
גם־בניהם עדי־עד ישבו לכסא־לך

Comment   The context is referring to the covenant with David. David's descendants will sit
on his throne if they keep the covenant. Parallel to "my covenant" is "my testimo-
nies which I teach them." Could this refer to the Mosaic covenant in the manner
of Deuteronomy 17, i.e., if they keep the Mosaic covenant, God will maintain
them on the throne?

Dan. 9:4

ואתפללה ליהוה אלהי ואתודה
ואמרה אנא אדני האל הגדול והנורא
שמר הברית והחסד לאהביו ולשמרי מצותיו

Comment   Daniel is beginning his famous prayer asking the Lord to bring the exile to an end.
After addressing God, his first acknowledgement of the character of God is as one
keeping "covenant and hesed" (cf. Neh. 1.5).

Neh. 1:5

ואמר אנא יהוה אלהי השמים האל הגדול והנורא
שמר הברית וחסד לאהביו ולשמרי מצותיו

Comment   Nehemiah is beginning his famous prayer beseeching the Lord concerning the
physical state of Jerusalem. After addressing God, his first acknowledgement of
the character of God is as one keeping "covenant and hesed." This pattern is identical to Daniel's prayer in 9.4.

Neh. 9:32

ועתה אלהינו האל הגדול הגבור והנורא
שומר הברית והחסד
אל־ימעט לפניך את כל־התלאה
אשר־מצאתנו למלכינו לשרינו ולכהנינו
ולנביאנו ולאבתינו ולכל־עמך

Comment   Nehemiah is beginning his famous prayer beseeching the Lord concerning the
spiritual state of Jerusalem. After addressing God, his first acknowledgement of
the character of God is as one keeping "covenant and hesed." This pattern is identical to Daniel's prayer in 9.4.

16. נצר ברית

Deut. 33:9

האמר לאביו ולאמו לא ראיתיו ואת־אחיו לא הכיר
ואת־בנו *בניו לא ידע
כי שמרו אמרתך ובריתך ינצרו

Comment The Levites guarded the word of God and protected his covenant. This may refer to the fact that they were in charge of caring for and protecting the tabernacle where the covenant was kept. Therefore "covenant" refers to the Mosaic covenant.

....

Ps. 25:10

כל־ארחות יהוה חסד ואמת
לנצרי בריתו ועדתיו

Comment The Lord is characterised by חסד and אמת, covenantal terms showing faithfulness and loyalty in the relationship. Those who keep his covenant and warnings are the ones experiencing his faithfulness and loyal love.

....

17. נאמן בברית

Ps. 78:37

ולבם לא־נכון עמו
ולא נאמנו בבריתו

Comment Asaph notes how frequently the people have not been faithful and loyal to the covenant. This must refer to the Mosaic covenant.

....

18. החזיק בברית

Isa. 56:4

כי־כה אמר יהוה לסריסים אשר ישמרו את־שבתותי
ובחרו באשר חפצתי ומחזיקים בבריתי

Comment Isaiah's vision depicts a future time in which foreigners are joined to the Lord. They are Sabbath keepers and firmly grasping and laying hold of the covenant, unlike those originally born into the covenant community, who were covenant breakers and Sabbath breakers.

Isa. 56:6

> ובני הנכר הנלוים על־יהוה
> לשרתו ולאהבה את־שם יהוה להיות לו לעבדים
> כל־שמר שבת מחללו ומחזיקים בבריתי

Comment   Isaiah's vision depicts a future time in which foreigners are joined to the Lord. They are Sabbath keepers and firmly grasping and laying hold of the covenant, unlike those originally born into the covenant community, who were covenant breakers and Sabbath breakers.

....

19. עזב ברית

Deut. 29.24

> ואמרו על אשר עזבו את־ברית יהוה אלהי אבתם
> אשר כרת עמם בהוציאו אתם מארץ מצרים

Comment   The book of Deuteronomy is "this book of the torah" which constitutes the covenant made between God and Israel when he brought them out of Egypt.

....

1 Kings 19:10
1 Kings 19:14

> [10] ויאמר קנא קנאתי ליהוה אלהי צבאות
> כי־עזבו בריתך בני ישראל את־מזבחתיך הרסו
> ואת־נביאיך הרגו בחרב
> ואותר אני לבדי ויבקשו את־נפשי לקחתה

> [14] ויאמר קנא קנאתי ליהוה אלהי צבאות
> כי־עזבו בריתך בני ישראל את־מזבחתיך הרסו
> ואת־נביאיך הרגו בחרב
> ואותר אני לבדי ויבקשו את־נפשי לקחתה

Comment   Elijah complains that the sons of Israel have abandoned, forsaken "your covenant."

Jer. 22:9

ואמרו על אשר עזבו את־ברית יהוה אלהיהם
וישתחוו לאלהים אחרים ויעבדום

Comment   Many nations will observe the destruction of Jerusalem and note that the reason
was that the people abandoned the covenant with Yahweh.

....

Dan. 11:30   (cf. Dan. 11.28, 30, 32 below)

ובאו בו ציים כתים ונכאה ושב וזעם על־ברית־קודש ועשה
ושב ויבן על־עזבי ברית קדש

....

20. הפר ברית

Gen. 17:14

וערל זכר אשר לא־ימול את־בשר ערלתו
ונכרתה הנפש ההוא מעמיה את־בריתי הפר

Comment   The person who is uncircumcised will be cut off from his people because he has
violated the covenant with God.

....

Lev. 26:15

ואם־בחקתי תמאסו ואם את־משפטי תגעל נפשכם
לבלתי עשות את־כל־מצותי להפרכם את־בריתי

Comment   The person who does not observe and practise the commands, refuses the statutes,
and abhors the Judgements by not practising the commands thus violates the covenant with God (Mosaic covenant).

Lev. 26:44

ואף־גם־זאת בהיותם בארץ איביהם
לא־מאסתים ולא־געלתים לכלתם להפר בריתי אתם
כי אני יהוה אלהיהם

Comment   When Israel experiences exile as a curse for violating the Mosaic covenant, God will not bring them to an end in the land of their enemies, which would violate his covenant with them. This reference is to the Abrahamic covenant (see Lev. 26.42).

Deut. 31:16

ויאמר יהוה אל־משה הנך שכב עם־אבתיך
וקם העם הזה וזנה אחרי אלהי נכר־הארץ אשר הוא בא־שמה בקרבו
ועזבני והפר את־בריתי אשר כרתי אתו

Comment   Israel will fornicate after the foreign gods of the land and forsake Yahweh and so violate his covenant.

....

Deut. 31:20

כי־אביאנו אל־האדמה אשר־נשבעתי לאבתיו
זבת חלב ודבש ואכל ושבע ודשן
ופנה אל־אלהים אחרים ועבדום ונאצוני והפר את־בריתי

Comment   Israel will enjoy a good life and turn to worship other gods and spurn Yahweh and so violate his covenant.

....

Judg. 2:1

ויעל מלאך־יהוה מן־הגלגל אל־הבכים ויאמר
אעלה אתכם ממצרים ואביא אתכם אל־הארץ
אשר נשבעתי לאבתיכם ואמר לא־אפר בריתי אתכם לעולם

Comment   Yahweh brought Israel to the land which he swore [to give] to their fathers. Yahweh said he would never break his covenant with them. This must be a reference to the Abrahamic covenant.

1 Kings 15:19

ברית ביני ובינך בין אבי ובין אביך
הנה שלחתי לך שחד כסף וזהב לך
הפרה את־בריתך את־בעשא מלך־ישראל ויעלה מעלי

Comment   Asa, king of Judah, empties the temple treasuries to bribe Ben-Hadad, son of
Tabrimmon, son of Hezion, king of Aram ruling in Damascus, and induce him
to make a treaty between the two of them and break his treaty with Baasha, king
of Israel. As part of this treaty Asa is asking Ben-Hadad to commence aggression
against Baasha so that Baasha will cease his hostilities against Asa and Judah.

Isa. 24:5

והארץ חנפה תחת ישביה
כי־עברו תורת חלפו חק הפרו ברית עולם

Comment   Destruction is promised for the entire earth because its inhabitants have "violated
the eternal covenant." This is not a reference to the law of Moses, which is never
called an everlasting covenant. Instead, it is a reference to the covenant made with
Noah, which in reality confirmed and reestablished the original covenant between
God and his creation.

Isa. 33:8

נשמו מסלות שבת עבר ארח
הפר ברית מאס ערים לא חשב אנוש

Comment   Zion will be delivered but the peoples punished. Some of the historical references are obscure. Apparently the attack of the Assyrians affects even most of
Judah as well as other nations. The broken treaty may refer to the large sums
paid by King Hezekiah to keep the Assyrians away. Now "he violated the treaty."
See 2 Kings 18.13–16.

Jer. 11:10

שבו על־עונת אבותם הראשנים אשר מאנו לשמוע את־דברי
והמה הלכו אחרי אלהים אחרים לעבדם
הפרו בית־ישראל ובית יהודה את־בריתי אשר כרתי את־אבותם

Comment   A clear reference to the covenant made at Sinai, which the house of Israel and the
house of Judah have violated (cf. Jer. 11.3–4).

Jer. 14:21

אל־תנאץ למען שמך אל־תנבל כסא כבודך
זכר אל־תפר בריתך אתנו

Comment   A back reference to the covenant with Abraham, Isaac, and Jacob; see Lev. 26.40–45.

....

Jer. 31:32

לא כברית אשר כרתי את־אבותם ביום
החזיקי בידם להוציאם מארץ מצרים
אשר־המה הפרו את־בריתי
ואנכי בעלתי בם נאם־יהוה

Comment   A back reference to the covenant made at Sinai.

....

Jer. 33:20
Jer. 33:20

כה אמר יהוה אם־תפרו את־בריתי היום ואת־בריתי הלילה
ולבלתי היות יומם־ולילה בעתם

Comment   A comparison is made between the inviolability of the covenant with day and night (i.e., the covenant with creation) and the covenant with David and the Levites; see Jer. 33.21, 25.

....

Ezek. 16:59

כי כה אמר אדני יהוה ועשית *ועשיתי אותך כאשר עשית
אשר־בזית אלה להפר ברית

Comment   According to the context (see 16.8 and 16.60) the covenant is probably the covenant made at Sinai (see Williamson, *Sealed with An Oath*, 167–168).

Ezek. 17:15
Ezek. 17:16
Ezek. 17:18
Ezek. 17:19

[15] וימרד־בו לשלח מלאכיו מצרים לתת־לו סוסים ועם־רב
היצלח הימלט העשה אלה והפר ברית ונמלט

[16] חי־אני נאם אדני יהוה אם־לא במקום המלך הממליך
אתו אשר בזה את־אלתו ואשר הפר את־בריתו

אתו בתוך־בבל ימות
[18] ובזה אלה להפר ברית
והנה נתן ידו וכל־אלה עשה לא ימלט

[19] לכן כה־אמר אדני יהוה חי־אני
אם־לא אלתי אשר בזה ובריתי אשר הפיר
ונתתיו בראשו

Comment   See Ezek. 17.14. If the king of Judah as a vassal of the king of Babylon breaks
the treaty by appealing to Egypt, he will not be successful but will die in Babylon.

....

Ezek. 44:7

בהביאכם בני־נכר ערלי־לב וערלי בשר
להיות במקדשי לחללו את־ביתי
בהקריבכם את־לחמי חלב ודם
ויפרו את־בריתי אל כל־תועבותיכם

Comment   The rebellious house of Israel brought foreigners into the sanctuary and so broke
the covenant. This is a clear reference to the Mosaic covenant.

....

Zech. 11:10

ואקח את־מקלי את־נעם ואגדע אתו
להפיר את־בריתי אשר כרתי את־כל־העמים

Comment   The passage is difficult to interpret. Apparently the covenant in the symbolic
drama represents an agreement between God and the nations to protect Judah
from being ravaged by the nations.

2 Chron. 16:3

ברית ביני ובינך ובין אבי ובין אביך
הנה שלחתי לך כסף וזהב לך
הפר בריתך את־בעשא מלך ישראל ויעלה מעלי

Comment   Baasha, king of Israel, fortifies Ramah so that he may prevent people from entering or exiting Judah. Asa, king of Judah, pays the king of Syria to attack Israel so
that Baasha may abandon his fortifications against Judah. This would result in the
king of Syria breaking his coalition treaty with Israel.

....

21. שכח ברית

Deut. 4:23

השמרו לכם פן־תשכחו את־ברית יהוה אלהיכם אשר כרת עמכם
ועשיתם לכם פסל תמונת כל אשר צוך יהוה אלהיך

Comment   Refers to forgetting the covenant, i.e., Mosaic covenant, and in particular to the
command concerning idol making.

....

Deut. 4:31

כי אל רחום יהוה אלהיך לא ירפך ולא ישחיתך
ולא ישכח את־ברית אבתיך אשר נשבע להם

Comment   The "fathers" had a covenant with Yahweh—he had made promises to them that
were solemnised in unilateral, unconditional covenants.

....

2 Kings 17.38
Jer. 50:5

ציון ישאלו דרך הנה פניהם
באו ונלוו אל־יהוה ברית עולם לא תשכח

Comment   The sons of Israel and the sons of Judah together will seek the Lord and ask the
way to Zion. They will say, "Come, that they may be joined to Yahweh in an
everlasting covenant that will not be forgotten." This is another reference to the
new covenant.

Prov. 2:17

העזבת אלוף נעוריה
ואת־ברית אלהיה שכחה

Comment   The noun phrase "covenant of her God" is a clear reference to the marriage vows made before God. Another interpretation is possible. In abandoning her marriage vows, she is committing adultery and thus violating the Sinai covenant.

....

22. חלל ברית

Mal. 2:10

הלוא אב אחד לכלנו הלוא אל אחד בראנו
מדוע נבגד איש באחיו לחלל ברית אבתינו

Comment   Malachi denounces divorce as a violation of the covenant of our fathers. Probably a reference to the Mosaic covenant, which is an extension of the Abrahamic covenant. See E. R. Clendenen, *Malachi*, 327–328.

....

Ps. 55:21

שלח ידיו בשלמיו חלל בריתו

Comment   In vv. 14–15 David complains of betrayal by a close friend with whom he enjoyed participation in divine worship. Verse 21 states that this companion has attacked his friends and profaned his covenant. Presumably the 3 m. sg. pronoun refers to the friend (and not, e.g., to God). The covenant, then, would be the basis of their close friendship.

....

Ps. 89:35

לא־אחלל בריתי
ומוצא שפתי לא אשנה

Comment   God promises he will not profane his covenant or alter what he has spoken. This refers to the covenant with David.

23. שחת ברית

Mal. 2:8

ואתם סרתם מן־הדרך הכשלתם רבים בתורה
שחתם ברית הלוי אמר יהוה צבאות

Comment   The expression "covenant of Levi" described in Mal. 2.4–9 refers to the setting apart of the Levites for special service to God as a result of their commitment to Yahweh expressed during the incident of the golden calf (Ex. 32.27–29 and Num. 8.5–26).

....

24. גאל ברית

Neh. 13:29

זכרה להם אלהי
על גאלי הכהנה וברית הכהנה והלוים

Comment   Nehemiah appeals to God because those who were priests in his time used their connections, power, and position for their own gain and interests and thus violated ("defiled") the covenant of the priesthood.

....

25. נאר ברית

Ps. 89:40

נארתה ברית עבדך
חללת לארץ נזרו

Comment   Ethan, the Ezrahite, in his great psalm on the Davidic covenant complains that Yahweh has renounced ("repudiated," "spurned") the covenant with David.

....

26. עבר ברית

Deut. 17:2

כי־ימצא בקרבך באחד שעריך אשר־יהוה אלהיך נתן לך
איש או־אשה אשר יעשה את־הרע בעיני יהוה־אלהיך לעבר בריתו

Comment   The text speaks of a person who does what is evil in the eyes of Yahweh "so as to transgress his covenant." This refers to the Mosaic covenant, either in Sinaitic or Deuteronomic form.

Josh. 7:11

חטא ישראל וגם עברו את־בריתי אשר צויתי אותם
וגם לקחו מן־החרם וגם גנבו וגם כחשו וגם שמו בכליהם

Comment   Achan's taking of the devoted things constituted a disobedience resulting in the charge that "Israel has sinned and transgressed my covenant." According to Lev. 27.28–29 and Deut. 20.16–18 the inhabitants of Canaan were to be devoted to destruction. Therefore Achan's disobedience constituted a violation of the Mosaic covenant.

Josh. 7:15

והיה הנלכד בחרם ישרף באש אתו ואת־כל־אשר־לו
כי עבר את־ברית יהוה וכי־עשה נבלה בישראל

Comment   The person caught in possession of devoted things has transgressed the covenant of Yahweh.

Josh. 23:17 (23:16 EV)

בעברכם את־ברית יהוה אלהיכם אשר צוה צוה אתכם
והלכתם ועבדתם אלהים אחרים והשתחויתם להם
וחרה אף־יהוה בכם ואבדתם מהרה מעל הארץ הטובה אשר נתן לכם

Comment   Serving and worshipping other gods constitutes transgression of the Mosaic covenant.

Judg. 2:20

ויחר־אף יהוה בישראל
ויאמר יען אשר עברו הגוי הזה את־בריתי
אשר צויתי את־אבותם ולא שמעו לקולי

Comment   The idolatry of Israel constituted violation of the Mosaic covenant.

2 Kings 18:12

על אשר לא־שמעו בקול יהוה אלהיהם
ויעברו את־בריתו את כל־אשר צוה משה עבד יהוה
ולא שמעו ולא עשׂו

Comment Another reference parallel to 2 Kings 17.15, where following mention of the last
king of Israel comes the description of the conquest by the Assyrians and a summary of the reasons why this happened: they refused the statutes and covenant
of the Lord. Here in 2 Kings 18.12 the expression is "they transgressed his covenant," and in apposition to this is "all that Moses the servant of Y. commanded."

Jer. 34:18

ונתתי את־האנשים העברים את־ברתי
אשר לא־הקימו את־דברי הברית אשר כרתו לפני
העגל אשר כרתו לשנים ויעברו בין בתריו

Comment King and people concluded (i.e., "cut") a covenant to free their slaves, i.e., they
made an agreement with one another to free their slaves. Yahweh announces that
the people have transgressed "my covenant" when they did not fulfill the obligations of the agreement made to free their slaves. This apparently refers to the
Mosaic covenant.

Hos. 6:7

והמה כאדם עברו ברית
שם בגדו בי

Comment Interpretation of this text is debated. See Williamson, *Sealed with an Oath*, 55–56,
who argues for an interpretation like "they as at Adam, transgressed a covenant."
He notes that "most interpreters . . . tak[e] the noun in its geographical sense—
referring to the first town Israel reached after crossing into the Promised Land
(Josh. 3.16)." Yet this is the name of the town where the waters of the Jordan
were heaped up, not a place reached by Israel upon entering the land. The presence of שם may support construing אדם as a geographical location, but the occurrences of Gilead (Hos. 6.8) and Shechem (Hos. 6.9) in the subsequent text do not.
Williamson does not explain what the text could *mean*. There is no reference in
the history of the people to any action at this obscure town. If אדם refers to the first
man, then the text speaks of violating a covenant in Eden.

Hos. 8:1

אל־חכך שפר כנשר על־בית יהוה
יען עברו בריתי ועל־תורתי פשעו

Comment   The prophet accuses the people of covenant violation. The covenant in view is the
Mosaic covenant; the parallel phrase is ועל־תורתי פשעו.

....

מאס ברית .27

2 Kings 17:15

וימאסו את־חקיו ואת־בריתו אשר כרת את־אבותם
ואת עדותיו אשר העיד בם
וילכו אחרי ההבל ויהבלו ואחרי הגוים אשר סביבתם
אשר צוה יהוה אתם לבלתי עשות כהם

Comment   Following mention of the last king of Israel comes the description of the conquest
and exile by the Assyrians and a summary of the reasons why this happened:
Israel refused the statutes and covenant of the Lord.

....

שקר בברית .28

Ps. 44:18

כל־זאת באתנו ולא שכחנוך
ולא־שקרנו בבריתך

Comment   The author claims that bad things happened to them although they had not been
false to the covenant. This must refer to the Mosaic covenant.

....

הרשיע ברית .29

Dan. 11:32

ומרשיעי ברית יחניף בחלקות
ועם ידעי אלהיו יחזקו ועשׂו

Comment   Predictions concerning Antiochus IV Epiphanes. Verse 28 shows him against "the
holy covenant," i.e., opposed to the culture of the Jewish people in Palestine. In a
military setback, he vents his wrath against the Jewish people and corrupts those
who violate the covenant (v. 32).

30. נשא ברית

Ps. 50:16

> ולרשע אמר אלהים מה־לך לספר חקי
> ותשא בריתי עלי־פיך

Comment   The guilty rebel has no right to speak of the Israelite covenant, i.e., to lift it up on his lips or rehearse the covenant statutes. See comments on Ps. 50:5 (above).

....

31. על ברית

Dan. 11:28

Dan. 11:30

(cf. Dan. 11.30 above, s.v. עזב ברית; and Dan. 11.32 below, s.v. הרשיע ברית)

> [28] וישב ארצו ברכוש גדול ולבבו על־ברית קדש
> ועשה ושב לארצו

> [30] ובאו בו ציים כתים ונכאה ושב וזעם על־ברית־קודש ועשה
> ושב ויבן על־עזבי ברית קדש

Comment   Predictions concerning Antiochus IV Epiphanes. Verse 28 shows him against "the holy covenant," i.e., opposed to the culture of the Jewish people in Palestine. In a military setback, he vents his wrath against the Jewish people and corrupts those who violate the covenant (v. 32).

....

EXPRESSIONS WITH ברית AS
SUBJECT OF THE VERB

Gen. 17:4

> אני הנה בריתי אתך
> והיית לאב המון גוים

Comment   God announces that his covenant is with Abraham, who will become a father of a multitude of nations. This is clearly connected to the promise in Genesis 12 that in him all the nations would be blessed.

Gen. 17:13

המול ימול יליד ביתך ומקנת כספך
והיתה בריתי בבשרכם לברית עולם

Comment   Circumcision is God's covenant in flesh with Abraham's family.

1 Kings 8:21

ואשם שם מקום לארון אשר־שם ברית יהוה
אשר כרת עם־אבתינו בהוציאו אתם מארץ מצרים

Comment   The temple that Solomon built was established as a place for the covenant of
Yahweh, which was initiated during the Exodus. The phrase "covenant of Yahweh"
refers to the Ten Commandments. The "genitive" seems to indicate possession or
source rather than the person with whom the covenant is made.

1 Kings 15:19

ברית ביני ובינך בין אבי ובין אביך
הנה שלחתי לך שחד כסף וזהב לך
הפרה את־בריתך את־בעשא מלך־ישראל ויעלה מעלי

Comment   Asa, king of Judah, empties the temple treasuries to bribe Ben-Hadad, son of
Tabrimmon, son of Hezion, king of Aram ruling in Damascus, and induce him
to make a treaty between the two of them and break his treaty with Baasha, king
of Israel. As part of this treaty Asa is asking Ben-Hadad to commence aggression
against Baasha so that Baasha will cease his hostilities against Asa and Judah.

Isa. 28:18

וכפר בריתכם את־מות וחזותכם את־שאול לא תקום
שוט שוטף כי יעבר והייתם לו למרמס

Comment   Interpretation is difficult due to a problem in the text: should וכפר be corrected
to ותפר even though no witnesses support this in the textual transmission, or
can an appropriate meaning for כפר be found? KB3 suggests "be covered" as a
primary meaning yielding "be dissolved" as a secondary meaning. This passage
corresponds to Isa. 28.15, where idolators boast that they have made a covenant
with death.

Jer. 33:21

גם־בריתי תפר את־דוד עבדי מהיות־לו בן מלך על־כסאו
ואת־הלוים הכהנים משרתי

Comment   If God's covenant with day and night (i.e., creation) can be violated, then so will
his covenant with David and the Levites.

....

Isa. 54:10

כי ההרים ימושו והגבעות תמוטנה
וחסדי מאתך לא־ימוש וברית שלומי לא תמוט אמר מרחמך יהוה

Comment   The new covenant, called here "my covenant of peace," is more permanent than
the hills and mountains; it will never be annulled.

....

Ezek. 37:26

וכרתי להם ברית שלום ברית עולם יהיה אותם
ונתתים והרביתי אותם ונתתי את־מקדשי בתוכם לעולם

Comment   Ezekiel announces a covenant of peace = new covenant.

....

Mal. 2:4

וידעתם כי שלחתי אליכם את המצוה הזאת
להיות בריתי את־לוי אמר יהוה צבאות

Comment   The passage refers to a covenant between God and the Levitical priesthood.

....

Mal. 2:5

בריתי היתה אתו החיים והשלום ואתנם־לו מורא וייראני
ומפני שמי נחת הוא

Comment   The passage refers to a covenant between God and the Levitical priesthood.

Ps. 25:14

סוד יהוה ליראיו
ובריתו להודיעם

Comment   On Psalm 25 see Lohfink and Zenger. God makes his covenant known to those who fear him. This passage extends the covenant beyond the Mosaic covenant to the nations. The basis must be the Abrahamic covenant. See, however, Ps. 25.10.

....

Ps. 89:29

לעולם אשמור *אשמר־לו חסדי
ובריתי נאמנת לו

Comment   God promises he will keep his obligation to David and his covenant will be firm for him. Strangely, the NIV employs a negative construction in translation.

....

Job 5:23

כי עם־אבני השדה בריתך
וחית השדה השלמה־לך

Comment   Eliphaz discourses on the blessings experienced by the person who is corrected by God. No harm will come to this man from stones (see Ps. 91.12, 121.3, where one could be injured by stumbling against a stone) and he need not fear harm from wild animals. This is expressed by saying that he has a covenant with stones in the field.

....

2 Chron. 6:11

ואשים שם את־הארון אשר־שם ברית יהוה
אשר כרת עם־בני ישראל

Comment   When Solomon dedicates the temple, just before his prayer of dedication he notes that he has placed the covenant in the ark. This is a clear reference to the "Ten Words" as the "short text" of the Mosaic covenant identified as the "covenant of Yahweh."

2 Chron. 16:3

ברית ביני וביניך ובין אבי ובין אביך
הנה שלחתי לך כסף וזהב לך
הפר בריתך את־בעשא מלך ישראל ויעלה מעלי

Comment   Baasha, king of Israel, fortifies Ramah so that he may prevent people from entering or exiting Judah. Asa, king of Judah, pays the king of Syria to attack Israel so
that Baasha may abandon his fortifications against Judah. This would result in the
king of Syria breaking his coalition treaty with Israel.

....

EXPRESSIONS WITH ברית AS NEITHER
OBJECT NOR SUBJECT
BOUND PHRASE: ברית *+ NOUN*

Gen. 14:13

ויבא הפליט ויגד לאברם העברי
והוא שכן באלני ממרא האמרי אחי אשכל ואחי ענר
והם בעלי ברית־אברם

Comment   Mamre, Eshcol, and Aner were parties in a treaty with Abram.

....

Ex. 31:16

ושמרו בני־ישראל את־השבת
לעשות את־השבת לדרתם ברית עולם

Comment   The Israelites are to celebrate or observe the Sabbath, thus making it an eternal
covenant.

....

Lev. 2:13

וכל־קרבן מנחתך במלח תמלח
ולא תשבית מלח ברית אלהיך מעל מנחתך
על כל־קרבנך תקריב מלח

Comment   The expression "covenant of your God" refers to the Sinai covenant.

1 Kings 20:34

ויאמר אליו הערים אשר־לקח־אבי מאת אביך אשיב
וחוצות תשים לך בדמשק כאשר־שם אבי בשמרון
ואני בברית אשלחך ויכרת־לו ברית וישלחהו

Comment   Ahab releases Ben-Hadad "on the basis of a treaty," i.e., if he will make a treaty with Ahab.

....

2 Kings 13:23

ויחן יהוה אתם וירחמם ויפן אליהם
למען בריתו את־אברהם יצחק ויעקב
ולא אבה השחיתם ולא־השליכם מעל־פניו עד־עתה

Comment   King Hazael of Damascus oppresses the northern tribal territories, but Yahweh has compassion because of his covenant with Abraham, Isaac, and Jacob.

....

Ezek. 16:61

וזכרת את־דרכיך ונכלמת בקחתך את־אחותיך
הגדלות ממך אל־הקטנות ממך
ונתתי אתהן לך לבנות ולא מבריתך

Comment   Judah's sisters are Samaria to the north and Sodom to the south. At the end, she will receive them, but not on the basis of a covenant with them, i.e., the gift of the nations will not be on the basis of the Mosaic covenant or on the basis of the new everlasting covenant. The former makes more sense in context.

....

Obad. 1:7

עד־הגבול שלחוך כל אנשי בריתך השיאוך יכלו לך אנשי שלמך
לחמך ישימו מזור תחתיך אין תבונה בו

Comment   Obadiah announces coming judgement upon Edom in the form of attack and conquest. Even her allies and friends will betray her. The expression for allies here is "the men of your covenant."

Zech. 9:11

גַּם־אַתְּ בְּדַם־בְּרִיתֵךְ שִׁלַּחְתִּי אֲסִירַיִךְ מִבּוֹר אֵין מַיִם בּוֹ

Comment   The prophet states that "because of the blood of my covenant" Yahweh will free the exiles. In the context of the larger story of the Old Testament, this must be a reference to the new covenant.

Mal. 2:14

וַאֲמַרְתֶּם עַל־מָה

עַל כִּי־יְהוָה הֵעִיד בֵּינְךָ וּבֵין אֵשֶׁת נְעוּרֶיךָ

אֲשֶׁר אַתָּה בָּגַדְתָּה בָּהּ וְהִיא חֲבֶרְתְּךָ וְאֵשֶׁת בְּרִיתֶךָ

Comment   Apparently when exiles returned under Ezra and Nehemiah they divorced their Jewish wives and married foreign women in order to advance their economic status. The "high-school sweetheart" they had originally married is called the "wife of your covenant," indicating that marriage is a covenant made before God.

Mal. 3:1

הִנְנִי שֹׁלֵחַ מַלְאָכִי וּפִנָּה־דֶרֶךְ לְפָנָי

וּפִתְאֹם יָבוֹא אֶל־הֵיכָלוֹ הָאָדוֹן אֲשֶׁר־אַתֶּם מְבַקְשִׁים

וּמַלְאַךְ הַבְּרִית אֲשֶׁר־אַתֶּם חֲפֵצִים הִנֵּה־בָא אָמַר יְהוָה צְבָאוֹת

Comment   The differences between Yahweh and his people will be resolved by the "messenger of the covenant." It seems that this may be in apposition to "the Lord whom the people are seeking" who will come "to his temple." This suggests that the messenger is a divine figure. It may be a reference like that in Isaiah 63.9 to the messenger God sent to help the people through the desert.

PHRASE = BAAL BERIT
Judg. 8:33

וַיְהִי כַּאֲשֶׁר מֵת גִּדְעוֹן וַיָּשׁוּבוּ בְּנֵי יִשְׂרָאֵל וַיִּזְנוּ אַחֲרֵי הַבְּעָלִים

וַיָּשִׂימוּ לָהֶם בַּעַל בְּרִית לֵאלֹהִים

Comment   After the death of Gideon the Israelites again commit idolatry and worship Baal-Berith as god.

Judg. 9:4

ויתנו־לו שבעים כסף מבית בעל ברית
וישכר בהם אבימלך אנשים ריקים ופחזים וילכו אחריו

Comment   This passage locates the temple of Baal-Berith in Shechem.

....

Judg. 9:46

וישמעו כל־בעלי מגדל־שכם
ויבאו אל־צריח בית אל ברית

Comment   The temple of Baal-Berith in Shechem is alternatively called the temple of El-Berith.

....

BOUND PHRASE: NOUN + ברית
Gen. 9:12
Gen. 9:13

[12] ויאמר אלהים זאת אות־הברית אשר־אני נתן ביני
וביניכם ובין כל־נפש חיה אשר אתכם לדרת עולם
[13] את־קשתי נתתי בענן
והיתה לאות ברית ביני ובין הארץ

Comment   The bow in the clouds is the sign of the covenant between God and every living being.

....

Gen. 9:17

ויאמר אלהים אל־נח
זאת אות־הברית אשר הקמתי ביני ובין כל־בשר אשר על־הארץ

Comment   The bow in the clouds is the sign of the covenant between God and every living being.

Gen. 17:7

[6] והפרתי אתך במאד מאד ונתתיך לגוים
ומלכים ממך יצאו
[7] והקמתי את־בריתי ביני ובינך ובין זרעך אחריך לדרתם
לברית עולם להיות לך לאלהים ולזרעך אחריך

Comment   Covenant with Abraham is an everlasting covenant.

....

Gen. 17:11

ונמלתם את בשׂר ערלתכם
והיה לאות ברית ביני וביניכם

Comment   Circumcision is the covenant sign between God and Abraham's family.

....

Gen. 17:13

המול ימול יליד ביתך ומקנת כספך
והיתה בריתי בבשׂרכם לברית עולם

Comment   Covenant with Abraham is an everlasting covenant.

....

Gen. 17:19

ויאמר אלהים אבל שׂרה אשתך ילדת לך בן וקראת את־שמו
יצחק והקמתי את־בריתי אתו לברית עולם לזרעו אחריו

Comment   Covenant with Abraham is an everlasting covenant.

....

Ex. 24:7

ויקח ספר הברית ויקרא באזני העם
ויאמרו כל אשר־דבר יהוה נעשׂה ונשמע

Comment   The expression "the Book of the Covenant" refers to the covenant about to be
concluded between God and Moses/Israel.

Ex. 24:8

ויקח משה את־הדם ויזרק על־העם
ויאמר הנה דם־הברית אשר כרת יהוה עמכם על כל־הדברים האלה

Comment   The expression "the blood of the covenant" refers to the covenant about to be
concluded between God and Moses/Israel.

....

Ex. 34:28

ויהי־שם עם־יהוה ארבעים יום וארבעים
לילה לחם לא אכל ומים לא שתה
ויכתב על־הלחת את דברי הברית עשׂרת הדברים

Comment   The expression "the words of the covenant" refers to the Ten Words as the stipulations of the Mosaic covenant.

....

Lev. 24:8

ביום השבת ביום השבת יערכנו לפני יהוה תמיד
מאת בני־ישׂראל ברית עולם

Comment   Bread is to be presented before Yahweh regularly, Sabbath by Sabbath, as an
"eternal covenant."

....

Lev. 26:25

והבאתי עליכם חרב נקמת נקם־ברית ונאספתם אל־עריכם
ושלחתי דבר בתוככם ונתתם ביד־אויב

Comment   Persistent refusal to accept correction from the Lord will result in an "avenging
sword," and in apposition to this is the expression, "vengeance of the covenant."
Thus, destruction by sword will constitute the judicial payback for covenant
violation.

Num. 18:19

כל תרומת הקדשים אשר ירימו בני־ישראל ליהוה
נתתי לך ולבניך ולבנתיך אתך לחק־עולם
ברית מלח עולם הוא לפני יהוה לך ולזרעך אתך

Comment   The holy offerings are given to Aaron and his sons and daughters. This permanent
statute is called "an eternal covenant of salt" before the Lord for Aaron and his
offspring. Cf. Lev. 2.13.

Num. 25:12

לכן אמר הנני נתן לו את־בריתי שלום

Num. 25:13

2 Chron. 13:5

הלא לכם לדעת כי יהוה אלהי ישראל נתן ממלכה
לדויד על־ישראל לעולם לו ולבניו ברית מלח

Comment   Describes a war between Abijah of Judah and Jeroboam of Israel. Abijah challenges his opponents, asking them, "Don't you know God gave the kingship to
David and his descendants as a covenant of salt?" Cf. Lev. 2.13.

והיתה לו ולזרעו אחריו ברית כהנת עולם
תחת אשר קנא לאלהיו ויכפר על־בני ישראל

Comment   Phinehas' action turned away the anger of Yahweh. As a result, God gave to him
a "covenant of peace," which is described as a "covenant of eternal priesthood."

Isa. 42:6

אני יהוה קראתיך בצדק ואחזק בידך
ואצרך ואתנך לברית עם לאור גוים

Isa. 49:8

כה אמר יהוה בעת רצון עניתיך וביום ישועה עזרתיך
ואצרך ואתנך לברית עם להקים ארץ להנחיל נחלות שממות

Comment　Normally, in a bound phrase where the bound member is ברית and the free member is a person, this person is the covenant partner. Here, in a unique expression,
the servant of Yahweh is himself the covenant between God and the people.

....

Isa. 59:21

ואני זאת בריתי אותם אמר יהוה
רוחי אשר עליך ודברי אשר־שמתי בפיך
לא־ימושו מפיך ומפי זרעך ומפי זרע זרעך
אמר יהוה מעתה ועד־עולם

Comment　This passage is another description of the new covenant in which the words of
Yahweh will not depart from the mouth of the people or from the mouths of their
descendants.

....

Ezek. 30:5

כוש ופוט ולוד וכל־הערב וכוב ובני ארץ הברית
אתם בחרב יפלו

Comment　The passage is a lament for Egypt and refers to groups of people and nations who
experience demise along with Egypt. Jer. 25.20 may be a parallel passage. This
appears to refer to non-Israelite peoples in the land of Israel, where the bound
noun phrase "land of the covenant" is a way of referring to Israel.

....

Dan. 11:22

וזרעות השטף ישטפו מלפניו וישברו
וגם נגיד ברית

Comment　Events in the Maccabean period are portrayed as events perpetrated by the king
of the North and the king of the South. In the sequence of things, a contemptible
person without royalty will gain power. A huge army will be swept away before
him along with a "covenant prince." This may refer to a Jewish leader.

Deut. 29:20

והבדילו יהוה לרעה מכל שבטי ישראל
ככל אלות הברית הכתובה בספר התורה הזה

Comment   The disobedient person will be singled out to receive all the curses of the covenant. Oath is employed in a positive sense in v. 11 and in a negative sense here.

....

PHRASE = "ARK OF THE COVENANT"

Num. 10:33

ויסעו מהר יהוה דרך שלשת ימים
וארון ברית־יהוה נסע לפניהם דרך שלשת ימים לתור להם מנוחה

Comment   The ark of the covenant of Yahweh journeyed before the people.

....

Num. 14:44

ויעפלו לעלות אל־ראש ההר
וארון ברית־יהוה ומשה לא־משו מקרב המחנה

Comment   The ark of the covenant of Yahweh did not accompany the excursion to the hill
country from Kadesh Barnea.

....

Jer. 3:16

והיה כי תרבו ופריתם בארץ בימים ההמה נאם־יהוה
לא־יאמרו עוד ארון ברית־יהוה ולא יעלה על־לב
ולא יזכרו־בו ולא יפקדו ולא יעשה עוד

Comment   A future time is described when the ark of the covenant will no longer be part of
the people of God.

PHRASE = "THE ARK OF THE COVENANT"
Josh. 3:6; Josh. 3:6

PHRASE = "THE ARK OF THE COVENANT OF YAHWEH"
Deut. 10:8; Josh. 4:7; Josh. 6:8; 1 Sam. 4:3; 1 Sam. 4:5; 1 Kings 6:19; 1 Kings 8:1; 1 Kings 8:6; 1 Chron. 15:25; 1 Chron. 15:28; 1 Chron. 15:29; 1 Chron. 16:37; 1 Chron. 17:1; 1 Chron. 22:19; 1 Chron. 28:2; 1 Chron. 28:18; 2 Chron. 5:2; 2 Chron. 5:7

*PHRASE = "THE ARK OF THE COVENANT
OF YAHWEH OF ARMIES"*
1 Sam. 4:4

PHRASE = "CARRIERS OF THE ARK OF THE COVENANT"
Josh. 3:8; Josh. 3:14; Josh. 4:9

*PHRASE = "CARRIERS OF THE ARK OF
THE COVENANT OF YAHWEH"*
Deut. 31:9; Deut. 31:25; 1 Chron. 15:26; Josh. 4:18; Josh. 8:33;
Josh. 3:17 (הכהנים נשׂאי הארון ברית־יהוה)

*PHRASE = "THE ARK OF THE COVENANT
OF YAHWEH YOUR GOD"*
Deut. 31:26; Josh. 3:3

PHRASE = "THE ARK OF THE COVENANT OF GOD"
Judg. 20:27; 1 Sam. 4:4; 2 Sam. 15:25; 1 Chron. 16:6

PHRASE = "THE ARK OF THE COVENANT OF THE LORD"
1 Kings 3:15

PHRASE = *"THE ARK OF THE COVENANT*
OF THE LORD OF ALL THE EARTH"
Josh. 3:11

PHRASE = *"THE ARK OF GOD"*
1 Sam. 3.3

PHRASE = *"WORDS OF THE COVENANT"*
Deut. 29:8 (29:9 EV)

ושמרתם את־דברי הברית הזאת ועשׂיתם אתם
למען תשׂכילו את כל־אשר תעשׂון

Comment   A reference to the terms of the covenant. The demonstrative shows that this is
equivalent to the book of Deuteronomy.

....

Jer. 11:2

שמעו את־דברי הברית הזאת
ודברתם אל־איש יהודה ועל־יׁשבי ירושלם

....

Jer. 11:3

ואמרת אליהם כה־אמר יהוה אלהי ישראל
ארור האיש אשר לא ישמע את־דברי הברית הזאת

....

Jer. 11:6

ויאמר יהוה אלי קרא את־כל־הדברים האלה
בערי יהודה ובחצות ירושלם לאמר
שמעו את־דברי הברית הזאת ועשׂיתם אותם

Jer. 11:8

ולא שמעו ולא־הטו את־אזנם וילכו איש בשרירות לבם הרע
ואביא עליהם את־כל־דברי הברית־הזאת אשר־צויתי לעשות ולא עשו

Comment   Four instances in Jeremiah 11 entail the expression "the words (i.e., terms) of this
covenant" and refer specifically to the terms of the Mosaic covenant. This is distinguished from the Abrahamic covenant, which is referred to as "the oath" in v. 5.

....

2 Chron. 34:30

ויעל המלך בית־יהוה וכל־איש יהודה וישבי ירושלם
והכהנים והלוים וכל־העם מגדול ועד־קטן
ויקרא באזניהם את־כל־דברי ספר הברית הנמצא בית יהוה

....

2 Chron. 34:31

ויעמד המלך על־עמדו ויכרת את־הברית לפני יהוה
ללכת אחרי יהוה ולשמור את־מצותיו ועדותיו וחקיו בכל־לבבו
ובכל־נפשו לעשות את־דברי הברית הכתובים על־הספר הזה

Comment   The passage relates the discovery of the Book of the Torah (34.14) during Josiah's
renovations of the temple and a renewal of commitment to this covenant (doubtless the book of Deuteronomy). The expression is that "he [the king] cut *the*
covenant before Yahweh to follow him and keep his commands . . . " One wonders why the word בירת is articulated here and what this may betoken? Does the
expression כרת ברית here refer to covenant renewal?

....

PHRASE = "THE TABLETS OF THE COVENANT"

Deut. 9:9

בעלתי ההרה לקחת לוחת האבנים לוחת הברית
אשר־כרת יהוה עמכם
ואשב בהר ארבעים יום וארבעים לילה
לחם לא אכלתי ומים לא שתיתי

Deut. 9:11

נתן יהוה אלי את־שני לחת האבנים לחות הברית

Comment   Reference is made to "the tablets of the covenant which Yahweh cut with you." This indicates the Ten Commandments written on the two stone tablets.

....

PHRASE = "THE BOOK OF THE COVENANT"

2 Kings 23:2

ויעל המלך בית־יהוה וכל־איש יהודה וכל־ישבי ירושלם אתו
והכהנים והנביאים וכל־העם למקטן ועד־גדול
ויקרא באזניהם את־כל־דברי ספר הברית הנמצא בבית יהוה

Comment   Here, "the words of the Book of the Covenant" found during the restoration of the temple are read during Josiah's revival.

....

2 Kings 23:21

ויצו המלך את־כל־העם לאמר עשו פסח ליהוה אלהיכם
ככתוב על ספר הברית הזה

Comment   Here, the king commands Passover to be celebrated according to "what is written in the Book of the Covenant" found during the restoration of the temple.

....

Listed Twice = Gen. 9.12 (ברית + Noun ,נתן)
Listed Twice = Ex. 24.8 (כרת, Noun + ברית)
Listed Twice = Deut. 4.23 (כרת, שכח)
Listed Twice = Deut. 29.24 (כרת, עזב)
Listed Twice = Deut. 31.16 (כרת, הפר)
Listed Twice = 2 Kings 17.38 (שכח, כרת)
Listed Twice = 1 Kings 8.21 (כרת, Subj)
Listed Twice = 2 Kings 17.15 (כרת, מאס)
Listed Twice = Jer. 11.10 (כרת, הפר)
Listed Twice = Zech. 11.10 (כרת, הפר)
Listed Twice = Ps. 105.8–9 (כרת, זכר)

Listed Twice = 1 Chron. 16.15 (כרת, זכר)
Listed Twice = Deut. 9.9 (כרת, לוחת)
Listed Twice = Deut. 29.11 (כרת, עבר ב)

PARALLEL EXPRESSIONS

1. הקים ברית = הקים השבעה
Gen. 26:3

גור בארץ הזאת ואהיה עמך ואברכך
כי־לך ולזרעך אתן את־כל־הארצת האל
והקמתי את־השבעה אשר נשבעתי לאברהם אביך

BIBLIOGRAPHY FOR
PARTS 1 AND 3

Alexander, T. D. "Beyond Borders: The Wider Dimensions of Land." In *The Land of Promise: Biblical, Theological, and Contemporary Perspectives*. Edited by Philip Johnston and Peter W. L. Walker. Downers Grove, IL: InterVarsity Press, 2000.

———. *From Eden to the New Jerusalem*. Nottingham, UK: Inter-Varsity Press, 2008.

———. "Seed." In *New Dictionary of Biblical Theology*. Edited by T. D. Alexander, Brian S. Rosner, D. A. Carson, and Graeme Goldsworthy. 769–773. Downers Grove, IL: InterVarsity Press, 2000.

———. *The Servant King*. Leicester, UK: Inter-Varsity Press, 1998.

Allen, David L. "The Atonement: Limited or Universal?" In *Whosoever Will: A Biblical-Theological Critique of Five-Point Calvinism*. Edited by David L. Allen and Steve W. Lemke. 68–109. Nashville: B&H, 2010.

Anderson, A. A. *2 Samuel*. Word Biblical Commentary 11. Waco, TX: Word, 1989.

Baker, David L. *Two Testaments, One Bible: The Theological Relationship between the Old and New Testaments,* 3rd ed. Downers Grove, IL: InterVarsity Press, 2010.

Barnes, Tom. *Atonement Matters*. Darlington, UK: Evangelical Press, 2008.

Barr, James. "Biblical Theology." In *Interpreter's Dictionary of the Bible: Supplementary Volume*. Edited by K. Crim. 104–106. Nashville: Abingdon, 1976.

———. *Fundamentalism*. London: SCM, 1977.

Bartholomew, Craig G., et al. *Canon and Biblical Interpretation*. Scripture and Hermeneutics Series 7: Grand Rapids, MI: Zondervan, 2006.

Bateman, Herbert W. IV, ed. *Three Central Issues in Contemporary Dispensationalism: A Comparison of Traditional and Progressive Views*. Grand Rapids, MI: Kregel, 1999.

Bauckham, Richard. *Jesus and the God of Israel:* God Crucified *and Other Studies on the New Testament's Christology of Divine Identity*. Grand Rapids, MI: Eerdmans, 2008.

Bavinck, Herman. *Reformed Dogmatics*. Edited by John Bolt. Translated by John Vriend. Grand Rapids, MI: Baker, 2006.

Beale, G. K. *The Book of Revelation: A Commentary on the Greek Text*. New International Greek Testament Commentary. Grand Rapids, MI: Eerdmans, 1999.

———. "Did Jesus and His Followers Preach the Right Doctrine from the Wrong Texts?" In *The Right Doctrine from the Wrong Texts: Essays on the Use of the Old Testament in the New*. Edited by G. K. Beale. Grand Rapids, MI: Baker, 1994.

———. *The Erosion of Inerrancy in Evangelicalism*. Wheaton, IL: Crossway, 2008.

———. "The Eschatological Conception of New Testament Theology." In *"The Reader Must Understand": Eschatology in Bible and Theology*. Edited by K. E. Brower and M. W. Elliott. 11–52. Leicester: Apollos, 1997.

———. *The Temple and the Church's Mission*. New Studies in Biblical Theology 17: Downers Grove, IL: InterVarsity Press, 2004.

———. *We Become What We Worship: A Biblical Theology of Idolatry*. Downers Grove, IL: InterVarsity Press, 2008.

Beale, G. K., and D. A. Carson, eds. *Commentary on the New Testament Use of the Old Testament.* Grand Rapids, MI: Baker, 2007.

Beasley-Murray, G. R. "Baptism." In *Dictionary of Paul and His Letters.* Edited by Gerald F. Hawthorne, et al. 60–66. Downers Grove, IL: InterVarsity Press, 1993.

———. *Baptism in the New Testament.* Grand Rapids, MI: Eerdmans, 1962.

———. "The Kingdom of God in the Old and New Testaments." In *Reclaiming the Prophetic Mantle: Preaching the Old Testament Faithfully.* Edited by George L. Kline. 179–201. Nashville: Broadman, 1992.

Berkhof, Louis. *Principles of Biblical Interpretation: Sacred Hermeneutics*, 2nd ed. Grand Rapids, MI: Baker, 1952.

———. *Systematic Theology.* 1941. Repr., Grand Rapids, MI: Eerdmans, 1982.

Bigalke, Ron J., Jr., ed. *Progressive Dispensationalism: An Analysis of the Movement and Defense of Traditional Dispensationalism.* Lanham, MD: University Press of America, 2005.

Bird, Chad L. "Typological Interpretation *within* the Old Testament: Melchizedekian Typology." *Concordia Journal* 26 (2000): 36–52.

Bird, Michael F. "Biblical Theology: An Endangered Species in Need of Defense." http://euangelizomai.blogspot.com/2008/01/biblical-theology-endangered-species-in.html.

———. "New Testament Theology Re-Loaded: Integrating Biblical Theology and Christian Origins." *Tyndale Bulletin* 60/2 (2009): 265–291.

Blaising, Craig A., and Darrell L. Bock, eds. *Dispensationalism, Israel, and the Church: A Search for Definition.* Grand Rapids, MI: Zondervan, 1992.

Blaising, Craig A., and Darrell L. Bock. *Progressive Dispensationalism.* Wheaton, IL: BridgePoint, 1993.

Blocher, Henri. *Original Sin: Illuminating the Riddle.* New Studies in Biblical Theology 5: Downers Grove, IL: InterVarsity Press, 2001.

Block, Daniel I. "My Servant David: Ancient Israel's Vision of the Messiah." In *Israel's Messiah in the Bible and the Dead Sea Scrolls.* Edited by Richard S. Hess and M. Daniel Carroll. 17–56. Grand Rapids, MI: Baker, 2003.

———. "Preaching Old Testament Apocalyptic to a New Testament Church." *Calvin Theological Journal* 41 (2006): 17–52.

Bock, Darrell L. "Covenants in Progressive Dispensationalism." In *Three Central Issues in Contemporary Dispensationalism: A Comparison of Traditional and Progressive Views.* Edited by Herbert W. Bateman IV. 169–203. Grand Rapids, MI: Kregel, 1999.

———. "Current Messianic Activity and OT Davidic Promise: Dispensationalism, Hermeneutics, and NT Fulfillment." *Trinity Journal* 15 (1994): 55–87.

———. "The Kingdom of God in New Testament Theology." In *Looking into the Future: Evangelical Studies in Eschatology.* Edited by David W. Baker. 28–60. Grand Rapids, MI: Baker, 2001.

Booth, Robert R. *Children of the Promise: The Biblical Case for Infant Baptism.* Phillipsburg, NJ: P&R, 1995.

Bowman, Robert M., Jr., and J. Ed. Komoszewski, *Putting Jesus in His Place: The Case for the Deity of Christ.* Grand Rapids, MI: Kregel, 2007.

Bray, Gerald. "Christology." In *New Dictionary of Theology.* Edited by Sinclair B. Ferguson, et al. Downers Grove, IL: InterVarsity Press, 1988.

Bromiley, Geoffrey W. "The Case for Infant Baptism." *Christianity Today*, October 9, 1964, 7–10.

Brower, K. E. "Eschatology." In *New Dictionary of Biblical Theology.* Edited by T. D. Alexander, Brian S. Rosner, D. A. Carson, and Graeme Goldsworthy. 459–464. Downers Grove, IL: InterVarsity Press, 2000.

Brown, Raymond E. *The Sensus Plenior of Sacred Scripture*. Baltimore: St. Mary's University, 1955.

Brueggemann, Walter. *The Land: Place as Gift, Promise, and Challenge in Biblical Faith*. London: SPCK, 1978.

Burns, J. Lanier. "Israel and the Church of a Progressive Dispensationalist." In *Three Central Issues in Contemporary Dispensationalism: A Comparison of Traditional and Progressive Views*. Edited by Herbert W. Bateman IV. 263–291. Grand Rapids, MI: Kregel, 1999.

Calvin, John. *Institutes of the Christian Religion*. Edited by John T. McNeil. Translated by Ford Lewis Battles, 2 vols. Philadelphia: Westminster, 1960.

Caneday, A. B. "Covenant Lineage Allegorically Prefigured: 'What Things Are Written Allegorically' (Galatians 4:21–31)." *Southern Baptist Journal of Theology* 14/3 (2010): 50–77.

Carson, D. A. *The Difficult Doctrine of the Love of God*. Wheaton, IL: Crossway, 2000.

———. "Evangelicals, Ecumenism, and the Church." In *Evangelical Affirmations*. Edited by Kenneth S. Kantzer and Carl F. H. Henry. 347–385. Grand Rapids, MI: Zondervan, 1990.

———, ed. *From Sabbath to Lord's Day: A Biblical, Historical, and Theological Investigation*. Grand Rapids, MI: Zondervan, 1982. Repr. Eugene, OR: Wipf & Stock, 2000.

———. *The Gagging of God: Christianity Confronts Pluralism*. Grand Rapids, MI: Zondervan, 1996.

———. *The Gospel according to John*. Pillar New Testament Commentary. Grand Rapids, MI: Eerdmans, 1991.

———. "Matthew." In *Matthew, Mark, Luke*. The Expositor's Bible Commentary 8. Edited by Frank E. Gaebelein. Grand Rapids, MI: Zondervan, 1984.

———. "Mystery and Fulfillment: Toward a More Comprehensive Paradigm of Paul's Understanding of the Old and the New." In *Justification and Variegated Nomism: Volume 2—The Paradoxes of Paul*. Edited by D. A. Carson, P. T. O'Brien, M. A. Seifrid. 393–436. Grand Rapids, MI: Baker, 2004.

———. "New Testament Theology." In *Dictionary of the Later New Testament and Its Developments*. Edited by Ralph P. Martin and Peter H. Davids. Downers Grove, IL: InterVarsity Press, 1997.

———. "Pauline Inconsistency: Reflections on 1 Corinthians 9.19–23 and Galatians 2.11–14." *Churchman* 100/1 (1986): 6–45.

———. *Showing the Spirit: A Theological Exposition of 1 Corinthians 12–14*. Grand Rapids, MI: Baker, 1987.

———. "Systematic Theology and Biblical Theology." In *New Dictionary of Biblical Theology*. Edited by T. D. Alexander, Brian S. Rosner, D. A. Carson, and Graeme Goldsworthy. 89–104. Downers Grove, IL: InterVarsity Press, 2000.

Carson, D. A., and John D. Woodbridge, eds. *Hermeneutics, Authority, and Canon*. Grand Rapids, MI: Zondervan, 1986.

———. *Scripture and Truth*. Grand Rapids, MI: Zondervan, 1983.

Chafer, Lewis S. "Dispensationalism." *Bibliotheca Sacra* 93 (1936): 390–449.

Chafer, Lewis Sperry. *Systematic Theology*. 1948. Repr., Grand Rapids, MI: Kregel, 1993.

Chapell, Bryan. "A Pastoral Overview of Infant Baptism." In *The Case for Covenantal Infant Baptism*. Edited by Gregg Strawbridge. Phillipsburg, NJ: P&R, 2003.

Charlesworth, J. H., et al., eds. *The Messiah: Developments in Earliest Judaism and Christianity*. Minneapolis: Fortress, 1992.

Clark, R. Scott. "A Contemporary Reformed Defense of Infant Baptism," http://public.csusm.edu/public/guests/rsclark/Infant_Baptism.html, 1–29.

———. "Theses on Covenant Theology." Accessed at http://www.wscal.edu/clark/covtheses.php.

Clowney, Edmund P. *The Church: Sacraments, Worship, Ministry, Mission.* Downers Grove, IL: InterVarsity Press, 1995.

———. *Preaching and Biblical Theology.* Grand Rapids, MI: Eerdmans, 1961.

Cole, Graham A. *He Who Gives Life: The Doctrine of the Holy Spirit.* Wheaton, IL: Crossway, 2007.

Collins, John J. *King and Messiah as Son of God: Divine, Human, and Angelic Messianic Figures in Biblical and Related Literature.* Grand Rapids, MI: Eerdmans, 2008.

Compton, Jared M. "Shared Intentions? Reflections on Inspiration and Interpretation in Light of Scripture's Dual Authorship." *Themelios* 33 (2008).

Cullmann, Oscar. *Christ and Time.* Translated by Floyd V. Filson. Philadelphia: Westminster, 1950.

Davidson, Richard. *Typology in Scripture: A Study of Hermeneutical TUPOS Structures.* Andrews University Seminary Doctoral Dissertation Series 2. Berrien Springs, MI: Andrews University, 1981.

Davies, W. D. *The Gospel and the Land: Early Christianity and Jewish Territorial Doctrine.* Berkeley: University of California Press, 1974.

Demarest, Bruce. *The Cross and Salvation.* Wheaton, IL: Crossway, 1997.

Dempster, Stephen G. *Dominion and Dynasty: A Biblical Theology of the Hebrew Bible.* New Studies in Biblical Theology 15. Downers Grove, IL: InterVarsity Press, 2003.

———. "An 'Extraordinary Fact:' *Torah* and Temple and the Contours of the Hebrew Canon, Part 1." *Tyndale Bulletin* 48/1 (1997): 23–56.

———. "An 'Extraordinary Fact:' *Torah* and Temple and the Contours of the Hebrew Canon, Part 2." *Tyndale Bulletin* 48/2 (1997): 191–218.

Douty, Norman. *Did Christ Die Only for the Elect?* Eugene, OR: Wipf & Stock, 1998.

Driscoll, Mark, and Gerry Breshears, *Death by Love.* Wheaton, IL: Crossway, 2008.

Dumbrell, William J. *Covenant and Creation: A Theology of the Old Testament Covenants.* Carlisle, UK: Paternoster, 1984.

———. *The Search for Order: Biblical Eschatology in Focus.* Grand Rapids, MI: Baker, 1994.

Dunn, James D. G. *Baptism in the Holy Spirit.* London: SCM, 1970.

Dunn, Matthew W. I. "Raymond Brown and the *Sensus Plenior* Interpretation of the Bible." *Studies in Religion* 36 (2007): 531–551.

Erickson, Millard. *Christian Theology.* 2nd ed. Grand Rapids, MI: Baker, 1998.

Feinberg, John S., ed. *Continuity and Discontinuity: Perspectives on the Relationship Between the Old and New Testaments.* Wheaton, IL: Crossway, 1988.

Feinberg, John S. "Systems of Discontinuity." In *Continuity and Discontinuity: Perspectives on the Relationship between the Old and New Testaments.* Edited by John S. Feinberg. 63–86. Wheaton, IL: Crossway, 1988.

Feinberg, Paul D. "Hermeneutics of Discontinuity." In *Continuity and Discontinuity: Perspectives on the Relationship between the Old and New Testaments.* Wheaton, IL: Crossway, 1988.

Ferguson, Sinclair B. *The Holy Spirit.* Downers Grove, IL: InterVarsity Press, 1996.

———. "How Does the Bible Look at Itself?" In *Inerrancy and Hermeneutic.* Edited by Harvie M. Conn. 47–66. Grand Rapids, MI: Baker, 1988.

Fesko, J. V. "On the Antiquity of Biblical Theology." In *Resurrection and Eschatology: Theology in Service of the Church.* Edited by L. G. Tipton and J. C. Waddington. 443–477. Phillipsburg, NJ: P&R, 2008.

Frame, John M. *The Doctrine of God.* Phillipsburg, NJ: P&R, 2002.

———. *The Doctrine of the Knowledge of God.* Phillipsburg, NJ: P&R, 1987.

———. *The Doctrine of the Word of God.* Phillipsburg, NJ: P&R, 2010.

———. "Scripture Speaks for Itself." In *God's Inerrant Word*. Edited by John W. Montgomery. 178–181. Minneapolis: Bethany, 1974.

Frei, Hans. *The Eclipse of Biblical Narrative: A Study in Eighteenth and Nineteenth Century Hermeneutics*. New Haven, CT: Yale University Press, 1980.

Fung, Ronald Y. K. *The Epistle to the Galatians*, New International Commentary on the New Testament. Grand Rapids, MI: Eerdmans, 1988.

Gaffin, Richard B., Jr., ed. *Redemptive History and Biblical Interpretation: The Shorter Writings of Geerhardus Vos*. Phillipsburg, NJ: P&R, 2001.

Gaffin, Richard B., Jr. "Systematic Theology and Biblical Theology." *Westminster Theological Journal* 38 (1976): 281–299.

Gathercole, Simon J. *The Preexistent Son: Recovering the Christologies of Matthew, Mark, and Luke*. Grand Rapids, MI: Eerdmans, 2006.

Geisler, Norman L. ed. *Inerrancy*. Grand Rapids, MI: Zondervan, 1979.

Golding, Peter. *Covenant Theology: The Key of Theology in Reformed Thought and Tradition*. Fearn, Ross-shire, UK: Mentor, 2004.

Goldsworthy, Graeme. *According to Plan: The Unfolding Revelation of God in the Bible*. Downers Grove, IL: InterVarsity Press, 2002.

———. *Gospel-Centered Hermeneutics: Foundations and Principles of Evangelical Biblical Interpretation*. Downers Grove, IL: InterVarsity Press, 2006.

———. "Kingdom of God." In *New Dictionary of Biblical Theology*. Edited by T. D. Alexander, Brian S. Rosner, D. A. Carson, and Graeme Goldsworthy. 615–620. Downers Grove, IL: InterVarsity Press, 2000.

———. *Preaching the Whole Bible as Christian Scripture: The Application of Biblical Theology to Expository Preaching*. Grand Rapids, MI: Eerdmans, 2000.

———. "Relationship of Old Testament and New Testament." In *New Dictionary of Biblical Theology*. Edited by T. D. Alexander, Brian S. Rosner, D. A. Carson, and Graeme Goldsworthy. 81–89. Downers Grove, IL: InterVarsity Press, 2000.

Goppelt, Leonhard, *Typos: The Typological Interpretation of the Old Testament in the New*. Translated by D. H. Madvig. Grand Rapids, MI: Eerdmans, 1982.

Grenz, Stanley J. *A Primer on Postmodernism*. Grand Rapids, MI: Eerdmans, 1996.

Grenz, Stanley J., and Roger Olson. *20th Century Theology: God and the World in a Transitional Age*. Downers Grove, IL: InterVarsity Press, 1992.

Grudem, Wayne. *1 Peter*. Tyndale New Testament Commentaries. Grand Rapids, MI: Eerdmans, 1988.

———. "Scripture's Self-Attestation and the Problem of Formulating a Doctrine of Scripture." In *Scripture and Truth*. Edited by D. A. Carson and John Woodbridge. 19–59. Grand Rapids, MI: Zondervan, 1983.

———. *Systematic Theology*. Grand Rapids, MI: Zondervan, 2000.

Gundry, Robert. "Why I Didn't Endorse 'The Gospel of Jesus Christ: An Evangelical Celebration' . . . Even though I Wasn't Asked To." *Books and Culture* 7/1 (2001): 6–9.

Hamilton, James M., Jr. *God's Glory in Salvation through Judgment: A Biblical Theology*. Wheaton, IL: Crossway, 2010.

———. *God's Indwelling Presence: The Holy Spirit in the Old and New Testaments*. Nashville: B&H, 2006.

Hannah, John D. ed. *Inerrancy and the Church*. Chicago: Moody, 1984.

Harris, Murray J. *Colossians and Philemon*. Exegetical Guide to the Greek New Testament. Grand Rapids, MI: Eerdmans, 1991.

————. *Jesus as God: The New Testament Use of* Theos *in Reference to Jesus*. Grand Rapids, MI: Baker, 1992.

————. *Three Crucial Questions about Jesus*. Grand Rapids, MI: Baker, 1994.

Hasel, Gerhard F. "The Nature of Biblical Theology: Recent Trends and Issues." *Andrews University Seminary Studies* 32/3 (1994): 211–214.

————. *Old Testament Theology: Basic Issues in the Current Debate*. 2nd ed. Grand Rapids, MI: Eerdmans, 1991.

————. "The Relationship between Biblical Theology and Systematic Theology." *Trinity Journal* 5 (1984): 113–127.

Hays, Richard B. *The Conversion of the Imagination*. Grand Rapids, MI: Eerdmans, 2005.

————. *Echoes of Scripture in the Letters of Paul*. New Haven, CT: Yale University Press, 1989.

Helseth, Paul Kjoss. *"Right Reason" and the Princeton Mind: An Unorthodox Proposal*. Phillipsburg, NJ: P&R, 2010.

Hester, James D. *Paul's Concept of Inheritance: A Contribution to the Understanding of Heilsgeschichte*. Scottish Journal of Theology Occasional Papers 14. Edinburgh: Oliver & Boyd, 1968.

Hoch, Carl B., Jr. *All Things New*. Grand Rapids, MI: Baker, 1995.

Hodge, Charles. *Systematic Theology*. 1852. Repr., Grand Rapids, MI: Eerdmans, 1982.

Hoekema, Anthony A. *The Bible and the Future*. Grand Rapids, MI: Eerdmans, 1994.

————. *Created in God's Image*. Grand Rapids, MI: Eerdmans, 1986.

Hoffecker, W. Andrew, ed. *Revolutions in Worldview: Understanding the Flow of Western Thought*. Phillipsburg, NJ: P&R, 2007.

Horton, Michael S. *The Christian Faith*. Grand Rapids, MI: Zondervan, 2011.

————. *Covenant and Eschatology: The Divine Drama*. Louisville: Westminster John Knox, 2002.

————. *God of Promise: Introducing Covenant Theology*. Grand Rapids, MI: Baker, 2006.

Hoskins, Paul M. *Jesus as the Fulfillment of the Temple in the Gospel of John*. Eugene, OR: Wipf & Stock Publishers, 2006.

House, H. Wayne, ed. *Israel: The Land and the People*. Grand Rapids, MI: Kregel, 1998.

House, Paul R. *Old Testament Theology*. Downers Grove, IL: InterVarsity Press, 1998.

Husbands, Mark, and Daniel J. Treier, eds. *Justification: What's at Stake in the Current Debates?* Downers Grove, IL: InterVarsity Press, 2005.

Jewett, Paul K. *Infant Baptism and the Covenant of Grace*. Grand Rapids, MI: Eerdmans, 1978.

Johnson, Elliott E. "Covenants in Traditional Dispensationalism." In *Three Central Issues in Contemporary Dispensationalism: A Comparison of Traditional and Progressive Views*. Edited by Herbert W. Bateman IV. 121–168. Grand Rapids, MI: Kregel, 1999.

Johnston, Philip, and Peter W. L. Walker, eds. *The Land of Promise: Biblical, Theological, and Contemporary Perspectives*. Downers Grove, IL: InterVarsity Press, 2000.

Kaiser, Walter C., Jr. "The Blessing of David: The Charter for Humanity." In *The Law and the Prophets*. Edited by John H. Skilton. Nutley, NJ: P&R, 1974.

————. "Israel and Its Land in Biblical Perspective." In *The Old Testament in the Life of God's People: Essays in Honor of Elmer A. Martens*. Edited by Jon Isaak. Winona Lake, IN: Eisenbrauns, 2009.

————. *The Messiah in the Old Testament*. Grand Rapids, MI: Zondervan, 1995.

————. *Toward Rediscovering the Old Testament*. Grand Rapids, MI: Zondervan, 1987.

Kaiser, Walter C., and Moisés Silva. *Introduction to Biblical Hermeneutics: The Search for Meaning*. 2nd ed. Grand Rapids, MI: Zondervan, 2007.

Kirk, J. R. Daniel. "The Sufficiency of the Cross (I): The Crucifixion as Jesus' Act of Obedience." *The Scottish Bulletin of Evangelical Theology* 24/1 (2006): 36–64.

———. "The Sufficiency of the Cross (II): The Law, the Cross, and Justification." *The Scottish Bulletin of Evangelical Theology* 24/2 (2006): 133–154.

Kline, Meredith G. *The Structure of Biblical Authority.* Grand Rapids, MI: Eerdmans, 1975.

Köstenberger, Andreas J. *John.* Baker Exegetical Commentary on the New Testament. Grand Rapids, MI: Baker, 2004.

Kulikovsky, Andrew S. *Creation, Fall, Restoration: A Biblical Theology of Creation.* Fearn, Ross-shire, UK: Mentor, 2009.

Ladd, G. E. "Biblical Theology, History of," and "Biblical Theology, Nature of." In *International Standard Bible Encyclopedia.* Rev. ed. 4 vols. 1:498–509. Grand Rapids, MI: Eerdmans, 1979.

———. "Kingdom of Christ, God, Heaven." In *Evangelical Dictionary of Theology.* Edited by W. A. Elwell. 607–611. Grand Rapids, MI: Baker, 1984.

———. *The Presence of the Future: The Eschatology of Biblical Realism.* Rev. ed. Grand Rapids, MI: Eerdmans, 1974.

LaHaye, Tim, and Jerry Jenkins, *Left Behind: A Novel of the Earth's Last Days.* Carol Stream, IL: Tyndale, 1996.

Lake, Donald. "He Died for All." In *Grace Unlimited.* Edited by Clark H. Pinnock. 31–50. Minneapolis: Bethany, 1975.

Lane, William L. *Hebrews 1–8.* Word Biblical Commentary 47a. Dallas: Word, 1991.

———. *Hebrews 9–13.* Word Biblical Commentary 47b. Dallas: Word, 1991.

Lehrer, Steven, ed. *Journal of New Covenant Theology.*

Letham, Robert. *The Holy Trinity: In Scripture, History, Theology, and Worship.* Phillipsburg, NJ: P&R, 2004.

———. *The Work of Christ.* Downers Grove, IL: InterVarsity Press, 1993.

Lightner, Robert. *The Death Christ Died.* 2nd ed. Grand Rapids, MI: Kregel, 1998.

Lindbeck, George A. *The Nature of Doctrine: Religion and Theology in a Postliberal Age.* 25th anniversary edition. Louisville: Westminster John Knox, 2009.

Lindsey, Hal. *The Late Great Planet Earth.* Grand Rapids, MI: Zondervan, 1973.

———. *There's a New World Coming.* Santa Ana, CA: Vision, 1974.

Lints, Richard. *The Fabric of Theology: A Prolegomenon to Evangelical Theology.* Grand Rapids, MI: Eerdmans, 1993.

Long, Gary D. *Definite Atonement.* Phillipsburg, NJ: P&R, 1977.

Longenecker, Richard N. *Galatians.* Word Biblical Commentary 41. Dallas: Word, 1990.

Lusk, Rich. "Do I Believe in Baptismal Regeneration?" Accessed at http://www.auburnavenue.org/Articles/DO%20I%20BELIEVE%20IN%20BAPTISMAL%20REGENERATION.htm.

Manson, W. "Eschatology in the New Testament." In *Eschatology,* Scottish Journal of Theology Occasional Papers 2. Edinburgh: Oliver & Boyd, 1953.

Marshall, I. Howard. *New Testament Theology.* Downers Grove, IL: InterVarsity Press, 2004.

———. "Universal Grace and Atonement in the Pastoral Epistles." In *The Grace of God, the Will of Man.* Edited by Clark H. Pinnock. Grand Rapids, MI: Zondervan, 1989.

Martin, Hugh. *The Atonement: In Its Relations to the Covenant, the Priesthood, the Intercession of Our Lord.* Edinburgh: James Gemmell, 1882.

Mathison, Keith A. *From Age to Age: The Unfolding of Biblical Eschatology.* Phillipsburg, NJ: P&R, 2009.

McCartney, Dan, and Charles Clayton. *Let the Reader Understand: A Guide to Interpreting and Applying the Bible.* 2nd ed. Phillipsburg, NJ: P&R, 2002.

McCartney, Dan G. "*Ecce Homo*: The Coming of the Kingdom as the Restoration of Human Viceregency." *Westminster Theological Journal* 56 (1994): 1–21.

McCormick, Micah J. *The Active Obedience of Jesus Christ.* PhD diss., The Southern Baptist Theological Seminary, 2010.

Mendenhall, George E. *Law and Covenant in Israel and the Ancient Near East.* Pittsburgh: The Biblical Colloquium, 1955.

Merrill, Eugene H. "Covenant and the Kingdom: Genesis 1–3 as Foundation for Biblical Theology." *Criswell Theological Review* 1/2 (1987): 295–308.

————. "The Covenant with Abraham: The Keystone of Biblical Architecture." *Journal of Dispensational Theology* 12 (2008): 5–17.

————. *Everlasting Dominion: A Theology of the Old Testament.* Nashville: B&H, 2006.

Metzger, Bruce M. *A Textual Commentary on the Greek New Testament.* 2nd ed. Peabody, MA: Hendrickson, 2005.

Meyer, Jason C. *The End of the Law: Mosaic Covenant in Pauline Theology.* Nashville: B&H Academic, 2009.

Miethe, Terry. "The Universal Power of the Atonement." In *The Grace of God, the Will of Man.* Edited by Clark H. Pinnock. 71–96. Grand Rapids, MI: Zondervan, 1989.

Millar, J. G. "Land." In *New Dictionary of Biblical Theology.* Edited by T. D. Alexander, Brian S. Rosner, D. A. Carson, and Graeme Goldsworthy. 623–627. Downers Grove, IL: InterVarsity Press, 2000.

Moo, Douglas J. *The Epistle to the Romans,* New International Commentary on the New Testament. Grand Rapids, MI: Eerdmans, 1996.

————. "The Law of Christ as the Fulfillment of the Law of Moses." In *The Law, the Gospel, and the Modern Christian: Five Views.* Edited by Wayne G. Strickland. Grand Rapids, MI: Zondervan, 1993.

————. "The Problem of Sensus Plenior." In *Hermeneutics, Authority, and Canon.* Edited by D. A. Carson and John D. Woodbridge. 179–211. Grand Rapids, MI: Zondervan, 1986.

Morgan, Christopher W., and Robert A. Peterson, eds. *The Deity of Christ.* Wheaton, IL: Crossway, 2011.

Motyer, J. Alec. *The Prophecy of Isaiah: An Introduction and Commentary.* Downers Grove, IL: InterVarsity Press, 1993.

Motyer, S. "Israel (nation)." In *New Dictionary of Biblical Theology.* Edited by T. D. Alexander, Brian S. Rosner, D. A. Carson, and Graeme Goldsworthy. 581–587. Downers Grove, IL: InterVarsity Press, 2000.

Muller, Richard. *Post-Reformation Reformed Dogmatics: The Rise and Development of Reformed Orthodoxy, ca. 1520 to ca. 1725.* 4 vols. Grand Rapids, MI: Baker, 2003.

Murray, John. "The Atonement." In *Collected Writings of John Murray.* 4 vols. 2:142–150. Carlisle, PA: Banner of Truth, 1977.

————. "Baptism." In *Collected Writings of John Murray.* 4 vols. 2:370–375. Carlisle, PA: Banner of Truth, 1977.

————. *Christian Baptism.* Phillipsburg, NJ: P&R, 1980.

————. "Covenant Theology." In *Collected Writings of John Murray.* 4 vols. 4:216–240. Carlisle, PA: Banner of Truth, 1982.

————. *Redemption Accomplished and Applied.* Grand Rapids, MI: Eerdmans, 1955.

Nelson, David. "The Design, Nature, and Extent of the Atonement." In *Calvinism: A Southern Baptist Dialogue.* Edited by E. Ray Clendenen and Brad Waggoner. Nashville: B&H, 2008.

Nelson, Richard. *Raising Up a Faithful Priest.* Louisville: Westminster John Knox, 1993.

Niehaus, Jeffrey J. "An Argument against Theologically Constructed Covenants." *Journal of the Evangelical Theological Society* 50/2 (2007): 259–273.

Niell, Jeffrey D. "The Newness of the New Covenant." In *The Case for Covenantal Infant Baptism.* Edited by Gregg Strawbridge. 127–155. Phillipsburg, NJ: P&R, 2003.

Ninow, Friedbert. *Indicators of Typology within the Old Testament: The Exodus Motif.* Berlin: Peter Lang, 2001.

Noble, Paul. *The Canonical Approach: A Critical Reconstruction of the Hermeneutics of Brevard S. Childs.* Leiden, Netherlands: Brill Academic, 1995.

O'Brien, Peter T. "Church." In *Dictionary of Paul and His Letters.* Edited by Gerald F. Hawthorne, et al. 123–131. Downers Grove, IL: InterVarsity Press, 1993.

———. *Colossians and Philemon.* Word Biblical Commentary 44. Dallas: Word, 1982.

———. *The Letter to the Hebrews.* Pillar New Testament Commentary. Grand Rapids, MI: Eerdmans, 2010.

Ortlund, Raymond C., Jr. *God's Unfaithful Wife.* New Studies in Biblical Theology 2. Downers Grove, IL: InterVarsity Press, 2003.

Osborne, Grant R. *The Hermeneutical Spiral: A Comprehensive Introduction to Biblical Interpretation.* 2nd ed. Downers Grove, IL: InterVarsity Press, 2006.

Oss, Douglas A. "Canon as Context: The Function of *Sensus Plenior* in Evangelical Hermeneutics." *Grace Theological Journal* 9 (1988): 105–127.

Owen, John. *The Death of Death in the Death of Christ.* 1648. Repr., Carlisle, PA: Banner of Truth, 1983.

Packer, J. I. *Concise Theology.* Wheaton, IL: Tyndale, 1993.

Parker, Brent E. "Paedocommunion, Paedobaptism, and Covenant Theology: A Baptist Critique and Assessment." Unpublished paper.

Patterson, Paige. "The Work of Christ." In *A Theology for the Church.* Edited by Daniel Akin. 545–602. Nashville: B&H, 2007.

Pennington, Jonathan. *Heaven and Earth in the Gospel of Matthew.* Novum Testamentum Supplements 126. Leiden, Netherlands: Brill, 2007.

Pinnock, Clark H., ed. *The Grace of God, the Will of Man.* Grand Rapids, MI: Zondervan, 1989.

———. *Grace Unlimited.* Minneapolis: Bethany, 1975.

Plantinga, Alvin. "Methodological Naturalism?" *Origins and Design* 18/1. Accessed at http://www.arn.org/docs/odesign/od181/methnat181.htm

———. "Methodological Naturalism? Part 2" *Origins and Design* 18/2. Accessed at http://www.arn.org/docs/odesign/od182/methnat182.htm.

Porter, Stanley, ed. *The Messiah in the Old and New Testaments.* Grand Rapids, MI: Eerdmans, 2007.

Poythress, Vern S. *The Shadow of Christ in the Law of Moses.* Phillipsburg, NJ: P&R, 1995.

———. *Understanding Dispensationalists.* 2nd ed. Phillipsburg, NJ: P&R, 1994.

Pratt, Richard L., Jr. "Infant Baptism in the New Covenant." In *The Case for Covenantal Infant Baptism.* Edited by Gregg Strawbridge. 156–174. Phillipsburg, NJ: P&R, 2003.

Radmacher, Earl D., and Robert D. Preus, eds. *Hermeneutics, Inerrancy, and the Bible.* Grand Rapids, MI: Zondervan, 1984.

Reisinger, John G. *Abraham's Four Seeds.* Frederick, MD: New Covenant Media, 1998.

Reventlow, H. G. "Theology (Biblical), History of." In *Anchor Bible Dictionary.* Edited by David Noel Freedman. 6 vols. 6:483–505. New York: Doubleday, 1992.

Reymond, Robert L. *Jesus, Divine Messiah: The New and Old Testament Witness.* Fearn, Ross-shire, UK: Mentor, 2003.

———. *A New Systematic Theology of the Christian Faith.* Nashville: Thomas Nelson, 1998.

Ridderbos, Herman. *Paul: An Outline of His Theology.* Translated by John Richard de Witt. Grand Rapids, MI: Eerdmans, 1975.

Robertson, O. Palmer. *The Christ of the Covenants.* Grand Rapids, MI: Baker, 1980.

———. *The Israel of God: Yesterday, Today, and Tomorrow.* Phillipsburg, NJ: P&R, 2000.

Roger, Jack B., and Donald K. McKim. *The Authority and Interpretation of the Bible.* San Francisco: Harper & Row, 1979.

Rosner, Brian. "Biblical Theology." In *New Dictionary of Biblical Theology.* Edited by T. D. Alexander, Brian S. Rosner, D. A. Carson, and Graeme Goldsworthy. 3–11. Downers Grove, IL: InterVarsity Press, 2000.

Ross, Hugh. *Creation and Time: A Biblical and Scientific Perspective on the Creation-Date Controversy.* Colorado Springs: NavPress, 1994.

Ross, Mark E. "Baptism and Circumcision as Signs and Seals." In *The Case for Covenantal Infant Baptism.* Edited by Gregg Strawbridge. 85–111. Phillipsburg, NJ: P&R, 2003.

Ryrie, Charles C. *Dispensationalism.* Rev. ed. Chicago: Moody, 2007.

Sailhamer, John H. *Introduction to Old Testament Theology: A Canonical Approach.* Grand Rapids, MI: Zondervan, 1995.

———. *The Pentateuch as Narrative: A Biblical-Theological Commentary.* Grand Rapids, MI: Zondervan, 1992.

Salter, Martin. "Does Baptism Replace Circumcision? An Examination of the Relationship between Circumcision and Baptism in Colossians 2:11–12." *Themelios* 35/1 (2010): 15–29.

Saucy, Robert L. *The Case for Progressive Dispensationalism.* Grand Rapids, MI: Zondervan, 1993.

Scalise, Charles J. "The 'Sensus Literalis': A Hermeneutical Key to Biblical Exegesis." *Scottish Journal of Theology* 42 (1989): 45–65.

Schaeffer, Francis A. *The God Who Is There.* Thirtieth anniversary ed. Downers Grove, IL: InterVarsity Press, 1998.

———. *He Is There and He Is Not Silent.* Carol Stream, IL: Tyndale, 1972.

Schilder, Klaas. *Christ Crucified.* Grand Rapids, MI: Eerdmans, 1940.

Schnabel, E. J. "Scripture." In *New Dictionary of Biblical Theology.* Edited by T. D. Alexander, Brian S. Rosner, D. A. Carson, and Graeme Goldsworthy. 34–43. Downers Grove, IL: InterVarsity Press, 2000.

Schreiner, Thomas R. *1, 2 Peter, Jude.* New American Commentary 37. Nashville: B&H, 2003.

———. *New Testament Theology: Magnifying God in Christ.* Grand Rapids, MI: Baker, 2008.

———. *Paul: Apostle of God's Glory in Christ.* Downers Grove, IL: InterVarsity Press, 2001.

———. *Romans.* Baker Exegetical Commentary on the New Testament. Grand Rapids, MI: Baker, 1998.

———. *Run to Win the Prize: Perseverance in the New Testament.* Wheaton, IL: Crossway, 2010.

Schreiner, Thomas R., and A. B. Caneday, *The Race Set before Us.* Downers Grove, IL: InterVarsity Press, 2001.

Schultz, Gary. "A Biblical and Theological Defense of a Multi-Intentional View of the Extent of the Atonement." PhD diss., The Southern Baptist Theological Seminary, 2008.

Scobie, C. H. H. "History of Biblical Theology." In *New Dictionary of Biblical Theology.* Edited by T. D. Alexander, Brian S. Rosner, D. A. Carson, and Graeme Goldsworthy. 11–20. Downers Grove, IL: InterVarsity Press, 2000.

Smith, Bill. "Infant Baptism, the New Man, and the New Creation: A Response to Stephen J. Wellum." Accessed at http://www.communitypca.org/wp-content/uploads/2007/11/infant-baptism-new-man-new-creation1.pdf.

Sproul, R. C. *Grace Unknown: The Heart of Reformed Theology.* Grand Rapids, MI: Baker, 1997.

Stein, Robert H. "Baptism and Becoming a Christian in the New Testament." *Southern Baptist Journal of Theology* 2/1 (1998): 6–17.

Stek, John H. "Biblical Typology Yesterday and Today." *Calvin Theological Journal* 5 (1970): 133–162.

Stott, John. *The Cross of Christ.* Downers Grove, IL: InterVarsity Press, 1986.

Strawbridge, Gregg. "Baptism and the Relationship between the Covenants: A Review." Accessed at www.paedobaptism.com/Wellum/pdf, 1–7.

———, ed. *The Case for Covenant Communion.* Monroe, LA: Athanasius, 2006.

———. "Introduction." In *The Case for Covenantal Infant Baptism.* Edited by Gregg Strawbridge. 4–5. Phillipsburg, NJ: P&R, 2003.

Streett, Daniel R. "As It Was in the Days of Noah: The Prophets' Typological Interpretation of Noah's Flood." *Criswell Theological Review* 5 (2007): 33–51.

Strickland, Wayne G., ed. *The Law, the Gospel, and the Modern Christian: Five Views.* Grand Rapids, MI: Zondervan, 1993.

Strong, A. H. *Outlines of Systematic Theology.* Valley Forge, PA: Judson, 1907.

Tidball, D. J. "Church." *New Dictionary of Biblical Theology.* Edited by T. D. Alexander, Brian S. Rosner, D. A. Carson, and Graeme Goldsworthy. 407–411. Downers Grove, IL: InterVarsity Press, 2000.

Treier, Daniel J. *Introducing Theological Interpretation of Scripture: Recovering a Christian Practice.* Grand Rapids, MI: Baker, 2008.

———. "Typology." In *Dictionary for Theological Interpretation of the Bible.* Edited by Kevin J. Vanhoozer. 823–827. Grand Rapids, MI: Baker, 2005.

Turner, David L. "The Continuity of Scripture and Eschatology: Key Hermeneutical Issues." *Grace Theological Journal* 6/2 (1985): 275–287.

Turner, Max. "Holy Spirit." In *New Dictionary of Biblical Theology.* Edited by T. D. Alexander, Brian S. Rosner, D. A. Carson, and Graeme Goldsworthy. 551–558. Downers Grove, IL: InterVarsity Press, 2000.

Turretin, Francis. *Institutes of Elenctic Theology.* Edited by James T. Dennison, Jr. Translated by George Musgrave Giger. 3 vols. Phillipsburg, NJ: P&R, 1994.

Van Court, Gregory A. *The Obedience of Christ.* Frederick, MD: New Covenant Media, 2005.

VanGemeren, Willem. "Israel as the Hermeneutical Crux in the Interpretation of Prophecy (II)." *Westminster Theological Journal* 46 (1984).

———. "Systems of Continuity." In *Continuity and Discontinuity: Perspectives on the Relationship between the Old and New Testaments.* 37–62. Wheaton, IL: Crossway, 1988.

Vanhoozer, Kevin J. *The Drama of Doctrine: A Canonical Linguistic Approach to Christian Doctrine.* Louisville: Westminster John Knox, 2005.

———. "Exegesis and Hermeneutics." In *New Dictionary of Biblical Theology.* Edited by T. D. Alexander, Brian S. Rosner, D. A. Carson, and Graeme Goldsworthy. 52–64. Downers Grove, IL: InterVarsity Press, 2000.

———. *First Theology: God, Scripture, and Hermeneutics.* Downers Grove, IL: InterVarsity Press, 2002.

———. "God's Mighty Speech-Acts: The Doctrine of Scripture Today." In *A Pathway into the Holy Scripture.* Edited by Philip E. Satterthwaite and David F. Wright. 143–182. Grand Rapids, MI: Eerdmans, 1994.

———. *Is There a Meaning in This Text? The Bible, the Reader and the Morality of Literary Knowledge.* Grand Rapids, MI: Zondervan, 1998.

———. "Wrighting the Wrongs of the Reformation? The State of the Union with Christ in St. Paul and Protestant Soteriology." In *Jesus, Paul and the People of God: A Theological Dialogue with N. T. Wright.* Edited by Nicholas Perrin and Richard B. Hays. Downers Grove, IL: InterVarsity Press, 2011.

Venema, Cornelius P. *Children at the Lord's Table?* Grand Rapids, MI: Reformation Heritage, 2009.

———. "Covenant Theology and Baptism." In *The Case for Covenantal Infant Baptism.* Edited by Gregg Strawbridge. Phillipsburg, NJ: P&R, 2003.

Vickers, Brian. *Jesus' Blood and Righteousness: Paul's Theology of Imputation.* Wheaton, IL: Crossway, 2006.

von Rad, Gerhard. *Genesis: A Commentary.* Translated by J. Marks. Philadelphia: Fortress, 1976.

Vos, Geerhardus. *Biblical Theology: Old and New Testaments.* Grand Rapids, MI: Eerdmans, 1948. Repr., Carlisle, PA: Banner of Truth, 2004.

———. "The Doctrine of the Covenant in Reformed Theology." In *Redemptive History and Biblical Interpretation: The Shorter Writings of Geerhardus Vos.* Edited by Richard B. Gaffin, Jr. Phillipsburg, NJ: P&R, 1979.

———. "The Eschatological Aspect of the Pauline Conception of the Spirit." In *Redemptive History and Biblical Interpretation: The Shorter Writings of Geerhardus Vos.* Edited by Richard B. Gaffin, Jr. 91–125. Phillipsburg, NJ: P&R, 1979.

———. *Pauline Eschatology.* Phillipsburg, NJ: P&R, 1979.

Waldron, Samuel, with Richard Barcellos. *A Reformed Baptist Manifesto.* Palmdale, CA: Reformed Baptist Academic Press, 2004.

Walker, Peter W. L. "The Land in the Apostles' Writings." In *The Land of Promise: Biblical, Theological, and Contemporary Perspectives.* Edited by Philip Johnston and Peter Walker. Downers Grove, IL: InterVarsity Press, 2000.

Waltke, Bruce K. "The Kingdom of God in Biblical Theology." In *Looking into the Future: Evangelical Studies in Eschatology.* Edited by David W. Baker. 15–27. Grand Rapids, MI: Baker, 2001.

———. "The Phenomenon of Conditionality within Unconditional Covenants." In *Israel's Apostasy and Restoration: Essays in Honor of Roland K. Harrison.* Edited by Avraham Gileadi. 123–139. Grand Rapids, MI: Baker, 1988.

Waltke, Bruce K. with Charles Yu. *An Old Testament Theology.* Grand Rapids, MI: Zondervan, 2007.

Walton, John H. *Covenant: God's Purpose, God's Plan.* Grand Rapids, MI: Zondervan, 1994.

Walvoord, John F. "Biblical Kingdoms Compared and Contrasted." In *Issues in Dispensationalism.* Edited by Wesley R. Willis, John R. Master, Charles C. Ryrie, et al. 75–91. Chicago: Moody, 1994.

Ward, Timothy. *Words of Life: Scripture as the Living and Active Word of God.* Downers Grove, IL: InterVarsity Press, 2009.

Ware, Bruce A. "The New Covenant and the People(s) of God." In *Dispensationalism, Israel, and the Church: A Search for Definition.* Edited by Craig A. Blaising and Darrell L. Bock. 68–97. Grand Rapids, MI: Zondervan, 1992.

Warfield, B. B. "The Spirit of God in the Old Testament." In *Biblical Doctrines.* 121–128. New York: Oxford University Press, 1929. Repr., Carlisle, PA: Banner of Truth, 1988.

Watts, R. E. "Exodus." In *New Dictionary of Biblical Theology.* Edited by T. D. Alexander, Brian S. Rosner, D. A. Carson, and Graeme Goldsworthy. 478–487. Downers Grove, IL: InterVarsity Press, 2000.

Webster, John. "Principles of Systematic Theology." *International Journal of Systematic Theology* 11/1 (2009): 56–71.

———. "Systematic Theology." In *The Oxford Handbook of Systematic Theology*. Edited by John Webster, Kathryn Tanner, and Iain Torrance. 1–18. Oxford: Oxford University Press, 2007.

Weinfeld, Moshe. *The Promise of the Land: The Inheritance of the Land of Canaan by the Israelites.* Berkeley: University of California Press, 1993.

Wells, David F. *God the Evangelist*. Grand Rapids, MI: Eerdmans, 1987.

———. *Losing Our Virtue*. Grand Rapids, MI: Eerdmans, 1999.

———. *The Person of Christ*. Wheaton, IL: Crossway, 1984.

Wells, Tom, and Fred Zaspel, *New Covenant Theology*. Frederick, MD: New Covenant Media, 2002.

Wellum, Stephen J. "Baptism and the Relationship between the Covenants." In *Believer's Baptism: Sign of the New Covenant in Christ*. Edited by Thomas R. Schreiner and Shawn D. Wright. 97–161. Nashville: B&H, 2006.

———. "The Inerrancy of Scripture." In *Beyond the Bounds: Open Theism and the Undermining of Biblical Christianity*. Edited by Paul K. Helseth, Justin Taylor, et al. 237–274. Wheaton, IL: Crossway, 2003.

———. "The New Covenant Work of Christ: Priesthood, Atonement, and Intercession." In *From Heaven He Came and Sought Her: Definite Atonement in Biblical, Theological, and Pastoral Perspective*. Edited by David Gibson and Jonathan Gibson. Wheaton, IL: Crossway, forthcoming.

Wenham, Gordon J. *Genesis 1–15*. Word Biblical Commentary 1. Waco, TX: Word, 1987.

Wenham, John. *Christ and the Bible*. 3rd ed. Grand Rapids, MI: Baker, 1994.

White, A. Blake. *The Newness of the New Covenant*. Frederick, MD: New Covenant Media, 2007.

White, James R. "The Newness of the New Covenant: Part 1" *Reformed Baptist Theological Review* 1/2 (2004): 144–152.

———. "The Newness of the New Covenant: Part 2." *Reformed Baptist Theological Review* 2/1 (2005).

White, R. F. "The Last Adam and His Seed: An Exercise in Theological Preemption." *Trinity Journal* n.s. 6/1 (1985).

Williams, Garry. "The Cross and the Punishment of Sin." In *Where Wrath and Mercy Meet: Proclaiming the Atonement Today*. Edited by David Peterson. 68–99. Carlisle, UK: Paternoster, 2001.

Williams, Michael D. *Far as the Curse Is Found: The Covenant Story of Redemption*. Phillipsburg, NJ: P&R, 2005.

———. *This World Is Not My Home: The Origins and Development of Dispensationalism*. Fearn, Ross-shire, UK: Mentor, 2003.

Williamson, Paul R. "Promise and Fulfillment: The Territorial Inheritance." In *The Land of Promise: Biblical, Theological, and Contemporary Perspectives*. Edited by Philip Johnston and Peter W. L. Walker. Downers Grove, IL: InterVarsity Press, 2000.

———. *Sealed with an Oath: Covenant in God's Unfolding Purpose*. New Studies in Biblical Theology 23; Downers Grove, IL: InterVarsity Press, 2007.

Willis, Wesley R., John R. Master, and Charles C. Ryrie, eds. *Issues in Dispensationalism.* Chicago: Moody, 1994.

Wilson, Alistair I., and Jamie A. Grant. "Introduction." In *The God of Covenant: Biblical, Theological, and Contemporary Perspectives*. Edited by Jamie A. Grant and Alistair I. Wilson. Leicester: Apollos, 2005.

Wilson, Douglas. *To a Thousand Generations: Infant Baptism—Covenant Mercy for the People of God*. Moscow, ID: Canon, 1996.

Woodbridge, John D. *Biblical Authority*. Grand Rapids, MI: Zondervan, 1982.

Wright, C. J. H. *God's People in God's Land: Family, Land, and Property.* Grand Rapids, MI: Eerdmans, 1994.

Wright, David F., ed. *A Pathway into the Holy Scriptures*. Grand Rapids, MI: Eerdmans, 1994.

Wright, David F. "Recovering Baptism for a New Age of Mission." In *Doing Theology for the People of God: Studies in Honor of J. I. Packer*. Edited by Donald Lewis and Alister McGrath. 51–66. Downers Grove, IL: InterVarsity Press, 1996.

Wright, N. T. "Jesus." In *New Dictionary of Theology*. Edited by Sinclair B. Ferguson, et al. Downers Grove, IL: InterVarsity Press, 1988.

―――. *The New Testament and the People of God*. Minneapolis: Fortress, 1992.

Yarbrough, Robert. *The Salvation Historical Fallacy? Reassessing the History of NT Theology*. Leiden, Netherlands: Deo, 2004.

BIBLIOGRAPHY FOR PART 2

Aejmelaeus, A. "Function and Interpretation of כי in Biblical Hebrew." *Journal of Biblical Literature* 105/2 (1986): 193–209.

Alexander, T. Desmond. *From Eden to the New Jerusalem: An Introduction to Biblical Theology.* Grand Rapids, MI: Kregel, 2008.

———. "Further Observations of the Term 'Seed' in Genesis." *Tyndale Bulletin* 48/1 (1997): 363–367.

———. "Genesis 22 and the Covenant of Circumcision." *Journal for the Study of the Old Testament* 25 (1983): 17–22.

———. "A Literary Analysis of the Abraham Narrative in Genesis." PhD diss., The Queen's University of Belfast, 1982.

———. "The Regal Dimension of the תולדות־יעקב: Recovering the Literary Context of Genesis 37–50." In *Reading the Law: Studies in Honour of Gordon J. Wenham.* Edited by J. G. McConville and Karl Möller. Library of Hebrew Bible/Old Testament Studies 461. 254–266. New York: T. & T. Clark, 2007.

Andersen, Francis I. "Yahweh, the Kind and Sensitive God." In *God Who Is Rich in Mercy: Essays Presented to Dr. D. B. Knox.* Edited by Peter T. O'Brien and David G. Peterson. 41–87. Homebush West, NSW, Australia: Lancer, 1986.

Anderson, Bernhard W. "Exodus Typology in Second Isaiah." In *Israel's Prophetic Heritage: Essays in Honor of James Muilenburg.* Edited by Bernhard W. Anderson and Walter Harrelson. 177–195. New York: Harper, 1962.

Arnold, Bill T. *Genesis.* Cambridge: Cambridge University Press, 2009.

Baden, Joel S. "The Morpho-Syntax of Genesis 12:1–3: Translation and Interpretation." *Catholic Biblical Quarterly* 72 (2010): 223–237.

Baltzer, Klaus. *Deutero-Isaiah*, Hermeneia. Minneapolis: Fortress, 2001.

Barr, James. "The Image of God in the Book of Genesis—A Study of Terminology." *Bulletin of the John Rylands Library* 51 (1968–1969): 11–26.

———. "The Image of God in Genesis—Some Linguistic and Historical Considerations." In *Proceedings of the Tenth Meeting (1967) of Die Ou-Testamentiese Werkgemeenskap in Suid-Afrika.* Edited by A. H. van Zyl. 5–13. Pretoria: Craft, 1971.

Barth, Karl. *Church Dogmatics, 3/1.* Authorised translation by J. W. Edwards, O. Bussey, and Harold Knight. Edinburgh: T. & T. Clark, 1958.

———. *Church Dogmatics, 3/2.* Authorised translation by Harold Knight, G. W. Bromiley, J. K. Reid, and R. H. Fuller. Edinburgh: T. & T. Clark, 1960.

Barthélemy, Dominique. *Critique Textuelle de L'Ancien Testament, 1.* Josué, Juges, Ruth, Samuel, Rois, Chroniques, Esdras, Néhémie, Esther. Rapport final du Comité pour l'analyse textuelle de l'Ancien Testament hébreu institué par l'Alliance Biblique Universelle, établi en coopération avec Alexander R. Hulst, Norbert Lohfink, William D. McHardy, H. Peter Rüger, coéditeur, James A. Sanders, coéditeur. Orbis Biblicus et Orientalis 50/1. Göttingen, Germany: Vandenhoeck & Ruprecht, 1982.

Bartholomew, Craig G. "Covenant and Creation: Covenant Overload or Covenantal Deconstruction, *Calvin Theological Journal* 30 (1995): 11–33.

————. "The Theology of Place in Genesis 1–3." In *Reading the Law: Studies in Honour of Gordon J. Wenham*. Edited by J. G. McConville and Karl Möller. Library of Hebrew Bible/Old Testament Studies 461. 173–195. New York: T. & T. Clark, 2007.

————. "A Time for War and a Time for Peace: Old Testament Wisdom, Creation, and O'Donovan's Theological Ethics." In *A Royal Priesthood? The Use of the Bible Ethically and Politically—A Dialogue with Oliver O'Donovan*. Edited by Craig Bartholomew, Jonathan Chaplin, Robert Song, and Al Wolters. Grand Rapids, MI: Zondervan, 2002.

Barton, John. *Reading the Old Testament: Method in Biblical Study*. Philadelphia: Westminster, 1984.

Batto, Bernard F. *Slaying the Dragon: Mythmaking in the Biblical Tradition*. Louisville, KY: Westminster/John Knox, 1992.

Baudissin, W. W. "Der Begriff der Heiligkeit im Alten Testament." In *Studien zu semitischen Religionsgeschichte*. 2:1–142. Leipzig, Germany: Grunow, 1878.

Bauer, H., and P. Leander. *Historische Grammatik der hebräischen Sprache des Alten Testaments*. Halle, Germany: Max Niemeyer, 1922. Repr., Hildesheim, Germany: Georg Olms, 1991.

Bauer, Walter. *A Greek-English Lexicon of the New Testament and Other Early Christian Literature*. Translated and revised by W. F. Arndt and F. W. Gingrich. 2nd ed. Revised by F. W. Gingrich and F.W. Danker. Chicago: University of Chicago Press, 1979.

————. *A Greek-English Lexicon of the New Testament and Other Early Christian Literature*. 3rd ed. Revised and edited by F. W. Danker. Chicago: University of Chicago Press, 1957, 1979, 2000.

————. *Griechisch-deutsches Wörterbuch zu den Schriften des Neuen Testaments und der frühchristlichen Literatur*. 6th ed. Revised and edited by K. Aland and B. Aland. Berlin: Walter de Gruyter, 1988.

Beckerleg, Catherine. "The 'Image of God' in Eden: the Creation of Mankind in Genesis 2:5–3:24 in Light of the *mīs pî pīt pî* and *wpt-r* Rituals of Mesopotamia and Ancient Egypt." PhD diss., Harvard University, 2009.

————. "New Light on Genesis 1–3 and Man as the Image of God." Paper presented at the annual meeting of the Evangelical Theological Society, Providence, RI, November 19, 2008.

Beckman, Gary. *Hittite Diplomatic Texts*. 2nd ed. Atlanta: Scholars Press, 1995, 1999.

Beckwith, Roger. "Daniel 9 and the Date of Messiah's Coming in Essene, Hellenistic, Pharisaic, Zealot, and Early Christian Computation." *Revue de Qumrân* 40 (1981): 521–542.

————. *The Old Testament Canon of the New Testament Church and Its Background in Early Judaism*. Grand Rapids, MI: Eerdmans, 1985.

Bernat, David A. *Sign of the Covenant: Circumcision in the Priestly Tradition*. Atlanta: Society of Biblical Literature, 2009.

Beuken, W. A. M. "Isaiah 55, 3–5: the Reinterpretation of David." *Bijdragen* 35 (1974): 49–64.

————. "Isaiah LIV: The Multiple Identity of the Person Addressed." *Oudtestamentische Studiën* 19 (1974): 29–70.

Bivin, Bill. "Translating IM." Paper presented at 2010 Genesis Workshop, SIL International, Dallas, Texas, October 20, 2010.

Blenkinsopp, Joseph. *Isaiah 40–55*. Anchor Bible 19. New York: Doubleday, 2000.

Blocher, H. *In the Beginning*. Downers Grove, IL: InterVarsity Press, 1984.

Block, Daniel I. "Bearing the Name of the Lord with Honor." In *How I Love Your Torah, O LORD! Studies in the Book of Deuteronomy*. Eugene, OR: Cascade, 2011. 61–72 (originally published in *Bibliotheca Sacra* 168) [2011]: 20–31).

————. "The Burden of Leadership: The Mosaic Paradigm of Kingship (Deuteronomy 17:14–20)." In *How I Love Your Torah, O LORD!* 118–139 (originally published in *Bibliotheca Sacra* 162 [July–September 2005]: 259–278).

————. *Deuteronomy*. NIV Application Commentary. Grand Rapids, MI: Zondervan, 2012.

————. "The Foundations of National Identity: A Study in Ancient Northwest Semitic Perceptions." PhD diss., University of Liverpool, 1981.

————. *The Gospel according to Moses: Theological and Ethical Reflections on the Book of Deuteronomy*. Eugene, OR: Cascade, 2012.

————. *How I Love Your Torah, O Lord! Studies in the Book of Deuteronomy*. Eugene, OR: Cascade, 2011.

————. "Introduction to the Old Testament, Part I: Pentateuch and Historiographic Literature 20200." Course notes, The Southern Baptist Theological Seminary, 2004.

————. "My Servant David: Ancient Israel's Vision of the Messiah." In *Israel's Messiah in the Bible and the Dead Sea Scrolls*. Edited by Richard S. Hess and M. Daniel Carroll. 17–56. Grand Rapids, MI: Baker, 2003.

————. "Reading the Decalogue Right to Left: The Ten Principles of Covenant Relationship in the Hebrew Bible." In *How I Love Your Torah, O Lord! Studies in the Book of Deuteronomy*. Eugene, OR: Cascade, 2011. 56–60.

————. "A Study in Deuteronomic Domestic Ideology." In *The Gospel according to Moses: Theological and Ethical Reflections on the Book of Deuteronomy*. Eugene, OR: Cascade, 2012. 137–168 (originally published in *Journal of the Evangelical Theological Society* 53 [2010]: 449–474).

Boda, Mark J., and Jamie Novotny, eds. *From the Foundations to the Crenellations: Essays on Temple Building in the Ancient Near East and Hebrew Bible*. Alter Orient und Altes Testament 366. Münster, Germany: Ugarit-Verlag, 2010.

Bogaert, P.-M. "La *vetus latina* de Jérémie: texte très court, témoin de la plus ancienne Septante et d'une forme plus ancienne de l'hébreu (Jer 39 et 52)." In *The Earliest Text of the Hebrew Bible: The Relationship between the Masoretic Text and the Hebrew Base of the Septuagint Reconsidered*. Edited by Adrian Schenker. Septuagint and Cognate Studies 52. 51–82. Atlanta: Scholars Press, 2003.

————, ed. *Le Livre de Jérémie: le Prophet et son Milieu, les Oracles et leur Transmission*. Bibliotheca Ephemeridum Theologicarum Lovaniensium 54. Leuven, Belgium: Peeters, 1981.

Boned Colera, Pilar, and Juan Rodríguez Somolinos. *Repertorio Bibliográfico de la Lexicografía Griega, Diccionario Griego-Español Anejo 3*. Madrid: Consejo Superior de Investagaciones Cientificas, 1998.

Bordreuil, P., ed. *Ras Shamra-Ougarit*. Publications de la Mission Française Archéologique de Ras Shamra-Ougarit. Paris: Éditions Recherche sur les Civilisations, 1991–.

Bordreuil, P. *Une bibliothèque au sud de la ville: Ras Shamra-Ougarit VII*. Paris: Éditions Recherche sur les Civilisations, 1991.

Bottéro, J. "The 'Code' of Hammurabi." In *Mesopotamia: Writing, Reasoning and the Gods*. 156–184. Chicago: University of Chicago Press, 1992.

————. "Intelligence and the Technical Function of Power: Enki/Ea." In *Mesopotamia: Writing, Reasoning and the Gods*. 232–250. Chicago: University of Chicago, 1992.

Bright, John *Jeremiah*. Anchor Bible 21. New York: Doubleday, 1984.

Brockelmann, C. *Hebräische Syntax*. Neukirchen-Vluyn, Germany: Neukirchener, 1956.

Brown, Francis, S. R. Driver, and C. A. Briggs. *A Hebrew and English Lexicon of the Old Testament*. Oxford: Clarendon, 1907, 1953.

Brueggemann, Walter. *Isaiah 40–66*. Louisville: Westminster John Knox, 1998.

Butterworth, Mike. *Structure and the Book of Zechariah*. Journal for the Study of the Old Testament: Supplement Series 130. Sheffield, UK: Sheffield Academic Press, 1992.

Callaham, Scott N. *Modality and the Biblical Hebrew Infinitive Absolute*. Wiesbaden: Harrassowitz, 2010.

Caquot, A. "Les «Graces de David». A Propos d'Isaie 55/3b." *Semitica* 15 (1965): 45–59.

Carson, Donald A. "Evangelicals, Ecumenism, and the Church." In *Evangelical Affirmations*. Edited by Kenneth S. Kantzer and Carl F. H. Henry. 359–360. Grand Rapids, MI: Zondervan, 1990.

Cassuto, Umberto. *A Commentary on the Book of Exodus*. Jerusalem: Magnes, 1976.

———. *A Commentary on the Book of Genesis I*. Jerusalem: Magnes, 1961.

———. *The Documentary Hypothesis: Eight Lectures*. Translated by I. Abrahams. Jerusalem: Magnes, 1961.

———. *La Questione della Genesi*. Florence: Felice le Monnier, 1934.

Christensen, Duane L. *Deuteronomy 1:1–21:9*. Rev. ed. Word Biblical Commentary 6a. Nashville: Thomas Nelson, 2001.

Clark, Gordon R. *The Word Hesed in the Hebrew Bible*. Journal for the Study of the Old Testament: Supplement Series 157. Sheffield, UK: JSOT Press, 1993.

Clark, W. M. "A Legal Background to the Yahwist's Use of 'Good and Evil' in Genesis 2–3." *Journal of Biblical Literature* 88 (1969): 266–278.

Claude Schaeffer, F.-A., ed. *Le Palais Royal d'Ugarit*. Mission de Ras Shamra 6–9. Paris: Klincksieck, 1955–.

———. *Ugaritica*. Paris: P. Geuthner, 1939–.

Clines, David J. A., ed. *The Dictionary of Classical Hebrew*. Sheffield, UK: Sheffield Phoenix, 1993–.

Clines, David J. A. "The Image of God in Man." *Tyndale Bulletin* 19 (1968): 53–103.

Cogan, M. *1 Kings*. Anchor Bible 10. New York: Doubleday, 2000.

Collins, C. John. "Galatians 3:16: What Kind of Exegete Was Paul?" *Tyndale Bulletin* 54/1 (2003): 75–86.

Collins, Jack. "A Syntactical Note (Genesis 3.15): Is the Woman's Seed Singular or Plural?" *Tyndale Bulletin* 48/1 (1997): 142–144.

Collins, John J. *Daniel: A Commentary on the Book of Daniel*. Hermeneia. Minneapolis: Fortress, 1993.

Costecalde, Claude-Bernard. *Aux origines du sacré biblique*. Paris: Letouzey & Ané, 1986.

Currid, John D. *Deuteronomy*. Darlington, UK: Evangelical Press, 2006.

Dahood, Mitchell. "Ugaritic Hebrew Parallel Pairs." In *Ras Shamra Parallels: The Texts from Ugarit and the Hebrew Bible*. Edited by Loren R Fisher. 3 vols. Analecta Orientalia, 49–51. 2:1–33. Rome: Pontifical Biblical Institute Press, 1975.

Dallaire, Hélène. "The Syntax of Volitives in Northwest Semitic Prose." PhD diss., Hebrew Union College, Cincinnati, OH, 2002.

Dancygier, Barbara, and Eve Sweetser. *Mental Spaces in Grammar: Conditional Constructions*. Cambridge Studies in Linguistics 108. Cambridge: Cambridge University Press, 2005.

Da Riva, Rocío. "A Note to the Nebuchadnezzar Inscription of Brisa." *Nouvelles Assyriologiques Bréves et Utilitaires* (2009/1): 15–16.

Davies, John A. *A Royal Priesthood: Literary and Intertextual Perspectives on an Image of Israel in Exodus 19:6*. Journal for the Study of the Old Testament: Supplement Series 395. London: T. & T. Clark, 2004.

Day, J. "Why Does God 'Establish' rather than 'Cut' Covenants in the Priestly Source?" In *Covenant as Context: Essays in Honour of E. W. Nicholson*. Edited by A. D. H. Mayes and R. B. Salters. 71–109. Oxford: Oxford University Press, 2003.

Day, John. "The Canaanite Inheritance of the Israelite Monarchy." In *King and Messiah in Israel and the Ancient Near East*. Edited by John Day. Journal for the Study of the Old Testament: Supplement Series 270. 72–90. Sheffield, UK: Sheffield Academic Press, 1998.

Dietrich, M., O. Loretz, and J. Sanmartín. *The Cuneiform Alphabetic Texts from Ugarit, Rab Ibn Hani and Other Places* (*KTU*: 2nd, enlarged edition.) Münster, Germany: Ugarit-Verlag, 1995.

del Olmo Lete, Gregorio, and Joaquín Sanmartín. *A Dictionary of the Ugaritic Language in the Alphabetic Tradition*. Translated by W. G. E. Watson. 2 vols. Handbook of Oriental Studies I: The Near and Middle East 67. Leiden, Netherlands: Brill, 2003.

Delitzsch, F. *Biblical Commentary on the Prophecies of Isaiah*. Translated by J. Martin. 2 vols. Grand Rapids, MI: Eerdmans, 1950.

Dell, J. "Covenant and Creation in Relationship." In *Covenant as Context: Essays in Honour of E. W. Nicholson*. Edited by A. D. H. Mayes and R. B. Salters. 111–133. Oxford: Oxford University Press, 2003.

Dempster, Stephen G. *Dominion and Dynasty: A Biblical Theology of the Hebrew Bible*. New Studies in Biblical Theology 15. Downers Grove, IL: InterVarsity Press, 2003.

———. "Linguistic Features of Hebrew Narrative: A Discourse Analysis of Narrative from the Classical Period." PhD diss., University of Toronto, 1985.

———. "The Servant of the Lord." In *Central Themes in Biblical Theology: Mapping Unity in Diversity*. Edited by Scott J. Hafemann and Paul R. House. 128–178. Grand Rapids, MI: Baker, 2007.

DeRouchie, Jason S. *A Call to Covenant Love: Text Grammar and Literary Structure in Deuteronomy 5–11*. Gorgias Dissertations 30. Piscataway, NJ: Gorgias, 2007.

———. "Circumcision in the Hebrew Bible and Targums: Theology, Rhetoric, and the Handling of Metaphor." *Bulletin for Biblical Research* 14/2 (2004): 175–203.

———. "Numbering the Decalogue: A Textlinguistic Reappraisal." Paper presented at the Upper Midwest Regional Meeting of the Society of Biblical Literature, April 2007.

Dietrich, M., and O. Loretz. "Die soziale Struktur von Alalah und Ugarit (II)." *Die Welt des Orients* 5 (1969): 57–93.

Dion, P. E. "Ressemblance et Image de Dieu." In *Suppléments aux Dictionnaire de la Bible*. Edited by H. Cazelles and A. Feuillet. Paris: Letouzey & Ané, 1985. 55:365–403.

Dumbrell, William J. *Covenant and Creation: A Theology of Old Testament Covenants*. Nashville: Thomas Nelson, 1984.

———. *The End of the Beginning: Revelation 21–22 and the Old Testament*. Homebush West, NSW, Australia: Lancer, 1985.

———. *The Search for Order*. Grand Rapids, MI: Baker, 1994.

Dupont, J. "ΤΑ ῞ΟΣΙΑ ΔΑΥΙΔ ΤΑ ΠΙΣΤΑ (Ac XIII 34 = Is LV 3)." *Revue Biblique* 68 (1961): 91–114.

Duriez, Colin. *Francis Schaeffer: An Authentic Life*. Wheaton, IL: Crossway, 2008.

Eaton, John. "The King as God's Witness." *Annual of the Swedish Theological Institute* 7 (1970): 25–40.

Eichrodt, Walther. *Theology of the Old Testament*. Translated by J. A. Baker. 2 vols. Old Testament Library. Philadelphia: Westminster, 1961/1967.

Eissfeldt, Otto. "The Promises of Grace to David in Isaiah 55:1–5." In *Israel's Prophetic Heritage: Essays in Honor of James Muilenburg*. Edited by Bernhard W. Anderson and Walter Harrelson. 196–207. New York: Harper, 1962.

Engnell, Ivan. "The 'Ebed Yahweh Songs and the Suffering Servant Messiah in 'Deutero-Isaiah'." *Bulletin of the John Rylands Library* 31 (1948): 54–93.

———. *Studies in Divine Kingship in the Ancient Near East*. 2nd ed. Oxford: Blackwell, 1967.

Fischer, Georg. *Jeremia 26–52*. Herders Theologischer Kommentar zum Alten Testament. Freiburg, Germany: Herder, 2005.

Fitzmyer, Joseph A. *The Aramaic Inscriptions of Sefire*. Rome: Pontifical Biblical Institute, 1967.

Fockner, Sven. "Reopening the Discussion: Another Contextual Look at the Sons of God," *Journal for the Study of the Old Testament* 32.4 (2008): 435–456.

Fokkelman, J. P. *Narrative Art and Poetry in the Books of Samuel: A Full Interpretation Based on Stylistic and Structural Analyses: Vol. III: Throne and City (II Sam. 2–8 & 21–24)*. Assen, Netherlands: Van Gorcum, 1990.

Frame, John M. *The Doctrine of the Christian Life*. Phillipsburg, NJ: P&R, 2008.

Frankena, R. "The Vassal-Treaties of Esarhaddon." *Oudtestamentische Studiën* 25 (1965): 122–154.

Frankfort, H. *Kingship and the Gods*. Chicago: University of Chicago Press, 1948.

Frantz-Szabó, G. "Hittite Witchcraft and Divination." In *Civilizations of the Ancient Near East*. Edited by Jack M. Sasson. New York: Charles Scribner's Sons, 1995.

Freedman, David Noel, and Jack R. Lundbom. "Haplography in Jeremiah 1–20." *Eretz-Israel* 26 (1999): 28*–38*.

Fretheim, Terence E. *Jeremiah*. Smyth and Helwys Bible Commentary. Macon, GA: Smyth & Helwys, 2002.

Friedman, Richard Elliott. "The Hiding of the Face: An Essay on the Literary Unity of Biblical Narrative." In *Judaic Perspectives on Ancient Israel*. Edited by Jacob Neusner, Baruch A. Levine, and Ernest S. Frerichs. Philadelphia: Fortress, 1987.

Gage, Warren Austin. *The Gospel of Genesis: Studies in Protology and Eschatology*. Winona Lake, IN: Carpenter, 1984.

Gakaru, Griphus. *An Inner-Biblical Exegetical Study of the Davidic Covenant and the Dynastic Oracle*. Mellen Biblical Press 58. Lewiston, NY: Edwin Mellen, 2000.

Gamberoni, J. "קוּם *qûm*." In *Theological Dictionary of the Old Testament*. Edited by G. Johannes Botterweck, Helmer Ringgren, and Heinz-Josef Fabry. 15 vols. 12:589–612. Grand Rapids, MI: Eerdmans, 2003.

Garlington, D. B. "Oath-Taking in the Community of the New Age (Matthew 5:33–37)." *Trinity Journal* n.s. 16/2 (1995): 139–170.

Garr, W. Randall. "'Image' and 'Likeness' in the Inscription from Tell Fakhariyeh." *Israel Exploration Journal* 50/3–4 (2003): 227–234.

———. *In His Own Image and Likeness: Humanity, Divinity, and Monotheism*. Culture and History of the Ancient Near East 15. Leiden, Netherlands: Brill, 2003.

Gentry, Peter J. "The Atonement in Isaiah's Fourth Servant Song (Isaiah 52:13–53:12)." *The Southern Baptist Journal of Theology* 11/2 (2007): 20–47.

———. "Daniel's Seventy Weeks and the New Exodus." *The Southern Baptist Journal of Theology* 14/1 (2010): 26–45.

———. "Kingdom through Covenant: Humanity as the Divine Image." *The Southern Baptist Journal of Theology* 12/1 (2008): 16–42.

———. "Rethinking the 'Sure Mercies of David' in Isaiah 55:3." *Westminster Theological Journal* 69 (2007): 279–304.

———. "The Son of Man in Daniel 7: Individual or Corporate?" In *Acorns to Oaks: The Primacy and Practice of Biblical Theology*. Edited by Michael A. G. Haykin. 59–75. Toronto: Joshua, 2003.

———. "Speaking the Truth in Love (Eph 4:15): Life in the New Covenant Community." *The Southern Baptist Journal of Theology* 10/2 (2006): 70–87.

———. "The System of the Finite Verb in Classical Biblical Hebrew." *Hebrew Studies* 39 (1998): 7–39.

Gibson, J. C. L. *Textbook of Syrian Semitic Inscriptions: Phoenician Inscriptions.* Vol. 3. Oxford: Clarendon, 1982.

Glenn, Donald. "Psalm 8 and Hebrews 2: A Case Study in Biblical Hermeneutics and Biblical Theology." In *Walvoord: A Tribute.* Edited by Donald K. Campbell. 39–51. Chicago: Moody, 1982.

Glueck, Nelson. Hesed *in the Bible.* Translated by Alfred Gottschalk. Edited by Elias L. Epstein. Cincinnati: Hebrew Union College, 1927, 1967.

Goldingay, John. *Isaiah.* New International Biblical Commentary. Peabody, MA: Hendrickson, 2001.

———. *The Message of Isaiah 40–55: A Literary-Theological Commentary.* London: T. & T. Clark, 2005.

———. *Old Testament Theology: Volume One—Israel's Gospel.* Downers Grove, IL: InterVarsity Press, 2003.

Gooding, David W. "The Literary Structure of the Book of Daniel and Its Implications." *Tyndale Bulletin* 32 (1981): 43–79.

Greenberg, Moshe. "Hebrew *segulla*: Akkadian *sikiltu.*" *Journal of the American Oriental Society* 71 (1951): 172–174.

Gröndahl, Frauke. *Die Personennamen der Texte aus Ugarit.* Studia Pohl 1. Rome: Pontifical Biblical Institute, 1967.

Grüneberg, Keith N. *Abraham, Blessing, and the Nations: A Philological and Exegetical Study of Genesis 12:3 in Its Narrative Context.* Berlin: Walter de Gruyter, 2003.

Guest, Steven W. "Deuteronomy 26:16–19 as the Central Focus of the Covenantal Framework of Deuteronomy." PhD diss., The Southern Baptist Theological Seminary, 2009.

Hafemann, Scott J. "The Covenant Relationship." In *Central Themes in Biblical Theology: Mapping Unity in Diversity.* Edited by Scott J. Hafemann and Paul R. House. Grand Rapids, MI: Baker, 2007.

Handy, Lowell. *Among the Host of Heaven.* Winona Lake, IN: Eisenbrauns, 1994.

Hasel, Gerhard F. "The Meaning of the Animal Rite in Genesis 15." *Journal for the Study of the Old Testament* 19 (1981): 61–78.

Heim, Knut M. "The (God-)forsaken King of Psalm 89: A Historical and Intertextual Enquiry." In *King and Messiah in Israel and the Ancient Near East: Proceedings of the Oxford Old Testament Seminar.* Edited by John Day. Journal for the Study of the Old Testament: Supplement Series 270. 296–322. Sheffield, UK: Sheffield Academic Press, 1998.

Heimpel, Wolfgang. *Letters to the King of Mari: A New Translation, with Historical Introduction, Notes, and Commentary.* Winona Lake, IN: Eisenbrauns, 2003.

Hess, R. "The Onomastics of Ugarit." In *Handbook of Ugaritic Studies.* Edited by W. G. E. Watson and N. Wyatt. Handbook of Oriental Studies I: The Near and Middle East 39. 499–528. Leiden, Netherlands: Brill, 1999.

Hess, Richard S. *Amarna Personal Names.* American Schools of Oriental Research Dissertation Series 9. Winona Lake, IN: Eisenbrauns, 1993.

———. "Amarna Proper Names." PhD dissertation, Hebrew Union College, 1984.

———. "The Slaughter of the Animals in Genesis 15: Genesis 15:8–21 and Its Ancient Near Eastern Context." In *He Swore an Oath: Biblical Themes from Genesis 12–50.* Edited by R. S. Hess, G. J. Wenham, and P. E. Satterthwaite. 2nd ed. 55–65. Cambridge: Tyndale House, 1993, 1994.

———. "Splitting the Adam: The Usage of *'ĀDĀM* in Genesis I-V." In *Studies in the Pentateuch.* Edited by J. A. Emerton. Supplements to Vetus Testamentum 41. 1–15. Leiden, Netherlands: Brill, 1990.

Hill, C. E. "The New Testament Canon: *Deconstructio ad Absurdum*?" *Journal of the Evangelical Theological Society* 52 (2009): 101–120.

————. *Who Chose the Gospels?* Oxford: Oxford University Press, 2010.

Hoehner, Harold W. *Chronological Aspects of the Life of Christ*. Grand Rapids, MI: Zondervan, 1977.

————. *Ephesians: An Exegetical Commentary*. Grand Rapids, MI: Baker, 2002.

Hoffmeier, J. K. "The King as God's Son in Egypt and Israel." *Journal of the Society for the Study of Egyptian Antiquities* 24 (1994): 28–38.

House, Paul R. *Old Testament Theology*. Downers Grove, IL: InterVarsity Press, 1998.

Höver-Johag, I. "טוֹב *ṭôḇ*." In *Theological Dictionary of the Old Testament*. Edited by G. Johannes Botterweck and Helmer Ringgren. 15 vols. 5:296–317. Grand Rapids, MI: Eerdmans, 1986.

Hugenberger, Gordon. *Marriage as a Covenant: A Study of Biblical Law and Ethics Governing Marriage Developed from the Perspective of Malachi*. Supplements to Vetus Testamentum 52. Leiden, Netherlands: Brill, 1994.

Hunger, Hermann. *Astrological Reports to Assyrian Kings*. State Archives of Assyria. Vol. 8. Helsinki: Helsinki University Press, 1992.

Hutter, M. "Adam als Gärtner und König (Gen. 2:8, 15)." *Biblische Zeitschrift* 30 (1985): 258–262.

Hwang, Jerry. "The Rhetoric of Remembrance: An Exegetical and Theological Investigation into the 'Fathers' in Deuteronomy." PhD diss., Wheaton College, 2009.

Jacobsen, T. "The Concept of Divine Parentage of the Ruler in the Stela of the Vultures." *Journal of Near Eastern Studies* 2 (1943): 119–121.

Janzen, J. G. *Genesis 12–50: Abraham and All the Families of the Earth*. International Theological Commentary. Grand Rapids/Edinburgh: Eerdmans/Handsel, 1993.

Jean, Charles-F. *Archives Royales de Mari*. Paris: Imprimerie Nationale, 1950.

Jenni, Ernst. *Die hebräischen Präpositionen, Band 1: Die Präposition Beth*. Stuttgart: Kolhammer, 1992.

————. *Die hebräischen Präpositionen, Band 2: Die Präposition Kaph*. Stuttgart: Kolhammer, 1994.

————. *Die hebräischen Präpositionen, Band 3: Die Präposition Lamed*. Stuttgart: Kolhammer, 2000.

Jenni, Ernst, and Claus Westermann. *Theological Lexicon of the Old Testament*. Translated by Mark E. Biddle. 3 vols. Peabody, MA: Hendrickson, 1997.

Jónsson, Gunnlauger A. *The Image of God: Genesis 1:26–28 in a Century of Old Testament Research*. Coniectanea Biblica: Old Testament Series 26. Lund, Sweden: Almqvist & Wiksell, 1988.

Joüon, Paul. *Grammaire de l'hébreu biblique*. Rome: Biblical Institute Press, 1923.

Kaiser, Walter C., Jr. "The Blessing of David: The Charter for Humanity." In *The Law and the Prophets: Old Testament Studies Prepared in Honor of Oswald Thompson Allis*. Edited by John H. Skilton, Milton C. Fisher, and Leslie W. Sloat. 311–312. Philadelphia: Presbyterian & Reformed, 1974.

————. *The Messiah in the Old Testament*. Grand Rapids, MI: Zondervan, 1995.

————. "The Unfailing Kindnesses Promised to David: Isaiah 55:3." *Journal for the Study of the Old Testament* 45 (1989): 91–98.

Kalluveettil, Paul. *Declaration and Covenant*. Analecta Biblica 88. Rome: Biblical Institute Press, 1982.

Kasari, Petri *Nathan's Promise in 2 Samuel 7 and Related Texts*. Helsinki: Finnish Exegetical Society, 2009.

Kaufman, Stephen A. "The Structure of the Deuteronomic Law." *Maarav* 1/2 (1978–1979): 105–158.

Kearney, Peter J. "Creation and Liturgy: The P Redaction of Exod 25–40." *Zeitschrift für die alttestamentliche Wissenschaft* 89 (1977): 375–387.

Kedar-Kopfstein, B. "תָּמַם *tāmam*; תָּם *tām*; תָּמִים*tāmîm*; תֹּם (תָּם) *tōm* (*tom-*); תֻּמָּה *tummâ*; תֻּמִּים *tummîm*." In *Theological Dictionary of the Old Testament*. Edited by G. Johannes Botterweck and Helmer Ringgren. 15 vols. 15:699–711. Grand Rapids, MI: Eerdmans, 2006.

Keel, Othmar. *The Symbolism of the Biblical World: Ancient Near Eastern Iconography and the Book of Psalms*. Translated by Timothy J. Hallett. New York: Seabury, 1978.

Keller, Timothy. *Counterfeit Gods: The Empty Promises of Money, Sex, and Power, and the Only Hope that Matters*. New York: Dutton, 2009.

Kim, Yoo-Ki. *The Function of the Tautological Infinitive in Classical Biblical Hebrew*. Harvard Semitic Studies 60. Winona Lake, IN: Eisenbrauns, 2009.

Kissane, E. J. *The Book of Isaiah: Translated from a Critically Revised Hebrew Text with Commentary*. 2 vols. Dublin: Browne & Nolan, 1943.

Kitchen, Kenneth A. *Ancient Orient and Old Testament*. Downers Grove, IL: InterVarsity Press, 1966.

———. *The Bible in Its World: The Bible and Archaeology Today*. Downers Grove, IL: InterVarsity Press, 1977.

———. "Egypt, Ugarit, Qatna and Covenant." *Ugarit-Forschung* 11 (1979): 453–464.

———. "The King List of Ugarit." *Ugarit Forschungen* 9 (1977): 131–142.

———. *On the Reliability of the Old Testament*. Grand Rapids, MI: Eerdmans, 2003.

Kittel, Gerhard, ed. *Theological Dictionary of the New Testament*. Translated and edited by Geoffrey W. Bromiley. Grand Rapids, MI: Eerdmans, 1964.

Kleven, T. "Kingship in Ugarit (*KTU* 1.16 I 1–23)." In *Ascribe to the Lord: Biblical and Other Studies in Memory of Peter C. Craigie*. Edited by L. Eslinger and G. Taylor. Journal for the Study of the Old Testament: Supplement Series 67. 29–53. Sheffield, UK: Sheffield Academic Press, 1988.

Kline, Meredith G. "The Covenant of the Seventieth Week." In *The Law and the Prophets: Old Testament Studies in Honor of Oswald T. Allis*. Edited by J. H. Skilton. 452–469. Nutley, NJ: Presbyterian & Reformed, 1974.

———. "Double Trouble." *Journal of the Evangelical Theological Society* 32/2 (1989): 171–179.

Knoppers, Gary N. "Ancient Near Eastern Royal Grants and the Davidic Covenant: A Parallel?" *Journal of the American Oriental Society* 116/4 (1996): 670–697.

Koehler, L., and W. Baumgartner. *Hebräisches und Aramäisches Lexikon zum Alten Testament*. 3rd ed. Edited by W. Baumgartner, J. J. Stamm, and B. Hartmann. Leiden, Netherlands: Brill, 1967–1995.

———. *Lexicon in Veteris Testamenti Libros*. 2nd. ed. Leiden, Netherlands: Brill, 1958, 1985.

Koehler, L., W. Baumgartner, et al. *The Hebrew and Aramaic Lexicon of the Old Testament*. Translated by M. E. J. Richardson. Study edition. 2 vols. Leiden, Netherlands: Brill, 2001.

Korošec, Viktor. *Hethitische Staatsverträge: Ein Beitrag zu ihrer juristischen Wertung*. Leipzig, Germany: T. Weicher, 1931.

Korpel, Marjo C. A. *A Rift in the Clouds: Ugaritic and Hebrew Descriptions of the Divine*. Münster, Germany: Ugarit-Verlag, 1990.

Kuen, Alfred. *Soixante-six en un: Introduction aux 66 livres de la Bible*. St-Légier: Editions Emmaüs, 2005.

Lambdin, Thomas O. *Introduction to Biblical Hebrew*. New York: Charles Scribner's Sons, 1971.

Lane, Daniel C. "The Meaning and Use of the Old Testament Term for 'Covenant' (*bᵉrît*): with Some Implications for Dispensationalism and Covenant Theology." PhD diss., Trinity International University, 2000.

Latto, A. "Second Samuel 7 and Ancient Near Eastern Royal Ideology." *Catholic Biblical Quarterly* 59 (1997): 244–269.

Leclerc, Thomas L. *Yahweh Is Exalted in Justice: Solidarity and Conflict in Isaiah.* Minneapolis: Fortress, 2001.

Lee, Chee-Chiew. "גוים in Genesis 35:11 and the Abrahamic Promise of Blessing for the Nations." *Journal of the Evangelical Theological Society* 52/3 (2009): 472.

Lee, Sung-Hun. "Lament and the Joy of Salvation in the Lament Psalms." In *The Book of Psalms: Composition and Reception.* Edited by Peter W. Flint and Patrick D. Miller, Jr. Supplements to Vetus Testamentum 94. Leiden, Netherlands: Brill, 2005.

Leithart, Peter J. *A House for My Name: A Survey of the Old Testament.* Moscow, ID: Canon, 2000.

Levenson, Jon D. *Creation and the Persistence of Evil: The Jewish Drama of Divine Omnipotence.* San Francisco: Harper & Row, 1988.

———. *Theology of the Program of Restoration of Ezekiel 40–48.* Harvard Semitic Museum 10. Missoula, MT: Scholars Press, 1976.

Lewis, C. S. *The Abolition of Man.* London: Geoffrey Bles, 1943, 1946.

Lichtheim, Miriam. *Ancient Egyptian Literature: A Book of Readings.* 3 vols. Berkeley: University of California Press, 1976.

Liddell, H. G., R. Scott, and H. S. Jones, *A Greek-English Lexicon.* 9th ed. with revised supplement. Oxford: Oxford University Press, 1996.

Lohfink, Norbert, and Erich Zenger, *The God of Israel and the Nations: Studies in Isaiah and the Psalms.* Collegeville, MN: Liturgical Press, 1994.

Lohr, Joel N. *Chosen and Unchosen: Conceptions of Election in the Pentateuch and Jewish-Christian Interpretation.* Shiphrut 2. Winona Lake, IN: Eisenbrauns, 2009.

Longacre, Robert E. "The Analysis of Preverbal Nouns in Biblical Hebrew Narrative: Some Overriding Concerns." *Journal of Translation and Textlinguistics* 5/3 (1992): 208–224.

———. "The Grammar of Discourse." In *Topics in Language and Linguistics.* Edited by Thomas A. Seboek and Albert Valdman. New York: Plenum, 1983.

———. "*Weqatal* Forms in Biblical Hebrew Prose." In *Biblical Hebrew and Discourse Linguistics.* Edited by Robert D. Bergen. 50–98. Dallas: SIL, 1994.

Lövestam, E. *Son and Saviour: A Study of Acts 13, 32–37. With an Appendix: 'Son of God' in the Synoptic Gospels.* Coniectanea Neotestamentica 18. Lund, Sweden: Gleerup, 1961.

Lundbom, J. "Haplography in the Hebrew *Vorlage* of Septuagint Jeremiah." Paper presented at the annual meeting of the Society of Biblical Literature, San Antonio, November 22, 2004.

Malamat, A. "'You Shall Love Your Neighbour as Yourself': A Case of Misinterpretation." In *Die Hebräische Bibel und ihre zweifache Nachgeschichte: Festschrift für Rolf Rendtorff zum 65.* Edited by E. Blum, C. Macholz, and E. W. Stegemann. 111–115. Neukirchen-Vluyn, Germany: Neukirchner Verlag, 1990.

Martens, Elmer A. *God's Design: A Focus on Old Testament Theology.* Grand Rapids, MI: Baker, 1981.

Mathews, Kenneth A. *Genesis 1–11:26.* New American Commentary 1A. Nashville: Broadman & Holman, 1996.

———. *Genesis 11:27–50:26.* New American Commentary 1B. Nashville: Broadman & Holman, 2005.

McConville, J. Gordon. "Abraham and Melchizedek: Horizons in Genesis 14." In *He Swore an Oath: Biblical Themes from Genesis 12–50.* 2nd ed. Edited by R. S. Hess, G. J. Wenham, and P. E. Satterthwaite. 93–118. Cambridge: Tyndale House, 1993, 1994.

McKenzie, Steven L. *Covenant.* St. Louis: Chalice, 2000.

McMarter, P. Kyle, Jr. *II Samuel.* Anchor Bible 9. New York: Doubleday, 1984.

———. "Two Bronze Arrowheads with Archaic Alphabetic Inscriptions." *Eretz-Israel* 26 (1999): 124*–128*.

Meade, John D. "The Meaning of Circumcision in Israel: A Proposal for a Transfer of Rite from Egypt to Israel." *Adorare Mente* 1 (2008): 14–29.

———. "OT Ḥesed in the NT." Unpublished paper presented to faculty of The Southern Baptist Theological Seminary, 2006.

Mendenhall, George E. "The Conflict between Value Systems and Social Control." In *Unity and Diversity: Essays in the History, Literature, and Religion of the Ancient Near East*. Edited by Hans Goedicke and J. J. M. Roberts. 169–180. Baltimore: Johns Hopkins University Press, 1975.

———. "Covenant Forms in Israelite Tradition." In *The Biblical Archaeologist Reader*. Vol. 3. Edited by Edward F. Campbell and David N. Freedman. New York: Doubleday, 1970.

———. *The Tenth Generation: The Origins of the Biblical Tradition*. Baltimore: Johns Hopkins University Press, 1973.

Merrill, Eugene H. *Kingdom of Priests: A History of Old Testament Israel*. Grand Rapids, MI: Baker, 1987.

———. "A Theology of the Pentateuch." In *A Biblical Theology of the Old Testament*. Edited by Roy B. Zuck. 7–87. Chicago: Moody, 1991.

Mettinger, T. N. D. *King and Messiah: The Civil and Sacral Legitimation of the Israelite Kings*. 259–274. Lund, Sweden: Gleerup, 1976.

Meyer, R., and H. Donner. *Wilhelm Gesenius Hebräisches und Aramäisches Handwörterbuch das Alte Testament*. 18th ed. 6 vols. Berlin: Springer, 1987–2010.

Meyer, Rudolf. "Auffallender Erzählungstil in einem angeblichen Auszug aus der 'Chronik der Konige von Juda'." In *Festschrift Friedrich Baumgärtel zum 70. Geburstag*. Edited by J. Herrmann and L. Rost. 115–122. Erlangen, Germany: Universitätsbund Erlangen, 1959.

Meyers, Carol L. *The Tabernacle Menorah: A Synthetic Study of a Symbol from the Biblical Cult*. American Schools of Oriental Research Dissertation Series 2. Missoula, MT: Scholars Press, 1976.

Milgrom, Jacob. *Leviticus 23–27*. Anchor Bible 3B. New York: Doubleday, 2001.

Millard, Alan. "The Tablets in the Ark." In *Reading the Law: Studies in Honour of Gordon J. Wenham*. Edited by J. G. McConville and Karl Möller. Library of Hebrew Bible/Old Testament Studies 461. 254–266. New York: T. & T. Clark, 2007.

Miller, Stephen R. *Daniel*. New American Commentary 18. Nashville: Broadman & Holman, 1994.

Min, Young-Jin "The Minuses and Pluses of the LXX Translation of Jeremiah as Compared with the Masoretic Text: Their Classification and Possible Origins." PhD diss., Hebrew University of Jerusalem, 1977.

Mirqin, M. A., ed. *Midrash Rabbah*. Tel-Aviv: Yavneh, 1956.

Mitchell, David C. *The Message of the Psalter: An Eschatological Programme in the Book of Psalms*. Journal for the Study of the Old Testament: Supplement Series 252. Sheffield, UK: Sheffield Academic Press, 1997.

Moberly, R. W. L. *The Bible, Theology, and Faith: Abraham and Jesus*. Cambridge Studies in Christian Doctrine 5. Cambridge: Cambridge University Press, 2000.

Moon, Joshua N. *Jeremiah's New Covenant: An Augustinian Reading*. Journal of Theological Interpretation Supplement 3. Winona Lake, IN: Eisenbrauns, 2011.

Moran, William L., ed. and trans. *The Amarna Letters*. Baltimore/London: John Hopkins University Press, 1987, 1992, 2002.

Morris, Henry M. *The Genesis Record: A Scientific and Devotional Commentary on the Book of Beginnings*. Grand Rapids, MI: Baker, 1976.

Morris, Leon. *Testaments of Love: A Study of Love in the Bible*. Grand Rapids, MI: Eerdmans, 1981.

Motyer, J. Alec. *Isaiah: An Introduction and Commentary*, Tyndale Old Testament Commentaries. Downers Grove, IL: InterVarsity Press, 1999.

————. *The Prophecy of Isaiah: An Introduction and Commentary*. Downers Grove, IL: InterVarsity Press, 1993.

Moulton, J. H., and W. F. Howard. *A Grammar of New Testament Greek, Vol. II: Accidence and Word-Formation*. Edinburgh: T. & T. Clark, 1929.

Muilenburg, James. "The Form and Structure of the Covenantal Formulations." *Vetus Testamentum* 9 (1959): 347–365.

Munch, Peter Andreas *The Expression Bajjôm Hāhū: Is It an Eschatological Terminus Technicus?* Oslo: I Kommisjon hos Jacob Dybwad, 1936.

Muraoka, T. *A Greek-English Lexicon of the Septuagint*. Leuven, Belgium: Peeters, 2009.

————. "The Tell-Fekherye Bilingual Inscription and Early Aramaic." *Abr-Nahrain* 22 (1983–1984): 79–117.

Murray, Donald F. *Divine Prerogative and Royal Pretension: Pragmatics, Poetics, and Polemics in a Narrative Sequence about David (2 Samuel 5.17–7.29)*. Journal for the Study of the Old Testament: Supplement Series 264. Sheffield, UK: Sheffield Academic Press, 1998.

Nash, Peter T. "The Hebrew Qal Active Participle: A Non-Aspectual Narrative Backgrounding Element." PhD diss., University of Chicago, 1992.

Newman, Robert C., John A. Bloom, and Hugh G. Gauch, Jr. "Public Theology and Prophecy Data: Factual Evidence that Counts for the Biblical World View." *Journal of the Evangelical Theological Society* 46/1 (2003): 79–110.

Niehaus, Jeffrey J. *Ancient Near Eastern Themes in Biblical Theology*. Grand Rapids, MI: Kregel, 2008.

————. "An Argument against Theologically Constructed Covenants." *Journal of the Evangelical Theological Society* 50/2 (2007): 259–273.

————. "Covenant: An Idea in the Mind of God." *Journal of the Evangelical Theological Society* 52/2 (2009): 225–246.

Noonan, Benjamin J. "Abraham, Blessing, and the Nations: A Reexamination of the Niphal and Hitpael of ברך in the Patriarchal Narratives." *Hebrew Studies* 51 (2010): 73–93.

O'Brien, Peter T. *The Letter to the Ephesians*. Pillar New Testament Commentary. Grand Rapids, MI: Eerdmans, 1999.

Olley, J. W. "'Righteous' and Wealthy? The Description of the *Ṣaddîq* in Wisdom Literature." *Colloquium* 22 (1990): 38–45.

Oppenheim, A. Leo, et al., eds. *The Assyrian Dictionary*. Chicago: Oriental Institute, 1968.

Oswalt, J. "משח." In *New International Dictionary of Old Testament Theology and Exegesis*. Edited by Willem A. VanGemeren. 5 vols. 2:1123–1127. Grand Rapids, MI: Zondervan, 1997.

Oswalt, John N. *The Book of Isaiah: Chapters 40–66*. Grand Rapids, MI: Eerdmans, 1998.

Parpola, Simo. *Letters from Assyrian Scholars to the Kings Esarhaddon and Assurbanipal, Part I: Texts*. Winona Lake, IN: Eisenbrauns, 2007.

————. *Letters from Assyrian Scholars to the Kings Esarhaddon and Assurbanipal, Part II: Commentary and Appendices*. Winona Lake, IN: Eisenbrauns, 2007.

Parpola, Simo, and Kazuko Watanabe. *Neo-Assyrian Treaties and Loyalty Oaths*. State Archives of Assyria 2. Helsinki: Helsinki University Press, 1988.

Parry, Jason. "Desolation of the Temple and Messianic Enthronement in Daniel 11:36–12:3." *Journal of the Evangelical Theological Society*, 54/3 (2011): 485–526.

Patrick, Dale. "The Covenant Code Source." *Vetus Testamentum* 27 (1977): 145–157.

Pietersma, A. "Greek Jeremiah and the Land of Azazel in *Studies in the Hebrew Bible, Qumran, and the Septuagint, Presented to Eugene Ulrich*. Edited by Peter W. Flint, Emanuel Tov, and James C. VanderKam. Supplements to Vetus Testamentum 101. 403–413. Leiden, Netherlands: Brill, 2006.

————. "Of Translation and Revision: From Greek Isaiah to Greek Jeremiah." In *Isaiah in Context: Studies in Honour of Arie van der Kooij on the Occasion of his Sixty-Fifth Birthday*. Edited by Michaël N. van der Meer, Percy van Keulen, Wido van Peursen, and Bas ter Haar Romeny. Supplements to Vetus Testamentum 138. 359–387. Leiden, Netherlands: Brill, 2010.

Porter, Stanley E. "The Concept of Covenant in Paul." In *The Concept of the Covenant in the Second Temple Period*. Edited by Stanley E. Porter and Jacqueline C. R. de Roo. Supplements to the Journal for the Study of Judaism 71. 269–285. Leiden, Netherlands: Brill, 2003.

Preuss, H. D. "דָּמָה *dāmāh*; דְּמוּת." In *Theological Dictionary of the Old Testament*. Edited by G. Johannes Botterweck and Helmer Ringgren. 15 vols. 3:250–260. Grand Rapids, MI: Eerdmans, 1978.

Pritchard, James B., ed. *Ancient Near Eastern Texts Relating to the Old Testament*. 3rd ed. with supplement. Princeton, NJ: Princeton University Press, 1969.

Qimron, E., and J. Strugnell. *Miqṣat Ma'aṣe Ha-Torah*. Qumran Cave 4. Vol. 5. Discoveries in the Judean Desert 10. Oxford: Clarendon, 1994.

Rae, Murray. "Texts in Context: Scripture in the Divine Economy." *Journal of Theological Interpretation* 1/1 (2007): 1–21,

Rendtorff, Rolf. *Die "Bundesformel": eine exegetisch-theologische Untersuchung*. Stuttgart: Katholisches Bibelwerk, 1995.

————. *The Covenant Formula: An Exegetical and Theological Investigation*. Trans. Margaret Kohl. Old Testament Studies. Edinburgh: T. & T. Clark, 1998.

Renz, Thomas. "The Use of the Zion Tradition in the Book of Ezekiel." In *Zion, City of Our God*. Edited by Richard S. Hess and Gordon J. Wenham. 86–87. Grand Rapids, MI: Eerdmans, 1999.

Ringgren, H. "שׁוֹפָר *šôpār*" In *Theological Dictionary of the Old Testament*. Edited by G. Johannes Botterweck, Helmer Ringgren, and Heinz-Josef Fabry. 15 vols. 14:541–542. Grand Rapids, MI: Eerdmans, 2004.

Robertson, O. Palmer. *The Christ of the Covenants*. Phillipsburg, NJ: Presbyterian & Reformed, 1980.

Rooker, Mark F. *Biblical Hebrew in Transition: The Language of Ezekiel*. Journal for the Study of the Old Testament: Supplement Series 90. Sheffield: JSOT Press, 1990.

Rose, Wolter H. *Zemah and Zerubbabel: Messianic Expectations in the Early Postexilic Period*. Journal for the Study of the Old Testament: Supplement Series 304. Sheffield, UK: Sheffield Academic Press, 2000.

Ross, Allen P. *Introducing Biblical Hebrew*. Grand Rapids, MI: Baker, 2001.

Ruprecht, Eberhard. "Der Traditionsgeschictliche Hintergrund der Einzelnen Elemente von Genesis XII 2–3." *Vetus Testamentum* 29 (1979): 444–464.

————. "Vorgegebene Tradition und Theologische Gestaltung in Genesis XII 1–3." *Vetus Testamentum* 29 (1979): 171–188.

Sailhamer, John H. *The Meaning of the Pentateuch: Revelation, Composition, and Interpretation*. Downers Grove, IL: InterVarsity Press, 2009.

Sakenfeld, Katharine D. *Faithfulness in Action: Loyalty in Biblical Perspective*. Philadelphia: Fortress, 1985.

————. *The Meaning of Hesed in the Hebrew Bible: A New Inquiry*. Harvard Semitic Monographs 17. Missoula, MT: Scholars Press, 1978.

Schenker, Adrian. *Das Neue am neuen Bund und das Alte am alten: Jer 31 in der hebräischen und griechischen Bibel*. Forschungen zur Religion und Literatur des Alten und Neuen Testaments 212. Göttingen, Germany: Vandenhoeck & Ruprecht, 2006.

————. "Est-ce que le livre de Jérémie fut publié dans une édition refondue au 2ᵉ siècle? La multiplcité textuelle peut-elle coexister avec l'édition unique d'un livre biblique?" In *Un Carrefour dans l'histoire de la Bible: Du texte à la théologie au IIᵉ siècle avant J.-C.* Edited by Innocent

Himbaza and Adrian Schenker. Orbis biblicus et orientalis 233. 58–74. Fribourg, Switzerland: Academic Press, 2008.

Schmidt, Werner. *The Faith of the Old Testament*. Philadelphia: Westminster, 1983.

Schniedewind, William M. *How the Bible Became a Book: The Textualization of Ancient Israel*. Cambridge: Cambridge University Press, 2004.

———. *Society and the Promise to David: The Reception History of 2 Samuel 7:1–17*. Oxford: Oxford University Press, 1999.

Schultz, Richard. "The King in the Book of Isaiah." In *The Lord's Anointed: Interpretation of Old Testament Messianic Texts*. Edited by P. E. Satterthwaite, Richard S. Hess, and Gordon J. Wenham. 141–165. Grand Rapids, MI: Baker, 1995.

Scofield, C. I., ed. *The New Schofield Reference Bible*. Oxford: Oxford University Press, 1970.

Seitz, Christopher. "The Call of Moses and the 'Revelation' of the Divine Name: Source-Critical Logic and Its Legacy." In *Theological Exegesis: Essays in Honor of Brevard S. Childs*. Edited by Christopher Seitz and Kathryn Greene-McCreight. Grand Rapids, MI: Eerdmans, 1991.

———. *Word Without End: The Old Testament as Abiding Theological Witness*. Grand Rapids, MI: Eerdmans, 1998.

Shulman, Ahouva. "The Use of Modal Verb Forms in Biblical Hebrew Prose." PhD diss., University of Toronto, 1996.

Sivan, Daniel. *Grammatical Analysis and Glossary of the Northwest Semitic Vocables in Akkadian Texts of the 15th–13th C.B.C. from Canaan and Syria*. Alter Orient und Altes Testament 214. Neukirchen-Vluyn, Germany: Neukirchener, 1984.

Smend, Rudolf. *Die Bundesformel*. Theologische Studien 68. Zürich: EVZ-Verlag, 1963.

Smith, George Adam. *The Book of Isaiah*. 2 vols. New York: Doubleday, 1927.

Smith, M. "God Male and Female in the Old Testament: Yahweh and His 'Asherah'." *Theological Studies* 48 (1987): 333–340.

Soderlund, Sven. *The Greek Text of Jeremiah. A Revised Hypothesis*. Journal for the Study of the Old Testament: Supplement Series 47. Sheffield, UK: JSOT Press, 1985.

Sommer, Benjamin D. *A Prophet Reads Scripture: Allusion in Isaiah 40–66*. Stanford, CA: Stanford University Press, 1998.

Spicq, Ceslas P. *Theological Lexicon of the New Testament*. Translated and edited by James D. Ernest. Peabody, MA: Hendrickson, 1994.

Stamm, Johann J., and Maurice E. Andrew. *The Ten Commandments in Recent Research*, Studies in Biblical Theology, Second Series 2. Naperville, IL: Alec R. Allenson, 1967.

Steinmann, Andrew E. *Daniel*. Concordia Commentary. Saint Louis: Concordia, 2008.

Stek, John H. "'Covenant' Overload in Reformed Theology." *Calvin Theological Journal* 29 (1994): 12–41.

Stendebach, F. J. "צֶלֶם *ṣelem*." In *Theological Dictionary of the Old Testament*. Edited by G. Johannes Botterweck, Helmer Ringgren, and Heinz-Josef Fabry. 15 vols. 12:386–396. Grand Rapids, MI: Eerdmans, 2003.

Sterchi, David A. "Does Genesis 1 Provide a Chronological Sequence?" *Journal of the Evangelical Theological Society* 39/4 (1996): 529–536.

Stipp, H.-J. *Das masoretische und alexandrinische Sondergut des Jeremiabuches—Textgeschichtlicher Rang, Eigenarten, Triebkräfte*. Orbis biblicus et orientalis 136. Fribourg, Switzerland: Éditions Universitaires/Göttingen, Germany: Vandenhoeck & Ruprecht, 1994.

Stoebe, Hans J. *Das zweite Buch Samuelis*. Kommentar zum Alten Testament VIII 2. Gutersloh, Germany: Gutersloher, 1994.

Stol, M. *Birth in Babylonia and the Bible: Its Mediterranean Setting*. Cuneiform Monographs 14. Groningen, Netherlands: Styx, 2000.

Stulman, Louis. *The Other Text of Jeremiah: A Reconstruction of the Hebrew Text Underlying the Greek Version of the Prose Sections of Jeremiah With English Translation*. Lanham, MD: University Press of America, 1985.

———. *The Prose Sermons of the Book of Jeremiah: A Redescription of the Correspondences with the Deuteronomistic Literature in the Light of Recent Textual Research*. SBL Dissertation Series 83. Atlanta: Scholars Press, 1986.

Thompson, J. A. *The Book of Jeremiah*. New International Commentary on the Old Testament. Grand Rapids, MI: Eerdmans, 1980.

Tigay, J. *The Evolution of the Gilgamesh Epic*. 152–156. Philadelphia: University of Pennsylvania Press, 1982.

Tov, Emanuel. "The Characterization of the Additional Layer of the Masoretic Text of Jeremiah." *Eretz-Israel* 26 (1999): 55–63.

———. "Exegetical Notes on the Hebrew *Vorlage* of the Septuagint of Jeremiah 27 (34)." In *The Greek and Hebrew Bible: Collected Essays on the Septuagint*. Edited by E. Tov. 315–332. Leiden, Netherlands: Brill, 1999.

———. "The Literary History of the Book of Jeremiah in Light of Its Textual History." In *The Greek and Hebrew Bible: Collected Essays on the Septuagint*. Edited by E. Tov. 363–384. Leiden, Netherlands: Brill, 1999.

———. "The Nature of the Large-Scale Differences between the LXX and MT S T V, Compared with Similar Evidence in Other Sources." In *The Earliest Text of the Hebrew Bible: The Relationship between the Masoretic Text and the Hebrew Base of the Septuagint Reconsidered*. Edited by Adrian Schenker. Septuagint and Cognate Studies 52. 121–144. Atlanta: Scholars Press, 2003.

———. "The Septuagint as a Source for the Literary Analysis of Hebrew Scripture." In *Exploring the Origins of the Bible: Canon Formation in Historical, Literary, and Theological Perspective*. Edited by Craig A. Evans and Emanuel Tov. 31–56. Grand Rapids, MI: Baker, 2008.

———. *The Septuagint Translation of Jeremiah and Baruch—A Discussion of an Early Revision of the LXX of Jeremiah 29–52 and Baruch 1:1–3:8*. Harvard Semitic Monographs 8. Missoula, MT: Scholars Press, 1976.

Trobisch, David. *The First Edition of the New Testament*. Oxford: Oxford University Press, 2000.

———. *Paul's Letter Collection*. Minneapolis: Fortress, 1994.

Vander Laan, Ray, with Judith Markham. *Echoes of His Presence: Stories of the Messiah from the People of His Day*. Colorado Springs: Focus on the Family, 1996.

van der Merwe, Christo H. J., Jackie A. Naudé, and Jan H. Kroeze. *A Biblical Hebrew Reference Grammar*. Biblical Languages: Hebrew 3. Sheffield, UK: Sheffield Academic Press, 1999.

van Soldt, Wilfred H. *Studies in the Akkadian of Ugarit: Dating and Grammar*. Alter Orient und Altes Testament 40. Neukirchen-Vluyn, Germany: Neukirchener, 1991.

Veijola, Timo. "The Witness in the Clouds: Ps 89:38." *Journal of Biblical Literature* 107/3 (1988): 413–417.

Vita, Juan-Pablo. "The Society of Ugarit." In *Handbook of Ugaritic Studies*. Edited by W. G. E. Watson and N. Wyatt. Handbook of Oriental Studies I: The Near and Middle East 39. 455–498. Leiden, Netherlands: Brill, 1999.

Wacholder, Ben Zion. "The Calendar of Sabbatical Cycles during the Second Temple and the Early Rabbinic Period." *Hebrew Union College Annual* 44 (1973): 153–196.

Walsh, Brian. "The Church in a Postmodern Age: Ten Things You Need to Know." In *Good Idea! A Resource Sheet on Evangelism and Church Growth* 3/4. Toronto: Wycliffe College Institute of Evangelism, 1996, 1–5.

Waltke, Bruce K. *The Book of Proverbs: Chapters 1–15*. New International Commentary on the Old Testament. Grand Rapids, MI: Eerdmans, 2004.

————. "The Book of Proverbs and Old Testament Theology." *Bibliotheca Sacra* 136 (1979): 302–317.

Waltke, Bruce K., with Cathi J. Fredricks, *Genesis: A Commentary*. Grand Rapids, MI: Zondervan, 2001.

Waltke, Bruce K., with Charles Yu, *An Old Testament Theology*. Grand Rapids, MI: Zondervan, 2007.

Waltke, Bruce K., and Michael P. O'Connor. *An Introduction to Biblical Hebrew Syntax*. Winona Lake, IN: Eisenbrauns, 1990.

Walton, John H. *Ancient Near Eastern Thought and the Old Testament*. Grand Rapids, MI: Baker, 2006.

————. *Covenant: God's Purpose, God's Plan*. Grand Rapids, MI: Zondervan, 1994, 72–73.

————. "Deuteronomy: An Exposition of the Spirit of the Law." *Grace Theological Journal* 8/2 (1987): 213–225.

————. *Genesis*. NIV Application Commentary. Grand Rapids, MI: Zondervan, 2001.

————. *Genesis One as Ancient Cosmology*. Winona Lake, IN: Eisenbrauns, 2011.

————. "Interpreting the Bible as an Ancient Near Eastern Document." In *Israel—Ancient Kingdom or Late Invention? Archaeology, Ancient Civilizations, and the Bible*. Edited by Daniel I. Block. 306–309. Nashville: Broadman & Holman, 2008.

————. *The Lost World of Genesis One: Ancient Cosmology and the Origins Debate*. Downers Grove, IL: InterVarsity Press, 2009.

Watson, W. G. E. "Ugaritic Onomastics (1)." *Aula Orientalis* 7 (1990): 113–127.

Weinfeld, M. "בְּרִית *bĕrît*." In *Theological Dictionary of the Old Testament*. Edited by G. Johannes Botterweck, Helmer Ringgren and Heinz-Josef Fabry. 15 vols. 2:253–279. Grand Rapids, MI: Eerdmans, 2003.

————. "Book of Deuteronomy." In *The Anchor Bible Dictionary*. Edited by David N. Freedman. New York: Doubleday, 1992.

————. "The Covenant of Grant in the Old Testament and in the Ancient Near East." *Journal of the American Oriental Society* 90 (1970): 184–203.

————. *Deuteronomy 1–11: A New Translation with Introduction and Commentary*. Anchor Bible 5. New York: Doubleday, 1991.

————. *Deuteronomy and the Deuteronomic School*. 1972. Repr., Winona Lake, IN: Eisenbrauns, 1992.

————. "Sabbath, Temple, and the Enthronement of the Lord—The Problem of the Sitz im Leben of Gen. 1:1–2:3." In *Melanges bibliques et orientaux en l'honneur de M. Henri Cazelles*. Edited by A. Caquot and M. Delcor. Alter Orient und Altes Testament 212. 501–512. Kevelaer, Germany: Butzon & Becker, 1981.

Wenham, Gordon J. *Exploring the Old Testament: A Guide to the Pentateuch*. Downers Grove, IL: InterVarsity Press, 2003.

————. *Genesis 1–15*. Word Biblical Commentary 1. Waco, TX: Word, 1987.

————. "Sanctuary Symbolism in the Garden of Eden Story." In *I Studied Inscriptions from before the Flood: Ancient Near Eastern, Literary, and Linguistic Approaches to Genesis 1–11*. Sources for Biblical and Theological Study 4. Edited by Richard S. Hess and David Toshio Tsumura. 399–404. Winona Lake, IN: Eisenbrauns, 1994.

Westermann, Claus. *Basic Forms of Prophetic Speech*. Translated by Hugh Clayton White. Louisville: Westminster/John Knox, 1991.

————. *Das Buch Jesaia: Kapitel 40–66*. 2nd ed. Göttingen, Germany: Vandenhoeck & Ruprecht, 1970.

Wheaton, Byron L. "Abraham, Land, and Stewardship: Reading the Abraham Narratives for their Contribution to Israel's Land Ethic." PhD diss., Westminster Theological Seminary, 2001.

Whitelam, K. W. "Israelite Kingship: The Royal Ideology and Opponents." In *The World of Ancient Israel*. Edited by R. E. Clements. 119–140. Cambridge: Cambridge University Press, 1989.

Wilcock, Michael. *I Saw Heaven Opened: The Message of Revelation*. The Bible Speaks Today. Downers Grove, IL: InterVarsity Press, 1975.

Williams, Ronald J. *Williams' Hebrew Syntax*. 3rd ed. Revised and expanded by John C. Beckman. Toronto: University of Toronto Press, 2007.

Williamson, H. G. M. "'The Sure Mercies of David': "Subjective or Objective Genitive?" *Journal of Semitic Studies* 23 (1978): 31–49.

———. *Variations on a Theme: King, Messiah and Servant in the Book of Isaiah*. Carlisle, UK: Paternoster, 1998.

Williamson, Paul R. *Abraham, Israel, and the Nations: The Patriarchal Promise and Its Covenantal Development in Genesis*. Journal for the Study of the Old Testament: Supplement Series 315. Sheffield, UK: Sheffield Academic Press, 2000.

———. *Sealed with an Oath: Covenant in God's Unfolding Purpose*. New Studies in Biblical Theology 23. Downers Grove, IL: InterVarsity Press, 2007.

Winston, David. *The Wisdom of Solomon*. Anchor Bible 43. New York: Doubleday, 1979.

Wolff, Hans Walter. *Anthropology of the Old Testament*. Philadelphia: Fortress, 1974.

———. "The Kerygma of the Yahwist." *Interpretation* 20 (1966): 131–158.

Wright, Christopher J. H. *Deuteronomy*. Peabody, MA: Hendrickson, 1996.

———. *The Mission of God: Unlocking the Bible's Grand Narrative*. Downers Grove, IL: InterVarsity Press Academic, 2006.

Wright, N. T. *The Climax of the Covenant*. Minneapolis: Fortress, 1991.

———. *Following Jesus: Biblical Reflections on Discipleship*. 57–59. Grand Rapids, MI: Eerdmans, 1995.

———. *Jesus and the Victory of God*. Christian Origins and the Question of God 2. Minneapolis: Fortress, 1996.

———. *The New Testament and the People of God*. Minneapolis: Fortress, 1992.

Youngblood, Kevin J. "Beyond Deuteronomism: Jeremiah's Unique Theological Contribution." Paper presented at Lipscomb University, 2009.

Younger, K. Lawson, Jr. "Shalmaneser III and Israel." In *Israel—Ancient Kingdom or Late Invention? Archaeology, Ancient Civilizations, and the Bible*. Edited by Daniel I. Block. 225–256. Nashville: Broadman & Holman, 2008.

Zobel, H.-J. "חֶסֶד *ḥesed*." In *Theological Dictionary of the Old Testament*. Edited by G. Johannes Botterweck and Helmer Ringgren. 15 vols. 6:44–64. Grand Rapids, MI: Eerdmans, 1986.

Zogbo, Lynell. "Interface entre l'exégèse et la traduction de la Bible: le cas de l'infinitif absolu en hébreu." Paper presented at 2010 International Symposium May 25–26, Montréal.

Zuckermann, Benedict. *Über Sabbathjahrcyclus und Jubelperiode*. Breslau, Germany: W. G. Korn, 1866.

GENERAL INDEX

"abomination of desolation" (Olivet discourse), 552, 561–562

Abraham, covenant with, 138, 155–156, 201, 247, 303–304, 304–305, 321, 433, 460–461, 465–466, 468, 511, 541, 630–635, 654; Abraham in the Genesis plot structure, 224; Abraham's obedience and God's mighty oath, 280–293; the call of Abraham, 230–231 (outline); the call of Abraham as a "new creation," 224–228; key grammatical issues and the literary structure of Genesis 12, 230–245; location of in the story line of Scripture, 630–632; the making of the covenant (promise of descendants and land), 248–256; nature of, 632–634; New Testament texts connecting the Abrahamic covenant with the coming of Jesus Christ, 296–297; as one covenant, not two, 275–280, 630; overview of God's dealings with Abraham, 228–230; parallels between the Abrahamic covenant and the Noahic covenant, 269 (table); purpose of, 295–299; in the Servant Songs, 438; sign of (circumcision), 258–275, 340; tensions in the metanarrative, 293–295; unconditional/unilateral and conditional/bilateral elements in, 634–635

Adam, covenant with, 138, 247, 302, 309n9, 321, 433, 611–628, 666–668; Adam as gardener, 210; comparison of the covenant with creation with the covenant with Noah, 168 (table); parallels between Adam and Noah, 176 (table)

Adam: role as the representative head of creation as defining what comes after him, 619 (figure); as a type of Christ, 105, 106–107, 616–618

'ādām (Hebrew: son of God, servant king), 184, 184n12, 194–196

Aejmelaeus, A., 318n34

'āh (Hebrew: brother), 166, 459–460

alētheuō (Greek: to act truthfully), 571–572

Alexander, T. Desmond, 115n78, 215, 235n20, 236, 236n23, 237n24, 269, 288–289, 467, 628n69, 710nn131–132

allegory, 102; the difference between allegory and typology, 102–103

Allen, David, 680n65

'am (Hebrew: people [of God, Israel]), 243

'āmēn (Hebrew: surely), 465

ancient Near East, 261 (map)

Andersen, Francis I., 142, 143

Anderson, A. A., 397n18

Anderson, Bernhard W., 437n5

Andrew, Maurice E., 329

Aquinas, Thomas, 171, 613n36

'ārar (Hebrew: curse), 242

Arnold, Bill T., 236

arrabōn (Greek: deposit, guarantee), 597, 597n10

atonement, the, extent of, 670–672, 671n38; Christ's work as mediator of the new covenant entails a particular redemption, 679–683; Christ's work as our great high priest is a unified work, 672–679

Augustine, 233, 467, 506

ba'ăbûr (Hebrew: on account of, in order that, for the sake of), 405–406

bā'ādām (Hebrew: by means of mankind, in exchange for the man), 166–167

Babel, 138, 225, 244, 303, 631

Baden, Joel S., 232n13

Baker, David L., 31n20, 104n49, 123

baptism: the baptismal divide, 694–703; covenant theology view of, 63, 76, 77–80, 695–703 (critique); meaning of (the believer's union, by grace, through faith, and all the benefits entailed), 697–700

bārā' (Hebrew: to create), 184, 467

bārak (Hebrew: to bless), 242; hithpael form of, 238–242, 286–287, 424, 466, 485–486; niphal form of, 238–242, 486

Barcellos, Richard, 679

Barnes, Tom, 678

Barr, James, 30n18, 84, 192n28, 198

Barth, Karl, 30, 185, 189n20, 209, 614n36

Bartholomew, Craig G., 154–155, 165, 178

Barton, John, 276

bāśār (Hebrew: flesh), 459

Batto, Bernard F., 214

Bauckham, Richard, 657n6, 659n11, 661n15

Baudissin, W. W., 324

Baur, F. C., 30n17

Bavinck, Herman, 32

Wenham, Gordon J., 185, 197, 198, 200, 209,
211n77, 213–214, 251–252, 256, 263,
291, 667n25
Wenham, John, 84n7
Westermann, Claus, 185–186, 364, 417
Westminster Confession of Faith, 57, 68, 331
Westminster Larger Catechism, 68
Westminster Shorter Catechism, 654
Westminster Theological Seminary, 32n26
Wheaton, Byron L., 261n15
White, Florence, 393n7
White, James R., 646n91, 649–650, 688n76,
689n79
White, R. Fowler, 693
Williams, Garry, 625n60
Williams, Michael D., 86n13
Williams, Ronald J., 380n44
Williamson, H. G. M., 403, 407–410, 413, 414,
415–417, 418, 515–516, 521, 528
Williamson, Paul R., 53n42, 59n63, 133n5,
153, 155n16, 156–158, 156n20, 163, 165,
171n56, 175, 177, 179–180, 217–218,
218n95, 220, 233–234, 239–240,
263–265, 266–267, 266n19, 269–270,
275–280, 543–544, 548n25, 550n32,
634, 707–708, 708n125, 709, 709n128,
710, 712
Wilson, Alistair, 21n1
Wilson, Douglas, 67n83, 74n104, 75, 77n111,
80n119
Winston, David, 418n86

Witsius, Herman, 57
Wolff, Hans Walter, 200, 242, 367, 369
Woodbridge, John D., 83n4
Wright, Christopher J. H., 206n65, 326–327,
333n66, 703n112
Wright, David F., 700n104
Wright, N. T., 224, 227, 553n36, 631, 661n15

yōneqet (Hebrew: shoot), 473
Youngblood, Kevin J., 507

Zechariah, book of, 438; allusions to earlier
portions of Scripture in, 576; apocalyptic
night visions in, 574 (table); chiastic
structure of Zechariah 7–8, 575 (table)
zemah (Hebrew: branch), 524–525, 525n39;
meanings of and corresponding lexical
fields, 524 (table)
Zenger, Erich, 298–299, 449, 452–453
zera' (Hebrew: seed), 288, 626–627, 626n64
Zion, 451–452; as the city of righteousness
in the book of Isaiah, 443–445; and the
Davidic covenant, 443; the new Zion,
501–502; transformation of in the book of
Isaiah, 446–447, 468–470
Zobel, H.-J., 407n46
Zogbo, Lynell, 314–315, 315
zō't tôrat hā'ādām (Hebrew: this is the instruction for humanity), 399–400
Zuckerman, Benedict, 547n24, 549, 549n28
Zwingli, Ulrich, 56

SCRIPTURE INDEX